CASES AND MATERIALS ON

BANKRUPTCY

Second Edition

By

Margaret Howard
Professor of Law
Vanderbilt University School of Law

Peter A. Alces
Professor of Law
College of William and Mary, Marshall-Wythe School of Law

AMERICAN CASEBOOK SERIES®

WEST
GROUP

ST. PAUL, MINN., 2001

610 Opperman Drive
P.O. Box 64526
St. Paul, MN 55164–0526
1–800–328–9352

Printed in the United States of America

ISBN 0–314–24092–6

*TEXT IS PRINTED ON 10% POST
CONSUMER RECYCLED PAPER*

FROM PROFESSOR HOWARD

to William Miller Howard, Jr.,
in memory.

FROM PROFESSOR ALCES

To Eileen
to Kelli
to Katherine.

Preface

We have yet to meet anyone who grew up wanting to be a bankruptcy lawyer. This just seems to be one of those fields that does not "sound interesting." It did not to us either, until we studied it for the first time. We are now hooked. Bankruptcy has it all: a long, tough statute that leaves huge and important issues unaddressed; rich case law development; sometimes an abundance and sometimes a dearth of legislative history; intriguing policy questions that go to the heart of what the law is and ought to be doing; theory as well as real-world practicality; economic analysis that enriches the debate on some issues and adds little on others; and even a constitutional issue or two poking around. What subject matter could be better for a lawyer? (Yes, a few of our students have thought we needed a reality check, but they have never doubted our sincerity!)

We discerned a gap (actually, a chasm) in the available teaching materials. Some books take either a purely problem-driven or wholly case-law approach, both equally unsatisfactory. Other books treat consumer and business bankruptcies separately. Still others proceed from an unremitting political or theoretical perspective. We could find no book of manageable length that comprehensively treats everything we believed students should learn in the basic bankruptcy course. Each of us used different books in the past and supplemented them extensively with our own materials. Thus are casebooks born.

We set out to write the perfect bankruptcy book, never giving a thought to the fact that authors who came before us, and to our minds missed the mark, undoubtedly did the same thing. We were also a natural pair, having concluded that we disagreed about so many things. What better way to produce teaching materials that would be all things to all people? We now know, of course, that we cannot please everyone (even each other) *all* of the time. We have come through the process with a deeper appreciation for the complexity of our subject, a new-found tolerance for those who view it differently, and an abiding respect for each other.

We are indebted to our research assistants for their invaluable hard work. In particular, we acknowledge Susan E. Sieger, Marshall-Wythe School of Law, The College of William and Mary, J.D. 1994, and Beth A. Dunning, Vanderbilt University School of Law, J.D. 1995.

P.A.A.,
Williamsburg, Virginia

M.H.,
Nashville, Tennessee

April, 1995

Preface to the Second Edition

Bankruptcy law has moved considerably in recent years, and we have learned a lot more about our subject, from our colleagues and—sometimes painfully!—from our students. We hope these materials reflect a little of that learning.

As we write, we still await amendments to the Bankruptcy Code. At some point, however, one must go forward. We have chosen to go ahead now, albeit with mixed feelings, in the sure knowledge that Congress will only add to our coverage, whenever and if ever it acts.

As before, we are indebted to the students who have helped us do this work. In particular, we acknowledge Andre J. Burba, Vanderbilt Law School, J.D. 2000.

M.H.,
Nashville, Tennessee

P.A.A.,
Williamsburg, Virginia

October, 2000

Acknowledgements

Alces, Peter A. & Luther M. Dorr, Jr., A Critical Analysis of the New Uniform Fraudulent Transfer Act, 1985 U. Ill. L. Rev. 527 (p. 439).

Alexander, Peter C., Bankruptcy Reorganizations Without The Bankruptcy Court: Reorganizations in Lieu of Bankruptcy, 7 J. Bank. L. & Prac. 81 (1997) (p. 15).

Andrew, Michael T., Executory Contracts in Bankruptcy: Understanding "Rejection," 59 U. Colo. L.Rev. 845 (1988) (p. 633).

Blumberg, Phillip I., Intragroup (Upstream, Cross-Stream, and Downstream) Guaranties Under the Uniform Fraudulent Transfer Act, 9 Cardozo L. Rev. 685 (1987) (p. 425).

Browne, Dik, *Hagar the Horrible* cartoon. Distributed by King Features Syndicate. Reprinted by permission. (p. 799).

Brubaker, Ralph, One Hundred Years of Federal Bankruptcy Law and Still Clinging To An In Rem Model of Bankruptcy Jurisdiction, 15 Bankr. Dev. J. 261 (1999) (p. 37).

Clark, Robert Charles, The Duties of the Corporate Debtor to Its Creditors, 90 Harv. L. Rev. 505 (1977) (p. 442).

Countryman, Vern, Executory Contracts in Bankruptcy: Part I, 57 Minn. L. Rev. 439 (1973) (p. 566).

Eisenberg, Theodore, Bankruptcy Law in Perspective, 28 UCLA L. Rev. 953 (1981) (p. 663).

Eisenberg, Theodore, The Unsecured Creditor in Reorganizations and the Nature of Security, 38 Vand. L. Rev. 931 (1985) (p. 276).

Eisenberg, Theodore & Lynn M. Lopucki, Shopping For Judges: An Empirical Analysis Of Venue Choice In Large Chapter 11 Reorganizations, 84 Cornell L. Rev. 967 (1999) (p. 41).

Guisewite, Cathy. *Cathy* cartoon (two). Distributed by Universal Press Syndicate. Reprinted by permission. (p. 715).

Heidt, Kathryn R., Environmental Obligations in Bankruptcy: A Fundamental Framework, 44 Fla. L. Rev. 153 (1992) (p. 156).

Howard, Margaret, A Theory of Discharge in Consumer Bankruptcy, 48 Ohio St. L.J. 1047 (1987) (p. 664).

Howard, Margaret, *Dewsnup*ping the Bankruptcy Code, 1 J. Bankr. L. & Prac. 513 (1992) (p. 349).

Jackson, Thomas H., The Logic and Limits of Bankruptcy Law (1986) (pp. 48, 247).

Keating, Daniel, Offensive Uses of the Bankruptcy Stay, 45 Vand. L. Rev. 71 (1991) (p. 69, 126).

Ketchum, Hank. "DENNIS THE MENACE" used by permission of Hank Ketchum and (c) by North America Syndicate. (p. xxxii).

Lazarus, Mell. *Miss Peach* cartoon. Creators Syndicate, Inc. Copyrighted by Mell Lazarus. (p. 363).

Markell, Bruce A., Toward True and Plain Dealing: A Theory of Fraudulent Transfers Involving Unreasonably Small Capital, 21 Ind. L. Rev. 469 (1988) (p. 439).

Ponoroff, Lawrence & F. Stephen Knippenberg, The Implied Good Faith Filing Requirement: Sentinel of an Evolving Bankruptcy Policy, 85 Nw. U.L. Rev. 919 (1991) (p. 47).

Riesenfeld, Stefan A., Enforcement of Money Judgments in Early American History, 71 Mich. L. Rev. 691 (1973). (p. 3).

Ryan, T. K., *Tumbleweeds* cartoon. (1989) Distributed by North American Syndicate, Inc. (p. 490).

Smyser, Kathryn V., Going Private and Going Under: Leveraged Buyouts and the Fraudulent Conveyance Problem, 63 Ind. L.J. 781 (1988) (p. 423).

Smythe, Reggie, *Andy Capp* cartoon (two). Reprinted by permission (pp. 5, 93).

Sullivan, Teresa A., Elizabeth Warren & Jay L. Westbrook, As We Forgive Our Debtors: Bankruptcy and Consumer Credit in America (1989) (p. 89).

Young, Dean & Drake, Stan, *Blondie* cartoon. Copyrighted by King Features Syndicate. Reprinted by permission. (p. 315).

Note on Citations

The Bankruptcy Code, 11 U.S.C. § 101 et seq., is generally referred to in this casebook by section number only.

Several subsections of the Code, principally found in § 101, were renumbered in 1984. When these subsections are cited in cases, we have omitted the original numbering and indicated the current numbers in brackets.

We have omitted citations in cases and quoted material without indication, but other omissions are noted with ellipses. We have moved and edited some citations for clarity and form. Numerous references are made in the cases to the Code's legislative history, principally the House Report, H.R. Rep. No. 595, 95th Cong., 1st Sess. (1977), and to the Senate Report, S. Rep. No. 989, 95th Cong., 2nd Sess. (1978), both of which are reprinted in U.S. Code Congressional and Administrative News (1978). We have edited almost all of those references to the following form: H.R. Rep. No. 95-595 at ___, *reprinted* in 1978 U.S.C.C.A.N. at ___; S. Rep. No. 95-989 at ___, *reprinted* in 1978 U.S.C.C.A.N. at ___.

We have retained the original footnote numbering found in the cases. Our own footnotes are indicated by letters.

Summary of Contents

Table of Contents

Table of Cases

Principal cases are in bold type. Cases cited or discussed in the text are in roman type. Cases cited in principal cases and within other quoted materials are not included. References are to pages.

Table of Statutes

UNITED STATES

UNITED STATES CONSTITUTION

UNITED STATES CODE ANNOTATED

11 U.S.C.A.--Bankruptcy

UNITED STATES CODE ANNOTATED

15 U.S.C.A.—Truth-in-Lending Act

UNITED STATES CODE ANNOTATED

26 U.S.C.A.—Internal Revenue Code

28 U.S.C.A.—Judiciary and Judicial Procedure

29 U.S.C.A.—Employee Retirement Income Security Act of 1974

42 U.S.C.A.—Social Security Act

POPULAR NAME ACTS

BANKRUPTCY ACT

BANKRUPTCY ACT

UNIFORM COMMERCIAL CODE

REVISED UNIFORM COMMERCIAL CODE

UNIFORM FRAUDULENT CONVEYANCE ACT

UNIFORM FRAUDULENT TRANSFER ACT

BANKRUPTCY RULES

RESTATEMENT OF CONTRACTS (2ND)

DENNIS THE MENACE
BY HANK KETCHAM
SO YOU BOYS WANT TO APPLY FOR A CREDIT CARD, EH?
YEAH, WE'RE BROKE!
ALLOWANCES DON'T LAST LONG THESE DAYS.
MY DAD SAYS IT'S INFLAYSHUN!
FIRST, YOU'LL HAVE TO FILL OUT THESE APPLICATIONS.
!
UH... WE DON'T WRITE VERY GOOD.
WE DON'T EVEN READ GOOD!
DO YOU BOYS HAVE A BANK ACCOUNT?
WE HAVE PIGGY BANKS... BUT OUR MOMS WON'T LET US BREAK 'EM.
HMMM.. FROZEN ASSETS, EH? WHAT YOU BOYS NEED IS A SHORT-TERM LOAN.
YOU CAN REPAY THIS LOAN WHEN YOU GET YOUR ALLOWANCES.
!
KNOW WHAT, JOEY? WE'RE ALMOST GROWN-UP!
WE ARE?
LOOK! WE'RE IN DEBT ALREADY!
?

Chapter 1

CREDITORS' RIGHTS AND REMEDIES

A. INTRODUCTION

We tend to think of obligations that debtors owe to creditors in contract terms—a loan or a purchase, each of which creates an obligation to pay that derives from the agreement between the debtor and creditor. In truth, the obligation imposed on one party (the "debtor") to pay money to another (the "creditor") may derive from many other sources. The careless driver of an automobile who plows into another car has just become a debtor. The taxpayer is a debtor, as is the parent who owes child support and the corporation that dumps toxic waste.

Debtors, whatever the source of the obligation, sometimes fail to pay. In that event, creditors can resort to collection devices made available under the contract between the parties, or under state or non-bankruptcy federal law. The nature of a particular creditor's collection choices depends upon whether that creditor is an unsecured (or general) creditor or the holder of some type of lien—that is, a collateral interest in property of the debtor. The second category includes creditors with judgment or execution liens, security interests and statutory liens—that is, liens that arise consensually, nonconsensually and by statute.

For each of these categories, we must be able to answer two important questions. First, what rights does the creditor enjoy against the debtor and the debtor's property? Second, what rights does the creditor enjoy against other creditors also seeking to be paid by this debtor? The former may be described as a question of *rights* and the latter as a question of *priority*.

1. RIGHTS

If a debtor fails to meet its obligation to a creditor, as in the case of a loan contract, or if an obligation must be established in the first instance, as in a tort case, the first step a creditor usually takes is to file a lawsuit. Successful prosecution of the suit only produces a judgment, however; it does not put money into the hands of the creditor. Here the creditor must turn to statutes that vary from state to state. These statutes are similar in broad outline, however, so we can generalize.

A debtor, of course, may choose to pay the judgment once the creditor obtains it. That happy possibility is legally uninteresting, as you might expect. Also, the debtor usually fails to pay in the first instance not because of unwillingness but because of inability. Thus, the creditor may need the resources of the state to turn the judgment into money. The two primary methods are judgment liens and execution liens.

Although a judgment lien is obtained automatically in some states when a judgment is entered, in most states a judgment must be "docketed" before a lien is created. In all but a handful of states, docketing creates a lien on any real property the debtor owns in the county in which the judgment was docketed. In three states—Alabama, Georgia and Mississippi—the judgment lien attaches to personal property as well. The judgment lien does not give the lienholder a right to immediate possession of the property. Rather, the lienholder must take whatever additional steps are required by state law, whether foreclosure or levy and sale under writ of execution.

The writ of execution, besides being the method for enforcing a judgment lien in some states, is the only method for reaching the debtor's personal property in states other than Alabama, Georgia and Mississippi. A writ of execution, which is addressed to the sheriff, directs the sheriff to seize and sell property of the debtor sufficient to satisfy the judgment creditor's claim. Levy by the sheriff creates an execution lien as of that date in most states, although in a few states the lien relates back either to the date the writ was issued by the clerk or to the date the writ was delivered to the sheriff.

These statutorily-based remedies developed from a series of common law writs that are today mostly anachronisms. The terms still appear from time to time, however, so Professor Riesenfeld's description of them is worthwhile:

The two principal collection remedies of judgment creditors under the classical English system were the writs *fieri facias*[a] and *elegit*. *Fieri facias* was a judicial writ, developed in the formative days of the common law, whose origins and early scope are still shrouded in mystery. At any rate, it came to have the form of a command to the sheriff, ordering him to raise the amount specified in the judgment from the "goods and chattels" of the judgment debtor, by the seizure and sale thereof. Freehold estates owned by the judgment debtor could not be reached by the writ of *fieri facias*. The proper procedure for seeking satisfaction of the judgment from real property owned by the debtor was the procurement and service of the writ of *elegit*, created by the Statute of Westminster II in 1285. This writ enabled the judgment debtor [sic] to obtain a term of years in one half of the debtor's lands for a period appraised to be long enough to satisfy the judgment debt from the rents and profits of the land thus "extended."

The subjection of real estate to the reach of judgment creditors resulted in the recognition of a new interest in land: the judgment lien. The Statute of Westminster II was construed to entitle the judgment creditor to a term for years in one half of the real property of the judgment debtor from the time of the judgment. Hence, the judgment was said to "bind" the lands or to create a "lien" thereon from that date. Since at common law, judgments related back to the first day of the term in which they were recovered, that date determined priorities between judgment creditors and purchasers as well as between judgment creditors *inter se*; in other words, all judgments recovered during the same term created liens of equal rank. * * * The protection of purchasers against latent judgment liens was enhanced by the Statute for the Better Discovery of Judgments in the Courts of Kings Bench, Common Pleas and Exchequer at Westminster. It provided that

> no Judgment not docketed and entered in the Books as aforesaid shall affect any Lands or Tenements as to Purchasers or Mortgagees or have any preference against Heirs Executors or Administrators in their Administration of their Ancestors Testators or Intestates Estates.

[a] Known affectionately as "fi-fa" to the cognoscente. Eds.

> The priorities between judgment creditors *inter se* were not affected by these enactments. It has been suggested, however, that, as between judgment creditors of equal rank, the first one to have the writ of *elegit* served thereby acquired priority.

Stefan A. Riesenfeld, *Enforcement of Money Judgments in Early American History*, 71 Mich. L. Rev. 691, 693–95 (1973) (footnotes omitted).

Although judgment and execution liens give a creditor the right to obtain the property subject to the lien, that right may be limited by the debtor's "exemptions." Every state, by statute, lists specific items of property that are immune from the reach of creditors. These lists vary from state to state and many of them are woefully outdated, but the idea behind each state's list is the same—to provide the debtor a minimum amount of property necessary for survival. This protects both the debtor and the society upon which the debtor would otherwise become dependent. (We will examine exemptions in bankruptcy in Chapter 2, Section D of this casebook.)

2. PRIORITIES

Since a debtor often defaults on payments to more than one creditor, multiple judgments may be taken against a single debtor. These judgments are likely to result in multiple judgment liens that encumber the same property. The priority of these competing liens is determined, generally, by statute. Priority is never determined by agreement between the debtor and creditor, because such an agreement would affect the rights of third parties.

When proper execution is accomplished, the collateral is sold and the proceeds made available to the lienholders. A lien with first priority is satisfied first out of the value of the collateral. If value is left over, the next lien is satisfied, and so on down the line until value is exhausted. The creditor holding a lien that is unpaid from the value of the collateral does not lose its rights against the debtor; the debt continues in existence, but the creditor has to find another way to collect. For example, assume that the debtor's real estate, worth \$60,000, is subject to two liens; the debtor owes the first lienholder \$50,000 and owes the second lienholder \$25,000. When the property is sold, the first lienholder will be paid in full and the second lienholder will receive \$10,000. The second lienholder retains a claim for the balance (\$15,000), but has no more collateral from which to seek payment.

The general priority rule is "first-in-time, first-in-right." In other words, the first lien to come into existence has first priority. (It is often referred to as a "senior" lien and liens having lower priority are "junior" liens.) A major exception to this general rule arises when some sort of public notice is required in order to "perfect" the lien. "Perfection" refers to the steps required to make a lien that is already enforceable against the debtor also enforceable against third parties, such as competing lienholders. These perfecting steps are designed to make third parties aware of the interest in the property claimed by the perfecting lienholder. If some sort of public notice is required for perfection, priority generally dates from the time the perfecting step is taken. The priority of judicial liens is normally measured from the date of docketing. Because execution liens usually arise only upon levy by the sheriff, that step accomplishes both creation of the lien and the public notice necessary to protect the executing creditor from competing claims. If the execution lien relates back to the date the writ is issued or delivered to the sheriff, however, priority problems may arise if a third party purchases the property or obtains a lien on the property before the sheriff takes possession.

A first-in-time perfected lien is not completely invulnerable. Certain types of third parties can take priority even though their interests arise later. For example, in some states a judicial lien attaches to the debtor's after-acquired real property, but that preexisting lien will be junior to a purchase money mortgagee whose loan made acquisition of the property possible.

B. CONSENSUAL LIENS

Judgment and execution liens are *nonconsensual*—that is, they arise in the absence of agreement between the debtor and creditor. The parties, however, may agree to the creation of a lien on specified items or types of the debtor's property. These *consensual* liens fall into two categories—security interests, which attach to personal property, and mortgages (including deeds of trust), which attach to real property.

1. SECURITY INTERESTS

a. Rights

A security interest is an interest in personal property, whether tangible or intangible, given to secure the performance of an obligation (typically, the repayment of a loan or the payment of the purchase price of goods). Security interests are governed by Article 9 of the Uniform Commercial Code (UCC). A security interest is enforceable between the debtor and the creditor ("secured party") when it "attaches." Attachment requires that: (1) the parties have a written "security agreement," which is the contract creating the security interest; (2) the debtor has acquired rights in the collateral subject to the security interest; and (3) the creditor has given value, as by making a loan or selling goods on credit. A written security agreement is not required if the creditor takes possession of the collateral.

A secured party has, upon the debtor's default, a cumulative assortment of remedies. Default is defined by the parties in the security agreement, rather than by Article 9, and usually includes such events as failing to make timely payments and failing to insure or otherwise properly care for collateral. Default also is often defined to include any event that increases the possibility of nonpayment, such as the filing of bankruptcy. Most security agreements accelerate the entire remaining obligation upon default.

One of the most important remedies under Article 9 is the right to take possession of the collateral without judicial process, as long as this so-called "self-help repossession" can be accomplished without a breach of the peace. After possession is obtained, whether by self-help or by judgment and execution, the collateral is sold and the proceeds applied to the expenses of sale and to the debt. The debtor is entitled to any surplus proceeds (which are as rare as the white rhino) and remains liable for any deficiency.

Collection pursuant to a security interest, unlike levy upon a writ of execution, is not limited by the debtor's exemptions. Exempt property can be collateral subject to a security interest and the exemptions statute will not insulate the debtor from the secured party's collection efforts. Because a security interest is *consensual*, the debtor is in no position to complain.

b. Priorities

In order to obtain priority against other claimants to the property of the debtor, a secured party must "perfect" its security interest. Perfection usually requires the filing of a "financing statement" in the place(s) specified in UCC § 9–401 (§ 9-501 of Revised Article 9), although perfection can also be accomplished by possession in most cases. A few types of Article 9 interests, however, are automatically perfected upon attachment. The most significant example of automatic perfection is purchase money security interests in consumer goods other than automobiles. Also, a few types of Article 9 interests, such as negotiable instruments, can only be perfected by possession.

Article 9 is largely concerned with priorities. It provides rules governing the priority between competing security interests, whether perfected or unperfected, and between security interests and other types of competing claims. Article 9 generally follows the first-in-time, first-in-right rule, but as with so many other areas of law, exceptions are omnipresent and important.

One of the most significant priority provisions in Article 9, for purposes of bankruptcy law, is § 9–301(1)(b):

> (1) Except as otherwise provided in subsection (2), an unperfected security interest is subordinate to the rights of
>
> * * *
>
> (b) a person who becomes a lien creditor before the security interest is perfected * * *.

Under § 9–301(1)(b) (as well as under the successor provision of Revised Article 9, § 9-317(a)(2)), an *unperfected* security interest is subordinate (i.e., junior) to a competing judicial lien. A secured party that fails to perfect its interest promptly after attachment, therefore, will be junior in priority to a creditor that obtains a judicial lien in the "gap" period before the security interest is perfected. It also follows from this subsection that a perfected security interest has priority over a judicial lien arising after the security interest was perfected.

As § 9–301(1) indicates, § 9–301(2) provides a different rule:

> If the secured party files with respect to a purchase money security interest before or within ten days after the deb-

tor receives possession of the collateral, he takes priority over the rights of a * * * lien creditor which arise between the time the security interest attaches and the time of filing.

Subsection (2) is a "relation back" provision. It allows a purchase money secured creditor to file a financing statement *after* a lien creditor has acquired rights, but to obtain priority nonetheless. The rule is justified by the favored position of a purchase money creditor, whose extension of value permitted the debtor to obtain the encumbered goods in the first place. (This rule is carried forward in § 9-317(e) of Revised Article 9.)

Note, too, *and remember* § 9–301(3), which provides that the bankruptcy trustee enjoys the same rights and powers as a judicial lien creditor. (Revised Article 9 defines "lien creditor" to include a trustee in bankruptcy, § 9-102(52)(C).)

2. MORTGAGES

A mortgage is an interest in real estate, given to secure the performance of an obligation (usually, the repayment of a loan). As with security interests, a mortgage is effective between the debtor (mortgagor) and creditor (mortgagee) upon execution of the mortgage documents. Effectiveness against third parties is of much more concern, however, and priority requires recording. The first-in-time, first-in-right rule also applies in this context, generally dating various interests from the time that public notice is placed in the real estate records. Most real estate recording systems are not pure "race" statutes, awarding priority to the first party to file, without regard to that party's knowledge of competing interests. Real estate recording systems, rather, are either "notice" or "race-notice" systems. Under the former, a subsequent purchaser without knowledge of a prior purchaser's interest has priority, as long as the prior purchaser's interest was not recorded; no recording by the subsequent purchaser is necessary. Under the latter, a subsequent purchaser without knowledge of a prior purchaser's interest has priority, but only if the subsequent purchaser records first.

As with security interests, a mortgagee has the right to realize against the property upon default by the mortgagor. Default is defined by the mortgage documents, just as the security agreement defines default for purposes of Article 9 security interests, and usually includes failure to make timely payments of principal and interest, failure to pay taxes and insurance, and waste.

The mortgagee's remedy is foreclosure. It usually requires a judicially-approved sale, although about half the states permit foreclosure by an out-of-court sale. As with security interests, the proceeds of sale are distributed to creditors in accordance with their priority; the mortgagor is entitled to any surplus and remains liable for any deficiency.

C. STATUTORY LIENS

Statutory liens are, unsurprisingly, interests in property created by state or federal statutes. A vast array of liens fall into this category: materialmen's and mechanic's liens, which secure compensation for parties who contribute materials and labor to make improvements on land; landlord's liens, which attach to tenants' property and secure their lease obligations; artisans' liens, which secure the payment of expenses to repair personal property; environmental liens, created by both state and federal environmental statutes to secure reimbursement of amounts spent in cleaning up contaminated property; and tax liens, which need no explanation. These liens are as varied as you might imagine, so generalizations are problematic. Some of the most interesting of the priority issues surround environmental "superliens," which take priority over all others.

D. COLLECTION UNDER NONBANKRUPTCY LAW

Bankruptcy is a creature of federal law. Before an entity (individual, corporate, or partnership) becomes the subject of a bankruptcy proceeding, state and nonbankruptcy federal law determine what a creditor must do to collect a debt. In order to appreciate bankruptcy's impact on a debtor-creditor relationship, one must first appreciate the panoply of state laws that may determine the rights of debtor and creditors before the initiation of an action in the bankruptcy court.

We have already reviewed some of these laws. Now let's consider the case of an individual who has, in fact, three legal identities so far as creditor-debtor law is concerned.

Janet Ward is a Conference Planner—a professional who attends to the details of arranging meetings for trade groups throughout the country. She is the part owner of Conferences, Inc., a corporation that typically handles logistics for meetings of more than 2,500 people at large hotels and resorts in the Eastern United States. Janet is in charge of planning, and works about 45 hours per week at that job.

Conferences, Inc. is a corporate entity, distinct from Janet Ward in the legal sense, with its own assets and liabilities. Janet owns 25% of the corporation's stock, and it has steadily increased in value as the business has grown. She is an integral part of the corporation. Without her, the corporation would not enjoy the same success and, in fact, might have to review its business plan and reduce the size of its customer base and areas of operation.

In her spare time, Janet acts as a consultant to smaller trade associations, helping them negotiate meeting space for groups of 500 or less. Janet is paid for that work at a rate of $250 per hour. She engages in that work with the knowledge and consent of the other owners of Conferences, Inc., who are happy to have her develop connections that will enhance her ability to attract new business to the corporation. Janet conducts her consulting business as a sole proprietorship, and scrupulously maintains financial records separate from her personal financial records. She uses "Janet Ward, Meeting Consultant" business cards and letterhead, and has a checking account in the name of the consulting business. All of the funds in that account are business funds and all of the checks drawn on that account are issued in payment of expenses of the sole proprietorship. She uses a business American Express card for many of the expenses of that consulting business.

Janet Ward is also, of course, an individual consumer. She never has more than $1,000 in her checking account and $2,500 in her savings account, both of which are maintained at a local credit union. She owns a car, subject to a security interest in favor of a local bank, a house, subject to a mortgage in favor of a local savings and loan, and personal effects that are unencumbered. She owes student loans and carries balances on three different Visa cards. She has a balance on her Sears card, which she recently used to purchase a new washing machine. Janet also has two retirement accounts: one funded by her employer, Conferences, Inc., and a separate Individual Retirement Account into which she has deposited $2,000 each year for the last five years.

In other words, Janet Ward is the typical young, upwardly mobile professional, living a life enhanced by relatively easy access to credit. She also has the capacity to increase her earnings as the fortunes of Conferences, Inc. improve and as she continues her private consulting business.

While it is not difficult to imagine the wealth that Janet Ward may accumulate as she grows professionally, it is also not difficult to imagine that personal and professional financial misfortunes could compromise both her current lifestyle and her future prospects. If all continues to go well, Janet will have no more than a passing interest in debtor-creditor law, state or federal. But if her financial fortunes take a turn for the worse, a panoply of laws will determine her lifestyle and prospects.

Because this book and course are concerned with the consequences of financial misfortune, focus on what can go wrong and how wrong it can all go even before the bankruptcy law is implicated.

If Janet were struck by a car and seriously injured during her daily commute, her life could change dramatically. A lengthy hospital stay followed by an extended period of rehabilitation could cost her thousands, even hundreds of thousands, of dollars. She might never recover this money, particularly if she has no insurance to cover expenses during her convalescence. Though it is not clear when her financial straits might become so dire as to make bankruptcy a (relatively) attractive option, it is clear that her personal creditors, as well as those of the corporation and of her consulting business, will take account of the rights provided them by state and federal law. Janet may have reason to learn more debtor protection law, state and federal, than she ever anticipated.

When a debtor is unable or unwilling to discharge her indebtedness (whether the debt arose in tort or contract), a creditor is generally free to pursue options designed to compel payment. So even though Janet's and her corporation's failure to pay their creditors in a timely manner was not a product of choice, creditors may pursue remedies available under state and federal law to recover on their claims.

While laws governing creditors' rights and debtors' protections vary from state to state, there is sufficient consistency to support some generalization.

1. REMEDIES AVAILABLE TO INDIVIDUAL CREDITORS

Remedies can be divided into two basic categories—provisional and post-judgment—although provisional remedies have post-judgment counterparts. Provisional remedies are available to a creditor who has not yet prosecuted its claim to judgment, but who has reason to believe that the delay involved with obtaining a judgment might compromise its ability to realize upon its claim, perhaps because the debtor is dissipating assets or presents a flight risk. Provisional remedies are designed to be temporary, to maintain the status quo pending judicial review of the claim.

Attachment: This statutory remedy (which in some states is available only to creditors with contract claims) permits a creditor to attach specific property prior to judgment if the creditor can demonstrate that its ability to collect on its claim would be in jeopardy otherwise. The creditor generally files a complaint in a court of competent jurisdiction and an affidavit alleging the appropriate grounds of attachment. The court, after notice to the debtor and an opportunity for a hearing, will issue a writ of attachment instructing the sheriff to levy on nonexempt property of the debtor sufficient in value to satisfy the creditor's claim. From the time of levy, the creditor obtains a lien on the attached property of the debtor.

In the case of Janet Ward and her corporation, three different groups of creditors may use attachment if they have the statutory prerequisites. Creditors with consumer credit claims against her individually (e.g., the issuer of her Visa card) and creditors of her unincorporated consulting business (e.g., American Express) could attach her real and personal property. Creditors of Conferences, Inc., who failed to receive timely payments for goods and services provided to the corporation, could attach any of the corporation's property. Janet's property, of course, would be immune from the claims of corporate creditors, under principles of limited liability.

Attachment may be either a provisional or post-judgment remedy.

Garnishment: This is a statutory third party action addressed to an entity that holds property of the debtor (typically wages or a deposit account). It instructs that third party (the garnishee) to hold the property for the garnishing creditor rather than turning it over to the debtor. That way, once the creditor obtains a judgment against the debtor, the creditor can recover from the property held by the garnishee. A garnishee who ignores the writ of garnishment and pays over property in its possession to the debtor will be liable to the judgment creditor. In most states, the writ of garnishment gives rise to a lien in favor of the garnishing creditor that dates from the time the writ is served on garnishee.

Personal creditors, both of Janet the consumer and Janet the consultant, would be able to garnish her wages from Conferences, Inc. and her bank accounts. They could also garnish any other property of hers held by third parties, such as fees earned for private consulting but not yet paid.

Federal law limits the extent to which Janet's wages are subject to garnishment, however, whatever the nature of the garnishing creditor's claim. Under Title III of the Truth-in-Lending Act, the amount subject to garnishment for any "workweek" may not exceed 25% of an individual's "disposable income for that week, or the amount by which [the individual's] disposable earnings for that week exceed thirty times the federal minimum hourly wage." 15 U.S.C. § 1673 (a)(1) & (2). That limitation complements but does not restrict state law limitations on garnishment.

Federal law does not insulate any property of the corporation, Conferences, Inc., that may be in the possession of a third party, because the corporation is not an individual. The federal limitation also extends only to wages, and thus would not insulate any account balances that Janet maintains. Other legislation, however, may limit the rights of creditors to reach certain accounts, such as those maintained by the Social Security Administration, 42 U.S.C. § 407, or those within the scope of pension and retirement funds protections, 29 U.S.C. §§ 1003(b) & 1144(a).

A creditor may use garnishment either as a provisional or as a post-judgment remedy.

Replevin: This statutory remedy, which operates only in favor of creditors with a lien against property of the debtor, authorizes the sheriff to seize the property. When used as a provisional remedy, it enables the sheriff to hold the property pending the outcome of litigation between the debtor and the creditor claiming rights in the property, serving to prevent the debtor from wasting the property meanwhile. The right to replevin is additional to any rights a creditor may have as a consensual secured creditor under Article 9 of the UCC.

In Janet's case, the creditor with the security interest in her car, who provided her the financing to purchase it, could replevy the car upon her default in payment. Replevin would also be available to any creditors of Conferences, Inc., who have an interest in particular property of the corporation. So if the company falls behind in the payments for its office furnishings or telephone system, for example, creditors with liens against those items could replevy them and have the sheriff hold them pending litigation on the corporation's indebtedness.

A creditor with the right to replevy may pursue that right either provisionally or after obtaining a judgment.

2. COLLECTIVE NONBANKRUPTCY REMEDIES

In addition to the collection rights available to individual creditors, state law provides a few procedures permitting creditors as a group to resolve their claims against a common debtor. Although these remedies are not used nearly as often as bankruptcy, you should appreciate these nonbankruptcy possibilities.

Receivership: A receivership *pendente lite*—a receiver appointed prior to judgment—is a device rarely invoked by the courts. More common is the post-judgment receiver, who is given the power to manage the debtor's financial affairs. The receiver will supervise (and usually liquidate and distribute) the debtor's property.

A receiver is usually appointed pursuant to the request of a creditor. The creditor obtaining the appointment, however, acquires no lien on any of the debtor's assets (although pre-existing liens are not impaired) and realizes no rights superior to those of other creditors who also benefit from the receiver's appointment.

Assignments for the Benefit of Creditors: This device enables a debtor voluntarily to liquidate its assets in order to pay creditors. The debtor conveys all nonexempt property to an assignee who liquidates it and distributes the proceeds to creditors. The device, like bankruptcy, divests the debtor of title to property in favor of an assignee who represents the interests of the debtor's creditors. Creditors often cooperate with debtors using this device, but the debtor need not obtain creditors' permission in order to make the assignment.

The remedy is generally statutory, but in states where it is not, principles of contract and trust law govern. It is generally less costly than bankruptcy, but the debtor cannot obtain a discharge of unpaid debts unless the creditors so agree as part of a composition agreement.

Composition and Extension Agreements: These are common law contractual, rather than statutory, devices that afford a debtor some debt relief without invoking the considerable, and cumbersome, power of the judiciary. Though generally utilized in the business context, they may be worthwhile devices in the consumer setting as well. In the following excerpt, Professor Alexander describes the functioning of this remedy.

PETER C. ALEXANDER, BANKRUPTCY REORGANIZATIONS WITHOUT THE BANKRUPTCY COURT: REORGANIZATIONS IN LIEU OF BANKRUPTCY

7 J. Bank. L. & Prac. 81, 88-95 (1997).

Many forms of out-of-court debt consolidations and workouts exist. Consumer credit counseling centers are present in most metropolitan areas, and finance companies regularly make debt consolidation loans. In addition, state courts appoint receivers to manage assets and to pay obligations, and parties enter into composition agreements to relieve a debtor from overwhelming financial burdens. One interesting form of composition is known as a "reorganization in lieu of bankruptcy."

A. Doctrine

In a reorganization in lieu of bankruptcy, as the author chooses to define that model, counsel for the debtor is to convene a meeting of the debtor's creditors, following adequate notice. Prior to the meeting, debtor's counsel is required to provide all creditors and interested parties with information about the debtor's finances. Then, at the meeting, debtor's counsel should explain the debtor's financial situation to the representatives gathered and predict the debtor's financial future. During the first part of the group's meeting, the debtor's attorney should explain to the creditors what caused the client's financial hardship, and counsel should advise the creditors about the steps the client would take in the future to avoid ending up in this situation again. In addition, debtor's counsel should prepare a Chapter 7 liquidation analysis so the creditors know what to expect in the event that the debtor finds it necessary to file bankruptcy (and, for comparison purposes, so the creditors can evaluate any proposal that is generated from the meeting).

During the first part of the meeting (the "asset" phase), the debtor's attorney and the creditors' attorneys are advocates, each trying to define the "pie" (the debtor's total asset pool) as small or as large as possible, respectively. Hopefully, all counsel will have prepared Chapter 7 liquidation analyses, based on the pre-hearing disclosures made by debtor's counsel, leaving the parties with little to argue about except arithmetic.

Once the size of the debtor's financial estate is agreed upon, debtor's counsel then serves as a "disinterested" facilitator, helping the creditors decide who was going to receive what portion of the estate and in what order. If there is any controversy at this point, it is not between the debtor and the creditors, because the focus of the discussion has changed. The discussion should no longer be about how much money the debtor has to pay his debts; the recipients should now be trying to distribute equitably the amount of money the parties had already agreed upon.

The role of debtor's counsel in the second part of the meeting—the "distribution" phase—is to provide direction for the creditors' discussion and to remind creditors' counsel what is available for distribution to the creditors now and what would be available in a bankruptcy. Debtors' counsel is now acting as merely a facilitator; it is for the creditors to decide who would receive how much and when. Debtor's counsel might be expected to remind the creditors what the debtor's options are in bankruptcy or counsel might merely act as "traffic cop," helping the creditors reach agreement in an orderly fashion.

This model of out-of-court debt restructuring is equally applicable to consumer bankruptcies as well as business cases; however, the more parties involved and the more complex the case (whether consumer or business in nature), the more time-consuming and costly the out-of-court proceeding will be.

B. Procedure

As with all forms of dispute resolution, those taking place inside or outside of the courtroom, notice and fairness to all concerned is the penultimate procedural concern. The reorganization in lieu of bankruptcy is no exception. Certain provisions must be incorporated into the overall plan in order to ensure that the process described above will succeed; those provisions include full disclosure of the debtor's assets and liabilities, a complete explanation of the cause(s) of the debtor's financial problems, adequate explanation of the step(s) the debtor intends to take to avoid future financial problems, and remedies for the creditors in the event of a default by the debtor.

1. Full Disclosure

At a minimum, the debtor must identify all of his or her creditors at the time a reorganization in lieu of bankruptcy is attempted. Failure to include a creditor will result in that creditor not being bound by the resulting agreement. While no particular format is urged, a notice of a reorganization in lieu of bankruptcy should contain essentially the same items that are disclosed in the Notice a bankruptcy court would send to creditors if the debtor had sought bankruptcy protection. That notice contains the name, address, and Social Security Number of the debtor(s), the name and address of debtor's counsel, and information adequate to enable the creditors to know why they are receiving the notice. * * *

In addition to the aforementioned notice provisions, the debtor must disclose all of his/her debts, assets, and monthly income and expenses. Again, there is no specific format for disclosure; however, it should follow a format similar to that required by the bankruptcy court. Full disclosure of the debtor's finances is essential for all creditors to be able to participate in the reorganization process equally.

The debtor's disclosure requirements, however, do not stop with a complete listing of the debtor's finances. The creditors are also entitled to receive some explanation of how the debtor ended up in his/her current financial situation and how the debtor intends to prevent the same result from occurring again. This information does not necessarily have to be reflected in the initial notice that is mailed to the creditors, but it should be shared early in the process, at the very least not later than the meeting of creditors. * * *

Once the date for the meeting of creditors is confirmed, or when it is actually convened, all creditors should be provided with a complete list of those creditors who have agreed to participate in the composition. This disclosure is very important as it provides participating creditors with some indication of what portion of the debtor's overall debt might still be subject to levy, garnishment, or attachment, notwithstanding the effort to reorganize outside of the bankruptcy court. It is also important because a composition agreement is binding on only those creditors who are parties to it. If a significant number of the debtor's creditors will not participate in the effort to reorganize outside of the bankruptcy court, the remaining creditors should be made aware of this fact and be given the opportunity to decide whether to continue participating in the reorganization effort.

2. Creditors' Remedies

In addition to full disclosure, all reorganization-in-lieu-of-bankruptcy agreements should contain adequate provisions to protect creditors in the event of a default by the debtor. All parties should initially be aware that, because an agreement as a result of a reorganization in lieu of bankruptcy is a contract, standard breach of contract remedies are available to the non-breaching parties. Additionally, agreements procured by fraud or misrepresentation will nullify the composition and subject the defrauding or misrepresenting party to all appropriate state court remedies. Also, the agreement should provide that if its terms are not complied with by the debtor, no release or discharge of debt will be effected.

The specific terms of the agreement must obviously reflect the careful negotiation of the parties, but it should generally include the figures used to form the basis of the agreement, what the parties agreed to do (or not to do), dates for performance and effective releases and payments, provisions for periodic reports from the debtor to the creditors (to ensure compliance), the effect of the agreement on secured creditors and their collateral, injunction or restraint provisions providing that each creditor will stop all pending actions, file no suits, and comply with the terms of the agreement, injunction or restraint provisions providing that the debtor will forbear seeking the protection of the bankruptcy court as long as the agreement remains in full force and effect, prohibitions against the debtor incurring any extraordinary debt without prior notice to creditors, provision for settlement or arbitration of claims arising out of a breach of the agreement, and signatures of all parties to be bound by the agreement.

E. OVERVIEW OF BANKRUPTCY

Bankruptcy law is a device for the resolution of the collective interests of creditors and for the relief of overburdened debtors. It is characterized by discharge, which means that creditors are forever barred from collecting any debts remaining unpaid at the end of the bankruptcy proceeding. We saw that several state law devices, such as assignments for the benefit of creditors and compositions, may provide alternatives to bankruptcy. These devices, however, do not permit the debtor to discharge any debts remaining unpaid. The availability of discharge under bankruptcy, therefore, may be its single most distinguishing feature.

Bankruptcy law is federal law. The current Bankruptcy Code appears at 11 U.S.C. §§ 101 et seq.

1. BANKRUPTCY IN HISTORY

American bankruptcy law can be traced back through the law of England to the laws of Italian city states in the fourteenth century that derived, in turn, from Roman law. The term "bankruptcy" is said to originate from "banca rupta," which was the medieval custom of breaking the bench of a defaulting merchant.

Early bankruptcy laws were entirely creditor-oriented. They were designed to prevent the debtor from hiding assets from creditors, and were purely punitive from the debtor's point of view. They were triggered by "acts of bankruptcy" that consisted of efforts by debtors to evade responsibility to their creditors. (Not until the Eighteenth Century did bankruptcy become a procedure applicable not only to dishonest debtors, but to unfortunate debtors as well.) These early bankruptcy laws permitted only involuntary cases and did not contemplate the discharge of debts remaining unpaid at the end of the proceeding. The notion of discharge came into English law only in the last three hundred years, first appearing in the Statute of 4 Anne ch. 17 (1705). This discharge did not have a debtor-protective or humanitarian purpose, however. Rather, it was designed to encourage debtors to cooperate with their creditors, thereby enabling the creditors to obtain more information about their debtors' assets. Early bankruptcy laws were also limited to certain classes of debtors, such as merchants and traders. Even from the beginning, however, bankruptcy laws had one characteristic still present today—they were collective remedies, enabling creditors to gather and divide a debtor's assets among themselves.

These antecedents are clearly visible in the first American bankruptcy laws. Congress was given the power to enact "uniform laws on the subject of bankruptcies" by Article I, § 8, clause 4 of the United States Constitution. Congress first exercised that power in 1800. This bankruptcy statute applied only to commercial parties (merchants, bankers, brokers, and the like), permitted only involuntary petitions, and required an "act of bankruptcy." Discharge was possible, but only if a designated percentage of creditors consented. The Bankruptcy Act of 1800 was repealed in 1803.

It was followed by two other short-lived statutes, both of which were enacted in response to periods of economic crisis. The Bankruptcy Act of 1841 was very debtor-favorable; it permitted voluntary petitions, was not limited to merchants and allowed discharge (unless a majority of creditors dissented). This statute survived only 18 months. The Bankruptcy Act of 1867 lasted longer—until 1878—but it was also unpopular.

A fourth bankruptcy statute, enacted in 1898, lasted. It was substantially revised by the Chandler Act in 1938, which added procedures for corporate reorganization and for wage-earner plans.

Gradually, the Act became hopelessly outdated and Congress began the process of reform. Congress appointed a National Bankruptcy Commission and the Commission's 1973 Report remains an important research source. Congress passed the Bankruptcy Reform Act of 1978, which became effective in October of 1979.[b] The 1978 Code is the most debtor-favorable bankruptcy law ever enacted in the United States and it immediately came under fire, chiefly from the credit industry. As a result, the Code was amended in 1984 to address some of the dissatisfactions. In addition, a new provision for family farmers was added in 1986. Additional amendments were passed in 1988 and 1990. The amendments of 1994 also created a new National Bankruptcy Review Commission. The Commission issued its report in 1997, but it has had little influence on the course of bankruptcy reform.

2. PURPOSES OF BANKRUPTCY

Bankruptcy is not the source of legal obligations. It creates no rights in one party against another. Instead, rights and obligations originating from other areas of law, such as contracts and torts, are brought into bankruptcy and processed according to its special procedural and substantive rules.

One of the striking differences between bankruptcy and the state law collection devices described above is the lack of a "race of diligence" in bankruptcy. Under state law, the first creditor to obtain a judgment and to collect on it will get the first bite from the debtor's assets. This creditor will be paid in full if the debtor's assets are sufficient, but the next creditor may not be so lucky.

---

[b] This legislation is, by consensus, referred to as the "Code," to distinguish it from the 1898 statute, which is called the "Act." These conventions will be observed in this casebook.

Bankruptcy stresses equality of distribution between similarly-situated creditors (although we will see the limits to this notion). Bankruptcy is also compulsory, in the sense that it presents the creditor's only chance to get paid. A creditor not paid in bankruptcy will not be paid at all, because bankruptcy offers the debtor a discharge from unpaid obligations at the end of the proceeding. The discharge is designed to facilitate the debtor's "fresh start" and is the primary reason that most individual debtors are attracted to bankruptcy. As the Supreme Court put it in *Local Loan Co. v. Hunt*, 292 U.S. 234, 244, 54 S.Ct. 695, 699, 78 L.Ed. 1230, 1235 (1934) (the most often quoted bankruptcy case ever decided), bankruptcy "gives to the honest but unfortunate debtor who surrenders for distribution the property which he owns *at the time of bankruptcy*, a new opportunity in life and a clear field for future effort, unhampered by the pressure and discouragement of preexisting debt."

In the process of accomplishing these objectives, bankruptcy is also intended to reduce overall collection costs and to preserve the estate in order to maximize the creditors' recovery. As we will see, all of these purposes cannot be achieved simultaneously.

3. STRUCTURE OF THE 1978 BANKRUPTCY CODE

The Bankruptcy Code is divided into chapters, all but one of which are odd-numbered. Chapters 1, 3 and 5 contain definitions and general provisions that apply to all bankruptcy proceedings. The remaining chapters (7, 9, 11, 12 and 13) govern the various types of bankruptcy proceedings. (Note that chapters are designated by Arabic numerals in the Code; the Act used Roman numerals.)

The trustee is charged with general administrative responsibility regarding the bankruptcy estate. In order to carry out that responsibility, the trustee has the power to bring back into the estate property that the debtor transferred before bankruptcy was filed. The most important of these "avoiding" powers permit recovery of fraudulent conveyances and preferences. Property recovered under one of the avoiding powers increases the size of the bankruptcy estate and becomes available for distribution to creditors holding unsecured claims. For this reason, the trustee is often described as the representative of unsecured creditors.

Two main types of bankruptcy are available—liquidation and reorganization. In liquidation, debts are paid from the value of currently owned assets. In reorganization, debtors keep their assets and pay debts out of future earnings, over the course of several years.

a. Chapter 7

Chapter 7 governs liquidation cases, also known as "straight bankruptcy." In these cases, a trustee is appointed and charged with the duty to collect the debtor's assets, reduce them to cash, and distribute the proceeds to creditors in accordance with the Code's distributional rules. The trustee learns about the debtor's financial affairs from schedules the debtor must file with the court. In addition, the debtor must appear at a meeting of creditors and answer questions under oath.

The individual debtor can keep some "exempt" property, but otherwise all assets the debtor owns at the time the case commences will be used to satisfy debts the debtor owes at that time. In "no asset" cases, nothing remains for creditors after the debtor's exemptions are set aside.

A creditor holding a valid lien will receive either the property itself or its value. That leaves only unencumbered property for unsecured creditors. This property is unlikely to be sufficient to pay all of the unsecured claims. Under the bankruptcy policy of equality, these creditors share pro rata.

In exchange for giving up nonexempt property, the individual debtor is discharged from liability for all debts remaining unpaid. Corporate debtors do not receive a discharge in bankruptcy, but they do not need one; liquidation leaves an empty corporate shell and state law's concept of limited liability protects shareholders from the corporate creditors' unpaid claims.

b. Chapter 13

Chapter 13 is a reorganization proceeding that is available only to individual debtors who have a steady source of income. Under Chapter 13, the debtor proposes a three- to five-year plan specifying amounts to be paid to each creditor from the debtor's postpetition income. Creditors need not be fully paid, but they must get at least as much as they would get if the debtor had filed a Chapter 7 instead. Chapter 13 debtors keep all their property; payments are made to creditors out of income net of necessary living expenses.

Unlike Chapter 7, only the debtor can file a Chapter 13 petition. No involuntary petitions are permitted. Also, Chapter 13 is not available to debtors with debts in excess of designated amounts. Finally, Chapter 13 has fewer restrictions on discharge than does Chapter 7, but Congress has made Chapter 13's discharge more restrictive with each successive amendment since enactment of the Code.

c. *Chapter 11*

Chapter 11 is also a reorganization proceeding, but it is more widely available than is Chapter 13. Chapter 11 is typically used by corporations, although it is not restricted to business use. A plan governs repayments to creditors in Chapter 11, as it does in 13, but the Code does not limit its duration to a specified number of years.

The Code provides a number of detailed requirements that a Chapter 11 plan must meet. As under 13, the plan must pay each creditor at least as much as that creditor would receive if the debtor had filed Chapter 7, unless the creditor agrees to accept less.

A Chapter 11 plan deals with similarly-situated creditors grouped together by classes. If any class of creditors refuses to accept the plan, it can nonetheless be confirmed ("crammed down") if it meets a two-part test: (1) it does not "discriminate unfairly;" and (2) it is "fair and equitable," i.e., either the dissenting class is paid in full or no class of creditors with a lower priority receives anything. The latter rule, known as the "absolute priority rule," means that the creditors usually become owners of a debtor corporation at the end of the bankruptcy case. This is true because shareholders, who have a lower priority than unsecured creditors, cannot retain any ownership interest unless unsecured creditors are paid in full.

Despite these rules, Chapter 11 plans are often negotiated under which creditors agree to accept less than full payment and to allow shareholders to retain some interest in the postbankruptcy enterprise.

A trustee is not typically appointed in a Chapter 11 case. Rather, the debtor remains in control of the property of the estate as debtor-in-possession and enjoys the powers of a trustee. The possibility that current management may retain control of a corporation may make Chapter 11 more attractive than Chapter 7. Since a liquidating plan can be proposed in Chapter 11, the liquidation/rehabilitation dichotomy is not perfect.

Chapter 11 debtors receive a discharge as soon as the plan is confirmed. (In Chapter 13, the discharge is delayed until the debtor completes performance under the plan.) Thus, upon confirmation, the creditors' rights are those specified in the plan.

Chapter 11 cases may be protracted. The Code does not regulate the length of time that may pass before a plan is proposed and confirmed, although it does grant the debtor a limited period within which only the debtor may propose a plan (the so-called "exclusivity period"). Provisions in the 1994 Amendments, designed to expedite the Chapter 11 process in small business cases, shorten the exclusivity period and require that all plans be proposed within 160 days of the filing.

d. Chapter 12

Chapter 12, which was added to the Code in 1986, is a reorganization provision for family farmers with a steady source of income. Although it incorporates some aspects of Chapter 11, its roots in Chapter 13 are quite evident: only the debtor may file; eligibility is subject to debt limits (although the limits are higher in 12 than in 13); the debtor remains in possession of property of the estate; payments to creditors are determined by the terms of the plan and only the debtor can propose a plan; and discharge is delayed until performance under the plan is completed.

Unlike Chapter 13, the debtor's regular income must derive from a particular source—farming—whether the debtor is an individual or corporation.

e. Chapter 9

Chapter 9, which governs the bankruptcy of municipalities, is used only occasionally. We will not cover it in this casebook.

F. JURISDICTION AND VENUE

1. JURISDICTION

Subsections (a) and (b) of 28 U.S.C. § 1334 govern the basic grant of jurisdiction in bankruptcy cases:

> (a) Except as provided in subsection (b) of this section, the district courts shall have original and exclusive jurisdiction of all cases under title 11.
>
> (b) Notwithstanding any Act of Congress that confers exclusive jurisdiction on a court or courts other than the district courts, the district courts shall have original but not exclusive jurisdiction of all civil proceedings arising under title 11, or arising in or related to cases under title 11.

The apparent contradiction in these subsections (one providing that jurisdiction is exclusive and the other that it is not) is explained by understanding the distinction between "cases" and "proceedings" in bankruptcy. The "case" is the entire bankruptcy that adjudicates the whole financial relationship between a debtor and all of its creditors. A "proceeding" is a subset of a case—a civil dispute that deals with particular legal issues and often involves the debtor and only an individual creditor. Each bankruptcy "case" may involve many "proceedings."

Note that the grant of jurisdiction is to district courts and not to bankruptcy courts. Bankruptcy courts originated as an administrative branch of district courts, governed by "referees." Bankruptcy judges today are Article I judges; they do not have the life tenure and protection from diminution in salary that is enjoyed by Article III judges, such as those appointed to the district and appellate courts.

This distinction was critical in *Northern Pipeline Construction Co. v. Marathon Pipe Line Co.*, 458 U.S. 50, 102 S.Ct. 2858, 73 L.Ed.2d 598 (1982), in which a debtor-in-possession brought suit in bankruptcy court for breach of a prepetition contract. The defendant asserted that the bankruptcy court lacked jurisdiction and that Congress could not authorize the bankruptcy court to hear such cases. The Supreme Court agreed, holding that the Constitution does not allow bankruptcy judges, who lack life tenure, to hear and determine cases such as the one at bar. The suit was neither directly related to the bankruptcy proceeding, nor a case in which a third party was suing the bankruptcy estate.

For practical purposes, *Marathon* voided bankruptcy court jurisdiction under the 1978 Bankruptcy Code. Congress had to amend the Code to revive the bankruptcy courts' power to hear bankruptcy cases. Simply making bankruptcy judges Article III judges—the easiest solution—was not a politically viable option. Congress, therefore, solved the *Marathon* dilemma by granting jurisdiction to the Article III judges of the district courts rather than to bankruptcy courts. Congress then provided, in 28 U.S.C. § 157(a), that district courts can delegate jurisdiction to the bankruptcy courts in "cases under" the Bankruptcy Code and in "proceedings arising under * * * or arising in or related to" the Code.

Subsection 157(b)(1) permits a bankruptcy judge to "hear and determine * * * all core proceedings arising under title 11, or arising in a case under title 11." Subsection 157(b)(2) provides a nonexclusive list of "core proceedings." The proceedings in the list, such as allowance of claims and objections to discharge, are ones that invoke substantial rights under the Code or can only arise in conjunction with a bankruptcy case. In other words, a core proceeding is "inextricably linked" to the bankruptcy case.

If a proceeding is "noncore," a bankruptcy judge may "hear and determine" it only if the parties consent. 28 U.S.C. § 157(c)(2). Otherwise, the bankruptcy judge may "hear" the matter, but cannot determine it; the bankruptcy judge must submit proposed findings of fact and conclusions of law to the district judge, who may enter those findings and conclusions "after consideration." The district judge must make a de novo review upon the record, or, if additional evidence is submitted, of any part of the bankruptcy judge's findings of fact or conclusions of law to which a party objected in accordance with Bankruptcy Rule 9033. The district judge may accept, reject, or modify the proposed findings of fact or conclusions of law, receive further evidence, or recommit the matter to the bankruptcy judge with instructions.

Congress determined that neither the district court nor the bankruptcy court should handle state law causes of action that are related to but that do not arise under title 11. Accordingly, 28 U.S.C. § 1334(c)(2) provides that a party to a proceeding based on a state law claim or cause of action may move the district court to abstain from hearing the proceeding if an action is commenced and can be timely adjudicated in an appropriate state forum. Section 1334(c) has been interpreted as a "clear congressional policy * * * to give state law claimants a right to have claims heard in state court." *Piombo Corp. v. Castlerock Properties (In re Castlerock Properties),* 781 F.2d 159, 163 (9th Cir.1986).

Though these jurisdictional rules are perhaps not a perfect solution, they have been effective thus far.

WOOD v. WOOD (MATTER OF WOOD)

United States Court of Appeals, Fifth Circuit, 1987.
825 F.2d 90.

WISDOM, Circuit Judge.

This appeal calls upon us to decipher the jurisdictional provisions of the Bankruptcy Amendments and Federal Judgeship Act of 1984. A brief history of the Act may cast some light on the nature of our task.

Years of effort to reform the bankruptcy laws culminated with the enactment of the Bankruptcy Reform Act of 1978. As part of its overall goal to create a more efficient procedure for administering bankruptcies, the 1978 Act vested broad powers in the bankruptcy courts. This reform was short-lived. In 1982 the Supreme Court decided *Marathon v. Northern Pipelines*.[2] The Court declared the jurisdictional provision of the 1978 Act unconstitutional because, in short, it vested Article III judicial power in Article I judges. Courts were left to their own devices while Congress deliberated a response to *Marathon*. With prompting from bench, bar, and law professors with expertise in bankruptcy, Congress responded with the Bankruptcy Amendments and Federal Judgeship Act of 1984. Essentially, Congress reenacted the 1978 Act, but divided its jurisdictional grant into "core" proceedings, over which the bankruptcy courts exercise full judicial power—and "otherwise related" or "non-core" proceedings—over which the bankruptcy courts exercise only limited power. In this case, we must decide two issues: first, whether bankruptcy jurisdiction exists; second, if jurisdiction does exist, whether the bankruptcy court may proceed over this matter as a "core" or a "non-core" proceeding.

I.

This case results from a dispute among the directors/ stockholders of a medical clinic. In 1981, Dr. James Wood and Dr. Arthur Wood, III, formed the Wayne Clinic, P.A., each becoming the owner of 1000 shares of stock. In March of 1984, Dr. James Wood and his wife, Carol Wood, filed a Chapter 11 bankruptcy petition in the Southern District Court of Mississippi. In May of 1985, Dr. Arthur Wood filed a complaint in the same court is alleging [sic] that in November of 1984, Dr. and Mrs. James Wood and Woodrow Barham,

---

[2] 458 U.S. 50, 102 S.Ct. 2858, 73 L.Ed.2d 598 (1982).

acting together as directors of the clinic, wrongfully issued additional stock to Dr. James Wood. The complaint stated that in the Spring of 1985, Dr. James Wood received a disproportionate distribution from the clinic as the result of the wrongful stock issuance in violation of the agreement between Dr. James Wood and Dr. Arthur Wood that they were to be equal partners in the clinic. The complaint seeks damages and declaratory relief.

The bankruptcy judge of the district denied the defendants' motion to dismiss for lack of subject-matter jurisdiction and held that the matter was a core proceeding. On appeal to the district court, the court held that the matter was neither a "core" proceeding, over which the bankruptcy judge had full judicial power, nor an "otherwise related" or "non-core" proceeding, over which the bankruptcy judge has limited judicial power. The court dismissed the complaint for lack of subject-matter jurisdiction. The plaintiffs appealed to this Court.

II.

The starting point in our analysis is 28 U.S.C. § 1334. [*The court quoted subsections (a) and (b).*] Section 1334 lists four types of matters over which the district court has jurisdiction:

1. "cases under title 11",

2. "proceedings arising under title 11",

3. proceedings "arising in" a case under title 11, and

4. proceedings "related to" a case under title 11.

The first category refers merely to the bankruptcy petition itself, over which district courts (and their bankruptcy units) have original and exclusive jurisdiction. Our concern, however, is with the other proceedings listed in subsection 1334(b), over which the district courts have original, but not exclusive, jurisdiction.

There is almost no legislative history to guide us in interpreting the 1984 Act. Subsection 1334(b), however, was taken verbatim from subsection 1471(b) of the 1978 Act. The legislative history and judicial interpretations of that Act therefore are instructive.

Legislative history indicates that the phrase "arising under title 11, or arising in or related to cases under title 11" was meant, not to distinguish between different matters, but to identify collectively a broad range of matters subject to the bankruptcy jurisdiction of federal courts. Congress was concerned with the inefficiencies of piecemeal adjudication of matters affecting the administration of bankruptcies and intended to give federal courts the power to adjudicate all matters having an effect on the bankruptcy. Courts have recognized that the grant of jurisdiction under the 1978 Act was broad.

Nothing in *Marathon* suggests that we should read the corresponding provisions of the 1984 Act differently. The jurisdictional provision of the 1978 Act, § 1471, accomplished two things. First, subsection (b) vested an expansive bankruptcy jurisdiction in the district courts. Second, subsection (c) conferred the power to exercise that jurisdictional grant in the bankruptcy courts.[10] The issue in *Marathon* was not the constitutionality of subsection (b), but the constitutionality of subsection (c). *Marathon* held that Congress could not vest the whole of bankruptcy jurisdiction in bankruptcy courts because the jurisdictional grant encompassed proceedings too far removed from the "core" of traditional bankruptcy powers to allow them to be adjudicated by non-Article III judges. The holding in *Marathon* suggests no concern over the constitutionality of the scope of bankruptcy jurisdiction defined by Congress; its concern is with the *placement* of that jurisdiction in non-Article III courts. In response to *Marathon*, Congress altered the placement of bankruptcy jurisdiction by creating a statutory distinction between core and non-core proceedings and restricting the power of bankruptcy courts to adjudicate the latter. Because *Marathon* did not compel Congress to reduce the scope of bankruptcy jurisdiction, it seems plain that Congress intended no change in the scope of jurisdiction set forth in the 1978 Act when it later enacted § 1334 of the 1984 Act.

The district court expressed its concern that an overbroad interpretation of § 1334 would bring into federal court matters that should be left to state courts to decide. We have also expressed the same concern. There is no necessary reason why that concern must be met by restrictive interpretations of the statutory grant of jurisdiction under

---

[10] Section 1471(c) of the 1978 Act read:

> The bankruptcy court for the district in which a case under title 11 is commenced shall exercise all of the jurisdiction conferred by this section on the district courts.

§ 1334. The Act grants the district court broad power to abstain whenever appropriate "in the interest of justice, or in the interest of comity with State courts or respect for State law". The abstention provisions of the Act demonstrate the intent of Congress that concerns of comity and judicial convenience should be met, not by rigid limitations on the jurisdiction of federal courts, but by the discretionary exercise of abstention when appropriate in a particular case. Here, the possibility of abstention was not raised in the district court.

For the purpose of determining whether a particular matter falls within bankruptcy jurisdiction, it is not necessary to distinguish between proceedings "arising under", "arising in a case under", or "related to a case under", title 11. These references operate conjunctively to define the scope of jurisdiction. Therefore, it is necessary only to determine whether a matter is at least "related to" the bankruptcy. The Act does not define "related" matters. Courts have articulated various definitions of "related", but the definition of the Court of Appeals for the Third Circuit appears to have the most support: "whether the outcome of that proceeding could *conceivably* have any effect on the estate being administered in bankruptcy."[15] This definition comports with the legislative history of the statutory predecessor to § 1334. Neither *Marathon* nor general concerns of comity counsel against its use. We adopt it as our own.

Applying this test to case before us, we find that the complaint is sufficiently related to the pending bankruptcy to allow the district court to exercise jurisdiction under § 1334. The complaint against the bankruptcy debtors could have a conceivable effect on their bankruptcy. The plaintiff seeks to recover stock and monies that the debtors allegedly appropriated from the clinic. They seek to resolve the disputed allocation of interest in the clinic. To the extent that the debtors' interest in the clinic, their stock holdings, or their withdrawals are now property of the estate, the complaint against them has a potential effect on their estate.

The debtors argue that the complaint raises a post-petition claim that will not affect their bankruptcy.[16] Generally, post-petition claims are not dischargeable in bankruptcy and, therefore, do not affect the

---

[15] *Pacor, Inc. v. Higgins*, 743 F.2d 984, 994 (3d Cir.1984) (emphasis added).

[16] The complaint challenges the issuance of stock in November of 1984 and the withdrawal of money in Spring of 1985, both of which occurred after the filing of the bankruptcy petition in March of 1984.

estate. To fall within the court's jurisdiction, the plaintiffs' claims must affect the estate, not just the debtor. Although we acknowledge the possibility that this suit may ultimately have no effect on the bankruptcy, we cannot conclude, on the facts before us, that it will have no *conceivable* effect. First, the complaint raises a dispute over the division of ownership of the clinic. Because the debtors held their stock in the clinic before filing for bankruptcy, the disputed share is now part of the estate. Second, the complaint seeks to recover stock and cash withdrawals made after the filing of the petition. Although post-petition acquisitions of the debtor are generally not part of the estate, they may be estate property in this case if considered income from pre-petition property. We raise these possibilities, not to resolve them, for that matter is left to the district and bankruptcy courts to decide under federal law, but to illustrate the conceivable effect of the complaint on the administration of the bankruptcy.

Defendant Woodrow Barham argues that even if the court has jurisdiction over the claims against Dr. James Wood and his wife, it does not have jurisdiction over him because he is not a debtor-in-bankruptcy. The Bankruptcy Rules incorporate the joinder provisions of the Federal Rules of Civil Procedure allowing the joinder of other defendants. Joinder is allowed, however, only if an independent basis of federal jurisdiction exists to support the joined claim. We find that the claim against Woodrow Barham is "related to" the Wood's bankruptcy and, thus, its joinder is jurisdictionally supported.

The plaintiff has filed one complaint against the defendants seeking liability for their joint conduct. Success against any of the defendants will have a potential effect on the estate. For example, if Dr. Wood and his wife are held liable but Barham is not, the bankrupt estate may bear the entire burden of the judgment. If, on the other hand, Barham is found jointly liable, the estate may bear only a portion of the judgment. Moreover, in filing the complaint, the plaintiff challenged the combined actions of both the debtors and Barham, a non-debtor. Resolution of the dispute will necessarily involve, therefore, consideration of Barham's involvement in those actions. * * *

III.

We have decided that subject-matter jurisdiction exists over this proceeding. We must now determine the placement of that jurisdiction. Our analysis turns to 28 U.S.C. § 157, the response of Congress to *Marathon* and its replacement for subsection 1471(c) of the 1978 Act. In contrast to subsection 1471(c), § 157 does not give bankruptcy courts full judicial power over all matters over which the district courts have jurisdiction under § 1334. With respect to proceedings other than the bankruptcy petition itself, § 157 divides all proceedings into two categories. Subsection 157(b)(1) gives bankruptcy judges the power to determine "all core proceedings arising under title 11, or arising in a case under title 11" and to enter appropriate orders and judgments. Subsection 157(c)(2) gives the bankruptcy judge the limited power to hear "a proceeding that is not a core proceeding but that is otherwise related to a case under title 11" and to submit proposed findings of fact and conclusions of law to the district court, subject to de novo review. The essential distinction that must be made, therefore, is whether this action is a core or non-core proceeding.

The statute does not define core proceedings. Subsection (b)(2) does provide a nonexclusive list of examples, three of which are arguably relevant here:

> (A) matters concerning the administration of the estate;
>
> (B) allowance or disallowance of claims against the estate * * *; and
>
> (O) other proceedings affecting the liquidation of the assets of the estate or the adjustment of the debtor-creditor or the equity security holder relationship * * * .

We note that the last example is broadly worded; indeed, "proceedings affecting * * * the estate" is similar in scope to the test of jurisdiction: proceedings having a "conceivable effect on the estate". We decline, however, to give such a broad reading to subsection 157(b)(2)(O); otherwise, the entire range of proceedings under bankruptcy jurisdiction would fall within the scope of core proceedings, a result contrary to the ostensible purpose of the 1984 Act. That purpose is to conform the bankruptcy statute to the dictates of *Marathon*.

Specifically, *Marathon*, involved an adversarial proceeding brought by the debtor-in-bankruptcy on a pre-petition claim arising under state substantive law against a defendant who had not filed a claim in bankruptcy. A plurality of the Supreme Court held that the proceeding could not be adjudicated by the bankruptcy court. The exact extent of *Marathon*'s holding is subject to debate. Certain principles can be extracted from its opinions, principles that apparently have been incorporated into the 1984 Act.

Justice Brennan, writing for the plurality, held that only controversies involving "public rights", rights provided to an individual by Congress under one of its exceptional powers under the Constitution, may be removed from Article III courts and delegated to non-Article III tribunals. Justice Brennan implicitly recognized that the exceptional powers of Congress under the bankruptcy clause may sometimes allow for such delegations of judicial power:

> But the restructuring of debtor-creditor relations, which is at the *core* of the federal bankruptcy power, must be distinguished from the adjudication of state-created private rights, such as the right to recover contract damages that is at issue in this case. The former may well be a "public right," but the latter obviously is not.[27]

Concerning the latter controversy, he noted:

> This claim may be adjudicated in federal court on the basis of its relationship to the petition for reorganization. But this relationship does not transform the state-created right into a matter between the Government and the petitioner for reorganization. Even in the absence of the federal scheme, the plaintiff would be able to proceed against the defendant on the state-law contractual claims.[28]

Two points are suggested by this language. First, bankruptcy judges may exercise full judicial power over only those controversies that implicate the peculiar rights and powers of bankruptcy or, in Justice Brennan's words, controversies "at the core of the federal bankruptcy power". Second, controversies that do not depend on the bankruptcy laws for their existence—suits that could proceed in another court even in the absence of bankruptcy—are not core proceedings. These points are echoed by Chief Justice Burger in his dissent in which he characterized the plurality opinion as follows:

> the Court's holding is limited to the proposition * * * that a "traditonal" [sic] state common-law action, not made subject to a federal rule of decision, and related only peripherally to an adjudication of bankruptcy under federal law, must, absent the

---

[27] 458 U.S. at 71 (emphasis added).

[28] *Id.* at 72 n.26.

consent of the litigants, be heard by an "Article III court".[29]

Justice White expressed concern, however, that the plurality's holding placed too much emphasis on the existence of state law issues in the proceeding before bankruptcy court:

> Second, the distinction between claims based on state law and those based on federal law disregards the real character of bankruptcy proceedings. * * * The crucial point to be made is that in the ordinary bankruptcy proceeding the great bulk of creditor claims are claims that have accrued under state law prior to bankruptcy—claims for goods sold, wages, rent, utilities, and the like. * * * Every such claim must be filed and its validity is subject to adjudication by the bankruptcy court. The existence and validity of such claims recurringly depend on state law. Hence, the bankruptcy judge is constantly enmeshed in state-law issues.[30]

Section 157 of the 1984 Act incorporates the principles suggested in the language of the *Marathon* opinions. The reference in the Act to "core" proceedings is taken directly from Justice Brennan's description of matters that involve the peculiar powers of bankruptcy courts. The Act describes non-core proceedings as "otherwise related", an apparent reference to Chief Justice Burger's description of the *Marathon* proceeding as "related only peripherally to an adjudication of bankruptcy". Mindful of the limitations of the plurality's holding and of Justice White's observations concerning state law, Congress added: "A determination that a proceeding is not a core proceeding shall not be made solely on the basis that its resolution may be affected by State law."[31]

The meaning of core proceedings is illuminated also by the textual context in which it appears. Subsection 157(b)(1) vests full judicial power in bankruptcy courts over "core proceedings *arising under title 11, or arising in a case under title 11.*" The prepositional qualifications of core proceedings are taken from two of the three categories of jurisdiction set forth in § 1334(b): proceedings "arising

---

29 *Id.* at 92 (Burger, C.J., dissenting).

30 *Id.* at 96-97 (White, J., dissenting).

31 28 U.S.C. § 157(b)(3).

under" title 11, "arising in" title 11 cases, and "related to" title 11 cases. Although the purpose of this language in § 1334(b) is to define conjunctively the scope of jurisdiction, each category has a distinguishable meaning. These meanings become relevant because § 157 apparently equates core proceedings with the categories of "arising under" and "arising in" proceedings.

Congress used the phrase "arising under title 11" to describe those proceedings that involve a cause of action created or determined by a statutory provision of title 11. Apparently, the phrase was taken from 28 U.S.C. § 1331, conferring federal question jurisdiction in which it carries a similar and well-accepted meaning. The meaning of "arising in" proceedings is less clear, but seems to be a reference to those "administrative" matters that arise *only* in bankruptcy cases. In other words, "arising in" proceedings are those that are not based on any right expressly created by title 11, but nevertheless, would have no existence outside of the bankruptcy.

As defined above, the phrases "arising under" and "arising in" are helpful indicators of the meaning of core proceedings. If the proceeding involves a right created by the federal bankruptcy law, it is a core proceeding; for example, an action by the trustee to avoid a preference. If the proceeding is one that would arise only in bankruptcy, it is also a core proceeding; for example, the filing of a proof of claim or an objection to the discharge of a particular debt. If the proceeding does not invoke a substantive right created by the federal bankruptcy law and is one that could exist outside of bankruptcy it is not a core proceeding; it may be *related* to the bankruptcy because of its potential effect, but under § 157(c)(1) it is an "otherwise related" or non-core proceeding.

Finally, the interpretation of core proceeding based on its equation with "arising under" and "arising in" proceedings comports with the interpretation suggested by *Marathon*. Justice Brennan's description of "core" matters parallels that of matters "arising under" title 11—matters invoking a substantive right created by federal bankruptcy law. Moreover, his comment that the matter could have proceeded absent the bankruptcy suggests a contrast with "arising in" proceedings—matters that could arise only in bankruptcy.

We hold, therefore, that a proceeding is core under § 157 if it invokes a substantive right provided by title 11 or if it is a proceeding that, by its nature, could arise only in the context of a bankruptcy case.

The proceeding before us does not meet this test and, accordingly, is a non-core proceeding. The plaintiff's suit is not based on any right created by the federal bankruptcy law. It is based on state created rights.[34] Moreover, this suit is not a proceeding that could arise only in the context of a bankruptcy. It is simply a state contract action that, had there been no bankruptcy, could have proceeded in state court.

The plaintiff argues that his action is literally a claim against the estate, which is expressly defined as a core proceeding by § 157-(b)(2)(B). We disagree. In determining the nature of a proceeding for purposes of determining core status, the court must look to both the form and the substance of the proceeding. The form of this action is not that of a "claim" as that term is used in bankruptcy law. A claim against the estate is instituted by filing a proof of claim as provided by the bankruptcy rules. The filing of the proof invokes the special rules of bankruptcy concerning objections to the claim, estimation of the claim for allowance purposes, and the rights of the claimant to vote on the proposed distribution. Understood in this sense, a claim filed against the estate is a core proceeding because it could arise only in the context of bankruptcy. Of course, the state-law right underlying the claim could be enforced in a state court proceeding absent the bankruptcy, but the nature of the state proceeding would be different from the nature of the proceeding following the filing of a proof of claim. Here, the plaintiff has not filed a proof of claim and has not invoked the peculiar powers of the bankruptcy court.

The substance of this action does not support a finding of core status. The essential issue in the proceeding is whether the defendants are liable to the plaintiff under state law. The suit does not raise as primary issues such matters as dischargeability, allowance of the claim, or other bankruptcy matters. Conceivably, a final judgment in this proceeding in the plaintiff's favor may lead to proceedings to allow the claim or to discharge the debt. At this juncture, however, these concerns are speculative and insubstantial issues in the proceeding. The plaintiff's suit is not a core proceeding.

The judgment of the district court is VACATED and the case is remanded to the district court for further proceedings consistent with this opinion.

---

[34] We are mindful that, alone, this circumstance should not be dispositive. 28 U.S.C. § 157(b)(3).

RALPH BRUBAKER, ONE HUNDRED YEARS OF FEDERAL BANKRUPTCY LAW AND STILL CLINGING TO AN IN REM MODEL OF BANKRUPTCY JURISDICTION

15 Bankr. Dev. J. 261, 269-77 (1999) (most footnotes omitted).

One of the primary targets of the bankruptcy reform efforts of the 1970s, of course, was the 1898 Act's *in rem* jurisdictional scheme. The federalism concerns that motivated the 1898 Act's restrictive federal bankruptcy jurisdiction had subsided considerably and, consequently, were dwarfed by the manifest inefficiencies and inequities produced by the summary/plenary dichotomy and its splintering of bankruptcy jurisdiction. The jurisdictional provisions of the resulting Bankruptcy Reform Act of 1978 were variously characterized in Congress as: "pervasive," "complete," "comprehensive," "as broad [a] jurisdiction as possible," and "as broad as can be conceived." This pervasive federal bankruptcy jurisdiction was explicitly designed to eliminate the summary/plenary dichotomy and its *in rem* confines, permitting the federal courts to "exercise in personam as well as in rem jurisdiction in order that they may handle everything that arises in a bankruptcy case."

Unfortunately, however, we are yet to fully realize this vision of complete, unrestricted *in personam* federal bankruptcy jurisdiction. A significant stumbling block standing in the way of full *in personam* bankruptcy jurisdiction is Congress's decision to not make the bankruptcy courts Article III courts. After the *Marathon* case and the ensuing Bankruptcy Amendments and Federal Judgeship Act (BAFJA) of 1984, we are left with federal bankruptcy jurisdiction that is divided between the non-Article III bankruptcy courts and the federal district courts, and that division predominately follows the lines of the 1898 Act's summary/plenary dichotomy which, of course, itself originated in the English *in rem* model of bankruptcy jurisdiction. That is an *in rem* aspect of bankruptcy jurisdiction with which we must suffer, however, at least until it becomes politically feasible to elevate the bankruptcy courts to Article III status. The objective of this essay, though, is to explore a less obvious realm of bankruptcy jurisdiction that remains haunted by *in rem* ghosts: the outermost limits of federal bankruptcy jurisdiction.

Marathon and the 1984 BAFJA amendments were concerned with an issue of separation of powers, and *Marathon*'s proscription, at its most basic level, was that the entirety of the 1978 Reform Act's pervasive federal bankruptcy jurisdiction cannot be assigned to non-Article III bankruptcy courts. That separation-of-powers holding speaks solely to the proper allocation of federal bankruptcy jurisdiction as between Article III and non-article III federal tribunals. *Marathon* and BAFJA, however, say nothing about the issue traced in this essay's historical overview, which pertains to the *scope* of federal bankruptcy jurisdiction. Irrespective of the type of federal judicial officer that will exercise it (Article III or non-Article III), what is the full extent of federal bankruptcy jurisdiction?

The scope of federal bankruptcy jurisdiction is, of course, a judicial federalism issue going to the allocation of judicial power as between the federal courts and the state courts. What disputes can we essentially take from the state courts and place before the federal courts through our pervasive federal bankruptcy jurisdiction? This essay will suggest that the scope of federal bankruptcy jurisdiction has been unnecessarily constricted by lingering *in rem* jurisdictional notions.

A. Pacor*'s* In Rem *Model of "Related To" Bankruptcy Jurisdiction*

The scope of federal bankruptcy jurisdiction is still defined by the same statutory grant as that of the 1978 Reform Act: federal bankruptcy jurisdiction over "all civil proceedings arising under [the Bankruptcy Code], or arising in or related to [bankruptcy] cases." The "related to" jurisdictional nexus is the most expansive portion of this grant and extends federal bankruptcy jurisdiction further than any of the prior bankruptcy statutes. Thus, "related to" bankruptcy jurisdiction goes beyond even Justice Story's image of a general federal bankruptcy jurisdiction over all claims by and against the bankruptcy estate. "Related to" bankruptcy jurisdiction creates federal jurisdiction over third-party disputes to which the bankruptcy estate is not a party, but that are nonetheless "related to" a bankruptcy case in some manner.

The dominant test that the courts have adopted to determine whether a third-party dispute is within "related to" bankruptcy jurisdiction is from the Third Circuit's opinion in *Pacor, Inc. v. Higgins*:

> The usual articulation of the test for determining whether a civil proceeding is related to bankruptcy is whether the outcome of that proceeding could conceivably have any effect on the estate being administered in bankruptcy. * * * An action is related to bankruptcy if the outcome could alter the debtor's rights, liabilities, options, or freedom of action (either

> positively or negatively) and which in any way impacts upon the handling and administration of the bankrupt estate.[53]

Under the *Pacor* test, then, there is "related to" bankruptcy jurisdiction over a third-party dispute whose outcome could conceivably affect the bankruptcy estate, even though the bankruptcy estate itself is not party to the dispute.

Pacor's "any conceivable effect" test is obviously a very broad test and in many respects is overly broad, to the point of permitting patently unconstitutional exercises of federal jurisdiction over non-diverse state-law claims. At the same time that the *Pacor* test is too broad, though, it is also excessively narrow—in a manner that betrays it as an *in rem* anachronism.

As an illustration of how *Pacor* is too narrow, take the example of a *Marathon*-like action: debtor with a state-law breach of contract cause against a defendant files a chapter 11 petition, becoming a chapter 11 debtor-in-possession whose bankruptcy estate succeeds to the breach of contract action. Debtor then brings suit against the defendant in federal court pursuant to federal bankruptcy jurisdiction. Federal jurisdiction over that suit on behalf of the debtor's bankruptcy estate, of course, fits comfortably within Justice Story's idea of a general federal bankruptcy jurisdiction over all claims by and against the estate, and the *Marathon* opinions presumed the propriety of federal jurisdiction over such a state-law claim as part of the 1978 Reform Act's pervasive federal bankruptcy jurisdiction.

Now, imagine that the debtor's state-law suit in federal court is against two defendants—against defendant-1 for breach of contract and against defendant-2 for tortious interference with debtor's contractual relations with defendant-1—and both defendants in that suit make state-law cross-claims against each other for contribution and indemnification, seeking reimbursement for any amounts they might be required to pay the debtor's estate in the suit. The Bankruptcy Rules expressly permit joinder of the debtor's claims against the two defendants and the defendants' cross-claims against each other in one action, and it makes perfect sense for the defendants' cross-claims to be heard in federal court in conjunction with the debtor's claims against the defendants that give rise to those cross-claims.

---

[53] 743 F.2d 984, 994 (3d Cir. 1984).

Indeed, the efficiency, fairness, and convenience of bundling such logically and factually related claims in one suit is the impetus for the doctrine of federal courts' supplemental jurisdiction (which now subsumes the subsidiary concepts of what were once known as ancillary and pendent jurisdiction). Supplemental jurisdiction permits a federal court to hear state-law claims that have no independent basis for federal jurisdiction, but that are nonetheless transactionally related to claims over which the federal court does have independent jurisdiction, and the federal courts routinely employ supplemental jurisdiction to entertain state-law cross-claims such as those in our hypothetical suit.

Using the *Pacor* test for "related to" bankruptcy jurisdiction of a third-party dispute, however, the courts have concluded that there is no jurisdiction over cross-claims such as those asserted in the suit by our chapter 11 debtor-in-possession. According to the *Pacor* test, the outcome of those cross-claims could have no effect on the debtor's chapter 11 estate, because the cross-claims will have no impact on the estate's recovery from the defendants. In fact, such a cross-claim presupposes that the bankruptcy estate has already successfully recovered from a particular defendant, and the cross-claim merely reallocates ultimate responsibility for that recovery between the defendants. Therefore, the cross-claims for contribution and indemnification are not "related to" the debtor's bankruptcy case under the *Pacor* test.

As this author argues elsewhere at length, such a result evidences an extremely myopic view of the intended function of "related to" bankruptcy jurisdiction.[63] In fact, the 1978 Reform Act's all-encompassing jurisdictional scheme was justified, as a policy matter, on precisely the same grounds of procedural convenience, fairness, and judicial economy that would commend an exercise of supplemental jurisdiction over such cross-claims.

Rather ironically, *Pacor*'s untoward repression of "related to" jurisdiction can largely be attributed to an *in rem* bias inherent in the *Pacor* test. *Pacor* essentially regards the bankruptcy estate as a jurisdictional *res*. A particular claim is within federal bankruptcy jurisdiction, according to *Pacor*, if the claim has a sufficient outcome-oriented, functional relationship to the jurisdictional *res*—*Pacor*'s "effect on the estate" test. *Pacor*, then, embraces the old English *in rem* model of bankruptcy jurisdiction and simply adopts a more expansive *in rem* nexus.

---

[63] Ralph Brubaker, *On the Nature of Federal Bankruptcy Jurisdiction: A General Statutory and Constitutional Theory*, 41 WM. & MARY L. REV. 743 (2000).

Pacor does not effectuate the shift from an *in rem* to an *in personam* model of bankruptcy jurisdiction envisioned by Congress in abandoning the 1898 Act's jurisdictional regime; it merely extends the *in rem* model.

2. VENUE

a. Venue of the Case

Proper venue for the entire bankruptcy *case*—that is, the court in which the petition under §§ 301, 302 or 303 should be filed—lies in the place where the debtor's domicile, residence, principal place of business or principal assets have been located for the greatest period of time in the six months preceding the filing of the petition. 28 U.S.C. § 1408. Since venue may be proper in more than one place in a given case, the party filing the bankruptcy petition may have a choice. This creates the potential for forum shopping.

Professors LoPucki and Whitford conducted an empirical study of the bankruptcy reorganization of the 43 largest publicly held companies to file and complete bankruptcy proceedings from 1979 to 1988. Lynn M. LoPucki & William C. Whitford, *Venue Choice and Forum Shopping in the Bankruptcy Reorganization of Large, Publicly Held Companies*, 1991 Wis. L. Rev. 11. The authors found extensive evidence of forum shopping in the course of their research. They found that when forum shopping occurred, either "a deliberate decision was made to proceed in a district other than the district in which the company was based" or the cases "proceeded at the venue of the company's headquarters, but those headquarters were located in a district where the company had little or no physical assets or operations, other than the headquarters itself." *Id.* at 13, 26–27. The authors suggested that reform should target the disparity of results between jurisdictions, however, rather than attempt to eliminate the opportunity for forum shopping in bankruptcy cases.

Professor LoPucki has continued his study of large corporate reorganizations and the persistent evidence of forum shopping in those cases. In the following excerpt, he and his co-author, Professor Eisenberg, discuss the evolution toward filing in the place of incorporation—often, Delaware:

> For almost two decades, an embarrassing pattern of forum shopping has been developing in the highly visible world of big-case bankruptcy reorganization. Forum shopping—defined here as

the act of filing in a court that does not serve the geographical area of the debtor's corporate headquarters—now occurs in more than half of all big-case bankruptcies.

Two jurisdictions have attracted most of the forum shoppers. During the 1980s, when a large portion of the shopping was to New York, the lawyers involved asserted that New York was a natural venue because of its role as the country's financial capital and because so many of the companies, creditors, and professionals involved had their offices there. In the early 1990s, however, when the favored destination shifted abruptly from New York to Delaware, these explanations wore thin. Delaware was then a sleepy, back-water bankruptcy district virtually devoid of bankruptcy professionals or corporate headquarters.

In response to widespread concern and the "troubling specter of courts competing for big-case bankruptcy business," the National Bankruptcy Review Commission recommended in the fall of 1997 that Congress amend the bankruptcy venue statute to prevent forum shoppers from filing in Delaware. One influential participant in the Commission's deliberations crystallized the sentiment for change, stating that "the effort to find debtor-friendly courts * * * demeaned the entire system by suggesting that bankruptcy courts were for sale." While the Commission deliberated, the Delaware federal court reacted by shifting the assignment of cases from the bankruptcy court to the district court.

This Article reports the results of a comprehensive study of big-case bankruptcy forum shopping from 1980 to 1997. A description of what has occurred helps explain both the causes of Delaware's rise as the preferred Chapter 11 forum and why embarrassment forced the system to take extraordinary countermeasures. The temporal coincidence of three major changes in Chapter 11 practice obscures those causes: (1) a nationwide increase in the rate of Chapter 11 forum shopping; (2) a national trend toward faster case-processing times; and (3) the rise of "prepackaged" bankruptcy cases in which the necessary majorities of creditors have accepted the reorganization plan before the debtor files the case. * * *

This Article casts doubt on the two common explanations for forum shoppers' attraction to Delaware: (1) that Delaware resolves bankruptcy cases more quickly, and (2) that Delaware has developed expertise in prepackaged cases. No statistically significant evidence exists that Delaware processes large Chapter 11 cases more quickly than other districts. The faster processing time * * * reported for Delaware, and thus Delaware's seeming comparative efficiency in resolving bankruptcy cases, is almost entirely a consequence of Delaware having a larger proportion of prepackaged cases than other districts. Moreover, Delaware does not process prepackaged cases significantly faster than other districts. We do find statistically significant evidence that New York processes cases slower than other bankruptcy courts. These findings cast further doubt on the argument that forum shopping targets the most efficient court.

Forum-shopping debtors must believe that the benefits of filing in Delaware outweigh the costs. The Delaware Bankruptcy Court requires that local counsel represent each party, adding an expense that the debtor usually would not incur when filing elsewhere. Because debtors who file in Delaware also incur travel expenses for nonlocal professionals and company personnel, the direct costs of forum shopping to Delaware are not trivial. Forum-shopping debtors must believe that the benefits of filing in Delaware are substantial.

* * *

Delaware's replacement of New York in 1990 as the forum shopper's destination of choice makes sense only in light of the political context in which it occurred. Changes in New York's judge-assignment mechanisms and a bankruptcy venue decision in Delaware, in combination with Delaware's recognized tradition of providing pro-corporate legal structures, may have triggered this shift to Delaware. Once Delaware gained a reputation as a shopping destination, this reputation probably persisted in part because the state had become a safe choice for bankruptcy lawyers and their clients. Nevertheless, for venue choice to become an issue, there first must exist some dissatisfaction with the home court.

* * *

Though the term "forum shopping" has a pejorative connotation, forum shopping is far from universally condemned. * * * One type of forum shopping, however, has received uniform condemnation and likely will lead to disciplinary proceedings against the attorney involved—shopping for judges. Observers seem to agree that judge shopping "breeds disrespect for and threatens the integrity of our judicial system" and undermines the aphorism that "ours is a government of laws, not men."

The principal means of preventing judge shopping within the same judicial panel is random case assignment. Shopping among the judges of different courts is more difficult to control, but holds less potential for embarrassment because the reason for inter-court shopping is ambiguous. The system's defenders plausibly can assert that the pattern of case filing observed demonstrates not judge shopping, but merely shopping for convenience, juries, or law.

These benign explanations, however, are not always available. Convenience cannot explain the forum shopping that this Article explores because this shopping has focused successively on two courts, New York and Delaware, neither of which is convenient to the filers. Nor can a search for friendly juries explain Chapter 11 forum shopping. Juries play no significant role in bankruptcy cases. Differences in law and procedure cannot drive the shopping because the governing law and procedure are federal. Theoretically, every significant aspect of Chapter 11 reorganization is uniform throughout the United States. Significant, persistent differences among bankruptcy courts that would make forum shopping the norm should be impossible. Contrary to these implausible explanations, the persistence of forum shopping demonstrates the importance of judges to litigants and, implicitly, the relative unimportance of law.

This discussion does not imply that bankruptcy judges are less likely to "follow the law" than other judges. Rather, it is easier to demonstrate in the context of bankruptcy that the principal purpose of forum shopping is to obtain or avoid the assignment of particular judges than it is to demonstrate the same in other contexts. The business of the bankruptcy courts is narrow and repetitive, allowing strategically minded lawyers to compare more easily the decisions and practices of one judge with those of another. When these lawyers express their preferences through forum shopping, they create the pattern that this Article documents. Strategically minded lawyers would have more difficulty discovering and comparing the views of judges who sit on courts of general jurisdiction and confront a much wider range of issues. These lawyers therefore would be less likely to have the knowledge base necessary to shop for nonbankruptcy judges in different jurisdictions.

* * *

> * * * The message of this forum-shopping pattern is troubling. Although bankruptcy law and procedure are uniform throughout the United States, the perception that case processing is different across cities induces forum shopping. Thus, the system's worst fears about the reasons for shopping are likely correct: debtors shopped to New York and now shop to Delaware in large part to secure particular judges or to avoid judges in their home districts.
>
> * * *
>
> Closing Delaware, the most visible manifestation of the nonuniformity that breeds forum shopping, would provide the system with a fig leaf. It arguably would reduce the aggregate level of forum shopping because no other district has proven to be as attractive as Delaware and no other district has so many large companies with a connection that would plausibly make the district an appropriate place to file. But this study's findings that Chapter 11 forum shopping is in significant part driven by judge shopping and by source-district conditions suggest that, even without Delaware, forum shopping would continue.

Theodore Eisenberg & Lynn M. Lopucki, *Shopping for Judges: An Empirical Analysis of Venue Choice in Large Chapter 11 Reorganizations*, 84 Cornell L. Rev. 967, 968-73, 1001-03 (1999) (footnotes omitted).

b. Venue of Proceedings

Under 28 U.S.C. § 1409(a), proper venue for a *proceeding* in a bankruptcy case lies in the district court in which the bankruptcy case is pending. In two specific instances, venue is *mandated* in the place that will prevent unfairness to third parties sued by a trustee or debtor-in-possession. First, if a bankruptcy trustee or debtor-in-possession attempts to collect a money judgment of less than $1,000, recover property worth less than $1,000 or collect a consumer debt of less than $5,000, venue lies in the district where the defendant resides. 28 U.S.C. § 1409(b). Second, if a claim arises from the debtor's business after commencement of the bankruptcy case, venue lies in the district in which a state or federal court would have had jurisdiction in the absence of bankruptcy. 28 U.S.C. § 1409(d).

If a claim arises from operation of the debtor's business after the filing and the plaintiff is the nondebtor, rather than the trustee or debtor-in-possession, then venue lies in the district court for the district in which either a state or federal court would have had jurisdiction under applicable nonbankruptcy law, or in the district in which the bankruptcy case is pending.

Finally, § 1409(c) provides an alternative venue for proceedings brought by the trustee or debtor-in-possession to claim property of the estate under § 541, or to avoid certain transfers under § 544(b). Such a proceeding can be brought in the district in which the suit could have been filed, either in state or federal court, in the absence of bankruptcy.

c. Change of Venue

Section 1412 of title 28 provides that "[a] district court may transfer a case or proceeding" in bankruptcy to another district court "in the interest of justice or for the convenience of the parties." If the original venue is proper, the party seeking a change of venue bears the burden of proving that a change of venue serves the interest of justice or eliminates inconvenience to the parties. Courts faced with a change of venue issue generally look to the following factors: (1) the economic harm to the debtor and creditors that would result from the change of venue; (2) the location of estate assets; (3) the economic administration of the estate; (4) the necessity for ancillary administration if liquidation should result; (5) the effect of the transfer on the parties' and witnesses' willingness and ability to participate in the case or proceeding; and (6) any interrelationship with another bankruptcy case involving the debtor's affiliate, general partner or partnership.

The result is much less clear if the original venue is improper. As enacted in 1978, the Code permitted the court in such a case, "in the interest of justice and for the convenience of the parties," either to retain or transfer the case or proceeding. The provision gave a court no authority to dismiss the matter. That section was repealed in 1984 and replaced by § 1412, quoted above. Section 1412 does not mention improper venue or authorize dismissal. Rule 1014(a)(2), which authorized a court to retain a case or proceeding despite improper venue, was amended in 1987. It now provides that a case "may be dismissed or transferred * * * in the interest of justice or for the convenience of the parties." Because no mention is made of retaining jurisdiction, it remains unclear whether a court can hear such a matter in the absence of waiver by the parties.

Chapter 2

THE FIRST CONSEQUENCES OF BANKRUPTCY

A. INTRODUCTION

Bankruptcy law effects a balance of interests, protecting the debtor, creditors, and the integrity of the bankruptcy court's jurisdiction. A bankruptcy proceeding, unlike state debt collection proceedings, brings together all of the debtor's creditors in a single forum, so that even the smallest creditor may participate. This, too, serves the debtor's interests. Only a proceeding that seeks to protect the interests of both debtors and creditors can achieve the Code's purpose of giving "honest but unfortunate" debtors a "fresh start."

As you read the cases and commentary throughout this chapter, keep in mind that bankruptcy policy is dynamic. Professors Ponoroff and Knippenberg noted that "legitimate questions remain about the limits of the bankruptcy process. * * * [M]uch about the scope of bankruptcy policy can be learned by observing courts' use of the good faith device in the decided case law. This information is valuable both in a descriptive sense and because of its powerful predictive capabilities." Lawrence Ponoroff & F. Stephen Knippenberg, *The Implied Good Faith Filing Requirement: Sentinel of an Evolving Bankruptcy Policy,* 85 Nw. U.L. Rev. 919, 938 n.59 (1991). The authors described two views regarding the purpose of bankruptcy:

> "Collectivism," as we use that term, should be taken to mean the set of shared fundamental assumptions and postulates

> of a group of scholars writing mainly from an economics-based perspective of the law. * * *
>
> For the Collectivists, * * * bankruptcy serves a single purpose: it is a federal debt collection system. Accordingly, bankruptcy is properly invoked only in response to a common pool problem, a term Jackson uses to describe the situation created when a debtor's assets are insufficient to satisfy the demands of a common pool of claimants. The purpose of bankruptcy—or, to use Jackson's term, the "first principle" of bankruptcy—is to serve as a debt collection device targeted to the common pool problem.
>
> * * * [In contrast, Professor Elizabeth Warren's Traditionalism proposes] that while debt collectivizing is always relevant in bankruptcy, it can be sacrificed when necessary to achieve other goals and purposes of the bankruptcy process. * * *
>
> By providing for the interests of non-creditors, the Traditional view recognizes that the financial collapse of a firm presents questions of loss allocation and community interest simply not implicated in individual debtor-creditor disputes. For this reason, the Traditionalist believes that the bankruptcy system is and should be designed to address a broad range of interests affected by the collapse of a debtor enterprise. This broad range should include, but not consist exclusively of, the interests of creditors with unpaid state law claims. Brought within the bankruptcy process, diverse interests can be taken into account and, perhaps, protected and accommodated collectively under the auspice of the proceeding itself.

Id. at 949–50, 959–61 (footnotes omitted).

The "common pool" problem to which Professors Ponoroff and Knippenberg referred, is an analytical analogy used to explain the purposes of bankruptcy law. It is well summarized in Thomas H. Jackson's book, The Logic and Limits of Bankruptcy Law (1986):

> Imagine that you own a lake. There are fish in the lake. You are the only one who has the right to fish in that lake, and no one constrains your decision as to how much fishing to do. You have it in your power to catch all the fish this year and sell them for, say, $100,000. If you did that, however, there would be no

fish in the lake next year. It might be better for you—you might maximize your total return from fishing—if you caught and sold some fish this year but left other fish in the lake so that they could multiply and you would have fish in subsequent years. Assume that, by taking this approach, you could earn (adjusting for inflation) $50,000 each year. Having this outcome is like having a perpetual annuity paying $50,000 a year. It has a present value of perhaps $500,000. Since (obviously, I hope) when all other things are equal, $500,000 is better than $100,000, you, as sole owner, would limit your fishing this year unless some other factor influenced you.

But what if you are not the only one who can fish in this lake? What if a hundred people can do so? The optimal solution has not changed: it would be preferable to leave some fish in the lake to multiply because doing so has a present value of $500,000. But in this case, unlike that where you have to control only yourself, an obstacle exists in achieving that result. If there are a hundred fishermen, you cannot be sure, by limiting *your* fishing, that there will be any more fish next year, unless you can also control the others. You may, then, have an incentive to catch as many fish as you can today because maximizing your take this year (catching, on average, $1,000 worth of fish) is better for you than holding off (catching, say, only $500 worth of fish this year) while others scramble and deplete the stock entirely. If you hold off, your aggregate return is only $500, since nothing will be left for next year or the year after. But that sort of reasoning by each of the hundred fishermen will mean that the stock of fish will be gone by the end of the first season. The fishermen will split $100,000 this year, but there will be no fish—and no money—in future years. Self-interest results in their splitting $100,000, not $500,000.

What is required is some rule that will make all hundred fishermen act as a sole owner would. That is where bankruptcy law enters the picture in a world not of fish but of credit. The grab rules of nonbankruptcy law and their allocation of assets on the basis of first-come, first-served create an incentive on the part of the individual creditors, when they sense that a debtor may have more liabilities than assets, to get in line today (by, for example, getting a sheriff to execute on the debtor's equipment), because if they do not, they run the risk of getting nothing. This decision by numerous individual creditors, however, may be the wrong decision for the creditors as a group.

> Even though the debtor is insolvent, they might be better off if they held the assets together. Bankruptcy provides a way to make these diverse individuals act as one, by imposing a *collective* and *compulsory* proceeding on them.

Id. at 11–13 (footnotes omitted).

B. INITIATING THE PROCEEDINGS

1. VOLUNTARY PROCEEDINGS

Section 301 of the Bankruptcy Code provides for the commencement of voluntary cases under any chapter of the Code, and § 302 governs joint cases. Under § 301, any debtor who meets the § 109 requirements may commence a bankruptcy action by filing a petition under the appropriate chapter of the Code. Read §§ 109, 301 and 302 (remembering to consult § 101 for pertinent definitions), and answer the following Problems.

Notes and Problems

1. Under which chapter(s) of the Code could each of the following debtors file a voluntary petition?

a. Last Federal Savings and Loan, which sustained substantial losses due to improvident loan policies.

b. Imprudential Insurance Company, which insured only property in the counties hardest hit by Hurricane Andrew.

c. Transylvania Railroad, which serviced mines that produced highly-polluting coal and that have gradually decreased their output.

d. Joe Farmer and his wife Jill, whose family farm has been unable to compete with larger, mechanized operations.

e. Mike Farmer and his brother Bob, who have been farming together on land they inherited from their parents.

f. Starcrossed Partnership, which developed real estate in an overdeveloped market.

2. Consider the circumstances of each of the following debtors and determine the chapter(s) of the Code under which each could file a bankruptcy petition.

a. Arnold Able incurred substantial hospital bills following an accident last year. Able has been unable to work since the accident and consequently cannot pay almost $70,000 in medical bills not covered by insurance.

b. Beta Construction Corporation has suffered considerable losses as a result of the sharp decline in new construction projects. Beta recently defaulted on a large bank loan and is unable to pay its suppliers. Beta's debts total over $1 million.

c. Clara Crumm is a big spender with a small (but regular) income. Crumm has charged purchases up to the limit of all thirteen of her credit cards. Those debts total approximately $95,000. Clara also has monthly rent, car payments, and other expenses, which absorb most of her income, leaving her unable to make even the minimum payments on her credit cards.

3. Among the obligations owed by Debtors, who operated a business as a sole proprietorship, were the following: a mortgage for $500,000 secured by land worth $600,000; a debt of $1,000,000 owed to the SBA, secured by a judgment lien in the land that was junior in priority to the mortgage; and debts to trade creditors totaling $150,000. All of the obligations were noncontingent and liquidated. Are Debtors eligible for Chapter 13? See *Soderlund v. Cohen (In re Soderlund)*, 236 B.R. 271 (9th Cir. BAP 1999).

4. Section 109(e) sets the Chapter 13 debt limits in terms of "noncontingent, liquidated" debts. The significance of these words is illustrated by *In re Solomon*, 166 B.R. 832 (Bankr. D.Md.1994), *rev'd on other grounds*, 67 F.3d 1128 (4th Cir. 1995). Several former patients brought lawsuits against Dr. Solomon alleging improper sexual conduct while the plaintiffs were in his care. The four lawsuits sought a total of $160 million in damages. Dr. Solomon filed a Chapter 13 petition that listed the claims as contingent, unliquidated and disputed, and assigned them zero value. The court held that Dr. Solomon was eligible for Chapter 13 because, as of the date of filing, the tort claims had not been reduced to judgment and the debtor had not admitted that any amount was due to those creditors. Dr. Solomon's later statement that he would not object to the claims did not retroactively liquidate the claims as of the date bankruptcy was filed. His statement merely "constituted a recognition that no interest of Debtor was served by objecting" because the tort claimants "would receive all plan payments, regardless of what was determined to be the amount of their claims, and the expense of litigation was likely to exceed what Debtor had concluded he should pay under his proposed plan." *Id.* at 838.

Does *Solomon* encourage debtors to file bankruptcy sooner rather than later? If so, is that a good thing? Is the court's interpretation of "noncontingent, liquidated" debts sound? These terms appear elsewhere in the Code; we will see them (and Dr. Solomon) again.

The following case, in the course of describing the availability of relief under different chapters of the Code, gives a sense of the differences among Chapters 7, 11 and 13. Note the strategic alternatives that the Supreme Court's opinion suggests.

TOIBB v. RADLOFF

United States Supreme Court, 1991.
501 U.S. 157, 111 S.Ct. 2197, 115 L.Ed.2d 145.

JUSTICE BLACKMUN delivered the opinion of the Court.

In this case we must decide whether an individual debtor not engaged in business is eligible to reorganize under Chapter 11 of the Bankruptcy Code.

I

From March 1983 until April 1985, petitioner Sheldon Baruch Toibb, a former staff attorney with the Federal Energy Regulatory Commission, was employed as a consultant by Independence Electric Corporation (IEC), a company he and two others organized to produce and market electric power. Petitioner owns 24 percent of the company's shares. After IEC terminated his employment, petitioner was unable to find work as a consultant in the energy field; he has been largely supported by his family and friends since that time.

On November 18, 1986, petitioner filed in the United States Bankruptcy Court for the Eastern District of Missouri a voluntary petition for relief under Chapter 7 of the Code. The Schedule of Assets and Liabilities accompanying petitioner's filing disclosed no secured debts, a disputed federal tax priority claim of $11,000, and unsecured debts of $170,605. Petitioner listed as nonexempt assets his IEC shares and a possible claim against his former business associates. He stated that the market value of each of these assets was unknown.

On August 6, 1987, the Chapter 7 trustee appointed to administer petitioner's estate notified the creditors that the Board of Directors of IEC had offered to purchase petitioner's IEC shares for $25,000. When petitioner became aware that this stock had such value, he decided to avoid its liquidation by moving to convert his Chapter 7 case to one under the reorganization provisions of Chapter 11.

The Bankruptcy Court granted petitioner's conversion motion and on February 1, 1988, petitioner filed a plan of reorganization. Under the plan, petitioner proposed to pay his unsecured creditors $25,000 less administrative expenses and priority tax claims, a proposal that would result in a payment of approximately 11 cents on the dollar. He further proposed to pay the unsecured creditors, for a period of six years, 50 percent of any dividends from IEC or of any proceeds from the sale of the IEC stock, up to full payment of the debts.

On March 8, 1988, the Bankruptcy Court on its own motion ordered petitioner to show cause why his petition should not be dismissed because petitioner was not engaged in business and, therefore, did not qualify as a Chapter 11 debtor. At the ensuing hearing, petitioner unsuccessfully attempted to demonstrate that he had a business to reorganize. Petitioner also argued that Chapter 11 should be available to an individual debtor not engaged in an ongoing business. On August 1, the Bankruptcy Court ruled that, under the authority of *Wamsganz v. Boatmen's Bank of De Soto*, 804 F.2d 503 (8th Cir.1986), petitioner failed to qualify for relief under Chapter 11.

The United States District Court for the Eastern District of Missouri, also relying on *Wamsganz*, upheld the Bankruptcy Court's dismissal of petitioner's Chapter 11 case. The United States Court of Appeals for the Eighth Circuit affirmed, holding that the Bankruptcy Court had the authority to dismiss the proceeding *sua sponte*, and that the Circuit's earlier *Wamsganz* decision was controlling. Because the Court of Appeals' ruling that an individual nonbusiness debtor may not reorganize under Chapter 11 clearly conflicted with the holding of the Court of Appeals for the Eleventh Circuit in *In re Moog*, 774 F.2d 1073 (11th Cir.1985), we granted certiorari to resolve the conflict.

II

A

In our view, the plain language of the Bankruptcy Code disposes of the question before us. Section 109 defines who may be a debtor under the various chapters of the Code. Section 109(d) provides: "Only a person that may be a debtor under chapter 7 of this title, except a stockbroker or a commodity broker, and a railroad may be a debtor under chapter 11 of this title." Section 109(b) states: "A person may be a debtor under chapter 7 of this title only if such person is not—(1) a railroad; (2) a domestic insurance company, bank, * * *; or (3) a foreign insurance company, bank, * * * engaged in such business in the

United States." The Code defines "person" as used in Title 11 to "includ[e] [an] individual." [§ 101(41)]. Under the express terms of the Code, therefore, petitioner is "a person who may be a debtor under chapter 7" and satisfies the statutory requirements for a Chapter 11 debtor.

The Code contains no ongoing business requirement for reorganization under Chapter 11, and we are loath to infer the exclusion of certain classes of debtors from the protection of Chapter 11, because Congress took care in § 109 to specify who qualifies—and who does not qualify—as a debtor under the various chapters of the Code. Section 109(b) expressly excludes from the coverage of Chapter 7 railroads and various financial and insurance institutions. Only municipalities are eligible for the protection of Chapter 9. § 109(c). Most significantly, § 109(d) makes stockbrokers and commodities brokers ineligible for Chapter 11 relief, but otherwise leaves that Chapter available to any other entity eligible for the protection of Chapter 7. Congress knew how to restrict recourse to the avenues of bankruptcy relief; it did not place Chapter 11 reorganization beyond the reach of a nonbusiness individual debtor.

B

The *amicus curiae* in support of the Court of Appeals' judgment acknowledges that Chapter 11 does not expressly exclude an individual nonbusiness debtor from its reach. He echoes the reasoning of those courts that have engrafted an ongoing-business requirement onto the plain language of § 109(d) and argues that the statute's legislative history and structure make clear that Chapter 11 was intended for business debtors alone. We find these arguments unpersuasive for several reasons.

First, this Court has repeated with some frequency: "Where, as here, the resolution of a question of federal law turns on a statute and the intention of Congress, we look first to the statutory language and then to the legislative history if the statutory language is unclear." *Blum v. Stenson*, 465 U.S. 886, 896 (1984). The language of § 109 is not unclear. Thus, although a court appropriately may refer to a statute's legislative history to resolve statutory ambiguity, there is no need to do so here.

Second, even were we to consider the sundry legislative comments urged in support of a congressional intent to exclude a nonbusiness debtor from Chapter 11, the scant history on this precise issue does not suggest a "clearly expressed legislative inten[t] * * * contrary * * *" to the plain language of § 109(d). See *Consumer Product Safety Comm'n v. GTE Sylvania, Inc.*, 447 U.S. 102, 108 (1980). The *amicus* does point to the following statement in a House Report:

> "Some consumer debtors are unable to avail themselves of the relief provided under chapter 13. For these debtors, straight bankruptcy is the only remedy that will enable them to get out from under the debilitating effects of too much debt." H.R. Rep. No. 95–595 at 125, *reprinted in* 1978 U.S.C.C.A.N. at 6086.

Petitioner responds with the following excerpt from a later Senate Report:

> "Chapter 11, Reorganization, is primarily designed for businesses, although individuals are eligible for relief under the chapter. The procedures of chapter 11, however, are sufficiently complex that they will be used only in a business case and not in the consumer context." S. Rep. No. 95–989 at 3, *reprinted in* 1978 U.S.C.C.A.N. at 5789.

These apparently conflicting views tend to negate the suggestion that the Congress enacting the current Code operated with a clear intent to deny Chapter 11 relief to an individual nonbusiness debtor.

Finally, we are not persuaded by the contention that Chapter 11 is unavailable to a debtor without an ongoing business because many of the Chapter's provisions do not apply to a nonbusiness debtor. There is no doubt that Congress intended that a business debtor be among those who might use Chapter 11. Code provisions like the ones authorizing the appointment of an equity security holders' committee, § 1102, and the appointment of a trustee "for cause, including fraud, dishonesty, incompetence, or gross mismanagement of the affairs of the debtor by current management," § 1104(a)(1), certainly are designed to aid in the rehabilitation of a business. It does not follow, however, that a debtor whose affairs do not warrant recourse to these provisions is ineligible for Chapter 11 relief. Instead, these provisions—like the references to debtor businesses in the Chapter's legislative history—reflect an understandable expectation that Chapter 11 would be used *primarily* by debtors with ongoing businesses; they do not constitute an additional prerequisite for Chapter 11 eligibility beyond those established in § 109(d).

III

Although the foregoing analysis is dispositive of the question presented, we deal briefly with *amicus'* contention that policy considerations underlying the Code support inferring a congressional intent to preclude a nonbusiness debtor from reorganizing under Chapter 11. First, it is said that bringing a consumer debtor within the scope of Chapter 11 does not serve Congress' purpose of permitting business debtors to reorganize and restructure their debts in order to revive the debtors' businesses and thereby preserve jobs and protect investors. This argument assumes that Congress had a single purpose in enacting Chapter 11. Petitioner suggests, however, and we agree, that Chapter 11 also embodies the general Code policy of maximizing the value of the bankruptcy estate. Under certain circumstances a consumer debtor's estate will be worth more if reorganized under Chapter 11 than if liquidated under Chapter 7. Allowing such a debtor to proceed under Chapter 11 serves the congressional purpose of deriving as much value as possible from the debtor's estate.

Second, *amicus* notes that allowing a consumer debtor to proceed under Chapter 11 would permit the debtor to shield both disposable income and nonexempt personal property. He argues that the legislative history of Chapter 11 does not reflect an intent to offer a consumer debtor more expansive protection than he would find under Chapter 13, which does not protect disposable income, or Chapter 7, which does not protect nonexempt personal assets. As an initial matter, it makes no difference whether the legislative history affirmatively reflects such an intent, because the plain language of the statute allows a consumer debtor to proceed under Chapter 11. Moreover, differences in the requirements and protection of each Chapter reflect Congress' appreciation that various approaches are necessary to address effectively the disparate situations of debtors seeking protection under the Code.

Amicus does not contend that allowing a consumer debtor to reorganize under Chapter 11 will leave the debtor's creditors in a worse position than if the debtor were required to liquidate. Nor could he. Section 1129(a)(7) provides that a reorganization plan may not be confirmed unless all the debtor's creditors accept the plan or will receive not less than they would receive under a Chapter 7 liquidation. Because creditors cannot be expected to approve a plan in which they would receive less than they would from an immediate liquidation of the debtor's assets, it follows that a Chapter 11 reorganization plan usually will be confirmed only when creditors will receive at least as much as if the debtor were to file under Chapter 7. Absent some showing of harm to the creditors of a nonbusiness debtor allowed to reorganize under Chapter 11, we see nothing in the allocation of "burdens" and "benefits" of Chapter 11 that warrants an inference that Congress intended to exclude a consumer debtor from its coverage.

Amicus also warns that allowing consumer debtors to proceed under Chapter 11 will flood the bankruptcy courts with plans of reorganization that ultimately will prove unworkable. We think this fear is unfounded for two reasons. First, the greater expense and complexity of filing under Chapter 11 likely will dissuade most consumer debtors from seeking relief under this Chapter. Second, the Code gives bankruptcy courts substantial discretion to dismiss a Chapter 11 case in which the debtor files an untenable plan of reorganization. See §§ 1112(b) and 1129(a).

Finally, *amicus* asserts that extending Chapter 11 to consumer debtors creates the risk that these debtors will be forced into Chapter 11 by their creditors under § 303(a), a result contrary to the intent reflected in Congress' decision to prevent involuntary bankruptcy proceedings under Chapter 13. In particular, he suggests that it would be unwise to force a debtor into a Chapter 11 reorganization, because an involuntary debtor would be unlikely to cooperate in the plan of reorganization—a point that Congress noted in refusing to allow involuntary Chapter 13 proceedings. See H.R. Rep. No. 95–595 at 120.

We find these concerns overstated in light of the Code's provisions for dealing with recalcitrant Chapter 11 debtors. If an involuntary Chapter 11 debtor fails to cooperate, this likely will provide the requisite "cause" for the bankruptcy court to convert the Chapter 11 case to one under Chapter 7. See § 1112(b). In any event, the argument overlooks Congress' primary concern about a debtor's being forced into bankruptcy under Chapter 13: that such a debtor, whose future wages are not exempt from the bankruptcy estate, § 1322(a)(1), would be compelled to toil for the benefit of creditors in violation of the Thirteenth Amendment's involuntary servitude prohibition. See H.R. Rep. No. 95–595 at 120. Because there is no comparable provision in Chapter 11 requiring a debtor to pay future wages to a creditor, Congress' concern about imposing involuntary servitude on a Chapter 13 debtor is not relevant to a Chapter 11 reorganization.

IV

The plain language of the Bankruptcy Code permits individual debtors not engaged in business to file for relief under Chapter 11. Although the structure and legislative history of Chapter 11 indicate that this Chapter was intended primarily for the use of business debtors, the Code contains no "ongoing business" requirement for Chapter 11 reorganization, and we find no basis for imposing one. Accordingly, the judgment of the Court of Appeals is reversed.

It is so ordered.

JUSTICE STEVENS, dissenting.

The Court's reading of the statute is plausible. It is supported by the omission of any prohibition against the use of Chapter 11 by consumer debtors and by the excerpt from the introduction to the Senate Report. Nevertheless, I am persuaded that the Court's reading is incorrect. Two chapters of the Bankruptcy Code—Chapter 7, entitled "Liquidation," and Chapter 13, entitled "Adjustment of Debts of an Individual With Regular Income,"—unquestionably and unambiguously authorize relief for individual consumer debtors. Chapter 11, entitled "Reorganization," was primarily designed to provide relief for corporate debtors but also unquestionably authorizes relief for individual proprietors of business enterprises. When the statute is read as a whole, however, it seems quite clear that Congress did not intend to authorize a "reorganization" of the affairs of an individual consumer debtor.

Section 109(d) places a limit on the class of persons who may be a debtor under Chapter 11, but it does not state that all members of that class are eligible for Chapter 11 relief. It states that "*only* a person that may be a debtor under Chapter 7 * * * may be a debtor under Chapter 11." (Emphasis added.) It does not, however, state that *every* person entitled to relief under Chapter 7 is also entitled to relief under Chapter 11. In my judgment, the word "only" introduces sufficient ambiguity to justify a careful examination of other provisions of the Act, as well as the legislative history.

This examination convinces me that consumer debtors may not avail themselves of Chapter 11. The repeated references to the debtor's "business," "the operation of the debtor's business," and the "current or former management of the debtor" make it abundantly clear that the principal focus of the chapter is upon business reorganizations. This conclusion is confirmed by the discussion of Chapter 11 in the Senate

Report, which describes the provision as a "chapter for *business* reorganization" and repeatedly refers to a "business" as the subject of Chapter 11 relief.

The House Report, however, is more significant because it emphasizes the relationship between different chapters of the Code. The Report unambiguously states that a Chapter 7 liquidation is "the only remedy" for "consumer debtors [who] are unable to avail themselves of the relief provided under chapter 13." H.R. Rep. No. 95–595 at 125. The accuracy of the statement in the House Report is confirmed by a comparison of the text of Chapter 11 with the text of Chapter 13.

Above, I noted the striking difference between the chapter titles—"Reorganization" for Chapter 11 as opposed to "Adjustment of Debts of an Individual With Regular Income" for Chapter 13. Also significant is the conspicuous omission from Chapter 11 of both an important limit and an important protection included in Chapter 13. Chapter 13 relief is only available to individuals whose unsecured debts amount to less than $100,000 and whose secured debts are less than $350,000.[a] Chapter 11 contains no comparable limit. Congress would have accomplished little in imposing this limit on the adjustment of individual consumer debt through Chapter 13 if Congress at the same time allowed the individual to avoid the limitation by filing under Chapter 11.

More important, the Code expressly provides that involuntary proceedings can only be instituted under Chapter 7 and Chapter 11. See § 303(a). A creditor therefore may not force an individual consumer debtor into an involuntary Chapter 13 proceeding. Under the Court's reading of the Act, however, a creditor could institute an involuntary proceeding under Chapter 11 against any individual with regular income. It seems highly unlikely that Congress intended to subject individual consumer debtors, such as pensioners, to involuntary Chapter 11 proceedings while at the same time prohibiting involuntary Chapter 13 proceedings against the same class of debtors.

For these reasons, notwithstanding the excerpt from the Senate Report on which the Court relies, I would, in accordance with the clear statement in the House Report, read the statute as a whole to limit Chapter 11 relief to business debtors. I therefore respectfully dissent.

---

[a] The debt limits for Chapter 13 have since been adjusted to $269,250 and $807,750 for unsecured and secured debts, respectively. Eds.

Notes and Questions

1. Justice Blackmun's opinion asserts that "the plain language of the Bankruptcy Code disposes of the question before us." Does the legislative history suggest that the plain language might not be dispositive? If it is not, what considerations should inform a court's interpretation of the scope of Chapter 11 relief? What leads Justice Stevens to conclude that § 109's meaning is not plain?

2. We know now that individual debtors may file Chapter 11, but why would they choose to do so? Would debtors choose Chapter 11 only if they, like Sheldon Toibb, have debts in excess of the Chapter 13 debt limits? Does Chapter 11 offer additional benefits to Sheldon Toibb that other chapters do not?

3. Could permitting individual debtors access to Chapter 11 result in the type of proceedings Congress wanted to avoid? Justice Stevens notes in his dissent that it would be incongruous for Congress to have barred involuntary Chapter 13 proceedings against individual debtors if it had contemplated that creditors could force individuals into involuntary Chapter 11 proceedings.

4. To what extent do the incongruities between Chapters 11 and 13 reveal Congress's preference that consumer debtors "reorganize" under Chapter 13 rather than Chapter 11? How would you take account of the dollar amount jurisdictional limits of Chapter 13 in that regard? *Toibb* is about alternative debt relief and creditor protection mechanisms. It seems to contemplate that Congress, or at least the congressional staff who wrote the Bankruptcy Code, thought carefully about and understood the coordination of the alternative chapters. Does the legislative history recounted in *Toibb* suggest that the alternative chapters are logically coordinated? If not, what does that intimate about the big bankruptcy picture?

2. INVOLUNTARY PROCEEDINGS

Section 303 of the Code provides for involuntary cases. Any entity that can file a voluntary petition under Chapter 7 or 11 can be the subject of an involuntary filing under that chapter, with two exceptions—farmers and not-for-profit corporations. § 303(a). Entities listed in § 109(b), therefore, cannot be forced into either Chapter 7 or Chapter 11 bankruptcy. Involuntary petitions are not permitted under Chapters 12 and 13.

The filing of the petition automatically constitutes an "order for relief" in a voluntary proceeding under § 301. The order for relief "is tantamount to an order approving the court's exercise of jurisdiction to grant relief pursuant to the provisions of the law." Frank R. Kennedy,

The Commencement of a Case Under the New Bankruptcy Code, 36 Wash. & Lee. L. Rev. 977, 983 (1979).

The filing of the involuntary petition, in contrast, does not constitute an order for relief. Thus, a "postpetition gap" exists between the date of the filing of an involuntary petition and entry of the order for relief. Section 303(f) permits the debtor to conduct business and to use, acquire or dispose of property during this gap period as if the petition had not been filed. Any new debts that the debtor acquires during this period are treated as if they arose prior to the petition, § 502(f), and they are given a higher priority claim status than debts that actually did arise before the petition was filed, § 507(a)(2). Further, the debtor may make transfers during the gap period that may not be later avoided by the bankruptcy trustee, as long as the transfers were in exchange for new value given after the petition was filed. A party in interest concerned that the bankruptcy estate will deteriorate during the gap period may move, pursuant to § 303(g), for appointment of an interim trustee to protect the estate until the order for relief is entered.

Section 303(b) imposes a two-part test that must be met by petitioning creditors in order to sustain the involuntary petition—a requisite number test and a requisite amount test. It also requires that the petitioning creditors hold claims that are "not contingent as to liability or the subject of a bona fide dispute." This is the second time we have encountered the requirement that a claim be noncontingent; the first time was in § 109(e), which identifies debtors who may file Chapter 13 petitions. The bona fide dispute requirement in § 303 protects debtors engaged in good faith disputes with creditors from being coerced into settling by the threat of an involuntary proceeding.

The Bankruptcy Code does not permit commencement of an involuntary petition merely because a debtor's liabilities exceed its assets. Rather, § 303(h) provides that when an involuntary petition is timely disputed, a bankruptcy court may order relief against the debtor after trial only if (1) "the debtor is generally not paying such debtor's debts as such debts become due unless such debts are the subject of a bona fide dispute;" or (2) within 120 days before the petition was filed a custodian was appointed and took possession of substantially all of the debtor's property. (Compare § 101(32), defining "insolvent" in the balance sheet sense of liabilities in excess of assets, with § 303(h), which is a variant of an "equitable insolvency" test.)

Bankruptcy courts articulate what amounts to a per se rule that failure to satisfy liability to a single creditor is insufficient to constitute "generally not paying such debtor's debts." Under this rule, involuntary petitions filed by the only unpaid creditor are not permissible. Courts employing the doctrine, however, recognize so many exceptions that they threaten to swallow the rule—that the debtor has behaved fraudulently, or is manipulating his or her income and transferring assets in an effort to evade the debt, or that the single unpaid obligation is extraordinarily large. In *Perez v. Feinberg (In re Feinberg)*, 238 B.R. 781 (8th Cir. BAP 1999), for example, the debtor, a doctor, paid all of his obligations except one—for $2.3 million—owed to his former partners. When their efforts to collect proved fruitless, they filed an involuntary Chapter 11 petition against him. The bankruptcy court granted the debtor's motion, ruling that the creditors had failed to show that he was generally not paying his debts as they became due. The bankruptcy appellate panel reversed. It acknowledged the single creditor rule, but concluded that "the exceptions override it." The court found an exception justified by the size of the obligation, and by the "debtor's actions in manipulating his and his wife's income, transferring assets, attempting to hinder and delay these creditors, while living lavishly." *Id.* at 784-85.

The court in *In re All Media Properties, Inc.*, 5 B.R. 126 (Bankr. S.D.Tex.1980), *affirmed mem.* 646 F.2d 193 (5th Cir.1981), in discussing the requirements for involuntary bankruptcy petitions, stated the leading test for determining whether a claim is contingent:

> The debtors here contend that the holder of a claim which is unmatured or disputed cannot be a qualified creditor as that establishes that such claims are contingent in the sense that they are not, at the time of the filing of the petition, fixed or liquidated or now owing but rather that such claims require further proceedings or the passage of time. The debtors' contention is summed up by the following statement in their brief: "if the claim asserted by the petitioners would require proof in order to establish the merits of the claim as to the debtor's liability or the amount of this claim, then such a claim could not be considered to be not contingent as to liability."
>
> * * *
>
> The court concludes that claims are contingent as to liability if the debt is one which the debtor will be called upon to pay only upon the occurrence or happening of an extrinsic event which will trigger the liability of the debtor to the alleged creditor and if such triggering event or occurrence was one

reasonably contemplated by the debtor and creditor at the time the event giving rise to the claim occurred.

Thus, in the case of the classic contingent liability of a guarantor of a promissory note executed by a third party, both the creditor and guarantor knew there would be liability only if the principal maker defaulted. No obligation arises until such default. In the case of a tort claim for negligence, the parties at the time of the alleged negligent act would be presumed to have contemplated that the alleged tort feasor would be liable only if it were so established by a competent tribunal. Such a tort claim is contingent as to liability until a final judgment is entered fixing the rights of the parties. On the other hand, in the ordinary debt arising from, for example, a sale of merchandise, the parties to the transaction would not at that time view the obligation as contingent. Subsequent events might lead to a dispute as to liability because of, for example, defective merchandise, but that would merely serve to render the debt a disputed one but would not make it a contingent one. A legal obligation arose at the time of the sale, although the obligation can possibly be avoided. Such a claim is disputed, but it is not contingent. A claim is contingent as to liability if the debtor's legal duty to pay does not come into existence until triggered by the occurrence of a future event and such future occurrence was within the actual or presumed contemplation of the parties at the time the original relationship of the parties was created. On the other hand, if a legal obligation to pay arose at the time of the original relationship, but that obligation is subject to being avoided by some future event or occurrence, the claim is not contingent as to liability, although it may be disputed as to liability for various reasons. Likewise, an unmatured obligation is not contingent as to liability. The obligation to pay existed from the outset; no outside event is necessary to bring the obligation into existence, but rather the obligation may be extinguished by payment. This does not render such a debt "contingent as to liability", but renders it only "unmatured".

* * *

[U]nder § 303(h)(1) of the Code the bankruptcy court shall enter an order for relief against a debtor only where "the debtor is generally not paying such debtor's debts as such debts become due." This phrase is not defined in the Code and the legislative history is not very helpful, but it seems reasonable to consider both the amount of the debt not being paid and the number of creditors not being paid in determining the answer to the issue.

During oral argument counsel for [the debtors] asserted that the term "generally" means usually or a majority of the time, and that the dividing line is one of simple mathematics. According to counsel for the alleged debtors, to be generally not paying his debts a debtor would have to be not paying at least 51% of his debts.

The court rejects this contention. The new test for involuntary petitions was adopted not to restrict and limit the involuntary process but was included to allow more flexibility. The legislative history describes § 303(h)(1) as the "most significant departure from present law concerning the present grounds for involuntary bankruptcy." Contrary to counsel's assertion at oral argument, this court believes that Congress contemplated that there would be a new and totally different approach to insolvency in involuntary cases when it passed the Code.

A hypothetical serves to illustrate the point. Consider a debtor who has 100 creditors, 15 of which hold 80% of the amount owed by the debtor. These 15 creditors also happen to be the only creditors not being paid by the debtor. Under the test suggested by [the debtors], the fact that only 15 creditors were not being paid would mean that involuntary relief would not be appropriate because a majority of the creditors were being paid. This court does not believe that Congress intended such a result. The term "generally" was not defined in order to avoid the result suggested by the mechanical test put forth by the alleged debtors and to give the bankruptcy courts enough leeway to be able to deal with the variety of situations that will arise.

Instead, the court believes that generally not paying debts includes regularly missing a significant number of payments to creditors or regularly missing payments which are significant in amount in relation to the size of the debtor's operation. Where the debtor has few creditors the number which will be significant will be fewer than where the debtor has a large number of creditors. Also, the amount of the debts not being paid is important. If the amounts of missed payments are not

> substantial in comparison to the magnitude of the debtor's operation, involuntary relief would be improper.

Id. at 131–32, 133, 142–43.

Questions and Problems

1. What is the difference between a *disputed* and a *contingent* claim, according to *All Media*? Give examples of each. What is the "jurisdictional" implication of concluding that a claim is noncontingent?

2. *All Media* suggested that both a prejudgment tort claim and a claim against a guarantor on a promissory note are "contingent." If so, what is the difference between a "contingent" claim and an "unliquidated" claim (which is an issue under § 109(e))?

3. According to the court, what policy is implicated by increasing the size of the potential pool of creditors who may join an involuntary petition? How is that policy consistent with drawing the line in terms of contingency as to liability?

4. First Marketing provided $8,000 in advertising services to Debtor, a radio broadcasting company. First Marketing asserts that it was to be paid cash for its services, but Debtor contends that the parties agreed that Debtor would provide advertising air time to First Marketing in exchange for its services. First Marketing joined two other creditors in filing an involuntary bankruptcy petition against Debtor, but Debtor argues that First Marketing's claim is disputed and contingent as to liability because the matter was being litigated in state court when the petition was filed. Is First Marketing an appropriate petitioning creditor?

5. Debtor owed Creditor $4,000 for goods sold on open account. After Creditor joined two other account creditors (each of which was owed a similar amount) in filing an involuntary petition against Debtor, Debtor paid the obligation. Debtor then argued that Creditor was an inappropriate petitioning creditor because the debt had been satisfied. What result?

6. Bank held a mortgage on Debtor's land, worth $25,000, securing an obligation of $40,000. Assuming that Debtor has fewer than 12 creditors, can Bank, acting alone, file an involuntary bankruptcy petition against Debtor?

3. DISMISSAL

A bankruptcy court has the power to dismiss the petition even though the eligibility requirements of § 109 (and § 303, for involuntary cases) have been met. As you work through the following three cases, note the various grounds that may lead to dismissal of the case.

PHOENIX PICCADILLY, LTD. v. LIFE INSURANCE CO. OF VIRGINIA (IN RE PHOENIX PICCADILLY, LTD.)

United States Court of Appeals, Eleventh Circuit, 1988.
849 F.2d 1393.

RONEY, Chief Judge.

* * *

The critical issue on this appeal is whether the bankruptcy court gave proper consideration to whether the debtor had equity in the secured property and had a prospect of a successful reorganization, after the court had made a finding that "the petition was not filed in good faith, but rather, for the purpose of delaying and frustrating the efforts of the Secured Creditors to enforce their rights in the property." We hold, as the district court did implicitly, that the prospects of a successful reorganization do not override, as a matter of law, the finding of bad faith in this case or compel, as a matter of fact, a contrary finding. A brief examination of the case clearly reflects sufficient evidentiary support of that finding under the clearly erroneous standard of review.

The debtor, Phoenix–Piccadilly, Ltd., is a limited partnership which owns the Piccadilly Square Apartments located in Louisville, Kentucky. Legal title to the property is held by Citizens Fidelity Bank and Trust Company of Louisville, under a deed of trust.

The property is comprised of four phases known as Phases I, II, III and IV. The three secured creditors, Meritor Savings Bank, Life Insurance Company of Virginia, and Future Federal Savings Bank, separately hold first mortgage liens on all four phases. In addition, Paul A. Evola and Ronald F. Heltinger hold a note which is secured by a "wraparound"[b] mortgage encumbering the entire property.

On June 19, 1987, mortgage foreclosure proceedings were instituted by Future Federal in Jefferson County, Kentucky. On June 29, 1987, an order was entered in the state court action appointing a receiver for Phase III of the property. The debtor filed this Chapter 11

[b] A "wraparound" mortgage is a second mortgage with a face amount equal to the amount advanced by the second mortgagee plus the outstanding balance on the first mortgage. Payments on the wraparound mortgage cover both obligations, with the wraparound mortgagee responsible for making the payments to the first mortgagee. Eds.

petition on November 19, 1987, the day before a hearing in the state court action to appoint a receiver for the other three phases of the property. After the automatic stay was lifted in this proceeding, a receiver was appointed for the entire property.

All three secured creditors filed motions for relief from the automatic stay provisions of the Bankruptcy Code, and subsequently filed motions to dismiss the Chapter 11 case. An automatic stay may be terminated for "cause" pursuant to § 362(d)(1) of the Bankruptcy Code if a petition was filed in bad faith. A case under Chapter 11 may be dismissed for cause pursuant to § 1112 of the Bankruptcy Code if the petition was not filed in good faith.

Although what amounts to bad faith is the same for both proceedings, there is no particular test for determining whether a debtor has filed a petition in bad faith. Instead, the courts may consider any factors which evidence "an intent to abuse the judicial process and the purposes of the reorganization provisions" or, in particular, factors which evidence that the petition was filed "to delay or frustrate the legitimate efforts of secured creditors to enforce their rights." *Albany Partners, Ltd. v. Westbrook (In re Albany Partners, Ltd.)*, 749 F.2d 670, 674 (11th Cir.1984).

The bankruptcy court's finding of bad faith is well supported by the record. The court held that many of the circumstantial factors which have been identified by the courts as evidencing a bad faith filing are present in this case:

(i) The Debtor has only one asset, the Property, in which it does not hold legal title;

(ii) The Debtor has few unsecured creditors whose claims are small in relation to the claims of the Secured Creditors;

(iii) The Debtor has few employees;

(iv) The Property is the subject of a foreclosure action as a result of arrearages on the debt;

(v) The Debtor's financial problems involve essentially a dispute between the Debtor and the Secured Creditors which can be resolved in the pending State Court Action; and

(vi) The timing of the Debtor's filing evidences an intent to delay or frustrate the legitimate efforts of the Debtor's secured creditors to enforce their rights.

The court held an evidentiary hearing and focused on certain evidence. Admissions of the debtor's agent, Lester N. Garripee, reveal the debtor's motive for filing its petition. In a letter to the debtor's limited partners dated July 16, 1987, Garripee detailed a plan "to fight Future Federal's foreclosure action" and, most tellingly, to posture the debtor "to make whatever legal defenses are appropriate to forestall Future Federal actions, including, if advisable, the filing of a Chapter 11 Bankruptcy Petition."

Additionally, Joey Bailey, President of Future Federal Savings Bank, testified that on July 21, 1987, another agent of the debtor, Claude Hesse, threatened to forestall Future Federal's foreclosure action "for years" by filing a Chapter 11 case in a location "far from Louisville, Kentucky." As of the petition date, the debtor had unsecured debt of less than $250,000 and less than $50,000, if its unsecured debt to its affiliated company is excluded. The only persons employed by the debtor, other than the general partner, were the 15 persons performing maintenance and related services at the property in Kentucky under the supervision of the debtor's affiliated management company.

Finally, the venue chosen by the debtor for its Chapter 11 filing was over 700 miles from Louisville, Kentucky,[c] where the apartment complex, its employees, its secured and unsecured creditors, and the pending state court proceedings were located. Although perhaps technically proper, the choice to file the petition so far from where the property and creditors are located may itself be evidence of bad faith.

Because the bankruptcy court found that a bad faith filing had occurred, it properly did not change the consequences of that finding simply because of the debtor's possible equity in the property or potential for successful reorganization. We reject the debtor's argument that the bankruptcy court cannot ever dismiss a case for bad faith if there is equity in the property because the presence of equity indicates the potential for a successful reorganization. Rather, as this Court stated in *Natural Land Corp. v. Baker Farms, Inc. (In re Natural Land Corp.)*, 825 F.2d 296 (11th Cir.1987):

[c] The bankruptcy petition was filed in the Middle District of Florida. Eds.

> the taint of a petition filed in bad faith must naturally extend to any subsequent reorganization proposal; thus, any proposal submitted by a debtor who filed his petition in bad faith would fail to meet § 1129's good faith requirement.

Id. at 298. The possibility of a successful reorganization cannot transform a bad faith filing into one undertaken in good faith.

AFFIRMED.

Notes and Questions

1. Is it "bad faith" to file a bankruptcy petition in order to take advantage of the automatic stay? Professor Daniel Keating, in *Offensive Uses of the Bankruptcy Stay*, 45 Vand. L. Rev. 71, 126, 128 (1991), asserted that "[t]he notion of discharge as insurance highlights the reality that discharge presents a moral hazard for debtors," as "those who are insured against certain risks have an incentive to use less than optimal care to avoid those risks * * *. [I]n individual cases, the reduction of collateral consequences of bankruptcy that result from offensive uses of the stay exacerbates the moral hazard that the discharge necessarily creates for individual debtors." What is the coincidence between such moral hazard and bad faith?

2. Can the debtor's choice of venue suggest bad faith? Recall the empirical studies, cited in Chapter 1, that found extensive evidence of forum shopping in large corporate bankruptcies. Theodore Eisenberg & Lynn M. LoPucki, *Shopping for Judges: An Empirical Analysis of Venue Choice in Large Chapter 11 Reorganizations*, 84 Cornell L. Rev. 967 (1999); Lynn M. LoPucki & William C. Whitford, *Venue Choice and Forum Shopping in the Bankruptcy Reorganization of Large, Publicly Held Companies*, 1991 Wis. L. Rev. 11.

IN RE JOHNS–MANVILLE CORP.

United States Bankruptcy Court, Southern District of New York, 1984.
36 B.R. 727.

BURTON R. LIFLAND, Bankruptcy Judge.

DECISION AND ORDER ON MOTIONS TO DISMISS MANVILLE'S CHAPTER 11 PETITION

I. Background and Issues Presented

Whether an industrial enterprise in the United States is highly successful is often gauged by its "membership" in what has come to be known as the "Fortune 500". Having attained this measure of financial achievement, Johns–Manville Corp. and its affiliated companies (collectively referred to as "Manville") were deemed a paradigm of success in corporate America by the financial community. Thus, Manville's filing for protection under Chapter 11 of Title 11 of the United States Code ("the Code or the Bankruptcy Code") on August 26, 1982 ("the filing date") was greeted with great surprise and consternation on the part of some of its creditors and other corporations that were being sued along with Manville for injuries caused by asbestos exposure. As discussed at length herein, Manville submits that the sole factor necessitating its filing is the mammoth problem of uncontrolled proliferation of asbestos health suits brought against it because of its substantial use for many years of products containing asbestos which injured those who came into contact with the dust of this lethal substance. According to Manville, this current problem of approximately 16,000 lawsuits pending as of the filing date is compounded by the crushing economic burden to be suffered by Manville over the next 20–30 years by the filing of an even more staggering number of suits by those who had been exposed but who will not manifest the asbestos-related diseases until some time during this future period ("the future asbestos claimants"). Indeed, approximately 6,000 asbestos health claims are estimated to have arisen in only the first 16 months since the filing date. This burden is further compounded by the insurance industry's general disavowal of liability to Manville on policies written for this very purpose. Indeed, the issue of coverage has been pending for years before a state court in California ("the California Coordinated Litigation").

It is the propriety of the filing by Manville which is the subject of the instant decision. Four separate motions to dismiss the petition pursuant to § 1112(b) of the Code have been lodged before this Court * * *.

Manville has opposed all four dismissal motions and has been joined in opposition to them by the Unofficial Committee of School Creditors and the Equity Holders Committee. The Unsecured Creditors Committee has filed a brief "in response" to the motions which advocates denial of the motions.

The Asbestos Committee, which is comprised with one exception of attorneys for asbestos victims, initially moved to dismiss this case on November 8, 1982 citing Manville's alleged lack of good faith in filing this petition. However, the Asbestos Committee did not press its motion before the Court until now, more than one year later. In the interim, while engaging in plan formulation negotiations, it has vigorously pursued discovery in order to bolster its factual contention that Manville knowingly perpetrated a fraud on this Court and on all its creditors and equity holders in exaggerating the profundity of its economic distress in 1981 so as to enable it to file for reorganization in 1982. Thus, the Asbestos Committee submitted in November 1983 a multitude of volumes of materials consisting of 55 days of depositions of Manville officers in alleged support of the inference that in 1981 a small Manville group "concocted" evidence to meet the requirements for filing a Chapter 11 petition. The Asbestos Committee alleges that this group manufactured evidence of crushing economic distress so as to demonstrate falsely that pursuant to required principles of accounting * * * Manville had to book a reserve of at least $1.9 billion for asbestos health liability, and thus had no alternative but to seek Chapter 11 protection. The booking of such a reserve would, in turn, have triggered the acceleration of approximately $450 million of outstanding debt, possibly resulting in a forced liquidation of key business segments. Thus, the multitudinous submissions by the Asbestos Committee are aimed at showing their challenge to the motive, methods and data used by Manville's accounting consultants, its management and its Litigation Advisory Group ("LAG") in determining whether relief under Chapter 11 should be sought.

Mindful that there is no insolvency requirement for Chapter 11 debtor status, the issue presented for determination by this Court is whether these allegations of error by the Asbestos Committee, even egregious error, in over-calculation of Manville's financial problems are relevant to establish the kind of bad faith in the sense of an abuse of this Court's jurisdiction which will vitiate the filing of a Chapter 11 petition. This opinion will thus elucidate whether the tomes of material submitted by the Asbestos Committee defeat the essential fact that as of August 26, 1982 Manville is a real company with real debt, real creditors and a compelling need to reorganize in order to meet these obligations.

The Whitman[, GAF and Co-defendants' motions] * * * are based on the theory that because the claims of future asbestos victims are not cognizable or dischargeable in bankruptcy, the *raison d'etre* for the filing is vitiated and thus the petition should be dismissed. However, this Court must bear in mind in determining the issues raised by these movants that even if the claims of future claimants are ultimately found not dischargeable, that finding does not necessarily preclude this Court from dealing with the interests of these "parties in interest" under Code § 1109(b), especially since blinding the reorganization process to their residual interests would doom this reorganization case to ineffectiveness. If future claimants are properly represented as parties in interest, the means for the emergence of a proper plan which fairly provides for the survival and just treatment of their interests post-petition will be better assured.

As background information, it should be noted that throughout the course of the past 16 months, all parties, including the movants herein, have participated to a substantial extent in negotiations aimed at formulating a consensual plan treating all interests justly and fairly. Indeed, it is interesting to note that some of the very co-defendants which now seek to dismiss the petition, notably Owens–Illinois and Keene Corp., have previously expressed on the record before this Court their fervent desire to engraft themselves onto any plan providing for a claims-handling facility with which to deal with asbestos claimants. They have related to the Court their arduous efforts at formulating a sharing arrangement whereby all co-defendants, including Manville, may apportion their relative liabilities to the victims as a first step toward full participation in and contribution to any claims-handling Manville reorganization plan to be funded by an industry "super fund".

In addition, Keene Corp., also one of the co-defendants seeking to dismiss the petition, is the proponent of the related motion to appoint a legal representative for future asbestos claimants proposed for the purported purpose of enabling this reorganization to deal effectively with this key constituency and thereby succeed. The shifting posture of many of the co-defendants is in no small measure impelled by their continued involvement in the nonbankruptcy asbestos litigation and the filing by Manville of a plan that as yet does not provide a sharing and contribution arrangement. In any event, whether or not the co-defendants may for the purpose of the dismissal motions deem it prudent to participate in the reorganization effort and effect a global solution to the asbestos problem, Manville should have the opportunity to attempt to successfully reorganize with or without them so long as it conforms to all Code requirements.

Throughout this 16–month period, the Asbestos Committee, at considerable expense to the debtor, has engaged its own counsel and epidemiologists and, jointly with the Unsecured Creditors Committee, engaged an investment banking firm to prepare projections of future income in aid of plan formulation. It is only now that negotiations have become seemingly deadlocked that the Asbestos Committee has reverted to its original position of attacking the filing. If there was merit in the motion to dismiss on grounds of lack of good faith, it could have been fervently pressed a year ago instead of tolerating this alleged misuse of the courts. This same assertion of untimeliness can be made regarding the other co-defendant proponents of dismissal of the petition because they too may be pressing these motions as a last resort as a result of frustrations at the bargaining table. This Court must therefore bear in mind the strategical motivations underlying the pursuit of these motions at this time as well as recognize the progress toward a successful, perhaps consensual, reorganization that has already taken place. It is against this backdrop of progress and achievement accomplished by the key constituencies toward a resolution on perhaps a sweeping basis of the asbestos problem that the instant motions are now placed before me for determination.

II. Discussion of Law

A. General Eligibility Requirements for Chapter 11 Status

The motions to dismiss Manville's petition filed by the Asbestos Committee, GAF, Whitman, and the Co-defendants must be denied. Preliminarily, it must be stated that there is no question that Manville is eligible to be a debtor under the Code's statutory requirements. Section 109 of the Code contains its eligibility requirements * * *.

Clearly, Manville meets the requirements contained in subsection (a) for debtors under all chapters of the Code in that it is domiciled and has its place of business in the United States. Also, the word "person" used in subsection (a), as defined in [§ 101(41)], includes an individual, a partnership, and a corporation, but not a governmental unit.

In addition, Manville meets the eligibility requirements contained in subsection (b) and made applicable to Chapter 11 debtors by subsection (d). Manville is obviously not any of the prohibited entities described in subsection (b).

Moreover, it should also be noted that neither § 109 nor any other provision relating to voluntary petitions by companies contains any insolvency requirement. * * * And, with specific regard to Chapter 11, the Code eliminates the requirement contained in * * * the Act that the debtor be insolvent or unable to pay his debts as they mature. This is in striking contrast to the requirement of insolvency contained in § 303[(h)] with regard to the commencement of involuntary cases. * * *

It is only with regard to Chapter 9 (Adjustment of Debts of a Municipality) that the Code mentions insolvency or inability to meet one's debts. *See* § 109(c)(3).

Accordingly, it is abundantly clear that Manville has met all of the threshold eligibility requirements for filing a voluntary petition under the Code. This Court will now turn to the issue of whether any of the movants have demonstrated sufficient "cause" pursuant to § 1112(b) to warrant the dismissal of Manville's petition.

B. The Standard of "Cause" for Dismissal of a Chapter 11 Petition

Section 1112(b) of the Code provides for conversion or dismissal of a case for "cause". It lists nine examples of cause, but the list is not exhaustive. One court has described the pertinent legislative history, declaring: "The court will be able to consider other factors as they arise, and use its equitable powers to reach an appropriate result in individual cases. What constitutes cause under § 1112(b) is subject to judicial discretion under the circumstances of each case." *In re Nancant, Inc.*, 8 B.R. 1005, 1006 (Bankr. D.Mass.1981). * * *

As is set forth in detail in part D *infra*, the interests of future claimants need not be discharged to be accounted for and fully and fairly represented in these proceedings. Indeed, under Manville's currently proposed plan, future claims would survive the Chapter 11 and would presumably be eligible to be liquidated by a claims handling facility or by another method as yet undetermined. Thus, the motions to dismiss filed by GAF, Whitman and the Codefendants premised on speculation as to the nondischargeability of future claims do not establish sufficient "cause" pursuant to § 1112(b) and must be denied in their entirety.

Furthermore, much of the argument in support of all of the motions to dismiss is pitched to the confirmability of Manville's proposed plan. This argument is misplaced. * * * The essential determination here is the propriety of the filing, and whether "cause" exists to vitiate it, not the confirmability of a particular plan. If Manville is unable to effectuate a particular plan, that is not tantamount to finding that no plan can be effectuated.

C. The Motion to Dismiss Filed by The Asbestos Committee

The motion to dismiss the petition filed by the Asbestos Committee must also be denied. The Asbestos Committee premises its motion to dismiss the petition on what it contends is Manville's "bad faith" in filing for protection under Chapter 11. * * *

Because the allegations of the Asbestos Committee are not supported by concrete facts and thus do not rebut the essential fact that Manville is a real company with a substantial amount of real debt and real creditors clamoring to enforce this real debt, the Asbestos Committee has not sustained its burden of demonstrating sufficient fraud to vitiate the filing *ab initio*. On balance, the inferences to be drawn from submissions by both Manville and the Asbestos Committee seem to favor Manville. This is because Manville has credibly analyzed its position in its counter to the Asbestos Committee's allegations of fraud * * * .

Manville's Compendium [of the Factual Record On the Issue of the Propriety of the Chapter 11 Filing] relates the testimony of Manville officers and supports the inference accepted herein that these petitions were filed only after Manville undertook lengthy, careful and detailed analysis. For example, Manville commissioned and strictly scrutinized the results of studies by two separate epidemiological groups * * *. [They] corroborated each other's projections of runaway asbestos health costs within the foreseeable future.

In addition, the Compendium cites to testimony of Manville officers which details the slow and deliberate process of data commissioning and review and "soul-searching" antedating the filing, including the employment and review of results of studies * * * regarding propensity to sue. The data submitted by Manville also supports the accepted inference that the $1.9 billion projected debt figure ratified by Manville was the result of careful, conservative and perhaps understated projections.

In so doing, Manville has succeeded in rebutting in general and in specific the Asbestos Committee's allegations of fraud regarding the size of its projected debt, including those of collusion, manipulation of figures, cover-up and falsification of data. That which therefore emerges from the voluminous submissions by both sides are unsubstantiated conclusory charges of fraud and misdeed and an expression by the Asbestos Committee of its disagreement with the methods used by Manville in projecting future asbestos health costs.

Manville was advised * * * that it was necessary to book a $1.9 billion reserve for contingent liability * * *. On balance, Manville's decision to follow this advice was neither unreasonable, illogical, nor in any sense fraudulent. * * *

Therefore, on balance, the Asbestos Committee has failed to sustain its burden of proof of fraud as to either the magnitude of the reserve to be booked or the necessity of so booking this reserve. * * *

1. The Code's Policies of Open Access and Liquidation Avoidance

In determining whether to dismiss under § 1112(b), a court is not necessarily required to consider whether the debtor has filed in "good faith" because that is not a specified predicate under the Code for filing. Rather, according to § 1129(a)(3), good faith emerges as a requirement for the confirmation of a plan. The filing of a Chapter 11 case creates an estate for the benefit of all creditors and equity holders of the debtor wherein all constituencies may voice their interests and bargain for their best possible treatment. * * * It is thus logical that the good faith of the debtor be deemed a predicate primarily for emergence out of a Chapter 11 case. It is after confirmation of a concrete and immutable reorganization plan that creditors are foreclosed from advancing their distinct and parochial interests in the debtor's estate.

A "principal goal" of the Bankruptcy Code is to provide "open access" to the "bankruptcy process". Report of the Commission on the Bankruptcy Laws of the United States, H.R. Doc. No. 137, Part II, 93rd Cong., 1st Sess. 75, 79 (1973). * * * Another major goal of the Code, that of "rehabilitation of debtors", requires that relief for debtors must be "timely". *Id.* at 79. Congress declared that it is essential to both the "open access" and "rehabilitation" goals that

> [i]nitiating relief should not be a death knell. The process should encourage resort to it, by debtors and creditors, that cuts short the dissipation of assets and the accumulation of debts. Belated commencement of a case may kill an opportunity for reorganization or arrangement.

Id. at 75.

Accordingly, the drafters of the Code envisioned that a financially beleaguered debtor with real debt and real creditors should not be required to wait until the economic situation is beyond repair in order to file a reorganization petition. The "Congressional purpose" in enacting the Code was to encourage resort to the bankruptcy process. This philosophy not only comports with the elimination of an insolvency requirement, but also is a corrollary [sic] of the key aim of Chapter 11 of the Code, that of avoidance of liquidation. * * *

In the instant case, not only would liquidation be wasteful and inefficient in destroying the utility of valuable assets of the companies as well as jobs, but, more importantly, liquidation would preclude just compensation of some present asbestos victims and all future asbestos claimants. This unassailable reality represents all the more reason for this Court to adhere to this basic potential liquidation avoidance aim of Chapter 11 and deny the motions to dismiss. Manville must not be required to wait until its economic picture has deteriorated beyond salvation to file for reorganization.

* * *

Manville's purported motivation in filing to obtain a breathing spell from asbestos litigation should not conclusively establish its lack of intent to rehabilitate and justify the dismissal of its petition. On the contrary, there has been submitted no evidence that Manville has not bargained to obtain a reorganization plan in good faith.

2. Manville's "Good Faith" Filing Is Measured By The Existence Of Massive Unmanageable Real Debt Owed To Real Claimants

It is this Court's belief that there is no strict and absolute "good faith" predicate to filing a Chapter 11 petition. Earlier bankruptcy laws, for example, former Chapter X relating to corporate debtors, specifically required that the court find that the petition "had been filed in good faith". However, the present Bankruptcy Code contains no such express requirement.

This Court, along with others, has opined that the concept of good faith is an elastic one which can be read into the statute on a limited *ad hoc* basis. *In re Eden Associates*, 13 B.R. 578, 584 (Bankr. S.D.N.Y.1981). However, in *Eden* this Court also cautioned that slavish adherence to a good faith concept may redound to the detriment of those non-debtor claimants who are or may putatively be beneficiaries of the reorganization process. * * * [A] Chapter 11 filing creates a bankruptcy estate which exists for the benefit not simply of the debtor, but rather also for the benefit of all of the debtor's creditors and equity holders. The filing triggers the springing into existence of important constituencies which, along with the debtor, must be protected by a reorganization court. Accordingly, the intense focus on the debtor's motives in filing is misplaced. * * *

Moreover, courts have generally held that the concept of good faith as of the filing date may only be applied where it is demonstrated that the jurisdiction of the bankruptcy court has been abused. * * *

* * * In *Manville*, it is undeniable that there has been no sham or hoax perpetrated on the Court in that Manville is a real business with real creditors in pressing need of economic reorganization. Indeed, the Asbestos Committee has belied its own contention that Manville has no debt and no real creditors by quantifying a benchmark settlement demand approaching one billion dollars for compensation of approximately 15,500 prepetition asbestos claimants, during the course of negotiations pitched toward achieving a consensual plan. This huge asserted liability does not even take into account the estimated 6,000 new asbestos health claims which have arisen in only the first 16 months since the filing date. The number of post-filing claims increases each day as "future claims back into the present."

Moreover, asbestos related property damage claims present another substantial contingent and unliquidated liability. Prior to the filing date, various schools initiated litigation seeking compensatory and punitive damages from, *inter alia*, Manville for their unknowing use of asbestos-containing products in ceilings, walls, structural members, piping, ductwork and boilers in school buildings. * * *

Accordingly, it is clear that Manville's liability for compensatory, if not punitive, damages to school authorities is not hypothetical, but real and massive debt. A range of $500 million to $1.4 billion is the total projected amount of Manville's real debt to the school creditors.

In addition, claims of $425 million of liquidated commercial debt have been filed in this proceeding. The filing also triggered the acceleration of more than $275 million in unsecured public and institutional debt which had not been due prior to the filing. Upon a dismissal of this petition, Manville may be liable in the amount of all of the above-described real debts, plus interest. Manville's present holdings of cash and liquid assets would be insufficient to pay these obligations and, as noted above, its insurance carriers have repeatedly expressed their unwillingness to contribute to the payment of this debt. Thus, upon dismissal, Manville would become a target for economic dismemberment, liquidation, and chaos, which would benefit no one except the few winners of the race to the courthouse. The economic reality of Manville's highly precarious financial position due to massive debt sustains its eligibility and candidacy for reorganization.

In short, there was justification for Manville to elect a course contemplating a viable court-supervised rehabilitation of the real debt owed by Manville to its real creditors. Manville's filing did not in the appropriate sense abuse the jurisdiction of this Court * * *. Thus, its petition must be sustained.

3. That Tort Claims Are Dischargeable In Bankruptcy Is Further Indication That Manville Has Not Abused This Court's Jurisdiction

* * * [U]nder the Code, unlike under the predecessor Act, state court tort claims are dischargeable in bankruptcy. * * * Section 502(c) requires that the bankruptcy court estimate all unliquidated claims regardless of delay to administration of the estate with a resulting discharge of these claims. *See* §§ 502(c)(1) (claims estimation), 524 (effect of discharge) and 1141 (discharge effect of plan confirmation). * * *

Moreover, District Judge Leval of the Southern District of New York has recently recognized the appropriateness of claims estimation of these tort claims in connection with appellate review of this Court's decision denying an expansion of the automatic stay to cover Manville's tort co-defendants. He declared that "the bankruptcy judge will undoubtedly seek to design, with the cooperation of the claimants and the debtor, procedures for the adjudication or settlement of those [tort] claims in a rational consolidated fashion, whether in the bankruptcy court or elsewhere." *Keene Corp. v. Johns–Manville Corp.*, 31 B.R. 627, 628 (S.D.N.Y.1983).

Indeed, Manville has lodged a motion before this Court seeking to accomplish this very purpose. This motion coupled with Manville's currently proposed plan seeks to establish a claims-handling facility whose purpose would be to estimate asbestos-related claims in an expeditious fashion. According to the unilateral reorganization plan filed by Manville on November 21, 1983, this facility would consist, *inter alia*, of a "no fault" system where victims would submit their claims to a medical screening panel and receive a predetermined amount for the injury specified with subsequent reevaluation not precluded. Thus, Manville recognizes that these traditionally state law tort claims may be liquidated pursuant to § 502(c) as part of its first-filed reorganization plan.

Accordingly, a filing so as to substitute bankruptcy court procedures for estimation of these claims in and of itself does not constitute an abuse of the bankruptcy court's jurisdiction. Because tort claims are now dischargeable under the Code, simply because a company's economic pressures are tort-related in nature instead of more traditional financial business woes does not demonstrate an abuse of jurisdiction. * * *

In sum, Manville is a financially beseiged [sic] enterprise in desperate need of reorganization of its crushing real debt, both present and future. The reorganization provisions of the Code were drafted with the aim of liquidation avoidance by great access to Chapter 11. Accordingly, Manville's filing does not abuse the jurisdictional integrity of this Court, but rather presents * * * reasons * * * for awaiting the determination of Manville's good faith until it is considered under § 1129(a)(3) as a prerequisite to confirmation * * *.

D. The GAF, Whitman, and Co-defendants' Motions to Dismiss the Petition Must Be Denied

The GAF, Whitman and Co-defendants' motions to dismiss must be denied because future claimants, whether or not they possess dischargeable "claims", possess a cognizable interest in these proceedings. This interest must be protected. The motion filed by GAF * * * is based on the theory that because the claims of future asbestos claimants are not cognizable and dischargeable in bankruptcy, the *raison d'etre* for the filing is vitiated and thus the petition should be dismissed. As GAF declares in its statement of the case within its brief: "Such future 'liability' is not cognizable under the bankruptcy laws, and hence the same cannot be adjusted and discharged in these proceedings. The factual and legal predicate for the petition is therefore rendered a nullity and the same should be dismissed."

It is just this concern that the [court in a separate decision] responds to in establishing that future claimants are parties in interest to this reorganization case who must have their own legal representative to safeguard this keen and compelling interest. Because this Court finds that the claims of these asbestos-exposed claimants may survive the bankruptcy and look to be liquidated post-confirmation, the rights of these claimants will be significantly impacted by these proceedings. It is undeniable that these proceedings will result in a delivery system for

Manville tort claimants, whether in the present questionably efficient tort system, a newly-created claims-estimation facility, or another form. Thus, the *raison d'etre* for the filing is not a nullity and these proceedings are not a useless exercise. * * *

The Co-defendants' motion to dismiss the petition similarly must be dismissed as it too is predicated on the theory that future claims are not dischargeable in a Chapter 11 proceeding. The Co-defendants declare: "[W]e demonstrate that the object and purpose of Manville's petition for reorganization are inconsistent with the Bankruptcy Code." The Equity Holders Committee's scathing criticism with regard to the Whitman motion that "only the author of Alice in Wonderland might simply declare future claims out of existence in the face of massive evidence to the contrary" applies equally to the Co-defendants' motion.

Regarding the GAF, Whitman and Co-defendants' motions, it should be noted that it is indeed possible that a liquidating plan will eventuate. As stated earlier, the type of plan which emerges, *i.e.*, whether or not it treats with future claimants fairly, if at all, is irrelevant to the threshold determination made by this Court today as to the propriety or "good faith" of Manville's filing. These pejorative considerations are more appropriately left to the decision on confirmability of a concrete plan, as applied to a plan proponent, under § 1129 of the Code.

IV. Conclusion

For the reasons set forth above * * *, all four of the motions to dismiss the Manville petition are denied in their entirety.

Notes and Questions

1. Are *Manville* and *Phoenix Piccadilly* consistent? Was Phoenix Piccadilly any less a real debtor with real debt than Manville?

2. Why did these petitioning creditors want Manville's bankruptcy petition dismissed? Was bankruptcy in the best interests of Manville's stockholders?

3. Does it make sense that insolvency not be a prerequisite for the filing of a bankruptcy petition?

4. Section 1112(b) allows dismissal "for cause." Is the debtor's solvency "cause" within § 1112(b)?

5. Section 1129(a)(3) requires that the plan be proposed in good faith. Does the Code require that a Chapter 11 case be *filed* in good faith? *Cf.* § 1112.

The court in *In re SGL Carbon Corp.*, 200 F.3d 154 (3d Cir. 1999), expressly adopted a good faith filing requirement for Chapter 11, relying on four factors: the permissive language of § 1112; other circuit-level decisions, such as *Phoenix Piccadilly*, finding that lack of good faith constitutes cause for dismissing a Chapter 11 petition; bankruptcy's equitable roots; and the purpose of Chapter 11 to balance the interests of debtors and creditors, preventing abuse of the process by debtors whose overriding motive is to delay creditors. The court then found lack of good faith and dismissed the Chapter 11 petition, for lack of a valid reorganizational purpose, of a financially healthy corporation that filed in anticipation of civil antitrust liability, in an effort to pressure those plaintiffs to accept the corporation's settlement terms.

Other courts have had harsh words for the good faith filing doctrine followed by *Phoenix Piccadilly* and *SGL Carbon*, and rejected by *Manville*. In *In re Victoria Ltd. Partnership*, 187 B.R. 54 (Bankr. D. Mass. 1995), the court slammed the doctrine as "in conflict with the Code, legislative history, Supreme Court precedent, and logic," even though admitting that "[g]ood faith, like apple pie, is difficult to oppose." *Id.* at 54. *Phoenix Piccadilly* came in for particular criticism: "Stripped of much of its window dressing, *Phoenix Piccadilly* stands for the startling proposition that it is an act of bad faith for a debtor to file under chapter 11 in order to prevent foreclosure upon its only asset." *Id.* at 59. The court also found deficiencies in the logic of the doctrine:

> The good faith filing doctrine * * * is a prime example of how courts should not formulate a rule of law.
>
> A rule of law should be susceptible to clear statement, so that the result of its application to particular facts can be predicted with reasonable certainty. The good faith filing doctrine fails this test miserably. Its application does not depend upon the presence of any particular circumstances the courts list as relevant. Moreover, although a filing on the eve of foreclosure is typically stated to be a factor in the doctrine, courts recognize, as they must, that invoking the automatic stay is not of itself bad faith. If that is so, it is difficult to see why filing to prevent foreclosure is an indicator of bad faith when combined with other factors. Also often stated as a factor in the doctrine is the debtor's perceived inability to reorganize. And yet, as demonstrated by *Phoenix Piccadilly*, not even this is an essential element.

* * *

> In sum, the good faith filing doctrine is an amorphous gestalt, devoid of reasoning and impenetrable to understanding.

Id. at 61-62.

As a parting shot, the court in *Victoria Ltd. Partnership* found the doctrine inconsistent with § 362(d)(3), which was added to the Code in 1994: "Congress obviously recognized the propriety of reorganization by single asset real estate debtors and their need for a reasonable period of time in which to file a plan of reorganization. The good faith filing doctrine all but bars them from reorganizing." *Id.* at 62.

6. Judge Lifland appointed a Wall Street attorney to protect the interests of future claimants in *Manville*, as an attorney would protect the interests of an unborn heir in a probate proceeding. As a result of the attorney's negotiations, Johns–Manville agreed to put certain assets, along with profits generated by them, in trust for the benefit of existing and future claimants. Though Judge Lifland did not treat the future claimants as creditors and so did not discharge their claims against Johns–Manville, he did identify them as "parties in interest" and permanently enjoined them from making claims against *other* assets of the corporation.

In 1994, Congress addressed the issue of claims that are to be paid through a trust in bankruptcy. An amendment to § 524 added a new subsection (g) that focuses directly on the rights of asbestosis victims, effectively codifying *Manville*'s trust device. The new provision allows a bankruptcy court to establish a trust from which future claimants may receive compensation, and it enjoins those future claimants from bringing an action against the reorganizing debtor.

The following case raises the issue of dismissal in a context very different from *Manville*—that is, an individual debtor's petition under Chapter 7.

FIRST USA v. LAMANNA (IN RE LAMANNA)

United States Court of Appeals, First Circuit, 1998.
153 F.3d 1.

LYNCH, Circuit Judge.

The question presented is the meaning of "substantial abuse" under § 707(b) of the Bankruptcy Code and the criteria by which it is measured. This is a question of first instance in this circuit. A Chapter

7 bankruptcy petition of an individual debtor whose debts are primarily consumer debts may be dismissed if the court finds that granting relief would be a "substantial abuse" of the Chapter.

Richard Lamanna sought relief from approximately $15,000 of primarily consumer debt by filing for bankruptcy under Chapter 7. The bankruptcy court sua sponte dismissed Lamanna's petition as a "substantial abuse" of Chapter 7 based on the finding that Lamanna had sufficient disposable income to pay off his debts under a Chapter 13 payment schedule. The Bankruptcy Appellate Panel (BAP) affirmed for the same reason.

On appeal, Lamanna argues that the BAP misconstrued § 707(b) as meaning that "substantial abuse" automatically exists where a debtor's income exceeds his expenses even minimally. Lamanna says that his expenses are artificially low because he has avoided normal expenses by living with his parents, and that it cannot constitute "substantial abuse" of the bankruptcy system for a debtor to live with parents who subsidize his needs. Lamanna also says that "substantial abuse" under § 707(b) refers only to acts of bad faith, and that there is no evidence of bad faith.

As amicus curiae, the United States Trustee argues that the court did not apply a per se future income test. He emphasizes that Lamanna's schedules show that he can repay 100% of his debts out of future disposable income and that, despite ample opportunity, Lamanna presented no evidence of countervailing factors which militated against dismissal. The Trustee invites this court to adopt the "totality of circumstances" test, employed by both the bankruptcy court and BAP, as the law of this circuit.

We adopt the "totality of the circumstances" test as the measure of "substantial abuse" under § 707(b) of the Bankruptcy Code. In doing so, we join the Fourth, Sixth, Eighth and Ninth Circuits in holding that a consumer debtor's ability to repay his debts out of future disposable [income] is not per se "substantial abuse" mandating dismissal. At the same time, we do not require a court to look beyond the debtor's ability to repay if that factor warrants the result. We explicitly reject the notion that "substantial abuse" refers only to bad faith acts, although a court may consider a debtor's bad faith acts in making its decision. Applying this test, we find that the BAP correctly decided that allowing Lamanna's petition would constitute a "substantial abuse" of Chapter 7, and affirm.

I.

Richard Lamanna, a Rhode Island resident, filed for bankruptcy under Chapter 7 on February 18, 1997.[1] Lamanna's schedules, filed with his voluntary petition, show that he has total unsecured debt of $15,911.96 which is primarily consumer debt, his monthly income is $1,350.96, and his monthly expenses are $580. Lamanna's income therefore exceeds his expenses by $770.96 per month, the amount of his disposable income.

On February 24, 1997, the bankruptcy court sua sponte ordered Lamanna to show cause why his petition should not be dismissed as a "substantial abuse" of Chapter 7 under § 707(b). In the show cause order, the court noted that Lamanna's schedules showed that he was capable of paying 100% of his debts over three years under a Chapter 13 payment plan.[5]

At the show-cause hearing, Lamanna argued that his expenses were artificially low because he was living with his parents. Without that subsidy, he said, he could not limit his expenses to $580 per month and would thus have no disposable income with which to pay his debts. Yet Lamanna acknowledged that his scheduled expenses and income were accurate and that he did not anticipate a change in living circumstances, i.e., moving out of his parents' house, that would precipitate a rise in living expenses.

The bankruptcy court, applying the "totality of the circumstances" test, found "substantial abuse" and dismissed the case. The BAP affirmed on the same grounds. Lamanna appeals.

II.

The question of whether allowing Lamanna's bankruptcy petition would constitute "substantial abuse" of Chapter 7 under § 707(b)

---

[1] Lamanna signed and dated his petition, along with his schedules, on November 22, 1996. During the four week period immediately prior to signing the documents, he charged $9,994.45 on credit cards and personal credit lines. This amounts to 63% of Lamanna's total debt. The Trustee suggests that this may be evidence of bad faith on Lamanna's part. We decline to decide that issue. The BAP did not make a finding regarding bad faith in deciding the case, and relied entirely on analysis of Lamanna's ability to repay.

[5] Lamanna could pay his debt over three years by making monthly payments of $491.10 to the Chapter 13 trustee. Lamanna could also pay his debt over five years by making monthly payments of $294.66.

contains two components: first, the proper test by which "substantial abuse" is measured; second, whether, applying that test, the BAP correctly decided the issue. The facts are undisputed, and we review de novo the BAP's conclusions of law.

A. *The "Totality of the Circumstances" Test*

Although "substantial abuse" is not self-defining, the history and policies underlying § 707(b) give content to its meaning and purpose. That history is well set out in previous opinions. See *In re Green*, 934 F.2d 568, 570 (4th Cir. 1991); *In re Krohn*, 886 F.2d 123, 125-26 (6th Cir. 1989); *In re Walton*, 866 F.2d 981, 983 (8th Cir. 1989); *In re Kelly*, 841 F.2d 908, 914 (9th Cir. 1988). We summarize the pertinent points.

Section 707(b) was added to the Bankruptcy Code as part of the Bankruptcy Amendments and Federal Judgeship Act of 1984. It authorizes a bankruptcy court, either sua sponte or on the motion of the United States Trustee, to dismiss the Chapter 7 petition of an individual debtor who owes primarily consumer debts where allowing the petition would be a "substantial abuse" of Chapter 7. Congress chose neither to define "substantial abuse" in the 1984 Act nor to leave specific guidance in legislative history. Congress thus left a flexible standard enabling courts to address each petition on its own merit.

The primary impetus for the enactment of § 707(b) was the credit industry's unhappiness with the fact that consumer debtors who were able to repay their debts had increasingly been filing for bankruptcy relief since the enactment of the 1978 Bankruptcy Act. "Prior to 1984, debtors enjoyed a virtually unfettered right to a 'fresh start' under Chapter 7, in exchange for liquidating their nonexempt assets for the benefit of their creditors." *Green*, 934 F.2d at 570. Section 707(b) was enacted to impose a restraint on consumer debtors' access to Chapter 7 discharge by interposing bankruptcy courts as gatekeepers who could examine the worthiness of debtor petitions and dismiss those petitions deemed abusive. As the *Walton* court summarized, § 707(b) was "aimed primarily at stemming the use of Chapter 7 by unneedy debtors." 866 F.2d at 983. "Substantial abuse" thus attempts to moderate the tension between "upholding creditors' interests in obtaining repayment where such repayment would not be a burden," *Kelly*, 841 F.2d at 914, and maintaining the ability of worthy debtors to gain access to Chapter 7's substantial protections. Section 707(b)'s ambiguity is inherent in its function as a guide to equitable discretion.

With "substantial abuse" lacking specific meaning, it has fallen to the courts to determine how "substantial abuse" ought to be measured. Although tests employed by various courts of appeals do not employ precisely the same language, they share common elements. First and foremost, it is agreed that a consumer debtor's ability to repay his debts out of future disposable income is strong evidence of "substantial abuse". *Kelly* and *Walton* focus primarily upon ability to repay, while *Green* and *Krohn* emphasize the need to consider the "totality of the circumstances." *Krohn* offers this test:

> In determining whether to apply § 707(b) to an individual debtor, * * * a court should ascertain from the totality of the circumstances whether he is merely seeking an advantage over his creditors, or is "honest," in the sense that his relationship with his creditors has been marked by essentially honorable and undeceptive dealings, and whether he is "needy" in the sense that his financial predicament warrants the discharge of his debts in exchange for liquidation of his assets. Substantial abuse can be predicated upon either lack of honesty or want of need.
>
> * * *
>
> Among the factors to be considered in deciding whether a debtor is needy is his ability to repay his debts out of future earnings. That factor alone may be sufficient to warrant dismissal. For example, a court would not be justified in concluding that a debtor is needy and worthy of discharge, where his disposable income permits liquidation of his consumer debts with relative ease. Other factors relevant to need include whether the debtor enjoys a stable source of future income, whether he is eligible for adjustments of his debts through Chapter 13 of the Bankruptcy Code, whether there are state remedies with the potential to ease his financial predicament, the degree of relief obtainable through private negotiations, and whether his expenses can be reduced significantly without depriving him of adequate food, clothing, shelter and other necessities.

Krohn, 886 F.2d at 126-27 (citations omitted). As described by *Krohn*, the "totality of the circumstances" test demands a comprehensive review of the debtor's current and potential financial situation.

We adopt the "totality of the circumstances" test largely as it is described in *Krohn*. In so doing, we reject any per se rules mandating dismissal for "substantial abuse" whenever the debtor is able to repay his debt out of future disposable income, or forbidding dismissal on that basis alone. Such strict interpretations cannot be squared with the open-textured nature of § 707(b) and are inconsistent with § 707(b)'s purpose of guiding, not constraining, bankruptcy courts in the exercise of their equitable discretion. We hold that a bankruptcy court may, but is not required to, find "substantial abuse" if the debtor has an ability to repay, in light of all of the circumstances.

In sum, in assessing the totality of a debtor's circumstances, courts should regard the debtor's ability to repay out of future disposable income as the primary, but not necessarily conclusive, factor of "substantial abuse." The factors recited in *Krohn* should be regarded as a nonexclusive list of relevant considerations.

B. *Application of the Standard*

Applying the "totality of the circumstances" test to Lamanna's case results in affirmance of the dismissal of his Chapter 7 petition for "substantial abuse." Lamanna's schedules showed that he has sufficient disposable income to repay his debts under a Chapter 13 repayment plan in three to five years. There is no evidence that Lamanna's living situation was unstable or likely to change in the near future. There is no evidence of other factors that cast doubt on the stability of Lamanna's future income and expenses. Although Lamanna's expenses are particularly low because he lives with his parents, this state of affairs, as the BAP noted, "is not artificial; it is actual." The court properly based its decision on the current and foreseeable facts. If Lamanna's circumstances dramatically change, he is free to seek relief anew.

Lamanna's argument that the court penalized him for living with his parents (and thus having exceptionally low monthly expenses) boils down to the notion that § 707 requires the bankruptcy court to impute a minimum cost of living to a debtor and then measure the debtor's actual income against the higher of the imputed minimum and the debtor's actual expenses. Section 707 does not contain such an implicit requirement, and this court will not write such a requirement into the statute.

Finally, we reject Lamanna's argument that the court imposed a "mechanically applied future income test" in determining that allowing Lamanna's petition would constitute "substantial abuse" of Chapter 7. The BAP's decision was not mechanical; it was simply uncomplicated.

III.

We adopt the "totality of the circumstances" test as the measure of "substantial abuse" under § 707(b) in this circuit. Applying this test, we hold that the court correctly decided to dismiss Lamanna's Chapter 7 petition. The decision is affirmed. Costs are awarded to the United States Trustee.

Questions

1. If Manville's solvency does not constitute a reason to dismiss, why does Lamanna's ability to pay something to his creditors support dismissal?

2. The court said that it rejected per se rules and that ability to repay is "the primary, but not necessarily conclusive, factor" under § 707(b). What are the other relevant factors? What more was present in this case?

3. Is *Lamanna* explained, at least in part, by negative assumptions about the nature and character of people who file bankruptcy? A path-breaking empirical study of bankruptcy debtors, which was conducted by two law professors and a sociologist, attempted to determine whether individuals who file bankruptcy can in fact repay their debts:

> Ultimately, the central question most people pose about bankruptcy is whether those who file could have repaid their debts if bankruptcy had not been available. Is the process one of humane discharge or sanctioned abuse?
>
> No single question has a more profound and direct influence on bankruptcy policy. If it is the needy who use bankruptcy, the bankruptcy system can focus on efficiency and fairness. The present system has a number of provisions directed at abuse and there will always be concern with abuse, but it would be a peripheral issue in a system perceived to serve the truly deserving. On the other hand, if the system is shot through with slick manipulation, bankruptcy should be structured around protections to weed out abusers even at greater cost to everyone, including the needy.
>
> * * * [I]n 1984 Congress passed amendments to the Bankruptcy Code that imposed substantial new restrictions on consumer bankruptcy. These amendments were adopted in response to a perceived problem of abuse. On a theoretical level, economists viewed bankruptcy as a very attractive alternative for the rational debtor and therefore theorized that many debtors would be eager to benefit from it. This theoretical proposition seemed to be confirmed by an empirical study done by Purdue University, which claimed that many Chapter 7 debtors could pay a "substantial" part of their debts.

Our data show that consumers in bankruptcy look very much like the rest of America in their work, but very different in their financial circumstances. The data for the debtors show that, on average, they are at the extreme end of the financial spectrum—earning less and owing more than most Americans, so that their overall financial condition makes them worse off than most of the population. But being at the bottom of the credit heap does not necessarily mean these debtors could not pay. If a substantial portion of debtors could repay, then bankruptcy policy must account for them. On the other hand, if the abusers are rare, the system may have braced for an onslaught that is not coming.

The Moral Definition of "Can Pay"

"How many debtors can pay?" is in part a normative question: the answer depends on moral and social value judgments. Some advocates mask this point in discussions of bankruptcy, speaking as if the ability to pay were an objective fact like height or weight. A debtor's ability to pay is a function of the level of sacrifice demanded. All of us might prefer to skip paying our monthly bills in favor of having a party or buying a new car, but we would hardly claim that this preference made us unable to pay. On the other hand, nearly all of us would agree that an elderly widow with few assets, living on her social security, "can't pay" the massive debts left by the failure of her late husband's business (a case in our files). Where to draw the line—how much sacrifice to require of people in debt—is the key question in bankruptcy.

[The authors described their methodology and their conclusions that only 3% of debtors could pay 100% of their unsecured debts by selling all of their assets, both real and personal. Only 10% of debtors could repay 100% of their unsecured debts out of future income over a three-year period, while living on the Bureau of Labor Statistics' low budget. Ninety percent of debtors could not pay their debts and simultaneously maintain a minimal standard of living.]

Policy Implications

To most people, abuse of the bankruptcy system means use of bankruptcy by those who could pay if they were willing to give up those assets that they had bought and now want to keep without paying. In the more sophisticated debates that have taken place in Congress, the assumed source of repayment is the debtor's future income, which would be ample to pay creditors if the debtor had a truly moral view of the obligation to keep promises. * * * We found very little capacity to repay in either way, although some will feel that the little we found justifies expending considerable resources to ferret out "can-pay" debtors and make them pay. We have sympathy with this point. But we also have great reservations.

We see bankruptcy as a social safety net. * * * [T]hose who use bankruptcy are not the underclass, the homeless, or the chronically unemployed. Not surprisingly, those in the worst economic circumstances are unlikely to gather sufficient credit to find themselves in bankruptcy. Instead, the debtors in bankruptcy are those who own homes, who work alongside other Americans, who participate in a middle-class lifestyle.

* * *

After an exhaustive (and exhausting) search for a sizable group of can-pay debtors, we find so few likely prospects for repayment that we conclude the effort to keep can-pay debtors out of bankruptcy or force them into Chapter 13 is a wasteful misdirection of energy. Out of 1202 wage earner debtors, only a handful could pay their debts by making payments from future income. The self-employed debtors, with their much higher debt/income ratios, were in worse shape with even lower repayment prospects. * * *

We conclude that bankruptcy laws should not be shaped around the can-pay question. When Congress responded to allegations of widespread abuse in 1984, it wrote a law to correct a problem that did not exist. The "solution" was costly to debtors who later used the system even though the changes would have little appreciable affect [sic] on actual abuse.

* * *

[Section 707(b)] permits the bankruptcy judge to examine a debtor's circumstances to see if the debtor's decision to file Chapter 7 is a substantial abuse of the bankruptcy system. If the court finds abuse, the debtor faces the choice of filing in Chapter 13 or staying out of bankruptcy altogether. It is likely that the scheme identifies some abusers, but no announced standards for the search exist and judges are supposed to make the investigation on their own without any prompting from the creditors.

The failure to use announced standards permits the court to pursue any "abuse" it finds, but it also has the potential to create a random system of justice. One leading case interpreting the new provision stated that there should be no finding of abuse unless the debtors could pay substantially all their debts in Chapter 13 [*In re Edwards*, 50 B.R. 933 (Bankr. S.D.N.Y.1985)], while another decision seems to bar from Chapter 7 everyone who could pay anything whatever to creditors under Chapter 13 [*In re Walton*, 69 B.R. 150 (E.D.Mo. 1986)]. * * *

On balance, we think that the mitigation of a relatively small level of clear abuse is not worth idiosyncratic, luck-of-the-draw justice. We have enough confidence in the operation of the consumer bankruptcy system to tolerate the occasional story of the local paper about a debtor who kept a mink coat, knowing that the debtor is rare and the details might reveal a very different picture.

* * * Chapter 13 has not turned out to be what was promised. For years participants in bankruptcy policy debates have talked about Chapter 13 as if it were a panacea, as if getting a debtor into Chapter 13 were virtually the same thing as getting all or most debts paid. Congress struggled in the 1978 Code to make Chapter 13 attractive, so debtors would file there and repay. The Purdue Study concluded that $1.1 billion would be repaid, if only those Chapter 7 debtors would take Chapter 13—their enthusiasm unencumbered by facts from a single Chapter 13 file.

Our data show the contrary. Debtors in Chapter 13 fail at extraordinary rates, with fewer than a third still making payments an average of two years after confirmation. On average, those who are paying have proposed plans that promise to pay only about half their debts. This is not surprising, considering how little they have. And some might say that a debtor who repays something is better than a debtor who does not. But with plans paying considerably less than 100%, it is not possible to know whether Chapter 13's pay creditors more than Chapter 7's. * * *

The implications of these findings for establishing policy are far reaching. In 1981 choosing Chapter 13 was an entirely voluntary act, with no legal bar to a Chapter 7 nor any creditor leverage to force a Chapter 13, which makes the failure rate in Chapter 13 all the more noteworthy. High failure rate among volunteers raises serious questions about the efficacy of proposals to force debtors into Chapter 13. If success eludes most debtors who evaluate their own finances and their own desire to pay their debts, and choose to try to pay, how much payment can we expect from those who are coerced into payment plans? We conclude that continued efforts to force more debtors into Chapter 13 may drive up Chapter 13 filings rates but will not necessarily add up to creditor repayment.

Teresa A. Sullivan, Elizabeth Warren & Jay L. Westbrook, As We Forgive Our Debtors: Bankruptcy and Consumer Credit in America 199–200, 219, 220, 221–22 (1989) (footnotes omitted).

Note on Voluntary Dismissal

What happens when debtors file for bankruptcy and then decide on their own initiative to dismiss the petition? In *In re Underwood*, 7 B.R. 936 (Bankr. W.Va.1981), debtors moved to dismiss their joint Chapter 7 petition so that they could refile and include a new debt incurred after the original filing. (During the case, the debtor-husband was involved in an automobile accident that gave rise to a $2,400 damages claim.) Although dismissal of a bankruptcy petition under § 707 requires a showing of cause, debtors cited precedent establishing that cause need not be shown when no party objects to dismissal. The court found, however, that debtors could not invoke that exception in the absence of proof that postpetition creditors had notice of debtors' plan to dismiss and refile.

In an attempt to establish cause, debtors argued that denial of their motion to dismiss would subvert the Bankruptcy Code's goal of furnishing them with a "fresh start." The court, however, likened the filing-dismissal-filing scheme to two separate discharges and cited § 727(a)(8), which prohibits a second Chapter 7 discharge within six years of the first. The court felt that dismissal of the first petition before a discharge was granted would present the same prejudice to postpetition creditors. To allow such dismissal would raise "the prospect of carefully timed dismissal requests which delay the entry of the discharge while new debts are being added" and would inequitably prejudice "the rights of those creditors who extended credit after the initial petition." *Id.* at 938. The court also took into account the administrative burden that such multiple filings and dismissals would place on the court system.

The court denied debtors' motion to dismiss, but noted that they could accomplish their goal by obtaining a discharge under the original Chapter 7 petition and then, with regard to any undischarged debts, filing a Chapter 13 petition. Section 727(a)(8) permits debtors to receive a discharge in Chapter 13 notwithstanding a Chapter 7 discharge in the past six years.

Contrary to the rule requiring a debtor to show cause for dismissal in a Chapter 7 case, other chapters seem to afford debtors a virtually absolute right to dismiss the petition. Section 1307(b) gives a debtor an absolute right to dismiss a Chapter 13 petition at any time before the case is converted to Chapter 7 or Chapter 11. Any waiver of that right is unenforceable. The rule does not apply, however, if the proceeding was converted to Chapter 13 from Chapters 7, 11 or 12. Similarly, § 1208(b) permits a debtor to dismiss a Chapter 12 petition at any time prior to the conversion of the case to a Chapter 7 or Chapter 11 case. Again, waiver of this right to dismiss is unenforceable.

Although a debtor's right to dismiss a Chapter 12 or 13 petition voluntarily seems almost absolute, a court may refuse dismissal on the basis of other Code sections. For instance, § 1208(d) allows a court to dismiss a debtor's Chapter 12 petition or convert the case to Chapter 7 upon the motion of a party in interest, if that party can show that the debtor committed fraud in connection with the Chapter 12 case. Similarly, § 1307(c) permits a court to dismiss or convert a debtor's Chapter 13 petition for cause. These provisions have lead to inconsistent results when debtors have sought voluntary dismissal of Chapter 12 or 13 petitions. In *Graven v. Fink (In re Graven)*, 936 F.2d 378 (8th Cir.1991), for example, a farmer who had filed for Chapter 12 reorganization sought to have the petition dismissed pursuant to § 1208(b). Before the petition could actually be dismissed, however, one of the farmer's creditors sought conversion to Chapter 7, alleging with the support of overwhelming evidence that the farmer had fraudulently transferred all of his assets to family members and closely held corporations prior to filing the Chapter 12 petition. Notwithstanding the farmer's § 1208(b) motion to dismiss, the bankruptcy court converted the case as requested by the creditor. The district court affirmed and the farmer appealed to the Eighth Circuit, arguing that § 1208(b) requires immediate dismissal upon a debtor's request, regardless of motions filed by other parties or allegations of fraud.

The Court of Appeals recognized that the language of § 1208(b) seems to give a debtor an absolute right to dismiss a Chapter 12 petition voluntarily, and that § 1208(d) does not specifically state that a motion to convert by a creditor overrides a debtor's motion to dismiss. The court concluded, however, that Congress enacted the Bankruptcy Code to provide protection for honest debtors, "not to provide a shield for those who exploit the code's protection then seek to escape judicial authority when their fraudulent schemes are exposed." *Id.* at 385. To permit § 1208(b) to give debtors an absolute right to dismiss would render meaningless a court's power under § 1208(d), which was enacted to protect against exactly the types of abuses that had occurred in the case. The court upheld conversion of the case to a Chapter 7 proceeding pursuant to § 1208(d).

In a similar fact pattern, however, the court in *Barbieri v. RAJ Acquisition Corp (In re Barbieri)*, 199 F.3d 616 (2d Cir. 1999), permitted dismissal. The debtor, who had contracted to sell an apartment building, filed a Chapter 13 petition in an effort to escape her contractual obligations when she found another buyer willing to pay a higher price. The bankruptcy court expressed its intention to convert the case to Chapter 7, but the debtor's attorney requested dismissal before the court's order was actually issued. The Second

Circuit held that § 1307(b) gives debtors an absolute right to dismiss, as long as the case has not been converted, that is not limited by § 1307(c). The court said that "concerns about abuse of the bankruptcy system do not license us to redraft the statute," and listed a number of other ways that abuse of the bankruptcy process, if it occurs, can be curbed.

C. PROPERTY OF THE ESTATE

Section 541(a) provides that the filing of a bankruptcy petition creates an estate that is comprised of "all legal or equitable interests of the debtor in property." Congress intentionally enacted a broad definition. Only property of the estate is subjected to bankruptcy administration. Thus, whether particular property is included in the estate is especially important in Chapter 7 cases, because only estate property is liquidated and its proceeds distributed to creditors.

Notes and Problems

1. Determine whether the following assets would be property of the bankruptcy estate under § 541:

a. Right to use the name of a company that was in business for twenty-five years before filing a petition in bankruptcy.

b. Copyrights owned in full by a bankrupt publisher.

c. Copyrights a bankrupt publisher shares with various authors.

d. Residential lease for a rent-controlled apartment in New York City, occupied by the debtor.

e. Commercial lease for warehouse space under which a bankrupt shipping company is lessee. *Cf.* § 541(b)(2).

2. Heavenly Hamburgers rents the small shop from which it sells the biggest, greasiest burgers in town. Sales have fallen since a local TV news story reported the cholesterol count in HH's burgers. HH filed bankruptcy with six years left to run on its lease. One of the terms of the lease provides for immediate termination upon the filing of any insolvency proceeding. Will HH's interest in the remaining lease term become property of its bankruptcy estate? See § 541(c)(1).

3. One of the most important principles in bankruptcy—that property rights created by state law are respected in bankruptcy—derives from two important pre-Code Supreme Court cases.

In *Board of Trade of the City of Chicago v. Johnson*, 264 U.S. 1, 44 S.Ct. 232, 68 L.Ed. 533 (1924), the debtor had a seat on the Board of Trade. Members could, under Board rules, transfer their memberships only if debts owed to other members were paid in full, but sale of memberships in order to pay debts could not be compelled. The debtor owed $60,000 to other members at the time bankruptcy was filed. Although the membership was not property under state law, the Supreme Court refused to limit "property" for bankruptcy purposes to correspond with state law and held that the membership became property of the estate.

What is "property" within § 541(a) remains a bankruptcy, not a state law, issue. Section 541(a)(1) provides, however, that only the debtor's interest in property becomes property of the estate. *Chicago Board of Trade* is relevant to that question as well, because the Court also held that the $60,000 owed to other members "must be satisfied before the trustee can realize anything on the transfer of the seat for the general estate." 264 U.S. at 15. In other words, the debtor's interest in his seat on the Board was encumbered by an obligation to pay debts to other members before the membership could be transferred; thus, the property in the trustee's hands was similarly encumbered. Under *Chicago Board of Trade*, therefore, what is "property" is determined by federal bankruptcy law, but the nature of the property rights (that is, the *attributes* of "property") are governed by state law.

The Court reiterated in *Butner v. United States*, 440 U.S. 48, 99 S.Ct. 914, 59 L.Ed.2d 136 (1979), that state law rights will be respected in bankruptcy unless bankruptcy policy mandates a different rule. In *Butner*, a mortgagee asserted a right to postpetition rents generated by the debtor's real property. The Court of Appeals held that the mortgagee had not taken the steps required by state law to create an entitlement to rents. The Supreme Court expressly declined to decide whether the Court of Appeals had applied state law correctly. Instead, the Court sought to decide the "proper approach" to such disputes—specifically, whether state law should determine entitlement to rents. The Court held that it should: "Property interests are created and defined by state law. Unless some federal interest requires a different result, there is no reason why such interests should be analyzed differently simply because an interested party is involved in a bankruptcy proceeding. Uniform treatment of property interests by both state and federal courts within a State serves to reduce uncertainty, to discourage forum shopping, and to prevent a party from receiving 'a windfall merely by reason of the happenstance of bankruptcy.'" 440 U.S. at 55 (citation omitted).

Congress passed the Employee Retirement Income Security Act of 1974 (ERISA), 29 U.S.C. §§ 1001 et seq., in order to provide nationally-uniform protection for workers' pension benefits. In order to be "ERISA-qualified," and thus eligible for favorable tax treatment, a plan must provide that plan benefits "may not be assigned or alienated." With such a provision, an ERISA-qualified plan appears to be excluded from the bankruptcy estate by § 541(c)(2). The legislative history, however, stated that (c)(2) was intended to preserve "restrictions on transfer of a spendthrift trust" if such restrictions are enforceable under nonbankruptcy law. Under state spendthrift trust law, self-settled trusts—*i.e.*, those created by a debtor for his or her own benefit—cannot be insulated from the reach of creditors. The problem arises because a pension plan may be both ERISA-qualified and self-settled. The question became whether § 541(c)(2) excludes from the bankruptcy estate only those plans that meet the stringent requirements of state spendthrift trust law, or whether ERISA-qualified plans, with their transfer restrictions, are also covered. The circuit courts divided on the issue.

PATTERSON v. SHUMATE

United States Supreme Court, 1992.
504 U.S. 753, 112 S.Ct. 2242, 119 L.Ed.2d 519.

JUSTICE BLACKMUN delivered the opinion of the Court.

The Bankruptcy Code excludes from the bankruptcy estate property of the debtor that is subject to a restriction on transfer enforceable under "applicable nonbankruptcy law." § 541(c)(2). We must decide in this case whether an anti-alienation provision contained in an ERISA-qualified pension plan constitutes a restriction on transfer enforceable under "applicable nonbankruptcy law," and whether, accordingly, a debtor may exclude his interest in such a plan from the property of the bankruptcy estate.

I

Respondent Joseph B. Shumate, Jr., was employed for over 30 years by Coleman Furniture Corporation, where he ultimately attained the position of president and chairman of the board of directors. Shumate and approximately 400 other employees were participants in the Coleman Furniture Corporation Pension Plan (Plan). The Plan satisfied all applicable requirements of the Employee Retirement Income Security Act of 1974 (ERISA) and qualified for favorable tax treatment under the Internal Revenue Code. In particular, Article 16.1 of the Plan contained the anti-alienation provision required for qualification under § 206(d)(1) of ERISA, 29 U.S.C. § 1056(d)(1) ("Each pension plan shall provide that benefits provided under the plan may not be assigned or alienated"). Shumate's interest in the plan was valued at $250,000.

In 1982, Coleman Furniture filed a petition for bankruptcy under Chapter 11 of the Bankruptcy Code. The case was converted to a Chapter 7 proceeding and a trustee, Roy V. Creasy, was appointed. Shumate himself encountered financial difficulties and filed a petition for bankruptcy in 1984. His case, too, was converted to a Chapter 7 proceeding, and petitioner John R. Patterson was appointed trustee.

Creasy terminated and liquidated the Plan, providing full distributions to all participants except Shumate. Patterson then filed an adversary proceeding against Creasy in the Bankruptcy Court for the Western District of Virginia to recover Shumate's interest in the Plan for the benefit of Shumate's bankruptcy estate. Shumate in turn asked the United States District Court for the Western District of Virginia, which already had jurisdiction over a related proceeding, to compel Creasy to pay Shumate's interest in the Plan directly to him. The bankruptcy proceeding subsequently was consolidated with the district court action.

The District Court rejected Shumate's contention that his interest in the Plan should be excluded from his bankruptcy estate. The court held that § 541(c)(2)'s reference to "nonbankruptcy law" embraced only state law, not federal law such as ERISA. Applying Virginia law, the court held that Shumate's interest in the Plan did not qualify for protection as a spendthrift trust. The District Court also rejected Shumate's alternative argument that even if his interest in the Plan could not be excluded from the bankruptcy estate under § 541(c)(2), he was entitled to an exemption under § 522(b)(2)(A), which allows a debtor to exempt from property of the estate "any property that is exempt under Federal law." The District Court ordered Creasy to pay Shumate's interest in the Plan over to his bankruptcy estate.

The Court of Appeals for the Fourth Circuit reversed. The court relied on its earlier decision in *Anderson v. Raine (In re Moore)*, 907 F.2d 1476 (1990), in which another Fourth Circuit panel was described as holding, subsequent to the District Court's decision in the instant case, that "ERISA-qualified plans, which by definition have a non-alienation provision, constitute 'applicable nonbankruptcy law' and contain enforceable restrictions on the transfer of pension interests." Thus, the Court of Appeals held that Shumate's interest in the Plan should be excluded from the bankruptcy estate under § 541(c)(2). The court then declined to consider Shumate's alternative argument that his interest in the Plan qualified for exemption under § 522(b).

We granted certiorari to resolve the conflict among the Courts of Appeals as to whether an anti-alienation provision in an ERISA-qualified pension plan constitutes a restriction on transfer enforceable under "applicable nonbankruptcy law" for purposes of the § 541(c)(2) exclusion of property from the debtor's bankruptcy estate.

II

A

In our view, the plain language of the Bankruptcy Code and ERISA is our determinant. Section 541(c)(2) provides the following exclusion from the otherwise broad definition of "property of the estate" contained in § 541(a)(1) of the Code:

> "A restriction on the transfer of a beneficial interest of the debtor in a trust that is enforceable under *applicable nonbankruptcy law* is enforceable in a case under this title" (emphasis added).

The natural reading of the provision entitles a debtor to exclude from property of the estate any interest in a plan or trust that contains a transfer restriction enforceable under any relevant nonbankruptcy law. Nothing in § 541 suggests that the phrase "applicable nonbankruptcy law" refers, as petitioner contends, exclusively to *state* law. The text contains no limitation on "applicable nonbankruptcy law" relating to the source of the law.

Reading the term "applicable nonbankruptcy law" in § 541(c)(2) to include federal as well as state law comports with other references in the Bankruptcy Code to sources of law. The Code reveals, significantly, that Congress, when it desired to do so, knew how to restrict the scope of applicable law to "state law" and did so with some frequency. See, *e.g.*, § 109(c)(2) (entity may be a debtor under chapter 9 if authorized "by State law"); § 522(b)(1) (election of exemptions controlled by "the State law that is applicable to the debtor"); § 523(a)(5) (a debt for alimony, maintenance, or support determined "in accordance with State or territorial law" is not dischargeable); § 903(1) ("a State law prescribing a method of composition of indebtedness" of municipalities is not binding on nonconsenting creditors); see also §§ 362(b)(12) and 1145(a). Congress' decision to use the broader phrase "applicable nonbankruptcy law" in § 541(c)(2) strongly suggests that it did not intend to restrict the provision in the manner that petitioner contends.

The text of § 541(c)(2) does not support petitioner's contention that "applicable nonbankruptcy law" is limited to state law. Plainly read, the provision encompasses any relevant nonbankruptcy law, including federal law such as ERISA. We must enforce the statute according to its terms.

B

Having concluded that "applicable nonbankruptcy law" is not limited to state law, we next determine whether the anti-alienation provision contained in the ERISA-qualified plan at issue here satisfies the literal terms of § 541(c)(2).

Section 206(d)(1) of ERISA, which states that "[e]ach pension plan shall provide that benefits provided under the plan may not be assigned or alienated," 29 U.S.C. § 1056(d)(1), clearly imposes a "restriction on the transfer" of a debtor's "beneficial interest" in the trust. The coordinate section of the Internal Revenue Code, 26 U.S.C. § 401(a)(13), states as a general rule that "[a] trust shall not constitute a qualified trust under this section unless the plan of which such trust is a part provides that benefits provided under the plan may not be assigned or alienated," and thus contains similar restrictions.

Coleman Furniture's pension plan complied with these requirements. Article 16.1 of the Plan specifically stated: "No benefit, right or interest" of any participant "shall be subject to alienation, sale, transfer, assignment, pledge, encumbrance or charge, seizure, attachment or other legal, equitable or other process."

Moreover, these transfer restrictions are "enforceable," as required by § 541(c)(2). Plan trustees or fiduciaries are required under ERISA to discharge their duties "in accordance with the documents and instruments governing the plan." 29 U.S.C. § 1104(a)(1)(D). A plan participant, beneficiary, or fiduciary, or the Secretary of Labor may file a civil action to "enjoin any act or practice" which violates ERISA or the terms of the plan. 29 U.S.C. §§ 1132(a)(3) and (5). Indeed, this Court itself vigorously has enforced ERISA's prohibition on the assignment or alienation of pension benefits, declining to recognize any implied exceptions to the broad statutory bar.

The anti-alienation provision required for ERISA qualification and contained in the Plan at issue in this case thus constitutes an enforceable transfer restriction for purposes of § 541(c)(2)'s exclusion of property from the bankruptcy estate.

III

Petitioner raises several challenges to this conclusion. Given the clarity of the statutory text, however, he bears an "exceptionally heavy" burden of persuading us that Congress intended to limit the § 541(c)(2) exclusion to restrictions on transfer that are enforceable only under state spendthrift trust law. *Union Bank v. Wolas*, 112 S.Ct. 527, 530 (1991).

A

Petitioner first contends that contemporaneous legislative materials demonstrate that § 541(c)(2)'s exclusion of property from the bankruptcy estate should not extend to a debtor's interest in an ERISA-qualified pension plan. Although courts "appropriately may refer to a statute's legislative history to resolve statutory ambiguity," *Toibb v. Radloff*, 501 U.S. 157, 162 (1991), the clarity of the statutory language at issue in this case obviates the need for any such inquiry.

Even were we to consider the legislative materials to which petitioner refers, however, we could discern no "clearly expressed legislative intention" contrary to the result reached above. In his brief, petitioner quotes from House and Senate reports accompanying the Bankruptcy Reform Act of 1978 that purportedly reflect "unmistakable" congressional intent to limit § 541(c)(2)'s exclusion to pension plans that qualify under state law as spendthrift trusts. Those reports contain only the briefest of discussions addressing § 541(c)(2). The House Report states: "Paragraph (2) of subsection (c) * * * preserves restrictions on transfer of a spendthrift trust to the extent that the restriction is enforceable under applicable nonbankruptcy law." H.R. Rep. No. 95–595 at 369, *reprinted in* 1978 U.S.C.C.A.N. at 6325. A general introductory section to the House Report contains the additional statement that the new law "continues over the exclusion from property of the estate of the debtor's interest in a spendthrift trust to the extent the trust is protected from creditors under applicable State law." *Id.* at 176, *reprinted in* 1978 U.S.C.C.A.N. at 6136. These meager excerpts reflect at best congressional intent to *include* state spendthrift trust law within the meaning of "applicable nonbankruptcy law." By no means do they provide a sufficient basis for concluding, in derogation of the statute's clear language, that Congress intended to *exclude* other state and federal law from the provision's scope.

B

Petitioner next contends that our construction of § 541(c)(2), pursuant to which a debtor may exclude his interest in an ERISA-qualified pension plan from the bankruptcy estate, renders § 522(d)(10)(E) of the Bankruptcy Code superfluous. Under § 522(d)(10)(E), a debtor who elects the federal exemptions set forth in § 522(d) may exempt from the bankruptcy estate his right to receive "a payment under a stock bonus, pension, profitsharing, annuity, or similar plan or contract * * *, to the extent reasonably necessary for the support of the debtor and any dependent of the debtor." If a debtor's interest in a pension plan could be *excluded* in full from the bankruptcy estate, the argument goes, then there would have been no reason for Congress to create a limited *exemption* for such interests elsewhere in the statute.

Petitioner's surplusage argument fails, however, for the reason that § 522(d)(10)(E) exempts from the bankruptcy estate a much broader category of interests than § 541(c)(2) excludes. For example, pension plans established by governmental entities and churches need not comply with Subchapter I of ERISA, including the anti-alienation requirment of § 206(d)(1). So, too, pension plans that qualify for preferential tax treatment under 26 U.S.C. § 408 (individual retirement accounts) are specifically excepted from ERISA's anti-alienation requirement. Although a debtor's interest in these plans could not be excluded under § 541(c)(2) because the plans lack transfer restrictions enforceable under "applicable nonbankruptcy law," that interest nevertheless could be exempted under § 522(d)(10)(E). Once petitioner concedes that § 522(d)(10)(E)'s exemption applies to more than ERISA-qualified plans containing anti-alienation provisions, his argument that our reading of § 541(c)(2) renders the exemption provision superfluous must collapse.

C

Finally, petitioner contends that our holding frustrates the Bankruptcy Code's policy of ensuring a broad inclusion of assets in the bankruptcy estate. As an initial matter, we think that petitioner mistakes an admittedly broad definition of includable property for a "policy" underlying the Code as a whole. In any event, to the extent that policy considerations are even relevant where the language of the statute is so clear, we believe that our construction of § 541(c)(2) is preferable to the one petitioner urges upon us.

First, our decision today ensures that the treatment of pension benefits will not vary based on the beneficiary's bankruptcy status. See *Butner v. United States*, 440 U.S. 48, 55 (1978) (observing that "[u]niform treatment of property interests" prevents "a party from 'receiving a windfall merely by reason of the happenstance of bankruptcy,' " quoting *Lewis v. Manufacturers National Bank*, 364 U.S. 603, 609 (1961)). We previously have declined to recognize any exceptions to ERISA's anti-alienation provision outside the bankruptcy context. Declining to recognize any exceptions to that provision *within* the bankruptcy context minimizes the possibility that creditors will engage in strategic manipulation of the bankruptcy laws in order to gain access to otherwise inaccessible funds.

Our holding also gives full and appropriate effect to ERISA's goal of protecting pension benefits. This Court has described that goal as one of ensuring that "if a worker has been promised a defined pension benefit upon retirement—and if he has fulfilled whatever conditions are required to obtain a vested benefit—he actually will receive it." *Nachman Corp. v. Pension Benefit Guaranty Corp.*, 446 U.S. 359, 375 (1980). In furtherance of these principles, we recently declined in *Guidry v. Sheet Metal Workers Pension Fund*, 493 U.S. 365 (1990), notwithstanding strong equitable considerations to the contrary, to recognize an implied exception to ERISA's anti-alienation provision that would have allowed a labor union to impose a constructive trust on the pension benefits of a corrupt union official. We explained:

> "Section 206(d) reflects a considered congressional policy choice, a decision to safeguard a stream of income for pensioners (and their dependents, who may be, and perhaps usually are, blameless), even if that decision prevents others from securing relief for the wrongs done them. If exceptions to this policy are to be made, it is for Congress to undertake that task." *Id.* at 376.

These considerations apply with equal, if not greater, force in the present context.

Finally, our holding furthers another important policy underlying ERISA: uniform national treatment of pension benefits. Construing "applicable nonbankruptcy law" to include federal law ensures that the security of a debtor's pension benefits will be governed by ERISA, not left to the vagaries of state spendthrift trust law.

* * *

The judgment of the Court of Appeals is affirmed.

It is so ordered.

JUSTICE SCALIA, concurring.

The Court's opinion today, which I join, prompts several observations.

When the phrase "applicable nonbankruptcy law" is considered in isolation, the phenomenon that three Courts of Appeals could have thought it a synonym for "state law" is mystifying. When the phrase is considered together with the rest of the Bankruptcy Code (in which Congress chose to refer to state law as, logically enough, "state law"), the phenomenon calls into question whether our legal culture has so far departed from attention to text, or is so lacking in agreed-upon methodology for creating and interpreting text, that it any longer makes sense to talk of "a government of laws, not of men."

Speaking of agreed-upon methodology: It is good that the Court's analysis today proceeds on the assumption that use of the phrases "state law" and "applicable nonbankruptcy law" in *other* provisions of the Bankruptcy Code is highly relevant to whether "applicable nonbankruptcy law" means "state law" in § 541(c)(2), since consistency of usage within the same statute is to be presumed. This application of a normal and obvious principle of statutory construction would not merit comment, except that we explicitly rejected it, in favor of a one-subsection-at-a-time approach, when interpreting another provision of this very statute earlier this Term. See *Dewsnup v. Timm*, 112 S.Ct. 773, 777--78 (1992). "[W]e express no opinion," our decision said, "as to whether the words [at issue] have different meaning in other provisions of the Bankruptcy Code." *Id.* at 778 n.3. I trust that in our search for a neutral and rational interpretive methodology we have now come to rest, so that the symbol of our profession may remain the scales, not the see-saw.

Notes and Questions

1. Note that, as in *Toibb,* both the *Patterson* majority and Justice Scalia in concurrence rely on the Code's "plain meaning."

2. What policy is suggested by the language in § 541(c)(2) and the Court's construction of it? Who are the ultimate winners and losers?

3. How do state spendthrift trusts differ from ERISA? Is there any reasoned basis to distinguish between federal and state law as "otherwise applicable nonbankruptcy law"? In any context?

4. Assume that a debtor makes voluntary after-tax contributions to the plan and, because the restriction on alienation required by ERISA only affects third parties, the debtor has immediate access to those funds. Are those amounts property of the estate notwithstanding § 541(c)(2) and *Patterson*? See *Barkley v. Conner (In re Conner)*, 73 F.3d 258 (9th Cir.), *cert. denied*, 519 U.S. 817, 117 S.Ct. 68, 136 L.Ed.2d 29 (1996).

JESS v. CAREY (IN RE JESS)

United States Court of Appeals, Ninth Circuit, 1999.
169 F.3d 1204.

DAVID R. THOMPSON, Circuit Judge.

Chapter 7 debtor Paul Clayton Jess ("Jess"), an attorney, appeals a Bankruptcy Appellate Panel ("BAP") decision affirming a bankruptcy court decision that granted, following a bench trial, the bankruptcy trustee's request that Jess turn over to the estate a portion of a contingent-fee payment attributable to pre-petition legal work performed by Jess. Jess argues that the fee is not property of the estate because he had no right to collect it until services which he rendered post-petition were completed and a recovery was made for the benefit of his client.

* * *

BACKGROUND

On June 24, 1994, Jess, an attorney acting pro se, filed a Chapter 11 bankruptcy petition.[3] Prior to filing this petition, Jess had entered into a contingent-fee contract with a client in what became known as

[3] Jess's case was converted to a Chapter 7 case on December 4, 1994.

the "Klouds-Pacey litigation." Under that contract, Jess was to receive one-third of any recovery obtained for his client by settlement before arbitration or trial, and forty percent of any recovery obtained after commencement of arbitration or trial.

Jess worked on the case both pre-petition and post-petition, and he kept track of his time. In June 1995, he collected a contingent fee of $156,000. He kept the full amount of the fee, and spent most of it.

In July 1996, the bankruptcy trustee ("Trustee") filed a complaint claiming part of Jess's contingent fee. Jess answered, contending that he wouldn't have collected any fee at all if he hadn't made a recovery for his client, and because that recovery was made after he filed his Chapter 11 petition, the entire recovery belonged to him as post-petition earnings under § 541(a)(6).

The bankruptcy court conducted a trial to resolve the dispute. During the proceeding, Jess conceded (and the Trustee stipulated) that 78% of Jess's work on the Klouds-Pacey litigation was completed prior to his Chapter 11 bankruptcy filing. The bankruptcy court awarded the Trustee a judgment based upon a calculation that 78% of Jess's contingent fee belonged to the estate. Jess filed a motion for a new trial, and that motion was denied.

Jess then appealed to the Bankruptcy Appellate Panel. The BAP affirmed the bankruptcy court's decision, holding that the portion of Jess's contingent-fee payment attributable to pre-petition work was includable in his bankruptcy estate even though he had to perform additional post-petition services to collect the fee. Jess then filed this timely appeal.

* * *

DISCUSSION

A. Contingent Fee Payments

* * *

Jess contends that all of the Klouds-Pacey contingent fee he received is excludable from property of the estate under § 541(a)(6) because the fee constitutes earnings from services he performed after the commencement of his bankruptcy case. Relying on *In re Sloan*, 32 B.R. 607, 611 (Bankr. E.D.N.Y. 1983), he contends that earnings received post-petition are not part of the bankruptcy estate unless all of the debtor's services necessary to produce those earnings are rooted in pre-petition acts. We disagree. Payments for pre-petition services are not excludable from the estate solely because post-petition services are required to receive payment. See *In re Ryerson*, 739 F.2d 1423, 1425-26 (9th Cir. 1984); *In re Wu*, 173 B.R. 411, 414-15 (9th Cir. BAP 1994) (rejecting explicitly *Sloan*'s "all or nothing" approach). The estate is entitled to recover the portion of post-petition payments attributable to pre-petition services.

Jess argues this should not be the result in his case, because his post-petition receipt of the contingent fee was dependent upon his post-petition continued services. He relies on *In re Tully*, 202 B.R. 481, 482 (9th Cir. BAP 1996). There, the court stated: "Where a debtor derives post-petition commissions under a pre-petition contract, and such commissions are dependent upon the continued services of the debtor, they do not constitute property of the estate." *Id.* at 483 (citations and internal quotations omitted). Jess argues his right to receive any part of the Klouds-Pacey compensation was dependent upon his post-petition continued services, and thus the entire contingent fee should be excluded from the estate because it was earned post-petition.

We reject this argument. Jess mischaracterizes the precedent upon which he relies. *Tully* is inapposite because the earnings paid post-petition in that case, unlike here, were solely for post-petition services. Jess's earnings, on the other hand, represented compensation for both pre-petition and post-petition services.

Finally, Jess argues he had no cause of action under California law to recover from his client any portion of his fees based on a theory of *quantum meruit* as of June 23, 1994, the day he filed his Chapter 11 petition in bankruptcy. Therefore, he contends, the Trustee could not have collected any portion of the fee on the date Jess filed his Chapter 11 petition, and as a result the entire fee which was received post-petition belongs to him. This argument also fails.

The BAP correctly recognized that Jess's *quantum meruit* argument "does not affect whether the prepetition earnings are property of the estate under § 541(a). While state law may ultimately determine whether an asset is property of the estate, in the final analysis § 541(a) supplies the basic definition." Moreover, Jess concedes that at the time he filed his Chapter 11 petition, he would have been entitled to part of the fee if he had been fired and another lawyer successfully finished the case. Although Jess may not have been able to sue his client for a portion of his fee at the time he filed his bankruptcy petition, he had an interest in the fee attributable to pre-petition work on the case. Such an interest is clearly property of the estate under § 541(a)(1). *See In re Ryerson*, 739 F.2d at 1425-26 (holding that a "contract value" payable to an employee upon termination was property of the estate when the employee was fired after filing a bankruptcy petition even though the employee had no right to collect this contract value pre-petition).

The Fifth Circuit has addressed the specific issue before us. In *Turner v. Avery*, 947 F.2d 772, 772-73 (5th Cir. 1991), the debtor, an attorney, had contingent-fee cases pending when he filed a Chapter 7 bankruptcy petition. The Fifth Circuit held that the portion of the contingent fee earned pre-petition was property of the estate because a contract on a case subsequently settled or successfully litigated has value on the date of a bankruptcy filing. The court stated:

> Very frequently, as a consequence of the dismissal or withdrawal of counsel, or the death or divorce of a married attorney * * * or the voluntary or involuntary dissolution of a partnership, it becomes necessary to place a value on services rendered under a contingent fee contract as of a certain target date. This assessment has proven to be "doable" both factually and legally. Perhaps the most typical example of a quantum meruit division of attorney's fees results from the situation where one attorney begins representation which is completed by a second attorney. Fair and equitable divisions routinely are reached.

Id. at 774 (citations omitted).

We agree with the Fifth Circuit's analysis. The bankruptcy court and the BAP applied the proper analysis in concluding that Jess earned a portion of his contingent fee pre-petition. In this circuit, a court must

> first determine whether any postpetition services are necessary to obtaining the payments at issue. If not, the payments are entirely "rooted in the pre-bankruptcy past," and the payments will be included in the estate. If some postpetition services are necessary, then courts must determine the extent to which the payments are attributable to the postpetition services and the extent to which the payments are attributable to prepetition services. That portion of the payments allocable to postpetition services will not be property of the estate.

In Re Wu, 173 B.R. at 414-15 (quoting *Ryerson*, 739 F.2d 1423 at 1426).

Jess conceded, and the Trustee stipulated, that 78% of Jess's work on the Klouds-Pacey litigation was performed pre-petition.[4] The bankruptcy court allocated the contingent fee on that basis—78% to the estate and 22% percent to Jess. The court did not err in so doing. * * *

Notes and Problems

1. Bruce Clark, a football player for the New Orleans Saints, signed three one-year contracts on the form in use by all NFL teams. Under the 1988–89 contract, his salary of $575,000 was payable in sixteen equal installments over the course of the regular season. The contract contained the following clauses: a "skill guarantee," effective upon passing the club physical, providing that the full salary would be paid despite unsatisfactory performance; a clause providing for incremental forgiveness of a $725,000 loan, over the course of the season, conditional on Clark's "fulfilling his contractual obligations by playing or being available to play"; and clauses requiring Clark to report promptly and participate, to devote his best efforts, to maintain his physical condition, and to permit examinations by the club doctor. Clark filed a Chapter 7 petition after seven of the sixteen games had been played. Is his salary for the next nine games property of the bankruptcy estate? See *Clark v. First City Bank (Matter of Clark)*, 891 F.2d 111 (5th Cir.1989).

2. Vera Rash was overwhelmed by her credit card obligations and filed bankruptcy on August 1, 2000. Her case was still pending in June of 2001 when she received a $600 tax refund from the IRS, relating to the 2000 taxable year. Is any or all of the refund property of the estate? See *Knight v. Cofield (In re Rash)*, 22 B.R. 323 (Bankr. D.Kan.1982).

3. Joel, who is a prolific writer, published a popular antitrust casebook. Unfortunately, Joel is also a prolific spender and he had to file bankruptcy the very next year. He received a royalty check for $1,000 three months after his bankruptcy filing, for sales of his antitrust book. Is any or all of the $1,000 property of the estate?

4. Debtor retired after a career as an insurance agent. During his career, he was paid solely by commissions on the policies he sold. He received a commission whenever one of his policies was renewed, even after

---

[4] We should note that Jess made no attempt in the bankruptcy court to place a greater value on his post-petition hours than on his pre-petition hours. Thus, all of Jess's hours were valued equally. We recognize that in a different context it might be possible to establish that hours worked at different stages of a case may have different values. We express no opinion on this question.

retirement. Are those commissions property of his bankruptcy estate? See *In re Braddy*, 226 B.R. 479 (Bankr. N.D.Fla. 1998).

5. Debtor owned season tickets to the Pittsburgh Steelers' games. Tickets ordinarily carried rights to annual renewal and to transfer, upon request in writing and payment of $5. Debtor's bankruptcy trustee decided to sell the tickets. The Steelers' organization objected to sale of the renewal rights (but not to sale of the rights to attend that season's games) on the grounds of unfairness to those who had been on the waiting list for tickets, some for as long as ten years. What result? See *In re I.D. Craig Service Corp.*, 138 B.R. 490 (Bankr. W.D.Pa.1992).

6. Liquor licenses have created interesting difficulties under § 541(a). In *In re Nejberger*, 934 F.2d 1300 (3d Cir.1991), the issue was whether a debtor's right to seek renewal of his liquor license was property of his estate. The state Liquor Control Board rejected debtor's renewal application, pursuant to state law, for failure to pay certain state taxes, but granted debtor a one-year grace period in which to pay the taxes and to reapply. Debtor filed Chapter 11 during the grace period. At the end of the period, the Board issued a final termination of debtor's license because debtor had failed to satisfy his tax obligation.

Debtor sought to compel the Board to renew his application, arguing that the tax liability was stayed automatically by his Chapter 11 petition. The bankruptcy court concluded that debtor's expectation of renewal was property of the estate and that nonrenewal was based solely on debtor's failure to pay taxes that constituted prepetition claims. Thus, the bankruptcy court ordered the Board to renew debtor's license. The district court agreed that the expectation created by the renewal grace period was property of the estate, but found that reasons other than nonpayment of taxes might have influenced the decision not to renew. The district court, therefore, ordered debtor to reapply for the license and directed the Board to consider the application without regard to the unpaid taxes.

The Third Circuit affirmed, agreeing that the expectation of consideration for renewal constituted property of the estate and that the bankruptcy court's order was too much of an intrusion on the Board's authority under state law. Therefore, the court ordered that the Board make an appropriate decision regarding debtor's renewal application, based on any factors other than nonpayment of taxes that state law allowed the Board to consider.

7. Generally, whatever the debtor owns at the moment a Chapter 7 petition is filed becomes property of the estate and is used to satisfy obligations that the debtor owes as of the same moment. Section 541(a)(5), however, includes certain property that the debtor acquires within six months after the filing—specifically, property obtained by inheritance, through a property settlement, or as beneficiary of a life insurance policy. Chapter 13, in contrast, includes all property the debtor acquires after the filing. § 1306.

These distinctions created difficulties when a Chapter 13 case was converted to a Chapter 7, as often happens. Before the 1994 Amendments, some courts held that the Chapter 7 estate included all property acquired after the filing, even though it would not have been property of the estate if Chapter 7 had been filed initially; other courts held that the converted case consisted of property held at the time of the original bankruptcy filing. The 1994 Amendments added § 348(f), which adopts the latter view.

D. EXEMPTIONS

"Exempt" property cannot be reached by creditors through judicial enforcement proceedings. Thus, such property is retained by the debtor free from the claims of creditors. Exemptions, which are available only to individual debtors, are intended to prevent a debtor from falling into financial ruin and to provide an opportunity for a "fresh start."

Section 522 of the Bankruptcy Code governs exemptions. Subsection (b) gives a debtor a choice of law regarding exemptions. The debtor may choose the exemptions provided by the law of his or her domicile (as well as exemptions provided by certain nonbankruptcy federal law), or the exemptions provided in § 522(d).

State schemes frequently benefit debtors who own real property more than those who do not, because the "homestead" exemption is often the most generous in amount and is available only to owners of residential real property. The federal scheme was designed with an eye toward equality for persons who do not own real property (although it got only half way there). Section 522(d)(5) allows debtors who do not use the $16,150 homestead exemption provided by § 522(d)(1) to apply up to $8,075 of the unused amount to other property. Section 522(d)(5) also allows debtors to exempt up to $850 of any property, without regard to whether it is otherwise exemptable. Thus, this catch-all provision enables debtors who do not own real property or do not use their entire homestead exemption to protect additional property from the reach of creditors. Section 104(b), which was added in 1994, requires that all of the dollar amounts in the federal exemptions (and a few other places in the Code) be adjusted every three years.

The choice between the federal scheme or a state scheme is not available to many debtors, however. Section 522(b)(1) allows the individual states to "opt out" of the federal scheme. In other words, states may require their residents who file bankruptcy to use only the state exemption scheme. Over two-thirds of the states have opted out of the federal scheme.

Notes and Problems

1. The federal exemptions provided by § 522(d), like many state exemptions, contain specific maximum dollar amounts. For instance, subsection (d)(3) allows a debtor to exempt up to $8,625 worth of household goods, but the value of each particular item must not exceed $425. Section 522(d)(4) allows a debtor to exempt up to $1,075 worth of jewelry.

What is the appropriate method of valuation to be used when determining the amount of actual property permitted to be exempted by these sections? Section 522(a) defines "value" to mean the fair market value as of the date of the filing of the petition. Because personal property often has a depressed value in bankruptcy, the market value of such property is usually its liquidation value, or the amount that the property would draw if it were the subject of a forced sale such as a public auction. See David L. Buchbinder, Fundamentals of Bankruptcy, A Lawyer's Guide § 9.3 at 158–64 (1991). Not surprisingly, the parties in interest to a bankruptcy proceeding do not always agree on the proper value to assign to a debtor's assets for purposes of determining exemptions. At the request of a party, the bankruptcy court will order a valuation hearing to determine the value of items the debtor has scheduled as exempt.

Valuation is a pervasive problem in bankruptcy, and we will return to it, in varying contexts, several times.

2. Consider the circumstances of the following debtors. Which assets may each exempt under the federal scheme set out in § 522(d)?

a. Anna is unmarried, with no dependents, and rents an apartment. Her material possessions are comprised of the following: jewelry worth approximately $4,000 (including her great-grandmother's engagement ring); furniture for which she paid $6,000 two years ago; vacuum cleaners and other equipment worth approximately $3,000 that she uses in her housecleaning business; and a 1995 automobile on which she still owes $6,000. The car is subject to a security interest held by GMAC and is currently worth $7,000.

b. Bernie and his wife Beth have filed for bankruptcy jointly. They own their condominium, worth $85,000, all of the furniture in their home, a painting appraised at $50,000 (which has been in Beth's family for over a century), a ten-year-old pickup truck, which they own free and clear, and a late model sports car on which they owe $14,000. Both Bernie and Beth are retired and receive Social Security. They raise exotic birds as pets, though they sometimes sell them to local pet stores. Bernie and Beth disagree as to which exemption scheme benefits them most. May Bernie opt for the federal exemptions, while Beth uses the state exemptions?

c. Clara Clotheshorse lives in a home, worth $200,000, that she inherited from her parents. The home is fully furnished, though the valuable antiques were inherited by Clara's brother, who is merely storing them in Clara's home while he is out of the country. Clara has over 150 pairs of shoes, several of which she purchased for more than $200 a pair. The aggregate value of her shoes was approximately $25,000 when they were purchased, though she has owned and worn most for more than a year. Additionally, Clara has several closets full of clothing, now worth approximately $75,000. Clara has insured her life for $250,000 and her brother is the beneficiary of the policy.

d. Douglas receives monthly alimony payments from his former wife of $800 and child support payments of $400 per month, which he uses to raise his daughter. Douglas is an independent contractor and owns a truck worth $8,000 that he uses in his business, and tools also used in the business that are worth $3,000. When Douglas obtained a loan several years ago, the bank took a security interest in his business tools. He still owes the bank $2,000. He also owns a home worth $95,000, that is subject to a first mortgage of $80,000 and a second mortgage of $25,000.

3. The Pattersons, who are dairy farmers, want to exempt their breeding bulls under their state's $5,000 exemption for tools of the trade. May they do so? Would it affect your answer if the state also provided a separate exemption for "one cow, two goats, 10 sheep, 10 chickens, and feed sufficient to keep the specified livestock through one winter"? Compare *Matter of Patterson*, 825 F.2d 1140 (7th Cir.1987), with *Parrotte v. Sensenich (In re Parrotte)*, 22 F.3d 472 (2d Cir.1994).

4. Debtor was in three separate prepetition accidents. After settlements were reached in each case, she became entitled to compensation of more than $20,000 for each accident. How much can she claim as exempt under § 522(d)(11)(D)? See *Christo v. Yellin (In re Christo)*, 192 F.3d 36 (1st Cir. 1999).

5. Section 522(d)(10)(E) exempts from a debtor's bankruptcy estate "a payment under a stock bonus, pension, profitsharing, annuity, or similar plan or contract on account of illness, disability, death, age, or length of service, to the extent reasonably necessary for the support of the debtor." The debtor need not worry about exempting ERISA-qualified pension plans, since the Supreme Court decided in *Patterson v. Shumate* that such funds are not property of the estate under § 541(c)(2). (Recall the trustee's argument in *Patterson* that the Court's interpretation of § 541(c)(2) rendered § 522(d)(10)(E) "superfluous.") Plans that qualify as state spendthrift trusts will also be excluded from the estate under § 541(c)(2). The exemption provision, how-

ever, remains applicable to pension plans that do not qualify as spendthrift trusts because, as is usually the case, they are self-settled or the debtor exercises too much control.

6. In reorganization, unlike liquidation, the debtor keeps his or her property and pays creditors out of future income. What, then, is the relevance of exemptions in Chapter 13s and individual Chapter 11s?

The following case, which is one-of-a-kind, raises some fundamental questions about the nature and purpose of exemptions.

MATTER OF SZEKELY

United States Court of Appeals, Seventh Circuit, 1991.
936 F.2d 897.

POSNER, Circuit Judge.

This bankruptcy appeal raises a surprisingly fundamental, and difficult, question * * * on which we are unable to find any authority. The question is whether if a debtor continues to occupy his home after declaring bankruptcy, the trustee can charge rent to him, notwithstanding the homestead exemption. The debtors in this case—a married couple named Szekely, living in Zion, Illinois—declared bankruptcy (originally under Chapter 13, later converted to Chapter 7—liquidation) on December 5, 1988. One of the assets of the bankrupt estate was the couple's home, on which there were both a first and a second mortgage. The Bankruptcy Code allows a state to require debtors to use the state's exemptions rather than the exemptions set forth in the Code itself. § 522(b)(1). Illinois has taken up this option, and as a result each of the Szekelys was "entitled to an estate of homestead to the extent in value of $7,500," for a total of $15,000.

The Szekelys continued living in their home, though they made no payments on either mortgage. In April, the trustee asked the bankruptcy judge to order the couple to pay rent. Two months later the bankruptcy judge granted the trustee's request and fixed the rent at $600 a month, though it was understood that since the Szekelys couldn't pay, the rent would accrue, and would be deducted from their homestead exemption when the house was sold. In September, although the house hadn't been sold yet, the Szekelys vacated it, owing eight months' accrued rent—$4,800. In February of the following year, the district judge affirmed the bankruptcy judge's rent order. The Szekelys now appeal the district judge's order to us. We were told at argument that the house has now been sold, for about $135,000, which is $30,000 more than the amount owing on the two mortgages and therefore enough to cover the entire homestead exemption. Yet if we affirm, the trustee will give the Szekelys only $10,200 ($15,000–$4,800).

* * *

In defending the judgment that he won below, the trustee points out correctly that the debtors' home became an asset of the bankrupt estate upon the declaration of bankruptcy. § 541. Thus, by continuing to live in the house, the Szekelys were using an asset that belonged to the bankrupt estate, not to them. Therefore—the trustee argues—they should be required to pay rent for its use, just as anyone else leasing assets of the estate would be required to pay rent to the trustee. The argument is fine as far as it goes, but it doesn't leave much in the way of a homestead exemption. Imagine a case—this case, in fact—in which the debtors live in a relatively expensive home. They go broke, and naturally they want to live more modestly. If they move out, then under the trustee's view of the case they get nothing until the house is sold, at which time they get their $15,000. But since they get nothing till then, they will find it hard to arrange for substitute accommodations if they move out now. (Of course they can rent housing out of their current income, if they have any. But this would be true even if there were no homestead exemption, so it is a better argument against the exemption—though not an argument properly addressed to us, for we of course have no authority to abolish the exemption—than it is in favor of allowing the trustee to charge rent.) If, therefore, they decide to remain in their house—their house that was, now the property of the estate—they will, if the trustee prevails, be forced to pay rent based on the value of the house, a value geared to the debtors' standard of living before they went bankrupt. As the months pass, the accruing rent will dig a deeper and deeper hole in the homestead exemption; in this case it reduced it by a third. When the debtors finally move out they will have substantially diminished resources with which to find alternative housing.

This is looking at the case from the debtors' point of view, and thus emphasizing the "fresh start" rationale of bankruptcy—that is, bankruptcy as a debtor's cushion against the effects of financial misfortune. Bankruptcy is equally a creditor's remedy, however, in particular a remedy of unsecured creditors, represented by the trustee. The house *was* an asset of the estate and *did* have a positive rental value that the debtors impaired by continuing to live in the house. If the house had been sold right after the Szekelys had declared bankruptcy, they would have gotten $15,000, period. If they prevail on this appeal, they will have got $15,000—plus free housing (well, almost free) for eight months. This overstates the windfall, because the present receipt of $15,000 is worth more in real terms than the receipt of $15,000 eight months later. Nevertheless the Szekelys *are* seeking a windfall. And the more valuable the house, the greater the windfall (for the greater the housing value is). But some degree of inequity is built into the homestead exemption: people too poor to own a house have no homestead exemption. This may be an argument against the exemption; and another argument, one not even limited to the homestead exemption, is that anything which impairs creditors' rights in bankruptcy drives up interest rates (for creditors will seek compensation in advance for any added risks of default), to the ultimate detriment of the debtor class. Indeed, the higher that interest rates are (other things being equal), the greater the risk of bankruptcy is, since interest is a fixed expense. But these are academic speculations, because we are not authorized to restructure bankruptcy law.

The competing thrusts of that law, as a debtor's and as a creditor's remedy respectively (though, as we have just said, it may only be in the short run that bankruptcy is *really* a debtor's remedy), are mirrored in the competing characterizations of the homestead exemption that the parties press on us. The Szekelys conceive of the exemption as a right to remain in one's home, rent-free, until the trustee either through sale or otherwise can pay the debtor the value of the exemption. They point out that Illinois law describes the exemption as an "*estate* of homestead," rather than using the humbler designation "homestead exemption," which is the formula in the list of federal statutory exemptions applicable in states that do not want their own exemptions applied in bankruptcy, § 522(d)(1), and is also the formula found in most state statutes. They cite cases which hold that even though the title of the Illinois statute is "Exemption of Homestead," the term in the body of the statute, "estate of homestead," is not an archaic sonority but denotes a right to possession.

The trustee argues that the homestead exemption (or "estate") is not a possessory interest at all, but merely a lien—a claim to $15,000 if and when the house is sold or the claim, which is freely alienable, is otherwise transferred.

The cases support the debtors' characterization. But none involves the precise issue here, the trustee's right to receive rent for the debtors' occupancy of their (former) house. Not even *Mix v. King*, 55

Ill. 434 (1870), on which the debtors principally rely. That case holds that the homestead exemption is possessory, all right; but it was not an insolvency case; it was a case of improper ejectment of the holder of an express right of homestead, and thus was analogous to the wrongful eviction of a tenant. The trustee does not contest the Szekelys' right to occupy the house until it is sold or he pays them the amount of the homestead exemption; all he wants is rent; and since the cases are emphatic that the "estate" is limited by the value of the exemption, it is a little hard to see why the debtors should obtain in effect the full rental value of the house, over and above the exemption, without paying rent for that surplus comfort. On the other hand, the case on which the trustee principally relies holds only that if there is a right of ejectment (as there was not in *Mix*), the owner must pay off the homestead exemption before ejecting the homesteader. *Hotchkiss v. Brooks*, 93 Ill. 386 (1879). That is common ground among the parties to this suit.

Precedent does not decide our case. We must consider principle.

Because the house belongs to the estate, the trustee can pay the Szekelys their $15,000 and tell them to skedaddle, and then rent the house to whomever he pleases until he sells it. That much is clear. And he can raise the $15,000 either by liquidating other assets of the bankrupt estate or, if there are insufficient other assets (as we may assume to be the case here), by taking out another mortgage on the house. The Szekelys' house, though, was already encumbered by two mortgages, and although in the end the house was sold for an amount that yielded enough equity over and above the mortgages (with all their arrearages) to pay the homestead exemption in full, the value of the house may have been too uncertain for the trustee to have been able to obtain a third mortgage, for $15,000, at a tolerable rate of interest. In that event he would (under the Szekelys' view of the case) have had to let them stay there rent free until he sold the house.

Some brokers believe that it is more difficult to sell a house with a tenant in it than with the house vacant, partly because it is easier to show a house when no one is living there and it is uncluttered with personal possessions and partly because the presence of a tenant will make it difficult for the owner to promise immediate possession to the buyer. (The argument *contra* is that a vacant house is uninviting.) So the trustee may not have wanted the Szekelys living there and paying rent, but may instead have wanted them out, and of course they were more likely to leave if they had to pay rent (eventually they did leave, perhaps for that reason, before the house was sold). If this is right, then had they moved out the trustee would not have rented the house to someone else. It would have stood vacant, yielding no income to him until he sold it. This suggests that he too is seeking a windfall, and that the real purpose of his charging rent was to induce the Szekelys to leave, so that the house could be sold more easily. To cast them out into the cold, as it were, without giving them the $15,000 to which the homestead exemption entitled them, undermined the purpose of the exemption, which is to assure the debtor adequate housing despite the economic disaster that has overtaken him. The harm to the debtor depends on how long it takes to sell the house. If it is sold right off, he gets the cash value of the exemption; but if there is a delay in selling it, he must arrange for substitute housing without the assistance that Illinois meant him to have through the homestead exemption.

We are just speculating that the trustee wanted the Szekelys out (though they did move out eventually, before the house was sold). But the speculation is not critical to our decision. The important thing is that whether they paid rent and stayed, or left before being cashed out of the homestead exemption, the value of the exemption to them was diminished. And while it is true that if the debtor can live rent-free in the house until it is sold he will have an incentive to delay the sale if he can, by the same token if the debtor can't live there rent-free the trustee has no incentive to sell the house as quickly as possible, and in addition the bankruptcy court must step in and fix a reasonable rental. The hardship to the debtor should have the greater weight in decision. The homestead exemption, perhaps especially when as here it is capped at a relatively modest sum of money, is designed to assist the debtor *to the extent of the exemption* to obtain more modest living quarters. That aim is blunted if the trustee can in effect expel the debtor from the homestead (whether directly or by charging a rent geared to a standard of living that the debtor no longer can maintain) without giving him a penny of benefit from the homestead exemption.

There is an analogy to tenancy in common. Neither tenant can charge the other rent, but either can demand that the property be partitioned between them. The interaction of bankruptcy law and the homestead exemption made the Szekelys in effect cotenants, with the trustee, of the Szekelys' former house. The trustee was entitled to obtain sole rights to the property by paying off the homestead exemption—in effect a partition of the property in which the Szekelys would receive $15,000—but until then he had no right to disturb the Szekelys in their possession of the property. We hold that the homestead exemption in Illinois entitles the debtor to remain in his home rent free until he receives the cash value of the exemption. We therefore reverse the decisions below with directions to allow the debtors their full $15,000 from the proceeds of the sale of the house.

TAYLOR v. FREELAND & KRONZ

United States Supreme Court, 1992.
503 U.S. 638, 112 S.Ct. 1644, 118 L.Ed.2d 280.

JUSTICE THOMAS delivered the opinion of the Court.

Section 522(*l*) of the Bankruptcy Code requires a debtor to file a list of the property that the debtor claims as statutorily exempt from distribution to creditors. Bankruptcy Rule 4003 affords creditors and the bankruptcy trustee 30 days to object to claimed exemptions. We must decide in this case whether the trustee may contest the validity of an exemption after the 30–day period if the debtor had no colorable basis for claiming the exemption.

I

[The debtor, Emily Davis, filed bankruptcy while pursuing an employment discrimination suit in state court. She claimed the proceeds she expected to win as exempt and listed the value as "unknown." Her trustee, Taylor, asked for more information about the suit and the lawyers representing her, Freeland and Kronz, expressed the opinion that it might settle for as much as $110,000. Taylor decided not to object to the exemption because he did not believe Davis's suit had any value. The case later settled for $110,000 and Freeland and Kronz received $71,000 in fees. Taylor sought turnover of the money from Freeland and Kronz, arguing that it was property of the estate. Freeland and Kronz argued that they could keep it because Davis had exempted it.]

The Bankruptcy Court sided with Taylor. It concluded that Davis had "no statutory basis" for claiming the proceeds of the lawsuit as exempt and ordered respondents to "return" approximately $23,000 to Taylor, a sum sufficient to pay off all of Davis' unpaid creditors. The District Court affirmed, but the Court of Appeals for the Third Circuit reversed. The Court of Appeals held that the Bankruptcy Court could not require respondents to turn over the money because Davis had claimed it as exempt, and Taylor had failed to object to the claimed exemption in a timely manner. We granted certiorari and now affirm.

II

When a debtor files a bankruptcy petition, all of his property becomes property of a bankruptcy estate. § 541. The Code, however, allows the debtor to prevent the distribution of certain property by claiming it as exempt. Section 522(b) allowed Davis to choose the exemptions afforded by state law or the federal exemptions listed in § 522(d). Section 522(*l*) states the procedure for claiming exemptions and objecting to claimed exemptions * * *. Although § 522(*l*) itself does not specify the time for objecting to a claimed exemption, Bankruptcy Rule 4003(b) provides in part:

> "The trustee or any creditor may file objections to the list of property claimed as exempt within 30 days after the conclusion of the meeting of creditors held pursuant to Rule 2003(a) * * * unless, within such period, further time is granted by the court."

In this case, as noted, Davis claimed the proceeds from her employment discrimination lawsuit as exempt by listing them in the schedule that she filed under § 522(*l*). The parties agree that Davis did not have a right to exempt more than a small portion of these proceeds either under state law or under the federal exemptions specified in § 522(d). Davis in fact claimed the full amount as exempt. Taylor, as a result, apparently could have made a valid objection under § 522(*l*) and Rule 4003 if he had acted promptly. We hold, however, that his failure to do so prevents him from challenging the validity of the exemption now.

A

Taylor acknowledges that Rule 4003(b) establishes a 30–day period for objecting to exemptions and that § 522(*l*) states that "[u]nless a party in interest objects, the property claimed as exempt * * * is exempt." He argues, nonetheless, that his failure to object does not preclude him from challenging the exemption at this time. In Taylor's view, § 522(*l*) and Rule 4003(b) serve only to narrow judicial inquiry into the validity of an exemption after 30 days, not to preclude judicial inquiry altogether. In particular, he maintains that courts may invalidate a claimed exemption after expiration of the 30–day period if the debtor did not have a good-faith or reasonably disputable basis for claiming it. In this case, Taylor asserts, Davis did not have a colorable basis for claiming all of the lawsuit proceeds as exempt and thus lacked good faith.

Taylor justifies his interpretation of § 522(*l*) by arguing that requiring debtors to file claims in good faith will discourage them from claiming meritless exemptions merely in hopes that no one will object. Taylor does not stand alone in this reading of § 522(b). Several Courts of Appeals have adopted the same position upon similar reasoning.

We reject Taylor's argument. Davis claimed the lawsuit proceeds as exempt on a list filed with the Bankruptcy Court. Section 522(*l*), to repeat, says that "[u]nless a party in interest objects, the property claimed as exempt on such list is exempt." Rule 4003(b) gives the trustee and creditors 30 days from the initial creditors' meeting to object. By negative implication, the Rule indicates that creditors may not object after 30 days "unless, within such period, further time is granted by the court." The Bankruptcy Court did not extend the 30–day period. Section 522(*l*) therefore has made the property exempt. Taylor cannot contest the exemption at this time whether or not Davis had a colorable statutory basis for claiming it.

Deadlines may lead to unwelcome results, but they prompt parties to act and they produce finality. In this case, despite what respondents repeatedly told him, Taylor did not object to the claimed exemption. If Taylor did not know the value of the potential proceeds of the lawsuit, he could have sought a hearing on the issue, see Rule 4003(c), or he could have asked the Bankruptcy Court for an extension of time to object, see Rule 4003(b). Having done neither, Taylor cannot now seek to deprive Davis and respondents of the exemption.

Taylor suggests that our holding will create improper incentives. He asserts that it will lead debtors to claim property exempt on the chance that the trustee and creditors, for whatever reason, will fail to object to the claimed exemption on time. He asserts that only a requirement of good faith can prevent what the Eighth Circuit has termed "exemption by declaration." *In re Peterson*, 920 F.2d 1389, 1393 (8th Cir.1990). This concern, however, does not cause us to alter our interpretation of § 522(*l*).

Debtors and their attorneys face penalties under various provisions for engaging in improper conduct in bankruptcy proceedings. See, *e.g.*, § 727(a)(4)(B) (authorizing denial of discharge for presenting fraudulent claims); Rule 1008 (requiring filings to "be verified or contain an unsworn declaration" of truthfulness under penalty of perjury); Rule 9011 (authorizing sanctions for signing certain documents not "well grounded in fact and * * * warranted by existing law or a good faith argument for the extension, modification, or reversal of existing law"); 18 U.S.C. § 152 (imposing criminal penalties for fraud in bankruptcy cases). These provisions may limit bad-faith claims of exemptions by debtors. To the extent that they do not, Congress may enact comparable provisions to address the difficulties that Taylor predicts will follow our decision. We have no authority to limit the application of § 522(*l*) to exemptions claimed in good faith.

* * *

The judgment of the Court of Appeals is

Affirmed.

JUSTICE STEVENS, dissenting.

The Court states that it has "no authority to limit the application of § 522(*l*) to exemptions claimed in good faith." It does not deny, however, that it has ample authority to hold that the doctrine of equitable tolling applies to the 30–day limitations period in Bankruptcy Rule 4003(b). In my view, such a result is supported not only by strong equitable considerations, but also by the common law, the widespread practice of the bankruptcy courts, and the text of § 522(b).

I

Rule 4003, which is derived from § 522(*l*) of the Code and in part from former Bankruptcy Rule 403, shifted the emphasis of the earlier rule, placing the burden on the debtor to list her exemptions and the burden on the parties in interest to raise objections. Rule 4003(b) in particular fills a gap that remains in § 522(*l*), which is silent as to the time in which parties in interest must file their objections. Rule 4003(b) provides for a 30–day period for objections. Although the adoption of Rule 4003 has furthered the interest in orderly administration, there is no suggestion that it was put into effect in order to avoid prejudice to the debtor. Thus, there is no identifiable reason why ordinary tolling principles that apply in other contexts should not also apply in bankruptcy proceedings; indeed, the generally equitable character of bankruptcy makes it especially appropriate to apply such rules in this context.

It is familiar learning that the harsh consequences of federal statutes of limitation have been avoided at times by relying on either fraudulent concealment or undiscovered fraud to toll the period of limitation. * * *

In this case, even if there was no fraud, and even if it is assumed that the trustee failed to exercise due diligence, it remains true that the parties injured by the trustee's failure to object within the 30–day period are innocent creditors. Moreover, it is apparently undisputed that there was no legitimate basis for the claim of an exemption for the entire award. Under these circumstances, unless the debtor could establish some prejudice caused by the trustee's failure to object promptly, I would hold that the filing of a frivolous claim for an exemption is tantamount to fraud for purposes of deciding when the 30–day period begins to run.

II

This, in essence, is also the position adopted by numerous bankruptcy courts and three Courts of Appeals. Over a period of years, they have held that the failure to make a timely objection is not dispositive, Rule 4003(b) notwithstanding. * * *

The equitable principles that motivated these bankruptcy courts are best encapsulated by the court in *In re Bennett*, 36 B.R. 893 (Bankr. W.D.Ky.1984). There, the court explained that to apply Rule 4003(b) rigidly would be to encourage a debtor to claim that all of her property was exempt, thus leaving it to the trustee and creditors to sift through the myriad claimed exemptions to assess their validity. Such a policy would result in reversion to "the law of the streets, with bare possession constituting not nine, but ten, parts of the law; orderly administration of estates would be replaced by uncertainty and constant litigation if not outright anarchy." *Id.* at 895.

Although several Courts of Appeals and bankruptcy courts did not go as far as these courts, preferring instead in the case of an untimely objection to examine a claimed exemption to determine if there was a "good-faith statutory basis" for the exemption, they nevertheless eschewed the literal reading of the statute and rule adopted by the Court today. They did so because they believed it was important to strike a proper balance between avoiding the undesirable effect of "exemption by declaration" and yet not permitting a trustee "another bite at the debtor's apple where the debtor has claimed certain property exempt in good faith." *In re Peterson*, 920 F.2d 1389, 1393–94 (8th Cir.1990).

Here, the trustee would succeed under either approach. Whether the court is always permitted to entertain an objection to a claimed exemption (at least until the case is closed) when the claimed exemption is invalid or whether the court can do so only if the claimed exemption lacks a good-faith statutory basis, would mean that in this case the court could review the debtor's claimed exemption. Here, the parties acknowledge that the debtor could not claim a statutory basis for her claimed exemption for the full award because neither backpay nor tort recovery is exempt under § 522(d)(5).

III

The practice of these lower courts has been motivated not only by equitable considerations, but also by the requirement set forth in § 522(b). Section 522(*l*) explicitly provides that "[t]he debtor shall file a list of property that the debtor claims as exempt under subsection (b) of this section." Subsection (b) limits exemptions claimed by the debtor to "any property that is exempt under federal law * * * or State or local law that is applicable on the date of the filing of the petition." § 522(b)(2)(A). When a debtor claims exemptions that do not even arguably satisfy this condition, there is good reason to hold that the filing does not comply with § 522 and therefore the 30–day objection period does not begin to run. * * *

IV

The Court's disposition of this case is straightforward. Because it regards the meaning of the statute and rule as "plain," that is the end of the case. I have no doubt, however, that if the debtor or the trustee were guilty of fraud, the Court would readily ignore what it now treats as the insurmountable barrier of "plain meaning." * * * In my view, it is a mistake to adopt a "strict letter" approach when justice requires a more searching inquiry. Accordingly, I respectfully dissent.

Questions

1. Is there any good faith reason why the debtor's attorneys filed this exemption claim in the first place? Are you satisfied that the tools available for policing the behavior of debtors and their attorneys, listed at the end of the majority opinion, are sufficient for the task?

2. Why did the trustee not pursue the $40,000 of the award that was paid to the debtor?

3. Justice Stevens pointed out, in an omitted footnote, that the debtor failed to amend her schedules after settlement of the suit. Is that failure relevant, given that settlement was reached after the 30–day period?

4. Justice Stevens also argued that innocent creditors were the parties injured by the trustee's failure to object. Is the fact that creditors have a right to object to the debtor's exemptions claims, equal to the trustee's, relevant to this point?

E. AUTOMATIC STAY

1. SCOPE OF THE STAY

Section 362 of the Code provides for an "automatic stay" that suspends nearly all activities of almost all creditors regarding any financial obligations of the debtor. The stay operates at the moment a voluntary or involuntary petition is filed, without the need for notice or for a formal court order.

The stay provides an opportunity to assess the debtor's financial situation and to prepare a reorganization or distribution plan without interference or harassment from creditors. The stay also fixes the relationship of each creditor to the debtor, as of the date of the filing of the bankruptcy petition. In this sense, the stay protects creditors as well as the debtor, by preventing individual creditors from pursuing their own remedies at the expense of other creditors.

Exceptions to the stay are listed in § 362(b) and include activities such as collection of alimony or child support, and continuation of a criminal proceeding against the debtor. The exceptions reflect a balance of public policies. When one of the exceptions applies, the affected creditor may continue otherwise-prohibited activity without first obtaining relief from the stay, just as if the debtor had never filed for bankruptcy.

The automatic stay does not destroy creditors' claims; it merely suspends them. Secured creditors do not lose their right to collect against their collateral even after discharge of the debtor's obligations. In addition, these creditors can obtain relief from the stay if their claim against the property is jeopardized. We will save examination of relief from the stay, which is governed by § 362(d), for Chapter 4 of this text.

Most courts regard the stay as a "shield" that protects a debtor from creditor pressure during a bankruptcy proceeding. You should be alert in studying the materials that follow for so-called "offensive" or "strategic" uses of the automatic stay. For example, a debtor whose sole asset is an overencumbered residence can file bankruptcy the day before a foreclosure proceeding is scheduled, in order to prevent dispossession. Professor Keating noted these possibilities: "In a number of important and recurring cases courts regularly are allowing both individual and corporate debtors to use the stay offensively as a means of extracting a future benefit from a nondebtor party to whom the debtor owes a prepetition debt." Daniel Keating, *Offensive Uses of the Automatic Stay*, 45 Vand. L. Rev. 71, 73 (1991). Does such an "offensive" use of bankruptcy constitute a bad faith filing?

Problems

1. Determine whether the following actions, taken after Debtor initiates a bankruptcy proceeding, violate the automatic stay of § 362(a):

a. Prior to bankruptcy, Debtor obtained a $15,000 loan from Bank, at which Debtor maintains a checking account. There is now $2,500 in Debtor's checking account. Upon Debtor's default, Bank applies the $2,500 to the amount Debtor owes Bank on the loan.

b. A representative of Charge Card Company to which Debtor owes $750, calls Debtor at work and suggests that Debtor get a cash advance from another credit card in order to pay the debt to Charge Card Company.

c. Secured Creditor repossesses Debtor's car after the trustee determines that the car is of no value to the estate and abandons it. (See § 554.)

d. Local Electric shuts off Debtor's power because Debtor failed to pay for service used in the three months after the petition was filed.

e. The State Bar continues a proceeding, begun before Debtor's bankruptcy petition was filed, to revoke Debtor's license to practice law.

f. An account creditor sends a very polite letter stating the amount of the debt and that "prompt payment would be very much appreciated."

g. An accident victim attempts to collect from Debtor's insurance company on a judgment against Debtor arising from an automobile accident that took place two years prior to the bankruptcy.

h. Lender attempts to collect payment from Debtor's parents, who signed a loan agreement for Debtor as guarantors. See §§ 1201 and 1301.

2. John and Jill Smith filed Chapter 7. Eleven days later, Southwest Auto Finance, which held a security interest in the Smiths' two cars, repossessed one of them. Southwest had no knowledge of the Smiths' bankruptcy petition at the time of the repossession, but still refused to return the car even after it learned the facts from the Smiths' attorney. Has Southwest violated the automatic stay? If so, can the Smiths recover damages and attorneys fees under § 362(h)?

3. Sportfame, a sporting goods retailer, fell behind on payments to its primary supplier, Wilson Sporting Goods. Consequently, Wilson ceased shipping inventory to Sportfame. After filing for reorganization under Chapter 11, Sportfame attempted to have inventory shipments resumed by offering to pay cash for all goods shipped. Wilson refused to supply any additional inventory until Sportfame brought its accounts current or made arrangements to pay 100% of the arrearage. Has Wilson violated the automatic stay? See *Sportfame of Ohio, Inc. v. Wilson Sporting Goods Co. (In re Sportfame of Ohio, Inc.)*, 40 B.R. 47 (Bankr. N.D. Ohio 1984).

4. Lumber Company received a default judgment against Debtor in the amount of $7,000. Six years later, in February, Lumber Company sought to enforce the judgment by filing continuing garnishment proceedings against Debtor and his employer, City. Debtor filed bankruptcy on March 19 and his attorney sent letters to both Lumber Company and City on that day, informing them of Debtor's bankruptcy. Lumber Company's attorney received the letter on March 20 and the City Attorney received the letter on March 25. On April 20, the Clerk of the Bankruptcy Court mailed the usual notice of bankruptcy to each of Debtor's creditors, including Lumber Company. Because City was not a creditor in Debtor's bankruptcy, it received no notice from the Clerk. On April 10 and again on May 25, City sent $300 to the Superior Court, to be paid to Lumber Company in accordance with the garnishment. Has Lumber Company or City violated the automatic stay? If so, was the violation willful? See *Elder v. City of Thomasville, Ga. (In re Elder)*, 12 B.R. 491 (Bankr. M.D.Ga. 1981).

5. Debtor filed a petition in bankruptcy, listing on the schedules filed with the bankruptcy court two debts owed to Creditor. One of the debts was a $4,000 car loan secured by Debtor's car; the other was a $500 unsecured loan. Debtor sought to reaffirm the car loan so that she could retain possession of the car. Creditor refused to allow Debtor to reaffirm the car loan without also reaffirming the unsecured loan. Has Creditor violated the automatic stay? What if Creditor threatened repossession of the car if Debtor did not reaffirm the unsecured debt?

6. Sears sent a letter to Debtor's attorney offering to give Debtor a modest amount of postpetition credit if he chose to reaffirm the debt. Sears sent a copy of the letter to Debtor, marked "for information purposes only." Has Sears violated the stay? See *Matter of Duke*, 79 F.3d 43 (7th Cir. 1996).

7. Debtor, whose business was the management of a commercial office building, owed Bank $4 million on a note secured by a mortgage on the building. Following a default, the parties negotiated a modification agreement under which Bank extended the due date on the note and Debtor agreed that it would not object to any motion to lift stay filed by Bank in any subsequent bankruptcy proceeding. Debtor filed a Chapter 11 petition a year later and Bank sought relief from the stay. Is Debtor's agreement not to contest such a motion enforceable? Does it matter what other creditors may think? See *In re Atrium High Point Ltd. Partnership*, 189 B.R. 599 (Bankr. M.D.N.C. 1995).

2. EXCEPTIONS TO THE STAY

The automatic stay bars *any* actions against the debtor or the property of the estate by *any* party of *any* character—almost. As with many rules, the mandate of § 362(a)'s automatic stay has exceptions, which are provided in § 362(b). The subsections of § 362 strike a balance between aiding the debtor's rehabilitation and allowing socially desirable actions against the debtor to proceed.

Problems

Determine whether the following actions, taken after Debtor files bankruptcy, violate the automatic stay under § 362(a) and, if they do, whether they are excepted under § 362(b):

a. The state tax department sends Debtor a notice of property tax due on Debtor's car.

b. Debtor's spouse attempts to collect alimony payments owed by Debtor.

c. Appliance store files a financing statement two days after Debtor's bankruptcy filing, in order to perfect its security interest in a refrigerator Debtor bought the week before.

d. The local district attorney's office files charges against Debtor for criminal fraud, despite Debtor's pleas that he cannot fund his Chapter 13 plan unless he can stay out of prison and continue working.

A "governmental unit" may enforce its "police or regulatory power," including a non-money judgment obtained in such an action, under § 362(b)(4). This exception, which is intended to protect the public health, safety and welfare, permits governmental actions undertaken to prevent or stop violation of laws regulating fraud, environmental protection, consumer protection, safety, and other similar police or regulatory laws, in addition to actions to fix damages for violations of such laws.

At the time the following cases were decided, this "police power" exception was covered by two subsections, §§ 362(b)(4) and (b)(5). They provided that the filing of a bankruptcy petition did not operate as a stay—

> (4) under subsection (a)(1) of this section, of the commencement or continuation of an action or proceeding by a governmental unit to enforce such governmental unit's police or regulatory power;
>
> (5) under subsection (a)(2) of this section, of the enforcement of a judgment, other than a money judgment, obtained in an action or proceeding by a governmental unit to enforce such governmental unit's police or regulatory power * * * .

The two provisions were combined into a new subsection (b)(4) in 1998 and subsection (b)(5) was deleted. The remaining subsections of § 362(b) were not renumbered.

MISSOURI v. UNITED STATES BANKRUPTCY COURT FOR THE EASTERN DISTRICT OF ARKANSAS

United States Court of Appeals, Eighth Circuit, 1981.
647 F.2d 768, *cert denied*, 454 U.S. 1162, 102 S.Ct. 1035, 71 L.Ed.2d 318 (1982).

BRIGHT, Circuit Judge.

This case presents the question of whether the State of Missouri or the federal bankruptcy court for the Eastern District of Missouri [sic] has jurisdiction over grain located in Missouri grain storage warehouses. The bankruptcy court asserts that it has exclusive jurisdiction over the grain warehouses pursuant to a bankruptcy proceeding instituted by Arkansas debtors, operators of warehouses in Missouri and Arkansas. The State of Missouri asserts that the grain should be liquidated in accordance with provisions of the Missouri Code, under the aegis of the Missouri Department of Agriculture.

The State of Missouri applies here for a writ of prohibition to prevent the bankruptcy court from exercising jurisdiction over the grain. The State also appeals from the district court's denial of its application for a similar writ of prohibition.

After carefully reviewing the record and the contentions of the various parties, we sustain the authority of the bankruptcy judge. We hold that the Bankruptcy Reform Act of 1978 vests the bankruptcy court with exclusive jurisdiction over the grain and grain warehouses in question, subject, of course, to the court's and trustee's obligation to protect the interests of farmers and others who have ownership rights in the grain. *See* § 361. Accordingly, we deny the writ of prohibition and affirm the order of the district court.

I. BACKGROUND

Robert James, Don James, and G. E. James (the debtors), residents of Arkansas, operated public grain elevators in Missouri and Arkansas under various partnership identities, including elevators located at Holcomb, New Madrid (Ristine), Caruthersville, and Naylor, Missouri. An affiliated corporation, James Agri–Center, Inc., operates a public grain warehouse at Neelyville, Missouri.

On August 11, 1980, these debtors, including the corporation, filed bankruptcy proceedings in the bankruptcy court for the Eastern District of Arkansas. The partnership liquidations were originally filed under chapter 7 of the Bankruptcy Code, and subsequently were converted into reorganization proceedings under chapter 11 of the Code. The corporation operates as a debtor in possession under chapter 11 of the Code. The bankruptcy court appointed Robert P. Lindsey initially as the interim trustee on August 15, 1980, and later as permanent trustee for the purpose of operating and liquidating the various partnerships.

Three days prior to the filing of the bankruptcy proceedings, the debtors authorized the Missouri Department of Agriculture to assume control of the grain in their Missouri warehouses, pursuant to Missouri law empowering the State to operate and liquidate insolvent grain warehouses. The Missouri Department of Agriculture filed receivership petitions for the debtors' grain warehouses in the state circuit courts for the counties in which the warehouses are located. On August 12, 1980, subsequent to the filing of the bankruptcy petitions, the Missouri courts appointed John G. Runyan, then Director of the Department, as receiver of each warehouse and ordered him to

> make an audit and full investigation of the financial circumstances of respondents [debtors] and carry out such operation or liquidation of said public grain warehouse[s] in order to protect the best interests of those individuals storing grain in said facilit[ies].

On August 29, the bankruptcy court entered an order directing the trustee to assume certain grain purchase contracts with farmers, executed by the debtors prior to bankruptcy. A number of farmers, believing this action deprived them of their rightful possession of their grain, barricaded the New Madrid (Ristine) grain warehouse. The bankruptcy court ordered United States Marshals to intercede and break the blockade.

On September 3, 1980, the State requested that the bankruptcy court determine the ownership of the grain located in the Missouri partnership warehouses. The State subsequently voluntarily withdrew the request; thus the question of the ownership of the grain remains in dispute. Missouri concedes that the debtors own at least 2.3 percent of the grain. Other parties claiming ownership of the grain include Missouri and Arkansas farmer-producers, the Commodity Credit Corporation, and the First Tennessee Bank, N.A., Memphis. The State and the trustee dispute whether the amount of grain on hand exceeds the outstanding warehouse receipts. The trustee estimates the value of the Missouri grain at approximately $5,000,000.

On September 11, 1980, the bankruptcy court issued an order approving the trustee's application for a grain dealer and warehouse operator's license. The court also fixed the trustee's bond at $1,000,000 and ordered the trustee to comply to the extent possible with Missouri laws and regulations concerning the licensing of grain dealers and warehouses.

The drama escalated when, on September 23, 1980, the trustee filed a request in bankruptcy court to sell the grain free and clear of all liens. The trustee alleged that the grain should be sold because of the cost of storage, the high market price, the danger of deterioration, and the financial benefits of investing the proceedings [sic] pending eventual distribution. The trustee asserted authority to sell the grain pursuant to § 363(f)(4), which permits the sale of property owned by an entity other than the bankruptcy estate if the ownership is in bona fide dispute. Here, the trustee alleged a genuine dispute between the estate and other parties concerning ownership of the grain.

In response to the petition to sell grain, the Missouri authorities brought an action in Missouri state court against the trustee and the debtors for enforcement of the Missouri grain laws. On October 20, 1980, the state court issued a temporary restraining order, coupled with an order to show cause, directing Missouri's Director of Agriculture to take possession of the grain warehouses and restraining the trustee from interfering in any way with the Director's control, operation, and liquidation of the Missouri grain.

Needless to say, the order produced an immediate response from the trustee and the bankruptcy court. On the same day the state order issued, the bankruptcy judge telephoned counsel for Missouri's Director of Agriculture and advised him that contempt proceedings would be heard against the Director.

The Missouri officials immediately sought a writ of prohibition in this court. We denied that petition on October 21, 1980, without prejudice to the filing of a petition for such a writ in the district court for the Eastern District of Arkansas. We also stayed certain bankruptcy proceedings, including the contempt proceeding, pending a further order of this court. The Missouri officials then unsuccessfully sought prohibitory relief in the federal district court.

The district court ruled that the bankruptcy court possessed exclusive jurisdiction over the estate of the debtors, which included all legal and equitable interests in property of the debtors wherever located as of the commencement of the action. The court also observed that, although state law defines the "interests" in property, federal law controls the issue of whether property, as so defined, becomes property of the debtor's estate. The court recognized that competing claims against the property existed, and, therefore, the bankruptcy court had jurisdiction at least to determine whether the grain is part of the estate as defined by the Code.

Missouri also argued that the legal proceedings brought in state court under the Missouri grain laws, as an exercise of the state's police and regulatory power, fall within the exception to the automatic stay provision of the Code, § 362(b)(4). The district court rejected this contention, concluding that:

> It is plain Petitioners are not endeavoring to prevent a violation of consumer protection, environmental protection, fraud or a similar police or regulatory law involving the safety, health, morals and the general welfare of society, but on the

contrary, Petitioners' sole objective is to protect the pecuniary interests in property of purported depositors. Consequently, Petitioners' action does not fall within the exception to the jurisdiction of the Bankruptcy Court where a governmental unit is enforcing a police or regulatory power.

The State of Missouri appeals from the district court order and renews its motion for a writ of prohibition in this court * * *.

We affirm the district court and deny the petition for a writ of prohibition.

II. DISCUSSION

* * *

B. Automatic Stay of State Court Proceedings

We next examine Missouri's contention that a writ of prohibition should issue based on the "police or regulatory power" exception to the automatic stay provision of the Bankruptcy Code. Section 362 provides that upon the filing of a bankruptcy petition, all judicial and other proceedings are stayed. This section also lists certain exceptions to the automatic stay, including § 362(b)(4) * * *.

Missouri asserts that this exception applies to the enforcement of its grain regulatory laws, and, therefore (1) the automatic stay provisions do not bar the Missouri state court proceedings; and (2) the bankruptcy court lacks the power to prevent Missouri from enforcing its grain laws by taking possession of the debtors' Missouri warehouses. Missouri essentially argues:

> [T]he enforcement of grain laws is a valid exercise of a state's police and regulatory powers. Section 362(b)(4) of the Bankruptcy Code permits enforcement proceedings initiated by state regulatory authorities to continue even though a bankruptcy petition has been filed. The case law is overwhelming that bankruptcy courts do not have *subject matter jurisdiction* to enjoin enforcement proceedings initiated by state regulatory authorities. The Bankruptcy Court here is attempting to enjoin Missouri's enforcement of its grain laws. The Bankruptcy Court is powerless to thwart the Circuit Court's exclusive jurisdiction over such enforcement proceedings. The October 20, 1980 law-

> suit now pending in the Circuit Court of New Madrid County should continue.

We reject these contentions.

The present stay provisions amplify and clarify provisions of the former bankruptcy law and bankruptcy rules providing for an automatic stay of certain proceedings against debtors. These automatic stays did not apply generally to proceedings affecting the public health and safety or certain governmental regulatory activity.

In explaining the § 362(b)(4) exception, the Congressional House Report comments:

> Paragraph (4) excepts commencement or continuation of actions and proceedings by governmental units to enforce police or regulatory powers. Thus, where a governmental unit is suing a debtor to prevent or stop violation of fraud, environmental protection, consumer protection, safety, or similar police or regulatory laws, or attempting to fix damages for violation of such a law, the action or proceeding is not stayed under the automatic stay. Paragraph (5) makes clear that the exception extends to permit an injunction and enforcement of an injunction, and to permit the entry of a money judgment, but does not extend to permit enforcement of a money judgment. Since the assets of the debtor are in the possession and control of the bankruptcy court, and since they constitute a fund out of which all creditors are entitled to share, enforcement by a governmental unit of a money judgment would give it preferential treatment to the detriment of all other creditors. [H.R. Rep. No. 95–595 at 343, *reprinted in* 1978 U.S.C.C.A.N. at 6299.]

Additionally, Congressman Don Edwards, Chairman of a subcommittee of the Judiciary Committee considering the Bankruptcy Code, observed:

> This section [§ 362(b)(4)] is intended to be given a narrow construction in order to permit governmental units to pursue actions to protect the public health and safety and not to apply to actions by a governmental unit to protect a pecuniary interest in property of the debtor or property of the estate. [124 Cong. Rec. H11089, *reprinted in* 1978 U.S.C.C.A.N. at 6436, 6444–45.]

In light of the legislative history and court decisions under the earlier bankruptcy act, we believe that the term "police or regulatory power" refers to the enforcement of state laws affecting health, welfare, morals, and safety, but not regulatory laws that directly conflict with the control of the *res* or property by the bankruptcy court. The pertinent provision of Missouri law relied on by the State, which concerns insolvency of grain warehouses, provides:

> If at any time, the director, whether or not he or his authorized agent has possession as authorized by this section, has evidence that a warehouseman is insolvent or is unable to satisfy the claims of all depositors, the director may petition the circuit court for the appointment of a receiver *to operate or liquidate* the business of the warehouseman in accordance with law. [Mo. Rev. Stat. § 411.519.6 (1979) (emphasis added).]

We conclude that Missouri's grain laws, although regulatory in nature, primarily relate to the protection of the pecuniary interest in the debtors' property and not to matters of public safety and health. Missouri's laws, by governing the operation and liquidation of grain warehouses, directly conflict with the control of the property by the bankruptcy court and, therefore, do not fall within the § 362(b)(4) exception.

Alternatively, even if Missouri's liquidation proceedings come within the exception, the State's attempted enforcement of its insolvency laws does not oust the bankruptcy court of jurisdiction.

It is well settled that a bankruptcy action preempts state insolvency proceedings. "The bankruptcy law is paramount, and the jurisdiction of the Federal courts in bankruptcy, when properly invoked, in the administration of the affairs of insolvent persons and corporations, is essentially exclusive." *In re Watts & Sachs*, 190 U.S. 1, 27 (1903). The bankruptcy court could take appropriate steps to protect its jurisdiction over the estate, regardless of whether a proceeding falls within the § 362(b)(4) exception. For example, the court may "issue any order, process, or judgment that is necessary or appropriate to carry out the provisions of this title." § 105(a).

Thus, even if the automatic stay provisions did not apply to the Missouri proceedings, the bankruptcy court possesses power in its discretion to enjoin state courts, officials, and agencies from interfering with assets in custody of the bankruptcy court. In other words, the exception of § 362(b)(4), even if applicable in this case, in no way deprives the bankruptcy court of jurisdiction over assets of the bankrupt's estate, and therefore, § 362(b)(4) cannot serve as a basis for issuing a writ of prohibition.

* * *

Notes and Questions

1. According to the opinion in the principal case, when may a bankruptcy court use § 105 to supplement the automatic stay? What effect does that have on the delicate balance struck by subsections (a) and (b) of § 362? Does the court suggest any constraints on the § 105 power?

2. Compare the result in *Missouri* with *Brock v. Rusco Industries, Inc.*, 842 F.2d 270 (11th Cir.1988). The debtor, Rusco Industries, failed to pay its employees for their final two weeks of work immediately preceding its Chapter 11 filing. The Secretary of Labor filed suit against Rusco for violation of the Fair Labor Standards Act (FLSA) and sought an injunction to prevent the sale of all goods produced by the workers during the last two weeks until Rusco paid the Secretary the minimum wages for the employees' work. The district court held that the automatic stay barred the action and dismissed the Secretary's suit. The Secretary appealed to the Eleventh Circuit.

The Court of Appeals recognized that to require Rusco to pay the wages before selling the goods would effectively give the employees a higher claim priority than Rusco's other creditors, thus creating a tension between the FLSA and the Bankruptcy Code. Nevertheless, the court found that § 362(b)(4) allowed the Secretary's action to continue. The court concluded that the Secretary's suit was filed to protect legitimate businesses from unfair competition and to enforce federal minimum wage laws. Accordingly, the suit was a proper exercise of the Secretary's police power. The court noted that a governmental unit may obtain a money judgment against a bankrupt debtor, but that the judgment cannot be enforced until the stay is lifted. The court held, however, that § 362(b)(5) (which was still in the Code) permitted enforcement of an *injunction* obtained against a bankrupt debtor. Consequently, Rusco could be enjoined from selling the goods until the employees were paid the minimum wage. The court, finally, held that Congress intended the "taint" to be removed from goods manufactured by employees making less than the minimum wage before the goods can be sold in commerce and that this intent extends to goods held by a bankrupt debtor. The court entered an order requiring Rusco to pay the minimum wage to its employees before selling the goods for the benefit of other creditors.

Is *Brock* consistent with *Missouri*? Does the kind of relief sought by the government distinguish the cases?

3. Courts are often urged to use § 105 injunctions to override § 362(b)(1), most commonly to enjoin criminal proceedings pursued for the

purpose of collecting debt. Although some courts believe that § 105 may be used, in appropriate circumstances, to stay criminal actions, requests for injunctive relief under § 105 are rarely granted.

The Supreme Court addressed whether state criminal actions may be stayed by federal injunction in *Younger v. Harris*, 401 U.S. 37, 91 S.Ct. 746, 27 L.Ed.2d 669 (1971). The *Younger* doctrine generally limits federal injunctive relief against state criminal prosecutions to rare cases in which a threat of great and immediate irreparable injury exists that is related to "federally protected rights" and that "cannot be eliminated by * * * defense in a single criminal prosecution." *Id.* at 46. The usual prerequisites for a finding of irreparable harm are "bad faith or harassment" in the prosecution. *Id.* at 50.

In determining whether bad faith exists, some courts rely on the "principal motivation test," which looks to the creditor's main reason for pursuing the criminal action, regardless of whether the action was initiated in good faith. Courts applying the principal motivation test attempt to determine whether a state criminal prosecution is being used to "vindicate the public good" or whether it is "to collect the debt for one of its residents." *Brinkman v. City of Edina (In re Brinkman)*, 123 B.R. 318, 322 (Bankr. D.Minn.1991).

4. Scott Hucke pleaded guilty to rape and, in lieu of a three-year prison sentence, was placed on probation for five years and ordered to pay $20,000 in compensation to his victim. He immediately filed a Chapter 13 petition and proposed a plan that would pay a 20% dividend to his unsecured creditors. The state began probation revocation proceedings and, at the hearing, the debtor offered to modify the plan to pay 100% to his victim. The state judge rejected the offer, finding that the state court no longer had to ability to fashion such a sentence, and ordered his incarceration. Was the automatic stay violated? See *Hucke v. Oregon (In re Hucke)*, 992 F.2d 950 (9th Cir.), *cert. denied*, 510 U.S. 862, 114 S.Ct. 178, 126 L.Ed.2d 137 (1993). Compare *In re Barboza*, 211 B.R. 450 (Bankr. D.R.I. 1997).

5. Any unit of government, including the United States, a state, a municipality, a public agency or a foreign state, can benefit from the stay exceptions for "governmental units" enumerated in § 362(b)(4). See § 101(27). The term is limited, however, to "actual governmental groups" and does not include "organizations acting in a governmental capacity." See *In re Colin, Hochstin Co.*, 41 B.R. 322, 324–25 (Bankr. S.D.N.Y. 1984) (holding that § 362(b)(4) does not apply to the New York Stock Exchange).

Environmental cases raise several important problems in bankruptcy. One of them is the proper interpretation of § 362(b)(4) (and, at the time these cases were decided, § 362(b)(5)), which provides an exception to the automatic stay for certain actions by governmental units to enforce their police or regulatory power. The following two cases deal with this issue.

OHIO v. KOVACS (IN RE KOVACS)

United States Court of Appeals, Sixth Circuit, 1982.
681 F.2d 454, *vacated*, 459 U.S. 1167, 103 S.Ct. 810, 74 L.Ed.2d 1010 (1983).

PER CURIAM.

In 1979, William Kovacs, along with Chem–Dyne Corporation and other business entities, were engaged in the industrial waste disposal business in Hamilton, Ohio. The state of Ohio sued Kovacs individually and as an officer of the defendant corporations, alleging that the defendants had caused water pollution, nuisance conditions and fish kills in violation of Ohio law. Kovacs signed a Stipulation and Judgment Entry in the Butler County Common Pleas Court on July 18, 1979, which enjoined him from causing further pollution and required him to remove all industrial wastes from the premises of Chem–Dyne Corporation within twelve months.

On February 1, 1980, because of noncompliance with the court's earlier judgment, the Common Pleas Court granted Ohio's motion appointing a receiver of Kovacs's non-exempt property and assets along with the assets of related corporate entities. The receiver was also directed to effect the clean-up of the Chem–Dyne site.

Among other things, the state court's order contained the following provisions:

> It is further ordered that Mr. Jack Zettler be appointed receiver of all property or assets, wherever situated, whether real or personal, tangible or intangible, and all interests, whether legal or equitable, in property or assets, of William Kovacs, except to the extent of any property exempt from the control of a receiver by operation of law;
>
> * * *
>
> The receiver shall have power and authority to receive and collect any and all sums of money due or owing to the defendant business entities or defendant Kovacs in any manner,

whether the same are now due or shall hereafter become due and payable. * * *

* * *

It is further ordered * * * that each of the business entities and defendant Kovacs, and all officers, agents, and employees of the Defendant business entities and defendant Kovacs be enjoined and ordered to cooperate fully with the receiver in the performance of such duties or the exercise of such powers.

Kovacs filed a personal petition in bankruptcy under Chapter 11 of the Bankruptcy Act on July 17, 1980. This action was converted to a straight bankruptcy under Chapter 7 on September 2, 1980, by order of the United States Bankruptcy Court for the Southern District of Ohio.

On September 13, 1980, Ohio filed a motion in the Butler County Court of Common Pleas for a hearing to determine Kovacs's current employment status and income. In response, Kovacs filed a motion with the bankruptcy court, seeking to restrain the proceedings in the Ohio state court. The bankruptcy judge concluded that the State sought the information in state court about Kovacs's current income "as a preliminary to requesting an order from that court which would require that part of debtor's current income be applied" to the receiver's efforts to complete Kovacs's unfulfilled obligation to clean up the industrial wastes from the Chem–Dyne location. The bankruptcy judge determined that Kovacs was entitled to an automatic stay of the state court proceedings under § 362, and accordingly enjoined the state of Ohio on October 31, 1980 from proceeding further in state court in its attempt to levy on Kovacs's post-petition earnings. The bankruptcy court's judgment was affirmed on appeal to the United States District Court for the Southern District of Ohio, Judge Spiegel presiding, on April 30, 1981.

[The court quoted §§ 362(a)(2) and (b)(5).]

The bankruptcy court concluded that the issue of whether Kovacs's obligation to clean up the Chem–Dyne site under the Ohio state court's judgment was dischargeable in bankruptcy was not properly before it, since an adversary proceeding is required to discharge a debtor's obligation; therefore, it assumed for purposes of argument that it was not dischargeable. The bankruptcy court determined:

> The question presented to us is whether what the State is attempting in [its motion in state court to determine Kovacs's current income] is exempted from the automatic stay of § 362(a)(2) by reason of § 362(b)(5). We hold that it is not, even though in its express language § 362(b)(5) says only that enforcement of a money judgment is subject to the § 362(a)(2) stay, while other enforcement actions obtained by a governmental unit to enforce its regulatory power are excepted from the stay. Neither prior order of the Butler County Common Pleas Court, it is true, gives the State a money judgment with respect to cleaning up the Chem–Dyne premises, but there is no difference in substance between efforts to collect money from a debtor by securing a court order, and efforts to enforce a money judgment against him. We hold, therefore, that the State is estopped to deny that it is seeking to enforce a money judgment against debtor.

* * *

We concur with the bankruptcy court's conclusion that § 362 indicates a clear intent to permit governmental units to continue to enforce their police power through mandatory injunctions despite the filing of a bankruptcy petition, but to deny those units the power to collect money in their enforcement efforts. We further concur with the conclusion of the bankruptcy court and the district court that the state of Ohio in its state court proceedings was seeking what in essence amounted to a money judgment against Kovacs, which was properly subject to the automatic stay. We note that the state court's order appointing a receiver also ordered that Kovacs turn over all his non-exempt assets to the receiver, and authorized the receiver to collect any sums of money that would become payable to Kovacs in the future. There is very little in substance to distinguish that order and a money judgment. As noted in In re *Canarico Quarries, Inc.*, 466 F.Supp. 1333, 1340 (D.P.R.1979), § 362 "is intended to be given a narrow construction in order to permit governmental units to pursue actions to protect the public health and safety and not to apply to actions by a governmental unit to protect a pecuniary interest in property of the debtor or property of the estate." To permit the state of Ohio to proceed with its state court action would subvert the purpose of the Bankruptcy Act to rehabilitate debtors and to give them relief from harassing creditors.

AFFIRMED.

PENN TERRA LTD. v. DEPARTMENT OF ENVIRONMENTAL RESOURCES

United States Court of Appeals, Third Circuit, 1984.
733 F.2d 267.

GARTH, Circuit Judge.

This case demonstrates the difficulty encountered when two governmental policies—one federal and one state—come into arguable conflict. On the one hand, the federally created bankruptcy policy requires that the assets of a debtor be preserved and protected, so that in time they may be equitably distributed to all creditors without unfair preference. On the other hand, the environmental policies of the Commonwealth of Pennsylvania require those within its jurisdiction to preserve and protect natural resources and to rectify damage to the environment which they have caused. The potential conflict between these two policies is presented in this case, in which the Commonwealth has attempted to force a company which has petitioned in bankruptcy to correct violations of state antipollution laws, even though this action would have the effect of depleting assets which would otherwise be available to repay debts owed to general creditors.

Both the bankruptcy court and the district court found that the actions by the Commonwealth to compel the debtor to correct the environmental damage were prohibited by the automatic stay provision of the Bankruptcy Code, § 362, which generally acts to halt the commencement or continuation of any legal proceedings against a debtor while a bankruptcy administration is pending. The Commonwealth was therefore enjoined from enforcing a state court order which it had obtained, which mandated remedial action on the part of the debtor company. Because we find that the courts below did not give adequate consideration to the statutory exception contained within the automatic stay provision which exempts certain actions by a governmental unit, we reverse and direct that, to the extent that the § 362 stay remains operative, it be vacated together with the November 4, 1982 permanent injunction against the Commonwealth Court order of May 24, 1982.

I.

The facts in this case are largely undisputed. Penn Terra Limited was the operator of coal surface mines in Armstrong County in western Pennsylvania. The Commonwealth's Department of Environmental Resources (hereafter "DER") found that Penn Terra was operating its mines in violation of various state environmental protection statutes. In February 1981, DER served Penn Terra with a total of 36 citations, both against the corporation and against Harvey Taylor, the president of Penn Terra, for these violations. Penn Terra apparently never contested that these violations existed. On November 9, 1981, DER and Mr. Taylor entered into a consent order and agreement to rectify these infractions and thus place Penn Terra in compliance with the state statutes. The consent agreement listed the violations, and established a schedule for corrective measures to be taken. Penn Terra, however, apparently did not comply with that schedule.

On March 15, 1982, Penn Terra filed a Petition for Bankruptcy under Chapter 7 of the Bankruptcy Code, having previously ceased all operations. In its schedule of assets, Penn Terra listed total property worth $14,000. Of this, $13,500 was designated as "certificates of deposit with DER," which Penn Terra had furnished as bonds for the backfilling operation. The schedule further noted that the cost of reclamation, as required under the consent agreement, would greatly exceed the market and book value of those bonds. The total amount of debts listed was $660,000.

On April 14, 1982, DER brought an equitable action in the Commonwealth Court of Pennsylvania, seeking a preliminary injunction against Penn Terra and Harvey Taylor to correct the violations of the state statutes and to enforce the terms of the consent order. DER apparently did not receive a notice of Penn Terra's bankruptcy petition until April 29, 1982. A hearing was conducted on DER's application in Commonwealth Court on May 24, 1982, as previously scheduled; Harvey Taylor appeared but Penn Terra did not, nor did the Trustee. After taking testimony, the Commonwealth Court granted injunctive relief to DER.

On May 28, 1982, Penn Terra filed a Petition for Contempt in the bankruptcy court against DER and two of its attorneys, Patti J. Saunders and Diana J. Stares, for proceeding with the Commonwealth Court hearing. Penn Terra contended that this proceeding violated the automatic stay provision of § 362(a). DER responded that the proceedings and the resulting injunction fell within the exception to the automatic stay which exempts actions by governmental units performed pursuant to the police power of the government. §§ 362(b)(4)-(5).

The bankruptcy court found that the actions by DER were, in its opinion, actions to enforce a money judgment, which do not fall within the exception to § 362(a). The bankruptcy judge opined that, given the "obvious insolvency" of the debtor, DER's pursuit of its action in state court has resulted in the entry of a "meaningless order." Pursuant to that ruling, on June 29, 1982, the bankruptcy court preliminarily enjoined DER from enforcing the Commonwealth Court injunction. On November 4, 1982, the preliminary injunction was made permanent.

On appeal, the district court affirmed the bankruptcy court's injunction. The district court noted that

> [i]n the instant case, although the DER's action was ostensibly undertaken to enforce state environmental laws, the effect of the action, in light of the disparity between the costs and funds available to do the reclamation work, was to collect a money judgment against Penn Terra; the purpose was not only to enforce a regulation, but to exhaust the debtor's assets.

Appeal to this court ensued. DER argues that the courts below misconstrued the Bankruptcy Code's automatic stay provision by applying it to the Commonwealth of Pennsylvania, and thus it was error to issue an injunction forbidding DER from enforcing the order obtained from the Commonwealth Court.

II.

A. The Statutory Framework

The crux of this case depends on an interpretation of § 362 * * *.

The general policy behind this section is to grant complete, immediate, albeit temporary relief to the debtor from creditors, and also to prevent dissipation of the debtor's assets before orderly distribution to creditors can be effected. Indeed, this relief is available even against those claims which in the end are found to be secured and therefore payable in full. Penn Terra claims that this section operates to remove from the Commonwealth the power to enforce its antipollution laws while the automatic stay is in effect.

The statute does clearly intend to limit State action at least to some extent. Section 362(a) provides that the automatic stay shall operate against "all entities." The legislative history is clear that, in general, this was intended to extend to governmental entities as well as private ones:

> With respect to stays issued under other powers, or the application of the automatic stay, to government actions, this section and the other sections mentioned are intended to be an express waiver of sovereign immunity of the Federal Government, *and an assertion of the bankruptcy power over State governments under the supremacy clause notwithstanding a State's sovereign immunity.*

H.R. Rep. No. 95–595 at 342, *reprinted in* 1978 U.S.C.C.A.N. at 6299 (emphasis added). Indeed, the fact that Congress created an exception to the automatic stay for certain actions by governmental units itself implies that such units are otherwise affected by the stay.

Subsections 362(b)(4) & (5), however, return to the States with one hand some of what was taken away by the other. The purpose of this exception is also explained in the legislative history of the Code:

> Paragraph (4) excepts commencement or continuation of actions and proceedings by governmental units to enforce police or regulatory powers. *Thus, where a government unit is suing a debtor to prevent or stop violation of fraud, environmental protection,* consumer protection, safety, or similar police or regulatory laws, or attempting to fix damages for violation of such law, the action or proceeding is not stayed under the automatic stay.

Id. at 343, *reprinted in* 1978 U.S.C.C.A.N. at 6299 (emphasis added).

Subsection 362(b)(5), however, creates a further "exception to the exception," in that actions to enforce money judgments *are* affected by the automatic stay, even if they otherwise were in furtherance of the State's police powers. As the legislative history explains:

> Paragraph (5) makes clear that the exception extends to permit an injunction and enforcement of an injunction, and to permit the entry of a money judgment, but does not extend to permit enforcement of a money judgment. Since the assets of the debtor are in the possession and control of the bankruptcy court, and since they constitute a fund out of which all creditors are entitled to share, enforcement by a government unit of a money judgment would give it preferential treatment to the detriment of all other creditors.

Id.

Our task is to determine: (1) whether DER's actions come within the police or regulatory power of the state; if so, then it must further be determined (2) whether DER's actions are an attempt to enforce a money judgment.

B. General Principles of Construction

* * *

Given the general rule that pre-emption is not favored, and the fact that, in restoring power to the States, Congress intentionally used such a broad term as "police and regulatory powers," we find that the exception to the automatic stay provision contained in subsections 362(b)(4)-(5) should itself be construed broadly, and no unnatural efforts be made to limit its scope. The police power of the several States embodies the main bulwark of protection by which they carry out their responsibilities to the People; its abrogation is therefore a serious matter. Congress should not be assumed, therefore, to have been miserly in its refund of that power to the States. Where important state law or general equitable principles protect some public interest, they should not be overridden by federal legislation unless they are inconsistent with explicit congressional intent such that the supremacy clause mandates their supersession. For the same policy reasons, the "exception to the exception" created by subsection 362(b)(5), rendering "enforcement of a money judgment" by a government unit susceptible to the automatic stay, should be construed *narrowly* so as to leave to the States as much of their police power as a fair reading of the statute allows.

There is another reason, specific to this case, why the automatic stay provision should, whenever possible, be read in favor of the States. Concededly, in some individual situations, the exercise of State power, even for the protection of the public health and safety, may run so contrary to the policy of the Bankruptcy Code that it should not be permitted. The statute provides for such exigencies, however. The bankruptcy court, in its discretion, may issue an appropriate injunction, even if the automatic stay is not operative. § 105. Congress explicitly took note of this provision when it excepted government regulation from the automatic stay:

> Subsection (b) lists seven exceptions to the automatic stay. The effect of an exception is not to make the action immune from injunction.

> The court has ample other powers to stay actions not covered by the automatic stay. Section 105, of the proposed title 11, derived from the Bankruptcy Act § 2a(15), grants the power to issue orders necessary or appropriate to carry out the provisions of title 11. The district court and the bankruptcy court as its adjunct have all the traditional injunctive powers of a court of equity [statutory citations omitted]. Stays or injunctions issued under these other sections will not be automatic upon commencement of the case, but will be granted or issued under the usual rules for the issuance of injunctions. By excepting an act or action from the automatic stay, the bill simply requires that the trustee move the court into action, rather than requiring the stayed party to request relief from the stay. There are some actions, enumerated in the exceptions, that generally should not be stayed automatically upon commencement of the case, for reasons of either policy or practicality. Thus, the court will have to determine whether a particular action which may be harming the estate should be stayed.

H.R. Rep. No. 95–595 at 342, *reprinted in* 1978 U.S.C.C.A.N. at 6298.

Therefore, little harm is done to congressional purpose in allowing some latitude in favor of State regulatory powers when interpreting § 362(b), since if, in a particular case, that latitude results in an impermissible dilution of federal bankruptcy policy, then the bankruptcy court may always issue an injunction tailored to fit those circumstances. Such an injunction, however, would be based upon traditional equitable standards, and its propriety would also be reviewable on an abuse of discretion standard. The automatic stay, on the other hand, is not discretionary and must remain in effect unless and until the bankruptcy court later grants relief.

We find that the foregoing considerations favoring liberal construction of the exception to the automatic stay provisions found in subsections 365(b)(4)-(5) outweigh the contrary considerations, relied upon by Penn Terra and the bankruptcy court below, favoring a more restrictive construction.

C. DER's Suit as an Exercise of Police Power

Turning now to the specific issues in this case, it first is clear to us that the actions taken by DER in obtaining and attempting to enforce the Commonwealth Court's injunction falls squarely within Pennsylvania's police and regulatory powers. DER seeks to force Penn

Terra to rectify harmful environmental hazards. No more obvious exercise of the State's power to protect the health, safety, and welfare of the public can be imagined. Indeed, both the Senate and the House committee reports on the Bankruptcy Reform Act explicitly acknowledge environmental protection as a part of the State's police power.[7]

D. Definition of the Term "Enforcement of a Money Judgment"

Having found that DER's actions constitute an exercise of the Commonwealth's police power, the dispositive issue in this case is whether the Commonwealth Court injunction ordering Penn Terra to perform reclamation work is in fact an attempt to enforce a money judgment. The Bankruptcy Court found that it was, as did the district court. Our analysis suggests otherwise.

In using the words "enforcement of a money judgment," Congress did not provide any definition for that term. Its meaning must therefore be gleaned from the commonly accepted usage and from whatever indications of congressional intent we find persuasive. "Where Congress uses terms that have accumulated settled meaning under either equity or common law, a court must infer, unless the statute otherwise dictates, that Congress means to incorporate the established meaning of these terms." *NLRB v. Amax Coal Co.*, 453 U.S. 322, 329 (1981). In attempting to arrive at a working definition of "enforcement of a money judgment," therefore, we must look to legal custom and practice to determine what was *traditionally* understood to be a recovery for money damages. This empirical approach is mandated by the fact that, in using the term "enforcement of a money judgment," Congress left us with a term whose words, standing alone, do not convey the legislative intent, and indeed are merely a shorthand notation for common practice as it has gradually developed in our legal history.

---

[7] We also acknowledge that exercise of a State's police powers may, depending on the circumstances, take the form of an execution on a money judgment. For example, if a coal mining company conducted operations in violation of applicable surface reclamation laws, then the assessment and *collection* of a civil penalty to serve as a punishment and deterrence against future violations would be no less an exercise of the police power than if the State had ordered the company to cease operations entirely. It is important to remember that § 362(b)(5), which prohibits governmental units from enforcing money judgments while the automatic stay is in effect, does not *exclude* such enforcement by definition from the meaning of "police power," or imply that when a state seeks to execute a money judgment it is not acting for the public health, safety, or welfare. Section 362(b)(5) is merely an *exception* to the rule that the exercise of police power by a State is not affected by the automatic stay.

In common understanding, a money judgment is an order entered by the court or by the clerk, after a verdict has been rendered for plaintiff, which adjudges that the defendant shall pay a sum of money to the plaintiff. Essentially, it need consist of only two elements: (1) an identification of the parties for and against whom judgment is being entered, and (2) a *definite* and *certain* designation of the amount which plaintiff is owed by defendant. It need not, and generally does not, contain provisions for its enforcement. As the legislative history explicitly notes, the mere *entry* of a money judgment by a governmental unit is not affected by the automatic stay, provided of course that such proceedings are related to that government's police or regulatory powers.

Quite separate from the entry of a money judgment, however, is a proceeding to *enforce* that money judgment. The paradigm for such a proceeding is when, having obtained a judgment for a sum certain, a plaintiff attempts to seize property of the defendant in order to satisfy that judgment. It is this seizure of a defendant-debtor's property, to satisfy the judgment obtained by a plaintiff-creditor, which is proscribed by subsection 362(b)(5).

At least as a matter of form, it is clear to us that the proceeding initiated by DER in Commonwealth Court was not to enforce a money judgment. Indeed, it could not have resulted even in the mere entry of a money judgment. DER brought its action in equity to compel the performance of certain remedial acts by Penn Terra. It did not seek the payment of compensation to the Commonwealth's coffers, and the injunction actually issued by the Commonwealth Court did not direct such payment. This proceeding, therefore, could never have resulted in the adjudication of liability for a sum certain, an essential element of a money judgment. Since this action was in form and substance (*see* discussion *infra*), not one to obtain a money judgment, it follows that it could not be one to *enforce* the payment of such a judgment.

Penn Terra contends, however, that whatever the appearance in form of DER's suit may have been, it was in substance an action to obtain and enforce a money judgment, and therefore was affected by the automatic stay. We generally agree, of course, that the legislative intent behind subsection 362(b)(5) should not be defeated by artful pleading that depends on form rather than substance. We must therefore determine whether, although not facially resembling an enforcement of a money judgment, DER's action in Commonwealth Court sought to achieve in actuality what a money judgment was traditionally intended to accomplish and no more.

* * * [A]n important factor in identifying a proceeding as one to enforce a money judgment is whether the remedy would compensate for *past* wrongful acts resulting in injuries already suffered, or protect against potential *future* harm. Thus, it is unlikely that any action which seeks to prevent culpable conduct *in futuro* will, in normal course, manifest itself as an action for a money judgment, or one to enforce a money judgment. This is consistent with our earlier observations, since a traditional money judgment requires *liquidated* damages, i.e. a sum certain, and one cannot liquidate damages which have not yet been suffered due to conduct not yet committed. Nor can one calculate such a sum with any certainty. Indeed, the very nature of injunctive relief is that it addresses injuries which may not be compensated by money.

The bankruptcy court adopted a totally different functional definition of money judgment, however. In its opinion, it apparently reasoned that a money judgment is anything which costs money to enforce. The court stated:

> Although DER characterizes its action as a governmental action in the exercise of its police or regulatory powers, it seeks a mandatory injunction requiring the debtor's expenditure of funds for the correction of violations. This Court concludes that the mandatory injunction sought by DER requiring the expenditure of funds is in essence the attempted enforcement of a money judgment. As such, it is subject to the automatic stay by virtue of § 362(b)(5).

The court below drew support from *In re Kovacs*, 681 F.2d 454 (6th Cir.1982), *vacated and remanded*, 459 U.S. 1167 (1983) (*Kovacs I*). There, as here, the debtor had not complied with various environmental control laws. A state court had ordered him to cease pollution and remove hazardous wastes from the premises. When Kovacs did not comply, the state court appointed a receiver to take possession of the debtor's property and effect a clean-up of the site. The Court of Appeals for the Sixth Circuit found that such action amounted to enforcement of a money judgment and was therefore automatically stayed.

To the extent that it found that a state effort to force a debtor to clean up his waste was in essence a money judgment, *Kovacs* lends support to the bankruptcy court's position.[11] We find, however, that the

[11] The Sixth Circuit itself recognizes that the original *Kovacs I* opinion has no authoritative value, since it had been vacated by the Supreme Court. *In re Kovacs*, 717 F.2d 984, 987 (6th Cir.1983) (on remand from Supreme Court), [*aff'd sub nom. Ohio v.*

definition of "money judgment" implied in *Kovacs* and adopted by the bankruptcy court is unduly broad. Were we to find that any order which requires the expenditure of money is a "money judgment," then the exception to § 362 for government police action, which should be construed broadly, would instead be narrowed into virtual nonexistence. Yet we cannot ignore the fundamental fact that, in contemporary times, almost everything costs something. An injunction which does not compel some expenditure or loss of monies may often be an effective nullity.[12]

It appears that, in defining the scope of the exception to the automatic stay, the Bankruptcy Court in this case placed too much weight on the value of preserving the corpus of the debtor's funds and estate under its own exclusive control. Admittedly, that goal is normally central to the statutory scheme of the Bankruptcy Code. As noted at the beginning of this opinion, however, in some instances this policy is in inexorable conflict with other, no less salutary, governmental goals.

Kovacs, 469 U.S. 274 (1985) (Kovacs II)]. *Kovacs II* did not address the issue of a money judgment in the context of a § 362 automatic stay. Because of the Supreme Court remand, the Sixth Circuit has not yet been afforded an opportunity to address that issue. *Kovacs II* was concerned with whether Kovacs' obligation under the state court order met the statutory definitions of "claim or debt" as set forth in [§§ 101(5) & (12)]. The State of Ohio contended that the obligation did not qualify as a claim or debt and therefore was not dischargeable in bankruptcy. *Kovacs II* held that Ohio essentially was seeking to obtain a money payment from Kovacs and affirmed Kovacs' discharge. Thus, since different sections of the Bankruptcy Code are at issue which involve different policies and considerations, we are not prepared to declare that our decision is in conflict with *Kovacs II*. Nor are we prepared to predict that the Sixth Circuit, if confronted with the issue that is presented in this case, would hold that the Commonwealth was enforcing a money judgment by requiring compliance with an environmental injunction. We would disagree with such a result if it did so, for the reasons we have expressed in text.

[12] The distinction between mandatory and prohibitory injunctions advanced by Penn Terra draws no support from the statute. Had Congress intended to restore to the States only the power to enforce prohibitory injunctions, it could have said so, yet no such distinctions are contained in the statute. Moreover, the distinction itself is misleading. Not all mandatory injunctions cost money to perform, and not all prohibitory injunctions are free from cost.

Moreover, it is sometimes difficult to distinguish between a mandatory injunction and a prohibitory one. An order requiring that Company X cease discharging pollutants into the river could be interpreted as a prohibitory injunction. It might also be perceived as a mandatory injunction because such an injunction would have the effect of forcing the Company to transport the wastes elsewhere. While the terms "mandatory" and "prohibitory" may, in general, be useful terms of art for some purposes, if they are to be used as definitional terms which limit the power of States, then they have little utility.

We believe that the resolution of this conflict is contained in the statute itself. In enacting the exceptions to § 362, Congress recognized that in some circumstances, bankruptcy policy must yield to higher priorities. Indeed, if the policy of preservation of the estate is to be invariably paramount, then one could not have exceptions to the rule. Since Congress did provide for exceptions, however, we may assume that the goal of preserving the debtor's estate is not always the dominant goal.

We believe that the inquiry is more properly focused on the nature of the injuries which the challenged remedy is intended to redress—including whether plaintiff seeks compensation for past damages or prevention of future harm—in order to reach the ultimate conclusion as to whether these injuries are traditionally rectified by a money judgment and its enforcement. Here, the Commonwealth Court injunction was, neither in form nor substance, the type of remedy traditionally associated with the conventional money judgment. It was not intended to provide compensation for past injuries. It was not reducible to a sum certain. No monies were sought by the Commonwealth as a creditor or obligee. The Commonwealth was not seeking a traditional form of damages in tort or contract, and the mere payment of money, without more, even if it could be estimated, could not satisfy the Commonwealth Court's direction to complete the backfilling, to update erosion plans, to seal mine openings, to spread topsoil, and to implement plans for erosion and sedimentation control. Rather, the Commonwealth Court's injunction was meant to prevent future harm to, and to restore, the environment. Indeed, examining the state order, it is clear that erosion control, backfilling, and reseeding were additionally meant to preserve the soil conditions from further deterioration (as well as to rectify a safety hazard).

Absent some other clear indication that these proceedings, although appearing in the guise of a request for equitable relief, are actually aimed toward the enforcement of a money judgment, we decline to equate DER's actions, which are those of a governmental unit enforcing the Commonwealth's police power, with those affected by the automatic stay of § 362(a). We therefore conclude that the suit brought by DER to compel Penn Terra to remedy environmental hazards was properly brought as an equitable action to prevent future harm, and did not constitute an action to enforce a money judgment. The automatic stay provision of § 362 is therefore inapplicable.

* * *

Notes and Questions

1. Although *Kovacs* was vacated, as footnote 11 in *Penn Terra* explains, the analysis it presents remains viable and worthy of attention.

2. *Kovacs* and *Penn Terra* illustrate that a court's definition of "money judgment" effectively determines whether a governmental unit's action will be within the exception of § 362(b)(4). One end of the spectrum was seen in *Kovacs*, which found that there is "very little in substance to distinguish" an order requiring Kovacs to turn over all of his nonexempt assets to a receiver and authorizing the receiver to collect any sums payable to Kovacs in the future, from a "money judgment." Consequently, the State of Ohio was stayed from enforcing the order. Conversely, *Penn Terra* defined money judgment narrowly, as "an order entered by the court or by the clerk, after a verdict has been entered for the plaintiff, which adjudges that the defendant shall pay a sum of money to the plaintiff." The proceeding DER initiated, therefore, was not to enforce a money judgment.

3. Be sure you appreciate *whose* interests are in the balance when a state seeks to escape the automatic stay in order to enforce its environmental protection laws. Who loses if the stay is applicable? Who loses if it is not? Does the governmental police power exception to the stay effect the best balance of interests?

4. Should "money judgment" be construed to focus on enforcement or on impairment of the estate's ability to pay creditors? If the latter, when would governmental action not constitute "enforcement of a money judgment"? Is that impairment construction supported by *Penn Terra*? If not, how does the *Penn Terra* court's construction differ in substance? What is the object of drawing a distinction between past and future harm?

5. According to the courts, the 1998 amendment to former §§ 362(b)(4) and (b)(5), previously noted, made three changes: (1) the two subsections were combined into one; (2) language was added to make the exception applicable to §§ 362(a)(1), (2), (3) and (6), rather than only to (a)(1) (to which former (b)(4) applied) and to (a)(2) (to which former (b)(5) applied); and (3) organizations exercising authority under the Chemical Weapons Convention were given the benefit of the exception. See, e.g., *In re Nelson*, 240 B.R. 802 (Bankr. D. Me. 1999).

Are the courts correct? Do you see another possible interpretation, based on the language of new § 362(b)(4)? See *In re PMI-DVW Real Estate Holdings, L.L.P.*, 240 B.R. 24 (Bankr. D. Ariz. 1999).

Chapter 3

UNSECURED CLAIMS IN BANKRUPTCY

A. INTRODUCTION

Bankruptcy law, as we will see, draws few distinctions among different types of creditors. All of them, regardless of the source of the debtor's obligation, are holders of claims. The source of the obligation can be important, however. A contract creditor is in a position to plan for possible default and to take precautions that will minimize the risk upon default. The creditor can assess the debtor's creditworthiness and adjust the terms of the contract on that basis. The parties can, and usually do, agree on terms defining default, accelerating the loan upon default and requiring the payment of collection costs. Nonconsensual creditors, such as tort victims, do not choose to become holders of claims owed by a particular debtor, and are not in a position to protect themselves from the risk of default. Bankruptcy, as a matter of policy, generally ignores these distinctions; all of these creditors are merely holders of claims.

The concept of "claim" is fundamentally important in bankruptcy: only holders of "claims" are entitled to receive payment (along with equityholders in certain Chapter 11 cases); "claims" are subject to the automatic stay; and "claims" are discharged.

A claim must be "allowed" if its holder is to receive a payment from the bankruptcy estate. Allowance simply means that the claim is recognized as valid. Section 502 governs allowance of claims. Because most claims are not disputed, a claim is "deemed allowed" by § 502 if it is filed (see § 501) and no objection to it is raised. Section

1111(a), which applies only to Chapter 11 cases, states that no proof of claim need be filed as long as the claim is included in the debtor's schedules and the debtor does not list it as disputed, contingent or unliquidated.

The Bankruptcy Rules impose fairly strict deadlines on the filing of claims, but permit late filings in instances of "excusable neglect." The Supreme Court held in *Pioneer Investment Services Co. v. Brunswick Associates Limited Partnership*, 507 U.S. 380, 113 S.Ct. 1489, 123 L.Ed.2d 74 (1993), that "excusable neglect" is not limited to intervening circumstances beyond a party's control, but also includes cases in which the failure to file on time is due to carelessness, inadvertence or mistake. The Court did not open the safety net widely, however, because notice of the bar date had been given in an unusual manner in *Pioneer Investment*, and neither the debtor nor efficient judicial administration was prejudiced by allowing the tardy claim.

If a party in interest objects to a claim, the court must determine if the claim falls into one of the categories of claims not allowable in bankruptcy. These categories are listed in § 502(b). Chief among the reasons why a claim might be disallowed in bankruptcy is that the claim is unenforceable against the debtor under nonbankruptcy law (see § 502(b)(1)). Sensibly, such a claim is not magically transformed into an enforceable claim by the filing of a bankruptcy petition. Another frequently-encountered reason for disallowing a claim in bankruptcy is that the claim is for unmatured interest (see § 502(b)(2)).

The universe of claims breaks down into two rough categories—secured and unsecured. Holders of secured claims have a legally recognized property interest in collateral of the debtor; holders of unsecured claims have a legally recognized right to payment by the debtor, but no property interests to support that right.

Section 506(a) determines an important category of unsecured claims. Under that subsection, a creditor with collateral worth less than the amount of the debt is treated as the holder of two claims—a secured claim, measured by the value of the collateral; and an unsecured claim, measured by the difference between the value of the collateral and the debt. For example, a creditor owed $125,000 that has a security interest in property worth $100,000 has a secured claim of $100,000 and an unsecured claim of $25,000. This concept, known as "bifurcation," is basic to bankruptcy and will appear again and again throughout the course.

The identity of holders of claims comes from the schedule of assets and liabilities that a debtor must file as part of the bankruptcy petition. The list of liabilities will include the names and addresses of creditors.

Read §§ 502(a) and (b) and answer the following Problems.

Problems and Questions

1. Debtor Corp. borrowed $120,000 from Bank on August 1. Debtor Corp. signed a note that obligated it to pay $1,000 in interest on the first of every month, beginning September 1, for one year, at which time principal was payable in full. Debtor made two interest payments and, on October 10, filed bankruptcy. What is the amount of Bank's allowable claim? Would the amount of Bank's claim change if no payments had been made?

2. Debtor Corp. borrowed $120,000 from Bank on August 1 at 10%. Debtor Corp. signed a note promising to pay $10,000 in principal and $1,000 in interest each month for one year, beginning September 1. Debtor made two payments of $11,000 each and, on October 10, filed bankruptcy. What is the amount of Bank's allowable claim? If Bank is not paid by the trustee until April of the next year, can Bank claim an additional $6,000 in interest?

3. The purchasing agent for Buyer Company telephoned Seller, Inc. and ordered 100 cases of widgets at $15 per case, for delivery in three weeks. Seller, Inc. confirmed the order over the phone, but did not mail an acknowledgment of the sale. A week after the call, Buyer Company repudiated the deal and filed bankruptcy. What is the amount of Seller, Inc.'s allowable claim?

4. Debtor leased commercial premises from Landlord. Five years remained in the lease term at the time Debtor filed bankruptcy and vacated the premises. Rent was $1,000 per month. Landlord has been unable to relet the premises despite its best efforts to do so. What is the amount of Landlord's allowable claim?

5. Assume the same facts as in Problem # 4, except that ten years remained in the lease term. What is the amount of Landlord's allowable claim? Does the result change in either Problem if Landlord is able to relet the premises for the remaining term for $500 per month?

6. Debtor bought a VCR from Electronics Galore on credit for $400. The VCR was, in fact, assembled without several necessary parts. Debtor, however, was distracted by his deteriorating financial situation. He never got around to returning the VCR or asserting a warranty claim. Debtor filed bankruptcy and Electronics Galore filed a proof of claim for $400. No one

objected to the claim. Unsecured creditors will get a 10% dividend in this case. Is Electronics Galore entitled to $40?

7. Debtor owes an obligation to Creditor that is not dischargeable in bankruptcy. Does Creditor have any reason to file a proof of claim? If Creditor does not file a proof of claim, does Debtor have any reason to do so? (See § 501(c), which allows a debtor to file a proof of claim if the creditor does not.)

B. WHAT CONSTITUTES A "CLAIM" IN BANKRUPTCY

Because bankruptcy revolves around the disposition of "claims" held by the debtor's various creditors, the question of what constitutes a claim is fundamental. This question arises in at least four important contexts. First, it is critical to a determination of the scope of the automatic stay, which bars, inter alia, any action "to recover a claim against the debtor that arose before" bankruptcy. § 362(a)(1). Second, it affects discharge, which covers "all debts" arising "before the date of the order for relief." § 727(b). A "debt," in turn, is defined in § 101(12) as "liability on a claim." Third, only "claims" are entitled to receive payment in bankruptcy, regardless of the chapter under which the case is filed. §§ 726(a), 1123(a)(1)-(4), 1325(a)(4)-(5). And finally, only creditors with allowed claims are entitled to vote on a Chapter 11 plan. § 1126(a).

A number of important bankruptcy cases have addressed whether a particular party holds a "claim" against the debtor. These cases involve different contexts, such as the automatic stay or discharge, but they are unified by the need to address the same ultimate issue of what constitutes a "claim."

Two of the next three principal cases involve environmental issues, which, as we have already seen in the automatic stay materials, have been particularly difficult to deal with in bankruptcy proceedings. Note the analytical approach to environmental obligations in bankruptcy outlined by Professor Heidt:

> [F]ederal courts hearing [environmental cleanup] cases have had to address two issues essential to understanding the appropriate treatment of environmental obligations in bankruptcy: (1) Is the particular obligation a "claim" within the meaning of the Bankruptcy Code and, (2) If so, when did the claim "arise?" If a cleanup obligation is held to be a claim that arose before the

> debtor filed for bankruptcy (a pre-petition claim), then the holder of the obligation may participate in the bankruptcy proceeding and share in any distribution of assets. However, the obligation holder will not be allowed to pursue the debtor post-bankruptcy. On the other hand, if a court holds the cleanup obligation either not to be a claim or not to have arisen pre-petition, then the obligation holder will not be allowed to participate in the bankruptcy proceeding or share in any distribution. However, the obligation holder will be allowed to seek redress from the debtor post-bankruptcy.

Kathryn R. Heidt, *Environmental Obligations in Bankruptcy: A Fundamental Framework*, 44 Fla. L. Rev. 153, 154-55 (1992).

We have already encountered William Kovacs in Chapter 2's discussion of exceptions to the automatic stay. The following case—which is *Kovacs II*, referred to in *Penn Terra*'s footnote 11—grew out of the same facts and raises the different but related question whether environmental obligations are dischargeable. (You may recall that non-dischargeability was assumed in *Kovacs I*, to which the Supreme Court refers in footnote 2.) Dischargeability turns on the definition of "claim."

OHIO v. KOVACS

United States Supreme Court, 1985.
469 U.S. 274, 105 S.Ct. 705, 83 L.Ed.2d 649.

JUSTICE WHITE delivered the opinion of the Court.

Petitioner State of Ohio obtained an injunction ordering respondent William Kovacs to clean up a hazardous waste site. A receiver was subsequently appointed. Still later, Kovacs filed a petition for bankruptcy. The question before us is whether, in the circumstances present here, Kovacs' obligation under the injunction is a "debt" or "liability on a claim" subject to discharge under the Bankruptcy Code.

I

Kovacs was the chief executive officer and stockholder of Chem–Dyne Corp., which with other business entities operated an industrial and hazardous waste disposal site in Hamilton, Ohio. In 1976, the State sued Kovacs and the business entities in state court for polluting public waters, maintaining a nuisance, and causing fish kills, all in violation of state environmental laws. In 1979, both in his individual capacity and on behalf of Chem–Dyne, Kovacs signed a stipulation and judgment entry settling the lawsuit. Among other things, the stipulation enjoined the defendants from causing further pollution of the air or public waters, forbade bringing additional industrial wastes onto the site, required the defendants to remove specified wastes from the property, and ordered the payment of $75,000 to compensate the State for injury to wildlife.

Kovacs and the other defendants failed to comply with their obligations under the injunction. The State then obtained the appointment in state court of a receiver, who was directed to take possession of all property and other assets of Kovacs and the corporate defendants and to implement the judgment entry by cleaning up the Chem–Dyne site. The receiver took possession of the site but had not completed his tasks when Kovacs filed a personal bankruptcy petition. Seeking to develop a basis for requiring part of Kovacs' postbankruptcy income to be applied to the unfinished task of the receivership, the State then filed a motion in state court to discover Kovacs' current income and assets. Kovacs requested that the Bankruptcy Court stay those proceedings, which it did.[2] The State also filed a complaint in the Bankruptcy Court seeking a declaration that Kovacs' obligation under the stipulation and judgment order to clean up the Chem–Dyne site was not dischargeable in bankruptcy because it was not a "debt," a liability on a "claim," within the meaning of the Bankruptcy Code. In addition, the complaint sought an injunction against the bankruptcy trustee to restrain him from pursuing any action to recover assets of Kovacs in the hands of the receiver. The Bankruptcy Court ruled against Ohio, as did the District Court. The Court of Appeals for the Sixth Circuit affirmed, holding that Ohio essentially sought from Kovacs only a monetary payment and that such a required payment was a liability on a claim that was dis-

---

[2] The Bankruptcy Court held that the requested hearing was an effort to collect money from Kovacs in violation of the automatic stay provision. See § 362. It entered a specific stay as well. The District Court affirmed, ruling that Ohio was trying to enforce a judgment obtained before filing of the bankruptcy petition. The Court of Appeals for the Sixth Circuit also found the hearing barred. *In re Kovacs*, 681 F.2d 454 (1982). In that court's view, while § 362(b) allowed governmental units to continue to enforce police powers through mandatory injunctions, it denied them the power to collect money in their enforcement efforts. Because of the later filing by Ohio of a complaint to declare that Kovacs' obligations were not claims under bankruptcy, we granted certiorari, vacated the judgment of the Court of Appeals, and remanded to that court to consider whether the dispute over the stay was moot. As far as we are advised, the Court of Appeals has taken no action on the remand.

chargeable under the bankruptcy statute. We granted certiorari to determine the dischargeability of Kovacs' obligation under the affirmative injunction entered against him.

* * *

III

Except for the nine kinds of debts saved from discharge by § 523(a), a discharge in bankruptcy discharges the debtor from all debts that arose before bankruptcy. § 727(b). It is not claimed here that Kovacs' obligation under the injunction fell within any of the categories of debts excepted from discharge by § 523. Rather, the State submits that the obligation to clean up the Chem–Dyne site is not a debt at all within the meaning of the bankruptcy law.

For bankruptcy purposes, a debt is a liability on a claim. [§ 101(12)]. A claim is defined by [§ 101(5)] * * *. The provision at issue here is [§ 101(5)(B)]. For the purposes of that section, there is little doubt that the State had the right to an equitable remedy under state law and that the right has been reduced to judgment in the form of an injunction ordering the cleanup. The State argues, however, that the injunction it has secured is not a claim against Kovacs for bankruptcy purposes because (1) Kovacs' default was a breach of the statute, not a breach of an ordinary commercial contract which concededly would give rise to a claim; and (2) Kovacs' breach of his obligation under the injunction did not give rise to a right to payment within the meaning of [§ 101(5)(B)]. We are not persuaded by either submission.

There is no indication in the language of the statute that the right to performance cannot be a claim unless it arises from a contractual arrangement. The State resorted to the courts to enforce its environmental laws against Kovacs and secured a negative order to cease polluting, an affirmative order to clean up the site, and an order to pay a sum of money to recompense the State for damage done to the fish population. Each order was one to remedy an alleged breach of Ohio law; and if Kovacs' obligation to pay $75,000 to the State is a debt dischargeable in bankruptcy, which the State freely concedes, it makes little sense to assert that because the cleanup order was entered to remedy a statutory violation, it cannot likewise constitute a claim for bankruptcy purposes. Furthermore, it is apparent that Congress desired a broad definition of a "claim" and knew how to limit the application of a provision to contracts when it desired to do so.[4] Other provisions cited by Ohio refute, rather than support, its strained interpretation.[5]

The courts below also found little substance in the submission that the cleanup obligation did not give rise to a right to payment that renders the order dischargeable under § 727. The definition of "claim" in H.R. 8200 as originally drafted would have deemed a right to an equitable remedy for breach of performance a claim even if it did not give rise to a right to payment. The initial Senate definition of claim was narrower, and a compromise version, [§ 101(5)], was finally adopted. In that version, the key phrases "equitable remedy," "breach of performance," and "right to payment" are not defined. Nor are the differences between the successive versions explained. The legislative history offers only a statement by the sponsors of the Bankruptcy Reform Act with respect to the scope of the provision:

> "Section [101(5)(B)] * * * is intended to cause the liquidation or estimation of contingent rights of payment for which there may be an alternative equitable remedy with the result that the equitable remedy will be susceptible to being discharged in bankruptcy. For example, in some States, a judgment for specific performance may be satisfied by an alternative right to payment in the event performance is refused; in that event, the creditor entitled to specific performance would have a 'claim' for purposes of a proceeding under title 11."[8]

We think the rulings of the courts below were wholly consistent with the statute and its legislative history, sparse as it is. The Bankruptcy Court ruled as follows:

> "There is no suggestion by plaintiff that defendant can render performance under the affirmative obligation other than by the payment of money. We therefore conclude that plaintiff

---

4 See § 365 (assumption or rejection of executory contracts and leases).

5 Congress created exemptions from discharge for claims involving penalties and forfeitures owed to a governmental unit, § 523(a)(7), and for claims involving embezzlement and larceny. § 523(a)(4). If a bankruptcy debtor has committed larceny or embezzlement, giving rise to a remedy of either damages or equitable restitution under state law, the resulting liability for breach of an obligation created by law is clearly a claim which is nondischargeable in bankruptcy.

8 124 Cong. Rec. 32393 (1978) (remarks of Rep. Edwards); see also *id.* at 33992 (remarks of Sen. DeConcini).

> has a claim against defendant within the meaning of [§ 101(5)], and that defendant owes plaintiff a debt within the meaning of [§ 101(12)]. Furthermore, we have concluded that that debt is dischargeable."

The District Court affirmed, primarily because it was bound by and saw no error in the Court of Appeals' prior opinion holding that the State was seeking no more than a money judgment as an alternative to requiring Kovacs personally to perform the obligations imposed by the injunction. To hold otherwise, the District Court explained, "would subvert Congress' clear intention to give debtors a fresh start." The Court of Appeals also affirmed, rejecting the State's insistence that it had no right to, and was not attempting to enforce, an alternative right to payment:

> "Ohio does not suggest that Kovacs is capable of personally cleaning up the environmental damage he may have caused. Ohio claims there is no alternative right to payment, but when Kovacs failed to perform, state law gave a state receiver total control over all Kovacs' assets. Ohio later used state law to try and discover Kovacs' post-petition income and employment status in an apparent attempt to levy on his future earnings. In reality, the only type of performance in which Ohio is now interested is a money payment to effectuate the Chem–Dyne cleanup.
>
> * * *
>
> "The impact of its attempt to realize upon Kovacs' income or property cannot be concealed by legerdemain or linguistic gymnastics. Kovacs cannot personally clean up the waste he wrongfully released into Ohio waters. He cannot perform the affirmative obligations properly imposed upon him by the State court except by paying money or transferring over his own financial resources. The State of Ohio has acknowledged this by its steadfast pursuit of payment as an alternative to personal performance."

As we understand it, the Court of Appeals held that, in the circumstances, the cleanup duty had been reduced to a monetary obligation.

We do not disturb this judgment. The injunction surely obliged Kovacs to clean up the site. But when he failed to do so, rather than prosecute Kovacs under the environmental laws or bring civil or criminal contempt proceedings, the State secured the appointment of a receiver, who was ordered to take possession of all of Kovacs' nonexempt assets as well as the assets of the corporate defendants and to comply with the injunction entered against Kovacs. As wise as this course may have been, it dispossessed Kovacs, removed his authority over the site, and divested him of assets that might have been used by him to clean up the property. Furthermore, when the bankruptcy trustee sought to recover Kovacs' assets from the receiver, the latter sought an injunction against such action. Although Kovacs had been ordered to "cooperate" with the receiver, he was disabled by the receivership from personally taking charge of and carrying out the removal of wastes from the property. What the receiver wanted from Kovacs after bankruptcy was the money to defray cleanup costs. At oral argument in this Court, the State's counsel conceded that after the receiver was appointed, the only performance sought from Kovacs was the payment of money. Had Kovacs furnished the necessary funds, either before or after bankruptcy, there seems little doubt that the receiver and the State would have been satisfied. On the facts before it, and with the receiver in control of the site, we cannot fault the Court of Appeals for concluding that the cleanup order had been converted into an obligation to pay money, an obligation that was dischargeable in bankruptcy.[11]

IV

It is well to emphasize what we have not decided. First, we do not suggest that Kovacs' discharge will shield him from prosecution for having violated the environmental laws of Ohio or for criminal contempt for not performing his obligations under the injunction prior to bankruptcy. Second, had a fine or monetary penalty for violation of state law been imposed on Kovacs prior to bankruptcy, § 523(a)(7) forecloses any suggestion that his obligation to pay the fine or penalty would be discharged in bankruptcy. Third, we do not address what the legal consequences would have been had Kovacs taken bankruptcy

---

[11] The State relies on *Penn Terra, Ltd. v. Department of Environmental Resources*, 733 F.2d 267 (3d Cir. 1984). There, the Court of Appeals for the Third Circuit held that the automatic stay provision of § 362 did not apply to the State's seeking an injunction against a bankrupt to require compliance with the environmental laws. This was held to be an effort to enforce the police power statutes of the State, not a suit to enforce a money judgment. But in that case, there had been no appointment of a receiver who had the duty to comply with the state law and who was seeking money from the bankrupt. The automatic stay provision does not apply to suits to enforce the regulatory statutes of the State, but the enforcement of such a judgment by seeking money from the bankrupt—what the Court of Appeals for the Sixth Circuit concluded was involved in this case—is another matter.

before a receiver had been appointed and a trustee had been designated with the usual duties of a bankruptcy trustee. Fourth, we do not hold that the injunction against bringing further toxic wastes on the premises or against any conduct that will contribute to the pollution of the site or the State's waters is dischargeable in bankruptcy; we here address, as did the Court of Appeals, only the affirmative duty to clean up the site and the duty to pay money to that end. Finally, we do not question that anyone in possession of the site—whether it is Kovacs or another in the event the receivership is liquidated and the trustee abandons the property, or a vendee from the receiver or the bankruptcy trustee—must comply with the environmental laws of the State of Ohio. Plainly, that person or firm may not maintain a nuisance, pollute the waters of the State, or refuse to remove the source of such conditions. As the case comes to us, however, Kovacs has been dispossessed and the State seeks to enforce his cleanup obligation by a money judgment.

The judgment of the Court of Appeals is

Affirmed.

JUSTICE O'CONNOR, concurring.

I join the Court's opinion and agree with its holding that the cleanup order has been reduced to a monetary obligation dischargeable as a "claim" under § 727 of the Bankruptcy Code. I write separately to address the petitioner's concern that the Court's action will impede States in enforcing their environmental laws.

To say that Kovacs' obligation in these circumstances is a claim dischargeable in bankruptcy does not wholly excuse the obligation or leave the State without any recourse against Kovacs' assets to enforce the order. Because "Congress has generally left the determination of property rights in the assets of a bankrupt's estate to state law," *Butner v. United States*, 440 U.S. 48, 54 (1979), the classification of Ohio's interest as either a lien on the property itself, a perfected security interest, or merely an unsecured claim depends on Ohio law. That classification—a question not before us—generally determines the priority of the State's claim to the assets of the estate relative to other creditors. Thus, a State may protect its interest in the enforcement of its environmental laws by giving cleanup judgments the status of statutory liens or secured claims.

The Court's holding that the cleanup order was a "claim" within the meaning of [§ 101(5)] also avoids potentially adverse consequences for a State's enforcement of its order when the debtor is a corporation, rather than an individual. In a Chapter 7 proceeding under the Bankruptcy Code, a corporate debtor transfers its property to a trustee for distribution among the creditors who hold cognizable claims, and then generally dissolves under state law. Because the corporation usually ceases to exist, it has no postbankruptcy earnings that could be utilized by the State to fulfill the cleanup order. The State's only recourse in such a situation may well be its "claim" to the prebankruptcy assets.

For both these reasons, the Court's holding today cannot be viewed as hostile to state enforcement of environmental laws.

Two distinct problems have arisen regarding the definition of "claim." The first is a timing problem, which is presented whenever some of the factual events pertinent to the claim occur after the bankruptcy filing. Two of the introductory Problems in Section A illustrate a straightforward timing question—the treatment of unmatured debts. More difficult timing questions are presented, however, when some period of time has passed between the debtor's conduct and the creditor's injury. This happens primarily in tort cases.

The second problem is determining when a right to an equitable remedy gives rise to a claim. This problem is encountered most often in the context of environmental injunctions, but it also arises when the creditor seeks to enforce other types of equitable remedies, such as covenants not to compete.

Claims are determined as of the date the petition is filed. See § 502(b) (claims are allowed in the amount owed "as of the date of the filing of the petition."). Conduct by the debtor that gives rise to an asserted claim may not produce cognizable consequences for some time, however. In addition, the nature of the connection between the debtor and the tort victim varies; the more attenuated that connection, the more difficult it becomes for a court to find that the tort victim has a claim in the debtor's bankruptcy.

The following opinion discusses this timing question in the context of a well-known mega-tort case.

GRADY v. A.H. ROBINS CO.

United States Court of Appeals, Fourth Circuit, 1988.
839 F.2d 198, *cert. dismissed*, 487 U.S. 1260, 109 S.Ct. 201, 101 L.Ed.2d 972 (1988).

WIDENER, Circuit Judge.

Rebecca Grady and the Legal Representative of the Future Claimants appeal an order of the district court deciding that Mrs. Grady's claim against A.H. Robins Co., Inc. (Robins) arose prior to the date Robins sought protection under the Bankruptcy Code and therefore was subject to the automatic stay provision of § 362(a)(1). We affirm.

Robins, a pharmaceutical company, was the manufacturer and marketer of the Dalkon Shield, an interuterine [sic] contraceptive device, from 1971 to 1974. Production was discontinued in 1974 because of mounting concerns about the device's safety. Because of the overwhelming number of claims filed against it because of the Dalkon Shield, Robins filed a petition for reorganization under Chapter 11 of the Bankruptcy Code on August 21, 1985.

Mrs. Grady had had inserted a Dalkon Shield some years before but thought that the device had fallen out. On August 21, 1985, she was admitted to Salinas Valley Memorial Hospital, Salinas, California, complaining of abdominal pain, fever and chills. X-rays and sonograms revealed the presence of the Dalkon Shield. On August 28, 1985, the Dalkon Shield was surgically removed. Mrs. Grady was discharged from the hospital but not long after returned to her physician, complaining of persistent pain, fever and chills. She was again admitted to the hospital on November 14, 1985, on which admission she was diagnosed as having pelvic inflammatory disease, and underwent a hysterectomy. She blames the Dalkon Shield for those injuries.

On October 15, 1985 (almost two months after Robins filed its petition for reorganization), Mrs. Grady filed a civil action against Robins in the United States District Court for the Northern District of California. The case was subsequently transferred to the Eastern District of Virginia.

Mrs. Grady then filed a motion in the bankruptcy court, seeking a decision that her claim did not arise before the filing of the petition so that it would not be stayed by the automatic stay provision of the Code. If the claim arose when the Dalkon Shield was inserted into her, the district court reasoned, then it would be considered a claim under the Bankruptcy Code and its prosecution would be stayed by the provisions of § 362(a)(1). If, however, the claim was found to arise when the injuries became apparent, then it might not be a claim for bankruptcy purposes and the automatic stay provision would be inapplicable.

The bankruptcy court determined that Mrs. Grady's claim against Robins arose when the acts giving rise to Robins' liability were performed, not when the harm caused by those acts was manifested. The court rejected Mrs. Grady's contention that the court must look to state law to determine when her cause of action accrued and equate that with a right to payment. It concluded that the court must follow federal law in determining when the claim arose. It held that the right to payment under [§ 101(5)(A)] of Mrs. Grady's claim arose when the acts giving rise to the liability were performed and thus the claim was prepetition under § 362(a)(1).

We emphasize the narrowness of the district court's holding. It held only that the automatic stay provision of § 362 applied, and we have recited its reasoning to arrive at that conclusion. It did not decide whether or not Mrs. Grady's claim would constitute an administrative expense under §503(b)(1)(A), and it also did not decide whether or not the Future Tort Claimants would have a dischargeable claim within the reorganization case. We affirm, although our reasoning may vary somewhat from that of the district court.

[The court quoted § 362(a)(1).]

The legislative history of the Code reveals the importance of [the] § 362 stay provision:

> The automatic stay is one of the fundamental debtor protections provided by the bankruptcy laws. It gives the debtor a breathing spell from his creditors. It stops all collection efforts, all harassment, and all foreclosure actions. It permits the debtor to attempt a repayment or reorganization plan, or simply to be relieved of the financial pressures that drove him into bankruptcy.

H.R. Rep. No. 95–595 at 340–41, *reprinted in* 1978 U.S.C.C.A.N. at 6296–97; S. Rep. No. 95–989 at 54–55, *reprinted in* 1978 U.S.C.C.A.N. at 5840–41.

The district court correctly noted that the automatic stay is particularly critical to a debtor seeking to reorganize under Chapter 11 because he needs breathing room to restructure his affairs. While the importance of § 362 cannot be over-emphasized, its coverage extends only to claims against the debtor that arose prior to the filing of its petition.

Section [§ 101(5)] * * * defines a claim * * *.

Congress intended that the definition of claim in the Code be as broad as possible, noting that "the bill contemplates that all legal obligations of the debtor, no matter how remote or contingent, will be able to be dealt with in the bankruptcy. It permits the broadest possible relief in the bankruptcy court." H.R. Rep. No. 95–595 at 309, *reprinted in* 1978 U.S.C.C.A.N. at 6266; S. Rep. No. 95–989 at 21–22, *reprinted in* 1978 U.S.C.C.A.N. at 5807–08. The courts have consistently recognized the very broad definition to be given to claims.

While the parties agree that the term claim is broadly defined under the Bankruptcy Code, they disagree over whether Mrs. Grady's suit falls within that definition. Mrs. Grady primarily relies upon *Matter of M. Frenville Co.*, 744 F.2d 332 (3d Cir.1984), cert. denied, 469 U.S. 1160 (1985), to support her contention that her claim falls outside the protection of the automatic stay.

Prior to filing its petition, Frenville, an independent auditing firm, had employed Avellina and Bienes (A & B), an accounting firm, to prepare its financial statement. After the bankruptcy petition was filed, several banks which had received the financial statement sued A & B, claiming that the statement was negligently prepared. A & B moved for relief from the automatic stay in order that it could bring Frenville into those lawsuits as a third-party defendant for their indemnification.

The court concluded that a pre-petition act by a debtor giving rise to later liability is not enough to bring an action within the definition of a claim. It held that the right to payment must exist pre-petition before a claim can exist. Because the Bankruptcy Code does not provide when a right to payment arises, the court turned to state law for its answer.[3] Because A & B had had no right under state law to seek indemnification from Frenville before the banks filed their suit, the claim

[3] The court did comment that application of federal law might be appropriate in instances where the bankruptcy stems from a mass tort. *Frenville*, 744 F.2d at 337 n.8.

was held to arise post-petition and therefore was not barred by the automatic stay provision of § 362(a)(1).

Mrs. Grady argues that her cause of action against Robins did not accrue until after Robins had filed its reorganization petition and therefore the stay provision is inapplicable. Under California law, she argues that she could not have sued Robins until she knew the nature of her injuries. The argument goes that because she had no right to payment from Robins under state law until she was injured, and since that injury occurred after the reorganization petition was filed, the stay provision of § 362 should not bar her case from its prosecution. While not agreeing that state law necessarily controls, the Future Tort Claimants agree that Mrs. Grady had no pre-petition right of payment from Robins and therefore no claim under the Bankruptcy Code.

Robins argues that the district court was correct in declining to apply the reasoning of *Frenville* and in its conclusion that Mrs. Grady's claim falls within the definition set out in [§ 101(5)(A)] because the tortious conduct occurred prior to the filing of the petition. * * *

We have found no court outside the Third Circuit which has followed the reasoning and holding of *Frenville*. All of the cases coming to our attention which have considered the issue have declined to follow *Frenville* 's limiting definition of claim. We likewise decline to follow *Frenville*, and our reasoning follows.

We commence with the proposition that "except where federal law, fully apart from bankruptcy, has created obligations by the exercise of power granted to the federal government, a claim implies the existence of an obligation created by State law." *Vanston Committee v. Green*, 329 U.S. 156, 167, 170 (1946) (Justice Frankfurter concurring), and further, from that concurring opinion, that "[b]ankruptcy legislation is superimposed upon rights and obligations created by the laws of the States." *Id.* at 171. The opinion of the court in *Vanston* further stands for the proposition that "In determining what claims are allowable and how a debtor's assets are to be distributed, a bankruptcy court does not apply the law of the State where it sits." *Id.* at 162. So, the bankruptcy Code is superimposed upon the law of the State which has created the obligation. Congress has the undoubted power under the bankruptcy article, U.S. Const. Art. I, § 8 cl. 4, to define and classify claims against the estate of a bankrupt. In the case of a claim as noted above, the legislative history shows that Congress intended that all legal obligations of the debtor, no matter how remote or contingent, will be able to be dealt with in bankruptcy. The Code contemplates the broadest possible relief in the bankruptcy court. Also, that history tells us that the automatic stay is one of the fundamental debtor protections provided by the bankruptcy laws. It provides a breathing spell to the debtor to restructure his affairs, which could hardly be done with hundreds or thousands of creditors persevering in different courts all over the country for a first share of a debtor's assets. Absent a stay of litigation against the debtor, dismemberment rather than reorganization would, in many or even most cases, be the inevitable result.

With those thoughts in mind, we turn to the pertinent parts of the statutes at hand. Section 362(a)(1) provides for an automatic stay of, among other things, judicial action against the debtor "to recover a claim against the debtor that arose before the commencement of the case under this title." Section [101(5)(A)] defines a claim to be a "right to payment whether or not such right is reduced to judgment, liquidated, unliquidated, fixed, contingent, matured, unmatured, disputed, undisputed, legal, equitable, secured or unsecured."

The *Frenville* case, in construing these two sections, identified the crucial issue as "when did [the] right to payment arise." It found that a right to payment must exist prior to the filing of the petition, and by that the court obviously meant the right to the payment of money immediately, for it distinguished cases involving sureties which it reasoned involved a right to payment immediately upon the signing of a contract of suretyship, but contingent upon the occurrence of a future event. The court obviously was of the view, which is that espoused by Mrs. Grady and the Future Tort Claimants, that, so far as § 362 is concerned, there is no such thing as a contingent tort claim.

While we do not dispute that the result obtained in *Frenville* is not irrational, with respect, we decline to follow it, and while the numerous cases which have declined to follow *Frenville* * * * have done so for a variety of reasons, we draw our conclusion largely from the words of the statute.

Shortly after the commencement of this case, the bankruptcy court created a class of claimants called "Future Tort Claimants." * * *

Section [101(5)(A)] provides for a "right to payment" whether or not "such right" is "contingent."

BLACK'S LAW DICTIONARY, 5th Ed., 1979, defines "contingent" as follows, and we adopt this definition, there being no indication that Congress meant to use the word in any other sense:

> **Contingent**. Possible, but not assured; doubtful or uncertain; conditioned upon the occurrence of some future event which is itself uncertain, or questionable. Synonymous with provisional. This term, when applied to a use, remainder, devise, bequest, or other legal right or interest, implies that no present interest exists, and that whether such interest or right ever will exist depends upon a future uncertain event.

Mrs. Grady's claim, as well as whatever rights the other Future Tort Claimants have, is undoubtedly "contingent." It depends upon a future uncertain event, that event being the manifestation of injury from use of the Dalkon Shield. We do not believe that there must be a right to the immediate payment of money in the case of a tort or allied breach of warranty or like claim, as present here, when the acts constituting the tort or breach of warranty have occurred prior to the filing of the petition, to constitute a claim under § 362(a)(1). It is at once apparent that there can be no right to the immediate payment of money on account of a claim, the existence of which depends upon a future uncertain event. But it is also apparent that Congress has created a contingent right to payment as it has the power to create a contingent tort or like claim within the protection of § 362(a)(1). We are of opinion that it has done so.

Not only do we think that a literal reading of the statute requires the result we have reached, our reading is fortified by other considerations. The broad reading of the word "claim" required by the legislative history and the cases is considerable support. That the legislative history contemplates "the broadest possible relief in the bankruptcy court" also enters our reasoning. If Mrs. Grady and the Future Tort Claimants, who had no right to the immediate payment of money at the time of the filing of the petition, were participants in a Chapter 7 proceeding, the chances are that they would receive nothing, for no compensable result had manifested itself prior to the filing of the petition.

We also find persuasive the fact that the district court probably had authority to achieve the same result by staying Mrs. Grady's suit under § 105(a) in the use of its equitable powers to assure the orderly conduct of reorganization proceedings.

We emphasize, as did the district court, that we do not decide whether or not Mrs. Grady's claim or those of the Future Tort Claimants are dischargeable in this case. Neither do we decide whether or not post-petition claims constitute an administrative expense. We hold only that the Dalkon Shield claim in the case before us, when the Dalkon

Shield was inserted in the claimant prior to the time of filing of the petition, constitutes a "claim" "that arose before the commencement of the case" within the meaning of § 362(a)(1).

The order appealed from is

AFFIRMED.

Notes and Questions

1. What is Grady attempting to accomplish? Would she have taken the same position if Robins had been liquidating under Chapter 7?

2. Is it as clear to you, as it was to the court, that the court was not deciding issues of priority and discharge?

3. Bankruptcy effectively stayed any product liability suits against Robins arising from its manufacture of the Dalkon Shield. Many of the original suits were brought against Robins along with nonbankrupt co-defendants, such as Robins's insurance carriers and officers of Robins that were entitled to indemnity from Robins's insurers. After Robins filed for bankruptcy, several of the plaintiffs in these suits sought to sever Robins from the other co-defendants and continue their actions against the co-defendants. Would continuation of those actions violate the automatic stay even though Robins was no longer named as a defendant?

4. Cases involving parties seeking to avoid § 362(a)(1)'s bar often turn, as did *Grady*, on the question whether the action "*could have been* commenced before" bankruptcy.

Recall the plight of Johns–Manville Corporation, which filed Chapter 11 in response to the staggering number of personal injury lawsuits arising from the company's manufacture of asbestos. After Manville filed bankruptcy, Carpenter and Kowalski attempted to sue Manville for allegedly defective materials, other than asbestos, supplied to them by Manville. They were themselves being sued for their use of the faulty materials and they sought to hold Manville liable as a third party defendant. Because the suits against Carpenter and Kowalski were not brought until after Manville filed bankruptcy, they argued that their suits against Manville were for postpetition causes of action that were not stayed.

The bankruptcy court rejected Carpenter's and Kowalski's argument and held that the key issue was when the "claim" arose rather than when the cause of action was initiated. *In re Johns–Manville Corp.*, 57 B.R. 680 (Bankr. S.D.N.Y. 1986). The court concluded that the word "claim," as defined by § 101(5)(A), was meant to be given the broadest interpretation possible so as to encompass "all legal obligations of the debtor, no matter how remote or contingent." Because the evidence indicated that Carpenter and Kowalski knew of the problems with the materials well in advance of Manville's Chapter 11 petition, and that they intended all along to hold Manville liable for any damages they suffered, the court held that the claim arose pre-petition. The fact that the specific "causes of action" giving rise to the lawsuits did not arise until Carpenter and Kowalski actually became defendants was irrelevant.

A judgment for money damages is not the only remedy available to an aggrieved party. Injunctions are often sought as a way to force a debtor to conform its conduct to some particular standard. It is sometimes difficult, however, for courts to determine when a right to an equitable remedy gives rise to a claim.

The next case discusses both problems of timing as well those related to equitable remedies. It illustrates the interconnectedness of these two issues.

IN RE CHATEAUGAY CORP.

United States Court of Appeals, Second Circuit, 1991.
44 F.2d 997.

JON O. NEWMAN, Circuit Judge.

This appeal presents important issues at the intersection of bankruptcy law and environmental law. The issues arise on an appeal and a cross-appeal from the March 26, 1990, judgment of the District Court for the Southern District of New York (John E. Sprizzo, Judge) in connection with the Chapter 11 reorganization of the LTV Corporation and its related companies (collectively "LTV"). The United States, New York, and the Committee of Equity Security Holders of the LTV Corporation ("Equity Holders") appeal from the judgment to the extent that it holds that "response costs" incurred by the United States Environmental Protection Agency ("EPA") under the Comprehensive Environmental Response, Compensation and Liability Act ("CERCLA"), 42 U.S.C. § 9601 *et seq.*, are pre-petition "claims," dischargeable in bankruptcy, regardless of when such costs are incurred, as long as they concern a release or threatened release of hazardous substances that occurred before the debtor filed its Chapter 11 petition. LTV Corporation, LTV Steel Company, Inc., and the Committee of Unsecured Creditors of LTV Steel Company, Inc. ("Unsecured Creditors") cross-appeal from the judgment to the extent that it holds that the debtor's obligation to operate and maintain facilities it owns or operates as required by environmental laws, regardless of when the offending condition arose, is not dischargeable * * *. We affirm.

BACKGROUND

LTV is a diversified steel, aerospace, and energy corporation with operations in several states. LTV filed a bankruptcy petition under Chapter 11 on July 16, 1986. The debtor's schedule of liabilities included 24 pages of claims, labeled "contingent," that were held by EPA and the environmental enforcement officers of all fifty states and the District of Columbia. The schedule provided no details concerning these claims. EPA filed a proof of claim for approximately $32 million, representing response costs incurred pre-petition at 14 sites where LTV had been identified as a "potentially responsible party" ("PRP") under CERCLA. EPA alleges that only one of these sites has reached the point where no further response costs are anticipated, and that the 14 sites are not necessarily all of the sites for which LTV might ultimately be determined to be a PRP. Thus, the $32 million in incurred response costs might be only a small fraction of the total CERCLA liability that EPA will ultimately assert against LTV.

Appreciating the distinction between the listed contingent claims and the claim for incurred response costs requires some understanding of the framework for recovery of CERCLA response costs. Section 104 of CERCLA authorizes EPA to take "any * * * response measure consistent with the national contingency plan which [EPA] deems necessary to protect the public health or welfare or the environment" whenever "any hazardous substance is released or there is a substantial threat of such a release into the environment." Upon identification of a release or threatened release, EPA makes an investigation to determine if the environmental risk is of sufficient severity to warrant inclusion of the site on the National Priorities List. Thereafter, EPA selects an appropriate remedy and can either order the potentially responsible party to take the remedial action under § 106(a), or take the remedial action itself, using so-called Superfund money, and seek reimbursement for such response costs under § 107(a) after the costs have been incurred.

With respect to the listed contingent claims, *i.e.*, those for which response costs had not been incurred pre-petition, LTV informed the Government that it expected confirmation of a reorganization plan to discharge all obligations of LTV concerning environmental liabilities that are traceable to pre-petition conduct of LTV, including obligations for response costs that are incurred post-confirmation. In disagreement with that position, the Government brought an adversary proceeding for a declaratory judgment that response costs incurred post-confirmation are not dischargeable because they do not arise from pre-petition claims. In the Government's view, it does not have a "claim" within the meaning of the Bankruptcy Code, [§ 101(5)], for reimbursement of CERCLA response costs until those costs have been incurred.

On the primary issue between the parties, the District Court ruled substantially in favor of LTV. Judge Sprizzo did not go quite so far as to consider response cost claims to be dischargeable whenever based on LTV's pre-petition conduct, a position that would have included LTV's pre-petition conduct of placing hazardous substances in sealed containers, followed by release of the substances into the environment years after confirmation. However, he agreed with LTV to the extent of ruling that an obligation to reimburse EPA for response costs is a dischargeable claim whenever based upon a pre-petition release or threatened release of hazardous substances. This ruling covers releases that have occurred pre-petition, even though they have not then been discovered by EPA (or anyone else).

The Court then considered which environmental claims based on injunctions were dischargeable. Applying that portion of the Code definition of "claim" that includes a "right to an equitable remedy for breach of performance if such breach gives rise to a right to payment," Judge Sprizzo stated that claims for injunctive relief based on a pre-petition release or threatened release would be dischargeable if the injunctive relief was an option EPA was electing to use in lieu of incurring response costs itself and thereafter seeking reimbursement; on the other hand, he continued, "where there is no right to such payment for cleanup or other remedial costs, claims for injunctive relief do not fall within the Bankruptcy [Code] and are not dischargeable."

* * *

DISCUSSION

* * * All the parties, to varying degrees, point to a conflict between the Bankruptcy Code and CERCLA and urge that one statute or the other be accorded primacy, depending on which statute supports the position they assert in this litigation.

We agree that the Bankruptcy Code and CERCLA point toward competing objectives. The Code aims to provide reorganized debtors with a fresh start, an objective made more feasible by maximizing the scope of a discharge. CERCLA aims to clean up environmental damage, an objective that the enforcement agencies in this litigation contend will be better served if their entitlement to be reimbursed for CERCLA response costs based on pre-petition pollution is not considered to be a "claim" and instead may be asserted at full value against the reorganized corporation. Preliminarily, we note that the conflict in objectives might not be quite as stark as the parties contend. Cleaning up the environment will not necessarily be aided by agreeing with the agencies that they do not yet have "claims." A determination that the CERCLA response costs ultimately to be incurred are not now claims might impair the prospects of achieving a viable reorganization, with the result that the debtor, instead of reorganizing, liquidates under Chapter 7 or dissolves under state law, and the assets of the corporation are either unavailable for environmental cleanup costs because such costs are not yet "claims" entitled to pro rata payment, or available only to the limited extent that such costs are considered unaccrued claims for which reserves must be established under state law.

But to whatever extent the Code and CERCLA point in different directions, we do not face in this context a conflict between two statutes, each designed to focus on a discrete problem, which happen to conflict in their application to a specific set of facts. Here, we encounter a bankruptcy statute that is intended to override many provisions of law that would apply in the absence of bankruptcy—especially laws otherwise providing creditors suing promptly with full payment of their claims. * * * If the Code, fairly construed, creates limits on the extent of environmental cleanup efforts, the remedy is for Congress to make exceptions to the Code to achieve other objectives that Congress chooses to reach, rather than for courts to restrict the meaning of across-the-board legislation like a bankruptcy law in order to promote objectives evident in more focused statutes.

With these considerations in mind, we turn to the specific issues.

1. *Unincurred* CERCLA *response costs for pre-petition releases as "claims."* * * *

Defining claims to include any ultimate right to payment arising from pre-petition conduct by the debtor comports with the theoretical model of assuring that all assets of the debtor are available to those seeking recovery for pre-petition conduct. But such an interpretation of "claim" yields questionable results. Consider, for example, a company that builds bridges around the world. It can estimate that of 10,000 bridges it builds, one will fail, causing 10 deaths. Having built 10,000 bridges, it becomes insolvent and files a petition in bankruptcy. Is there a "claim" on behalf of the 10 people who will be killed when they drive across the one bridge that will fail someday in the future? If the only test is whether the ultimate right to payment will arise out of the debtor's pre-petition conduct, the future victims have a "claim." Yet it must be obvious that enormous practical and perhaps constitutional problems would arise from recognition of such a claim. The potential victims are not only unidentified, but there is no way to identify them. Sheer fortuity will determine who will be on that one bridge when it crashes. What notice is to be given to these potential "claimants"? Or would it suffice to designate a representative for future victims and authorize the representative to negotiate terms of a binding reorganization plan?

To expect "claims" to be filed by those who have not yet had any contact whatever with the tort-feasor has been characterized as "'absurd.'"

Even where a tort victim has had some pre-petition contact with the tort-feasor, such as purchasing a product or working in proximity to hazardous materials, some courts have declined to recognize a "claim" in advance of some manifestation of injury. Yet other courts, construing the broad definition of "claim" under the Bankruptcy Code, have ruled that those exposed to a hazardous product like asbestos do have claims, despite the absence of manifest injury. * * *

Accepting as claimants those future tort victims whose injuries are caused by pre-petition conduct but do not become manifest until after confirmation, arguably puts considerable strain not only on the Code's definition of "claim," but also on the definition of "creditor"—an "entity that has a claim against the debtor that *arose* at the time of or before the order for relief concerning the debtor." [§ 101(10)(A)] (emphasis added). It has been suggested that the "arose" limitation is an inartfully drafted provision not intended to exclude tort victims injured by pre-petition conduct, but designed instead to make sure that those supplying goods and services to the debtor during reorganization do not fall within the category of claimants who have their claims reduced pro rata. *See* Mark Roe, *Bankruptcy and Mass Tort*, 84 Colum. L. Rev. 846, 895–96 (1984). Indeed, reading the "creditor" definition too narrowly risks undue limitation of the deliberately broad definition of "claim," especially the express inclusion of unmatured and contingent claims.

We need not decide how the definition of "claim" applies to tort victims injured by pre-petition conduct, especially as applied to the difficult case of pre-petition conduct that has not yet resulted in detectable injury, much less the extreme case of pre-petition conduct that has not yet resulted in any tortious consequence to a victim. We deal here with the far more manageable problem of sums ultimately to be owed to EPA at such time as it incurs CERCLA response costs. When such costs are incurred, EPA will unquestionably have what can fairly be called a "right to payment." That right is currently unmatured and will not mature until the response costs are incurred. In the context of contract claims, the Code's inclusion of "unmatured" and "contingent" claims is usually said to refer to obligations that will become due upon the happening of a future event that was "within the actual or presumed contemplation of the parties at the time the original relationship between the parties was created." *In re All Media Properties, Inc.*, 5 B.R. 126, 133 (Bankr. S.D.Tex.1980), *aff'd mem.*, 646 F.2d 193 (5th Cir.1981). The concepts of "maturity" and "contingency" are not readily transferable from the context of contracts to that of tort and statutory claims.

Yet the evident intent of Congress to apply broadly the definition of "claim" counsels against the narrow reading urged by EPA, especially in the context of obligations arising out of public regulation. Though there does not yet exist between EPA and LTV the degree of relationship between claimant and debtor typical of an existing though unmatured contract claim, the relationship is far closer than that existing between future tort claimants totally unaware of injury and a tortfeasor. EPA is acutely aware of LTV and vice versa. The relationship between environmental regulating agencies and those subject to regulation provides sufficient "contemplation" of contingencies to bring most ultimately maturing payment obligations based on pre-petition conduct within the definition of "claims." True, EPA does not yet know the full extent of the hazardous waste removal costs that it may one day incur and seek to impose upon LTV, and it does not yet even know the location of all the sites at which such wastes may yet be found. But the location of these sites, the determination of their coverage by CERCLA, and the incurring of response costs by EPA are all steps that may fairly be viewed, in the regulatory context, as rendering EPA's claim "contingent," rather than as placing it outside the Code's definition of "claim."

Judge Sprizzo recognized that "before a contingent claim can be discharged, it must result from pre-petition conduct fairly giving rise to that contingent claim." Though relying on pre-petition conduct, the District Court did not go so far as to include CERCLA response costs attributable to any action of the debtor that occurred pre-petition, such as the construction of a storage facility. Instead, the Court carefully limited its ruling to pre-petition releases or threatened releases of hazardous substances.

We think the District Court properly applied the Bankruptcy Code's definition of "claim." * * *

Moreover, we are not unmindful of the observations of Justice O'Connor concerning the disadvantage to environmental claimants if "claim" is interpreted to exclude items like unincurred CERCLA response costs. *See Ohio v. Kovacs*, 469 U.S. 274, 285–86 (1985) (O'Connor, J., concurring). Accepting EPA's argument in this Chapter 11 reorganization case would leave EPA without any possibility of even partial recovery against a dissolving corporation in a Chapter 7 liquidation case. Indeed, while EPA obviously prefers in this case to keep its CERCLA claim outside of bankruptcy so that it may present it, without reduction, against the reorganized company that it anticipates will emerge from bankruptcy, one may well speculate whether, if unincurred CERCLA response costs are not claims, some corporations facing substantial environmental claims will be able to reorganize at all.

We see no merit in EPA's contention that holding unincurred CERCLA response costs to be "claims" so long as a release or threatened release of hazardous wastes has occurred pre-petition is precluded by CERCLA itself. Specifically, EPA points to the 1986 amendment to § 113 of CERCLA, prohibiting pre-enforcement judicial review. * * *

The assumption that appears to underlie EPA's concern that the bankruptcy proceeding amounts to pre-enforcement judicial review of CERCLA claims is that extensive factual inquiry will have to be undertaken. EPA contends that it "would be forced to litigate in the bankruptcy proceedings to liquidate and fix any claims it might conceivably have against [LTV] for post-confirmation response costs" at numerous sites. This is not necessarily so. Contingent claims may be estimated if their liquidation "would unduly delay the administration of the case." § 502(c). Though EPA fears that even an estimation process would "embroil the parties and the bankruptcy court in disputes over the wisdom and scope of possible remedies," nothing prevents the speedy and rough estimation of CERCLA claims for purposes of determining EPA's voice in the Chapter 11 proceedings, with ultimate liquidation of the claims to await the outcome of normal CERCLA enforcement proceedings in which EPA will be entitled to collect its allowable share (full or pro rata, depending on the reorganization plan) of incurred response costs.

* * *

2. *Injunctive remedies as "claims."* * * *

Professors Baird and Jackson advance the thesis that injunctions imposing an equitable obligation should be dischargeable claims whenever a non-bankrupt corporation could have effectively escaped from the burden of the obligation through dissolution under state law. In making the argument, they purport to divide the universe of environmental injunctions into (a) those that impose obligations "that arise because of the debtor's continued existence and that would disappear if the debtor were to cease operations" and (b) those that impose obligations "that result from activities engaged in before the filing of the petition and whose consequences *continue* to exist even if the debtor goes out of business." Douglas G. Baird & Thomas H. Jackson, Kovacs *and Toxic Wastes in Bankruptcy*, 36 Stan. L. Rev. 1199, 1204 (1984) (emphasis in original). In their view, obligations in the first category are not dischargeable claims; those in the second category are. Their point is that this classification achieves the desirable result of mirroring non-bankruptcy consequences under prevailing substantive law (whether state or federal). If a corporation dissolves in the absence of bankruptcy, its obligations in the first category cease to have meaning; therefore, obligations of this sort should not be affected by bankruptcy and are properly considered non-dischargeable. On the other hand, obligations in the second category would be claims upon a debtor in dissolution; therefore, the governmental enforcers of the obligation should share in the assets of the corporation and this result is achieved if the obligations are recognized as claims.

An initial difficulty with the argument, before we even consider whether it squares with the Bankruptcy Code as written, is that the two categories are not as mutually exclusive as the argument suggests. For Baird and Jackson, the distinction is simply between an injunction "to cease polluting" (non-dischargeable) and an injunction "to clean up toxic wastes that already have been deposited" (dischargeable). For some injunctions, the distinction is clear. An order to stop burning high-sulphur fuel is clearly in the first category, and an order to remove containers of radioactive waste, feared to become insecure in the future, is clearly in the second category. But what of an order, typical of CERCLA orders, to clean up a toxic waste site from which hazardous substances are leaching into nearby water supplies? To some extent the order requires the defendant to "stop polluting," *i.e.*, to stop the run-off of hazardous substances from its property, and to some extent the order requires the defendant to "clean up toxic wastes that have already been deposited," *i.e.*, to pay for the removal of the hazardous substances.

We will return to the classification problem shortly, but for now, assuming that some orders can be divided as suggested, we consider whether the Bankruptcy Code makes the distinction that has been urged. Manifestly, the Code does not say expressly that dischargeable orders are those that impose mandatory obligations to remedy past misconduct and that non-dischargeable orders are those that impose prohibitions against future misconduct. Instead, the Code defines "claim" to include "an equitable remedy for breach of performance if such breach gives rise to a right to payment." That wording, Baird and Jackson argue, is merely an "inartful[]" way of capturing the distinction they endorse.

We think we must endeavor to apply the "claim" definition as written, mindful of the purposes of bankruptcy law but without the prerogative of rewriting it to maximize bankruptcy objectives that Congress might not have fully achieved. Thus, we must determine whether the injunctions, alleged to give rise to dischargeable "claims," impose a remedy for a performance breach that gives rise to a right of payment. A clear example of such an order may help to focus our inquiry. A seller of a unique property has an enforceable duty to convey the property to a buyer. For breach of that duty, a court may order the remedy of specific performance. In some states, however, the specific performance obligation may be satisfied by an alternative right to payment, in which event the specific performance creditor has a "claim" in bankruptcy. This was the example used in Congress in explaining the reach of section [§ 101(5)(B)].

While this example illustrates the type of injunction that gives rise to a dischargeable claim, its simplicity contrasts with the more typical injunctions encountered in environmental cases, and therein lies our problem. These injunctions, as we have noted, frequently combine an obligation as to which the enforcing agency has an alternative right to payment with an obligation as to which no such alternative exists. An injunction that does no more than impose an obligation entirely as an alternative to a payment right is dischargeable. Thus, if EPA directs

LTV to remove some wastes that are not currently causing pollution, and if EPA could have itself incurred the costs of removing such wastes and then sued LTV to recover the response costs, such an order is a "claim" under the Code. On the other hand, if the order, no matter how phrased, requires LTV to take any action that ends or ameliorates current pollution, such an order is not a "claim."

We think that is precisely the distinction the District Court was endeavoring to achieve when it ruled that injunctions sought as an option to EPA's (or a state's) right to incur and sue for response costs are within section [§ 101(5)], but that "where there is no right to such payment for cleanup or other remedial costs, claims for injunctive relief" are not dischargeable. In any event, it is the distinction we believe is made by the "claim" definition of the Code. EPA is entitled to seek payment if it elects to incur cleanup costs itself, but it has no authority to accept a payment from a responsible party as an alternative to continued pollution. Thus, a cleanup order that accomplishes the dual objectives of removing accumulated wastes and stopping or ameliorating ongoing pollution emanating from such wastes is not a dischargeable claim. It is true that, if in lieu of such an order, EPA had undertaken the removal itself and sued for the response costs, its action would have both removed the accumulated waste and prevented continued pollution. But it is only the first attribute of the order that can be said to remedy a breach that gives rise to a right to payment. Since there is no option to accept payment in lieu of continued pollution, any order that to any extent ends or ameliorates continued pollution is not an order for breach of an obligation that gives rise to a right of payment and is for that reason not a "claim." But an order to clean up a site, to the extent that it imposes obligations distinct from any obligation to stop or ameliorate ongoing pollution, is a "claim" if the creditor obtaining the order had the option, which CERCLA confers, to do the cleanup work itself and sue for response costs, thereby converting the injunction into a monetary obligation. We recognize that most environmental injunctions will fall on the non-"claim" side of the line. On this understanding, we affirm the District Court's ruling concerning injunctions.

In reaching this conclusion, we have reckoned with the Supreme Court's decision in *Ohio v. Kovacs*, 469 U.S. 274 (1985), and agree with Judge Sprizzo that it does not preclude the ruling he has made. *Kovacs* involves an individual debtor rather than a corporate debtor and a Chapter 7 liquidation rather than a Chapter 11 reorganization, but neither distinction appears to affect the Court's determination that the cleanup order obtained by Ohio was a dischargeable claim. What seems to have been decisive was the fact that Ohio obtained the appointment of a receiver, precluded Kovacs from taking any steps to comply with the injunction, and was seeking from Kovacs only the payment of money. The Court expressly noted that it was not deciding "what the legal consequences would have been had Kovacs taken bankruptcy before a receiver had been appointed and a trustee had been designated with the usual duties of a bankruptcy trustee." *Id.* at 284. The Court also emphasized that it was "not question[ing] that anyone in possession of the site * * * must comply with the environmental laws of the State of Ohio." *Id.* at 285.

To some extent *Kovacs* involves the same dilemma we face in determining what aspects of an environmental injunction give rise to a right of payment. The order in *Kovacs* enjoined the defendants "from causing further pollution of the air or public waters" and "required the defendants to remove specified wastes from the property." *Id.* at 276. Like most environmental decrees, it thus contained "a negative order to cease polluting" and "an affirmative order to clean up the site." *Id.* at 279. However, the Court was spared the need to determine precisely which obligations of the order, as entered, could be said to constitute a "claim" because, by virtue of Ohio's actions, "the cleanup order had been converted into an obligation to pay money." *Id.* at 283. To the extent that CERCLA affords EPA and others a right to payment in lieu of an order directed solely at cleanup, *Kovacs* indicates that such an order is a "claim." And to the extent that an order is obtained under CERCLA or any other environmental statute that seeks to end or ameliorate pollution, we are satisfied that nothing in *Kovacs* permits a discharge of such obligation. As the Court concluded, a person or firm in possession of a site "may not maintain a nuisance, pollute the waters of the State, or refuse to remove the source of such conditions." *Id.* at 285.

We recognize that in the context of environmental remedies the line between "claim" injunctions and non-"claim" injunctions could arguably be drawn somewhat differently, for example, by placing on the non-"claim" side only those injunctions ordering a defendant to stop current activities that add to pollution (*e.g.*, depositing new hazardous substances), while leaving on the "claim" side all other injunctions, including those that direct the cleanup of sites from which hazardous substances, previously deposited, are currently contributing to pollution. But we believe that placing on the non-"claim" side all injunctions that seek to remedy on-going pollution is more faithful to the Supreme Court's teachings in both *Kovacs* and *Midlantic National Bank v. N.J. Dep't of Environmental Protection*, 474 U.S. 494 (1986). It is difficult to understand how any injunction directing a property owner to remedy on-going pollution could be a dischargeable "claim" if, as *Kovacs* instructs, the owner "may not maintain a nuisance, pollute the waters of the State, or refuse to remove the source of such conditions." Moreover, leaving such injunctions outside the category of dischargeable "claims" is entirely consistent with *Midlantic's* holding that the Bankruptcy Code does not entitle a debtor to abandon property in violation of an environmental regulation "that is reasonably designed to protect the public health or safety from identified hazards." 474 U.S. at 507 (footnote omitted).

* * *

Notes and Questions

1. How are the "claims" being asserted by the state in *Kovacs* different from those being asserted by the federal government in *Chateaugay*?

2. The filing of bankruptcy does not enable a debtor to ignore the requirements of generally applicable law regulating how business operations are to be conducted. Under 28 U.S.C. § 959(b), a trustee or debtor in possession is required to manage and operate property "according to the requirements of the valid laws of the State in which such property is situated, in the same manner that the owner or possessor thereof would be bound to do if in possession thereof."

3. The court in *Kewanee Boiler Corp. v. Smith (In re Kewanee Boiler Corp.)*, 198 B.R. 519 (Bankr. N.D. Ill. 1996), referred to *Chateaugay*'s bridge hypothetical, as well as to *Grady* and other opinions, in its discussion of timing problems.

Kewanee Boiler manufactured a boiler that was installed in a school in Bar Harbor, Maine in 1952. Smith began working at the school as a maintenance man in 1969 and, in November 1989, he was injured while working on the boiler. He filed suit in state court in January 1991. Kewanee Boiler had filed bankruptcy in 1986, however, and its plan of reorganization was confirmed in March 1988. It emerged from bankruptcy under the name OakFabCo. The plan provided for unsecured claims to be paid out of a sinking fund to which OakFabCo would contribute 60% of its net cash flow for six years. By the time the case was decided, the fund was fully funded and was expected to pay unsecured creditors about 6% of their claims. The plan made no provision for persons injured post-confirmation by defective boilers.

In a wide-ranging opinion, the court explained the competing policies at work in these cases:

> One such policy consideration is the influence that future liability has on a debtor's assets. Being able to account for injuries caused by a debtor's product and limit collection to assets devoted to

the bankruptcy estate effectively frees debtor's assets not committed to the reorganization from liability for tortious acts. It is argued that such a cleansing of assets enhances their value by reducing liability exposure of reorganized debtors. Enhancing value of assets raises the chances that such assets will be kept together as a going concern thereby arguably raising the amount that creditors, including tort victims, can recover for their claims. A broad interpretation of "claim" is said to give debtors a more effective reorganization by shielding reorganized businesses or their purchasers from future lawsuits. Moreover, the continued flow of cash may increase the distribution that creditors may get on their claims. If a debtor is forced into liquidation because the burden of liability prevents a reorganization, persons injured by a debtor's products after the liquidation is complete cannot recover anything. It is said that such persons should get no better treatment than those injured pre-petition. Accordingly, it is argued that as many claims as possible should be resolved in the bankruptcy proceeding in order to enhance value of Debtor's assets and permit the Debtor to reorganize and remain viable.

Equality and fairness among creditors is another policy cited in support of dealing with all persons holding future tort claims arising out of pre-petition conduct in one bankruptcy proceeding. Indeed, assuring that similarly situated creditors receive equal pro-rata distributions is a fundamental concept in the Bankruptcy Code. Allowing tort claimants to sue the reorganized debtor because, by fortuity, their injury occurred post-petition or post confirmation would give these creditors different and likely higher distributions on their claims. The instant case is [a] good example of this. Had Smith been injured before the bankruptcy filing, he would have been given an opportunity to file a claim and would have had to participate in the Kewanee bankruptcy in order to collect anything on his claim. As such, he would have been an unsecured creditor and would have recovered only about 6% of the amount of his claim as liquidated.

By chance Smith was injured later. Also by chance he was injured by a boiler manufactured pre-bankruptcy. If successful in Maine, he may be able to recover the whole amount of his liquidated claim against OakFabCo. Absent insurance, such recovery will come out of current profit or assets. It is argued that this result would be unfair to pre-petition claimants who must be satisfied out of the unsecured creditors' sinking fund.

Such "unfairness," however, is more apparent than real. Life is filled with fortuities. It was a fortuity that the boiler involved in that accident was manufactured pre-petition, and it was a fortuity that Smith was hurt at all. The law must deal with events as they actually occurred. In this case, Smith had no § 101(5) "right to payment" at all under non-bankruptcy law at any time prior to Debtor's confirmation

> and therefore had no pre-petition or pre-confirmation "claim" under that provision. His future claim was therefore not "contingent" or "unmatured" in any legal sense pre-petition or pre-confirmation. Debtor had no debt to him at all, even if (as asserted in the Maine suit) it had a duty under tort law to warn of some possible danger. In short, until the accident, Smith had no "claim" under § 101(5) against Debtor.

Id. at 527-28.

The court recognized the differences in fact patterns in these difficult timing cases—those in which the debtor's pre-petition conduct causes post-confirmation injury.

> Some may already be injured through some physical contact with a dangerous product with their bodies, but have not shown any symptoms and may not know of any illness in early stages. This category is synonymous with mass tort litigation arising out of injuries related to asbestos inhalation and is argued to be the case with defective breast implants and intrauterine devices. Another model comprises those who have not been injured through contact with debtor's products, although they came in close proximity to such products but escaped any injury at all until after debtor's reorganization plan had been confirmed. Mr. Smith's case falls in the latter category.

Id. at 530-31. The court reviewed two tests developed in previous cases for dealing with these fact patterns. The "conduct test," applied in *Grady*, focuses on when the debtor's culpable conduct occurred. The "pre-petition relationship test," adopted in *Chateaugay*, requires that some relationship have existed between the debtor and the potential future claimant at the time of injury. "Thus, if their injury occurs post-petition, only if they purchased, used, operated, or came in contact with debtor's defective product in their ordinary activity pre-petition, were they found to have a pre-petition claim." *Id.* at 531.

According to the court in *Kewanee Boiler*, *Chateaugay*'s bridge hypothetical illustrates the weakness in both tests. It shows that "[t]he 'conduct test' is not helpful in bankruptcies of manufacturing debtors in isolating and specifying those who may hold future claims against the estate." *Id.* at 532. It also reveals that under the "relationship test" "it remains impossible to predict the identity of persons who will be harmed by a debtor's defective products unless injury occurs prior to confirmation and special notice is given to such injured persons in time to permit them to participate in the bankruptcy process." *Id.*

Kewanee Boiler adopted a test that depends upon the nature of the notice that can be, and is, given to prospective claimants:

> The Bankruptcy Code encourages businesses to reorganize through rewriting debt. However, the Code cannot justify disregard-

ing due process concerns and bankruptcy notice requirements to the detriment of persons affected and benefit of businesses seeking to eliminate liability and their known creditors who receive notice.

The extent to which notice can be given may well determine the extent to which future debt can be managed. Different products and circumstances may require different outcomes. One rule does not fit all cases where future claims may arise.

For example, in the case of defective automobiles, the purchasers can easily be found and noticed to file claims. However, no notice can reach future victims of an airplane crash that will injure passengers or of a boiler explosion that will injure people fortuitously in the vicinity. Even though the manufacturer may be able to estimate its liability, problems of notice in such cases seem insurmountable. Notice to the purchasers will not reach future victims. Notice by publication would be meaningless in these cases where there is no relationship between the product and a set of specific persons. Notice of any form is not sufficient there, even in the unlikely event the manufacturer would acknowledge and publish notice of great danger for any persons near its product as by posting a sign to that effect on every airplane or boiler.

* * *

* * * Identifying persons who might come in close proximity to any of Kewanee's boilers that were manufactured imperfectly would have been impossible at time of confirmation here. While a list could have been compiled of those who had purchased all the boilers, it is doubtful that notice to such parties and their employees could have reached all future victims of malfunctioning boilers or that anyone would have known what to do with notice of a bankruptcy as to which they then had no claim of injury. It is also doubtful that notice to the buyers of the boilers and their employees would motivate them to participate meaningfully in the proceeding. But apart from all this, it is clear that Debtor made no attempt to reach such endangered persons with any notice. It cannot obtain the benefit of notice that was not even attempted.

* * *

* * * [T]he Kewanee confirmed Plan did not take steps to limit its liability to future tort victims through the bankruptcy either by any attempt to notice them or through any special provision for them in the Plan. No fund was provided for distribution to these future claimants. No claims were ever filed on behalf of possible future claimants and never was a legal representative appointed. The Plan itself never expressly provided for payment to a future class of

claimants who had at that time not been injured by Kewanee's products manufactured before bankruptcy was filed, but would or might be injured thereafter.

Because no such provision was made in the Plan, and because future victims of torts were not represented in the bankruptcy or noticed, these persons cannot be forced into participating in the limited distribution that unsecured creditors are entitled to receive under the Plan here. Whether Smith had a "claim" under § 101(5) is doubtful because he had no right to payment prior to confirmation. But even if he did, his right to notice under bankruptcy law and the Constitution were not met.

Moreover, it is clear from the disclosure statement in this case that known pre-petition unsecured creditors were not told that their recovery from a fixed pot could be diluted by possible future post-confirmation claimants being injured. Indeed, the Debtor's position, if adopted, would make the whole Plan illusory. The OakFabCo position has no limit in time. If Smith is barred by the confirmed Plan, then why not someone injured by a boiler explosion next year? Or five years from now? How can the sinking fund ever be distributed if injured parties from post-confirmation explosions must be covered? If Debtor's approach here were correct, the unsecured creditors voted on an illusory plan from which they can never finally recover what they were promised. In the absence of anything in the Plan to warrant such a result, the absence of special treatment to future claimants must be read to mean that they were not treated at all in the confirmed Plan.

* * *

Even where confirmed Chapter 11 plans have dealt with future liability, no case has been found that forced persons injured entirely post-petition to be bound by the bankruptcy because they were merely in the vicinity of the product manufactured pre-petition. *A.H. Robins* and *Johns-Manville* are cases where such proximity to a defective and harmful product forced a post-petition claimant to share in past bankruptcy settlement. There some physical contact between the victim and the product actually occurred with some injury pre-petition. In those cases, however, exhaustive procedures were undertaken in an effort to assure constitutionality of trusts created for future claimants.

In all cases found where a trust was created out of which future claims against the estate were to be paid, some assertedly injurious contact between the future victim and the product occurred pre-petition. Only the manifestation of a disease was lacking. In those cases, the existence of pre-petition physical contact, such as inhalation

> of asbestos, *Johns-Manville*, or insertion of a contraceptive, *A.H. Robins*, or implantation of a breast implant, *Dow-Corning*, more or less fixed the class of potential victims. In cases like * * * the case at bar, where absolutely no physical harm was suffered pre-bankruptcy and only some proximity to the product could be shown, a different practical and constitutional issue is presented.
>
> Should Kewanee's Plan be read to apply to post-confirmation injuries, enjoining of Smith's efforts to liquidate his claim against the reorganized debtor and forcing him to partake in Kewanee's bankruptcy would be an inadmissible deprivation of his property interest in that claim, wholly without prior due process notice or bankruptcy notice. Even if due process concerns and absence of bankruptcy notice did not foreclose Debtor's position, there was never any attempt in the confirmed Plan to adjudicate what future injured victims were to collect for their injuries. Anyone seeking a finding that a future injured party holds a claim in a Chapter 11 bankruptcy must at least show that such future claimant's rights were actually and specifically adjudicated in that bankruptcy.

Id. at 536-37, 538, 539-40 (footnote omitted).

4. Is the court in *Kewanee Boiler* saying that tort victims in Smith's position can be foreclosed from recovering their full claims against the reorganized debtor as long as the plan establishes a fund from which such claims can receive a dividend, however small? At least one case suggests that no such fund will be permitted. In *Epstein v. Official Committee of Unsecured Creditors (In re Piper Aircraft Corp.)*, 58 F.3d 1573 (11th Cir. 1995), the prospective buyer of the debtor's assets required the appointment of a representative of future claimants to supervise the set-aside of a fund for their claims. The representative filed a claim for $100,000,000, which was based on statistical assumptions as to the number of people likely to be injured, after confirmation, by the debtor's pre-confirmation manufacture of aircraft and spare parts. The bankruptcy and district courts disallowed the claim on the basis of the pre-petition relationship test. The Eleventh Circuit modified the test by moving the "cut-off" date from the time of the petition to the date of confirmation. Thus, under *Piper Aircraft*, an individual has a claim against the debtor if the events occurring before confirmation create a relationship, such as contact, exposure, impact or privity, between the claimant and the debtor's product, and the basis for liability is the debtor's pre-petition conduct in designing, manufacturing and selling the allegedly defective product. No representative is permitted otherwise.

The next case discusses the treatment of a different type of equitable remedy—the covenant not to compete.

MAIDS INTERNATIONAL, INC. v. WARD (IN RE WARD)

United States Bankruptcy Court, District of Massachusetts, 1996.
194 B.R. 703.

JAMES F. QUEENAN, JR., Bankruptcy Judge.

Seeking to enforce a noncompetition clause in its franchise agreement, The Maids International, Inc. ("Maids") has brought this complaint to enjoin Michael E. Ward and Angela L. Ward (the "Debtors") from owning or operating a maintenance and cleaning service within a fifty mile radius of the franchised territory. Maids contends neither the Debtors' bankruptcy filing nor rejection of their covenant not to compete affects its right to an injunction against the Debtors' competition. I am thus faced with the question of whether Maids' right to injunctive relief is a "claim" within the meaning of the Bankruptcy Code and hence subject to being discharged. At the hearing on Maids' motion for a temporary restraining order, I ruled its right to an injunction is a claim. I therefore dismissed the complaint and ordered Maids to file a proof of claim, reserving jurisdiction to issue the present opinion. Set forth here are my findings of fact and conclusions of law in support of the order of dismissal.

I. FACTS

The facts are not in dispute. Maids has developed a system for establishing and operating a household maintenance and cleaning service. Having a principal office in Omaha, Nebraska, Maids franchises its rights in the system to numerous parties throughout the United States.

On April 10, 1989, Maids signed a franchise agreement with a corporation owned and operated by the Debtors named Award Services, Inc. ("Award"). In addition to signing on behalf of Award, the Debtors signed the agreement personally as guarantors of Award's performance thereunder. The agreement also includes the Debtors within the meaning of the term "Franchise", thereby making them jointly responsible with Award. Under the agreement, Maids gave Award the exclusive right to use its system and the name "Maids" in Concord, Massachusetts and in several nearby towns. In return, Award paid Maids $15,900 and obligated itself (and the Debtors) to pay Maids a royalty based on a percentage of its gross sales at rates which range from 4.5%

to 7%, depending upon the amount of weekly gross sales. The agreement was for an initial term of five years.

* * *

The franchisee agreement expired on April 9, 1994, the end of its five year term. Thereafter, the Debtors commenced operation of a cleaning service within the franchised territory. They operate the business under the name "Mops" and do not hold themselves out as operating a franchise of Maids.

Maids responded to this competition with a series of legal actions. It first commenced an arbitration proceeding in Omaha with the American Arbitration Association. This was uncontested by the Debtors. On March 31, 1995, the arbitrator awarded Maids damages (including interest) of $29,232. He also ordered the Debtors to cease and desist the ownership or operation of a maintenance and cleaning service until April 9, 1996, within a radius of fifty miles from the franchised area or within a radius of fifty miles from any Maids franchise existing on April 9, 1994. Maids then brought suit in the District Court of Douglas County, Nebraska. On July 20, 1995, that court entered a default judgment against the Debtors in the sum of $61,056. Apparently this was in part a confirmation of the arbitration award. At no time has any court entered an injunction against the Debtors competing, in confirmation of the arbitration award or otherwise. Maids next brought its attack closer to home. On November 1, 1995, it filed suit on the judgment in the District Court of Concord, Massachusetts. That court authorized attachments of the Debtors' residence and bank accounts.

Shortly thereafter, on November 13, 1995, the Debtors filed a petition with this court requesting entry of an order for relief under chapter 7 of the Bankruptcy Code. Undeterred, Maids on January 25, 1996 filed its complaint commencing the present adversary proceeding. In its complaint Maids requested an injunction against the Debtors owning or operating a maintenance and cleaning establishment within a fifty mile radius of the franchised territory. At the same time, Maids filed a motion for a temporary restraining order and asked for an emergency hearing. At the hearing on February 5, 1996, I denied the motion, dismissed the complaint and ordered Maids to file a proof of claim. Maids thereafter filed a proof of claim within the permissible filing period.

* * *

III. MAIDS' INJUNCTIVE RIGHTS AS A "CLAIM"

The Debtors are clearly in breach of their covenant not to compete. Breach of the ordinary contract gives rise only to a claim for damages. Maids, however, has the additional right under state law to obtain an injunction against the Debtors' competition, without regard to the provision in the agreement permitting such relief. * * * [B]reach of a covenant not to compete presents a question which has proven difficult for the courts: Do the nondebtor's injunctive rights constitute a "claim" so as to be subject to discharge? The Debtors' discharge hinges upon this issue. A discharge in bankruptcy releases a debtor only as to liability on a "debt," which is defined as "liability on a claim."

[The court quoted § 101(5)].

Maids unquestionably has a "right to an equitable remedy" for breach of the Debtors' covenant. But does the breach also give rise to a "right to payment" within the meaning of the statute? That question is not answered by Maids having obtained a damage judgment. As shall be explained, the damages available for breach of the covenant must be an alternative to an equitable remedy if "a right to payment" is to be present. For all we know, the arbitration award and default judgment Maids obtained were only for damages accrued to the date of the hearings, and did not include the future damages that are an alternative to equitable relief.

The only order issued against the Debtors competing is the arbitrator's cease and desist order. No court has entered an injunction against the competition. Even if one had, it would make no difference on the claim issue. The inclusion of an equitable remedy within the definition of "claim" applies "whether or not such right to an equitable remedy is reduced to judgment."

The Supreme Court's decision in *Ohio v. Kovacs* did not involve a covenant not to compete, but it deals with the meaning of the phrase "right to payment" in the context of paragraph (B) of the claim definition. *Kovacs* has been influential in cases involving covenants not to compete. * * *

* * *

Kovacs bears close study. The Court made no attempt to analyze the statutory definition of claim, except to note that the phrases "equitable remedy," "breach of performance" and "right to payment" are undefined.[14] For an equitable remedy to be a claim, the definition requires only that the breach giving rise to the equitable remedy also give rise to a "right" to payment. It imposes no requirement that the claimant exercise his right to payment or show an intent to exercise it. Yet, without pointing to statutory language, the Court saw significance in the State's intention to seek reimbursement for cleanup costs. Nor does the statute say compliance with a court decree granting the equitable remedy must involve an expenditure of money. The Court nevertheless quotes with apparent approval from the opinion of the bankruptcy court requiring such linkage. Indeed, the Court took pains to tie its opinion to all the various views of the lower courts. This makes the decision vague. The Court also seemed intent on confining its rationale to the particular facts before it. It apparently took this approach because of the inherent difficulty in meshing the compelling environmental concerns before it with a Bankruptcy Code which promotes a fresh start and gives no priority to prepetition environmental claims. The reasoning employed in *Kovacs* should therefore not be binding in cases involving covenants not to compete.

Some courts nevertheless rely upon *Kovacs* or its progeny in cases dealing with covenants. They hold that a right to injunctive relief against the debtor's competition is not a claim, and hence is not dischargeable, because compliance with the injunction involves no monetary expenditure.

There is also case law rejecting application of the *Kovacs* reasoning to these covenants. In *In re Kilpatrick*,[17] before the bankruptcy filing a state court had enjoined the debtor from breaching his covenant not to compete. In discussing *Kovacs*, the court observed that the statutory definition of "claim" speaks only of a "right" to payment, without imposing any requirement that the claimant pursue that right or disavow the equitable remedy. Because under state law the beneficiary of a covenant can elect to receive either damages or an injunction, the court held injunctive rights are a claim.

* * *

---

14 Of these phrases, only the meaning of "breach of performance" was contested. The Court held this phrase encompassed breach of an obligation imposed by law as well as by private contract. *Id.* at 279.

17 160 Bankr. 560 (Bankr. E.D. Mich. 1993).

Focussing more on the statutory definition, some courts hold the nondebtor party's injunctive right is not a claim because it is present only if the remedy at law is "inadequate," or only if the threatened harm is "irreparable," concluding from this that the nondebtor has no right to payment within the meaning of the statutory definition. Although these courts are correct in ruling a right to payment must exist under non-bankruptcy law, their holding that there is no right to payment for breach of a covenant not to compete conflicts with the damage rights of the beneficiary of a covenant as well as with the general standard employed by courts in determining whether a party's remedy at law is adequate. This requires some explanation.

An injunction against breach of the covenant is a grant of specific performance. As a result of the historical separation of courts of law and equity, such an equitable remedy is available only if the remedy at law, typically damages, is "inadequate." Courts take into account a number of factors in determining whether damages are inadequate. Principal among them are difficulty in proving the existence and amount of damages with reasonable certainty, difficulty in collecting a monetary judgment, and uncertainty that the benefits of a monetary judgment would be equivalent to the promised performance. * * *

Courts thus compare the remedies at law and equity to see which is more effective in serving the ends of justice. Difficulty in fixing damages is only one factor in that equation. In any event, damages need only be difficult, not impossible, to prove for equitable relief to be available. Comparison of the two remedies usually leads to the grant of equitable relief. Doubts as to the adequacy of the remedy at law are resolved in favor of granting equitable relief. In sum, courts look quite favorably upon equitable relief. This has led one author to conclude that the adequate remedy rule is essentially dead.[30]

Loss of future profits is typically a principal element of damages for breach of a covenant not to compete. The evidentiary problems here for Maids and other covenant beneficiaries are obvious. The proof involves futuristic projections which are especially subject to contest. Courts therefore readily grant an injunction for breach of a covenant not to compete. Indeed, the injured party invariably requests injunctive relief because an injunction gives strong assurance he will receive precisely what was bargained for. This avoids the trauma of future injury, the need to prove damages, and problems in collecting a

[30] Douglas Laycock, *The Death of the Irreparable Injury Rule*, 103 HARV. L. REV. 688 (1990).

money judgment. The request for equitable relief has historically been regarded as the election of a preferred remedy.

If the beneficiary of a covenant not to compete elects to receive damages for loss of future profits, he gets the lost profits. Lost profits are a proper element of damages for any breach of contract so long as at the time of the contract the breaching party had reason to know they would be the probable result of breach. The Debtors certainly had that knowledge. The purpose of their covenant was to protect Maids' business. Although damages must be established with reasonable certainty, an approximation rather than mathematical accuracy is all that is required. The perceived difficulty in proving lost profits is less present today because of the receptive attitude of modern courts toward proof of sophisticated financial data through expert testimony. The award of damages for lost future profits is now a commonplace remedy for breach of all kinds of contracts.

Maids therefore has the right to obtain either damages for the Debtors' future competition or an injunction against the competition. As a result, in the words of the statute, Maids has a "right to an equitable remedy for breach of performance * * * [which] breach gives rise to a right to payment." As an alternative remedy, this right to payment permits a dollar sign to be placed on the equitable remedy, as is done with other claims. Including equitable remedies within the statute's definition of "claim" is therefore supported by a strong bankruptcy policy—equal treatment of similar rights. And because a "claim" is subject to discharge, another important bankruptcy policy is promoted—the policy favoring a debtor's fresh start, unencumbered by past commitments.

In *In re Udell*,[42] the Seventh Circuit came to the opposite conclusion, and in the process added greatly to the confusion in this troubled area of the law. The debtor there had signed an agreement not to compete with his former employer, Standard Carpetland USA, Inc. The covenant was for three years, commencing on termination of employment, and covered a fifty mile radius from the store where the debtor worked. It further provided: "In the event of [the debtor's] actual or threatened breach of the [covenant], Carpetland shall be entitled to an injunction restraining [the debtor] as well as reimbursement for reasonably [sic] attorneys fees incurred in securing said judgment and stipulated damages in the sum of $25,000." Soon after leaving his employment, the debtor purchased a carpet store which he

[42] 18 F.3d 403 (7th Cir. 1994).

claimed did not compete in the same market as Carpetland's. He sued Carpetland in state court, seeking past due commissions and other compensation. Contending the debtor had breached his agreement not to compete, Carpetland counterclaimed for damages and an injunction against the debtor operating his new store. The state court issued the requested preliminary injunction. The debtor appealed and then filed a chapter 13 petition. Carpetland moved for relief from the automatic stay in order to pursue the state court litigation.

In approving relief from stay as a proper exercise of discretion, the Seventh Circuit in *Udell* held Carpetland's injunctive rights were not a "claim" and hence were not dischargeable in bankruptcy.[43] Although not finding the statutory definition of claim ambiguous, the court nevertheless looked to the legislative history that accompanied the final version of the definition, which reconciled differences in the House and Senate bills. It saw significance in the following statement made on the floors of both houses of Congress:

> Section [101(5)(B)] represents a modification of the House-passed bill to include [sic] the definition of "claim" a right to an equitable remedy for breach of performance if such breach gives rise to a right to payment. This is intended to cause the liquidation or estimation of contingent rights of payment for which there may be an alternative equitable remedy with the result that the equitable remedy will be susceptible to being discharged in bankruptcy. For example, in some States, a judgment for specific performance may be satisfied by an alternative right to payment, in the event performance is refused; in that event the creditor entitled to specific performance would have a "claim" for purposes of proceeding under title 11.
>
> On the other hand, rights to an equitable remedy for breach of performance with respect to which such breach does

43 In so holding, the Seventh Circuit reversed the district court, which had ruled Carpetland's injunctive rights constituted a claim because the $25,000 liquidated damage clause gave it a "right to payment" within the meaning of the statutory definition of "claim." To qualify as the grant of a right to payment within the meaning of the statute, the district court reasoned, the liquidated damage clause must provide compensation for both past and future damage and hence be the monetary equivalent of an injunction. It concluded the clause qualified because it was stated to be compensation for "actual or threatened harm." This is questionable. There is no reason to require that the clause provide compensation for both past and future damages. The parties apparently intended liquidated damages to be compensation for past damages and an injunction to be protection against incurring future damages.

not give rise to a right to payment are not "claims" and would therefore not be susceptible to discharge in bankruptcy.[46]

The *Udell* court constructed a confusing alternative test from this floor statement. It seized on the awkward phrase "with respect to which such breach does not give rise to a right to payment" appearing in the last sentence. Because the phrase arguably modifies "equitable remedy" rather than "breach of performance," the court concluded equitable rights are a claim if payment arises from their exercise. This is opposed to the wording of the statute, which clearly requires that the breach, not the equitable remedy, give rise to a right to payment. And the test makes no sense because equitable remedies are typically designed to provide nonmonetary relief. Having thus created a virtually unpassable test, the court ruled it was flunked by the facts before it because the right to obtain liquidated damages arose from the contract, not from an equitable remedy under it.

The *Udell* court also fashioned another test which, if passed, would make an equitable remedy a claim. It here focussed on the reference in the floor statement to a right to payment being an "alternative" to the equitable remedy. From this the court concluded *all* right to payment must be an alternative to the equitable remedy. Because state courts would enforce the parties' agreement by granting both damages and an injunction, the court ruled an alternative right to payment was not present, so Carpetland's rights failed this test as well. This reasoning ignores Carpetland's right to damages for future loss, which *is* an alternative to its equitable remedy. The floor statement's reference to a right to payment being an alternative to equitable relief is understandable because the claim for future loss is the monetary equivalent to the right to an injunction against further competition. Nor is there any reason to believe Congress intended that this alternative right to payment be the only right to payment. The statute does not say so. The injured party is obviously entitled to compensation for damages already incurred by the time of trial, as well as to an injunction against future competition. The liquidated damage clause before the court was presumably designed to provide this compensation because the parties also agreed upon an injunction to prevent future loss. *Udell* thus commits the double sin of elevating legislative history above the statute's plain wording and then misunderstanding the legislative history.

---

[46] 124 Cong. Rec. H11090 (daily ed. Sept. 28, 1978); S17406 (daily ed. Oct. 6, 1978) (statements of Rep. Edwards and Sen. DeConcini).

The real basis for the *Udell* court's holding emerges from the concurring opinion of Judge Raum. He thought the majority opinion "dodges this statute's plain language in an effort to reach a sensible result." To Judge Raum, and one suspects to the other panel members, discharge in bankruptcy of an injunction against competition is like a bankruptcy discharge of an injunction against trespassing, polluting, stalking or battering. Because he thought the debtor's discharge would have similar "patently absurd consequences," Judge Raum believed the plain language of the statute should not be followed.

Judge Raum's reasoning leaves much to be desired as well, quite apart from his willingness to elide what he admits to be the statute's plain wording. The case concerned breach of contract, not trespass, pollution, stalking or battery. Moreover, trespass and the like is prohibited by law, without regard to the existence of an injunction. So a bankruptcy discharge does not terminate the obligation to refrain from such conduct. In the final analysis, the decision in *Udell* comes down to this: The court could not bring itself to equate an injunction against breach of contract with a monetary judgment for breach of contract which is routinely discharged in bankruptcy.

IV. CONCLUSION

In summary, although the decisions are in disarray, Maids' alternative right to damages from the Debtors' future competition in breach of their covenant not to compete is a "right to payment" within the meaning of the statutory definition of an equitable claim. Hence, under the definition, Maids' injunctive rights constitute a claim. That state courts consider damages inadequate when compared to the equitable remedy of an injunction is beside the point. Although damages for breach of the covenant, particularly damages for lost future profits, are difficult to fix, courts are perfectly capable of doing so. This alternative right to damages fits into the statutory definition of an equitable claim very well. The same breach, a debtor's competition and threat of further competition, "gives rise" to both a damage claim and injunctive rights. The definition imposes no requirement that the claimant elect to receive a monetary payment, that compliance with the injunction require an expenditure of funds, or that the equitable remedy, as opposed to the breach, give rise to a right to payment. Following the statute's plain meaning promotes two fundamental policies of the Bankruptcy Code—the policy favoring a debtor's fresh start and the policy favoring equality among holders of similar rights.

Notes and Questions

1. Has *Maids* gutted the distinction between an injunctive remedy and a damages remedy?

2. Is Maids consistent with *Chateaugay*?

C. PAYMENT OF UNSECURED CLAIMS IN CHAPTER 7

Chapter 7 is conceptually simple. The trustee collects the debtor's assets, liquidates them, and distributes the proceeds in accordance with the Code's directions. See §§ 704(1) & 726. Nonexempt assets owned on the date of filing are used to pay the debts owed on that date. For example, assume that after the trustee collects and liquidates the debtor's assets (and the expenses of doing so are deducted), $5,000 remains. If twenty unsecured creditors are owed $500 each, a total of $10,000 in claims is being asserted against an estate worth half that amount. Each claim will receive 50 cents on the dollar.

Reality is slightly more complicated (isn't it always?), because certain distributions are made from property of the estate ahead of unsecured creditors. Some of the debtor's assets may be subject to valid liens. The lienholder, who is the holder of a secured claim, is entitled to the property that is collateral for its lien (§ 725), thus removing it from the pot of assets available to unsecured creditors. In addition, the debtor may exempt certain types of property, again removing those assets from the reach of creditors. Finally, certain claims, although unsecured, enjoy priority status and are entitled to be paid before general unsecured claims are satisfied. We examined exemptions in Chapter 2 of this text. Priorities are examined later in this Chapter. The rights of secured creditors are the subject of the next Chapter.

D. PAYMENT OF UNSECURED CLAIMS IN CHAPTERS 12 AND 13

In Chapter 7, payments to holders of general unsecured claims are determined by the amount remaining in the estate after secured claims, estate expenses, exemptions and priorities are satisfied. In Chapters 12 and 13, payments to holders of unsecured claims are determined by the plan proposed by the debtor. Sections 1225(a)(4) and 1325(a)(4) set a floor, however. They require that the plan provide an amount "not less than the amount that would be paid on such claim if the estate of the debtor were liquidated under chapter 7." This is known as the "best interests" test. It necessitates a hypothetical Chapter 7 calculation.

Since unsecured creditors receive nothing in many Chapter 7 cases (generally referred to as "no asset" cases), the best interests test frequently does not provide an effective floor for payments to unsecured creditors in Chapter 13 cases. Courts troubled by this result often seized upon the "good faith" requirement of § 1325(a)(3), reading it to require minimum payment amounts. Then, in 1984, Congress added § 1325(b) to the Code, which imposes a disposable income test.

IN RE GREER

United States Bankruptcy Court, Central District of California, 1986.
60 B.R. 547.

SAMUEL L. BUFFORD, Bankruptcy Judge.

ORDER CONFIRMING CHAPTER 13 PLAN

I. FACTS

Debtors Phillip and Judy Greer filed this joint Chapter 13 case on February 21, 1986. They filed their Chapter 13 statement and proposed plan on the same date. Mr. Greer is a staff sergeant in the United States Marine Corps, in which he has served for eighteen years. Mrs. Greer is a secretary/office manager at Jacoby and Meyers Law Offices, which is counsel for debtors. They have two teen-age children.

As of the date of filing, the debtors owned their family residence, which had a fair market value of approximately $98,000, and which was encumbered by a first trust deed with an outstanding balance of approximately $88,000 and a second trust deed with an outstanding balance of approximately $3,800. On the date of filing the debtors owed arrearages of $6,000 on the first trust deed and $790 on the second trust deed.

The debtors own two automobiles, on which payments were current at the time of filing. Their 1977 Ford is worth $2,100, and is encumbered by a loan of $2,800, leaving $700 as an unsecured claim. Their 1983 Toyota is worth $8,600, and is fully encumbered. Three other creditors are partially secured on loans for the purchase of home furnishings. Apart from the Chapter 13 Trustee, there are no priority creditors. In addition to the secured debt, at the time of filing the debtors owed unsecured debts totalling more than $18,000 to more than thirty creditors.

The debtors' budget discloses that they receive $3,200 per month in net income. Their monthly expense budget is as follows:

Real estate payments	$1255
Utilities	241
Food	300
Clothing	100
Laundry and cleaning	75
Auto insurance	146
Transportation	300
Total	$2,417

This budget leaves a surplus of $783, of which the debtors propose to pay $707.43 per month for 36 months to their creditors under their Chapter 13 plan. This will cover the arrearages on the secured debt, plus interest at the rate of 12% per annum. These payments, plus the trustee's fees, take up all but $5.73 per month of the payments. The debtors propose to pay unsecured creditors a total of $206.22 under the plan, which is approximately one percent of the outstanding unsecured debt.

The principal effect of the plan is to cure the arrearages on the home, to discharge one-quarter of the debt on the Ford automobile, and to discharge all of the unsecured debt. The debtors will retain their automobiles, and pay the secured debt on them.

No creditor has objected to the plan. Elsie Davis, the Chapter 13 Trustee objects to the termination of the plan after 36 months, and argues (1) that the payments should be larger, and (2) that the plan should be extended beyond 36 months to permit a significant payment to the unsecured creditors.

II. Issues Presented

This case presents two related issues: (1) whether a three-year Chapter 13 plan can be confirmed where all of the payments thereunder go to the priority and secured creditors and the trustee's fees, and the general unsecured creditors receive nothing; (2) whether there is "cause" for a Chapter 13 plan to extend more than three years, if the unsecured creditors would otherwise receive nothing thereunder.

Apart from adequate protection and relief from the automatic stay, this is apparently the most litigated issue under the Bankruptcy Code. The vast majority of reported opinions (virtually all of which have been reviewed by the Court), however, involve at least some payments to the general unsecured creditors.

The Court would normally be reluctant to add to the multiplicity of voices on this issue. However, the Court finds two reasons to write yet another opinion on this subject. First, despite the multitude of opinions on this issue, there is no settled law on this subject. Second, one out of every twelve Chapter 13 cases filed in the United States is filed in this district: In 1985 there were 108,059 Chapter 13 cases filed, of which 9,067 were filed in the Central District of California.

The Court holds that such a plan is not disqualified under Chapter 13 solely on the grounds that the general unsecured creditors receive nothing, and that the plan before the Court must be confirmed. The Court further holds that the lack of any payment to the general unsecured creditors in the first three years is not alone cause to extend the plan beyond three years.

III. ANALYSIS

The benefit to a debtor of proposing a plan of repayment under Chapter 13, rather than opting for liquidation under Chapter 7, is that it permits the debtor to protect his assets. In a liquidation case, the debtor must surrender his nonexempt assets, as of the date of filing, for liquidation and sale by the trustee. Under Chapter 13, the debtor may retain his property by agreeing to repay his creditors from his disposable income over a period of time.

A. Pre–1984 Law

In the early days of the Bankruptcy Code there were a large number of reported cases on this subject, and several appellate level cases. Cases went both ways at the bankruptcy Court level. However, the circuit courts took a skeptical view of a requirement of substantial repayment to general unsecured creditors. A number of courts, including the Ninth Circuit, came to the view that, if a minimum payment to unsecured creditors was to be required, it should be mandated by Congress, and not imposed by the courts. *In re Goeb*, 675 F.2d 1386, 1389 (9th Cir.1982).

In 1984 Congress adopted the Bankruptcy Amendments and Federal Judgeship Act ("BAFJA"), which, in this Court's opinion, resolved the issues raised in this case.

1. Statute

Prior to 1984, § 1325(a) in substance required a court to confirm a Chapter 13 plan if it satisfied six conditions: (1) it complied with Chapter 13 and the other provisions of the Bankruptcy Code; (2) the filing fees had been paid; (3) the plan was proposed in good faith; (4) the unsecured creditors were to receive as much as they would under a Chapter 7 liquidation; (5) the secured creditors were appropriately provided for; (6) the plan was feasible. The language of § 1325(a) was mandatory: If the six conditions were satisfied, the Court was required to confirm the Chapter 13 plan.

The statute does not define "good faith," and its meaning cannot be discerned from the legislative history.

2. Lower Court Cases

The Bankruptcy Code went into effect on October 1, 1979. By early 1980, the Bankruptcy courts were already faced with the issue of whether a plan under Chapter 13 of the new Code could provide for little or no payment to unsecured creditors.

Because the language of § 1325(a) was mandatory, the courts were required to find any grounds for denial of confirmation within the four corners of § 1325(a). This led the courts to focus upon the "good faith" provision of § 1325(a)(3) as a basis for rejecting plans that violated the basic intent of Chapter 13.

Of the reported pre–1984 cases, only one has been discovered approving a plan of 36 months or less that provided zero payment to general unsecured creditors. * * * In contrast, a number of courts held that the good faith requirement of § 1325(a)(3) imposed a higher threshold for the minimum payment to unsecured creditors than that imposed by § 1325(a)(4).

The issue became particularly pointed when debtors began to propose plans of rather short duration that provided zero payment to unsecured creditors. In *In re Estus*, 695 F.2d 311 (8th Cir.1982), for example, the Eighth Circuit reversed the confirmation of a 15–month Chapter 13 plan that provided zero payment to unsecured creditors. In

In re Ali, 33 B.R. 890 (Bankr. D. Kan.1983), the debtor proposed a plan to pay zero percent to unsecured creditors over 25 months. The court confirmed the plan, but required its extension to 36 months, which provided a repayment of approximately three percent to the unsecured creditors.

3. Ninth Circuit Cases

While courts in other circuits debated whether a Chapter 13 plan must provide substantial repayment to the unsecured creditors, the Ninth Circuit took the view that good faith did not require substantial repayment.

The leading Ninth Circuit case was *In re Goeb*, 675 F.2d 1386 (9th Cir.1982), where the plan proposed payment of one percent of the general unsecured claims. The bankruptcy court had denied confirmation on the grounds that a plan that did not propose substantial payment to the unsecured creditors was proposed in bad faith. The Ninth Circuit reversed, and held that the purpose of the "good faith" standard of § 1325 was to require that a debtor act equitably in proposing a Chapter 13 plan. This included such issues as whether the debtor has misrepresented facts in the plan, or unfairly manipulated the Bankruptcy Code. The minimum repayment required by § 1325(a)(4) (at least what a creditor would receive in a Chapter 7 liquidation) strongly suggested, in the Ninth Circuit's view, that Congress did not intend the general good faith requirement to be used to impose a more rigorous standard.

A zero percent plan came before the Ninth Circuit in *Lawrence Tractor Co. v. Gregory (In re Gregory)*, 705 F.2d 1118 (9th Cir.1983). However, the unsecured creditor had failed to object at the confirmation hearing, or to appeal the order of confirmation. Instead, two months after the confirmation the creditor filed a dischargability [sic] complaint alleging that its debt was not "provided for" in the plan, and thus was not dischargeable. While the Ninth Circuit found that the legality of zero payment plans was not before it (because the order confirming the plan had become final), it stated, "If the bankrupt [sic] can show good faith, it seems almost pointless to distinguish between nominal-payment and zero-payment plans. In fact, the view from the trenches appears to be that zero-payment plans are administratively preferable." *Id.* at 1121. The Ninth Circuit further noted with apparent approval the representation of counsel at oral argument that the Bankruptcy Court in Fresno (which had confirmed the plan) had confirmed more than 300 zero-payment plans.

Prior to BAFJA, however, the Ninth Circuit had no occasion to consider a case such as *In re Estus* or *In re Ali*, *supra*, proposing no payment to unsecured creditors in a plan shorter than 36 months or where not all of the disposable income was allocated to the plan.

B. BAFJA—Best Efforts Requirement

Among the amendments to the Bankruptcy Code enacted in 1984 in BAFJA was a new subsection of § 1325. The confirmation mandate of § 1325(a) was qualified by a new subsection (b), which provides in substance that, upon objection of the trustee or an unsecured creditor, all of the debtor's projected disposable income for three years must be applied to the plan (alternatively, in the case of an objecting creditor, such creditor may be paid in full). "Disposable income" is defined in § 1325(b)(2) to include all income "not reasonably necessary to be expended * * * for the maintenance or support of the debtor or a dependent of the debtor."

This statutory provision solves both the problem of excess disposable income and the problem of unreasonably short plans. Under this provision an unsecured creditor cannot be compelled to accept zero payment unless the plan extends at least 36 months, and all of the disposable income is allocated to the plan.

In this case the debtors' budget shows $783 in unallocated income, of which $707.43 is to be paid to the Chapter 13 Trustee for creditors under the plan, which leaves a cushion of approximately $75 per month for contingencies.

Does § 1325(b)(1)(B) authorize a contingency reserve? If a contingency reserve is "reasonably necessary * * * for the maintenance or support of the debtor or a dependent of the debtor", it is excepted from the § 1325(b)(2) definition of disposable income. The Court considers such a reserve to be reasonably necessary. As the court stated in *In re Otero*, 48 B.R. 704, 708 (Bankr. E.D. Va.1985):

> [A] difference of $117.00 a month is not a significant or substantial amount to be extracted from the debtors. It was not intended to take the last son. A cushion of money is necessary in Chapter 13 budgeting to guard against life's unexpectancies. It is not in the public interest to squeeze the last dollar from Chapter 13 debtors to fund a Chapter 13 plan.

Indeed, such a cushion may be required for compliance with § 1325(a)(6), which requires confirmation of a plan if, inter alia, "the debtor will be able to make all payments under the plan." *In re Goodavage*, 41 B.R. 742, 745–46 (Bankr. E.D.Va.1984).

This Court's Chapter 13 relief from stay calendar, which averages more than 100 such motions per week in Los Angeles, indicates that debtors in general have been cutting their budgets too thinly to be able to meet their post-petition obligations, including plan payments. While improvident spending doubtless accounts for a certain portion of post-petition defaults, it appears that most of the relief from stay litigation results from debtors' simple inability to live within their proposed budgets.

The contingency reserve in this case is particularly appropriate, in the view of the Court, because the budget is quite austere. No funds are budgeted for medical or dental expenses, for insurance (except for the automobiles), for recreation or for newspapers and periodicals. The food and clothing budgets are both tight for a family of four adults. While $75 per month for laundry and cleaning may be unusual, Mr. Greer's uniforms and the clothing required for Mrs. Greer's professional employment must be dry cleaned regularly. In fact, the only budgetary item that may be unreasonably generous is an allocation of $150 for heating, which is required in Southern California only for two or three months of the year. In view of the overall leanness of the budget, this item should not hinder confirmation of the plan. Thus the best efforts requirement of § 1325(b) is met by the plan in this case.

However, the Court does not consider it practical to pay $5.73 per month to unsecured creditors. Even if the Chapter 13 Trustee makes a single final distribution to unsecured creditors, only three or four unsecured creditors would qualify for the minimum payment of $15.00 provided by Bankruptcy Rule 3010(b). For this reason, the Court orders that the plan be amended by striking the $206.22 to be distributed to unsecured creditors, and orders that the plan payments be reduced accordingly. No notice to unsecured creditors of this change is required, because the change is de minimis.

C. Minimum Payment to Unsecured Creditors

The minimum payment to general unsecured creditors under a Chapter 13 plan is governed by § 1325(a)(4). Congress could have required that a Chapter 13 plan provide that unsecured creditors to [sic] be paid in full. It could also have provided that unsecured creditors be paid 70%, or 30%, or some other minimum amount of their claim. However, Congress decided against this approach.

Instead of fixing a minimum percentage payment to unsecured creditors, Congress provided in § 1325(a)(4) that the minimum payment to unsecured creditors should be determined by what they would get under a Chapter 7 liquidation. A Chapter 13 plan may be confirmed if:

> the value, as of the effective date of the plan, of property to be distributed under the plan on account of each unsecured claim is not less than the amount that would be paid on such claim if the estate of the debtor were liquidated under Chapter 7.

Thus, if a Chapter 7 case would provide payment to unsecured creditors of 100% of their claims, a Chapter 13 plan must provide 100% also. Similarly, if a Chapter 7 plan would provide 50%, the Chapter 13 plan must provide 50%. On the other hand, if the unsecured creditors would receive nothing under a Chapter 7 case (which is often true for Chapter 13 cases filed in this Court), § 1325 does not require that they receive more under a Chapter 13 plan.

The Chapter 13 Trustee's argument, that some payment to unsecured creditors should be required, should be addressed to Congress, not to the Court.

Part V of the proposed plan in this case provides a comparison with what the unsecured creditors would receive under Chapter 7. This comparison shows that, after application of the exemptions available to a Chapter 7 debtor, the unsecured creditors would receive nothing in a Chapter 7 case. Although the unsecured creditors are to receive nothing under this Chapter 13 plan, this is not less than the amount that they would receive in a Chapter 7 case.

D. Good Faith

BAFJA relieved the § 1325(a)(3) good faith provision of the "best efforts" excess baggage of certain pre-BAFJA cases. This result was foreshadowed in the *Goeb* decision. The "good faith" requirement of § 1325(a)(3) was thus left to fill its proper role in the evaluation of a Chapter 13 plan.

Goeb provides the guidance for the determination of whether the Chapter 13 plan in this case was proposed in good faith: "The proper inquiry is whether [the debtors] acted equitably in proposing their Chapter 13 plan." 675 F.2d at 1390. More recently, the Ninth Circuit stated, "A good faith test * * * should examine the intentions of the debtor and the legal effect of the confirmation of a Chapter 13 plan in light of the spirit and purposes of Chapter 13." *Chinichian v. Campolongo (In re Chinichian)*, 784 F.2d 1440, 1444 (9th Cir.1986) (bad faith to file a plan for the purpose of avoiding specific performance of a real estate sales contract). This determination must be made on a case by case basis, and all relevant factors must be considered. No complete list of the relevant considerations has been made. However, relevant factors may include whether the debtor has misrepresented the facts to the court or failed to disclose relevant facts (such as prior bankruptcies), and whether the debtor has unfairly manipulated the Bankruptcy Code.

Nominal or zero payment to general unsecured creditors may be evidence of bad faith. However, other evidence of bad faith is required to justify the denial of confirmation of a proposed Chapter 13 plan. In this case neither the Chapter 13 Trustee nor any creditor has brought forth any other evidence of bad faith. In consequence, the Court finds that the plan has been proposed in good faith.

E. Cause

A distinction of perhaps more substantial importance between this case and *Goeb* is that *Goeb* involved a five-year plan, while the plan before the Court is a three-year plan. The Chapter 13 Trustee urges that the plan be extended to four or five years to provide a modest payment to unsecured creditors.

The limits on the length of a Chapter 13 plan are provided by [§ 1322(d)]:

> The plan may not provide for payments over a period that is longer than three years, unless the court, *for cause*, approves a longer period, but the court may not approve a period that is longer than five years (emphasis added).

Under Chapter XIII of the Bankruptcy Act, plans frequently extended as long as seven to ten years. Congress was concerned that this amounted to involuntary servitude. H.R. Rep. No. 95–595 at 117, *reprinted in* 1978 U.S.C.C.A.N. at 6078. In consequence, in the Bankruptcy Code Congress limited the duration of a plan to three years, except upon a finding of "cause." "Cause" under [§ 1322(d)] is not defined in the Bankruptcy Code: Congress left it to the courts to determine its dimensions in the light of experience and in the context of particular cases.

Case law has not developed a comprehensive definition of "cause" under [§ 1322(d)], and perhaps none should be expected. Three typical examples of "cause" to extend a plan more than three years have emerged.

First, the payment of 100% of a debtor's unsecured debts provides cause for a plan longer than three years for two reasons: (1) it provides a better credit rating to the debtor; (2) under § 727(a)(9), it does not disqualify the debtor from a Chapter 7 discharge within the ensuing six years.

Second, the payment of 70% of the debtor's unsecured debts also prevents disqualification, under § 727(a)(9), from a Chapter 7 discharge within six years, provided that the plan is proposed in good faith and is the debtor's best effort. In consequence, a 70% payment to unsecured creditors is generally recognized as cause for a Chapter 13 plan to extend beyond three years.

A third category of "cause" may arise after confirmation, if a debtor is unable to make plan payments for a period of time. The debtor may then request a suspension of plan payments and an extension of the plan beyond 36 months to permit full payment of the plan. However, this option is not available if the original plan already extends for 60 months. [§ 1322(d)].

A more substantial payment to unsecured creditors, on the other hand, does not qualify as "cause" for a Chapter 13 plan to extend more than three years. Every three-year plan providing less than full repayment to unsecured creditors can be extended to provide more substantial payment to them. If such payment were to qualify as "cause," the Chapter 13 Trustee could routinely object to all such plans, and the three-year Chapter 13 plan would become the exception, rather than the rule. This is surely not a legitimate interpretation of [§ 1322(d)], which contemplates that the three-year plan will be the rule.

This interpretation of [§ 1322(d)] is bolstered by BAFJA's addition of the new § 1325(b) to the Bankruptcy Code. If the proposed plan is less than 36 months, it must be extended to 36 months upon objection of a creditor or the Chapter 13 Trustee. However, in limiting § 1325(b) to 36 months, Congress chose not to require a plan to be extended further to solve low payment problems. If the Chapter 13

Trustee or a creditor contends that a debtor is not proposing sufficient payment to unsecured creditors, such objector should examine carefully the income and expense projections of a debtor to assure that the debtor meets the best efforts requirement of § 1325(b).

Thus low or zero payment to general unsecured creditors is not cause to extend a plan beyond 36 months, and in this case there is no cause for the plan to last more than three years.

IV. CONCLUSION

The Court concludes that the Chapter 13 plan in this case is proposed in good faith, that it satisfies the "best efforts" requirement, and that there is no cause for it to extend more than 36 months.

The Court does not suggest that Chapter 13 plans that provide zero payment to general unsecured creditors should become the rule, or even that they should be frequent. In the vast majority of cases, the best efforts requirements of § 1325(b) will provide at least some payments to unsecured creditors. In most of the remaining cases the debtor will not be able to repay secured debt arrearages (because the Court requires debtors to repay arrearages on secured debt over 36 months), and confirmation must be denied under § 1325(a)(6). Only the most marginal Chapter 13 case will involve a 36–month plan that provides zero payment to general unsecured creditors.

For the foregoing reasons, the plan is confirmed.

If an interested party objects to the debtor's plan, § 1325-(b)(1)(B) requires that the debtor devote all "projected disposable income" for the next three years to payments under the plan. The term is defined in § 1325(b)(2) as income not reasonably necessary for support of the debtor and his or her family. Application of these provisions requires two determinations: what is to be counted as income, and what expenses are reasonably necessary.

The following case focuses on the first of these issues, as well as on § 1325(a)(4)'s best interest test and § 1325(a)(3)'s good faith requirement. We have already encountered this debtor, in the Notes and Problems at the beginning of Chapter 2, Section B.1. of this text. There, the issue was his eligibility to file a Chapter 13 petition in the first place. Here, the primary issue is calculation of his disposable income under § 1325(b).

SOLOMON v. COSBY (IN RE SOLOMON)

United States Court of Appeals, Fourth Circuit, 1995.
67 F.3d 1128.

WILKINSON, Circuit Judge.

This case presents the question whether a Chapter 13 debtor must include in his "disposable income" some portion of funds invested in various individual retirement accounts ("IRAs"). The bankruptcy court denied confirmation of the debtor's proposed Chapter 13 plan for failure to include hypothetical distributions from the IRAs in the disposable income to be paid under the plan. Because we believe that funds held in the debtor's IRAs but not distributed to the debtor do not constitute "disposable income" under § 1325, we reverse.

I.

The debtor herein, Neil Solomon, M.D., filed a Chapter 13 bankruptcy petition on September 20, 1993; he filed his proposed Chapter 13 plan shortly thereafter. Dr. Solomon's only creditors are three former patients (and the spouse of one) who have sued him in tort for alleged sexual misconduct during the course of their treatment as his medical patients.* The plaintiffs claimed compensatory and punitive damages totaling approximately $160 million. Solomon scheduled each plaintiff's claim as contingent, unliquidated, and disputed and listed the amount of each claim as zero. Although these debts were arguably non-dischargeable under Chapter 7 since they arose from "willful and malicious injury by the debtor," § 523(a)(6), the claims could be discharged under the broader "super-discharge" available to Chapter 13 debtors. § 1328(a).

Solomon scheduled assets valued at $2,184,645, of which he claimed $2,140,501.25 to be exempt from the claims of his creditors. Of the assets claimed exempt, $1,413,888 is held in three individual retirement accounts. Federal law does not require that income be withdrawn from these accounts until the recipient reaches age 70½. Solomon, currently age 62, informed the bankruptcy court that he had

* Solomon apparently paid all his other creditors in full before filing his Chapter 13 petition.

no intention of withdrawing any funds from the IRAs during the term of the plan. Moreover, under Maryland law, the IRAs are exempt from execution by creditors. Solomon was thus left with approximately $40,000 in non-exempt assets.

After his petition was filed, Solomon voluntarily surrendered his medical license and ceased practicing medicine. As a result, his net monthly income decreased substantially from the $14,800 initially disclosed in Schedule I to approximately $2,650, which consisted primarily of monthly mandatory distributions from his Maryland state pension. According to the plan, Solomon proposed to pay the Trustee $750 per month for an extended term of five years, § 1322(d), for a total payout to the creditors of $45,000. Solomon planned to use the remainder of his monthly income, together with income from investments and exempt assets other than his IRAs, to pay his normal living expenses.

In February 1994, the Chapter 13 Trustee and the creditors filed various objections to the proposed plan. Only the treatment of Solomon's three IRAs is relevant to this appeal. According to the Trustee, the IRAs should have been taken into account in determining the minimum amount Solomon should be required to pay under his Chapter 13 plan. *See* § 1325(b)(1)(B) (upon objection by trustee or unsecured creditor, when plan proposes less than full payment of unsecured claims, debtor must devote all his projected disposable income for typical three-year term to payments under the plan). The Trustee also objected to the plan on the ground that it did not satisfy the "good faith" requirement of § 1325(a)(3), but the bankruptcy court declined to address this fact-dependent issue, preferring to decide questions such as the disposable income requirement that could be resolved as a matter of law.

The bankruptcy court agreed with the Trustee and denied confirmation on the ground that Solomon's plan failed to provide for payment of all his projected disposable income when it failed to include some minimum amount attributable to allowed distributions from his IRAs. Under applicable non-bankruptcy law, the bankruptcy court noted, Solomon has the right to receive periodic distributions from these accounts without suffering a tax "penalty," despite his stated intention not to take such distributions. On appeal, the district court affirmed. Solomon appeals, and the Trustee cross-appeals, arguing that confirmation should be denied since the plan was not filed in good faith.

II.

A.

The Trustee objected to confirmation of Solomon's Chapter 13 plan on the ground that the plan did not meet the "disposable income" requirement of § 1325(b) since it failed to include hypothetical withdrawals from the IRAs in the calculation of Solomon's monthly income. We hold, however, that the funds invested in Solomon's IRAs are not "disposable income" within the meaning of § 1325(b)(2).

The statute defines "disposable income" as "income which is received by the debtor and which is not reasonably necessary to be expended * * * for the maintenance or support of the debtor or a dependent of the debtor." § 1325(b)(2). If the trustee or the holder of an allowed unsecured claim objects to the confirmation of a Chapter 13 plan and the plan proposes less than full payment of unsecured claims, the plan may be confirmed only if it provides for payment of "all of the debtor's projected disposable income" to be received during the life of the plan. § 1325(b)(1)(B).

Solomon's IRAs are not "income" under the clear terms of this section. Both the statutory definition of "disposable income" as income that is received by the debtor as well as the requirement that projected income must be calculated over the life of the plan contemplate income that a debtor is actually receiving at the time of confirmation. Projected disposable income typically is calculated by multiplying a debtor's monthly income at the time of confirmation by 36 months, the normal duration of a Chapter 13 plan, then determining the portion of that income which is "disposable" according to the statutory definition. It is undisputed that, at the time of the confirmation hearing on Solomon's plan, he was not actually receiving any disbursements from his IRAs; he further insisted that he had no intention of withdrawing funds from the IRAs during the life of the plan.

On these facts, we cannot sanction the bankruptcy court's inclusion of some hypothetical amount of income from the IRAs in the calculation of disposable income. "[R]ather than engaging in hopeless speculation about the future," a court should determine projected disposable income by calculating a debtor's "present monthly income and expenditures" and extending those amounts over the life of the plan. *In re Crompton*, 73 B.R. 800, 808 (Bankr. E.D.Pa.1987). Solomon's present, regular monthly income does not include distributions from his

IRAs, and the bankruptcy court's imputation of amounts from such speculative distributions in its calculation of disposable income is contrary to the plain terms of the statutory definition.

Cases such as *In re Schnabel*, 153 B.R. 809 (Bankr. N.D.Ill. 1993), and *In re Hagel*, 171 B.R. 686 (Bankr. D. Mont. 1994), are distinguishable: they involved debtors who, at the time the bankruptcy petition was filed, were receiving regular monthly pension or social security payments. In this case, by contrast, Solomon receives no regular distributions from his IRAs, has indicated no intent to take such distributions during the life of the Chapter 13 plan, and is not required to do so by the Internal Revenue Code until he reaches age 70½. *Schnabel* and *Hagel* thus do not require that these accounts be treated as a source of hypothetical income regularly received by Solomon.

B.

Although they are not a source of regular, periodic income, Solomon's IRAs are assets of the estate, much like a checking or savings account. In fact, Solomon listed each of his IRAs as personal property in the schedules submitted to the bankruptcy court. In this regard, the IRAs are relevant not to the "disposable income" requirement, but rather to the "best interests of creditors" prerequisite for confirmation of a Chapter 13 plan. *See* § 1325(a)(4) (unsecured creditors must receive no less in a Chapter 13 proceeding than they would in a Chapter 7 liquidation proceeding).

Here, the debtor's IRAs would be "exempt" assets and thus unavailable to creditors in a Chapter 7 liquidation. Maryland has elected to opt out of the federal exemptions and instead has established specific exemptions under state law. Solomon relies on one of these state-law exemptions * * * . Solomon's IRAs * * * fall within the terms of the Maryland exemption.

Because the IRAs would be unavailable to creditors in a Chapter 7 proceeding by virtue of the state law exemption, creditors would receive nothing from those accounts if Solomon's non-exempt assets were to be liquidated. Thus, preserving the IRAs from the claims of Solomon's creditors in this Chapter 13 proceeding is both logically sound and in keeping with the Code. In fact, in a Chapter 7 proceeding, Solomon's creditors would be entitled to the proceeds from liquidation of non-exempt assets worth approximately $40,000. The $45,000 he proposes to pay the creditors under his Chapter 13 plan thus appears to satisfy the "best interests of creditors" prerequisite for confirmation. The Supreme Court has emphasized that the mere happenstance of bankruptcy should not result in a windfall to creditors. *Patterson v. Shumate*, 504 U.S. 753 (1992). Nor, we think, should a debtor's choice to proceed under Chapter 13 invariably entitle creditors to more than they would receive in Chapter 7, contrary to the mandate of the Bankruptcy Code.

Our holding today is consistent with the treatment accorded IRAs by the Internal Revenue Code. Subject to certain limitations, a taxpayer's contribution to an IRA is tax deductible, and the account accrues interest tax-free. As a general matter, only when the account holder takes a distribution from the account is the payment subject to tax. Moreover, a taxpayer need not take a distribution until he reaches age 70½. In light of these provisions, we do not believe that the funds held in the accounts but not distributed to Solomon constitute "income" as that term is commonly understood. "Income is not a gain accruing to capital or a growth in the value of the investment, but is a gain, a profit, something of exchangeable value, proceeding from the property, severed from the capital, however invested or employed, and coming in, being derived, that is, received or drawn by the recipient for his separate use, benefit, and disposal." *Black's Law Dictionary* 687 (5th ed. 1979).

In sum, we do not think it a condition of invoking the protections of Chapter 13 that one withdraw pension or retirement income to fund a plan that otherwise meets the § 1325 prerequisites for confirmation. A contrary holding could have devastating results for pension and retirement savings. By requiring an otherwise eligible Chapter 13 debtor to withdraw such monies to fund a Chapter 13 plan, we would effectively undercut the very purpose of retirement and pension plans: to ensure that workers have sufficient funds with which to support themselves and their dependents during their retirement years. We agree with the Third Circuit that "Congress has expressed a deep and continuing interest in the preservation of pension plans, and in encouraging retirement savings, as reflected in the statutes which have given us ERISA, Keogh plans and IRAs," *Velis v. Kardanis*, 949 F.2d 78, 82 (3d Cir. 1991). We decline to undercut this clear congressional purpose by conditioning the availability of Chapter 13 relief on a debtor's agreement to withdraw funds from an IRA prior to the distribution date mandated by the Internal Revenue Code and its accompanying regulations.

III.

Our holding does not mean, however, that Solomon is entitled to invoke the protections of Chapter 13. Whether his Chapter 13 plan will be confirmed hinges upon a finding by the bankruptcy court on remand that the debtor has proposed this plan in good faith. *See* § 1325(a)(3) (plan may be confirmed only if "proposed in good faith and not by any means forbidden by law").

In *Neufeld v. Freeman*, 794 F.2d 149 (4th Cir. 1986), this court addressed the elements that inform the good faith determination. This totality-of-the-circumstances inquiry focuses on such factors as the percentage of proposed repayment to creditors, the debtor's financial situation, the period of time over which creditors will be paid, the debtor's employment history and prospects, the nature and amount of unsecured claims, the debtor's past bankruptcy filings, the debtor's honesty in representing the facts of the case, the nature of the debtor's pre-petition conduct that gave rise to the debts, whether the debts would be dischargeable in a Chapter 7 proceeding, and any other unusual or exceptional problems the debtor faces. On remand, the bankruptcy court should consider relevant factors in its § 1325(a)(3) analysis of Solomon's plan, mindful of the fact that the good faith inquiry is intended to prevent abuse of the provisions, purpose, or spirit of Chapter 13.

It is here that the concerns of our dissenting brother are addressed. The dissent vents its understandable displeasure with the nature of the acts of which Solomon stands accused. It fashions on appeal a "Solomon Rule" which, however attractive in the particular case, would thwart the general intent of Congress to safeguard pension and retirement plans. The better approach is to require triers of fact in bankruptcy cases to review the good faith with which individual debtors attempt to invoke Chapter 13 protections. This good faith inquiry is expressly mandated under § 1325(a)(3) of the Bankruptcy Code and has been expressly held by this circuit to encompass "both prepetition conduct and prior bankruptcy filings by the debtor." *Neufeld*, 794 F.2d at 150. Having the trier of fact determine whether Solomon failed to exercise good faith is preferable to reworking the law of Chapter 13 based on the circumstances of a single debtor. Our dissenting brother would do just that, however—in reaching the distasteful situation here, the dissent would compel debtors to prematurely withdraw and make available pension savings which they had no intention of using during the life of a Chapter 13 plan.

IV.

For the foregoing reasons, the judgment of the district court is reversed and the case is remanded for further proceedings.

MICHAEL, Circuit Judge, dissenting.

I respectfully dissent.

Facing tort claims of sexual misconduct made by several former medical patients who seek damages of $160 million, the debtor, Neil Solomon, filed a bankruptcy petition. In an attempt to wipe out these claims under the broader "super-discharge" available under Chapter 13, Solomon proposes a plan that offers his former patients (his only creditors) a total of just $45,000, payable in monthly installments of $750 over the next five years. But Solomon, who has retired, refuses to make available to his creditors any income (which is readily accessible without penalty) from three exempt IRAs worth more than $1.4 million. He does not need any income from the IRAs for the reasonable maintenance and support of himself or any dependent. I would hold that income he could elect to receive without penalty from his IRAs may be counted as projected disposable income for purposes of his Chapter 13 plan. This result best comports with the language of § 1325(b) and the overall purposes of Chapter 13, which gives a debtor such as Solomon an enormous break under the "super-discharge."

I.

A.

* * * "Super-discharge," however, does not come without a price, and indeed it should not. The debtor must be willing to sacrifice his projected disposable income for three years. * * * [I]f a Chapter 13 debtor has retired and is old enough to take distributions from his IRA without penalty under the federal tax laws, his projected IRA distributions should be included in the disposable income calculation.[1] Including social security, pension or IRA payments in the disposable income calculation does not mean that the Chapter 13 debtor is thrown into the streets to beg or forced onto the public assistance rolls. Section 1325(b)(2) defines "disposable income" as "income which is received

[1] The language of § 1325(b) makes no distinction between income from exempt assets (such as pension funds and IRAs) and income from non-exempt assets (such as marketable securities). This was not an oversight on the part of Congress. * * *

by the debtor and which is not reasonably necessary to be expended for the maintenance or support of the debtor or a dependent of the debtor." Thus, even under Chapter 13, the claims of creditors are secondary to the reasonable needs of the debtor and his dependents. Yet once those needs are met, the creditors are entitled to the remaining income in the three-year period.

Although § 1325(b)(2) defines "disposable income" as "income which is received by the debtor," § 1325(b)(1)(B) calls for a "projection" of income for three years into the future. The court, not the debtor, has the final say in projecting the debtor's disposable income. In the usual case, the projection is relatively straightforward. This, however, is not the usual case.

* * *

The point here is simple: Solomon has retired. One would, therefore, expect (and could reasonably project) that Solomon would start to draw income from his IRAs. They are, after all, called *retirement* accounts.

* * * Because Solomon is 62, has retired, and can never return to the practice of medicine, it is reasonable to project that his disposable income during the next three years will include income from his IRAs.

Under Chapter 13 Solomon can still shield all of his assets, including exempt assets such as his IRAs. And he can obtain a "super-discharge" and free himself of the sexual misconduct claims. In return, Solomon must do one thing: pay *all* of his projected disposable income (including that from exempt assets) to his creditors during the relatively short life of his plan. This is a small price to pay for any debtor in such trouble, regardless of his disposable income level. The bankruptcy and district courts were right to refuse confirmation of a plan that did not project income from Solomon's IRAs.

B.

The majority says that requiring a Chapter 13 debtor such as Solomon to contribute disposable IRA income "could have devastating results for pension and retirement savings." I respectfully disagree for three reasons. First, the statutory definition of "disposable income" under § 1325(b)(2)(A) ensures that during the life of his plan Solomon (or any other Chapter 13 debtor) would always have sufficient funds for the maintenance and support of himself and his dependents. All of the reasonable living expenses of the debtor and his family come off the top before a penny is paid to creditors.

Second, § 1325(b) does not require that all of the funds in the IRAs be used to fund the Chapter 13 plan. Far from it. A retired Chapter 13 debtor would simply be required to include the amount he would reasonably be expected to withdraw as retirement income for three years. Section 1325(b)(1)(B) gives the bankruptcy court the ultimate responsibility to make the projection, and there exists an ample basis for making a logical and sensible one. Here, the bankruptcy court suggested applying the *minimum* distribution formulas established by the Internal Revenue Code and regulations. For example, "[o]ne alternative measure of the minimum [yearly] withdrawal is the actuarially determined amount needed to exhaust the fund during the lifetimes of the owner and the primary beneficiary." In any event, the IRS's formulas ensure a steady income stream from the IRA throughout a person's retirement years. In addition, the formulas produce a ready projection of future income. * * * Thus, under the bankruptcy court's suggestion, a minimum annual IRA distribution would be dedicated to the payment of Solomon's creditors during the life of his plan. Thereafter, Solomon (or any other Chapter 13 debtor) would get all of his IRA distributions for the rest of his (projected) lifetime.

Third, persons who are not retired would not be required to include projected income from their IRAs. They would have the disposable income from their jobs to pay their creditors. However, if a retiree voluntarily invokes Chapter 13, it is only reasonable to require him to use any excess pension or IRA income to fund his plan.

C.

The majority notes that paying projected IRA income to creditors goes beyond what is required by the "best interests of creditors" test for confirmation of a Chapter 13 plan. Thus, according to the majority, because Solomon's IRAs would be exempt from liquidation in a Chapter 7 proceeding, his failure to include IRA income in his Chapter 13 plan "appears to satisfy the 'best interests of creditors' prerequisite for confirmation." Perhaps it does, but this does not dispose of the question before us today.

Satisfaction of the "best interests" test is but one prerequisite for confirmation of a Chapter 13 plan. The creditor must also satisfy the "disposable income" test. Therefore, I cannot accept the majority's suggestion that satisfaction of the "best interests" test results in satisfaction of the "disposable income" test. Using the "best interests" test to set the minimum or "floor" for payments to creditors under Chapter 13 would completely eviscerate the "disposable income" test of § 1325(b)(1)(B).

Finally, allowing creditors to share in a retired debtor's projected disposable IRA income (for three years) under Chapter 13 does not violate the Supreme Court's admonition in *Patterson v. Shumate*, 504 U.S. 753, 764 (1992), that the mere happenstance of bankruptcy should not result in a windfall to creditors. I reemphasize that Solomon himself voluntarily chose to seek the protection of "super-discharge" under Chapter 13. That choice subjected his plan to the "disposable income" test of § 1325(b)(1)(B) and placed his IRA income at risk. That choice was not happenstance; it was Solomon's considered decision. In fact, to hold that Solomon's projected disposable income does not include projected income from his IRAs results in a windfall to Solomon. It is a windfall that nullifies Congress's determination that "Chapter 13 proceedings * * * look to [the debtor's] future income * * * as a source of repayment of debt." S. Rep. No. 65, 98th Cong. 1st Sess. 20 (1983).

II.

The majority remands for proceedings under § 1325(a)(3) to determine whether Solomon proposed his plan in good faith. Perhaps his creditors will ultimately achieve relief under that section. That possibility, however, does not change the fact that the bankruptcy and district courts have already correctly refused to confirm Solomon's Chapter 13 plan because it fails to meet the "disposable income" test under § 1325(b). I would let the judgment stand and put an end to the matter right now.

Questions and Problems

1. If you were the judge on remand, how would you decide the case? Keep this case in mind when you read *Handeen v. LeMaire*, in Chapter 7, Section A, of this text.

2. What is the relationship between the best interests test of § 1325(a)(4) and the disposable income test of § 1325(b)(2)?

3. If the debtor wants to continue his or her country club membership, will the payments of dues be considered necessary for support under § 1325(b)(2)? What if the debtor is a lawyer who meets potential clients there and entertains current clients on the club's golf course?

4. What if the payments are for private school tuition for the debtor's children? Does it matter if the private school is a parochial school and the debtor believes that such religious training is mandatory?

5. Debtor has equity in her residence of $105,000 and is entitled to an exemption of $45,000 under state law. Debtor proposed a plan requiring payment of all her excess disposable income to the trustee for three years, but a total of only $14,000 would be paid to unsecured creditors. One of them argued that unsecured creditors should receive at least $60,000. Debtor countered with the argument that if the property were sold in a Chapter 7, capital gains taxes and costs of sale would consume $46,000 and, therefore, that § 1325(a)(4) is satisfied by her plan. Assuming that Debtor's numbers are correct, who wins? See *In re Card*, 114 B.R. 226 (Bankr. N.D.Cal.1990).

6. Debtor embezzled $57,000 from her employer, Corporation One, and was placed in a pretrial diversion program that required restitution. Debtor obtained employment with Corporation Two and embezzled $105,000, using part of the proceeds to repay Corporation One. Debtor was caught again and this time sentenced to jail. Upon her release, Debtor found a job (!) but never offered or attempted to repay Corporation Two. Instead, when Corporation Two began collection proceedings, Debtor filed Chapter 13. She listed three creditors: 1) Bank, with an $8,000 secured claim in Debtor's car; 2) Visa, with a $1,000 unsecured claim; and 3) Corporation Two, with an unsecured claim of $105,000. Debtor's three-year plan proposed to pay 100% to Bank and 3% to the unsecured creditors. Does the plan meet the good faith requirement of § 1325(a)(3)? See *In re Zelnar*, 91 B.R. 448 (Bankr. N.D. Ohio 1988).

7. Debtor, who had been a homemaker for 19 years, filed for an automobile dealer's license "in order to put food on the table" when her husband lost his license for rolling back odometers. Debtor knew nothing about the business, but her husband promised that he would help her and that he would not do anything dishonest. Despite those promises, he altered odometers and bribed state officials. Debtor was held civilly liable under agency principles for $200,000. She filed Chapter 13 in an effort to discharge that debt. Does Debtor's plan lack § 1325(a)(3) good faith? See *In re Hughes*, 98 B.R. 784 (Bankr. S.D. Ohio 1989).

E. PAYMENT OF UNSECURED CLAIMS IN CHAPTER 11

Payments to unsecured creditors in Chapter 11 are governed by the plan, as they are in Chapter 13, but Chapter 11 imposes no disposable income test. Classes of creditors in Chapter 11 get to vote on the plan, with each creditor in the class voting in proportion to the dollar amount of debt owed to that creditor. (A case later in this Chapter,

Kane v. Johns–Manville Corp., discusses Chapter 11's voting requirements in further detail.) Any treatment under the plan is permissible if the affected creditors agree to it. If a creditor votes against the plan, however, Chapter 11 imposes a "best interests" test much like the one in Chapter 13—the plan must pay the individual dissenting creditor as much as that creditor would have received in a Chapter 7. See § 1129-(a)(7)(A)(ii). The Code also permits the debtor to confirm a plan over the objection of certain *classes* of creditors; when the dissenting class is unsecured, the "absolute priority rule" requires the debtor either to pay those claims in full or leave shareholders with nothing. All of these provisions are covered in detail in Chapter 8 of this casebook.

Note on Original Issue Discount and § 502(b)(2)

In today's financial market, debt instruments are often issued for less than their face values. These instruments include zero coupon bonds, which are issued with a deep discount and no stated interest rate, and junk bonds, which are issued for less than the face amount in order to compensate the purchaser for the risk of nonpayment not fully covered by the stated interest rate. The difference between the amount received by the issuer and the face amount the issuer must pay upon maturity is called "original issue discount" (OID). OID is additional interest, paid when the stated rate of interest, if any, is too low to compensate the purchaser for the risks associated with the particular issue.

Assume, for example, that a one-year debt instrument with a face amount of $1,000 is issued for $910. Even if no interest is stated, as with a zero coupon note, the additional $90 is obviously interest and the rate is clearly close to 10%. The bankruptcy problem arises because § 502(b)(2) bars claims for unmatured interest. If bankruptcy is filed immediately after issue of the note, does the purchaser have a claim for $1,000 or only for $910? If bankruptcy is filed six months after issue, is the claim $1,000 or only $955?

The Second Circuit examined OID in *Official Committee of Unsecured Creditors of LTV Steel Co. v. Valley Fidelity Bank & Trust Co. (In re Chateaugay Corp.)*, 961 F.2d 378 (2d Cir.1992). In that case, the debtor replaced old debentures with new notes, prepetition, receiving 89% of the face value of the old debentures. The debtor sought an order disallowing claims for unamortized OID. The Second Circuit agreed with the debtor that § 502(b)(2) is applicable to OID:

> Original issue discount results when a bond is issued for less than its face value. The discount, which compensates for a stated interest rate that the market deems too low, equals the difference between a bond's face amount (stated principal amount) and the proceeds, prior to issuance expenses, received by the issuer. OID is amortized, for accounting and tax purposes, over the life of the bond,

with the face value generally paid back to the bondholders on the maturity date. If the debtor meets with financial trouble and turns to the bankruptcy court for protection, as in the present case, then OID comes into play as one of the factors determining the amount of the bondholder's allowable claim in bankruptcy.

* * * The first question we face is whether unamortized OID is "unmatured interest" within the meaning of § 502(b)(2). We conclude that it is. As a matter of economic definition, OID constitutes interest. Moreover, the Bankruptcy Code's legislative history makes inescapable the conclusion that OID is interest within the meaning of § 502(b)(2). The House committee report on that section explains:

> Interest disallowed under this paragraph includes postpetition interest that is not yet due and payable, and any portion of prepaid interest that represents an original discounting of the claim, yet that would not have been earned on the date of bankruptcy. For example, a claim on a $1,000 note issued the day before bankruptcy would only be allowed to the extent of the cash actually advanced. If the original issue discount was 10% so that the cash advanced was only $900, then notwithstanding the face amount of [the] note, only $900 would be allowed. If $900 was advanced under the note some time before bankruptcy, the interest component of the note would have to be pro-rated and disallowed to the extent it was for interest after the commencement of the case.

H.R. Rep. No. 95–595 at 352–53, *reprinted in* 1978 U.S.C.C.A.N. at 6308–09.

* * *

A debtor in financial trouble may seek to avoid bankruptcy through a consensual out-of-court workout. Such a recapitalization, when it involves publicly traded debt, often takes the form of a debt-for-debt exchange, whereby bondholders exchange their old bonds for new bonds. The debtor hopes that the exchange, by changing the terms of the debt, will enable the debtor to avoid default. The bondholders hope that by increasing the likelihood of payment on their bonds, the exchange will benefit them as well. The debtor and its creditors share an interest in achieving a successful restructuring of the debtor's financial obligations in order to avoid the uncertainties and daunting transaction costs of bankruptcy.

An exchange offer made by a financially troubled company can be either a "fair market value exchange" or a "face value exchange." In a fair market value exchange, an existing debt instrument is exchanged for a new one with a reduced principal amount, determined by the market value at which the existing instrument is trading. By offering a fair market value exchange, an issuer seeks to reduce its overall debt obligations. Usually, this is sought only by companies in severe financial distress. A face value exchange, by contrast, involves the substitution of new indebtedness for an existing debenture, modifying terms or conditions but not reducing the principal amount of the debt. A relatively healthy company faced with liquidity problems may offer a face value exchange to obtain short-term relief while remaining fully liable for the original funds borrowed.

The question is whether a face value exchange generates new OID. The bankruptcy court, in an opinion endorsed by the district court, held that it does. The court reasoned that, by definition, OID arises whenever a bond is issued for less than its face amount, and that in LTV's debt-for-debt exchange, the issue price of the New Notes was the fair market value of the Old Debentures. The court therefore concluded that the New Notes were issued at a discount equaling the difference between their face value and the fair market value of the Old Debentures.

The bankruptcy court's reasoning leaves us unpersuaded. While its application of the definition of OID to exchange offers may seem irrefutable at first glance, we believe the bankruptcy court's logic ignores the importance of context, and does not make sense if one takes into account the strong bankruptcy policy in favor of the speedy, inexpensive, negotiated resolution of disputes, that is an out-of-court or common law composition. If unamortized OID is unallowable in bankruptcy, and if exchanging debt increases the amount of OID, then creditors will be disinclined to cooperate in a consensual workout that might otherwise have rescued a borrower from the precipice of bankruptcy. We must consider the ramifications of a rule that places a creditor in the position of choosing whether to cooperate with a struggling debtor, when such cooperation might make the creditor's claims in the event of bankruptcy smaller than they would have been had the creditor refused to cooperate. The bankruptcy court's ruling places creditors in just such a position, and unreversed would likely result in fewer out-of-court debt exchanges and more Chapter 11 filings. Just as that ruling creates a disincentive for creditors to cooperate with a troubled debtor, it grants a corresponding windfall both to holdouts who refuse to cooperate and to an issuer that files for bankruptcy subsequent to a debt exchange.

The bankruptcy court's decision might make sense in the context of a fair market value exchange, where the corporation's overall debt obligations are reduced. In a face value exchange such as LTV's, however, it is unsupportable.

Id. at 380–82.

F. TREATMENT OF UNLIQUIDATED AND CONTINGENT CLAIMS

Although the Code defines "claim" broadly, to include obligations that are "contingent," "disputed" and "unliquidated," it does not define these terms. Consider a lawsuit brought against the debtor that has not been resolved by the time bankruptcy is filed. Because the debtor's obligation to the creditor, if any, has not been fixed, the claim is "unliquidated." If the debtor takes the position that nothing is owed the creditor at all, that claim is also "disputed." Some obligations depend upon the happening of a future event. For example, the debtor may have endorsed a promissory note as an accommodation party; liability does not arise unless the maker fails to pay. Because the debtor's liability arises only if a condition precedent occurs, the holder of the note has a "contingent" claim. (We have already seen the requirement that a claim be noncontingent in connection with Chapter 13 eligibility, § 109(e), and in connection with the filing of involuntary petitions, § 303(b)(1).)

Under pre-Code law, courts excluded most claims that were not fixed and undisputed. The holders of such claims could not share in the distribution of the debtor's assets, although they could pursue their rights against the debtor after the case was closed. This result was unfair to both the debtor and the creditor. A corporation that successfully reorganized or an individual with post-bankruptcy assets would be forced to pay the creditor 100% of its claim after the case, rather than the pro rata share the creditor would have received in bankruptcy. That jeopardized the fresh start Congress intended bankruptcy to provide. If the debtor was a corporation that liquidated or an individual with no post-bankruptcy assets, then the creditor at issue would receive no pro rata share during the case and nothing thereafter, and other creditors in the case would receive a dividend undiminished by the additional claim.

The Code drafters responded with § 101(5), which we have already seen, and with § 502(c), which directs the bankruptcy court to estimate contingent or unliquidated claims for the purpose of allowance if fixing or liquidating such claims would unduly delay administration of the case. The major practical effect of allowing a claim in Chapter 11 is to permit the creditor to vote on confirmation of the debtor's Chapter 11 reorganization plan and to receive payments under the confirmed plan. Once a plan is confirmed, debts that arose before bankruptcy are discharged under § 1141(d). Estimation under § 502(c), therefore, appears to constitute a final adjudication of the claim.

Courts have consistently asserted otherwise, however, stating that estimation does not fix ultimate liability:

> At an estimation hearing, the bankruptcy court would not decide liability or assign a permanently fixed value for the claim. Rather, [the court] would estimate the *likelihood* of liability and the *probable* value of that liability. The estimated amount would be the amount that claimants would be entitled to vote for or against confirmation of [the debtor's] reorganization plan. If the plan is confirmed the estimated amount would be set aside pending the determination of liability and the liquidation of the claim, which would not occur in a bankruptcy court. If liability is ultimately found, claimants would then be able to receive payment up to the amount of the judgment or the estimated value, whichever is lower.

In re Baldwin–United Corp., 57 B.R. 751, 758 (S.D. Ohio 1985). Although the court in *Baldwin-United* suggested that the estimated value may provide a *ceiling* on the claim, estimation may be for the purposes of confirmation and voting, but not for the purposes of distribution.

Another common § 502(c) challenge is to the method by which the bankruptcy court estimates a contingent or unliquidated claim. Estimation, as the following cases illustrate, is anything but simple.

These cases address two issues—the procedure a bankruptcy court should use to estimate contingent and unliquidated claims, and the purposes for which a claim is estimated.

BITTNER v. BORNE CHEMICAL CO.

United States Court of Appeals, Third Circuit, 1982.
691 F.2d 134.

GIBBONS, Circuit Judge.

Stockholders of The Rolfite Company appeal from the judgment of the district court, affirming the decision of the bankruptcy court to assign a zero value to their claims in the reorganization proceedings of Borne Chemical Company, Inc. (Borne) under Chapter 11 of the Bankruptcy Code (Code). Since the bankruptcy court neither abused its discretionary authority to estimate the value of the claims pursuant to § 502(c)(1) nor relied on clearly erroneous findings of fact, we affirm.

I.

Prior to filing its voluntary petition under Chapter 11 of the Code, Borne commenced a state court action against Rolfite for the alleged pirating of trade secrets and proprietary information from Borne. The Rolfite Company filed a counterclaim, alleging, *inter alia*, that Borne had tortiously interfered with a proposed merger between Rolfite and the Quaker Chemical Corporation (Quaker) by unilaterally terminating a contract to manufacture Rolfite products and by bringing its suit. Sometime after Borne filed its Chapter 11 petition, the Rolfite stockholders sought relief from the automatic stay so that the state court proceedings might be continued. Borne then filed a motion to disallow temporarily the Rolfite claims until they were finally liquidated in the state court. The bankruptcy court lifted the automatic stay but also granted Borne's motion to disallow temporarily the claims, extending the time within which such claims could be filed and allowed if they should be eventually liquidated.

Upon denial of their motion to stay the hearing on confirmation of Borne's reorganization plan, the Rolfite stockholders appealed to the district court, which vacated the temporary disallowance order and directed the bankruptcy court to hold an estimation hearing. The parties agreed to establish guidelines for the submission of evidence at the hearing, and, in accordance with this agreement, the bankruptcy court relied on the parties' choice of relevant pleadings and other documents related to the state court litigation, and on briefs and oral argument. After weighing the evidence, the court assigned a zero value to the Rolfite claims and reinstated its earlier order to disallow temporarily the claims until such time as they might be liquidated in the state court, in effect requiring a waiver of discharge of the Rolfite claims from Borne. Upon appeal, the district court affirmed.

II.

Section 502(c) of the Code * * * [and] the Rules of Bankruptcy Procedure * * * are silent as to the manner in which contingent or unliquidated claims are to be estimated. Despite the lack of express direction on the matter, we are persuaded that Congress intended the procedure to be undertaken initially by the bankruptcy judges, using whatever method is best suited to the particular contingencies at issue. The principal consideration must be an accommodation to the underlying purposes of the Code. It is conceivable that in rare and unusual cases arbitration or even a jury trial on all or some of the issues may be necessary to obtain a reasonably accurate evaluation of the claims.

Such methods, however, usually will run counter to the efficient administration of the bankrupt's estate and where there is sufficient evidence on which to base a reasonable estimate of the claim, the bankruptcy judge should determine the value. In so doing, the court is bound by the legal rules which may govern the ultimate value of the claim. For example, when the claim is based on an alleged breach of contract, the court must estimate its worth in accordance with accepted contract law. However, there are no other limitations on the court's authority to evaluate the claim save those general principles which should inform all decisions made pursuant to the Code.

* * *

According to the Rolfite stockholders, the estimate which § 502(c)(1) requires is the present value of the probability that appellants will be successful in their state court action. Thus, if the bankruptcy court should determine as of this date that the Rolfite stockholders' case is not supported by a preponderance or 51% of the evidence but merely by 40%, they apparently would be entitled to have 40% of their claims allowed during the reorganization proceedings, subject to modification if and when the claims are liquidated in state court. The Rolfite stockholders contend that instead of estimating their claims in this manner, the bankruptcy court assessed the ultimate merits and, believing that they could not establish their case by a preponderance of the evidence, valued the claims at zero.

We note first that the bankruptcy court did not explicitly draw the distinction that the Rolfite stockholders make. Assuming however that the bankruptcy court did estimate their claims according to their ultimate merits rather than the present value of the probability that they would succeed in their state court action, we cannot find that such a valuation method is an abuse of the discretion conferred by § 502(c)(1).

The validity of this estimation must be determined in light of the policy underlying reorganization proceedings. In Chapter 11 of the Code, Congress addressed the complex issues which are raised when a corporation faces mounting financial problems.

> The modern corporation is a complex and multi-faceted entity. Most corporations do not have a significant market share of the lines of business in which they compete. The success, and even the survival, of a corporation in contemporary markets depends on three elements: First, the ability to attract and hold skilled management; second, the ability to obtain credit; and third, the

> corporation's ability to project to the public an image of vitality. * * *
>
> One cannot overemphasize the advantages of speed and simplicity to both creditors and debtors. Chapter XI allows a debtor to negotiate a plan outside of court and, having reached a settlement with a majority in number and amount of each class of creditors, permits the debtor to bind all unsecured creditors to the terms of the arrangement. From the perspective of creditors, early confirmation of a plan of arrangement: first, generally reduces administrative expenses which have priority over the claims of unsecured creditors; second, permits creditors to receive prompt distributions on their claims with respect to which interest does not accrue after the filing date; and third, increases the ultimate recovery on creditor claims by minimizing the adverse effect on the business which often accompanies efforts to operate an enterprise under the protection of the Bankruptcy Act.

124 Cong. Rec. H 11101–H 11102 (daily ed. Sept. 28, 1978) (statement of Rep. D. Edwards of California, floor manager for bankruptcy legislation in the House of Representatives). Thus, in order to realize the goals of Chapter 11, a reorganization must be accomplished quickly and efficiently.

If the bankruptcy court estimated the value of the Rolfite stockholders' claims according to the ultimate merits of their state court action, such a valuation method is not inconsistent with the principles which imbue Chapter 11. Those claims are contingent[5] and unliquidated. According to the bankruptcy court's findings of fact, the Rolfite stockholders' chances of ultimately succeeding in the state court action are uncertain at best. Yet, if the court had valued the Rolfite stockholders' claims according to the present probability of success, the Rolfite stockholders might well have acquired a significant, if not controlling, voice in the reorganization proceedings. The interests of those creditors with liquidated claims would have been subject to the Rolfite interests, despite the fact that the state court might ultimately decide against those interests after the reorganization. The bankruptcy court may well have decided that such a situation would at best unduly complicate the reorganization proceedings and at worst undermine Borne's

[5] The Rolfite stockholders assert that the claims are not contingent since they are not dependent on some future event which may never occur. In as much as the very existence of the claims in the reorganization proceeding is dependent on a favorable decision by the state court, the Rolfite stockholders are clearly mistaken.

attempts to rehabilitate its business and preserve its assets for the benefit of its creditors and employees.[7] By valuing the ultimate merits of the Rolfite stockholders' claims at zero, and temporarily disallowing them until the final resolution of the state action, the bankruptcy court avoided the possibility of a protracted and inequitable reorganization proceeding while ensuring that Borne will be responsible to pay a dividend on the claims in the event that the state court decides in the Rolfite stockholders' favor. Such a solution is consistent with the Chapter 11 concerns of speed and simplicity but does not deprive the Rolfite stockholders of the right to recover on their contingent claims against Borne.

III.

* * *

[T]he Rolfite counterclaim in the state action lacked legal merit. Faced with only the remote possibility that the state court would find otherwise, the bankruptcy court correctly valued the claims at zero. On the basis of the court's subsidiary findings, such an estimation was consistent both with the claims' present value and with the court's assessment of the ultimate merits.

* * *

Questions

1. What sort of procedure does *Bittner* contemplate for purposes of estimation?

2. Is the court correct, as it asserted in footnote 5, that a claim is contingent if it has not yet been ruled upon favorably by a state court?

3. Do you agree that a claim should be disallowed if, in the bankruptcy court's judgment, the creditor has only a 49% chance of winning the state court suit?

4. For what purpose(s) did the court value the claims at zero? Did the court disallow the claims forever and for all purposes? What if the creditors

---

[7] Certainly this consideration played a role in the bankruptcy court's initial decision to disallow the claims. According to the court, "[T]o allow the hotly disputed claims, both present and prospective, herein referenced, would be for all practical purposes to doom Borne's rehabilitation efforts, now nearing their final stages, defeating the very purpose of reorganization."

obtained relief from the stay and later won the state suit? After this ruling, would the creditors have any reason to continue prosecution of the state suit?

KANE v. JOHNS–MANVILLE CORP.

United States Court of Appeals, Second Circuit, 1988.
843 F.2d 636.

JON O. NEWMAN, Circuit Judge.

This appeal challenges the lawfulness of the reorganization plan of the Johns–Manville Corporation ("Manville"), a debtor in one of the nation's most significant Chapter 11 bankruptcy proceedings. Lawrence Kane, on behalf of himself and a group of other personal injury claimants, appeals from an order of the District Court for the Southern District of New York (Whitman Knapp, Judge) affirming an order of the Bankruptcy Court (Burton R. Lifland, Chief Judge) that confirmed a Second Amended Plan of Reorganization (the "Plan"). Kane and the group of 765 individuals he represents (collectively "Kane") are persons with asbestos-related disease who had filed personal injury suits against Manville prior to Manville's Chapter 11 petition. The suits were stayed, and Kane and other claimants presently afflicted with asbestos-related disease were designated as Class–4 creditors in the reorganization proceedings. Kane now objects to confirmation of the reorganization Plan on [the grounds that] the voting procedures used in approving the Plan violated the Bankruptcy Code and due process requirements * * *. [W]e reject on the merits * * *. The order of the District Court affirming the Bankruptcy Court's confirmation of the Plan is affirmed.

BACKGROUND

* * *

Because future asbestos-related liability was the *raison d'etre* of the Manville reorganization, an important question at the initial stages of the proceedings concerned the representation and treatment of what were termed "future asbestos health claimants" ("future claimants"). The future claimants were persons who had been exposed to Manville's asbestos prior to the August 1982 petition date but had not yet shown any signs of disease at that time. Since the future claimants were not yet ill at the time the Chapter 11 proceedings were commenced, none had filed claims against Manville, and their identities were unknown. An Asbestos Health Committee was appointed to represent all personal injury claimants, but the Committee took the position that it represented the interests only of "present claimants," persons who, prior to the petition date, had been exposed to Manville asbestos and had already developed an asbestos-related disease. The Committee declined to represent the future claimants. Other parties in the proceedings, recognizing that an effective reorganization would have to account for the future asbestos victims as well as the present ones, moved the Bankruptcy Court to appoint a legal guardian for the future claimants. The Bankruptcy Court granted the motion, reasoning that regardless of whether the future claimants technically had "claims" cognizable in bankruptcy proceedings, *see* [§ 101(5)], they were at least "parties in interest" under § 1109(b) of the Code and were therefore entitled to a voice in the proceedings. The Court appointed a Legal Representative to participate on behalf of the future claimants. Additionally, the Court invited any person who had been exposed to Manville's asbestos but had not developed an illness to participate in the proceedings, and two such persons appeared.

The Second Amended Plan of Reorganization resulted from more than four years of negotiations among Manville, the Asbestos Health Committee, the Legal Representative, the Equity Security Holders' Committee, and other groups interested in the estate. The cornerstone of the Plan is the Asbestos Health Trust (the "Trust"), a mechanism designed to satisfy the claims of all asbestos health victims, both present and future. The Trust is funded with the proceeds from Manville's settlements with its insurers; certain cash, receivables, and stock of the reorganized Manville Corporation; long term notes; and the right to receive up to 20% of Manville's yearly profits for as long as it takes to satisfy all health claims. According to the terms of the Trust, individuals with asbestos-related disease must first try to settle their claims by a mandatory exchange of settlement offers with Trust representatives. If a settlement cannot be reached, the claimant may elect mediation, binding arbitration, or traditional tort litigation. The claimant may collect from the Trust the full amount of whatever compensatory damages he is awarded. The only restriction on recovery is that the claimant may not obtain punitive damages.

The purpose of the Trust is to provide a means of satisfying Manville's ongoing personal injury liability while allowing Manville to maximize its value by continuing as an ongoing concern. To fulfill this purpose, the Plan seeks to ensure that health claims can be asserted only against the Trust and that Manville's operating entities will be protected from an onslaught of crippling lawsuits that could jeopardize the entire reorganization effort. To this end, the parties agreed that as a condition precedent to confirmation of the Plan, the Bankruptcy Court would issue an injunction channeling all asbestos-related personal injury claims to the Trust (the "Injunction"). The Injunction provides that asbestos health claimants may proceed only against the Trust to satisfy their claims and may not sue Manville, its other operating entities, and certain other specified parties, including Manville's insurers. Significantly, the Injunction applies to all health claimants, both present and future, regardless of whether they technically have dischargeable "claims" under the Code. The Injunction applies to any suit to recover "on or with respect to any Claim, Interest or Other Asbestos Obligation." "Claim" covers the present claimants, who are categorized as Class–4 unsecured creditors under the Plan and who have dischargeable "claims" within the meaning of [§ 101(5)]. The future claimants are subject to the Injunction under the rubric of "Other Asbestos Obligation," which is defined by the Plan as asbestos-related health liability caused by pre-petition exposure to Manville asbestos, regardless of when the individual develops clinically observable symptoms. Thus, while the future claimants are not given creditor status under the Plan, they are nevertheless treated identically to the present claimants by virtue of the Injunction, which channels all claims to the Trust.

The Plan was submitted to the Bankruptcy Court for voting in June of 1986. At that time relatively few present asbestos health claimants had appeared in the reorganization proceedings. Approximately 6,400 proofs of claims had been filed for personal injuries, which accounted for less than half of the more than 16,000 persons who had filed pre-petition personal injury suits against Manville. Moreover, Manville estimated that there were tens of thousands of additional present asbestos victims who had neither filed suits nor presented proofs of claims. Manville and the creditor constituencies agreed that as many present claimants as possible should be brought into the proceedings so that they could vote on the Plan. However, the parties were reluctant to embark on the standard Code procedure of establishing a bar date, soliciting proofs of claims, resolving all disputed claims on notice and hearing, and then weighting the votes by the amounts of the claims, as such a process could delay the reorganization for many years. To avoid this delay, the Bankruptcy Court adopted special voting procedures for Class 4. Manville was directed to undertake a comprehensive multi-media notice campaign to inform persons with present health claims of the pendency of the reorganization and their opportunity to participate. Potential health claimants who responded to the campaign were given a combined proof-of-claim-and-voting form in which each could present a medical diagnosis of his asbestos-related disease and vote to accept or reject the Plan. For voting purposes only, each claim was valued in the amount of one dollar. Claimants were informed that the proof-of-claim-and-voting form would be used only for voting and that to collect from the Trust, they would have to execute an additional proof of claim establishing the actual value of their damages.

The notice campaign produced a large number of present asbestos claimants. In all, 52,440 such claimants submitted proof-of-claim-and-voting forms. Of these, 50,275 or 95.8% approved the Plan, while 2,165 or 4.2% opposed it. In addition to these Class–4 claimants, all other classes of creditors also approved the Plan. Class 8, the common stockholders, opposed the Plan.

A confirmation hearing was held on December 16, 1986, at which Manville presented evidence regarding the feasibility and fairness of the Plan. Objections to confirmation were filed by several parties, including Kane. On December 18, 1986, the Bankruptcy Court issued a Determination of Confirmation Issues in which it rejected all objections to confirmation. With respect to Kane's challenge to the Injunction and the voting procedures, the Court relied primarily on its broad equitable powers to achieve reorganizations. * * * The Court entered an order confirming the Plan on December 22, 1986. Kane and others appealed. By order dated July 15, 1987, the District Court affirmed the Bankruptcy Court's confirmation order "for substantially the reasons set forth" in the Bankruptcy Judge's Determination of Confirmation Issues. This appeal followed.

DISCUSSION

* * *

B. Voting Procedures

Consideration of Kane's challenge to the voting procedures requires a brief outline of pertinent provisions of the Bankruptcy Code. A plan of reorganization must either be accepted by each impaired class of claims or interests, § 1129(a)(8), or meet certain rigid requirements with respect to each non-accepting class, § 1129(b) (so-called "cram down" provision). A class of creditors has accepted a plan under the Code "if such plan has been accepted by creditors * * * that hold at least two-thirds in amount and more than one-half in number of the allowed claims of such class held by creditors * * * that have accepted or rejected such plan." § 1126(c). Claims are "allowed" in the amount filed unless they are objected to by a party in interest, including the debtor or another creditor. § 502(a). * * *

Kane contends that the special Class–4 voting procedures adopted by the Bankruptcy Court violated his rights under the Code in several ways. First, since proofs of claims and votes were simultaneously solicited from present claimants in a combined mailing form, no creditor had an opportunity to object to the Class–4 members' claims before their votes were cast. Kane argues that this lack of opportunity to object prejudiced him because some of the claims might have been invalid and counting votes of those with invalid claims diluted his own vote. Second, Kane argues that the Bankruptcy Court improperly "allowed" claims for voting purposes in the arbitrary amount of one dollar, thereby depriving him of the opportunity to vote his claim weighted in the amount indicated in his proof of claim. By weighting all Class–4 votes equally, the Bankruptcy Court, in Kane's view, failed to adhere to the Code's voting scheme whereby a minority of class members with just over one third of the value of the total claims may reject a plan. Finally, Kane suggests that by assigning the one dollar value to all of the claims, the Bankruptcy Court might have discouraged Plan opponents with large claims from casting their votes since such opponents might have believed that, without the benefit of weighted voting, their opposition to the Plan would be futile.

Appellees respond that the Code is sufficiently flexible to accommodate the creative voting scheme used in this case. They argue primarily that the Code evinces a strong preference for facilitating reorganizations and that strict adherence to a weighted voting scheme would have been impractical in this case. Appellees point out that either the reorganization would have been delayed for years while the dollar value of every disputed health claim was determined or the vote would have been taken without contacting present health claimants other than the few who had voluntarily submitted proofs of claims, leaving a large group of important creditors disenfranchised. * * *

We need not decide whether the special Class–4 voting procedures violate the Code because, in view of the outcome of the vote, the alleged irregularities were at most harmless error. * * *

None of the procedures that Kane contends were required would have changed the outcome of the vote. With respect to denial of the opportunity to object to the Class–4 claims before they were voted, no substantial rights were impaired because Kane is unable to show that, had he been afforded a chance to object, any of the present health claims would have been excluded. The only objection Kane contends that he would have asserted is that the combined proof-of-claim-and-voting form approved by the Bankruptcy Court permitted a filing supported only by a written medical diagnosis of an asbestos-related condition without evidence that the claimant was exposed to Manville's product, as opposed to the product of some other company. However, it is clear from the record that this objection would have been unavailing. The combined proof-of-claim-and-voting form required anyone who had not already filed a lawsuit against Manville to submit a diagnosis of his disease *and* to represent that he had been exposed to Manville's product. Such a representation would have sufficed to warrant accepting the claim for voting purposes, especially in the absence of any particularized contrary evidence from Kane. In any event, since 95.8% of those Class–4 members who voted approved the Plan, the result would not have been different unless more than 90% of those who voted in favor had invalid claims, an improbable circumstance.

Similarly, Kane was not prejudiced by the assignment of a one dollar value to each claim. If we make the reasonable assumption that the percentage of claims that are valid is the same for "yes" votes and "no" votes, then the "no" votes would have to be at least ten times larger, on average, than the "yes" votes in order to change the result from what occurred with equal weighting of each vote. Nothing in the record gives any indication that such a large variation in claims existed, much less that the "no" votes were the larger claims. Indeed, it is safe to assume that if the procedures insisted upon by Kane had been used, all the votes would have still been weighted roughly the same since significant variations would not likely occur in the damages sustained by similar groups of people from similar kinds of injuries. Even if Kane is correct that some Plan opponents with larger claims were discouraged from voting, no prejudice occurred. Even if we make the unlikely assumption, favorable to Kane, that Plan opponents in Class 4, on average, had claims twice the size of the claims of Plan proponents, the number of "no" votes in this class would have had to increase nearly six times, from 2,165 to 12,569, in order to change the result. If there really were 12,569 Class–4 claimants opposed to the Plan, it is highly unlikely that 10,404 or 83% of them would have been discouraged from voting.

* * *

MINER, Circuit Judge, concurring.

* * *

By the time of the June 23, 1986 hearing held to consider the Disclosure Statement and the Second Amended and Restated Plan of

Reorganization filed by the debtors, approximately 6,400 proofs of claim had been submitted by asbestos health claimants for personal injuries. It was apparent at that juncture in the proceedings that the administration of the case would be delayed unduly if each of those unliquidated claims were to be considered separately for allowance purposes. Referring to the number of actual lawsuits then pending on behalf of asbestos health claimants, the bankruptcy judge observed that more than 16,500 hearings would be necessary "to treat each individual claim discretely." In the words of the debtors' attorney, "the practical effect of having to value each and every claim individually would * * * be delay[ ] beyond anybody's reasonable expectations and probably life-time." The problem of delay was even more apparent at the conclusion of the notice campaign, when proof-of-claim-and-voting forms had been received from 52,440 claimants.

Under the circumstances, the bankruptcy judge properly exercised his authority to estimate each of the claims at $1.00. The asbestos health claims were especially suited to estimation because of the uncertain nature of both liability and damages. Moreover, the very purpose of the reorganization would be defeated if each claim were to be considered separately for purposes of allowance and voting. Indeed, the delay entailed by such an approach would not only be fatal to the entire plan but might very well be fatal to any recovery for the claimants. Section 502(c)(1) is designed to forestall these types of consequences.

In any event, the assignment of a value of $1.00 per claim is merely the temporary allowance contemplated by Rule 3018(a), with the right reserved to each claimant to seek actual damages from the Asbestos Health Trust. Although the Rule calls for objections to the claims, followed by notice and hearing, before temporary allowances for voting purposes are made, there was substantial compliance with this requirement here. * * *

Notes and Problems

1. For what purpose(s) did the court set asbestosis victims' claims at $1.00? Is the court holding that they cannot be paid more than that? Is the court opening the door to trumped-up claims filed by people never exposed to asbestos?

2. Estimation under § 502(c) is mandatory only if liquidation in the usual way—by trial in a nonbankruptcy forum—would unduly delay the bankruptcy case. If resolution outside of bankruptcy is imminent, the bankruptcy court will lift the stay so that the nonbankruptcy court can complete its adjudi-

cation. See *Apex Oil Co. v. Stinnes Interoil, Inc. (In re Apex Oil Co.),* 107 B.R. 189 (E.D.Mo.1989).

3. The procedural rules granting bankruptcy judges jurisdiction over core proceedings arguably permit estimation of claims for purposes of distribution as well as allowance. The explicit prohibition against estimating personal injury tort and wrongful death claims for purposes of distribution, found in 28 U.S.C. § 157(b)(5), may be an implicit grant of jurisdiction to estimate all other claims for purposes of distribution. See *Matter of Poole Funeral Chapel, Inc.*, 63 B.R. 527, 533 (Bankr. N.D.Ala.1986).

4. *Kane* highlights the conflict between the rights of future claimants and the continued viability of a company made possible by a bankruptcy reorganization plan that binds all creditors with claims against the company. While binding future claimants to a Chapter 11 reorganization plan raises significant due process issues, the alternative may have far graver consequences. For example, if not included within a reorganization plan, future claimants may be shut off from recovery due to a lack of assets on the part of the debtor. On the other hand, a debtor whose assets are not depleted could be subjected to ongoing and unlimited liability far into the future. The experience of Johns–Manville, with 130,000 claimants filing suit against it by 1990 and an estimated liability of $8.8 billion, makes the former possibility far more likely than the latter. *Kane* describes the trust device, along with the channeling injunction, created to deal with the debtor's mass tort liabilities. These innovations alone would have made *Manville* one of the most important bankruptcy cases ever filed.

Congress recognized the creativity and utility of the *Manville* trust device. The 1994 Amendments adopted the trust device in § 524(g), which applies only to asbestos cases. The trust device remains available in other types of cases, however, through reasoned extensions of *Manville.*

5. Bank made an unsecured loan of $100,000 to Debtor Corporation. Paula Debtor, the president and sole shareholder of Debtor Corporation, guaranteed payment of the debt. Debtor Corporation defaulted on the obligation and filed a Chapter 7 case. It has assets sufficient to pay 25% of unsecured claims. Answer the following questions, using §§ 502(e) and 509.

a. Assume that Bank has been paid nothing on the debt and files a claim for $100,000. Paula Debtor also files a claim for $100,000. How are the claims handled?

b. Assume that Paula paid Bank in full before bankruptcy was filed. Which of them has an allowable claim in bankruptcy and for how much?

c. Assume that Paula paid Bank only $50,000 before bankruptcy was filed. Which of them has an allowable claim in bankruptcy and for how much?

ANDY CAPP

G. PRIORITIES

Despite bankruptcy's equality principle, some creditors are more equal than others. We already know that secured creditors are paid first, leaving unsecured creditors to share whatever is left. But some unsecured creditors are paid before the rest. These favored creditors are "priority" creditors. Bankruptcy's priorities are listed in § 507.

Under § 507, each level of claims is paid in full before any payment is made to the next lower priority level, as long as funds are sufficient. When funds are insufficient to pay all of the claims at a particular priority level, those claims are paid pro rata. Any claims at a lower priority level, as well as general unsecured claims having no priority, will get nothing.

In Chapter 11, priority claims in the first two levels must be paid in full and in cash on the effective date of the plan, unless the individual claimholder waives this requirement. The remaining priority claims must also be paid in full in cash on the plan's effective date unless the class of claimholders votes to accept payment over time. § 1129(a)(9). In Chapter 13, priority claims must be paid in full, although payment can be made over time, unless the claimholder agrees to different treatment. § 1322(a)(2).

Read § 507(a) and answer the following Problems.

Problems

1. Joe Debtor, who practiced law as a professional corporation, had one office employee who earned $30,000 per year. When Debtor, P.C. filed

Chapter 11, it owed $5,000 in wages to the employee for work performed in the two months immediately preceding the filing. How much, if any, of the wage claim is entitled to a priority?

2. Assume that the employee from Problem # 1 continued to work for Debtor, P.C. for two months after bankruptcy was filed, but that the employee then quit in disgust because no wages were paid. What priority, if any, will the employee's claim for $5,000 in post-petition wages enjoy? See § 503(b).

3. Customer ordered a custom-made sofa for his den from Furniture Manufacturer, Inc. The price of the sofa was $2,200 and Customer paid 50% down. Before the sofa was delivered, Furniture Manufacturer, Inc. filed Chapter 7. Customer received neither refund nor sofa. What priority, if any, will Customer's claim enjoy in Furniture Manufacturer, Inc.'s bankruptcy?

4. Debtor owed federal income taxes for the tax years 1995, 1996, 1997 and 1998. The taxes for each year were due on April 15th of the next year. Debtor received no extensions and the IRS filed no notice of tax lien. What priority, if any, will the tax claims enjoy if Debtor files bankruptcy on April 10, 2000? Does it matter whether Debtor filed no returns at all, or filed returns but included no checks?

Administrative expenses, *i.e.*, expenses of bankruptcy itself, are paid first under § 507(a). You should not be surprised to learn that fees for the trustee and for attorneys enjoy a first priority. Given the favorable relative position administrative expenses enjoy, creditors with a possible entitlement to that status have a strong incentive to press their argument.

Although the following case arose under the Bankruptcy Act, it is the seminal case on this issue and maintains its vitality.

READING CO. v. BROWN

Supreme Court of the United States, 1968.
391 U.S. 471, 88 S.Ct. 1759, 20 L.Ed.2d 751.

MR. JUSTICE HARLAN delivered the opinion of the Court.

On November 16, 1962, I. J. Knight Realty Corporation filed a petition for an arrangement under Chapter XI of the Bankruptcy Act. The same day, the District Court appointed a receiver, Francis Shunk Brown, a respondent here. The receiver was authorized to conduct the debtor's business, which consisted principally of leasing the debtor's only significant asset, an eight-story industrial structure located in Philadelphia.

On January 1, 1963, the building was totally destroyed by a fire which spread to adjoining premises and destroyed real and personal property of petitioner Reading Company and others. On April 3, 1963, petitioner filed a claim for $559,730.83 in the arrangement, based on the asserted negligence of the receiver. It was styled a claim for "administrative expenses" of the arrangement. Other fire loss claimants filed 146 additional claims of a similar nature. The total of all such claims was in excess of $3,500,000, substantially more than the total assets of the debtor.

On May 14, 1963, Knight Realty was voluntarily adjudicated a bankrupt and respondent receiver was subsequently elected trustee in bankruptcy. The claims of petitioner and others thus became claims for administration expenses in bankruptcy which are given first priority under § 64a(1) of the Bankruptcy Act.[a] The trustee moved to expunge the claims on the ground that they were not for expenses of administration. It was agreed that the decision whether petitioner's claim is provable as an expense of administration would establish the status of the other 146 claims. It was further agreed that, for purposes of deciding whether the claim is provable, it would be assumed that the damage to petitioner's property resulted from the negligence of the receiver and a workman he employed. The United States, holding a claim for unpaid prearrangement taxes admittedly superior to the claims of general creditors and inferior to claims for administration expenses, entered the case on the side of the trustee.

The referee disallowed the claim for administration expenses. He also ruled that petitioner's claim was not provable as a general claim against the estate, a ruling challenged by neither side. On petition for review, the referee was upheld by the District Court. On appeal, the Court of Appeals for the Third Circuit, sitting *en banc*, affirmed the decision of the District Court by a 4–3 vote. We granted certiorari because the issue is important in the administration of the bankruptcy laws and is one of first impression in this Court. For reasons to follow, we reverse.

* * *

[a] Section 64a of the Bankruptcy Act was the predecessor to § 507(a)(1) of the Code. The two provisions are substantially alike. Eds.

The question in this case is whether the negligence of a receiver administering an estate under a Chapter XI arrangement gives rise to an "actual and necessary" cost of operating the debtor's business. The Act does not define "actual and necessary," nor has any case directly in point been brought to our attention. We must, therefore, look to the general purposes of § 64a, Chapter XI, and the Bankruptcy Act as a whole.

The trustee contends that the relevant statutory objectives are (1) to facilitate rehabilitation of insolvent businesses and (2) to preserve a maximum of assets for distribution among the general creditors should the arrangement fail. He therefore argues that first priority as "necessary" expenses should be given only to those expenditures without which the insolvent business could not be carried on. For example, the trustee would allow first priority to contracts entered into by the receiver because suppliers, employees, landlords, and the like would not enter into dealings with a debtor in possession or a receiver of an insolvent business unless priority is allowed. The trustee would exclude all negligence claims, on the theory that first priority for them is not necessary to encourage third parties to deal with an insolvent business, that first priority would reduce the amount available for the general creditors, and that first priority would discourage general creditors from accepting arrangements.

In our view the trustee has overlooked one important, and here decisive, statutory objective: fairness to all persons having claims against an insolvent. Petitioner suffered grave financial injury from what is here agreed to have been the negligence of the receiver and a workman. It is conceded that, in principle, petitioner has a right to recover for that injury from their "employer," the business under arrangement, upon the rule of *respondeat superior*. Respondents contend, however, that petitioner is in no different position from anyone else injured by a person with scant assets: its right to recover exists in theory but is not enforceable in practice.

That, however, is not an adequate description of petitioner's position. At the moment when an arrangement is sought, the debtor is insolvent. Its existing creditors hope that by partial or complete postponement of their claims they will, through successful rehabilitation, eventually recover from the debtor either in full or in larger proportion than they would in immediate bankruptcy. Hence the present petitioner did not merely suffer injury at the hands of an insolvent business: it had an insolvent business thrust upon it by operation of law. That business will, in any event, be unable to pay its fire debts in full. But the question is whether the fire claimants should be subordinated to, should share equally with, or should collect ahead of those creditors for whose benefit the continued operation of the business (which unfortunately led to a fire instead of the hoped-for rehabilitation) was allowed.

* * *

The trustee contends that if the present claims are not provable in bankruptcy they would survive as claims against the shell. He also suggests that petitioner may be able to recover from the receiver personally, or out of such bond as he posted. Without deciding whether these possible avenues are indeed open, we merely note that they do not serve the present purpose. The "master," liable for the negligence of the "servant," in this case was the business operating under a Chapter XI arrangement for the benefit of creditors and with the hope of rehabilitation. That benefit and that rehabilitation are worthy objectives. But it would be inconsistent both with the principle of *respondeat superior* and with the rule of fairness in bankruptcy to seek these objectives at the cost of excluding tort creditors of the arrangement from its assets, or totally subordinating the claims of those on whom the arrangement is imposed to the claims of those for whose benefit it is instituted.

* * *

In any event, we see no reason to indulge in a strained construction of the relevant provisions, for we are persuaded that it is theoretically sounder, as well as linguistically more comfortable, to treat tort claims arising during an arrangement as actual and necessary expenses of the arrangement rather than debts of the bankrupt. In the first place, in considering whether those injured by the operation of the business during an arrangement should share equally with, or recover ahead of, those for whose benefit the business is carried on, the latter seems more natural and just. Existing creditors are, to be sure, in a dilemma not of their own making, but there is no obvious reason why they should be allowed to attempt to escape that dilemma at the risk of imposing it on others equally innocent.

More directly in point is the possibility of insurance. An arrangement may provide for suitable coverage, and the court below recognized that the cost of insurance against tort claims arising during an arrangement is an administrative expense payable in full under § 64a(1) before dividends to general creditors. It is of course obvious that proper insurance premiums must be given priority, else insurance could not be obtained; and if a receiver or debtor in possession is to be encouraged to obtain insurance in adequate amounts, the claims against which insurance is obtained should be potentially payable in full. In the present case, it is argued, the fire was of such incredible magnitude that adequate insurance probably could not have been obtained and in any event would have been foolish; this may be true, as it is also true that allowance of a first priority to the fire claimants here will still only mean recovery by them of a fraction of their damages. In the usual case where damages are within insurable limits, however, the rule of full recovery for torts is demonstrably sounder.

Although there appear to be no cases dealing with tort claims arising during Chapter XI proceedings, decisions in analogous cases suggest that "actual and necessary costs" should include costs ordinarily incident to operation of a business, and not be limited to costs without which rehabilitation would be impossible. It has long been the rule of equity receiverships that torts of the receivership create claims against the receivership itself; in those cases the statutory limitation to "actual and necessary costs" is not involved, but the explicit recognition extended to tort claims in those cases weighs heavily in favor of considering them within the general category of costs and expenses.

In some cases arising under Chapter XI it has been recognized that "actual and necessary costs" are not limited to those claims which the business must be able to pay in full if it is to be able to deal at all. For example, state and federal taxes accruing during a receivership have been held to be actual and necessary costs of an arrangement. The United States, recognizing and supporting these holdings, agrees with petitioner that costs that form "an integral and essential element of the continuation of the business" are necessary expenses even though priority is not necessary *to* the continuation of the business. Thus the Government suggests that "an injury to a member of the public—a business invitee—who was injured while on the business premises during an arrangement would present a completely different problem [i.e., could qualify for first priority]" although it is not suggested that priority is needed to encourage invitees to enter the premises.

The United States argues, however, that each tort claim "must be analyzed in its own context." Apart from the fact that it has been assumed throughout this case that all 147 claimants were on an equal footing and it is not very helpful to suggest here for the first time a rule by which lessees, invitees, and neighbors have different rights, we perceive no distinction. No principle of tort law of which we are aware offers guidance for distinguishing, within the class of torts committed by receivers while acting in furtherance of the business, between those "integral" to the business and those that are not.

We hold that damages resulting from the negligence of a receiver acting within the scope of his authority as receiver give rise to "actual and necessary costs" of a Chapter XI arrangement.

The judgment of the Court of Appeals is reversed, and the case remanded for further proceedings consistent with this opinion.

It is so ordered.

MR. CHIEF JUSTICE WARREN, with whom MR. JUSTICE DOUGLAS joins, dissenting.

In my opinion, the Court has misinterpreted the term "costs and expenses of administration" as intended by § 64a(1) of the Bankruptcy Act and, by deviating from the natural meaning of those words, has given the administrative cost priority an unwarranted application. The effect of the holding in this case is that the negligence of a workman may completely wipe out the claims of all other classes of public and private creditors. I do not believe Congress intended to accord tort claimants such a preference. Accordingly, I would affirm the judgment below.

On other occasions, this Court has observed that "[t]he theme of the Bankruptcy Act is 'equality of distribution'; and if one claimant is to be preferred over the others, the purpose should be clear from the statute." *Nathanson v. NLRB*, 344 U.S. 25, 29 (1952). More particularly, the Act expressly directs that eligible negligence claims are to share *equally* with the unsecured claims in a pro rata distribution of the debtor's nonexempt assets. Departing from this statutory scheme, the Court today singles out one class of tort claims for special treatment. After today's decision, the status of a tort claimant depends entirely upon whether he is fortunate enough to have been injured after rather than before a receiver has been appointed. And if the claimant is in the select class, he may be permitted to exhaust the estate to the exclusion of the general creditors as well as of the wage claims and government tax claims for which Congress has shown an unmistakable preference. In my view, this result frustrates rather than serves the underlying purposes of a Chapter XI proceeding, and I would not reach it without a clear indication that Congress so intended.

Congress enacted Chapter XI as an alternative to straight bankruptcy for individuals and small businesses which might be successfully rehabilitated instead of being subjected to economically wasteful liquidation. The success of a Chapter XI proceeding depends largely on two factors: first, whether creditors will take the chance of permitting an arrangement; second, whether other businesses will continue to deal with the distressed business. With respect to the first of these considerations, today's decision will undoubtedly discourage creditors from permitting arrangements, because it subjects them to unpredictable and probably uninsurable tort liability. I do not believe the statutory language requires such an interpretation. I would construe § 64a(1) with reference to the second consideration mentioned above. In my opinion, the Court would reach a result more in line with congressional intent and the Bankruptcy Act generally by regarding as administrative costs only those costs required for a smooth and successful arrangement. Accordingly, the administrative cost priority should be viewed as a guaranty to the receiver and those who deal with or are employed by him that they will be paid for their goods and services. Any broader interpretation will discourage creditors from permitting use of the rehabilitative machinery of Chapter XI and tend to force distressed businesses into straight bankruptcy.

It is equitable, the Court believes, that the general creditors (and wage and tax claimants) bear the loss in this case because they have "thrust" an insolvent business upon petitioner for their own benefit. I respectfully submit that this is a most unfair characterization of arrangements. An economically distressed businessman seeks an arrangement for his own and not for his creditors' benefit. Of course the creditors will benefit if the arrangement is successful, just as they would have benefited if the businessman had been successful without resorting to an arrangement. But a business in arrangement is no more thrust on the public than is any other business enterprise which is conducted for the mutual prosperity of the owners, the wage earners and the creditors. Realistically, the only difference is that a business administered under Chapter XI has not been prosperous. If the arrangement is successful, the owners, wage earners and creditors will all benefit; if it is not, they will all be injured. Thus, I would not distinguish in this case between petitioner and the other general creditors, none of whom was responsible for the catastrophe for which all of them must sustain some loss. Instead, in deciding this case, I would adhere to the Act's basic theme of equality of distribution.

The Court states that its decision will encourage Chapter XI receivers to obtain "adequate" insurance. The Court fairly well concedes, however, that in this case "adequate" insurance "probably could not have been obtained and in any event would have been foolish." In other words, so far as this Court knows, the insurance taken out by the receiver in this case was in fact "adequate," in the sense that no reasonable receiver could or should obtain fire insurance in the amount of $3,500,000 on the assumption that his workman might accidentally cause a fire of the proportions which occurred here. Moreover, quite apart from the case at bar, there is absolutely no indication that today's decision is needed to encourage receivers to obtain insurance. I see no basis in the Act or in sound policy for a ruling that the creditors of an estate under a Chapter XI arrangement become involuntary insurers against a liability which probably would not and should not be insurable by more traditional means.

The Court also relies, in my opinion mistakenly, upon analogies to equity receiverships. In reorganizations under Chapter X and § 77, Congress has directed the courts to apply the rules of priority developed in equity. However, arrangements under Chapter XI are governed strictly by the statutory priorities fixed by § 64a. These statutory priorities differ in many respects from those applicable to equity receiverships, and they have been amended repeatedly to narrow the class of claimants which may participate ahead of the general creditors. Furthermore, even in the case of § 77 reorganizations where the priorities developed in equity are controlling, Congress has specifically provided for one exception to the rule that tort claimants are to be treated as general creditors. That exception is in favor of a narrowly defined class of claimants. Congress has not expressly provided a similar exception to cover petitioner's tort claim, and I would not infer one.

* * *

I see no basis in equity or in the statutory language or purpose for subjecting every class of creditors except petitioner's to a loss caused by the negligence of a workman. Consequently, I would construe "actual and necessary costs" as limited to those costs actually and necessarily incurred in preserving the debtor's estate and administering it for the benefit of the creditors. I would not include ordinary negligence claims within this class.

Notes and Problems

1. Thomas H. Jackson analyzed the viewpoints of the majority and dissent as follows:

> It is fruitful to recharacterize the underlying dispute in *Reading Co. v. Brown* as essentially one of whether the transfer of ownership of the corporation to its creditors should be deemed to occur at the moment bankruptcy is filed or at the moment the process is over. Consider, first, the case of a liquidating corporation. Such a corporation, if it were to dissolve outside bankruptcy, would parcel out its assets as the final step in the dissolution process. Tort claims that accrued after the decision to dissolve but before the actual dissolution would presumably share pro rata with the other general creditors in the distribution. No postdissolution torts would be committed by the corporation because by definition the corporation would no longer exist.
>
> This analogy supports the dissenting view of Chief Justice Warren. The bankruptcy process may be part of a *decision* to dissolve, but its commencement is not tantamount to a dissolution. Justice Harlan's view is supported by a slightly different analogy whereby the decision to invoke bankruptcy is itself a triggering event that transfers ownership of the corporation to its creditors. The general creditors are treated as the new equity owners of the corporation. The corporation in bankruptcy is then like a corporation held by shareholders. Any debts that the corporation incurs during the bankruptcy proceeding have priority over prepetition unsecured claims because debts take priority over equity claims. Upon completion of the bankruptcy process and dissolution of the corporation the tort claims that arose during the bankruptcy proceeding would have priority over the prepetition claims of the general creditors, which are viewed, for purposes of bankruptcy law, as equity owners.
>
> * * *
>
> The selection between these competing scenarios should be based on minimizing the costs of a transition to the collective regime. The closest nonbankruptcy analogy in the case of business entities seems to be that in which the commencement of bankruptcy is viewed as the beginning of the process of dissolution or negotiation over the change of ownership, not its end. This conclusion would avoid the possibility that creditors would reject the collective procedure because they would fare worse than they would if they remained outside of bankruptcy. If, when creditors avoid using bankruptcy in converting ownership of the assets to themselves, tort claims that accrue during

> the transitional process share pro rata, use of bankruptcy to occasion that conversion should have no different attributes.
>
> This argument for pro rata treatment, however, only applies—as does Chief Justice Warren's dissent—to nonconsensual claims. The costs of bankruptcy procedures themselves are properly charged against the creditors. * * *
>
> Thus, although there is much to be said for Justice Harlan's analogy to a business with an all common capital stock structure—and hence for his conclusion that postpetition tort claimants are entitled to administrative expense priority—the analogy ultimately seems the less persuasive one.

Thomas H. Jackson, The Logic and Limits of Bankruptcy Law 154–56 (1986).

2. Debtor operated a network of convenience stores and gas stations, each of which had one or more underground storage tanks (USTs). Debtor failed to comply with state environmental laws requiring each owner of a UST to provide proof of financial responsibility, by obtaining insurance or meeting a self-insurance standard. The state environmental protection agency obtained an order for civil penalties of $200,000 and sought administrative expense priority for that amount, all of which was attributable to the postpetition period. Is the claim entitled to priority? See *Cumberland Farms, Inc. v. Florida Dep't of Environmental Protection*, 116 F.3d 16 (1st Cir. 1997).

3. Several employees of Debtor, Inc. cashed their payroll checks at Brooks Supermarket. None of the checks was for more than $4,000. Debtor, Inc. filed bankruptcy and the checks were dishonored for insufficient funds when Brooks presented them. Brooks filed a claim in Debtor, Inc.'s bankruptcy and now seeks priority for its claim under § 507(a)(3). Is the claim entitled to priority, given § 507(d)? See *Wilson v. Brooks Supermarket, Inc. (In re Missionary Baptist Foundation of America, Inc.)*, 667 F.2d 1244 (5th Cir.1982); *In re All American Manufacturing Corp.*, 185 B.R. 79 (Bankr. S.D. Fla. 1995).

4. Jartran is in the business of leasing trucks to consumers on a nationwide basis. In September, Jartran placed orders with an advertising agency for ads in Yellow Pages across the country. Under the advertising agreement, Jartran became liable to the agency immediately and it, in turn, was liable to publishers of the various directories. Neither party was to be billed until after publication. Jartran filed bankruptcy under Chapter 11 before publication but after the closing date, on which ads could no longer be withdrawn. The agency claims administrative expense priority for the cost of the ads. Should priority be granted? See *Matter of Jartran, Inc.*, 732 F.2d 584 (7th Cir.1984).

MATTER OF NORTHWEST ENGINEERING CO.

United States Court of Appeals, Seventh Circuit, 1988.
863 F.2d 1313.

EASTERBROOK, Circuit Judge.

Firms often require their employees to work a full year to accumulate vacation time that can be enjoyed the next. Northwest Engineering Co. used that system. Employees who worked a minimum number of hours in one calendar year (the work requirement) and one day in the next year (the vesting requirement) became entitled to a paid vacation (or cash in lieu of leave) during that year. The length of the vacation depended on the number of years the employee had been with the firm and the number of hours worked in the accumulation year; these details are unimportant.

Northwest filed a petition in bankruptcy on April 1, 1983, and laid off 116 employees. The firm paid all wages due, but most of these employees also are entitled to vacation pay on account of work performed in 1982. The firm acknowledges the obligations, aggregating $258,000, but wants to treat vacation pay as general unsecured debt. Unsecured creditors of the firm, which remains in business, will receive some cash plus equity under the approved plan of reorganization. The former employees prefer all cash. They contend that the vacation pay should be paid before other debts because of § 507(a), which provides:

> The following expenses and claims have priority in the following order:
>
> * * *
>
> (3) Third, allowed unsecured claims for wages, salaries, or commissions, including vacation, severance, and sick leave pay—
>
> > (A) earned by an individual within 90 days before the date of the filing of the petition or the date of the cessation of the debtor's business, whichever occurs first; but only
> >
> > (B) to the extent of $2,000 for each such individual.

Section 507(a)(3) gives a priority to vacation pay "earned" within 90 days of the bankruptcy, and each side plays on this word. Northwest observes that the vacation pay in question depends on work done in 1982. The collective bargaining agreement says that "[v]acation granted in this Agreement will be earned in the year prior to the year in which taken." Vacation therefore was "earned" in 1982, Northwest submits, and none qualifies for priority distribution since the firm filed the bankruptcy petition more than 90 days after the end of 1982. The employees reply that their entitlement to vacation pay depended on working at least one day in 1983, and they submit that all of the vacation pay was "earned" for bankruptcy purposes on that day of vesting, within the 90–day period.

The bankruptcy judge bridled at this all-or-nothing choice. "Earned" is a statutory term, the court noted, which may not be defined by contract. Congress gave priority to 90 days' worth of vacation pay, and the bankruptcy court therefore treated one-fourth of the 1982 vacation pay as a debt covered by the third priority. The district court reversed. Believing that the parties' options are the only possible ones—because either the whole amount was "earned" early in 1983 when the right to receive vacation pay vested, or none was "earned" in 1983—the district court concluded that the employees' position better fits the language of § 507(a)(3). * * *

"Earned" could take any of at least four meanings. (i) Vacation pay may be earned as work is done, with or without regard to the vesting rules in a given firm's contracts. (ii) Vacation pay may be earned as work is done, but only if the right to receive pay has vested (that is, if there is a contractual debt). (iii) Vacation pay may be earned on the day the right to receive it vests. (iv) Vacation pay may be earned on the date payment is due. The choice is easy if vacation pay accrues so many hours per week or month, for then it vests as soon as the work is done and is due on demand; the definitions coalesce. This is a common method of awarding vacation pay—treating vacation pay as no different in principle from an immediately-available bonus on wages—and must have been the model on which § 507(a)(3) was based. The statute uses a single word, "earned", to refer to wages and vacation pay, and the continual-accrual method, which the national government uses for its own employees, is well known in Washington. No legislative history suggests a different meaning of "earned". Indeed no legislative history suggests any meaning of "earned". The committee reports and other material relate only that the maximum priority amount has been raised and that vacation pay has been expressly included with wages; everyone assumed that "earned" has an obvious meaning.

What, then, is to be done when the employer separates work from vesting, which the drafters assumed are one? The structure of the statute suggests treating "earned" as a work rather than a vesting requirement, parallel to the treatment of wages. This eliminates possibility (iv), for ordinary wages are earned before payment comes due, and a firm can't avoid its obligations by closing its doors the day before payday. A fundamental principle of bankruptcy law disposes of possibility (i), if it means disregarding the contractual terms for the creation of a debt: the bankruptcy case is a collective proceeding to settle the rights of creditors. The bankruptcy court starts with obligations under state law, *Butner v. United States*, 440 U.S. 48 (1979), before deciding where the obligation stands in the queue. If there is no debt (because an event essential to liability never took place), then there is nothing to which a priority can attach. "When there is not enough to go around, the bankruptcy judge must establish priorities and apportion assets among creditors with the same priority, but the starting point is legal entitlements that exist outside of bankruptcy." *In re American Reserve Corp.*, 840 F.2d 487, 489 (7th Cir.1988).

In choosing among the remaining possible definitions, we attempt to conform with the treatment given to similar problems in bankruptcy law and to avoid drifting too far from the principal function of § 507(a)(3)—to assure employees that they will be paid at least $2,000 for their last days of work at the firm. If employees were treated in all respects as unsecured creditors, they would be inclined to desert a leaky ship, speeding up the firm's collapse; other creditors might be inclined to propel the firm into bankruptcy on the day before payday, obtaining greater security for themselves (and producing substantial hardship for the employees, who unlike creditors with diversified portfolios of loans may have no other source of income).

Two analogous situations are instructive. One is the treatment of vacation and severance pay as an administrative expense. The day of vesting may precede or follow the petition in bankruptcy. If it follows the petition, the employees are sure to contend that they are entitled to 100 cents on the dollar on the ground that vacation pay is a first-priority administrative expense, see § 507(a)(1). Administrative expenses include "wages, salaries, or commissions for services rendered after the commencement of the case". § 503(b)(1)(A). If vacation and sick pay, bonuses, and the like are "earned" on the day of vesting—and if "services [are] rendered" on that date—then the full amount of the pay is an administrative expense. It would come ahead of all other debt, including the claims of secured creditors, even though much of the vacation pay or bonus represents a deferred payment for work preceding the petition. Courts routinely conclude, however, that vacation pay and bonuses may be paid out as administrative expenses only to the extent they reflect work done after the commencement of the case.

A second related problem is the treatment of vacation pay under § 507(a)(3) when vesting comes after the bankruptcy. Take the facts of *United States v. Munro–Van Helms Co.*, 243 F.2d 10 (5th Cir.1957). The contract provided that the right to receive vacation pay vested on July 1, and the firm closed its doors on June 30. (Since the firm was defunct, there was no subsequent work and no administrative priority for vacation pay.) The debtor's plan—unlike that of Northwest Engineering—did not require the employees to work on or after the vesting date, so that an employee on layoff nonetheless could acquire a legal entitlement to vacation pay. If vacation pay is "earned" on the vesting date, then no vacation pay is earned in the 90 days preceding it, and so none was entitled to the priority under the predecessor of § 507(a)(3). The Fifth Circuit distinguished, however, between the vesting requirement and the work requirement. Vesting is essential to the existence of a debt, and addressing this requirement the court remarked that "[t]he rights of the employees * * * were conditional, contingent or inchoate prior to July 1. On that day their rights became unconditional and absolute and these rights then accrued." *Id.* at 13. So there was a debt. But when had the pay been "earned"? The court remarked that "it is wages which are earned and the right to receive them which accrues." *Id.* at 12. Vacation pay was "earned" continuously as work was done, even though the right to receive a year's worth "accrued" on a single date. Consequently "the vacation pay of those entitled to it under the contract constituted wages earned over the period of a year but such wages are entitled to priority only to the extent of one-fourth of the annual vacation pay." *Id.* at 13.

The parallel to the treatment of vacation pay for administrative priority, the parallel to the treatment of vacation pay with vesting after the date of bankruptcy, and the aim of § 507(a)(3) all point to separating the work requirement from the vesting requirement. The vesting rules determine whether there *is* a debt; if there is, the timing of the work determines "earning" for purposes of § 507(a)(3). Yet this approach, so apt in *Munro–Van Helms*, seems to lead straight to Northwest Engineering's conclusion here: because the work needed to qualify for vacations in 1983 occurred in 1982, no vacation pay was "earned" within 90 days of bankruptcy. That conclusion surely would defeat the function of § 507(a)(3) by denying the employee any return on the portion of the work in the last 90 days that was going toward the vacation pay entitlement. If forced to choose between that outcome and the district court's, we would pick the latter.

We are not forced to choose, however. It is congruent with the resolution of related problems, and consistent with the function of § 507(a), to hold that vacation pay is "earned" continuously. During January to March 1983, the employees of Northwest Engineering "earned" three months' vacation pay, because they did the work required for that boon. True, the entitlement to receive vacation for work in 1983 would not vest until 1984—and for these 116 employees it never did vest, because they were gone. Northwest Engineering nonetheless owed them a year's vacation pay (less any taken before April 1, 1983). The question is how much of this acknowledged debt is to be paid at the third priority. Section 507(a)(3) sets up a measuring rod—90 days' earnings—without implying that the acts of the 90 days before the petition establish a debt. If the employee works during that time but the firm is not indebted to him—perhaps because the firm has paid him already, perhaps because a condition subsequent such as a vesting rule is never satisfied—then there can be work without a debt, and hence no priority. So, too, there can be a priority without a new debt, just so long as the firm is indebted to the worker in that amount or more. In other words, the debt can come from the 1982 vacation pay, and the measure of priority can come from the work done in the 90 days before the bankruptcy. This approach leads to a sensible outcome, in accord with the statute's goal: the employee gets a priority equal to the value of services rendered in the 90 days before bankruptcy.

Doubtless the approach has a jerry-built look, but it is difficult to see how any of the alternatives could be better. The employer's proposal sends workers away empty-handed even though the firm owes a year's vacation pay as a debt, and even though the employees built up more (potential) entitlements in the 90 days before the filing. Employees on vacation between March 15 and April 1 would not receive their last pay check (because that pay had been "earned" in 1982), while employees who worked those weeks would be paid or have a third priority claim. The employer's approach gives firms an incentive to defer filing for bankruptcy until 90 days after the vesting date, for doing so cuts off the employees' claims. Vacation pay can be a significant claim against the firm (the vacation pay claims come to about 6% of Northwest's total debt), giving other creditors reason to delay to the workers' disadvantage. Even if employers and creditors do not behave strategically, the employer's proposed rule gives workers much less, on average, than 90 days' priority. If a petition on one date is equally likely as a petition on another, then ¾ of all petitions will be filed after March 30, and employees will get no priority for vacation pay. In the remaining ¼ of cases, employees will obtain, on average, a priority for 45 days of pay. (Employees of all firms taken together, then, would receive on average about 10 days' vacation pay as a priority.) On the employer's approach, a filing on March 30 would yield priority for a single day's pay, a filing on March 29 for two days' vacation pay, and so on. No conceivable function would be served by such a treatment. Both the divergence between this result and the aim of the statute, and the incentives the rule would create for strategic conduct, are sufficient reasons to reject it.

The employees' preferred position, which the district court accepted, is slightly preferable but not much so. In today's case, the rule "Treat vacation pay as earned on the date the entitlement to receive it vests" gives the workers a priority for 365 days' vacation pay. If Northwest Engineering had filed its petition on April 15 rather than April 1, however, the rule would give the employees nothing—for the vesting date (and hence the date on which 100% of the vacation pay was "earned") would have come more than 90 days before April 15. The rule could give employees of firms taken together priority for an average of 91 days' vacation pay: in ¾ of the business failures (those with petitions after April 1) the employees would get no priority, and in ¼ of the failures the employees would get 365 days' priority. This would be fine on average—other creditors' claims are subordinated to the extent Congress anticipated, and workers as a group get the priority Congress planned—but it is wrong in *every* individual case. Workers do not have diversified portfolios of employment. One business failure is all they care about. They want to receive their entitlements today and are not mollified by the fact that missing the mark in 100% of the cases will produce the correct average as other creditors see things.

Too, the rule the district court applied creates a strategic incentive in the same direction, but greater in magnitude, than the employer's favored rule. Waiting a single day can have large consequences. Employers and their creditors will be tempted to wait until April 2 or later to file their petitions, if they know that by waiting they can demote the priority of what may be (and in this case is) a substantial debt for vacation pay. If creditors wait, then more than ¾ of business bankruptcies will be filed after April 1, and employees will receive on average less than 90 days' worth of priority for vacation pay. Probably a good deal less, because we have reckoned so far without the effect of § 507(a)(3)(B), which limits the priority to $2,000. An entitlement to a year's priority in a quarter of the cases, and no priority in the rest, averages out to 90 days' worth only if the employee receives the whole priority whenever it is available. This won't happen; the $2,000 limit will prevent it. Suppose firms owe employees, on average, two weeks' wages and three weeks' vacation pay when they file for bankruptcy. Five weeks' pay exceeds $2,000 whenever the annual wage exceeds $20,800—in other words, for a majority of industrial employees. Employees with higher wages (or more weeks of pay in arrears) will find the full year's priority useless to them. If, however, every employee is entitled to a priority for two weeks' wages and four days' vacation pay (a quarter of an annual accumulation), the $2,000 limit will impose a ceiling only if the annual wage exceeds $37,143, a significantly smaller fraction of workers.

In the end, we must choose among unsatisfactory options. The employer's option is unsatisfactory because it almost never gives employees a full 90 days of priority, because it gives them on average only 10 days' priority, and because it creates unacceptable incentives for strategic conduct. The employees' option, which the district court chose, is unacceptable because it gives employees a year's priority or none, missing the statutory mark in every case; because given the $2,000 limit even the average priority will be less than 90 days' worth; and because it, too, creates opportunities for strategic conduct. The option of awarding 90 days' priority in every case is jarring because it sets up a disjunction between the debt (which may be attributable to work done more than 90 days before the filing) and the standard of priority (which depends on the work done in the last 90 days). But of these unsatisfactory choices, the least bad is the one divorcing the work requirement from the vesting requirement, exactly as the Fifth Circuit did in *Munro–Van Helms*.

Vacation pay is "earned" continuously as work is done. The worker receives third priority treatment for benefits "earned" in the 90 days before filing—provided always that the employer is indebted to the worker in at least this sum, a question that depends on the contract and state law. The debt in this case is conceded; only the priority is debated. That priority is, as § 507(a)(3) provides, for 90 days' worth of vacation pay.

REVERSED AND REMANDED.

Notes and Problems

1. Section 507(a)(3) was amended in 1994 to increase the amount entitled to priority from $2,000 per employee to $4,000, and has since been further amended to reflect the cost-of-living adjustment required by § 104(b).

The 1994 amendment also clarified that the debtor's independent sales representatives are entitled to the same priority as employees.

2. Does "earned" have a necessary meaning? Is the result reached by the court consistent with the language of the statute?

3. Debtor operated two separate sole proprietorships—a mine and a restaurant. The mine ceased operating in 1996, but the restaurant remained open until Debtor filed bankruptcy in June of 2000. Debtor owed more than $4,300 per employee in wages earned at the mine within 90 days of its close, and those former employees sought priority under § 507(a)(3) to the extent of $4,300 per individual. Are they entitled to priority? See *Boatwright v. Rau (In re Rau),* 113 B.R. 619 (9th Cir. BAP 1990).

4. Debtor owed the State Insurance Fund $190,000 in premiums for workers' compensation coverage attributable to the 180 days preceding bankruptcy. Is that amount entitled to priority under § 507(a)(4)? Is it relevant that § 507(a)(4) was enacted in order to recognize that fringe benefits are often wage substitutes, negotiated as part of collective bargaining agreements? See *State Insurance Fund v. Southern Star Foods, Inc. (In re Southern Star Foods, Inc.)*, 144 F.3d 712 (10th Cir.), *cert. denied sub nom. State Insurance Fund v. Mather*, 525 U.S. 978, 119 S.Ct. 438, 142 L.Ed.2d 357 (1998).

5. Debtor Corp. had 20 employees who were covered by two benefit plans—a retirement plan and a medical plan. At the time bankruptcy was filed, Debtor Corp. owed a total of $30,000 in back wages for work performed by its employees in the three months before filing. Debtor Corp. also owed $40,000 in contributions to the retirement plan and $60,000 to the medical plan, based on work performed during the same period. What priority, if any, can the retirement and medical plans enjoy?

H. EQUITABLE SUBORDINATION

A claim will not take its usual place in the bankruptcy distribution line if the claimholder has agreed to subordinate its position to another creditor. Such contracts are enforced in bankruptcy, under § 510(a). Similarly, claims arising from securities fraud are subordinated under § 510(b).

Other claims may not take their usual distributive position for reasons of fairness or equity. Section 510(c) recognizes the inherent equitable power of the bankruptcy court to subordinate the claim of a creditor that has misbehaved in some way. This is a codification of the equitable subordination doctrine articulated in *Pepper v. Litton*, 308 U.S. 295, 60 S.Ct. 238, 84 L.Ed. 281 (1939). In *Pepper*, a corporation's dominant shareholder caused the corporation to confess judgment, pre-petition, on a dormant wage claim held by the shareholder. Justice Douglas, writing for the Court, noted that the shareholder had manipulated the corporation's affairs in such a way that unsecured creditors would receive nothing. Justice Douglas concluded that the transaction did not carry "the earmarks of an arm's length bargain," *id.* at 306–07, 60 S.Ct. at 245, 84 L.Ed. at 289, and approved subordination in priority of the shareholder's claim relative to the claims of other creditors.

The Code does not specify the standards that bankruptcy courts should apply in deciding equitable subordination issues. Rather, the legislative history states that § 510(c) was intended to codify existing case law, such as *Pepper*, and was "not intended to limit the court's power in any way." H.R. Rep. No. 95–595 at 359, *reprinted in* 1978 U.S.C.C.A.N. at 6315.

Pepper was an insider case. As the next case reveals, equitable subordination is a bit more difficult in a noninsider context.

SMITH v. ASSOCIATES COMMERCIAL CORP. (IN RE CLARK PIPE & SUPPLY CO.)

United States Court of Appeals, Fifth Circuit, 1990.
893 F.2d 693.

E. GRADY JOLLY, Circuit Judge.

ON SUGGESTION FOR REHEARING EN BANC

Treating the suggestion for rehearing en banc filed in this case by Associates Commercial Corporation ("Associates"), as a petition for panel rehearing, we hereby grant the petition for re-hearing. After re-examining the evidence in this case and the applicable law, we conclude that our prior opinion was in error. We therefore withdraw our prior opinion[b] and substitute the following:

In this bankruptcy case we are presented with two issues arising out of the conduct of the bankrupt's lender during the ninety days prior to the bankrupt's filing for protection from creditors. * * * [T]he second question is whether the lender engaged in such inequitable conduct that would justify subordination of the lender's claims to the extent that the conduct harmed other creditors. * * *

[b] 870 F.2d 1022 (5th Cir.1989). Eds.

I

Clark Pipe and Supply Company, Inc., ("Clark") was in the business of buying and selling steel pipe used in the fabrication of off-shore drilling platforms. In September 1980, Associates and Clark executed various agreements under which Associates would make revolving loans secured by an assignment of accounts receivable and an inventory mortgage. Under the agreements, Clark was required to deposit all collections from the accounts receivable in a bank account belonging to Associates. The amount that Associates would lend was determined by a formula, i.e., a certain percentage of the amount of eligible accounts receivable plus a certain percentage of the cost of inventory. The agreements provided that Associates could reduce the percentage advance rates at any time at its discretion.

When bad times hit the oil fields in late 1981, Clark's business slumped. In February 1982 Associates began reducing the percentage advance rates so that Clark would have just enough cash to pay its direct operating expenses. Clark used the advances to keep its doors open and to sell inventory, the proceeds of which were used to pay off the past advances from Associates. Associates did not expressly dictate to Clark which bills to pay. Neither did it direct Clark not to pay vendors or threaten Clark with a cut-off of advances if it did pay vendors. But Clark had no funds left over from the advances to pay vendors or other creditors whose services were not essential to keeping its doors open.

One of Clark's vendors, going unpaid, initiated foreclosure proceedings in February and seized the pipe it had sold Clark. Another attempted to do so in March. The resulting priority dispute was resolved only in litigation. ([Five vendors] had valid vendors' privileges in the goods they had sold Clark that, under Louisiana law, primed Associates' inventory mortgage). When a third unpaid creditor initiated foreclosure proceedings in May, Clark sought protection from creditors by filing for reorganization under Chapter 11 of the Bankruptcy Code.

The case was converted to a Chapter 7 liquidation on August 31, 1982, and a trustee was appointed. In 1983, the trustee brought this adversary proceeding against Clark's lender, Associates. The trustee sought * * * equitable subordination of Associates' claims. Following a one-day trial on August 28, 1986, the bankruptcy court entered judgment on April 10, 1987, and an amended judgment on June 9, 1987.

The court * * * subordinated Associates' claims. The district court affirmed on May 24, 1988.

* * *

III

The second issue before us is whether the bankruptcy court was justified in equitably subordinating Associates' claims. This court has enunciated a three-pronged test to determine whether and to what extent a claim should be equitably subordinated: (1) the claimant must have engaged in some type of inequitable conduct, (2) the misconduct must have resulted in injury to the creditors of the bankrupt or conferred an unfair advantage on the claimant, and (3) equitable subordination of the claim must not be inconsistent with the provisions of the Bankruptcy Code. Three general categories of conduct have been recognized as sufficient to satisfy the first prong of the three-part test: (1) fraud, illegality or breach of fiduciary duties; (2) undercapitalization; and (3) a claimant's use of the debtor as a mere instrumentality or alter ego.

In essence, the bankruptcy court found that once Associates realized Clark's desperate financial condition, Associates asserted total control and used Clark as a mere instrumentality to liquidate Associates' unpaid loans. Moreover, it did so, the trustee argues, to the detriment of the rights of Clark's other creditors.

Associates contends that its control over Clark was far from total. Associates says that it did no more than determine the percentage of advances as expressly permitted in the loan agreement; it never made or dictated decisions as to which creditors were paid. Thus, argues Associates, it never had the "actual, participatory, total control of the debtor" required to make Clark its instrumentality * * *. If it did not use Clark as an instrumentality or engage in any other type of inequitable conduct * * *, argues Associates, then it cannot be equitably subordinated.

A

We first consider whether Associates asserted such control over the activities of Clark that we should consider that it was using Clark as its mere instrumentality. In our prior opinion, we agreed with the district court and the bankruptcy court that, as a practical matter, Associates asserted total control over Clark's liquidation, and that it used its control in a manner detrimental to the unsecured creditors. Upon reconsideration, we have concluded that we cannot say that the sort of control Associates asserted over Clark's financial affairs rises to the level of unconscionable conduct necessary to justify the application of the doctrine of equitable subordination. We have reached our revised conclusion primarily because we cannot escape the salient fact that, pursuant to its loan agreement with Clark, Associates had the right to reduce funding, just as it did, as Clark's sales slowed. We now conclude that there is no evidence that Associates exceeded its authority under the loan agreement, or that Associates acted inequitably in exercising its rights under that agreement.

We think it is important to note at the outset that the loan and security agreements between Associates and Clark, which are at issue here, were executed in 1980, at the inception of their relationship. There is no evidence that Clark was insolvent at the time the agreements were entered into. Clark was represented by counsel during the negotiations, and there is no evidence that the loan documents were negotiated at anything other than arm's length or that they are atypical of loan documents used in similar asset-based financings.

The loan agreement between Associates and Clark established a line of credit varying from \$2.2 million to approximately \$2.7 million over the life of the loan. The amount that Associates would lend was determined by a formula: 85% of the amount of eligible accounts receivables plus 60% of the cost of inventory. Under the agreement, Clark was required to deposit all collections from the accounts receivable in a bank account belonging to Associates. Associates would, in turn, re-advance the agreed-upon portion of those funds to Clark on a revolving basis. The agreement provided that Associates could reduce the percentage advance rates at any time in its discretion.

When Clark's business began to decline, along with that of the oil patch generally, Associates advised Clark that it would reduce the advance ratio for the inventory loan by 5% per month beginning in January 1982. After that time, the company stopped buying new inventory and, according to the Trustee's expert witness, Clark's monthly sales revenues amounted to less than one-fifth of the company's outstanding accounts payable. Clark prepared a budget at Associates' request that indicated the disbursements necessary to keep the company operating. The budget did not include payment to vendors for previously shipped goods. Associates' former loan officer, Fred Slice, testified as to what he had in mind:

> If he [the comptroller of Clark] had had the availability [of funds to pay a vendor or other trade creditor] that particular day, I would have said, "Are you sure you've got that much availability, Jim," because he shouldn't have that much. The way I had structured it, he wouldn't have any money to pay his suppliers.
>
> * * *
>
> But you know, the possibility that—this is all hypothetical. I had it structured so that there was no—there was barely enough money—there was enough money, if I did it right, enough money to keep the doors open. Clark could continue to operate, sell the inventory, turn it into receivables, collect the cash, transfer that cash to me, and reduce my loans.
>
> And, if he had ever had availability for other things, that meant I had done something wrong, and I would have been surprised. To ask me what I would have done is purely hypothetical[;] I don't think it would happen. I think it's so unrealistic, I don't know.

Despite Associates' motive, which was, according to Slice, "to get in the best position I can prior to the bankruptcy, i.e., I want to get the absolute amount of dollars as low as I can by hook or crook," the evidence shows that the amount of its advances continued to be based on the applicable funding formulas. Slice testified that the lender did not appreciably alter its original credit procedures when Clark fell into financial difficulty.

In our original opinion, we failed to focus sufficiently on the loan agreement, which gave Associates the right to conduct its affairs with Clark in the manner in which it did. In addition, we think that in our previous opinion we were overly influenced by the negative and inculpatory tone of Slice's testimony. Given the agreement he was working under, his testimony was hardly more than fanfaronading about the power that the agreement afforded him over the financial affairs of Clark. Although his talk was crass (e.g., "I want to get the absolute dollars as low as I can, by hook or crook"), our careful examination of the record does not reveal any conduct on his part that was inconsistent with the loan agreement, irrespective of what his personal motive may have been.

Through its loan agreement, every lender effectively exercises "control" over its borrower to some degree. A lender in Associates' position will usually possess "control" in the sense that it can foreclose or drastically reduce the debtor's financing. The purpose of equitable subordination is to distinguish between the unilateral remedies that a creditor may properly enforce pursuant to its agreements with the debtor and other inequitable conduct such as fraud, misrepresentation, or the exercise of such total control over the debtor as to have essentially replaced its decision-making capacity with that of the lender. The crucial distinction between what is inequitable and what a lender can reasonably and legitimately do to protect its interests is the distinction between the existence of "control" and the exercise of that "control" to direct the activities of the debtor. As the Supreme Court stated in *Comstock v. Group of Institutional Investors*, 335 U.S. 211, 229 (1948): "It is not mere existence of an opportunity to do wrong that brings the rule into play; it is the unconscionable use of the opportunity afforded by the domination to advantage itself at the injury of the subsidiary that deprives the wrongdoer of the fruits of his wrong."

In our prior opinion, we drew support from *In re American Lumber Co.*, 5 B.R. 470 (D.Minn.1980), to reach our conclusion that Associates' claims should be equitably subordinated. Upon reconsideration, however, we find that the facts of that case are significantly more egregious than we have here. In that case, the court equitably subordinated the claims of a bank because the bank "controlled" the debtor through its right to a controlling interest in the debtor's stock. The bank forced the debtor to convey security interests in its remaining unencumbered assets to the bank after the borrower defaulted on an existing debt. Immediately thereafter, the bank foreclosed on the borrower's accounts receivable, terminated the borrower's employees, hired its own skeleton crew to conduct a liquidation, and selectively honored the debtor's payables to improve its own position. The bank began receiving and opening all incoming mail at the borrower's office, and it established a bank account into which all amounts received by the borrower were deposited and over which the bank had sole control. The bankruptcy court found that the bank exercised control over all aspects of the debtor's finances and operation including: payments of payables and wages, collection and use of accounts receivable and contract rights, purchase and use of supplies and materials, inventory sales, a lumber yard, the salaries of the principals, the employment of employees, and the receipt of payments for sales and accounts receivable.

Despite its decision to prohibit further advances to the debtor, its declaration that the debtor was in default of its loans, and its decisions to use all available funds of the company to offset the company's obligations to it, the bank in *American Lumber* made two specific representations to the American Lumbermen's Credit Association that the debtor was not in a bankruptcy situation and that current contracts would be fulfilled. Two days after this second reassurance, the bank gave notice of foreclosure of its security interests in the company's inventory and equipment. Approximately two weeks later the bank sold equipment and inventory of the debtor amounting to roughly $450,000, applying all of the proceeds to the debtor's indebtedness to the bank.

Associates exercised significantly less "control" over the activities of Clark than did the lender in *American Lumber*. Associates did not own any stock of Clark, much less a controlling block. Nor did Associates interfere with the operations of the borrower to an extent even roughly commensurate with the degree of interference exercised by the bank in *American Lumber*. Associates made no management decisions for Clark, such as deciding which creditors to prefer with the diminishing amount of funds available. At no time did Associates place any of its employees as either a director or officer of Clark. Associates never influenced the removal from office of any Clark personnel, nor did Associates ever request Clark to take any particular action at a shareholders meeting. Associates did not expressly dictate to Clark which bills to pay, nor did it direct Clark not to pay vendors or threaten a cut-off of advances if it did pay vendors. Clark handled its own daily operations. The same basic procedures with respect to the reporting of collateral, the calculation of availability of funds, and the procedures for the advancement of funds were followed throughout the relationship between Clark and Associates. Unlike the lender in *American Lumber*, Associates did not mislead creditors to continue supplying Clark. Perhaps the most important fact that distinguishes this case from *American Lumber* is that Associates did not coerce Clark into executing the security agreements after Clark became insolvent. Instead, the loan and security agreements between Clark and Associates were entered into at arm's length prior to Clark's insolvency, and all of Associates' activities were conducted pursuant to those agreements.

Associates' control over Clark's finances, admittedly powerful and ultimately severe, was based solely on the exercise of powers found in the loan agreement. Associates' close watch over Clark's affairs does not, by itself, however, amount to such control as would justify equitable subordination. "There is nothing inherently wrong with a creditor carefully monitoring his debtor's financial situation or with suggesting what course of action the debtor ought to follow." *In re Teltronics Services, Inc.*, 29 B.R. 139, 172 (Bankr. E.D.N.Y.1983) (citations omitted). Although the terms of the agreement did give Associates potent leverage over Clark, that agreement did not give Associates total control over Clark's activities. At all material times Clark had the power to act autonomously and, if it chose, to disregard the advice of Associates; for example, Clark was free to shut its doors at any time it chose to do so and to file for bankruptcy.

Finally, on reconsideration, we are persuaded that the rationale of *In re W.T. Grant Co.*, 699 F.2d 599 (2d Cir.1983), should control the case before us. In that case, the Second Circuit recognized that

> a creditor is under no fiduciary obligation to its debtor or to other creditors of the debtor in the collection of its claim. The permissible parameters of a creditor's efforts to seek collection from a debtor are generally those with respect to voidable preferences and fraudulent conveyances proscribed by the Bankruptcy Act; apart from these there is generally no objection to a creditor's using his bargaining position, including his ability to refuse to make further loans needed by the debtor, to improve the status of his existing claims.

699 F.2d at 609–10. Associates was not a fiduciary of Clark, it did not exert improper control over Clark's financial affairs, and it did not act inequitably in exercising its rights under its loan agreement with Clark.

* * *

We therefore conclude that the district court erred in affirming the bankruptcy court's decision to subordinate Associates' claims.

* * *

Questions

1. Why is it so important that the contract between Associates and Clark provided for the actions Associates took?

2. A transferee cannot escape responsibility for a fraudulent conveyance by pointing to a contract clause permitting such actions. Why, then, should a creditor escape the subordination of its claim by relying on contractual terms?

3. Assume that the contract between Associates and Clark authorized Associates to require additional collateral in the event of Clark's default, to foreclose on it immediately, to conduct a liquidation sale using its own employees, and to decide whether purchases would be made or other creditors paid. If Associates took those authorized actions, would its claim be equitably subordinated?

4. Will a creditor escape subordination as long as the debtor has retained control over the decision to remain open or to shut its doors?

5. The legislative history to § 510(c) states that "a claim is generally subordinated only if [the] holder of such claim is guilty of inequitable conduct, *or the claim itself is of a status susceptible to subordination, such as a penalty* * * * ." 124 Cong. Rec. 32398 (1978) (statement of Rep. Edwards); *id.* at 33998 (statement of Sen. DeConcini) (emphasis added). Relying on this language, a number of courts equitably subordinated tax penalties, which do not represent pecuniary losses, to secured and unsecured claims held by creditors who extended value to the debtor. The Supreme Court put a stop to this in *United States v. Nolan*, 517 U.S. 535, 116 S.Ct. 1524, 134 L.Ed.2d 748 (1996). The government's priority claim had been subordinated not because of inequitable conduct, but solely because of status. The Court stated that if § 510(c)

> authorized a court to conclude on a general, categorical level that tax penalties should not be treated as administrative expenses to be paid first, it would empower a court to modify the operation of the priority statute at the same level at which Congress operated when it made its characteristically general judgment to establish the hierarchy of claims in the first place. That is, the distinction between characteristic legislative and trial court functions would simply be swept away, and the statute would delegate legislative revision, not authorize equitable exception.

Id. at 540, 116 S.Ct. at 1527, 134 L.Ed.2d at 755. Because the Court held categorical subordination inappropriate, it found no need to decide "whether a bankruptcy court must always find creditor misconduct before a claim may be equitably subordinated." *Id.* at 543, 116 S.Ct. at 1528, 134 L.Ed.2d at 756. See also *United States v. Reorganized CF&I Fabricators of Utah, Inc.*, 518 U.S. 213, 116 S.Ct. 2106, 135 L.Ed.2d 506 (1996) (holding *Nolan* applicable to subordination of a tax penalty not entitled to priority).

I. CLASSIFICATION OF CLAIMS IN REORGANIZATION CASES

As noted above, payments to unsecured creditors in Chapters 11 and 13 depend to a large degree on the provisions in the plan. The statute provides minimum payment amounts, but does not otherwise dictate a rigid distribution scheme.

Payments under the reorganization chapters are made to *classes* of creditors. Thus, how a claim is classified by the plan is crucial. The relevant statutory provisions are §§ 1122, 1123(a), 1222(b)(1) and 1322(b)(1).

Section 1123(a)(1) requires a Chapter 11 plan to designate classes of claims (with certain exceptions we can ignore for now) and requires that the designation comport with § 1122. Section 1122(a), in turn, provides that "a plan may place a claim or an interest in a particular class only if such claim or interest is substantially similar to the other claims or interests of such class." In other words, only like claims can be classified together.

Section 1322(b)(1) provides, in pertinent part, that a Chapter 13 plan may designate classes "as provided in section 1122 of this title, but may not discriminate unfairly against any class so designated." By the cross-reference to § 1122, Chapter 13 also requires that only like claims be classified together. *See also* § 1222(b)(1).

None of these statutory provisions addresses what attributes make claims similar, or whether similar claims can be classified separately.

1. CLASSIFICATION IN CHAPTER 13

IN RE HARRIS

United States Bankruptcy Court, Eastern District of Michigan, 1986.
62 B.R. 391.

ARTHUR J. SPECTOR, Bankruptcy Judge.

The debtors filed their joint petition for relief under Chapter 13 on August 19, 1985. In their petition, they list their unsecured debts in two separate categories: one for debts incurred during the operation of their bookstore, The Mustard Seed; the other for unsecured consumer debts. According to their schedules, the business debts are in the amount of $19,697.80, plus a debt of $50,438 to Old Kent Bank–Central representing the unsecured portion of its claim, for a total of $70,135.80; the consumer debts total $1,920.70.

The debtors' proposed Chapter 13 plan continues this distinction between business and consumer unsecured debt. Consumer debts are listed as "Class 3" debts, on which the debtors propose to pay 100%

over three years. "Class 5" debts constitute the unsecured business debts. The debtors estimated that there will be no distribution to this class. Moreover, as counsel for the debtors stated on the record, it was their intention not to pay business creditors when they formulated their plan. However, it appears that there may in fact be some distribution to Class 5 creditors due to the failure of some Class 3 creditors to file proofs of claim. In their confirmation worksheet filed after the confirmation hearing on April 16, 1986, the debtors state that filed unsecured consumer claims total $1,521.62, and filed unsecured business claims total $57,426. Assuming that these figures are correct, consumer creditors would still receive 100% payment, and business creditors would receive 4.82% on their claims. By way of comparison, if all unsecured creditors are paid without regard to how the debt was incurred, each would receive 7.28% of its claim.

On March 29, 1986, Spring Arbor Distributors, an unsecured business creditor of the debtors, filed an objection to the debtors' plan. The basis of its objection is that the above classification of unsecured creditors unfairly discriminates against the business creditors, and that such treatment is barred by the Bankruptcy Code. After a hearing on April 16, the Court took the matter under advisement.

The debtors' authority to classify unsecured claims separately is contained in § 1322(b)(1). * * *

Section 1122, to which § 1322 refers, does not offer much guidance. It provides that a debtor may designate various classes of creditors, so long as each member of that class holds a claim or interest that is "substantially similar" to the claims or interests of other class members. There is, unfortunately, no statutory definition of what makes claims or interests "substantially similar" to each other. Section 1122(a) has been characterized as "not a model of statutory clarity", *In re Wolff*, 22 B.R. 510, 515 (9th Cir. BAP 1982) (concurring opinion), and we are therefore reluctant to rely on it.

Fortunately, there have been a considerable number of cases discussing what sorts of classifications of unsecured claims are permissible under § 1322. The debtors rely on *In re Cook*, 26 B.R. 187 (D.N.M.1982). There, the debtor sought to pay unsecured debts guaranteed by a co-signor and claims for child support, but nothing to other unsecured creditors. The court adopted the "emergent majority view" that "[a] classification is not *ipso facto* unfairly discriminatory because it provides for a greater percentage of payment to some unsecured creditors than to others." *Id.* In order to determine whether a particular classification was fair, the court went on to espouse a four-factor test developed by other courts. Those factors are:

> (1) Whether the discrimination has a reasonable basis;
>
> (2) Whether the debtor can carry out a plan without such discrimination;
>
> (3) Whether such discrimination is proposed in good faith; and
>
> (4) The treatment of the class discriminated against.

These factors are not rigid rules, but are simply flexible guidelines to assist courts in deciding whether a debtor's plan ought to be confirmed. Each plan should be decided on its own merits. Although to a large extent these guidelines overlap, the reasoning of these opinions is sound and we adopt it.

The standards are consistent with two underlying purposes of the Bankruptcy Code. On the one hand, the remedies provided debtors in the Bankruptcy Code, including Chapter 13, are intended to provide debtors with the opportunity to emerge from bankruptcy with the famous "fresh start." Chapter 13 gives debtors wide latitude to propose a plan which will allow them to pay their debts without undue hardship, yet exit from bankruptcy in sounder financial shape than when they filed for relief. Thus, § 1322(b)(1) allows debtors to discriminate among unsecured creditors where it is beneficial to the debtor to do so. However, the objective of providing debtors with a fresh start is counter-balanced by the Congress' intent that the debtor's creditors be treated fairly. More precisely, it is fundamental to the operation of the Code that creditors of an equal status—e.g. priority, administrative and unsecured—be treated equally and equitably. *See* § 726(b). Accordingly, while the debtor may classify unsecured creditors differently, they cannot do so in such a fashion that any single class is treated unfairly, that is, inequitably. As the Code presumes that creditors of like position will be treated equally, the debtor has the burden of persuading us that a deviation from that norm is not unfair to creditors.

Applying the four-part test to the facts of this case, we find that the debtor has failed to show that the proposed discrimination is fair. The first factor is whether the discrimination has a reasonable basis. We interpret this to be an inquiry into whether there is any logical or rational foundation for the classification. For example, classifying creditors alphabetically would have no rational basis in the context of a

Chapter 13. Here, the debtors have divided their creditors into those who extended credit to them in the operation of their prior business, and those who extended credit for personal consumer purposes. Simply put, the debtors have closed their bookstore and have no further interest in paying the debts incurred therefrom or of maintaining an ongoing debtor-creditor relationship with their business creditors. Conversely, they wish to repay those parties who lent them money or extended them credit for personal needs, and who the debtors will likely encounter post-bankruptcy. The classification thus is rational at least from the debtors' perspective.

The proposed classification makes less sense when evaluated in terms of recourse available to the unsecured creditors. Legally, all of the unsecured creditors in this case, business and consumer, would have the same remedies under state law to pursue collection of their debts. After obtaining a judgment for the balance due, they could attempt to satisfy it through garnishment of wages and deposit accounts or by execution on the debtors' property. In reducing their claims to hard cash, the law cares not whether credit was extended to the debtors for an ill-fated business enterprise or for the debtors' personal needs. Of course, we realize that in practical terms the ability of creditors to pursue their legal remedies may differ; however, it is not the purpose for which the debts were incurred that makes them different. For example, some creditors may hold claims against the debtor for which there may be a co-obligor. Against the debtor, that creditor has the same rights as any unsecured creditor; but the creditor's ability to seek payment from a third-party (often a member of the debtor's family) gives that creditor added leverage against the debtor. Thus, § 1322(b)(1) expressly allows debtors to establish a separate class for unsecured consumer debts on which a non-debtor is liable. Additionally, some claimants may possess claims so small that it is impractical for the creditor to pursue its legal remedies. Suppose a creditor holds an unsecured claim for $100.00; even if that creditor could find counsel willing to litigate the matter, it would probably cost more than $100.00 to do so. Because creditors so situated may have *fewer* remedies against the debtor, § 1122(b), and by reference § 1322, provides that such creditors may be separately classified. As *Colliers* has noted, in enacting an amendment to § 1322(b) in 1984,

> Congress has recognized that practical necessity can be a proper reason for separate classification of claims. In doing so, it has apparently rejected the view that unsecured claims may be separately classified only if they would receive differing distributions in chapter 7 and allowed the court to consider the

practical justifications for proposed classifications on a case-by-case basis.

5 *Collier on Bankruptcy*, ¶ 1322.01[3][A](i), 1322–8 (15th ed. 1979).

Thus some classifications among unsecured creditors may be found to be fair. Suppose, for example, a debtor was compelled to pay a criminal restitution debt or risk imprisonment. There, the debtor would certainly benefit by paying that debt in full and perhaps in advance of other unsecured creditors; but this would likely inure to the benefit of the "lesser" class, because they might receive nothing if the debtor goes to jail. Or, a debtor who wished to continue his or her business might want to pay business creditors *more* as a means of maintaining good relations with essential suppliers, for if those suppliers are not made happy the business might fail, causing both the debtor and the less favored creditors to lose out. Separately classifying these creditors may be reasonable. *See also In re Perskin*, 9 B.R. 626 (Bankr. N.D. Tex.1980) (traveling salesman permissibly discriminated in favor of credit card creditors).

Although the unhappy creditor there was partially secured, in *Memphis Bank & Trust Co. v. Whitman*, 692 F.2d 427 (6th Cir.1982), the Court of Appeals implicitly authorized different treatment of otherwise similar claims based on the manner in which the claims were incurred. There, the debtor had obtained a car loan by inflating her statement of income on the loan application. One of the issues was whether the debtor's plan was filed in good faith when the debt might have been incurred fraudulently. In remanding the case for further determinations, the Court of Appeals stated that the bankruptcy court could, as we do here, deny confirmation. However, the court went on to provide another alternative: it could require that the debt which was incurred under questionable circumstances be paid in full. If the court has authority to order separate treatment for such debts, it follows that the debtor could offer such a plan in good faith. Similarly, it has been held that otherwise nondischargeable debts may be separately classified from other unsecured debts for favored treatment.

In the case at bar, the classification suggested by the debtors was not proposed with any regard to the ability of the various creditors to collect their debts. So far as we can tell, there are no debts on which there is a co-obligor with either of the debtors. Furthermore, the proposed classification has no correlation to the size of the various claims. According to the debtors' schedules, the unsecured business claims range in size from $10.96 to $8,500.00; the consumer claims range from $154.04 to $988.00. In the instant case, the business creditors would receive no benefit as a result of the proposed classification, either directly or indirectly, nor is there any moral justification for preferring any of the consumer creditors. We also reject the debtors' unsubstantiated assertion that business creditors are more able to take care of themselves than consumer creditors. In short, we find that while the proposed classification may have a rational basis from the debtors' position, it is arbitrary when examined from the creditors' viewpoint. This makes the proposed classification suspect.

The second factor is whether the debtors could consummate a plan without the proposed classification. We find that they could do so. As noted above, assuming the same level of funding and duration of plan as has been proposed, if unsecured creditors are not classified, each would receive 7.28% on its claim. Although plans paying an unusually low percentage may draw closer scrutiny than 100% plans, they may be confirmed if the plan otherwise complies with the standards for confirmation in § 1325. Although the debtors might be able to consummate a non-discriminatory plan, it is not necessarily fatal to their plan that they have not done so.

The third factor is whether the discrimination is proposed in good faith. This is where the debtors' plan fails. As we have stated above, the debtors are attempting to wash their hands of their business and the debts they accumulated in its operation. Their stated intent was to pay their business creditors nothing, and it is only because some creditors neglected to timely file proofs of claim that creditors of the business might receive any distribution at all. In attempting to obtain a discharge of these debts without making any payment thereon, the debtors are essentially seeking to file a Chapter 7 petition for their business and a Chapter 13 petition for their personal, preferred creditors. This flies in the face of the policy that similarly situated creditors receive equal treatment under the Bankruptcy Code, and cannot be held to constitute a good faith proposal. We agree with the statement made in *In re Bowles*, 48 B.R. 502, 508 (Bankr. E.D.Va.1985), that "Chapter 13 is not an unbridled 'market' in which the debtor may, even with some justification, pick and choose which creditors he seeks to prefer." The debtors bear the burden of showing that their plan is filed in good faith. Because the debtors have failed to persuade us that their proposed classification satisfies this standard, § 1325(a)(3), their plan cannot be confirmed.

Although the above finding makes consideration of the impact of the classification on the adversely effected [sic] creditors superfluous, we will discuss it briefly. While the good faith requirement may be regarded as a test of whether the plan is consistent with the spirit underlying Chapter 13 relief, this last factor measures the practical consequences to the affected creditors. Here, the result is obviously unfair. The debtors' consumer creditors will receive full payment; however, their business creditors will receive nothing, or, at best, an inadvertent and insignificant amount. Nonetheless, the debtors' discharge will *not* discriminate between business and consumer debts—each will be discharged. Indeed, because this is a Chapter 13 case, the effect of a Chapter 13 discharge would be more severe than if the debtors filed a Chapter 7 petition, because the business creditors would have no opportunity to seek to have their debts excepted from discharge under § 523.[6] On these facts, the harm visited upon the adversely affected class far outweigh[s] any legitimate benefit to be gained by the debtors, thus providing another reason for denying confirmation.

The result we reach here is consistent with the holding in a prior unpublished [sic] opinion by this Court, *In re Shands*, 63 B.R. 121 (Bankr. E.D.Mich.1985). There, the debtor filed a petition for relief under Chapter 7. However, because the debtor stated her intention to reaffirm several debts, and her current husband assumed payments on several other obligations, the result was that the only significant creditor not being paid was the debtor's ex-husband, who was owed some $6,000 pursuant to a divorce property settlement. In an answer filed in an adversary proceeding, and in a hearing held to determine whether the case was a substantial abuse of the Bankruptcy Code, § 707(b), the debtor admitted that her primary purpose in filing a Chapter 7 petition was to discharge the debt to her ex-husband.

We dismissed the debtor's case as a substantial abuse, pursuant to § 707(b). By filing a Chapter 7 petition, then reaffirming or otherwise paying essentially all debts except those to her ex-husband, she was effectively filing a Chapter 7 as to him and a Chapter 13 as to her other creditors. We held such discriminatory treatment to be a substantial abuse of Chapter 7 and dismissed the case. It is equally abusive to attempt to manipulate Chapter 13 to file bankruptcy against only some of a debtor's creditors. When debtors seek to take advantage of the benefits contained in the Bankruptcy Code, one of the conditions placed upon that relief—a "fresh start"—is that they must treat all their creditors fairly.

---

6 It is unlikely that any of the business debts were incurred for alimony, support or maintenance, and thus are nondischargeable under § 1328(a)(2).

In the instant case, the debtors' plan fails to treat all similarly situated creditors equally, and thus is not proposed in good faith. Accordingly, confirmation of their plan must be denied. An order consistent with this opinion will be entered contemporaneously herewith.

Notes and Questions

1. Why in *Harris* is the creditors' viewpoint, rather than the debtors', determinative?

2. The court says that a debtor who wants to remain in business may separately classify essential suppliers in a Chapter 13 plan and pay them *more*. Given the disposable income requirement of § 1325(b)(1)(B), the bankruptcy will be a zero sum game and other creditors will necessarily receive less as a result of this permissible discrimination. Why, then, can a debtor quitting business not separately classify business creditors and pay them *less*?

3. Is it appropriate to allow the creditor in *Harris* to endanger the debtors' postpetition consumer credit rating for an additional 2.5% of its claim?

4. Does the court in *Harris* import § 707(b) into Chapter 13?

5. Consider the following statement from *In re Young*, 102 B.R. 1022, 1023 (Bankr. W.D.Mo.1989):

> [This Court concludes] that while the amendments to Chapter 13 allow certain latitude in discriminating between some claims that latitude is circumscribed still by the measurements of equity and fairness. Neither allow totally different treatment of *identical* claims. One unsecured, cosigned, consumer claim must be treated comparably to another unsecured, cosigned, consumer claim. To rule otherwise is to undermine the entire structure and concept of equal treatment. A debtor has never been allowed, in bankruptcy, to pick and choose between his creditors—the statute instead outlines any priority to be afforded his creditors.

Is *Young* correct? Isn't it plain that the Code permits some differences in treatment of classes under the plan?

6. Debtor cosigned a loan for her son, so that he could buy a car. May Debtor separately classify the loan in her Chapter 13 plan and propose to pay it 50% if her other unsecured claims are to receive 5%?

7. Debtor was convicted of a crime and, as a condition of probation, was required to pay $1,000. That obligation is not dischargeable in bankruptcy. Debtor filed a Chapter 13 petition and proposed a three-year plan under which $100 a month would be paid on the restitution obligation, for the first

ten months of the plan. Other unsecured creditors were to receive a total of 5% of their claims over the remaining term of the plan. Is that difference in treatment permissible? See *In re Williams*, 231 B.R. 280 (Bankr. S.D. Ohio 1999).

2. CLASSIFICATION IN CHAPTER 11

Section 1129(a) imposes two apparently inconsistent requirements that must be met before a plan can be confirmed—each impaired class must accept the plan, § 1129(a)(8), and at least one impaired class must accept the plan, § 1129(a)(10). The apparent inconsistency melts away when § 1129(b) is consulted—a plan can be confirmed despite its failure to win acceptance by each impaired class as required by (a)(8) if the requirements of § 1129(b) (having to do with minimum payments and the order of payments) are satisfied. This is "cram down." It permits a debtor to impose a plan on dissenting creditors, as long as certain payment requirements are met. But cram down cannot be attempted unless all the requirements of § 1129(a) other than (a)(8) are satisfied. Among those requirements of § 1129(a) that must still be met is (a)(10)—at least one impaired class must accept the plan. In other words, at least one impaired class must vote for the plan before it can be crammed down the throats of the others.

You should now be able to guess that a substantial number of Chapter 11 classification cases involve the debtor's attempt to gerrymander classes so as to obtain the one vote necessary to satisfy § 1129(a)(10). This issue is treated in more detail in Chapter 8 of this casebook.

Chapter 4

SECURED CLAIMS IN BANKRUPTCY

A. INTRODUCTION

According to § 506(a), as we have seen, a claim "secured by a lien on property in which the estate has an interest * * * is a secured claim to the extent of the value of such creditor's interest in the estate's interest in such property." It "is an unsecured claim to the extent that the value of such creditor's interest * * * is less than the amount of such allowed claim."

Although one might wish that the plain-English school of legal writing had enlightened the Code's drafters, § 506(a) operates fairly straightforwardly. Consider two fact patterns. First, assume that Debtor, Inc. borrows $100,000 from Bank and grants a mortgage on its factory to secure repayment of the obligation. Assume in addition that the property is worth $130,000 at the time Debtor, Inc.'s Chapter 7 bankruptcy is filed. Under § 506(a), Bank has a secured claim in the amount of $100,000. If Debtor, Inc. liquidates, the property will be sold and Bank will be paid $100,000 from the proceeds. The excess value of the property ($30,000) will remain in the estate to be distributed to unsecured creditors.

Assume, on the other hand, that the property is worth only $80,000 when bankruptcy is filed. Under § 506(a), Bank's security interest is measured by the value of the property. Because only $80,000 in value is available from the property, Bank's secured claim is only $80,000. Bank also has an unsecured claim of $20,000. This is known as "bifurcation" of an undersecured claim. The undersecured creditor is treated as the holder of two claims, one secured and one unsecured.

Because no value is available to the bankruptcy estate from overencumbered property, the creditor should readily obtain relief from the stay under § 362(d)(2) in a liquidation case. (Reorganizations are different, as we will see, because the property may be necessary to the reorganization effort.) The creditor may not have to bother with relief from stay efforts, however, because the trustee usually abandons property that has no economic value to the estate. § 554. (In addition, § 725 requires the trustee to dispose of property in which another party holds an interest, before the estate is distributed under § 726.) Once property is abandoned it reverts to the debtor and those provisions of the automatic stay prohibiting acts to collect prepetition debts from property of the estate no longer apply, § 362(c)(1). The creditor will have to seek relief from the stay nonetheless, because § 362(a)(5) also stays efforts to enforce prepetition obligations against property of the debtor.

Note that *by definition* assets are available to pay holders of secured claims.

A secured claim is one secured by a "lien." Section 101(37) defines lien as a "charge against or interest in property to secure payment of a debt or performance of an obligation." This includes in the single category of secured claims many types of interests distinct under state law—security interests, mortgages, tax liens, judicial liens and statutory liens.

One of bankruptcy's fundamental policy decisions is that property rights created under nonbankruptcy law will be respected in bankruptcy. The Code's drafters believed this to be constitutionally necessary, although that premise is debatable. See James Steven Rogers, *The Impairment of Secured Creditors' Rights in Reorganization: A Study of the Relationship Between the Fifth Amendment and the Bankruptcy Clause*, 96 Harv. L. Rev. 973 (1983). Acceptance of the premise that lienholders' rights are respected in bankruptcy does not, however, require that the rights themselves be recognized. Professor Theodore Eisenberg articulated an "alternative, scaled-down view of the nature of a secured creditor's right in bankruptcy." Under Professor Eisenberg's view, the *value* of a secured creditor's rights is respected rather than the in rem rights themselves. The significance of secured status, therefore, is the priority afforded its holder:

> This view translates secured status into a priority claim equal to the value of the creditor's collateral, which alone is the measure of the value of the creditor's secured status in bankruptcy.

> Under the priority approach, secured creditors have merely a right to be paid ahead of other creditors to the extent of the value of the secured creditors' collateral. They have no right to force surrender of specific property.

Theodore Eisenberg, *The Undersecured Creditor in Reorganizations and the Nature of Security*, 38 Vand. L. Rev. 931, 952 (1985). This tension between the value of rights and the rights themselves is pervasive in bankruptcy.

Problems

1. Debtor owns a house that is subject to two purchase money mortgages. The first mortgage is for $100,000 and the second is for $50,000. If the house is worth $175,000, what claims are held by the first and second mortgagees?

2. Assume the same facts as in Problem # 1, except that the house is only worth $130,000. What claims are held by the first and second mortgagees?

3. Assume the same first and second mortgagees as above and that the house is worth $130,000. Assume also that another creditor, to whom Debtor owes $45,000, obtains a third-priority judicial lien against the house. What claims are held by the first and second mortgagees and by the judicial lienholder?

B. RELIEF FROM THE STAY AND ADEQUATE PROTECTION

The automatic stay applies in all types of bankruptcy cases and to all claims. The impact of the stay is very different under the various chapters, however. In a Chapter 11, for example, the debtor is operating the business while formulating and negotiating the plan. The debtor must use property of the estate while holding off creditors who have interests in that property. Those creditors assume an increased risk of loss while the debtor tries to reorganize. If the reorganization fails (and most never culminate in a confirmed plan) and the case is converted to a liquidation, secured creditors may suffer damage as a result of depreciation in the value of their collateral during the reorganization effort. The Code provides that, if creditors are subjected to this risk, they are entitled to "adequate protection" of their interests. § 363(e).

A secured creditor facing the risk of deterioration in the value of its collateral is likely to want to obtain relief from the stay in order to take the collateral immediately. Section 362(d) applies to a creditor's effort to obtain relief from the stay. Subsections (1), (2) and (3) state alternative grounds for relief from the stay.

Relief is granted under § 362(d)(1) "for cause, including the lack of adequate protection." Although the Code provides no definition, courts have found cause if the debtor abuses the bankruptcy process (for example, by repeated filings in order to stave off a foreclosure) or if the debtor defaults under a plan.

Relief is granted under § 362(d)(2) if property is fully encumbered and is not needed in an effort to reorganize. Subsection (2) applies in a case like the hypothetical presented above, in which collateral worth $80,000 secures a debt of $100,000 and the debtor files a Chapter 7.

Subsection (3), which was added in 1994, provides for the lifting of the stay in a single asset real estate case if the debtor fails to file a feasible reorganization plan within 90 days of the bankruptcy filing or if the debtor has not begun making monthly payments to the creditor holding an interest in the real estate. Notice that both of the principal cases in this section are, apparently, single asset real estate cases. Such cases are treated in more detail in Chapter 8 of this casebook.

Section 362(e) puts a short fuse on motions for relief from the stay.

BANKERS LIFE INSURANCE COMPANY OF NEBRASKA v. ALYUCAN INTERSTATE CORP. (IN RE ALYUCAN INTERSTATE CORP.)

United States Bankruptcy Court, District of Utah, 1981.
12 B.R. 803.

RALPH R. MABEY, Bankruptcy Judge.

INTRODUCTION AND BACKGROUND

This case raises the question whether an "equity cushion" is necessary to provide adequate protection under § 362(d)(1). This Court concludes that it is not.

On January 14, 1981, Alyucan Interstate Corporation (debtor), a construction and real estate development firm, filed a petition under Chapter 11 of the Code. On May 4, Bankers Life Insurance Company of Nebraska (Bankers Life), holder of a trust deed on realty owned by debtor, brought this action for relief from the automatic stay under § 362(d). The complaint alleges that the realty secures a debt in the principal amount of $1,220,000 and that Bankers Life is not adequately protected. On May 20, the preliminary hearing contemplated by § 362(e) was held. After receiving evidence, the Court fixed the value of the realty on the date of the petition at $1,425,000 and found that there had been no erosion in that value as of the hearing. The debt owing was $1,297,226 as of the petition, and with interest accruing at roughly $8,000 per month,[a] had increased to $1,330,761 as of the hearing. Thus, there was an "equity cushion" of $127,774 or approximately nine percent of the value of the collateral, as of the petition, which had decreased to $94,239, or approximately six and one half percent of the value of the collateral, as of the hearing. As interest accumulates, and if no payments are made, this cushion will dissipate within a year.

THE MEANING OF ADEQUATE PROTECTION

Section 362(d)(1) mandates relief, in some form, from the stay "for cause, including the lack of adequate protection of an interest in property." The only cause asserted in this proceeding is a lack of adequate protection.

Adequate protection is not defined in the Code. This omission was probably deliberate. Congress was aware of the turbulent rivalry of interests in reorganization. It needed a concept which would mediate polarities. But a carefully calibrated concept, subject to a brittle construction, could not accommodate the "infinite number of variations possible in dealings between debtors and creditors." H.R. Rep. No. 95–595 at 339, *reprinted in* 1978 U.S.C.C.A.N. at 6295. This problem required, not a formula, but a calculus, open-textured, pliant, and versatile, adaptable to "new ideas" which are "continually being implemented in this field" and to "varying circumstances and changing modes of financing." *Id.* Adequate protection was requisitioned to meet these needs. Its meaning, therefore, is born afresh out of the

[a] See § 506(b). Eds.

"reflective equilibrium"[2] of each decision, understood through analysis of the reorganization context and the language of § 362(d).

A. The Reorganization Context

Relief from the stay cannot be viewed in isolation from the reorganization process. Bankruptcy in general and Chapter 11 in particular are "procedural devices" for the rehabilitation of financially embarrassed enterprises. The process presupposes dynamic rather than static uses of property and denouement in a plan which accommodates the many, not just the few.

The automatic stay, within this framework, is designed "to prevent a chaotic and uncontrolled scramble for the debtor's assets in a variety of uncoordinated proceedings in different courts." *Fidelity Mortgage Investors v. Camelia Builders, Inc.*, 550 F.2d 47, 55 (2d Cir.1976). It grants a "breathing spell" for debtors to regroup. It shields creditors from one another by replacing "race" and other preferential systems of debt collection with a more equitable and orderly distribution of assets. It encourages rehabilitation: debtors may seek its asylum while recovery is possible rather than coasting to the point of no return; creditors, realizing that foreclosure is useless, may rechannel energies toward more therapeutic ends.

Although self-help and other unilateral recourse against debtors are forbidden, creditors are not left remediless. They may act through committees with professional assistance, often at the expense of the estate, or by seeking appointment of a trustee or examiner. Conversion to Chapter 7 and dismissal are options. Within certain time constraints, they may file a plan.

In short, the adequate protection vouchsafed creditors in Chapter 11 is interim protection, designed not as a purgative of all creditor ailments, but as a palliative of the worst: reorganization, dismissal, or liquidation will provide the final relief. During this interim, the policies favoring rehabilitation and the benefits derived from the stay should not be lightly discarded. Alternative remedies are available to creditors. Indeed, even relief from the stay need not mean termination of the stay. Section 362(d) provides for relief, *such as* "terminating,

---

[2] This phrase is coined in J. Rawls, A Theory of Justice 20–21 (1971), to describe a hypothetical deliberative process.

annulling, modifying, or conditioning" the stay. Thus, relief may be fashioned to suit the exigencies of the case.

B. The Language of § 362(d)

Turning from Chapter 11 at large to § 362(d) in specific, several issues must be addressed. First, what is the "interest in property" being protected? Second, what aspects of the "interest in property" require protection? Third, from what is the "interest in property" being protected? Fourth, what is the method of protection?

(1) What is the "interest in property" being protected? The legislative history mentions only "the interest of a secured creditor or co-owner of property with the debtor" in connection with adequate protection. H.R. Rep. No. 95–595 at 338. Within these classes of creditors, however, "the interests of which the court may provide protection * * * include equitable as well as legal interests. For example, a right to redeem under a pledge or a right to recover property under a consignment are both interests that are entitled to protection.' *Id.* This classification is important because adequate protection depends upon the interest *and* property involved. Protection afforded a lessor, for example, may be different from that afforded a secured creditor. Treatment of a secured creditor who faces turnover may be different from treatment of a secured creditor who has not repossessed. Treatment of a senior lienholder may be different from treatment of a junior lienholder. Similarly, protection may vary if the property is real or personal, tangible or intangible, perdurable or perishable, or if its value is constant, depreciating, or subject to sudden or extreme fluctuations. Also relevant is the proposed use or idleness of the property.

(2) What aspects of the "interest in property" require protection? Adequate protection is concerned with the value of the interest in property. The legislative commentary to § 361 underscores this point: "Though the creditor might not receive his bargain in kind, the purpose of the section is to insure that the secured creditor receives *in value* essentially what he bargained for." *Id.* at 339 (emphasis supplied). The legislative history reemphasizes this point by noting that adequate protection is "derived from the fifth amendment protection of property interests," *id.*, citing *Wright v. Union Central Insurance Co.*, 311 U.S. 273 (1940), and *Louisville Bank v. Radford*, 295 U.S. 555 (1935). In *Wright*, Justice Douglas held that the bank received "the value of the [interest in] property" and that "there is no constitutional claim of a creditor to more than that." 311 U.S. at 278. Debtors were allowed to redeem the property at its appraised price, despite an obligation which

exceeded the value of the collateral by $10,000. Thus, the "interest in property" entitled to protection is not measured by the amount of the debt but by the value of the lien. A mushrooming debt, through accrual of interest or otherwise, may be immaterial, if the amount of the lien is not thereby increased, while vicissitudes in the market, loss of insurance or other factors affecting the value of the lien are relevant to adequate protection. The purpose of adequate protection is to assure the recoverability of this value during the hiatus between petition and plan, or in the event the reorganization is stillborn, between petition and dismissal.[11]

(3) From what is the "interest in property" being protected? The short answer is from any impairment in value attributable to the stay. The stay does not cause, but it may forestall a creditor from preventing or mitigating, a decline in value. Some harm to collateral, however, may be unavoidable with or without the stay. Likewise, creditors may acquiesce in some harm to collateral for business or other reasons notwithstanding the stay. In these situations, and others which may arise, any impairment in value may not be attributable to the stay.

---

[11] Some cases have interpreted adequate protection more in terms of contractual benefits than economic values. They have focused on language in the legislative history suggesting that secured creditors must receive the "benefit of their bargain." H.R. Rep. No. 95–595 at 339. Congress, however, was not referring to the *contractual* bargain between creditors and debtors because the next portion of the House Report acknowledges "there may be situations in bankruptcy where giving a secured creditor an absolute right to his bargain may be impossible or seriously detrimental to the bankruptcy laws. Thus, this section [§ 361] recognizes the availability of alternate means of protecting a secured creditor's interest. Though the creditor might not receive his bargain in kind, the purpose of the section is to insure that the secured creditor receives in value essentially what he bargained for." *Id.* Whether and to what extent noncontractual or business elements of a bargain may be factored into the adequate protection equation is problematical. Some courts, employing an equity cushion analysis (discussed below), insist that a ratio of debt to collateral is "bargained for" between debtor and creditor and must be considered in determining adequate protection. The stream of inquiry along this path, however, may be difficult to contain. Many business motives, which may or may not be expressed in the documents memorializing a transaction, could then become relevant to adequate protection. As a practical matter, for example, foreclosure may not be an attractive prospect for some lenders who are, after all, in the business of loaning money not managing properties. Hence, their bargain is primarily for payment with interest and, as a last resort, for liquidation with its burdens of custodial care and costs. Foreclosure may likewise pose regulatory complications. Banks and insurance companies are traditionally limited in the amount of illiquid assets, such as realty, which they can carry at any given time in their portfolio.

Hence, not every decline in value must be recompensed, only those which, but for the stay, could be and probably would be prevented or mitigated.

(4) What is the method of protection? The method of affording adequate protection, as noted above, will vary with the interest in property to be protected. In some cases, the debtor need do nothing, either because the value of the interest in property is not declining or because the decline in value is not attributable to the stay. If the stay is responsible for a decline in value, § 361 states three illustrative methods for providing adequate protection. Some courts, however, have not looked beyond its trilogy of alternatives. Others have insisted on a showing of indubitable equivalence. These approaches miss the mark: they violate the nonprescriptive character of § 361, and may simply exchange one imponderable for another. Indubitable equivalence is not a method; nor does it have substantive content. Indeed, something "indubitable" is more than "adequate;" "equivalent" is more than "protection;" hence, the illustration may eclipse the concept. At best, it is a semantic substitute for adequate protection and one with dubious, not indubitable, application to the question of relief from the stay.

C. Application to This Proceeding

In this proceeding, the "interest in property" is the lien of Bankers Life on the realty of debtor. It is a trust deed and therefore may be peremptorily foreclosed. It is a first lien with ample collateral to protect Bankers Life. The collateral and therefore the lien are not declining or subject to sudden depreciation in value. Bankers Life is suffering no pain cognizable under § 362 as a result of the stay, and relief from the stay is therefore, at this juncture, unnecessary.

Moreover, this property is essential to the reorganization of the debtor. Foreclosure and liquidation of the property would run counter to this need and would deprive debtor and other creditors of its going concern value. If liquidation is allowed, it should occur under the aegis of the Court and in the interests of all. Bankers Life is no better qualified to handle this liquidation than the debtor or the trustee. Indeed, Bankers Life may be ill-equipped to undertake this task, both because its interests are parochial and because, for regulatory or other reasons, it may be a reluctant caretaker. *See* discussion *supra* note 11. In any event, Bankers Life has other remedies under the Code. A trustee has been appointed. It may work with him or with creditor committees to negotiate a sale of the property. It can seek dismissal or conversion to Chapter 7. It can propose a plan of liquidation. In short, the application of adequate protection to the facts of this case avoids the trauma of relief from the stay and maintains the equilibrium of interests in this reorganization.

THE EQUITY CUSHION ANALYSIS

In contrast to these principles, there is a trend toward defining adequate protection in terms of an "equity cushion": the difference between outstanding debt and the value of the property against which the creditor desires to act. Where the difference is substantial, a cushion is said to exist, adequately protecting the creditor. As interest accrues, or depreciation advances, and the margin declines, the cushion weakens and the stay may be lifted. Naturally, courts disagree on what is an acceptable margin. The emerging view, however, may be that the stay should be terminated when the cushion will be absorbed through interest, commissions, and other costs of resale. The cushion analysis enjoys practical appeal and ease of application.

This Court rejects a cushion analysis upon four grounds: (1) It is inconsistent with the purpose of adequate protection. (2) It is inconsistent with the illustrations of adequate protection found in § 361. (3) It is inconsistent with the statutory scheme of § 362(d). (4) It has no basis in the historical development of relief from stay proceedings.

(1) The cushion analysis, by focusing on the ratio of debt to collateral, obscures the purpose of adequate protection, *viz.*, to guard against impairment of a lien. This blurring of objectives may produce improper results. If Bankers Life had been undersecured at the petition, for example, the absence of cushion would have dictated relief from the stay, even though the stay did not impair its lien and notwithstanding the usual appreciation in the value of realty.

(2) Since the thrust of adequate protection is to assure maintenance of the value of the lien, it is largely compensatory. Sections 361(1) and (2) therefore speak not in terms of preserving equity but in terms of compensating for any "decrease in the value of [an] interest in property." Moreover, the cushion analysis, because it is confined to the relationship between debt and collateral in a specific property, ignores the recoverability of value, not only from the property at stake but also from other sources. Sections 361(1) and (2), which provide for interim payments and replacement liens, contemplate that value from other assets held by debtors may be appropriated to supply any needed protection. Indeed, the legislative history to § 361 suggests the use of sureties or guarantors for this purpose. Even if the debtor has no other

assets, it is nevertheless conceivable that an enterprise valuation, which approaches value in terms of capitalized earnings, could show an income potential sufficient to meet the adequate protection standard.

(3) Under § 362(d)(2) a lack of equity, absent a further showing that the property is unnecessary to an effective reorganization, does not warrant relief from the stay. This statutory provision expresses a legislative judgment, first, that it is the *absence* of equity rather than any particular cushion which is the criterion for relief from stay, and second, that the absence of equity is not alone dispositive—the court must still weigh the necessity of the property to an effective reorganization. The cushion analysis is inconsistent with this judgment. It makes surplusage out of § 362(d)(2) which speaks in terms of equity *and* reorganization. Indeed, this dual requirement emphasizes the role of equity, when present, not as a cushion, but to underwrite, through sale or credit, the rehabilitation of debtors.

(4) The cushion analysis is alien to the development of stay litigation. The stay provisions in Chapter proceedings in the Act * * * allowed relief "for cause shown." This was interpreted to require consideration of a number of factors, including the presence of equity, the likelihood of harm to the creditor, prospects for reorganization, and essentiality of the property in the operation of the estate. *See, e.g.*, Peitzman and Smith, "The Secured Creditor's Complaint: Relief from the Automatic Stays in Bankruptcy Proceedings," 65 Cal. L. Rev. 1216, 1226 (1977).

Although the "idea of equity" became "something of a totem for courts," *id.* at 1227, it was equity in the sense contemplated under § 362(d)(2), not an equity cushion. Thus, it was acknowledged that "deciding whether to continue or vacate the stay solely on the ground of the debtor's equity in the property may produce an unjust result," for example where "the encumbered property is so vital to the operation of debtor's business that foreclosure will simply not be allowed." *Id.*

* * *

CONCLUSION

Adequate protection is a concept designed to balance the rights of creditors and debtors in the preliminary stages of reorganization. It is, in each case, *ad hoc*. For this reason the cushion analysis, which may be helpful in general, falls short in the particular. It is not fully alert to the legislative directive that "the facts," in each hearing under

§ 362(d), "will determine whether relief is appropriate under the circumstances." H.R. Rep. No. 95–595 at 344. The facts of each case, thoughtfully weighed, not formularized, define adequate protection.

Questions and Problems

1. According to *Alyucan*, exactly what property interests of the secured creditor are entitled to adequate protection?

2. The court asserted that "[a] mushrooming debt, through accrual of interest or otherwise, may be immaterial, if the amount of the lien is not thereby increased." When, factually, will that occur?

3. Loan agreements frequently require a debt-to-equity ratio of a designated percentage. This means that the debt cannot exceed that percentage of the value of the collateral, and assures the creditor of a continuous equity cushion. What if such an agreement had been present in *Alyucan*?

4. Assume the same facts as in *Alyucan*, except that the collateral is depreciating at the rate of $200 per month rather than holding its value. What rights to adequate protection would the secured creditor have?

5. Debtor owned an apartment building worth $300,000. It was subject to a first purchase money mortgage of $150,000 and a second purchase money mortgage of $50,000. Debtor later gave a third lien on the property to a bank, in exchange for a loan of $70,000, and a fourth priority judgment lien for $130,000 was taken by a previously unsecured creditor. Debtor filed bankruptcy and the holder of the first mortgage sought relief from the stay under § 362(d)(2). Debtor argued that the requirements of (d)(2)(A) were not satisfied because the property had a value of $150,000 in excess of movant's lien. Movant argued that "equity" is the difference between the property's value and the total amount of liens encumbering it. Who prevails? See *Nantucket Investors II v. California Federal Bank (In re Indian Palms Assocs., Ltd.)*, 61 F.3d 197, 206-08 (3d Cir. 1995).

UNITED SAVINGS ASSOCIATION OF TEXAS v. TIMBERS OF INWOOD FOREST ASSOCIATES, LTD.

United States Supreme Court, 1988.
484 U.S. 365, 108 S.Ct. 626, 98 L.Ed.2d 740.

JUSTICE SCALIA delivered the opinion of the Court.

Petitioner United Savings Association of Texas seeks review of an en banc decision of the United States Court of Appeals for the Fifth

Circuit, holding that petitioner was not entitled to receive from respondent debtor, which is undergoing reorganization in bankruptcy, monthly payments for the use value of the loan collateral which the bankruptcy stay prevented it from possessing. We granted certiorari to resolve a conflict in the Courts of Appeals regarding application of §§ 361 and 362(d)(1) of the Bankruptcy Code. Compare *Grundy Nat'l Bank v. Tandem Mining Corp.*, 754 F.2d 1436, 1440–41 (4th Cir.1985); *In re American Mariner Industries, Inc.*, 734 F.2d 426, 432–35 (9th Cir.1984); see also *In re Briggs Transp. Co.*, 780 F.2d 1339, 1348–51 (8th Cir.1985).

I

On June 29, 1982, respondent Timbers of Inwood Forest Associates, Ltd., executed a note in the principal amount of $4,100,000. Petitioner is the holder of the note as well as of a security interest created the same day in an apartment project owned by respondent in Houston, Texas. The security interest included an assignment of rents from the project. On March 4, 1985, respondent filed a voluntary petition under Chapter 11 of the Bankruptcy Code in the United States Bankruptcy Court for the Southern District of Texas.

On March 18, 1985, petitioner moved for relief from the automatic stay of enforcement of liens triggered by the petition, see § 362(a), on the ground that there was lack of "adequate protection" of its interest within the meaning of § 362(d)(1). At a hearing before the Bankruptcy Court, it was established that respondent owed petitioner $4,366,388.77, and evidence was presented that the value of the collateral was somewhere between $2,650,000 and $4,250,000. The collateral was appreciating in value, but only very slightly. It was therefore undisputed that petitioner was an undersecured creditor. Respondent had agreed to pay petitioner the postpetition rents from the apartment project (covered by the after-acquired property clause in the security agreement), minus operating expenses. Petitioner contended, however, that it was entitled to additional compensation. The Bankruptcy Court agreed and on April 19, 1985, it conditioned continuance of the stay on monthly payments by respondent, at the market rate of 12% per annum, on the estimated amount realizable on foreclosure, $4,250,000—commencing six months after the filing of the bankruptcy petition, to reflect the normal foreclosure delays. The court held that the postpetition rents could be applied to these payments. Respondent appealed to the District Court and petitioner cross-appealed on the amount of the adequate protection payments. The District Court affirmed but the Fifth Circuit en banc reversed.

We granted certiorari to determine whether undersecured creditors are entitled to compensation under § 362(d)(1) for the delay caused by the automatic stay in foreclosing on their collateral.

II

When a bankruptcy petition is filed, § 362(a) of the Bankruptcy Code provides an automatic stay of, among other things, actions taken to realize the value of collateral given by the debtor. The provision of the Code central to the decision of this case is § 362(d) * * *. The phrase "adequate protection" in paragraph (1) of [§ 362(d)] is given further content by § 361 of the Code * * *.

It is common ground that the "interest in property" referred to by § 362(d)(1) includes the right of a secured creditor to have the security applied in payment of the debt upon completion of the reorganization; and that that interest is not adequately protected if the security is depreciating during the term of the stay. Thus, it is agreed that if the apartment project in this case had been declining in value petitioner would have been entitled, under § 362(d)(1), to cash payments or additional security in the amount of the decline, as § 361 describes. The crux of the present dispute is that petitioner asserts, and respondent denies, that the phrase "interest in property" also includes the secured party's right (suspended by the stay) to take immediate possession of the defaulted security, and apply it in payment of the debt. If that right is embraced by the term, it is obviously not adequately protected unless the secured party is reimbursed for the use of the proceeds he is deprived of during the term of the stay.

The term "interest in property" certainly summons up such concepts as "fee ownership," "life estate," "co-ownership," and "security interest" more readily than it does the notion of "right to immediate foreclosure." Nonetheless, viewed in the isolated context of § 362-(d)(1), the phrase could reasonably be given the meaning petitioner asserts. Statutory construction, however, is a holistic endeavor. A provision that may seem ambiguous in isolation is often clarified by the remainder of the statutory scheme—because the same terminology is used elsewhere in a context that makes its meaning clear or because only one of the permissible meanings produces a substantive effect that is compatible with the rest of the law. That is the case here. Section 362(d)(1) is only one of a series of provisions in the Bankruptcy Code dealing with the rights of secured creditors. The language in those other provisions, and the substantive dispositions that they effect, persuade us that the "interest in property" protected by § 362(d)(1) does not include a secured party's right to immediate foreclosure.

Section 506 of the Code defines the amount of the secured creditor's allowed secured claim and the conditions of his receiving postpetition interest. * * * In subsection (a) of this provision the creditor's "interest in property" obviously means his security interest without taking account of his right to immediate possession of the collateral on default. If the latter were included, the "value of such creditor's interest" would increase, and the proportions of the claim that are secured and unsecured would alter, as the stay continues—since the value of the entitlement to use the collateral from the date of bankruptcy would rise with the passage of time. No one suggests this was intended. The phrase "value of such creditor's interest" in § 506(a) means "the value of the collateral." H.R. Rep. No. 95–595 at 181, 356. We think the phrase "value of such entity's interest" in § 361(1) and (2), when applied to secured creditors, means the same.

Even more important for our purposes than § 506's use of terminology is its substantive effect of denying undersecured creditors postpetition interest on their claims—just as it denies *over* secured creditors postpetition interest to the extent that such interest, when added to the principal amount of the claim, will exceed the value of the collateral. Section 506(b) provides that "*[t]o the extent that* an allowed secured claim is secured by property the value of which * * * is greater than the amount of such claim, there shall be allowed to the holder of such claim, interest on such claim." (Emphasis added.) Since this provision permits postpetition interest to be paid only out of the "security cushion," the undersecured creditor, who has no such cushion, falls within the general rule disallowing postpetition interest. See § 502(b)(2). If the Code had meant to give the undersecured creditor, who is thus denied interest on his *claim*, interest on the value of his *collateral*, surely this is where that disposition would have been set forth, and not obscured within the "adequate protection" provision of § 362(d)(1). Instead of the intricate phraseology set forth above, § 506(b) would simply have said that the secured creditor is entitled to interest "on his allowed claim, or on the value of the property securing his allowed claim, whichever is lesser." Petitioner's interpretation of § 362(d)(1) must be regarded as contradicting the carefully drawn disposition of § 506(b).

Petitioner seeks to avoid this conclusion by characterizing § 506(b) as merely an alternative method for compensating oversecured creditors, which does not imply that no compensation is available to undersecured creditors. This theory of duplicate protection for oversecured creditors is implausible even in the abstract, but even more so in light of the historical principles of bankruptcy law. Section 506(b)'s denial of postpetition interest to undersecured creditors merely codified pre-Code bankruptcy law, in which that denial was part of the conscious allocation of reorganization benefits and losses between undersecured and unsecured creditors. "To allow a secured creditor interest where his security was worth less than the value of his debt was thought to be inequitable to unsecured creditors." *Vanston Bondholders Protective Committee v. Green*, 329 U.S. 156, 164 (1946). It was considered unfair to allow an undersecured creditor to recover interest from the estate's unencumbered assets before unsecured creditors had recovered any principal. We think it unlikely that § 506(b) codified the pre-Code rule with the intent, not of achieving the principal purpose and function of that rule, but of providing oversecured creditors an alternative method of compensation. Moreover, it is incomprehensible why Congress would want to favor undersecured creditors with interest if they move for it under § 362(d)(1) at the inception of the reorganization process—thereby probably pushing the estate into liquidation—but not if they forbear and seek it only at the completion of the reorganization.

Second, petitioner's interpretation of § 362(d)(1) is structurally inconsistent with § 552. Section 552(a) states the general rule that a prepetition security interest does not reach property acquired by the estate or debtor postpetition. Section 552(b) sets forth an exception, allowing postpetition "proceeds, product, offspring, rents, or profits" of the collateral to be covered only if the security agreement expressly provides for an interest in such property, and the interest has been perfected under "applicable nonbankruptcy law."[b] Section 552(b) therefore makes possession of a perfected security interest in postpetition rents or profits from collateral a condition of having them applied to satisfying the claim of the secured creditor ahead of the claims of unsecured creditors. Under petitioner's interpretation, however, the undersecured creditor who lacks such a perfected security interest in effect achieves the same result by demanding the "use value" of his collateral under § 362. It is true that § 506(b) gives the *over* secured creditor, despite lack of compliance with the conditions of § 552, a similar priority over unsecured creditors; but that does not compromise the principle of § 552, since the interest payments come only out of the

---

[b] In 1994, § 552(b) was renumbered § 552(b)(1), the reference to "rents" was deleted, and § 552(b)(2) was added. The new subsection now treats rents separately. Eds.

"cushion" in which the oversecured creditor *does have* a perfected security interest.

Third, petitioner's interpretation of § 362(d)(1) makes nonsense of § 362(d)(2). On petitioner's theory, the undersecured creditor's inability to take immediate possession of his collateral is always "cause" for conditioning the stay (upon the payment of market rate interest) under § 362(d)(1), since there is, within the meaning of that paragraph, "lack of adequate protection of an interest in property." But § 362(d)(2) expressly provides a different standard for relief from a stay "of an act against property," which of course includes taking possession of collateral. It provides that the court shall grant relief "if * * * (A) the debtor does not have an equity in such property [*i.e.*, the creditor is undersecured]; *and* (B) such property is not necessary to an effective reorganization." (Emphasis added.) By applying the "adequate protection of an interest in property" provision of § 362(d)(1) to the alleged "interest" in the earning power of collateral, petitioner creates the strange consequence that § 362 entitles the secured creditor to relief from the stay (1) if he is undersecured (and thus not eligible for interest under § 506(b)), *or* (2) if he is undersecured *and* his collateral "is not necessary to an effective reorganization." This renders § 362(d)(2) a practical nullity and a theoretical absurdity. If § 362(d)(1) is interpreted in this fashion, an undersecured creditor would seek relief under § 362(d)(2) only if his collateral was not depreciating (or he was being compensated for depreciation) and it was receiving market rate interest on his collateral, but nonetheless wanted to foreclose. Petitioner offers no reason why Congress would want to provide relief for such an obstreperous and thoroughly unharmed creditor.

Section 362(d)(2) also belies petitioner's contention that undersecured creditors will face inordinate and extortionate delay if they are denied compensation for interest lost during the stay as part of "adequate protection" under § 362(d)(1). Once the movant under § 362(d)(2) establishes that he is an undersecured creditor, it is the burden of the *debtor* to establish that the collateral at issue is "necessary to an effective reorganization." See § 362(g). What this requires is not merely a showing that if there is conceivably to be an effective reorganization, this property will be needed for it; but that the property is essential for an effective reorganization *that is in prospect*. This means, as many lower courts, including the en banc court in this case, have properly said, that there must be "a reasonable possibility of a successful reorganization within a reasonable time." The cases are numerous in which § 362(d)(2) relief has been provided within less than a year from the filing of the bankruptcy petition. And while the bankruptcy courts demand less detailed showings during the four months in which the debtor is given the exclusive right to put together a plan, see §§ 1121(b), (c)(2), even within that period lack of any realistic prospect of effective reorganization will require § 362(d)(2) relief.

III

A

Petitioner contends that denying it compensation under § 362-(d)(1) is inconsistent with sections of the Code other than those just discussed. Petitioner principally relies on the phrase "indubitable equivalent" in § 361(3), which also appears in § 1129(b)(2)(A)(iii). Petitioner contends that in the latter context, which sets forth the standards for confirming a reorganization plan, the phrase has developed a well-settled meaning connoting the right of a secured creditor to receive present value of his security—thus requiring interest if the claim is to be paid over time. It is true that under § 1129(b) a secured claimant has a right to receive under a plan the present value of his collateral. This entitlement arises, however, not from the phrase "indubitable equivalent" in § 1129(b)(2)(A)(iii), but from the provision of § 1129-(b)(2)(A)(i)(II) that guarantees the secured creditor "deferred cash payments * * * of a value, *as of the effective date of the plan*, of at least the value of such [secured claimant's] interest in the estate's interest in such property." (Emphasis added.) Under this formulation, even though the undersecured creditor's "interest" is regarded (properly) as solely the value of the collateral, he must be rendered payments that assure him that value *as of the effective date of the plan*. In § 361(3), by contrast, the relief pending the stay need only be such "*as will result in the realization* * * * of the indubitable equivalent" of the collateral. (Emphasis added.) It is obvious (since §§ 361 and 362(d)(1) do not entitle the secured creditor to immediate payment of the principal of his collateral) that this "realization" is to "result" not at once, but only upon completion of the reorganization. It is *then* that he must be assured "realization * * * of the indubitable equivalent" of his collateral. To put the point differently: similarity of outcome between § 361(3) and § 1129 would be demanded only if the former read "such other relief * * * as will give such entity, *as of the date of the relief*, the indubitable equivalent of such entity's interest in such property."

Nor is there merit in petitioner's suggestion that "indubitable equivalent" in § 361(3) connotes reimbursement for the use value of collateral because the phrase is derived from *In re Murel Holding*

Corp., 75 F.2d 941 (2d Cir.1935), where it bore that meaning. *Murel* involved a proposed reorganization plan that gave the secured creditor interest on his collateral for 10 years, with full payment of the secured principal due at the end of that term; the plan made no provision, however, for amortization of principal or maintenance of the collateral's value during the term. In rejecting the plan, *Murel* used the words "indubitable equivalence" with specific reference not to interest (which was assured), but to the jeopardized principal of the loan:

> "Interest is indeed the common measure of the difference [between payment now and payment 10 years hence], but a creditor who fears the safety of his principal will scarcely be content with that; he wishes to get his money or at least the property. We see no reason to suppose that the statute was intended to deprive him of that in the interest of junior holders, unless by a substitute of the most indubitable equivalence." *Id.* at 942.

Of course *Murel*, like § 1129, proceeds from the premise that in the confirmation context the secured creditor is entitled to present value. But no more from *Murel* than from § 1129 can it be inferred that a similar requirement exists as of the time of the bankruptcy stay. The reorganized debtor is supposed to stand on his own two feet. The debtor in process of reorganization, by contrast, is given many temporary protections against the normal operation of the law.

Petitioner also contends that the Code embodies a principle that secured creditors do not bear the costs of reorganization. It derives this from the rule that general administrative expenses do not have priority over secured claims. See §§ 506(c), 507(a). But the general principle does not follow from the particular rule. That secured creditors do not bear one kind of reorganization cost hardly means that they bear none of them. The Code rule on administrative expenses merely continues pre-Code law. But it was also pre-Code law that undersecured creditors were not entitled to postpetition interest as compensation for the delay of reorganization. Congress could hardly have understood that the readoption of the rule on administrative expenses would work a change in the rule on postpetition interest, which it also readopted.

Finally, petitioner contends that failure to interpret § 362(d)(1) to require compensation of undersecured creditors for delay will create an inconsistency in the Code in the (admittedly rare) case when the debtor proves solvent. When that occurs, § 726(a)(5) provides that postpetition interest is allowed on unsecured claims. Petitioner contends it would be absurd to allow post-petition interest on unsecured claims but not on the secured portion of undersecured creditors' claims. It would be disingenuous to deny that this is an apparent anomaly, but it will occur so rarely that it is more likely the product of inadvertence than are the blatant inconsistencies petitioner's interpretation would produce. Its inequitable effects, moreover, are entirely avoidable, since an undersecured creditor is entitled to "surrender or waive his security and prove his entire claim as an unsecured one." *United States Nat'l Bank v. Chase Nat'l Bank*, 331 U.S. 28, 34 (1947). Section 726(a)(5) therefore requires no more than that undersecured creditors receive post-petition interest from a solvent debtor on equal terms with unsecured creditors rather than ahead of them—which, where the debtor is solvent, involves no hardship.

B

Petitioner contends that its interpretation is supported by the legislative history of §§ 361 and 362(d)(1), relying almost entirely on statements that "[s]ecured creditors should not be deprived of the benefit of their bargain." H.R. Rep. No. 95–595 at 339, *reprinted in* 1978 U.S.C.C.A.N. at 6295; S. Rep. No. 95–989 at 53, *reprinted in* 1978 U.S.C.C.A.N. at 5839. Such generalizations are inadequate to overcome the plain textual indication in §§ 506 and 362(d)(2) of the Code that Congress did not wish the undersecured creditor to receive interest on his collateral during the term of the stay. If it is at all relevant, the legislative history tends to subvert rather than support petitioner's thesis, since it contains not a hint that § 362(d)(1) entitles the undersecured creditor to postpetition interest. Such a major change in the existing rules would not likely have been made without specific provision in the text of the statute; it is most improbable that it would have been made without even any mention in the legislative history.

Petitioner makes another argument based upon what the legislative history does *not* contain. It contends that the pre-Code law gave the undersecured creditor relief from the automatic stay by permitting him to foreclose; and that Congress would not have withdrawn this entitlement to relief without any indication of intent to do so in the legislative history, unless it was providing an adequate substitute, to wit, interest on the collateral during the stay.

The premise of this argument is flawed. As petitioner itself concedes, the undersecured creditor had no absolute entitlement to foreclosure in a Chapter X or XII case; he could not foreclose if there was a reasonable prospect for a successful rehabilitation within a reasonable time. Thus, even assuming petitioner is correct that the undersecured creditor had an absolute entitlement to relief under Chapter XI, Congress would have been faced with the choice between adopting the rule from Chapters X and XII or the asserted alternative rule from Chapter XI, because Chapter 11 of the current Code "replaces chapters X, XI and XII of the Bankruptcy Act" with a "single chapter for all business reorganizations." S. Rep. No. 95–989 at 9. We think § 362(d)(2) indicates that Congress adopted the approach of Chapters X and XII. In any event, as far as the silence of the legislative history on the point is concerned, that would be no more strange with respect to alteration of the asserted Chapter XI rule than it would be with respect to alteration of the Chapters X and XII rule.

Petitioner's argument is further weakened by the fact that it is far from clear that there was a distinctive Chapter XI rule of absolute entitlement to foreclosure. At least one leading commentator concluded that "a Chapter XI court's power to stay lien enforcement is as broad as that of a Chapter X or XII court and that the automatic stay rules properly make no distinctions between the Chapters." Countryman, Real Estate Liens in Business Rehabilitation Cases, 50 Am. Bankr. L.J. 303, 315 (1976). Petitioner cites dicta in some Chapter XI cases suggesting that the undersecured creditor was automatically entitled to relief from the stay, but the courts in those cases uniformly found in addition that reorganization was not sufficiently likely or was being unduly delayed. Moreover, other Chapter XI cases held undersecured creditors not entitled to foreclosure under reasoning very similar to that used in Chapters X and XII cases. The at best divided authority under Chapter XI removes all cause for wonder that the alleged departure from it should not have been commented upon in the legislative history.

The Fifth Circuit correctly held that the undersecured petitioner is not entitled to interest on its collateral during the stay to assure adequate protection under § 362(d)(1). Petitioner has never sought relief from the stay under § 362(d)(2) or on any ground other than lack of adequate protection. Accordingly, the judgment of the Fifth Circuit is

Affirmed.

Notes and Questions

1. Are *Alyucan* and *Timbers* consistent?

2. What would be the practical impact of a contrary result in *Timbers*?

3. Outside of bankruptcy, the secured creditor could have foreclosed on the collateral, sold it, and reinvested the proceeds. Doesn't the result in *Timbers* essentially force the creditor to make an interest-free loan to the debtor for the duration of the bankruptcy case? Does the Court give sufficient consideration to the rights of the creditor under state law?

4. Does *Timbers* give the debtor and junior creditors an incentive to procrastinate? Would that incentive have been removed by a contrary decision?

5. The Court's answer to "inordinate and extortionate delay" is § 362(d)(2), which requires that relief from the stay be granted if the collateral is not necessary to an effective reorganization. According to the Court, this means a "reorganization *that is in prospect.*" Do you think this protection is really reassuring to an undersecured creditor?

6. If the debtor anticipates a liquidating plan in Chapter 11, is the property still "necessary to an effective reorganization" within § 362(d)(2)?

7. Section 1205(a) provides that § 361 does not apply in a Chapter 12 case. Congress included that subsection in Chapter 12 because *Grundy* and *American Mariner*, which were noted in *Timbers*, had held that an undersecured creditor's lost opportunity costs were an interest entitled to adequate protection under § 361. Now that *Timbers* has overruled those cases, the reason for § 1205(a) has been eliminated.

8. Apex purchased a gas station from Robert and Susan Neier, paying $165,000 in cash and giving a note for the $450,000 balance. The note was fully secured by a mortgage on the property. When Apex filed Chapter 11, it stopped making payments on the note. The Neiers sought relief from the stay, on the grounds that the monthly payments on the note were their primary source of income and were needed in order to support their family. (They had two children with special needs and were responsible for three elderly aunts.) Does the creditor's neediness constitute "cause" within § 362(d)(1)? See *Neier v. Clark Oil & Refining Corp. (In re Apex Oil)*, 85 B.R. 538 (Bankr. E.D.Mo.1988).

C. RIGHTS OF SECURED CREDITORS TO POSTPETITION INTEREST

The secured creditor's claim in *Alyucan* was increasing after the filing of bankruptcy because § 506(b) allows postpetition interest to oversecured creditors. In *Alyucan*, the creditor's claim arose out of a prepetition contract with the debtor. But what of the nonconsensual secured creditor, whose rights against the debtor arise by operation of law? Does such a creditor also have a right to postpetition interest under § 506(b)?

UNITED STATES v. RON PAIR ENTERPRISES, INC.

United States Supreme Court, 1989.
489 U.S. 235, 109 S.Ct. 1026, 103 L.Ed.2d 290.

JUSTICE BLACKMUN delivered the opinion of the Court.

In this case we must decide the narrow statutory issue whether § 506(b) of the Bankruptcy Code of 1978 entitles a creditor to receive postpetition interest on a nonconsensual oversecured claim allowed in a bankruptcy proceeding. We conclude that it does, and we therefore reverse the judgment of the Court of Appeals.

I

Respondent Ron Pair Enterprises, Inc., filed a petition for reorganization under Chapter 11 of the Bankruptcy Code on May 1, 1984, in the United States Bankruptcy Court for the Eastern District of Michigan. The Government filed timely proof of a prepetition claim of $52,277.93, comprised of assessments for unpaid withholding and Social Security taxes, penalties, and prepetition interest. The claim was perfected through a tax lien on property owned by respondent. Respondent's First Amended Plan of Reorganization, filed October 1, 1985, provided for full payment of the prepetition claim, but did not provide for postpetition interest on that claim. The Government filed a timely objection, claiming that § 506(b) allowed recovery of postpetition interest, since the property securing the claim had a value greater than the amount of the principal debt. At the Bankruptcy Court hearing, the parties stipulated that the claim was oversecured, but the court subsequently overruled the Government's objection. The Government appealed to the United States District Court for the Eastern District of Michigan. That court reversed the Bankruptcy Court's judgment, concluding that the plain language of § 506(b) entitled the Government to postpetition interest.

The United States Court of Appeals for the Sixth Circuit, in its turn, reversed the District Court. While not directly ruling that the language of § 506(b) was ambiguous, the court reasoned that reference to pre-Code law was appropriate "in order to better understand the context in which the provision was drafted and therefore the language itself." The court went on to note that under pre-Code law the general rule was that postpetition interest on an oversecured prepetition claim was allowable only where the lien was consensual in nature. In light of this practice, and of the lack of any legislative history evincing an intent to change the standard, the court held that § 506(b) codified the pre-existing standard, and that postpetition interest was allowable only on consensual claims. Because this result was in direct conflict with the view of the Court of Appeals for the Fourth Circuit, see *Best Repair Co. v. United States*, 789 F.2d 1080 (1986), and with the views of other courts, we granted certiorari to resolve the conflict.

II

Section 506, enacted as part of the extensive 1978 revision of the bankruptcy laws, governs the definition and treatment of secured claims, *i.e.*, claims by creditors against the estate that are secured by a lien on property in which the estate has an interest. Subsection (a) of § 506 provides that a claim is secured only to the extent of the value of the property on which the lien is fixed; the remainder of that claim is considered unsecured. Subsection (b) is concerned specifically with oversecured claims, that is, any claim that is for an amount less than the value of the property securing it. Thus, if a $50,000 claim were secured by a lien on property having a value of $75,000, the claim would be oversecured, provided the trustee's costs of preserving or disposing of the property were less than $25,000. Section 506(b) allows a holder of an oversecured claim to recover, in addition to the prepetition amount of the claim, "interest on such claim, and any reasonable fees, costs, or charges provided for under the agreement under which such claim arose."

The question before us today arises because there are two types of secured claims: (1) voluntary (or consensual) secured claims, each created by agreement between the debtor and the creditor and called a "security interest" by the Code, [§ 101(51)], and (2) involuntary secured claims, such as a judicial or statutory lien, see [§§ 101(36) and (53)], which are fixed by operation of law and do not require the consent of the debtor. The claim against respondent's estate was of this latter kind. Prior to the passage of the 1978 Code, some Courts of Appeals drew a distinction between the two types for purposes of determining postpetition interest. The question we must answer is whether the 1978 Code recognizes and enforces this distinction, or whether Congress intended that all oversecured claims be treated the same way for purposes of postpetition interest.

III

Initially, it is worth recalling that Congress worked on the formulation of the Code for nearly a decade. It was intended to modernize the bankruptcy laws, see H.R. Rep. No. 95–595 at 3, *reprinted in* 1978 U.S.C.C.A.N. at 5965 (Report), and as a result made significant changes in both the substantive and procedural laws of bankruptcy. In particular, Congress intended "significant changes from current law in * * * the treatment of secured creditors and secured claims." Report at 180. In such a substantial overhaul of the system, it is not appropriate or realistic to expect Congress to have explained with particularity each step it took. Rather, as long as the statutory scheme is coherent and consistent, there generally is no need for a court to inquire beyond the plain language of the statute.

A

The task of resolving the dispute over the meaning of § 506(b) begins where all such inquiries must begin: with the language of the statute itself. In this case it is also where the inquiry should end, for where, as here, the statute's language is plain, "the sole function of the courts is to enforce it according to its terms." *Caminetti v. United States*, 242 U.S. 470, 485 (1917). The language before us expresses Congress' intent—that postpetition interest be available—with sufficient precision so that reference to legislative history and to pre-Code practice is hardly necessary.

The relevant phrase in § 506(b) is: "[t]here shall be allowed to the holder of such claim, interest on such claim, and any reasonable fees, costs, or charges provided for under the agreement under which such claim arose." "Such claim" refers to an oversecured claim. The natural reading of the phrase entitles the holder of an oversecured claim to postpetition interest and, in addition, gives one having a secured claim created pursuant to an agreement the right to reasonable fees, costs, and charges provided for in that agreement. Recovery of postpetition interest is unqualified. Recovery of fees, costs, and charges, however, is allowed only if they are reasonable and provided for in the agreement under which the claim arose. Therefore, in the absence of an agreement, postpetition interest is the only added recovery available.

This reading is also mandated by the grammatical structure of the statute. The phrase "interest on such claim" is set aside by commas, and separated from the reference to fees, costs, and charges by the conjunctive words "and any." As a result, the phrase "interest on such claim" stands independent of the language that follows. "[I]nterest on such claim" is not part of the list made up of "fees, costs, or charges," nor is it joined to the following clause so that the final "provided for under the agreement" modifies it as well. The language and punctuation Congress used cannot be read in any other way.[4] By the plain language of the statute, the two types of recovery are distinct.[5]

B

The plain meaning of legislation should be conclusive, except in the "rare cases [in which] the literal application of a statute will produce a result demonstrably at odds with the intentions of its drafters." *Griffin v. Oceanic Contractors, Inc.*, 458 U.S. 564, 571 (1982). In such cases, the intention of the drafters, rather than the strict language, controls. It is clear that allowing postpetition interest on nonconsensual oversecured liens does not contravene the intent of the framers of the Code. Allowing such interest does not conflict with any other section of the Code, or with any important state or federal interest; nor is a contrary view suggested by the legislative history. Respondent has not articulated, nor can we discern, any significant reason why Congress would have intended, or any policy reason would compel, that the two

---

[4] The United States Court of Appeals for the Fourth Circuit pointed out in *Best Repair Co.* that, had Congress intended to limit postpetition interest to consensual liens, § 506(b) could have said: "there shall be allowed to the holder of such claim, as provided for under the agreement under which such claim arose, interest on such claim and any reasonable fees, costs or charges." 789 F.2d at 1082, n.2. A less clear way of stating this, closer to the actual language, would be: "there shall be allowed to the holder of such claim, interest on such claim and reasonable fees, costs, and charges provided for under the agreement under which such claim arose."

[5] It seems to us that the interpretation adopted by the Court of Appeals in this case not only requires that the statutory language be read in an unnatural way, but that it is inconsistent with the remainder of § 506 and with terminology used throughout the Code. Adopting the Court of Appeals' view would mean that § 506(b) is operative only in regard to consensual liens, *i.e.*, that only a holder of an oversecured claim arising from an agreement is entitled to any added recovery. But the other portions of § 506 make no distinction between consensual and nonconsensual liens. Moreover, had Congress intended § 506(b) to apply only to consensual liens, it would have clarified its intent by using the specific phrase, "security interest," which the Code employs to refer to liens created by agreement. [§ 101(51)]. When Congress wanted to restrict the application of a particular provision of the Code to such liens, it used the term "security interest." See, *e.g.*, §§ 362(b)(12) and (13), 363(a), 547(c)(3), (5), 552, 752(c), 1110(a), 1168(a), 1322(b)(2).

types of secured claims be treated differently in allowing postpetition interest.

C

Respondent urges that pre-Code practice drew a distinction between consensual and nonconsensual liens for the purpose of determining entitlement to postpetition interest, and that Congress' failure to repudiate that distinction requires us to enforce it. It is respondent's view, as it was the view of the Court of Appeals, that *Midlantic National Bank v. New Jersey Dept. of Environmental Protection*, 474 U.S. 494 (1986), and *Kelly v. Robinson*, 479 U.S. 36 (1986), so require. We disagree.

In *Midlantic* we held that § 554(a) of the Code, which provides that "the trustee may abandon any property of the estate that is burdensome to the estate," does not give a trustee the authority to violate state health and safety laws by abandoning property containing hazardous wastes. In reaching that conclusion, we noted that according to pre-Code doctrine the trustee's authority to dispose of property could be limited in order "to protect legitimate state or federal interests." 474 U.S. at 500. But we did not rest solely, or even primarily, on a presumption of continuity with pre-Code practice. Rather, we concluded that a contrary result would render abandonment doctrine inconsistent with other provisions of the Code itself, which embody the principle that "the trustee is not to have *carte blanche* to ignore nonbankruptcy law." *Id.* at 502. We also recognized that the outcome sought would be not only a departure from pre-Code practice, but also "an extraordinary exemption from nonbankruptcy law," *id.* at 501, requiring some clearer expression of congressional intent. We relied as well on Congress' repeated emphasis in environmental legislation "on its 'goal of protecting the environment against toxic pollution.'" *Id.* at 505, quoting *Chemical Manufacturers Assn. v. Natural Resources Defense Council, Inc.*, 470 U.S. 116, 143 (1985). To put it simply, we looked to pre-Code practice for interpretive assistance, because it appeared that a literal application of the statute would be "demonstrably at odds with the intentions of its drafters." *Griffin v. Oceanic Contractors, Inc.*, 458 U.S. at 571.

A similar issue presented itself in *Kelly v. Robinson*, where we held that a restitution obligation, imposed as part of a state criminal sentence, was not dischargeable in bankruptcy. We reached this conclusion by interpreting § 523(a)(7) of the Code as "preserv[ing] from discharge any condition a state criminal court imposes as part of a criminal sentence." 479 U.S. at 50. We noted that the Code provision was "subject to interpretation" and considered both legislative history and pre-Code practice in aid of that interpretation. But in determining that Congress had not intended to depart from pre-Code practice in this regard, we did not rely on a pale presumption to that effect. We concluded that the pre-Code practice had been animated by "a deep conviction that federal bankruptcy courts should not invalidate the results of state criminal proceedings," *id.* at 47, which has its source in the basic principle of our federalism that "the States' interest in administering their criminal justice systems free from federal interference is one of the most powerful of the considerations that should influence a court considering equitable types of relief." *Id.* at 49. In *Kelly*, as in *Midlantic*, pre-Code practice was significant because it reflected policy considerations of great longevity and importance.

Kelly and *Midlantic* make clear that, in an appropriate case, a court must determine whether Congress has expressed an intent to change the interpretation of a judicially created concept in enacting the Code. But *Midlantic* and *Kelly* suggest that there are limits to what may constitute an appropriate case. Both decisions concerned statutory language which, at least to some degree, was open to interpretation. Each involved a situation where bankruptcy law, under the proposed interpretation, was in clear conflict with state or federal laws of great importance. In the present case, in contrast, the language in question is clearer than the language at issue in *Midlantic* and *Kelly*: as written it directs that postpetition interest be paid on all oversecured claims. In addition, this natural interpretation of the statutory language does not conflict with any significant state or federal interest, nor with any other aspect of the Code. Although the payment of postpetition interest is arguably somewhat in tension with the desirability of paying all creditors as uniformly as practicable, Congress expressly chose to create that alleged tension. There is no reason to suspect that Congress did not mean what the language of the statute says.

D

But even if we saw the need to turn to pre-Code practice in this case, it would be of little assistance. The practice of denying postpetition interest to the holders of nonconsensual liens, while allowing it to holders of consensual liens, was an exception to an exception, recognized by only a few courts and often dependent on particular circumstances. It was certainly not the type of "rule" that we assume Congress was aware of when enacting the Code; nor was it of such significance that Congress would have taken steps other than enacting statutory language to the contrary.

There was, indeed, a pre-Code rule that the running of interest ceased when a bankruptcy petition was filed. Two exceptions to this rule had been recognized under pre-Code practice. The first allowed postpetition interest when the debtor ultimately proved to be solvent; the second allowed dividends and interest earned by securities held by the creditor as collateral to be applied to postpetition interest. Neither of these exceptions would be relevant to this case. A third exception was of more doubtful provenance: an exception for oversecured claims. At least one Court of Appeals refused to apply this exception, and there was some uncertainty among courts which did recognize it as to whether this Court ever had done so.

What is at issue in this case is not the oversecured claim exception *per se*, but an exception to that exception. Several Courts of Appeals refused to apply the oversecured claim exception to an over-secured federal tax claim. It is this refusal to apply the exception that the Court of Appeals thought constituted a well-established judicially created rule.

The fact that this Court never clearly has acknowledged or relied upon this limitation on the oversecured-claim exception counsels against concluding that the limitation was well recognized. Also arguing against considering this limitation a clear rule is the fact that all the cases that limited the third exception were tax-lien cases. Each gave weight to *City of New York v. Saper*, 336 U.S. 328 (1949), where this Court had ruled that postpetition interest was not available on *unsecured* tax claims, and reasoned that the broad language of that case denied it for all tax claims. The rule articulated in these cases never was extended to other forms of nonconsensual liens. Obviously, there is no way to read § 506(b) as allowing postpetition interest on all over-secured claims except claims based on unpaid taxes. For this reason, the statute Congress wrote is simply not subject to a reading that would harmonize it with the supposed pre-Code rule.

More importantly, this "rule," in the few cases where it was recognized, was only a guide to the trustee's exercise of his powers in the particular circumstances of the case. We have noted that "the touchstone of each decision on allowance of interest in bankruptcy * * * has been a balance of equities between creditor and creditor or between creditors and the debtor." *Vanston Bondholders Protective Committee v. Green*, 329 U.S. 156, 165 (1946). All the exceptions to the denial of postpetition interest "are not rigid doctrinal categories. Rather, they are flexible guidelines which have been developed by the courts in the exercise of their equitable powers in insolvency proceedings." *In re Boston & Maine Corp.*, 719 F.2d 493, 496 (1st Cir.1983), cert. denied *sub nom. City of Cambridge v. Meserve*, 466 U.S. 938 (1984). None of the cases cited by the Court of Appeals states that the doctrine does anything more than provide a bankruptcy court with guidance in the exercise of its equitable powers. As such, there is no reason to think that Congress, in enacting a contrary standard, would have felt the need expressly to repudiate it. The contrary view, which is the view we adopt today, is more consistent with Congress' stated intent, in enacting the Code, to "codif[y] creditors' rights *more clearly than the case law* * * * by defin[ing] the protections to which a secured creditor is entitled, and the means through which the court may grant that protection." Report at 4–5 (emphasis added). Whether or not Congress took notice of the pre-Code standard, it acted with sufficient clarity in enacting the statute.

The judgment of the Court of Appeals is reversed.

It is so ordered.

JUSTICE O'CONNOR, with whom JUSTICE BRENNAN, JUSTICE MARSHALL, and JUSTICE STEVENS join, dissenting.

The Court's decision is based on two distinct lines of argument. First, the Court concludes that the language of § 506(b) of the Bankruptcy Code is clear and unambiguous. Second, the Court takes a very narrow view of *Midlantic National Bank v. New Jersey Dept. of Environmental Protection*, 474 U.S. 494 (1986), and its progeny. I disagree with both aspects of the Court's opinion, and with the conclusion to which they lead.

The relevant portion of § 506(b) provides that "there shall be allowed to the holder of [an oversecured] claim, interest on such claim, and any reasonable fees, costs, or charges provided for under the agreement under which such claim arose." The Court concludes that the only natural reading of § 506(b) is that recovery of postpetition interest is "unqualified." As Justice Frankfurter remarked some time ago, however, "[t]he notion that because the words of a statute are plain, its meaning is also plain, is merely pernicious oversimplification." *United States v. Monia*, 317 U.S. 424, 431 (1943) (dissenting opinion).

Although "the use of the comma is exceedingly arbitrary and indefinite," *United States v. Palmer*, 3 Wheat. 610, 638 (1818) (separate opinion of Johnson, J.), the Court is able to read § 506(b) the way that it does only because of the comma following the phrase "interest on such claim." Without this "capricious" bit of punctuation, *In re Newbury Cafe, Inc.*, 841 F.2d 20, 22 (1st Cir.1988), cert. pending, the relevant portion of § 506(b) would read as follows: "there shall be allowed to the holder of [an oversecured] claim, interest on such claim and any reasonable fees, costs, or charges provided for under the agreement under which such claim arose." The phrase "interest on such claim" would be qualified by the phrase "provided for under the agreement under which such claim arose," and nonconsensual liens would not accrue postpetition interest. This conclusion is not altered by the fact that the words "and any" follow the phrase "interest on such claim." Those words simply indicate that interest accrues only on the amount of the claim, and not on "fees, costs, or charges" that happen to be incurred by the creditor.

The Court's reliance on the comma is misplaced. "Punctuation is not decisive of the construction of a statute." *Costanzo v. Tillinghast*, 287 U.S. 341, 344 (1932). Under this rule of construction, the Court has not hesitated in the past to change or ignore the punctuation in legislation in order to effectuate congressional intent.

Although punctuation is not controlling, it can provide useful confirmation of conclusions drawn from the words of a statute. The Court attempts to buttress its interpretation of § 506(b) by suggesting that any other reading would be inconsistent with the remaining portions of § 506, which "make no distinction between consensual and nonconsensual liens." But § 506(b), regardless of how it is read, does distinguish between types of liens. The phrase "provided for under the agreement under which such claim arose" certainly refers to consensual liens, and must qualify some preceding language. Even under the Court's interpretation, "reasonable fees, costs, or charges" can only be awarded if provided for in a consensual lien. Thus, limiting postpetition interest to consensual liens simply reinforces a distinction that already exists in § 506(b). For the same reason, I find unavailing the Court's assertion that Congress would have used the phrase "security interest" if it wanted to limit postpetition interest to consensual liens.

Even if I believed that the language of § 506(b) were clearer than it is, I would disagree with the Court's conclusion, for *Midlantic* counsels against inferring congressional intent to change pre-Code bankruptcy law. * * *

The Court characterizes *Midlantic* as involving "a situation where bankruptcy law, under the proposed interpretation, was in clear conflict with state or federal laws of great importance." Though I agree with that characterization, I think there is more to *Midlantic* than conflict with state or federal laws. Contrary to the Court's intimation, *Midlantic* did not "concern[] statutory language which was open to interpretation." The language of § 554(a) is "absolute in its terms," 474 U.S. at 509 (REHNQUIST, J., dissenting), and the Court in *Midlantic* did not attempt to argue otherwise. Nonetheless, the Court concluded that such clear language was insufficient to demonstrate specific congressional intent to change pre-Code law. The rule of *Midlantic* is that bankruptcy statutes will not be deemed to have changed pre-Code law unless there is some indication that Congress thought that it was effecting such a change.

The first step under *Midlantic* is to ascertain whether there was an established pre-Code bankruptcy practice. That question is easily answered here. Prior to the 1978 enactment of the Code, this Court, as well as every Court of Appeals to address the question, had refused to allow postpetition interest on nonconsensual liens such as the tax lien involved in this case. In order to deflect this line of cases, the Court refers to the practice "of denying postpetition interest to the holders of nonconsensual liens, while allowing it to holders of consensual liens," as "an exception to an exception." Regardless of how it is labeled, the practice was more widespread and more well established than the practice in *Midlantic*, and was certainly one that Congress "would have been aware of when enacting the Code."

The denial of postpetition interest on nonconsensual liens was based on the distinction between types of liens as well as equitable considerations. Unlike consensual liens, to which the parties voluntarily agree, nonconsensual liens depend for their existence only on legislative fiat. Thus, the justification for the allowance of postpetition interest on consensual liens—"that when the creditor extended credit, he relied upon the particular security given as collateral to secure both the principal of the debt and interest until payment and, if the collateral is sufficient to pay him, the contract between the parties ought not be abrogated by bankruptcy," *United States v. Harrington*, 269 F.2d 719, 724 (4th Cir.1959)—has no application to nonconsensual liens. The allowance of interest on nonconsensual liens is akin to a penalty on the debtor for the nonpayment of taxes or other monetary obligations imposed by law. Permitting postpetition interest on nonconsensual liens drains the pool of assets to the detriment of lower priority creditors who are not responsible for the debtor's inability to pay and who cannot avoid the imposition of postpetition interest. Indeed, the Court acknowledges that "the payment of postpetition interest is arguably somewhat in tension with the desirability of paying all creditors as uniformly as possible."

The second step under *Midlantic* is to look for some indicia that Congress knew it was changing pre-Code law. As the Court said only last Term, "it is most improbable that [a change in the existing bankruptcy rules] would have been made without even any mention in the legislative history." *United Savings Ass'n of Texas v. Timbers of Inwood Forest Associates, Ltd.*, 484 U.S. 365, 380 (1988). * * * Because there is no evidence whatsoever that § 506(b) was meant to allow postpetition interest on nonconsensual liens, it should not be assumed that Congress "silently abrogated" the pre-Code law.

For the reasons set forth above, I respectfully dissent.

Questions and Problems

1. In grammatical terms, what is the issue in *Ron Pair*?

2. If the IRS is entitled to interest as the holder of an oversecured nonconsensual lien, from whose pocket does the money come? Does that make good sense as a matter of bankruptcy policy?

3. Debtor gave a lien on Blackacre to secure a promissory note for $600,000. Under the terms of the note, Debtor was to pay $100,000 per year, plus 10% interest, for six years. Debtor defaulted before making any payments and filed Chapter 11. Because Blackacre was worth $750,000, Creditor sought postpetition interest at the contract rate. Debtor argued that interest should be measured either by the statutory judgment rate of 6% or by the then-current market rate for similar loans, which was 7%. What rate is appropriate?

4. Assume the same facts as in Problem # 3, except that the property is also encumbered by a second lien of $150,000. When the first lienholder sought postpetition interest, the second lienholder objected, arguing that the interest would come directly out of its pocket. Which creditor prevails?

5. Debtor's home, which was worth $150,000, was encumbered by a purchase money mortgage. The mortgage documents permitted Bank to accelerate the obligation if Debtor missed a payment, but neither the documents nor state law provided for interest on arrearages. When the debt was $120,000, Debtor missed several payments (totaling $2,750) and Bank accelerated. Debtor filed Chapter 13 before Bank could begin foreclosure proceedings. Under Debtor's proposed plan, Debtor would make regular monthly payments in accordance with the loan documents and pay the arrearage over

the life of the plan. The plan did not provide for interest, either before or after confirmation, on the $2,750 arrearage. Bank argued it was entitled to pre- and postconfirmation interest, under § 506(b) and *Ron Pair,* because it was oversecured. What result? See § 1322(e).

D. RIGHTS OF SECURED CREDITORS WHO REPOSSESS BEFORE BANKRUPTCY

Debtors sliding into financial crisis frequently default on one or more of their obligations to various creditors. A secured creditor who finds itself among the ranks of the unpaid is likely to respond by repossessing or seizing the property subject to its lien. Such a repossession or seizure may spell financial doom if the debtor is a business enterprise that needs the property in order to continue operating. Can such a debtor find some strategic help in the Bankruptcy Code?

UNITED STATES v. WHITING POOLS, INC.

United States Supreme Court, 1983.
462 U.S. 198, 103 S.Ct. 2309, 76 L.Ed.2d 515.

JUSTICE BLACKMUN delivered the opinion of the Court.

Promptly after the Internal Revenue Service (IRS or Service) seized respondent's property to satisfy a tax lien, respondent filed a petition for reorganization under the Bankruptcy Reform Act of 1978, hereinafter referred to as the "Bankruptcy Code." The issue before us is whether § 542(a) of that Code authorized the Bankruptcy Court to subject the IRS to a turnover order with respect to the seized property.

I

A

Respondent Whiting Pools, Inc., a corporation, sells, installs, and services swimming pools and related equipment and supplies. As of January 1981, Whiting owed approximately $92,000 in Federal Insurance Contribution Act taxes and federal taxes withheld from its employees, but had failed to respond to assessments and demands for payment by the IRS. As a consequence, a tax lien in that amount attached to all of Whiting's property.

On January 14, 1981, the Service seized Whiting's tangible personal property—equipment, vehicles, inventory, and office supplies—pursuant to the levy and distraint provision of the Internal Revenue Code of 1954. According to uncontroverted findings, the estimated liquidation value of the property seized was, at most, $35,000, but its estimated going-concern value in Whiting's hands was $162,876. The very next day, January 15, Whiting filed a petition for reorganization, under the Bankruptcy Code's Chapter 11 in the United States Bankruptcy Court for the Western District of New York. Whiting was continued as debtor-in-possession.

The United States, intending to proceed with a tax sale of the property, moved in the Bankruptcy Court for a declaration that the automatic stay provision of the Bankruptcy Code, § 362(a), is inapplicable to the IRS or, in the alternative, for relief from the stay. Whiting counterclaimed for an order requiring the Service to turn the seized property over to the bankruptcy estate pursuant to § 542(a) of the Bankruptcy Code. Whiting intended to use the property in its reorganized business.

B

The Bankruptcy Court determined that the IRS was bound by the automatic stay provision. Because it found that the seized property was essential to Whiting's reorganization effort, it refused to lift the stay. Acting under § 543(b)(1) of the Bankruptcy Code, rather than under § 542(a), the court directed the IRS to turn the property over to Whiting on the condition that Whiting provide the Service with specified protection for its interests.[7]

The United States District Court reversed, holding that a turnover order against the Service was not authorized by either § 542(a) or § 543(b)(1). The United States Court of Appeals for the Second Circuit, in turn, reversed the District Court. It held that a turnover order could issue against the Service under § 542(a), and it remanded the case for reconsideration of the adequacy of the Bankruptcy Court's protection conditions. The Court of Appeals acknowledged that its

---

[7] * * * Pursuant to [§ 363(e)], the Bankruptcy Court set the following conditions to protect the tax lien: Whiting was to pay the Service $20,000 before the turnover occurred; Whiting also was to pay $1,000 a month until the taxes were satisfied; the IRS was to retain its lien during this period; and if Whiting failed to make the payments, the stay was to be lifted.

ruling was contrary to that reached by the United States Court of Appeals for the Fourth Circuit in *Cross Electric Co. v. United States*, 664 F.2d 1218 (1981), and noted confusion on the issue among bankruptcy and district courts. We granted certiorari to resolve this conflict in an important area of the law under the new Bankruptcy Code.

II

By virtue of its tax lien, the Service holds a secured interest in Whiting's property. We first examine whether § 542(a) of the Bankruptcy Code generally authorizes the turnover of a debtor's property seized by a secured creditor prior to the commencement of reorganization proceedings. Section 542(a) requires an entity in possession of "property that the trustee may use, sell, or lease under § 363" to deliver that property to the trustee. Subsections (b) and (c) of § 363 authorize the trustee to use, sell, or lease any "property of the estate," subject to certain conditions for the protection of creditors with an interest in the property. Section 541(a)(1) defines the "estate" as "comprised of all the following property, wherever located: * * * all legal or equitable interests of the debtor in property as of the commencement of the case." Although these statutes could be read to limit the estate to those "interests of the debtor in property" at the time of the filing of the petition, we view them as a definition of what is included in the estate, rather than as a limitation.

A

In proceedings under the reorganization provisions of the Bankruptcy Code, a troubled enterprise may be restructured to enable it to operate successfully in the future. Until the business can be reorganized pursuant to a plan under §§ 1121–1129, the trustee or debtor-in-possession is authorized to manage the property of the estate and to continue the operation of the business. See § 1108. By permitting reorganization, Congress anticipated that the business would continue to provide jobs, to satisfy creditors' claims, and to produce a return for its owners. H.R. Rep. No. 95–595 at 220, *reprinted in* 1978 U.S.C.C.A.N. at 5787. Congress presumed that the assets of the debtor would be more valuable if used in a rehabilitated business than if "sold for scrap." The reorganization effort would have small chance of success, however, if property essential to running the business were excluded from the estate. Thus, to facilitate the rehabilitation of the debtor's business, all the debtor's property must be included in the reorganization estate.

This authorization extends even to property of the estate in which a creditor has a secured interest. §§ 363(b) and (c); see H.R. Rep. No. 95–595 at 182. Although Congress might have safeguarded the interests of secured creditors outright by excluding from the estate any property subject to a secured interest, it chose instead to include such property in the estate and to provide secured creditors with "adequate protection" for their interests. § 363(e). At the secured creditor's insistence, the bankruptcy court must place such limits or conditions on the trustee's power to sell, use, or lease property as are necessary to protect the creditor. The creditor with a secured interest in property included in the estate must look to this provision for protection, rather than to the nonbankruptcy remedy of possession.

Both the congressional goal of encouraging reorganizations and Congress' choice of methods to protect secured creditors suggest that Congress intended a broad range of property to be included in the estate.

B

The statutory language reflects this view of the scope of the estate. As noted above, § 541(a)(1) provides that the "estate is comprised of all the following property, wherever located: * * * all legal or equitable interests of the debtor in property as of the commencement of the case." The House and Senate Reports on the Bankruptcy Code indicate that § 541(a)(1)'s scope is broad. Most important, in the context of this case, § 541(a)(1) is intended to include in the estate any property made available to the estate by other provisions of the Bankruptcy Code. Several of these provisions bring into the estate property in which the debtor did not have a possessory interest at the time the bankruptcy proceedings commenced.[10]

Section 542(a) is such a provision. It requires an entity (other than a custodian) holding any property of the debtor that the trustee can use under § 363 to turn that property over to the trustee. Given the broad scope of the reorganization estate, property of the debtor repossessed by a secured creditor falls within this rule, and therefore may be drawn into the estate. While there are explicit limitations on

[10] See, *e.g.*, §§ 543, 547, and 548. These sections permit the trustee to demand the turnover of property that is in the possession of others if that possession is due to a custodial arrangement, § 543, to a preferential transfer, § 547, or to a fraudulent transfer, § 548. * * *

the reach of § 542(a),[12] none requires that the debtor hold a possessory interest in the property at the commencement of the reorganization proceedings.

As does all bankruptcy law, § 542(a) modifies the procedural rights available to creditors to protect and satisfy their liens.[14] In effect, § 542(a) grants to the estate a possessory interest in certain property of the debtor that was not held by the debtor at the commencement of reorganization proceedings. The Bankruptcy Code provides secured creditors various rights, including the right to adequate protection, and these rights replace the protection afforded by possession.

C

This interpretation of § 542(a) is supported by the section's legislative history. Although the legislative reports are silent on the precise issue before us, the House and Senate hearings from which § 542(a) emerged provide guidance. Several witnesses at those hearings noted, without contradiction, the need for a provision authorizing the turnover of property of the debtor in the possession of secured creditors. Section 542(a) first appeared in the proposed legislation shortly after these hearings. The section remained unchanged through subsequent versions of the legislation.

Moreover, this interpretation of § 542 in the reorganization context is consistent with judicial precedent predating the Bankruptcy Code. Under Chapter X, the reorganization chapter of the Bankruptcy Act of 1878 [sic], as amended, the bankruptcy court could order the

---

[12] Section 542 provides that the property be usable under § 363, and that turnover is not required in three situations: when the property is of inconsequential value or benefit to the estate, § 542(a), when the holder of the property has transferred it in good faith without knowledge of the petition, § 542(c), or when the transfer of the property is automatic to pay a life insurance premium, § 542(d).

[14] One of the procedural rights the law of secured transactions grants a secured creditor to enforce its lien is the right to take possession of the secured property upon the debtor's default. Uniform Commercial Code § 9–503. A creditor's possessory interest resulting from the exercise of this right is subject to certain restrictions on the creditor's use of the property. See § 9–504. Here, we address the abrogation of the Service's possessory interest obtained pursuant to its tax lien, a secured interest. We do not decide whether any property of the debtor in which a third party holds a possessory interest independent of a creditor's remedies is subject to turnover under § 542(a). For example, if property is pledged to the secured creditor so that the creditor has possession prior to any default, § 542(a) may not require turnover.

turnover of collateral in the hands of a secured creditor. Nothing in the legislative history evinces a congressional intent to depart from that practice. Any other interpretation of § 542(a) would deprive the bankruptcy estate of the assets and property essential to its rehabilitation effort and thereby would frustrate the congressional purpose behind the reorganization provisions.[17]

We conclude that the reorganization estate includes property of the debtor that has been seized by a creditor prior to the filing of a petition for reorganization.

III

A

We see no reason why a different result should obtain when the IRS is the creditor. The Service is bound by § 542(a) to the same extent as any other secured creditor. The Bankruptcy Code expressly states that the term "entity," used in § 542(a), includes a governmental unit. [§ 101(15)]. Moreover, Congress carefully considered the effect of the new Bankruptcy Code on tax collection, see generally S. Rep. No. 95–1106 (1978) (Report of Senate Finance Committee), and decided to provide protection to tax collectors, such as the IRS, through grants of enhanced priorities for unsecured tax claims, [§ 507(a)(8)], and by the nondischarge of tax liabilities, § 523(a)(1). S. Rep. No. 95–989 at 14–15. Tax collectors also enjoy the generally applicable right under § 363(e) to adequate protection for property subject to their liens. Nothing in the Bankruptcy Code or its legislative history indicates that Congress intended a special exception for the tax collector in the form of an exclusion from the estate of property seized to satisfy a tax lien.

B

Of course, if a tax levy or seizure transfers to the IRS ownership of the property seized, § 542(a) may not apply. The enforcement provisions of the Internal Revenue Code of 1954 do grant to the Service powers to enforce its tax liens that are greater than those

---

[17] Section 542(a) also governs turnovers in liquidation and individual adjustment of debt proceedings under Chapters 7 and 13 of the Bankruptcy Code. See § 103(a). Our analysis in this case depends in part on the reorganization context in which the turnover order is sought. We express no view on the issue whether § 542(a) has the same broad effect in liquidation or adjustment of debt proceedings.

possessed by private secured creditors under state law. But those provisions do not transfer ownership of the property to the IRS.

The Service's interest in seized property is its lien on that property. The Internal Revenue Code's levy and seizure provisions are special procedural devices available to the IRS to protect and satisfy its liens and are analogous to the remedies available to private secured creditors. See Uniform Commercial Code § 9–503. They are provisional remedies that do not determine the Service's rights to the seized property, but merely bring the property into the Service's legal custody. At no point does the Service's interest in the property exceed the value of the lien. The IRS is obligated to return to the debtor any surplus from a sale. Ownership of the property is transferred only when the property is sold to a bona fide purchaser at a tax sale. In fact, the tax sale provision itself refers to the debtor as the owner of the property after the seizure but prior to the sale. Until such a sale takes place, the property remains the debtor's and thus is subject to the turnover requirement of § 542(a).

IV

When property seized prior to the filing of a petition is drawn into the Chapter 11 reorganization estate, the Service's tax lien is not dissolved; nor is its status as a secured creditor destroyed. The IRS, under § 363(e), remains entitled to adequate protection for its interests, to other rights enjoyed by secured creditors, and to the specific privileges accorded tax collectors. Section 542(a) simply requires the Service to seek protection of its interest according to the congressionally established bankruptcy procedures, rather than by withholding the seized property from the debtor's efforts to reorganize.

The judgment of the Court of Appeals is affirmed.

It is so ordered.

Notes and Questions

1. The Court did not decide whether its analysis applies in a Chapter 7 or a Chapter 13 case. Does it? Should it?

2. Does *Whiting Pools* apply when the collateral is real estate upon which the creditor has foreclosed?

3. At what point is it too late for the debtor to file bankruptcy in order to force the return of repossessed and foreclosed collateral? See § 1322(c)(1); *Homeside Lending, Inc. v. Denny (In re Denny)*, 242 B.R. 593 (Bankr. D. Md. 1999).

4. To the extent that § 542 and *Whiting Pools* apply, they provide a powerful tool for debtors seeking to undo collection actions taken by creditors. Debtors have no other way, short of paying the full debt, of forcing creditors to return collateral seized through levy, foreclosure or repossession. Once you understand this, you will see why the threat of bankruptcy may be a persuasive negotiating strategy for obligors.

E. CHARGES AGAINST A SECURED CREDITOR'S COLLATERAL

Section 506(c) permits expenses of preserving or disposing of property subject to a lien to be charged against the property. For example, assume that a reorganizing debtor has a fleet of trucks that is subject to a security interest, but that is also necessary to the reorganization. The trustee must spend money for maintenance and insurance in order to keep the trucks on the road. These expenditures are of benefit to the secured creditor also, since they serve to protect the value of the collateral. Thus, § 506(c) permits the trustee to "surcharge" the collateral in order to reimburse the estate for these expenses.

That is an easy, prototypical § 506(c) case. But what if the estate has enjoyed the value of goods and services for which payment has not been made? These claims enjoy an administrative expense priority—a status that is of little comfort when the estate is administratively insolvent. Can the claimant look to § 506(c)?

HARTFORD UNDERWRITERS INSURANCE CO. v. UNION PLANTERS BANK, N. A.

United States Supreme Court, 2000.
___ U.S. ___, 120 S.Ct. 1942, 147 L.Ed.2d 1.

JUSTICE SCALIA delivered the opinion of the Court.

In this case, we consider whether § 506(c) allows an administrative claimant of a bankruptcy estate to seek payment of its claim from property encumbered by a secured creditor's lien.

I

This case arises out of the bankruptcy proceedings of Hen House Interstate, Inc., which at one time owned or operated several restaurants and service stations, as well as an outdoor-advertising firm. On September 5, 1991, Hen House filed a voluntary petition under Chapter 11 of the Bankruptcy Code in the United States Bankruptcy Court for the Eastern District of Missouri. As a Chapter 11 debtor-in-possession, Hen House retained possession of its assets and continued operating its business.

Respondent had been Hen House's primary lender. At the time the Chapter 11 petition was filed, it held a security interest in essentially all of Hen House's real and personal property, securing an indebtedness of over $4 million. After the Chapter 11 proceedings were commenced, it agreed to lend Hen House an additional $300,000 to help finance the reorganization. The Bankruptcy Court entered a financing order approving the loan agreement and authorizing Hen House to use loan proceeds and cash collateral to pay expenses, including workers' compensation expenses.

During the attempted reorganization, Hen House obtained workers' compensation insurance from petitioner Hartford Underwriters (which was unaware of the bankruptcy proceedings). Although the policy required monthly premium payments, Hen House repeatedly failed to make them; Hartford continued to provide insurance nonetheless. The reorganization ultimately failed, and on January 20, 1993, the Bankruptcy Court converted the case to a liquidation proceeding under Chapter 7 and appointed a trustee. At the time of the conversion, Hen House owed Hartford more than $50,000 in unpaid premiums.

Hartford learned of Hen House's bankruptcy proceedings after the conversion, in March 1993.

Recognizing that the estate lacked unencumbered funds to pay the premiums, Hartford attempted to charge the premiums to respondent, the secured creditor, by filing with the Bankruptcy Court an "Application for Allowance of Administrative Expense, Pursuant to § 503 and Charge Against Collateral, Pursuant to § 506(c)." The Bankruptcy Court ruled in favor of Hartford, and the District Court and an Eighth Circuit panel affirmed. The Eighth Circuit subsequently granted en banc review, however, and reversed, concluding that § 506(c) could not be invoked by an administrative claimant. We granted certiorari.

II

Petitioner's effort to recover the unpaid premiums involves two provisions, §§ 503(b) and 506(c). Section 503(b) provides that "the actual, necessary costs and expenses of preserving the estate, including wages, salaries, or commissions for services rendered after the commencement of the case" are treated as administrative expenses, which are, as a rule, entitled to priority over prepetition unsecured claims, see §§ 507(a)(1), 726(a)(1), 1129(a)(9)(A). Respondent does not dispute that the cost of the workers' compensation insurance Hen House purchased from petitioner is an administrative expense within the meaning of this provision. Administrative expenses, however, do not have priority over secured claims, see §§ 506, 725–726, 1129(b)(2)(A), and because respondent held a security interest in essentially all of the estate's assets, there were no unencumbered funds available to pay even administrative claimants.

Petitioner therefore looked to § 506(c), which constitutes an important exception to the rule that secured claims are superior to administrative claims. *[The Court quoted § 506(c).]* Petitioner argued that this provision entitled it to recover from the property subject to respondent's security interest the unpaid premiums owed by Hen House, since its furnishing of workers' compensation insurance benefited respondent by allowing continued operation of Hen House's business, thereby preserving the value of respondent's collateral; or alternatively, that such benefit could be presumed from respondent's consent to the postpetition financing order. Although it was contested below whether, under either theory, the workers' compensation insurance constituted a "benefit to the holder" within the meaning of § 506(c), that issue is not before us here; we assume for purposes of this decision that it did, and consider only whether petitioner—an administrative claimant—is a proper party to seek recovery under § 506(c).

In answering this question, we begin with the understanding that Congress "says in a statute what it means and means in a statute what it says there," *Connecticut Nat. Bank* v. *Germain,* 503 U.S. 249, 254 (1992). As we have previously noted in construing another provision of § 506, when "the statute's language is plain, 'the sole function of the courts'"—at least where the disposition required by the text is not absurd—"'is to enforce it according to its terms.'" *United States* v. *Ron Pair Enterprises, Inc.,* 489 U.S. 235, 241 (1989) (quoting *Caminetti* v. *United States,* 242 U.S. 470, 485 (1917)). Here, the statute appears quite plain in specifying who may use § 506(c)—"[t]he trustee." It is true, however, as petitioner notes, that all this actually "says" is that the trustee may seek recovery under the section, not that others may not. The question thus becomes whether it is a proper inference that the trustee is the only party empowered to invoke the provision.[7] We have little difficulty answering yes.

Several contextual features here support the conclusion that exclusivity is intended. First, a situation in which a statute authorizes specific action and designates a particular party empowered to take it is surely among the least appropriate in which to presume nonexclusivity. * * * Second, the fact that the sole party named—the trustee—has a unique role in bankruptcy proceedings makes it entirely plausible that Congress would provide a power to him and not to others. Indeed, had no particular parties been specified—had § 506(c) read simply "[t]here may be recovered from property securing an allowed secured claim the reasonable, necessary costs and expenses, etc."—the trustee is the most obvious party who would have been thought empowered to use the provision. It is thus far more sensible to view the provision as answering the question "Who may use the provision?" with "only the trustee" than to view it as simply answering the question "May the trustee use the provision?" with "yes."

Nor can it be argued that the point of the provision was simply to establish that certain costs may be recovered from collateral, and not to say anything about who may recover them. Had that been Congress's intention, it could easily have used the formulation just sug-

[7] Debtors-in-possession may also use the section, as they are expressly given the rights and powers of a trustee by § 1107.

gested. Similarly, had Congress intended the provision to be broadly available, it could simply have said so, as it did in describing the parties who could act under other sections of the Code. Section 502(a), for example, provides that a claim is allowed unless "a party in interest" objects, and § 503(b)(4) allows "an entity" to file a request for payment of an administrative expense. The broad phrasing of these sections, when contrasted with the use of "the trustee" in § 506(c), supports the conclusion that entities other than the trustee are not entitled to use § 506(c).

Petitioner's primary argument from the text of § 506(c) is that "what matters is that § 506(c) does not say that 'only' a trustee may enforce its provisions." To bolster this argument, petitioner cites other provisions of the Bankruptcy Code that do use "only" or other expressly restrictive language in specifying the parties at issue. See, *e.g.*, § 109(a) ("[O]nly a person that resides or has a domicile, a place of business, or property in the United States, or a municipality, may be a debtor under this title"); § 707(b) (providing that a case may be dismissed for substantial abuse by "the court, on its own motion or on a motion by the United States trustee, but not at the request or suggestion of any party in interest"). Petitioner argues that in the absence of such restrictive language, no party in interest is excluded. This theory—that the expression of one thing indicates the inclusion of others unless exclusion is made explicit—is contrary to common sense and common usage. Many provisions of the Bankruptcy Code that do not contain an express exclusion cannot sensibly be read to extend to all parties in interest. See, *e.g.*, § 363(b)(1) (providing that "[t]he trustee, after notice and a hearing, may use, sell, or lease * * * property of the estate"); § 364(a) (providing that "the trustee" may incur debt on behalf of the bankruptcy estate); § 554(a) (giving "the trustee" power to abandon property of the bankruptcy estate).

Petitioner further argues that § 1109 evidences the right of a nontrustee to recover under § 506(c). We are not persuaded. That section, which provides that a "party in interest" "may raise and may appear and be heard on any issue in a case under [Chapter 11]," is by its terms inapplicable here, since petitioner's attempt to use § 506(c) came after the bankruptcy proceeding was converted from Chapter 11 to Chapter 7. In any event, we do not read § 1109(b)'s general provision of a right to be heard as broadly allowing a creditor to pursue substantive remedies that other Code provisions make available only to other specific parties.

III

Because we believe that by far the most natural reading of § 506(c) is that it extends only to the trustee, petitioner's burden of persuading us that the section must be read to allow its use by other parties is "'exceptionally heavy.'" *Patterson* v. *Shumate,* 504 U.S. 753, 760 (1992) (quoting *Union Bank* v. *Wolas,* 502 U.S. 151, 156 (1991)). To support its proffered reading, petitioner advances arguments based on pre-Code practice and policy considerations. We address these arguments in turn.

A

Section 506(c)'s provision for the charge of certain administrative expenses against lienholders continues a practice that existed under the Bankruptcy Act of 1898. It was not to be found in the text of the Act, but traced its origin to early cases establishing an equitable principle that where a court has custody of property, costs of administering and preserving the property are a dominant charge. It was the norm that recovery of costs from a secured creditor would be sought by the trustee. Petitioner cites a number of lower court cases, however, in which—without meaningful discussion of the point—parties other than the trustee were permitted to pursue such charges under the Act, sometimes simultaneously with the trustee's pursuit of his own expenses. Petitioner also relies on early decisions of this Court allowing individual claimants to seek recovery from secured assets, see *Louisville, E. & St. L. R. Co.* v. *Wilson,* 138 U.S. 501, 506 (1891); *Burnham* v. *Bowen,* 111 U.S. 776, 779, 783 (1884); *New York Dock Co.* v. *S. S. Poznan,* 274 U.S. 117, 121 (1927). *Wilson* and *Burnham* involved equity receiverships, and were not only pre-Code, but predate the Bankruptcy Act of 1898 that the Code replaced; while *New York Dock* was a case arising in admiralty.

It is questionable whether these precedents establish a bankruptcy practice sufficiently widespread and well recognized to justify the conclusion of implicit adoption by the Code. We have no confidence that the allowance of recovery from collateral by nontrustees is "the type of 'rule' that * * * Congress was aware of when enacting the Code." *United States* v. *Ron Pair Enterprises, Inc.,* 489 U.S. at 246. In any event, while pre-Code practice "informs our understanding of the language of the Code," *Kelly* v. *Robinson,* 479 U.S. 36, 44 (1986), it cannot overcome that language. It is a tool of construction, not an extratextual supplement. We have applied it to the construction of provisions which were "subject to interpretation," *id.*, at 50, or contained "ambiguity in the text," *Dewsnup* v. *Timm,* 502 U.S. 410, 417 (1992). "[W]here the meaning of the Bankruptcy Code's text is itself clear * * * its operation is unimpeded by contrary * * * prior practice," *BFP* v. *Resolution Trust Corporation,* 511 U.S. 531, 546 (1994) (internal quotation marks omitted).

In this case, we think the language of the Code leaves no room for clarification by pre-Code practice. If § 506(c) provided only that certain costs and expenses could be recovered from property securing a secured claim, without specifying any particular party by whom the recovery could be pursued, the case would be akin to those in which we used prior practice to fill in the details of a pre-Code concept that the Code had adopted without elaboration. See, *e.g.*, *United States* v. *Noland,* 517 U.S. 535, 539 (1996) (looking to pre-Code practice in interpreting Code's reference to "principles of equitable subordination"); *Midlantic Nat. Bank* v. *New Jersey Dept. of Environmental Protection,* 474 U.S. 494, 501 (1986) (codification of trustee's abandonment power held to incorporate established exceptions). Here, however, it is not the unelaborated concept but only a specifically narrowed one that has been adopted: a rule allowing the charge of costs to secured assets *by the trustee*. Pre-Code practice cannot transform § 506(c)'s reference to "the trustee" to "the trustee and other parties in interest."

B

Finally, petitioner argues that its reading is necessary as a matter of policy, since in some cases the trustee may lack an incentive to pursue payment. Section 506(c) must be open to nontrustees, petitioner asserts, lest secured creditors enjoy the benefit of services without paying for them. Moreover, ensuring that administrative claimants are compensated may also serve purposes beyond the avoidance of unjust enrichment. To the extent that there are circumstances in which the trustee will not use the section although an individual creditor would, allowing suits by nontrustees could encourage the provision of postpetition services to debtors on more favorable terms, which would in turn further bankruptcy's goals.

Although these concerns may be valid, it is far from clear that the policy implications favor petitioner's position. The class of cases in which § 506(c) would lie dormant without nontrustee use is limited by the fact that the trustee is obliged to seek recovery under the section whenever his fiduciary duties so require. And limiting § 506(c) to the trustee does not leave those who provide goods or services that benefit secured interests without other means of protecting themselves as against other creditors: They may insist on cash payment, or contract directly with the secured creditor, and may be able to obtain super-priority under § 364(c)(1) or a security interest under §§ 364(c)(2), (3) or § 364(d). And of course postpetition creditors can avoid unnecessary losses simply by paying attention to the status of their accounts, a protection which, by all appearances, petitioner neglected here.

On the other side of the ledger, petitioner's reading would itself lead to results that seem undesirable as a matter of policy. In particular, expanding the number of parties who could use § 506(c) would create the possibility of multiple administrative claimants seeking recovery under the section. Each such claim would require inquiry into the necessity of the services at issue and the degree of benefit to the secured creditor. Allowing recovery to be sought at the behest of parties other than the trustee could therefore impair the ability of the bankruptcy court to coordinate proceedings, as well as the ability of the trustee to manage the estate. Indeed, if administrative claimants were free to seek recovery on their own, they could proceed even where the trustee himself planned to do so.[5] Further, where unencumbered assets were scarce, creditors might attempt to use § 506(c) even though their claim to have benefited the secured creditor was quite weak. The possibility of being targeted for such claims by various administrative claimants could make secured creditors less willing to provide post-petition financing.

In any event, we do not sit to assess the relative merits of different approaches to various bankruptcy problems. It suffices that the natural reading of the text produces the result we announce. Achieving a better policy outcome—if what petitioner urges is that—is a task for Congress, not the courts.

* * *

---

[5] We do not address whether a bankruptcy court can allow other interested parties to act in the trustee's stead in pursuing recovery under § 506(c). *Amici* American Insurance Association and National Union Fire Insurance Co. draw our attention to the practice of some courts of allowing creditors or creditors' committees a derivative right to bring avoidance actions when the trustee refuses to do so, even though the applicable Code provisions, see §§ 544, 545, 547(b), 548(a), 549(a), mention only the trustee. Whatever the validity of that practice, it has no analogous application here, since petitioner did not ask the trustee to pursue payment under § 506(c) and did not seek permission from the Bankruptcy Court to take such action in the trustee's stead. Petitioner asserted an independent right to use § 506(c), which is what we reject today.

We have considered the other points urged by petitioner and find them to be without merit. We conclude that § 506(c) does not provide an administrative claimant an independent right to use the section to seek payment of its claim. The judgment of the Eighth Circuit is affirmed.

It is so ordered.

Questions

1. Is it relevant that the Bank, although undersecured, had a security interest in everything Debtor owned, so that the benefits of Debtor's reorganization effort, had there been any, would have flowed first and foremost to Bank?

2. Was Hartford lax in looking after its own interests, as the Court suggested?

F. SATISFACTION OF SECURED CLAIMS IN CHAPTER 7

If the value of collateral exceeds the total amount owed to creditors with liens against the collateral, the trustee will sell the property, pay secured claims in full from the proceeds, and put the equity in the pot to be divided among unsecured claims. If the value of collateral is entirely consumed by the claims of creditors with liens against the collateral, the trustee will abandon the property and leave the creditors to fight it out among themselves under state law.

More difficult questions arise when the debtor wants to keep the collateral. Necessarily, something has to be done about the lien. One possibility, for Chapter 7 debtors, is redemption under § 722. Redemption requires a lump sum payment, however; installment payments are not an option. *GMAC v. Bell (In re Bell)*, 700 F.2d 1053 (6th Cir. 1983). Although postpetition earnings are not property of the Chapter 7 estate, the debtor may not have accumulated sufficient funds to make such a payment. Another possibility is reaffirmation under § 524(c), which contemplates the signing of a new contract by the debtor and creditor. That requires the consent of both parties, and creditors are often unwilling to continue dealing with a borrower who has filed bankruptcy. It will also almost always require the debtor's agreement to repay the *entire* debt, since creditors are unlikely to accept anything less. (We will return to the issue of reaffirmations in Chapter 7, Section E of this casebook.)

One other strategy has been used by Chapter 7 debtors, but it has produced a deep split among the Courts of Appeal. The next case elaborates.

CAPITAL COMMUNICATIONS FEDERAL CREDIT UNION v. BOODROW (IN RE BOODROW)

United States Court of Appeals, Second Circuit, 1997.
126 F.3d 43, *cert. denied*, 522 U.S. 1117, 118 S.Ct. 1055,
140 L.Ed.2d 140 (1998).

FEINBERG, J.

This case presents an issue of first impression in this circuit: whether a bankruptcy court may allow a debtor, who files for bankruptcy and is "current" on a car-purchase loan, to retain the collateral securing the loan and continue making monthly payments under the original loan agreement. Creditor Capital Communications Federal Credit Union (Capital) moved in the United States Bankruptcy Court for the Northern District of New York for, among other things, relief from the automatic stay imposed by § 362 when debtor Brian K. Boodrow filed for bankruptcy under Chapter 7 of the Bankruptcy Code. In December 1995, Bankruptcy Judge Littlefield, Jr. denied that motion. In June 1996, the United States District Court for the Northern District of New York, Thomas J. McAvoy, C.J., affirmed the decision of the bankruptcy court. Capital appeals from that ruling; for reasons stated below, we affirm.

I. Facts and Prior Proceedings

The material facts in this case are not in dispute. In May 1995, Boodrow filed for relief pursuant to Chapter 7. Prior to filing, Boodrow had borrowed $15,900 from Capital to purchase a 1992 Pontiac Grand Am. As of the petition date, Boodrow owed Capital $8,820, which sum was secured by a first priority lien on the vehicle. Capital agrees that the market value of the vehicle on that date was $9,650.

After filing his Chapter 7 petition, Boodrow filed a statement of intention pursuant to § 521(2), indicating that he intended to retain the vehicle and reaffirm his debt to Capital. However, Boodrow, who had been receiving workmen's compensation and disability payments for an injury, discovered sometime thereafter that he was permanently disabled and would not be able to return to full-time employment. For this reason, Boodrow says, he did not execute a reaffirmation agreement with Capital but rather retained the car, remained "current" on his monthly installment payments and maintained adequate insurance on the car. Apparently, as part of the loan contract with Capital, Boodrow had purchased disability insurance, which was the source of the monthly payments due under the loan. Indeed, it is undisputed that at all times up to the argument of this case before us, Boodrow has remained current on his payments and maintained adequate insurance for the vehicle.

In July 1995, Capital moved to lift the automatic stay and for other relief on the ground that Boodrow had not complied with § 521(2), and that this failure constituted cause under § 362(d)(1) for lifting the stay to enable Capital to recover the vehicle. Capital maintained that Boodrow was required under § 521(2) to either enter into a reaffirmation agreement, surrender the vehicle to Capital, or redeem it by immediately paying Capital the market value of the vehicle.

Bankruptcy Judge Littlefield conducted a hearing on Capital's motion in August 1995 and reserved decision. In September, he granted Boodrow a discharge from bankruptcy. Thereafter in December, Judge Littlefield denied Capital's motion for relief from the automatic stay. The court held that Capital had not demonstrated cause for lifting the stay because § 521(2) allowed a debtor in Boodrow's position to retain the collateral and continue making monthly payments. The court concluded that Capital had not demonstrated that it would suffer harm if the stay was not lifted.

Capital appealed to the district court, and Chief Judge McAvoy affirmed. * * * The judge held that § 521(2) allowed Boodrow to retain the collateral and continue to perform under the original loan agreement, and therefore the bankruptcy court had properly denied Capital's motion. This appeal followed.

II. Discussion

* * *

[The majority first held, in response to the dissent, that the case had not been rendered moot by the grant of discharge to the debtor three months earlier.]

B. The Merits

* * *

Capital argues that "cause" existed pursuant to § 362(d)(1) for lifting the automatic stay. * * * Although a bankruptcy court has discretion to lift the stay in various situations, the "most common basis for granting relief for cause," and the one most applicable here, is a lack of adequate protection of a party's interest in property. * * *

Capital argues primarily that it did show cause to lift the stay because Boodrow violated § 521(2) by not electing to reaffirm the debt or surrender or redeem[4] the vehicle. In other words, Boodrow could not simply retain the vehicle and continue to make monthly payments. Courts in several circuits have taken the position that § 521(2) confines a debtor to the options specifically listed in that section. E.g, *In re Edwards*, 901 F.2d 1383, 1387 (7th Cir. 1990); *Taylor v. Age Federal Credit Union (In re Taylor)*, 3 F.3d 1512, 1517 (11th Cir.1993); *Johnson v. Sun Finance Co. (In re Johnson)*, 89 F.3d 249, 252 (5th Cir.1996); cf. *General Motors Acceptance Corp. v. Bell (In re Bell)*, 700 F.2d 1053, 1058 (6th Cir.1983) (case decided before § 521(2) added to Code).

Boodrow responds that no cause existed to modify the stay because he complied with § 521(2) by indicating to Capital that he would retain the vehicle and continue making payments due under the loan agreement. Courts in other circuits have held that, consistent with § 521(2), a debtor who is current on a loan may follow this course of action. E.g., *Home Owners Funding Corp. v. Belanger (In re Belanger)*, 962 F.2d 345, 348-49 (4th Cir.1992); *Lowry Federal Credit Union v. West*, 882 F.2d 1543, 1547 (10th Cir.1989); *Sears Roebuck & Co. v. Lamirande*, 199 B.R. 221, 224 (D.Mass.1996); *In re Hunter*, 121 B.R. 609, 617 (Bankr. N.D.Ala.1990); *In re Crouch*, 104 B.R. 770, 772-73 (Bankr. S.D.W.Va.1989). Boodrow also argues that Capital alleged no affirmative harm justifying the lifting of the stay.

It is not clear to us that violation of § 521(2) would automatically require a bankruptcy court to lift the automatic stay. However, even assuming that such violation constitutes cause for lifting the stay,

[4] Section 521(2)(A) also states that a debtor can "specify[] that such property is claimed as exempt," but in response to Capital's motion Boodrow made no claim of exemption.

we find, for reasons discussed below, that Capital has not shown that Boodrow violated § 521(2).

(1) Text of § 521(2)

Section 521(2) * * * was added to the Bankruptcy Code by the Bankruptcy Amendment and Federal Judgeship Act of 1984 and states in relevant part that

> the debtor shall file with the clerk a statement of his intention with respect to the retention or surrender of such property and, *if applicable*, specifying that such property is claimed as exempt, that the debtor intends to redeem such property, or that the debtor intends to reaffirm debts secured by such property.

§ 521(2)(A) (emphasis added). As Capital points out, surrender requires a debtor to return the collateral to the creditor. Redemption is governed by § 722. * * * That section allows a debtor to retain the collateral by paying the creditor the value of the property. Most courts require a debtor to pay the creditor in one "lump sum" payment rather than in installments, unless the creditor agrees otherwise. Alternatively, a debtor can reaffirm a debt by entering into a new loan agreement with the creditor, a legal obligation that survives the debtor's discharge from bankruptcy. *See* § 524(c). Capital observes, however, that in a reaffirmation agreement the parties can negotiate new terms to supplant those in the original loan agreement, and that the creditor's acceptance of the agreement must be voluntary.

* * *

The bankruptcy and district courts in this case both held that the language of § 521(2)(A) * * * did not prevent the bankruptcy court from allowing Boodrow to retain the collateral and continue to perform under the loan agreement. (This course of action has been described as "reinstatement," a term we use at times hereafter in this opinion.) Both courts relied on *Belanger*, where the Fourth Circuit explained that

> the fact that the statutory options are stated in the disjunctive shows that the words "if applicable" are unnecessary under a construction of the statute that makes the options exclusive. But if the phrase "if applicable" is given effect, it plays an important role. * * * The debtor must specify a choice of the options if applicable. But if these options are not applicable, the debtor need not specify them.

962 F.2d at 348 (internal citations omitted).

In support of this interpretation, Collier states that "nothing in § 521(2) requires the debtor to choose redemption, reaffirmation or surrender of the property to the exclusion of all other alternatives. Section 521(2) merely requires a statement of whether the debtor intends to choose any of those options, if applicable." Collier on Bankruptcy, ¶ 521.10, at 521-34 to 521-35 (Lawrence P. King ed., 15th ed. rev. 1996) (footnote omitted). One court has held that the options listed in § 521(2) were not exclusive and explained that in Chapter 7 bankruptcies the trustee often sells encumbered property, using the proceeds to settle creditors' claims. *In re Parker*, 142 B.R. 327, 330 (Bankr. W.D. Ark. 1992). The court noted that "in this common scenario, none of the three so-called mandatory alternatives listed in [§ 521(2)(A)] have occurred." *Id.*

Capital counters that the plain language of § 521(2)(A) shows that Congress intended the options set forth to be the only ones available to a debtor. Capital relies on the reasoning of *Taylor*, where the Seventh Circuit explained the meaning of the phrase "if applicable" as follows:

> It is clear when the options of redemption and reaffirmation would not be applicable. This language does not apply to a debtor's surrender of the property; it therefore must apply to a debtor's retention of property. If a debtor retains secured property, then the options of redemption and reaffirmation are applicable and the debtor is required to redeem or reaffirm.

3 F.3d at 1516. Capital argues that § 521(2)(A) would be confusing without "if applicable" because it would require a debtor who decides to surrender the collateral to indicate an intention to reaffirm or redeem, two choices that do not logically apply if the debtor is giving back the collateral.[7]

---

[7] The Tenth Circuit has taken the position that a bankruptcy court may allow reinstatement despite the court's belief that the "plain English of the section" required the debtor to select one of the options listed. *Lowry*, 882 F.2d at 1545 n.2 (deeming the phrase "if applicable" to be "gratuitous"). The court held that the debtor's "failure to comply fully with § 521(2)" did not warrant relief from the automatic stay so that the creditor could repossess the collateral. *Id.* at 1546. As will be seen below, although we agree with the outcome in *Lowry* we disagree with its view that the language of § 521(2)(A) plainly restricts a debtor to redemption, surrender or reaffirmation.

Both parties assert that their interpretation of § 521(2)(A) better comports with other subsections of § 521(2). Capital maintains that reinstatement cannot be reconciled with § 521(2)(B), which states in relevant part that "within forty-five days after the filing of a notice of intent * * * the debtor shall perform his intention with respect to such property." Admittedly, retaining the collateral and continuing to make scheduled payments is not action that typically can be performed within 45 days. Capital also insists that the options listed in § 521(2)(A) must be exclusive because nowhere else does the Code provide for additional options.

Boodrow argues, on the other hand, that his interpretation of § 521(2)(A) is reinforced by § 521(2)(C), which states that "nothing in subparagraphs (A) and (B) of this paragraph shall alter the debtor's or the trustee's rights with regard to such property under this title." The district court here agreed, relying on *Belanger*, where the Fourth Circuit noted that, before the enactment of § 521(2), one bankruptcy court had held that a debtor who was not in default on a loan was entitled to retain the collateral securing the loan as long as he remained current on the loan payments. *In re Belanger*, 962 F.2d at 347 (citing *In re Ballance*, 33 B.R. 89 (Bankr. E.D.Va. 1983)).

Although § 521(2)(A) clearly imposes a mandatory obligation on a debtor to state whether he intends to retain or surrender collateral, we find the section to be ambiguous as to whether Congress intended the options there listed to be exclusive, and we believe that the "plain" language arguably supports either of the interpretations described above. We thus turn to other sources for evidence of congressional intent as to the meaning of § 521(2).

(2) Legislative History and Policy

The bankruptcy court in this case concluded that review of the legislative history of § 521(2) did "not assist resolution of this matter," noting that no Senate or House report became part of the record regarding § 521(2). Nevertheless, the district court found that the "limited legislative history points to the general conclusion that § 521(2) is meant to be a notice provision." Judge Small, the bankruptcy judge in *Belanger*, came to the same conclusion based on detailed statements made at a congressional subcommittee hearing by "a coalition of bankers, credit unions, finance companies, oil companies and retailers." *In re Belanger*, 118 B.R. 368, 370. Those statements indicate that § 521(2)(A) was intended specifically to eliminate the problem that secured creditors could not determine what a debtor who had filed for bankruptcy was going to do with collateral securing a debt. Instead of the creditor having to spend time and money obtaining this information through judicial proceedings, § 521(2) placed on a debtor "the responsibility of giving creditors information * * * as to what they intend to do with the collateral." *Id.* at 370 n.5.

We agree that § 521(2) appears to serve primarily a notice function, not necessarily to restrict the substantive options available to a debtor who wishes to retain collateral securing a debt. With respect to Capital's argument that the time limit in § 521(2)(B) precludes such a conclusion, the district court here reasoned that "obviously, under such a scheme it is appropriate to set a time limit for action upon such a statement, but that limit does not necessarily change the nature of the section" as one aimed at providing notice to creditors of a debtor's intentions. We note also that a bankruptcy court has discretion under § 521(2)(B) to give a debtor "additional time * * * for cause" beyond the 45-day deadline to perform a stated intention.

Moreover, we believe that the interpretation advocated by Boodrow and adopted by the courts below better comports with the policies behind the Bankruptcy Code. The bankruptcy court viewed Boodrow's interpretation of § 521(2) as "most consistent with balancing the 'fresh start' policy underlying the Code and the rights of the * * * secured creditors." * * *

Confining an individual Chapter 7 debtor to the choices of surrender, redemption or reaffirmation can severely interfere with providing the debtor a fresh start. As Judge Butzner explained in *Belanger*, a debtor is "unlikely to be able to redeem the collateral in a lump sum as required by § 722," and "reaffirmation requires the consent of the creditor in order to comply with § 524(c)." 962 F.2d at 348. Thus, if the options listed in § 521(2) were exclusive, a debtor's only real choices would be either to reaffirm the debt under whatever new terms the creditor requires or to surrender the property. Because reaffirmation involves negotiation between parties with unequal bargaining power and requires voluntary agreement by both debtor and creditor, it gives a creditor an effective veto on the "fresh start." Yet, surrender may deprive a debtor of much needed property, such as disabled debtor Boodrow's vehicle in this case.

Capital responds that a creditor faces the possibility of "substantial financial danger" and "very real loss" when a bankruptcy court allows a debtor to retain property without redeeming or reaffirming. Capital explains that because bankruptcy discharges a debtor from personal liability on outstanding loans, Capital's only remedy if Boodrow defaulted on the loan after discharge would be to commence legal action to recover the vehicle. Capital would not then be entitled to recover the difference, if any, between the outstanding balance on the loan and the value of the vehicle. Further, Capital argues that a debtor whose personal liability is discharged through bankruptcy has no incentive to maintain the collateral in good condition or to continue making payments if the value of the collateral drops below the amount outstanding on the loan. Finally, Capital contends that Boodrow's interpretation of § 521(2) would in effect negate reaffirmation because no debtor would reaffirm personal liability rather than simply continue to make payments on the loan and retain the collateral. Capital asserts, as the court stated in *Taylor*, that this additional option gives the debtor "not a 'fresh start' but a 'head start.'" 3 F.3d at 1516.

It is true that a debtor's discharge from bankruptcy eliminates personal liability on the loan, thereby theoretically limiting the amount a creditor could recover if the debtor defaults. However, we disagree with Capital's assumption that a creditor will necessarily or even probably suffer financial injury when a debtor who is current on a loan retains the collateral and continues to make the payments required under the loan agreement. As the court in *Crouch* observed, because a creditor can recover the collateral from a discharged debtor who defaults on a loan, the creditor's main concern should be that, upon default, the value of the collateral exceeds the amount outstanding on the loan. 104 B.R. at 773. The bankruptcy court here characterized Capital's suggestion that Boodrow would not have any incentive to maintain the collateral as "uninformed with regard to the realities of the typical Chapter 7 case." Boodrow argues that "there is a great incentive for [him] to maintain current on the debt and to preserve the auto since he has no means to acquire another auto." Indeed, the bankruptcy court explained that a

> debtor's ability to obtain credit on the same (or comparable) terms as nondebtors, is generally impaired by filing bankruptcy. If a debtor fails to maintain or permits a waste of collateral, such as an automobile, he is therefore less able than a nondebtor to obtain financing required to replace the collateral. As a result, debtors are generally likely to have a *greater* incentive than nondebtors to stay current on payments and to maintain the value of the collateral.

In any event, other courts have noted that a debtor's failure, after discharge, to insure or maintain collateral typically permits a creditor to

> accelerate the indebtedness and repossess the collateral. In fact default clauses which permit the lender to declare a default in the event that the creditor deems its security interest insecure are specifically authorized by the Uniform Commercial Code and may be exercised by a secured lender if it has a good faith belief that the prospect for payment is impaired.

In re Belanger, 118 B.R. at 372. We thus disagree that a creditor invariably, or even probably, will lose the benefit of its bargain under the original loan agreement when a bankruptcy court permits reinstatement.

With regard to Capital's contention that Boodrow's interpretation of § 521(2) reads reaffirmation out of the statute, amicus NACBA[c] points out that sometimes a debtor has an incentive to reaffirm a debt. The NACBA brief explains that a debtor may seek to reaffirm in order to reestablish credit standing after a bankruptcy discharge or, if the debtor was not current on the loan when the bankruptcy petition was filed, to obtain a new agreement that would provide for the right to cure the arrearage and avoid default. The brief also notes that sometimes a debtor may want to reaffirm in order to retain the benefit of certain consumer protection provisions contained in the original loan agreement. They thus challenge Capital's assumption that no debtor would choose reaffirmation.

In any event, Capital's argument misapprehends the scope of the holding that we review in this case. The district court explained that a bankruptcy court must exercise its discretion in determining whether a debtor may retain collateral and keep making payments by considering the debtor's "previous payment record, a comparison of the value of the collateral and the amount of debt, and other relevant facts." *See Lowry*, 882 F.2d at 1547 (holding that bankruptcy court has such discretion only when "evidence indicates neither the debtor nor the creditor would be prejudiced"). Thus, a debtor in default on a loan at the time of the bankruptcy petition or whose behavior indicates that he will not be able to continue making scheduled payments might well suffer a lifting of the stay. In fact, Judge Littlefield—the bankruptcy

---

[c] National Association of Consumer Bankruptcy Attorneys. Eds.

judge in this case—recently granted summary judgment to a creditor because a debtor not current on his loan obligation had not reaffirmed the loan or redeemed or surrendered the collateral. *Beneficial N.Y., Inc. v. Bushey (In re Bushey)*, 204 B.R. 661, 663-64 (Bankr. N.D.N.Y. 1997).

After considering the text of § 521(2), its legislative history and the policies informing the Bankruptcy Code, we hold that § 521(2) does not prevent a bankruptcy court from allowing a debtor who is current on loan obligations to retain the collateral and keep making payments under the original loan agreement.

(3) Exercise of Discretion

We turn now to whether the bankruptcy court abused its discretion in refusing to grant Capital the relief it sought. We agree with both courts below that Capital had the burden of showing that "continuation of the stay [would] cause some affirmative harm" to its interest in the vehicle. As noted above, Boodrow was current on his loan payments when the bankruptcy petition was filed. We have no information to indicate that Boodrow has, at any time since then, failed to make required payments. We agree with the district court that because Boodrow's disability insurance was making the monthly loan payments, there was little chance that Boodrow would default.

* * *

Affirmed.

SHADUR, District Judge, dissenting.

There are two respects in which my analysis diverges from that of my colleagues. First and most fundamentally, I believe that the most basic jurisprudential principles teach that the case now before us is not only moot but—somewhat astonishingly—was moot even before the Bankruptcy Court rendered its decision. Second, if that problem were not present, so that we were in a position to reach the merits, I believe that the unambiguous language of § 521(2) renders it inappropriate for this Court to fashion a "reinstatement" remedy for debtors in Boodrow's position. Hence I am constrained to dissent with all respect.

* * *

The Merits

As a matter of pure logic, what I have said to this point ought to prevent me from going on to the merits of the proper reading and application of § 521(2). But because I also depart from the panel's treatment of those subjects, in the interest of full disclosure I believe that I should explain my dissent on that score as well.

My colleagues, finding particularly persuasive the Fourth Circuit's decision in *Belanger*, deem the language of § 521(2) to be ambiguous. And having so found, they embark on a rather extensive review of which interpretation of § 521(2) best comports with the general "fresh start" policy of the Bankruptcy Code. When they determine that limiting Boodrow's options to the three articulated possibilities of § 521(2)(A) might "severely interfere" with his opportunity for a fresh start, my colleagues read the statute as providing a debtor with a so-called "fourth option" of retaining secured collateral and keeping current on the debtor's installment loan payments.

* * * In that respect, I believe that all but one of the Courts of Appeals that have examined the matter—the Fifth Circuit (*Johnson*, 89 F.3d at 252), the Seventh Circuit (*In re Edwards*, 901 F.2d 1383, 1385-87 (7th Cir. 1990), the Tenth Circuit (*Lowry*, 882 F.2d at 1545) and the Eleventh Circuit (*Taylor*, 3 F.3d at 1516) have properly read the plain language of that section in a totally different way from *Belanger* and the panel opinion here.

As stated in *Taylor*:

> The Taylors urge us to adopt the Fourth Circuit's holding in [*Belanger*], which permits a debtor to retain his or her property and keep current on his or her obligation under the existing contract. They also rely on several bankruptcy opinions from this circuit. Most of these courts focused upon the phrase "if applicable" and reasoned that if a debtor wishes to retain secured property but does not want to redeem or reaffirm, then those options are not "applicable." This reasoning does not comport with the plain language of § 521 which states that "the debtor shall file with the clerk a statement of his intention with respect to the retention or surrender of such property, and if applicable * * * ." Referring to the language preceding the phrase "if applicable," it is clear when the options of redemption and reaffirmation would not be applicable. This language does not apply to a debtor's surrender of the property; it there-

> fore must apply to a debtor's retention of property. If a debtor retains secured property, then the options of redemption and reaffirmation are applicable and the debtor is required to redeem or reaffirm.

And though the Tenth Circuit in *Lowry*, 882 F.2d at 1545-46, found difficulties posed by the absence of a stated enforcement mechanism for § 521(2), the court there expressed its conclusion as to the unambiguous language of that section even more forcefully:

> The creditor argues that the requirements of § 521(2) are mandatory. That is obvious. There is no room within the direct language of the section to presume otherwise.

* * *

But like all of the other Courts of Appeals except for the Fourth Circuit, I consider that such a reading of the "if applicable" phrase—to connote the existence of an unexpressed "fourth option"—demands an inordinately awkward use of the statutory language. That construction reads the statute both (1) as though Congress had said that the statutorily identified options of exemption, redemption, or reaffirmation would be the only ones available solely *if the debtor decides* that one of those "is applicable" (something that Congress certainly did not say) and (2) as though Congress had also said (as it also certainly did not) that some alternative other than those three choices was available if the debtor decided on such other alternative. By contrast, it is perfectly conventional usage—and perfectly good English—for someone to employ the "if applicable" language in the statute as a shorthand way of calling for a choice between A and B and, only if B "is applicable," then a further choice among subsets of B.

Further, as my colleagues recognize, limiting a debtor to one of those three expressly stated options is most consistent with the language of the very next subpart of § 521(2), § 521(2)(B). * * * As recognized in such cases as *Taylor*, 3 F.3d 15 1516, that obligation of a debtor to "perform his intention" within 45 days after filing the notice of intent is totally at odds with any concept of Congress having contemplated a "fourth option" involving a continued and extended payout schedule that would run the length of the underlying consumer debt contract—a period of many months (or years) in most cases. And my colleagues' position that the bankruptcy court's discretion to extend that 45-day period "for cause" might equate with a permissible period of performance extending over several years really fabricates that "fourth option" out of whole cloth, particularly when no other language in the Bankruptcy Code would support such a result.

* * *

But far more significant, I submit, is the total absence from the Bankruptcy Code of any provision that would expressly permit the "fourth option" now recognized by my colleagues. Any practitioner possessing even a modicum of familiarity with bankruptcy proceedings knows that this so-called "fourth option" would be by far the most advantageous option for many Chapter 7 debtors who, though insolvent, file for bankruptcy while they are current on their secured consumer loans. For unlike a § 722 redemption, the debtor need not raise funds sufficient to pay the full "amount of the allowed secured claim" in one lump-sum payment. And unlike a § 524(c) reaffirmation, the debtor need not negotiate with creditors—from a disadvantaged bargaining-power position—while facing the likely prospect of having to reaffirm otherwise dischargeable debt. Rather, the "fourth option," if it were to be judicially created, would "give[] the debtor not a 'fresh start' but a 'head start' since the debtor effectively converts his secured obligation from recourse to nonrecourse with no downside risk for failing to maintain or insure the lender's collateral" (*Taylor*, 3 F.3d at 1516). That option allows the debtor to strip from his or her obligation any debt that would in future turn out not to be fully secured by the value of the creditor's collateral, while at the same time avoiding any risk of future personal liability.[9]

Yet despite the clear surface attractiveness of that prospect to innumerable Chapter 7 debtors, Congress has simply not seen fit to insert (or even to recognize) such a "reinstatement" option in the Code—whether by a separate explicit provision (as it has in the cases of § 722 for redemption and § 524(c) for reaffirmation), or even by reference in the text of § 521(2)(A). * * *

In sum, even if we were somehow able to overcome the mootness hurdle to proceed with the merits, I believe that the power simply does not lie in this Court to devise a new Chapter 7 remedy where

[9] It is scarcely necessary to observe that the volatility of the market for used consumer goods, automobiles representing a good example, is such that the first-time imposition of that unbargained-for risk on a secured lender such as Capital is extraordinarily unfair. And any judicial creation of that risk for all future cases, by the inexorable operation of the Coase Theorem, will drive the cost of obtaining credit upward. Whose interests does that serve?

Congress has opted not to act. For this reason too I part company with my colleagues.

As stated at the outset, I respectfully dissent.

Note

1. The split of authority continues. Since *Boodrow* was decided, two other circuits have weighed in. *McClellan Federal Credit Union v. Parker (In re Parker)*, 139 F.3d 668 (9th Cir.), *cert. denied*, 525 U.S. 1041, 119 S.Ct. 592, 142 L.Ed.2d 535 (1998) (agreeing with *Boodrow*); *Bank of Boston v. Burr (In re Burr)*, 160 F.3d 843 (1st Cir. 1998) (disagreeing with *Boodrow*).

2. Which side of this debate has the better statutory argument? Which view is most sensible in terms of bankruptcy policy?

The debtor in *Boodrow* presumably was unable to redeem the collateral by lump-sum payment under § 722. Other debtors do have access to funds, often through the generosity of family or friends, and want to keep property by paying off the amount of the secured claim and requiring the creditor to release the lien. If the property falls within § 722, there is no problem. The following case deals with debtors' efforts to keep property not within § 722.

DEWSNUP v. TIMM

United States Supreme Court, 1992.
502 U.S. 410, 112 S.Ct. 773, 116 L.Ed.2d 903.

JUSTICE BLACKMUN delivered the opinion of the Court. [THOMAS, J. took no part in the consideration or decision of the case.]

We are confronted in this case with an issue concerning § 506(d) of the Bankruptcy Code. May a debtor "strip down" a creditor's lien on real property to the value of the collateral, as judicially determined, when that value is less than the amount of the claim secured by the lien?

I

On June 1, 1978, respondents loaned $119,000 to petitioner Aletha Dewsnup and her husband, T. LaMar Dewsnup, since deceased.

The loan was accompanied by a Deed of Trust granting a lien on two parcels of Utah farmland owned by the Dewsnups.

Petitioner defaulted the following year. Under the terms of the Deed of Trust, respondents at that point could have proceeded against the real property collateral by accelerating the maturity of the loan, issuing a notice of default, and selling the land at a public foreclosure sale to satisfy the debt.

Respondents did issue a notice of default in 1981. Before the foreclosure sale took place, however, petitioner sought reorganization under Chapter 11 of the Bankruptcy Code. That bankruptcy petition was dismissed, as was a subsequent Chapter 11 petition. In June 1984, petitioner filed a petition seeking liquidation under Chapter 7 of the Code. Because of the pendency of these bankruptcy proceedings, respondents were not able to proceed to the foreclosure sale. See § 362.

In 1987, petitioner filed the present adversary proceeding in the Bankruptcy Court for the District of Utah seeking, pursuant to § 506, to "avoid" a portion of respondents' lien. Petitioner represented that the debt of approximately $120,000 then owed to respondents exceeded the fair market value of the land and that, therefore, the Bankruptcy Court should reduce the lien to that value. According to petitioner, this was compelled by the interrelationship of the security-reducing provision of § 506(a) and the lien-voiding provision of § 506(d). Under § 506(a) * * * respondents would have an "allowed secured claim" only to the extent of the judicially determined value of their collateral. And under § 506(d) * * * the court would be required to void the lien as to the remaining portion of respondents' claim, because the remaining portion was not an "allowed secured claim" within the meaning of § 506(a).

The Bankruptcy Court refused to grant this relief. After a trial, it determined that the then value of the land subject to the Deed of Trust was $39,000. It indulged in the assumption that the property had been abandoned by the trustee pursuant to § 554, and reasoned that once property was abandoned it no longer fell within the reach of § 506(a), which applies only to "property in which the estate has an interest," and therefore was not covered by § 506(d).

The United States District Court, without a supporting opinion, summarily affirmed the Bankruptcy Court's judgment of dismissal with prejudice.

The Court of Appeals for the Tenth Circuit, in its turn, also affirmed. Starting from the "fundamental premise" of § 506(a) that a claim is subject to reduction in security only when the estate has an interest in the property, the court reasoned that because the estate had no interest in abandoned property, § 506(a) did not apply (nor, by implication, did § 506(d)). The court then noted that a contrary result would be inconsistent with § 722 under which a debtor has a limited right to redeem certain personal property.

Because the result reached by the Court of Appeals was at odds with that reached by the Third Circuit in *Gaglia v. First Federal Savings & Loan Ass'n*, 889 F.2d 1304, 1306–11 (1989), and was expressly recognized by the Tenth Circuit as being in conflict, we granted certiorari.

II

As we read their several submissions, the parties and their *amici* are not in agreement in their respective approaches to the problem of statutory interpretation that confronts us. Petitioner-debtor takes the position that § 506(a) and § 506(d) are complementary and to be read together. Because, under § 506(a), a claim is secured only to the extent of the judicially determined value of the real property on which the lien is fixed, a debtor can void a lien on the property pursuant to § 506(d) to the extent the claim is no longer secured and thus is not "an allowed secured claim." In other words, § 506(a) bifurcates classes of claims allowed under § 502 into secured claims and unsecured claims; any portion of an allowed claim deemed to be unsecured under § 506(a) is not an "allowed secured claim" within the lien-voiding scope of § 506(d). Petitioner argues that there is no exception for unsecured property abandoned by the trustee.

Petitioner's *amicus* argues that the plain language of § 506(d) dictates that the proper portion of an undersecured lien on property in a Chapter 7 case is void whether or not the property is abandoned by the trustee. It further argues that the rationale of the Court of Appeals would lead to evisceration of the debtor's right of redemption and the elimination of an undersecured creditor's ability to participate in the distribution of the estate's assets.

Respondents primarily assert that § 506(d) is not, as petitioner would have it, "rigidly tied" to § 506(a). They argue that § 506(a) performs the function of classifying claims by true secured status at the time of distribution of the estate to ensure fairness to unsecured claimants. In contrast, the lien-voiding § 506(d) is directed to the time at which foreclosure is to take place, and, where the trustee has abandoned the property, no bankruptcy distributional purpose is served by voiding the lien.

In the alternative, respondents, joined by the United States as *amicus curiae*, argue more broadly that the words "allowed secured claim" in § 506(d) need not be read as an indivisible term of art defined by reference to § 506(a), which by its terms is not a definitional provision. Rather, the words should be read term-by-term to refer to any claim that is, first, allowed, and, second, secured. Because there is no question that the claim at issue here has been "allowed" pursuant to § 502 of the Code and is secured by a lien with recourse to the underlying collateral, it does not come within the scope of § 506(d), which voids only liens corresponding to claims that have *not* been allowed and secured. This reading of § 506(d), according to respondents and the United States, gives the provision the simple and sensible function of voiding a lien whenever a claim secured by the lien itself has not been allowed. It ensures that the Code's determination not to allow the underlying claim against the debtor personally is given full effect by preventing its assertion against the debtor's property.

Respondents point out that pre-Code bankruptcy law preserved liens like respondents' and that there is nothing in the Code's legislative history that reflects any intent to alter that law. Moreover, according to respondents, the "fresh-start" policy cannot justify an impairment of respondents' property rights, for the fresh start does not extend to an *in rem* claim against property but is limited to a discharge of personal liability.

III

The foregoing recital of the contrasting positions of the respective parties and their *amici* demonstrates that § 506 of the Bankruptcy Code and its relationship to other provisions of that Code do embrace some ambiguities. Hypothetical applications that come to mind and those advanced at oral argument illustrate the difficulty of interpreting the statute in a single opinion that would apply to all possible fact situations. We therefore focus upon the case before us and allow other facts to await their legal resolution on another day.

We conclude that respondents' alternative position, espoused also by the United States, although not without its difficulty, generally is the better of the several approaches. Therefore, we hold that

§ 506(d) does not allow petitioner to "strip down" respondents' lien, because respondents' claim is secured by a lien and has been fully allowed pursuant to § 502. Were we writing on a clean slate, we might be inclined to agree with petitioner that the words "allowed secured claim" must take the same meaning in § 506(d) as in § 506(a).[3] But, given the ambiguity in the text, we are not convinced that Congress intended to depart from the pre-Code rule that liens pass through bankruptcy unaffected.

1. The practical effect of petitioner's argument is to freeze the creditor's secured interest at the judicially determined valuation. By this approach, the creditor would lose the benefit of any increase in the value of the property by the time of the foreclosure sale. The increase would accrue to the benefit of the debtor, a result some of the parties describe as a "windfall."

We think, however, that the creditor's lien stays with the real property until the foreclosure. That is what was bargained for by the mortgagor and the mortgagee. The voidness language sensibly applies only to the security aspect of the lien and then only to the real deficiency in the security. Any increase over the judicially determined valuation during bankruptcy rightly accrues to the benefit of the creditor, not to the benefit of the debtor and not to the benefit of other unsecured creditors whose claims have been allowed and who had nothing to do with the mortgagor-mortgagee bargain.

Such surely would be the result had the lienholder stayed aloof from the bankruptcy proceeding (subject, of course, to the power of other persons or entities to pull him into the proceeding pursuant to § 501), and we see no reason why his acquiescence in that proceeding should cause him to experience a forfeiture of the kind the debtor proposes. It is true that his participation in the bankruptcy results in his having the benefit of an allowed unsecured claim as well as his allowed secured claim, but that does not strike us as proper recompense for what petitioner proposes by way of the elimination of the remainder of the lien.

2. This result appears to have been clearly established before the passage of the 1978 Act. Under the Bankruptcy Act of 1898, a lien

[3] Accordingly, we express no opinion as to whether the words "allowed secured claim" have different meaning in other provisions of the Bankruptcy Code.

on real property passed through bankruptcy unaffected. This Court recently acknowledged that this was so. See *Farrey v. Sanderfoot*, 500 U.S. 291, 297 (1991) ("Ordinarily, liens and other secured interests survive bankruptcy"); *Johnson v. Home State Bank*, 501 U.S. 78, 84 (1991) ("Rather, a bankruptcy discharge extinguishes only one mode of enforcing a claim—namely, an action against the debtor *in personam*—while leaving intact another—namely, an action against the debtor *in rem*.").

3. Apart from reorganization proceedings, no provision of the pre-Code statute permitted involuntary reduction of the amount of a creditor's lien for any reason other than payment on the debt. Our cases reveal the Court's concern about this. In *Long v. Bullard*, 117 U.S. 617, 620–21 (1886), the Court held that a discharge in bankruptcy does not release real estate of the debtor from the lien of a mortgage created by him before the bankruptcy. And in *Louisville Joint Stock Land Bank v. Radford*, 295 U.S. 555 (1935), the Court considered additions to the Bankruptcy Act effected by the Frazier–Lemke Act, 48 Stat. 1289 (1934). There the Court noted that the latter Act's "avowed object is to take from the mortgagee rights in the specific property held as security; and to that end 'to scale down the indebtedness' to the present value of the property." 295 U.S. at 594. The Court invalidated that statute under the Takings Clause. It further observed: "No instance has been found, except under the Frazier–Lemke Act, of either a statute or decision compelling the mortgagee to relinquish the property to the mortgagor free of the lien unless the debt was paid in full." *Id.* at 579.

Congress must have enacted the Code with a full understanding of this practice. See H.R. Rep. No. 95–595 at 357, *reprinted in* 1978 U.S.C.C.A.N. at 6313 ("Subsection (d) [of § 506] permits liens to pass through the bankruptcy case unaffected").

4. When Congress amends the bankruptcy laws, it does not write "on a clean slate." See *Emil v. Hanley*, 318 U.S. 515, 521 (1943). Furthermore, this Court has been reluctant to accept arguments that would interpret the Code, however vague the particular language under consideration might be, to effect a major change in pre-Code practice that is not the subject of at least some discussion in the legislative history. Of course, where the language is unambiguous, silence in the legislative history cannot be controlling. But, given the ambiguity here, to attribute to Congress the intention to grant a debtor the broad new remedy against allowed claims to the extent that they become "unsecured" for purposes of § 506(a) without the new remedy's being mentioned somewhere in the Code itself or in the annals of Congress is

not plausible, in our view, and is contrary to basic bankruptcy principles.

The judgment of the Court of Appeals is affirmed.

It is so ordered.

JUSTICE SCALIA, with whom JUSTICE SOUTER joins, dissenting.

With exceptions not pertinent here, § 506(d) of the Bankruptcy Code provides: "To the extent that a lien secures a claim against the debtor that is not an allowed secured claim, such lien is void." Read naturally and in accordance with other provisions of the statute, this automatically voids a lien to the extent the claim it secures is not both an "allowed claim" and a "secured claim" under the Code. In holding otherwise, the Court replaces what Congress said with what it thinks Congress ought to have said—and in the process disregards, and hence impairs for future use, well-established principles of statutory construction. I respectfully dissent.

I

This case turns solely on the meaning of a single phrase found throughout the Bankruptcy Code: "allowed secured claim." Section 506(d) unambiguously provides that to the extent a lien does not secure such a claim it is (with certain exceptions) rendered void. See § 506(d). Congress did not leave the meaning of "allowed secured claim" to speculation. Section 506(a) says that an "allowed claim" (the meaning of which is obvious) is also a "secured claim" "to the extent of *the value of [the] creditor's interest in the estate's interest in [the securing] property.*" (This means, generally speaking, that an allowed claim "is secured only to the extent of the value of the property on which the lien is fixed; the remainder of that claim is considered unsecured." *United States v. Ron Pair Enterprises, Inc.*, 489 U.S. 235, 239 (1989).) When § 506(d) refers to an "allowed secured claim," it can only be referring to that allowed "secured claim" so carefully described two brief subsections earlier.

The phrase obviously bears the meaning set forth in § 506(a) when it is used in the subsections of § 506 other than § 506(d)—for example, in § 506(b), which addresses "allowed secured claim[s]" that are oversecured. Indeed, as respondents apparently concede, even when the phrase appears outside of § 506, it invariably means what § 506(a) describes: the portion of a creditor's allowed claim that is secured after the calculations required by that provision have been performed. See, *e.g.*, § 722 (permitting a Chapter 7 debtor to redeem certain tangible personal property from certain liens "by paying the holder of such lien the amount of the *allowed secured claim* of such holder that is secured by such lien"); § 1225(a)(5) (prescribing treatment of "*allowed secured claim[s]*" in family farmer's reorganization plan); § 1325(a)(5) (same with respect to "*allowed secured claim[s]*" in individual reorganizations) (emphases added). The statute is similarly consistent in its use of the companion phrase "*allowed unsecured claim*" to describe (with respect to a claim supported by a lien) that portion of the claim that is treated as "unsecured" under § 506(a). See, *e.g.*, [§ 507(a)(8)] (fixing priority of "*allowed unsecured claims* of governmental units"); § 726(a)(2) (providing for payment of "*allowed unsecured claim[s]*" in Chapter 7 liquidation); § 1225(a)(4) (setting standard for treatment of "*allowed unsecured claim[s]*" in Chapter 12 plan); § 1325(a)(4) (setting standard for treatment of "*allowed unsecured claim[s]*" in Chapter 13 plan) (emphases added). When, on the other hand, the Bankruptcy Code means to refer to a secured party's entire allowed claim, *i.e.*, to both the "secured" and "unsecured" portions under § 506(a), it uses the term "*allowed claim*"—as in § 363(k), which refers to "a lien that secures an allowed claim." Given this clear and unmistakable pattern of usage, it seems to me impossible to hold, as the Court does, that "the words 'allowed secured claim' in § 506(d) need not be read as an indivisible term of art defined by reference to § 506(a)." * * *

The Court makes no attempt to establish a textual or structural basis for overriding the plain meaning of § 506(d), but rests its decision upon policy intuitions of a legislative character, and upon the principle that a text which is "ambiguous" (a status apparently achieved by being the subject of disagreement between self-interested litigants) cannot change pre-Code law without the imprimatur of "legislative history." Thus abandoning the normal and sensible principle that a term (and especially an artfully defined term such as "allowed secured claim") bears the same meaning throughout the statute, the Court adopts instead what might be called the one-subsection-at-a-time approach to statutory exegesis. "[W]e express no opinion," the Court amazingly says, "as to whether the words 'allowed secured claim' have different meaning in other provisions of the Bankruptcy Code." "We * * * focus upon the case before us and allow other facts to await their legal resolution on another day."

* * *

III

Although the Court makes no effort to explain why petitioner's straightforward reading of § 506(d) is textually or structurally incompatible with other portions of the statute, respondents and the United States do so. They point out, to begin with, that the two exceptions to § 506(d)'s nullifying effect both pertain to *the disallowance of claims*, and not to *the inadequacy of security*, see §§ 506(d)(1) and (2)—from which they conclude that the applicability of § 506(d) turns only on the allowability of the underlying claim, and not on the extent to which the claim is a "secured claim" within the meaning of § 506(a). But the fact that the statute makes no exceptions to invalidation by reason of inadequate security in no way establishes that such (plainly expressed) invalidaion does not exist. The premise of the argument—that if a statute qualifies a noun with two adjectives ("allowed" and "secured"), and provides exceptions with respect to only one of the adjectives, then the other can be disregarded—is simply false. The most that can be said is that the two exceptions in § 506(d) do not *contradict* the United States' and respondents' interpretation; but they in no way suggest or support it.

Respondents and the United States also identify supposed inconsistencies between petitioner's construction of § 506(d) and other sections of the Bankruptcy Code; they are largely illusory. The principal source of concern is § 722, which enables a Chapter 7 debtor to "redeem" narrow classes of exempt or abandoned personal property from "a lien securing a dischargeable consumer debt." The price of redemption is fixed as "the amount of the *allowed secured claim* of [the lienholder] that is secured by such lien" (emphasis added). This provision, we are told, would be largely superfluous if § 506(d) automatically stripped liens securing undersecured claims to the value of the collateral, *i.e.*, to the value of the allowed secured claims.

This argument is greatly overstated. Section 722 is necessary, and not superfluous, because § 506(d) is not a *redemption* provision. It reduces the value of a lienholder's equitable interest in a debtor's property to the property's liquidation value, but it does not insure the debtor an opportunity to "redeem" the property at that price, *i.e.*, to "free [the] property * * * from [the] mortgage or pledge by paying the debt for which it stood as security." Black's Law Dictionary 1278 (6th ed. 1990). Congress had good reason to be solicitous of the debtor's right to redeem personal property (the exclusive subject of § 722), since state redemption laws are typically less generous for personalty than for real property. The most that can be said regarding § 722 is that petitioner's construction of § 506(d) would permit a more concise formulation: Instead of describing the redemption price as "the amount of the allowed secured claim * * * that is secured by such lien" it would have been *possible* to say simply "the amount of the claim * * * that is secured by such lien"—since § 506(d) would automatically have cut back the lien to the amount of the allowed secured claim. I would hardly call the more expansive formulation a redundancy—not when it is so far removed from the section that did the "cutting back" that the reader has likely forgotten it.

Respondents and their *amicus* also make much of the need to avoid giving Chapter 7 debtors a better deal than they can receive under the other Chapters of the Bankruptcy Code. They assert that, by enabling a Chapter 7 debtor to strip down a secured creditor's liens and pocket any postpetition appreciation in the property, petitioner's construction of § 506(d) will discourage debtors from using the preferred mechanisms of reorganization under Chapters 11, 12, and 13. This evaluation of the "finely reticulated" incentives affecting a debtor's behavior rests upon critical—and perhaps erroneous—assumptions about the meaning of provisions in the reorganization chapters. Respondents assume, for example, that a debtor in Chapter 13 cannot strip down a mortgage placed on the debtor's home; but that assumption may beg the very question the Court answers today. True, § 1322(b)(2) provides that Chapter 13 filers may not "modify the rights of holders of secured claims" that are "*secured only by a security interest in real property that is the debtor's principal residence*," § 1322(b)(2) (emphasis added). But this can be (and has been) read, in light of § 506(a), to prohibit modification of the mortgagee's rights only with respect to the portion of his claim that is deemed secured under the Code.[d] If petitioner's construction of § 506(d) were applied consistently in this fashion to the Code's various chapters, see § 103(a) (providing that "chapters 1, 3, and 5 * * * [shall] apply in a case under chapter 7, 11, 12, or 13"), Chapter 7 would not appear unduly attractive. In any event, reorganization contains other enticements to lure a debtor away from Chapter 7. It not only permits him to maintain control over his personal and business assets, but affords a broader discharge from pre-petition *in personam* liabilities. Compare, *e.g.*, § 523 (listing numerous exceptions to Chapter 7 discharge) with § 1328(a) (listing two exceptions to Chapter 13 discharge).

---

[d] But see *Nobelman v. American Savings Bank*, 508 U.S. 324, 113 S.Ct. 2106, 124 L.Ed.2d 228 (1993), which appears later in this Chapter. Eds.

Finally, respondents and the United States find it incongruous that Congress would so carefully protect secured creditors in the context of reorganization while allowing them to be fleeced in a Chapter 7 liquidation by operation of § 506(d). This view mistakes the generosity of treatment that creditors can count upon in reorganization. There, no more than under Chapter 7, can they demand the benefit of postevaluation increases in the value of property given as security. See §§ 1129(b)(2)(A) and 1325(a)(5) (permitting "cram-down" of reorganization plan over objections of secured creditors if creditors are to receive payments equal in present value to the cash value of the collateral, and if creditors retain liens securing such payments).

* * *

V

As I have said, the Court does not trouble to make or evaluate the foregoing arguments. Rather, in Part II of its opinion it merely describes (uncritically) "the contrasting positions of the respective parties and their *amici*" concerning the meaning of § 506(d) and concludes, because the positions are contrasting, that there is "ambiguity in the text." (This mode of analysis makes every litigated statute ambiguous.) Having thus established "ambiguity," the Court is able to summon down its *deus ex machina*: "the pre-Code rule that liens pass through bankruptcy unaffected"—which cannot be eliminated by an ambiguous provision, at least where the "legislative history" does not mention its demise.

We have, of course, often consulted pre-Code behavior in the course of interpreting gaps in the express coverage of the Code, or genuinely ambiguous provisions. And we have often said in such cases that, absent a textual footing, we will not presume a departure from longstanding pre-Code practice. But we have *never* held pre-Code practice to be determinative in the face of what we have here: contradictory statutory text. * * *

* * * Congress's careful reexamination *and entire rewriting* of [the secured claims] provisions supports the conclusion that, regardless of whether pre-Code practice is retained or abandoned, the text means precisely what it says. Indeed, the rewriting here is so complete that, no matter how deeply one admires and venerates "pre-Code law," it is impossible to interpret § 506(d) in a manner that entirely preserves it—and the Court itself, for all its protestation of fealty, does not do so. No provision of the former Bankruptcy Act, nor any pre-Code doctrine,

purported to invalidate—across the board—liens securing claims disallowed in bankruptcy, yet that is precisely what § 506(d), as interpreted by the Court today, accomplishes.

It is even more instructive to compare today's opinion with our decision a few years ago in *United States v. Ron Pair Enterprises, Inc.*, 489 U.S. 235 (1989), which involved another subsection of § 506 itself. The issue was whether § 506(b) made post-petition interest available even to those oversecured creditors whose liens were nonconsensual. * * * The opinion for the Court began "where all such inquiries must begin: with the language of the statute itself." We did not recite the contentions of the parties and declare "ambiguity," but entered into our own careful consideration of "[t]he natural reading of the [relevant] phrase," the "grammatical structure of the statute," and the "terminology used throughout the Code." Having found a "natural interpretation of the statutory language [that] does not conflict with any significant state or federal interest, nor with any other aspect of the Code," we deemed the pre-Code practice to be irrelevant. * * * Almost point for point, today's opinion is the methodological antithesis of *Ron Pair*—and I have the greatest sympathy for the Courts of Appeals who must predict which manner of statutory construction we shall use for the next Bankruptcy Code case.

The principal harm caused by today's decision is not the misinterpretation of § 506(d) of the Bankruptcy Code. The disposition that misinterpretation produces brings the Code closer to prior practice and is, as the Court irrelevantly observes, probably fairer from the standpoint of natural justice. (I say irrelevantly, because a bankruptcy law has little to do with natural justice.) The greater and more enduring damage of today's opinion consists in its destruction of predictability, in the Bankruptcy Code and elsewhere. * * * Having taken this case to resolve uncertainty regarding one provision, we end by spawning confusion regarding scores of others. I respectfully dissent.

Notes and Questions

1. Now that you have read part of Justice Scalia's dissent in *Dewsnup*, reread his concurring opinion in *Patterson v. Shumate*, Chapter 2, Section C.

2. What amount will the respondents receive from the property? How does that differ from the amount the Dewsnups offered to pay?

3. Do the respondents still have an unsecured claim of $81,000?

4. Assume that the debtor's residence, which the debtor very much wants to keep, is encumbered by a fully secured first mortgage and an under-secured second mortgage. Can you devise a strategy, based on *Dewsnup*, that the second mortgagee can use to get paid *more* than the value of its interest in the property?

5. Does *Dewsnup* apply to judicial liens? To mortgages that are completely underwater? Compare *In re Yi*, 219 B.R. 394 (E.D. Va. 1998), with *Laskin v. First Nat'l Bank of Keystone (In re Laskin)*, 222 B.R. 872 (9th Cir. BAP 1998), and *Cunningham v. Homecomings Financial Network (In re Cunningham)*, 246 B.R. 241 (Bankr. D. Md. 2000).

MARGARET HOWARD, *DEWSNUP*PING THE BANKRUPTCY CODE

1 J. Bankr. L. & Prac. 513, 524–25, 526, 528–29, 530 (1992) (footnotes omitted).

In *Dewsnup* the Court made much over pre-Code practice and concluded that Congress indicated no intent to change that practice when it passed the Bankruptcy Code in 1978 * * *. The Court made two mistakes in this discussion: It erroneously implied by its citation of *Radford* that strip down raises constitutional concern, and it misunderstood the history of bankruptcy's treatment of liens.

Constitutional Rights of Secured Creditors

By citing only *Radford* and not referring to subsequent cases and their interpretations of *Radford*, the Court gives a misleading impression of its holdings relevant to bankruptcy's treatment of secured claims. The version of the Frazier–Lemke Act at issue in *Radford* applied only retroactively. Its "avowed purpose" was, admittedly, "'to scale down the indebtedness' to the present value of the property," but the act did not, in fact, do merely that. Rather, it permitted debtors to purchase property by making deferred payments having a present value of less than the value of the property. It was retroactive application coupled with purchase for less than fair market value that led to invalidation in *Radford*. The Court approved the Frazier–Lemke Act when it was amended to give the creditor the value of the collateral. [*Wright v. Vinton Branch of the Mountain Trust Bank*, 300 U.S. 440 (1937).] The constitutionality of strip down, which also gives the creditor the value of the collateral, is not placed in question by *Radford* and its progeny.

* * *

Bankruptcy History and the Treatment of Liens

The statement that "[a]part from reorganization proceedings * * * no provision of the pre-Code statute permitted involuntary reduction of the amount of a creditor's lien for any reason other than payment on the debt" reveals the Court's ignorance of the history of bankruptcy's treatment of liens. Citation of *Long v. Bullard* immediately after this assertion gives the impression that bankruptcy law is accurately captured by the phrase, often used as shorthand for *Long*'s holding, that "liens pass through bankruptcy." It is not, and *Long* does not stand for that proposition.

Long held, as the Court put it, that "discharge in bankruptcy does not release real estate of the debtor from the lien of a mortgage created by him before the bankruptcy." The issue in *Long* was whether discharge in bankruptcy eliminates only a creditor's in personam rights against the debtor or in rem rights as well. The Court's holding that only in personam rights are affected by discharge is still good law. Thus, while it is inaccurate to say that *Long* has been legislatively overruled, it is also inaccurate to baldly assert that liens pass through bankruptcy unaffected. A more accurate statement is that liens pass through bankruptcy unaffected only if none of bankruptcy's powers to affect liens have been brought to bear.

* * *

The Code shifted focus away from in rem rights toward protection of the value of those rights, and bankruptcy experts understood as much at the time of enactment. According to one commentator, the Code "illustrated the changing nature of collateral—from 'property rights' in specific items that a secured party can 'possess' and sell to something more like a prior claim against a debtor's fungible assets."

The value being protected is the value of the secured claim (as measured under § 506(a)). Significantly, every single provision affecting the rights of secured creditors in bankruptcy (other than those few allowing destruction of secured status entirely and until *Dewsnup*) is consistent with the proposition that bankruptcy protects only the value of the postbifurcation secured claim and nothing more. * * *

In addition, the Supreme Court's decision in *United Savings Association of Texas v. Timbers of Inwood Forest Associates* held that adequate protection, which is required for a debtor to keep and use collateral, protects only the secured claim. *Timbers* rejected the argument that a secured creditor's "interest in property" includes the right to seize and realize on collateral or, if such action is prohibited by the automatic stay, to receive compensation for the use of proceeds that foreclosure would otherwise have made available. *Timbers* rests on the conclusion that bankruptcy protects only the *value* of the postbifurcation secured claim. * * *

Dewsnup's suggestion that certain in rem rights are unaffected by bankruptcy is inconsistent with *Timbers*' premise that the value of rights, but not the rights themselves, are protected in bankruptcy. Now only § 506(d) as interpreted by *Dewsnup* stands counter to the proposition that a secured creditor's protection in bankruptcy is limited to the value of the postbifurcation secured claim. *Dewsnup*, therefore, is much more inconsistent with the evolution of bankruptcy's treatment of lienors than the Court knew.

Note on Special Treatment for Tax Liens in Chapter 7—§ 724(b)

Debtors sliding into bankruptcy almost always owe substantial tax obligations. In addition, tax debts are frequently secured by liens that attach to "all property and rights to property, whether real or personal, belonging to" the taxpayer. 26 U.S.C. § 6321. Congress was concerned that these often sizeable tax liens, secured by everything the debtor owns, would swamp bankruptcy estates and leave disproportionately small amounts available to priority unsecured creditors. Thus, the Code's drafters included § 724(b). It subordinates unavoidable[e] tax liens to unsecured claims having a higher priority under § 507(a) than unsecured tax claims. Section 724(b) is an exception to the general rule that priority among secured creditors is determined among secured creditors is determined by nonbankruptcy law. Read § 724(b) and solve the following Problems.

1. A security interest in the amount of $70,000 is perfected against assets of Debtor Corp. on January 15th and a federal tax lien for $80,000 is recorded on February 1st. A second security interest of $25,000, on the same collateral as the first, is perfected on March 1st. Debtor Corp. files Chapter 7 six months later. At that time, Debtor Corp. owes $20,000 in wages to ten employees who worked during the pay period immediately preceding bankruptcy and $80,000 to holders of general unsecured claims. The estate has assets of $150,000 and costs of administration of the case are $10,000. How is this estate distributed?

---

[e] In Chapter 5 of this casebook, we will examine provisions that permit certain liens to be avoided in bankruptcy.

2. Assume the same facts as in Problem # 1, except that the tax lien is $20,000. How is this estate distributed?

3. Assume the same facts as in Problem # 1, except that the estate has assets of $200,000. How is this estate distributed?

G. SATISFACTION OF SECURED CLAIMS IN CHAPTER 13

As you recall, the theory of Chapter 7 is that debtors exchange all nonexempt property owned at the time of filing for a discharge of debts owed at that time. The theory of Chapter 13, on the other hand, is that debtors keep their property and creditors are paid out of the debtors' future earnings. Debtors frequently choose Chapter 13 because it allows them to keep their homes and cars.

A Chapter 13 plan may deal with a secured creditor in one of three ways. First, the debtor may obtain the creditor's acceptance of its treatment under the plan. § 1325(a)(5)(A). Any treatment is permissible if the affected creditor agrees to it. Second, the debtor may surrender the collateral to the creditor. § 1325(a)(5)(C). Third, the plan may provide that the secured creditor retain its lien and that "the value, as of the effective date of the plan, of property to be distributed under the plan on account of such claim is not less than the allowed amount of such claim." § 1325(a)(5)(B). This is a "present value" requirement. See *Williams v. Tower Loan of Mississippi (In re Williams)*, 168 F.3d 845 (5th Cir. 1999) (holding that a debtor cannot surrender part of a creditor's collateral under (C) and pay the present value of the remaining collateral under (B); the choices are mutually exclusive.)

Two determinations must be made under § 1325(a)(5)(B)—the value of the collateral and the proper discount rate. We will postpone the second of those issues for a moment and begin with valuation. As the next case demonstrates, valuation of collateral in Chapter 13, as in other chapters, is crucial legally but uncertain factually. Lower courts were deeply divided on this issue when the Supreme Court agreed to hear the case. Ask yourself, as you read, whether the Court succeeded in providing certainty in this important area.

While the case arose in Chapter 13, be aware that it is equally applicable to Chapter 11. (As you will see in Section H of this chapter, § 1129(b)(2)(A)(i) sets out requirements similar to those of § 1325(a)(5)(B).)

ASSOCIATES COMMERCIAL CORP. v. RASH

United States Supreme Court, 1997.
520 U.S. 953, 117 S. Ct. 1879, 138 L. Ed. 2d 148.

JUSTICE GINSBERG delivered the opinion of the Court.*

We resolve in this case a dispute concerning the proper application of § 506(a) of the Bankruptcy Code when a bankrupt debtor has exercised the "cram down" option for which Code § 1325(a)(5)(B) provides. Specifically, when a debtor, over a secured creditor's objection, seeks to retain and use the creditor's collateral in a Chapter 13 plan, is the value of the collateral to be determined by (1) what the secured creditor could obtain through foreclosure sale of the property (the "foreclosure-value" standard); (2) what the debtor would have to pay for comparable property (the "replacement-value" standard); or (3) the midpoint between these two measurements? We hold that § 506(a) directs application of the replacement-value standard.

I

In 1989, respondent Elray Rash purchased for $73,700 a Kenworth tractor truck for use in his freight-hauling business. Rash made a down payment on the truck, agreed to pay the seller the remainder in 60 monthly installments, and pledged the truck as collateral on the unpaid balance. The seller assigned the loan, and its lien on the truck, to petitioner Associates Commercial Corporation (ACC).

In March 1992, Elray and Jean Rash filed a joint petition and a repayment plan under Chapter 13 of the Bankruptcy Code (Code). At the time of the bankruptcy filing, the balance owed to ACC on the truck loan was $41,171. Because it held a valid lien on the truck, ACC was listed in the bankruptcy petition as a creditor holding a secured claim. Under the Code, ACC's claim for the balance owed on the truck was secured only to the extent of the value of the collateral; its claim over and above the value of the truck was unsecured.

To qualify for confirmation under Chapter 13, the Rashes' plan had to satisfy the requirements set forth in § 1325(a) of the Code. The Rashes' treatment of ACC's secured claim, in particular, is governed by subsection (a)(5). Under this provision, a plan's proposed treatment of

* Justice Scalia joins all but footnote 4 of this opinion.

secured claims can be confirmed if one of three conditions is satisfied: the secured creditor accepts the plan, § 1325(a)(5)(A); the debtor surrenders the property securing the claim to the creditor, § 1325(a)(5)(C); or the debtor invokes the so-called "cram down" power, § 1325-(a)(5)(B). Under the cram down option, the debtor is permitted to keep the property over the objection of the creditor; the creditor retains the lien securing the claim, § 1325(a)(5)(B)(i), and the debtor is required to provide the creditor with payments, over the life of the plan, that will total the present value of the allowed secured claim, *i.e*, the present value of the collateral, § 1325(a)(5)(B)(ii). The value of the allowed secured claim is governed by § 506(a) of the Code.

The Rashes' Chapter 13 plan invoked the cram down power. It proposed that the Rashes retain the truck for use in the freight-hauling business and pay ACC, over 58 months, an amount equal to the present value of the truck. That value, the Rashes' petition alleged, was $28,500. ACC objected to the plan and asked the Bankruptcy Court to lift the automatic stay so ACC could repossess the truck. ACC also filed a proof of claim alleging that its claim was fully secured in the amount of $41,171. The Rashes filed an objection to ACC's claim.

The Bankruptcy Court held an evidentiary hearing to resolve the dispute over the truck's value. At the hearing, ACC and the Rashes urged different valuation benchmarks. ACC maintained that the proper valuation was the price the Rashes would have to pay to purchase a like vehicle, an amount ACC's expert estimated to be $41,000. The Rashes, however, maintained that the proper valuation was the net amount ACC would realize upon foreclosure and sale of the collateral, an amount their expert estimated to be $31,875. The Bankruptcy Court agreed with the Rashes and fixed the amount of ACC's secured claim at $31,875; that sum, the court found, was the net amount ACC would realize if it exercised its right to repossess and sell the truck. The Bankruptcy Court thereafter approved the plan, and the United States District Court for the Eastern District of Texas affirmed.

A panel of the Court of Appeals for the Fifth Circuit reversed. On rehearing en banc, however, the Fifth Circuit affirmed the District Court, holding that ACC's allowed secured claim was limited to $31,875, the net foreclosure value of the truck.

In reaching its decision, the Fifth Circuit highlighted, first, a conflict it perceived between the method of valuation ACC advanced, and the law of Texas defining the rights of secured creditors. See Tex. Bus. & Com. Code Ann. §§ 9.504(a), (c), 9.505 (1991). In the Fifth

Circuit's view, valuing collateral in a federal bankruptcy proceeding under a replacement-value standard—thereby setting an amount generally higher than what a secured creditor could realize pursuing its state-law foreclosure remedy—would "change the extent to which ACC is secured from what obtained under state law prior to the bankruptcy filing." Such a departure from state law, the Fifth Circuit said, should be resisted by the federal forum unless "clearly compelled" by the Code.

The Fifth Circuit then determined that the Code provision governing valuation of security interests, § 506(a), does not compel a replacement-value approach. Instead, the court reasoned, the first sentence of § 506(a) requires that collateral be valued from the creditor's perspective. And because "the creditor's interest is in the nature of a security interest, giving the creditor the right to repossess and sell the collateral and nothing more[,] * * * the valuation should start with what the creditor could realize by exercising that right." This foreclosure-value standard, the Fifth Circuit found, was consistent with the other relevant provisions of the Code, economic analysis, and the legislative history of the pertinent provisions. Judge Smith, joined by five other judges, dissented, urging that the Code dictates a replacement-value standard.

Courts of Appeals have adopted three different standards for valuing a security interest in a bankruptcy proceeding when the debtor invokes the cram down power to retain the collateral over the creditor's objection. In contrast to the Fifth Circuit's foreclosure-value standard, a number of Circuits have followed a replacement-value approach. See, *e.g.*, *In re Taffi*, 96 F.3d 1190, 1191-1192 (CA9 1996) (en banc), cert. pending *sub nom. Taffi v. United States*, No. 96-881;[2] *In re Winthrop Old Farm Nurseries, Inc.*, 50 F.3d 72, 74-75 (CA1 1995); *In re Trimble*, 50 F.3d 530, 531-532 (CA8 1995). Other courts have settled on the midpoint between foreclosure value and replacement value. See *In re Hoskins*, 102 F.3d 311, 316 (CA7 1996); cf. *In re Valenti*, 105 F.3d 55, 62 (CA2 1997) (bankruptcy courts have discretion to value at midpoint between replacement value and foreclosure value). We

[2] In *In re Taffi*, the Ninth Circuit contrasted replacement value with fair-market value and adopted the latter standard, apparently viewing the two standards as incompatible. By using the term "replacement value," we do not suggest that a creditor is entitled to recover what it would cost the debtor to purchase the collateral brand new. Rather, our use of the term replacement value is consistent with the Ninth Circuit's understanding of the meaning of fair-market value; by replacement value, we mean the price a willing buyer in the debtor's trade, business, or situation would pay a willing seller to obtain property of like age and condition. See also *infra* n. 6.

granted certiorari to resolve this conflict among the Courts of Appeals, and we now reverse the Fifth Circuit's judgment.

II

The Bankruptcy Code provision central to the resolution of this case is § 506(a) * * *. Over ACC's objection, the Rashes' repayment plan proposed, pursuant to § 1325(a)(5)(B), continued use of the property in question, *i.e.*, the truck, in the debtor's trade or business. In such a "cram down" case, we hold, the value of the property (and thus the amount of the secured claim under § 506(a)) is the price a willing buyer in the debtor's trade, business, or situation would pay to obtain like property from a willing seller.

Rejecting this replacement-value standard, and selecting instead the typically lower foreclosure-value standard, the Fifth Circuit trained its attention on the first sentence of § 506(a). In particular, the Fifth Circuit relied on these first sentence words: a claim is secured "to the extent of the value of such *creditor's interest* in the estate's interest in such property." (Emphasis added). The Fifth Circuit read this phrase to instruct that the "starting point for the valuation [is] what the creditor could realize if it sold the estate's interest in the property according to the security agreement," namely, through "repossessing and selling the collateral."

We do not find in the § 506(a) first sentence words—"the creditor's interest in the estate's interest in such property"—the foreclosure-value meaning advanced by the Fifth Circuit. Even read in isolation, the phrase imparts no valuation standard: A direction simply to consider the "value of such creditor's interest" does not expressly reveal *how* that interest is to be valued.

Reading the first sentence of § 506(a) as a whole, we are satisfied that the phrase the Fifth Circuit considered key is not an instruction to equate a "creditor's interest" with the net value a creditor could realize through a foreclosure sale. The first sentence, in its entirety, tells us that a secured creditor's claim is to be divided into secured and unsecured portions, with the secured portion of the claim limited to the value of the collateral. To separate the secured from the unsecured portion of a claim, a court must compare the creditor's claim to the value of "such property," *i.e.*, the collateral. That comparison is sometimes complicated. A debtor may own only a part interest in the property pledged as collateral, in which case the court will be required to ascertain the "estate's interest" in the collateral. Or, a creditor may hold a junior or subordinate lien, which would require the court to ascertain the creditor's interest in the collateral. The § 506(a) phrase referring to the "creditor's interest in the estate's interest in such property" thus recognizes that a court may encounter, and in such instances must evaluate, limited or partial interests in collateral. The full first sentence of § 506(a), in short, tells a court what it must evaluate, but it does not say more; it is not enlightening on how to value collateral.

The second sentence of § 506(a) does speak to the *how* question. "Such value," that sentence provides, "shall be determined in light of the purpose of the valuation and of the proposed disposition or use of such property." By deriving a foreclosure-value standard from § 506(a)'s first sentence, the Fifth Circuit rendered inconsequential the sentence that expressly addresses how "value shall be determined."

As we comprehend § 506(a), the "proposed disposition or use" of the collateral is of paramount importance to the valuation question. If a secured creditor does not accept a debtor's Chapter 13 plan, the debtor has two options for handling allowed secured claims: surrender the collateral to the creditor, § 1325(a)(5)(C); or, under the cram down option, keep the collateral over the creditor's objection and provide the creditor, over the life of the plan, with the equivalent of the present value of the collateral, § 1325(a)(5)(B). The "disposition or use" of the collateral thus turns on the alternative the debtor chooses—in one case the collateral will be surrendered to the creditor, and in the other, the collateral will be retained and used by the debtor. Applying a foreclosure-value standard when the cram down option is invoked attributes no significance to the different consequences of the debtor's choice to surrender the property or retain it. A replacement-value standard, on the other hand, distinguishes retention from surrender and renders meaningful the key words "disposition or use."

Tying valuation to the actual "disposition or use" of the property points away from a foreclosure-value standard when a Chapter 13 debtor, invoking cram down power, retains and uses the property. Under that option, foreclosure is averted by the debtor's choice and over the creditor's objection. From the creditor's perspective as well as the debtor's, surrender and retention are not equivalent acts.

When a debtor surrenders the property, a creditor obtains it immediately, and is free to sell it and reinvest the proceeds. We recall here that ACC sought that very advantage. If a debtor keeps the property and continues to use it, the creditor obtains at once neither the property nor its value and is exposed to double risks: The debtor may again default and the property may deteriorate from extended use. Adjustments in the interest rate and secured creditor demands for more "adequate protection," § 361, do not fully offset these risks.[3]

Of prime significance, the replacement-value standard accurately gauges the debtor's "use" of the property. It values "the creditor's interest in the collateral in light of the proposed [repayment plan] reality: no foreclosure sale and economic benefit for the debtor derived from the collateral equal to * * * its [replacement] value." *In re Winthrop Old Farm Nurseries*, 50 F.3d at 75. The debtor in this case elected to use the collateral to generate an income stream. That actual use, rather than a foreclosure sale that will not take place, is the proper guide under a prescription hinged to the property's "disposition or use."

The Fifth Circuit considered the replacement-value standard disrespectful of state law, which permits the secured creditor to sell the collateral, thereby obtaining its net foreclosure value "and nothing more." In allowing Chapter 13 debtors to retain and use collateral over the objection of secured creditors, however, the Bankruptcy Code has reshaped debtor and creditor rights in marked departure from state law. See, *e.g.*, Uniform Commercial Code §§ 9-504, 9-505. The Code's cram down option displaces a secured creditor's state-law right to obtain immediate foreclosure upon a debtor's default. That change, ordered by federal law, is attended by a direction that courts look to the "proposed disposition or use" of the collateral in determining its value. It no more disrupts state law to make "disposition or use" the guide for valuation than to authorize the rearrangement of rights the cram down power entails.

Nor are we persuaded that the split-the-difference approach adopted by the Seventh Circuit provides the appropriate solution. See *In re Hoskins*, 102 F.3d at 316. Whatever the attractiveness of a standard that picks the midpoint between foreclosure and replacement values, there is no warrant for it in the Code.[5] Section 506(a) calls for

---

[3] On this matter, *amici curiae* supporting ACC contended: "'Adequate protection' payments under §§ 361, 362(d)(1) typically are based on the assumption that the collateral will be subject to only ordinary depreciation. Hence, even when such payments are made, they frequently fail to compensate adequately for the usually more rapid depreciation of assets retained by the debtor." Brief for American Automobile Manufacturers Association, Inc., et al. as *Amici Curiae* 21, n.9.

[5] As our reading of § 506(a) makes plain, we also reject a ruleless approach allowing use of different valuation standards based on the facts and circumstances of individual

the value the property possesses in light of the "disposition or use" in fact "proposed," not the various dispositions or uses that might have been proposed. The Seventh Circuit rested on the "economics of the situation," only after concluding that the statute suggests no particular valuation method. We agree with the Seventh Circuit that "a simple rule of valuation is needed" to serve the interests of predictability and uniformity. We conclude, however, that § 506(a) supplies a governing instruction less complex than the Seventh Circuit's "make two valuations, then split the difference" formulation.

In sum, under § 506(a), the value of property retained because the debtor has exercised the § 1325(a)(5)(B) "cram down" option is the cost the debtor would incur to obtain a like asset for the same "proposed * * * use."[6]

For the foregoing reasons, the judgment of the Court of Appeals is reversed, and the case is remanded for further proceedings consistent with this opinion.

It is so ordered.

JUSTICE STEVENS, dissenting.

Although the meaning of § 506(a) is not entirely clear, I think its text points to foreclosure as the proper method of valuation in this case. The first sentence in § 506(a) tells courts to determine the value of the "*creditor's* interest in the estate's interest" in the property. (Em-

---

cases. Cf. *In re Valenti*, 105 F.3d 55, 62-63 (CA2 1997) (permissible for bankruptcy courts to determine valuation standard case-by-case).

6 Our recognition that the replacement-value standard, not the foreclosure-value standard, governs in cram down cases leaves to bankruptcy courts, as triers of fact, identification of the best way of ascertaining replacement value on the basis of the evidence presented. Whether replacement value is the equivalent of retail value, wholesale value, or some other value will depend on the type of debtor and the nature of the property. We note, however, that replacement value, in this context, should not include certain items. For example, where the proper measure of the replacement value of a vehicle is its retail value, an adjustment to that value may be necessary: A creditor should not receive portions of the retail price, if any, that reflect the value of items the debtor does not receive when he retains his vehicle, items such as warranties, inventory storage, and reconditioning. Nor should the creditor gain from modifications to the property—*e.g.*, the addition of accessories to a vehicle—to which a creditor's lien would not extend under state law.

phasis added). This language suggests that the value should be determined from the creditor's perspective, *i.e.*, what the collateral is worth, on the open market, in the creditor's hands, rather than in the hands of another party.

The second sentence explains that "such value shall be determined in light of the purpose of the valuation and of the proposed disposition or use of such property." In this context, the "purpose of the valuation" is determined by § 1325(a)(5)(B). Commonly known as the Code's "cram down" provision, this section authorizes the debtor to keep secured property over the creditor's objections in a Chapter 13 reorganization, but, if he elects to do so, directs the debtor to pay the creditor the "value" of the secured claim. The "purpose" of this provision, and hence of the valuation under § 506(a), is to put the creditor in the same shoes as if he were able to exercise his lien and foreclose.*

It is crucial to keep in mind that § 506(a) is a provision that applies *throughout* the various chapters of the bankruptcy code; it is, in other words, a "utility" provision that operates in many different contexts. Even if the words "proposed disposition or use" did not gain special meaning in the cram down context, this would not render them surplusage because they have operational significance in their many other Code applications. In this context, I also think the foreclosure standard best comports with economic reality. Allowing any more than the foreclosure value simply grants a general windfall to undersecured creditors at the expense of unsecured creditors. Cf. *In re Hoskins*, 102 F.3d 311, 320 (CA7 1996) (Easterbrook, concurring in judgment). As Judge Easterbrook explained in rejecting the split-the-difference approach as a general rule, a foreclosure-value standard is also consistent with the larger statutory scheme by keeping the respective

* The Court states that "surrender and retention are not equivalent acts" from the creditor's perspective because he does not receive the property and is exposed to the risk of default and deterioration. I disagree. That the creditor does not receive the property is irrelevant because, as § 1325(a)(5)(B)(ii) directs, he receives the present value of his security interest. Present value includes both the underlying value and the time-value of that interest. The time value component similarly vitiates the risk concern. Higher risk uses of money must pay a higher premium to offset the same opportunity cost. In this case, for instance, the creditor was receiving nine percent interest, well over the prevailing rate for an essentially risk-free loan, such as a United States Treasury Bond. Finally, the concern with deterioration is addressed by another provision of the Code, § 361, which authorizes the creditor to demand "adequate protection," including increased payments, to offset any derogation of his security interest during a cram down.

recoveries of secured and unsecured creditors the same throughout the various bankruptcy chapters.

Accordingly, I respectfully dissent.

Notes and Questions

1. From whose perspective, debtor or creditor, does the Code require that value be determined?

2. Is there a tension between the first and second sentences of § 506(a)?

3. Has the Court provided sufficient guidance for lower courts called upon in the future to determine the value of collateral? Is there still room to argue, on behalf of debtors, for a value close to wholesale?

4. A similar valuation issue, albeit in a very different context, arose in *Brown & Co. Securities Corp. v. Balbus (In re Balbus)*, 933 F.2d 246 (4th Cir. 1991). *Balbus* involved a challenge brought under § 109(e) to a Chapter 13 filing. At the time of the case, § 109(e) restricted Chapter 13 to debtors owing less than $100,000 of unsecured debt and $350,000 of secured debt. Debtor's schedules listed secured debts of $324,000 and unsecured debts of $58,000. The parties agreed that the collateral for the secured debts was worth $287,000. The secured creditors were undersecured, therefore, and had $37,000 in postbifurcation unsecured claims. Addition of those claims to the other unsecured claims gave a total of $95,000 in unsecured debts. An undersecured creditor argued, however, that the value of the collateral should be reduced by 6% to account for the costs of selling it. That would increase the postbifurcation unsecured claims by approximately $17,000, to a total of $54,000, and would put debtor over § 109(e)'s then-applicable $100,000 debt limit for unsecured claims. Debtor resisted this argument because he intended to keep the property and no costs of sale would be incurred.

The court noted that the precedents disagree on how to interpret "value" within § 506(a) when the debtor intends to keep the collateral. The court believed that the conflict in the cases derives from conflict between the two sentences in § 506(a)—the first sentence focusing on the amount the creditor would realize if liquidation were necessary, and the second sentence focusing on the debtor's intended use.

The court joined an "emerging majority" and held that hypothetical costs should not be deducted because to do so would read the second sentence out of § 506(a). In addition, a contrary result could permit manipulation of Chapter 13 eligibility, depending on the amount of hypothetical costs found to be reasonable. Finally, the court found support in *Timbers*'s statement that "[t]he phrase 'value of such creditor's interest' in § 506(a) means 'the value of the collateral.'"

The dissent found that the "emerging majority" was neither "emerging" nor a "majority," and that the court's holding did not solve § 506(a)'s internal conflict:

> One may conclude from the line of cases in the "emerging majority" cited by my brothers that the courts involved construed § 506(a) by placing their emphasis on the value of the property to the *debtor* and thus on the "disposition and use" language found in the section's second sentence. Of course, the argument can be made that such inordinate focus on the statute's second sentence simply renders the first sentence "mere surplusage," and moves us no closer to divining Congress' intent. (Likewise, attention to the first sentence with equal force could be said to render the second sentence "mere surplusage.")

Id. at 253–54. The dissent believed that the two sentences of § 506(a) can be read together in the way suggested by an earlier decision:

> The emphasis to be placed upon the concept of "use" or "disposition" of property should not be placed in the context of collateral retention by the debtor via a reorganization plan, but rather ought to focus on a use or disposition of collateral that is either destructive or unanticipated in the sense that it would increase the risk of loss to the creditors' interest in the collateral. Illustrative of such use in a Chapter 12 treatment context might be a post-confirmation proposal to use a combine for custom work where previously it had been used seasonally to harvest the debtor's own crop.

Id. at 254, quoting *In re Claeys*, 81 B.R. 985, 992 (Bankr. D.N.D.1987).

Interestingly, the debtor in *Balbus* argued that the secured claim was *higher* in amount than the undersecured creditor asserted. Does this make sense in light of § 1325(a)(5)(B)? If costs of sale should not be taken into account in determining the debtor's eligibility for Chapter 13, should they also not be taken into account in other contexts requiring determination of the amount of a creditor's secured claim, regardless of the purpose of the determination—*e.g.*, entitlement to postpetition interest, motions for relief from the stay, whether plan provisions meet the minimum payment requirements of the Code, etc.?

Note on Present Value

"Present value" is based on the time value of money. Assume, for example, that a creditor has a secured claim of $100 and that the debtor's plan proposes to pay that creditor $100 in a year. Section 1325(a)(5)(B) is not satisfied because receiving $100 in a year is not equivalent to receiving $100 today. A creditor with $100 today could invest that money and have a larger sum in a year. (At 10%, the creditor would have $110 in a year.)

To arrive at the present value of $100 to be paid in a year, you must determine how much it would require today to produce $100 in a year. That, in turn, depends upon the rate of return an investment will earn over the course of a year. At 6%, $94 will grow to $100 (almost) in a year. At 10%, $91 will grow to $100 in a year. Thus, you should be indifferent to receiving $91 today or $100 in a year, if 10% is the correct rate of return.

If the debtor proposes to pay a creditor $100 next year, that is equivalent to a claim of $91 today (at 10%). If the creditor's claim is more than $91, $100 to be paid in a year is not enough to constitute the claim's present value.

Section 1325(a)(5)(B)(ii) requires that the stream of payments the creditor is to receive under the plan be worth, at the time the plan goes into effect, the value of the creditor's allowed secured claim. Thus, the total payments proposed under the plan must be *discounted* to present worth. That is like paying interest on the secured claim, only viewed from the end of the plan looking backward, rather than from the inception of the plan looking forward.

Thus, after the collateral's value has been determined, the second problem is setting an appropriate interest or discount rate.

GMAC v. JONES

United States Court of Appeals, Third Circuit, 1993.
999 F.2d 63.

STAPLETON, Circuit Judge.

These chapter 13 bankruptcy cases require us to determine the rate of interest which will assure that a secured creditor receives payments under a chapter 13 plan having a present value equal to the value of its allowed secured claim, as required by § 1325(a)(5)(B)(ii). This is a question of first impression in this Circuit. We hold that the rate of interest under § 1325(a)(5)(B)(ii) is that which the secured creditor would charge, at the effective date of the plan, for a loan similar in character, amount and duration to the credit which the creditor will be required to extend under the plan. We will reverse the district court's judgment upholding the order of the bankruptcy court and will remand these cases for proceedings consistent with this opinion.

I.

Appellee Jones possessed a Chevy pickup truck which he purchased pursuant to a financing agreement with appellant General Motors Acceptance Corporation (GMAC). Jones filed a voluntary petition and a plan under chapter 13 of the bankruptcy code. The value of the truck, as collateral, was less than the amount Jones owed to GMAC on the date of the filing, and Jones was able to reduce the amount of GMAC's secured claim down to the value of the collateral. Jones's plan proposed to reduce the secured claim due to GMAC as of the filing date from $15,713.98 at 11.98% annual rate of interest, to $11,500.00 at 10% interest. Appellee Jordan also possessed a GMC pickup truck purchased pursuant to a financing agreement with GMAC. The value of the truck as collateral also was less than the amount Jordan owed to GMAC. Jordan filed a plan proposing to reduce the secured claim owed to GMAC from $15,115.79 at 13%, to $9,700.00 at 10%. In both cases, GMAC objected to the interest rate, contending that a 10% rate was too low to provide GMAC with the present value of its allowed secured claim over the time of the plan, as required by § 1325-(a)(5)(B)(ii).

* * *

III.

Chapter 13 of the Bankruptcy Code provides for the adjustment of debts for individual debtors with regular income. A chapter 13 case begins when the debtor files a voluntary petition of bankruptcy. This petition will stay most proceedings by creditors against the debtor and his property. Generally, the debtor must propose a plan for payment of his debts within fifteen days of the filing of the petition. Creditors with an interest in the plan are given twenty-five days' notice before the plan comes before the bankruptcy court for confirmation.

In situations known as "cramdowns", the plan may be confirmed over the objection of a secured creditor if certain conditions are met. Specifically, in a chapter 13 "cramdown", a debtor may retain property in which a secured creditor has a security interest, even if the secured creditor would prefer to repossess and liquidate the property as it would be entitled to do in the absence of a bankruptcy filing. In exchange for giving the debtor a right to continue possession of the property, § 1325(a)(5)(B) directs two things: (i) the secured creditor shall retain a continuing lien on the property; and (ii) the secured creditor shall receive from the debtor "the value, as of the effective date of the plan, of such property to be distributed under the plan on account of such claim [which shall be] not less than the allowed amount of such claim." § 1325(a)(5)(B)(ii).

In order for the secured creditor to get payments over time under the plan having a present value equal to the allowed amount, as the above quoted statutory language directs, the debtor normally pays interest on the allowed amount. Unfortunately, the statute is silent about how to determine the interest rate.

IV.

The concept of present value recognizes that money received after a given period is worth less than the same amount received today. This is the case in part because money received today can be used to generate additional value in the interim. How much additional value can be generated depends on who is investing the money received today and in what market. It necessarily follows that determining the present value of money to be received in the future requires a selection of the relevant investor and the relevant market. That selection should be made on the basis of the purpose for which one is determining present value. In this context, we look to the purpose of § 1325-(a)(5)(B)(ii) which, as we understand it, seeks to put the secured creditor in an economic position equivalent to the one it would have occupied had it received the allowed secured amount immediately, thus terminating the relationship between the creditor and the debtor. In determining present value, we therefore look to the additional value that the secured creditor could be expected to generate in the regular course of its business if the plan provided for an immediate, rather than a deferred, payment of the allowed secured amount.

A.

Some courts, including the bankruptcy court in the cases we are here reviewing, have suggested a "cost of funds" theory which would determine present value by looking to the creditor and the market in which the creditor borrows capital. According to the "cost of funds" theory, a creditor in a cramdown is deprived of the right to immediately repossess and liquidate the collateral and thus realize an immediate inflow of cash. The creditor, under this view, can cover for this loss, however, by borrowing funds equivalent in value to the funds it would have realized had it been allowed to repossess and liquidate its secured interest. Accordingly, a secured creditor can be protected against any loss occasioned by delayed payment under the plan if it is paid interest on the allowed secured amount at the interest rate it would pay in the market in order to borrow the funds needed to replace those being temporarily withheld.

We view the "cost of funds" approach as falling short of the statutory objective. Paying the creditor the cost of the funds unavailable to it during the period of the plan will partially compensate the creditor for the loss of opportunity it would have had if it had been able to repossess the collateral. There is more involved, however, than the mere cost of funds. When a cramdown plan calling for payments to a secured creditor over time is confirmed, the creditor is forced both to absorb the costs of deferred payment *and* to continue a lending relationship with the debtor past the point contemplated in the original agreement. A plan under Chapter 13 thus effectively coerces a new extension of credit in which the creditor is required to assume not only the cost of capital over the deferral period but also the cost of sustaining the lending relationship over that period. The "cost of funds" approach inappropriately compensates the creditor for only the former category of cost.

Any creditor extending credit anticipates that over the course of the loan it will recover, in interest, its cost of capital and its cost of service, as well as a profit. When we focus on the present value of chapter 13 deferred payments to a secured creditor who has been forced to extend this new credit, this fact should not be ignored. It is only by acknowledging the coerced loan aspects of a cramdown and by compensating the secured creditor at the rate it would voluntarily accept for a loan of similar character,[4] amount and duration that the creditor can

[4] By a loan of "similar character" we mean a loan that the creditor regularly extends to other debtors who are not in bankruptcy but who are otherwise similarly situated to the

be placed in the same position he would have been in but for the cramdown.

B.

We think that the model of a coerced loan presents a more complete picture of what happens in a cramdown, and should provide the starting point for determining the appropriate interest rate under § 1325(a)(5)(B)(ii). The Sixth Circuit has stated tersely and well the basic idea of the "coerced loan" theory: "In effect the law requires the creditor to make a new loan in the amount of the value of the collateral rather than repossess it, and the creditor is entitled to interest on his loan." *Memphis Bank & Trust Co. v. Whitman*, 692 F.2d 427, 429 (6th Cir.1982). Courts have implemented the "coerced loan" approach by determining the appropriate interest rate to be equal to the interest rates of "similar loans" made in the region. Some have made specific reference to the interest rates of similar loans made in the region by the actual creditor who is effectively being coerced into extending the loan by the chapter 13 proceeding. While the difference between the rates charged by the particular creditor in the regular course of its business in a competitive market will not differ materially from those charged by competing creditors in that market, we believe the theory behind § 1325(a)(5)(B)(ii) indicates that the appropriate rate is that charged by the particular creditor forced to extend credit. If that creditor receives interest at a rate equal to the rate it charges in the regular course of its business in the region for loans of similar character, amount and duration, that creditor will be placed in approximately the same position it would have occupied had it been able simply to repossess the collateral at the time of the bankruptcy.

We say "approximately", because we realize that the "loan" coerced from a creditor in GMAC's position is not the precise equivalent of a new loan that GMAC would extend to a client. In particular, since GMAC had already extended loans to Jones and Jordan, GMAC incurs no costs of actually issuing new loans. Additionally, the trustee, who collects payments from the debtor and distributes them to the creditors, fulfills some of GMAC's monitoring function and is paid by the debtor. GMAC, however, retains some monitoring and other relational costs in its dealings with the trustee and the bankruptcy court, and it is unclear as an empirical matter whether GMAC's net costs in this area increase or decrease with the introduction of a cramdown.

---

debtor who is the recipient of the loan coerced by the chapter 13 proceeding and who are seeking the same kind of credit (*e.g.*, auto loan, home equity loan, etc.).

Both the absence of a "new loan" cost and the diminution, if any, of monitoring and other relational costs make the "coerced loan" somewhat less costly to GMAC than a voluntarily elected new loan.

Other factors, however, tend to make "coerced loans" more costly to the secured creditor than new loans would be. For example, loans coerced in cramdown proceedings are frequently loans without an "equity cushion". An equity cushion exists when the appraised value of the collateral is greater than the value of the loan. A lender seeks to lend on an equity cushion, among other reasons, in order to hedge against the depreciation in the value of the collateral. In these cases, the allowed amount of GMAC's claim has been made equivalent to the appraised value of the collateral, thus depriving the creditor of an equity cushion and making these "coerced loans" more costly than new loans that the creditor would have voluntarily extended. In a free, rather than a coerced, market the creditor would increase the lending rate to compensate for the absence of an equity cushion. Additionally, if the creditor had been allowed to freely construct and extend the loans coerced by the cramdown proceedings, it would have increased the lending rate based on the debtors' demonstrably poor credit history.

Both the "equity cushion" and the practice of gauging the lending rate to the debtor's credit history are important to a creditor trying to decrease the costs to itself of anticipated debtor default. At the same time, we acknowledge that some courts may have overestimated the degree to which risk of loss from default is increased in a cramdown even where there is no equity cushion and the lending rate does not reflect the debtor's bad credit rating. There are aspects of the bankruptcy process itself that counterbalance the factors of the debtor's credit history and the absence of an equity cushion.[8] Nevertheless, we are persuaded that the elements that would tend to make "coerced loans" more costly to the secured creditor than new loans, and the elements that would tend to make "coerced loans" less costly to the secured creditor than new loans will generally balance out and that it would be difficult or impossible to empirically demonstrate and quantify the cost differential between new and coerced loans. More important, while determining present value by reference to the creditor's rate for new credit in analogous situations produces only an approximation and may not always put the creditor in precisely the same position as it would have been in absent the plan, it is preferable to the competing "cost of

---

[8] The debtor has both demonstrated commitment and increased incentive not to default once in bankruptcy. Moreover, the plan of repayment will have been reviewed and approved by the court as feasible in the light of the debtor's repayment capacity.

funds" approach which ignores the fact that a coerced loan is being made and that the creditor will incur costs in connection with that loan.[9]

It is true that treating a cramdown as a coerced loan will result in a § 1325 interest rate that includes an element of profit that the creditor typically hopes to make on its loans. Some courts have objected that "profit is not an appropriate factor to consider in determining present value in a chapter 13 case." *Matter of Jordan*, 130 B.R. 185, 189 (Bankr. D.N.J.1991). On the contrary, because the objective of § 1325(a)(5)(B)(ii) is to put the creditor in the same position it would have been in if it had been allowed to end the lending relationship at the point of the bankruptcy filing by repossessing the collateral, we believe that it would be inappropriate to attempt to exclude consideration of "profit" from a determination of the § 1325 interest rate. Moreover, we perceive no unfairness in including the profit component that anyone lending money in a commercial context expects. The effect of chapter 13 is to extend, in modified form, the lending relationship that creditor and debtor created by contract. The instant lending relationship always included a mutual anticipation of profit; specifically, GMAC (as the financing arm of General Motors) valued the monetary gain more than the trucks, and the appellees valued the trucks more than the money. For a court to order the disgorgement of the creditor's profit, while laboring to preserve the profit of the debtor, would be a distortion of the lending relationship which we believe the bankruptcy code did not intend.

* * *

Moreover, we believe the coerced loan approach has appeal from a pragmatic perspective as well. Since chapter 13 cases adjust the debts of the individual wage earner, such cases tend to be rather high in volume and low in absolute value, making a reduction of the litigation and transactions costs of chapter 13 cases an important prudential consideration. We believe that in most instances, regularly maintained

---

[9] Some courts, rather than looking to the creditor's cost of making a loan (the "coerced loan" theory) or the creditor's cost of getting a loan (the "cost of funds" theory), have looked to the debtor's cost of getting a loan. In an attempt to calculate the appropriate interest rate, these cases have typically fashioned formulas designed to approximate the cost of the debtor's borrowing. One of the more common formulas is to take a "riskless" rate of interest, such as the rate of return on a treasury instrument, and tack on a point or two for consideration of risk of the debtor's default. We decline to follow these cases both because of the problems associated with judicial creation of interest rates, and because the rationale behind § 1325(a)(5)(B)(ii) links the interest rate to the present value of the deferred payments to the creditor.

documents of the creditor should make it possible for the debtor and creditor to stipulate on the interest rate the creditor would charge for a new loan of similar character, amount and duration.

In sum, because the effect of the instant cramdowns was to force GMAC to extend loans to appellees for the duration of the plans, we hold that the appropriate interest rate under § 1325(a)(5)(B)(ii) is the interest rate that GMAC would charge, at the time of the effective date of the plans, for a loan of similar character, amount and duration.

V.

As we have indicated, our selection of the coerced loan approach is based on our understanding of the objective of § 1325(a)(5)(B)(ii) and our view of the importance of minimizing the expense of getting a chapter 13 plan formulated and approved. We conclude that it would be consistent with the statutory objective and would reduce litigation expenses if we imposed an additional rule of practice in this area. The contract rate of interest is, of course, the rate that the creditor voluntarily agreed to accept at an earlier date. While in some cases the passage of time will have seen a material increase or decrease in the lending rate of the creditor, the contract rate is a fair place to begin. In the absence of a stipulation regarding the creditor's current rate for a loan of similar character, amount and duration, we believe it would be appropriate for bankruptcy courts to accept a plan utilizing the contract rate if the creditor fails to come forward with persuasive evidence that its current rate is in excess of the contract rate.[11] Conversely, utilizing the same rebuttable presumption approach, if a debtor proposes a plan with a rate less than the contract rate, it would be appropriate, in the absence of a stipulation, for a bankruptcy court to require the debtor to come forward with some evidence that the creditor's current rate is less than the contract rate.[12]

---

[11] Some courts have adopted the contract rate of interest as a cap on the interest rate to be required under § 1325(a)(5)(B)(ii). We decline to impose such a cap because we believe it would be inconsistent with the coerced loan theory to do so. A cap would give a debtor the benefit of interest rates that fall after the original contract, but deny a creditor compensation on its coerced loan for interest rates that climb after the original contract. In those situations where a cap would deny the creditor the benefit of rising rates, it would frustrate the purpose of § 1325(a)(5)(B)(ii) by potentially making the creditor worse off than it would have been had it been able to levy on the collateral at the time of the bankruptcy.

[12] Because the issue is not before us, we take no position on whether the contract rate should constitute a cap on the interest rate where the creditor is not undersecured and,

VI.

We hold that the bankruptcy and district courts erred in utilizing the prime rate to determine whether the proposed plan, as required by § 1325(a)(5)(B)(ii), provided for payments to the creditor having a present value equal to the value of its allowed secured claim. The appropriate interest rate for this purpose is the rate of interest currently being charged by the creditor in the regular course of its business for loans similar in character, amount and duration to the loan being coerced in the cramdown. It is further appropriate, we hold, for a bankruptcy court to treat the contract rate as a proxy for the creditor's current rate in the absence of a stipulation or evidence to the contrary. Accordingly, we will reverse and remand to the district court with instructions that it vacate its judgment and remand to the bankruptcy court for proceedings consistent with this opinion.

Notes and Questions

1. The court said that "Jones's plan proposed to reduce the secured claim due to GMAC as of the filing date from $15,713.98 at 11.98% annual rate of interest, to $11,500.00 at 10% interest." In other words, Jones's debt of $15,713.98, plus contract interest at 11.98%, was secured by a truck worth $11,500. Jones bifurcated the claim under § 506(a) and proposed to pay the amount of the postbifurcation secured claim plus 10% interest.

2. Can you make an argument that the contract rate should constitute a cap on interest under the plan when the creditor is oversecured, but not when the creditor is undersecured? See footnote 12 to the court's opinion.

3. What is the appropriate rate of interest for a judgment lien?

The next case illustrates a creative use of bankruptcy that enabled the debtor, by filing under Chapter 7 and Chapter 13 in rapid succession, to obtain results that could not have been reached in either Chapter alone. This sort of filing is known in the trade as a "Chapter 20."

This case also revisits the question of what constitutes a "claim," this time in a secured credit context.

---

accordingly, has not had its expectations frustrated through the "bifurcation" provisions of § 506(a).

JOHNSON v. HOME STATE BANK

United States Supreme Court, 1991.
501 U.S. 78, 111 S.Ct. 2150, 115 L.Ed.2d 66.

JUSTICE MARSHALL delivered the opinion of the Court.

The issue in this case is whether a debtor can include a mortgage lien in a Chapter 13 bankruptcy reorganization plan once the personal obligation secured by the mortgaged property has been discharged in a Chapter 7 proceeding. We hold that the mortgage lien in such a circumstance remains a "claim" against the debtor that can be rescheduled under Chapter 13.

I

This case arises from the efforts of respondent Home State Bank (Bank) to foreclose a mortgage on the farm property of petitioner. Petitioner gave the mortgage to secure promissory notes to the Bank totaling approximately $470,000. When petitioner defaulted on these notes, the Bank initiated foreclosure proceedings in state court. During the pendency of these proceedings, petitioner filed for a liquidation under Chapter 7 of the Bankruptcy Code. Pursuant to § 727, the Bankruptcy Court discharged petitioner from personal liability on his promissory notes to the Bank. Notwithstanding the discharge, the Bank's right to proceed against petitioner *in rem* survived the Chapter 7 liquidation. After the Bankruptcy Court lifted the automatic stay protecting petitioner's estate, see § 362, the Bank reinitiated the foreclosure proceedings. Ultimately, the state court entered an *in rem* judgment of approximately $200,000 for the Bank.

Before the foreclosure sale was scheduled to take place, petitioner filed the Chapter 13 petition at issue here. In his Chapter 13 plan, petitioner listed the Bank's mortgage in the farm property as a claim against his estate and proposed to pay the Bank four annual installments and a final "balloon payment" equal in total value to the Bank's *in rem* judgment. Over the Bank's objection, the Bankruptcy Court confirmed the Chapter 13 plan. The Bank appealed to the District Court, arguing that the Code does not allow a debtor to include in a Chapter 13 plan a mortgage used to secure an obligation for which personal liability has been discharged in Chapter 7 proceedings; the Bank argued in the alternative that the Bankruptcy Court had erred in finding that petitioner had proposed the plan in good faith and that the plan was feasible. The District Court accepted the first of these arguments and disposed of the case on that ground.

The Court of Appeals affirmed. Emphasizing that petitioner's personal liability on the promissory notes secured by the mortgage had been discharged in the Chapter 7 proceedings, the court reasoned that the Bank no longer had a "claim" against petitioner subject to rescheduling under Chapter 13. Like the District Court, the Court of Appeals disposed of the case without considering the Bank's contentions that Johnson's plan was not in good faith and was not feasible.

In contrast to the decision of the Tenth Circuit in this case, two other Circuit Courts of Appeals have concluded that a debtor *can* include a mortgage lien in a Chapter 13 plan even after the debtor's personal liability on the debt secured by the property has been discharged in a Chapter 7 liquidation. Having granted certiorari to resolve this conflict, we now reverse.

II

Chapter 13 of the Bankruptcy Code provides a reorganization remedy for consumer debtors and proprietors with relatively small debts. So long as a debtor meets the eligibility requirements for relief under Chapter 13, see § 109(e), he may submit for the bankruptcy court's confirmation a plan that "modif[ies] the rights of holders of secured claims * * * or * * * unsecured claims," § 1322(b)(2), and that "provide[s] for the payment of all or any part of any [allowed] claim," § 1322(b)(6). The issue in this case is whether a mortgage lien that secures an obligation for which a debtor's personal liability has been discharged in a Chapter 7 liquidation is a "claim" subject to inclusion in an approved Chapter 13 reorganization plan.

To put this question in context, we must first say more about the nature of the mortgage interest that survives a Chapter 7 liquidation. A mortgage is an interest in real property that secures a creditor's right to repayment. But unless the debtor and creditor have provided otherwise, the creditor ordinarily is not limited to foreclosure on the mortgaged property should the debtor default on his obligation; rather, the creditor may in addition sue to establish the debtor's *in personam* liability for any deficiency on the debt and may enforce any judgment against the debtor's assets generally. A defaulting debtor can protect himself from personal liability by obtaining a discharge in a Chapter 7 liquidation. See § 727. However, such a discharge extinguishes *only* "the personal liability of the debtor." § 524(a)(1). Codifying the rule of *Long v. Bullard*, 117 U.S. 617 (1886), the Code provides that a creditor's right to foreclose on the mortgage survives or passes through the bankruptcy. See § 522(c)(2).

Whether this surviving mortgage interest is a "claim" subject to inclusion in a Chapter 13 reorganization plan is a straightforward issue of statutory construction to be resolved by reference to "the text, history, and purpose" of the Bankruptcy Code. *Farrey v. Sanderfoot*, 500 U.S. 291, 298 (1991). * * * We have previously explained that Congress intended by [§ 101(5)] to adopt the broadest available definition of "claim." See *Pennsylvania Dept. of Public Welfare v. Davenport*, 495 U.S. 552, 558 (1990). In *Davenport*, we concluded that "'right to payment' [means] nothing more nor less than an enforceable obligation." *Id.* at 559.[4]

Applying the teachings of *Davenport*, we have no trouble concluding that a mortgage interest that survives the discharge of a debtor's personal liability is a "claim" within the terms of § 101(5). Even after the debtor's personal obligations have been extinguished, the mortgage holder still retains a "right to payment" in the form of its right to the proceeds from the sale of the debtor's property. Alternatively, the creditor's surviving right to foreclose on the mortgage can be viewed as a "right to an equitable remedy" for the debtor's default on the underlying obligation. Either way, there can be no doubt that the surviving mortgage interest corresponds to an "enforceable obligation" of the debtor.

The Court of Appeals thus erred in concluding that the discharge of petitioner's *personal liability* on his promissory notes constituted the complete termination of the Bank's *claim* against petitioner. Rather, a bankruptcy discharge extinguishes only one mode of enforcing a claim—namely, an action against the debtor *in personam*—while leaving intact another—namely, an action against the debtor *in rem*. Indeed, but for the codification of the rule of *Long v. Bullard*, *supra*, there can be little question that a "discharge" under Chapter 7 would

[4] Using this definition, we held in *Davenport* that restitution orders imposed as a condition of probation in state criminal proceedings were "claims" dischargeable in a Chapter 13 reorganization. Congress subsequently overruled the result in *Davenport*. See Criminal Victims Protection Act of 1990, Pub. L. 101–581, § 3, 104 Stat. 2865. It did so, however, by expressly withdrawing the Bankruptcy Court's power to discharge restitution orders under § 1328(a), not by restricting the scope of, or otherwise amending, the definition of "claim" under § 101(5). Consequently, we do not view the Criminal Victims Protection Act as disturbing our general conclusions on the breadth of the definition of "claim" under the Code.

have the effect of extinguishing the *in rem* component as well as the *in personam* component of any claim against the debtor. And because only "claims" are discharged under the Code,[5] the very need to codify *Long v. Bullard* presupposes that a mortgage interest is otherwise a "claim."

The conclusion that a surviving mortgage interest is a "claim" under § 101(5) is consistent with other parts of the Code. Section 502(b)(1), for example, states that the bankruptcy court "shall determine the amount of [a disputed] claim * * * and shall allow such claim in such amount, except to the extent that * * * such claim is unenforceable against the debtor *and property of the debtor*" (emphasis added). In other words, the court must allow the claim if it is enforceable against *either* the debtor *or* his property. Thus, § 502(b)(1) contemplates circumstances in which a "claim," like the mortgage lien that passes through a Chapter 7 proceeding, may consist of nothing more than an obligation enforceable against the debtor's property. Similarly, § 102(2) establishes, as a "[r]ul[e] of construction," that the phrase "'claim against the debtor' includes claim against property of the debtor." A fair reading of § 102(2) is that a creditor who, like the Bank in this case, has a claim enforceable only against the debtor's property nonetheless has a "claim against the debtor" for purposes of the Code.

* * *

The Bank * * * contends that even if an obligation enforceable only against the debtor's property might normally be treated as a "claim" subject to inclusion in a Chapter 13 plan, such an obligation should not be deemed a claim against the debtor when it is merely the remainder of an obligation for which the debtor's personal liability has been discharged in a Chapter 7 liquidation. Serial filings under Chapter 7 and Chapter 13, respondent maintains, evade the limits that Congress intended to place on these remedies.

We disagree. Congress has expressly prohibited various forms of serial filings. See, *e.g.*, § 109(g) (no filings within 180 days of dismissal); § 727(a)(8) (no Chapter 7 filing within six years of a Chapter

[5] A bankruptcy discharge extinguishes "the personal liability of the debtor with respect to any *debt*." § 524(a)(1) (emphasis added). As we explained in *Davenport*, "debt," which is defined under the Code as "liability on a claim," § 101(12), has a meaning coextensive with that of "claim" as defined in § 101(5). 495 U.S. at 558. Hence, a discharge under the Code extinguishes the debtor's personal liability on his creditor's claims.

7 or Chapter 11 filing); § 727(a)(9) (limitation on Chapter 7 filing within six years of Chapter 12 or Chapter 13 filing). The absence of a like prohibition on serial filings of Chapter 7 and Chapter 13 petitions, combined with the evident care with which Congress fashioned these express prohibitions, convinces us that Congress did not intend categorically to foreclose the benefit of Chapter 13 reorganization to a debtor who previously has filed for Chapter 7 relief.

The Bank's contention also fails to apprehend the significance of the full range of Code provisions designed to protect Chapter 13 creditors. A bankruptcy court is authorized to confirm a plan only if the court finds, *inter alia*, that "the plan has been proposed in good faith," § 1325(a)(3); that the plan assures unsecured creditors a recovery as adequate as "if the estate of the debtor were liquidated under chapter 7," § 1325(a)(4); that secured creditors either have "accepted the plan," obtained the property securing their claims, or "retain[ed] the[ir] lien[s]" where "the value * * * of property to be distributed under the plan * * * is not less than the allowed amount of such claim[s]," § 1325(a)(5); and that "the debtor will be able to make all payments under the plan and to comply with the plan," § 1325(a)(6). In addition, the bankruptcy court retains its broad equitable power to "issue any order, process, or judgment that is necessary or appropriate to carry out the provisions of [the Code]." § 105(a). Any or all of these provisions may be implicated when a debtor files serially under Chapter 7 and Chapter 13. But given the availability of these provisions, and given Congress' intent that "claim" be construed broadly, we do not believe that Congress intended the bankruptcy courts to use the Code's definition of "claim" to police the Chapter 13 process for abuse.

III

The Bank renews here its claim that the Bankruptcy Court erred in finding petitioner's plan to be in good faith for purposes of § 1325(a)(3) and feasible for purposes of § 1325(a)(6) of the Code. Because the District Court and Court of Appeals disposed of this case on the ground that the Bank's mortgage interest was not a "claim" subject to inclusion in a Chapter 13 plan, neither court addressed the issues of good faith or feasibility. We also decline to address these issues and instead leave them for consideration on remand.

The judgment of the Court of Appeals is reversed, and the case is remanded for further proceedings consistent with this opinion.

It is so ordered.

Notes and Questions

1. *Johnson* was decided before *Dewsnup*. Does *Dewsnup* undercut the reasoning in *Johnson*?

2. Is a strategy similar to the one used by the debtor in *Johnson* a solution for the post-*Dewsnup* debtor who wants to keep overencumbered property?

3. On remand, the bankruptcy court confirmed the plan, explicitly finding good faith and feasibility. The district court affirmed, finding the result not clearly erroneous. 1991 U.S. Dist. LEXIS 18769 (D. Kan. 1991).

NOBELMAN v. AMERICAN SAVINGS BANK

United States Supreme Court, 1993.
508 U.S. 324, 113 S.Ct. 2106, 124 L.Ed.2d 228.

JUSTICE THOMAS delivered the opinion of the Court.

This case focuses on the interplay between two provisions of the Bankruptcy Code. The question is whether § 1322(b)(2) prohibits a Chapter 13 debtor from relying on § 506(a) to reduce an undersecured homestead mortgage to the fair market value of the mortgaged residence. We conclude that it does and therefore affirm the judgment of the Court of Appeals.

I

In 1984, respondent American Savings Bank loaned petitioners Leonard and Harriet Nobelman $68,250 for the purchase of their principal residence, a condominium in Dallas, Texas. In exchange, petitioners executed an adjustable rate note payable to the bank and secured by a deed of trust on the residence. In 1990, after falling behind in their mortgage payments, petitioners sought relief under Chapter 13 of the Bankruptcy Code. The bank filed a proof of claim with the Bankruptcy Court for $71,335 in principal, interest, and fees owed on the note. Petitioners' modified Chapter 13 plan valued the residence at a mere $23,500—an uncontroverted valuation—and proposed to make payments pursuant to the mortgage contract only up to that amount (plus prepetition arrearages). Relying on § 506(a) of the Bankruptcy Code, petitioners proposed to treat the remainder of the bank's claim as unsecured. Under the plan, unsecured creditors would receive nothing.

The bank and the Chapter 13 trustee, also a respondent here, objected to petitioners' plan. They argued that the proposed bifurcation of the bank's claim into a secured claim for $23,500 and an effectively worthless unsecured claim modified the bank's rights as a homestead mortgagee, in violation of § 1322(b)(2). The Bankruptcy Court agreed with respondents and denied confirmation of the plan. The District Court affirmed, as did the Court of Appeals. We granted certiorari to resolve a conflict among the Courts of Appeals.

II

Under Chapter 13 of the Bankruptcy Code, individual debtors may obtain adjustment of their indebtedness through a flexible repayment plan approved by a bankruptcy court. Section 1322 sets forth the elements of a confirmable Chapter 13 plan. The plan must provide, *inter alia*, for the submission of a portion of the debtor's future earnings and income to the control of a trustee and for supervised payments to creditors over a period not exceeding five years. See §§ 1322(a)(1) and 1322(c). Section 1322(b)(2), the provision at issue here, allows modification of the rights of both secured and unsecured creditors, subject to special protection for creditors whose claims are secured only by a lien on the debtor's home. * * *

The parties agree that the "other than" exception in § 1322(b)(2) proscribes modification of the rights of a homestead mortgagee. Petitioners maintain, however, that their Chapter 13 plan proposes no such modification. They argue that the protection of § 1322(b)(2) applies only to the extent the mortgagee holds a "secured claim" in the debtor's residence and that we must look first to § 506(a) to determine the value of the mortgagee's "secured claim." Section 506(a) provides that an allowed claim secured by a lien on the debtor's property "is a secured claim to the extent of the value of [the] property"; to the extent the claim exceeds the value of the property, it "is an unsecured claim." Petitioners contend that the valuation provided for in § 506(a) operates automatically to adjust downward the amount of a lender's undersecured home mortgage before any disposition proposed in the debtor's Chapter 13 plan. Under this view, the bank is the holder of a "secured claim" only in the amount of $23,500—the value of the collateral property. Because the plan proposes to make $23,500 worth of payments pursuant to the monthly payment terms of the mortgage contract, petitioners argue, the plan effects no alteration of the bank's rights as the holder of that claim. Section 1322(b)(2), they assert, allows unconditional modification of the bank's leftover "unsecured claim."

This interpretation fails to take adequate account of § 1322-(b)(2)'s focus on "rights." That provision does not state that a plan may modify "claims" or that the plan may not modify "a claim secured only by" a home mortgage. Rather, it focuses on the modification of the "*rights of holders*" of such claims. By virtue of its mortgage contract with petitioners, the bank is indisputably the holder of a claim secured by a lien on petitioners' home. Petitioners were correct in looking to § 506(a) for a judicial valuation of the collateral to determine the status of the bank's secured claim. It was permissible for petitioners to seek a valuation in proposing their Chapter 13 plan, since § 506(a) states that "[s]uch value shall be determined * * * in conjunction with any hearing * * * on a plan affecting such creditor's interest." But even if we accept petitioners' valuation, the bank is still the "holder" of a "secured claim," because petitioners' home retains $23,500 of value as collateral. The portion of the bank's claim that exceeds $23,500 is an "unsecured claim componen[t]" under § 506(a), *United States v. Ron Pair Enterprises, Inc.*, 489 U.S. 235, 239 n.3 (1989) (internal quotation marks omitted); however, that determination does not necessarily mean that the "rights" the bank enjoys as a mortgagee, which are protected by § 1322(b)(2), are limited by the valuation of its secured claim.

The term "rights" is nowhere defined in the Bankruptcy Code. In the absence of a controlling federal rule, we generally assume that Congress has "left the determination of property rights in the assets of a bankrupt's estate to state law," since such "[p]roperty interests are created and defined by state law." *Butner v. United States*, 440 U.S. 48, 54–55 (1979). Moreover, we have specifically recognized that "[t]he justifications for application of state law are not limited to ownership interests," but "apply with equal force to security interests, including the interest of a mortgagee." *Id.* at 55. The bank's "rights," therefore, are reflected in the relevant mortgage instruments, which are enforceable under Texas law. They include the right to repayment of the principal in monthly installments over a fixed term at specified adjustable rates of interest, the right to retain the lien until the debt is paid off, the right to accelerate the loan upon default and to proceed against petitioners' residence by foreclosure and public sale, and the right to bring an action to recover any deficiency remaining after foreclosure. These are the rights that were "bargained for by the mortgagor and the mortgagee," *Dewsnup v. Timm*, 112 S.Ct. 773, 778 (1992), and are rights protected from modification by § 1322(b)(2).

This is not to say, of course, that the contractual rights of a home mortgage lender are unaffected by the mortgagor's Chapter 13 bankruptcy. The lender's power to enforce its rights—and, in particular, its right to foreclose on the property in the event of default—is checked by the Bankruptcy Code's automatic stay provision. § 362. In addition, § 1322(b)(5) permits the debtor to cure prepetition defaults on a home mortgage by paying off arrearages over the life of the plan "notwithstanding" the exception in § 1322(b)(2). These statutory limitations on the lender's rights, however, are independent of the debtor's plan or otherwise outside § 1322(b)(2)'s prohibition.

Petitioners urge us to apply the so-called "rule of the last antecedent," which has been relied upon by some Courts of Appeals to interpret § 1322(b)(2) the way petitioners favor. According to this argument, the operative clause "other than a claim secured only by a security interest in * * * the debtor's principal residence" must be read to refer to and modify its immediate antecedent, "secured claims." Thus, § 1322(b)(2)'s protection would then apply only to that subset of allowed "secured claims," determined by application of § 506(a), that are secured by a lien on the debtor's home—including, with respect to the mortgage involved here, the bank's secured claim for $23,500. We acknowledge that this reading of the clause is quite sensible as a matter of grammar. But it is not compelled. Congress chose to use the phrase "claim secured * * * by" in § 1322(b)(2)'s exception, rather than repeating the term of art "secured claim." The unqualified word "claim" is broadly defined under the Code to encompass any "right to payment, whether * * * secure[d] or unsecured" or any "right to an equitable remedy for breach of performance if such breach gives rise to a right to payment, whether * * * secure[d] or unsecured." § 101(5). It is also plausible, therefore, to read "a claim secured only by a [homestead lien]" as referring to the lienholder's entire claim, including both the secured and the unsecured components of the claim. Indeed, § 506(a) itself uses the phrase "claim * * * secured by a lien" to encompass both portions of an undersecured claim.

This latter interpretation is the more reasonable one, since we cannot discern how § 1322(b)(2) could be administered under petitioners' interpretation. Petitioners propose to reduce the outstanding mortgage principal to the fair market value of the collateral, and, at the same time, they insist that they can do so without modifying the bank's rights "as to interest rates, payment amounts, and [other] contract terms." That appears to be impossible. The bank's contractual rights are contained in a unitary note that applies at once to the bank's overall claim, including both the secured and unsecured components. Petitioners cannot modify the payment and interest terms for the unsecured component, as they propose to do, without also modifying the terms of the secured component. Thus, to preserve the interest rate and the amount of each monthly payment specified in the note after having reduced the principal to $23,500, the plan would also have to reduce the term of the note dramatically. That would be a significant modification of a contractual right. Furthermore, the bank holds an adjustable rate mortgage, and the principal and interest payments on the loan must be recalculated with each adjustment in the interest rate. There is nothing in the mortgage contract or the Code that suggests any basis for recalculating the amortization schedule—whether by reference to the face value of the remaining principal or by reference to the unamortized value of the collateral. This conundrum alone indicates that § 1322(b)(2) cannot operate in combination with § 506(a) in the manner theorized by petitioners.

In other words, to give effect to § 506(a)'s valuation and bifurcation of secured claims through a Chapter 13 plan in the manner petitioners propose would require a modification of the rights of the holder of the security interest. Section 1322(b)(2) prohibits such a modification where, as here, the lender's claim is secured only by a lien on the debtor's principal residence.

The judgment of the Court of Appeals is therefore

Affirmed.

JUSTICE STEVENS, concurring.

At first blush it seems somewhat strange that the Bankruptcy Code should provide less protection to an individual's interest in retaining possession of his or her home than of other assets. The anomaly is, however, explained by the legislative history indicating that favorable treatment of residential mortgagees was intended to encourage the flow of capital into the home lending market. It therefore seems quite clear that the Court's literal reading of the text of the statute is faithful to the intent of Congress. Accordingly, I join its opinion and judgment.

Notes and Questions

1. Does § 1322(b)(2), as interpreted by *Nobelman*, prohibit bifurcation and strip down when the creditor holds collateral in addition to the debtor's home? See *Hammond v. Commonwealth Mortgage Corp. of America (In re Hammond),* 27 F.3d 52 (3d Cir. 1994). What if the property is a multi-unit dwelling, with debtor living in one unit and renting out the others? Compare *Lomas Mortgage, Inc. v. Louis*, 82 F.3d 1 (1st Cir.1996), with *Brunson v.*

Wendover Funding, Inc. (In re Brunson), 201 B.R. 351 (Bankr. W.D.N.Y. 1996).

2. If the debtor is unable to confirm a plan that pays the full amount of the debt and, instead, gives the undersecured creditor the keys to the house, is the deficiency discharged?

3. Debtor's house is encumbered by two mortgages—a first mortgage securing a debt of $120,000 and a second mortgage securing a debt of $50,000. Debtor's home is worth $100,000 and Debtor wants to keep it. Debtor's Chapter 13 plan proposes to continue paying the first mortgagee in accordance with the parties' contract, with the lien to remain in place until completion of payments. Debtor wants to put the second mortgagee in the class of unsecured creditors, pay a pro rata share on that claim, and void the second mortgagee's lien. Does § 1322(b)(2), as interpreted by *Nobelman*, prohibit this treatment of the second mortgagee? Compare *McDonald v. Master Financial, Inc. (In re McDonald)*, 205 F.3d 606 (3d Cir.2000), and *Bartee v. Tara Homeowners Assoc. (In re Bartee)*, 212 F.3d 277 (5th Cir.2000), with *In re Lane*, 248 B.R. 534 (Bankr. E.D.Tenn.2000), and *Boehmer v. Essex (In re Boehmer)*, 240 B.R. 837 (Bankr. E.D.Pa.1999).

4. Debtor owed Bank $22,000 on a note secured by a mobile home, in which Debtor lived, worth $15,000. The note was due in 2004. Debtor filed a Chapter 13 petition in 2001 and proposed a five-year plan. Under the plan, Bank would be paid $15,000 in 60 monthly installments, with appropriate interest. The balance of Bank's obligation would be treated as unsecured. Bank objected to confirmation of the plan, citing § 1322(b)(2). Debtor countered by pointing to § 1322(c)(2), which was added to the Code after *Nobelman*. Does § 1322(c)(2) apply in this case and, if so, does it affect *Nobelman*? See *Witt v. United Companies Lending Corp. (In re Witt)*, 113 F.3d 508 (4th Cir.1997).

5. Debtors in *Di Pierro v. Taddeo (In re Taddeo)*, 685 F.2d 24 (2d Cir.1982), defaulted on their residential mortgage. The mortgagee accelerated in accordance with state law and began foreclosure proceedings. Debtors filed Chapter 13 before the mortgagee could obtain a final judgment of foreclosure and sale. Debtors proposed to cure the default and to reinstate the mortgage under § 1322(b)(5). The mortgagee objected to the plan, arguing that once she had accelerated the mortgage, the debtors had to pay the full amount in accordance with state law. She sought relief from the stay in order to pursue foreclosure. The court rejected the creditor's arguments and held that debtors can use Chapter 13 to "de-accelerate" residential mortgages:

> When Congress empowered Chapter 13 debtors to "cure defaults," we think Congress intended to allow mortgagors to "de-accelerate" their mortgage and reinstate its original payment schedule. We so hold for two reasons. First, we think that the power to cure must comprehend the power to "de-accelerate." This follows from the

concept of "curing a default." A default is an event in the debtor-creditor relationship which triggers certain consequences—here, acceleration. Curing a default commonly means taking care of the triggering event and returning to pre-default conditions. The consequences are thus nullified. This is the concept of "cure" used throughout the Bankruptcy Code. * * *

Policy considerations strongly support this reading of the statute. Conditioning a debtor's right to cure on its having filed a Chapter 13 petition prior to acceleration would prompt unseemly and wasteful races to the courthouse. Worse, these would be races in which mortgagees possess an unwarranted and likely insurmountable advantage: wage earners seldom will possess the sophistication in bankruptcy matters that financial institutions do, and often will not have retained counsel in time for counsel to do much good. In contrast, permitting debtors in the Taddeos' position to de-accelerate by payment of the arrearages will encourage parties to negotiate in good faith rather than having to fear that the mortgagee will tip the balance irrevocably by accelerating or that the debtor may prevent or at least long postpone this by filing a Chapter 13 petition.

Secondly, we believe that the power to "cure any default" granted in § 1322(b)(3) and (b)(5) is not limited by the ban against "modifying" home mortgages in § 1322(b)(2) because we do not read "curing defaults" under (b)(3) or "curing defaults and maintaining payments" under (b)(5) to be *modifications* of claims.

It is true that § 1322(b)(5)'s preface, "notwithstanding paragraph (2)," seems to treat the power to cure in (b)(5) as a subset of the power to modify set forth in (b)(2), but that superficial reading of the statute must fall in the light of legislative history and legislative purpose. The "notwithstanding" clause was added to § 1322(b)(5) to emphasize that defaults in mortgages could be cured notwithstanding § 1322(b)(2). But the clause was not necessary. The Senate protected home mortgages from *modification* in its last bill; it evinced no intent to protect these mortgages from *cure*.

Id. at 26–28. Under the authority of *Taddeo*, Chapter 13 is an attractive alternative for debtors faced with the loss of their residences. Does anything in *Nobelman* affect *Taddeo*?

6. Debtor's home, which was worth $150,000, was encumbered by a purchase money mortgage securing an obligation of $100,000. When Debtor missed several payments, Bank accelerated and obtained a foreclosure judgment. Debtor filed Chapter 13 before Bank could hold its foreclosure sale. Under the plan, Debtor proposed to make regular monthly payments in accordance with the loan documents and to pay the arrearage over the life of the plan. The plan did not provide for interest on the arrearage or reimbursement for

Bank's collection costs. Debtor would thereby be back on the regular payment schedule by the end of the plan. Bank objected to the plan, arguing that it impermissibly modified Bank's rights and that Debtor's right to cure had expired. What result? See §§ 1322(c)(1) and (e).

7. Subsection 1123(b)(5), which was added by the 1994 Amendments, provides protections for the residential mortgagee in Chapter 11 that parallel § 1322(b)(2). This has effectively extended *Nobelman* to individual Chapter 11 cases.

H. SATISFACTION OF SECURED CLAIMS IN CHAPTER 11

Section 1129, which governs payments under Chapter 11 plans, is similar to § 1325(a), which applies to Chapter 13 plans. In both chapters, a plan may impose any degree of disadvantage if the creditor agrees to that treatment. A creditor's decision is formed against a background of the alternatives—that is, what can be imposed on an unwilling creditor. In Chapter 11, § 1129 provides that background.

The "best interests" test of § 1129(a)(7) applies to all creditors, whether secured or unsecured, and requires that the plan give each nonconsenting creditor at least as much as that creditor would have received if a Chapter 7 case had been filed. (It is analogous to § 1325-(a)(4), which sets out a best interests test for Chapter 13.) Valuation is centrally important in Chapter 11 as it is in other chapters, but may be more complicated when large businesses are involved.

If the plan is to be crammed down, § 1129(b)(2)(A) sets out the requirements relating to secured claims. The most important subpart for current purposes, which is much like § 1325(a)(5)(B), is § 1129-(b)(2)(A)(i). It requires that the creditor retain its lien and receive a stream of payments that meets a two-part test: 1) "deferred cash payments totaling at least the allowed amount of such claim"—a "principal amount" test; and 2) "of a value, as of the effective date of the plan, of at least the value of such holder's interest in the estate's interest in such property"—a "present value" test.

Assume, for example, that Debtor owes Creditor $15,000 and that the obligation is secured by a lien on collateral worth $10,000. (Obviously, Creditor's allowed secured claim, under § 506(a), is $10,000.) Debtor proposes a plan that provides for Creditor to retain its lien and to receive payments of $917 per month for 12 months. The "principal amount" test requires that the stream of payments total at least as much as the secured claim—$10,000. The payments proposed here total $11,004, so the principal amount test is met. Under the "present value" test, the right to receive $917 a month for 12 months must have a present value of $10,000. The test is met if the appropriate discount rate is 10% or less. (Or one could say that, in order to satisfy an obligation of $10,000 at 10% interest, a one-year plan must pay at least $11,000.) If the court finds that a higher discount rate should be used, however, the present value test is not met and the plan cannot be confirmed.

These requirements are treated in more detail in Chapter 8 of this casebook.

Questions

Now that you know how secured claims are paid in Chapters 11 and 13, recall *Dewsnup v. Timm*, which held that a Chapter 7 debtor cannot strip down an undersecured lien and retain the property by paying the amount of the postbifurcation secured claim. Does *Dewsnup* apply in a Chapter 11 case? A Chapter 13 case? If so, what prospect do you see for effective reorganizations in the future?

Even when the Code is fairly clear about the rights of secured creditors in reorganization cases, plans occasionally include provisions that are contrary to the Code's requirements. In other situations, plans may contain provisions the legal effect of which is unclear, or omit provisions that should be included. If the affected creditor is paying attention, a properly raised objection to confirmation of the plan should result in removal of the offending provision, resolution of the uncertainty or addition of the missing provisions. But what if the creditor is not paying attention and fails to raise these matters before confirmation?

MATTER OF PENROD

United States Court of Appeals, Seventh Circuit, 1995.
50 F.3d 459.

POSNER, Chief Judge.

This appeal raises an issue of bankruptcy law that one might have supposed had been settled long ago. It is whether, when a plan of reorganization makes provision for the payment of a secured creditor's claim but does not say whether the creditor's security interest (lien) is extinguished, the security interest survives, in accordance with the old saw that "liens pass through bankruptcy unaffected."

Hog farmers named Penrod executed a promissory note to Mutual Guaranty Corporation (actually to its predecessor, but we can ignore that detail) for $150,000, secured by the Penrods' hogs. A year later, the Penrods filed for bankruptcy under Chapter 11, owing Mutual Guaranty $132,000. Mutual Guaranty filed a proof of claim in the bankruptcy proceeding. The Penrods, neither objecting to the claim nor questioning the validity of Mutual Guaranty's lien, filed a plan of reorganization which designated Mutual Guaranty as a "Class 3 creditor"—in fact as the only Class 3 creditor. Class 3 creditors, the plan states, "will be paid in full, with interest at the rate of eleven percent (11 percent) per annum. Payments to this Class shall be paid on a monthly basis commencing sixty (60) days after Confirmation. Furthermore, said payments shall be based upon a seven (7) year amortization." That is all that the plan, or the order confirming it, says about Mutual Guaranty's interest.

Shortly after the plan went into effect, the Penrods' hogs became infected with "pseudo-rabies" virus, a disease of the reproductive system that causes the females infected with it to miscarry. Hogs so stricken cannot be kept for breeding purposes; all they are good for is food (human food, we note with some anxiety). So the Penrods sold their hogs for slaughter—without remitting the proceeds to Mutual Guaranty, as the security agreement accompanying the promissory note had required. Mutual Guaranty brought suit in a state court to enforce a lien in the proceeds. The Penrods responded by asking the bankruptcy court to hold Mutual Guaranty in contempt for violating the order confirming the plan of reorganization, which the Penrods claim extinguished Mutual Guaranty's lien. The bankruptcy court agreed that the lien had been extinguished and enjoined (the court's term was "precluded," but as far as we can tell it meant the same thing) Mutual Guaranty from attempting to enforce it. The district court affirmed.

A secured creditor can bypass his debtor's bankruptcy proceeding and enforce his lien in the usual way, which would normally be by bringing a foreclosure action in a state court. This is the principle that liens pass through bankruptcy unaffected. *Long v. Bullard*, 117 U.S. 617 (1886); *Dewsnup v. Timm*, 502 U.S. 410 (1992); *In re James Wilson Associates*, 965 F.2d 160, 167 (7th Cir. 1992). If the creditor follows this route, the discharge in bankruptcy will not impair his lien. *Dewsnup v. Timm, supra*, 112 S. Ct. at 778; *In re Tarnow*, 749 F.2d

464 (7th Cir. 1984). Alternatively, he may decide to collect his debt in the bankruptcy proceeding, and to this end may file a proof of claim in that proceeding. § 501(a). He will do this if he is undersecured, for in that case merely enforcing his lien would not enable him to collect the entire debt owed him. His only chance of recovering any part of the amount by which the debt exceeds the value of the lien would be to share in the distribution of the debtor's estate to the unsecured creditors.

A secured creditor may be dragged into the bankruptcy involuntarily, because the trustee or debtor (if there is no trustee), or someone who might be liable to the secured creditor and therefore has an interest in maximizing the creditor's recovery, may file a claim on the creditor's behalf. §§ 501(b), (c). He may participate in the bankruptcy in order to try to get the automatic stay lifted to the extent of allowing him to enforce his lien; for the stay applies to the enforcement of liens. He may want to participate in the bankruptcy proceeding (and so may decide to file a claim) simply because he wants to make sure that the debtor's estate is not administered in a way that will diminish the value, as distinct from threatening the existence, of his lien.

The secured creditor does not, by participating in the bankruptcy proceeding through filing a claim, surrender his lien. But this is not to say that the lien is sure to escape unscathed from the bankruptcy. We have mentioned the automatic stay. If the secured creditor's claim is challenged in the bankruptcy proceeding and the court denies the claim, the creditor will lose the lien by operation of the doctrine of collateral estoppel. § 506(d). He may be forced in the plan of reorganization to swap his lien for an interest that is an "indubitable equivalent" of the lien. § 1129(b)(2)(A)(iii). And in some circumstances he may even be compelled to surrender his lien without receiving anything in return. *See* §§ 1126(d), 1129(a)(10), (b)(1). And, of course, he can consent to its discharge. The right is implicit in § 1126, and is anyway obvious. It is a frequent element of a plan of reorganization, as we are about to see.

Nothing we have said so far is controversial, and we can take one more step without inviting controversy. A plan of reorganization can expressly preserve preexisting liens, such as that of Mutual Guaranty in this case. § 1123(b)(1). Conversely, it can expressly abrogate some or all of those liens with the full consent of the lienholders; and this is common. * * * By now it should be clear that like most generalizations about law, the principle that liens pass through bankruptcy unaffected cannot be taken literally.

The question we must decide in this case is whether preexisting liens survive a reorganization when the plan (or the order confirming it) does not mention the liens. What in other words is the default rule when the plan is silent? We acknowledge this to be a difficult question. Liens are property rights and the forfeiture of such rights is disfavored. But when lienholders participate in a bankruptcy proceeding, and especially in a reorganization, they know that their liens are likely to be affected, and indeed altered. The issue here, moreover, is what the proper rule for interpreting silence is rather than in what circumstances a lien can be taken away from someone who has expressed his desire to retain it.

We have concluded that the default rule for secured creditors who file claims for which provision is made in the plan of reorganization is extinction and is found in the Code itself. Section 1141(c) provides with immaterial exceptions that "except as provided in the plan or in the order confirming the plan, after confirmation of a plan, the property dealt with by the plan is free and clear of all claims and interests of creditors, equity security holders, and of general partners in the debtor." The term "interest" is not defined in the Code, but a lien is defined as an interest in property, § 101(37), and there is no doubt that a security interest is an interest, and it is defined as a "lien created by an agreement." § 101(51). So § 1141(c) must cover liens, and must mean, therefore, that unless the plan of reorganization, or the order confirming the plan, says that a lien is preserved, it is extinguished by the confirmation. This is provided, we emphasize, that the holder of the lien participated in the reorganization. If he did not, his lien would not be "property dealt with by the plan," and so the section would not apply. One could argue that the quoted phrase should be equated to "property of the estate," defined in § 541 to include "all legal or equitable interests of the debtor in property *as of the commencement of the case*" (emphasis added), and that at the start of the bankruptcy proceeding the liens of the secured creditors are not the debtor's property—which indeed they are not. *Moody v. Amoco Oil Co.*, 734 F.2d 1200, 1213 (7th Cir. 1984); *In re Interstate Motor Freight System*, 86 Bankr. 500, 505 (Bankr. W.D. Mich. 1988). But the suggested equation is not especially plausible. Property dealt with by the plan is property dealt with by the plan, whether it was part of the debtor's estate when bankruptcy was first declared or was tossed into the pot later. As we have said, secured creditors commonly give up their preexisting liens for other interests in the reorganized firm. A plan of reorganization that does this "deals with" the liens. Or does it? For it could be argued that the plan in this case dealt with the secured creditor's *claim*, but not with its *lien*. But this interpretation would be inconsistent with the rest of

§ 1141(c)—that the property dealt with by the plan is, after confirmation of the plan, to be "free and clear of all claims and interests of creditors" (and others). On the view pressed by Mutual Guaranty, the assets of the reorganized entity would continue to be burdened by secured creditors' claims by virtue of their liens even if the plan made provision for those claims.

Our suggested interpretation reconciles the language of § 1141(c) with the principle, which we have pointed out cannot be maintained without careful qualification, that liens pass through bankruptcy unaffected. They do—unless they are brought into the bankruptcy proceeding and dealt with there. The interpretation makes practical sense as well. It lowers the costs of transacting with the reorganized firm, thus boosting the chances that the reorganization will succeed. By studying the plan of reorganization a prospective creditor of or investor in the reorganized firm can tell whether any liens that creditors whose interests in the new entity are defined in the plan may have had against its bankrupt predecessor survive as encumbrances on the assets of the new firm. The cases that support a contrary interpretation are cases in which the courts were, we respectfully suggest, mesmerized by a formula ("liens pass through bankruptcy unaffected"). They are none of them appellate cases, and there are plenty of cases that take our view. Oddly, none of the cases on either side is an appellate case, the ones cited by Mutual Guaranty being readily distinguishable. The secured creditor in *Tarnow, supra,* did not participate in the reorganization, except to file a late claim against the debtor. The bankruptcy court disallowed the lien because the claim was late—an excessive punishment—not because the plan of reorganization had dealt with the property constituted by the creditor's lien. It had not; in fact no plan had yet been confirmed. Nor had the plan in *Estate of Lellock v. Prudential Ins. Co.*, 811 F.2d 186, 188-89 (3d Cir. 1987), made provision for the secured creditor; the debtor had never even listed the property subject to the lien as an asset of the estate. In *General Electric Credit Corp. v. Nardulli & Sons Inc.*, 836 F.2d 184, 188-89 (3d Cir. 1988), the plan denominated the creditor as a "secured creditor" and explicitly recognized its security interest. *In re Simmons*, 765 F.2d 547 (5th Cir. 1985), not cited by Mutual Guaranty—no doubt because it did not involve a plan of reorganization or cite § 1141(c)—is nevertheless its best case. It arose under an analogous provision of the Code, § 1327(c), which governs plans under Chapter 13—a counterpart to Chapter 11, only for individuals rather than firms. *Simmons* relied heavily on our decision in *Tarnow*, but *Tarnow* did not involve the interpretation of a plan of reorganization: there was none.

There is nothing to Mutual Guaranty's suggestion that our interpretation raises a question under the due process or takings clauses of the Fifth Amendment because a lien is property within the meaning of the clause. It is, *United States v. Security Industrial Bank*, 459 U.S. 70, 76-77 (1982), but Mutual Guaranty could have protected it by appealing from the order confirming the plan of reorganization. We recognize that since the law was not clear with respect to the survival of the lien of a creditor who is provided for in the plan without mention of his lien, Mutual Guaranty may not have realized when the plan was adopted that its lien was in jeopardy. Conceivably this might give Mutual Guaranty an equitable defense to the complete extinction of the lien, but it has not presented such a defense. It has staked its all on persuading us that its lien survived the bankruptcy proceeding intact.

AFFIRMED.

Chapter 5

AVOIDING POWERS

A. INTRODUCTION

Transfers of the debtor's property that occur pre- or postpetition may make the goals of bankruptcy—equality of distribution for creditors and a fresh start for the debtor—more difficult to achieve. These transfers may take out of the estate property that should be available to all the creditors or to the debtor. In order to reverse these effects, the Code gives the trustee (and, in limited circumstances, the debtor) the power to *avoid* or undo certain transfers.

"Transfer" is defined in § 101(54) to include "every mode * * * of disposing of or parting with property or with an interest in property." This includes an outright disposition, such as a gift or sale, as well as the creation of an encumbrance or lien. When an outright disposition is avoided, the property is recovered from the transferee and, under § 541(a)(3), becomes property of the bankruptcy estate. When a lien is avoided, the property is freed from encumbrance. The secured creditor whose lien is avoided becomes an unsecured creditor. Because involuntary as well as voluntary transfers are included, avoiding powers apply equally to judicial liens and to security interests.

Existence of the avoiding powers serves to regulate the conduct of parties operating in the shadow of bankruptcy. Because certain transfers can be undone in bankruptcy, the threat of a bankruptcy filing can be a powerful negotiating tool.

Although benefit to the debtor is occasionally the purpose of avoidance, the benefit most often goes to creditors because property is pulled back into the estate and into the pot of assets divided among holders of unsecured claims. For that reason, the trustee is often referred to as the representative of unsecured creditors.

This chapter deals with a number of avoiding powers, including fraudulent conveyances, preferences and the "strong-arm" power.

B. FRAUDULENT CONVEYANCES

1. INTRODUCTION

To avoid having property seized by creditors, a debtor might transfer it to a friend or relative in exchange for little or no consideration. Or the debtor might transfer property to another with the understanding that the debtor will continue to have the use and benefit of the property. Such attempts to insulate property from creditors' claims are generally rendered ineffective by fraudulent conveyances law.

Fraudulent conveyances law, which draws upon state law as well as the Bankruptcy Code, covers two types of transfers—those intended to delay or defraud creditors and those made for inadequate consideration by an insolvent transferor. The clearest example of the former is my decision to hide my personal assets, in order to keep my creditors from getting them. The second branch of fraudulent conveyances law, which prevents an insolvent person from making gifts, is summed up in the maxim that a debtor must be "just before generous." Transfers covered by the second branch of fraudulent conveyances law are "constructively fraudulent."

Modern fraudulent conveyances law is rooted in the Statute of 13 Elizabeth, enacted in 1570, which provided for the avoidance of fraudulent transfers made by debtors with actual intent to hinder, delay or defraud creditors. *Twyne's Case*, 3 Coke 80b, 76 Eng. Rep. 809 (Star Chamber 1601), decided under the Statute, is the basis of contemporary fraudulent dispositions law. The debtor in *Twyne's Case*, Pierce, was indebted to Twyne for four hundred pounds and to C for two hundred pounds. C brought an action against Pierce to recover the debt. While the action was pending, Pierce secretly conveyed all of his property, worth three hundred pounds, to Twyne by a deed of gift. Despite the "gift," Pierce kept some sheep in his possession and treated them as his own. After C obtained a judgment against Pierce, the sheriff sought to levy on the sheep; he was prevented from doing so by friends of Pierce, who asserted that the sheep actually belonged to Twyne. C sued Twyne to set aside the conveyance.

The court held that the transfer to Twyne was in fact fraudulent and enumerated "badges of fraud" to support its holding. These "badges of fraud"—circumstances indicative of an intent to defraud—were used to meet the Statute's requirement of proof of "intent to delay, hinder or defraud." *Twyne's Case* involved the following badges of fraud: (1) the conveyance consisted of all of Pierce's property, (2) the property remained in Pierce's possession and he treated it as his own, (3) the conveyance was made while a suit was pending against Pierce, (4) the transaction was secret, and (5) Twyne held the property in trust for Pierce. Contemporary courts use similar indicia of an intent to defraud creditors.

Although the Statute of Elizabeth was recognized in many American jurisdictions as part of the common law inherited from England, most states have enacted their own statutory provisions. Many states adopted the Uniform Fraudulent Conveyance Act (UFCA), adopted the Uniform Fraudulent Transfer Act (UFTA), or based their fraudulent conveyance statutes, at least in part, on one of the uniform laws. The UFCA was officially withdrawn in 1984 by the National Conference of Commissioners on Uniform State Laws in favor of the UFTA. Like the Statute of Elizabeth, both model statutes condemn transfers that are *actually* fraudulent because the debtor had an actual, subjective intent to hinder, defraud or delay creditors. See UFCA § 7, UFTA § 4(a)(1). In addition, the uniform statutes deem *constructively* fraudulent certain transfers that prejudice creditors because of circumstances existing at the time of the transfer, regardless of the debtor's intent.

The Bankruptcy Code contains its own fraudulent conveyance provision, § 548, after which the UFTA was patterned. Section 548 authorizes the trustee (*not* a creditor) to avoid any transfer of the debtor's property that was fraudulently made or any obligation of the debtor that was fraudulently incurred. The two branches of fraudulent conveyances law are found in subsections (a)(1)(A) and (a)(1)(B). For a transfer to be deemed actually "fraudulent," § 548(a)(1)(A) requires the trustee to show that (1) an interest in the debtor's property was transferred, (2) the transfer was made with actual intent to hinder, delay or defraud a creditor, and (3) the transfer occurred within one year before the bankruptcy petition was filed. Obviously, a debtor will rarely admit fraudulent intent, so meeting the requirements of subsection (a)(1)(A) is no simple task.

The trustee may avoid a transfer as constructively fraudulent under § 548(a)(1)(B) if the trustee can show that (1) an interest in the debtor's property was transferred, (2) the transfer occurred within one year before the bankruptcy petition was filed, (3) the debtor received less than reasonably equivalent value in exchange for the transfer, and (4) the debtor was insolvent at the time of the transfer or became insolvent as a result of it. Because proving the elements of subsection (a)(1)(B) is easier than proving those of (a)(1)(A), (a)(1)(B) is more often asserted. The trustee usually invokes subsection (a)(1)(A) only if insolvency, as required by subsection (a)(1)(B), cannot be proved.

The Bankruptcy Code also enables the trustee to use *state* fraudulent conveyances law. This alternative, found in § 544(b), allows the trustee to avoid any transfer that an unsecured creditor of the debtor could avoid under applicable nonbankruptcy law. This route is particularly useful when the targeted transfer occurred more than a year before the bankruptcy petition was filed, because state statutes of limitation tend to be longer than one year. In order for the trustee to use § 544(b), however, an unsecured creditor with power to avoid the transfer *actually must exist*. The trustee, in essence, is subrogated to the actual creditor's nonbankruptcy avoiding power.

Section 544(b) follows the rule in *Moore v. Bay*, 284 U.S. 4, 52 S.Ct. 3, 76 L.Ed. 133 (1931), that a transfer is entirely avoidable by a trustee regardless of the amount of the creditor's claim relied upon by the trustee. The effect of this rule is illustrated by the following hypothetical: Debtor made a $500 gift to Friend when Debtor was insolvent. Trustee cannot avoid it under § 548 because the gift was made more than a year before Debtor filed bankruptcy. Creditor has a $25 unsecured claim against Debtor that would allow Creditor to avoid the gift, under state law, to the extent necessary to repay Creditor—$25. Trustee is subrogated to Creditor's avoiding power under § 544(b) and, under the rule in *Moore v. Bay*, may avoid the entire $500 transfer. Trustee is not limited to the recovery of $25; it is irrelevant that Creditor's claim, asserted by Trustee, is considerably smaller than the amount of the transfer. In addition, Creditor shares equally with the other unsecured creditors in bankruptcy, despite the fact that Creditor's state law avoiding power was used by Trustee to avoid the transfer in the first place.

2. CONSTRUCTIVELY FRAUDULENT DISPOSITIONS

Problems

Assume the following transactions take place within a year of the date the debtor files a bankruptcy petition. Determine whether the transactions are constructively fraudulent and avoidable by the trustee under § 548(a)(1)(B):

1. Aunt Nellie transferred her home, worth approximately $150,000, to her nephew, Joe, in exchange for Joe's promise to care for Aunt Nellie for the rest of her life. At the time Aunt Nellie transferred her home, she owed Mercy Hospital $5,000 and had credit card debts totaling $45,000. Aunt Nellie's home was her only significant asset.

2. Steve owed his grocer $1,000, not including interest, as a result of the grocer's allowing Steve to charge his groceries to his account while Steve was between jobs. Steve's debts increased steadily while he was without an income, and he failed to pay many of his bills. After Steve had been out of work for many months, he gave the grocer his stereo system, worth about $1,100, in exchange for cancellation of his debt.

3. Tom, who was entitled to a tax refund by reason of overpayment of his 2000 taxes, opted to have the overpayment applied to his 2001 estimated tax. Tom figured that this would provide him a greater benefit than accepting the refund, since the amount of the refund would not be enough to pay most of the debts he owed to various creditors.

4. Corporation decided to pay its president a large bonus at the end of its fiscal year. Corporation's board of directors felt that the president deserved the bonus for his hard work, despite the fact that Corporation was no longer able to pay its suppliers and had not paid its shareholders a dividend in five years.

5. Father was very proud of his daughter for graduating from medical school and so, as a graduation gift, he paid off her $50,000 loan balance. Father also thought of the payment as a good investment, as he was sure that his daughter would be willing to return the favor when she started making a good salary. Unfortunately, by paying off the medical school debt, Father became unable to pay his own bills.

6. Debtors took a trip to Las Vegas, hoping to win enough to pay their mounting bills. Unfortunately, they lost the last money they had—several thousand dollars—gambling at Casino's black jack tables. See *Allard v. Flamingo Hilton (In re Chomakos)*, 69 F.3d 769 (6th Cir.1995), *cert. denied*, 517 U.S. 1168, 116 S.Ct. 1568, 134 L.Ed.2d 667 (1996).

7. Debtor, who had a gross income of $44,000, made a first-time contribution of $10,000 to his college. The gift rendered Debtor unable to meet his obligations to his creditors. See *Murray v. Louisiana State University Foundation (In re Zohdi)*, 234 B.R. 371 (Bankr. M.D.La.1999).

The following case examines the operation of fraudulent conveyances law in the context of real property foreclosures. In that context, a sale will not be set aside on the grounds of low price unless the price is so low as to "shock the conscience."

BFP v. RESOLUTION TRUST CORP.

United States Supreme Court, 1994.
511 U.S. 531, 114 S.Ct. 1757, 128 L.Ed.2d 556.

JUSTICE SCALIA delivered the opinion of the Court.

This case presents the question whether the consideration received from a noncollusive, real estate mortgage foreclosure sale conducted in conformance with applicable state law conclusively satisfies the Bankruptcy Code's requirement that transfers of property by insolvent debtors within one year prior to the filing of a bankruptcy petition be in exchange for "a reasonably equivalent value." [§ 548(a)(1)(B)(i)].

I

Petitioner BFP is a partnership, formed by Wayne and Marlene Pedersen and Russell Barton in 1987, for the purpose of buying a home in Newport Beach, California, from Sheldon and Ann Foreman. Petitioner took title subject to a first deed of trust in favor of Imperial Savings Association (Imperial)[1] to secure payment of a loan of $356,250 made to the Pedersens in connection with petitioner's acquisition of the home. Petitioner granted a second deed of trust to the Foremans as security for a $200,000 promissory note. Subsequently, Imperial, whose loan was not being serviced, entered a notice of default under the first deed of trust and scheduled a properly noticed foreclosure sale. The foreclosure proceedings were temporarily delayed by the filing of an involuntary bankruptcy petition on behalf of petitioner. After the dismissal of that petition in June 1989, Imperial's foreclosure proceeding was completed at a foreclosure sale on July 12, 1989. The home was purchased by respondent Paul Osborne for $433,000.

In October 1989, petitioner filed for bankruptcy under Chapter 11 of the Bankruptcy Code. Acting as a debtor in possession, petitioner

---

[1] Respondent Resolution Trust Corporation (RTC) acts in this case as receiver of Imperial Federal Savings Association (Imperial Federal) * * *. For convenience we refer to all respondents other than RTC and Imperial as the private respondents.

filed a complaint in bankruptcy court seeking to set aside the conveyance of the home to respondent Osborne on the grounds that the foreclosure sale constituted a fraudulent transfer under § 548 of the Code. Petitioner alleged that the home was actually worth over $725,000 at the time of the sale to Osborne. Acting on separate motions, the bankruptcy court dismissed the complaint as to the private respondents and granted summary judgment in favor of Imperial. The bankruptcy court found, *inter alia*, that the foreclosure sale had been conducted in compliance with California law and was neither collusive nor fraudulent. In an unpublished opinion, the District Court affirmed the bankruptcy court's granting of the private respondents' motion to dismiss. A divided bankruptcy appellate panel affirmed the bankruptcy court's entry of summary judgment for Imperial. Applying the analysis set forth in *In re Madrid*, 21 B.R. 424 (BAP 9th Cir.1982), affirmed on other grounds, 725 F.2d 1197 (9th Cir.), cert. denied, 469 U.S. 833 (1984), the panel majority held that a "non-collusive and regularly conducted nonjudicial foreclosure sale * * * cannot be challenged as a fraudulent conveyance because the consideration received in such a sale establishes 'reasonably equivalent value' as a matter of law."

Petitioner sought review of both decisions in the Court of Appeals for the Ninth Circuit, which consolidated the appeals. The Court of Appeals affirmed. BFP filed a petition for certiorari, which we granted.

II

* * *

Section 548 applies to any "transfer," which includes "foreclosure of the debtor's equity of redemption." § 101(54). Of the three critical terms "reasonably equivalent value," only the last is defined: "value" means, for purposes of § 548, "property, or satisfaction or securing of a * * * debt of the debtor," § 548(d)(2)(A). The question presented here, therefore, is whether the amount of debt (to the first and second lien holders) satisfied at the foreclosure sale (viz., a total of $433,000) is "reasonably equivalent" to the worth of the real estate conveyed. The Courts of Appeals have divided on the meaning of those undefined terms. In *Durrett v. Washington Nat. Ins. Co.*, 621 F.2d 201 (1980), the Fifth Circuit, interpreting a provision of the old Bankruptcy Act analogous to [§ 548(a)(1)(B)], held that a foreclosure sale that yielded 57% of the property's fair market value could be set aside, and indicated in dicta that any such sale for less than 70% of fair market value should be invalidated. This "*Durrett* rule" has continued to be applied by some courts under § 548 of the new Bankruptcy Code. In *In re Bundles*, 856 F.2d 815, 820 (1988), the Seventh Circuit rejected the *Durrett* rule in favor of a case-by-case, "all facts and circumstances" approach to the question of reasonably equivalent value, with a *rebuttable* presumption that the foreclosure sale price is sufficient to withstand attack under [§ 548(a)(1)(B)]. In this case the Ninth Circuit * * * adopted the position first put forward in *In re Madrid* that the consideration received at a noncollusive, regularly conducted real estate foreclosure sale constitutes a reasonably equivalent value under [§ 548-(a)(1)(B)(i)]. The Court of Appeals acknowledged that it "necessarily part[ed] from the positions taken by the Fifth Circuit in *Durrett* * * * and the Seventh Circuit in *Bundles*."

In contrast to the approach adopted by the Ninth Circuit in the present case, both *Durrett* and *Bundles* refer to fair market value as the benchmark against which determination of reasonably equivalent value is to be measured. In the context of an otherwise lawful mortgage foreclosure sale of real estate,[3] such reference is in our opinion not consistent with the text of the Bankruptcy Code. The term "fair market value," though it is a well-established concept, does not appear in § 548. In contrast, § 522, dealing with a debtor's exemptions, specifically provides that, for purposes of that section, " 'value' means fair market value as of the date of the filing of the petition." § 522(a)(2). "Fair market value" also appears in the Code provision that defines the extent to which indebtedness with respect to an equity security is not forgiven for the purpose of determining whether the debtor's estate has realized taxable income. § 346(j)(7)(B). Section 548, on the other hand, seemingly goes out of its way to avoid that standard term. It might readily have said "received less than fair market value in exchange for such transfer or obligation," or perhaps "less than a reasonable equivalent of fair market value." Instead, it used the (as far as we are aware) entirely novel phrase "reasonably equivalent value." "[I]t is generally presumed that Congress acts intentionally and purposely when it includes particular language in one section of a statute but omits it in another," *Chicago v. Environmental Defense Fund*, 114 S.Ct. 1588, 1593 (1994) (internal quotation marks omitted), and that presumption is even stronger when the omission entails the replacement of standard legal terminology with a neologism. One must suspect the language means that fair market value cannot—or at least cannot *always*—be the benchmark.

---

3 We emphasize that our opinion today covers only mortgage foreclosures of real estate. The considerations bearing upon other foreclosures and forced sales (to satisfy tax liens, for example) may be different.

That suspicion becomes a certitude when one considers that market value, as it is commonly understood, has no applicability in the forced-sale context; indeed, it is the very *antithesis* of forced-sale value. "The market value of * * * a piece of property is the price which it might be expected to bring if offered for sale in a fair market; not the price which might be obtained on a sale at public auction or a sale forced by the necessities of the owner, but such a price as would be fixed by negotiation and mutual agreement, after ample time to find a purchaser, as between a vendor who is willing (but not compelled) to sell and a purchaser who desires to buy but is not compelled to take the particular * * * piece of property." Black's Law Dictionary 971 (6th ed. 1990). In short, "fair market value" presumes market conditions that, by definition, simply do not obtain in the context of a forced sale.

Neither petitioner, petitioner's *amici*, nor any federal court adopting the *Durrett* or the *Bundles* analysis has come to grips with this glaring discrepancy between the factors relevant to an appraisal of a property's market value, on the one hand, and the strictures of the foreclosure process on the other. Market value cannot be the criterion of equivalence in the foreclosure-sale context. The language of [§ 548-(a)(1)(B)(i)] ("received less than a reasonably equivalent value in exchange") requires judicial inquiry into whether the foreclosed property was sold for a price that approximated its worth at the time of sale. An appraiser's reconstruction of "fair market value" could show what similar property would be worth if it did not have to be sold within the time and manner strictures of state-prescribed foreclosure. But property that *must* be sold within those strictures is simply *worth less*. No one would pay as much to own such property as he would pay to own real estate that could be sold at leisure and pursuant to normal marketing techniques. And it is no more realistic to ignore that characteristic of the property (the fact that state foreclosure law permits the mortgagee to sell it at forced sale) than it is to ignore other price-affecting characteristics (such as the fact that state zoning law permits the owner of the neighboring lot to open a gas station). Absent a clear statutory requirement to the contrary, we must assume the validity of this state-law regulatory background and take due account of its effect. * * *

There is another artificially constructed criterion we might look to instead of "fair market price." One might judge there to be such a thing as a "reasonable" or "fair" forced-sale price. Such a conviction must lie behind the *Bundles* inquiry into whether the state foreclosure proceedings "were calculated * * * to return to the debtor-mortgagor his equity in the property." And perhaps that is what the courts that follow the *Durrett* rule have in mind when they select 70% of fair market value as the outer limit of "reasonably equivalent value" for forecloseable property (we have no idea where else such an arbitrary percentage could have come from). The problem is that such judgments represent policy determinations which the Bankruptcy Code gives us no apparent authority to make. How closely the price received in a forced sale is likely to approximate fair market value depends upon the terms of the forced sale—how quickly it may be made, what sort of public notice must be given, etc. But the terms for foreclosure sale are not *standard*. They vary considerably from State to State, depending upon, among other things, how the particular State values the divergent interests of debtor and creditor. To specify a federal "reasonable" foreclosure-sale price is to extend federal bankruptcy law well beyond the traditional field of fraudulent transfers, into realms of policy where it has not ventured before. * * *

* * *

Fraudulent transfer law and foreclosure law enjoyed over 400 years of peaceful coexistence in Anglo–American jurisprudence until the Fifth Circuit's unprecedented 1980 decision in *Durrett*. To our knowledge no prior decision had ever applied the "grossly inadequate price" badge of fraud under fraudulent transfer law to set aside a foreclosure sale. To say that the "reasonably equivalent value" language in the fraudulent transfer provision of the Bankruptcy Code requires a foreclosure sale to yield a certain minimum price beyond what state foreclosure law requires, is to say, in essence, that the Code has adopted *Durrett* or *Bundles*. Surely Congress has the power pursuant to its constitutional grant of authority over bankruptcy to disrupt the ancient harmony that foreclosure law and fraudulent-conveyance law, those two pillars of debtor-creditor jurisprudence, have heretofore enjoyed. But absent clearer textual guidance than the phrase "reasonably equivalent value"—a phrase entirely compatible with pre-existing practice—we will not presume such a radical departure.[7]

---

[7] We are unpersuaded by petitioner's argument that the 1984 amendments to the Bankruptcy Code codified the *Durrett* Rule. Those amendments expanded the definition of "transfer" to include "foreclosure of the debtor's equity of redemption," § 101(54), and added the words "voluntarily or involuntarily" as modifiers of the term "transfer" in § 548(a). The first of these provisions establishes that foreclosure sales fall within the general definition of "transfers" that may be avoided under several statutory provisions, including (but not limited to) § 548. The second of them establishes that a transfer may be avoided as fraudulent even if it was against the debtor's will. Neither of these consequences has any bearing upon the meaning of "reasonably equivalent value" in the context of a foreclosure sale.

Nor does our reading render these amendments "superfluous," as the dissent

* * *

For the reasons described, we decline to read the phrase "reasonably equivalent value" in [§ 548(a)(1)(B)] to mean, in its application to mortgage foreclosure sales, either "fair market value" or "fair foreclosure price" (whether calculated as a percentage of fair market value or otherwise). We deem, as the law has always deemed, that a fair and proper price, or a "reasonably equivalent value," for foreclosed property, is the price in fact received at the foreclosure sale, so long as all the requirements of the State's foreclosure law have been complied with.

This conclusion does not render [§ 548(a)(1)(B)] superfluous, since the "reasonably equivalent value" criterion will continue to have independent meaning (ordinarily a meaning similar to fair market value) outside the foreclosure context. Indeed, [§ 548(a)(1)(B)] will even continue to be an exclusive means of invalidating some foreclosure sales. Although *collusive* foreclosure sales are likely subject to attack under § 548(a)(1)[(A)], which authorizes the trustee to avoid transfers "made * * * with actual intent to hinder, delay, or defraud" creditors, that provision may not reach foreclosure sales that, while not intentionally fraudulent, nevertheless fail to comply with all governing state laws. Any irregularity in the conduct of the sale that would permit judicial invalidation of the sale under applicable state law deprives the sale price of its conclusive force under [§ 548(a)(1)(B)(i)], and the transfer may be avoided if the price received was not reasonably equivalent to the property's actual value at the time of the sale (which we think would be the price that would have been received if the foreclosure sale had proceeded according to law).

III

A few words may be added in general response to the dissent. We have no quarrel with the dissent's assertion that where the "meaning of the Bankruptcy Code's text is itself clear," its operation is unimpeded by contrary state law or prior practice. Nor do we contend that Congress must override historical state practice "expressly or not at all." The Bankruptcy Code can of course override by implication when the implication is unambiguous. But where the intent to override is doubt-

---

contends. Prior to 1984, it was at least open to question whether § 548 could be used to invalidate even a *collusive* foreclosure sale. It is no superfluity for Congress to clarify what had been at best unclear, which is what it did here by making the provision apply to involuntary as well as voluntary transfers and by including foreclosures within the definition of "transfer."

ful, our federal system demands deference to long established traditions of state regulation.

The dissent's insistence that here no doubt exists—that our reading of the statute is "in derogation of the *straightforward language* used by Congress" (emphasis added)—does not withstand scrutiny. The problem is not that we disagree with the dissent's proffered "plain meaning" of [§ 548(a)(1)(B)(i)] ("the bankruptcy court must compare the price received by the insolvent debtor and the worth of the item when sold and set aside the transfer if the former was substantially ('[un]reasonabl[y]') 'less than' the latter"—which indeed echoes our own framing of the question presented ("whether the amount of debt * * * satisfied at the foreclosure sale * * * is 'reasonably equivalent' to the worth of the real estate conveyed"). There is no doubt that this provision directs an inquiry into the relationship of the value received by the debtor to the worth of the property transferred. The problem, however, as any "ordinary speaker of English would have no difficulty grasping," is that this highly generalized reformulation of the "plain meaning" of "reasonably equivalent value" continues to leave unanswered the one question central to this case, wherein the ambiguity lies: *What is a foreclosed property worth?* Obviously, until that is determined, we cannot know whether the value received in exchange for foreclosed property is "reasonably equivalent." We have considered three (not, as the dissent insists, only two) possible answers to this question—fair market value, reasonable forced-sale price, and the foreclosure sale price itself—and have settled on the last. We would have expected the dissent to opt for one of the other two, or perhaps even to concoct a fourth; but one searches JUSTICE SOUTER'S opinion in vain for any alternative response to the question of the transferred property's worth. Instead, the dissent simply reiterates the "single meaning" of "reasonably equivalent value" (with which we entirely agree): "a court should discern the 'value' of the property transferred and determine whether the price paid was, under the circumstances, 'less than reasonabl[e].'" Well and good. But what *is* the "value"? The dissent has no response, evidently thinking that, in order to establish that the law is clear, it suffices to show that "the eminent sense of the natural reading" provides an unanswered question.

* * *

We take issue with the dissent's characterization of our interpretation as carving out an "exception" for foreclosure sales or as giving "two different and inconsistent meanings" to "reasonably equivalent value." As we have emphasized, the inquiry under [§ 548-

(a)(1)(B)(i)]—whether the debtor has received value that is substantially comparable to the worth of the transferred property—is the same for all transfers. But as we have also explained, the fact that a piece of property is legally subject to forced sale, like any other fact bearing upon the property's use or alienability, necessarily affects its worth. *Unlike* most other legal restrictions, however, foreclosure has the effect of completely redefining the market in which the property is offered for sale; normal free-market rules of exchange are replaced by the far more restrictive rules governing forced sales. Given this altered reality, and the concomitant inutility of the normal tool for determining what property is worth (fair market value), the only legitimate evidence of the property's value at the time it is sold is the foreclosure sale price itself.

For the foregoing reasons, the judgment of the Court of Appeals for the Ninth Circuit is

Affirmed.

JUSTICE SOUTER, with whom JUSTICE BLACKMUN, JUSTICE STEVENS, and JUSTICE GINSBURG join, dissenting.

The Court today holds that by the terms of the Bankruptcy Code Congress intended a peppercorn paid at a noncollusive and procedurally regular foreclosure sale to be treated as the "reasonabl[e] equivalent" of the value of a California beachfront estate. Because the Court's reasoning fails both to overcome the implausibility of that proposition and to justify engrafting a foreclosure-sale exception onto [§ 548(a)(1)(B)(i)], in derogation of the straightforward language used by Congress, I respectfully dissent.

I

A

The majority presents our task of giving meaning to [§ 548-(a)(1)(B)(i)] in this case as essentially entailing a choice between two provisions that Congress might have enacted, but did not. One would allow a bankruptcy trustee to avoid a recent foreclosure-sale transfer from an insolvent debtor whenever anything less than fair market value was obtained, while the second would limit the avoidance power to cases where the foreclosure sale was collusive or had failed to comply with state-prescribed procedures. The Court then argues that, given the unexceptionable proposition that forced sales rarely yield as high a price as sales held under ideal, "market" conditions, Congress's "omission" from [§ 548(a)(1)(B)(i)] of the phrase "fair market value" means that the latter, narrowly procedural reading of [§ 548(a)(1)(B)(i)] is the preferable one.

If those in fact were the interpretive alternatives, the majority's choice might be a defensible one. The first, equating "reasonably equivalent value" at a foreclosure sale with "fair market value" has little to recommend it. Forced-sale prices may not be (as the majority calls them) the "very antithesis" of market value, but they fail to bring in what voluntary sales realize, and rejecting such a reading of the statute is as easy as statutory interpretation is likely to get. On the majority's view, laying waste to this straw man necessitates accepting as adequate value whatever results from noncollusive adherence to state foreclosure requirements. Because properties are "simply worth less" on foreclosure sale, the Court posits, they must have been "worth" whatever price was paid. That, however, is neither a plausible interpretation of the statute, nor its only remaining alternative reading.

The question before the Court is whether the price received at a foreclosure sale after compliance with state procedural rules in a non-collusive sale must be treated conclusively as the "reasonably equivalent value" of the mortgaged property and in answering that question, the words and meaning of § 548(a)(1)(B)(i) are plain. A trustee is authorized to avoid certain recent pre-bankruptcy transfers, including those on foreclosure sales, that a bankruptcy court determines were not made in exchange for "a reasonably equivalent value." Although this formulation makes no pretense to mathematical precision, an ordinary speaker of English would have no difficulty grasping its basic thrust: the bankruptcy court must compare the price received by the insolvent debtor and the worth of the item when sold and set aside the transfer if the former was substantially ("[un]reasonabl[y]") "less than" the latter.[3] Nor would any ordinary English speaker, concerned to determine whether a foreclosure sale was collusive or procedurally irregular (an enquiry going exclusively to the process by which a transaction was consummated), direct an adjudicator, as the Court now holds Congress did, to ascertain whether the sale had realized "less than a reasonably equivalent value" (an enquiry described in quintessentially substantive terms).[4]

---

[3] Indeed, it is striking that this is what the Court says the statute (probably) does mean, with respect to almost every transfer other than a sale of property upon foreclosure.

[4] The Court protests that its formulation deviates only subtly from the reading

Closer familiarity with the text, structure, and history of the disputed provision (and relevant amendments), confirms the soundness of the plain reading. Before 1984, the question whether foreclosure sales fell within bankruptcy courts' power to set aside transfers for "too little in return" was, potentially, a difficult one. Then, it might plausibly have been contended that § 548 was most concerned with "fraudulent" conduct by debtors on the brink of bankruptcy, misbehavior unlikely to be afoot when an insolvent debtor's property is sold, against his wishes, at foreclosure. Indeed it could further have been argued, again consonantly with the text of the earlier version of the Bankruptcy Code, that Congress had not understood foreclosure to involve a "transfer" within the ambit of § 548, on the theory that the "transfer" from mortgagor to mortgagee occurs, once and for all, when the security interest is first created. See generally *In re Madrid*, 725 F.2d 1197 (9th Cir.), cert. denied, 469 U.S. 833 (1984).

In 1984, however, Congress pulled the rug out from under these previously serious arguments, by amending the Code in two relevant respects. One amendment provided expressly that "involuntar[y]" transfers are no less within the trustee's § 548 avoidance powers than "voluntar[y]" ones, and another provided that the "foreclosure of the debtor's equity of redemption" itself is a "transfer" for purposes of bankruptcy law. See § 101(54).[6] Thus, whether or not one believes (as the majority seemingly does not) that foreclosure sales rightfully belong within the historic domain of "fraudulent conveyance" law, that is exactly where Congress has now put them, and our duty is to give effect to these new amendments, along with every other clause of the Bankruptcy Code. The Court's attempt to escape the plain effect of [§ 548(a)(1)(B)(i)] opens it to some equally plain objections.

---

advanced here and purports not to disagree that the statute compels an enquiry "into the relationship of the value received and the worth of the property transferred." Reassuring as such carefully chosen words may sound, they can not obscure the fact that the "comparison" the majority envisions is an empty ritual.

6 [A]n earlier version of the Senate Bill contained a provision that would have added to § 548 the conclusive presumption the Court implies here. See S. 445, 98th Cong., 1st Sess. § 360 (1983) ("A secured party or third party purchaser who obtains title to an interest of the debtor in property pursuant to a good faith prepetition foreclosure, power of sale, or other proceeding or provision of nonbankruptcy law permitting or providing for the realization of security upon default of the borrower under a mortgage, deed of trust, or other security agreement takes for reasonably equivalent value within the meaning of this section"). The provision was deleted from the legislation enacted by Congress.

The first and most obvious of these objections is the very enigma of the Court's reading. If a property's "value" is conclusively presumed to be whatever it sold for, the "less than reasonabl[e] equivalen[ce]" question will never be worth asking, and the bankruptcy avoidance power will apparently be a dead letter in reviewing real estate foreclosures. The Court answers that the section is not totally moribund: it still furnishes a way to attack collusive or procedurally deficient real property foreclosures, and it enjoys a vital role in authorizing challenges to other transfers than those occurring on real estate foreclosure. The first answer, however, just runs up against a new objection. If indeed the statute fails to reach noncollusive, procedurally correct real estate foreclosures, then the recent amendments discussed above were probably superfluous. There is a persuasive case that collusive or seriously irregular real estate sales were already subject to avoidance in bankruptcy, and neither the Court nor the respondents and their amici identify any specific case in which a court pronounced itself powerless to avoid a collusive foreclosure sale. It would seem peculiar, then, that for no sound reason, Congress would have tinkered with these closely-watched sections of the Bankruptcy Code, for the sole purpose of endowing bankruptcy courts with authority that had not been found wanting in the first place.

The Court's second answer to the objection that it renders the statute a dead letter is to remind us that the statute applies to all sorts of transfers, not just to real estate foreclosures, and as to all the others, the provision enjoys great vitality, calling for true comparison between value received for the property and its "reasonably equivalent value." (Indeed, the Court has no trouble acknowledging that something "similar to" fair market value may supply the benchmark of reasonable equivalence when such a sale is not initiated by a mortgagee.) This answer, however, is less tenable than the first. A common rule of construction calls for a single definition of a common term occurring in several places within a statute, and the case for different definitions within a single text is difficult to make. But to give a single term two different and inconsistent meanings (one procedural, one substantive) for a single occurrence is an offense so unlikely that no common prohibition has ever been thought necessary to guard against it. Unless whimsy is attributed to Congress, the term in question cannot be exclusively procedural in one class of cases and entirely substantive in all others. To be sure, there are real differences between sales on mortgage foreclosures and other transfers, as Congress no doubt understood, but these differences may be addressed simply and consistently with the statute's plain meaning.

The "neologism" "reasonably equivalent value" (read in light of the amendments confirming that foreclosures are to be judged under the same standard as are other transfers) has a single meaning in the one provision in which it figures: a court should discern the "value" of the property transferred and determine whether the price paid was, under the circumstances, "less than reasonabl[e]." There is thus no reason to rebuke the courts of appeals for having failed to "come to grips" with the implications of the fact that foreclosure sales cannot be expected to yield fair market value. The statute has done so for them. As courts considering nonforeclosure transfers often acknowledge, the qualification "reasonably equivalent" itself embodies both an awareness that the assets of insolvent debtors are commonly transferred under conditions that will yield less than their optimal value and a judgment that avoidance in bankruptcy (unsettling as it does the expectations of parties who may have dealt with the debtor in good faith) should only occur when it is clear that the bankruptcy estate will be substantially augmented.

* * *

C

What plain meaning requires and courts can provide, indeed, the policies underlying a national bankruptcy law fully support. This case is a far cry from the rare one where the effect of implementing the ordinary meaning of the statutory text would be "patent absurdity" or "demonstrably at odds with the intentions of its drafters," *United States v. Ron Pair Enterprises, Inc.*, 489 U.S. 235, 244 (1989) (internal quotation marks omitted).[15] Permitting avoidance of procedurally regular foreclosure sales for low prices (and thereby returning a valuable asset to the bankruptcy estate) is plainly consistent with those policies of obtaining a maximum and equitable distribution for creditors and ensuring a "fresh start" for individual debtors, which the Court has often said are at the core of federal bankruptcy law. They are not, of course, any less the policies of federal bankruptcy law simply because state courts will not, for a mortgagor's benefit, set aside a foreclosure sale for "price inadequacy" alone. The unwillingness of the state courts to upset a foreclosure sale for that reason does not address the question

[15] Tellingly, while the Court's opinion celebrates fraudulent conveyance law and state foreclosure law as the "twin pillars" of creditor-debtor regulation, it evinces no special appreciation of the fact that this case arises under the Bankruptcy Code, which, in maintaining the national system of credit and commerce, embodies policies distinct from those of state debtor-creditor law, and which accordingly endows trustees with avoidance power beyond what state law provides.

of what "reasonably equivalent value" means in bankruptcy law, any more than the refusal of those same courts to set aside a contract for "mere inadequacy of consideration" would define the scope of the trustee's power to reject executory contracts. On the contrary, a central premise of the bankruptcy avoidance powers is that what state law plainly allows as acceptable or "fair," as between a debtor and a particular creditor, may be set aside because of its impact on other creditors or on the debtor's chances for a fresh start.

When the prospect of such avoidance is absent, indeed, the economic interests of a foreclosing mortgagee often stand in stark opposition to those of the debtor himself and of his other creditors. At a typical foreclosure sale, a mortgagee has no incentive to bid any more than the amount of the indebtedness, since any "surplus" would be turned over to the debtor (or junior lienholder), and, in some states, it can even be advantageous for the creditor to bid less and seek a deficiency judgment. And where a property is obviously worth more than the amount of the indebtedness, the lending mortgagee's interests are served best if the foreclosure sale is poorly attended; then, the lender is more likely to take the property by bidding the amount of indebtedness, retaining for itself any profits from resale. While state foreclosure procedures may somewhat mitigate the potential for this sort of opportunism (by requiring for publication of notice, for example), it surely is plausible that Congress, in drafting the Bankruptcy Code, would find it intolerable that a debtor's assets be wasted and the bankruptcy estate diminished, solely to speed a mortgagee's recovery.

* * *

III

Like the Court, I understand this case to involve a choice between two possible statutory provisions: one authorizing the trustee to avoid "involuntar[y] * * * transfers [including foreclosure sales] * * * [for] less than a reasonably equivalent value," see § 548(a), and another precluding such avoidance when "[a] secured party or third party purchaser * * * obtains title to an interest of the debtor in property pursuant to a good faith prepetition foreclosure * * * proceeding * * * permitting * * * the realization of security upon default of the borrower," see S. 445, 98th Cong., 1st Sess. § 360 (1983). But that choice is not ours to make, for Congress made it in 1984, by enacting the former alternative into law and not the latter. Without some indication that doing so would frustrate Congress's clear intention or yield patent absurdity, our obligation is to apply the statute as Congress wrote it. Doing that in this case would produce no frustration or absurdity, but quite the opposite.

Notes and Questions

1. To what must the value given by the creditor be "reasonably equivalent"? From whose perspective—the creditor who gives the value, the debtor, or the debtor's other creditors?

2. Would Justice Scalia be satisfied that the price received at a state foreclosure sale is reasonably equivalent value if the state foreclosure law actually encouraged low sales prices? That is, does the federal bankruptcy law have any interest in reasonably equivalent value beyond the foreclosing creditor's compliance with state foreclosure procedures? If sales procedures are the only concern of the reasonably equivalent value requirement, isn't the term "reasonably equivalent value" a curious formulation? Keep in mind that Article 9 of the UCC requires only that a foreclosure sale be "commercially reasonable." Does Justice Scalia's opinion effectively equate "reasonably equivalent value" with "commercially reasonable" disposition? See *Case v. TBAC-Prince Gardner, Inc. (In re Prince Gardner, Inc.)*, 220 B.R. 63 (Bankr. E.D.Mo.1998).

3. Justice Scalia concludes that "[t]o specify a federal 'reasonable' foreclosure-sale price is to extend federal bankruptcy law well beyond the traditional field of fraudulent transfers, into realms of policy where it has not ventured before." Would the result in the case have been different, then, if the bankruptcy court had avoided the foreclosure sale on the basis of state fraudulent conveyance law? A trustee in bankruptcy, under § 544(b) of the Code, may use state fraudulent conveyance law to avoid a fraudulent transfer, and this is not limited to § 548 avoidance.

4. The Court asserted, in an omitted footnote, that the dissent "ignores the fact that it is not state authority over debtor-creditor law *in general* that is at stake in this case, but the essential sovereign interest in the security and stability of title to land." Why is the state's interest in real property title more "essential" than state interests vindicated by debtor-creditor law? Is the tension the type of zero-sum game Justice Scalia describes? Could you argue that the *Durrett* doctrine ultimately served the state's "sovereign interest in the security and stability of title to land"?

3. CORPORATE CONTEXTS

a. Leveraged Buyouts

Although the following case does not involve a debtor in bankruptcy, it is one of the leading opinions dealing with leveraged buyouts.

The statute at issue, the Uniform Fraudulent Conveyance Act (UFCA), has provisions that parallel the Bankruptcy Code's two branches of fraud. Because the bankruptcy trustee can use state law through § 544(b), this opinion is of great significance in bankruptcy despite its nonbankruptcy setting. It has, in fact, become an important precedent case in bankruptcy.

UNITED STATES v. TABOR COURT REALTY CORP.

United States Court of Appeals, Third Circuit, 1986.
803 F.2d 1288, *cert. denied sub nom.* McClellan Realty Co. v. United States, 483 U.S. 1005, 107 S.Ct. 3229, 97 L.Ed.2d 735 (1987).

ALDISERT, Chief Judge.

We have consolidated appeals from litigation involving one of America's largest anthracite coal producers that emanate from a district court bench trial that extended over 120 days and recorded close to 20,000 pages of transcript. Ultimately, we have to decide whether the court erred in entering judgment in favor of the United States in reducing to judgment certain federal corporate tax assessments made against the coal producers, in determining the priority of the government liens, and in permitting foreclosure on the liens. To reach these questions, however, we must examine a very intricate leveraged buy-out and decide whether mortgages given in the transaction were fraudulent conveyances within the meaning of the constructive and intentional fraud sections of the Pennsylvania Uniform Fraudulent Conveyances Act (UFCA), 39 Pa. Stat. §§ 354–357, and if so, whether a later assignment of the mortgages was void as against creditors.

The district court made 481 findings of facts and issued three separate published opinions: *United States v. Gleneagles Investment Co.*, 565 F.Supp. 556 (M.D.Pa.1983) (*Gleneagles I*); 571 F.Supp. 935 (1983) (*Gleneagles II*); and 584 F.Supp. 671 (1984) (*Gleneagles III*). We are told that this case represents the first significant application of the UFCA to leveraged buy-out financing.

* * *

We will summarize a very complex factual situation and then discuss these issues seriatim.

I.

These appeals arise from an action by the United States to reduce to judgment delinquent federal income taxes, interest, and penalties assessed and accrued against Raymond Colliery Co., Inc. and its subsidiaries (the Raymond Group) for the fiscal years of June 30, 1966 through June 30, 1973 and to reduce to judgment similarly assessed taxes owed by Great American Coal Co., Inc. and its subsidiaries for the fiscal year ending June 30, 1975.

The government sought to collect these tax claims from surface and coal lands owned by the Raymond Group as well as from lands formerly owned by it but which, as a result of allegedly illegal and fraudulent county tax sales, were later owned by Gleneagles Investment Co., Inc. In addition, the government sought to assert the priority of its liens over liens held by others. The district court held in favor of the government on most of its claims and concluded the litigation by promulgating an order of priority of liens on Raymond Group lands.

[Raymond Colliery was a closely-held corporation that owned real property used for mining. It was also the parent of several subsidiaries engaged in the coal mining business. In the early 1970s, Raymond began experiencing "serious and chronic cash flow problems" that resulted in Raymond's failure to pay both local and federal taxes. Tension caused by financial difficulties prompted the principals of Raymond to seek a buyer for their interests in the corporation. They granted James Durkin, Raymond's president, an option to buy Raymond's stock. Durkin incorporated Great American as a holding company and assigned the option to it. In November 1973, some of the companies in the Raymond Group borrowed $8,530,000 from Institutional Investors Trust (IIT) to finance the acquisition of Raymond stock. The loan was secured by mortgages on assets of Raymond and its wholly owned subsidiaries. Some of the subsidiaries were borrowing companies (Blue Coal, Glen Nan and Olyphant) and others were guarantor companies, but all hypothecated their assets, either to secure the loan made to them or to secure guaranties of loans made to the borrowing companies. Of the loan proceeds, $7 million was paid to the borrowing companies, $1.53 million was placed in escrow for the payment of interest, $.7 million went for closing costs, and $2.2 million was used to pay an obligation to Chemical Bank guaranteed by one of Raymond's shareholders. The borrowing companies transferred $4,085,000 to Great American, which obtained additional funds elsewhere and purchased the Raymond stock for $6.7 million. The shareholders received $6.2 million in cash and a $500,000 promissory note.

This constituted a "leveraged buy-out." As the court summarized it, "[s]hareholders of the Raymond Group sold the corporation to a small group of investors headed by Raymond's president; these investors borrowed substantially all of the purchase price at an extremely high rate of interest secured by mortgages on the assets of the selling company and its subsidiaries and those of additional entities that guaranteed repayment."

The closing left the Raymond Group unable to pay its routine operating expenses and in a deteriorating financial condition. In December 1976, the IIT mortgages were assigned to Pagnotti Enterprises, another large anthracite coal producer. Pagnotti and IIT agreed that Tabor Court Realty and McClellan Realty should be formed as nominee corporations to bid on Raymond properties at upcoming county tax sales. Pagnotti paid Lackawanna County taxes that predated IIT's mortgages and later assigned the mortgages to McClellan Realty.]

II.

The instant action was commenced by the United States on December 12, 1980 to reduce to judgment certain corporate federal tax assessments made against the Raymond Group and Great American. The government sought to assert the priority of its tax liens and to foreclose against the property that Raymond had owned at the time of the assessments as well as against properties currently owned by Raymond. The United States argued that the IIT mortgages executed in November 1973 should be set aside under the Uniform Fraudulent Conveyance Act and further that the purported assignment of these mortgages to Pagnotti should be voided because at the inception Pagnotti had purchased the mortgages with knowledge that they had been fraudulently conveyed.

As heretofore stated, after a bench trial, the district court issued three separate published opinions. In *Gleneagles I*, the court concluded, *inter alia*, that the mortgages given by the Raymond Group to IIT on November 26, 1973 were fraudulent conveyances within the meaning of the constructive and intentional fraud sections of the Pennsylvania Uniform Fraudulent Conveyances Act, 39 Pa. Stat. §§ 354–357. In *Gleneagles II*, the court further held that the mortgages to McClellan Realty were void as against the other Raymond Group creditors. In its third opinion, the court set out the priority of the creditors. The court granted McClellan and Tabor Court an equitable lien ahead of the creditors for the Pennsylvania municipal taxes they paid in Raymond's behalf prior to the 1976 Lackawanna county tax sale of Raymond's properties. However, the court placed McClellan, as assignee of the IIT mortgages, near the bottom of the list of creditors. The trustee in bankruptcy of Blue Coal and Glen Nan argues that McClellan's rights are totally invalidated and that McClellan has no standing whatsoever as a creditor.

The Raymond Group—four coal mining companies that executed the mortgages (Raymond Colliery, Blue Coal, Glen Nan, and Olyphant Associates) as well as interrelated associated companies that had placed guarantee mortgages and subsidiaries of such associated companies—has appealed. As heretofore stated, all these mortgages, subsequently invalidated by the district court, had been granted to IIT on November 26, 1973 and assigned by IIT to appellant McClellan. For the purpose of this appeal, we shall refer to the Raymond Group as "appellants", or "McClellan".

* * *

III.

McClellan initially challenges the district court's application of the Pennsylvania Uniform Fraudulent Conveyances Act (UFCA), 39 Pa. Stat. §§ 351–363, to the leveraged buy-out loan made by IIT to the mortgagors, and to the acquisition of the mortgages from IIT by McClellan. The district court determined that IIT lacked good faith in the transaction because it knew, or should have known, that the money it lent the mortgagors was used, in part, to finance the purchase of stock from the mortgagors' shareholders, and that as a consequence of the loan, IIT and its assignees obtained a secured position in the mortgagors' property to the detriment of creditors. Because this issue involves the interpretation and application of legal precepts, review is plenary.

In applying § 353(a) of the UFCA, the district court stated:

> The initial question * * * is whether the transferee, IIT, transferred its loan proceeds in good faith. * * * IIT knew or strongly suspected that the imposition of the loan obligations secured by the mortgages and guarantee mortgages would probably render insolvent both the Raymond Group and each individual member thereof. In addition, IIT was fully aware that no individual member of the Raymond Group would receive fair consideration within the meaning of the Act in exchange for the

> loan obligations to IIT. Thus, we conclude that IIT does not meet the standard of good faith under § 353(a) of the Act.

Gleneagles I, 565 F.Supp. at 574.

McClellan argues that "the only reasonable and proper application of the good faith criteria as it applies to the lender in structuring a loan is one which looks to the lender's *motives* as opposed to his *knowledge*." McClellan argues that good faith is satisfied when "the lender acted in an arms-length transaction without ulterior motive or collusion with the debtor to the detriment of creditors."

Section 354 of the UFCA is a "constructive fraud" provision. It establishes that a conveyance made by a person "who is or will be thereby rendered insolvent, is fraudulent as to creditors, without regard to his actual intent, if the conveyance is made * * * without a fair consideration." Section 353 defines fair consideration as an exchange of a "fair equivalent * * * in good faith." Because § 354 excludes an examination of intent, it follows that "good faith" must be something other than intent; because § 354 also focuses on insolvency, knowledge of insolvency is a rational interpretation of the statutory language of lack of "good faith." McClellan would have us adopt "without ulterior motive or collusion with the debtor to the detriment of creditors" as the good faith standard. We are uneasy with such a standard because these words come very close to describing intent.

* * *

We have decided that the district court reached the right conclusion here for the right reasons. It determined that IIT did not act in good faith because it was aware, first, that the exchange would render Raymond insolvent, and second, that no member of the Raymond Group would receive fair consideration. We believe that this determination is consistent with the statute and case law.

McClellan and amicus curiae also argue that as a general rule the UFCA should not be applied to leveraged buy-outs. They contend that the UFCA, which was passed in 1924, was never meant to apply to a complicated transaction such as a leveraged buy-out. The Act's broad language, however, extends to any "conveyance" which is defined as "every payment of money * * * and also the creation of any lien or incumbrance." This broad sweep does not justify exclusion of a particular transaction such as a leveraged buy-out simply because it is innovative or complicated. If the UFCA is not to be applied to leveraged buy-outs, it should be for the state legislatures, not the courts, to decide.

In addition, although appellants' and amicus curiae's arguments against general application of the Act to leveraged buy-outs are not without some force, the application of fraudulent conveyance law to certain leveraged buy-outs is not clearly bad public policy.[2] In any event, the circumstances of this case justify application. Even the policy arguments offered against the application of fraudulent conveyance law to leveraged buy-outs assume facts that are not present in this case. For example, in their analysis of fraudulent conveyance law, Professors Baird and Jackson assert that their analysis should be applied to leveraged buy-outs only where aspects of the transaction are not hidden from creditors and the transaction does not possess other suspicious attributes. *See* Baird and Jackson, *Fraudulent Conveyance Law and Its Proper Domain*, 38 Vand. L. Rev. 829, 843 (1985). In fact, Baird and Jackson conclude their article by noting that their analysis is limited to transactions in which "the transferee parted with value when he entered into the transaction and that transaction was entered in the ordinary course." In the instant case, however, the severe economic circumstances in which the Raymond Group found itself, the obligation, without benefit, incurred by the Raymond Group, and the small number of shareholders benefited by the transaction suggest that the transaction was not entered in the ordinary course, that fair consideration was not exchanged, and that the transaction was anything but unsuspicious. The policy arguments set forth in opposition to the application of fraudulent conveyance law to leveraged buy-outs do not justify the exemption of transactions such as this.[3]

---

[2] A major premise of the policy arguments opposing application of fraudulent conveyance law to leveraged buy-outs is that such transactions often benefit creditors and that the application of fraudulent conveyance law to buy-outs will deter them in the future. *See* Baird and Jackson, *Fraudulent Conveyance Law and Its Proper Domain*, 38 Vand. L. Rev. 829, 855 (1985). An equally important premise is that creditors can protect themselves from undesirable leveraged buy-outs by altering the terms of their credit contracts. *Id.* at 835. This second premise ignores, however, cases such as this one in which the major creditors (in this instance the United States and certain Pennsylvania municipalities) are involuntary and do not become creditors by virtue of a contract. The second premise also ignores the possibility that the creditors attacking the leveraged buy-out (such as many of the creditors in this case) became creditors before leveraged buy-outs became a common financing technique and thus may not have anticipated such leveraged transactions so as to have been able to adequately protect themselves by contract. These possibilities suggest that Baird and Jackson's broad proscription against application of fraudulent conveyance law to leveraged buy-outs may not be unambiguously correct.

[3] It should also be noted that another basic premise of the Baird and Jackson analysis

IV.

McClellan next argues that under § 359(2) of the UFCA, it is entitled to a lien superior to all other creditors on Raymond's property. * * *

A.

Section 359 establishes a two-tier system to protect certain purchasers from the effects of the UFCA. Section 359(1) permits a purchaser who has paid "fair consideration without knowledge of the fraud at the time of the purchase" to maintain the conveyance as valid against a creditor. Section 359(2) of the Act specifies that a "purchaser who, without actual fraudulent intent, has given less than a fair consideration for the conveyance or obligation may retain the property or obligation as security for repayment."

In *Gleneagles II*, the district court found that Pagnotti, who purchased the IIT mortgages for $4,047,786 and transferred them to McClellan Realty, was not entitled to protection under § 359(1). The court determined that although Pagnotti had given a "fair equivalent" for the IIT mortgages, it did not do so without knowledge of the fraud at the time of the purchase.

In *Gleneagles III*, the district court concluded that McClellan, Pagnotti's assignee, was not entitled to the partial protection of § 359(2). The court stated that although it had found in *Gleneagles II* that Pagnotti had not acted in good faith in acquiring the IIT mortgages, this was not equivalent to a finding that Pagnotti had given "less than fair consideration." The court, however, also implied that notwithstanding its finding that Pagnotti had not acted with "actual fraudulent intent," it had not "purchased the IIT mortgages in good faith." The court ruled that good faith is at least required to merit protection under § 359(2). The court therefore found that Pagnotti was not entitled to such protection.

---

is that as a general matter fraudulent conveyance law should be applied only to those transactions to which a rational creditor would surely object. Although a rational creditor might under certain circumstances consent to a risky but potentially beneficial leveraged buy-out of a nearly insolvent debtor, no reasonable creditor would consent to the intentionally fraudulent conveyance the district court correctly found this transaction to be. Thus, the application of fraudulent conveyance law to the instant transaction appears consistent even with Baird and Jackson's analysis.

McClellan faults this reasoning with an argument that, at least facially, seems persuasive. It argues that the district court's finding that Pagnotti acted with knowledge of the fraud means that Pagnotti acted without good faith and therefore paid "less than fair consideration" as defined by § 353 of the Act. Therefore, McClellan reasons, absent a finding of "actual fraudulent intent," it is entitled to protection under § 359(2).

Admittedly, § 359(2) is inartfully drafted and a literal reading of the section could conceivably command this result. We believe, however, that the public policy behind the UFCA compels a different interpretation. The Act protects both *purchasers* and *third parties*. We see a distinction here. The Act protects those *purchasers*, who, without actual fraudulent intent and without a lack of good faith, have paid less than a fair equivalent for the property received. Conversely, the Act does not protect purchases [sic] having a fraudulent intent or a lack of good faith. We are not satisfied that the UFCA affords third parties greater protection than purchasers. The purposes of the Act would be nullified if third parties who in bad faith paid less than a fair equivalent could take the property in a better position than an original purchaser who at the outset had engaged in a fraudulent transfer.

* * *

B.

Moreover, we find support in analogizing to the federal bankruptcy laws. Section 548(c) of the Bankruptcy Code—the successor to § 67(d)(6) of the Bankruptcy Act—provides that a transferee or obligee of a fraudulent transfer or obligation who takes for value and in good faith may retain the interest transferred or the obligation incurred. § 548(c). This section of the Bankruptcy Code thus closely tracks § 359(2) of the UFCA. * * *

In two cases similar to the one at bar, courts have denied protection to lenders under § 67(d) of the Bankruptcy Act because, although their conduct was not intentionally fraudulent, the lenders exhibited a lack of good faith. The same principles should apply here to deny protection to Pagnotti where the record supports the district court's findings that Pagnotti lacked good faith.

C.

McClellan next challenges the district court's finding that as Pagnotti's assignee, it too, lacked good faith, and therefore was disqualified from protection under the Act. McClellan states that "[t]he District Court never suggests, much less finds, that McClellan's dealings with IIT concerning its purchase of the mortgages were anything but at arms-length." The district court's determination that McClellan lacked good faith is a factual finding reviewed on the clearly erroneous standard.

Although McClellan attempts to distance itself from Pagnotti, the party that purchased the mortgages from IIT and assigned them to McClellan, it cannot do this successfully. A well-recognized rule provides that an assignee gets only those rights held by its assignor and no more. The district court clearly held that Pagnotti did not obtain the mortgages in good faith. The court supported its findings with facts from the record. Because McClellan's rights as an assignee are no greater than Pagnotti's and because McClellan does not show how the district court's finding of Pagnotti's lack of good faith was clearly erroneous, McClellan is charged with the same quality of faith.

* * *

E.

McClellan next contends that the district court erred in not crediting McClellan for that portion of the IIT loan that was not passed through to Raymond's shareholders: although "the District Court acknowledged that $2,915,000, or approximately 42 percent, of the IIT loan proceeds originally went for the benefit of * * * creditors, IIT and McClellan received no credit therefor in regard to the partial validity of their liens." McClellan argues the district court determined that "[t]he wrong committed upon the creditors * * * [was] the diversion of some 58 percent of the loan proceeds from the IIT loan to [Raymond's] shareholders." It concludes that to invalidate the entire mortgage would be to provide Raymond's creditors with a "double recovery." We understand the dissent to agree with McClellan's analysis when noting that "'creditors have causes of action in fraudulent conveyance law only to the extent they have been damaged.'"

McClellan and, by implication, the dissent mischaracterize the district court's findings and conclusions regarding the fraudulent nature of the IIT loans. The district court did not determine that the loan transaction was only partially—or, to use McClellan's formulation, 58%—fraudulent. Nor did the district court conclude that Raymond's creditors had been wronged by only a portion of the transaction. Instead, the district court stated that:

> McClellan Realty's argument rests on the incorrect assumption that some portions of the IIT mortgages are valid as against the Creditors. In *Gleneagles I*, this Court found that IIT and Durkin engaged in an intentionally fraudulent transaction on November 26, 1973. The IIT mortgages are therefore invalid in their entirety as to creditors.

Gleneagles III, 584 F.Supp. at 683. In essence, the district court ruled that the *aggregate* transaction was fraudulent, notwithstanding the fact that a portion of the loan proceeds was allegedly used to pay existing creditors.

This determination is bolstered by the fact that most of the $2,915,000 allegedly paid to the benefit of Raymond's creditors went to only one creditor—Chemical Bank. In *Gleneagles I*, the district court found that $2,186,247 of the IIT loan proceeds were paid to Chemical Bank in satisfaction of the mortgage that Raymond had taken to purchase Blue Coal (a Raymond subsidiary). The purpose of this payment is of critical significance:

> The Gillens and the Clevelands [Raymond's shareholders] required satisfaction of the Chemical Bank mortgage as a condition of the sale of their Raymond Colliery stock at least in part because Royal Cleveland had personally guaranteed repayment of that loan.

Gleneagles I, 565 F.Supp. at 571. McClellan does not challenge this finding on appeal. Thus, of the $2.9 million allegedly paid to benefit Raymond's creditors, $2.2 million were actually intended to benefit Raymond's shareholders and to satisfy a condition for the sale. The remaining amounts allegedly paid to benefit Raymond's creditors were applied to the closing costs of the transaction.

On this record, the district court's characterization of the transaction as a whole as fraudulent cannot reasonably be disputed. The court's consequent determination that the "IIT mortgages are * * * invalid in their entirety as to creditors" is supported by precedent.

* * *

The district court determined that "[t]he Creditors * * * would not be placed in the same or similar position which they held with respect to the Raymond Group in 1973 merely by replacing the $4,085,500 of IIT loan proceeds that were misused on November 26, 1973." * * * Here, the district court found that only by voiding the entire amount could the creditors be placed in the same position they held before the November 26, 1973 misuse of the loans. To the extent that this determination was based on facts, we do not view them as clearly erroneous; to the extent the conclusion was based on law, we find no error. Consequently, we do not believe that the district court's equitable remedy was "arbitrary, fanciful, or unreasonable," or the product of "improper standards, criteria, or procedures."

For the above reasons, therefore, we will not disturb the district court's determination that McClellan is not entitled to a "lien superior to all other creditors" as the assignee of all or part of the IIT mortgages.

V.

McClellan, joined by the amicus, next argues that the district court erred "by collapsing two separate loans into one transaction." The loan arrangement was a two-part process: the loan proceeds went from IIT to the borrowing Raymond Group companies, which immediately turned the funds over to Great American, which used the funds for the buy-out. McClellan contends that the district court erred by not passing on the fairness of the transaction between IIT and the Raymond Group mortgagors. Review of this issue is plenary.

Contrary to McClellan's contentions, the district court did examine this element of the transaction, stating: "[W]e find that the obligations incurred by the Raymond Group and its individual members to IIT were not supported by fair consideration. The mortgages and guarantee mortgages to secure these obligations were *also* not supported by fair consideration." *Gleneagles I,* 565 F.Supp. at 577 (emphasis supplied).

Admittedly, in the course of its determination that the IIT–Raymond Group transaction was without fair consideration under § 353(a), the court looked beyond the exchange of funds between IIT and the Raymond Group. But there was reason for this. The two exchanges were part of one integrated transaction. As the court concluded: "[t]he $4,085,000 in IIT loan proceeds which were lent immediately by the borrowing companies to Great American were merely passed through the borrowers to Great American and ultimately to the selling stockholders and cannot be deemed consideration received by the borrowing companies." *Id.* at 575.

The district court's factual findings support its treatment of the IIT–Raymond Group–Great American transaction as a single transaction. For example, Durkin, president of Great American, solicited financing from IIT for the purchase. The loan negotiations included representatives of all three parties. The first closing was aborted by IIT's counsel because of, *inter alia*, concern about "unknown individuals" involved with Great American. The $7 million loaned by IIT to the borrowing companies was "immediately placed in an escrow account"; "simultaneously" with the receipt of the IIT proceeds, the borrowing companies loaned Great American the cash for the buy-out and received in return "an unsecured note promising to repay the loans to the borrowing companies on the same terms and at the same interest rate as pertained to the loans to the borrowing companies from IIT." *Id.* at 570.

Appellant cannot seriously challenge these findings of fact. We are satisfied with the district court's conclusion that the funds "merely passed through the borrowers to Great American." This necessitates our agreement with the district court's conclusion that, for purposes of determining IIT's knowledge of the use of the proceeds under § 353(a), there was one integral transaction.[8]

* * *

VII.

McClellan next argues that the district court erred in holding that the mortgages were invalid under § 357 of the UFCA. Review of this issue is plenary.

As distinguished from the "constructive fraud" sections of the UFCA discussed *supra*, § 357 invalidates conveyances made with an intent to defraud creditors * * *. Under Pennsylvania law, an intent to

---

[8] Admittedly, McClellan's and amicus' arguments could have some validity where the lender is unaware of the use to which loans proceeds are to be put. That is not the case here. IIT was intimately involved with the formulation of the agreement whereby the proceeds of its loan were funnelled into the hands of the purchasers of the stock of a corporation that was near insolvency. Try as they might to distance themselves from the transaction now, they cannot rewrite history.

hinder, delay, or defraud creditors may be inferred from transfers in which consideration is lacking and where the transferer and transferee have knowledge of the claims of creditors and know that the creditors cannot be paid. Direct evidence is not necessary to prove "actual intent." In Pennsylvania, the existence of actual intent is a question of fact; therefore, the court's determination is reviewed on the clearly erroneous standard.

A.

The evidence recited by the district court supports its finding of an intent to hinder creditors. McClellan does not challenge the sufficiency of this evidence, but rather its application, arguing that from this evidence the court inferred intent, and that inferences and presumptions are proscribed by § 357. This argument was rejected by the Pennsylvania courts in *Godina v. Oswald*, 206 Pa. Super. 51, 211 A.2d 91 (1965). There, the court ruled that "'[s]ince fraud is usually denied, it must be inferred from all facts and circumstances surrounding the conveyance, including subsequent conduct.'" This is precisely what the district court did here.

* * *

C.

We conclude that the court's finding on intent was not clearly erroneous.

* * *

A. LEON HIGGINBOTHAM, JR., Circuit Judge, concurring in part and dissenting in part.

I concur in the majority's judgment that Pennsylvania's fraudulent conveyance laws may be applied to a leveraged buyout where, as here, a few shareholders seek to use it as a device to benefit themselves and take advantage of the creditors of a clearly faltering corporation. Since I find that the purposes underlying Pennsylvania's fraudulent conveyance law dictate that only a portion of the disputed transfer of funds be set aside, however, I must dissent from that part of the majority's opinion which declares the IIT mortgage loans wholly void.

The basic objective of fraudulent conveyance law is to preserve estates and to prevent them from being wrongfully drained of assets.

Fraudulent conveyance law is not intended to add to estates for the unjustified benefit of creditors. In fact, "creditors have causes of action in fraudulent conveyance law only to the extent they have been damaged." IIT made four separate loans totaling $8,530,000. Of this, $4,085,000 was passed through Raymond Group companies to shareholders and $1,530,000 was retained by IIT as an interest reserve as part of the invalid transaction. However, $2,915,000 was used to pay existing debts (including an existing mortgage loan owned by Chemical Bank). To the extent that the IIT funds were used to pay existing creditors, the assets available to creditors generally were not diminished and the Raymond Group's estate was not improperly depleted. I would therefore hold that only the transfer of the $4,085,000 between IIT and the Raymond Group's shareholders and the creation of the $1,530,000 interest reserve for IIT should be set aside.

Notes and Questions

1. What relationship among the elements of actual fraud and the savings provisions of state and federal fraudulent transfer law emerges from *Tabor Court* 's analysis?

2. In order for a transfer, such as a leveraged buyout, to be set aside, the trustee must meet the requirements of a two-part test, regardless of the fraudulent conveyance law applied. First, the trustee must show that "fair consideration" was not given for the transfer (under the UFCA) or that the transfer was not made for "reasonably equivalent value" (under the Bankruptcy Code or the UFTA). Second, the trustee must establish that the debtor was either insolvent or rendered insolvent at the time of the transfer, or that the debtor was left with unreasonably small capital. UFCA §§ 4, 5; § 548(a)(2)(B); UFTA §§ 5(a), 4(a)(2)(i). If the trustee can make these showings, a leveraged buyout is vulnerable to avoidance as a fraudulent conveyance.

Professors Baird and Jackson, who believe that leveraged buyouts should not fall within the realm of fraudulent conveyance law, acknowledge that "[e]ven under the narrowest view of fraudulent conveyance law, the leveraged buyout may be a fraudulent conveyance." Douglas G. Baird & Thomas H. Jackson, *Fraudulent Conveyance Law and Its Proper Domain,* 38 Vand. L. Rev. 829, 851 (1985).

Professor Smyser criticized Baird and Jackson for failing "to comprehend fully the distinctive potential for harm to creditors in those leveraged buyout transactions occurring under circumstances which trigger the application of fraudulent conveyance statutes." Kathryn V. Smyser, *Going Private and Going Under: Leveraged Buyouts and the Fraudulent Conveyance Problem,* 63 Ind. L.J. 781, 784 (1988). Professor Smyser argued that the use of fraudulent conveyance law in the context of leveraged buyouts is "consistent with the policies underlying traditional applications of fraudulent conveyance statutes and is both necessary and appropriate to afford creditors protection against transactions which are the fundamental equivalent of transactions generally prohibited under state corporation laws." *Id.* She concluded that leveraged buyouts are within the "proper domain" of fraudulent conveyance law:

> Where corporate debtors are concerned, the application of fraudulent conveyance laws to leveraged buyouts serves as an essential complement to the statutory protections afforded to corporate creditors by restrictions on shareholder distributions contained in the corporation laws. Unless one is prepared to argue for the abolition of statutory restrictions to shareholders as inconsistent with creditors' desires and best interests, there is no reason to believe that creditors do not consistently and rationally desire to limit leveraged buyouts of insolvent or nearly insolvent companies. Whatever the evidence may ultimately indicate concerning the economic benefit of leveraged buyouts generally, the limited marginal categories of buyouts involving financially ailing ventures, and of buyouts of otherwise healthy companies which are so highly leveraged in the course of the buyout as to threaten the company's solvency are probably not so beneficial that the traditional policies of creditor protection embodied in the fraudulent conveyance laws should be sacrificed.

Id. at 824.

3. In another important leveraged buyout case, *Kupetz v. Continental Illinois National Bank & Trust Co.*, 77 B.R. 754 (Bankr. C.D.Cal.1987), *affirmed sub nom. Kupetz v. Wolf*, 845 F.2d 842 (9th Cir.1988), the court was swayed by the Baird and Jackson view that application of fraudulent conveyance law to leveraged buyouts is not in the best interests of creditors. In *Kupetz*, the owners of a company that manufactured mannequins decided to sell the company in order to finance their retirement. Purchase of the company was financed by a $1.1 million loan secured by the company's assets. Unable to service its debts, the company filed bankruptcy two and one-half years later. The bankruptcy trustee attempted to set aside the purchase agreement as a fraudulent conveyance because the way the purchase was financed left the company's creditors without a chance of collecting their debts. The district court found that the owners did not know the buyer intended to secure repayment of acquisition financing by causing the acquired company to grant the bank a collateral interest in its real and personal property. The district court noted "the broader questions posed by Baird and Jackson of whether the fraudulent conveyance laws should be applied to buyouts entered in the ordinary course." 77 B.R. at 760 n.5.

b. Intragroup Transactions

Corporate enterprises made up of affiliated companies operate to promote the welfare of the enterprise as a whole, rather than as separate unrelated corporations. Frequently, one member of the corporate group guarantees the obligations of another. The guaranty by a parent of a subsidiary's obligations is known as a "downstream" guaranty. The opposite, a guaranty by a subsidiary of a parent's obligations, is an "upstream" guaranty. When one subsidiary guarantees the obligations of another, it is a "cross-stream" guaranty. Because a guarantor incurs an obligation, the undertaking may constitute a fraudulent conveyance. (As you recall, § 548 applies to "any obligation incurred by the debtor," as well as to "any transfer of an interest of the debtor in property.")

Professor Blumberg maintained that the provisions of the Bankruptcy Code and the Uniform Fraudulent Transfer Act reflect the trend toward viewing corporate affiliates within a group as a single entity rather than viewing affiliates as separate entities:

> Upstream and cross-stream guaranties occupy an important place in the process. They represent the inevitable response of lenders and corporate groups in fashioning group financing to harness the economic strength of a group to support the financing which will effectuate the objectives of the group, although it may not affect all constituent companies, or even all guarantor-constituents, to the same degree. It is important that this process be encouraged in order to permit the more effective functioning of the economic system. It is equally important to provide equivalent protection for creditors dealing with group constituents against insider manipulation to their detriment as well as against economic consequences from legal rules contrary to their expectations. This is a continuing challenge to the law. The UFTA and the changes it incorporates with respect to insider transactions are, notwithstanding minor areas of disagreement, a considerable step forward in helping meet that challenge.

Phillip I. Blumberg, *Intragroup (Upstream, Cross–Stream, and Downstream) Guaranties Under the Uniform Fraudulent Transfer Act,* 9 Cardozo L. Rev. 685, 728 (1987).

The following case was decided under § 67(d) of the Bankruptcy Act, the predecessor to § 548. The two provisions are similar, although § 67(d) uses the phrase "fair consideration" while § 548 refers to "reasonably equivalent value."

RUBIN v. MANUFACTURERS HANOVER TRUST CO.

United States Court of Appeals, Second Circuit, 1981.
661 F.2d 979.

KEARSE, Circuit Judge.

This appeal arises from the collapse and ultimate bankruptcy of two affiliated firms, U.S.N., Inc. ("USN"), and Universal Money Order Co., Inc. ("UMO"), companies in the business of issuing money orders. Plaintiffs Herbert Rubin and Eliot H. Lumbard, bankruptcy trustees of USN and UMO, respectively, appeal from a judgment of the United States District Court for the Southern District of New York * * * dismissing their claims to recover the value of certain funds and securities of the bankrupts from defendant Manufacturers Hanover Trust Co. ("MHT"). The trustees contend that MHT took these assets pursuant to fraudulent conveyances within the meaning of § 67(d) of the Bankruptcy Act of 1898, in satisfaction of debts arising from defaulted loans made, at the behest of the bankrupts, to companies that acted as sales agents for the bankrupts. The district court held, after a bench trial, that the loans against which MHT applied the bankrupts' property were supported by fair consideration and did not render the bankrupts insolvent, so that the transactions could not be set aside pursuant to § 67(d). Because we conclude that the district court did not apply the proper legal standards in considering the issues of fair consideration and insolvency, we vacate its judgment and remand the matter for further proceedings.

I. History of the Bankrupts' Business

[John Trent and Eugene Skowron controlled a system of interrelated corporations that offered financial services mainly to lower-income individuals without regular checking accounts. USN and UMO issued money orders through subsidiaries of TWO and National that cashed checks and sold food stamps. The court summarized the relationships among the various corporations with the following schematic diagram:

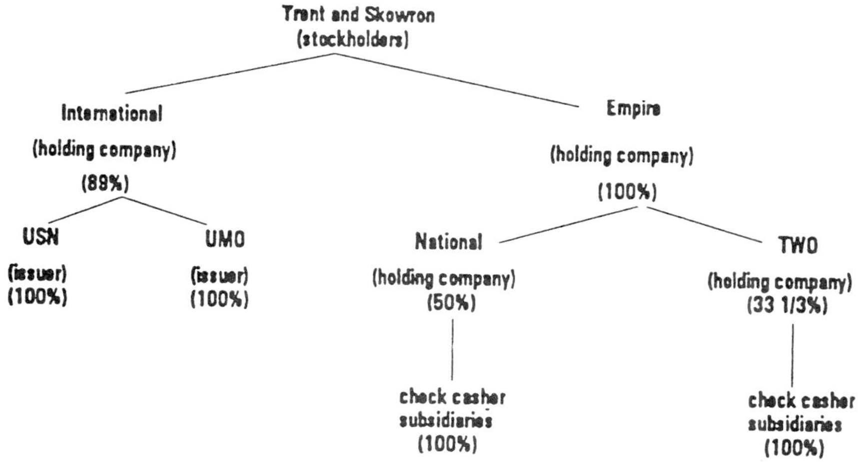

Manufacturers Hanover began financing the Trent–Skowron enterprises in 1964. In November 1972, MHT obtained a series of guaranties and cross-guaranties that enabled MHT to look to the assets of any of the Trent–Skowron entities, including USN and UMO, in the event of a default by the check cashers. The guaranties were secured by liens against accounts at MHT, including the accounts of USN and UMO. UMO pledged 44,000 shares of stock in July 1975 to guarantee Trent and Skowron's debts. UMO re-executed the guaranties in September 1976 to reflect substitutions of collateral since July of 1975 and the addition of a $187,000 certificate of deposit.

The check cashers failed to remit food stamp proceeds to the government and MHT increased its loan lines to TWO and National to enable their subsidiaries to settle the arrearages. The system of guaranties made the other affiliated entities, including USN and UMO, responsible for repaying the increased loan obligation.

The empire began to collapse when the California Banking Department issued a report finding UMO insolvent. A few months later, MHT discontinued extensions of credit to all of UMO's check casher sales agents except one, Propper. Several banks at which USN and UMO maintained checking accounts stopped honoring checks drawn on uncollected funds. USN and UMO immediately became unable to redeem money orders presented for collection. Both entities filed bankruptcy in January 1977.

Meanwhile, MHT looked to the assets of USN and UMO that had been encumbered to guarantee Trent and Skowron's debts. Pre-

petition, MHT had seized $295,000 and $80,000 from the checking accounts of USN and UMO, respectively, and applied the proceeds to loan balances of National's check casher subsidiaries. MHT also sold securities pledged by UMO to guarantee Trent and Skowron's debts. The $1,387,000 proceeds were applied as follows: $78,000 to National's loans; $318,000 to loans made to TWO affiliates; $531,000 to Propper's debts; and the $459,000 balance to UMO's bankruptcy trustee.]

II. The Proceedings Below

[Only two counts of the trustees' complaint were at issue in the case. In Count 2, UMO's trustee argued that the liens and pledges of collateral given by UMO in 1972 and 1976 were fraudulent conveyances. He sought to recover the balance of the proceeds from the sale of securities ($1,387,000) and the amount seized from the checking account ($80,000). In Count 10, both trustees asserted that the guaranties and related liens incurred to enable National and TWO to settle their food stamp accounts were fraudulent conveyances. They sought to recover the same amounts as in Count 2, plus the $295,000 seized from USN's account and $186,000 in other proceeds from the sale of securities owned by USN and UMO.

The lower court held for MHT, concluding that the trustees had failed to prove lack of fair consideration. Because the Trent–Skowron enterprises were "one ball of wax," application of UMO's assets to satisfy the debts of National, TWO and Propper produced an "indirect benefit" to UMO. In addition, the entire enterprise was benefitted by settling the delinquent food stamp accounts. Alternatively, the court held that UMO's trustee failed to show that it was insolvent or lacking sufficient capital as of the pertinent time.]

III. Discussion

When an overburdened debtor perceives that he will soon become insolvent, he will often engage in a flurry of transactions in which he transfers his remaining property, either outright or as security, in exchange for consideration that is significantly less valuable than what he has transferred. Although such uneconomical transactions are sometimes merely final acts of recklessness, the calculating debtor may employ them as a means of preferring certain creditors or of placing his assets in friendly hands where he can reach them but his creditors cannot. Whatever the motivation, the fraudulent conveyance provisions of § 67(d) of the Bankruptcy Act recognize that such transactions may operate as a constructive fraud upon the debtor's innocent creditors, for they deplete the debtor's estate of valuable assets without bringing in property of similar value from which creditors' claims might be satisfied. In addition, § 67(d) recognizes that the incurring of an obligation chargeable against the debtor's property, as distinguished from the actual grant of an interest in that property, may unfairly deplete the debtor's estate if the debtor does not receive in exchange a consideration roughly equal in value to the obligation incurred. Thus, § 67(d)(2) provides in relevant part as follows:

> Every transfer made and every obligation incurred by a debtor within one year prior to the filing of a petition initiating a proceeding under this title by or against him is fraudulent (a) as to creditors existing at the time of such transfer or obligation, if made or incurred without fair consideration by a debtor who is or will be thereby rendered insolvent, without regard to his actual intent; or (b) as to then existing creditors and as to other persons who become creditors during the continuance of a business or transaction, if made or incurred without fair consideration by a debtor who is engaged or is about to engage in such business or transaction, for which the property remaining in his hands is an unreasonably small capital, without regard to his actual intent * * *.

Section 67(d)(6) of the Act empowers the bankruptcy trustee to set aside transfers made or obligations incurred on uneconomical terms, and to recover for the benefit of creditors the value of the property removed from the debtor's estate through such transactions.

In the present case, in order to prove their claims that UMO's and USN's guarantees of the obligations of National, TWO, and Propper were constructively fraudulent, and therefore voidable under criteria set forth in § 67(d)(2)(a) and (b), the trustees were required to show: (1) that USN and UMO made transfers or incurred obligations to MHT within one year of the January 1977 filings of their bankruptcy petitions, (2) that these transactions were entered into without "fair" consideration to USN and UMO, and (3) that the bankrupts were, or were rendered, insolvent or insufficiently capitalized as a result.[14] We discuss these issues in turn.

---

[14] In addition, § 67(d)(2) required the trustees to prove the existence of creditors at the time when the obligations were incurred. MHT asserts that the trustees have failed to do so, reasoning that the one unredeemed UMO money order placed in evidence by the trustees was issued on January 7, 1977, after the disputed transactions occurred. This argument is baseless. The trustees showed that USN and UMO issued an average of

A. The Timing of the Transactions

Subsections 67(d)(2)(a) and (b) apply only to transfers and obligations made or incurred "within one year prior to the filing" of a bankruptcy petition. With respect to both counts 2 and 10, the trustees contend that USN and UMO incurred obligations as guarantors of the debts of National, TWO, and Propper whenever those firms drew on the loan lines, and that because National, TWO, and Propper drew on the loan lines in September and December 1976, within one year of the January 1977 filings of their bankruptcy petitions, the statutory timing requirement was met. MHT responds that USN and UMO made transfers and incurred obligations only in 1972 and 1975, when they executed their principal guarantees and created the various security interests under them, *i.e.*, more than one year before the January 1977 filing dates. The district court expressed some doubt about the soundness of the trustees' position, but did not reach the issue in view of its ruling that the trustees had failed to show lack of fair consideration and, in the case of UMO, insolvency. We think the trustees' position is correct.

At the outset, we note that there are certain factual difficulties with MHT's position on this point. As recounted above, USN and UMO executed their initial guarantees in 1972, giving as security liens on their checking accounts and other assets held or to be held by MHT; UMO executed a second guarantee in 1975, pledging certain stocks and bonds as collateral. Although these transactions occurred more than one year before the January 1977 filing dates, USN and UMO each executed an additional guarantee and gave additional security at times well within the one year period: in September 1976, UMO guaranteed the debts of Trent and Skowron, specifically pledging as collateral many of the securities already pledged under the 1975 agreement, pledging as new collateral a $187,000 certificate of deposit, and, as it had done in 1972, granting MHT a lien on all cash and other property of UMO held, actually or constructively, by MHT at that time or in the future; and on December 31, 1976, USN guaranteed the debts of National and TWO in connection with the loans made that day to those firms' check casher subsidiaries, granting as security a lien on all cash and other property of USN actually or constructively held by MHT at that time or in the future, precisely as it had done in the 1972 agreement. Thus, even if we were to agree with MHT that the execution of the guarantees constituted the operative statutory events, we would probably conclude that

900,000 money orders per month. Holders of unredeemed money orders were obviously creditors of the firms. It strains reason to suppose that USN and UMO, whose business was based on the float created by unredeemed money orders, had no money orders outstanding in September or December of 1976.

those events occurred when the last guarantees were executed late in 1976, well within the one-year period, and that the issuers "made" "transfer[s]" at those times, at least to the extent that they gave new collateral.

Nonetheless, and regardless of the significance under § 67(d) of the execution of the 1976 guarantees, we conclude that both USN and UMO "incurred" "obligation[s]" within the meaning of the Act on or about September 16, 1976, when National and TWO drew an additional $500,000 against their increased credit line to cover their food stamp arrearages, and in December 1976, when National, TWO, and Propper last drew on the loan lines. Whenever National, TWO, and Propper borrowed under the loan lines, they of course incurred an obligation of repayment under the terms of their financing agreements with MHT. At the same time, as principal guarantors of the loan line debts under the system of guarantees, Trent and Skowron became contingently liable to discharge the check cashers' obligations if those firms defaulted. Similarly, USN and UMO, as secondary guarantors, became contingently liable if both the principal debtors and the principal guarantors defaulted. Undoubtedly, therefore, USN and UMO "incurred" an "obligation" of repayment, although admittedly a contingent one, whenever National, TWO, and Propper borrowed under the loan line, as they did in September and December 1976.

That the obligations thus incurred by USN and UMO were contingent on others' defaults does not remove them from the scope of § 67(d)(2). The statute does not distinguish between fixed and contingent obligations; rather, it applies to "*every* obligation incurred" within one year of filing, regardless of its nature. (Emphasis added.) * * *

Thus we conclude that USN and UMO "incurred" "obligation[s]" within the meaning of the Act when MHT loaned money to National, TWO, and Propper in December 1976. This event of course occurred within the one-year period dealt with by the statute.

B. "Fair" Consideration

Even if the debtor has transferred property or incurred an obligation within one year of filing a bankruptcy petition, the trustee cannot set aside the transaction under § 67(d)(2), (a), (b) if the debtor received "fair" consideration for his property or obligation. "Fair" consideration under the Bankruptcy Act, which is defined in § 67(d)(1)(e), means more than just the "good and valuable" consideration needed to support a simple contract:

> [C]onsideration given for the property or obligation of a debtor is "fair" (1) when, in good faith, in exchange and as a fair equivalent therefor, property is transferred or an antecedent debt is satisfied, or (2) when such property or obligation is received in good faith to secure a present advance or antecedent debt in an amount not disproportionately small as compared with the value of the property or obligation obtained.

The reason for this requirement is obvious: if the debtor receives property or discharges or secures an antecedent debt that is substantially equivalent in value to the property given or obligation incurred by him in exchange, then the transaction has not significantly affected his estate and his creditors have no cause to complain. By the same token, however, if the benefit of the transaction to the debtor does not substantially offset its cost to him, then his creditors have suffered, and, in the language of § 67(d), the transaction was not supported by "fair" consideration.

Three-sided transactions such as those at issue here present special difficulties under the § 67(d)(1)(e) definition of fair consideration. On its face, the statute appears to sanction, as supported by "fair" consideration, a transaction in which the debtor transfers property or incurs an obligation as security for the debt of a third person, provided that the debt is "not disproportionately small" in comparison to that property or obligation. Nonetheless, if the debt secured by the transaction is not the debtor's own, then his giving of security will deplete his estate without bringing in a corresponding value from which his creditors can benefit, and his creditors will suffer just as they would if the debtor had simply made a gift of his property or obligation. Accordingly, courts have long recognized that "[t]ransfers made to benefit third parties are clearly not made for a 'fair' consideration," and, similarly, that "a conveyance by a corporation for the benefit of an affiliate [should not] be regarded as given for fair consideration as to the creditors of the conveying corporations." 4 Collier on Bankruptcy ¶ 67.33, at 514.1–14.2 (14th ed. 1978).

The cases recognize, however, that a debtor may sometimes receive "fair" consideration even though the consideration given for his property or obligation goes initially to a third person. As we have recently stated, although "transfers *solely* for the benefit of third parties do not furnish fair consideration" under § 67(d)(1)(e), the transaction's benefit to the debtor "need not be direct; it may come indirectly through benefit to a third person." *Klein v. Tabatchnick*, 610 F.2d 1043, 1047 (2d Cir.1979) (emphasis added). If the consideration given to the third person has ultimately landed in the debtor's hands, or if the giving of the consideration to the third person otherwise confers an economic benefit upon the debtor, then the debtor's net worth has been preserved, and § 67(d) has been satisfied—provided, of course, that the value of the benefit received by the debtor approximates the value of the property or obligation he has given up. * * * Thus, although these "indirect benefit" cases frequently speak as though an "identity of [economic] interest" between the debtor and the third person sufficed to establish fair consideration, the decisions in fact turn on the statutory purpose of conserving the debtor's estate for the benefit of creditors.

With these principles in mind, we turn to the parties' contentions concerning the obligations assumed by USN and UMO to repay the debts of National, TWO, and Propper.

The trustees' position is very simple. Pointing out that USN and UMO incurred obligations under their guarantees as security for advances made not to themselves but to National, TWO, and Propper, they argue that the advances did not confer any benefit upon USN and UMO, and that the money order issuers' obligations to repay those advances were therefore unsupported by fair consideration. MHT, seizing on the indirect benefit cases, adopts a subtler position. With respect to count 2, which pertained only to UMO, MHT contends that its loans to National, TWO, and Propper provided fair consideration for UMO's guarantee of their debts because the loans enabled the check cashers to settle their accounts with USN and UMO more quickly, thus increasing both the pool of funds available to redeem UMO money orders and the "float" from which UMO's profits were derived. Similarly, with respect to count 10, which pertained to both issuers, MHT asserts that there was fair consideration to both USN and UMO for the food stamp-related increase in the loans to National and TWO because the increased loans replaced the food stamp "float" as a source of working capital for the check cashers, enabling them to stay in business and securing the stream of money order sales proceeds relied on by both issuers. Finding that there was an "identity of interest" between USN and UMO on the one hand and National and TWO on the other, the district court agreed with MHT. We conclude that the district court should reconsider the matter after additional factfinding on remand.

Initially, we note that the trustees take too narrow a view of the fair consideration requirement of § 67(d). As was explained above, the fact that a third party initially receives the consideration given for the debtor's property or obligation does not automatically mean that fair consideration was lacking. Thus the simple fact that National, TWO, and Propper, rather than USN and UMO, received the loan line advances need not compel a ruling in favor of the trustees on this point. The relationships among the Trent/Skowron firms and Propper were such that the advances to National, TWO, and Propper very likely did facilitate transfers of funds from those firms to the bank account shared by USN and UMO, benefiting each of those firms to some degree. Accordingly, the district court did not err in rejecting the trustees' argument that the corporate separateness of the loan recipients from their guarantors necessarily precluded a finding of fair consideration.

On the other hand, the district court did err in accepting MHT's argument that the existence of any indirect benefit whatever to USN and UMO from the advances to National, TWO, and Propper meant that the issuers' obligations as guarantors were necessarily supported by fair consideration. In a transfer for security, § 67(d)(1)(e) requires that the present advance or antecedent debt be "not disproportionately small as compared with the value of the property or obligation" given by the bankrupt to secure it. In a three-sided transaction such as that presented here, it is not enough merely to compare the absolute amount of the third person's debt with the amount of security given by the bankrupt. The trustee, who has the burden of proving that the transaction was "without fair consideration," could establish lack of fair consideration under § 67(d) by proving that the value of what the *bankrupt* actually received was disproportionately small compared to the value of what it gave. Accordingly, the court must attempt to measure the economic benefit, if any, that accrued to each bankrupt as a result of the third person's indebtedness, and it must then determine whether that benefit was "disproportionately small" when compared to the size of the security that that bankrupt gave and the obligations that it incurred.

The district court did not * * * attempt to quantify the indirect benefits to either issuer or to compare those benefits with the obligations assumed by the issuers under the guarantees. Without such an analysis, it was impossible for the court to determine whether the estate of either issuer had been conserved in accordance with the principles of § 67(d), and it was therefore error for the court to conclude that those purposes had been satisfied.[16] Since the court's alternative ground for

---

[16] Nor should the court have concluded that the money order issuers necessarily received fair consideration by virtue of the benefit to them of the loans made directly to UMO and its check casher sales agents, and of the guarantees of the debts of USN and UMO given by other Trent/Skowron affiliates. The loans to UMO were fully collateralized, and we may assume that UMO's giving of collateral to secure them was supported by fair consideration; but this does not mean that there was fair consideration for UMO's guarantee of the debts of other companies. The loans made

dismissal was also flawed, *see* Part C *infra*, we vacate the judgment of the district court and remand the matter for review of the fair consideration issue under the proper legal standards.

Given the complexity of the transactions and relationships at issue here, we think it advisable to detail the inquiry to be pursued on remand. First, the court must attempt to determine the extent to which the December 1976 loans to National and TWO increased remittances from those firms to USN, their principal in the money order business. Next, it must attempt to determine the extent to which UMO shared in the increased remittances to USN by virtue of the pooling of the issuers' funds. Similarly, it must attempt to determine the extent to which the December 1976 loans to Propper increased remittances from Propper to UMO, and the extent to which USN shared in any such increases by virtue of the pooling arrangement. The court must then compare its estimate of the value thus received by each issuer with the magnitude of the obligation charged against that issuer under its guarantee. If the value received by either issuer is found to be disproportionately small as compared with its obligation, then, to that extent, the trustee for that issuer will have proved lack of fair consideration, and the court must proceed to consider the insolvency issue, discussed below. However, if either trustee fails to establish that the value is disproportionately small, the court must rule for MHT against that trustee.

In making the determinations and comparisons called for above, the court need not strive for mathematical precision. Section 67(d) requires only "fair" consideration, not a penny-for-penny exchange. * * *

C. Insolvency or Insufficiency of Capital

As the third principal element of their causes of action under § 67(d)(2)(a), (b), the trustees were required to show that USN and UMO were, or were rendered, insolvent or insufficiently capitalized when they incurred obligations under their guarantees in September or December 1976. Under § 67(d)(1)(d), a person is insolvent "when the present fair salable value of his property is less than the amount re-

---

to UMO's sales agent Propper may have facilitated remittances from Propper to UMO, but would only constitute fair consideration to UMO if the amount of money passing to it as a result of the loan was "not disproportionately small" in comparison with its obligation of repayment. Finally, while the various cross-guarantees of USN and UMO may have induced MHT to loan money to the check cashers, the crucial issues are whether any of that money found its way to USN and UMO and, if it did, whether its amount was "not disproportionately small" as compared to the issuers' respective obligations.

quired to pay his debts." The statute does not define insufficiency of capital, and the amount of capital deemed sufficient under § 67(d)(2)(b) for the carrying on of a particular business will of course depend on its nature and size. We take up these issues separately with respect to the two debtors.

1. Financial Status of UMO

The evidence concerning UMO's financial health was conflicting. Trustee Lumbard's principal proof of UMO's insolvency was the report of the California Banking Department, which opined that as of March 31, 1976, UMO had a negative net worth of at least $561,000, and perhaps as much as $3.6 million. In addition, Lumbard adduced testimony of John Waters, an accountant and partner in Arthur Andersen & Co., who supervised an audit of UMO conducted shortly after it petitioned in bankruptcy; Waters testified that UMO had a capital deficit of approximately $6 million as of January 31, 1977, and that the results of his examination of UMO's finances were consistent with the conclusions drawn in the California report. On examination by the court, however, Waters stated that Arthur Andersen had ultimately disclaimed any opinion as to UMO's solvency "[b]ecause of significant uncertainties [concerning efforts 'to reach the holders of money orders to firmly establish the liability,' and concerning the outcome of the present and other litigation] that could not be resolved at that particular time." In addition, Sparago testified that UMO's books showed a net worth of some $2.4 million throughout 1976, and that the company's net worth was some $900,000 even if one of the most significant adjustments sought by the California authorities were made on its books. Similarly, Trent testified that UMO had "a positive net worth" until January 1977.

Reviewing this evidence, the court stated that the trustee, and the California report, had "artificially segregated [UMO] * * * from the overall [Trent/Skowron] enterprise," and that the solvency or insolvency of the enterprise had not been shown. The court chose to credit the testimony of Trent and Sparago over the conclusions of the California report, and observed that UMO's "books * * * showed a positive net worth at all relevant times well into 1977." The court discounted the testimony of Waters as to UMO's negative net worth, on the grounds that Waters had ultimately disclaimed any opinion respecting UMO's solvency and that his initial conclusions concerning UMO's financial position as of January 31, 1977 were "unhelpful in ascertaining the solvency of UMO at the time (months, even years earlier) when the guarantees were made, or even as of December 1976," when the disputed loans were made. Accordingly, the district court concluded that UMO's trustee had failed to meet his burden of proving insolvency "at the time the guarantees were made." We are persuaded that this ruling was made in the context of incorrect legal standards, and that we must vacate the court's judgment and remand for further consideration in light of the principles set forth below.

First, we think the district court placed undue emphasis on the financial health of the Trent/Skowron enterprise as a whole as a determinant of UMO's solvency. Section 67(d)(2) condemns as fraudulent conveyances transactions entered into "*by a debtor* who is or will be thereby rendered insolvent * * * [or] *by a debtor* who is engaged or is about to engage in [a] business or transaction, for which the property remaining in *his* hands is an unreasonably small capital." (Emphasis added.) Thus the insolvency issue hinges on the financial position of the debtor, not on that of related entities. Admittedly, the solvency or insolvency of controlling stockholders and related corporations may often shed some light on the fiscal soundness of a corporate debtor, and the district court did not err in considering the finances of Trent, Skowron, USN, and other affiliates in its effort to gauge the status of UMO. Nonetheless, the trustees were not required to prove that all of the Trent/Skowron entities were insolvent or insufficiently capitalized, or that as a whole the enterprise was in that condition. That burden pertained only to the debtor, UMO.

Second, to the extent that the court focused on UMO alone, its emphasis on the testimony concerning book value suggests that the court lost sight of the statutory definition of insolvency, which is cast in terms of "the present fair salable value of [the debtor's] property." The market value of particular property may of course differ substantially from its book value, and the market value of certain of UMO's assets may have been greater or less than their book value. While it was the parties' responsibility to bring any such disparities to the court's attention and to establish market value if the need arose, we think that the court may have overlooked the possibility of such disparities in reviewing the welter of figures with which it was presented.

Finally, we think the court's uncertainty concerning the time when the relevant obligations were incurred may have impeded its examination of the questions of insolvency and insufficiency of capital. The district court stated that UMO's trustee had failed to prove that UMO was insolvent "at the time the guarantees were made." As discussed above, however, UMO's incurring of obligations as guarantor must also be tested as of December 1976, when the loans for which it was charged were made. Accordingly, the question for decision was whether UMO was, or was rendered, insolvent or insufficiently capitalized as of December 1976, not just as of September 1976, when it executed its third guarantee in connection with the food stamp loans, or as of any earlier time.

In view of the court's misapprehensions of the legal framework within which proof as to UMO's insolvency should have been evaluated, the dismissal of Trustee Lumbard's claims for failure of proof of insolvency or insufficiency of capitalization cannot stand. On remand the district court should reconsider the matter, taking additional evidence if necessary, under the proper standards.

2. Financial Status of USN

The question of USN's insolvency presents us with a rather different problem. As nearly as we can tell, Trustee Rubin did not offer proof that USN was insolvent or insufficiently capitalized; certainly the district court did not purport to rule on the issue, and the matter has not been mentioned at any time in this appeal. Possibly Rubin sought to establish USN's insolvency simply by showing the proximity in time between, on the one hand, USN's assumption of obligations in connection with loans to National, TWO, and Propper in December 1976 and, on the other hand, its debarment from the money order business by the New York State Banking Department on January 10, 1977, and its adjudication as a bankrupt on January 21, 1977. If this was his intention, however, he apparently has not yet invited any court to consider the theory. Accordingly, we must consider whether Rubin should be given an opportunity to pursue this issue on remand, or whether we should simply affirm the district court's dismissal of Rubin's claims on the ground of failure to prove this crucial element of his cause of action.

Ordinarily, of course, strong policies favoring finality in litigation and conservation of judicial resources lead an appellate court to disregard contentions that a party has not asserted at trial or has failed to raise on appeal. Were Rubin suing in his own right, we would not hesitate to levy this most appropriate sanction for inattention to vital detail. In the present case, however, Rubin appears not as an entirely self-interested private litigant, but as a trustee, representing the interests of the creditors of USN. Undoubtedly numerous, these creditors—primarily purchasers of USN money orders—possess relatively small individual claims, but are likely to have suffered with disproportionate severity during the long period that those claims have remained unsatisfied. We exercise our discretion in their favor and instruct the district court to consider the issue of USN's insolvency on remand, if trustee Rubin wishes to pursue it. Otherwise, we instruct the court to enter judgment in favor of MHT with respect to Rubin's claims.

CONCLUSION

We vacate the judgment of the district court and remand the matter for further consideration of the issues of fair consideration and insolvency in accordance with this opinion.

Notes and Problems

1. The UFTA uses an "unreasonably small assets" test in § 4(a)(2)(i) and an insolvency standard in § 5(a). A problem with using both standards is that "the objective indicia of § 5 may overcome the more subjective inquiry of § 4 and may insulate some transfers by creating a safe harbor." Peter A. Alces & Luther M. Dorr, Jr., *A Critical Analysis of the New Uniform Fraudulent Transfer Act,* 1985 U. Ill. L. Rev. 527, 560:

> [T]he fact that the unsecured creditors of the debtor/guarantor are in court challenging the [upstream or cross-stream] guaranty makes the argument that the debtor retained unreasonably small assets easy, even tautological. If the debtor had sufficient assets, then the complaining creditors would have satisfied their claims without judicial intervention. To preclude such circular analysis, courts may have to construe the unreasonably small assets language by referring to objective criteria: the balance sheets of the debtor/guarantor. * * * [H]owever, the "certainty" offered by financial statements is ephemeral at best, manipulable at worst.

Professor Markell disagrees with that criticism, however. He views the unreasonably small capital section

> as an auxiliary and adjunct to the section of the fraudulent conveyance law on transfers by insolvents. It is also a tool to distinguish and discredit at least two unwarranted *per se* rules [that a pledge of all or substantially all of a company's assets *ipso facto* leaves the transferor with unreasonably small capital and that a finding of insolvency is automatically a finding of unreasonably small capital] that have developed in the unreasonably small capital jurisprudence.

Bruce A. Markell, *Toward True and Plain Dealing: A Theory of Fraudulent Transfers Involving Unreasonably Small Capital,* 21 Ind. L. Rev. 469, 508 (1988).

2. Corporation-A sought a loan of $5,000,000 from Bank. Despite Corporation-A's strong financial position, Bank required Corporation-A to ob-

tain a guaranty from its affiliate, Corporation-D, as a condition of loan approval. Corporation-D's product line had fallen out of fashion with the public and it was not as strong financially as Corporation-A, having net assets at the time of the transaction of only $2,500,000. Nonetheless, the guaranty was given and Bank made the loan. Within a few months, Corporation-D's business collapsed and it filed a bankruptcy petition. Is Corporation-D's guaranty avoidable as a fraudulent conveyance? Can you think of an argument that it is not? Cf. *Matter of Xonics Photochemical, Inc.*, 841 F.2d 198 (7th Cir.1988).

C. PREFERENCES

1. INTRODUCTION

Unlike state law's condemnation of fraudulent transfers, state law generally does not condemn preferences. A debtor may treat some creditors more favorably than others. In other words, if Debtor has $1,000 in assets and owes $500 to each of five creditors, state law allows Debtor to pay two of them in full and not to pay the remaining three anything at all. The Bankruptcy Code, however, does not allow such preferred treatment of creditors. The objects of preference law are to assure that all those with claims against the debtor share in an equitable fashion, as determined by the nature of their claims, and that creditors do not rush in on a shaky debtor, thus propelling the debtor into bankruptcy. While a solvent debtor is free to pay creditors in any order whatever, preference law assures that the insolvent debtor does not favor one creditor over another. Preference law constitutes a conclusion that each of Debtor's five creditors should realize $200, rather than two receiving the full $500 owed them and the other three receiving nothing.

Preferences are an important part of bankruptcy law. "Probably none of [the trustee's avoidance] powers is of more concern to prebankruptcy transferees than the trustee's power to avoid preferential transfers." Vern Countryman, *The Concept of a Voidable Preference in Bankruptcy*, 38 Vand. L. Rev. 713 (1985).

The elements of a preference are found in § 547(b). (Exceptions, to which we will turn shortly, are listed in § 547(c).) In order to find a preference, *every single one* of the elements must be satisfied. Read §§ 547(b), (e) and (f) and decide which of the following fact patterns present preferences. In each case, assume that unsecured creditors will be paid less than 100% of their claims.

Problems

1. Debtor borrowed $25,000 from Bank on May 1 on an unsecured basis. Debtor repaid the loan on June 15 and filed bankruptcy on September 1. Can the trustee avoid the payment as a preference?

2. Would your answer to Problem # 1 change if Debtor filed bankruptcy on October 1?

3. Paul made an unsecured loan of $15,000 to Corporation on February 1. Because Paul was president of Corporation, he was aware that Corporation was encountering financial problems. Corporation repaid Paul's loan on April 20 and filed bankruptcy on November 1. Can the trustee avoid the payment as a preference?

4. Creditor obtained a judgment against Debtor on June 5 for $6,000 and docketed it in the county where Debtor lived. Debtor's house, which was worth $100,000, was already encumbered by a mortgage of $70,000 and a prior judgment lien of $15,000. Debtor filed bankruptcy on September 1. Has a preferential transfer occurred?

5. Debtor borrowed $20,000 from Bank on October 1 and signed a security agreement granting Bank a security interest in equipment Debtor already owned, which was worth $10,000, to secure repayment of the loan. Bank did not file the financing statement until October 8. Debtor filed bankruptcy on January 5 of the next year. Has a preferential transfer occurred?

6. Would your answer to Problem # 5 change if Bank filed its financing statement on October 25? If Bank failed to file the financing statement at all?

7. Would your answer to Problem # 5 change if Debtor used the funds borrowed from Bank to buy the equipment that served as collateral for the loan?

8. Debtor borrowed $20,000 from Bank, in order to purchase a luxury car; Bank perfected a security interest in the car immediately. When Debtor filed bankruptcy 18 months later, the car was worth $12,000 and Debtor still owed $15,000 to Bank. In the 90 days before bankruptcy, Debtor paid Bank three loan installments of $350 each. Are the payments preferential transfers?

9. Would your answer to Problem # 8 change if the car were worth $18,000?

10. Debtor Corp. borrowed $50,000 from Bank. The loan was guaranteed by Debtor Corp.'s president, who had substantial personal assets. Debtor Corp. made a $20,000 payment to Bank and filed bankruptcy 10 days later. Can the trustee avoid the payment as a preference?

2. THE RELATIONSHIP BETWEEN PREFERENCES AND FRAUDULENT CONVEYANCES

Fraudulent transfers and preferences may appear to be distinct transactions in commercial insolvency law. For a transfer to be fraudulent, the debtor must either receive less than reasonably equivalent value or the transfer must have been infected with an actual intent to hinder, delay or defraud creditors. Neither of those circumstances is necessarily the case when the debtor prefers one creditor over another. The two avoiding powers, however, may apply to the same transaction. Indeed, the most noteworthy case in the fraudulent conveyance jurisprudence, *Twyne's Case*, actually involved a preference: Pierce preferred Twyne as a creditor over C and did so with an intent to hinder his other creditors. Preferences and fraudulent transfers also share a policy affinity, as Dean Robert Clark recognized:

> The law of fraudulent conveyances, together with the law of voidable preferences, implicates a coherent set of conceptually distinct moral principles that should govern the conduct of debtors toward their creditors. These principles of Truth, Respect and Evenhandedness, which may be grouped under the more general duty of Nonhindrance, are so related to one another in practice and under the standard "rules" of fraudulent conveyance actions that courts understandably have trouble, at times, distinguishing fraudulent conveyances from preferences.

Robert Charles Clark, *The Duties of the Corporate Debtor to Its Creditors,* 90 Harv. L. Rev. 505, 560–61 (1977). As you work through the materials in this part of the chapter, be sensitive to the fundamental affinity among fraudulent transfer and preference principles. Try to determine whether any of the fraudulent transfer cases in the first part of the chapter would have also supported recovery on a preference theory.

The conclusion that no creditor should be preferred is not unassailable, as a matter of policy. Arguably, the insolvent debtor should be just as free as the solvent debtor to prefer some creditors over others—by preferring one to another the debtor may be compensating the preferred creditor for some favor or relationship that was of greater value to the debtor (and, more or less directly, to the other creditors) than was the value extended to the debtor by creditors who were not preferred. Even if preferences are allowed, however, a potential fraud problem remains: the law cannot be certain that the preferred creditor has not engaged in some type of over-reaching inimical to the object of debtor-creditor law. At that juncture—the fraud risk—an affinity between fraudulent transfer law and preference principles is manifest. The following case concerns that fraud affinity. (As you will note, § 547(b) differs in some respects from the preference provision in the Bankruptcy Act, under which the case was decided.)

DEAN v. DAVIS

United States Supreme Court, 1917.
242 U.S. 438, 37 S.Ct. 130, 61 L.Ed. 419.

MR. JUSTICE BRANDEIS delivered the opinion of the Court.

The Bankruptcy Act, as amended Feb. 5, 1903, provides in § 60b that if a debtor has within four months before the filing of the petition in bankruptcy made a transfer which the person receiving the same has reason to believe was intended to give a preference, the transfer shall be voidable, and the trustee in bankruptcy may recover the property or its value. The act also provides in § 67e that if a debtor within four months before the filing of the petition in bankruptcy makes any transfer "with the intent and purpose on his part to hinder, delay, or defraud his creditors, or any of them," it shall be null and void except as to purchasers in good faith and for a present fair consideration; and that it shall be the duty of the trustee to recover the same.

R. Crawley Jones was a farmer and owner of a country store. A bank having discounted his notes bearing endorsements which it later concluded had been forged, demanded that Jones take up the notes. Fearing arrest he appealed through his father to his brother-in-law, Dean, for a loan of $1,600, promising to secure it by a mortgage of all his property, which he represented was worth more than five times that amount. Dean provided the money, and on September 3, 1909, acting in conjunction with Jones' father, "took up" the notes. Most of them were not yet due. A mortgage deed of trust dated September 3 was executed September 10, and recorded September 11. It covered practically all of Jones' property, including the stock in trade and accounts, store furnishings and fixtures, household furniture and goods, live stock, crops standing and cut and the farm itself, the last subject to a prior deed of trust. Four mortgage notes were given, payable respectively in seven, thirty, sixty and ninety days; with a proviso that upon default on any one all should become payable. The first note—and hence all—were overdue when the mortgage was recorded. On that day Dean directed that possession of the property be taken, which was done on September 13 (the twelfth being Sunday). Jones was at the time deeply insolvent and had many unsecured creditors. Some of these immediately challenged the validity of the mortgage. Within a few days an involuntary petition in bankruptcy was filed and Jones was adjudicated a bankrupt. The mortgaged property was converted into cash under an agreement with general creditors that it should be deposited to await the ultimate determination of the rights of the parties. It yielded only $1,634—leaving nothing for the general creditors, if the mortgage is held valid.

Davis, the trustee in bankruptcy, brought a bill in equity to set aside the mortgage. The District Court granted the relief prayed for; and its decree was affirmed by the Circuit Court of Appeals. Both courts found the facts to be in substance as above stated and held the mortgage void under § 67e as having been made by Jones "with the intent and purpose on his part to hinder, delay, or defraud his creditors" to one not a "purchaser in good faith" within the meaning of the act. The Circuit Court of Appeals held the mortgage void also as a preference under § 60b. The case comes to this court upon appeal; Dean contending that the mortgage is not invalid under either § 60b or § 67e.

The mortgage was not voidable as a preference under § 60b. Preference implies paying or securing a preexisting debt of the person preferred. The mortgage was given to secure Dean for a substantially contemporary advance. The bank, not Dean, was preferred. The use of Dean's money to accomplish this purpose could not convert the transaction into a preferring of Dean, although he knew of the debtor's insolvency. Mere circuity of arrangement will not save a transfer which effects a preference from being invalid as such. But a transfer to a third person is invalid under this section as a preference, only where that person was acting on behalf of the creditor. Here Dean acted on the debtor's behalf in providing the money and taking up the notes.

But under § 67e the basis of invalidity is much broader. It covers every transfer made by the bankrupt "within four months prior to the filing of the petition, with the intent and purpose on his part to hinder, delay, or defraud his creditors, or any of them" "except as to purchasers in good faith and for a present fair consideration." As provided in § 67d, only "liens given or accepted in good faith and not in contemplation of or in fraud upon this Act" are unassailable. A transfer, the intent (or obviously necessary effect) of which is to deprive creditors of the benefits sought to be secured by the Bankruptcy Act "hinders, delays or defrauds creditors" within the meaning of § 67e. *Van Iderstine* v. *National Discount Co.*, 227 U.S. 575, 582 [(1913)], points out the distinction between the intent to prefer and the intent to defraud. A transaction may be invalid both as a preference and as a fraudulent transfer. It may be invalid only as a preference or only as a fraudulent transfer. Making a mortgage to secure an advance with which the insolvent debtor intends to pay a preexisting debt does not necessarily imply an intent to hinder, delay or defraud creditors. The mortgage may be made in the expectation that thereby the debtor will extricate himself from a particular difficulty and be enabled to promote the interest of all other creditors by continuing his business. The lender who makes an advance for that purpose with full knowledge of the facts may be acting in perfect "good faith." But where the advance is made to enable the debtor to make a preferential payment with bankruptcy in contemplation, the transaction presents an element upon which fraud may be predicated. The fact that the money advanced is actually used to pay a debt does not necessarily establish good faith. It is a question of fact in each case what the intent was with which the loan was sought and made.

We cannot say that the facts found by the District Court and affirmed by the Circuit Court of Appeals were not supported by the evidence, nor that these courts erred in concluding upon this evidence that the mortgage was made with the purpose and intent to hinder, delay or defraud Jones' creditors, and that Dean was not as against general creditors "a purchaser in good faith." Jones knew that he was insolvent. He knew that he was making a preferential payment. He must have known that suspension of his business and bankruptcy would result from giving and recording a mortgage of all his property to secure a note which had matured before the mortgage was executed. The lower courts were justified in concluding that he intended the necessary consequences of his act; that he willingly sacrificed his property and his other creditors to avert a threatened criminal prosecution; and that Dean, who, knowing the facts, cooperated in the bankrupt's fraudulent purpose, lacked the saving good faith.

* * *

Decree affirmed.

Questions and Problems

1. Even though the Court found no preferential transfer in *Dean v. Davis*, are preference policies implicated on the facts of the case?

2. The affinity between fraudulent transfers and preferences is also illustrated by *Kidder Skis International v. Williams*, 60 B.R. 808 (W.D.Mo.

1985). Debtor owed Kidder $8,900 for water ski equipment purchased from Kidder for resale to consumers. All of Debtor's inventory was subject to a blanket security interest in favor of Community Bank. When it became apparent that Debtor's business was collapsing, Debtor returned the skis to Kidder in complete satisfaction of the outstanding indebtedness. Kidder resold the skis for $3,200. Kidder received the last reshipment of skis 91 days before Debtor filed bankruptcy. The bankruptcy court characterized the return of the skis as an intentionally fraudulent transfer. Kidder did not appeal that finding, but argued that its good faith defense under § 548(c) should not have been rejected. The district court found no error, however: "Kidder cancelled an $8,900.00 debt for $3,200.00 worth of merchandise. A prudent businessman would not have cancelled such a large debt for such small consideration unless it knew that the debtor was in financial trouble. Kidder was obviously trying to cut its losses to a minimum." *Id.* at 810.

3. Debtor contracted to purchase a hotel in the Caribbean for $5.2 million. Under the contract, Debtor was to make a 10% down payment and pay the balance in five months. The contract further provided that the down payment was forfeited if Debtor failed to pay the balance. Debtor made the initial down payment, but was unable to pay the balance. Subsequently, Debtor filed a petition in bankruptcy under Chapter 7. May the trustee avoid the forfeiture of Debtor's down payment as a fraudulent conveyance? As a preference? See *Sullivan v. Willock (Matter of Wey)*, 854 F.2d 196 (7th Cir.1988).

3. ELEMENTS OF A PREFERENCE

We often speak of the five elements of a preference, referring to §§ 547(b)(1) through (b)(5). The preamble to (b)(1), however, contains an additional two requirements—that there be a "transfer" and that the transfer be "of an interest of the debtor in property." The following case deals with the second of those additional elements.

BEGIER v. INTERNAL REVENUE SERVICE

Supreme Court of the United States, 1990.
496 U.S. 53, 110 S.Ct. 2258, 110 L.Ed.2d 46.

JUSTICE MARSHALL delivered the opinion of the Court.

This case presents the question whether a trustee in bankruptcy may "avoid" (*i.e.*, recover) from the Internal Revenue Service payments of certain withholding and excise taxes that the debtor made before it filed for bankruptcy. We hold that the funds paid here were not the property of the debtor prior to payment; instead, they were held in trust by the debtor for the IRS. We accordingly conclude that the trustee may not recover the funds.

I

American International Airways, Inc., (AIA) was a commercial airline. As an employer, AIA was required to withhold federal income taxes and to collect Federal Insurance Contributions Act (FICA) taxes from its employees' wages. As an airline, it was required to collect excise taxes from its customers for payment to the IRS. Because the amount of these taxes is "held to be a special fund in trust for the United States," they are often called "trust-fund taxes." By early 1984, AIA had fallen behind in its payments of its trust-fund taxes to the Government. In February of that year, the IRS ordered AIA to deposit all trust-fund taxes it collected thereafter into a separate bank account. AIA established the account, but did not deposit funds sufficient to cover the entire amount of its trust-fund tax obligations. It nonetheless remained current on these obligations through June 1984, paying the IRS $695,000 from the separate bank account and $946,434 from its general operating funds. AIA and the IRS agreed that all of these payments would be allocated to specific trust-fund tax obligations.

On July 19, 1984, AIA petitioned for relief from its creditors under Chapter 11 of the Bankruptcy Code. AIA unsuccessfully operated as a debtor in possession for three months. Accordingly, on September 19, the Bankruptcy Court appointed petitioner Harry P. Begier, Jr., trustee, and a plan of liquidation in Chapter 11 was confirmed. Among the powers of a trustee is the power under § 547(b) to avoid certain payments made by the debtor that would "enabl[e] a creditor to receive payment of a greater percentage of his claim against the debtor than he would have received if the transfer had not been made and he had participated in the distribution of the assets of the bankrupt estate." H.R. Rep. No. 95–595 at 177. Seeking to exercise his avoidance power, Begier filed an adversary action against the Government to recover the entire amount that AIA had paid the IRS for trust-fund taxes during the 90 days before the bankruptcy filing.

The Bankruptcy Court found for the Government in part and for the trustee in part. It refused to permit the trustee to recover any of the money AIA had paid out of the separate account on the theory that AIA had held that money in trust for the IRS. It allowed the trustee to avoid most of the payments that AIA had made out of its general accounts, however, holding that "only where a tax trust fund is actually established by the debtor and the taxing authority is able to trace funds segregated by the debtor in a trust account established for the purpose of paying the taxes in question would we conclude that such funds are not property of the debtor's estate." The District Court affirmed. On appeal by the Government, the Third Circuit reversed, holding that *any* prepetition payment of trust-fund taxes is a payment of funds that are not the debtor's property and that such a payment is therefore not an avoidable preference. We * * * affirm.

II

A

Equality of distribution among creditors is a central policy of the Bankruptcy Code. According to that policy, creditors of equal priority should receive pro rata shares of the debtor's property. Section 547(b) furthers this policy by permitting a trustee in bankruptcy to avoid certain preferential payments made before the debtor files for bankruptcy. This mechanism prevents the debtor from favoring one creditor over others by transferring property shortly before filing for bankruptcy. Of course, if the debtor transfers property that would not have been available for distribution to his creditors in a bankruptcy proceeding, the policy behind the avoidance power is not implicated. The reach of § 547(b)'s avoidance power is therefore limited to transfers of "property of the debtor."

The Bankruptcy Code does not define "property of the debtor." Because the purpose of the avoidance provision is to preserve the property includable within the bankruptcy estate—the property available for distribution to creditors—"property of the debtor" subject to the preferential transfer provision is best understood as that property that would have been part of the estate had it not been transferred before the commencement of bankruptcy proceedings. For guidance, then, we must turn to § 541, which delineates the scope of "property of the estate" and serves as the postpetition analog to § 547(b)'s "property of the debtor."

Section 541(a)(1) provides that the "property of the estate" includes "all legal or equitable interests of the debtor in property as of the commencement of the case." Section 541(d) provides:

> "Property in which the debtor holds, as of the commencement of the case, only legal title and not an equitable interest * * * becomes property of the estate under subsection (a) of this section only to the extent of the debtor's legal title to such property, but not to the extent of any equitable interest in such property that the debtor does not hold."

Because the debtor does not own an equitable interest in property he holds in trust for another, that interest is not "property of the estate." Nor is such an equitable interest "property of the debtor" for purposes of § 547(b). As the parties agree, then, the issue in this case is whether the money AIA transferred from its general operating accounts to the IRS was property that AIA had held in trust for the IRS.

B

We begin with the language of 26 U.S.C. § 7501, the Internal Revenue Code's trust-fund tax provision: "Whenever any person is required to collect or withhold any internal revenue tax from any other person and to pay over such tax to the United States, the amount of tax so collected or withheld shall be held to be a special fund in trust for the United States." The statutory trust extends, then, only to "the amount of tax so collected or withheld." Begier argues that a trust-fund tax is not "collected or withheld" until specific funds are either sent to the IRS with the relevant return or placed in a segregated fund. AIA neither put the funds paid from its general operating accounts in a separate account nor paid them to the IRS before the beginning of the preference period. Begier therefore contends that no trust was ever created with respect to those funds and that the funds paid to the IRS were therefore property of the debtor.

We disagree. The Internal Revenue Code directs "every person receiving any payment for facilities or services" subject to excise taxes to "collect the amount of the tax from the person making such payment." § 4291. It also requires that an employer "collec[t]" FICA taxes from its employees "by deducting the amount of the tax from the wages *as and when paid*." § 3102(a) (emphasis added). Both provisions make clear that the act of "collecting" occurs at the time of payment—the recipient's payment for the service in the case of excise taxes and the employer's payment of wages in the case of FICA taxes. The mere fact that AIA neither placed the taxes it collected in a segregated fund nor paid them to the IRS does not somehow mean that AIA never collected the taxes in the first place.

The same analysis applies to taxes the Internal Revenue Code requires that employers "withhold." Section 3402(a)(1) requires that "every employer making payment of wages shall deduct and withhold *upon such wages* [the employee's federal income tax]." (Emphasis added.) Withholding thus occurs at the time of payment to the employee of his net wages. S. Rep. No. 95–1106 at 33 (1978) ("[A]ssume that a debtor owes an employee $100 for salary on which there is required withholding of $20. If the debtor paid the employee $80, there has been $20 withheld. If, instead, the debtor paid the employee $85, there has been withholding of $15 (which is not property of the debtor's estate in bankruptcy)"). See *Slodov* v. *United States*, 436 U.S. 238, 243 (1978) (stating that "[t]here is no general requirement that the withheld sums be segregated from the employer's general funds," and thereby necessarily implying that the sums are "withheld" whether or not segregated). The common meaning of "withholding" supports our interpretation. See Webster's Third New International Dictionary 2627 (1981) (defining "withholding" to mean "the act or procedure of deducting a tax payment from income *at the source* ") (emphasis added).

Our reading of § 7501 is reinforced by § 7512, which permits the IRS, upon proper notice, to require a taxpayer who has failed timely "to collect, truthfully account for, or pay over [trust-fund taxes]," or who has failed timely "to make deposits, payments, or returns of such tax," § 7512(a)(1), to "deposit such amount in a separate account in a bank * * * and * * * keep the amount of such taxes in such account until payment over to the United States," § 7512(b). If we were to read § 7501 to mandate segregation as a prerequisite to the creation of the trust, § 7512's requirement that funds be segregated in special and limited circumstances would become superfluous. Moreover, petitioner's suggestion that we read a segregation requirement into § 7501 would mean that an employer could avoid the creation of a trust simply by refusing to segregate. Nothing in § 7501 indicates, however, that Congress wanted the IRS to be protected only insofar as dictated by the debtor's whim. We conclude, therefore, that AIA created a trust within the meaning of § 7501 at the moment the relevant payments (from customers to AIA for excise taxes and from AIA to its employees for FICA and income taxes) were made.

C

Our holding that a trust for the benefit of the IRS existed is not alone sufficient to answer the question presented by this case: whether the *particular dollars* that AIA paid to the IRS from its general operating accounts were "property of the debtor." Only if those particular funds were held in trust for the IRS do they escape characterization as "property of the debtor." All § 7501 reveals is that AIA at one point created a trust for the IRS; that section provides no rule by which we can decide whether the assets AIA used to pay the IRS were assets belonging to that trust.

In the absence of specific statutory guidance on how we are to determine whether the assets transferred to the IRS were trust property, we might naturally begin with the common-law rules that have been created to answer such questions about other varieties of trusts. Unfortunately, such rules are of limited utility in the context of the trust created by § 7501. Under common-law principles, a trust is created *in property*; a trust therefore does not come into existence until the settlor identifies an ascertainable interest in property to be the trust res. A § 7501 trust is radically different from the common-law paradigm, however. That provision states that "the *amount* of [trust-fund] tax * * * collected or withheld shall be held to be a special fund in trust for the United States." (Emphasis added.) Unlike a common-law trust, in which the settlor sets aside particular *property* as the trust res, § 7501 creates a trust in an abstract "amount"—a dollar *figure* not tied to any particular assets—rather than in the actual dollars withheld. Common-law tracing rules, designed for a system in which particular property is identified as the trust res, are thus unhelpful in this special context.

Federal law delineating the nature of the relationship between the § 7501 trust and preferential transfer rules is limited. The only case in which we have explored that topic at any length is *United States* v. *Randall*, 401 U.S. 513 (1971), a case dealing with a post-petition transfer of property to discharge trust-fund tax obligations that the debtor had accrued prepetition. There, a court had ordered a debtor in possession to maintain a separate account for its withheld federal income and FICA taxes, but the debtor did not comply. When the debtor was subsequently adjudicated a bankrupt, the United States sought to recover from the debtor's general assets the amount of withheld taxes ahead of the expenses of the bankruptcy proceeding. The Government argued that the debtor held the amount of taxes due in trust for the IRS and that this amount could be traced to the funds the debtor had in its accounts when the bankruptcy petition was filed. The trustee maintained that no trust had been created because the debtor had not segregated the funds. The Court declined directly to address either of these contentions. Rather, the Court simply refused to permit the IRS to recover the taxes ahead of administrative expenses, stating that "the statutory policy of subordinating taxes to costs and expenses of administration would not be served by creating or enforcing trusts which eat up an estate, leaving little or nothing for creditors and court officers whose goods and services created the assets." *Id.* at 517.

In 1978, Congress fundamentally restructured bankruptcy law by passing the new Bankruptcy Code. Among the changes Congress decided to make was a modification of the rule this Court had enunciated in *Randall* under the old Bankruptcy Act. The Senate bill attacked *Randall* directly, providing in § 541 that trust-fund taxes withheld or collected prior to the filing of the bankruptcy petition were not "property of the estate." See S. Rep. No. 95–1106 at 33 ("These amounts will not be property of the estate regardless of whether such amounts have been segregated from other assets of the debtor by way of a special account, fund, or otherwise, or are deemed to be a special fund in trust pursuant to provisions of applicable tax law") (footnote omitted). The House bill did not deal explicitly with the problem of trust-fund taxes, but the House Report stated that "property of the estate" would not include property held in trust for another. See H.R. Rep. No. 95–595 at 368, *reprinted in* 1978 U.S.C.C.A.N. at 6324. Congress was unable to hold a conference, so the Senate and House floor managers met to reach compromises on the differences between the two bills. See 124 Cong. Rec. 32392 (1978) (remarks of Rep. Edwards); Klee, Legislative History of the New Bankruptcy Law, 28 DePaul L. Rev. 941, 953–54 (1979). The compromise reached with respect to the relevant portion of § 541, which applies to postpetition transfers, was embodied in the eventually enacted House amendment and explicitly provided that "in the case of property held in trust, the property of the estate includes the legal title, but not the beneficial interest in the property." 124 Cong. Rec. at 32417 (remarks of Rep. Edwards). Accordingly, the Senate language specifying that withheld or collected trust-fund taxes are not part of the bankruptcy estate was deleted as "unnecessary since property of the estate does not include the beneficial interest in property held by the debtor as a trustee. Under [§ 7501], the amounts of withheld taxes are held to be a special fund in trust for the United States." *Id.*

Representative Edwards discussed the effects of the House language on the rule established by *Randall*, indicating that the House amendment would supplant that rule:

> "[A] serious problem exists where 'trust fund taxes' withheld from others are held to be property of the estate where the withheld amounts are commingled with other assets of the debtor. The courts should permit the use of reasonable assumptions under which the Internal Revenue Service, and other tax authorities, can demonstrate that amounts of withheld taxes are still in the possession of the debtor at the commencement of the case." *Ibid.*

The context of Representative Edwards' comment makes plain that he was discussing whether a *post*petition payment of trust-fund taxes involved "property of the estate." This focus is not surprising given that *Randall*, the case Congress was addressing, involved a postpetition demand for payment by the IRS. But Representative Edwards' discussion also applies to the question whether a *pre*petition payment is made from "property of the debtor." We have explained that "property of the debtor" is that property that would have been part of the estate had it not been transferred before the commencement of bankruptcy proceedings. The same "reasonable assumptions" therefore apply in both contexts.

The strict rule of *Randall* thus did not survive the adoption of the new Bankruptcy Code. But by requiring the IRS to "demonstrate that amounts of taxes withheld are still in the possession of the debtor at the commencement of the case [*i.e.*, at the filing of the petition]," 124 Cong. Rec. at 32417 (remarks of Rep. Edwards), Congress expected that the IRS would have to show *some* connection between the § 7501 trust and the assets sought to be applied to a debtor's trust-fund tax obligations. See *United States* v. *Whiting Pools, Inc.*, 462 U.S. 198, 205, n.10 (1983) (IRS cannot exclude funds from the estate if it cannot trace them to § 7501 trust property). The question in this case is how extensive the required nexus must be. The Bankruptcy Code provides no explicit answer, and Representative Edwards' admonition that courts should "permit the use of reasonable assumptions" does not add much. The House Report does, however, give sufficient guidance regarding those assumptions to permit us to conclude that the nexus requirement is satisfied here. That Report states:

> "A payment of withholding taxes constitutes a payment of money held in trust under Internal Revenue Code § 7501(a), and thus will not be a preference because the beneficiary of the trust, the taxing authority, is in a separate class with respect to those taxes, if they have been properly held for payment, as they will have been if the debtor is able to make the payments." H.R. Rep. No. 95–595 at 373, *reprinted in* 1978 U.S.C.C.A.N. at 6329.

Under a literal reading of the above passage, the bankruptcy trustee could not avoid *any* voluntary prepetition payment of trust-fund taxes, regardless of the source of the funds. As the House Report expressly states, the limitation that the funds must "have been properly held for payment" is satisfied "if the debtor is able to make the payments." The debtor's act of voluntarily paying its trust-fund tax obligation therefore is alone sufficient to establish the required nexus between the "amount" held in trust and the funds paid.

We adopt this literal reading. In the absence of any suggestion in the Bankruptcy Code about what tracing rules to apply, we are relegated to the legislative history. The courts are directed to apply "reasonable assumptions" to govern the tracing of funds, and the House Report identifies one such assumption to be that any voluntary prepetition payment of trust-fund taxes out of the debtor's assets is not a transfer of the debtor's property. Nothing in the Bankruptcy Code or its legislative history casts doubt on the reasonableness of that assumption. Other rules might be reasonable, too, but the only evidence we have suggests that Congress preferred this one. We see no reason to disregard that evidence.

III

We hold that AIA's payments of trust-fund taxes to the IRS from its general accounts were not transfers of "property of the debtor," but were instead transfers of property held in trust for the Government pursuant to § 7501. Such payments therefore cannot be avoided as preferences. The judgment of the Court of Appeals is

Affirmed.

JUSTICE SCALIA, concurring in the judgment.

* * *

If the Court had applied to the text of the statute the standard tools of legal reasoning, instead of scouring the legislative history for some scrap that is on point (and therefore *ipso facto* relevant, no matter how unlikely a source of congressional reliance or attention), it would have reached the same result it does today, as follows: § 7501 obviously intends to give the United States the advantages of a trust beneficiary with respect to collected and withheld taxes. Unfortunately, it does not always succeed in doing so. A trust without a res can no more be created by legislative decree than can a pink rock-candy mountain. In the nature of things no trust exists until a res is identified. Ordinarily the res is identified by the settlor of the trust; in the case of § 7501 it is initially identified (if at all) by the statute, subject * * * to later reidentification by the taxpayer. Where the taxes subject to the trust-fund provision of § 7501 are *collected* taxes, the statute plainly identifies the res: it is the collections. There may be difficulty in tracing them, but there is no doubt that they exist. Where, however, the taxes subject to the trust-fund provision are *withheld* taxes, the statute provides no clear identification. When I pay a worker $90 there is no clearly identifiable locus of the $10 in withheld taxes that I do *not* pay him. Indeed, if my total assets at the time of the payment are $90 there is no conceivable locus.

We may have to grapple at some later date with the question whether the lack of immediate identification means that no trust arises, or rather that § 7501 creates some hitherto unheard-of floating trust in an unidentified portion of the taxpayer's current or later-acquired assets. We do not have to reach that question today, because even though identification was not made by the statute immediately, it *was* made by the taxpayer when it wrote a check upon a portion of a designated fund to the Government. * * *

The designation here, however, occurred within the 90–day preference period. Ordinarily, the debtor's alienation of his equitable interest by declaring a trust would constitute a preference. It seems to me, however, that one must at least give this effect to § 7501's clearly expressed but sometimes ineffectual intent to create an *immediate* trust: If and when the trust res is identified from otherwise unencumbered assets, the trust should be deemed to have been in existence from the time of the collection or withholding. Thus, the designation of res does not constitute a preference, and the funds paid were not part of the debtor's estate.

For these reasons, I concur in the judgment of the Court.

Notes and Questions

1. Does the Court's conclusion in *Begier* take sufficient account of the prejudice to creditors affected by its holding? What conception of the interests vindicated by preference law emerges from *Begier*'s construction of § 547?

2. A similar question regarding whether a transfer *of the debtor's property* had occurred for preference purposes was presented in *Matter of Coppie*, 728 F.2d 951 (7th Cir.1984), *cert. denied sub nom. Gouveia v. Hammond Clinic,* 469 U.S. 1105, 105 S.Ct. 777, 83 L.Ed.2d 772 (1985). *Coppie* focused on whether garnishment actions instituted prior to the preference period, but reaching salary payable during the preference period, were dispositions of the debtor's property. The *Coppie* court held that, since under Indiana law a garnishee is accountable, from the date the garnishment summons is served, to the judgment creditor for any money the garnishee owes the judgment debtor, the garnished wages paid to the creditor during the preference period were not property of the debtor. In other words, on the date a court orders that liens on a debtor's future salary be continuous, the debtor no

longer has an interest in those future earnings to be paid to the creditor. The employer instead owes the specified portion of the debtor's salary to the garnishment plaintiff.

The next case deals with the requirement that the transfer be "of an interest of the debtor in property," as did *Begier*. Here we encounter a judicially-created gloss on the Code, known as the "earmarking" doctrine.

MCCUSKEY v. NATIONAL BANK OF WATERLOO (IN RE BOHLEN ENTERPRISES, LTD.)

United States Court of Appeals, Eighth Circuit, 1988.
859 F.2d 561.

IRVING HILL, Senior District Judge, sitting by designation.

In this opinion we reverse a judgment of the district court in a bankruptcy case because it erroneously applied the doctrine of "earmarking" to justify rejection of a claim that a transfer of funds to a pre-existing creditor was a voidable preference.

FACTS

Bohlen Enterprises Ltd. ("debtor") was a retail office equipment business in Waterloo, Iowa. Mr. William F. Bohlen was its president. In late April 1986 the debtor owed two separate obligations to the National Bank of Waterloo, Iowa ("bank"). One obligation was a short-term inventory loan dating from November, 1985, in the principal amount of $189,000. The other obligation was a longstanding arrangement for an open line of credit in the principal amount of $125,000. Both obligations were secured by a single security agreement.

In late April, 1986 the bank was insisting that the $189,000 obligation, which was overdue, be repaid by the end of that month. Mr. Bohlen went to the John Deere Community Credit Union ("credit union") in Waterloo and applied for a $200,000 loan. He disclosed to the credit union the debtor's $125,000 obligation to the bank but failed to disclose its $189,000 obligation. Mr. Bohlen told the credit union that if it provided the $200,000 loan, $125,000 of the proceeds would be used to repay the $125,000 obligation to the bank and the rest would be used for miscellaneous purposes. The credit union agreed to those arrangements.

Although the credit union's formal approval of the loan did not occur until May 1, 1986, it apparently determined on April 30, 1986 that the loan would be granted. On that date the credit union opened a share draft account[1] in the debtor's name and gave Mr. Bohlen some blank share drafts to use in drawing on the share draft account.

The opening of the share draft account on April 30, the day before the approval and funding of the loan, is a critical fact in the rather bizarre series of transactions which followed that event. The transcript does not disclose why the share draft account was opened in advance of the loan's being approved and funded, or why the borrower was given the blank share drafts before there was any money in the account.

In any event, Mr. Bohlen on April 30, 1986, purported to utilize and draw upon the share draft account despite the fact that on that date it had nothing in it. That day he issued a share draft on that account in the sum of $192,000 payable to the bank, which he then deposited in the debtor's checking account at the bank. He then immediately wrote three checks on the debtor's checking account at the bank totalling $191,777.27. All three checks were payable to the bank.

The three checks collectively constitute the transfer which is alleged to be the voidable preference. One was for $189,000 to repay the entire principal of the debtor's larger loan obligation. The second was for $1,708.77 which paid the interest on that obligation to date. The third check was for $1,068.50 which paid the interest on the debtor's $125,000 obligation to date. The principal of the $125,000 loan obligation remained unpaid.

The conclusion is inescapable that Mr. Bohlen on his own had decided to pay off the $189,000 obligation to the bank, which he was being pressured to retire at once, and to leave the $125,000 obligation unpaid. The conclusion is likewise inescapable that Mr. Bohlen expected his $192,000 share draft to be made good by the credit union's depositing the entire $200,000 of loan proceeds in the share draft account so that he could freely draw upon the account as he saw fit.

[1] The record does not disclose the exact nature of a "share draft account" or the exact nature of a "share draft". So far as we can determine they are indistinguishable from the usual bank checking account and the usual form of checks used in connection with such an account.

But the credit union did not put the entire proceeds of the loan at Mr. Bohlen's disposal. Instead it deposited only $74,931.50 of the loan proceeds in the share draft account. It funded the rest of the loan on May 1, 1986 by issuing a check for $125,068.50[2] jointly payable to the debtor and the bank.

The credit union obviously intended the joint payee check to be endorsed to the bank to pay off the $125,000 obligation as Mr. Bohlen had promised. If Mr. Bohlen endorsed that check and turned it over to the bank, the bank would clearly use it as repayment of the $125,000 loan and this would leave Mr. Bohlen without funds to cover the unauthorized payment already made of the $189,000 obligation. Mr. Bohlen was apparently unable to solve that dilemma and the joint payee check was never negotiated.

So on the morning of May 2, 1986, Mr. Bohlen realized that his attempt to pay off the $189,000 obligation to the bank without ever disclosing that obligation to the credit union would fail because the full $200,000 had not been put at his disposal. Only $75,000 was available to him to pay the $192,000 share draft he had written. The remaining $125,000 of new proceeds were embodied in the joint payee check and not available to him. He needed another $125,000 to cover. So on May 2, 1986, at 8:05 A.M., utilizing a drive-thru window at the credit union, Mr. Bohlen purported to deposit into the debtor's share draft account at the credit union, a check for $125,000 which he wrote on the debtor's checking account at the bank. That check, having been written on an account with no funds in it, was eventually dishonored. It seems clear that that check was written in a desperate check-kiting scheme in which Mr. Bohlen was playing for time.

In the meantime, during the night of May 1, 1986, the share draft of $192,000 was presented to the credit union for payment by the normal electronic process. It cleared electronically, i.e., it was honored and paid. The next morning, May 2, 1986, a clerk in the operations department of the credit union noted the electronic clearance but took no action because of Mr. Bohlen's deposit in the share draft account that morning of the debtor's $125,000 check drawn on the bank account. The clerk was also apparently relying on the approximately $75,000 of the loan proceeds which the credit union was transferring into the share

2 The odd sum of $68.50 was computed as interest due to date on the $125,000 loan. As noted *supra*, the debtor calculated the interest due as $1,068.50. We are unable to reconcile the difference.

draft account that day. The two sums together would cover the $192,000 share draft.

As of Monday, May 5 then, the picture was as follows: The credit union and the debtor had made a deal for a new $200,000 loan to the debtor with the credit union stipulating that $125,000 of the proceeds be used to retire the debtor's $125,000 obligation to the bank, the only obligation of the debtor to the bank known to the credit union. Through the share draft account, the credit union had advanced $192,000. None of that money had been used to pay the $125,000 obligation. Instead, the bulk of the money was used to pay the $189,000 obligation which was still unknown to the credit union.

The debtor filed a Chapter 11 bankruptcy petition on July 21, 1986. On August 19, 1986, the bankruptcy trustee commenced this adversary proceeding against the bank. The trustee asserted that the three checks written by Mr. Bohlen on April 30, 1986, totalling $191,777.27 in favor of the bank, constituted a voidable preference and that the said sum should be disgorged by the bank and made a part of the debtor's estate.

The bank contended that the entire sum of $191,777.27 was protected from treatment as a voidable preference by the doctrine of earmarking. * * *

Following a trial, the bankruptcy judge in a lengthy written opinion, held that $125,068.50 of the $191,777.27 was not a voidable preference because of earmarking. He * * * ordered the bank to disgorge the remainder, $66,708.77.

Both sides appealed the bankruptcy court's decision to the district judge, who affirmed the bankruptcy court in all respects.

Both sides have appealed to us from the judgment below. The trustee argues that the application of the earmarking doctrine to any of the funds in issue is an error of law. The bank contends that the lower court's application of the earmarking doctrine was legally correct but did not go far enough. The bank argues that the doctrine should be extended to protect the entire $191,777.27. * * *

THE MERITS

The prerequisites for a voidable preference are set forth in § 547(b). * * * The major dispute in the case centers around the threshold requirement that the transfer being attacked be a transfer of an interest of the debtor in property.

A. THE EARMARKING DOCTRINE

We first turn to the question of whether the earmarking doctrine was properly applied to any of the funds in this case. In so doing, it is appropriate for us to consider the origins and rationale of the doctrine and its various applications.

The earmarking doctrine is entirely a court-made interpretation of the statutory requirement that a voidable preference must involve a "transfer of an interest of the debtor in property". Equivalent language has existed in the Bankruptcy Act for many decades. However, neither the Act, nor the present Code, have apparently ever defined when a transfer involves "property of the debtor", leaving definition of the term entirely to the courts.

In every earmarking situation there are three necessary dramatis personae. They are the "old creditor", (the pre-existing creditor who is paid off within the 90–day period prior to bankruptcy), the "new creditor" or "new lender" who supplies the funds to pay off the old creditor, and the debtor.

When new funds are provided by the new creditor to or for the benefit of the debtor for the purpose of paying the obligation owed to the old creditor, the funds are said to be "earmarked" and the payment is held not to be a voidable preference.

The earliest enunciation of the doctrine occurred in cases where the new creditor providing new funds to pay off the old creditor, was himself also obligated to pay that prior debt. In other words, the new creditor was a guarantor of the debtor's obligation, such as a surety, a subsequent endorser or a straight contractual guarantor. Where such a guarantor paid the debtor's obligation directly to the old creditor, the courts rejected the claim that such payment was a voidable preference. The holding rested on a finding that the new creditor's payment to the old creditor did not constitute a transfer of the debtor's property. The courts buttressed this conclusion with the rationale that no diminution of the debtor's estate had occurred since the new funds and new debt were equal to the preexisting debt and the amount available for general creditors thus remained the same as it was before the payment was made. A possible additional rationale may have been the view that such a result was needed to avoid unfairness and inequity to the new creditor. If his direct payment to the old creditor was voided, and the money was ordered placed in the bankruptcy estate, the new creditor, as guarantor, would have to pay a second time.

Where the guarantor, instead of paying the old creditor directly, entrusted the new funds to the debtor with instructions to use them to pay the debtor's obligation to the old creditor, the courts quite logically reached the same result.

In this latter type of case, the courts have been willing to overlook the fact that the method chosen by the guarantor to pay off the old creditor was one in which the debtor was given some control of the new funds. The courts have said that even when the guarantor's new funds are placed in the debtor's possession before payment to the old creditor, they are not within the debtor's "control". In some instances the language used has been that the debtor was holding the new funds "in trust" or in a "fiduciary capacity". In other cases the courts have said they would not let form control over substance. Finally, as in the direct payment situations, almost every opinion emphasizes that the result involves "no diminution" in the debtor's estate.

The courts have extended the doctrine beyond the guarantor situations and have applied it to situations where the new creditor is not a guarantor but merely loans funds to the debtor for the purpose of enabling the debtor to pay the old creditor. The same rationales have been used to justify the results where the doctrine has been so extended, i.e., that the debtor held the new money "in trust", that the debtor did not have "control" of the new money and that the transaction did not diminish the debtor's estate. Earmarking has been held to exist where the new lender himself directly pays the old creditor, and even in cases where the new lender entrusts the funds to the debtor with instructions to use them to pay the old creditor.

As a matter of first impression, it would seem that the doctrine should not have been so extended. The equities in favor of a guarantor or surety, the risk of his having to pay twice if the first payment is held to be a voidable preference, are not present where the new lender is not a guarantor himself. Yet the courts, without much detailed anlaysis [sic] of the differences, have routinely made the extension to non-guarantors.

Where there is no guarantor, the earmarking doctrine does not help either the new creditor or the debtor. In fact the new creditor is harmed. He is a general creditor whose recovery must come from a debtor's estate which is diminished to the extent that the payment made to the old creditor cannot be recovered as a preference. The only person aided by the doctrine is the old creditor, who had nothing to do with earmarking the funds, and who, in equity, deserves no such benefit. We can see no basis for preferring this old creditor to another who was paid with non-earmarked funds.

It is not necessary for us to decide whether the earmarking doctrine, as thus far enunciated in non-guarantor situations, should be preserved, limited, or even rejected entirely. The instant case involves an extension of the doctrine beyond situations in which it has heretofore been applied. Recognizing the important public policy behind the entire scheme of voidable preferences, and recognizing that the earmarking doctrine is an exclusion from the general applicability of voidable preferences, we see no basis for extending the doctrine at all and particularly to the instant facts.

In our view, the transaction should meet the following requirements to qualify for the earmarking doctrine:

(1) the existence of an agreement[11] between the new lender and the debtor that the new funds will be used to pay a specified antecedent debt,

(2) performance of that agreement according to its terms, and

(3) the transaction viewed as a whole (including the transfer in of the new funds and the transfer out to the old creditor) does not result in any diminution of the estate.

In the instant case it is crystal clear that the second requirement is not met. The agreement was not performed according to its terms and we therefore deem the decision below to be an unjustified extension of the earmarking doctrine beyond its previous boundaries. It cannot be disputed that the agreement between the parties was that part of the proceeds of the credit union's new loan would be used to pay the $125,000 obligation. For reasons of its own, the debtor did not perform that agreement. It used the funds to pay a different antecedent debt

[11] Where a guarantor pays the old creditor directly, the requirement of an agreement between the new lender-guarantor and the debtor is inapplicable. For the reasons discussed *supra*, no voidable preference can exist even in the absence of a specific agreement.

which happened to be owed to the same creditor, and of which the new lender was completely unaware. The joint payee check for $125,068.50, which could be characterized as evidence of an attempted or contemplated earmarking, was never negotiated.

To be sure, the instant case involves a very unusual situation, i.e., two separate debts being owed to the same old creditor and the new funds being used to discharge a debt to that very creditor but a debt other than the one the parties agreed would be discharged. Suppose that the debtor in the instant case had violated the agreement by using the new loan proceeds to pay an antecedent debt owed to an outsider, someone other than the bank. There is no doubt that that payment would be held to be a voidable preference despite the attempted earmarking. We see no rational basis for reaching a different result in the instant case where the debtor likewise violated his agreement with the new lender and failed to pay off the designated debt as promised.

Even if we apply the frequently invoked test of whether the debtor had "control" over the funds provided by the new lender, the instant facts nevertheless require a holding that a voidable preference has occurred. One cannot conceive of greater or more telling "control" of the new funds by the debtor than to have the debtor use them for its own purposes and in violation of its agreement with the new lender.

The bankruptcy judge apparently recognized that his decision involved an extension of the earmarking doctrine as previously applied. He invoked general equitable principles to justify the extension. As he put it, a court of equity should "look through form to substance" and should "act to achieve the intended result [of the parties]." Failure to do so, he argued, would "result in unjust enrichment to the estate and the general creditors."

We disagree. In our view, extending the doctrine to the instant facts is not required by equitable principles. We fail to see how holding this transfer to be a voidable preference could produce "unjust enrichment" to the debtor's estate or to anyone else. The recovery of voidable preferences has not been viewed as unjustly enriching the debtor's estate or the general creditors in any sense. We also fail to see how bringing the instant facts within the earmarking doctrine can be said to achieve the parties' "intended result." The general equitable concept of carrying out the parties' intent is of dubious applicability in this context, where none of the parties contemplated the debtor's bankruptcy, the unwinding of transactions, and the division of the estate. Moreover, the bank's only intention was that its $189,000 loan would somehow be repaid, regardless of the source of the funds. Finally, the transaction as consummated by the debtor, i.e., the failure to pay the $125,000 obligation and using the loan proceeds to pay off a $189,000 debt which had not been revealed to the new lender, is certainly not the result which the new lender intended. Equity does not require a court to construct a hypothetical transaction which did not occur in order to allow what is really a preference to remain in the old creditor's hands.

* * *

Notes and Questions

1. The court was reluctant to "extend" the earmarking doctrine to non-guarantor situations. Why? What harm would have been caused by such an extension?

2. Is it only the second criterion for earmarking that is not met, or is the third also not satisfied under the facts of this case? If only the second, why should it be decisive?

3. The bankruptcy judge in this case concluded that failure to apply the earmarking doctrine would "result in unjust enrichment to the estate and the general creditors." The Eighth Circuit disagreed. Which court had it right? Given the facts of this case, won't there be unjust enrichment no matter what outcome is reached?

Note on Avoidability of Payments by Check

A debtor who pays a creditor by check may unwittingly enter the preference period. The debtor may draw a check and deliver it to the creditor several days before the 90–day period. The creditor then deposits the check, but a few days pass before the check reaches the debtor's bank and is honored. If the check is honored within the preference period, the question is whether the operative transfer for preference purposes occurred when the check was delivered to the payee or when the drawee bank honored it.

In *Barnhill v. Johnson*, 503 U.S. 393, 112 S.Ct. 1386, 118 L.Ed.2d 39 (1992), the trustee argued that the transfer occurred on the date the bank honored the check. The creditor, on the other hand, argued for a "date of delivery" rule. The bankruptcy court agreed with the creditor, but the Tenth Circuit reversed.

The Supreme Court looked to commercial paper law, which gives the holder of a checking account a claim against the bank in an amount equal to the account balance. The check is an order to the drawee bank to pay, but it gives the recipient of the check no rights against the drawee bank if the bank refuses to honor the check. See UCC § 3–409. The disappointed recipient may sue the drawer either on the check or on the underlying obligation for which the check was given, but the recipient may not sue the bank. The Court concluded, in light of these state law rules, "that no transfer of any part of the debtor's claim against the bank occurred until the bank honored the check." 503 U.S. at 399.

The creditor then made an argument based on the definition of "transfer" found in § 101(54):

> Petitioner urges that rather than viewing the transaction as involving two distinct actions—delivery of the check, with no interest in property thereby being transferred, and honoring of the check, with an interest being transferred—that we instead should view delivery of the check as a "conditional" transfer. We acknowledge that § 101(54) adopts an expansive definition of transfer, one that includes "every mode * * * absolute or conditional * * * of disposing of or parting with property or with an interest in property." There is thus some force in petitioner's claim that he did, in fact, gain something when he received the check. But at most, what petitioner gained was a chose in action against the debtor. Such a right, however, cannot fairly be characterized as a conditional right to "property or an interest in property," § 101(54), where the property in this case is the account maintained with the drawee bank. For as noted above, until the moment of honor the debtor retains full control over disposition of the account and the account remains subject to a variety of actions by third parties. To treat petitioner's nebulous right to bring suit as a "conditional transfer" of the property would accomplish a near-limitless expansion of the term "conditional." In the absence of any right against the bank or the account, we think the fairer description is that petitioner had received no interest in debtor's property, not that his interest was "conditional."
>
> Finally, we note that our conclusion that no transfer of property occurs until the time of honor is consistent with § 547(e)(2)(A). That section provides that a transfer occurs at the time the transfer "takes effect between the transferor and the transferee." For the reasons given above, and in particular because the debtor in this case retained the ability to stop payment on the check until the very last, we do not think that the transfer of funds in this case can be said to have "taken effect between the debtor and petitioner" until the moment of honor.

Id. at 400-01. The creditor also argued that the legislative history calls for a date-of-delivery rule, but the Court disagreed:

> [The legislative history applies] only to § 547(c), not § 547(b). Section 547(c), in turn, establishes various exceptions to § 547(b)'s

> general rule permitting recovery of preferential transfers. Subsection (c)(1) provides an exception for transfers that are part of a contemporaneous exchange of new value between a debtor and creditor; subsection (c)(2) provides an exception for transfers made from debtor to creditor in the ordinary course of business. These sections are designed to encourage creditors to continue to deal with troubled debtors on normal business terms by obviating any worry that a subsequent bankruptcy filing might require the creditor to disgorge as a preference an earlier received payment. But given this specialized purpose, we see no basis for concluding that the legislative history, particularly legislative history explicitly confined by its own terms to § 547(c), should cause us to adopt a "date of delivery" rule for purposes of § 547(b).

Id. at 402. Because the drawer's underlying obligation on a check is suspended pro tanto under UCC § 3–802, the two dissenters concluded that delivery was the operative event for preference purposes.

The Court's holding leaves open the possibility that a date-of-honor rule might apply for purposes of determining whether a preference occurred, but that a date-of-delivery rule might govern the preference exceptions.

4. PREFERENCE EXCEPTIONS

As you work through the following materials on the preference exceptions, keep in mind the commercial policies that inform preference law. Are the "exceptions" really exceptional or do they, rather, clarify the preference elements? That is, do the excepted transfers compromise preference principles in any way?

Preference law is not intended to interfere with the ordinary, everyday payments commonly made by every individual or business entity. One of the most important preference exceptions, therefore, is the "ordinary course" exception, dealt with in the next two cases.

UNION BANK v. WOLAS

United States Supreme Court, 1991.
502 U.S. 151, 112 S.Ct. 527, 116 L.Ed.2d 514.

JUSTICE STEVENS delivered the opinion of the Court.

Section 547(b) of the Bankruptcy Code authorizes a trustee to avoid certain property transfers made by a debtor within 90 days before bankruptcy. The Code makes an exception, however, for transfers made in the ordinary course of business, § 547(c)(2). The question presented is whether payments on long-term debt may qualify for that exception.

On December 17, 1986, ZZZZ Best Co., Inc. (Debtor) borrowed seven million dollars from petitioner, Union Bank (Bank). On July 8, 1987, the Debtor filed a voluntary petition under Chapter 7 of the Bankruptcy Code. During the preceding 90–day period, the Debtor had made two interest payments totalling approximately $100,000 and had paid a loan commitment fee of about $2,500 to the Bank. After his appointment as trustee of the Debtor's estate, respondent filed a complaint against the Bank to recover those payments pursuant to § 547(b).

The Bankruptcy Court found that the loans had been made "in the ordinary course of business or financial affairs" of both the Debtor and the Bank, and that both interest payments as well as the payment of the loan commitment fee had been made according to ordinary business terms and in the ordinary course of business. As a matter of law, the Bankruptcy Court concluded that the payments satisfied the requirements of § 547(c)(2) and therefore were not avoidable by the trustee. The District Court affirmed the Bankruptcy Court's summary judgment in favor of the Bank.

Shortly thereafter, in another case, the Court of Appeals held that the ordinary course of business exception to avoidance of preferential transfers was not available to long-term creditors. *In re CHG International, Inc.*, 897 F.2d 1479 (9th Cir.1990). In reaching that conclusion, the Court of Appeals relied primarily on the policies underlying the voidable preference provisions and the state of the law prior to the enactment of the 1978 Bankruptcy Code and its amendment in 1984. Thus, the Ninth Circuit concluded, its holding in *CHG International, Inc.* dictated a reversal in this case. The importance of the question of law decided by the Ninth Circuit, coupled with the fact that the Sixth Circuit had interpreted § 547(c)(2) in a contrary manner, *In re Finn*, 909 F.2d 903 (1990), persuaded us to grant the Bank's petition for certiorari.

I

We shall discuss the history and policy of § 547 after examining its text. In subsection (b), Congress broadly authorized bankruptcy trustees to "avoid any transfer of an interest of the debtor in property" *if* five conditions are satisfied and *unless* one of seven exceptions defined in subsection (c) is applicable. * * * In this case, it is undisputed that

* * * the interest and loan commitment fee payments were voidable preferences unless excepted by subsection (c)(2).

The most significant feature of subsection (c)(2) that is relevant to this case is the absence of any language distinguishing between long-term debt and short-term debt.[7]

* * *

Instead of focusing on the term of the debt for which the transfer was made, subsection (c)(2) focuses on whether the debt was incurred, and payment made, in the "ordinary course of business or financial affairs" of the debtor and transferee. Thus, the text provides no support for respondent's contention that § 547(c)(2)'s coverage is limited to short-term debt, such as commercial paper or trade debt. Given the clarity of the statutory text, respondent's burden of persuading us that Congress intended to create or to preserve a special rule for long-term debt is exceptionally heavy. As did the Ninth Circuit, respondent relies on the history and the policies underlying the preference provision.

II

The relevant history of § 547 contains two chapters, one of which clearly supports, and the second of which is not inconsistent with, the Bank's literal reading of the statute. Section 547 was enacted in 1978 when Congress overhauled the Nation's bankruptcy laws. The section was amended in 1984. For purposes of the question presented in this case, the original version of § 547 differed in one significant respect from the current version: it contained a provision that the ordinary course of business exception did not apply unless the payment was made within 45 days of the date the debt was incurred.[8] That provision

---

[7] Nor does the definitional section of the Bankruptcy Code, which defines the term "debt" broadly as a "liability on a claim," [§ 101(12)], distinguish between short-term debt and long-term debt.

[8] As enacted in 1978, § 547(c) provided, in relevant part:

"The trustee may not avoid under this section a transfer—

* * *

"(2) to the extent that such transfer was—

"(A) in payment of a debt incurred in the ordinary course of

presumably excluded most payments on long-term debt from the exception.[9] In 1984 Congress repealed the 45–day limitation but did not substitute a comparable limitation.

Respondent contends that this amendment was intended to satisfy complaints by issuers of commercial paper and by trade creditors that regularly extended credit for periods of more than 45 days. Furthermore, respondent continues, there is no evidence in the legislative history that Congress intended to make the ordinary course of business exception available to conventional long-term lenders. Therefore, respondent argues, we should follow the analysis of the Ninth Circuit and read § 547(c)(2) as protecting only short-term debt payments.

We need not dispute the accuracy of respondent's description of the legislative history of the 1984 amendment in order to reject his conclusion. For even if Congress adopted the 1984 amendment to redress particular problems of specific short-term creditors, it remains true that Congress redressed those problems by entirely deleting the time limitation in § 547(c)(2). The fact that Congress may not have foreseen all of the consequences of a statutory enactment is not a sufficient reason for refusing to give effect to its plain meaning.

Respondent also relies on the history of voidable preferences prior to the enactment of the 1978 Bankruptcy Code. The text of the preference provision in the earlier Bankruptcy Act did not specifically include an exception for payments made in the ordinary course of business. The courts had, however, developed what is sometimes described as the "current expense" rule to cover situations in which a debtor's payments on the eve of bankruptcy did not diminish the net estate because

---

business or financial affairs of the debtor and the transferee;

"(B) *made not later than 45 days after such debt was incurred*;

"(C) made in the ordinary course of business or financial affairs of the debtor and the transferee; and

"(D) made according to ordinary business terms." (Emphasis added.)

[9] We use the term "presumably" because it is not necessary in this case to decide whether monthly interest payments on long-term debt were protected by the initial version of § 547(c)(2). Cf. *In re Iowa Premium Service Co., Inc.*, 695 F.2d 1109 (8th Cir.1982) (en banc) (holding that interest obligations are "incurred" when they become due, rather than when the promissory note is signed). We refer to "most" instead of "all" long-term debt payments because of the possibility that a debtor's otherwise avoidable payment was made within 45 days of the date the long-term loan was made.

tangible assets were obtained in exchange for the payment. Without such an exception, trade creditors and other suppliers of necessary goods and services might have been reluctant to extend even short-term credit and might have required advance payment instead, thus making it difficult for many companies in temporary distress to have remained in business. Respondent argues that Congress enacted § 547(c)(2) in 1978 to codify that exception, and therefore the Court should construe § 547(c)(2) as limited to the confines of the current expense rule.

This argument is not compelling for several reasons. First, it is by no means clear that § 547(c)(2) should be construed as the statutory analogue of the judicially crafted current expense rule because there are other exceptions in § 547(c) that explicitly cover contemporaneous exchanges for new value.[13] Those provisions occupy some (if not all) of the territory previously covered by the current expense rule. Nor has respondent directed our attention to any extrinsic evidence suggesting that Congress intended to codify the current expense rule in § 547(c)(2).[14]

The current expense rule developed when the statutory preference provision was significantly narrower than it is today. To establish a preference under the Bankruptcy Act, the trustee had to prove that the challenged payment was made at a time when the creditor had "reasonable cause to believe that the debtor [was] insolvent." When Congress rewrote the preference provision in the 1978 Bankruptcy Code, it substantially enlarged the trustee's power to avoid preferential transfers by eliminating the reasonable cause to believe requirement for transfers made within 90 days of bankruptcy and creating a presumption of insolvency during that period. At the same time, Congress created a new exception for transfers made in the ordinary course of business, § 547(c)(2). This exception was intended to "leave undisturbed normal financial relations, because it does not detract from the general policy of the preference section to discourage unusual action by either the debtor or his creditors during the debtor's slide into bankruptcy." H.R. Rep. No. 95–595 at 373, *reprinted in* 1978 U.S.C.C.A.N. at 6329.

---

[13] Thus, for example, § 547(c)(1) exempts a transfer to the extent that it was a "contemporaneous exchange for new value given to the debtor," and § 547(c)(4) exempts a transfer to a creditor "to the extent that, after such transfer, such creditor gave new value to or for the benefit of the debtor."

[14] In fact, the legislative history apparently does not even mention the current expense rule. See Broome, Payments on Long–Term Debt as Voidable Preferences: The Impact of the 1984 Bankruptcy Amendments, 1987 Duke L.J. 78, 97.

In light of these substantial changes in the preference provision, there is no reason to assume that the justification for narrowly confining the "current expense" exception to trade creditors before 1978 should apply to the ordinary course of business exception under the 1978 Code. Instead, the fact that Congress carefully reexamined and entirely rewrote the preference provision in 1978 supports the conclusion that the text of § 547(c)(2) as enacted reflects the deliberate choice of Congress.

III

The Bank and the trustee agree that § 547 is intended to serve two basic policies that are fairly described in the House Committee Report. The Committee explained:

> "A preference is a transfer that enables a creditor to receive payment of a greater percentage of his claim against the debtor than he would have received if the transfer had not been made and he had participated in the distribution of the assets of the bankrupt estate. The purpose of the preference section is two-fold. First, by permitting the trustee to avoid prebankruptcy transfers that occur within a short period before bankruptcy, creditors are discouraged from racing to the courthouse to dismember the debtor during his slide into bankruptcy. The protection thus afforded the debtor often enables him to work his way out of a difficult financial situation through cooperation with all of his creditors. Second, and more important, the preference provisions facilitate the prime bankruptcy policy of equality of distribution among creditors of the debtor. Any creditor that received a greater payment than others of his class is required to disgorge so that all may share equally. The operation of the preference section to deter 'the race of diligence' of creditors to dismember the debtor before bankruptcy furthers the second goal of the preference section—that of equality of distribution." *Id.* at 177–78, *reprinted in* 1978 U.S.C.C.A.N. at 6138.

As this comment demonstrates, the two policies are not entirely independent. On the one hand, any exception for a payment on account of an antecedent debt tends to favor the payee over other creditors and therefore may conflict with the policy of equal treatment. On the other hand, the ordinary course of business exception may benefit all creditors by deterring the "race to the courthouse" and enabling the struggling debtor to continue operating its business.

Respondent places primary emphasis, as did the Court of Appeals, on the interest in equal distribution. When a debtor is insolvent, a transfer to one creditor necessarily impairs the claims of the debtor's other unsecured and undersecured creditors. By authorizing the avoidance of such preferential transfers, § 547(b) empowers the trustee to restore equal status to all creditors. Respondent thus contends that the ordinary course of business exception should be limited to short-term debt so the trustee may order that preferential long-term debt payments be returned to the estate to be distributed among all of the creditors.

But the statutory text—which makes no distinction between short-term debt and long-term debt—precludes an analysis that divorces the policy of favoring equal distribution from the policy of discouraging creditors from racing to the courthouse to dismember the debtor. Long-term creditors, as well as trade creditors, may seek a head start in that race. Thus, even if we accept the Court of Appeals' conclusion that the availability of the ordinary business exception to long-term creditors does not directly further the policy of equal treatment, we must recognize that it does further the policy of deterring the race to the courthouse and, as the House Report recognized, may indirectly further the goal of equal distribution as well. Whether Congress has wisely balanced the sometimes conflicting policies underlying § 547 is not a question that we are authorized to decide.

IV

In sum, we hold that payments on long-term debt, as well as payments on short-term debt, may qualify for the ordinary course of business exception to the trustee's power to avoid preferential transfers. We express no opinion, however, on the question whether the Bankruptcy Court correctly concluded that the Debtor's payments of interest and the loan commitment fee qualify for the ordinary course of business exception, § 547(c)(2). In particular, we do not decide whether the loan involved in this case was incurred in the ordinary course of the Debtor's business and of the Bank's business, whether the payments were made in the ordinary course of business, or whether the payments were made according to ordinary business terms. These questions remain open for the Court of Appeals on remand.

The judgment of the Court of Appeals is reversed and the case is remanded for further proceedings consistent with this opinion.

It is so ordered.

JUSTICE SCALIA, concurring.

I join the opinion of the Court, including Parts II and III, which respond persuasively to legislative-history and policy arguments made by respondent. It is regrettable that we have a legal culture in which such arguments have to be addressed (and are indeed credited by a Court of Appeals), with respect to a statute utterly devoid of language that could remotely be thought to distinguish between long-term and short-term debt. Since there was here no contention of a "scrivener's error" producing an absurd result, the plain text of the statute should have made this litigation unnecessary and unmaintainable.

Notes and Problems

1. The debtor in *Wolas*, ZZZZ Best Co., was a carpet cleaning and disaster restoration company begun by Barry Minkow when he was 16 years old. It became one of the most sensational frauds in Southern California history, raking in $100 million on the basis of almost totally fabricated paper profits. The fraud was uncovered in 1987, soon after publication of Minkow's ghost-written autobiography, "Making It In America." (A book about the scheme, entitled "Faking It In America," was written by Joe Domanick.)

Minkow was sentenced to a 25-year prison sentence at the age of 23. He served 7½ years, during which he earned a degree from Liberty University and started a prison Bible-study group called "Barry's Boys." When he got out of prison, he began doing anti-fraud seminars for the FBI. He also began a "Consumer Hotline" radio show, with profits going toward the $26 million he owes to his victims.

When Minkow was sentenced in 1989, he said, "Today is a great day for this country. The system works. * * * They got the right guy." District Judge Tevrizian, who sentenced him, was unimpressed: "El toro poo-poo, that's what I'm hearing. * * * Is he trying to clean my carpet or what?"

2. *Wolas* endeavors to come to terms with fundamental preference policies in order to discern the fit between subsections 547(b) and (c)(2). How are the interests of the debtor weighed in the balance? What are the interests of the debtor, as distinct from the interests of the debtor's creditors?

3. Justice Stevens referred to the "current expense" rule, which was used before the ordinary course of business exception came into existence. The current expense rule, according to Justice Stevens, covered "situations in which a debtor's payments on the eve of bankruptcy did not diminish the net estate because tangible assets were obtained in exchange for the payment." Is such a "no harm, no foul" rule within the bounds of the earmarking doctrine? Recall *McCuskey*'s narrow construction of the earmarking doctrine. In light of Justice Stevens's opinion, is the *McCuskey* construction correct? That is, does

the earmarking doctrine, as applied in *McCuskey,* serve the purpose articulated by Justice Stevens?

4. Debtor Corp. hired Attorney to represent an employee of Debtor. Debtor's usual practice was to send payment at least a month after Debtor received Attorney's bill for services. Later, Attorney demanded assurance of payment *before* he would proceed with a deposition. Consequently, Debtor sent payment less than a week after Attorney billed it. Debtor Corp. filed bankruptcy a month later and the trustee sought to recover the payment made for the deposition. Attorney maintained that the payment was made in the ordinary course of business and was therefore not avoidable as a preference. Who wins? See *Boone v. Marlatt (In re Day Telecommunications, Inc.)*, 70 B.R. 904 (Bankr. E.D.N.C.1987).

MATTER OF TOLONA PIZZA PRODUCTS CORP.

United States Court of Appeals, Seventh Circuit, 1993.
3 F.3d 1029.

POSNER, Circuit Judge.

When, within 90 days before declaring bankruptcy, the debtor makes a payment to an unsecured creditor, the payment is a "preference," and the trustee in bankruptcy can recover it and thus make the creditor take pot luck with the rest of the debtor's unsecured creditors. § 547. But there is an exception if the creditor can show that the debt had been incurred in the ordinary course of the business of both the debtor and the creditor, § 547(c)(2)(A); that the payment, too, had been made and received in the ordinary course of their businesses, § 547(c)(2)(B); and that the payment had been "made according to ordinary business terms." § 547(c)(2)(C). The first two requirements are easy to understand: *of course* to defeat the inference of preferential treatment the debt must have been incurred in the ordinary course of business of both debtor and creditor and the payment on account of the debt must have been in the ordinary course as well. But what does the third requirement—that the payment have been "made according to ordinary business terms"—add? And in particular does it refer to what is "ordinary" between this debtor and this creditor, or what is ordinary in the market or industry in which they operate? The circuits are divided on this question, the scholarly literature inconclusive, our court undecided, the bankruptcy judges divided.

Tolona, a maker of pizza, issued eight checks to Rose, its sausage supplier, within 90 days before being thrown into bankruptcy by its creditors. The checks, which totaled a shade under $46,000, cleared and as a result Tolona's debts to Rose were paid in full. Tolona's other major trade creditors stand to receive only 13¢ on the dollar under the plan approved by the bankruptcy court, if the preferential treatment of Rose is allowed to stand. Tolona, as debtor in possession, brought an adversary proceeding against Rose to recover the eight payments as voidable preferences. The bankruptcy judge entered judgment for Tolona. The district judge reversed. He thought that Rose did not, in order to comply with § 547(c)(2)(C), have to prove that the terms on which it had extended credit to Tolona were standard terms in the industry, but that if this was wrong the testimony of Rose's executive vice-president, Stiehl, did prove it. The parties agree that the other requirements of § 547(c)(2) were satisfied.

Rose's invoices recited "net 7 days," meaning that payment was due within seven days. For years preceding the preference period, however, Tolona rarely paid within seven days; nor did Rose's other customers. Most paid within 21 days, and if they paid later than 28 or 30 days Rose would usually withhold future shipments until payment was received. Tolona, however, as an old and valued customer (Rose had been selling to it for fifteen years), was permitted to make payments beyond the 21-day period and even beyond the 28-day or 30-day period. The eight payments at issue were made between 12 and 32 days after Rose had invoiced Tolona, for an average of 22 days; but this actually was an improvement. In the 34 months before the preference period, the average time for which Rose's invoices to Tolona were outstanding was 26 days and the longest time was 46 days. Rose consistently treated Tolona with a degree of leniency that made Tolona (Stiehl conceded on cross-examination) one of a "sort of exceptional group of customers of Rose * * * fall[ing] outside the common industry practice and standards."

It may seem odd that paying a debt late would ever be regarded as a preference to the creditor thus paid belatedly. But it is all relative. A debtor who has entered the preference period—who is therefore only 90 days, or fewer, away from plunging into bankruptcy—is typically unable to pay all his outstanding debts in full as they come due. If he pays one and not the others, as happened here, the payment though late is still a preference to that creditor, and is avoidable unless the conditions of § 547(c)(2) are met. One condition is that payment be in the ordinary course of both the debtor's and the creditor's business. A late payment normally will not be. It will therefore be an avoidable preference.

This is not a dryly syllogistic conclusion. The purpose of the preference statute is to prevent the debtor during his slide toward bankruptcy from trying to stave off the evil day by giving preferential treatment to his most importunate creditors, who may sometimes be those who have been waiting longest to be paid. Unless the favoring of particular creditors is outlawed, the mass of creditors of a shaky firm will be nervous, fearing that one or a few of their number are going to walk away with all the firm's assets; and this fear may precipitate debtors into bankruptcy earlier than is socially desirable.

From this standpoint, however, the most important thing is not that the dealings between the debtor and the allegedly favored creditor conform to some industry norm but that they conform to the norm established by the debtor and the creditor in the period before, preferably well before, the preference period. That condition is satisfied here—if anything, Rose treated Tolona more favorably (and hence Tolona treated Rose less preferentially) before the preference period than during it.

But if this is all that the third subsection of 547(c)(2) requires, it might seem to add nothing to the first two subsections, which require that both the debt and the payment be within the ordinary course of business of both the debtor and the creditor. For, provided these conditions are fulfilled, a "late" payment really isn't late if the parties have established a practice that deviates from the strict terms of their written contract. But we hesitate to conclude that the third subsection, requiring conformity to "ordinary business terms," has no function in the statute. We can think of two functions that it might have. One is evidentiary. If the debtor and creditor dealt on terms that the creditor testifies were normal for them but that are wholly unknown in the industry, this casts some doubt on his (self-serving) testimony. Preferences are disfavored, and subsection C makes them more difficult to prove. The second possible function of the subsection is to allay the concerns of creditors that one or more of their number may have worked out a special deal with the debtor, before the preference period, designed to put that creditor ahead of the others in the event of bankruptcy. It may seem odd that allowing late payments from a debtor would be a way for a creditor to make himself more rather than less assured of repayment. But such a creditor does have an advantage during the preference period, because he can receive late payments then and they will still be in the ordinary course of business for him and his debtor.

The functions that we have identified, combined with a natural reluctance to cut out and throw away one-third of an important provision of the Bankruptcy Code, persuade us that the creditor must show that the payment he received was made in accordance with the ordinary business terms in the industry. But this does not mean that the creditor must establish the existence of some single, uniform set of business terms, as Tolona argues. Not only is it difficult to identify the industry whose norm shall govern (is it, here, the sale of sausages to makers of pizza? The sale of sausages to anyone? The sale of anything to makers of pizza?), but there can be great variance in billing practices within an industry. Apparently there is in this industry, whatever exactly "this industry" is; for while it is plain that neither Rose nor its competitors enforce payment within seven days, it is unclear that there is a standard outer limit of forbearance. It seems that 21 days is a goal but that payment as late as 30 days is generally tolerated and that for good customers even longer delays are allowed. The average period between Rose's invoice and Tolona's payment during the preference period was only 22 days, which seems well within the industry norm, whatever exactly it is. The law should not push businessmen to agree upon a single set of billing practices; antitrust objections to one side, the relevant business and financial considerations vary widely among firms on both the buying and the selling side of the market.

We conclude that "ordinary business terms" refers to the *range* of terms that encompasses the practices in which firms similar in some general way to the creditor in question engage, and that only dealings so idiosyncratic as to fall outside that broad range should be deemed extraordinary and therefore outside the scope of subsection C. *In re SPW Corp.*, 96 B.R. 676, 681-82 (Bankr.N.D.Tex.1989); *In re White*, 64 B.R. 843, 850 (Bankr.E.D.Tenn.1986); *In re Economy Milling Co.*, 37 B.R. 914, 922 (D.S.C.1983). Stiehl's testimony brought the case within the scope of "ordinary business terms" as just defined. Rose and its competitors pay little or no attention to the terms stated on their invoices, allow most customers to take up to 30 days to pay, and allow certain favored customers to take even more time. There is no single set of terms on which the members of the industry have coalesced; instead there is a broad range and the district judge plausibly situated the dealings between Rose and Tolona within it. These dealings are conceded to have been within the normal course of dealings between the two firms, a course established long before the preference period, and there is no hint either that the dealings were designed to put Rose ahead of other creditors of Tolona or that other creditors of Tolona would have been surprised to learn that Rose had been so forbearing in its dealings with Tolona.

* * *

The judgment reversing the bankruptcy judge and dismissing the adversary proceeding is

AFFIRMED.

[JUDGE FLAUM agreed that § 547(c)(2)(C) requires the creditor to show that the debtor's payments were made in accordance with the industry's ordinary business terms. He dissented, however, because he did not find that Rose had made the requisite showing.]

Note on "Enabling Loans"

Section 547(c)(3) sets forth the so-called "enabling loan" exception. It applies to extensions of credit that enable a debtor to purchase property that then serves as collateral for its own purchase price. This is the Bankruptcy Code version of the "purchase money security interest" that may be familiar to you from UCC § 9-107 (§ 9-103(a)(2) in Revised Article 9). That provision defines purchase money security interests to include those created in favor of the seller of goods on credit, as well as those given to lenders who make loans for the purpose of permitting the borrower to buy goods, as long as the loan funds are "in fact so used." Clearly, these same concepts are imbedded in § 547(c)(3), despite differences in wording.

This preference exception is designed to mesh with state-law provisions giving priority to purchase money secured parties who perfect their interests within a few days of the time the debtor takes possession of the encumbered property. Most states provide, in their version of UCC § 9-301(2), that secured parties who perfect within 20 days after the debtor gets possession of the property have priority over competing claimants who had obtained rights in the debtor's property before the secured party's perfection. (In this respect, most states deviated from the official 1972 version of Article 9, which gives a 10-day grace period in § 9-301(2). Under § 9-317(e) of Revised Article 9, a 20-day rule is made standard.) Section 547(c)(3)(B) mimics these state law grace periods with the 20-day provision of § 547(c)(3)(B).

A few states have enacted a grace period longer than 20 days, however. In those states, creditors may be able to perfect within the state law's grace period but outside the safe harbor of § 547(c)(3). Creditors argued in several cases that they were entitled to a preference exception under § 547-(c)(3) as long as their perfection related back, under state law, to a point in time within the 20-day period under (c)(3). The Supreme Court rejected that argument in *Fidelity Financial Services, Inc. v. Fink*, 522 U.S. 211, 118 S.Ct. 651, 139 L.Ed.2d 571 (1998), extending the protection of (c)(3) only to creditors who perfect within 20 days after the debtor gets possession of the property, regardless of the length of the state's grace period.

In revolving credit arrangements, such as the "open account," the debtor's payments are not coordinated with the creditor's extensions of new credit (*e.g.*, accomplished by the shipment of additional goods). Payments during the 90–day period will be preferences and, if the new value is not given in exchange for the preferential transfer, the preferences will not be saved by § 547(c)(1). Another exception—§ 547(c)(4)—may apply in these cases.

Read § 547(c)(4) and apply it to each of the following fact patterns.

Problems

1. Creditor made an unsecured $10,000 loan to Debtor on August 1. Debtor paid Creditor $2,500 on September 15 and borrowed an additional $1,000 on October 1. Debtor filed a bankruptcy petition on November 15.

2. Creditor made an unsecured $10,000 loan to Debtor on August 1 and loaned an additional $1,000 on September 15. Debtor paid Creditor $2,500 on October 1 and filed a bankruptcy petition on November 15.

3. Creditor made an unsecured $10,000 loan to Debtor on August 1. Debtor paid Creditor $2,500 on September 15. Debtor sought an additional $1,000 from Creditor on October 1, but Creditor refused to lend without security. In exchange for the additional funds, therefore, Debtor gave Creditor a security interest in personal property worth $5,000 to secure the new loan. Creditor filed a financing statement immediately. Debtor filed a bankruptcy petition on November 15.

4. Does your answer to Problem # 3 change if Creditor failed to file a financing statement?

5. Creditor sold Debtor $10,000 worth of widgets on open account on August 1, with payment due in 15 days. Debtor paid only $2,500 and paid it late—on September 1. Then, on September 10, Debtor ordered $1,000 worth of thingamajigs. Creditor refused to sell without immediate payment and Debtor agreed. Creditor shipped the thingamajigs on September 15 and Debtor issued a check on September 20. Creditor received the check on September 22 and Debtor's bank honored it on October 1. Debtor filed a bankruptcy petition on November 15.

A so-called "floating lien" is one that attaches to types of collateral, such as inventory and accounts receivable, that constantly turn over. Such liens normally secure lines of credit, which consist of numerous extensions of value over time, rather than one-shot loans. Thus, the collateral needs to be replenished in order to protect the creditor. The solution is an after-acquired property clause that enables the lien to "float" over the collateral and to attach to new items as soon as the debtor acquires an interest in them. This will occur long after value was first extended and the security interest first attached and was perfected.

The floating lien raises special problems in bankruptcy. If the security interest in the newly-acquired property arises within the 90 days before bankruptcy, it looks suspiciously like a preference.

Arguments concerning the treatment of floating liens under the 1898 Act centered around § 60a(2):

> [A] transfer of property other than real property shall be deemed to have been made or suffered at the time when it became so far perfected that no subsequent lien upon such property obtainable by legal or equitable proceedings on a simple contract could become superior to the rights of the transferee.

Trustees made a straightforward argument based on § 60a(2): First, a security interest has priority over a lien creditor only when the security interest is perfected; second, a security interest must attach before it can be perfected; third, a security interest cannot attach until the debtor has rights in the collateral; fourth, the debtor does not have rights in inventory and accounts until inventory is received and accounts come into existence. Therefore, the transfer is deemed made for preference purposes at the time inventory is received or accounts arise.

Two important cases decided in 1969 rejected this reasoning and held that floating liens do not create preferences. The court in *DuBay v. Williams*, 417 F.2d 1277 (9th Cir.1969), held that a "transfer" occurs for bankruptcy purposes when the secured creditor will take priority over lien creditors under state law, and not when the security interest attaches to the newly-acquired inventory or accounts. Thus, the "transfer" occurs when the financing statement is first filed.

The court in *Grain Merchants v. Union Bank & Savings Co.*, 408 F.2d 209 (7th Cir.), *cert. denied sub nom. France v. Union Bank & Savings Co.*, 396 U.S. 827, 90 S.Ct. 75, 24 L.Ed.2d 78 (1969), agreed with *DuBay*'s time-of-transfer theory and advanced two others. First, a floating lien is not taken in individual components of accounts or inventory, but in the entity as a whole. The analogy is to a river that retains its identity even though the water constantly changes. Under this "entity theory," the transfer occurred when the interest in the entity was transferred—*i.e.*, when the financing statement was originally filed. Second, the interest in new components of accounts or inventory is merely a substitute for the old accounts that are collected or items of inventory that are sold. Floating liens, therefore, fit within the long-standing substitution-of-collateral exception to preferences.

Section 547(e)(3) was included in the 1978 Code in order to eliminate the time-of-transfer argument adopted by *DuBay* and *Grain Merchants*. According to the legislative history, "[t]his provision, more than any other in the section, overrules *DuBay* and *Grain Merchants*." H.R. Rep. No. 95–595 at 374, *reprinted in* 1978 U.S.C.C.A.N. at 6330. Now, a transfer for preference purposes cannot occur until the debtor has rights in the collateral—that is, when new shipments of inventory are received or when new accounts arise.

The drafters also included a new preference exception in § 547(c)(5) that imposes a "two-point net improvement test." It applies only to inventory and accounts—the types of collateral that turn over—and avoids as a preference only those transfers that improve the creditor's position during the preference period.

Although § 547(c)(5) appears nightmarish upon first reading, it is not really so bad. It requires determining the amount by which the creditor's position has improved from one point in time to another. The later of those two points in time is always the time the petition was filed. The earlier one varies from case to case. For most cases, it is 90 days before the filing. In an insider case, it is one year before the filing. If, however, the creditor first extended value to the debtor after whichever of those dates is otherwise applicable, then the earlier point in time is the date on which the creditor first gave value.

You must, for each of the two points in time, determine the amount by which the creditor was undersecured—that is, the "amount by which the debt secured by such security interest exceeded the value of all security interests for such debt." The amount by which the creditor's position has improved between the two points in time—that is, the "reduction" of the creditor's undersecurity—is the amount of the preference.

Section 547(c)(5) is intended to prevent build-up of the creditor's collateral at the expense of the estate. Improvements in the creditor's position just before bankruptcy are often due to illicit, but disguised, overreaching by the benefited creditor. These improvements in position will be undone by § 547(c)(5).

Read § 547(c)(5) and determine the amount of the avoidable preference in each of the following fact patterns.

Problems

1. Debtor owes Creditor $200,000 90 days before bankruptcy. Creditor has a security interest in inventory worth $150,000 at that time. When the bankruptcy petition is filed, the debt is still $200,000 but the inventory is worth $175,000.

2. Debtor owes Creditor $200,000 90 days before bankruptcy. Creditor has a security interest in inventory worth $150,000 at that time. When the bankruptcy petition is filed, the debt is $175,000 and the inventory is worth $100,000.

3. Debtor owes Creditor $30,000 90 days before bankruptcy. Creditor has a security interest in Debtor's inventory of baseball cards, which is worth $15,000 at that time. Although Debtor does not acquire any new cards before bankruptcy, the value of the cards in Debtor's inventory increases to $20,000 by the time the bankruptcy petition is filed. Debtor still owes Creditor $30,000.

4. Debtor borrowed $15,000 from Bank and gave Bank a security interest in accounts worth $25,000 at that time. Under their security agreement, the accounts were collateral for "any and all obligations of Debtor to Bank, whenever arising." A month later, when bankruptcy appeared imminent, Bank bought an unsecured debt from Trade Creditor to whom Debtor owed $5,000. Trade Creditor, who expected to get nothing in bankruptcy, received $1,000 from Bank for the claim. Debtor filed a bankruptcy petition two weeks later, and Bank filed a secured claim of $20,000.

The following case makes two important points for purposes of § 547(c)(5). First, it illustrates how courts reconstruct the value of inventory collateral as of the appropriate date, which is usually 90 days before bankruptcy. This reconstruction is necessary because no one is likely to have "taken inventory" as of the day that later turns out to have been critical. Second, the opinion discusses the appropriate standard for valuation—an issue we have seen repeatedly, in many different contexts.

SAMSON v. ALTON BANKING & TRUST CO. (IN RE EBBLER FURNITURE & APPLIANCES, INC.)

United States Court of Appeals, Seventh Circuit, 1986.
804 F.2d 87.

FLAUM, Circuit Judge.

This suit involves an issue of first impression in this circuit. We are asked to define the word "value" as used in § 547(c)(5). We affirm the bankruptcy court and district court in their use of "cost" as the proper measurement in this case. However, we remand this case for further proceedings to determine the precise amount of the preference payment that the defendant received.

I.

The present action is by the trustee in bankruptcy under §§ 547(b) and (c)(5), to recover preference payments received by the defendant. Ebbler Furniture and Appliance, Inc. ("Ebbler"), filed a voluntary petition for relief pursuant to the Chapter 7 liquidation provisions of the Bankruptcy Code.

The appellant, Alton Bank & Trust Co. ("the Bank"), was the inventory financier for Ebbler. Although the security agreement is not in the record, it appears that the security agreement granted the Bank a security interest in Ebbler's inventory, and accounts receivable. The record is unclear as to whether the security interest covered proceeds and whether it was properly perfected.

The bankruptcy court made the following factual findings. Purchases made by the debtor within ninety days prior to bankruptcy totaled $170,911.33. The cost of goods sold during the ninety day period equaled $214,065.19. The ending inventory, as of the date of filing bankruptcy, was $67,000.00. The cost of the beginning inventory ninety days prior to the filing of the bankruptcy was calculated by the bankruptcy court in the following manner.

cost of goods sold	$214,065.19
+ ending inventory	$67,000.00
- purchases	$170,911.33
beginning inventory	$110,000.00

The bankruptcy court also found that there were $19,000 worth of accounts receivable, subject to the Bank's security interest. These receivables were added to beginning inventory. The bankruptcy court then concluded:

> 12. On the basis on [sic] the foregoing figures, the creditor Bank received a preference as described in § 547(c)(5) of approximately $75,000.00, *i.e.*, the difference between what the Bank received on account of the debt it was owed ($204,571.61), less the debtor's beginning inventory ($110,000.00) and its accounts receivable ($19,000).

The bankruptcy court noted that a discrepancy existed in the amount of $15,000 as to the value of the ending inventory. Consequently, the bankruptcy court reduced the preference by $15,000.00, and found a preference of $60,000.00.

Beginning approximately three to four months before filing its petition, Ebbler conducted a going out of business sale. Ebbler ceased doing business on November 30, 1983. At that time Ebbler was indebted to the Bank in the amount of $50,000 and had $67,000 in inventory (valued on a cost basis). The Bank repossessed $50,000 worth of inventory and sold it at cost applying the $50,000 proceeds to the debt.

Finally, and perhaps most important for purposes of this appeal, the bankruptcy court determined that the parties "were relying on the cost basis of the inventory in evaluating the security for the indebtedness."

II.

* * *

B.

The issue presented is the interpretation of "value" as used in § 547(c)(5) of the Bankruptcy Code. Section 547(c)(5) applies to situations where a secured creditor does not have sufficient collateral to cover his outstanding debt. Subparagraph five * * * prevents a secured creditor from improving its position at the expense of an unsecured creditor during the 90 days prior to filing the bankruptcy petition.

The first step in applying § 547(c)(5) is to determine the amount of the loan outstanding 90 days prior to filing and the "value" of the collateral on that day. The difference between these figures is then computed. Next, the same determinations are made as of the date of filing the petition. A comparison is made, and, if there is a reduction during the 90-day period of the amount by which the initially existing debt exceeded the security, then a preference for § 547(c)(5) purposes exists. The effect of § 547(c)(5) is to make the security interest voidable to the extent of the preference. Of course, if the creditor is fully secured 90 days before the filing of the petition, then that creditor will never be subject to a preference attack.

C.

The language of § 547(c)(5), the "value of all security interest[s] for such debt," was purposely left without a precise definition. *See generally* H.R. Rep. No. 95–595 at 216, *reprinted in* 1978 U.S.C.C.A.N. at 6176; N. Cohen, *"Value" Judgments: Account[s] Receivable Financing and Voidable Preferences Under the New Bankruptcy Code*, 66 Minn. L. Rev. 639, 653 (1982) (hereinafter "Cohen"). Furthermore, it has been persuasively argued that the other Bankruptcy Code sections' definitions of "value" would not be useful for § 547(c)(5) purposes. Cohen, *supra*, at 651–54. Thus, the only legislative guidance is "that we are to determine value on a case-by-case basis, taking into account the facts of each case and the competing interests in the case." *Matter of Lackow Bros., Inc.*, 752 F.2d 1529, 1532 (11th Cir.1985), *citing* H.R. Rep. No. 95–595 at 356, *reprinted in* 1978 U.S.C.C.A.N. at 6312.

The method used to value the collateral is crucial in determining whether or not the bank received a preference. The Bank urges that we adopt an "ongoing concern" value standard, which, in this case, would be cost plus a 60% mark-up. The Bank relies on *Lackow Bros.* as authority for the use of this definition of value. We find *Lackow Bros.* readily distinguishable. There, the only evidence of value before the court was ongoing concern value. As the Eleventh Circuit stated: "The only evidence in the record of value for the ninetieth day prior to the filing of the bankruptcy is the ongoing concern value; therefore, this is the *only* standard of valuation that can be applied to determine if Creditor's position improved." 752 F.2d at 1532.

Another view as to how value should be defined is proposed by Professor Cohen. He proposes an after-the-fact determination of value. In his article discussing accounts receivable, Cohen argues that the courts should look at the actual manner in which the collateral was liquidated, i.e. cost or ongoing concern. Whatever method is used to dispose of the collateral, Cohen argues, should be used to value the collateral 90 days before the filing of the bankruptcy petition. *Cohen*, *supra*, at 664. At least one circuit has found Cohen's reasoning useful, though not necessarily adopting it as a rigid rule. *Matter of Missionary Baptist Foundation*, 796 F.2d 752, 761–62 (5th Cir.1986).

In *Missionary Baptist Foundation*, the appellate court remanded to the district court for factual determinations as to whether or not the bank improved its position during the preference period. The court noted, however, that merely remanding for factual findings may not be sufficient in light of the ambiguous meaning of "value" in § 547(c)(5). *Id.* at 761–62. The Fifth Circuit quoted with approval Cohen's admonition of an individualized approach in defining value and his hindsight solution of the problem. We follow the Fifth Circuit's lead and hold that under § 547(c)(5) value should be defined on a case by case basis, with the factual determinations of the bankruptcy court controlling.

D.

In the present case we affirm the bankruptcy court's use of cost as the method for valuing the collateral for 547(c)(5) purposes. The bankruptcy court found that the parties were using a cost basis for valuing the security. Furthermore, when the Bank removed inventory with a *cost* of approximately $50,000, about a week before the petition was filed, Ebbler was given credit for that amount—$50,000. We do not find the bankruptcy court's factual findings so clearly erroneous as to warrant reversal.

Using these factual findings the bankruptcy court applied cost as the legal definition of "value." We affirm the use of this definition as applied to these facts.

III.

We remand to the bankruptcy court, however, for a determination as to the amount of the preference. The bankruptcy court found, weighing the conflicting evidence, that a preference of $60,000 existed. It is not clear why the bankruptcy court did not consider the $43,000 in cash which the debtor had in hand at the time of filing the bankruptcy petition.

The bankruptcy court held that the Bank had a security interest in the inventory and accounts receivable. The bankruptcy court's opinion is silent as to whether or not this security agreement covered cash proceeds, and whether or not the $43,000 in actuality was cash proceeds of the inventory. It must also be determined if these interests were properly perfected. The only evidence in the record is Mr. Ebbler's testimony that all the proceeds from sales of inventory were deposited into an account at the Bank. The bank statement shows that on the 90th day prior to the bankruptcy the account contained $43,000. Depending on the court's findings on these issues an adjustment downward in the amount of the preference might be appropriate.

IV.

For the reasons set forth we affirm the use of cost as a basis for defining value in § 547(c)(5) of the Bankruptcy Code. We remand, however, for a determination as to how the debtor's cash on hand affected the preference amount.

EASTERBROOK, Circuit Judge, concurring.

This case involves the meaning of "value" under § 547(c)(5). I join the court's opinion, which concludes that the statute does not require bankruptcy judges to use one universal definition. The history of condemnation litigation shows that a single definition of "value" is not within judicial grasp. Still, we need not leave bankruptcy judges and litigants adrift. Security interests must be appraised with some frequency in bankruptcy litigation. The greater the uncertainty in the legal rule, the harder it is to settle pending cases. "Anything goes" is not a durable rule. The parties cannot know their entitlements until bankruptcy, district, and appellate courts have spoken. One important function of appellate courts is to provide additional clarity, when that is reasonably possible. It is possible here. The bankruptcy judge did better than to avoid an abuse of discretion. He decided the case correctly.

"Value" is defined for a purpose, which sets limits on the admissible standards of appraisal even though it does not govern all cases. Section 547(c)(5) requires the court to find whether the secured creditor improved its position at the expense of other investors during the 90 days before the filing of the petition in bankruptcy. This calls for two appraisals, one on the day of filing and one 90 days earlier, using the same method each time, to see whether there was an improvement in position. The only standard that might plausibly be used in this case is wholesale cost of goods, because that is the only standard that could have been applied on both dates.

Wholesale cost is also the appropriate standard as a rule because wholesale and retail goods are different things. A furniture store, a supermarket, or the manufacturer of a product (the three situations are identical) uses raw materials purchased at wholesale to produce a new item. In the retailing business the difference between the wholesale price and the retail price is the "value added" of the business. It is the amount contributed by storing, inspecting, displaying, hawking, collecting for, delivering, and handling warranty claims on the goods. This difference covers the employees' wages, rent and utilities of the premises, interest on the cost of goods, bad debts, repairs, the value of entrepreneurial talent, and so on. The increment of price is attributable to this investment of time and other resources. The Bank does not have a security interest in these labors. It has an interest only in its merchandise and cash on hand.* The value of its interest depends on what the Bank could do, outside of bankruptcy, to realize on its security. What it could do is seize and sell the inventory. It would get at most the wholesale price—maybe less because the Bank would sell the goods "as is" and would not offer the wholesaler's usual services to its customer. The Bank does not operate its own furniture store, and if it did it would still incur all the costs of retailing the goods, costs that would have to be subtracted from the retail price to determine the "value" of the inventory on the day the Bank seized it.

To give the Bank more than the wholesale value is to induce a spate of asset-grabbing among creditors, which could make all worse off. If the Bank gets the whole increment of value (from wholesale to retail) during the last 90 days, other creditors may respond by watching the debtor closely and propelling it into bankruptcy when it has a lower inventory (and therefore less "markup" for the Bank to seize). The premature filing may reduce the value of the enterprise. There are other defensive measures available to creditors. The principal function of § 547(c)(5) is to reduce the need of unsecured creditors to protect themselves against the last-minute moves of secured creditors. It would serve this function less well if goods subject to a security interest were appraised at their retail price.

---

* The Bank's interest in the proceeds of sales is not the same as an interest in the whole retail price for unsold inventory. An ongoing financing arrangement provides for operating expenses, too, to come out of proceeds. The security interest on any given day covers only identified proceeds, an asset that is identifiable and significantly smaller than the wholesale or retail value of the entire inventory.

Too, the Bank's security interest does not reach the "going concern" value of the debtor; it had security in the *goods*, not in the *firm*. To value the inventory in a way that reflects "going concern" value is to give the Bank something for which it did not contract. At all events, this wrinkle does not make a difference. If Ebbler had been sold as a going venture 90 days before the filing of the bankruptcy petition, the buyer of the business would have paid only wholesale price for Ebbler's inventory. If Ebbler had been at the peak of health, the buyer would have paid no more for inventory. A buyer would not have paid retail, because it would have had to invest the additional time and money necessary to obtain the retail price. So whether Ebbler is valued as a defunct business or as a going business sold to a hypothetical buyer on the critical date, wholesale is the right valuation, because it reflects the price that a willing buyer would pay after arms'-length negotiation. (The "going concern" value of Ebbler is reflected in its name, reputation, customer list, staff, and so on—things in which the Bank did not have a security interest.)

To put this differently, a willing buyer of a flourishing retail or manufacturing business will not pay more than the wholesale price for inventory of goods or parts on hand, because this buyer could purchase the same items on the market from the original sellers. Why pay Ebbler $500 for a sofa when you can get the same item for $200 from its manufacturer? Nothing would depend on whether Ebbler planned to stay in business. The court therefore properly does not allow the outcome of this case to turn on the fact that Ebbler chose a Chapter 7 liquidation rather than a Chapter 11 reorganization. Chapter titles are of little use in valuing assets under § 547(c)(5). A "liquidation" may be a sale of the business en bloc as an ongoing concern, and a "reorganization" may be a transition from one line of business to another.

The difference between the wholesale and retail prices of the inventory is the compensation that the other factors of production—the employees, landlords, utilities, etc.—obtain for their services. To appraise Ebbler's inventory at "retail" is to award to the Bank the entire value of the work done during the last 90 days by these other creditors of Ebbler. It is to allow the Bank to improve its position at their expense. Because a valuation at "retail" would produce exactly the consequence that § 547(c)(5) is designed to avert, the bankruptcy court wisely chose to appraise the goods at wholesale. The court leaves to another day the question whether retail price is ever an appropriate measure of value under § 547(c)(5). The observation that the bankruptcy court has leeway, however, does not imply that the court's discretion should be exercised without reference to the function of § 547(c)(5) and the limits of the security interest.

Questions

Is Judge Easterbrook's concurring opinion in *Ebbler Furniture* at odds with the Supreme Court's decision in *Rash*, which appears in Chapter 4, Section G of this casebook? Does his opinion give you some ideas about how to frame some debtor-favorable arguments under footnote 6 of *Rash*?

D. RECOVERY OF AVOIDED TRANSFERS

Section 550 specifies from whom property that was the subject of an avoidable transfer may be recovered. Under § 550(a), a trustee may recover property transferred from the initial transferee or beneficiary of the transfer, or any immediate or mediate transferee of the initial transferee. Consider the following example: Debtor transfers property to *X* and the trustee of Debtor's estate avoids the transfer under §§ 544, 545, 547, 548, 549, 553(b) or 724(a). *X*, who still possesses the property, is liable under § 550(a)(1) as the initial transferee. A debtor's initial transferee is always, and any succeeding transferee is typically, held accountable to the trustee. Section 550(b), however, prevents the trustee from recovering from any succeeding good faith transferee who takes without knowledge of the voidability of the transfer.

Add some facts to the previous example: Assume that after *X* received the property from Debtor, *X* sold it to *Y*, who subsequently transferred the property to *Z*. Nothing has happened to affect *X* 's liability. *Y* is now liable, under § 550(a)(2), as the immediate transferee, and *Z* also is liable as the mediate transferee. *Y* and *Z*, however, have the defense of § 550(b) available to them. If *Y* gave *X* value in good faith for the property, and *Y* was unaware that the initial transfer was voidable, *Y* will be protected from liability by § 550(b)(1). If *Y* is protected, then so too is *Z*, under § 550(b)(2), if *Z* took the property in good faith.

Section 550 further provides that a good faith transferee from whom the trustee recovers is entitled to a lien on the recovered property in the amount of the lesser of (1) the amounts expended to improve the property, or (2) the increase in value of the transferred property due to such improvements. Assume in the above examples that *X* was a good faith transferee. If *X* made repairs to the property after he received it from Debtor, then *X* has a claim against Debtor's estate for the amount the property increased in value due to the repairs. If the cost of making the repairs was less than the increase in the property's value, then *X* is only entitled to a claim in the amount he spent to make the repairs.

The following cases and notes deal with the appropriate target of the trustee's recovery powers. Although they arise under different avoiding powers, each of them involves the proper interpretation of § 550.

BONDED FINANCIAL SERVICES, INC. v. EUROPEAN AMERICAN BANK

United States Court of Appeals, Seventh Circuit, 1988.
838 F.2d 890.

EASTERBROOK, Circuit Judge.

Michael Ryan controlled a number of currency exchanges in Illinois. He also owned quite a few horses, doing business as Shamrock Hill Farm. Ryan had borrowed $655,000 from European American Bank to run this business. One of the currency exchanges, Bonded Financial Services, put $200,000 at Ryan's disposal in January 1983. Bonded sent the Bank a check payable to the Bank's order on January 21 with a note directing the Bank to "deposit this check into Mike [Ryan]'s account." The Bank did this. On January 31 Ryan instructed the Bank to debit the account $200,000 in order to reduce the outstanding balance of the Shamrock loan. The Bank did this. Ryan paid off the loan in two more installments, on February 11 and 14, 1983. The Bank released its security interest in the horses.

The currency exchanges and Ryan paid visits to the judicial system. Bonded filed a petition in bankruptcy on February 10, 1983, along with about 65 other entities that Ryan controlled. Creditors later filed involuntary proceedings against Ryan. Ryan was convicted of mail fraud on account of his irregular administration of the currency exchanges (Bonded was not, for starters) and is in prison. The transfer of $200,000 out of Bonded on January 21, 1983, was a fraudulent conveyance, see § 548(a), and the trustee may recover for the benefit of creditors the value of such a conveyance. The trustee seeks to recover from the Bank, which unlike Ryan is solvent.

The right of recovery depends on § 550 * * *. Bonded's trustee contends in this adversary proceeding that the Bank is the "initial transferee" under § 550(a)(1) because it was the payee of the check it received on January 21; that the Bank is in any event the "entity for whose benefit such transfer was made" because Ryan intended to pay off the loan when he caused Bonded to write the check; that if the Bank is a subsequent transferee under § 550(a)(2) it did not give "value" under § 550(b)(1) because Bonded received nothing; and that the Bank loses even if it gave value because it should have known that something was amiss, given the substantial sum Bonded was transferring to a corporate officer. The bankruptcy court granted summary judgment to the Bank without explicitly discussing § 550. The district court affirmed on appeal under 28 U.S.C. § 158(a). It held that the Bank handled the check of January 21 as a "mere conduit" and so was not the initial transferee; that Ryan was the person "for whose benefit the transfer was made" because he got the benefit of the reduction in the balance of the loan; that the Bank's giving value to Ryan satisfied § 550(b)(1); and that because the trustee presented no evidence that the Bank knew or should have known of Bonded's impending collapse, the Bank took in good faith. * * *

I

If the note accompanying Bonded's check had said: "use this check to reduce Ryan's loan" instead of "deposit this check into [Ryan]'s account", § 550(a)(1) would provide a ready answer. The Bank would be the "initial transferee" and Ryan would be the "entity for whose benefit [the] transfer was made". The trustee could recover the $200,000 from the Bank, Ryan, or both, subject to the rule of [§ 550(d)] that there may be but one recovery. The trustee contends that the apparently formal difference—depositing the check in Ryan's account and then debiting that account—should not affect the outcome. In either case the Bank is the payee of the check and ends up with the money, while Ryan gets the horses free of liens and Bonded is left holding the bag. From a larger perspective, however, the two cases are different.

Fraudulent conveyance law protects creditors from last-minute diminutions of the pool of assets in which they have interests. They accordingly need not monitor debtors so closely, and the savings in monitoring costs make businesses more productive. See Douglas G. Baird & Thomas H. Jackson, *Fraudulent Conveyance Law and its Proper Domain*, 38 Vand. L. Rev. 829 (1985); Robert Charles Clark, *The Duties of the Corporate Debtor to its Creditors*, 90 Harv. L. Rev. 505, 554–60 (1977). The original rule, in 13 Eliz. ch. 5 (1571), dealt with debtors who transferred property to their relatives, while the debtors themselves sought sanctuary from creditors. The family enjoyed the value of the assets, which the debtor might reclaim if the creditors stopped pursuing him. In the last 400 years the principle has been generalized to address transfers without either sufficient consideration or bad intent, for they, no less than gifts, reduce the value of the debtor's estate and thus the net return to creditors as a group.[1] The trustee

[1] The fraudulent conveyance must be distinguished from a preferential transfer to a creditor, which does not diminish the total payoff for the group, but which may be undone to reduce the incentive individual creditors have to rush to dismember the debtor before rival creditors can do so. The collective bankruptcy proceeding solves

reverses, for the benefit of all creditors, un- or under-compensated conveyances within a specified period before the bankruptcy.

There have always been limits on the pursuit of transfers. If the recipient of a fraudulent conveyance uses the money to buy a Rolls Royce, the auto dealer need not return the money to the bankrupt even if the trustee can identify the serial numbers on the bills. The misfortune of the firm's creditors is not a good reason to mulct the dealer, who gave value for the money and was in no position to monitor the debtor. Some monitoring is both inevitable and desirable, and the creditors are in a better position to carry out this task than are auto dealers and the many others with whom the firm's transferees may deal. The considerations behind the holder in due course rule for commercial paper, Uniform Commercial Code § 3–302, and the bona fide purchaser rule for chattels, UCC § 2–403(1)—the waste that would be created if people either had to inquire how their transferors obtained their property or to accept a risk that a commercial deal would be reversed for no reason they could perceive at the time—also apply to subsequent holders of assets fraudulently conveyed out of bankrupts. Just as the holder in due course rule requires the transferor of commercial paper to bear the risk and burden of inquiry, increasing the liquidity of paper, so § 550(b) leaves with the initial transferee the burden of inquiry and the risk if the conveyance is fraudulent. The initial transferee is the best monitor; subsequent transferees usually do not know where the assets came from and would be ineffectual monitors if they did.

The potential costs of monitoring and residual risk are evident when the transferees include banks and other financial intermediaries. The check-clearing system processes more than 100 million instruments every day; most pass through several banks as part of the collection process; each bank may be an owner of the instrument or agent for purposes of collecting at a given moment. Some of these instruments represent funds fraudulently conveyed out of bankrupts, yet the cost of checking back on the earlier transferors would be staggering. Bonded's trustee dismisses financial intermediaries on the ground that they obviously are not initial transferees, but this is not so clear. Hundreds of thousands of wire transfers occur every day. The sender of money on a wire transfer tells its bank to send instructions to the Federal Reserve System (for a Fedwire transfer) or to a correspondent bank to make money or credit available through still another bank. The Fed or the receiving bank could be called the "initial transferee" of the funds if

---

the common pool problem, which otherwise may produce a reduction in the value of the productive assets taken jointly.

we disregarded the function of fraudulent conveyance law. Similarly, an armored car company might be called the "initial transferee" if the bankrupt gave it valuables or specie to carry. Exposing financial intermediaries and couriers to the risk of disgorging a "fraudulent conveyance" in such circumstances would lead them to take precautions, the costs of which would fall on solvent customers without significantly increasing the protection of creditors.

The functions of fraudulent conveyance law lead us to conclude that the Bank was not the "initial transferee" of Bonded's check even though it was the payee. The Bank acted as a financial intermediary. It received no benefit. Ryan's loan was fully secured and not in arrears, so the Bank did not even acquire a valuable right to offset its loan against the funds in Ryan's account. Under the law of contracts, the Bank had to follow the instructions that came with the check. The Uniform Commercial Code treats such instructions as binding to the extent any contract binds (see UCC § 3–119). The Bank therefore was no different from a courier or an intermediary on a wire transfer; it held the check only for the purpose of fulfilling an instruction to make the funds available to someone else.

Although the Bankruptcy Code does not define "transferee", and there is no legislative history on the point, we think the minimum requirement of status as a "transferee" is dominion over the money or other asset, the right to put the money to one's own purposes. When A gives a check to B as agent for C, then C is the "initial transferee"; the agent may be disregarded. This perspective had impressive support under the 1898 Code and has been employed under the 1978 Code as well.

As the Bank saw the transaction on January 21, it was Ryan's agent for the purpose of collecting a check from Bonded's bank. Cf. UCC § 4–201(1) (giving a collecting bank a presumption of agency status unless "a contrary intent clearly appears"). It received nothing from Bonded that it could call its own; the Bank was not Bonded's creditor, and Ryan owed the Bank as much as ever. The Bank had no dominion over the $200,000 until January 31, when Ryan instructed the Bank to debit the account to reduce the loan; in the interim, so far as the Bank was concerned, Ryan was free to invest the whole $200,000 in lottery tickets or uranium stocks. As the Bank saw things on January 31, it was getting Ryan's money. It would be at risk if Ryan were defrauding his other creditors or preferring the Bank, but the Bank would perceive no reason to investigate Bonded or sequester the money for the benefit of Bonded's creditors. So the two-step transaction is indeed different from the one-step transaction we hypothesized at the beginning of this discussion.

We are aware that some courts say that an agent (or a bank in a case like ours) is an "initial transferee" but that courts may excuse the transferee from repaying using equitable powers. This is misleading. "Transferee" is not a self-defining term; it must mean something different from "possessor" or "holder" or "agent". To treat "transferee" as "anyone who touches the money" and then to escape the absurd results that follow is to introduce useless steps; we slice these off with Occam's Razor and leave a more functional rule.

There is a related, and more nettlesome, question about the use of equitable powers under § 550(a). Genuine transferees can be caught in a time warp as a result of the special treatment of inside guarantors. Suppose Firm borrows money from Lender, with Guarantor as surety. When Firm pays off the debt, Lender is the "initial transferee" and Guarantor is an "entity for whose benefit [the] transfer was made". The payment of a debt benefits the guarantor. Each may have received a preference voidable under § 547 (and therefore recoverable under § 550). If Guarantor is a stranger to Firm, the trustee may recover only preferences within 90 days of the petition. § 547(b)(4)(A). If Guarantor is an "insider" at the time of the transfer, the preference period lasts a year. § 547(b)(4)(B). Section 547(b)(4) distinguishes according to the status of Guarantor, but § 550 does not. It says that if a transfer is recoverable by the trustee, it may be recovered from *either* the "initial transferee" (Lender) or the "entity for whose benefit such transfer was made" (Guarantor). This creates a situation that several courts have perceived to be "inequitable": Lender must satisfy the trustee (if Firm goes bankrupt between 91 days and a year after the preference) when Guarantor is an insider, but not when Guarantor is a stranger, yet, it seems, this has nothing to do with any proper theory of Lender's liability. Most bankruptcy courts that have addressed this question conclude that "equity" will relieve Lender from a literal construction of § 550. Commentators, whose articles collect and discuss the cases, are divided. We have serious doubts both about the amount of equity in Lender's position (for Firm may have paid Lender preferentially only to assist Guarantor, the insider, and Lender is in a good position to monitor the performance of its debtor; if Firm collects from Lender, Lender may collect in turn from Guarantor, bearing the risk of Firm's insolvency it planned to bear all along) and about the propriety of judges' declining to enforce statutes that produce inequitable results. Bankruptcy statutes are not special cases. We mention the problem not to resolve it (for it is not before us) but to show that this appeal to "equity"—to deny recovery against an "initial transferee" within the statute—is different in source and scope from the way in which we have employed considerations of policy to *define* "transferee" under § 550(a)(1). Doubts about this use of equity do not imply that courts should take "transferee" for all it could be worth rather than for what a sensible policy implies it is worth.

II

If the Bank is not the "initial transferee", the trustee insists, it is at least the "entity for whose benefit such transfer was made". The Bank ultimately was paid and therefore, one might think, it got the "benefit" of the transfer—though the Bank cancelled the note and gave up a security interest in horses that, the trustee concedes, was sufficient to cover the balance. Kenneth Kortas, Bonded's day-to-day manager, filed an affidavit stating that he prepared the check in question at Ryan's request as part of Ryan's program "to put the horse business in a position where it could function and sustain itself for at least several months even if his other business ventures ran into financial difficulty. * * * At the request of Ryan, I routinely prepared checks payable to banks where Ryan had personal accounts and loan accounts to finance his horse business." This may show that Ryan intended all along to wash the $200,000 through his personal account and pay the Bank; at a minimum, the argument would run, questions of intent prevent summary judgment.

The Bank responds that *it* did not "intend" to be the beneficiary of the transfer; it was not in cahoots with Ryan or Bonded and did not know of their plans. Moreover, the Bank insists that it did not receive a "benefit" because it gave value for the $200,000. The only beneficiary on this view was Ryan, who increased his equity position in Shamrock Hill Farm and obtained clear title to the horses. As both initial transferee and ultimate beneficiary, Ryan is the only person covered by § 550(a)(1), the Bank insists. The distinction is important, because entities covered by § 550(a)(1) cannot use the value-and-good-faith defense provided by § 550(b).

This exchange seems to raise difficult questions. To what extent does "intent" matter under § 550(a)(1)? If intent matters, whose? To what extent must courts find the true economic benefits of a transaction? If the Bank were undersecured, would the transfer make the Bank the beneficiary by the amount of the difference between the loan and the security? Suppose Ryan planned to, and did, buy a Rolls Royce with the money; would the dealer be the beneficiary by the difference between the wholesale and retail price of the car? How are bankruptcy courts to determine "intent" and compute the benefit in transactions of this nature?

These questions need not be answered, because a subsequent transferee cannot be the "entity for whose benefit" the initial transfer was made. The structure of the statute separates initial transferees and beneficiaries, on the one hand, from "immediate or mediate transferee[s]", on the other. The implication is that the "entity for whose benefit" is different from a transferee, "immediate" or otherwise. The paradigm "entity for whose benefit such transfer was made" is a guarantor or debtor—someone who receives the benefit but not the money. In the Firm–Guarantor–Lender example at the end of Part I, when Firm pays the loan, Lender is the initial transferee and Guarantor, which no longer is exposed to liability, is the "entity for whose benefit". If Bonded had sent a check to the Bank with instructions to reduce Ryan's loan, the Bank would have been the initial transferee and Ryan the "entity for whose benefit". Section 550(a)(1) recognizes that debtors often pay money to A for the benefit of B; that B may indeed have arranged for the payment (likely so if B is an insider of the payor); that but for the payment B may have had to make good on the guarantee or pay off his own debt; and accordingly that B should be treated the same way initial recipients are treated. If B gave value to the bankrupt for the benefit, B will receive credit in the bankruptcy, see § 547(c)(1)(A), § 548(c), and if not, B should be subject to recovery to the same extent as A—sometimes ahead of A, although § 550 does not make this distinction. Someone who receives the money later on is not an "entity for whose benefit such transfer was made"; only a person who receives a benefit from the initial transfer is within this language.

The legislative history of § 550(a) might show that a transferee also could be an "entity for whose benefit"—but it does not. There is no legislative history concerning the "entity for whose benefit" language and little legislative history for the rest of § 550. The section was extensively revised after the bill had been reported by the committees in both houses of Congress. Senator DiConcini and Representative Edwards read into the Congressional Record identical statements about the effect of the amendment, 124 Cong. Rec. 32400 (1978) (Edwards), 124 Cong. Rec. 34000 (DiConcini):

> Section 550(a)(1) of the House amendment has been modified in order to permit recovery from an entity for whose benefit an avoided transfer is made in addition to a recovery from the initial transferee of the transfer. Section [550(d)]

> would still apply, and the trustee is entitled only to a single satisfaction. The liability of a transferee under § 550(a) applies only "to the extent that a transfer is avoided." This means that liability is not imposed on a transferee to the extent that a transferee is protected under a provision such as § 548(c) which grants a good faith transferee for value of a transfer that is avoided only as a fraudulent transfer, a lien on the property transferred to the extent of value given.

This is the only discussion of the enacted version of § 550(a) in the legislative history of the 1978 Code, and it does not address the problems our case presents. We are left with the inference from structure: § 550 distinguishes transferees (those who receive the money or other property) from entities that get a benefit because someone else received the money or property.

To say that the categories "transferee" and "entity for whose benefit such transfer was made" are mutually exclusive does not necessarily make it easy to determine in which category a given entity falls. The method we employed in Part I of this opinion to decide that the Bank was not an "initial" transferee governs the question whether entities are subsequent transferees, too. The answer is not difficult in this case, however. The Bank did not obtain a benefit from the transfer to Ryan on January 21; it obtained dominion over the funds on January 31. The Bank is a transferee.

III

A trustee may not recover from a subsequent transferee who "takes for value, including satisfaction * * * of a present or antecedent debt, in good faith, and without knowledge of the voidability of the transfer avoided," § 550(b)(1). The Bank took for value on January 31. It had extended $655,000 in credit to Ryan, and the payment satisfied $200,000 of this debt; the Bank also released a share of its security interest. Bonded's trustee contends, however, that a subsequent transferee must give value to the debtor; the Bank gave value only to Ryan.

The statute does not say "value to the debtor"; it says "value." A natural reading looks to what the transferee gave up rather than what the debtor received. Other portions of the Code require value to the debtor. Section 548(c), for example, gives the initial recipient of a fraudulent conveyance a lien against any assets it hands back, "to the extent that such transferee * * * gave value to the debtor in exchange for such transfer." The difference between "value" in § 550(b)(1) and "value to the debtor" in § 548(c) makes sense. Section 550(b)(1) implements a system well known in commercial law, in which a transferee of commercial paper or chattels acquires an interest to the extent he purchased the items without knowledge of a defect in the chain. These recipients receive protection because monitoring of earlier stages is impractical, and exposing them to risk on account of earlier delicts would make commerce harder to conduct. Benefits to the commercial economy, and not to the initial transferors (who may be victims of fraud), justify this approach.

Transferees and other purchasers generally deal only with the previous person in line; they give value, if at all, to their transferors (or the transferors' designees). The statute emulates the pattern of other rules protecting good faith purchasers. All of the courts that have considered this question have held or implied that value to the transferor is sufficient. We agree with these cases. * * *

IV

The final question is whether the Bank received the $200,000 "in good faith, and without knowledge of the voidability of the transfer avoided." The trustee does not contend that the Bank knew of Bonded's precarious condition or Ryan's plan to use Bonded's money to pay his personal debts. He does not say that the Bank acted in bad faith—or even that there is a difference between "good faith" and "without knowledge of the voidability of the transfer." See Lawrence P. King, 4 *Collier on Bankruptcy* ¶ 550.03[1] p. 550–10 (15th ed. 1987) (treating the two as redundant). (We need not decide whether there is a difference.) And the trustee does not try to show that this transaction satisfies the test suggested by the legislative history of § 550(b)(1):

> The phrase "good faith" in [§ 550(b)] is intended to prevent a transferee from whom the trustee could recover from transferring the recoverable property to an innocent transferee, and receiving a retransfer from him, that is, "washing" the transaction through an innocent third party. In order for the transferee to be excepted from liability * * * he himself must be a good faith transferee.

H.R. Rep. No. 95–595 at 376, *reprinted in* 1978 U.S.C.C.A.N. at 6332; S. Rep. No. 95–989 at 90, *reprinted in* 1978 U.S.C.C.A.N. at 5876. The trustee contends, instead, that the Bank should have known about Bonded's distress and Ryan's chicanery; had it investigated the deposit on January 21, it would have found out; and because it should have known, this is as good as knowledge.

Imputed knowledge is an old idea, employed even in the criminal law. Venerable authority has it that the recipient of a voidable transfer may lack good faith if he possessed enough knowledge of the events to induce a reasonable person to investigate. No one supposes that "knowledge of voidability" means complete understanding of the facts and receipt of a lawyer's opinion that such a transfer is voidable; some lesser knowledge will do. Some facts strongly suggest the presence of others; a recipient that closes its eyes to the remaining facts may not deny knowledge. But this is not the same as a duty to investigate, to be a monitor for creditors' benefit when nothing known so far suggests that there is a fraudulent conveyance in the chain. "Knowledge" is a stronger term than "notice." A transferee that lacks the information necessary to support an inference of knowledge need not start investigating on his own.

Nothing in the record of this case suggests that the Bank knew of Bonded's financial peril or Ryan's plan. Bonded was not the Bank's customer. The transfer from Ryan to the Bank on January 31 was innocuous. The Bank thought it got Ryan's money; its loan was fully secured; it perceived Ryan as a well-heeled horse breeder, with a balance sheet in the millions, current on his loan payments.

The transfer from Bonded to Ryan on January 21 was only slightly more problematic from the Bank's perspective. A corporation was transferring $200,000 to one of its executives. This does not hint at a fraudulent conveyance by a firm on the brink of insolvency; for all the Bank knew, Bonded had plenty more where the $200,000 came from. Banks frequently receive large checks from corporations to their officers; think of the annual bonus checks General Motors issues, or the check to repurchase a bloc of shares. A $200,000 check is not a plausible bonus for a currency exchange, however. It could hint at embezzlement. Several Illinois cases say that a bank should inquire when a firm's employee signs a large check with himself as payee.

Since those cases were decided, Illinois adopted the Uniform Fiduciaries Act, which relieves banks of such a duty to inquire into the authority of the fiduciary signing the check on the maker's behalf. At all events, the Bank had no reason to think Ryan an embezzler. The check was accompanied by a memorandum from Kenneth Kortas, Bonded's manager, demonstrating that Ryan was not keeping other corporate officers in the dark. The Kortas memorandum would have led a reasonable bank to conclude that Bonded as a corporate entity wanted to make the transfer—and a bank drawing that inference here would have been right. Had the Bank called Kortas (or anyone else at Bonded) to inquire about the check, the Bank would have learned that the instrument was authorized by the appropriate corporate officials. Since the inquiry would have turned up nothing pertinent to voidability, the Bank's failure to make it does not permit a court to attribute to it the necessary knowledge.

The Bank is a subsequent transferee covered by § 550(b)(1). It took for value and without knowledge of the voidability of the initial transaction.

AFFIRMED.

Notes and Questions

1. This case would have turned out differently, according to the court, if the note accompanying Bonded's check had said "use this check to reduce Ryan's loan" instead of "deposit this check into [Ryan]'s account." Did the court promote form over substance, despite its protestation to the contrary? If not, what is the substantive difference between the two? Does the court's conclusion give bad actors like Michael Ryan too much flexibility to structure transfers so that they cannot be avoided even though designed to defraud creditors?

2. Was the court so influenced by the "functions of fraudulent conveyance law" that it disregarded the plain meaning of the statute?

3. *Bonded Financial*'s "dominion and control" test for determining whether an entity is an "initial transferee" under § 550 has been widely adopted. See *Bowers v. Atlanta Motor Speedway, Inc. (In re Southeast Hotel Properties Ltd. Partnership)*, 99 F.3d 151 (4th Cir.1996).

4. In *Bonded Financial*, Judge Easterbrook anticipated a fact pattern in which Firm pays all or part of its debt to Lender more than 90 days but less than a year before filing bankruptcy. If the debt is guaranteed by a noninsider, the payment is not recoverable. If Guarantor is an insider, however, Lender remains the "initial transferee" under § 550(a), but Guarantor is an "entity for whose benefit [the] transfer was made." That may allow recovery from Lender.

That very fact pattern came before Judge Easterbrook the next year in *Levit v. Ingersoll Rand Financial Corp.*, 874 F.2d 1186 (7th Cir.1989) (which is often referred to as the *Deprizio* case). In that case, V.N. Deprizio Construction Co. had borrowed money from a number of lenders, including

Ingersoll Rand Financial. The loans were guaranteed by the Deprizio brothers, all of whom were insiders of the corporation. After the corporation filed bankruptcy, the trustee sought to recover from the lenders, as preferences, payments made in the year before the filing, including those made more than 90 days previously.

The court held the payments recoverable, using reasoning based on a multitude of Code sections. An "insider" (§ 101(21)(B)(ii)) Guarantor has a "claim" (§ 101(5)(A)), because he has a contingent right of payment, and is therefore a "creditor" of the debtor Firm (§ 101(10)). Every payment made by Firm to Lender is a "transfer" (§ 101(54)) that is "for the benefit of a creditor" (§ 547(b)(1)), Guarantor, because it reduces the amount Guarantor might be called upon to pay in the event of Firm's default. That makes the transfer avoidable under § 547(b)(4)(B). Once a transfer is found avoidable under § 547, § 550 determines from whom recovery can be obtained. Section 547 distinguishes insiders from noninsiders, but § 550 does not. It permits recovery from either the "initial transferee," Lender, or from the "entity for whose benefit such transfer was made," Guarantor. Thus, Lender may be required to repay the preferential transfer even though it is not an insider.

Levit caused a substantial negative reaction in the lending community, which saw itself made *more* vulnerable in its borrowers' bankruptcies, due to the presence of guarantors, rather than less. Congress responded by passing § 550(c), which provides that, in fact patterns like *Levit*, the trustee may not recover from the non-insider.

The game is not up, however. Consider a case in which a creditor perfects a security interest long enough after attachment that the perfection constitutes a preference, and that perfection occurs less than a year, but more than 90 days, before the debtor files bankruptcy. That fact pattern arose in *Roost v. Associates Home Equity Services, Inc. (In re Williams)*, 234 B.R. 801 (Bankr. D.Ore.1999). In that case, the trustee argued that § 550(c) was inapplicable because no "recovery" was necessary. The court agreed, holding that when

> the property is already property of the estate pursuant to § 541 and the property has not been transferred to the creditor or some other third party prior to the filing of the bankruptcy, the trustee has no need for "recovery". In such a case, where the trustee seeks merely to avoid a security interest, the security interest is avoided and automatically preserved for the benefit of the estate pursuant to § 551.

Id. at 805.

5. In *Bonded Financial*, the Seventh Circuit talked about the "common pool" problem. Recall the description of it, from Thomas H. Jackson's book, The Logic and Limits of Bankruptcy Law (1986), set out in Chapter 2, Section A of this casebook.

KELLOGG v. BLUE QUAIL ENERGY, INC. (MATTER OF COMPTON CORP.)

United States Court of Appeals, Fifth Circuit, 1987.
831 F.2d 586.

JERRE S. WILLIAMS, Circuit Judge.

This is a bankruptcy preference case in which a bankruptcy trustee seeks to recover a transfer made via a letter of credit for the benefit of one of the debtor's unsecured creditors on the eve of bankruptcy. The bankruptcy court and the district court found there to be no voidable preference. We reverse.

I. FACTUAL BACKGROUND

In March 1982, Blue Quail Energy, Inc., delivered a shipment of oil to debtor Compton Corporation. Payment of $585,443.85 for this shipment of oil was due on or about April 20, 1982. Compton failed to make timely payment. Compton induced Abilene National Bank (now MBank–Abilene) to issue an irrevocable standby letter of credit in Blue Quail's favor on May 6, 1982. Under the terms of the letter of credit, payment of up to $585,443.85 was due Blue Quail if Compton failed to pay Blue Quail this amount by June 22, 1982. Compton paid MBank $1,463.61 to issue the letter of credit. MBank also received a promissory note payable on demand for $585,443.85. MBank did not need a security agreement to cover the letter of credit transaction because a prior 1980 security agreement between the bank and Compton had a future advances provision.[1] This 1980 security agreement had been perfected as to a variety of Compton's assets through the filing of several financing statements. The most recent financing statement had been filed a year before, May 7, 1981. The letter of credit on its face noted that it was for an antecedent debt due Blue Quail.

On May 7, 1982, the day after MBank issued the letter of credit in Blue Quail's favor, several of Compton's creditors filed an involuntary bankruptcy petition against Compton. On June 22, 1982, MBank paid Blue Quail $569,932.03 on the letter of credit after Compton failed to pay Blue Quail.

---

[1] A future advances clause in a security agreement subjects the specified collateral to any future loan made by the creditor in addition to the current loans.

In the ensuing bankruptcy proceeding, MBank's aggregate secured claims against Compton, including the letter of credit payment to Blue Quail, were paid in full from the liquidation of Compton's assets which served as the bank's collateral. Walter Kellogg, bankruptcy trustee for Compton, did not contest the validity of MBank's secured claim against Compton's assets for the amount drawn under the letter of credit by Blue Quail. Instead, on June 14, 1983, trustee Kellogg filed a complaint in the bankruptcy court against Blue Quail asserting that Blue Quail had received a preferential transfer under § 547 through the letter of credit transaction. The trustee sought to recover $585,443.85 from Blue Quail pursuant to § 550.

Blue Quail answered and filed a third party complaint against MBank. On June 16, 1986, Blue Quail filed a motion for summary judgment asserting that the trustee could not recover any preference from Blue Quail because Blue Quail had been paid from MBank's funds under the letter of credit and therefore had not received any of Compton's property. On August 27, 1986, the bankruptcy court granted Blue Quail's motion, agreeing that the payment under the letter of credit did not constitute a transfer of debtor Compton's property but rather was a transfer of the bank's property. The bankruptcy court entered judgment on the motion on September 10, 1986. Trustee Kellogg appealed this decision to the district court. On December 11, 1986, the district court affirmed the bankruptcy court ruling, holding that the trustee did not establish two necessary elements of a voidable transfer under § 547. The district court agreed with Blue Quail and the bankruptcy court that the trustee could not establish that the funds transferred to Blue Quail were ever property of Compton. Furthermore, the district court held that the transfer of the increased security interest to MBank was a transfer of the debtor's property for the sole benefit of the bank and in no way benefitted Blue Quail. The district court therefore found no voidable preference as to Blue Quail. The trustee is appealing the decision to this Court.

II. THE LETTER OF CREDIT

It is well established that a letter of credit and the proceeds therefrom are not property of the debtor's estate under § 541. When the issuer honors a proper draft under a letter of credit, it does so from its own assets and not from the assets of its customer who caused the letter of credit to be issued. As a result, a bankruptcy trustee is not entitled to enjoin a post petition payment of funds under a letter of credit from the issuer to the beneficiary, because such a payment is not a transfer of debtor's property (a threshold requirement under § 547(b)). A case apparently holding otherwise, *In re Twist Cap, Inc.*, 1 B.R. 284 (Bankr. D.Fla.1979), has been roundly criticized and otherwise ignored by courts and commentators alike.

Recognizing these characteristics of a letter of credit in a bankruptcy case is necessary in order to maintain the independence principle, the cornerstone of letter of credit law. Under the independence principle, an issuer's obligation to the letter of credit's beneficiary is independent from any obligation between the beneficiary and the issuer's customer. All a beneficiary has to do to receive payment under a letter of credit is to show that it has performed all the duties required by the letter of credit. Any disputes between the beneficiary and the customer do not affect the issuer's obligation to the beneficiary to pay under the letter of credit.

Letters of credit are most commonly arranged by a party who benefits from the provision of goods or services. The party will request a bank to issue a letter of credit which names the provider of the goods or services as the beneficiary. Under a standby letter of credit, the bank becomes primarily liable to the beneficiary upon the default of the bank's customer to pay for the goods or services. The bank charges a fee to issue a letter of credit and to undertake this liability. The shifting of liability to the bank rather than to the services or goods provider is the main purpose of the letter of credit. After all, the bank is in a much better position to assess the risk of its customer's insolvency than is the service or goods provider. It should be noted, however, that it is the risk of the debtor's insolvency and not the risk of a preference attack that a bank assumes under a letter of credit transaction. Overall, the independence principle is necessary to insure "the certainty of payments for services or goods rendered regardless of any intervening misfortune which may befall the other contracting party." *In re North Shore & Central Ill. Freight Co.*, 30 B.R. 377, 378 (Bankr. N.D.Ill.1983).

The trustee in this case accepts this analysis and does not ask us to upset it. The trustee is not attempting to set aside the post petition payments by MBank to Blue Quail under the letter of credit as a preference; nor does the trustee claim the letter of credit itself constitutes debtor's property. The trustee is instead challenging the earlier transfer in which Compton granted MBank an increased security interest in its assets to obtain the letter of credit for the benefit of Blue Quail. Collateral which has been pledged by a debtor as security for a letter of credit is property of the debtor's estate. The trustee claims that the direct transfer to MBank of the increased security interest on May 6, 1982, also constituted an indirect transfer to Blue Quail which occurred one day prior to the filing of the involuntary bankruptcy petition and is voidable as a preference under § 547. This assertion of a preferential transfer is evaluated in Parts III and IV of this opinion.

It is important to note that the irrevocable standby letter of credit in the case at bar was not arranged in connection with Blue Quail's initial decision to sell oil to Compton on credit. Compton arranged for the letter of credit after Blue Quail had shipped the oil and after Compton had defaulted in payment. The letter of credit in this case did not serve its usual function of backing up a contemporaneous credit decision, but instead served as a back up payment guarantee on an extension of credit already in jeopardy. The letter of credit was issued to pay off an antecedent unsecured debt. This fact was clearly noted on the face of the letter of credit. Blue Quail, the beneficiary of the letter of credit, did not give new value for the issuance of the letter of credit by MBank on May 6, 1982, or for the resulting increased security interest held by MBank. MBank, however, did give new value for the increased security interest it obtained in Compton's collateral: the bank issued the letter of credit.

When a debtor pledges its assets to secure a letter of credit, a transfer of debtor's property has occurred under the provisions of § 547. By subjecting its assets to MBank's reimbursement claim in the event MBank had to pay on the letter of credit, Compton made a transfer of its property. The broad definition of "transfer" under [§ 101(54)] is clearly designed to cover such a transfer. Overall, the letter of credit itself and the payments thereunder may not be property of debtor, but the collateral pledged as a security interest for the letter of credit is.

Furthermore, in a secured letter of credit transaction, the transfer of debtor's property takes place at the time the letter of credit is issued (when the security interest is granted) and received by the beneficiary, not at the time the issuer pays on the letter of credit.

The transfer to MBank of the increased security interest was a direct transfer which occurred on May 6, 1982, when the bank issued the letter of credit. Under § 547(e)(2)(A), however, such a transfer is deemed to have taken place for purposes of § 547 at the time such transfer "takes effect" between the transferor and transferee if such transfer is perfected within 10 days. The phrase "takes effect" is undefined in the Bankruptcy Code, but under Uniform Commercial Code Article 9 law, a transfer of a security interest "takes effect" when the security interest attaches. Because of the future advances clause in MBank's 1980 security agreement with Compton, the attachment of the

MBank's security interest relates back to May 9, 1980, the date the security agreement went into effect. The bottom line is that the direct transfer of the increased security interest to MBank is artifically [sic] deemed to have occurred at least by May 7, 1981, the date MBank filed its final financing statement, for purposes of a preference attack against the bank. This date is well before the 90 day window of § 547-(b)(4)(A). This would protect the bank from a preference attack by the trustee even if the bank had not given new value at the time it received the increased security interest. MBank is therefore protected from a preference attack by the trustee for the increased security interest transfer under either of two theories: under § 547(c)(1) because it gave new value and under the operation of the relation back provision of § 547-(e)(2)(A). The bank is also protected from any claims of reimbursement by Blue Quail because the bank received no voidable preference.

The relation back provision of § 547(e)(2)(A), however, applies only to the direct transfer of the increased security interest to MBank. The indirect transfer to Blue Quail that allegedly resulted from the direct transfer to MBank occurred on May 6, 1982, the date of issuance of the letter of credit. The relation back principle of § 547(e)(2)(A) does not apply to this indirect transfer to Blue Quail. Blue Quail was not a party to the security agreement between MBank and Compton. So it will not be able to utilize the relation back provision if it is deemed to have received an indirect transfer resulting from the direct transfer of the increased security interest to MBank. Blue Quail, therefore, cannot assert either of the two defenses to a preference attack which MBank can claim. Blue Quail did not give new value under § 547(c)(1), and it received a transfer within 90 days of the filing of Compton's bankruptcy petition.

III. DIRECT/INDIRECT TRANSFER DOCTRINE

The federal courts have long recognized that "[t]o constitute a preference, it is not necessary that the transfer be made directly to the creditor." *National Bank of Newport v. National Herkimer County Bank*, 225 U.S. 178, 184 (1912). "If the bankrupt has made a transfer of his property, the *effect* of which is to enable one of his creditors to obtain a greater percentage of his debt than another creditor of the same class, circuity of arrangement will not avail to save it." *Id.* (Emphasis added.) To combat such circuity, the courts have broken down certain transfers into two transfers, one direct and one indirect. The direct transfer to the third party may be valid and not subject to a preference attack. The indirect transfer, arising from the same action by the debtor, however, may constitute a voidable preference as to the creditor who indirectly benefitted from the direct transfer to the third party.

This is the situation presented in the case before us. The term "transfer" as used in the various bankruptcy statutes through the years has always been broad enough to cover such indirect transfers and to catch various circuitous arrangements. The new Bankruptcy Code implicitly adopts this doctrine through its broad definition of "transfer." Examining the case law that has developed since the *National Bank of Newport* case yields an understanding of what types of transfers the direct/indirect doctrine is meant to cover.

In *Palmer v. Radio Corporation of America*, 453 F.2d 1133 (5th Cir.1971), a third party purchased from the debtor a television station for $40,000 cash and the assumption of certain liabilities of the debtor, including unsecured claims by creditor RCA. This Court found the direct transfer from the debtor to the third party purchaser constituted an indirect preferential transfer to creditor RCA. We found that the assumption by the third party purchaser of the debt owed by the debtor to RCA and the subsequent payments made thereunder constituted a voidable transfer as to RCA. The court noted that such indirect transfers as this had long been held to constitute voidable preferences under bankruptcy laws.

Although the *Palmer* court did not elaborate its reasoning behind this holding, such reasoning is self evident. A secured creditor was essentially substituted for an unsecured creditor through the transfer of the television station to the third party purchaser and the assumption of the unsecured debt by the purchaser. The third party purchaser was in effect secured because it had the television station. Creditor RCA would receive payments directly from the solvent third party without having to worry about its original debtor's financial condition. The original debtor's other unsecured creditors were harmed because a valuable asset of the debtor, the television station, was removed from the debtor's estate. The end result of the *Palmer* case was that the third party's payments on the RCA debt were to be made to the debtor's estate instead of to RCA. RCA would then recover the same percentage of its unsecured claim from the estate as the other unsecured creditors.

* * *

In *Virginia National Bank v. Woodson*, 329 F.2d 836 (4th Cir.1964), the debtor had several overdrawn accounts with his bank.[8] The debtor talked his sister into paying off $8,000 of the overdrafts in exchange for an $8,000 promissory note and an assignment of some collateral as security. The debtor's sister made the $8,000 payment directly to the bank. The $8,000 technically was never part of the debtor's estate. The court, however, held that the payment of the $8,000 by the sister to the bank was a preference as to the bank to the extent of the value of the collateral held by the sister. The court noted that the measure of the value of a voidable preference is diminution of the debtor's estate and not the value of the transfer to the creditor.

In the *Woodson* case the sister was secured only to the extent the pledged collateral had value; the remainder of her loan to her brother was unsecured. Swapping one unsecured creditor for another unsecured creditor does not create any kind of preference. The court held that a preference in such a transaction arises only when a secured creditor is swapped for an unsecured creditor. Only then is the pool of assets available for distribution to the general unsecured creditors depleted because the secured creditor has priorty [sic] over the unsecured creditors. Furthermore, the court held that the bank and not the sister had received the voidable preference and had to pay back to the trustee an amount equal to the value of the collateral.

* * *

IV. The Direct/Indirect Doctrine in the Context of a Letter of Credit Transaction

The case at bar differs from the cases discussed in Part III *supra* only by the presence of the letter of credit as the mechanism for paying off the unsecured creditor. Blue Quail's attempt to otherwise distinguish the case from the direct/indirect transfer cases does not withstand scrutiny.

In the letter of credit cases discussed in Part II *supra*, the letters of credit were issued contemporaneously with the initial extension of credit by the beneficiaries of the letters. In those cases the letters of credit effectively served as security devices for the benefit of the creditor beneficiaries and took the place of formal security interests. The courts in those cases properly found there had been no voidable transfers, direct or indirect, in the letter of credit transactions involved. New

[8] Unsecured antecedent debts.

value was given contemporaneously with the issuance of the letters of credit in the form of the extensions of credit by the beneficiaries of the letters. As a result, the § 547(c)(1) preference exception was applicable.

The case at bar differs from these other letter of credit cases by one very important fact: the letter of credit in this case was issued to secure an antecedent unsecured debt due the beneficiary of the letter of credit. The unsecured creditor beneficiary gave no new value upon the issuance of the letter of credit. When the issuer paid off the letter of credit and foreclosed on the collateral securing the letter of credit, a preferential transfer had occurred. An unsecured creditor was paid in full and a secured creditor was substituted in its place.

The district court upheld the bankruptcy court in maintaining the validity of the letter of credit issued to cover the antecedent debt. The district court held that MBank, the issuer of the letter of credit, could pay off the letter of credit and foreclose on the collateral securing it. We are in full agreement. But we also look to the impact of the transaction as it affects the situation of Blue Quail in the bankrupt estate. We hold that the bankruptcy trustee can recover from Blue Quail, the beneficiary of the letter of credit, because Blue Quail received an indirect preference. This result preserves the sanctity of letter of credit and carries out the purposes of the Bankruptcy Code by avoiding a preferential transfer. MBank, the issuer of the letter of credit, being just the intermediary through which the preferential transfer was accomplished, completely falls out of the picture and is not involved in this particular legal proceeding.

MBank did not receive any preferential transfer—it gave new value for the security interest. Furthermore, because the direct and indirect transfers are separate and independent, the trustee does not even need to challenge the direct transfer of the increased security interest to MBank, or seek any relief at all from MBank, in order to attack the indirect transfer and recover under § 550 from the indirect transferee Blue Quail.

We hold that a creditor cannot secure payment of an unsecured antecedent debt through a letter of credit transaction when it could not do so through any other type of transaction. The purpose of the letter of credit transaction in this case was to secure payment of an unsecured antecedent debt for the benefit of an unsecured creditor. This is the only proper way to look at such letters of credit in the bankruptcy context. The promised transfer of pledged collateral induced the bank to issue the letter of credit in favor of the creditor. The increased security interest held by the bank clearly benefitted the creditor because the bank would not have issued the letter of credit without this security. A secured creditor was substituted for an unsecured creditor to the detriment of the other unsecured creditors.

We also hold, therefore, that the trustee can recover under § 550(a)(1) the value of the transferred property from "the entity for whose benefit such transfer was made." In the case at bar, this entity was the creditor beneficiary, not the issuer, of the letter of credit even though the issuer received the direct transfer from the debtor. The entire purpose of the direct/indirect doctrine is to look through the form of a transaction and determine which entity actually benefitted from the transfer.

The fact that there was a prior security agreement between the issuing bank and the debtor containing the future advances clause does not alter this conclusion. As we pointed out in Part II *supra*, this prior security agreement gave MBank an additional shield from preferential attack because of the relation back mechanism of § 547(e)(2)(A). Section 547(e)(2)(A), however, does not avail Blue Quail to shield it from a preferential attack for the indirect transfer. The indirect transfer to Blue Quail occurred on May 6, 1982, when the letter of credit was issued and the increased security interest was pledged. This was the day before the involuntary bankruptcy petition was filed. For purposes of § 547, a transfer of Compton's property for the benefit of Blue Quail did occur within 90 days of the bankruptcy filing. The bankruptcy and district courts erred in failing to analyze properly the transfer of debtor's property that occurred when Compton pledged its assets to obtain the letter of credit. This transfer consisted of two aspects: the direct transfer to MBank which is not a voidable preference for various reasons and the indirect transfer to Blue Quail which is a voidable preference.

All of the requirements of § 547(b) have been satisfied in the trustee's preferential attack against Blue Quail. * * * The net effect of the indirect transfer to Blue Quail was to remove $585,443.85 from the pool of assets available to Compton's unsecured creditors and substitute in its place a secured claim for the same amount.

The precise holding in this case needs to be emphasized. We do not hold that payment under a letter of credit, or even a letter of credit itself, constitute preferential transfers under § 547(b) or property of a debtor under § 541. The holding of this case fully allows the letter of credit to function. We preserve its sanctity and the underlying independence doctrine. We do not, however, allow an unsecured creditor to avoid a preference attack by utilizing a letter of credit to secure payment of an antecedent debt. Otherwise the unsecured creditor would receive an indirect preferential transfer from the granting of the security for the letter of credit to the extent of the value of that security. Our holding does not affect the strength of or the proper use of letters of credit. When a letter of credit is issued contemporaneously with a new extension of credit, the creditor beneficiary will not be subject to a preferential attack under the direct/indirect doctrine elaborated in this case because the creditor will have given new value in exchange for the indirect benefit of the secured letter of credit. Only when a creditor receives a secured letter of credit to cover an unsecured antecedent debt will it be subject to a preferential attack under § 547(b).

V. LIABILITY OF MBANK FOR THE PREFERENTIAL TRANSFER

Blue Quail has no valid claim against MBank for reimbursement for any amounts Blue Quail has to pay the trustee under the trustee's preference claim, just as the trustee has no preference challenge against MBank. Blue Quail received the preferential transfer, not MBank. MBank gave new value in exchange for the increased security interest in its favor. Thus, it is insulated from any assertion of a voidable preference. The bank in no way assumed the risk of a preference attack by issuing the letter of credit. For these reasons, we affirm the district court's dismissal of Blue Quail's request to proceed against MBank for reimbursement.

In addition, the trustee may not set aside the $1,463.61 fee Compton paid MBank to issue the letter of credit. This payment is not a preferential transfer. MBank has fully performed its duties under the terms of the letter of credit and has earned this fee. The services MBank rendered in issuing and executing the letter of credit constitute new value under the § 547(c)(1) preference exception.

VI. CONCLUSION

Blue Quail Energy received an indirect preferential transfer from Compton Corporation on May 6, 1982, one day prior to the filing of Compton's bankruptcy petition. We reverse the district court and render judgment in favor of Trustee Kellogg against Blue Quail Energy, Inc. in the amount of $585,443.85 plus interest to be fixed by the district court pursuant to §§ 547, 550. The district court's dismissal of Blue Quail's claim against MBank for reimbursement is affirmed.

Questions

1. Recall Problem # 4 following the materials on § 547(c)(5) in Section C.4 of this chapter. Does *Kellogg* suggest an argument the trustee could use in an effort to avoid the transfer under those facts?

2. Look again at *Dean v. Davis*, which appears in Section C.2 of this chapter, and Question 1 following the case. Now that you have read *Kellogg*, do you see a preference in *Dean v. Davis* despite the Supreme Court's conclusion to the contrary?

Note on Recovery From Governmental Units

As we have seen, the avoiding powers are designed to further several of bankruptcy's fundamental principles—namely, that creditors should be discouraged from "rushing in" and hastening a shaky debtor's economic demise, and that similarly situated creditors should be treated equally. States and other governmental units are often among those creditors in bankruptcy cases who have taken avoidable transfers before bankruptcy filing. They may also have violated the automatic stay with postpetition efforts to collect, in contravention of the principle that debtors should be afforded a "breathing space" through the automatic stay. Until a few years ago, trustees simply relied on § 106—a broadly-worded abrogation of sovereign immunity—to hold states accountable in such situations.

All of that began to change with *Seminole Tribe v. Florida*, 517 U.S. 44, 116 S.Ct. 1114, 134 L.Ed.2d 252 (1996). The case dealt with the Indian Gaming Regulatory Act, which permits an Indian tribe to conduct certain gaming activities within a state if the tribe and the state have first agreed on conditions governing the conduct of those activities. The Seminole Tribe sued Florida in federal court, asserting that the state failed to negotiate such an agreement in good faith. The state sought dismissal on the grounds of sovereign immunity. The Supreme Court agreed with the state, holding that Congress cannot abrogate a state's immunity under the Eleventh Amendment by enacting legislation pursuant to powers enumerated in Article I of the Constitution.

Although *Seminole* did not involve bankruptcy, the case clearly rendered § 106(a) unconstitutional when used by trustees to haul states into bankruptcy court to account for avoidable transfers or violations of the stay. The option remaining for trustees seeking to call states to account under the Bankruptcy Code was to bring suit in state court. While state courts are not as attractive to trustees as bankruptcy courts for a number of reasons, *Seminole* did not foreclose that alternative.

Then, in June of 1999, the Supreme Court decided three more sovereign immunity cases. Although none of them involved bankruptcy, their applicability is evident and they cast serious doubt on the power of trustees to demand state compliance with the mandates of the Bankruptcy Code. In *Alden v. Maine*, 527 U.S. 706, 119 S.Ct. 2240, 144 L.Ed.2d 636 (1999), the Court held that states may assert sovereign immunity as a defense to suits brought in state court to enforce legislation enacted under Article I of the Constitution. The Court held in *Florida Prepaid Postsecondary Education Expense Board v. College Savings Bank*, 527 U.S. 627, 119 S.Ct. 2199, 144 L.Ed.2d 575 (1999), that a federal statute authorizing patent infringement suits against states was unconstitutional. And, in *College Savings Bank v. Florida Prepaid Postsecondary Education Expense Board*, 527 U.S. 666, 119 S.Ct. 2219, 144 L.Ed.2d 605 (1999), the Court invalidated the doctrine of constructive waiver of sovereign immunity. Taken together, these cases leave trustees very little power to rectify abuse of the bankruptcy process by states.

All is not entirely lost, however. First, express waiver remains a viable doctrine, because the Eleventh Amendment prohibits suits against unconsenting states only. Thus, §§ 106(b) and (c) can be constitutionally applied to some counterclaims and setoffs asserted against state entities that file proofs of claim in bankruptcy cases. Second, Eleventh Amendment protection extends only to states and their instrumentalities. Other governmental units, such as local jurisdictions, are not protected. Finally, suits against state officials under the doctrine of *Ex parte Young*, 209 U.S. 123, 28 S.Ct. 441, 52 L.Ed. 714 (1908), remain a possibility. Under *Young*, a federal judge can issue a prospective injunction to enjoin continuing violations of the Bankruptcy Code. Such injunctions, however, will not be effective in recovering avoided transfers or in remedying violations of the automatic stay.

This is a rapidly changing area of law and one of considerable importance to the bankruptcy system.

E. THE "STRONG ARM" POWER

Section 544(a), which is known as the "strong arm clause," is designed primarily to permit avoidance of unrecorded security interests and mortgages. Under § 544(a)(1), the trustee has the rights of a judicial lien creditor. Those rights, as far as unrecorded security interests are concerned, are specified in Article 9 of the Uniform Commercial Code. Under UCC § 9-301(1)(b), "an unperfected security interest is subordinate to the rights of * * * a person who becomes a lien creditor before the security interest is perfected." Similarly, under § 9-317(a)(2) of Revised Article 9, "[a] security interest * * * is subordinate to the rights of * * * a person that becomes a lien creditor before the earlier of the time the security interest * * * is perfected or a financing statement covering the collateral is filed." In other words, a judicial lien creditor has priority over an unperfected security interest. The trustee, therefore, can avoid an unperfected security interest under § 544(a).

In most states, an unrecorded mortgage has priority over judicial lien creditors, but not over subsequent bona fide purchasers. Because § 544(a)(3) gives the trustee the power of a bfp, the trustee can also avoid an unrecorded mortgage under the strong arm clause.

The key to § 544(a) is the avoiding power of specified entities—judicial lien creditors, judgment lien creditors and bona fide purchasers—under state law. We hypothesize such an entity as of the moment bankruptcy is filed. The trustee has, under § 544(a), whatever avoiding power that hypothetical entity would have under state law.

Problems

1. Debtor bought residential real estate on May 1, giving Creditor a mortgage on the property to secure the purchase money loan of $120,000. Creditor failed to record its interest and Debtor filed bankruptcy on October 15. Is the mortgage avoidable under § 544(a)?

2. Does your answer to Problem # 1 change if Creditor properly recorded its interest in the real estate records on October 13?

3. Debtor obtained a loan of $20,000 on May 1, giving Creditor a security interest in Debtor's equipment. Creditor failed to file a financing statement and Debtor filed bankruptcy on October 15. Is the security interest avoidable under § 544(a)?

BELISLE v. PLUNKETT

United States Court of Appeals, Seventh Circuit, 1989.
877 F.2d 512, *cert. denied sub nom.* Belisle v. Anzivino, 493 U.S. 893, 110 S.Ct. 241, 107 L.Ed.2d 191.

EASTERBROOK, Circuit Judge.

May the trustee in a bankruptcy case bring into the estate property that the debtor holds in constructive trust for victims of fraud? Oliver Plunkett organized partnerships that provided funds to buy a 50–year leasehold interest in a shopping center, Pan–Am Pavilion in Christiansted, St. Croix, Virgin Islands. Plunkett treated the leasehold as his own—including making a collateral assignment to secure a loan of $100,000 that Plunkett put to personal use. Invoking the strong-arm powers of § 544, the Trustee claimed the status of a bona fide purchaser for value. Both the bankruptcy court and the district court held that § 544(a)(3) allows the Trustee to claim the leasehold for the estate, leaving the partners to participate as creditors. The partners contend that § 541(d) keeps the leasehold out of the estate and that the Trustee may not employ § 544(a) to fetch into the estate something that § 541(d) excludes.

Stripped of irrelevant detail, the facts are that in March 1979 Plunkett (a real estate entrepreneur operating out of Milwaukee) signed a contract, in his own name, to buy the leasehold from W.O.F. Associates for $1.2 million. Through the spring and summer of 1979 Plunkett formed five partnerships to raise the money for the acquisition. After getting the cash, Plunkett closed the deal in October 1979—in his own name, despite using partnership funds. He recorded the assignment of the leasehold in the St. Croix real estate records, again in his own name. Although Plunkett recognized the partnerships for tax purposes—he reported a share between 5% and 7%—and informed the partners of the income and deductions they should report on their own returns, he dealt with tenants and creditors as if he owned the leasehold.

Plunkett and his wife filed petitions under the Bankruptcy Code in 1982. After the Trustee asserted that the leasehold is an asset of the estate, the partners filed an adversary proceeding, seeking to quiet title in the partnerships. Chief Judge Clevert of the bankruptcy court granted the Trustee's motion for summary judgment, and the district judge affirmed on appeal * * *.

Plunkett bamboozled the partners and used for his own benefit the leasehold acquired with partnership funds. Virgin Islands law impresses a constructive trust on the leasehold and its fruits. A constructive trust ordinarily survives bankruptcy: the property may not be used to satisfy the debtor's obligations to other creditors, and the debts to the victims of the fraud may not be discharged. § 523(a)(2), (4). The Trustee acknowledges all of this but relies on § 544(a)(3) * * * . A bona fide purchaser of the leasehold interest, without notice of the earlier claim, would take ahead of a person who has not recorded his entitlement. Not only Virgin Islands real estate law, but also the Uniform Partnership Act, adopted in both the Virgin Islands and Wisconsin, provides this. So the Trustee submits that the Plunkett estate includes the Pan–Am leasehold, "as of the commencement of the case", without need for action on his part.

Not so fast!, the partners rejoin. The estate can't contain the leasehold "as of the commencement of the case" because § 541(d) says that it does not contain property in which the debtor holds bare legal title. * * * If this were not enough, the partners continue, § 544(a)(3) speaks of a "transfer," yet Plunkett did not transfer the Pan–Am leasehold, and there is therefore nothing for the Trustee to avoid. As the partners see things, §§ 541(d) and 544(a)(3) allow a trustee to recover property transferred out of the estate before the filing, but not to claim for the estate property held in a constructive trust. Several courts have perceived a "conflict" between § 541(d) and § 544(a)(3). E.g., *In re General Coffee Corp.*, 828 F.2d 699, 704–06 (11th Cir.1987); *In re Quality Holstein Leasing*, 752 F.2d 1009, 1013–14 (5th Cir.1985). The parties ask us to decide which statute prevails. We believe, however, that there is no conflict.

Section 544(a)(3) pulls into the debtor's estate property that ostensibly was there all along. Dealing with ostensible ownership is not, however, the statute's objective—at least not its only one—because the benefits are not limited to those who relied on the asset in extending credit. Section 544(a)(3) complements §§ 544(a)(1) and (2), which give the trustee the status of a judgment creditor vis-à-vis chattels in the debtor's possession. If one creditor had (or could get) a judgment effective against the chattels, the trustee secures the same advantage for all—which reduces any creditor's incentive to try to be first in line, a rush that may reduce the value of the debtor's assets. Sections 544(a)(1) and (2) follow state law, however, in giving the trustee no *greater* rights than the judgment creditor would have. If the debtor possesses a stolen diamond ring, the real owner's rights would trump those of a judgment creditor, and under the Code therefore would defeat the claims of all of the debtor's creditors. Whether or not we say that the debtor holds the ring in "constructive trust" for the owner is a detail. Under state law the owner's claims are paramount; the debtor could not defeat those rights by pledging or selling the ring, and the creditors in bankruptcy receive only what state law allows them. *Butner v. United States*, 440 U.S. 48 (1979). Under most states' laws, however, the buyer in good faith of *real* property can obtain a position superior to that of the rightful owner, if the owner neglected to record his interest in the filing system. Section 544(a)(3) gives the trustee the same sort of position.

A bona fide purchaser from Plunkett would have taken ahead of the partners under local law. They neglected to record the partnerships' interest, though recording is easy. (The partners could, and in retrospect should, have refused to invest funds except through an escrow agent, who would have held the cash until good title had been recorded in the partnerships' names.) * * *

Nothing in the text or function of § 544(a)(3) makes the force of this claim turn on whether Plunkett once owned the leasehold and then sold it to the partnerships (but failed to record their interest) or whether, instead, Plunkett acquired the leasehold through the partnerships. The sequence W.O.F. to Plunkett (perhaps with a bridge loan) to Pan–Am partnerships, with Plunkett retaining ostensible ownership, is identical in every respect to the sequence W.O.F. to Pan–Am partnerships to Plunkett, with Plunkett obtaining ostensible ownership. Identical from the perspective of Plunkett, of the partners, and of Plunkett's (other) creditors—and identical from the perspective of § 544(a)(3). Section 544(a)(3) allows the trustee to have a bona fide purchaser's rights *or* avoid a transfer, so a "transfer" by the debtor cannot be a necessary condition of the exercise of the strong-arm power. The statute mentions "transfer" only in the sense of the *hypothetical* transfer that measures the trustee's rights: if a hypothetical bona fide transferee from the debtor would come ahead of the "true" owner's rights, then the trustee takes ahead of the true owner.

Section 541(d) does not have anything to say about the effects of § 544(a)(3). It forbids including property in the debtor's estate "under subsection (a) of this section" and does not address whether property may be included under some other part of the Code. The courts that have perceived a conflict between §§ 541(d) and 544(a)(3) did not discuss this limitation on the domain of § 541(d). Moreover, even if we confine attention to the estate defined by § 541(a), § 541(d) carves out only "an equitable interest in such property that the debtor does not hold." This could mean, as the partners treat it, "an equitable *interest* * * * that the debtor does not hold" (here, because subject to constructive trust), but perhaps the statute addresses "*property* that the debtor does not hold", on which, therefore, lenders were unlikely to rely in extending credit. If read to exclude any "equitable interest * * * that the debtor does not hold", the statute would remove from the estate even the Plunketts' house, if it had been mortgaged to secure a loan. Estates commonly include such property.

Section 541(d) was designed, its text and history reveal, to deal with persons with title to property who had sold the equitable interests. E.g., S. Rep. No. 95–989 at 83-84, *reprinted in* 1978 U.S.C.C.A.N. at 5869-70. This is a common arrangement in secondary mortgage markets: a person with many titles sells certificates representing shares in the pool of income generated by the notes. Section 541(d) ensures that the creditors of the service corporation stand in line behind the owners of the income stream. The bankruptcy court thought that because the legislative history speaks only of secondary mortgage markets, § 541(d) is limited to such cases. Legislative history does not carry so much force. Mortgage markets may have been the impetus for § 541(d), but statutes often create rules that reach beyond the immediate concerns that spawned them. "It is not the law that a statute can have no effects which are not explicitly mentioned in its legislative history". *Pittston Coal Group v. Sebben*, 488 U.S. 105, 115 (1988). Section 541(d)'s genesis helps us understand, however, that reading the law as limited to inclusions in the estate under § 541(a) makes legal as well as linguistic sense.

Although our reading of § 541(d) and § 544(a)(3) does not conflict with the holding of any other court of appeals, there is some tension between the course we believe appropriate and statements in other opinions. The Fifth Circuit said in *Quality Holstein Leasing*, 752 F.2d at 1013 (note omitted) that "[a]s a general rule, it must be held that § 541(d) prevails over the trustee's strong-arm powers. * * * Congress did not mean to authorize a bankruptcy estate to benefit from property that the debtor did not own." With all respect to the Fifth Circuit, we believe that allowing the estate to "benefit from property that the debtor did not own" is exactly what the strong-arm powers are about: they give the trustee the status of a bona fide purchaser for value, so that the estate contains interests to which the debtor lacked good title. The estate gets what the debtor could *convey* under local law rather than only what the debtor *owned* under local law—a critical distinction that the Fifth Circuit did not mention. The discussion of § 541(d) in *Quality Holstein Leasing* is dictum, however, because the court held that state law did not impress a constructive trust on the property, and the trustee prevailed under § 544(a)(3).

The Eleventh Circuit took a course opposite to that of the Fifth. It said in *General Coffee*, 828 F.2d at 704, "that § 544(a) would bring the [constructive] trust property into the estate in spite of § 541(d)." But having proclaimed the supremacy of the strong-arm power, the court retreated to neutrality and then held that a bona fide purchaser for value would not have defeated the interest in question under state law. So in *Quality Holstein Leasing*, which proclaimed the supremacy of § 541(d), the trustee won, and in *General Coffee*, which treated § 544(a) as the victor, the trustee lost. For the reasons already canvassed, we believe that both the Fifth and Eleventh Circuits got off on the wrong foot by finding a "conflict" in need of resolution.

Section 544(a)(3) gives the Trustee the status of a bona fide purchaser for value. The bankruptcy and district courts reached the same conclusion. The partners' remaining contentions were waived or are insubstantial, so the judgment is

AFFIRMED.

F. DELAYED RECORDING

Nonbankruptcy law requires that certain types of property interests, both real and personal, be publicly recorded. These requirements are based generally on the notion that an unrecorded interest can be misleading to other creditors who are not aware that the common debtor's property is subject to someone else's preexisting claims. This is an "ostensible ownership" problem, because the appearance that assets are unencumbered might lead others to extend credit in reliance on those assets. Nonbankruptcy law, therefore, protects certain categories of creditors from the perils of "secret liens."

The bankruptcy trustee has the power to avoid liens that are either never recorded or not recorded in a timely fashion. The avoiding powers that apply to these fact patterns are ones that we have seen before, so this section of the casebook can serve as a review. The unifying theme here is the fact pattern of delayed (or nonexistent) recording.

Problems

Determine whether the following can be avoided by a trustee using §§ 544(a) or 547. Does § 544(b) provide any help to the trustee?

1. Corporation obtained a $100,000 line of credit from Bank six months ago, secured by a security interest in Corporation's assets, consisting primarily of films in which Corporation owns a copyright. Bank failed to comply with federal copyright law to perfect its security interest in the films. Corporation made several payments on the loan, including two payments the month before Corporation filed a Chapter 11 petition.

2. Debtor obtained a $50,000 loan from Bank. The loan is secured by a mortgage on Debtor's home. Debtor began making regular loan payments, but soon fell behind. Debtor filed a petition in bankruptcy one month after making a payment of $1,000. At the time the petition was filed, Bank had not yet recorded the mortgage. Under the law of the state, an unrecorded conveyance of real property is void against a good faith purchaser.

3. Tortfeasor filed a petition in bankruptcy with a state law suit pending against her. As a result of the pending lawsuit, Victim secured an attachment lien on Tortfeasor's property. Victim cannot enforce the lien unless he wins the lawsuit, but state law provides that an attachment lien has priority over a subsequent judicial lien.

4. Dealer obtained a $200,000 loan from Bank. The loan was secured by a security interest in Dealer's inventory, and Bank properly recorded its

interest. Dealer's business subsequently slowed considerably and Dealer was able to make only erratic payments to Bank. Bank allowed the perfection to lapse and Dealer filed a bankruptcy petition the following day.

5. Debtor obtained a $200,000 loan from Bank on July 1, signing a security agreement giving a security interest in property Debtor already owned. On July 25, Trade Creditor shipped Debtor $50,000 in goods on open account. Bank filed its financing statement in the appropriate place on August 1. Debtor filed a bankruptcy petition on December 1.

6. Debtor obtained a $20,000 loan from Creditor on October 10 to buy equipment, giving Creditor a security interest in the purchased equipment. Debtor filed a bankruptcy petition on October 15 and Creditor filed its financing statement on October 17. Is the security interest avoidable under § 544(a)? See § 546(b) and UCC § 9–301(2) (Revised § 9–317(a)(2) & (e)). Does your answer change if the security interest is not purchase money?

7. Has Creditor in Problem # 6 violated the automatic stay by filing the financing statement after commencement of the bankruptcy case? See § 362(b)(3). Does your answer depend on whether the security interest is purchase money?

G. AVOIDING POWERS INTENDED TO PROTECT EXEMPTIONS

By the time the bankruptcy petition is filed, any property the debtor owns is likely to be encumbered by one or more liens. Real estate may have been purchased with borrowed funds and therefore be subject to a purchase money mortgage. Disappointed creditors may have sued to judgment and taken judgment liens that attach to real estate. In addition, personalty may be covered by security interests, both purchase money and not. Inevitably, these liens will encumber property that Congress or the debtor's state legislature deemed important to a fresh start. (Remember § 522(c).)

Section 522(f) is intended to protect that fresh start. Subsection (f)(1)(B), which allows the debtor to avoid nonpossessory, nonpurchase money security interests on designated categories of property, was intended to prevent creditor overreaching:

> Frequently, creditors lending money to a consumer debtor take a security interest in all of the debtor's belongings, and obtain a waiver by the debtor of his exemptions. In most of these cases, the debtor is unaware of the consequences of the forms he signs. The creditor's experience provides him with a substantial

> advantage. If the debtor encounters financial difficulty, creditors often use threats of repossession of all the debtor's household goods as a means of obtaining payment.
>
> In fact, were the creditor to carry through on his threat and foreclose on the property, he would receive little, for household goods have little resale value. They are far more valuable to the creditor in the debtor's hands, for they provide a credible basis for the threat, because the replacement costs of the goods are generally high. Thus, creditors rarely repossess, and the debtors, ignorant of the creditors' true intentions, are coerced into payments they simply cannot afford to make.
>
> The exemption provision allows the debtor, after bankruptcy has been filed, and creditor collection techniques have been stayed, to undo the consequences of a contract of adhesion, signed in ignorance, by permitting the invalidation of nonpurchase money security interests in household goods. Such security interests have too often been used by over-reaching creditors. The bill eliminates any unfair advantage creditors have.

H.R. Rep. No. 95–595 at 127, *reprinted in* 1978 U.S.C.C.A.N. at 6088 (footnote omitted).

The justification for subsection (f)(1)(A), which permits the debtor to avoid judicial liens, is more difficult to identify. The legislative history says that the subsection

> allows the debtor to undo the actions of creditors that bring legal action against the debtor shortly before bankruptcy. Bankruptcy exists to provide relief for an overburdened debtor. If a creditor beats the debtor into court, the debtor is nevertheless entitled to his exemptions.

Id. at 126–27, *reprinted in* 1978 U.S.C.C.A.N. at 6087–88. This justification overlooks § 547, which already serves the function of avoiding judicial liens taken within the preference period. Section 522(f)(1)(A) is hardly needed to undo a judicial lien taken by a creditor who "shortly before bankruptcy * * * beats the debtor into court." Perhaps the policy behind § 522(f)(1)(A) looks to the nature of the creditor—one who initially dealt with the debtor on an unsecured basis, not bargaining for security on the front end and not relying on the availability of particular assets from which to seek repayment. This may not be the sort of creditor who should be protected from the debtor's power to claim exemptions.

As originally enacted, § 522(f)(1) referred only to judicial liens and (f)(2) dealt with nonpossessory, nonpurchase money security interests. These subsections were redesignated (f)(1)(A) and (f)(1)(B), respectively, in 1994, when a formula for determining impairment was added as § 522(f)(2). Language prohibiting avoidance of judicial liens securing debts for alimony, maintenance or support was also added in 1994. This and similar language added elsewhere in the Code—§ 101(12A), defining a "debt for child support"; § 362(b)(2), broadening the stay exception applicable to support obligations; § 507(a)(7), granting priority for support obligations; § 523(a)(15), excepting nonsupport obligations from discharge; and § 547(c)(7), excepting support payments from preference avoidance—was intended to prevent use of bankruptcy to escape marital and parental obligations.

Read § 522(f) and review § 522(d). In answering the following Problems, assume that the debtor selects the federal exemptions.

Problems

1. Debtors' home is subject to two liens—a first priority mortgage for $50,000 and a second priority judgment lien of $10,000. The property is worth $70,000. Debtors file a joint Chapter 7 petition. Is either lien avoidable? If so, in what amount? What is the amount of the exemption Debtors can claim in the property?

2. Assume the same facts as in Problem # 1, except that the property is worth $55,000. Is either lien avoidable? If so, in what amount? What is the amount of the exemption Debtors can claim in the property?

3. Debtor bought a piano and a stereo from a music store in early December, using proceeds of a $3,000 loan from Consumer Finance. Debtor granted Consumer Finance a security interest in all of Debtor's household goods, including the piano and stereo, to secure repayment of the loan. Debtor filed a bankruptcy petition in May of the next year. Can Debtor avoid all or part of the security interest in the piano? The stereo? Debtor's remaining household goods (assuming that their aggregate value does not exceed the cap under § 522(d)(3))?

4. Assume the same facts as in Problem # 3, except that Debtor did not file a bankruptcy petition in May. Rather, when Debtor had trouble making the payments on the loan, Debtor and Consumer Finance refinanced it. Consumer Finance made a new loan and used its proceeds to pay off the old loan, to pay additional finance charges and insurance, and to give Debtor $60

in cash. The new loan was for a longer period than the old loan, and required smaller monthly payments. Debtor eventually was unable to pay this loan, too, and filed a bankruptcy petition in October. Can Debtor avoid all or part of the security interest in the piano? The stereo? Debtor's remaining household goods? See *Matthews v. Transamerica Financial Services* (*In re Matthews*), 724 F.2d 798 (9th Cir.1984).

Divorce courts often permit one spouse to keep the couple's house, and require that spouse to make payments to the other in order to even up the division of assets. The obligation to make the stream of payments is usually secured by a lien on the retained property. In a number of cases, obligor spouses later filed bankruptcy and argued that the lien was a judicial lien, avoidable under § 522(f). Courts divided on the question whether avoidance was permissible in this fact pattern, and many commentators lamented the misuse of bankruptcy when the strategy met with success. The Supreme Court decided the issue in the next case. (Remember that subsection (f)(1) has been renumbered (f)(1)(A) and that language regarding support obligations has been added since the date of this decision.)

FARREY v. SANDERFOOT

United States Supreme Court, 1991.
500 U.S. 291, 111 S.Ct. 1825, 114 L.Ed.2d 337.

JUSTICE WHITE delivered the opinion of the Court.

In this case we consider whether § 522(f) of the Bankruptcy Code allows a debtor to avoid the fixing of a lien on a homestead, where the lien is granted to the debtor's former spouse under a divorce decree that extinguishes all previous interests the parties had in the property, and in no event secures more than the value of the non-debtor spouse's former interest. We hold that it does not.

I

Petitioner Jeanne Farrey and respondent Gerald Sanderfoot were married on August 12, 1966. The couple eventually built a home on 27 acres of land in Hortonville, Wisconsin, where they raised their three children. On September 12, 1986, the Wisconsin Circuit Court for Outagamie County entered a bench decision granting a judgment of divorce and property division that resolved all contested issues and terminated the marriage. A written decree followed on February 5, 1987.

The decision awarded each party one-half of their net $60,600.68 marital estate. This division reflected Wisconsin's statutory presumption that the marital estate "be divided equally between the parties." The decree granted Sanderfoot sole title to all the real estate and the family house, which was subject to a mortgage and which was valued at $104,000, and most of the personal property. For her share, Farrey received the remaining items of personal property and the proceeds from a court-ordered auction of the furniture from the home. The judgment also allocated the couple's liabilities. Under this preliminary calculation of assets and debts, Sanderfoot stood to receive a net award of $59,508.79, while Farrey's award would otherwise have been $1,091.90. To insure that the division of the estate was equal, the court ordered Sanderfoot to pay Farrey $29,208.44, half the difference in the value of their net assets. Sanderfoot was to pay this amount in two installments: half by January 10, 1987, and the remaining half by April 10, 1987. To secure this award, the decree provided that Farrey "shall have a lien against the real estate property of [Sanderfoot] for the total amount of money due her pursuant to this Order of the Court, i.e. $29,208.44, and the lien shall remain attached to the real estate property * * * until the total amount of money is paid in full."

Sanderfoot never made the required payments nor complied with any other order of the state court. Instead, on May 4, 1987, he voluntarily filed for Chapter 7 bankruptcy. Sanderfoot listed the marital home and real estate on the schedule of assets with his bankruptcy petition and listed it as exempt homestead property. Exercising his option to invoke the state rather than the federal homestead exemption, § 522(b)(2)(A), Sanderfoot claimed the property as exempt "to the amount of $40,000." * * * He also filed a motion to avoid Farrey's lien under the provision in dispute, § 522(f)(1), claiming that Farrey possessed a judicial lien that impaired his homestead exemption. Farrey objected to the motion, claiming that § 522(f)(1) could not divest her of her interest in the marital home. The Bankruptcy Court denied Sanderfoot's motion, holding that the lien could not be avoided because it protected Farrey's pre-existing interest in the marital property. The District Court reversed, concluding that the lien was avoidable because it "is fixed on an interest of the debtor in the property."

A divided panel of the Court of Appeals affirmed. The court reasoned that the divorce proceeding dissolved any pre-existing interest Farrey had in the homestead and that her new interest, "created in the dissolution order and evidenced by her lien, attached to Mr. Sanderfoot's interest in the property." Noting that the issue had caused a split among the Courts of Appeals, the court expressly relied on those decisions that it termed more "faithful to the plain language of § 522(f)."

Judge Posner, in dissent, argued that to avoid a lien under § 522(f), a debtor must have an interest in the property at the time the court places the lien on that interest. Judge Posner concluded that because the same decree that gave the entire property to Sanderfoot simultaneously created the lien in favor of Farrey, the lien did not attach to a pre-existing interest of the husband. * * *

We granted certiorari to resolve the conflict of authority. We now reverse the Court of Appeals' judgment and remand.

II

* * *

Section 522(f)(1) provides in relevant part:

> "Notwithstanding any waiver of exemptions, the debtor may avoid the fixing of a lien on an interest of the debtor in property to the extent that such lien impairs an exemption to which the debtor would have been entitled under subsection (b) of this section, if such lien is—
>
> "(1) a judicial lien * * *."

The provision establishes several conditions for a lien to be avoided, only one of which is at issue. Farrey does not challenge the Court of Appeals' determination that her lien was a judicial lien, nor do we address that question here. The Court of Appeals also determined that Farrey had waived any challenge as to whether Sanderfoot was otherwise entitled to a homestead exemption under state law and we agree. The sole question presented in this case is whether § 522(f)(1) permits Sanderfoot to avoid the fixing of Farrey's lien on the property interest that he obtained in the divorce decree.

The key portion of § 522(f) states that "the debtor may avoid the fixing of a lien on an interest in * * * property." Sanderfoot, following several Courts of Appeals, suggests that this phrase means that a lien may be avoided so long as it is currently fixed on a debtor's interest.

Farrey, following Judge Posner's lead, reads the text as permitting the avoidance of a lien only where the lien attached to the debtor's interest at some point after the debtor obtained the interest.

We agree with Farrey. No one asserts that the two verbs underlying the provision possess anything other than their standard legal meaning: "avoid" meaning "annul" or "undo," see Black's Law Dictionary 136 (6th ed. 1990); H.R. Rep. No. 95–595 at 126–27, *reprinted in* U.S.C.C.A.N. at 6087–88, and "fix" meaning to "fasten a liability upon," see Black's Law Dictionary, *supra*, at 637. The statute does not say that the debtor may undo a lien on an interest in property. Rather, the statute expressly states that the debtor may avoid "the fixing" of a lien on the debtor's interest in property. The gerund "fixing" refers to a temporal event. That event—the fastening of a liability—presupposes an object onto which the liability can fasten. The statute defines this pre-existing object as "an interest of the debtor in property." Therefore, unless the debtor had the property interest to which the lien attached at some point *before* the lien attached to that interest, he or she cannot avoid the fixing of the lien under the terms of § 522(f)(1).

This reading fully comports with the provision's purpose and history. Congress enacted § 522(f) with the broad purpose of protecting the debtor's exempt property. Ordinarily, liens and other secured interests survive bankruptcy. In particular, it was well settled when § 522(f) was enacted that valid liens obtained before bankruptcy could be enforced on exempt property, see *Louisville Joint Stock Land Bank* v. *Radford*, 295 U.S. 555, 582–83 (1935), including otherwise exempt homestead property, *Long* v. *Bullard*, 117 U.S. 617, 620–21 (1886). Congress generally preserved this principle when it comprehensively revised bankruptcy law with the Bankruptcy Reform Act of 1978. But Congress also revised the law to permit the debtor to avoid the fixing of some liens. See, *e.g.*, § 545 (statutory liens).

Section 522(f)(1), by its terms, extends this protection to cases involving the fixing of judicial liens onto exempt property. What specific legislative history exists suggests that a principal reason Congress singled out judicial liens was because they are a device commonly used by creditors to defeat the protection bankruptcy law accords exempt property against debts. As the House Report stated:

> "The first right [§ 522(f)(1)] allows the debtor to undo the actions of creditors that bring legal action against the debtor shortly before bankruptcy. Bankruptcy exists to provide relief for an

> overburdened debtor. If a creditor beats the debtor into court, the debtor is nevertheless entitled to his exemptions." H.R. Rep. No. 95–595 at 126–27, *reprinted in* 1978 U.S.C.C.A.N. at 6087–88.

One factor supporting the view that Congress intended § 522(f)(1) to thwart a rush to the courthouse is Congress' contemporaneous elimination of § 67 of the 1898 Bankruptcy Act. Prior to its repeal, § 67(a) invalidated any lien obtained on an exempt interest of an insolvent debtor within four months of the bankruptcy filing. The Bankruptcy Reform Act eliminated the insolvency and timing requirements. It is possible that Congress simply decided to leave exemptions exposed despite its longstanding policy against doing so. But given the legislative history's express concern over protecting exemptions, it follows instead that § 522(f)(1) was intended as a new device to handle the old provision's job by "giv[ing] the debtor certain rights not available under current law with respect to exempt property." H.R. Rep. No. 95–595 at 126-27, *reprinted in* 1978 U.S.C.C.A.N. at 6087.

Conversely, the text, history, and purpose of § 522(f)(1) also indicate what the provision is *not* concerned with. It cannot be concerned with liens that fixed on an interest before the debtor acquired that interest. Neither party contends otherwise. Section 522(f)(1) does not state that any fixing of a lien may be avoided; instead, it permits avoidance of the "fixing of a lien on an interest of the debtor." If the fixing took place before the debtor acquired that interest, the "fixing" by definition was not on the debtor's interest. Nor could the statute apply given its purpose of preventing a creditor from beating the debtor to the courthouse, since the debtor at no point possessed the interest without the judicial lien. There would be no fixing to avoid since the lien was already there. To permit lien avoidance in these circumstances, in fact, would be to allow judicial lienholders to be defrauded through the conveyance of an encumbered interest to a prospective debtor. For these reasons, it is settled that a debtor cannot use § 522(f)(1) to avoid a lien on an interest acquired after the lien attached. As before, the critical inquiry remains whether the debtor ever possessed the interest to which the lien fixed, before it fixed. If he or she did not, § 522(f)(1) does not permit the debtor to avoid the fixing of the lien on that interest.

III

We turn to the application of § 522(f)(1) to this case.

Whether Sanderfoot ever possessed an interest to which the lien fixed, before it fixed, is a question of state law. Farrey contends that prior to the divorce judgment, she and her husband held title to the real estate in joint tenancy, each possessing an undivided one-half interest. She further asserts that the divorce decree extinguished these previous interests. At the same time and in the same transaction, she concludes, the decree created new interests in place of the old: for Sanderfoot, ownership in fee simple of the house and real estate; for Farrey, various assets and a debt of $29,208.44 secured by a lien on the Sanderfoot's new fee simple interest. Both in his briefs and at oral argument, Sanderfoot agreed on each point.

On the assumption that the parties characterize Wisconsin law correctly, Sanderfoot must lose. Under their view, the lien could not have fixed on Sanderfoot's pre-existing undivided half interest because the divorce decree extinguished it. Instead, the only interest that the lien encumbers is debtor's wholly new fee simple interest. The same decree that awarded Sanderfoot his fee simple interest simultaneously granted the lien to Farrey. As the judgment stated, he acquired the property "free and clear" of any claim "except as expressly provided in this [decree]." Sanderfoot took the interest and the lien together, as if he had purchased an already encumbered estate from a third party. Since Sanderfoot never possessed his new fee simple interest before the lien "fixed", § 522(f)(1) is not available to void the lien.

The same result follows even if the divorce decree did not extinguish the couple's pre-existing interests but instead merely reordered them. The parties' current position notwithstanding, it may be that under Wisconsin law the divorce decree augmented Sanderfoot's previous interest by adding to it Farrey's prior interest. If the court in exchange sought to protect Farrey's previous interest with a lien, § 522(f)(1) could be used to undo the encumbrance to the extent the lien fastened to any portion of Sanderfoot's previous surviving interest. This follows because Sanderfoot would have possessed the interest to which that part of the lien fixed, before it fixed. But in this case, the divorce court did not purport to encumber any part of Sanderfoot's previous interest even on the assumption that state law would deem that interest to have survived. The decree instead transferred Farrey's previous interest to Sanderfoot and, again simultaneously, granted a lien equal to that interest minus the small amount of personal property she retained. Sanderfoot thus would still be unable to avoid the lien in this case since it fastened only to what had been Farrey's pre-existing interest, and this interest Sanderfoot would never have possessed without the lien already having fixed.[4]

The result, on either theory, accords with the provision's main purpose. As noted, the legislative history suggests that Congress primarily intended § 522(f)(1) as a device to thwart creditors who, sensing an impending bankruptcy, rush to court to obtain a judgment to defeat the debtor's exemptions. That is not what occurs in a divorce proceeding such as this. Farrey obtained the lien not to defeat Sanderfoot's pre-existing interest in the homestead but to protect her own pre-existing interest in the homestead that was fully equal to that of her spouse. The divorce court awarded the lien to secure an obligation the court imposed on the husband in exchange for the court's simultaneous award of the wife's homestead interest to the husband. We agree with Judge Posner that to permit a debtor in these circumstances to use the Code to deprive a spouse of this protection would neither follow the language of the statute nor serve the main goal it was designed to address.

IV

We hold that § 522(f)(1) of the Bankruptcy Code requires a debtor to have possessed an interest to which a lien attached, before it attached, to avoid the fixing of the lien on that interest. Accordingly, the judgment of the Court of Appeals is reversed, and the case is remanded for further proceedings consistent with this opinion.

It is so ordered.

JUSTICE KENNEDY, with whom JUSTICE SOUTER joins, concurring.

I agree with the Court's holding that a debtor cannot use § 522(f)(1) of the Bankruptcy Code to avoid a lien on an interest the debtor acquired after the lien attached. I agree also with the Court's determination that respondent conceded what we all now know to be the key point in the case. In describing the effect of the Outagamie County Circuit Court's decree on the real property in question, the husband stated in his brief before this Court:

> "Prior to the judgment of divorce, the parties held title to the real estate in joint tenancy, each holding a pre-existing undivided one-half interest. At the point that the divorce court

---

[4] Justice Scalia does not join in this paragraph.

issued its property division determination, those property rights were wholly extinguished and new rights were put into place."

This concession is fatal to the argument respondent must make to prevail here, which is that the judicial lien fixed upon his pre-existing interest in the property. With the case in this posture, though, the possibility arises that later cases, whether from Wisconsin or from some other jurisdiction, could yield a different result. This would depend upon the relevant state laws defining the estate owned by a spouse who had a pre-existing interest in marital property and upon state laws governing awards of property under a decree settling marital rights.

In this case, prior to the Circuit Court decree ordering the property division, respondent had a vested, present, and undivided interest in one-half the marital property. The relevant Wisconsin statutes, enacted when the State adopted substantial parts of the Uniform Marital Property Act, provide that "[a]ll property of spouses is presumed to be marital property," and "[e]ach spouse has a present undivided one-half interest in each item of marital property." Absent respondent's concession, it would seem that the state court did not divest him of his pre-existing interest. At no place in its "Findings of Fact, Conclusions of Law, and Judgment of Divorce" did the court declare that respondent's predecree interests were extinguished. Rather, the decree declared that upon its effective date sole title to the property vested in respondent. It also gave respondent's wife a lien against the home to secure the debt he owed her to equalize the property settlement. Finally, it divested each party of "any and all right, title and interest in and to the property awarded to the other." As I read these provisions, respondent obtained from his wife her one-half interest in the home, while always retaining his one-half interest as well. Because no interest in the home, other than the lien, was awarded to respondent's wife, respondent was never divested of any interest.

This interpretation conforms to the result mandated if a marriage terminates without any decree for property division. Wisconsin law provides that "[a]fter a dissolution each former spouse owns an undivided one-half interest in the former marital property as a tenant in common." So too, if one spouse were to make a voluntary transfer of his or her one-half interest to the other spouse, I should not think it could be said that the transferee's prior interest had been extinguished. Rather, the transferee would retain his or her own interest, and the two interests would be merged into a single estate. A state-law scheme in this pattern is to be distinguished, of course, from a regime in which a tenancy by the entirety is recognized and is deemed a single interest owned by the marital entity, a regime in which the estate dissolves when the marriage does. Thus, it is not at all clear that as a matter of state law the judicial lien could not attach to the husband's predecree interest in his one-half of the marital property. If so, respondent could use § 522(f)(1) to avoid at least part of his wife's lien.

The result the Court reaches consists with fairness and common sense. Since the Outagamie County Circuit Court had the power to strip the husband of his interest altogether, it can be reasoned that the court granted him the entire property on the condition that his prior interest would terminate and that a lien would attach to a new interest in the whole. The problem with this argument, however, is that there is no indication in the record that the husband consented to the decree. A waiver of this sort may also be contrary to the nonwaiver provision of § 522(f).

Following this analysis, I believe the Bankruptcy Code may be used in some later case to allow a spouse to avoid otherwise valid obligations under a divorce court decree. Though adept drafting of property decrees or the use of court orders directing conveyances in a certain sequence might resolve the problem, it appears that congressional action may be necessary to avoid in some future case the perhaps unjust result the Court today avoids having to consider only because of the fortuity of a litigant's concession. With these observations, I concur in the opinion and the judgment of the Court.

Notes and Questions

1. *Farrey* was decided before the 1994 Amendments created § 522-(f)(1)(A), which protects liens securing support obligations. The legislative history indicates that the new subsection was intended to "supplement the reach of *Farrey*." In what way does it "supplement" *Farrey*? Would it have controlled the result in *Farrey* if it had been in effect when the case arose?

2. Note the Court's reliance on § 522's "purpose and history" and its assertion that "Congress enacted § 522(f) with the broad purpose of protecting the debtor's exempt property." Note also that the Court used dictionary definitions to guide its construction of the statute.

3. The concurrence acknowledged that the majority's opinion is consistent "with fairness and common sense," but recognized as well that the decision was dependent on Sanderfoot's stipulation regarding the effect of the family court's order. Would the concurrence be comfortable with the 1994 amendment creating § 522(f)(1)(A)?

4. If Sanderfoot's concessions were fatal to his case, why were they made?

5. Judgment lienholders typically are nonreliance creditors, having first dealt with the debtor on an unsecured basis. Does the lien at issue in *Farrey* more nearly resemble a judgment lien or a purchase money mortgage?

Section 522(f)(1) allows avoidance of a lien "to the extent that" it impairs an exemption. In some states, exemptions are defined in terms of the debtor's equity in property, so there is no exemption to the extent that the property is encumbered. Creditors in those states argued that their liens were not avoidable because the debtor had no exemption that could be impaired by the lien. That argument, if successful, would effectively eliminate the debtor's avoiding power under § 522(f)(1). The Supreme Court addressed that argument in the next case.

OWEN v. OWEN

United States Supreme Court, 1991.
500 U.S. 305, 111 S.Ct. 1833, 114 L.Ed.2d 350.

JUSTICE SCALIA delivered the opinion of the Court.

The Bankruptcy Code allows the States to define what property a debtor may exempt from the bankruptcy estate that will be distributed among his creditors. § 522(b). The Code also provides that judicial liens encumbering exempt property can be eliminated. § 522(f). The question in this case is whether that elimination can operate when the State has defined the exempt property in such a way as specifically to exclude property encumbered by judicial liens.

I

In 1975, Helen Owen, the respondent, obtained a judgment against petitioner Dwight Owen, her former husband, for approximately $160,000. The judgment was recorded in Sarasota County, Florida, in July 1976. Petitioner did not at that time own any property in Sarasota County, but under Florida law, the judgment would attach to any after-acquired property recorded in the county. In 1984, petitioner purchased a condominium in Sarasota County; upon acquisition of title, the property became subject to respondent's judgment lien.

One year later, Florida amended its homestead law so that petitioner's condominium, which previously had not qualified as a homestead, thereafter did. Under the Florida Constitution, homestead property is "exempt from forced sale * * * and no judgment, decree or execution [can] be a lien thereon." Fla. Const., Art. 10, § 4(a). The Florida courts have interpreted this provision, however, as being inapplicable to pre-existing liens, *i.e.*, liens that attached before the property acquired its homestead status. Pre-existing liens, then, are in effect an exception to the Florida homestead exemption.

In January 1986, petitioner filed for bankruptcy under Chapter 7 of the Code, and claimed a homestead exemption in his Sarasota condominium. The condominium, valued at approximately $135,000, was his primary asset; his liabilities included approximately $350,000 owed to the respondent. The bankruptcy court discharged petitioner's personal liability for these debts, and sustained, over respondent's objections, his claimed exemption.

The condominium, however, remained subject to respondent's pre-existing lien, and after discharge, petitioner moved to reopen his case to avoid the lien pursuant to § 522(f)(1). The Bankruptcy Court refused to decree the avoidance; the District Court affirmed, finding that the lien had attached before the property qualified for the exemption, and that Florida law therefore did not exempt the lien-encumbered property. The Court of Appeals for the Eleventh Circuit affirmed on the same ground. We granted certiorari.

II

An estate in bankruptcy consists of all the interests in property, legal and equitable, possessed by the debtor at the time of filing, as well as those interests recovered or recoverable through transfer and lien avoidance provisions. An exemption is an interest withdrawn from the estate (and hence from the creditors) for the benefit of the debtor. Section 522 determines what property a debtor may exempt. Under § 522(b), he must select between a list of federal exemptions (set forth in § 522(d)) and the exemptions provided by his State, "unless the State law that is applicable to the debtor * * * specifically does not so authorize," § 522(b)(1)—that is, unless the State "opts out" of the federal list. If a State opts out, then its debtors are limited to the exemptions provided by state law. Nothing in subsection (b) (or elsewhere in the Code) limits a State's power to restrict the scope of its exemptions; indeed, it could theoretically accord no exemptions at all.

Property that is properly exempted under § 522 is (with some exceptions) immunized against liability for prebankruptcy debts. § 522(c). No property can be exempted (and thereby immunized), however, unless it first falls *within* the bankruptcy estate. Section 522(b) provides that the debtor may exempt certain property "from property of the estate"; obviously, then, an interest that is not possessed by the estate cannot be exempted. Thus, if a debtor holds only bare legal title to his house—if, for example, the house is subject to a purchase-money mortgage for its full value—then only that legal interest passes to the estate; the equitable interest remains with the mortgage holder, § 541(d). And since the equitable interest does not pass to the estate, neither can it pass to the debtor as an exempt interest in property. Legal title will pass, and can be the subject of an exemption; but the property will remain subject to the lien interest of the mortgage holder. This was the rule of *Long* v. *Bullard*, 117 U.S. 617 (1886), codified in § 522. Only where the Code empowers the court to avoid liens or transfers can an interest originally not within the estate be passed to the estate, and subsequently (through the claim of an exemption) to the debtor.

It is such an avoidance provision that is at issue here, to which we now turn. Section 522(f) reads as follows:

> "(f) Notwithstanding any waiver of exemptions, the debtor may avoid the fixing of a lien on an interest of the debtor in property to the extent that such lien impairs an exemption to which the debtor would have been entitled under subsection (b) of this section, if such lien is—
>
> "(1) a judicial lien; or
>
> "(2) a nonpossessory, nonpurchase-money security interest * * *."

The lien in the present case is a judicial lien, and we assume without deciding that it fixed "on an interest of the debtor in property." See *Farrey* v. *Sanderfoot*, 500 U.S. 291 (1991). The question presented by this case is whether it "impairs an exemption to which [petitioner] would have been entitled under subsection (b)." Since Florida has chosen to opt out of the listed federal exemptions, the only subsection (b) exemption at issue is the Florida homestead exemption described above. Respondent suggests that, to resolve this case, we need only ask whether the judicial lien impairs that exemption. It obviously does not, since the Florida homestead exemption is not assertable against pre-existing judicial liens. To permit avoidance of the lien, respondent urges, would not *preserve* the exemption but would *expand* it.

At first blush, this seems entirely reasonable. Several Courts of Appeals in addition to the Eleventh Circuit here have reached this result with respect to built-in limitations on state exemptions, though others have rejected it. What must give us pause, however, is that this result has been widely *and uniformly* rejected with respect to built-in limitations on the *federal* exemptions. Most of the federally listed exemptions (set forth in § 522(d)) are explicitly restricted to the "debtor's aggregate interest" or the "debtor's interest" up to a maximum amount. See §§ 522(d)(1)-(6), (8). If respondent's approach to § 522(f) were applied, all of these exemptions (and perhaps others as well) would be limited by unavoided encumbering liens, see § 522(c). The federal homestead exemption, for example, allows the debtor to exempt from the property of the estate "[t]he debtor's aggregate interest, not to exceed $7,500 in value, in * * * a residence." § 522(d)(1). If respondent's interpretation of § 522(f) were applied to this exemption, a debtor who owned a house worth $10,000 that was subject to a judicial lien for $9,000 would not be entitled to the full homestead exemption of $7,500. The judicial lien would not be avoidable under § 522(f), since it does not "impair" the exemption, which is limited to the debtor's "aggregate interest" of $1,000. The uniform practice of bankruptcy courts, however, is to the contrary. To determine the application of § 522(f) they ask not whether the lien impairs an exemption to which the debtor is in fact entitled, but whether it impairs an exemption to which he *would have been* entitled but for the lien itself.

As the preceding italicized words suggest, this reading is more consonant with the text of § 522(f)—which establishes as the baseline, against which impairment is to be measured, not an exemption to which the debtor "*is* entitled," but one to which he "*would have been* entitled." The latter phrase denotes a state of affairs that is conceived or hypothetical, rather than actual, and requires the reader to disregard some element of reality. "Would have been" *but for what*? The answer given, with respect to the federal exemptions, has been *but for the lien at issue*, and that seems to us correct.

* * *

This reading must also be accepted, at least with respect to the federal exemptions, if § 522(f) is not to become an irrelevancy with respect to the most venerable, most common, and most important exemptions. The federal exemptions for homestead (§ 522(d)(1)), for motor vehicles (§ 522(d)(2)), for household goods and wearing apparel (§ 522(d)(3)), and for tools of the trade (§ 522(d)(6)), are all defined by reference to the debtor's "interest" or "aggregate interest," so that if respondent's interpretation is accepted, no encumbrances of these could be avoided. Surely § 522(f) promises more than that—and surely it would be bizarre for the federal scheme to prevent the avoidance of liens on those items, but to permit it for the less crucial items (for example, an "unmatured life insurance contract owned by the debtor," § 522(d)(7)) that are not described in such fashion as unquestionably to exclude liens.

We have no doubt, then, that the lower courts' unanimously agreed-upon manner of applying § 522(f) to federal exemptions—ask first whether avoiding the lien would entitle the debtor to an exemption, and if it would, then avoid and recover the lien—is correct. The question then becomes whether a different interpretation should be adopted for state exemptions. We do not see how that could be possible. Nothing in the text of § 522(f) remotely justifies treating the two categories of exemptions differently. The provision refers to the impairment of "exemption[s] to which the debtor would have been entitled under subsection (b)," and that includes federal exemptions and state exemptions alike. Nor is there any overwhelmingly clear policy impelling us, if we possessed the power, to create a distinction that the words of the statute do not contain. Respondent asserts that it is inconsistent with the Bankruptcy Code's "opt-out" policy, whereby the States may define their own exemptions, to refuse to take those exemptions with all their built-in limitations. That is plainly not true, however, since there is no doubt that a state exemption which purports to be available "unless waived" will be given full effect, *even if it has been waived*, for purposes of § 522(f)—the first phrase of which, as we have noted, recites that it applies "[n]otwithstanding any waiver of exemptions." Just as it is not inconsistent with the policy of permitting state-defined exemptions to have another policy disfavoring waiver of exemptions, whether federal- or state-created; so also it is not inconsistent to have a policy disfavoring the impingement of certain types of liens upon exemptions, whether federal- or state-created. We have no basis for pronouncing the opt-out policy absolute, but must apply it along with whatever other competing or limiting policies the statute contains.

On the basis of the analysis we have set forth above with respect to federal exemptions, and in light of the equivalency of treatment accorded to federal and state exemptions by § 522(f), we conclude that Florida's exclusion of certain liens from the scope of its homestead protection does not achieve a similar exclusion from the Bankruptcy Code's lien avoidance provision.[6]

III

The foregoing conclusion does not necessarily resolve this case. Section 522(f) permits the avoidance of the "fixing of a lien on an interest of the debtor." Some courts have held it inapplicable to a lien that was already attached to property when the debtor acquired it, since in such a case there never was a "*fixing* of a lien" on *the debtor's* interest. Under Florida law, the lien may have attached simultaneously with the acquisition of the property interest. If so, it could be argued that the lien did not fix "on an interest of the debtor." See *Farrey* v. *Sanderfoot*, 500 U.S. 291 (1991). The Court of Appeals did not pass on this issue, nor on the subsidiary question of whether the Florida statute extending the homestead exemption was a taking, cf. *United States* v. *Security Industrial Bank*, 459 U.S. 70 (1982). We express no opinion on these points, and leave them to be considered by the Court of Appeals on remand.

The judgment of the Court of Appeals is reversed, and the case remanded for proceedings consistent with this opinion.

It is so ordered.

JUSTICE STEVENS, dissenting.

The Court's analysis puts the cart before the horse. As I read the statute at issue, it is not necessary to reach the issue the majority addresses. In construing the lien avoidance provisions of the Bankruptcy Code, it is important to recognize a distinction between two classes of cases: those in which the lien attached to the exempt property *before* the debtor had any right to claim an exemption, and those in which the lien attached *after* the debtor acquired that right. This case falls in the former category. As I shall explain, I believe it was correctly decided by the Bankruptcy Court, the District Court, and the Court of Appeals, and that the judgment should be affirmed.

---

[6] In the dissent's view, the question is whether the lien impairs an "exemption to which the debtor would have been entitled at the time the lien 'fixed'." Under the Code, however, the question is whether the lien impairs an "exemption to which the debtor would have been entitled under subsection (b)," and under subsection (b), exempt property is determined "on the date of the filing of the petition," not when the lien fixed. §§ 522(f), (b)(2)(A). We follow the language of the Code.

I

The facts raise a straight forward issue: whether the lien avoidance provisions in § 522(f) of the Bankruptcy Code apply to a judicial lien that attached before the debtor had any claim to an exemption. It is undisputed that respondent's judicial lien attached to petitioner's Sarasota condominium when he acquired title to the property in November 1984. It is also undisputed that petitioner was not entitled to a homestead exemption when he acquired title because he was single. At that time, the exemption was available only to a "head of a household" under Article 10, § 4, of the Florida Constitution. An amendment that became effective in 1985 broadened the exemption to extend to "a natural person." On the effective date of this amendment petitioner became entitled to the homestead exemption at issue in this case. Thus, it is undisputed that petitioner had an exemption on his condominium when he filed his bankruptcy petition in 1986, but did not have a right to that exemption in 1984 when respondent's judicial lien attached.

As I read the text of § 522(f), it does not authorize the avoidance of liens that were perfected at a time when the debtor could not claim an exemption in the secured property. * * *

As it applies to judicial liens, § 522(f) raises two questions: (1) whether the exemption provides a basis for avoidance of the lien; and (2) if so, to what extent should the lien be avoided? The first question concerns the relative priority of conflicting claims on the same asset; on such issues, the timing of the claims is often decisive. The second question—I shall call it the "impairment question"—concerns the distribution of the proceeds of sale after the issue of priority has been resolved. This second question need not be reached unless the first question has been answered positively.

In determining whether the exemption provides a basis for avoiding the lien, § 522(f) turns our attention towards the exemption to which the debtor would have been entitled at the time the lien "fixed." In *United States* v. *Security Industrial Bank*, 459 U.S. 70 (1982), this Court was presented with the question whether applying [§ 522(f)(1)(B)] to avoid nonpossessory liens perfected before the enactment of the Bankruptcy Reform Act of 1978 would be a taking of property without compensation in violation of the Fifth Amendment of the Constitution. The Court avoided deciding that precise question by holding that § 522(f) did not apply retroactively to liens that had been perfected before the Bankruptcy Reform Act was enacted. Although there is no such constitutional question presented here, *Security Industrial Bank* establishes that the critical date for determining whether a lien may be avoided under the statute is the date of the fixing of that lien.

The date of the fixing of the respondent's lien on petitioner's condominium is therefore controlling in this case. Because it is undisputed that petitioner was not entitled to an exemption when the lien attached, the subsequently acquired exemption does not provide a basis for avoidance of the respondent's lien. Thus, the priority question in this case was correctly decided by the Court of Appeals and its judgment should be affirmed.

* * *

Notes and Questions

1. The Supreme Court remanded *Owen* for a determination whether there was a "fixing" of a lien on the debtor's interest—the *Farrey* issue. On remand, the court held that *Farrey* requires the debtor to have had an interest in the property *before* the lien attaches. Thus, the lien was not avoidable. *In re Owen*, 961 F.2d 170 (11th Cir.1992).

2. Does it make sense, as a matter of policy, to deny avoidance when a judgment is docketed before the debtor acquires the property, but to permit avoidance when the debtor acquires the property first?

Several subsections of § 522 enable the debtor, in certain circumstances, to exempt property recovered by virtue of the trustee's avoiding powers, or to exercise the avoiding powers, if the trustee does not, when exemptable property could be recovered thereby. These provisions, although a bit complicated, are intended to protect the debtor's exemptions.

Begin with a straightforward case. Assume that a previously unsecured creditor obtains a judgment for $18,000 and a judicial lien against the debtor's residence. The home, which is worth $90,000, was already encumbered by a first priority mortgage of $72,000. A month after the judgment lien attaches, the debtor files bankruptcy. The trustee avoids the judicial lien as a preference under § 547, thus freeing the property of encumbrance. Under § 522(g), the debtor can take the homestead exemption out of the $18,000 in value brought into the estate; the transfer was not voluntary and the debtor did not conceal the property. If any amount remains after satisfaction of the homestead exemption, it goes into the estate, to be distributed to unsecured creditors.

Assume, however, that the trustee fails to avoid the judicial lien, deciding that the remainder for the estate is not worth the trouble. Sections 522(h) and (i) allow the debtor to exercise the avoiding power so that the exemption will not be lost. Ordinarily, avoided liens are preserved for the benefit of the estate, § 551. Subsection 522(i)(2) allows the debtor to enjoy the benefit of the avoided lien when exemptions are at stake.

Read subsections (g), (h) and (i) and apply them to the following Problems.

Problems

1. Debtor owed $30,000 on a signature loan obtained from First National Bank. When Debtor defaulted, First National sued to judgment and obtained a judgment lien on Debtor's house. A month after the lien attached, Debtor filed bankruptcy. The house is worth $100,000 and is also subject to a first mortgage (which is senior to the judgment lien) of $80,000. The trustee avoided First National's interest as a preference. Can Debtor claim a homestead exemption out of the value that avoidance brought into the estate? See § 522(g).

2. Last year, Debtor borrowed $4,500 from Finance Company to pay some medical bills and granted a security interest in Debtor's car. Finance Company failed to perfect its interest until two weeks before Debtor filed a bankruptcy petition, but the trustee has made no move to avoid the security interest because the car is only worth $2,000. Can Debtor avoid the security interest and then claim an exemption in the car?

3. Debtor's home, which was worth $60,000, was encumbered by the following liens, in descending order of priority: a first mortgage of $25,000; a judgment lien of $13,500; and a second mortgage of $80,000. Can Debtor use § 522(f) to obtain the benefit of the homestead exemption? If so, what liens remain in place after conclusion of the bankruptcy case?

H. SETOFFS

Assume that Borrower obtains an unsecured loan from Bank for $10,000 and that Borrower also maintains a checking account there. On the loan transaction, Borrower is the debtor and Bank is the creditor. The checking account, however, represents Bank's obligation to Borrower. As far as the checking account is concerned, Borrower is the creditor and Bank is the debtor. Borrower and Bank owe each other mutual debts. If Borrower fails to pay the loan when it is due, Bank has the right under state law to set off the account against the loan balance. If the account has a balance of $7,500, then the loan balance is reduced to $2,500 and the account balance is reduced to zero. If the account has a balance of $12,000, then the loan balance is reduced to zero and the account balance is reduced to $2,000.

Bankruptcy law does not create the right of setoff, but recognizes it. Section 553(a) provides that bankruptcy "does not affect" a creditor's right to set off mutual prepetition debts. The Code, however, limits the exercise of setoff. Setoff can be either pre- or postpetition, but the latter is subject to the automatic stay. See § 362(a)(7).

Subsections (a)(1), (a)(2) and (a)(3) of § 553, which apply to both pre- and postpetition setoffs, provide circumstances under which setoff will be denied. Subsection (a)(1) prohibits setoff when the creditor's claim against the debtor is not allowed, thus preventing indirect recovery of claims that cannot be recovered directly.

Subsections (a)(2) and (a)(3) prevent efforts to increase the right to setoff. Subsection (a)(2) prevents a creditor from amassing claims against the debtor for the purpose of exercising setoff rights. It prohibits the setoff of claims obtained from another creditor after bankruptcy was filed, or obtained during the 90 days preceding bankruptcy if the debtor was insolvent at the time. (And the debtor is presumed to have been insolvent during that period, § 553(c).)

Subsection (a)(3) applies when the creditor incurs a debt to the bankruptcy debtor, rather than acquiring a claim against the debtor. It would apply if Bank in the hypothetical above, knowing that bankruptcy was imminent and that any payment would be a preference, "encouraged" Borrower to build up the checking account balance instead of making a direct payment on the loan.

A fourth limitation on setoff in bankruptcy is found in § 553(b), which applies only to prepetition setoffs. It imposes an improvement-in-position test patterned after § 547(c)(5). The kinship between setoff and preferences is clear (hence the placement of setoff in this casebook's chapter on avoiding powers), and Congress was concerned that creditors in a position to exercise the right of setoff would "rush in" on faltering debtors by decreasing the amount of their "insufficiency." See § 553(b)(2). Thus, § 553(b) prohibits setoff to the extent it reduces the "insufficiency." This improvement-in-position test applies only to setoffs that occur during the 90 days before bankruptcy; the reason for the rule is not implicated if the creditor waits until after the petition is filed and then seeks relief from the stay in order to exercise its right of setoff.

The 1994 Amendments added a specialized sort of setoff by creating § 546(h). It allows a buyer to return goods shipped before bankruptcy, if the seller consents and return would be in the best interests of the estate. The buyer can then set off the price of the unsold goods against the seller's claim. Return of goods under § 546(h) requires a motion by the trustee (which, of course, includes the debtor in possession), made within 120 days of the filing, and approval by the court.

Read § 553 and solve the following Problems.

Problems

1. Debtor, a subcontractor, owed $22,000 to Materialman for construction materials. Contractor owed Debtor $18,000 for subcontracting services. Under local law, a general contractor is surety for a subcontractor's debts to material suppliers. Thus, Contractor was obligated to pay Materialman $22,000. When Contractor paid Materialman, Contractor acquired Materialman's claim against Debtor. After Debtor entered bankruptcy, Contractor sought to set off that claim against the $18,000 it owed Debtor. Is the setoff proper? See *In re Flanagan Bros., Inc.*, 47 B.R. 299 (Bankr. D.N.J.1985).

2. Bank made Corporation an unsecured loan of $125,000 and Corporation's President personally guaranteed repayment. When Corporation began to experience financial problems, President made several deposits of corporate funds in Corporation's checking account at Bank, increasing the balance from $10,000 to $100,000 during the 90 days before bankruptcy. Bank sought relief from the stay in order to set off the checking account against the loan. Is setoff proper? See *Katz v. First National Bank of Glen Head*, 568 F.2d 964 (2d Cir.1977), *cert. denied* 434 U.S. 1069, 98 S.Ct. 1250, 55 L.Ed.2d 771 (1978).

3. Corporation owed Bank $100,000 on the 90th day before bankruptcy. At that time, Corporation's checking account at Bank had a balance of $40,000. When Bank exercised its right of setoff two days before filing, the balance in the account was $50,000. The loan balance was unchanged. How much, if anything, can the trustee recover under § 553?

4. Corporation owed Bank $30,000 throughout the 90 days before bankruptcy. The amounts in Corporation's checking account at Bank fluctuated during that period as follows: $30,000 on the 90th day; $20,000 on the 85th day; $15,000 on the 80th day; and $29,000 on the 25th day, which was the day of setoff. How much, if anything, can the trustee recover under § 553?

5. Assume the same facts as in Problem # 4, except that the amount in Corporation's checking account on the 90th day is $29,998. Does your answer change?

The following cases illustrate two important aspects of § 553. The first is § 553's status as a "legalized preference." The second is the requirement of "mutuality."

DURHAM v. SMI INDUSTRIES CORP.

United States Court of Appeals, Fourth Circuit, 1989.
882 F.2d 881.

WILKINS, Circuit Judge.

SMI Industries, Inc., a creditor of Continental Commodities, Inc., appeals from the district court judgment affirming a bankruptcy court ruling that its receipt of a check as part of a check exchange by the two companies constituted an avoidable preferential transfer under the Bankruptcy Code, § 547(b). We reverse and remand.

I.

SMI and Continental are scrap metal dealers that until November 1983 engaged in a substantial amount of business with each other, selling each other materials on open account. Although the total dollar figures of the open account invoices often grew quite large, the net balance due either party at any one time was relatively small. Periodically, in order to reduce these account debts, SMI and Continental would either make mutual accounting entries cancelling corresponding debts and credits, or they would exchange checks for the outstanding balances. The check exchanges were carefully coordinated to allow simultaneous deposits in their respective bank accounts to ensure that the checks would clear.

In late August 1983 SMI and Continental made such a check exchange. Continental sent SMI 17 checks totalling $273,137.62 from August 25 to August 26, representing amounts it owed SMI for invoiced deliveries from September 3, 1982 to June 28, 1983. On August 29 SMI sent Continental its check for $271,967.20 for invoiced deliveries by Continental from February 22, 1983 through August 16,

1983. Both parties deposited the checks into their bank accounts on August 30.

On November 18, 1983, less than 90 days later, Continental filed a petition in bankruptcy under Chapter 7. In November 1985 Continental's Trustee filed an adversary action against SMI seeking to recover $273,137.62, which represented the total amount of the checks Continental had sent SMI as part of the check exchange. The bankruptcy court held in favor of the Trustee, finding that Continental's remittance of the checks to SMI constituted avoidable preferential transfers, § 547(b), that were not part of a valid setoff under § 553. * * *

The district court affirmed, finding that SMI's payment constituted a transfer under the Code, which defines "transfer" very broadly in [§ 101(54)], and was a preference under § 547. * * *

II.

Section 547(b) provides that a trustee may avoid, and proceed to seek recovery of, any transfer made by a debtor to a creditor within 90 days prior to filing for bankruptcy that has the effect of enabling that creditor to receive more than it would in the bankruptcy proceeding had the transfer not been made. However, under § 553(b), a valid setoff executed within 90 days of the date of the filing of a bankruptcy petition is nonetheless protected from avoidance under § 547, except for any insufficiency. Where a pre-petition setoff is asserted in defense to a proceeding brought by a trustee the court must first determine whether the setoff is valid under § 553. Only if the court finds the setoff invalid, and further concludes that no right of setoff exists in bankruptcy, is § 547 applied. We hold that the lower courts erred by attempting to resolve this case under § 547 after SMI asserted that it and Continental had completed a pre-petition setoff of their mutual debts.

* * *

B.

Section 553(b)(1) provides, in pertinent part, that except as to circumstances not relevant here:[4]

[4] The right of pre-petition setoff is further limited by the "improvement-in-position" test designed to ensure that a creditor will not improve its position during the 90–day period before bankruptcy and then protect its position by completing a setoff prior to the debtor's filing of a petition. This improvement-in-position test is "in essence, a miniature preference provision akin to § 547(d)(5) [sic]." *In re Balducci Oil Co.*, 33

> [I]f a creditor offsets a mutual debt owing to the debtor against a claim against the debtor on or within 90 days before the date of the filing of the petition, then the trustee may recover from such creditor the amount so offset to the extent [of] any insufficiency on the date of such setoff. * * *

"Insufficiency" is defined in § 553(b)(2) as the amount by which a party's credit against the debtor exceeded its mutual debt to the debtor at the time the setoff was effected. Where there is no improvement in position found, a setoff within 90 days of the filing of a bankruptcy petition as to mutual debts incurred more than 90 days prior to the filing of the petition is effective as between the impending bankrupt debtor and a creditor except to the extent that the creditor receives more in the setoff than it pays.

Section 553 does not create a right of setoff or prescribe the means by which a setoff must be executed in order to be effective. It merely preserves any right of setoff accorded by state law, subject to certain limitations. North Carolina has long recognized the right of setoff where mutual debts exist between parties. North Carolina has not, however, prescribed any method by which a setoff must be executed to be valid.

The United States Supreme Court, applying the former Bankruptcy Act, recognized that a pre-petition setoff may be effected where parties with mutual debts have "themselves given checks, charged notes, made book entries, or stated an account whereby the smaller obligation is applied on the larger." *Studley v. Boylston Nat'l Bank*, 229 U.S. 523, 528 (1913). The Trustee concedes that had the parties executed this setoff by corresponding accounting entries it would have been valid, but he argues that a setoff may not be effected by exchanging checks. We see no reason to distinguish between the two practices. Indeed, the exchange of checks, with the resulting endorsements each made on the other's checks before depositing them, provided better documentation of satisfaction of the debt than mere book entries. We hold that the check exchange constituted an effective exercise of setoff pursuant to North Carolina law and § 553(b).

B.R. 847, 852 (Bankr. D.Colo.1983).

Since the mutual debts Continental and SMI extinguished by the check swap represented only shipments delivered more than 90 days before Continental filed its petition, and there has been no allegation that SMI improved its position as to these debts prior to completing the setoff, the improvement-in-position test does not limit this setoff.

The lower courts used "hypothetical facts" to ignore the intent of the parties at the time of the check exchange and to view each party's act of sending a check as the independent payment of a valid debt. Under these "facts," the Trustee argues, SMI should be seen as merely having decided to pay a valid debt without a cognizable expectation that its corresponding debt from Continental would be paid. If SMI and Continental's payments of their unrelated debts could be seen as unrelated occurrences that just happened to coincide, then Continental's payment could be found to be a preference avoidable under § 547.

However, the clear intent of the parties, as expressed through their overt acts, may not be so readily ignored. As part of their general and longstanding business practice SMI and Continental customarily accrued and then set off, sometimes by accounting entries and sometimes by check exchange, debts to the other. In the check exchange in question SMI and Continental took every step possible to ensure that their checks would cross in the collection process since neither had funds sufficient to cover their checks. As neither intended a substantial amount of money to change hands, there was no need to have sufficient funds on hand, apart from the coordinated deposits of the other's check, to ensure that their own check would clear. Although checks were used, in essence the exchange constituted an accounting exercise to clear their books of mutual debts.

SMI would have been entitled to assert its right of setoff under § 553(a) post-petition if the check exchange had not been executed before Continental's petition was filed since both debts were incurred pre-petition. Where a creditor fails "to exercise its right of setoff prior to the filing of the petition" it does not lose the right, but must "proceed in the bankruptcy court by means of a complaint to lift the automatic stay so as to be allowed to exercise its already existing right to offset." *In re Compton Corp.,* 22 B.R. 276, 278 (Bankr.N.D.Tex.1982). And, as the Trustee concedes, there is no evidence that the debt SMI extinguished in the setoff was incurred either fraudulently or " 'for the purpose of obtaining a right of setoff against the debtor.' " *In re Southern Indus. Banking Corp.*, 809 F.2d 329, 332 (6th Cir.1987) (quoting § 553(a)(3)(C)). It would be inequitable to construe § 553(b) to prevent "the parties from voluntarily doing, before the petition is filed, what the law itself requires to be done after proceedings in bankruptcy are instituted." *Studley*, 229 U.S. at 528–29.

III.

Since the debts the two parties eliminated with the setoff were not exactly the same, the resulting checks were not equal. The check exchange was a proper setoff only up to the amount that SMI and Continental owed each other equivalent amounts. Since SMI sent Continental $271,967.20 while receiving from Continental $273,137.62, an insufficiency of $1,170.42, recoverable from SMI, was created pursuant to §§ 553(b)(1) and (b)(2). SMI must return this insufficiency to Continental's estate. The district court judgment is reversed, and the case is remanded for entry of an appropriate judgment in favor of the estate consistent with this opinion.

Notes and Questions

1. What type of creditor is most likely to have an available right of setoff? Would that explain the formulation of the setoff provision? Is a setoff a form of preference? Or is the setoff right the functional equivalent of a security interest generally? Read § 506(a) again.

2. To what extent was the intent of the parties pertinent to the *Durham* court's application of § 553? Does the court suggest that intent determines whether § 553 or § 547 is applicable?

3. In footnote 4, the court asserted that § 553(b)(1) is "a miniature preference provision akin to" § 547(c)(5). In what way is that true? How are the two subsections different? What explains their different formulations? Consider the following example as you answer these questions.

> Ninety days before bankruptcy, Debtor owes Creditor $10,000, repayment of which is fully secured by a floating lien on inventory and receivables collateral. Forty-five days before bankruptcy, the outstanding indebtedness is still $10,000, but the collateral has decreased in value to $6,000. On the day before bankruptcy, the outstanding indebtedness still has not changed, but the collateral has increased in value to $9,000.
>
> Assume Creditor sets off Debtor's loan against the collateral on the day before bankruptcy. Under § 553(b)(1), the trustee may recover $3,000 from Creditor, as Day 45 was the first date on which there was an insufficiency and the insufficiency on the setoff day had decreased by $3,000.
>
> Conversely, the trustee may not avoid Creditor's security interest under § 547(c)(5)'s improvement of position test, because Creditor was fully secured and could not improve its position.

MATTER OF ELCONA HOMES CORP.

United States Court of Appeals, Seventh Circuit, 1988.
863 F.2d 483.

POSNER, Circuit Judge.

This appeal requires us to examine the Bankruptcy Code's provision on set offs, which states that the Code "does not affect any right of a creditor to offset a [prebankruptcy] mutual debt owing by such creditor to the debtor * * * against a [prebankruptcy] claim of such creditor against the debtor." § 553(a). The debtor, Elcona Homes Corporation, was (and still is, for this is a reorganization case) a manufacturer of mobile homes. Shortly before it went broke, Linda Markle had ordered a mobile home from one of its dealers, Monro Homes, Inc. The price was $36,700. Markle paid $14,000 down, and Elcona agreed to sell the home to Monro for $22,700. This was, of course, the difference between the retail price and the amount of the down payment; so the latter amount represented Monro's profit.

Payment of the balance was to be due when Monro delivered the home to Markle and set it up for her. Green Tree Acceptance, Inc., the creditor in the case, agreed to finance Markle's purchase by giving Monro $22,700 in exchange for an assignment of the installment contract that Monro had signed with Markle. So instead of making her monthly payments to Monro, Markle would make them to Green Tree, and Green Tree's profit would come from the interest it charged Markle. Upon receipt of the $22,700 from Green Tree, Monro would remit an equal amount to Elcona to pay for the mobile home. The parties refer to the type of arrangement by which Green Tree financed Monro's business as "retail proceeds" financing. It bears a family resemblance to the more common "floor-planning" system of dealer financing, but there the lender takes a security interest in the goods before the dealer sells them and here it was afterward.

This was not the first time that Green Tree had financed Monro's sales of Elcona homes; and a practice had developed of Green Tree's paying Elcona directly rather than paying Monro for remittance to Elcona. This meant that instead of Green Tree's paying Monro $22,700 for the installment contract and Monro's then turning around and paying Elcona $22,700 for the mobile home, Green Tree would be expected simply to pay $22,700 to Elcona. Elcona preferred this arrangement, since it protected it (how far we shall see) against the risk of Monro's defaulting. This was not only the practice between the parties but also, they have stipulated, the practice generally followed in the mobile home industry.

Elcona's bankruptcy occurred after the sale to Markle but before Green Tree had paid Elcona. Now it happened that Elcona owed Green Tree $16,000 (more or less) on an earlier transaction. Green Tree decided to set off this debt against the $22,700 that normally it would have sent directly to Elcona, and therefore sent Elcona only the difference between $22,700 and $16,000 (actually somewhat less, but like the exact amount owed Green Tree in the earlier transaction, that is a detail of no importance to this appeal). The bankruptcy judge did not consider this a proper set off. Since the $22,700 was not a debt that Green Tree owed Elcona but a debt it owed Monro, there was no mutual indebtedness between Elcona and Green Tree, as the statute requires. (Elcona adds that Green Tree was really just an escrow agent of Monro, Elcona's real debtor.) The district judge * * * reversed the bankruptcy judge. He thought the evidence showed "a mutuality of obligations between Green Tree and Elcona and vice versa because it was both the industry practice and the practice between the parties for the lender (Green Tree) to pay the manufacturer (Elcona) directly the amount due the manufacturer from the dealer. That being the case, Green Tree was entitled to setoff the debt owed it by Elcona." Elcona appeals.

The set-off provision in the Bankruptcy Code seems at first glance inconsistent with the usual result in bankruptcy, which is that all unsecured creditors are treated alike ("equity is equality"). But it is no more than the usual result precisely because the principle that unsecured creditors shall be treated alike is riddled with exceptions. There are all sorts of preferences (for the Internal Revenue Service, for employees having wage claims, for persons who extend credit to the debtor after the petition for bankruptcy is filed, etc.) and discriminations (e.g., against creditors treated preferentially on the eve of bankruptcy). And it might be more accurate to say not that there is a principle (however qualified) of equal treatment among creditors but that bankruptcy provides a mechanism for enforcing pre-bankruptcy entitlements given by state or federal law, with some exceptions. But the idea of equal treatment is a useful as well as persistent one. An important purpose of bankruptcy law is to prevent individual creditors from starting a "run" on the debtor by assuring them that they will be treated equally if the debtor is precipitated into bankruptcy, rather than being given either preferential treatment for having jumped the gun or disadvantageous treatment for having hung back.

The principle is not absolute, as we have stressed, but its exceptions generally are intelligible; and we will be helped in determining the scope of the set-off exception—which on its face is arbitrary—if we can understand its rationale, too.

Set offs outside of bankruptcy are in no wise anomalous or problematic; no third party's rights comparable to those of unsecured creditors in bankruptcy are affected, and circuitous proceedings are avoided. But in bankruptcy an unsecured creditor fortunate enough to owe his debtor as much as or more than the debtor owes him can, by setting off his debt against the debtor's, in effect receive 100 cents on the dollar, while the other unsecured creditors, who have nothing to set off against the debtor, might be lucky to collect 10 cents on the dollar. The difference in treatment seems based on a fortuitous difference among the unsecured creditors, and therefore arbitrary. Let us inquire further.

Although the right of set off has been a part of Anglo–American bankruptcy law since 1705, see Act of 4 Anne, ch. 17, § 11, its rationale has never been made clear. To say that it "recognize[s] the possible injustice in compelling a creditor to file its claim in full and accepting possible dividends thereon, while at the same time paying in full its indebtedness to the estate," 4 Collier on Bankruptcy ¶ 553.02, at p. 553–10 (King 15th ed. 1988) (footnote omitted), is to say very little; for why is it not an equal or greater injustice to advance one unsecured creditor over another merely because the first happens also to owe money to their common debtor? Nor is it helpful to point out that "it is only the balance which is the real and just sum owing by or to the bankrupt," *Prudential Ins. Co. v. Nelson*, 101 F.2d 441, 443 (6th Cir.1939), for if the set off is allowed, the other unsecured creditors will not receive "the real and just sum owing" to them.

The only sense we can make of the rule is that it recognizes that the creditor who owes his debtor money is like a secured creditor; indeed, the mutual debts, to the extent equal, secure each party against the other's default. This reasoning figured in Congress's decision to retain the right of set off in the 1978 overhaul of bankruptcy law. The reasoning may seem circular, however, for it is only by virtue of the Bankruptcy Code's preserving the right of set off that the creditor has, in the event of his debtor's bankruptcy, a form of security for the debt he is owed. (But of course not all defaulting debtors are bankrupt.) And one might suppose that if the theory of the set off is that it provides the creditor with security, the creditor would have to prove that the parties had intended a right of set off as a means of securing the creditor—that is, would have to prove that the creditor had been counting on the right in extending credit to the debtor on the terms he did. But such proof is not in fact required.

Banks argue that the right to set off deposits (a bank deposit is a debt of the bank to the depositor) against the depositor's debts to the bank facilitates the provision of bank credit and lowers the rate of interest, by giving the bank security in the event of the depositor's going broke. But the more secure the bank is, the less secure the depositor's other creditors will be, so they will charge higher interest rates. This, however, is a general characteristic of secured lending. The secured lender faces a lower risk of loss in the event of default and therefore will lend at a lower interest rate, but unsecured lenders, facing a higher risk of loss because fewer assets will be available to satisfy their claims in the event of default, will charge higher interest rates. Nevertheless secured financing is so firmly established a commercial practice that it is hard to believe it does not serve important commercial purposes, and it is apparent what they might be: lenders differ in their ability to monitor their borrowers (in order to prevent the borrower from increasing the riskiness of its activities) and to bear risk, and thus a combination of secured and unsecured financing enables a borrower to appeal to the different capabilities and preferences of different lenders.

Yet if deposits are intended to secure the bank's loans, why not treat the bank as a secured creditor rather than creating a general right in all creditors to set off their debts against the bankrupt's debts to them? Maybe the answer is simply that set offs are just another form of secured financing that the Bankruptcy Code has decided to recognize, though under a different name and with different restrictions. But the underlying rights of creditors which are asserted in bankruptcy proceedings are the creation of state law, not of the Bankruptcy Code. * * * Maybe the right question to ask, therefore, is not why the Code allows set offs (for it also allows secured creditors to withdraw their collateral from the pool available to other creditors), but why it places restrictions on them. Against this view of set offs as a species of secured financing, however, it can be argued that, apart perhaps from such special situations as that of banks dealing with their depositor-borrowers, set offs are recognized in state law for their procedural convenience—the consolidation of offsetting claims in the same suit—and that this convenience should receive little weight in bankruptcy. Professor Gilmore thought the express exemption of set offs from the filing requirements in Article 9 (secured financing) of the Uniform Commercial Code, see § 9–104(i), absurd: "Of course a right of setoff is not a security interest and has never been confused with one: the statute might as appropriately exclude fan dancing." 1 Gilmore, Security Interests in Personal Property § 10.7, at pp. 315–16 (1965). This view seems extreme and has been questioned, but certainly there is no evidence here that the existence of mutual debts (if that is what they were) between Elcona and Green Tree reflected a desire by the parties to secure each other's obligations; it appears to have been an accident.

But we need not resolve these questions, or press our inquiry into the rationale for the Bankruptcy Code's treatment of set offs further, in order to decide this case. Whether that treatment reflects a felt tension between the right of set off and the normal practice in bankruptcy of treating unsecured creditors equally, or whether one denies the tension, points out that the recognition by state law of a right of set off makes the set off a form of secured financing, and argues (contrary to our earlier point) that there really is no policy of treating unsecured creditors in bankruptcy equally, the statute itself speaks of "a *mutual* debt" (emphasis ours) and therefore precludes "triangular" set offs. See, e.g., *In re Berger Steel Co.*, 327 F.2d 401 (7th Cir.1964); *Depositors Trust Co. v. Frati Enterprises, Inc.*, 590 F.2d 377, 379 (1st Cir.1979).

Two recurrent cases should be noted. In the first and easier, illustrated by *In re Southern Industrial Banking Corp.*, 809 F.2d 329 (6th Cir.1987), the creditor of a bankrupt buys a debt owed by someone else to the debtor in order to offset the debt that the bankrupt debtor owes him and so gain an advantage over the other unsecured creditors. This is plainly evasive and easily rebuffed. Indeed, it will normally violate § 553(a)(3), which was added in 1978 to close a loophole that had allowed preferences in the form of set offs, and which forbids a set off where the debt was incurred within 90 days before bankruptcy, while the debtor was insolvent, and for the purpose of obtaining a set off against him.

In the second case, illustrated by both *Berger Steel* and *Depositors Trust*, a subsidiary or other affiliate of the creditor owes money to the bankrupt and the two affiliates ask that they be treated as a single entity. This is rebuffed by pointing out that, save in exceptional circumstances, corporate and commercial law treat affiliated corporations as separate enterprises.

Our case follows neither of these familiar patterns. It is neither a transaction in contemplation of bankruptcy (the timing suggests it may be but Elcona does not argue the point, and it is therefore waived) nor an attempt by affiliated corporations to lift the corporate veil that separates them. Nevertheless there can be no set off unless the $22,700 was in fact a debt owed by Green Tree to Elcona.

The district court's opinion does not deal satisfactorily with this issue. The court inferred the existence of a mutual debt from the practice of the parties and of the industry; indeed, he equated obligation to practice. He said, "there was a mutuality of obligation between Green Tree and Elcona and vice versa *because* it was both the industry practice and the practice between the parties for the lender (Green Tree) to pay the manufacturer (Elcona) directly the amount due the manufacturer from the dealer. *That being the case*, Green Tree was entitled to setoff the debt owed it by Elcona." (Emphasis added.) In other words, a practice equals or creates an obligation. It does not. Suppose the practice of a landlord is to accept late payment from his tenant. That practice does not entitle the tenant to pay late; it does not modify the contract. If every forbearance to enforce a contract to its hilt operated to modify the contract against the party exercising forbearance, such forbearance would become rare; promisees would always insist on exact performance of the promisor's obligation, and defaults and litigation would become more frequent. A practice may be evidence of an obligation, may give meaning to vague terms, and so on; but it is not the equivalent of it.

The question can be put this way: if, instead of remitting $22,700 directly to Elcona, Green Tree had remitted the money to Monro, and Monro had absconded with the money without paying Elcona, could Elcona have sued Green Tree? Possibly so, since as we said the practice of Green Tree in remitting directly to Elcona provided both parties with security against a default by the dealer, and the security would be less if the contract were interpreted to allow either party to disregard the practice. Maybe, then, the practice was also an implied term of the contract. If so—and if, therefore, Elcona could have sued Green Tree (and won) in our hypothetical case—this would show that Green Tree was indeed indebted to Elcona, and then the debts were mutual and could be offset. The case must be remanded for a determination whether there was not only a practice of direct payment from the finance company to the manufacturer but an obligation to make such payments.

* * *

The decision of the district court is vacated and the case remanded for further proceedings consistent with this opinion.

[The dissenting opinion of Senior District Judge Will, sitting by designation, is omitted. The district court, in Judge Will's view, had already determined that Green Tree was obligated to pay Elcona directly. Thus, Judge Will would have affirmed, rather than remanded.]

As was noted at the beginning of this Section, setoff often arises in the context of loans made by banks to their depositors. The amount in the deposit account can be set off against the loan balance if the depositor-borrower fails to pay. That is all well and good, but how does the bank protect its setoff rights if the depositor-borrower files a bankruptcy petition and then attempts to clean out the account? Can the bank refuse to permit the withdrawal or refuse to honor checks as they are presented? If it does, has it violated the automatic stay?

CITIZENS BANK OF MARYLAND v. STRUMPF

United States Supreme Court, 1995.
516 U.S. 16, 116 S.Ct. 286, 133 L.Ed.2d 258.

JUSTICE SCALIA delivered the opinion of the Court.

We must decide whether the creditor of a debtor in bankruptcy may, in order to protect its setoff rights, temporarily withhold payment of a debt that it owes to the debtor in bankruptcy without violating the automatic stay imposed by § 362(a).

I

On January 25, 1991, when respondent filed for relief under Chapter 13 of the Bankruptcy Code, he had a checking account with petitioner, a bank conducting business in the State of Maryland. He also was in default on the remaining balance of a loan of $5,068.75 from the bank. Under § 362(a), respondent's bankruptcy filing gave rise to an automatic stay of various types of activity by his creditors, including "the setoff of any debt owing to the debtor that arose before the commencement of the [bankruptcy case] against any claim against the debtor." § 362(a)(7).

On October 2, 1991, petitioner placed what it termed an "administrative hold" on so much of respondent's account as it claimed was subject to setoff—that is, the bank refused to pay withdrawals from the account that would reduce the balance below the sum that it claimed was due on respondent's loan. Five days later, petitioner filed in the Bankruptcy Court, under § 362(d), a "Motion for Relief from Automatic Stay and for Setoff." Respondent then filed a motion to hold petitioner in contempt, claiming that petitioner's administrative hold violated the automatic stay established by § 362(a).

The Bankruptcy Court ruled on respondent's contempt motion first. It concluded that petitioner's "administrative hold" constituted a "setoff" in violation of § 362(a)(7) and sanctioned petitioner. Several weeks later, the Bankruptcy Court granted petitioner's motion for relief from the stay and authorized petitioner to set off respondent's remaining checking account balance against the unpaid loan. By that time, however, respondent had reduced the checking account balance to zero, so there was nothing to set off.

The District Court reversed the judgment that petitioner had violated the automatic stay, concluding that the administrative hold was not a violation of § 362(a). The Court of Appeals reversed. "An administrative hold," it said, "is tantamount to the exercise of a right of setoff and thus violates the automatic stay of § 362(a)(7)." We granted certiorari.

II

The right of setoff (also called "offset") allows entities that owe each other money to apply their mutual debts against each other, thereby avoiding "the absurdity of making A pay B when B owes A." *Studley v. Boylston Nat. Bank*, 229 U.S. 523, 528 (1913). Although no federal right of setoff is created by the Bankruptcy Code, § 553(a) provides that, with certain exceptions, whatever right of setoff otherwise exists is preserved in bankruptcy. Here it is undisputed that, prior to the bankruptcy filing, petitioner had the right under Maryland law to set off the defaulted loan against the balance in the checking account. It is also undisputed that under § 362(a) respondent's bankruptcy filing stayed any exercise of that right by petitioner. The principal question for decision is whether petitioner's refusal to pay its debt to respondent upon the latter's demand constituted an exercise of the setoff right and hence violated the stay.

In our view, petitioner's action was not a setoff within the meaning of § 362(a)(7). Petitioner refused to pay its debt, not permanently and absolutely, but only while it sought relief under § 362(d) from the automatic stay. Whether that temporary refusal was otherwise wrongful is a separate matter—we do not consider, for example, respondent's contention that the portion of the account subjected to the "administrative hold" exceeded the amount properly subject to setoff. All that concerns us here is whether the refusal *was a setoff*. We think it was not, because—as evidenced by petitioner's "Motion for Relief from Automatic Stay and for Setoff"—petitioner did not purport permanently to reduce respondent's account balance by the amount of the defaulted loan. A requirement of such an intent is implicit in the rule followed by a majority of jurisdictions addressing the question, that a setoff has not occurred until three steps have been taken: (i) a decision to effectuate a setoff, (ii) some action accomplishing the setoff, and (iii) a recording of the setoff. But even if state law were different, the question whether a setoff *under § 362(a)(7)* has occurred is a matter of federal law, and other provisions of the Bankruptcy Code would lead us to embrace the same requirement of an intent permanently to settle accounts.

Section 542(b) of the Code, which concerns turnover of property to the estate, requires a bankrupt's debtors to "pay" to the trustee (or on his order) any "debt that is property of the estate and that is matured, payable on demand, or payable on order * * * *except to the extent that such debt may be offset under § 553 of this title against a claim against the debtor*." § 542(b) (emphasis added). Section 553(a), in turn, sets forth a general rule, with certain exceptions, that any right of setoff that a creditor possessed prior to the debtor's filing for bankruptcy is not affected by the Bankruptcy Code. It would be an odd construction of § 362(a)(7) that required a creditor with a right of setoff to do immediately that which § 542(b) specifically excuses it from doing as a general matter: pay a claim to which a defense of setoff applies.

Nor is our assessment of these provisions changed by the fact that § 553(a), in generally providing that nothing in the Bankruptcy Code affects creditors' prebankruptcy setoff rights, qualifies this rule with the phrase "except as otherwise provided in this section and in sections 362 and 363." This undoubtedly refers to § 362(a)(7), but we think it is most naturally read as merely recognizing that provision's restriction upon *when* an *actual setoff* may be effected—which is to say, not during the automatic stay. When this perfectly reasonable reading is available, it would be foolish to take the § 553(a) "except" clause as indicating that § 362(a)(7) requires immediate payment of a debt subject to setoff. That would render § 553(a)'s general rule that the Bankruptcy Code does not affect the right of setoff meaningless, for by forcing the creditor to pay *its* debt immediately, it would divest the creditor of the very thing that supports the right of setoff. Furthermore, it would, as we have stated, eviscerate § 542(b)'s exception to the duty to pay debts. It is an elementary rule of construction that "the act cannot be held to destroy itself." *Texas & Pacific R. Co. v. Abilene Cotton Oil Co.*, 204 U.S. 426, 446 (1907).

Finally, we are unpersuaded by respondent's additional contentions that the administrative hold violated §§ 362(a)(3) and 362(a)(6). Under these sections, a bankruptcy filing automatically stays "any act to obtain possession of property of the estate or of property from the estate or to exercise control over property of the estate," § 362(a)(3), and "any act to collect, assess, or recover a claim against the debtor that arose before the commencement of the case under this title," § 362(a)(6). Respondent's reliance on these provisions rests on the false premise that petitioner's administrative hold took something from respondent, or exercised dominion over property that belonged to respondent. That view of things might be arguable if a bank account consisted of money belonging to the depositor and held by the bank. In fact, however, it consists of nothing more or less than a promise to pay, from the bank to the depositor, and petitioner's temporary refusal to pay was neither a taking of possession of respondent's property nor an exercising of control over it, but merely a refusal to perform its promise. In any event, we will not give § 362(a)(3) or § 362(a)(6) an interpretation that would proscribe what § 542(b)'s "exception" and § 553(a)'s general rule were plainly intended to permit: the temporary refusal of a creditor to pay a debt that is subject to setoff against a debt owed by the bankrupt.

The judgment of the Court of Appeals for the Fourth Circuit is reversed.

It is so ordered.

Notes and Questions

1. The Court did not point to two other sections of the Code that could have bolstered its conclusion: § 363(c)(2), which prohibits a debtor from using cash collateral without permission from the court or the affected creditor; and § 506(a), which treats a creditor's right to setoff as a secured claim.

2. The Court stressed that the bank's administrative hold was temporary. How long is "temporary"? Is it necessary that a bank using an administrative hold also immediately seek relief from the automatic stay?

I. STATUTORY LIENS

Section 545 enables the trustee to avoid statutory liens—that is, involuntary liens that arise solely by statute, without the necessity for legal or equitable proceedings. Its reach is limited.

Subsection (1) avoids liens that arise only upon the happening of one of the events listed, all of which relate to the debtor's financial condition. It was enacted to prevent states from circumventing bankruptcy priorities by creating statutory liens for favored creditors that would arise only when a debtor filed bankruptcy or suffered a similar financial indignity. States have gotten the message, so § 545(1) will seldom apply.

Subsection (2) avoids liens that are vulnerable to a bona fide purchaser because of nonrecording. This provision overlaps to some extent with § 544(a)'s strong arm power, and will seldom apply because most statutory liens are enforceable against bfps.

Subsection (3) avoids liens for rent, and will apply even if the lien is invulnerable under § 544(a) (because perfected) and under § 547(b) (because outside the 90–day period).

Subsection (4) applies to a lien of distress for rent, which is actually a common law lien rather than statutory. It is treated for bankruptcy purposes as a statutory lien, however.

Any statutory lien not within the preceding categories is invulnerable to the trustee under § 545. It may, however, be vulnerable under one of the other avoiding powers, with one exception—§ 547. One of the preference exceptions, § 547(c)(6), protects a statutory lien from avoidance as a preference if it is not avoidable under § 545.

J. POSTPETITION TRANSFERS

All of the avoiding powers that we have seen so far are applicable to *prepetition* transfers of an interest in the debtor's property. (Please never make the mistake, on a bankruptcy exam or in front of a judge, of thinking that a transfer made after the filing of the petition is possibly a preference!) Once the petition is filed, all of the debtor's property becomes property of the estate and its disposition should be in accordance with the Code's directions.

The debtor does not lose possession and control of estate property in a Chapter 11, however, and it takes time to put a trustee in place in a Chapter 7 or 13 case. Thus, the debtor will have the opportunity, though not the right, to transfer estate property.

Section 549 governs postpetition transfers. That the trustee can avoid unauthorized postpetition transfers, § 549(a)(2)(B), comes as no surprise. But the trustee can, under § 549(a)(2)(A), avoid certain *authorized* transfers as well—those authorized *only* under § 303(f) or § 542(c). Since § 549(a) is subject to §§ 549(b) and (c), avoidance of these transfers under (a) has the effect of testing them under (b) and (c). Section 303(f) permits the debtor to continue to operate its business during the "involuntary gap period" (that is, the time between the filing of an involuntary petition and the hearing under § 303(h)). Section 542(c) protects an entity who, without knowledge of the bankruptcy, transfers property of the estate or pays a debt owed to the debtor to someone other than the trustee. The legislative history to § 542(c) indicates that it codifies *Bank of Marin v. England*, 385 U.S. 99, 87 S.Ct. 274, 14 L.Ed.2d 197 (1966), which held that a drawee bank is not liable for honoring a debtor's checks postpetition unless the bank knew of the bankruptcy. But § 542(c) only protects the bank; the payee will be tested under § 549(b).

Read § 549 and answer the following:

Questions and Problems

1. A few days after filing a bankruptcy petition, Debtor sold her car to Neighbor for the amount listed in the National Automobile Dealer Association's "Blue Book" as the car's wholesale value. Neighbor knew that Debtor was in bankruptcy. Can the trustee recover the car?

2. Would it matter under the facts of Problem # 1 if the car had been sold for its listed retail value?

3. Would it matter under the facts of Problem # 1 if Neighbor had been unaware of the bankruptcy?

4. A few days after filing a bankruptcy petition, Debtor sold a lot on which she had hoped to build a vacation home to Purchaser for $45,000, its fair market value. No notice of the bankruptcy had been filed in Distant County, where the lot was located, and Purchaser was unaware of the bankruptcy case. Is the transfer avoidable? What is the relationship between §§ 362(a) and 549(c)? See *Glendenning v. Third Federal Savings Bank (In re Glendenning)*, 243 B.R. 629 (Bankr. E.D.Pa.2000).

5. Debtor, a wholesaler of women's clothing, received an order for evening dresses from one of its regular customers a few days after filing a petition under Chapter 11. Debtor sent the dresses to its customer with payment due in 15 days. Bank, to which Debtor owes a large unsecured obligation, wants to use § 549 to recover the shipment of dresses. Assuming Bank can get the court's permission to pursue this action, will it succeed? See § 363(c)(1).

6. In *Harris v. McCauley* (*In re McCauley*), 814 F.2d 1350 (9th Cir.1987), Debtor and his parents each owned a parcel of real estate. Debtor's parents owned the Susanville property, which they had bought in 1979 for $16,500. Debtor owned the Truckee property, which he had bought in 1981 and in which he had equity of $35,000. In October of 1981, Debtor quitclaimed the Truckee property to his parents; they quitclaimed the Susanville property to him, as consideration for conveyance of the Truckee property, in February of 1982. Debtor filed bankruptcy in June of 1982. Four days later, the parties quitclaimed the properties back to each other, on advice of counsel, believing that the original exchange would be avoided "due to lack of consideration."

The court held the postpetition transfer of the Susanville property avoidable under § 549(a). The court rejected the parents' argument that this gave the trustee more than a single satisfaction, contrary to § 550(d), because the trustee would keep both parcels. If the parents had been good faith purchasers for value, without knowledge of the bankruptcy, either the transfer would not have been avoided or they would have had a lien on the property. They knew of the bankruptcy, however, and voluntarily transferred the Truckee property back to the estate, accepting an avoidable transfer in return. Thus, *both* parcels came into the hands of the bankruptcy trustee.

Could this debtor and his parents have traded parcels immediately before bankruptcy and prevented this result?

K. RECLAMATION

A seller of goods to the debtor has only an unsecured claim. The unpaid seller cannot take back the goods under state law, except to the extent that UCC § 2-702(2) applies. That provision gives sellers, under certain circumstances, a right to reclaim the goods:

> Where the seller discovers that the buyer has received goods on credit while insolvent he may reclaim the goods upon demand made within ten days after the receipt, but if misrepresentation of solvency has been made to the particular seller in writing within three months before delivery the ten day limitation does not apply. Except as provided in this subsection the seller may not base a right to reclaim goods on the buyer's

> fraudulent or innocent misrepresentation of solvency or of intent to pay.

This right of reclamation is akin to a lien, since the seller can take back the goods and apply their value to the unpaid purchase price.

The Bankruptcy Code contains a reclamation provision that was patterned after UCC § 2-702(2). Section 546(c) makes the trustee's avoiding powers subject to the seller's right of reclamation. As with setoff, bankruptcy does not create a substantive right of reclamation; rather, it recognizes the state-law right of reclamation.

Section 546(c), however, imposes requirements that do not exactly track those of UCC § 2-702(2). Furthermore, § 546(c) does not assure the recovery of goods to a seller meeting the requirements of both state law and § 546(c)(1).

Subsection 546(c)(1) was extensively revised in 1994. Before the revision, it read as follows:

> (1) such seller may not reclaim any such goods unless such seller demands in writing reclamation of such goods before ten days after receipt of such goods by the debtor; and * * *.

Read the old and new versions of § 546(c) and solve the following Problems.

Problems

1. Neighbor sold her used lawnmower to Debtor when Neighbor bought a new one. She agreed to accept payment in 30 days. Five days after the sale, however, one of Debtor's other creditors knocked on Neighbor's door while looking for Debtor and told Neighbor a tale of default, pursuit and evasion. Neighbor telephoned Debtor that evening and demanded return of the lawnmower. Debtor filed a bankruptcy petition the next day. Is Neighbor entitled to reclaim the lawnmower?

2. Retailer received a shipment of hairdryers from Wholesaler on September 1, with payment due in 45 days. Retailer filed a bankruptcy petition on September 8 and, on the 15th, Wholesaler sent a written reclamation demand. Is Wholesaler entitled to reclaim the goods?

3. Debtor, a farmer, sought to purchase goods on credit from Seller, a retailer of farm equipment. Debtor provided Seller a financial statement

reflecting marginal solvency. Seller, relying on that information, sold Debtor $18,000 worth of equipment. Debtor never paid for the goods and, four months later, Seller learned that the financial statement was inaccurate—Debtor had been hopelessly insolvent all along. Seller sent a written reclamation demand immediately thereafter and, a week later, Debtor entered bankruptcy. What are Seller's rights under § 546(c)?

4. Seller was a manufacturer of tow tractors, used to haul cargo to and from airplanes. Seller delivered three tow tractors to Debtor less than a week before Debtor filed Chapter 11. The price for the tow tractors was $86,000. Seller learned of Debtor's bankruptcy the day it was filed and immediately sent a written reclamation demand. Debtor refused to turn over the tow tractors, asserting that they were needed in the reorganization effort. Seller filed a reclamation action in the bankruptcy court. What result? See *Eagle Industrial Truck Manufacturing, Inc. v. Continental Airlines, Inc. (In re Continental Airlines, Inc.)*, 125 B.R. 415 (Bankr. D.Del.1991).

5. Has Seller in Problem # 4 violated the automatic stay by its post-petition reclamation demand?

6. Seller, a retailer of computers, sold two computers to Debtor, an accounting firm. Debtor failed to pay for the computers and, six days after delivery, Seller sent a written reclamation demand. Instead of returning the goods, Debtor resold them to an advertising agency that knew nothing about these events. Debtor filed a bankruptcy petition several weeks later. What are Seller's rights under § 546(c)?

Chapter 6

EXECUTORY CONTRACTS AND UNEXPIRED LEASES

A. INTRODUCTION

Section 365 of the Code provides special treatment for the debtor's executory contracts and unexpired leases (which are, after all, just a species of executory contract), carrying rights and powers not available to the debtor outside of bankruptcy. Determining when § 365 applies is important because of its special rules. To help focus you on the types of transactions that are of concern, consider the following fact patterns:

1. Debtor ordered a case of widgets from Seller that is delivered on Day 1. A case of widgets costs $500, but Debtor has not yet paid. Debtor files a bankruptcy petition on Day 10.

2. Debtor ordered a case of widgets from Seller on Day 1 and included a check for $500 along with the order. Debtor files a bankruptcy petition on Day 10 and the widgets have not yet been delivered.

3. Debtor ordered a case of widgets from Seller on Day 1, which is to be delivered and paid for on Day 15. Debtor files a bankruptcy petition on Day 10.

What are the bankruptcy consequences of each of these fact patterns? Do you see what sets an executory contract apart from other contracts?

What to do with these contracts, on which some future performance is due, is a question of considerable importance in bankruptcy. It is particularly important in reorganization cases, in which the debtor needs to retain the benefits of favorable bargains and to escape the burdens of unfavorable ones.

B. TRANSACTIONS TO WHICH § 365 APPLIES

The first question is to determine what transactions fall within the category of "executory contracts and unexpired leases." The most-cited authority on this question is an article written by Professor Vern Countryman before the Code was enacted:

VERN COUNTRYMAN, EXECUTORY CONTRACTS IN BANKRUPTCY: PART I

57 Minn. L. Rev. 439, 450–52, 456–61 (1973) (most footnotes omitted).

II. WHAT IS AN EXECUTORY CONTRACT?

As Professor Williston has said, "All contracts to a greater or less extent are executory. When they cease to be so, they cease to be contracts." But that expansive meaning can hardly be given to the term as used in the Bankruptcy Act or even to the Act's occasional alternative reference to contracts "executory in whole or in part." The concept of the "executory contract" in bankruptcy should be defined in the light of the purpose for which the trustee is given the option to assume or reject. Similar to his general power to abandon or accept other property, this is an option to be exercised when it will benefit the estate. A fortiori, it should not extend to situations where the only effect of its exercise would be to prejudice other creditors of the estate.

A. Contracts Performed by the Nonbankrupt

Executory contracts, in the sense in which Professor Williston spoke, abound in a bankruptcy proceeding. One example is the contract under which the nonbankrupt party has fully rendered the performance to which the bankrupt is entitled, but which the bankrupt has performed only partially or not at all. Such a contract will give the nonbankrupt party a provable claim in the bankruptcy proceeding, whether it is liquidated or unliquidated and whether it is absolute or contingent as to liability. The trustee's option to assume or reject should not extend to such contracts. The estate has whatever benefit it can obtain from the other party's performance and the trustee's rejection would neither add to nor detract from the creditor's claim or the estate's liability. His assumption, on the other hand, would in no way benefit the estate and would only have the effect of converting the claim into a first priority expense of administration and thus of preferring it over all claims not assumed—a prerogative which the Bankruptcy Act has never been supposed to have vested in either the trustee or the court.

* * *

It seems clear, therefore, that a contract which is executory only in the sense that it provides the fully performed nonbankrupt party with a claim against the bankrupt estate is not one which may be assumed or rejected. * * * Of course, the nonbankrupt party who has fully performed may have provided an asset which comes into the bankrupt estate and which the trustee will have the option to abandon or accept, quite apart from the bankrupt's liability with respect to it. But if the trustee does accept the property, he accepts it *cum onere*, taking its burdens with its benefits, whether the burden be a liability imposed upon the owner by law solely by virtue of his ownership, a condition to full enjoyment imposed by a contract valid against the trustee, or a lien which the trustee cannot avoid. But the trustee's acceptance of such property should not amount to assumption of a contract of sale so as to elevate an unsecured obligation for the purchase price to the level of a first priority administration expense. Nor should his abandonment of the property, or even his mistaken attempt to reject the contract of sale, have any effect on a seller's unsecured claim for the price.

Of course, to speak of a contract under which the nonbankrupt party has "fully performed" is to draw an extremely fine line, one which would include among the executory contracts which the trustee can accept or reject some which should be excluded. What of the nonbankrupt building contractor who has fully performed save that he has failed to connect the water or has made a defective connection? Such a failure, even if not cured, would entitle the bankrupt to damages but would not be sufficiently material to permit him to refuse to accept the building or to excuse his performance. The trustee's rejection of such a contract would neither add to nor detract from the estate's benefits or its liabilities; his assumption of it, which likewise would not benefit the estate, should therefore not convert the contractor's claim into a first priority administration expense. Hence, a contract so nearly performed by the nonbankrupt party that failure to complete performance would not be sufficiently material to excuse performance by the bankrupt should not be treated as an executory contract in bankruptcy.

B. Contracts Performed by the Bankrupt

Another example of a contract executory in the Willistonian sense which should not be treated as an executory contract within the meaning of the Bankruptcy Act is a contract which the bankrupt has fully performed, but which the nonbankrupt party has performed only partially or not at all. The bankrupt's claim to further performance under such a contract obviously is an asset which in most instances will pass to the trustee * * *.

Since the bankrupt's claim against the other party is an asset which will pass to the trustee, it is one which the trustee can accept or abandon just as he can accept or abandon noncontractual claims. But his acceptance of the asset merely leaves the other party's liability where § 70a of the Act[a] has already transferred it, while his abandonment of it merely leaves the other party liable to the bankrupt as he was before bankruptcy.

Indeed, this is the manner in which the Act and the courts have treated such contracts when questions have arisen as to the treatment of actions on them which the bankrupt had pending at bankruptcy. Section 11c of the Act provides that the trustee may, with approval of the court, prosecute any suit commenced by the bankrupt prior to adjudication.[b] This section has been construed by the courts, which follow the statute in making no distinction between suits based on contract and others, as meaning that the trustee has three choices: (1) he may take over the bankrupt's suit; (2) he may allow the bankrupt to continue it for the benefit of the estate; or (3) he may abandon the claim to the bankrupt.

Here again, the concept of a nonexecutory contract should accommodate the contract so nearly performed by the bankrupt that his failure to complete performance would not constitute a material breach which would excuse performance by the nonbankrupt party. Rejection of such a contract by the trustee should not be treated as a material breach excusing the other party's performance. Nor should the trustee's assumption of such a contract require either that performance of the

[a] Section 541 of the Code, which governs property of the estate, is the successor to § 70a of the Act. Eds.

[b] Section 11c of the Act was not carried over into the Code. Eds.

bankrupt's obligation be completed at the expense of the estate or that the nonbankrupt party's damage claim be elevated to a first priority expense of administration.

C. Contracts Unperformed on Both Sides

Thus, by a process similar to one method of sculpting an elephant,[85] we approach a definition of executory contract within the meaning of the Bankruptcy Act: a contract under which the obligation of both the bankrupt and the other party to the contract are so far unperformed that the failure of either to complete performance would constitute a material breach excusing the performance of the other.

Such a contract, similar to the contract under which the other party has fully performed but the bankrupt has not, represents a claim against the estate. But here that claim may be reduced or totally eliminated if the trustee rejects the contract, because the other party is required to mitigate damages by an amount approximating the value of the performance he is spared by the trustee's rejection. In addition, such a contract, like the one under which the bankrupt has fully performed but the other party has not, represents an asset of the estate to the extent that it carries the unperformed obligation of the other party. But if the trustee elects to assume the contract, as when he accepts other assets to which he takes the title of the bankrupt under § 70a, he takes it *cum onere* and must render that performance which the bankrupt had contracted to perform as a condition to receiving the benefits of the contract. Whether in a given case the trustee will assume or reject depends, presumably, on his comparative appraisal of the value of the remaining performance by the other party and the cost to the estate of the unperformed obligation of the bankrupt, although the Act is silent on that point.

As you will see, many of the cases that consider issues arising under § 365 begin with a discussion of whether an executory contract is presented by the facts at hand, often citing the Countryman test. Keep the issue of § 365's applicability in mind as you progress through this chapter.

---

85 Obtain a large piece of stone. Take hammer and chisel and knock off everything that doesn't look like an elephant.

IN RE BOOTH

United States Bankruptcy Court, District of Utah, 1982.
19 B.R. 53.

RALPH R. MABEY, Bankruptcy Judge.

INTRODUCTION AND FACTUAL BACKGROUND

This case asks whether debtor, who is vendee under a contract for deed, has rights in an "executory contract" within the meaning of § 365.

Debtor is a debtor in possession under Chapter 11. He is a broker and dealer in real property. His schedules show land worth $2,641,550, most of which has been bought or sold on contracts for deed.

Lewis and Edris Calvert (sellers) made a contract to sell land to debtor at a price of $97,200, with $1,100 down, and the balance payable over time with interest. Sellers must convey title when debtor completes performance. They may forfeit his interest if he defaults. Debtor has resold the property, again using a contract, to a third party, John Collett.

Sellers moved for an order, pursuant to § 365(d)(2), directing debtor to assume or reject their contract. Debtor demurred, arguing that the contract is not executory and therefore § 365 is inapplicable. After denying the motion orally on the record, the court files this explanatory memorandum.

EXECUTORY CONTRACTS AND BANKRUPTCY POLICY

Sellers point to the definition of executory contract formulated by Professor Countryman: "a contract under which the obligations of both the bankrupt and the other party to the contract are so far unperformed that the failure of either to complete performance would constitute a material breach excusing the performance of the other." Countryman, "Executory Contracts in Bankruptcy: Part I," 57 Minn. L. Rev. 439, 460 (1973).[2] This definition embraces the contract for deed, they

---

[2] The Countryman definition is mentioned in the legislative history. The Commission Report quotes Countryman, Report of the Commission on the Bankruptcy Laws of the United States, H. Doc. No. 93–137, Part II, at 198–99 (1973), while the House and Senate Reports contain an abridgement of his test, H.R. Rep. No. 95–595 at 347,

maintain, because both sides have unperformed obligations, *viz*. Payment by debtor and delivery of title by sellers. Failure of either to complete performance would constitute a material breach excusing the performance of the other.

Countryman propounded a definition of executory contract which was "functional," that is, "defined in the light of the purpose for which the trustee is given the option to assume or reject. Similar to his general power to abandon or accept other property, this is an option to be exercised when it will benefit the estate." Countryman, *supra*, at 450. From this premise, he framed his test of performance due on both sides. If the creditor has performed, rejection would be meaningless, since "the estate has whatever benefit it can obtain * * * and * * * rejection would neither add to nor detract from the creditor's claim or the estate's liability." *Id*. at 451. Assumption likewise would be meaningless, and further, would transform the obligation of debtor into a cost of administration, "a prerogative which the Bankruptcy Act has never been supposed to have vested in either the trustee or the court." *Id*. at 452. If the debtor has performed, assumption adds nothing to his right to performance. Rejection, on the other hand, would not constitute a breach. In short, the Countryman test is an index to when assumption or rejection of a contract will "benefit the estate" and therefore of when a contract is executory.

Section 365, however, reflects a number of policies, including not only benefit to the estate but also protection of creditors. The Countryman test may often define the benefit to the estate, but does it always? And does it speak to the protection of creditors? These questions underlie the refusal of the Commission to define executory contract, Report of the Commission on the Bankruptcy Laws of the United States, H. Doc. No. 93–137, Part I, at 199 (1973) ("any succinct statutory language risks an unintended omission or inclusion"), especially in relation to the contract for deed.

Sections 365(i) and 365(j), for example, give special treatment to nondebtor vendees of land sale contracts. They were passed in response to the plight of nondebtor vendees under former law. In *In re New York Investors Mutual Group*, 143 F.Supp. 51 (S.D.N.Y.1956), the debtor had contracted to sell land to a buyer for $105,000. There was a down payment of $15,000 with the balance due at closing in 18 months. Prior to closing, debtor was adjudicated bankrupt. The trustee sought

reprinted in 1978 U.S.C.C.A.N. at 6303–04, and S. Rep. No. 95–989 at 58, *reprinted in* 1978 U.S.C.C.A.N. at 5844.

and the referee ordered rejection of the contract with buyer. This order was affirmed on appeal. The court ruled that the interest of buyer was subject to rejection by the trustee and that the remedy of buyer "is a claim for damages for breach of the agreement." *Id.* at 54. Thus buyer, who under state law may have owned the land, was relegated to the status of an unsecured creditor. *New York Investors* was followed. But there was uneasiness over its result, and some courts moved to soften its impact.

Meanwhile, reformers sought change. The Commission spearheaded this movement and §§ 365(i) and 365(j) evolved from its report, which in turn was derived from a working paper, later published as Lacy, "Land Sale Contracts in Bankruptcy," 21 U.C.L.A. L. Rev. 477 (1973).

The method for apportioning the benefits and burdens of insolvency, Lacy wrote, cannot be found through "definitions of 'executory' * * *. Instead, the search should be for a policy which defines those interests of present or potential value which may properly be taken from others for the benefit of the bankrupt or his estate." *Id.* at 482. Nondebtor vendees deserve special treatment, not because their contract is executory in the sense that performance remains due on both sides, but because "the purchaser in this kind of contract is likely to be the buyer of a home or farm or small business who has adjusted to a new location. Very often, especially in the case of a residential buyer, he will be poor. Certainly, modern American bankruptcy policy places as high a value on relieving the poor from the consequences of their own and others' improvidence as in doing perfect justice between creditors." *Id.* at 484.

He criticized the assumption that "the purchaser whose contract is rejected after he has paid a part of the price will have only an unsecured claim" but that "he may get the land if he has paid the entire price on the ground that the contract is no longer 'executory.' * * * The suggested distinction between paid-in-part and paid-in-full seems utterly capricious. Instead, one should not speculate about the meaning of 'executory' but rather should consider what ought to be thrown into the pot for general creditors and when it is fair to recognize special claims to certain assets." *Id.* at 487.

Others echoed Lacy. One, emphasizing the "economic consequences" of rejection, argued that the nondebtor vendee should not be "used as a resource by the trustee to increase the bankrupt's estate and the cost of the bankruptcy [should] be completely borne by commercial creditors. This would increase the creditors' incentive to deal only with sound vendors and would entirely remove this 'policing' function from the vendees, who occupy the poorest position to exercise such control. Moreover, the commercial creditors are capable of distributing the risks of a vendor's bankruptcy, but the vendees are not. The creditors can simply pass on the increased costs of vendor bankruptcy by raising the cost of credit. Most likely, the vendees would ultimately pay for most of this increase in the cost of credit. But they would be paying as a group, and therefore the risks of bankruptcy would be distributed evenly and rationally—rather than falling completely on a small and arbitrary group of vendees." Note, "Bankruptcy and the Land Sale Contract," 23 Case Wes. Res. L. Rev. 393, 410–11 (1972).

Thus, §§ 365(i) and 365(j), far from representing the Countryman test, are a tonic for the consequence of its application. This suggests that, in the final analysis, executory contracts are measured not by a mutuality of commitments but by the nature of the parties and the goals of reorganization. A debtor as vendee is free from the constraints of § 365, and is thereby afforded flexibility in proposing a plan, but meanwhile must provide, upon request, adequate protection to vendors. A debtor as vendor may use § 365 as a springboard to rehabilitation but not at the expense of vendees. Thus, it is the consequences of applying § 365 to a party, especially in terms of benefit to the estate and the protection of creditors, not the form of contract between vendor and vendee, which controls. This conclusion is supported by many statutory provisions and much judicial gloss.[6]

---

[6] There are many examples of the use of "policy," rather than a rule like the Countryman test, in determining what is an "executory contract" within the scope of § 365 under the Code and § 70(b) under the Act.

* * *

This approach may be criticized for being result oriented. Result-orientation, however, is endemic to the policymaking which has determined what is an executory contract and when it is rejectable within the scope of §§ 365 and 70(b). Indeed, the Countryman test, which is predicated on the policy of benefit to the estate, is result oriented. Some commentators and courts have frankly admitted as much. *See, e.g., In re Jolly*, 574 F.2d 349, 351 (6th Cir.1978) ("such definitions [as the Countryman test] are helpful, but do not resolve this problem. The key, it seems, to deciphering the meaning of the executory contract rejection provisions, is to work backward, proceeding from an examination of the purposes rejection is expected to accomplish. If those objectives have already been accomplished, or if they can't be accomplished through rejection, then the contract is not executory within the meaning of the Bankruptcy Act").

EXECUTORY CONTRACTS AND THE POLICIES OF BENEFIT TO THE ESTATE AND THE PROTECTION OF CREDITORS

The contract for deed, where debtor is vendee, benefits the estate more when viewed as a lien than as an executory contract. This is because treatment of the contract for deed as a lien enlarges the value of the estate and furthers the rehabilitation of the debtor. This treatment likewise makes adequate protection available to creditors.

1. *Enlarging the Value of the Estate.* The assumption or rejection of executory contracts, like the strong-arm and other avoiding powers, "is a valuable weapon * * * in the armory of the trustee," meant to free "his estate to pay a larger dividend to general creditors." Silverstein, "Rejection of Executory Contracts In Bankruptcy and Reorganization," 31 U. Chi. L. Rev. 467, 468 (1964). If the contract for deed is viewed as an executory contract, it may be assumed or rejected, but if assumed, it must be taken *cum onere*, that is, debtor must take the contract as written, with its benefits and burdens.

In practical terms this means that, absent assumption of the contract, vendor may enforce his remedy of forfeiture. Vendor, although in substance a mortgagee, may receive an advantage over other lienors, and the estate may be deprived of whatever equity exists in the property. The bankruptcy court, as a court of equity, regards substance over form, demands equality of treatment among creditors, and loathes a forfeiture. The contract should be treated as a lien; the vendor is thereby placed on a par with other lienors; forfeiture and the loss of equity are prevented.

This result is analogous to the treatment of security interests disguised as leases. The lessor is entitled to assumption and performance of the lease or rejection and return of the property, with any equity lost to the estate. The security interest disguised as a lease, however, is treated as a lien, with any equity available to the estate.

2. *Furthering the Rehabilitation of the Debtor.* Executory contracts should be handled to "assist in the debtor's rehabilitation." H.R. Rep. No. 95–595 at 348, *reprinted in* 1978 U.S.C.C.A.N. at 6304. If the contract is executory, and if it is assumed during the interim between petition and plan, defaults must be cured, damages must be paid, and adequate assurance of performance must be given, all as costs of administration. If the contract is assumed in a plan, the same conditions must be satisfied with the accumulated costs of administration

payable on the effective date of the plan. The same burdens are imposed if the contract is assigned, in or without a plan. * * *

If the contract is a lien, assumption is irrelevant, and no administrative costs are incurred.[14] Instead of taking the contract *cum onere*, the lien may be "dealt with" in a plan, *viz.*, by scaling down the debt, reducing the interest rate, and extending maturities. With or without a plan, the property may be sold free of the lien.

Debtor, like most dealers in the contract for deed, uses that instrument because other financing is unavailable. He can afford little down, and hopes to subdivide and resell in order to meet payments. Chapter 11 has not improved his cash flow. Treating the contract as a lien thus allows more latitude in proposing a plan and thereby furthers the rehabilitation of the debtor.

3. *Adequate Protection of Creditors*. Vendors have two rights under a contract for deed: the right to payment, which is not adequately protected, and the right to hold title as security, which is adequately protected. While the right to payment is suspended, the interest in property is adequately protected. This strikes a balance between vendors, other creditors, and the estate. Vendors are not preferred, for example, in terms of administrative claims, but are treated on a par with other mortgagees, who are protected against any decrease in the value of their liens.

THE BASIS FOR DISTINGUISHING BETWEEN DEBTORS AS VENDORS AND AS VENDEES

Sellers contend that §§ 365(i) and 365(j) mean that contracts for deed are executory contracts. They argue that because §§ 365(i) and 365(j) treat some contracts for deed as executory contracts, all contracts for deed must be executory contracts. Put differently, it would be anomalous if contracts where the debtor *sells* realty are executory but contracts where the debtor *buys* realty are not. This would result in the contract between debtor and Collett being executory and the contract between debtor and sellers being nonexecutory although both are identical in form. Consistency in the treatment of contracts for deed, whether debtor is vendor or vendee, is necessary for a sensible construction of the Code.

---

[14] The exception to this rule would be any payments required adequately to protect lienors. This is improbable, however, where the collateral is land. *Cf. In re Alyucan Interstate Corp.*, 12 B.R. 803 (Bankr. D.Utah 1981).

Seller's argument founders, however, on at least two shoals. First, treatment of the contract for deed as an executory contract, where debtor is vendee, ignores the reasons for enacting §§ 365(i) and 365(j). They were passed to give nondebtor vendees the protection of mortgagors. Viewing the contract for deed as a lien, where debtor is vendee, therefore is consistent with the spirit of these provisions. Second, consistency in terminology, that is treating contracts for deed as executory contracts under § 365 in every instance, favors nondebtor vendees over debtor vendees and debtor vendors over debtor vendees in bankruptcy. Particularized treatment of the contract for deed is necessary to avoid these consequences.

First. Sections 365(i) and 365(j), as discussed above, were enacted to prevent harm which had occurred under prior law to nondebtor vendees. They accomplish this purpose, where the vendee is in possession, by allowing him to stay, continue payments, and receive title. In short, he is treated as a mortgagor, an analogy frequently drawn by proponents of §§ 365(i) and 365(j).

Countryman notes that mortgages are not executory contracts and "where the vendor of land is himself the purchase money mortgagee, including those cases where applicable nonbankruptcy law will treat the land sale contract as a mortgage, the situation seems no different." Countryman, *supra*, at 472. Then what of a debtor as vendor in California where contracts for deed are deemed mortgages? Under the Countryman test this would not be an executory contract. But this interpretation would deprive homeowners of the protection of § 365(i). We afford them protection either by sacrificing the symmetry of sellers' argument or by recognizing that vendees are seen as mortgagors under § 365(i). What about the debtor as vendee? We can take Countryman at face value and call the contract a lien, bypassing § 365, but it will still be the same piece of paper, which under different circumstances, mandates special treatment to nondebtor vendees under § 365(i).

Second. Consistency in the characterization of the contract leads to disparity in the treatment of the parties for other reasons. Where debtor is vendor, vendees are protected at least with a lien for the amount paid on the contract under § 365(j). But where debtor is vendee, he has no protection under § 365(j). Absent cure and adequate assurance of performance, he stands to lose, through forfeiture, his equity in the property. Likewise, debtor as vendor, under some circumstances, may sell the property free of liens. Thus, unencumbered proceeds, or encumbered proceeds for which adequate protection is provided, may underwrite operations pending workout of a plan, or fund a plan. But debtor as vendee may have no similar option. He must find cash to cure and supply adequate assurance of performance before he may assume the contract. And assumption is a condition to assignment of the contract.

The upshot is that nondebtor vendees, by virtue of §§ 365(i) and 365(j), may receive more favorable treatment in bankruptcy than debtor vendees. And debtor vendors, because of other policies and provisions in the Code, may fare better than debtor vendees. It may be argued that this disparity in treatment is warranted because of the risk of default when debtor is vendor, or because the nondebtor, in each instance, is an innocent victim. But this argument admits that the reasons for calling a contract "executory" may have less to do with the terms of the "paper" than with the status of the parties and their interests in light of bankruptcy policies.

CONCLUSION

The court is reluctant to depart from a rule as workable as the Countryman test. But application of the rule in this case contradicts the reason for its existence. Classifying the contract for deed, where debtor is vendee, as a lien rather than an executory contract benefits the estate by enlarging the value of the estate and furthering the rehabilitation of the debtor. Sellers, as lienors, enjoy adequate protection. This is in harmony with the rationale for §§ 365(i) and 365(j). The blessings and burdens of reorganization are fairly distributed between creditors and the estate.

Notes and Questions

1. *Booth* was one of the first cases to raise questions about the Countryman test, and remains one of the most prominent. Are you persuaded by the court's reasoning? Do you agree that the question *whether* to apply § 365 should turn on the *result* of applying § 365?

2. The court, in footnote 6, quotes *In re Jolly*, 574 F.2d 349, 351 (6th Cir.1978), *cert. denied sub nom. Still v. Chattanooga Memorial Park*, 439 U.S. 929, 99 S.Ct. 316, 58 L.Ed.2d 322 (1978), which seems to call unabashedly for a result-oriented approach to the determination of executoriness. Although *Jolly* was decided under the Act, its statement was approved in a Code case, *Martin Bros. Toolmakers, Inc. v. Industrial Development Board (In re Martin Bros. Toolmakers, Inc.)*, 796 F.2d 1435, 1439 (11th Cir.1986). Is this result-driven decisionmaking sensible to you?

3. *Booth* suggests that its result was necessary to ameliorate the otherwise harsh consequences of § 365. Aren't these consequences really the product of state law's refusal to treat contracts for deed as secured transactions? If so, should bankruptcy provide the cure?

4. As *Booth* indicated, a large number of cases address the question whether a particular transaction constitutes a lease or a disguised security interest. The governing law is § 1–201(37) of the Uniform Commercial Code, which defines "security interest." It focuses on the functional characteristics of a transaction, looking particularly at whether an economically meaningful residual remains at the end of the term. See Corinne Cooper, *Identifying a Personal Property Lease Under the UCC*, 49 Ohio St. L.J. 195 (1988).

If a transaction is a disguised security interest rather than a lease, the nondebtor party is a secured creditor who is unlikely to have perfected its security interest. Thus, the nondebtor will be an unsecured creditor (after the trustee finishes wielding the avoiding powers) rather than a party to an executory contract entitled to performance according to the contract terms. That's a long way to fall.

MATTER OF CRIPPIN

United States Court of Appeals, Seventh Circuit, 1989.
877 F.2d 594.

MANION, Circuit Judge.

These consolidated appeals present the issue of whether debtors could treat their agreements to participate in an Employee Stock Ownership Plan (ESOP) as an executory contract and reject that contract in bankruptcy (and hence discontinue their participation) pursuant to § 365. The practical effect of rejection in these cases is to allow the debtors to rescind a 15 percent wage reduction they had agreed to as a condition of their eligibility to participate in the ESOP. The bankruptcy court and the district court allowed the debtors to reject their agreements to participate. We disagree with that conclusion and therefore reverse and remand.

In August 1985, after negotiations with its employees' collective bargaining agent, P*I*E Nationwide, Inc. (PIE) established the Ryder/P*I*E Employee Stock Investment Plan (the "SIP"). PIE established the SIP as an Employee Stock Ownership Plan (ESOP) under the Employee Retirement Income Security Act (ERISA), 29 U.S.C. §§ 1001–1461. The SIP was to run from October 7, 1985 through December 1, 1990.

To be eligible to participate in the SIP, an employee had to irrevocably agree to accept a 15 percent wage reduction over the SIP's life. (Some lower-paid employees were required to accept a smaller wage reduction but this detail is unimportant.) In return, PIE agreed to fund the SIP with common stock. Although the SIP participants had no right to back out of the SIP, PIE could terminate the SIP at any time (while allowing the employees to keep their right to shares they had already earned). If PIE decided to terminate the SIP (an event that, to our knowledge, has not occurred), the wage reduction would also end.

Participants were to earn stock on a daily basis; in other words, a participant could receive stock only for days he worked. Each participant had a separate account in the SIP. The SIP trustee was to allocate stock annually into each account based on the proportion that each participant's wage reduction for that year bore to the total wage reduction for all SIP participants. The value of the shares PIE contributed, however, was not directly tied to the amount that employee wages were reduced; in fact, PIE anticipated that the value of the stock it contributed would be substantially less than the value of the wages that the SIP participants relinquished (a fact that the parties confirmed at oral argument).

By establishing the SIP, PIE hoped to stanch substantial losses that it had suffered in 1984 and continued to suffer in 1985. By requiring employees to accept a wage reduction to participate in the SIP, PIE hoped to reduce substantially its payroll expenses, and thus reduce its overall operating expenses. PIE's management also hoped to increase productivity and efficiency by giving employees a stake in the company.

In October 1985, Steven Bruce and Thomas Crippin, PIE employees, elected to accept wage reductions and to participate in the SIP. Both, however, had difficulties making ends meet on their reduced wages. In October 1985 [sic], Bruce and his wife (who we shall refer to jointly as Bruce) filed a Chapter 13 bankruptcy petition. Crippin was able to hold out longer but in February 1987 he also filed a Chapter 13 petition.

Chapter 13 offers an alternative to liquidation under Chapter 7 by allowing a debtor with regular income to keep his assets and establish a plan to pay creditors out of his future income. As part of his plan, a debtor may include provisions rejecting executory contracts that he entered into before bankruptcy, § 1322(b)(7), subject to § 365, the general Bankruptcy Code provision authorizing rejection. As part of their Chapter 13 plans, Bruce and Crippin sought to reject their participation in the SIP as of the date they filed their bankruptcy petitions. By rejecting their future participation in the SIP, Bruce and Crippin sought to avoid the 15 percent wage reduction they had agreed to and to be paid the wages they would have received had they not agreed to the reduction. Bruce and Crippin maintained that the additional income they sought was necessary to fund their Chapter 13 plans. Despite PIE's objections, the bankruptcy court and, on appeal, the district court, allowed Bruce and Crippin to reject their future participation in the SIP as an executory contract and ordered PIE to restore Bruce's and Crippin's wages to pre-reduction levels.

We must decide whether Bruce and Crippin could reject their participation in the SIP as an executory contract and force PIE to restore their wages to pre-reduction levels. While Congress has provided that debtors may reject executory contracts in bankruptcy, Congress has not defined exactly what an executory contract is. Attempts to frame a precise definition have been somewhat vexing. A recurring theme in many courts' definitions, however, has been the idea of mutual obligations. The Bankruptcy Code's legislative history states that the term "executory contract" "generally includes contracts on which performance is due to some extent on both sides." H.R. Rep.No. 95–595 at 347, *reprinted in* 1978 U.S.C.C.A.N. at 6303. A common definition, which this court has cited with approval, states that a contract is executory for bankruptcy purposes where "'the obligation of both the bankrupt and the other party to the contract are so far unperformed that the failure to complete performance would be a material breach excusing the performance of the other.'" *In re Chicago, Rock Island & Pacific R. Co.*, 604 F.2d 1002, 1004 (7th Cir.1979) (quoting Countryman, *Executory Contracts in Bankruptcy: Part I*, 57 Minn. L. Rev. 439, 456 (1973)).

Viewed in isolation, the SIP looks like an executory contract under the mutual obligation approach. The bankruptcy and district courts reasoned that it was because performance remains due on both sides. If a participant did not work, he did not receive stock; and, if PIE did not credit a participant with stock, he would not have to continue working at the reduced wage. The courts below separated participation in the SIP from the overall employment relationship (despite the fact that both SIP participation and all other employment benefits depended upon a participant's continuing to work) and in effect treated the SIP simply as a contract to buy and sell stock in the future. In the bankruptcy court's and district court's view, all PIE employees received cash compensation; some (the SIP participants), however, agreed to take 15 percent of their wages and purchase stock from PIE.

We think, however, that it was error to treat the SIP as simply a contract to buy and sell stock. Instead, the SIP is a part of PIE's compensation system, and thus an integral part of the entire employment relationship. PIE provides a benefit to Bruce and Crippin by providing them jobs and paying them; Bruce and Crippin in return benefit PIE by working. Although the courts below thought that PIE was required to invest the 15 percent the SIP participants gave up in PIE stock, the stock's value bears no direct relationship to the value of wages the employees give. Also, when the SIP participants agreed to reduce their wages, they also agreed to reduce their wage-based fringe benefits—including incentive compensation, vacation and holiday pay, and short-term disability benefits—because PIE based those benefits on the participants' reduced wages, not on the wages they would have received if they had elected not to participate in the SIP. These facts indicate that the wage reduction really was a wage reduction and not simply part of a contract to purchase stock through payroll deductions. In other words, the SIP was an alternative form of compensation to straight wages.

Bruce and Crippin could not reject the SIP while accepting the other benefits their employment provided them. Allowing debtors to reject executory contracts frees them from burdensome future obligations and thus frees up more assets for creditors. At the same time, rejection constitutes a breach and gives the nonbankrupt party a claim against the debtor. But since rejection constitutes a breach, it also excuses performance by the nonbankrupt party. Thus, rejecting a contract allows a debtor to escape a contract's burdens; but, at the same time, the debtor must also give up any future benefit he might receive from the contract.

When a debtor rejects a contract he rejects his obligation to perform under the contract and to receive the benefits that go along with that performance because the burden of performing outweighs the benefits received. But Bruce and Crippin want to continue working and to receive all the benefits that go along with working (including having a job). By "rejecting" the SIP, they merely want to receive the wages they would have been receiving had they not elected to participate in the SIP. But at the time Bruce and Crippin elected to participate in the SIP, they had to choose how they wanted PIE to compensate them for their work: by not joining the SIP, they could choose to be compensated strictly in cash (to simplify things, we disregard any other benefits); by joining the SIP, they could choose to be compensated partly in cash and partly in stock to be held in trust for their future benefit. Bruce and Crippin chose to participate in the SIP and thus chose to be compensated in both cash and stock. Bruce and Crippin had no device outside of bankruptcy to force PIE to reinstate their old wage; the only way they could get out of the SIP would have been to stop working or to persuade PIE (through their union) to terminate the SIP. If PIE would not terminate the SIP, and Bruce and Crippin had to quit their jobs to escape the SIP, they would be rejecting much more than the SIP; they would be rejecting their jobs and all other benefits that go with them (including their cash wages). Bruce and Crippin are really asking the courts to change the form of their compensation (and, given the fact that the stock's value is less than the value of the wages they would have otherwise received, to in effect give them a raise). This the courts may not do. While bankruptcy courts have the power to allow debtors to *escape* burdensome contracts by rejecting them, bankruptcy courts do not have the power to rewrite contracts to allow debtors to continue to perform on more favorable terms. Once they chose to accept cash wages and stock as compensation, Bruce and Crippin could not unilaterally modify their agreement to choose straight wages.

It is true that if PIE terminates the SIP, the wage reduction will end and the SIP participants will receive higher cash wages. But that provision does not make the wage reduction any less a true wage reduction or the SIP any less an alternative compensation system. The termination provision is much like a statement by an employer who has agreed to pay an employee $10 per hour that he might at some time unilaterally decide to pay the employee $12 per hour. The employee in that case could not force the employer to raise his wages; neither may Bruce or Crippin force PIE to compensate them differently by terminating the SIP.

Because participation in the SIP was part of their overall employment relationship that depended upon their continued employment with PIE, Bruce and Crippin could not reject the SIP without rejecting that entire relationship. The bankruptcy court's and district court's decision to, in effect, allow Bruce and Crippin to unilaterally modify their employment agreement with PIE to change the form of compensation they received was error. Therefore, we reverse those courts' judgments allowing Bruce and Crippin to reject the SIP and ordering PIE to pay them higher wages and remand to the bankruptcy court to vacate or modify its orders confirming Bruce's and Crippin's Chapter 13 plans consistent with this opinion.

REVERSED AND REMANDED.

Questions

1. Does the Countryman definition, which the court endorsed, prove helpful on these facts?

2. What outcome would *Booth*'s approach to defining an "executory contract" have produced? That is, what result would have best served bankruptcy policies?

C. ASSUMPTION AND ASSIGNMENT

1. GENERAL RULES

Section 365 gives a trustee (or, often, a debtor-in-possession) three choices regarding an executory contract or lease—to assume and retain, to assume and assign, or to reject. Assumption turns the debtor's obligations under the agreement into obligations of the estate, entitled to administrative expense priority. Rejection of the agreement is treated as a breach of contract, and the nondebtor party acquires a claim for damages that is treated as if it arose before the petition. We will return to rejection in a moment, after we explore the meaning and consequences of assumption, as well as of assignment.

As you have already seen, if a contract is assumed it is assumed *cum onere*—with all its benefits and burdens. Thus, a debtor should assume only those executory contracts on which the benefits outweigh the burdens. Remember, a favorable contract can be assumed even if the debtor does not itself have any use for the benefits of the deal (because, for example, it is liquidating or streamlining its business in order to reorganize). In such a case, the debtor will realize the benefits of the favorable deal by assigning the contract to another party. For example, if the price of premises has risen above the lease price, the debtor will assume the lease and sell (assign) it at the higher market rate to a third party; the nondebtor lessor will receive the lease price and the debtor will retain the appreciation.

Subsections (a) and (b) of § 365 set out the requirements for assumption. Section 365(f)(2)(A) makes assumption a prerequisite for assignment. Read §§ 365(a) and (b) and solve the following Problems.

Problems

1. Debtor, Inc. filed a Chapter 11 petition on July 15 and wants to assume the lease of the premises on which its retail store is located. Debtor,

however, has not paid any rent since April. Is the arrearage an impediment to assumption of the lease?

2. Debtor, Inc.'s lease contains a so-called "ipso facto" clause, which provides that the filing of bankruptcy is a default under the lease that terminates the lease automatically. Debtor filed bankruptcy and sought to assume the lease. Lessor argued that no lease existed because of the termination provision. Can Debtor assume?

One of the requirements for assumption is that the debtor give "adequate assurance of future performance." § 365(b)(1)(C). Similarly, a requirement for assignment is that the nondebtor party get "adequate assurance of future performance by the assignee." § 365(f)(2)(B). Courts look to the same factors, whether adequate assurance is of the debtor's or of an assignee's future performance. The following case deals with adequate assurance when the assignee will violate a use provision in a lease.

MATTER OF U.L. RADIO CORP.

United States Bankruptcy Court, Southern District of New York, 1982.
19 B.R. 537.

JOHN J. GALGAY, Bankruptcy Judge.

Debtor, U.L. Radio Corp., has moved for an order, pursuant to Bankruptcy Code § 365(f), authorizing it to assume its lease ("Lease") with Jemrock Realty Company ("Jemrock"), the landlord, and authorizing U.L. Radio to assign the Lease to Just Heaven Restaurant, Ltd. ("Just Heaven"). U.L. Radio operates the leasehold as a television sales and service store. Just Heaven, the prospective assignee, will operate the premises as a small bistro. Jemrock opposes such an assignment, citing a use clause in the Lease which provides that the lessee shall use the premises only for television service and sale of electrical appliances. Jemrock asserts that the assignment of the Lease to Just Heaven would unlawfully modify the Lease by violating the use clause. Such modification, Jemrock avers, is not permitted under § 365 without the landlord's consent, which consent Jemrock withholds.

* * * The Court grants debtor's motion to assume and assign the Lease to Just Heaven.

I. Background

On September 17, 1979, the debtor entered into the Lease with Jemrock for a store located at 2656 Broadway, New York, New York. The store is located in a building which is also occupied by a grocery store, a Chinese restaurant, a liquor store, and 170 apartments. The term of the Lease is for ten years. The rent required to be paid is as follows: $9600 per year from November 1, 1979, to October 31, 1982; $10,800 from November 1, 1982, to October 31, 1985; and $12,000 from November 1, 1985 to October 31, 1989. Paragraph 43 of the Rider to the Lease provides that the tenant may assign the Lease with the written consent of the Landlord, which consent is not to be unreasonably withheld.

On May 20, 1981, the debtor filed an original petition under Chapter 11 of the Bankruptcy Code and continues to operate its business as debtor in possession. No creditors' committee has been formed. The debtor intends to propose a liquidation plan of reorganization. The debtor is current in the payment of rent and related charges required by the terms of the Lease and is not in default of any of the Lease terms.

In furtherance of its intention to liquidate all of its assets and to propose a plan of reorganization, the debtor, subject to the approval of this Court, entered into an assignment of the Lease to Just Heaven. The proposed assignment provides, *inter alia*, that Just Heaven will pay to the Debtor as consideration for the assignment as follows: for the period commencing three months after this Court's approval of the assignment to October 31, 1988, the sum of $2000 per month. Such payments will fund a plan paying unsecured creditors 100 percent of their claims. Rockwell International, the largest creditor, recommends the assignment.

The president of Just Heaven has executed a personal guarantee for the payment of rent in favor of the landlord for the first two years of the assignment, together with a statement that her net worth exceeds $50,000.

The Lease provides in paragraph 45 of the rider to the Lease that "any noise emanating from said premises shall be deemed a breach of the terms and conditions of this Lease." Just Heaven has allocated $20,000 for construction, including soundproofing. David Humpal St. James, Vice President and Secretary as well as a director and a shareholder of Just Heaven, is a noted interior designer including the design of commercial restaurants. His design work has involved soundproofing.

II. Issues

Two issues confront this Court:

(1) Have the provisions of § 365, regarding assumption and assignment of leases, been satisfied?

(2) Can deviation from a use clause prevent the assignment of a lease, when the assumption and assignment otherwise comport with the requirements of § 365?

III. Assumption and Assignment Under § 365

Code § 365 governs the assumption and assignment of executory contracts, providing broad authority to a trustee or debtor in possession to assume and assign an unexpired lease. The aim of this statutory authority to assume a lease is to "assist in the debtor's rehabilitation or liquidation." H.R. Rep. No. 95–595 at 348, *reprinted in* 1978 U.S.C.C.A.N. at 6304.

Assignment of a lease, which is at issue here, must comply with § 365(f) * * *.

Subsection (f)(1) "partially invalidates restrictions on assignment of contracts or leases by the trustee to a third party." H.R. Rep. No. 95–595 at 349, *reprinted in* 1978 U.S.C.C.A.N. at 6305. Subsection (f)(2) "imposes two restrictions on assignment by the trustee: (1) he must first assume the contract or lease, subject to all the restrictions found in the section; and (2) adequate assurance of future performance must be provided to the other contracting party." *Id.* at 349, *reprinted in* 1978 U.S.C.C.A.N. at 6305.[2] Finally, subsection (f)(3) "invalidates contractual provisions that permit termination or modification in the event of an assignment, as contrary to the policy of this subsection." *Id.* at 349, *reprinted in* 1978 U.S.C.C.A.N. at 6305.

---

[2] Code § 365(f) does not state which party must provide assurance. However, since Code § 365(k) relieves the debtor-assignor of liability under the lease after assignment, it is sensible that the assignee must provide the assurance of performance.

A. Requirements of Assumption

The first requirement of assignment under § 365(f)(2) is proper assumption under § 365. § 365(f)(2)(A). The broad authority of a trustee or debtor in possession to assume is limited in Code § 365 by subsections (b), (c), and (d).

Section[s] 365(b)(1) and (2) prescribe conditions to assumption of a lease if a default has occurred. "Subsection (b) requires the [debtor] to cure any default in the * * * lease and to provide adequate assurance of future performance * * * before he may assume." H.R. Rep. No. 95–595 at 347, *reprinted in* 1978 U.S.C.C.A.N. at 6304. No default exists under the Lease before this Court; therefore, the subsection (b) requirements for assignment are not applicable.

Section 365(c) prohibits a debtor from assuming a lease if applicable nonbankruptcy law "independent of any language in the contract or Lease itself " excuses the other party from giving performance to or receiving performance from someone other than the debtor. H.R. Rep. No. 95–595 at 348, *reprinted in* 1978 U.S.C.C.A.N. at 6304. Such "nondelegable" and, therefore, nonassumable contracts and leases include those for unique personal services, as well as those to extend credit, to make loans, and to issue securities. The Lease before this Court does not fall under the prohibition of § 365(c).

Section 365(d) sets time limits on the assumption of unexpired leases. The time requirements of subsection (d) have been met and are not at issue.

B. Adequate Assurance of Future Performance

The second requirement of assignment under § 365(f)(2) is adequate assurance of future performance. § 365(f)(2)(B). Adequate assurance also appears in § 365(b) as a requirement of assumption if an executory contract is in default. § 365(b)(1)(C). The phrase "adequate assurance of future performance" is not found in the Bankruptcy Act.

Adequate assurance is not defined in § 365(f) nor in the legislative history of § 365(f), but "[t]he definition should generally be the same as in § 365(b)." Fogel, *Executory Contracts and Unexpired Leases in the Bankruptcy Code*, 64 Minn. L. Rev. 341, 362 (1980). In the legislative history of § 365(b), Congress while discussing assumption under § 365(b) and the bankruptcy clause under § 365(f), provided this explanation of adequate assurance:

> If a trustee is to assume a contract or lease, the courts will have to insure that the trustee's performance under the contract or lease gives the other contracting party the full benefit of the bargain.

H.R. Rep. No. 95–595 at 348, *reprinted in* 1978 U.S.C.C.A.N. at 6304–05.

Beyond equating adequate assurance with the full benefit of the bargain, Congress offers no definition of adequate assurance except in the case of real property leases in shopping centers. The Lease at issue here is not located in a shopping center. Congress described a shopping center as "often a carefully planned enterprise, and though it consists of numerous individual tenants, the center is planned as a single unit, often subject to a master lease or financing agreement." *Id.* at 348, *reprinted in* 1978 U.S.C.C.A.N. at 6305. The building in which U.L. Radio is located is primarily a residential apartment building, with a liquor store, a grocery store, a restaurant, and U.L. Radio on the first floor. Thus the specific provisions of adequate assurance in the shopping center case do not apply to the assignment at issue here.

Apart from shopping center leases, Congress "entrusted the courts with the definition of adequate assurance of the performance of contracts and other leases." Fogel, *Executory Contracts* at 359. Adequate assurance of future performance are not words of art, but are to be given practical, pragmatic construction. What constitutes "adequate assurance" is to be determined by factual conditions. The broad authorization of the trustee or debtor to assume or assign unexpired leases, notwithstanding anti-assignment or bankruptcy clauses, prompted the admonition from Congress that the courts must "be sensitive to the rights of the nondebtor party to * * * unexpired leases." H.R. Rep. No. 95–595 at 348, *reprinted in* 1978 U.S.C.C.A.N. at 6304.

The phrase "adequate assurance of future performance" was adopted from Uniform Commercial Code § 2–609. U.C.C. § 2–609 provides that a party with reasonable grounds for insecurity regarding another party's performance may demand "adequate assurance." Official Comment 4 to § 2–609 * * * indicates that "adequate assurance" focuses on the financial condition of a contracting party and his ability to meet his financial obligations. Regarding adequate assurance under an assignment pursuant to § 365(f)(2), the Court in *In re Lafayette Radio Electronics* stated, "[T]he Court's primary focus will be on the ability of [the assignee] to comply with the financial obligations under the agreement." 9 B.R. 993, 998 (Bankr. E.D.N.Y.1981).[6]

In *In re Pin Oaks Apartments*, 7 B.R. 364 (Bankr. S.D.Tex. 1980), the Court found that changes in financial provisions of a lease, a percentage rental clause and a sublease provision which protected that rental clause, precluded a finding that adequate assurance had been provided because of the drastic effect the changes would have on rentals received.

Thus, the primary focus of adequate assurance is the assignee's ability to satisfy financial obligations under the lease. In this case, the president of the assignee has executed a personal guarantee of the payment of rent in favor of the landlord for the first two years of the assignment, together with a statement that her net worth exceeds $50,000. The assignee has budgeted $20,000 for construction, enhancing the chances of success of the assignee's enterprise. The assignee will have operating capital of an additional $30,000. Upon these facts, the Court rules that adequate assurance of future financial performance has been provided by the assignee.

IV. USE CLAUSE

However, adequate assurance of future financial performance is not the complete statutory requirement; adequate assurance of future performance is. The financial capability of an assignee may be sufficient for a finding of adequate assurance under an executory sales contract or a similar commercial transaction. In a landlord-tenant relationship, more than an assignee's ability to comply with the financial provisions of a lease may be required. More particularly, will compliance with a use clause be required in order to provide adequate assurance?

Congress indicates that adequate assurance will give the landlord the full benefit of his bargain. H.R. Rep. No. 95–595 at 348. In its case-by-case determination of those factors, beyond financial assurance, which constitute the landlord's bargain, the Court will generally consider the provisions of the lease to be assigned.

---

6 The *Lafayette Radio* Court found that the agreement in that case was a sublease not an assignment. Thus, the Court's inquiry was the debtor's ability to fulfill the financial obligations of the lease. Nonetheless, *financial* wherewithal is the key component of adequate assurance.

However, it is equally clear that, by requiring provision of adequate assurance under § 365, i.e., "the lessor's receipt of the 'full benefit of his bargain'," Congress did not require the Court to assure "literal fulfillment by the lessee of each and every term of the bargain." Simpson, *Leases and the Bankruptcy Code: The Protean Concept of Adequate Assurance of Future Performance* at 35 (unpublished draft in Bankruptcy Court, S.D.N.Y.).[c] Section 365, by its own terms, empowers the court to render unenforceable bankruptcy clauses and anti-assignment clauses which permit modification or termination of a lease for filing in bankruptcy or assignment of the lease. § 365(e), (f)(3). Section 365(k) relieves the estate of liability for future breaches of a lease after assignment, notwithstanding lease provisions to the contrary.

The Court in *In re Pin Oaks Apartments* argued that court authority to abrogate lease provisions extends only to those provisions expressly stated by Congress:

> If Congress intended to give this Court or the trustee the power to abrogate any contractual rights between a debtor and nondebtor contracting party other than anti-assignment and "ipso facto" [i.e. bankruptcy] clauses, it would have expressly done so.

7 B.R. at 367.

Such a narrow view of court authority is not supported by the statute or the legislative history. First, such a narrow view would frustrate the express policy of Congress favoring assignment. Under the *Pin Oaks* reasoning, lessors could employ very specific use clauses to prevent assignment and thus circumvent the Code. Section 365(f), in broad language, empowers the Court to authorize assignment of an unexpired lease and invalidate any lease provision which would terminate or modify the lease because of the assignment of that lease. § 365(f)(1), (3). Any lease provision, not merely one entitled "anti-assignment clause", would be subject to the court's scrutiny regarding its anti-assignment effect. The court could render unenforceable any provision whose sole effect is to restrict assignment, "as contrary to the policy of [subsection (f)(3)]." H.R. Rep. No. 95–595 at 349.

Further, when Congress intended that all terms and provisions of an agreement remain unaltered, it expressly stated such an intent. Section 1124 sets down stringent requirements to define unimpaired

---

[c] This article was published at 56 Am. Bankr. L.J. 233 (1982). Eds.

claims, requiring the cure of defaults and the unaltered maintenance of legal, equitable, and contractual rights. § 1124(2)(D). As one commentator points out, these expressed, stringent requirements for unimpaired claims differ from the requirement that Congress mandated under § 365—mere provision of adequate assurance. Simpson, *Leases* at 40–41. Under both §§ 1124 and 365, Congress expressly stated the requirements. Under § 365, literal compliance with all lease terms was not required. Even under the tightly drawn definition of adequate assurance in the shopping center case, Congress did not envision literal compliance with all lease provisions; insubstantial disruptions in, *inter alia*, tenant mix and insubstantial breaches in other leases or agreements were contemplated and allowed. § 365(b)(3)(C), (D).

Thus, provision of adequate assurance of future performance does not require an assignee's literal compliance with each and every term of the lease. The court may permit deviations from strict enforcement of any provision including a use clause.

One commentator suggested that the court render completely invalid any use clause in a nonshopping center lease because: (1) "the lessor is seeking to protect his tenant mix with the lease provision, and the Code does not require the court to provide such protection"; and (2) a use clause "invalidly conditions assignment." Fogel, *Executory Contracts* at 364 (footnote omitted). The Court rejects this "*per se* unenforceable" reading of a use clause.

However, the Court will not go to the other extreme and adopt the "insubstantial" breach or disruption standard for non-shopping center cases that is applicable only to shopping center leases. The insubstantial breaches and disruptions language of § 365(b)(3) "clearly reflects an attempt to limit the effects of what was understood—and feared—to be the more expansive authority conferred by the balance of § 365(a)." Simpson, *Leases* at 37–38. The Court's authority to waive strict enforcement of lease provisions in the non-shopping center cases will permit deviations which would exceed those permitted in the shopping center cases.

Within the range between unenforceability of a use clause and insubstantial breaches of a use clause, the Code provides no specific standard by which to measure permissible deviations in use. Whatever standard is applied must serve the policy aims of Congress.

Section 365 expresses a clear Congressional policy favoring assumption and assignment. Such a policy will insure that potential valuable assets will not be lost by a debtor who is reorganizing his affairs or liquidating assets for distribution to creditors. This policy parallels case law which disfavors forfeiture. To prevent an assignment of an unexpired lease by demanding strict enforcement of a use clause, and thereby contradict clear Congressional policy, a landlord or lessor must show that actual and substantial detriment would be incurred by him if the deviation in use was permitted.

In this case, the contemplated deviation in use is from an appliance store to a small bistro. The building in which the unexpired leasehold is located already contains a restaurant, a laundry, and a liquor store. The landlord has failed to demonstrate any actual and substantial detriment which he would incur if the proposed deviation in use is permitted. The Court also notes that the contemplated use, along with the planned soundproofing, will have no adverse effect on other tenants in the building. Thus, this Court rules that the use clause may not be enforced so as to block assignment of this lease to Just Heaven. The fact that Jemrock withholds its consent to the proposed assignment will not prevent the assignment. Consent is required only in leases governed by § 365(c). The lease here is not subject to § 365(c).

* * *

Congress, in § 365, has stated a general policy favoring assignment. Balanced against this general policy is the requirement that the non-debtor contracting party receive the full benefit of his bargain. Jemrock Realty will receive the full benefit of its bargain under the proposed assignment of the leasehold from U.L. Radio to Just Heaven. No defaults exist under the lease. The lease has properly been assumed and Just Heaven has provided adequate assurance of future performance. The landlord has shown no actual or substantial detriment to him from the proposed assignment. The statutory requirements have been satisfied. The assignment is authorized.

Problems

1. Standor Jewelers operated several retail jewelry stores. When bankruptcy became necessary, Standor decided to streamline its operation. It sought to assign the lease of one of its stores. A provision in the lease required the lessor's consent as a condition to assignment and, as a condition to consent, Standor was required to pay 75% of the appreciation in value of the premises to the lessor. Is Standor required to make that payment in order to assign the lease? See *South Coast Plaza v. Standor Jewelers W., Inc. (In re Standor Jewelers W., Inc.)*, 129 B.R. 200 (9th Cir. BAP 1991).

2. Debtor operated an automobile dealership under a franchise agreement with a seven-day "going dark" clause—*i.e.*, a provision permitting termination for failure to operate the business for a stated period. Debtor filed a Chapter 11 petition and sought to assume the franchise agreement. The franchisor argued that Debtor had committed a noncurable default and thus could not meet the requirements for assumption. Debtor countered that such a default need not be cured under § 365(b)(2)(D). What result? See *Claremont Acquisition Corp. v. General Motors Corp. (In re Claremont Acquisition Corp.)*, 113 F.3d 1029 (9th Cir.1997).

3. Debtor, Fashions by Evelyn, leased premises on Park Avenue in New York City where it sold high-fashion women's clothing. Fashions by Evelyn sought to assign the lease to Labels for Less, a discounter of designer dresses. The lease provided that "tenant shall use the premises for the sale of fine women's clothing and for no other purpose" and that "tenant shall conduct its business in a high grade and reputable manner." Lessor objected to assignment because Labels for Less appoints its stores with track lighting and chrome fixtures, rather than as a "salon" decorated like the living room of a home. Lessor argued that Labels for Less is just not "elegant." Will that argument suffice to prevent assignment? See *In re Evelyn Byrnes, Inc.*, 32 B.R. 825 (Bankr. S.D.N.Y.1983).

4. John's Adult Discotheque, Inc. operated under a lease limiting use to operation of a "lounge bar and discotheque." The lease also prohibited "any practices that may be a nuisance or objectionable to other local merchants." After filing a bankruptcy petition, John realized that he could attract a new audience because of Monday Night Football. Thus, John's Adult Discotheque began male striptease shows "for women only" on Monday nights. The dancers performed only after 10 p.m. and the shows were not advertised. A number of local merchants complained, but others said that their traffic increased because of the shows. If the lessor objects to assumption of the lease, will that objection succeed? See *In re Johns*, 5 B.C.D. 1074 (Bankr. D.Nev.1979).

5. Gardinier, Inc. contracted to sell land for over $5 million and to pay a 10% commission for brokerage services to the real estate agent who located the buyer. After a buyer was located, Gardinier filed a Chapter 11 petition and sought to assume the contract. Some of Gardinier's creditors objected to payment of the brokerage fee. If Gardinier assumes the contract, must it pay the fee? See *Byrd v. Gardinier, Inc. (In re Gardinier, Inc.)*, 831 F.2d 974 (11th Cir.1987), *cert. denied*, 488 U.S. 853, 109 S.Ct. 140, 102 L.Ed.2d 112 (1988).

As we have seen, debtors often use Chapter 13 to save their houses and cars. But what of debtors who rent? Can bankruptcy, through § 365, help them? The next case addresses that issue.

BRATTLEBORO HOUSING AUTHORITY v. STOLTZ (IN RE STOLTZ)

United States Court of Appeals, Second Circuit, 1999.
197 F.3d 625.

KATZMANN, Circuit Judge.

Brattleboro Housing Authority ("BHA"), creditor-appellant, appeals from a judgment of the United States District Court for the District of Vermont, reversing the decision of the United States Bankruptcy Court for the District of Vermont which: (1) denied the motion of Laura Stoltz, debtor-appellee, to assume her residential lease pursuant to § 365(d)(2), and (2) granted BHA's motions for relief from stay and co-debtor stay pursuant to § 362(d). BHA contends that the district court erred in holding that a debtor who has a possessory interest in leased residential property on the date the debtor files a Chapter 13 bankruptcy petition has an "unexpired" lease that may be assumed under the Bankruptcy Code. For the reasons that follow, we affirm the judgment of the district court and remand to the bankruptcy court for further proceedings consistent with this opinion.

BACKGROUND

Stoltz lives with her children and Shane Farrell, the co-debtor in this case, in an apartment (the "Apartment") owned and operated by BHA, an entity that offers federally funded public housing in Brattleboro, Vermont. The lease on the Apartment (the "Lease") requires Stoltz to pay $560 per month in rent on or before the first day of each month. In addition, section 2 of the Lease provides, in relevant part:

> MONTH-TO-MONTH LEASE. The terms of this lease shall commence on August 1, 1996, and shall continue for the remainder of said month of August and for the term of one month thereafter; provided, however, that in the absence of a notice to terminate, * * * the term of this lease shall be renewed for successive terms of one (1) calendar month upon payment each month of the rent * * * and upon compliance by the Tenant with all the provisions of this lease.

Stoltz failed to pay the rent for July and August 1997. On or about August 5, 1997, BHA sent Stoltz and Farrell a "Notice to Quit/NonPayment of Rent" (the "Notice"). The Notice advised them that:

> [T]he Brattleboro Housing Authority is terminating its Lease Agreement with you effective September 1, 1997 for nonpayment of rent. You may stop the proceedings if you pay the entire amount of arrears shown below on or before September 1, 1997.

When Stoltz did not pay the arrearage by September 1, 1997, BHA initiated eviction proceedings in the Windham Superior Court against her and Farrell. By Order dated December 22, 1997, the Windham Superior Court held that BHA was entitled to recover possession of the Apartment. The Order provided, pursuant to Vermont law, that a Writ of Possession was to be issued on December 31, 1997.

On December 26, 1997, after the judgment of possession was entered but before the writ of possession was issued, Stoltz filed a Chapter 13 bankruptcy petition in the United States Bankruptcy Court for the District of Vermont, thereby triggering an automatic stay of the eviction proceedings. In her bankruptcy plan, she proposed, among other things, to cure the default on her Lease by paying all back rent over a 36-month period beginning in January 1998, and to assume the Lease. On January 14, she filed a motion to assume lease in the bankruptcy court. BHA objected to the motion on various grounds and then moved for relief from automatic stay[3] and co-debtor stay pursuant to § 362(d).

The bankruptcy court denied Stoltz's motion to assume lease on the ground that the Lease had expired according to its own terms when she fell behind on her rent payments and therefore, no lease existed that could be assumed. Finding that the sole purpose of Stoltz's Chapter 13 reorganization plan was the assumption of the Lease, the bankruptcy court also denied Stoltz's motion to confirm the plan. It then granted BHA's motions for relief from stay and co-debtor stay because it determined that neither Stoltz nor Farrell had any equity in the leased property and the property was not necessary to an effective reorganization.

The district court conditionally reversed. To the extent that the bankruptcy court denied Stoltz's motion to assume lease on the ground that the Lease had expired before she filed her Chapter 13 petition, the district court reversed. The district court ruled that while a debtor's residential lease may be terminated under Vermont law, it is not

---

[3] Farrell has not filed for bankruptcy protection under the Bankruptcy Code. However, because he is a resident at the Apartment, the automatic stay created by Stoltz's Chapter 13 petition protects him as well.

"expired" for purposes of Chapter 13 until the writ of possession is executed. Where, as here, a debtor continues physically to occupy the leased premises, the debtor possesses an unexpired lease that may be assumed pursuant to § 365(d)(2). However, the district court remanded this case to the bankruptcy court to determine whether alternative bases supported the denial of the motion to assume lease. To the extent the district court held that the Lease may be assumed, its decision implicitly reversed the lifting of the automatic stay and co-debtor stay by the bankruptcy court. On remand, the bankruptcy court construed the district court's ruling as a final judgment and adjourned the hearing on the confirmation of Stoltz's Chapter 13 plan pending the resolution of this appeal.

DISCUSSION

* * *

Section 541 of the Bankruptcy Code enumerates the types of property interests that are included in the bankruptcy estate. The estate is defined broadly to include "all legal or equitable interests of the debtor in property as of the commencement of the case." § 541(a)(1). "Unexpired leasehold interests * * * constitute property of the bankrupt estate." *See 48th Street Steakhouse, Inc. v. Rockefeller Group, Inc. (In re 48th Street Steakhouse, Inc.)*, 835 F.2d 427, 430 (2d Cir.1987). Subject to court approval and with some exceptions, a Chapter 13 debtor may assume an unexpired lease of residential real property at any time before the confirmation of a reorganization plan. *See* § 365(d)(2). Only an "unexpired" lease may be assumed. The term "unexpired" is not defined in the Bankruptcy Code itself or in its legislative history. Instead, because property interests are created and defined by state law, federal courts have looked to state law to determine a debtor's interests, including leasehold interests, in the bankruptcy estate. Accordingly, we look to Vermont law to determine Stoltz's interests, if any, in her month-to-month tenancy.

Under Vermont law, a lease is "a contract between the landlord and the tenant wherein the landlord promises to deliver and maintain the demised premises in habitable condition and the tenant promises to pay rent for such habitable premises." *Hilder v. St. Peter*, 144 Vt. 150, 158-59, 478 A.2d 202, 208 (1984). Pursuant to Vermont statute, a landlord seeking to evict a residential tenant for failing to pay rent must: (1) give notice by certified mail or by having the notice served by a law enforcement officer at least fourteen days prior to the termination date in the notice; (2) wait for the termination date in the notice to pass; (3)

obtain a judgment of possession by filing an action of ejectment; (4) obtain a writ of possession; and (5) execute the writ of possession. *See* Vt. Stat. Ann. tit. ix, § 4467(a); Vt. Stat. Ann. tit. xii, § 4854.

Vermont law also expressly provides for redemption of a residential lease upon default for nonpayment of rent. A defaulting tenant can cause an action of ejectment for nonpayment of rent to be discontinued by paying, before final judgment, the rent in arrears with interest and the costs of suit. See Vt. Stat. Ann. tit. xii, § 4773. The Vermont Supreme Court has explained that "a judgment for possession is not final for purposes of § 4773 until the earlier of (a) the date of the issuance of the writ of possession, or (b) the date by which a notice of appeal must be filed." *Tucker v. Bushway*, 166 Vt. 592, 689 A.2d 426, 427 (Vt. 1996) (holding that tenants of a mobile home park had right to redeem lease by paying all back rent after judgment of possession was entered in favor of landlord). Thus, Vermont law recognizes the right of a tenant to redeem a residential lease by curing a default and to remain in possession of residential property even after the fourth step in the eviction process—issuance of a judgment of possession—is completed, provided the judgment has not become final.

In this case, Stoltz filed her Chapter 13 petition before the writ of possession was issued and before the time to appeal the judgment of possession had expired. Therefore, the judgment of possession against her had not become final as of the date her bankruptcy petition was filed. At that time, she had the right to vacate the judgment of possession by curing the default on rent and paying interest and costs. This right was preserved by the granting of the automatic stay under § 362. Thus, she continues to be in lawful possession of the Apartment.

Our Circuit has not squarely addressed the issue of whether, under applicable state law, a tenant-debtor with a possessory interest in leased residential property has an "unexpired" lease that may be assumed under § 365(d)(2). However, in determining when a judgment of possession becomes final, the Vermont Supreme Court reasoned that "[o]nce the landlord obtains a writ of possession, it would be irrational to allow the tenant to regain entry to the property." *Tucker*, 689 A.2d at 427. By implication, until the landlord obtains a writ of possession, a tenant who has lost possession may nonetheless regain entry by curing the default. We are therefore of the view that under Vermont law, a debtor who retains a possessory interest in a residential tenancy has an "unexpired" lease at least until the writ of possession is issued. On the facts of this case, it is unnecessary to decide whether a lease remains unexpired until the execution of the writ of possession. Accordingly, we hold that Stoltz possesses an unexpired lease which may be assumed provided she satisfies the requirements of § 365(b)(1) for assuming a lease.

BHA contends that the district court's holding is inconsistent with the plain language of the Lease. It argues that pursuant to section 2 of the Lease, the Lease had expired by its own terms when Stoltz failed to pay rent for July and August 1997, before she filed her Chapter 13 petition. However, section 2 of the Lease specifies that "in the absence of a notice to terminate," the Lease shall be renewed for successive one-month terms upon payment each month of rent. Consistent with statutory requirements for termination of a tenancy under Vermont law, section 2 of the Lease offers BHA the option to terminate in the event of nonpayment of rent by giving notice to the tenant. However, section 2 does not by its terms mean that the Lease automatically "expires" if rent is not timely paid.

We have considered all of BHA's other arguments and find them to be without merit. Therefore, the judgment of the district court is affirmed. We remand this case to the bankruptcy court to determine whether Stoltz's motion to assume lease should be denied on other grounds. If, on remand, the bankruptcy court finds that such alternative grounds exist, BHA may, of course, renew its motions for relief from stay and co-debtor stay. * * *

Notes

Under § 541(b)(2), property of the estate does not include a lease of nonresidential real property that has terminated before the filing of bankruptcy. Similarly, § 365(c)(3) provides that a trustee may not assume a lease of nonresidential real property that has terminated under state law before bankruptcy. Those provisions do not create a result for nonresidential leases that is inconsistent with *Stoltz*, despite appearances, because those subsections depend, as did *Stoltz*, on when a lease terminates under state law. Courts reached similar conclusions even before those provisions were added to the Code in 1984. *See, e.g., Omni International. Ltd. v. Mimi's of Atlanta, Inc. (In re Mimi's of Atlanta, Inc.)*, 5 B.R. 623 (Bankr. N.D.Ga.1980), *aff'd*, 11 B.R. 710 (N.D.Ga.1981).

Sections 365(c)(3) and 541(b)(2) only apply to termination of a lease at the end of a stated term. A lease terminated under an "ipso facto" clause (which provides for termination upon the happening of a particular event, such as bankruptcy filing) nevertheless becomes property of the estate and may be assumed. See § 365(e)(1).

2. SPECIAL RULES FOR SHOPPING CENTERS

Congress was concerned with the special problems faced by shopping center lessors, as well as other tenants, when lessees of space in shopping centers go into bankruptcy. In these cases, the economic interests of a number of nonbankrupt parties are implicated. Thus, Congress included § 365(b)(3), which governs adequate assurance of future performance when leased premises are in a shopping center. In such cases, a court has less latitude than it has in other cases to permit the debtor or an assignee to deviate from strict performance of lease provisions. It is important to determine, therefore, whether the premises are in a shopping center. Because the Code does not define "shopping center," courts have undertaken the task.

The following case deals with the definition of "shopping center" and with the heightened requirements for "adequate assurance" when a shopping center is involved.

IN RE JOSHUA SLOCUM, LTD.

United States Court of Appeals, Third Circuit, 1990.
922 F.2d 1081.

A. LEON HIGGINBOTHAM, JR., Chief Judge.

This case concerns the power of the bankruptcy court to excise a paragraph from a shopping center lease. On November 21, 1988 (the "Filing Date"), Joshua Slocum, Ltd., a Pennsylvania corporation (the "Debtor"), filed a voluntary petition for relief under chapter 11 of the United States Code with the bankruptcy court. On February 16, 1989, the bankruptcy court appointed Melvin Lashner (the "Trustee") to act as trustee in the case pursuant to § 1104. Appellant George Denney ("Denney") contends that the bankruptcy court erred in entering its orders excising paragraph 20 of the lease in question, and then authorizing the assumption and assignment of that lease, without paragraph 20, over his objections. He also maintains that the district court erred in affirming the bankruptcy court's decision. We agree with the appellant and therefore will reverse the district court's summary affirmance of the bankruptcy court's judgment.

I. FACTS AND PROCEDURAL HISTORY

The Debtor, Joshua Slocum, Ltd., d/b/a JS. Acquisition Corporation, began its relationship with Landlord, George Denney, in May of

1983 when Debtor signed a ten year lease for retail space at the Denney Block in Freeport, Maine. The Denney Block, which consisted of three buildings containing seven stores, was developed in two phases commencing in 1982 and completed in 1983. The first phase was undertaken by Cole Haan, a manufacturer and retailer of fine men's and women's shoes, of which Denney is the President. Cole Haan purchased and renovated a building on Main Street in Freeport, Maine, and gave Denney the option to purchase the building in the event that the stock of Cole Haan was acquired by a third person. When the capital stock of Cole Haan was purchased by Nike, George Denney exercised his option to purchase the Cole Haan building.

Shortly thereafter, Denney purchased the building immediately adjoining the Cole Haan building and a third building separated from the second building by a courtyard. Architectural plans to develop the two new buildings in a manner consistent with the Cole Haan building as a common scheme were commissioned by Denney and presented to the Freeport, Maine planning board for approval.

The buildings comprising Denney Block front on Main Street and are part of the downtown shopping district in Freeport. The shopping district consists of a number of streets lined with stores. In addition to the Landlord's three buildings, the Denney Block has a courtyard located between two of its buildings and a parking lot behind the stores. George Denney owns the parking lot which is primarily for the use of patrons of the Denney Block, although according to local ordinance it is also open to the public (thus, it can be used by all persons who shop in the stores along Main Street, Freeport).

Debtor's lease, signed in 1983, along with the leases of some or all of the other Denney Block tenants, contains an average sales clause. This clause allows for Debtor or Landlord to terminate the lease if, after six years, Debtor's average yearly sales are below $711,245. A similar option also existed after the third year of the lease. At that point, either party held the power to terminate the lease if the tenant's average yearly sales were below $602,750.

The lease also contains a percentage rent clause. For the years currently remaining in the lease, this clause requires the tenant to pay additional rent in the amount of four percent of gross sales in excess of $1,175,362. Otherwise, the base rent due in the final five years of the lease is $3,917.88 per month. The leases also require the tenants to provide Landlord with financial information concerning their business so that these lease provisions can be implemented.

Joshua Slocum, Ltd. filed a voluntary petition for relief under chapter 11 of the United States Bankruptcy Code with the bankruptcy court. By application to the bankruptcy court dated February 2, 1989 (the "Application"), the Trustee requested authorization to assume and assign the Lease pursuant to § 365. In March 1989, Denney filed written objections and a memorandum of law in opposition to the application with the bankruptcy court.

By opinion (the "opinion") and order both dated March 29, 1989 (the "interim order"), the bankruptcy court granted the relief requested in the Application and authorized the Trustee to assume and assign the Lease to European Collections, Inc. (the "assignee"). The bankruptcy court entered another Order on April 11, 1989 (the "final order"), setting forth fully the rights and obligations of the parties. In the opinion and the final order, the bankruptcy court held unenforceable and excised paragraph 20 of the Lease ("paragraph 20"), which provides that "in the event that Tenant's gross sales for the first six (6) lease-years of the term of this Lease do not average Seven Hundred Eleven Thousand Two Hundred Forty Five and 00/100 Dollars ($711,245.00) per lease-year either Landlord or Tenant may elect to terminate this Lease."

The court approved the assignment of the lease without paragraph 20 to European Collections. European Collection[s] has begun occupancy and operation of a store in George Denney's premises in Freeport, Maine. Denney's consolidated appeals followed.

On May 31, 1989, the Trustee filed a motion to dismiss George Denney's appeal as moot. By Order dated December 21, 1989 the district court affirmed without opinion the bankruptcy court's opinion and final order and denied Trustee's motion to dismiss. On January 22, 1990, Denney appealed the district court order.

II. DISCUSSION

* * *

B. Shopping Center

The Bankruptcy Code imposes heightened restrictions on the assumption and assignment of leases for shopping centers. * * *

George Denney, the landlord of the Denney Block, wishes to take advantage of these heightened restrictions in order to block the assignment of the lease to European Collections. Thus, appellant Denney contends that the Denney Block is a "shopping center" within the meaning of § 365(b)(3). We agree.

However, the bankruptcy court agreed with the appellee, Trustee, and found that Denney Block was not a "shopping center" within the meaning of § 365(b)(3). The court looked to *Collier on Bankruptcy* and two cases addressing the question of whether a particular arrangement of stores constitutes a "shopping center" for purposes of § 365(b)(3). *See In re Goldblatt Bros., Inc.*, 766 F.2d 1136, 1140–41 (7th Cir.1985); *In re 905 Int'l Stores, Inc.*, 57 B.R. 786, 788–89 (E.D. Mo.1985). Both of these appellate decisions affirm bankruptcy court determinations that the respective premises in question were not in "shopping centers."

In *Goldblatt*, although the court found the common ownership of contiguous parcels, the presence of an "anchor tenant" (Goldblatt) and joint off street parking adjacent to all stores was significant in deciding whether the arrangement at issue was a shopping center, those factors were not determinative. The court was persuaded by the absence of other typical indicia of shopping centers, i.e., a master lease, fixed hours during which the stores are all open, common areas and joint advertising, and particularly whether the stores were developed to be a shopping center.

In *905 Int'l*, the court, in finding that the arrangement at issue in that case was not a "shopping center," was impressed with "the absence of contractual interdependence among tenants." 57 B.R. at 788. That case, like *Goldblatt*, also sets out several objective criteria in determining whether an arrangement is a "shopping center." In addition to contractual interdependence, these factors include the existence of percentage rent clauses, anchor tenant clauses, joint contribution to trash and maintenance needs, contiguous grouping of stores, a tenant mix, and restrictive clauses. Relying on the indicia pointed to in *Goldblatt*, the court found that only one of the four, joint advertising, was satisfied, and concluded the stores did not comprise a shopping center.

The bankruptcy court utilized the correct criteria for determining what constitutes a "shopping center." The court's focus on the physical attributes of the Denney Block, however, i.e., the fact that it was located on a typical "Main St." in a downtown district, is not a factor laid out as dispositive in the Bankruptcy Code, Collier's treatise, or either of the above cited cases. Nor is there any intrinsic sense to the bankruptcy court's conclusion that the Denney Block's location makes it fall outside the purview of the definition of "shopping center." The court noted that "a shopping center brings to mind a configuration of stores which are not freestanding or detached in the sense that stores appear in a typical 'Main St.' downtown shopping district. Such a downtown shopping district is usually considered in many communities, as the *alternative* (emphasis in original) to the archetypal 'shopping center,' i.e., the large enclosed shopping mall." While it is true that the mall *is* the archetypal "shopping center," all shopping centers do not necessarily take the form of shopping malls.

Location is only one element in the determination of whether a group of stores can properly be described as a "shopping center." However, more significant are the following criteria sketched in Collier, *Goldblatt* and *905 Int'l*:

(a) A combination of leases;

(b) All leases held by a single landlord;

(c) All tenants engaged in the commercial retail distribution of goods;

(d) The presence of a common parking area;

(e) The purposeful development of the premises as a shopping center;

(f) The existence of a master lease;

(g) The existence of fixed hours during which all stores are open;

(h) The existence of joint advertising;

(j) Contractual interdependence of the tenants as evidenced by restrictive use provisions in their leases;

(k) The existence of percentage rent provisions in the leases;

(*l*) The right of the tenants to terminate their leases if the anchor tenant terminates its lease;

(m) Joint participation by tenants in trash removal and other maintenance;

(n) The existence of a tenant mix; and

(*o*) The contiguity of the stores.

We do not think that the bankruptcy court gave adequate consideration to all of the factors described above and gave undue weight to the testimony that the Denney Block does not look like a shopping center. The bankruptcy court placed what it termed "the physical configuration" of the Denney Block at the center of its analysis: "we find that the physical characteristics of the Denney Block *preclude* its characterization as a 'shopping center.'" We are not convinced that the physical configuration of the property plays such a prominent role. Indeed, Collier notes that "the most important characteristic will be a combination of leases held by a single landlord, leased to commercial retail distributors of goods, with the presence of a common parking area." 2 *Collier on Bankruptcy* ¶ 365.04[3]. Except for contiguity of stores criterion listed above, the appearance of premises or their location within a downtown shopping district has not been cited as a factor in the determination of whether a group of stores is a "shopping center." All of the stores of Denney Block, except to the extent that they are separated by common areas, are contiguous.

Moreover, George Denney is the sole landlord of all the stores in the Denney Block. Those stores share and provide support for the maintenance of common areas. The stores are all retail distributors of goods subject to substantially similar leases which include both percentage rent provisions and clauses for the benefit of other tenants that restrict the type of goods that a tenant may sell. There is a mix of tenants at Denney Block. Cole Haan primarily sells footwear, Laura Ashley sells a variety of goods including clothing, wall paper and linens, Jones New York sells men's and women's clothing, Benneton sells sports wear, Class Perfume sells perfume and Christmas Magic sells Christmas decorations and ornaments. The plot plan for Denney Block was presented to the Freeport planning board as a common scheme.

The bankruptcy court found that there was no common parking because customers of stores other than those shops in the Denney Block also use [the] parking lot located directly behind it. That common parking is available at the Denney Block is not obviated by the fact that according to local ordinance the public must also have access to that lot. Hence, the Denney Block satisfies, with the exception of joint advertising, the existence of a master lease and the right of a tenant to terminate the lease if the anchor tenant does so, all of the criteria for determining what constitutes a "shopping center," and all of the "most important" characteristics listed by Collier. Because the bankruptcy court did not adequately consider each of the factors enumerated above its reading of the Act was overly restrictive.

The provisions of § 365 are intended to remedy three "serious problems caused shopping centers and their solvent tenants by the administration of the bankruptcy code." 130 Cong. Rec. S8891 (statement by the Hon. Orrin G. Hatch, a ranking majority member of the Senate Committee on the Judiciary and a Senate conferee), *reprinted in* 1984 U.S.C.C.A.N. 590, 598. Congress wished to alleviate the hardship caused landlord and tenant resulting from vacancy or partial operation of the debtor's space in the shopping center. Section 365 also insures that the landlord will continue to receive payments due under the lease. Finally, the statute guarantees to the landlord and remaining tenants that the tenant mix will not be substantially disrupted. Each of these serious problems was faced by Denney and the remaining shops after Joshua Slocum, Ltd. went bankrupt. We conclude that in light of the harms § 365 was intended to remedy, and after application of all relevant criteria, denying Denney and his tenants the protections of § 365 would not further the congressional will.

Additionally, the legislative history of the Bankruptcy Reform Act of 1978 briefly addresses the definition of a "shopping center."

> A shopping center is often a carefully planned enterprise, and though it consists of numerous individual tenants, the center is planned as a single unit, *often* subject to a master lease or financing agreement. Under these agreements, the tenant mix in a shopping center may be as important to the lessor as the actual promised rental payments, because certain mixes will attract higher patronage of the stores in the center, and thus, a higher rental for the landlord from those stores that are subject to a percentage of gross receipts rental agreement.

H.R. Rep. No. 95–595 at 348, *reprinted in* 1978 U.S.C.C.A.N. at 6305 (emphasis added).

We think that the Denney Block fits within Congress' conceptualization of a shopping center. The use of the term "often" in the above quoted passage indicates that the existence of a master lease should not be determinative in this court's analysis. We also note that a "single unit" as described above does not have to be an enclosed mall as the bankruptcy court would have it, but rather could be properly conceived of as a cluster of three relatively contiguous buildings as with the Denney Block.

We conclude that Denney Block is a "shopping center" within the meaning of § 365(b)(3) and should be entitled to its special protections.

C. Bankruptcy Court's Power to Excise Paragraph 20 of the Lease

The bankruptcy court, in considering the motion of the Trustee, Melvin Lashner to allow the Debtor, Joshua Slocum, Ltd. to assume and assign its store lease with the Denney Block, held that the average sales clause in paragraph 20 of that lease [is] unenforceable because it is not material or economically significant to the landlord and/or landlord's other tenants. The bankruptcy court granted Trustee's motion to assume and assign the lease and deleted the average sales clause. Appellant, George Denney takes issue with the court's authority to excise paragraph 20 of his leasehold with Joshua Slocum, Ltd. We shall defer the issue of whether that clause was material until later in our discussion. However, we now turn our attention to the question of the bankruptcy court's authority to delete paragraph 20.

Paragraph 20 of Joshua Slocum, Ltd.'s lease at the Denney Block provides as follows:

> Paragraph 20 ("average sales"):
>
> *Option to Terminate.* In the event that Tenant's gross sales for the first three (3) lease-years of the term of this Lease do not average at lease [sic] Six Hundred Thousand Seven Hundred Fifty and 009/100 Dollars ($602,750.00) [sic] per lease-year, either Landlord or Tenant may elect to terminate this Lease; and in the event that Tenant's gross sales for the first six (6) lease-years of the term of this lease do not average Seven Hundred Eleven Thousand Two Hundred Forty Five Dollars and 00/100 Dollars ($711,245.00) per lease-year, either Landlord or Tenant may elect to terminate this Lease. Such election must be made, if at all, by written notice to the other party received within thirty (30) days from the date of receipt by Landlord of the accountant's statement described in Paragraph 4(b) hereinabove; and termination shall become effective ninety (90) days after receipt of such notice. * * *

The bankruptcy court viewed this average sales provision as a cleverly disguised anti-assignment clause. The court stated:

> Perhaps the most novel issue raised by this motion is the enforceability of the "minimum sales" provision which, if enforced, would probably allow Denney to terminate the Lease in July, 1989. If this provision were enforced, with EC having to incorporate the Debtor's sales record through February 20, 1989, the value of the Lease would obviously be nominal. EC's offer to pay $77,000 for the right to obtain an assignment of the Lessee was expressly predicated on its receiving the right to utilize the Debtor's former Freeport store for at least the remaining four years of the lease. It is certainly questionable whether, in the short time before EC could open the store and July, 1989, it could attain a sales volume, when combined with the Debtor's interrupted sales record, sufficient to meet that required as the minimum in the first six lease-years of the Debtor's lease.

Working from the premise that Denney Block is not a "shopping center," the bankruptcy court held that the heightened protection accorded to non-debtor contractual rights under § 365(b)(3) of the Bankruptcy Code does not apply and turned its attention to § 365(f) dealing with assumptions and assignments of lease in non-shopping center cases. However, as discussed above, Denney Block is a "shopping center" and thus, § 365(f) does not apply.

The bankruptcy court does have some latitude in waiving contractual provisions when authorizing a trustee to assume and assign an unexpired lease. Section 365(b)(2) on its face permits the court to ignore so-called *ipso facto* and forfeiture clauses. However, the court's authority to waive the strict enforcement of lease provisions in the context of shopping center cases like this one is further qualified by § 365(b)(3) of the Bankruptcy Code. Even under the tightly drawn definition of "adequate assurance" in the shopping center context, Congress did not envision literal compliance with all lease provisions; insubstantial disruptions in, *inter alia*, tenant mix, and insubstantial breaches in other leases or agreements were contemplated and allowed. § 365(b)(3)(C), (D).

In this case, however, the bankruptcy court did not have the authority to excise paragraph 20 of the shopping center lease which addresses the landlord and/or tenant's option to terminate dependent upon the average sales generated by the tenant. We note that even if the Denney Block were not a shopping center, the bankruptcy court's authority to excise paragraph 20 of the lease is questionable. That paragraph must be read in conjunction with paragraph 4, the percent rent clause of the lease which provides a formula requiring Joshua Slocum, Ltd. to pay a percentage of the lease as specified on any amount in excess of the designated gross sales threshold for a given lease-year. These two clauses taken together clearly indicate that a bargained for element in this contract was that tenant, Joshua Slocum, Ltd., average a certain volume of sales as specified in paragraph 20 of the lease so that the Landlord could accurately calculate the minimum total rent expected pursuant to paragraph 4 of the lease. Even standing alone, paragraph 20 is an essential bargained for element of this lease agreement because it governs occupancy. We also note that paragraph 20 of the lease falls within the statutory meaning of "other consideration due"[9] under the lease, and without this clause the trustee could not give adequate assurance as to its future performance.

Congress has suggested that the modification of a contracting party's rights is not to be taken lightly. Rather, a bankruptcy court in authorizing assumptions and assignment of unexpired leases must be sensitive to the rights of the non-debtor contracting party (here, George Denney) and the policy requiring that the non-debtor receive the full benefit of his or her bargain. Congress' solicitous attitudes toward shopping centers is reflected in the legislative history regarding § 365(b)(3), which states:

> A shopping center is often a carefully planned enterprise, and though it consists of numerous individual tenants, the center is planned as a single unit, often subject to a master lease or financing agreement. Under these agreements, the tenant mix in a shopping center may be as important to the lessor as the actual promised rental payments, because certain mixes will attract higher patronage of the stores in the center, and thus a higher rental for the landlord from those stores that are subject to a percentage of gross receipts rental agreement. Thus, in order to assure a landlord of his bargained for exchange, the court would have to consider such factors as the nature of the business to be conducted by the trustee or his assignee, whether that business complies with the requirements of any master agreement, whether the kind of business proposed will generate gross sales in an amount such that the percentage rent specified in the lease is substantially the same as what would have been provided by the debtor, and whether the business proposed to be

---

[9] *See* § 365(b)(3)(A).

> conducted would result in a breach of other causes [sic] in master agreements relating, for example to tenant mix and location.

H.R. Rep. No. 95–595 at 348–49, *reprinted in* 1978 U.S.C.C.A.N. 5963, 6305; *see also* S. Rep. No. 95–989, *reprinted in id.* at 5787, 5845.

In excising paragraph 20, the bankruptcy court undermined both the Congressional policy and the statutory requirement under § 365-(b)(3)(A) that the trustee give adequate assurance of "other consideration due" under an unexpired lease. We find that the bankruptcy court did not have the authority to excise paragraph 20 of the lease.

D. Materiality

Appellant takes issue with the bankruptcy court's conclusion that paragraph 20 of the lease at issue, allowing for the termination of the lease by either the landlord, Denney or the debtor-tenant, Joshua Slocum, Ltd., if certain minimum sales figure were not realized, was not enforceable. Central to the bankruptcy court's view was the notion that unless the landlord establishes that a leasehold is in a "shopping center," such a restrictive clause is only enforceable if the landlord is able to establish that such terms are material and jeopardize the economic position of the landlord and/or the landlord's other tenants. The bankruptcy court, working from the premise that the Denney Block is not a "shopping center," looked to case law interpreting § 365 of the Bankruptcy Code and distilled the concepts of "materiality and economic significance." Those cases state that "the [bankruptcy] court does retain some discretion in determining that lease provisions * * * may still be refused enforcement in a bankruptcy context in which there is no substantial economic detriment to the landlord shown, and in which enforcement would preclude the bankruptcy estate from realizing the intrinsic value of its assets." *In re Mr. Grocer, Inc.*, 77 B.R. 349, 354 (Bankr. D.N.H.1987).

[The bankruptcy court] was incorrect in finding that on these facts, paragraph 20 of the lease, addressing the right of the parties to terminate the leasehold is not "material or economically significant." That conclusion flies in the face of logic and simple common sense. * * *

We find that the average sales provision of paragraph 20 was not merely inserted as an escape hatch in the event that the location became unprofitable for the protection of the tenant. But rather, that particular clause is of financial import to the landlord in insuring occupancy by high volume sales, viable businesses, thus increasing the rent received under the percentage rent clause. The combination of paragraph 4 and paragraph 20 acts as a minimum income guarantee for the landlord. Certainly nothing could be as material or economically significant to landlords as some minimal assurance that there will be a positive return on their investments. The clause is also significant to landlord as well as the other tenants because customers will be attracted to stores where business is perceived as booming. We conclude, therefore, paragraph 20 is a material and economically significant clause in the leasehold at issue.

III. CONCLUSION

* * * [W]e hold that the Denney Block, a contiguous grouping of stores, is subject to the heightened restrictions on the assumption and assignment of leases of real property in shopping centers. We find that the district court erred in affirming the bankruptcy court's approval of the assignment of the leasehold at issue without paragraph 20, an average sales clause, to European Collections. The bankruptcy court did not have authority to excise paragraph 20, a material provision governing the terms of occupancy under the lease. Therefore, we will vacate the judgment of the district court and remand to the district court for further proceedings consistent with this opinion.

Questions

1. Did George Denney face the kinds of risks about which Congress was concerned when it enacted the special provisions in § 365 for shopping centers?

2. How many of the characteristics of a shopping center, listed by the court, were present in the Denney Block? What minimum is necessary?

3. Are physical characteristics, such as contiguity, or contractual characteristics, such as a master lease, more important in the court's view? Why?

4. Does *Joshua Slocum* effectively resurrect ipso facto clauses, as far as shopping centers are concerned?

3. NONASSIGNABLE CONTRACTS

Contract law prohibits assignments that might jeopardize the justifiable expectations of a party. If, for example, one party's obligations depend upon the discretion of the other party, substitution of an assignee for the other party might significantly change the obligor's duties. Or an assignment might increase the risk a party faces. Under circumstances such as these, contract law holds assignments ineffective.

Congress understood the policy reasons behind nonassignability, but also recognized that bankruptcy cases can be undermined if nondebtor contracting parties are able to stand aloof. (Evidence of the latter was readily available, since ipso facto clauses were enforceable under the Act.) Congress, therefore, sought to balance these competing considerations in § 365.

IN RE PIONEER FORD SALES, INC.

United States Court of Appeals, First Circuit, 1984.
729 F.2d 27.

BREYER, Circuit Judge.

The Ford Motor Company appeals a federal district court decision allowing a bankrupt Ford dealer (Pioneer Ford Sales, Inc.) to assign its Ford franchise over Ford's objection to a Toyota dealer (Toyota Village, Inc.). The district court decided the case on the basis of a record developed in the bankruptcy court. The bankruptcy court had approved the transfer, which ran from Pioneer to Fleet National Bank (Pioneer's principal secured creditor) and then to Toyota Village. Fleet sought authorization for the assignment because Toyota Village will pay $10,000 for the franchise and buy all parts and accessories in Pioneer's inventory at fair market value (about $75,000); if the franchise is not assigned, Ford will buy only some of the parts for between $45,000 and $55,000. Thus, the assignment will increase the value of the estate. Fleet is the appellee here.

The issue that the case raises is the proper application of § 365(c)(1)(A), an exception to a more general provision, § 365(f)(1), that allows a trustee in bankruptcy (or a debtor in possession) to assign many of the debtor's executory contracts even if the contract itself says that it forbids assignment. * * *

The words "applicable law" in this section [§ 365(c)(1)(A)] mean "applicable nonbankruptcy law." *See* H.R. Rep. No. 95–595 at 348, *reprinted in* 1978 U.S.C.C.A.N. at 6304. Evidently, the theory of this section is to prevent the trustee from assigning (over objection) contracts of the sort that contract law ordinarily makes nonassignable, *i.e.* contracts that cannot be assigned when the contract itself is silent about assignment. At the same time, by using the words in (1)(A) "whether *or not* the contract prohibits assignment," the section prevents parties from using contractual language to prevent the trustee from assigning contracts that (when the contract is silent) contract law typically makes assignable. *Id.* Thus, we must look to see whether relevant nonbankruptcy law would allow Ford to veto the assignment of its basic franchise contract "whether or not" that basic franchise contract itself specifically "prohibits assignment."

The nonbankruptcy law to which both sides point us is contained in Rhode Island's "Regulation of Business Practices Among Motor Vehicle Manufacturers, Distributors and Dealers" Act. It states that

> [N]o dealer * * * shall have the right to * * * assign the franchise * * * without the consent of the manufacturer, except that such consent shall not be unreasonably withheld.

The statute by its terms, allows a manufacturer to veto an assignment where the veto is reasonable but not otherwise. The statute's language also indicates that it applies "whether or not" the franchise contract itself restricts assignment. Thus, the basic question that the case presents is whether Ford's veto was reasonable in terms of the Rhode Island law.

Neither the district court nor the bankruptcy court specifically addressed this question. Their failure apparently arose out of their belief that § 365(c)(1)(A) refers only to traditional personal service contracts. But in our view they were mistaken. The language of the section does not limit its effect to personal service contracts. It refers *generally* to contracts that are not assignable under nonbankruptcy law. State laws typically make contracts for personal services nonassignable (where the contract itself is silent); but they make other sorts of contracts nonassignable as well. *See, e.g.*, N.Y. State Finance Law § 138 (1974) (making certain government contracts unassignable). The legislative history of § 365(c) says nothing about "personal services." To the contrary, it speaks of letters of credit, personal loans, and leases—instances in which assigning a contract may place the other party at a significant disadvantage. The history thereby suggests that (c)(1)(A) has a broader reach.

The source of the "personal services" limitation apparently is a bankruptcy court case, *In re Taylor Manufacturing, Inc.*, 6 B.R. 370

(Bankr. N.D.Ga.1980), which other bankruptcy courts have followed. The *Taylor* court wrote that (c)(1)(A) should be interpreted narrowly, in part because it believed that (c)(1)(A) conflicted with another section, (f)(1) * * * . As a matter of logic, however, we see no conflict, for (c)(1)(A) refers to state laws that prohibit assignment "whether or not" the contract is silent, while (f)(1) contains no such limitation. Apparently (f)(1) includes state laws that prohibit assignment only when the contract is *not* silent about assignment; that is to say, state laws that enforce contract provisions prohibiting assignment. These state laws are to be ignored. The section specifically excepts (c)(1)(A)'s state laws that forbid assignment even when the contract *is* silent; they are to be heeded. Regardless, we fail to see why a "conflict" suggests that (c)(1)(A) is limited to "personal services."

The *Taylor* court cites 2 *Collier on Bankruptcy* § 365.05 and the Commission Report, H.R. Doc. No. 93–137, 93rd Cong., 1st Sess. 199 (1973), in support. Both of these sources speak of personal services. However, they do not say that (c)(1)(A), was intended to be *limited* to personal services. Indeed, since it often is difficult to decide whether or not a particular duty can be characterized by the label "personal service," it makes sense to avoid this question and simply look to see whether state law would, or would not, make the duty assignable where the contract is silent. * * * Fleet concedes in its brief that "the exception to assignment [of § 365(c)(1)(A)] is not limited to personal services contracts." We therefore reject the district court's conclusion in this respect.

Although the district court did not explicitly decide whether Ford's veto was reasonable, it decided a closely related question. Under other provisions of § 365 a bankruptcy court cannot authorize assignment of an executory contract if 1) the debtor is in default, unless 2) there is "adequate assurance of future performance." § 365(b)(1)(C). Pioneer is in default, but the bankruptcy and district courts found "adequate assurance." For the sake of argument, we shall assume that this finding is equivalent to a finding that Ford's veto of the assignment was unreasonable. And, we shall apply a "clearly erroneous" standard in reviewing the factual element in this lower court finding. On these assumptions, favorable to Fleet, we nonetheless must reverse the district court, for, in our view, any finding of unreasonableness, based on this record, is clearly erroneous.

Our review of the record reveals the following critical facts. First, in accordance with its ordinary business practice and dealer guidelines incorporated into the franchise agreement, Ford would have required Toyota Village, as a dealer, to have a working capital of at least $172,000, of which no more than half could be debt. Toyota Village, however, had a working capital at the end of 1981 of $37,610; and its net worth was $31,747. Although the attorney for Fleet at one point in the bankruptcy proceedings said Toyota Village could borrow some of the necessary capital from a bank, he made no later reference to the point, nor did he ever specifically state how much Toyota Village could borrow. Since the tax returns of Toyota Village's owner showed gross income of $27,500 for 1981, there is no reason to believe that the owner could readily find the necessary equity capital.

Second, at a time when Japanese cars have sold well throughout the United States, Toyota Village has consistently lost money. The financial statements in the record show the following operating losses:

	1977	1978	1979	1980	1981
Loss	($7,522)	($7,552)	($13,938)	($12,684)	($21,317)

At the same time, the record contains no significant evidence tending to refute the natural inference arising from these facts. The bankruptcy court mentioned five factors that it said showed that Toyota Village gave "adequate assurance" that it could do the job.

1) Toyota Village was an established dealership.

2) Toyota Village was "located within 500 yards of the present Ford dealership."

3) Toyota Village had a proven track record for selling cars.

4) Toyota Village was willing and able to pay $15,000 that Pioneer still owed Ford.

5) The owner and sole stockholder of Toyota Village testified that he was willing and able to fulfill the franchise agreement.

The first of these factors (dealer experience), while favoring Toyota Village, is weak, given the record of continuous dealership losses. The second (location) proves little, considering that Pioneer went bankrupt at the very spot. The third (track record) cuts against Toyota Village, not in its favor, for its track record is one of financial loss. The fourth (willingness to pay a $15,000 debt that Pioneer owed Ford) is relevant, but it shows, at most, that Toyota Village *believed* it could make a success of the franchise. The fifth (ability to act as franchisee) is supported by no more than a simple statement by the owner of Toyota Village that he could do the job.

We do not see how the few positive features about Toyota Village that the record reveals can overcome the problem of a history of losses and failure to meet Ford's capital requirements. In these circumstances, Ford would seem perfectly reasonable in withholding its consent to the transfer. Thus, Rhode Island law would make the franchise unassignable.

* * *

One might still argue that under Rhode Island law the only "reasonable" course of action for Ford is to allow the transfer and then simply terminate Toyota Village if it fails to perform adequately. This suggestion, however, overlooks the legal difficulties that Ford would have in proving cause for termination under the Rhode Island "Regulation of Business Practices Among Motor Vehicle Manufacturers, Distributors and Dealers" Act. The very purpose of the statute—protecting dealer reliance—suggests that it ought to be more difficult for a manufacturer to terminate a dealer who has invested in a franchise than to oppose the grant of a franchise to one who has not. In any event, the law does not suggest a manufacturer is "unreasonable" in objecting to a transfer unless he would have "good cause" to terminate the transferee. And, to equate the two standards would tend to make the "unreasonable" provision superfluous. Thus, we conclude that the Rhode Island law would make the franchise unassignable on the facts here revealed. Therefore, neither the bankruptcy court nor the district court had the power to authorize the transfer.

* * *

For these reasons, the judgment of the district court is

Reversed.

Questions and Problems

1. Do you understand the nature of the "conflict" between §§ 365-(c)(1)(A) and (f)(1)? How did the court resolve this "conflict"?

2. Debtor was a member of Country Club, with full golfing privileges. Only 375 members of the Club had such privileges at any one time, and elaborate rules governed selection: members of the Club interested in golfing

privileges were required to pay a substantial fee to be placed on the waiting list; when a vacancy occurred, the member at the top of the list would be offered the option to obtain golfing privileges upon the payment of another substantial fee; and golfing privileges could not be sold or assigned. At the time of Debtor's bankruptcy filing, 70 members were on the waiting list for golfing privileges. Trustee sought to assume and assign Debtor's golfing privileges as an executory contract. Can Trustee do so? Would it matter if Trustee agreed to sell only to Club members on the waiting list? See *Rieser v. Dayton Country Club Co. (In re Magness)*, 972 F.2d 689 (6th Cir.1992).

3. West Electronics had a contract with the federal government to supply missile launchers to the Air Force. When West missed delivery deadlines, the government served an administrative notice on West to show cause why the contract should not be terminated. West promptly filed for bankruptcy protection and moved to assume the contract. The government objected to assumption, citing 41 U.S.C. § 15, which provides that "no [government] contract * * * shall be transferred by the party to whom such contract * * * is given to any other party, and any such transfer shall cause the annulment of the contract." Can West assume the contract in the absence of the government's consent? See *Matter of West Electronics Inc.*, 852 F.2d 79 (3d Cir.1988).

D. REJECTION

1. GENERAL RULES

As we have noted, a trustee or debtor-in-possession will reject an agreement if its burdens outweigh its benefits. For example, if the debtor has a contract for the purchase of computer equipment for $5,000, but the market price of such equipment has fallen to $4,000, then the debtor-in-possession will reject the contract and negotiate a new contract at the lower market price. Rejection, however, constitutes a breach by the debtor-in-possession under § 365(g). Although it is a postpetition event, the breach is treated as if it occurred "immediately before the date of the filing of the petition," in order to give the nondebtor party an unsecured claim in the bankruptcy. See § 502(g).

Thus, in our hypothetical contract case, the lessor will have a claim for $1,000. But where is the advantage of rejection if rejection creates a new claim against the estate in an amount equal to the estate's savings? The answer lies in the fact that the nondebtor-seller's claim is unsecured; it will be paid in "bankruptcy dollars," which are not worth 100 cents.

The effect of rejection is a matter of considerable debate. The Code provides an answer in a limited group of cases—when the debtor is a lessor or seller of certain real estate interests, or a licensor of rights to intellectual property. In those cases, §§ 365(h), (i), (j) and (n) protect the nondebtor party. In addition, § 365(o) provides special protection for certain governmental agencies, such as the FDIC, that are creditors in bankruptcy cases. The Code, however, leaves open the question of the effect of rejection when those subsections are inapplicable. The following cases present this issue in several contexts.

IN RE CARRERE

United States Bankruptcy Court, Central District of California, 1986.
64 B.R. 156.

GERALDINE MUND, Bankruptcy Judge.

STATEMENT OF FACTS

In August, 1985, Tia Carrere ("Carrere") entered into a personal services contract with American Broadcasting Company ("ABC") whereby she agreed to perform in the television series "General Hospital" from that time until August, 1988 ("ABC Contract"). Under the terms of the contract, Carrere was guaranteed employment on the average of 1½ performances per week. She was to be paid between $600 and $700 for each 60-minute program in which she performed.

While the contract with ABC was still in effect, Carrere agreed to make an appearance on the show "A Team." Under the terms of her agreement with Steven J. Cannell Productions ("A Team Contract"), if she became a regular on A Team, she would make considerably more money over the life of the contract than if she remained on General Hospital.

Although a state court suit was filed by ABC against Carrere for breach of contract due to her agreement with A Team, it appears that no actual breach of the ABC contract will take place until the option in the A Team Contract has been exercised.

On March 4, 1986, Carrere filed her voluntary petition under Chapter 11. The next day she filed a Notice of Rejection of Executory Contract, seeking to reject the ABC Contract. A motion to reject the ABC Contract was filed by the debtor and the matter was set for hearing.

In her declaration in support of the motion to reject, Carrere makes it clear that her primary motivation in seeking the protection of this Court was to reject the contract with ABC so as to enter into the more lucrative contract with A Team. In fact, she claims she did not enter into the contract with A Team until she had obtained advice that the bankruptcy would allow her to reject the contract with ABC. In her schedules she claims unsecured debt only. Her stated liabilities are $76,575 and her assets are $13,191. The amount of debts is disputed by ABC.

ABC vigorously opposed the rejection of its contract and has sought extensive discovery concerning Carrere's liabilities and motivations in filing this bankruptcy. ABC also brought a motion to dismiss the Chapter 11 proceeding on the grounds that it was filed in bad faith.

ANALYSIS

The key issue to be determined by this Court is whether a debtor, who is a performer under a personal services contract, is entitled to reject the contract by virtue of the provisions of § 365.[1] If so, what criteria must be applied?

A Personal Services Contract is not Property of the Estate in Chapters 7 or 11

* * *

Section 541(a)(6) states that property of the estate does not include "earnings from services performed by an individual debtor after the commencement of the case." This is limited to cases under Chapter 7 or 11, as post-petition earnings of the debtor become property of the estate in Chapter 13 cases (§ 1306). The post-petition earnings from personal services contracts are thus excluded from the Chapter 7 or Chapter 11 estate. Does this exclude the contract itself?

* * * The language of § 541(a)(6), which excludes post-petition proceeds from property of the estate, is an enactment of case law which specified that where an executory contract between the debtor and another is based upon the personal service or skill of the debtor, the Trustee does not take title to the debtor's rights in the contract.

---

1 The practical issue raised here is whether Carrere may deprive ABC of a cause of action for a negative injunction if she seeks further employment under the A Team Contract.

Under the Code, it has been held that a contract for personal services is excluded from the estate pursuant to both § 541(a)(6) and § 365(c). The foremost recent opinion on this matter is *In re Noonan*, 17 B.R. 793 (Bankr. S.D.N.Y.1982), which is cited by both sides in support of their respective positions. While *Noonan* is usually cited for the proposition that a debtor may not be forced to assume a personal services contract, it also deals with the personal services contract as property of the estate.

In *Noonan* the debtor was also a performer. He had entered into a personal services contract with a recording company, which wished to exercise its option and require him to record new albums. Noonan, a debtor-in-possession, sought to reject the contract. When the recording company vigorously opposed Noonan's motion, Noonan converted to Chapter 7, knowing that the trustee could not assume the contract, nor could he force the debtor to perform. Therefore the contract would be automatically rejected.

The recording company moved to reconvert to Chapter 11 and to be allowed to confirm a creditor's plan requiring Noonan to assume the contract and perform under it. The Court denied the motion. Among the grounds for denial was the holding that a personal services contract is not property of the estate.

The *Noonan* case did not deal with the issue of rejection of a personal services contract, for the debtor's motion to reject was never heard. But the case clearly held that a personal services contract is not property of the estate. The Court finds this line of reasoning to be persuasive.

Since the trustee has no interest in the contract, he has no standing to act at all under § 365. Therefore, he cannot assume or reject the contract.

The Rights of a Debtor-in-Possession are No Greater Than Those of a Trustee

An argument might be made that the debtor-in-possession, by virtue of the fact that she is also the individual who can perform the contract, has greater rights than the trustee and therefore can assume or reject the contract. The Court does not agree with this.

Upon the filing of a Chapter 11, Ms. Carrere created a new entity called a debtor-in-possession. That debtor-in-possession is not identical to the debtor herself. She is granted the rights and duties of a trustee (§ 323). Therefore while the debtor (Tia Carrere) may have duties under the ABC contract and may wish to reject those duties, the debtor-in-possession (who represents the estate of Tia Carrere) has no rights or duties whatsoever in the contract and therefore is a stranger to it.

In her role as debtor-in-possession, she has no interest in the proceeds of the personal services contract, nor in the contract itself. The contract never comes under the jurisdiction of the Bankruptcy Court. The Court has no interest, the estate has no interest, and even if the debtor-in-possession were allowed by consent of all parties to assume the contract under § 365, the assumption would not create an asset of the estate, for the proceeds would not be an asset of the estate, nor would the contract be assignable. Therefore, no rights of assumption are vested in the debtor-in-possession.

The only one who has rights or duties under the contract is the debtor herself. But the statutory scheme of § 365(d)(1) does not allow the debtor to reject an executory contract. It only allows the trustee to do so.

Therefore this Court finds that § 365 concerning assumption or rejection of a contract does not apply to a personal services contract in a bankruptcy case under Chapter 7 or 11, whether or not a trustee has been appointed.[4]

It Would be Inequitable to Allow the Contract to Be Rejected

Beyond the legal arguments described above, the Court is concerned about the good faith issue of allowing a debtor to file for the primary purpose of rejecting a personal services contract. A personal services contract is unique and money damages will often not make the employer whole. In weighing the rights of the employer to require performance against the rights of the performer to refuse to perform,

---

[4] The Court has no need at this time to deal with rejection of a contract under Chapter 13. Unlike Chapter 7 or 11, post-petition earnings from a personal services contract do become property of the estate under Chapter 13. Therefore the theories set forth to this point in the opinion are not applicable to Chapter 13. However, the Court does question the equity of allowing a Chapter 13 trustee to reject the contract, while denying the Chapter 13 [sic] trustee the power to assume it.

The issues of good faith, equity, and effect of rejection as described in the balance of this opinion apply equally to cases under all chapters.

California courts have allowed the employer to seek an injunction against the performer so that she could not breach the negative promises not to compete. It is this very remedy that Carrere seeks to avoid.

The Bankruptcy Court is a court of equity, as well as a court of law. It would be inequitable to allow a greedy debtor to seek the equitable protection of this Court when her major motivation is to cut off the equitable remedies of her employer.

For that reason this Court finds that there is not "cause" to reject this contract, if the major motivation of the debtor in filing the case was to be able to perform under the more lucrative A Team contract. It is clear that for Carrere this is the major motivation, even if it is not the sole motivation. Therefore, rejection is denied for lack of cause.

Rejection Would Not Relieve the Debtor of a Possible Negative Injunction

There is yet another issue that arises and impacts on the ultimate outcome of such cases: if rejection were permitted, what would be its effect on the creditor's right to seek a negative injunction against the debtor?

Rejection of an executory contract constitutes a breach, which is deemed to have occurred immediately before the date of the filing of the petition (§ 365(g)(1)). The claim for monetary damages thus becomes a claim in the estate (§ 502(g)).

But a rejection under the Bankruptcy Code only affects the monetary rights of the creditor. It does not disturb equitable, non-monetary rights that the creditor may have against the debtor because of the breach of contract.

This issue was raised in *In re Mercury Homes Development Co.*, 4 B.C.D. 837 (Bankr. N.D.Cal.1978). The debtor/vendor of a condominium rejected the land sale contract. The buyer requested specific performance; the trustee argued that the only remedy left to the buyer was his unsecured claim for monetary damages. The court rejected the trustee's argument and held that the buyer was entitled to enforce the equitable remedies given to it by state law.

While the *Mercury Homes* case does not differentiate between the equitable rights that the aggrieved party has against the debtor and those that he has against the trustee, the Court finds no reason in this situation to make any such distinction. California law has given ABC an equitable remedy: to seek a negative injunction against Carrere and thereby prevent her from performing elsewhere. Rejection of the ABC contract would not interfere with ABC's rights to seek that equitable remedy. Rejection would merely categorize any claim for monetary damages as a pre-petition debt. Therefore, whether this Court were to allow rejection or not, Carrere cannot use the Bankruptcy Code to protect her from whatever nonmonetary remedies are enforceable under state law.

On both the legal and equitable grounds set forth above, Carrere's Motion to Reject this contract is denied.

Notes and Questions

1. What about Tia Carrere's fresh start? Should the court have given some weight to that consideration?

2. In *Matter of Taylor*, 103 B.R. 511 (D.N.J.1989), James Taylor sought to reject a recording contract. (The debtor was not Sweet Baby James; he was J.T., lead singer in "Kool and the Gang.") The nondebtor argued that personal services contracts are not property of the estate and, therefore, that the trustee lacks power to affect them. The court, however, did not find § 541(a)(6) determinative:

> It is unclear at this stage whether personal service contracts themselves are to be included in the bankrupt's estate at the commencement of the case. However, it is logical to conclude that if the debtor's earnings under these contracts are not part of the estate, the contracts also should not be considered part of the estate at the commencement of the case.
>
> Pursuant to § 365(a), the trustee "subject to the court's approval, may assume or reject any executory contract or unexpired lease of the debtor." This language, by its express terms, permits the assumption or rejection of all executory contracts; no distinction is made between contracts which are part of the debtor's estate and those which are not so included at the time of commencement of the case. The trustee's general power to assume or reject any executory contract is limited only when additional restrictions or limitations have been established in the Bankruptcy Code.

Id. at 515–16 (footnote omitted). The court held that the contract was executory and subject to rejection, as long as the bankruptcy petition was filed in good faith:

> Implicit in the debtor's exercise of the option to reject executory personal service contracts is an obligation that the debtor's bankruptcy petition is filed in good faith with a valid reorganizational purpose. A requirement of good faith in the initial filing of a bankruptcy petition prevents abuse by debtors whose overriding motive is use of the bankruptcy process for reasons other than relief from overwhelming obligations. If the debtor's petition is filed in good faith with a proper reorganizational intent, the personal services executory contract may be rejected by the Bankruptcy Court.

Id. at 517–18 (footnotes omitted). Refusal to permit rejection, according to the court, would "force the debtor into involuntary servitude." *Id.* at 517. The court distinguished *Carrere* because that debtor filed in bad faith—that is, solely to enter another, more lucrative contract.

The next case deals with the effect of rejection on a covenant not to compete. We saw a similar issue in *Maids International, Inc. v. Ward (In re Ward)*, in Chapter 3, Section B of this casebook. There, the issue was whether a right to enjoin a debtor from competing is a "claim" in bankruptcy. In an omitted footnote, *Ward* declined to "waste ink and trees going through the usual protracted exercise for a determination of whether a covenant not to compete is an 'executory contract' within the meaning of § 365 of the Code." As the next case shows, another way of looking at the issue is to ask whether the covenant not to compete survives rejection.

SILK PLANTS, ETC. FRANCHISE SYSTEMS, INC. v. REGISTER (IN RE REGISTER)

United States Bankruptcy Court, Middle District of Tennessee, 1989.
95 B.R. 73, *affirmed* 100 B.R. 360 (M.D.Tenn.1989).

GEORGE C. PAINE, II, Chief Judge.

The issue presented is whether a covenant-not-to-compete contained in a franchise agreement is still enforceable after the debtors-franchisees rejected the executory franchise agreement. The plaintiff, Silk Plants, Etc. Franchise Systems, Inc., is seeking to enjoin the debtors from operating a business in apparent violation of the covenant-not-to-compete. * * *

On March 8, 1986, the Registers executed a franchise agreement with the plaintiff granting the Registers a franchise to operate a Silk Plants, Etc. specialty retail store offering artificial flowers, plants and related items. Under part of the franchise agreement the debtors covenanted not to engage in any capacity in a business offering to sell or selling merchandise or products similar to those sold in the Silk Plants, Etc. Systems business for a period of two years after the termination of the franchise agreement. The covenant-not-to-compete was also limited to business activities within a ten-mile radius of the Register's Silk Plants, Etc. store.

On March 15, 1988, the Registers filed their Chapter 13 bankruptcy petition. On May 18, 1988, the Registers rejected the franchise agreement through an agreed order with Silk Plants, Etc. Since then the Registers have operated a business very similar to their former Silk Plants, Etc. franchise. The plaintiffs then filed this adversary proceeding to enjoin the Registers from operating that store arguing that such activities violated the covenant-not-to-compete contained in the original franchise agreement.

Debtors in a bankruptcy proceeding may accept or reject executory contracts. The primary purposes behind allowing debtors to reject executory contracts are (1) to relieve the estate from burdensome obligations while the debtor is trying to recover financially, and (2) to effect a breach of contract allowing the injured party to file a claim.

Both of these goals are furthered by permitting debtors to reject covenants-not-to-compete with the rest of the executory contract. In fact, equitably enforcing such clauses in contracts that have been rejected would directly frustrate the purposes of relieving debtors from burdens that would hinder rehabilitation. For these reasons the debtor should be able to reject the covenant-not-to-compete along with the rest of the executory contract; Silk Plants, Etc. should then be able to file a claim for the injury resulting from that breach of contract under § 502(g) of the Bankruptcy Code. This is also consistent with the general rule that executory contracts must be accepted or rejected as a whole. The franchise agreement here clearly is an executory contract and as such may be rejected as it was in this case.

Silk Plants, Etc., however, argues that the covenant-not-to-compete was not executory and so cannot be rejected. According to Silk Plants, the covenant was severable from the executory parts of this contract and was based on a separate consideration which Silk Plants, Etc. had fully provided. This separate consideration according to Silk Plants, Etc. was the provision of training and information at the beginning of the franchise relationship. Silk Plants argues that it fully performed its portion of this severable agreement when it provided the promised training and information to the debtors.

The franchise agreement, when taken as a whole, however, shows that the debtors and Silk Plants Etc. contemplated that the covenant-not-to-compete would only be enforceable if Silk Plants performed on the entire franchise agreement, not just the sections requiring it to provide special training to the debtors. If Silk Plants had rejected the contract in a bankruptcy proceeding or had otherwise breached the franchising agreement the debtors clearly would not have had to honor the covenant-not-to-compete.

Silk Plants' reliance on *Leasing Service Corp. v. First Tennessee Bank, N.A.*, 826 F.2d 434 (6th Cir.1987), is misplaced. The question there was whether the granting and perfecting of a security interest was severable from the rest of a lease. A security interest is far different from a covenant-not-to-compete. Once perfected the security interest is a present interest in property; it establishes the priority of the holder of the security interest; and the existence of the security interest is not dependent on the holders' performance of the rest of the contract. For example, in *Leasing Service Corp.* if the lessor had breached, it would have been liable to the tenant for damages. If the lessor had some valid claim against the tenant, however, the security interest would have been available to satisfy that claim regardless of the lessor's breach. Here, however, the franchisor's ability to enforce the covenant-not-to-compete is totally dependent on his faithful performance of the entire agreement. Thus the covenant-not-to-compete is not severable from the rest of the executory contract.

Silk Plants, Etc. next argues that a covenant-not-to-compete is enforced by an injunction and other equitable relief and not by a suit for money damages. Therefore the breach of this covenant does not give rise to a claim as defined by [§ 101(5)]. Silk Plants, Etc.'s right to equitable relief then should not be affected by the bankruptcy.

In support of this claim Silk Plants, Etc. cites *In re Noco, Inc.*, 76 B.R. 839 (Bankr. N.D.Fla.1987), and *In re Carrere*, 64 B.R. 156 (Bankr. C.D.Cal.1986). Both of these cases may be distinguished from the instant case because in both cases the filing of bankruptcy had elements of bad faith. The bankruptcies seemed to have been filed solely for the purpose of avoiding the covenants not to compete. Such is not the case here. * * *

To the extent that these cases support Silk Plants, Etc.'s position, this court declines to follow them. For purposes of [§ 101(5)], the principle issue is whether this court is capable of reducing the injury that Silk Plant[s] incurs as a result of the breach of this covenant to a dollar amount. If it can, then Silk Plants has a claim under §§ [101(5)] and 502(g). Although state courts have ruled that they cannot put a value on the injury incurred for breach of these covenants this Court believes that it can. As the court in *In re Norquist*, 43 B.R. 224, 231 (Bankr. E.D.Wash.1984), noted, "The equitable configuration of this court may very well permit a just determination and treatment of [a breach of a covenant-not-to-compete] which would not be accomplished under the rigid application of evidentiary rules in state court." This approach furthers the underlying goals of § 365 by relieving the debtor completely of the burden of this executory contract and by granting the creditor a claim for the injury incurred.

The court holds that the covenant-not-to-compete terminated when the contract was rejected and that Silk Plants may file a claim for the breach of the entire franchise agreement, including the covenant-not-to-compete, under § 502(g).

The case law on post-rejection enforceability of covenants not to compete is deeply divided. See *In re Printronics, Inc.*, 189 B.R. 995 (Bankr. N.D.Fla.1995). Much of the disagreement stems from evolving concepts about the effect of rejection, which have followed from analysis of the next case and scholarly commentary it has generated. After reading the following materials, think again about *Register* and such covenants.

LUBRIZOL ENTERPRISES, INC. v. RICHMOND METAL FINISHERS, INC. (IN RE RICHMOND METAL FINISHERS, INC.)

United States Court of Appeals, Fourth Circuit, 1985.
756 F.2d 1043, *cert. denied sub nom.* Lubrizol Enterprises v. Canfield, 475 U.S. 1057, 106 S.Ct. 1285, 89 L.Ed.2d 592 (1986).

JAMES DICKSON PHILLIPS, Circuit Judge.

The question is whether Richmond Metal Finishers (RMF), a bankrupt debtor in possession, should have been allowed to reject as executory a technology licensing agreement with Lubrizol Enterprises (Lubrizol) as licensee. The bankruptcy court approved rejection pursuant to § 365(a); but the district court reversed on the basis that within contemplation of § 365(a), the contract was not executory and, alternatively, that rejection could not reasonably be expected substantially to benefit the bankrupt debtor. We reverse and remand for entry of judgment in conformity with that entered by the bankruptcy court.

I

In July of 1982, RMF entered into the contract with Lubrizol that granted Lubrizol a nonexclusive license to utilize a metal coating process technology owned by RMF. RMF owed the following duties to Lubrizol under the agreement: (1) to notify Lubrizol of any patent infringement suit and to defend in such suit; (2) to notify Lubrizol of any other use or licensing of the process, and to reduce royalty payments if a lower royalty rate agreement was reached with another licensee; and (3) to indemnify Lubrizol for losses arising out of any misrepresentation or breach of warranty by RMF. Lubrizol owed RMF reciprocal duties of accounting for and paying royalties for use of the process and of cancelling certain existing indebtedness. The contract provided that Lubrizol would defer use of the process until May 1, 1983, and in fact, Lubrizol has never used the RMF technology.

RMF filed a petition for bankruptcy pursuant to Chapter 11 of the Bankruptcy Code on August 16, 1983. As part of its plan to emerge from bankruptcy, RMF sought, pursuant to § 365(a), to reject the contract with Lubrizol in order to facilitate sale or licensing of the technology unhindered by restrictive provisions in the Lubrizol agreement. On RMF's motion for approval of the rejection, the bankruptcy court properly interpreted § 365 as requiring it to undertake a two-step inquiry to determine the propriety of rejection: first, whether the contract is executory; next, if so, whether its rejection would be advantageous to the bankrupt.

Making that inquiry, the bankruptcy court determined that both tests were satisfied and approved the rejection. But, as indicated, the district court then reversed that determination on the basis that neither test was satisfied and disallowed the rejection. This appeal followed.

II

We conclude initially that, as the bankruptcy court ruled, the technology licensing agreement in this case was an executory contract, within contemplation of § 365(a). Under that provision a contract is executory if performance is due to some extent on both sides. This court has recently adopted Professor Countryman's more specific test for determining whether a contract is "executory" in the required sense. By that test, a contract is executory if the "'obligations of both the bankrupt and the other party to the contract are so far unperformed that the failure of either to complete the performance would constitute a material breach excusing the performance of the other.'" *Gloria Manufacturing Corp. v. International Ladies' Garment Workers' Union*, 734 F.2d 1020, 1022 (4th Cir.1984) (quoting Countryman, *Executory Contracts in Bankruptcy: Part I*, 57 Minn. L. Rev. 439, 460 (1973). This issue is one of law that may be freely reviewed by successive courts.

Applying that test here, we conclude that the licensing agreement was at the critical time executory. RMF owed Lubrizol the continuing duties of notifying Lubrizol of further licensing of the process and of reducing Lubrizol's royalty rate to meet any more favorable rates granted to subsequent licensees. By their terms, RMF's obligations to give notice and to restrict its right to license its process at royalty rates it desired without lowering Lubrizol's royalty rate extended over the life of the agreement, and remained unperformed. Moreover, RMF owed Lubrizol additional contingent duties of notifying it of suits, defending suits and indemnifying it for certain losses.

The unperformed, continuing core obligations of notice and forbearance in licensing made the contract executory as to RMF. In *Fenix Cattle Co. v. Silver (In re Select–A–Seat Corp.)*, 625 F.2d 290, 292 (9th Cir.1980), the court found that an obligation of a debtor to refrain from selling software packages under an exclusive licensing agreement made a contract executory as to the debtor notwithstanding the continuing obligation was only one of forbearance. Although the license to Lubrizol was not exclusive, RMF owed the same type of unperformed continuing duty of forbearance arising out of the most favored licensee clause running in favor of Lubrizol. Breach of that duty would clearly constitute a material breach of the agreement.

Moreover, the contract was further executory as to RMF because of the contingent duties that RMF owed of giving notice of and defending infringement suits and of indemnifying Lubrizol for certain losses arising out of the use of the technology. Contingency of an obligation does not prevent its being executory under § 365. Until the time has expired during which an event triggering a contingent duty may occur, the contingent obligation represents a continuing duty to stand ready to perform if the contingency occurs. A breach of that duty once it was triggered by the contingency (or presumably, by anticipatory repudiation) would have been material.

Because a contract is not executory within the meaning of § 365(a) unless it is executory as to both parties, it is also necessary to determine whether the licensing agreement was executory as to Lubrizol. We conclude that it was.

Lubrizol owed RMF the unperformed and continuing duty of accounting for and paying royalties for the life of the agreement. It is true that a contract is not executory as to a party simply because the party is obligated to make payments of money to the other party. Therefore, if Lubrizol had owed RMF nothing more than a duty to make fixed payments or cancel specified indebtedness under the agreement, the agreement would not be executory as to Lubrizol. However, the promise to account for and pay royalties required that Lubrizol deliver written quarterly sales reports and keep books of account subject to inspection by an independent Certified Public Accountant. This promise goes beyond a mere debt, or promise to pay money, and was at the critical time executory. Additionally, subject to certain exceptions, Lubrizol was obligated to keep all license technology in confidence for a number of years.

Since the licensing agreement is executory as to each party, it is executory within the meaning of § 365(a), and the district court erred as a matter of law in reaching a contrary conclusion.

III

There remains the question whether rejection of the executory contract would be advantageous to the bankrupt. Courts addressing that question must start with the proposition that the bankrupt's decision upon it is to be accorded the deference mandated by the sound business judgment rule as generally applied by courts to discretionary actions or decisions of corporate directors.

As generally formulated and applied in corporate litigation the rule is that courts should defer to—should not interfere with—decisions of corporate directors upon matters entrusted to their business judgment except upon a finding of bad faith or gross abuse of their "business discretion." Transposed to the bankruptcy context, the rule as applied to a bankrupt's decision to reject an executory contract because of perceived business advantage requires that the decision be accepted by courts unless it is shown that the bankrupt's decision was one taken in bad faith or in gross abuse of the bankrupt's retained business discretion.

In bankruptcy litigation the issue is of course first presented for judicial determination when a debtor, having decided that rejection will be beneficial within contemplation of § 365(a), moves for approval of the rejection. The issue thereby presented for first instance judicial determination by the bankruptcy court is whether the decision of the debtor that rejection will be advantageous is so manifestly unreasonable that it could not be based on sound business judgment, but only on bad faith, or whim or caprice. That issue is one of fact to be decided as such by the bankruptcy court by the normal processes of fact adjudication. And the resulting fact determination by the bankruptcy court is perforce then reviewable up the line under the clearly erroneous standard.

Here, the bankruptcy judge had before him evidence not rebutted by Lubrizol that the metal coating process subject to the licensing agreement is RMF's principal asset and that sale or licensing of the technology represented the primary potential source of funds by which RMF might emerge from bankruptcy. The testimony of RMF's president, also factually uncontested by Lubrizol, indicated that sale or further licensing of the technology would be facilitated by stripping Lubrizol of its rights in the process and that, correspondingly, continued obligation to Lubrizol under the agreement would hinder RMF's capability to sell or license the technology on more advantageous terms to other potential licensees. On the basis of this evidence the bankruptcy court determined that the debtor's decision to reject was based upon sound business judgment and approved it.

On appeal the district court simply found to the contrary that the debtor's decision to reject did not represent a sound business judgment. The district court's determination rested essentially on two grounds:

that RMF's purely contingent obligations under the agreement were not sufficiently onerous that relief from them would constitute a substantial benefit to RMF; and that because rejection could not deprive Lubrizol of all its rights to the technology, rejection could not reasonably be found beneficial. We conclude that in both of these respects the district court's factual findings, at odds with those of the bankruptcy court, were clearly erroneous and cannot stand.

A

In finding that the debtor's contingent obligations were not sufficiently onerous that relief from them would be beneficial, the district court could only have been substituting its business judgment for that of the debtor. There is nothing in the record from which it could be concluded that the debtor's decision on that point could not have been reached by the exercise of sound (though possibly faulty) business judgment in the normal process of evaluating alternative courses of action. If that could not be concluded, then the business judgment rule required that the debtor's factual evaluation be accepted by the court, as it had been by the bankruptcy court.

B

On the second point, we can only conclude that the district court was under a misapprehension of controlling law in thinking that by rejecting the agreement the debtor could not deprive Lubrizol of all rights to the process. Under § 365(g), Lubrizol would be entitled to treat rejection as a breach and seek a money damages remedy; however, it could not seek to retain its contract rights in the technology by specific performance even if that remedy would ordinarily be available upon breach of this type of contract. Even though § 365(g) treats rejection as a breach, the legislative history of § 365(g) makes clear that the purpose of the provision is to provide only a damages remedy for the non-bankrupt party. H.R. Rep. No. 95–595 at 349, *reprinted in* 1978 U.S.C.C.A.N. at 6305. For the same reason, Lubrizol cannot rely on provisions within its agreement with RMF for continued use of the technology by Lubrizol upon breach by RMF. Here again, the statutory "breach" contemplated by § 365(g) controls, and provides only a money damages remedy for the non-bankrupt party. Allowing specific performance would obviously undercut the core purpose of rejection under § 365(a), and that consequence cannot therefore be read into congressional intent.

IV

Lubrizol strongly urges upon us policy concerns in support of the district court's refusal to defer to the debtor's decision to reject or, preliminarily, to treat the contract as executory for § 365(a) purposes. We understand the concerns, but think they cannot control decision here.

It cannot be gainsaid that allowing rejection of such contracts as executory imposes serious burdens upon contracting parties such as Lubrizol. Nor can it be doubted that allowing rejection in this and comparable cases could have a general chilling effect upon the willingness of such parties to contract at all with businesses in possible financial difficulty. But under bankruptcy law such equitable considerations may not be indulged by courts in respect of the type of contract here in issue. Congress has plainly provided for the rejection of executory contracts, notwithstanding the obvious adverse consequences for contracting parties thereby made inevitable. Awareness by Congress of those consequences is indeed specifically reflected in the special treatment accorded to union members under collective bargaining contracts, *see NLRB v. Bildisco & Bildisco*, 465 U.S. 513, 519–26 (1984), and to lessees of real property, see § 365(h). But no comparable special treatment is provided for technology licensees such as Lubrizol. They share the general hazards created by § 365 for all business entities dealing with potential bankrupts in the respects at issue here.

The judgment of the district court is reversed and the case is remanded for entry of judgment in conformity with that entered by the bankruptcy court.

Notes and Questions

1. Do you agree with the result in *Lubrizol*? Why should bankruptcy enable a debtor to take back rights already granted?

2. Do the decisions reached by the District Court and the Court of Appeals in *Lubrizol* reveal a fundamental disagreement about what "rejection" means?

3. Note *Lubrizol* 's statement of the standard for rejection.

4. *Register* and *Lubrizol* raise the problem of what rejection means in cases not susceptible to the usual formula of contract breach remedied by a judgment for money damages. In certain kinds of cases—those involving unique goods, covenants not to compete, technology licenses and the like—

state law provides injunctive relief or a decree for specific performance, not money damages. The decisions in *Register* and *Lubrizol* suggest that bankruptcy will provide the nondebtor only a damages claim. But what should bankruptcy do in these cases if *Register* and *Lubrizol* are wrong?

5. Largely in response to *Lubrizol*, Congress added § 365(n) to the Code in 1988. That subsection applies to agreements governing certain types of intellectual property and reverses the specific result in *Lubrizol*. Other cases, including those concerning covenants not to compete seen in *Register*, may follow *Lubrizol* 's analysis. For that reason, the case remains important.

6. Debtor entered into a 20–year licensing agreement under which Nondebtor, Inc. was given the exclusive right to manufacture and sell Debtor's inventions in Canada. Debtor filed Chapter 11 and sought to reject the agreement. Nondebtor, Inc. resisted the motion to reject, arguing that it was incorporated for the purpose of enjoying rights under the agreement and all of its business and income was based on the agreement. Should rejection be permitted when it will totally destroy Nondebtor, Inc.'s business? See *In re Petur U.S.A. Instrument Co.*, 35 B.R. 561 (Bankr. W.D.Wash.1983).

MICHAEL T. ANDREW, EXECUTORY CONTRACTS IN BANKRUPTCY: UNDERSTANDING "REJECTION"

59 U. Colo. L. Rev. 845, 848–49, 883–84, 901–02, 916–18, 920–22 (1988) (footnotes omitted).

In this article I suggest that much of the jurisprudence of "rejection" is profoundly confused, and that the strikingly simple concept embodied in that term has been all but lost in the confusion. As will be seen, rejection is not the revocation or repudiation or cancellation of a contract or lease, nor does it affect contract or lease liabilities. It is simply a bankruptcy estate's decision not to assume, because the contract or lease does not represent a favorable or appropriate investment of the estate's resources. Rejection does not change the substantive rights of the parties to the contract or lease, but merely means that the bankruptcy estate itself will not become a party to it. Simply put, the election to "assume or reject" is the election to assume or not assume; "rejection" is the name for the latter alternative.

Far from benign, the confusion over rejection has yielded wasteful litigation, absurd results, and dramatic distortions in bankruptcy law. Understanding that rejection does not affect contract liabilities demonstrates, for example, that litigation over whether rejection will be permitted is largely a pointless exercise. The understanding also makes clear that terminating rights in or to property arising under contracts that happen to be "executory" is fundamentally contrary to general bankruptcy principles, to the history and purpose of executory contracts doctrine itself, and to common sense. The most serious consequence of the confusion over rejection is that it has diverted attention away from important questions of bankruptcy policy, focusing it instead on the generally meaningless question of what constitutes an "executory" contract.

* * *

"Assumption" aptly describes what occurs when a bankruptcy estate elects to take on the obligations of a contract or lease as the price of obtaining the benefit of the non-debtor party's performance. By contrast, "rejection" is a particularly inapt term to describe the election *not* to assume. The reason: it suggests, misleadingly, that the trustee or debtor in possession is somehow rejecting (cancelling? repudiating? renouncing? rescinding?) *liabilities*. In fact, what the estate's representative is rejecting is the contract or lease *asset*, which conceivably could carry continuing obligations with it into the estate on an administrative basis. Rejection simply prevents the *estate* from unadvisedly stepping into such liabilities. The liabilities are not repudiated; to the contrary, as the rejection-as-breach doctrine is designed to insure, the contract or lease liabilities remain intact after rejection and give the non-debtor party a claim in the distribution of the estate.

The doctrinal labelling of rejection as a "breach" is also unfortunate, though, for two reasons. First, it undoubtedly exacerbates the confused view of rejection as a cancellation or repudiation of liabilities. A superficial reading of the doctrine can suggest the upside-down conclusion that bankruptcy law confers on bankruptcy trustees and debtors in possession a special "power" to breach contracts. That confused restatement of the doctrine at least implies that a trustee or debtor in possession can make obligations simply disappear, or can in some other way impair the rights of the non-debtor party, *just because the contract is "executory."* In fact, rejection-as-breach doctrine exists for precisely the opposite reason: It assures non-debtor parties to executory contracts and leases that, for purposes of the bankruptcy distribution, they will not be treated differently than other claimants and the obligations owed to them will *not* disappear.

Second, the use of "breach" terminology (particularly when coupled to rejection rather than bankruptcy itself) suggests that there is some discontinuity between the treatment of "executory" contracts and other liabilities. In fact, "breach" was used as an indirect way of saying that there is *no* discontinuity: For executory contracts, as for all other obligations, claims will be determined based upon the presumption that the debtor will not perform. To say that an executory contract is "breached" is merely to say what is already presumed to be true with respect to all other obligations. Again, it must be emphasized that the "breach" here is a presumed pre-bankruptcy breach *by the debtor*.

Much confusion would have been averted had the election to "assume or reject" been called, more comprehensibly but to identical effect, the election to "assume or decline" or, as in *Copeland* [*v. Stephens*, 106 Eng.Rep. (K.B. 1818)], the election to "accept or refuse." Similarly, the "breach" rule would have been eminently more understandable described as what it is: a presumption of the debtor's non-performance for claims allowance purposes.

* * *

Another more significant result of confusion about "rejection" has been the creation of a distinct doctrine—"avoiding-power" rejection, as I call it—only spuriously related to basic executory contracts doctrine. That separate doctrine, like bankruptcy's explicit avoiding powers, terminates the rights of third parties in or to property in which the debtor had an interest. It does so, however, without any of the justifications of the avoiding powers, but instead only because the third party's rights arise under a contract that happens to be "executory" when the bankruptcy commences.

* * *

The case that illustrates perhaps better than any other what is wrong with avoiding-power rejection, and how the Countryman test of an "executory" contract fuels it, is the Fourth Circuit's decision in *Lubrizol Enterprises, Inc. v. Richmond Metal Finishers, Inc.* There the debtor had licensed certain technology to Lubrizol non-exclusively, and sought in its chapter 11 case to reject the license and terminate Lubrizol's rights to the technology. The key issue, thought the court, was the hunt for mutual "executoriness."

Addressing first the debtor-licensor's side of the agreement, the court found executory aspects in the "continuing duties of notifying Lubrizol of further licensing of the process and of reducing Lubrizol's royalty rate to meet any more favorable rates granted to subsequent licensees." In addition, the debtor had the "additional contingent duties of notifying [Lubrizol] of suits, defending suits and indemnifying it for certain losses."

The "executoriness" of Lubrizol's side of the arrangement was more difficult, because the court thought the mutual performance test required remaining duties other than merely the payment of money. But the necessary "executory" obligations were found, as the court explained in this remarkable passage:

> [I]f Lubrizol had owed [the debtor] nothing more than a duty to make fixed payments or cancel specified indebtedness under the agreement, the agreement would not be executory as to Lubrizol. However, the promise to account for and pay royalties *required that Lubrizol deliver written quarterly sales reports and keep books of account subject to inspection by an independent Certified Public Accountant.* This promise goes beyond a mere debt, or promise to pay money, and was at the critical time executory.

The court went on to approve rejection of the license and termination of the licensee's interest, relying in part on the absence of any special protection for licensees in § 365.

The passage just quoted is one of the most noteworthy in the annals of avoiding-power rejection. Lubrizol had what everyone apparently believed was a perfectly valid license. Nothing suggests that the license was in any way subject to termination by any creditor of, or purchaser from, the debtor under non-bankruptcy law, or that it was in any other way avoidable under bankruptcy law. It also seems quite clear that if the license had been found to have been non-"executory," the court would have enforced it. *Lubrizol lost its right to the technology because it had the duty to "deliver written quarterly sales reports and keep books of account subject to inspection."*

The court did not pause to ask why the happenstance of "executoriness" should control an issue so important as the licensee's continued ability to use the technology. Its only real attempt at an explanation of the result was to observe that the "clear" purpose of § 365(g), the rejection-as-breach rule, "is to provide only a damages remedy for the non-bankrupt party" * * *.

* * *

Whether the debtor is a licensor, lessor, vendor, or mortgagor, or any other owner of real or personal property in or to which a third party has rights under a contract, the analysis should be the same. Rejection of the contract by the estate—the estate's decision not to assume—is not a rescission or cancellation of the contract. It is merely the estate's decision not to become obligated on it. Thus, rejection of the *contract* does not enhance the estate's rights to the *underlying asset*. The estate acquires that asset, like all other assets, in the "same plight and condition that the [debtor] himself held it, and subject to all the equities impressed upon it in the hands of the [debtor]," even though clearly the estate is not itself bound by the contract.

As a starting premise, therefore, the position of the estate is no different from that of any other ordinary transferee acquiring the underlying asset from the debtor without assuming the debtor's contract obligations. The proper inquiry is what the position of such a nonassuming transferee would be vis-a-vis the non-debtor party. To the extent that the non-debtor could enforce its rights as against such a transferee of the underlying asset—by specific performance, other injunctive relief, replevin, or some other remedy—it should be able to do so as against the estate despite the rejection of the contract. It is for precisely that reason that a lessee is entitled to remain in possession of property despite rejection of a lease by the lessor's bankruptcy estate.

It must be clearly understood, though, that this analysis does not somehow elevate the non-debtor party over other claimants. The non-debtor's right to the property or to some use of it, like any other right in or to property in bankruptcy, is good against the estate only if it survives the true avoiding powers. To that extent, the estate has *better* rights in the asset than would an ordinary transferee from the debtor. That means, among other things, that a right to property not good against a lien creditor of the debtor (or a bona fide purchaser of real property from the debtor) under state law would not be good as against the estate. Thus, the contract right in or to the property is enforced in bankruptcy only to the extent that it was a right *good against other claimants in the first place*.

That point also makes clear the error in arguing that recognition of the non-debtor's rights in or to property will somehow defeat a fundamental purpose of rejection—to insure that parties to executory contracts are treated the same as other claimants. Bankruptcy law distinguishes between *other* claimants on the basis of rights in or to property. Nothing in executory contracts doctrine remotely suggests a design to treat all parties to unassumed executory contracts as unsecured creditors, any more than bankruptcy law generally treats all other claimants as unsecured creditors, which it plainly does not. Rather, the design of executory contracts doctrine is to eliminate "executoriness" as a factor in determining the non-debtor party's rights when a contract is not assumed.

2. SPECIAL RULES FOR CERTAIN REAL ESTATE INTERESTS

The Code contains special protections when the party in bankruptcy is the lessor, the seller under a real estate sales contract, or the seller of a timeshare interest. Congress believed that the nondebtor party to these types of contracts is particularly vulnerable and in need of protection.

Read §§ 365(h), (i) and (j) and solve the following Problems.

Problems

1. Debtor Corp. owns an office building and leases space to Law Firm. The lease, which runs for 10 more years, requires Law Firm to pay $10,000 per month in rent. It also requires Debtor Corp. to heat and cool the building, to keep the building clean and to provide elevator service. The demand for office space has risen in the last year and Debtor Corp. wants to reject Law Firm's lease and relet the premises for more money. Can Debtor Corp. reject the lease? If so, can it dispossess Law Firm following rejection? What are Law Firm's options? See § 365(h).

2. Flowers-by-Florence leased space in Downtown Mall, which was owned by Debtor, Inc. Florence chose to remain in place when Debtor, Inc. filed bankruptcy and rejected the lease, but Florence later decided to close the shop and assign the balance of the lease term to Wilma's Wines. The lease provides that no more than one specialty store of any type can occupy premises in the Mall. Both Debtor, Inc. and Fred's Fine Wines, which is located on the other end of Downtown Mall, object to the assignment. What result? See § 365(h).

3. Debtor Corp. owned an apartment complex. Two years ago, facing severe financial problems, Debtor Corp. decided to convert the premises to condominiums. Mary Occupant agreed to purchase her unit and signed a contract requiring payments over a 10–year period, with title remaining in Debtor Corp. until payment of the last installment. Debtor Corp. filed Chapter 11 last month and notified Mary that it intended to reject her purchase contract. What are Mary's options? See § 365(i).

4. Developer sold a beachfront lot to Greg Greene under an installment sales contract requiring the payment of $7,500 per year for five years.

Title was to remain in Developer until completion of payments. After Greg made two annual payments, Developer filed bankruptcy and sought to reject the contract. Greg had looked forward to building a get-away cottage on the lot as soon as he could afford to, and he is very upset. What are Greg's options? See §§ 365(i) and (j).

5. Developer owned a tract of land on which Bank held a purchase money mortgage for $400,000. Developer contracted with Joe and Jane Homeowner to build them a house on the lot for $520,000. The Homeowners gave Developer a down payment of $60,000, which Developer used to pay for labor and materials. At the time Developer stopped work and filed bankruptcy, $50,000 remained owing to materials suppliers. The land and unfinished house were sold for $430,000. Claims against the proceeds were asserted by Bank, the materials suppliers and the Homeowners. How should the proceeds be distributed? See *Thompson Designs, Inc. v. Treasurer of Hamilton County (In re Thompson Designs, Inc.)*, 213 B.R. 725 (Bankr. S.D. Ind. 1997).

3. REJECTION OF PREVIOUSLY ASSUMED CONTRACTS AND LEASES

As we have seen, assumption turns the debtor's obligations under an executory contract or lease into obligations of the estate that enjoy administrative expense priority. A trustee or debtor-in-possession should assume only after determining that the lease or contract will benefit the estate enough to merit burdening the estate with the obligations that will flow from assumption. But what if those beneficial projections prove to have been overly optimistic, as happens all too often, and the lease or contract is later rejected? What is the status of the obligations under the contract or lease—do all of the remaining obligations enjoy administrative expense priority? And what about the cap on a long-term lessor's claim under § 502(b)(6)?

These issues were addressed in *Nostas Associates v. Costich (In re Klein Sleep Products, Inc.)*, 78 F.3d 18 (2d Cir.1996). The debtor, which leased retail premises from Nostas, filed a Chapter 11 petition in June, 1991 and assumed the lease shortly thereafter. The debtor continued to pay rent through October, 1992, at which point the reorganization failed and a trustee was appointed to liquidate the estate. The lease was rejected at the end of January, 1993 and Nostas relet the premises, at a reduced rental, in July. Nostas asserted an administrative expense priority for the arrearage (rent due for November 1992 through January 1993), for the full amount of future rent due after rejection and before the premises were relet (February through June, 1993), and for the difference between the amount it was receiving from its new tenant and the amount the debtor owed under the lease.

The bankruptcy court allowed administrative expense priority for the amount of the rent arrearage, but found that the claim for future damages was a general unsecured claim, subject to § 502(b)(6)'s cap. The district court affirmed, but the Second Circuit, in an opinion written by Judge Calabresi, reversed:

II. DISCUSSION

A. *Administrative Expense Status*

* * *

> Once the trustee gave the store back to Nostas, the [bankruptcy] court reasoned, Klein Sleep received no further benefit from the lease. As a result, the damages it sought for future rent did not meet the prerequisites for administrative expense status under § 503(b)(1)(A).
>
> At first glance, the bankruptcy court's approach has much to recommend it. By denying administrative expense status for all future rent under an assumed lease, the court followed our stated policy that priorities in bankruptcy should be narrowly construed and sparingly granted. And, the bankruptcy court's relegation of Nostas to the ranks of the unsecured creditors furthered this fundamental policy—based on the notion that individual creditors, whenever possible, should be prevented from seizing a disproportionate share of the estate—in a second way as well. Once future rent is treated merely as an unsecured claim, it is clearly capped by § 502(b)(6) at one year's worth of unpaid rent. As a result, the rent claims cannot absorb all the assets of the estate, no matter how long the lease.
>
> Yet this approach has several deficiencies. First, it relies on an unduly narrow view of the benefit conferred on an estate when a trustee assumes an unexpired lease. Second, it does not adequately account for the Code's timing provisions, which explicitly provide that claims arise "postpetition," and therefore during the administration of the estate, if they are based on breaches of assumed leases. And finally, even if these two considerations did not resolve the matter, the district court's approach does not accord with prior practice under the Bank-

ruptcy Act (practice which, in cases of ambiguity, stands as a decisive guidepost for interpreting today's Bankruptcy Code). Bankruptcy Act practice strongly directs us to treat the entire liability resulting from breach of an assumed lease as a cost of administering the estate.

1. *Benefit*

* * *

One sensible way to look at whether the estate was benefitted by assuming the lease is to ask whether the debtor's entry into the lease would have been a voidable preference had it occurred just prior to the bankruptcy filing. According to § 547(c)(1) of the Code, where the debtor transfers assets to a creditor and, through a substantially contemporaneous exchange, receives new value, there is no voidable preference. If the debtor had entered into the lease within 90 days before the filing of the petition, and if the rent for the entire term of the lease had been due and payable immediately, the estate would undoubtedly have received "new value." That value is the right to occupy the premises for the full term of the lease—an assignable right that has value, regardless of whether it is ever exercised or sold. By assuming the lease, the debtor retains an identical transferable right and therefore receives an "actual benefit" * * * .

The trustee argues that any inquiry as to "benefit" is foreclosed by the district court's factual finding that Klein Sleep did not benefit from its assumption of the lease. The opposite, however, is true: the bankruptcy court's earlier decision to let Klein Sleep assume the unexpired lease—a decision that was not appealed—precluded a subsequent finding that assuming the lease did not benefit Klein Sleep. That decision required a judicial finding—up-front—that it was in the best interests of the estate (and the unsecured creditors) for the debtor to assume the lease, pursuant to § 365(a). It is the same kind of finding that the bankruptcy court is required to make with regard to all *new* contracts entered into by the trustee without prior court approval during the administration of the estate in order for those contracts to qualify for priority pursuant to § 503(b).

* * *

In short, we decline to find that Klein Sleep did not benefit by assuming its lease simply because the lease was no longer profitable at the time it stopped displaying mattresses on the premises. Such a holding would mean that any postbankruptcy contract, entered into for the benefit of a bankrupt's estate, would cease to be entitled to priority the moment the deal turned sour. When the debtor-in-possession assumed the lease, it retained the right to occupy the leased premises immediately and in the future. Its ability to assign this immediate right of possession, as well as its ability to assign the future right of possession under the lease, had a present value at the time of assumption. Acquisition of those rights clearly constituted a benefit to the estate even if, later, the benefit turned to dust.

2. *Timing*

The Code's timing provisions also tilt in favor of Nostas's position that all future rent is an administrative expense. In allowing and assigning priority to claims arising from unexpired leases, the Code distinguishes between leases that have been assumed, and those that have not. Section 502(g) of the Code clearly instructs us that claims arising from *unassumed* leases are to be allowed as general unsecured claims. Section 502(g) has no analogue that tells us what to do with claims arising from *assumed* leases. But because § 502(g) limits its reach to unassumed leases, it is reasonable to infer that assumed leases are to be treated differently. Since it would be absurd to suppose that such leases would not qualify as claims at all, it follows that they must be considered administrative expenses of the estate.

This inference is further supported by § 365(g), which fixes the time at which a debtor's rejection of an unexpired lease is deemed to constitute a breach of the lease. When a debtor rejects an unassumed lease, breach is deemed to occur at the time the bankruptcy petition was filed. § 365(g)(1). If the lease has been assumed, however, breach is deemed to occur whenever the lease is later rejected. § 365(g)(2)(A). According to the Code's legislative history, the purpose of § 365(g) is to treat claims arising from unassumed leases "as prepetition claims." H.R. Rep. No. 595, 95th Cong., 2d Sess. 349 (1977); S. Rep. No. 989, 95th Cong., 2d Sess. 63 (1978), *reprinted in* 1978 U.S.C.C.A.N. 5787, 6305, 5849. But the only way in which prepetition claims are treated differently from postpetition claims is that the former are classified as general claims, whereas the latter—arising, for example, from torts committed by the estate in bankruptcy, or from contracts entered into by the trustee or debtor-in-possession—are entitled to administrative expense priority. It would seem to follow that rejection of an assumed lease—that is, breach of contract committed by the trustee or debtor-in-possession while administering the estate—gives rise to a debt entitled to the same administrative expense priority.

The timing provisions of the Code were not, however, directly designed to answer the question we are asking today, and so we are hesitant to read too much into them. Indeed, because all of our previous discussion has essentially required us to read between the lines of Congress's directives, we conclude that the Bankruptcy Code, though it clearly leans in favor of administrative status for assumed leases, is still ambiguous. When that is the case, we are required to turn for further guidance to the prior practice under the Bankruptcy Act.

3. Practice Under the Bankruptcy Act

* * *

* * * That practice strongly supports the conclusion that Nostas's claim was entitled to administrative expense status. This result, moreover, agrees with our earlier analysis that the Code's timing provisions, together with the rules governing "benefit," indicate that all future rent accruing under an assumed lease is entitled to the status of an administrative expense. Accordingly, we so hold.

B. *The § 502(b)(6) Cap on Damages for Future Rent*

Because it determined that Nostas's claim was not an administrative expense, the district court never reached the issue of whether § 502(b)(6) limits Nostas's claim arising from the assumed leases to one year's worth of future rent. Since we conclude that such future rent is an administrative expense, we must now decide whether § 502(b)(6) caps the rent.

* * * This cap is designed to prevent a landlord's single unsecured claim—which, depending on the length of the lease, may be enormous—to elbow aside the other unsecured credi-

tors. The trustee argues that "the policy underlying § 502(b)(6) applies equally to claims arising under leases that have been assumed and those that have not." Indeed, because the drafters of the Code took such care to prevent a monstrous *unsecured* claim from swallowing up the estate, it might seem odd not only to give an analogous type of claim priority over unsecured creditors, but also to allow such a claim in its entirety, merely because it arose from an assumed lease.

Sensible as this policy argument might be, we do not find the Code ambiguous on this point. Section 502, which contains the cap on future rent, applies only to "a claim or interest, proof of which is filed under § 501." Section 501 prescribes the method for filing proofs of prepetition claims against the debtor and certain postpetition claims that are deemed to have arisen prepetition. It does not apply to administrative expenses payable by the debtor, which must be requested pursuant to § 503. And because § 502 does not apply to administrative expenses, it cannot cap future rent due under an assumed lease.

The legislative history of § 502(b)(6) confirms that, at least on this score, Congress said what it meant. H.R. Rep. No. 595, 95th Cong., 2d Sess. 353 (1977); S. Rep. No. 989, 95th Cong., 2d Sess. 63 (1978), 1978 U.S.C.A.A.N. 5849, 6309 (stating that § 502(b)(6) "does not apply to limit administrative expense claims for use of the leased premises to which the landlord is otherwise entitled"); see also 2 Collier on Bankruptcy ¶ 365.08, at 365-67 (15th ed. 1995) ("The limitation upon the amount of an allowed claim arising from breach of a lease in § 502(b)(6) of the Code does not apply to leases assumed and thereafter rejected in the case.") (footnotes omitted).

III. CONCLUSION

It would surely have been better if Congress had spelled out its intentions as to assumed leases in the Code, rather than leaving it up to the courts to clean up the ambiguities. But, under the circumstances, clean them up we must. The trustee complains that the rule we pick—a rule that accords administrative priority to claims for all future rent under an assumed lease—is overly generous to landlords, since it gives them a lion's share of estates upon liquidation. While that may seem to be the case, we doubt that it will work out that way in practice. Under the rule we adopt, bankruptcy courts will rarely find that assuming liability for all future rent under a long-term lease is in the best interests of the estate—including the interest of the general creditors—unless the rental terms are highly advantageous. They will therefore block assumption of such leases except in unusual cases. As a result, landlords will find themselves with unsecured claims capped at one year's worth of future rent.

This may also seem undesirable, especially since in some such cases the tenant properly wishes to continue the rental. But this too is not quite the end of the story, for bankruptcy courts may have another option open to them. Faced with the unattractive choice of either requiring a bankrupt tenant to reject its long-term lease (and thereby possibly dooming the reorganization to failure) or letting it assume the lease (and leaving the general creditors with a paltry recovery should liquidation ensue), one bankruptcy court suggested that it could instead put off the decision on whether or not to assume a long-term lease. It could delay, the court stated, until the moment of confirmation, when the debtor's chances of rehabilitation would finally be clear. The uncertainty engendered by such an approach would give the bankruptcy court significant leverage over both tenant and landlord, and might well lead to a renegotiation of the long-term lease. The tenant who wishes to retain control over the premises has an interest—arising out of fear that the court will force rejection of the original lease—in renegotiating the lease, though perhaps for a shorter term. The landlord also has an interest in renegotiating the lease to escape the limbo between assumption and rejection. In such circumstances the landlord might well prefer to recover some guaranteed amount of future rent, as an administrative expense, under a new contract rather than risk having the lease rejected and the recovery limited to a fractional share of one year's worth of future rent, as an unsecured claim, under the pre-existing contract.

None of this is before us today. But we do note that the rule that we enunciate may not be quite as rigid as it looks. It may well operate, like so many other default rules in contract law, only as a backdrop against which the parties—here the landlord and tenant—can renegotiate to reach a satisfactory, middle solution.

Id. at 22-30.

E. TIME LIMITS FOR DECIDING WHETHER TO ASSUME OR REJECT

Because the interests of the nondebtor party to an executory contract can be seriously and adversely affected by delay, § 365 imposes time limits within which the trustee or debtor-in-possession must decide whether to assume or reject. The applicable time period depends, in the case of real estate leases, upon whether the premises are residential or nonresidential. The applicable time period also depends upon the chapter under which bankruptcy was filed. In the case of personal property leases, the applicable time period depends upon whether the case is filed under Chapter 7 or under another chapter, but the Code draws no distinctions based on whether the subject matter of the lease is commercial or consumer property.

Read § 365(d) and answer the following Problems.

Problems

1. Dan Debtor filed Chapter 7, largely as a result of bad financial management. Dan leased a beautiful apartment overlooking a river and the trustee thought the apartment might be worth a lot more than Dan was paying. How long does the trustee have to decide whether to assume or reject? Does the trustee have to keep paying rent while deciding?

2. Would your answers to Problem # 1 change if Dan filed under Chapter 13 instead?

3. Accounting Firm leased its premises from Landlord and all of its office machines from Supplier, Inc. If Accounting Firm files a Chapter 11 petition, how long does it have to decide whether to assume or reject the real estate lease? The lease of office equipment? Does Accounting Firm have to keep paying Supplier, Inc. and Landlord while deciding?

SOUTHWEST AIRCRAFT SERVICES, INC. v. CITY OF LONG BEACH (IN RE SOUTHWEST AIRCRAFT SERVICES, INC.)

United States Court of Appeals, Ninth Circuit, 1987.
831 F.2d 848, *cert. denied sub nom.* City of Long Beach v. Southwest Aircraft Services, Inc., 487 U.S. 1206, 108 S.Ct. 2848, 101 L.Ed.2d 885 (1988).

REINHARDT, Circuit Judge:

We are asked here to resolve a question of first impression in the circuit courts regarding the interpretation of § 365(d)(4) of the

Bankruptcy Code. The Code permits a debtor in bankruptcy to assume or reject any unexpired lease it may have. § 365(a). Under § 365(d)(4), a nonresidential lease is deemed rejected by a debtor-lessee unless that party assumes the lease within 60 days after filing for Chapter 11 protection or within such additional period as is fixed by the bankruptcy court. In the case before us, the debtor-lessee moved, before the initial 60–day period had expired, for an extension of time within which to assume or reject a commercial lease, but the bankruptcy court did not hear the motion until after that period had ended. The court held that the lease was deemed rejected immediately upon the expiration of the sixtieth day, and that it was without authority to grant the timely filed motion for extension. The bankruptcy appellate panel affirmed; we reverse.

I. FACTS

Southwest Aircraft Services, Inc., is an aircraft maintenance company located at the Long Beach Airport. Southwest leases its business premises from the City of Long Beach under a long-term lease it assumed in 1976. Several years later, commercial jet flights into the airport increased, and Long Beach leased a vacant parcel adjoining Southwest's to Atlantic Aviation, which built a jet facility on the newly leased property. Evidently the existence of the new facility resulted in a significant increase in the value of Southwest's parcel.

Southwest filed for Chapter 11 relief on April 18, 1985, and received permission to operate its business as debtor-in-possession. * * *

On June 14, 57 days after filing for Chapter 11, Southwest filed a motion to extend the 60–day deadline for assuming or rejecting its lease with Long Beach. The bankruptcy court did not hear Southwest's motion until July 17, 90 days after the bankruptcy filing, and 30 days after the 60–day period had ended. * * *

While the bankruptcy judge declared that he would be inclined to grant the extension motion, he concluded that he no longer had authority to do so, ruling that the lease was deemed rejected pursuant to § 365(d)(4) of the Bankruptcy Code. The court found that in order for a debtor-lessee to obtain an extension of time under that section, not only must that party move for an extension within 60 days of filing for Chapter 11 protection, but the court must hear and grant the motion within that period. Under the bankruptcy judge's view, rejection was automatic since the 60–day deadline passed before he had held any hearing or issued any ruling on the motion. The Bankruptcy Appellate Panel affirmed, holding that the language of § 365(d)(4) "is precise and leaves no room for arguing that an extension may be granted or confirmed after 60 days have elapsed." Southwest promptly appealed.

II. LEGAL DISCUSSION

A. The Proper Interpretation of § 365(d)(4)

* * *

Here, the meaning of the words of § 365(d)(4) is not entirely clear. The section is not plainly susceptible to only one interpretation, and bankruptcy courts are divided on how the statute should be applied. Section 365(d)(4) provides that any unexpired nonresidential lease is deemed rejected unless the debtor-lessee assumes it "within 60 days after the date of the order for relief, *or within such additional time as the court, for cause, within such 60–day period, fixes*." (Emphasis added.) Under the section, the court's ability to extend the 60–day period is limited by a clause which includes three successive terms: "for cause," "within such 60–day period," and "fixes." It is not entirely clear whether the second term—"within such 60–day period"—modifies the term that precedes it or the term that follows it. If we read it as modifying "fixes", then a bankruptcy court would not under the literal words of the statute have the authority to grant a timely motion to extend after the sixtieth day. That is the interpretation advanced by Long Beach, as well as by some bankruptcy courts in this and other cases. If, however, the 60–day term modifies "for cause," then while the cause must arise within 60 days (and implicitly the debtor must file its motion to show cause within that period), there is no express limit on when the bankruptcy court must hear and decide the motion. This more liberal reading of the statute would allow the bankruptcy courts to operate with greater freedom and flexibility. It is the one we adopt.

Several bankruptcy courts have held that the more restrictive interpretation of the statute would lead to arbitrary and fortuitous results and have rejected it for that reason. While we recognize that were we to look only to the face of the statute Long Beach's argument would by far be the stronger one, we cannot say with certainty that it is the only plausible interpretation of § 365(d)(4). There is another possible interpretation of the statutory language, one that permits a more reasonable construction—a construction that is more consistent with the normal concepts that govern the functioning of the judiciary. Thus, we turn to the legislative purpose and history for whatever guidance they may provide.

Like the language of § 365(d)(4), the legislative purpose and history of the section do not provide a definitive answer to the question before us; however, they do offer some support for Southwest's view. Before 1984, debtors in Chapter 11 reorganizations had no fixed deadline to assume or reject unexpired leases, although any party could request the court to fix a time limit. § 365(d)(2) (1983). Congress became concerned about the practical consequences of Chapter 11 filings by tenants of shopping centers. It was particularly concerned that mall operators were facing periods of extended vacancies, that would last until such time as the bankruptcy courts would finally decide to take the initiative and force debtors to make a choice whether to assume or reject the leases. It was also concerned about the effects the extended vacancies were having on other tenants.

To address this problem, Congress added two provisions dealing specifically with nonresidential leases in Chapter 11 proceedings. Subsection (d)(3) requires the debtor to perform all lease obligations while deciding whether to assume, but permits the court to delay the debtor's performance during the first 60 days after filing for reorganization. Subsection (d)(4) establishes the 60–day deadline for assumption or rejection, and imposes on the debtor the burden of petitioning the bankruptcy court for a change in the deadline.

According to the legislative history, the so-called Shopping Center Amendments were expressly intended to

> lessen the problems caused by extended vacancies and partial operation of tenant space by requiring that the trustee decide whether to assume or reject nonresidential real property lease [sic] within 60 days after the order for relief in a case under any chapter. This time period could be extended by the court for cause, such as in exceptional cases involving large numbers of leases.

1984 U.S.C.C.A.N. at 599. This is the sole passage in the legislative history that addresses extensions of time. The second sentence discusses the requirement that the court find "cause" for the extension; there is no reference to any requirement that the bankruptcy judge make his finding within any particular period of time. Congress' emphasis on cause for an extension, and its failure to mention any deadline within which the court must act, is fairly indicative of its intent. Congress was concerned that a properly supported motion for extension, i.e., one for good cause, should be permitted under the provision and not that the bankruptcy court should be stripped of its authority to grant an extension if it did not act within a prescribed time period.

We recognize that while the legislative history does not specifically mention that the debtor must file its motion for an extension within 60 days, such a requirement may be fairly implied in the section. It is frequently the case that if an act must be undertaken within a particular time period a request for an extension must be made before that period has expired. Such a rule can hardly be said to be unusual or worthy of special discussion in the legislative history. On the other hand, a rule that forfeits a party's rights, benefits, privileges or opportunities simply because a court fails to act within a particular time period would be quite extraordinary. We think that Congress would not adopt any such rule without clearly indicating in the legislative history its intention to do so and explaining its reasons.

* * *

Long Beach's interpretation of § 365(d)(4) would produce arbitrary and fortuitous results. Under the city's view, a diligent debtor with an unexpired lease—oftentimes an asset critical to a successful reorganization—who moved for an extension of time immediately upon filing his petition for relief would nevertheless automatically lose the lease if the bankruptcy court failed, for whatever reason, to decide the motion within a 60–day period. Also, a debtor who diligently attempted to determine whether he could prudently assume the lease, and sought an extension only after he had determined that more time was in actuality required, might find his leasehold interest forfeited if the bankruptcy judge took even a minimal amount of time to conduct a hearing and reach a decision. The results in both instances would be manifestly unjust—and so might the result here. The bankruptcy judge said that he was inclined to the view that Southwest *had* demonstrated cause for the grant of an extension; yet, under Long Beach's interpretation, the court would be unable to act, Southwest would be deprived of its place of doing business, and Long Beach might well obtain an undeserved windfall.

Bankruptcy courts, like district courts, may have numerous reasons that make it impractical or impossible for them to act within a fairly short time deadline. Construing Congress' action in adopting § 365(d)(4) as an attempt by the legislative branch to force bankruptcy courts to act at an earlier time than they would otherwise deem proper would not only result in hasty, ill-considered decisions by bankruptcy courts but might in addition exacerbate rather than alleviate the judicial backlog problem. Such an interpretation would also encourage debtors to make *pro forma* motions for extension of time before they had a full opportunity to consider whether an extension was necessary—conceivably as soon as the petition for reorganization was filed—simply to minimize the possibility that the vagaries of bankruptcy court scheduling would deny them a timely hearing. Bankruptcy courts would then be burdened with numerous unnecessary show cause hearings. Moreover, extensions would undoubtedly be granted in cases in which, but for the restrictive interpretation of the provision, requests for extensions would not ever have been made. The cumulative effect might well be even greater delays in deciding assumption of lease issues than previously existed. In any event, Long Beach's interpretation would impose an arbitrary and unreasonable restriction on bankruptcy courts as well as work an injustice on many debtors.

* * * [W]e are nevertheless influenced in our decision by the rule announced almost one hundred years ago by the Supreme Court: "If a literal construction of the words of a statute be absurd, the act must be so construed as to avoid the absurdity." *Church of the Holy Trinity v. United States*, 143 U.S. 457, 460 (1892). This is still good law today. "It is a familiar rule that a thing may be within the letter of the statute and yet not within the statute, because not within its spirit nor within the intention of its makers." *Philbrook v. Glodgett*, 421 U.S. 707, 714 (1975) (quoting *Church of the Holy Trinity*, 143 U.S. at 459).

* * *

For all the above reasons, we hold that if cause for an extension arises within the 60–day period and a motion for an extension is made within that period, a bankruptcy court may, even after the 60–day period has expired, consider the debtor's motion and, if it finds there was sufficient cause at the time the motion was filed, grant the requested extension.

* * *

III. CONCLUSION

Application of our views on the proper interpretation of §§ 365(d)(3) and 365(d)(4) to this case is a straightforward matter. The bankruptcy court retains the authority to decide Southwest's motion for an extension of time. We reverse and remand so that the court may hear that motion. Southwest's failure to make proper rental payments does not require that the bankruptcy court deem the lease rejected. That failure should, however, be considered at the hearing, along with all other relevant factors, including Southwest's previous tender of all sums due.

REVERSED and REMANDED.

ANDERSON, Circuit Judge, dissenting.

In my view, dissents should be sparing. We should strive for open-minded unanimity. In this case, try though I have, it is not possible to make that decision. Respectfully, my disagreement seems to demand a dissent from the majority opinion.

The Bankruptcy Appellate Panel was eminently correct when it observed that the language of § 365(d)(4) "is precise and leaves no room for arguing that an extension may be granted or confirmed after the 60 days has elapsed."

The majority attempts to find a "possible" ambiguity in order to allow more freedom and flexibility. That ambiguity simply does not exist. The majority ignores the plain meaning and the structure of the pertinent portions of § 365(d)(4). *Webster's Third International Dictionary, Unabridged*, 1978, defines "within" in several different ways: "on the inside or the inner side," "internally," "inside the bounds of a place or region," and "used as a function word to indicate enclosure or containment." In any definition of the word, in any application, there is not the slightest hint that something within the parameters of containment can also, at the same time, be "without." The majority complains that 60 days is a short period of time to act and uses that as a reason for creating an exception or extension that clearly was not contemplated by Congress. The assertion is also made that a plain reading renders the section harsh and inequitable.

Sixty days is really not that short. It is six times longer than that fixed to take a criminal appeal. It is twice as long as that fixed for taking a civil appeal. It is one-sixth of a year. Significant and important decisions are often made in those time frames. It may be safely assumed that debtors, their lawyers and accountants are familiar with this time frame and have (or should have) already assessed the pros and cons of accepting or rejecting a nonresidential lease prior to filing a bankruptcy petition so that they may act or advise the trustee.

In my experience, judges at all levels are quick to respond to urgent and emergency situations. An ex parte emergency motion for extension of time is clearly an option open to the debtor or the trustee in this situation. It simply was not done.

* * *

Notes and Questions

1. Do you agree with the dissenting opinion that § 365(d)(4) is unambiguous? Is it easier to explain the result in the case on the grounds of practicality than statutory interpretation?

2. Larry Lippman leased three apartments in the same building. He lived in one of them with his daughter and sublet the other two. Larry filed a Chapter 11 petition, but made no move to assume or reject any of the leases. Sixty-five days after bankruptcy was filed and before Larry had proposed a plan of reorganization, Lessor moved for relief from the stay on the grounds that the leases were deemed rejected. What result? See *In re Lippman,* 122 B.R. 206 (Bankr.S.D.N.Y.1990).

F. PRE–DECISION OBLIGATIONS OF THE PARTIES

Subsection 365(d)(3), which was added in 1984, requires the trustee to perform under a lease of nonresidential real property while deciding whether to assume or reject the lease. This obligation applies regardless of the chapter under which bankruptcy was filed. Subsection 365(d)(10) was added in 1994 and imposes similar requirements for nonconsumer personal property leases, but only in Chapter 11. The following case raises an interpretive problem under § 365(d)(3) that will also be encountered under (d)(10).

IN RE J.T. RAPPS, INC.

United States Bankruptcy Court, District of Massachusetts, 1998.
225 B.R. 257.

HENRY J. BOROFF, Bankruptcy Judge.

Before the Court for determination is the "Motion of Landlord for Order Directing Chapter 7 Trustee to Make Immediate Payment of Administrative Rent Claim" (the "Payment Motion") filed by Woburn Mall Associates (the "Landlord"). The issue for determination is whether § 365(d)(3) of the Bankruptcy Code requires that a commercial lessor's Chapter 11 administrative claim for postpetition, pre-rejection rent be paid immediately with priority over other unpaid Chapter 11 administrative claims and unpaid Chapter 7 administrative claims where the estate is administratively insolvent.

I. *Facts*

The facts are not in dispute. At the time of case commencement, J.T. Rapps, Inc., d/b/a J.T. Rapps Sports Closet (the "Debtor") was in the business of selling licensed sports apparel and sports novelties at retail. The Debtor's business operated out of several locations, including several shopping centers in the northeast United States.

On May 7, 1991, the Debtor entered into a lease agreement (the "Lease") with the Landlord to rent a store in the Woburn Mall, a shopping center in Woburn, Massachusetts, for a period of five years. The Lease provided that on the first day of each month the Debtor would pay a base rent of $1,705.17, in addition to monthly assessments for real estate taxes, insurance, and common area charges.

The Debtor filed Chapter 11 petition in this Court on January 21, 1994. Pursuant to § 365(d)(4), the deadline within which the Debtor was required to assume or reject the Lease (or seek an extension) was March 21, 1994. That deadline was later extended to May 20, 1994. The Lease was finally deemed rejected on May 20, 1994 when the Debtor failed to act to assume or reject it. § 365(d)(4). However, while occupying the premises, the Debtor had defaulted in rental payments for the months of February, March, April and May. On May 13, 1994, the Landlord filed a motion seeking immediate payment of the rental obligations, relief from the automatic stay to exercise its rights under the Lease, and an order compelling the Debtor to vacate the premises.

[The court entered an order granting the landlord an administrative expense claim in the amount of $8,990.27. Sometime later, the case was converted to Chapter 7 and the landlord sought an order compelling the Chapter 7 trustee to pay the administrative expense claim immediately.]

II. *Positions of the Parties*

The Landlord argues that the language of § 365(d)(3) requiring the "trustee" to "timely perform" requires that a debtor in possession, or Chapter 11 or 7 Trustee (hereinafter, jointly and severally, the "estate representative") pay a debtor's commercial lease obligations when they become due regardless of the administrative solvency of the bankruptcy estate. The Landlord, therefore, concludes that it is entitled to immediate payment in full of all accrued postpetition pre-rejection rent.

The Trustee argues that immediate payment of the Landlord's administrative claim is inappropriate because there are insufficient assets in the estate to pay all accrued administrative expenses. The Trustee explains that there is just over $30,000 on hand in the Chapter 7 bankruptcy estate, while the Chapter 7 administrative expenses are approximately $12,000 and the Chapter 11 administrative expenses approximate $47,500. The Trustee asserts that immediate payment of the Landlord's claim in full would constitute the granting of an improper superpriority for the Landlord's claim over Chapter 7 administrative claims and other Chapter 11 administrative claims, and reasons that because § 365(d)(3) does not explicitly grant commercial lessors a superpriority claim, one should not be read into the statute.

III. *Discussion*

[The court quoted § 365(d)(3).]

Section 365(d)(3) was added to the Bankruptcy Code by the Bankruptcy Amendments and Federal Judgment Act of 1984. Prior to the 1984 Amendments, debtors and trustees were not required to immediately pay rental obligations during the period between the filing of the case and the date of the assumption or rejection of a nonresidential real property lease. Therefore, a commercial lessor was forced to extend credit to the bankruptcy estate during the period in which the estate representative decided whether to assume or reject the lease. The lessor's rental claim was treated as an administrative claim, usually measured by the reasonable value of the estate's use and occupancy of the premises, and was paid, if at all, with other administrative claimants.

The amended § 365(d)(3) was intended to ease the immediate financial burden borne by the lessors of nonresidential real property by requiring the estate representative to "timely perform" the debtor's obligations under the lease. The legislative history of § 365(d)(3) evidences Congress' belief that, "[t]his timely performance requirement [would] insure that debtor/tenants pay their rent, common area, and other charges [at the time required in the lease] pending the trustee's assumption or rejection of the lease." *In re Longua*, 58 B.R. 503, 505 n.1 (Bankr. W.D.Wis.1986) (quoting H.R. Conf. Rep. No. 882, 98th Cong., 2d Sess. (1984), *reprinted in* 1984 U.S.C.C.A.N. 576). In interpreting the effect of the amended § 365(d)(3), courts have uniformly held that it requires that the estate representative pay the rent as it becomes due.

Nevertheless, while Congress clearly intended that commercial landlords receive timely postpetition pre-rejection rental payments, the language and legislative history of the statute do not specify the remedy for the estate representative's noncompliance, or the treatment of unpaid postpetition pre-rejection rental payment claims. As one court explained:

> If the lease were assumed, the trustee would have to bring the rental obligations current or make other arrangements with the landlord to cure the prior lease obligations, but in a case where the trustee has not made the post-petition, pre-rejection lease payments under § 365(d)(3), and then subsequently rejects the lease, there is a question as to how the unpaid rental payments should be treated by the court.

In re Amber's Stores, Inc., 193 B.R. 819, 822 (Bankr. N.D.Tex.1996). This failure to provide an express remedy to lessors in the event of a default under § 365(d)(3) has created much difference of opinion.

Most courts do agree on at least two aspects of § 365(d)(3). First, they acknowledge that its clause "notwithstanding § 503(b)(1) of this title" waives the requirement for an express order authorizing payment of the administrative rent claim. Second, they agree that the lessor is entitled to be paid the full amount of the rent and other charges due under the lease without reference to traditional § 503(b)(1) factors such as actual use and reasonable value.

This Court has already determined, and the parties have agreed, that the Landlord has a Chapter 11 administrative expense claim of $8,990.27 for the Debtor's postpetition pre-rejection rental obligation. The current dispute relates only to whether that claim is entitled to immediate payment; in other words, whether the Landlord's claim is entitled to be paid immediately with priority over Chapter 7 administrative claims and other Chapter 11 administrative claims, where the estate is administratively insolvent.

Courts faced with the issue are divided between those which have determined that the lessor's claim is entitled to ordinary administrative priority (and therefore to be treated as any other unpaid administrative claim) and those which would afford the claim priority over some or all other administrative claimants. The United States Court of

Appeals for the First Circuit has not yet addressed this question, and the decisions arising out of this district are split. *Compare In re Brennick*, 178 B.R. 305 (Bankr. D.Mass.1996) (finding that commercial landlord's unpaid postpetition, pre-rejection rent claim is entitled to superpriority); *In re McCabe*, 212 B.R. 21 (Bankr. D.Mass.1996) (same), *with In re MJ 500, Inc.*, 217 B.R. 93 (Bankr. D.Mass.1998) (commercial landlord's unpaid rent claim was not entitled to priority over chapter 7 administrative claims).

For the majority who reject any superpriority for a commercial lessor's unpaid postpetition pre-rejection administrative rent claim, the Code's failure to expressly authorize superpriority status for such claimants is deemed fatal. *In re Bryant Universal Roofing, Inc.*, 218 B.R. 948, 953 (Bankr. D.Ariz.1998) ("[Section] 507, which determines the priority status of administrative claimants, is noticeably silent as to any priority for claims arising under § 365(d)(3)."). Other courts also worry that granting superpriority status to a commercial lessor's claim particularly with respect to Chapter 7 administrative claims "undermines the incentive built into the priority that § 726 gives to Chapter 7 administrative claims." *MJ 500*, 217 B.R. at 95. Section 726(b) provides that administrative expenses incurred while a case is pending under Chapter 7 shall be paid prior to expenses of administration accrued under any other Chapter. § 726(b). The rationale for granting such a priority to Chapter 7 administrative claims is that "those who must wind up the affairs of a debtor's estate must be assured of payment, or else they will not participate in the liquidation or distribution of the estate." *In re Lochmiller Indust., Inc.*, 178 B.R. 241, 247 (Bankr. S.D.Cal.1995) (quoting H.R. Rep. No. 95-595, 95th Cong., 1st Sess. (1977) 186-87, *reprinted in* 1978 U.S.C.C.A.N. 5787, 6147). Therefore, according to these courts, granting priority status for a commercial lessor's rent claim over Chapter 7 administrative claims would violate the Bankruptcy Code's express priority scheme.

A separate line of cases, however, holds that unpaid postpetition pre-rejection lease payments are entitled to superpriority status over all Chapter 7 and 11 administrative claims. In fact, in the case of *In re Telesphere Communications, Inc.*, 148 B.R. 525 (Bankr. N.D.Ill.1992), that court argued that § 365(d)(3) claims should not be labeled administrative expenses at all, but should be more properly characterized as operational payments made during a Chapter 11 case under § 363(c)(1). *Id.* at 531.

In re Brennick, 178 B.R. 305 (Bankr. D.Mass.1996), a case heavily relied upon by the Landlord, agreed with *Telesphere*, ruling that

§ 365(d)(3) claims were entitled to superpriority status under the Code. In *Brennick*, the court determined that the "clear command" of § 365(d)(3)—that the trustee "timely perform" the obligations of the debtor—required the trustee to pay such expenses immediately, and ruled that "[t]he command must be obeyed even though to do so grants a priority as a practical matter." *Brennick*, 178 B.R. at 307-08. Agreeing with *Telesphere*, the court reasoned that it would be inequitable to treat certain parties paid during a Chapter 11 case in the ordinary course of business better than the lessor forced by § 365(d)(3) to rent its property to the debtor during at least the first sixty day period of the case. Relying on § 105(a), the court ordered immediate payment of the lessor's claim and held that the lessor would not be required to disgorge the payment if the estate funds later proved insufficient to pay other Chapter 11 and 7 administrative claimants.

This Court agrees that the language of § 365(d)(3) requires an estate representative to make immediate payment of nonresidential lease obligations where the estate representative can meet those obligations consistent with its obligations to others. However, where the estate is administratively insolvent and the estate representative fails to comply with § 365(d)(3), an *automatic* grant of superpriority status is more problematic. The difficulty with ordering immediate payment of the lessor's unpaid rent claim in every instance without regard to administrative solvency is that it mirrors a statutory superpriority (or subordination, depending on whether one is looking up or down) where none was explicated by § 365(d)(3).

In at least three sections of the Bankruptcy Code, Congress explicitly provides a claim with blanket priority over another class of claims. Section 726(b) provides such priority to Chapter 7 administrative claims over Chapter 11 administrative claims. Section 364(c)(1) allows the court to afford superpriority status to postpetition borrowings when the debtor is unable to obtain unsecured credit. And § 507(b) claims receive superpriority status when adequate protection under § 361 fails. Congress clearly understood how to provide superpriority status for claims it sought to prefer. "In absence of such Congressional direction with regard to § 365(d)(3) claimants 'it would be inappropriate to imply the existence of an automatic superpriority status.'" *In re Granada*, 88 B.R. 369, 373 (Bankr. D.Utah 1988) (quoting *In re Dieckhaus Stationers of King of Prussia, Inc.*, 73 B.R. 969, 973 (Bankr. E.D.Pa.1987)).

Further, denying a nonresidential real property lessor's claim superpriority status does not necessarily interfere with Congress' resolve to provide special protection for commercial lessors. If an estate representative does not comply with its obligations under § 365(d)(3), the lessor is not without a remedy. The lessor may: (1) file a motion seeking an order compelling the estate representative to immediately pay the rental obligations before rejection; (2) move for an order requiring the estate representative to immediately surrender the premises; (3) file a motion for relief from stay to have the estate representative evicted from the premises; or (4) move for an order to convert the case to one under Chapter 7 for failure to comply with § 365(d)(3).

An estate representative who defaults under § 365(d)(3) will run the risk that the automatic stay will be terminated, its right of possession of the premises will be terminated, or that its case will be converted to one under Chapter 7. See *In re Mr. Gatti's, Inc.*, 164 B.R. 929, 944 (Bankr. W.D.Tex.1994). Failure to comply with § 365(d)(3) also jeopardizes the estate representative's right to assume the lease later, thereby risking loss of a valuable asset in the early stages of the bankruptcy case. "Any rational thinking [estate representative] would be ill-advised to believe that intentional inaction provides them only with an upside position in light of the[] remedies available to the lessor." *Id.* at 944.

However, while it is true that Congress intended that estate representatives not exploit the involuntary post-bankruptcy performance of commercial lessors, and likely contemplated that non-compliance with § 365(d)(3) would have negative consequences for the estate representative, there is no evidence that Congress intended that the remedy for non-compliance be fashioned at the expense of those not responsible for the offense. Nor is it always true that other administrative creditors are necessarily benefited by an estate representative's failure to perform its § 365(d)(3) obligations. A failure to pay rent may conceal from creditors operational losses or an ongoing dissipation of estate assets. And, ironically, the combination of the failure to pay the rental obligations and the subsequent characterization of the lessor's claim as one with superpriority might unfairly benefit the lessor. If an early complaint by a lessor would generate rejection of the lease, leaving the lessor with no tenant and only rejection damages treated as a prepetition claim (§ 365(g)(1)), it might behoove a commercial lessor to sit idly by, accruing a superpriority claim outside of the viewing screen of most other creditors while the claims of the latter are correspondingly reduced. By appearing to "drop the ball," the lessor might be better off than if it had timely acted.[10]

[10] Presumably, the "infield fly rule" was adopted to address analogous concerns.

On the other hand, if a commercial lessor, upon discovering a payment default, must immediately act to demand its rights under § 365(d)(3), other creditors will be provided with appropriate notice of the problem and any proposed solution, including, if determined by the court to be of benefit to the estate, payment or superpriority for some or all of the lessor's claims. And in that case, should the court order the estate representative to make payment to the lessor (or order superpriority of the lessor's administrative claims to effectuate an order for payment) as a condition of the estate representative's right to remain in possession of the premises, other creditors would have no cause for complaint.

This Court very much agrees with Judge Kenner's observation in *McCabe* that after examining the different positions taken by various courts on this issue, one is left with the conclusion that none is "completely satisfactory." *McCabe*, 212 B.R. at 22. The same could properly be said of the position taken here. Nonetheless, this Court's refusal to accord automatic superpriority status to all postpetition pre-rejection commercial lease claims appears to more closely conform to the distribution scheme of § 726 of the Bankruptcy Code and to draw least upon § 105(a) to achieve the result intended by Congress.

IV. *Conclusion*

Based on the foregoing analysis, this Court holds that § 365(d)(3) does not afford automatic superpriority status to post-petition pre-rejection nonresidental real property rent claims. Accordingly, the Payment Motion is DENIED.

Questions and Problems

1. The court in *J.T. Rapps* referred to *Telesphere*, which reached the opposite outcome regarding payment of § 365(d)(3) obligations when the estate is or is likely to be administratively insolvent. The court in *Telesphere* relied in part on the "operational payments" reasoning to which *J.T. Rapps* referred:

> The Bankruptcy Code contains two distinct procedures for the payment of administrative expenses. One of these procedures—the one that involves § 503(b)(1)—is supervised by the court, and requires application, notice and hearing. The court supervised procedure requires pro rata payment of administrative claims, pursuant to § 726(b), unless the claim involved is given an express superpriority.

The other procedure for payment of administrative expenses does not involve § 503(b)(1) or any court supervision. Section 1108 of the Code authorizes the trustee (and hence the debtor in possession under § 1107) to operate the business of a Chapter 11 debtor unless otherwise ordered by the court. Section 363(c)(1) allows a trustee or debtor in possession, authorized to operate the debtor's business, to "use property of the estate in the ordinary course of business without notice or a hearing." Thus, a trustee or debtor in possession may expend unencumbered cash (property of the estate), in the ordinary course of the debtor's business, to pay providers of goods and services to the estate. This alternative to court supervised payment of administrative expenses may be referred to as "operational payment."

In contrast to payments made pursuant to the court supervised procedure, there is no requirement that operational payments be made pro rata with other administrative expenses; operational payments are final. * * * Although it appears that no other decision to date has addressed the question, vendors who receive payments from the trustee or debtor in possession, for value in the ordinary course of business under § 363(c)(1), need not fear that the money they receive is subject to disgorgement. Thus, operational payments, by their nature, enjoy a de facto priority over other administrative expenses, without any express provision for superpriority.

Given this structure of the Code, the language of § 365(d)(3) should be read as requiring that rental payments be made according to the procedure for operational payments under § 363(c)(1). There is nothing in the language of § 365(d)(3) suggesting that it involves any of the procedures for court supervised payment. To the contrary, § 365(d)(3) provides that its terms apply "notwithstanding § 503(b)(1)"—the section providing a right to court supervised payment—and it requires the trustee or debtor in possession to act without application and without court review. Consequently, and contrary to the reasoning of the majority decisions, there would have been no reason for Congress to have provided any express grant of superpriority for § 365(d)(3) rent payments—such a "superpriority" is implicit in the direction that the debtor make the payments without court involvement. The absence of an express grant of superpriority cannot, then, be a basis for disregarding the plain language of § 365(d)(3).

148 B.R. at 530-31. *Telesphere* reasoned that the rental payments at issue were "administrative expenses," but they were not paid pursuant to § 503-(b)(1). Rather, they were "operational payments" pursuant to § 363(c)(1). Therefore, the rents were payable despite potential administrative insolvency. Is this reasoning supported by the phrase in § 365(d)(3) "notwithstanding § 503(b)(1)"? Could that phrase be referring to something else entirely?

(Hint: What if the rents had not been an actual cost of preserving the estate because the debtor had not used the leased premises postpetition?)

2. Which court, *J.T. Rapps* or *Telesphere*, has the better statutory argument? Which viewpoint reflects the better bankruptcy policy?

3. Whitcomb & Keller, Inc. is a mortgage banker that is also in the business of servicing mortgage accounts for investors. W & K contracted with Data–Link for the computer services necessary to maintain its customer accounts. The contract provided that, upon termination, W & K would pay any outstanding balance in full and Data–Link would return all master files to W & K. W & K filed Chapter 11, owing Data–Link $13,000 for prepetition computer services. While W & K was looking for a buyer for its mortgage account servicing operation, and before it decided whether to assume or reject the contract, Data–Link terminated its services. That paralyzed W & K's operation. Can W & K obtain a court order forcing Data–Link to resume performance on this contract? See *Data-Link Systems, Inc. v. Whitcomb & Keller Mortgage Co. (Matter of Whitcomb & Keller Mortgage Co.)*, 715 F.2d 375 (7th Cir.1983).

4. Debtor leased several gas station and convenience store locations from Lessor. The leases, which had an initial term of ten years, permitted renewal for an additional ten-year term, but the option to renew could not be exercised if any lease was in default. Debtor filed a Chapter 11 petition six months before expiration of the original term and obtained an extension of time within which to assume or reject the leases. Debtor sought to exercise the renewal option during that period, but Lessor objected because Debtor's pre-petition defaults had not been cured. Can Debtor renew the leases, without first deciding whether to assume or reject and without curing the defaults? See *Coleman Oil Co. v. Circle K Corp. (In re Circle K Corp.)*, 127 F.3d 904 (9th Cir.1997), *cert. denied*, 522 U.S. 1148, 118 S.Ct. 1166, 140 L.Ed.2d 176 (1998).

Chapter 7

DISCHARGE

A. INTRODUCTION

Discharge, which effectuates the "fresh start," is the reason most individual debtors file bankruptcy. The Code as enacted in 1978 contained the most liberal discharge provisions ever enacted in American bankruptcy law. Ever since that time, lobbying efforts have been directed toward retrenchment. These efforts have met with some success, as we will see; numerous amendments, beginning in 1984, have cut back the generosity of discharge. Political support for curtailment has come primarily from the credit industry lobby. Theoretical justification for curtailment has come largely from economically-oriented bankruptcy analysts who argue that liberal discharge results in the pass-along of increased credit costs to debtors:

> [I]f one assumes that by increasing interest rates lenders are economically as well placed as debtors to bear the added risk inherent in a discharge system that prevents access to future wages, * * * the existing discharge system can be said to have a questionable interdebtor effect. Those debtors who pay their debts bear the assumed increased credit costs. Nonpaying debtors, to whose defaults the increased cost of credit is attributable, do not fully share in that increased cost. Liberal discharge provisions thus increase the extent to which those who repay their debts subsidize those who do not.

Theodore Eisenberg, *Bankruptcy Law in Perspective*, 28 UCLA L. Rev. 953, 983 (1981). Does this make sense to you? Read the following excerpt and see if you still agree.

MARGARET HOWARD, A THEORY OF DISCHARGE IN CONSUMER BANKRUPTCY

48 Ohio St. L.J. 1047, 1066–68 (1987) (footnotes omitted).

The concern with which we should greet this potential pass-along of costs depends in part on its likelihood. That, in turn, depends upon the elasticity of the supply of funds available for lending. If the supply is perfectly elastic, increased costs will be borne completely by borrowers; if the supply is not perfectly elastic, creditors will bear part of these increased costs. "But only if the elasticity of supply is zero * * * will the full costs of increases in bad-debt losses be borne entirely by creditors, and only then will the wealth transfer be entirely from creditors to debtors."

Empirical evidence, such as it is, suggests that the supply of credit funds is not perfectly elastic. First, bad-debt losses may be taken as a tax deduction (which is, in effect, a pass-along to each of us), so only the loss not recouped through the reduced tax is passed to borrowers. Second, other legal changes, akin to changes in discharge availability, that should have increased lenders' costs have had little or no measurable effect on consumer credit. For example, more liberal state exemption laws are not associated with increased cost or reduced availability of consumer credit; states that prohibit wage garnishment do not experience increased cost or reduced availability of consumer credit; and states that permit debtors to waive their right to exemptions do not experience decreased cost or increased availability of consumer credit. Thus, even if we are prepared to concede that the costs of some credit losses are passed along, "we simply do not know" if these additional costs are significant.

Commentators who assert that more liberal bankruptcy discharge raises the cost of borrowing for those who repay their debts argue that this increased cost of borrowing forces some potential borrowers out of the credit market entirely, either because of increased interest rates or more stringent credit screenings. This argument made sense in the mid–1970s when it was advanced in opposition to passage of more liberalized discharge provisions. Today, however, when the effort is to restrict rather than liberalize discharge, the argument necessarily implies that some debtors who are *not* now in the credit market, should be—*i.e.*, that restriction of discharge will lower credit costs in the future, thus including in the credit market persons not currently able to borrow. One problem with this argument is that no empirical support exists for the proposition that persons (obviously of high risk) are currently excluded from the credit market who should not be. Furthermore, the argument is hard to square with the commonly held belief that credit is too easy to get. Finally, entry of these high risk borrowers into the credit market would surely result in an increased incidence of default and discharge in bankruptcy, thus compounding the problem of nonrepayment that troubles opponents of liberalized discharge.

The concern with which we should greet the potential pass-along of costs also depends on whether it is viewed as inappropriate. One way of viewing the added cost is as an insurance premium, paid by all users of credit to insure their own access to bankruptcy relief in the event of financial disaster. Viewed in this way, the "bankruptcy premium" is no more an undesirable deadweight economic loss than is insurance generally. In addition, empirical evidence about the relationship between bankruptcy discharge and bad debts generally would have to be adduced to determine whether the availability of discharge has any effect on the amount or distribution of this "insurance premium."

Last, the concern with which we should greet this potential pass-along of costs depends in part on the group to whom costs will be passed. Commentators who argue that this cost will be passed on in the form of increased costs for borrowers who repay their debts do not agree as to the category of borrowers to whom these costs will be passed. The outcome turns on whether lenders are able to, and do, stratify borrowers into various risk groups. If lenders are able to isolate the group of borrowers that poses the highest risk of bankruptcy, lenders will pass increased costs attributable to more liberal bankruptcy discharge on to that group. The result would be to place the cost of the system on those who use it. Unless the consequence would be exclusion of those persons from the credit market altogether, which does not seem to be the case, this outcome seems perfectly acceptable both economically and ethically.

Commentators engaged in the debate about the group to which costs will be passed assume, apparently, that these costs will be passed, in the form of higher interest rates, only to borrowers—either solely to those who default, or to both those who default and those who repay. None of the commentators has discussed the possibility that costs may be spread even more broadly—that is, to all purchasers, whether for cash or on credit—in the form of increased prices of goods and services. At least two factors suggest this possibility. First, putting aside certain gasoline stations that offer "discounts" for cash, sellers typically do not price products differently for users of credit than for users of cash. Second, credit sellers do not typically carry their own notes;

rather, they discount their commercial paper to institutional lenders. The discount rate must be accounted for by the seller in setting the price of his goods and services. Since the discount rate reflects, in part, the risk that the obligation will not be repaid, setting prices to account for the discount automatically passes on the cost of default by some credit purchasers to all buyers, including those who pay cash.

If this broader pass-along of costs in fact occurs, then it reduces the extent to which any one group bears the cost and, therefore, reduces the force of the argument that some borrowers will be forced out of the credit market. A broader pass-along also invites the argument that increased costs for cash purchasers, attributable to defaults by credit buyers, will exclude cash buyers from the market by raising the prices of goods and services to levels these cash buyers can no longer afford to pay on a cash basis. (Whether they will then become credit buyers is another issue.) In the absence of empirical evidence to the contrary (and there are, apparently, no empirical data for any of this), one can only speculate that any such price increase would be spread so broadly that the incremental difference would not be sufficiently great to affect any decision to purchase.

Before tinkering with bankruptcy rules in the name of economic efficiency, we should admit our limitations. First, if costs are passed along when creditors bear the risk, so that paying debtors subsidize nonpayers, this pass-along will occur without regard to the rules in bankruptcy. Those who pay subsidize those who *default*, not just those who default and obtain a discharge in bankruptcy. A change in the rules of discharge to reach a debtor's future income would make a difference in this pass-along of costs only to the extent that consumer debtors end up in bankruptcy, are able to pay out of future income and in fact pay through the vehicle of mandatory 13. Second, economic analysis requires a great many assumptions. Before we make major changes in the scope of bankruptcy in order to benefit commercial lenders and sellers, we need substantially more empirical data.

The following case captures in microcosm questions about why we allow discharge of debts at all. As you study the majority and dissenting opinions, think about whether the benefits of granting discharge outweigh the costs to creditors who remain unpaid and, perhaps, the costs to society as a whole. The statutory key to understanding the case is that § 523(a)(6) applies only in Chapter 7; because this discharge exception is not among those made applicable in Chapter 13 by § 1328-

(a)(2), debtors facing nondischargeability under § 523(a)(6) may be tempted to file Chapter 13 instead. We present the case at this point not because of its statutory issue, however. Rather, we think that the two opinions, as well as your reaction to them, may turn not so much on exegesis of the Code as on unstated views regarding the reasons for and the appropriate scope of discharge.

HANDEEN v. LEMAIRE (IN RE LEMAIRE)

United States Court of Appeals, Eighth Circuit, 1990.
898 F.2d 1346 (en banc).

JOHN R. GIBSON, Circuit Judge.

The issue before us is whether a civil judgment awarded to the victim of an intentional shooting may be discharged under Chapter 13 of the Bankruptcy Act. Paul Handeen, the victim of the assault and subsequently a judgment creditor, asks this court to hold, as a matter of law, that the judgment arising out of criminal conduct may not be discharged. Alternatively, he argues that the bankruptcy court's holding that the debtor Gregory LeMaire proposed his Chapter 13 plan in good faith was clearly erroneous. We conclude that the court's finding of good faith was clearly erroneous and therefore reverse and remand for further proceedings consistent with this opinion.

On July 9, 1978, at about noon, Handeen went to pick up his son and found LeMaire waiting for him. When Handeen got out of his car, LeMaire shot at him nine times with a bolt action rifle. The first two shots missed Handeen, but the third struck him on the left side of his neck. Handeen then attempted to hide behind the car. LeMaire circled the car, shot at and missed Handeen twice more, and then hit him inside of his left knee. LeMaire circled again and Handeen jerked his head back to avoid the bullet at the time he thought LeMaire would pull the trigger of the rifle aimed at his head. LeMaire fired, and the bullet went through Handeen's right nostril, shattering the roof of his mouth and going through his tongue. LeMaire then fired a shot at Handeen's left arm. The bullet went through Handeen's arm and lodged on his spine. LeMaire fired a final shot through Handeen's ankle. In all, five of the nine shots fired by LeMaire struck Handeen. LeMaire declared that he had intended to kill Handeen. He pled guilty to a charge of aggravated assault and was sentenced to imprisonment for a term of one to ten years. He served twenty-seven months of his sentence and was released in 1981. LeMaire then returned to graduate school at the

University of Minnesota and received his doctorate in experimental behavioral pharmacology in January 1986.

Handeen brought a civil suit against LeMaire and obtained a consent judgment. LeMaire paid $3,000 of the judgment, but made no further payments, prompting Handeen to commence garnishment proceedings to collect the $50,362.50 balance on the judgment. Soon after, on January 16, 1987, LeMaire filed this bankruptcy petition under Chapter 13.

Handeen objected to the bankruptcy court confirming LeMaire's Chapter 13 plan; the bankruptcy court, however, rejected his assertion that the civil judgment arising out of the crime was not dischargeable. The court instead confirmed LeMaire's plan, which provided that his creditors be paid approximately 42% on their claims. The plan listed three claims: (1) Handeen's judgment; (2) a student loan; and (3) a claim by LeMaire's parents for loans to LeMaire, including $3,600 expended on his legal fees, $3,000 spent in partial payment on the judgment, and $2,172 lent to buy a computer. The record reveals that LeMaire's debt to his parents was evidenced by a promissory note he signed the day before he filed his Chapter 13 petition.

Handeen appealed to the district court from the bankruptcy court's order confirming LeMaire's Chapter 13 plan. The district court affirmed and, upon appeal, a panel of this court also affirmed. We granted rehearing en banc, vacated the panel opinion, and heard oral argument. We now reverse.

I.

Handeen vigorously argues that, as a matter of law, his civil judgment cannot be discharged because it arose from a criminal act. The panel rejected this argument and we do likewise.

Handeen's argument is based upon § 523(a)(6), which provides that a debt arising from infliction of "willful and malicious injury by the debtor to another entity" may not be discharged under specified sections of the Bankruptcy Code. As the panel observed, there is no question that LeMaire's assault inflicted a "willful and malicious" injury upon Handeen. Handeen's reliance upon § 523(a)(6) is unavailing, however, because LeMaire filed his petition under Chapter 13, which does not include § 523(a)(6) in its list of nondischargeable debts. See § 1328(a). Although § 523(a)(6) does by its express statutory terms apply to a petition for bankruptcy under Chapter 7, its applicability does not extend to a filing under Chapter 13. Therefore, a debt which falls within the scope of § 523(a)(6), such as the debt owed to Handeen, which may not be discharged under Chapter 7, may nevertheless be discharged if the debtor meets the requirements of Chapter 13.

II.

Alternatively, Handeen argues that the bankruptcy court should not have confirmed LeMaire's Chapter 13 plan because LeMaire did not propose it in good faith. Section 1325(a) of Title 11 of the Bankruptcy Code establishes six criteria which a debtor must meet in order to have his Chapter 13 plan confirmed by a bankruptcy court. The critical requirement, for present purposes, is that "the plan has been proposed in good faith and not by any means forbidden by law." § 1325(a)(3).

In deciding whether LeMaire has met the good faith criterion, we recognize that legislative amendments to § 1325 have affected judicial interpretation of the phrase "good faith," which is defined neither in the Bankruptcy Code nor in its legislative history. Prior to the Bankruptcy Amendments and Federal Judgeship Act of 1984, our analysis focused upon "whether the plan constitutes an abuse of the provisions, purpose or spirit of Chapter 13." *In re Estus*, 695 F.2d 311, 316 (8th Cir.1982). This required looking to the totality of circumstances to discern whether good faith existed, a task aided by the *Estus* court listing a number of factors it considered relevant to this analysis.[4] This approach was widely used in other circuits.

---

[4] As enumerated by the *Estus* court, these factors include:

> (1) the amount of the proposed payments and the amount of the debtor's surplus;
>
> (2) the debtor's employment history, ability to earn and likelihood of future increases in income;
>
> (3) the probable or expected duration of the plan;
>
> (4) the accuracy of the plan's statements of the debts, expenses and percentage repayment of unsecured debt and whether any inaccuracies are an attempt to mislead the court;
>
> (5) the extent of preferential treatment between classes of creditors;
>
> (6) the extent to which secured claims are modified;
>
> (7) the type of debt sought to be discharged and whether any such debt is nondischargeable in Chapter 7;

After *Estus*, the Bankruptcy Amendments and Federal Judgeship Act of 1984 added a new § 1325(b) which authorizes courts to confirm a plan in which all of the debtor's disposable income for three years is applied to make payments under the plan. In *Education Assistance Corp. v. Zellner*, 827 F.2d 1222 (8th Cir.1987), we considered the effect of the new § 1325(b) on the *Estus* analysis of good faith. We stated that the new section's "ability to pay" criteria subsumed most of the *Estus* factors and thus narrowed the focus of the good faith inquiry. We described the narrower focus as depending upon "whether the debtor has stated his debts and expenses accurately; whether he has made any fraudulent misrepresentation to mislead the bankruptcy court; or whether he has unfairly manipulated the Bankruptcy Code."

Although *Zellner* modified the good faith determination in response to the new § 1325(b), it is recognized that *Zellner* preserved the traditional "totality of circumstances" approach with respect to *Estus* factors not addressed by the legislative amendments. Thus, in considering whether LeMaire proposed his plan in good faith, factors such as the type of debt sought to be discharged and whether the debt is nondischargeable in Chapter 7, and the debtor's motivation and sincerity in seeking Chapter 13 relief are particularly relevant. * * *

In its order confirming LeMaire's plan, the bankruptcy court examined in detail each of the eleven factors enumerated by the *Estus* court to assess whether a plan has been proposed in good faith. We are particularly concerned with the court's treatment of two of these factors:[5] (1) whether the debt is nondischargeable in Chapter 7; and (2) the debtor's motivation and sincerity in seeking Chapter 13 relief.

---

(8) the existence of special circumstances such as inordinate medical expenses;

(9) the frequency with which the debtor has sought relief under the Bankruptcy Reform Act;

(10) the motivation and sincerity of the debtor in seeking Chapter 13 relief; and

(11) the burden which the plan's administration would place upon the trustee.

695 F.2d at 317.

[5] We are also concerned with the bankruptcy court's treatment of other *Estus* factors. *Estus* directs the bankruptcy court to determine the extent of preferential treatment between classes of creditors and the court here found that LeMaire's proposed plan did not discriminate among his creditors. There was evidence in the record, however, that

A.

Estus directs a bankruptcy court to consider whether the debt would be nondischargeable in a Chapter 7 filing, and the court did so here, observing that this factor is closely linked to the debtor's motivation and sincerity. Although the court was correct in this observation, our review of the record convinces us that the court accorded insufficient weight to this factor. The specific evidence in the record which persuades us that the bankruptcy court was clearly erroneous in finding that LeMaire proposed his plan in good faith is discussed below in the context of another *Estus* factor, LeMaire's motivation and sincerity in seeking Chapter 13 relief. At this point, we need only observe that this debt could not be discharged under Chapter 7.

B.

In evaluating LeMaire's motivation and sincerity, the bankruptcy court balanced Handeen's desire to be compensated for his injuries against LeMaire's desire to have a fresh start and found the latter to outweigh the former in importance. The court noted that, while LeMaire had been unable to pay his debt to his victim, he had paid his debt to society by serving a prison sentence and had attempted to reorder his life and make a fresh start. The court found that forcing LeMaire to be burdened the rest of his life with a judgment which would continue to accrue interest, result in endless garnishments, and prevent him from accumulating property would be inimical to such a fresh start. The court concluded that LeMaire had made a wholehearted attempt to pay Handeen as much as possible, and that LeMaire's motivation was proper and his sincerity real.

We are convinced that the court's analysis here fails to properly consider the strong public policy factors, inherent in the Bankruptcy Code, which are implicated in discharging this debt and gives undue emphasis to the fact that the statutory terms governing Chapter 13 petitions do not expressly make a debt resulting from a willful and mali-

---

LeMaire's petition failed to disclose a contingent debt in the amount of $30,000 to $50,000 which he would have to pay back to the United States Public Health Service if he failed to fulfill the terms of this fellowship stipend. * * * Since LeMaire failed to include this contingent debt in his plan, it would not be discharged after he completed payments to other creditors under the plan. Since the debt would be accorded different treatment than LeMaire's other debts, there would be discrimination among creditors.

Another *Estus* factor, the accuracy of LeMaire's statements of debts and expenses, is also affected by this failure to disclose. * * *

cious injury nondischargeable. In light of the court's clear errors both in according insufficient weight to the nondischargeability of this debt in Chapter 7, and in finding that LeMaire's motivation and sincerity in seeking Chapter 13 relief were proper, we do not believe that LeMaire has fulfilled the good faith requirement of Chapter 13. We are "left with the definite and firm conviction that a mistake has been committed." *Anderson v. City of Bessemer City*, 470 U.S. 564, 573 [(1985)] (quoting *United States v. United States Gypsum Co.*, 333 U.S. 364, 395 (1948)).

After reviewing the bankruptcy court's findings here, according due deference to its credibility determinations, we are compelled to conclude that the bankruptcy court's finding was clearly erroneous because the evidence before the court regarding LeMaire's good faith was so "implausible on its face that a reasonable factfinder would not credit it." *Id.* at 575. The record here very clearly indicates that LeMaire intended to kill Handeen, he shot at him nine times, he hit him with five of the bullets, and he nearly succeeded in his intention. The record also reveals that LeMaire sought the protection of bankruptcy when Handeen tried to collect his judgment. Ironically, LeMaire listed the $3000 which he actually paid on the judgment as a debt owed to his parents, as evidenced by a promissory note signed the day before he sought bankruptcy protection.[6] The record shows that LeMaire received his doctorate from the University of Minnesota and was appointed as a postdoctoral research fellow at the University. Handeen argues that LeMaire's fellowship, which pays him a relatively low wage, is essentially a means of repaying a debt of $30,000 to $50,000 owed to the United States Public Health Service. As we have observed, this debt was not included in the plan but LeMaire testified freely that he was aware of it and of his obligation to pay it back if he failed to comply with his obligations to the Public Health Service. The bank-

---

6 We are troubled by the circumstances surrounding LeMaire's obligations to his parents. The record shows that LeMaire signed a promissory note evidencing a debt to his parents of $12,722 only one day prior to filing his bankruptcy petition. Prior to this filing, LeMaire had never made any payments on his debts to his parents, even though he had incurred some of them years earlier and he was receiving a regular stipend from his fellowship. LeMaire's plan also listed as an expense a monthly rental payment of $240 to his parents. The record shows that he had never paid rent while living at home in the past.

Despite this evidence in the record, the bankruptcy court found that LeMaire's financial dealings with his parents did not indicate bad faith on his part. We need not review these findings more closely, however, because we believe that there is other evidence in the record which persuades us that the bankruptcy court's finding of good faith was clearly erroneous.

ruptcy court did not address this argument. We believe, however, that the court should have discussed whether LeMaire's failure to disclose this contingent debt when he filed his petition and his testimony of the continuing obligation demonstrated a lack of good faith and unfair manipulation of the Bankruptcy Code. The bankruptcy court's order does not specifically discuss whether LeMaire has attempted to unfairly manipulate the Bankruptcy Code, despite the fact that this inquiry has been identified as central to the court's task of determining whether the plan "constitutes an abuse of the provisions, purpose or spirit of Chapter 13." *Zellner*, 827 F.2d at 1227 (quoting *Estus*, 695 F.2d at 316).

We recognize that "a Chapter 13 plan may be confirmed despite even the most egregious pre-filing conduct where *other factors* suggest that the plan nevertheless represents a good faith effort by the debtor to satisfy his creditors' claims." *Neufeld v. Freeman*, 794 F.2d 149, 153 (4th Cir.1986) (emphasis added). While pre-filing conduct is not determinative of the good faith issue, it is nevertheless relevant. When we consider the pre-filing conduct here, including the maliciousness of the injury which LeMaire inflicted upon Handeen, in light of the lack of "other factors" sufficient to establish good faith, we are persuaded that the bankruptcy court clearly erred in finding that LeMaire proposed his plan in good faith.

Our decision does not rest solely on considerations of public policy; we believe, however, that it is appropriate to note that our decision is consistent with the policies underlying the Bankruptcy Code. "[T]he primary purpose of the bankruptcy statute * * * is the collection and distribution of the debtor's estate to his creditors." *In re May*, 12 B.R. 618, 621 (N.D.Fla.1980). A secondary purpose is to discharge the debtor's financial obligations and is "designed to give the honest debtor the opportunity to reinstate himself in the business world; it is not intended to be available to a dishonest debtor." *Id.*[8]

---

[8] The dissent takes issue with our consideration of policy factors in holding that LeMaire did not propose his bankruptcy plan in good faith. We believe, however, that Congress did not intend to replace the discretion of courts with a rigid, mechanistic checklist to assess good faith. We are to bear in mind that the good faith requirement is "the only safety valve available through which plans attempting to twist the law to malevolent ends may be cast out." *In re Waldron*, 785 F.2d 936, 939 (11th Cir.1986). Thus, our task is to consider the totality of the circumstances, in light of the policies inherent in the Bankruptcy Code, to determine whether a court's finding of good faith was clearly erroneous. The Eleventh Circuit has explained the role of policy analysis in this determination:

> [W]ith § 1325(a)(3) Congress intended to provide bankruptcy courts with a *discretionary means to preserve the bankruptcy process for its intended pur-*

While the bankruptcy court correctly recognized that the exceptions to discharge specified in § 523(a)(6) do not expressly apply to a Chapter 13 petition, the court's analysis falls short by failing to examine the public policies promoted by not discharging the debts enumerated there. It is valuable to compare § 523(a)(6), stating that debts resulting from willful and malicious injury may not be discharged, with the other debts which § 523 states may not be discharged. The section exempts from discharge debts for a tax or customs duty; for money obtained by false pretenses; for embezzlement or larceny; for support of a spouse, former spouse, or child; for governmental fines or penalties; and for educational loans guaranteed by the government. While there is a strong public policy prohibiting the discharge of each of these types of debts, we believe that there is a particularly strong policy prohibiting the discharge of a debt resulting from a willful and malicious injury following an attempted murder.

We recognize that Congress intentionally expanded the scope of the debtor's discharge in Chapter 13 after he completes his plan in order to "encourage more debtors to attempt to pay their debts under bankruptcy court supervision." *Estus*, 695 F.2d at 313. "The fact that a discharge would not be available in a [chapter 7] liquidation case should furnish a greater incentive for the debtor to perform under the [Chapter 13] plan." H.R. Rep. No. 95–595 at 129, *reprinted in* 1978 U.S.C.C.A.N. at 6090. But we believe that the public policies promoted by not discharging a debt resulting from willful or malicious injury in any Chapter 7 case are also implicated in this particular Chapter 13 case, and that the bankruptcy court's decision was clearly erroneous in not according these policies sufficient weight. Our decision should not be read as a broad declaration extending beyond the facts before us. We simply hold that the circumstances surrounding this particular debt reveal that Lemaire did not demonstrate the requisite good faith to seek Chapter 13 protection and that refusing to discharge this particular debt, because of his lack of good faith, is consistent with the policies which the Bankruptcy Code seeks to advance.

> *pose*. Accordingly, whenever a Chapter 13 petition appears to be tainted with a questionable purpose, it is incumbent upon the bankruptcy courts to examine and question the debtor's motives. If the court discovers unmistakable manifestations of bad faith, as we do here, confirmation must be denied.
>
> Unmistakable manifestations of bad faith need not be based upon a finding of actual fraud, requiring proof of malice, scienter or an intent to defraud. *We simply require that the bankruptcy courts preserve the integrity of the bankruptcy process by refusing to condone its abuse.*

Id. at 941 (emphasis added).

* * *

We remand this case to the district court with instructions to remand, in turn, to the bankruptcy court for further proceedings consistent with this opinion.

MAGILL, CIRCUIT JUDGE, with whom LAY, CHIEF JUDGE, and MCMILLIAN, CIRCUIT JUDGE, join, dissenting.

I respectfully dissent. Although it purports to consider the totality of the circumstances and give due deference to the bankruptcy court's credibility determinations, the majority ultimately relies on its own view of "public policy" to hold clearly erroneous the bankruptcy court's finding that LeMaire proposed his plan in good faith. I reject the idea that this court's own policy preference is a legitimate basis for reversing the bankruptcy court's decision.

I.

Despite the disclaimer that its decision does not rest on "public policy" alone, the majority concludes that "the public policies promoted by not discharging a debt resulting from willful or malicious injury in any Chapter 7 case are also implicated in this particular Chapter 13 case, and that the bankruptcy court's decision was clearly erroneous in not according these policies sufficient weight." The majority's holding is contrary to the law of this circuit, *In re Estus*, 695 F.2d 311 (8th Cir.1982), and the many other circuits which have held that good faith under § 1325(a)(3) must be judged on the totality of the circumstances. Section 1328(a) expressly states that, except for alimony, child support, and certain long-term obligations, "all debts" provided for in a Chapter 13 plan "shall" be discharged after the completion of payments under the plan. Thus, "[a]lthough the debtor's motive in invoking Chapter 13 solely to obtain discharge of a[n] [otherwise] non-dischargeable debt, as well as the circumstances under which that debt arose, may be factors to consider as part of the totality of the circumstances, they cannot, as a matter of law, suffice to show bad faith." *In re Chaffin*, 816 F.2d 1070, 1074 (5th Cir.1987), *modified on reconsideration on other grounds*, 836 F.2d 215 (5th Cir.1988). Section 1325(a)(3) requires that the plan be "'*proposed* in good faith' * * *, not that the debt was incurred in good faith." *In re Smith*, 848 F.2d 813, 819 (7th Cir.1988). As a result, "'a Chapter 13 plan may be confirmed despite even the most egregious pre-filing conduct where other factors suggest that the plan nevertheless represents a good faith effort by the debtor to satisfy his creditors' claims.'"[10] *Id.* (quoting *Neufeld v. Freeman*, 794 F.2d 149, 153 (4th Cir.1986)). Along with every other circuit that has addressed the issue, this circuit has held that a Chapter 13 debtor's attempt to discharge a debt nondischargeable in Chapter 7 is not *per se* bad faith under § 1325(a)(3), but rather is simply *one* of many factors to be considered in applying the totality of the circumstances standard. *Education Assistance Corp. v. Zellner*, 827 F.2d 1222, 1227 (8th Cir.1987); *Estus*, 695 F.2d at 317.

Despite the express terms of §§ 1328(a) and 1325(a)(3) and the overwhelming weight of the case law, Handeen argues that a Chapter 13 plan paying less than one hundred percent of a debt incurred as the result of a heinous crime can never be proposed in good faith.[11] On appeal, the district court correctly rejected this argument, as did a panel of this court.[12] Under the guise of the clearly erroneous standard, the majority now effectively applies the bright line rule urged by Handeen. It concludes that a finding of good faith is precluded in this case because of a strong "public policy" against the discharge of debts arising from crimes as heinous as that committed by LeMaire. This position is directly contrary to the express terms of Chapter 13 and has no support in the statute's legislative history. In my view, this court is not free to declare its own notion of justice as "public policy" where Congress has clearly spoken to the contrary. * * *

The bankruptcy court carefully considered each of the relevant factors set forth in *Estus* and, in light of all the circumstances of the case, determined that LeMaire's plan was proposed in good faith. The majority ignores many of the findings underlying the bankruptcy court's

---

[10] The majority acknowledges the existence of this well-established principle, but finds a lack of other factors indicating a good faith effort only by ignoring many of the factors underlying the bankruptcy court's decision and rejecting its treatment of others on the basis of "public policy." Because of the heinous nature of LeMaire's crime, the majority is simply unwilling in this case to recognize that "[i]t is not conclusively bad faith for a debtor to seek to discharge a debt incurred through his own criminal or tortious conduct." *In re Caldwell*, 895 F.2d 1123, 1127 (6th Cir.1990).

[11] The majority states that Handeen makes two separate arguments, one based on § 523(a)(6), and the other based on § 1325(a)(3). Actually, Handeen makes an argument that involves both sections, i.e., because § 523(a)(6) makes the debt arising out of LeMaire's heinous criminal act nondischargeable in Chapter 7, his Chapter 13 plan was not proposed in good faith under § 1325(a)(3) as a matter of law.

[12] The panel rejected Handeen's argument for a bright line rule because "[s]uch a rule would effectively extend the nondischargeability provision of § 523(a)(6) to Chapter 13 proceedings, a result directly contrary to Chapter 13's terms and unsupported by the statute's legislative history."

determination. The court found the proposed percentage of payment (42.3 percent of each unsecured debt) was "significant." In addition, the plan provided for payments over a period of five years, the maximum period allowable under Chapter 13. See § 1322(c). After examining the terms of the proposed plan in detail, the court was "convinced that the debtor has made substantial financial sacrifices and that his parents have made significant financial sacrifices, which they are not required to do." Indeed, the court found that "[t]he debtor already has excess expenses over income which will have to made up [sic] by sacrifices in other places or by continued financial support from his parents. He has already foregone such things as entertainment and budgets a minimal amount for clothing." The court found that there had been no attempt to mislead the court and that LeMaire had not previously sought relief under the Bankruptcy Code. The plan imposed no particular administrative burden on the trustee. The court also found that LeMaire had been offered employment to commence at the end of his three-year fellowship, and specifically noted that the plan would be subject to modification under § 1329(a) if LeMaire's income increased significantly.

The bankruptcy court recognized that the debt to Handeen would be nondischargeable in Chapter 7 and that this was a factor to "weigh carefully" before confirming Lemaire's plan. Accordingly, the court carefully took into account the dischargeability factor, along with other relevant considerations, when it evaluated LeMaire's motivation and sincerity in seeking Chapter 13 relief:

> I can certainly understand Handeen's feelings; he has been grievously wronged, seriously injured, and now may receive only part of the agreed on compensation for that injury. However, it is the very essence of bankruptcy to provide a debtor with a fresh start. *The concept of fresh start is one that is very much overworked, but is one which applies in this case.* The debtor pled guilty to the crime that he committed and has paid his debt to society but, unfortunately, has not been able to pay his debt to his victim. It appears that he has made *every* attempt to reorder his life and obtain the fresh start that bankruptcy promises. Having to live the rest of his life with a significant judgment which would forever accrue interest and result in endless garnishments against his wages and keep him from accumulating any property would be inimical to such a fresh start. *I feel that he has made a wholehearted attempt to pay Handeen as much as he is able, which turns out to be a significant amount.*

> *Under these circumstances, I find that his motivation is proper and his sincerity real.*

The majority misreads the nature of the bankruptcy court's evaluation and, in so doing, disregards an essential basis for the court's ultimate determination with respect to LeMaire's motivation and sincerity. The majority fails to recognize that the key to the court's determination was its finding that LeMaire "has made a wholehearted attempt to pay Handeen as much as he is able." It is clear the bankruptcy court made a separate finding that LeMaire was making such an attempt, and it was this finding that in large part led the court to conclude LeMaire was entitled to have the fresh start principle, the cornerstone of bankruptcy law, weigh significantly in his favor. This finding obviously rests primarily on an assessment of LeMaire's credibility. * * *

The majority concludes that the bankruptcy court's evaluation of LeMaire's motivation and sincerity in seeking Chapter 13 relief is clearly erroneous because the court's evaluation "fails to properly consider the strong public policy factors, inherent in the Bankruptcy Code, which are implicated in discharging [the] debt [to Handeen] and gives undue emphasis to the fact that the statutory terms governing Chapter 13 petitions do not expressly make a debt resulting from a willful and malicious injury nondischargeable."[14] The majority asserts that in reaching this conclusion it "accord[ed] due deference to [the bankruptcy court's] credibility determinations." "Public policy," however, has nothing to do with an assessment of the credibility of LeMaire's testimony. Nor is it relevant to determining whether any of the other evidence before the bankruptcy court "was so 'implausible on its face that a reasonable factfinder would not credit it.'" (Quoting *Bessemer City*, 470 U.S. at 575.) The majority does not explain how the testimony and other evidence before the court was so facially implausible that a reasonable factfinder could not find, for instance, that LeMaire has made every attempt to reorder his life, substantial financial sacrifices, and a wholehearted attempt to pay Handeen as much as he is able. Instead, it simply focuses on the undisputed facts of LeMaire's attack on Handeen. This apparently is the "specific evidence" which compels the majority to conclude that the bankruptcy court's determination of LeMaire's motivation and sincerity in seeking Chapter 13 relief is clearly erroneous. * * *

---

[14] Contrary to the majority's view, the *express* terms of § 1328(a) make debts for willful and malicious injury *dischargeable* in Chapter 13. To conclude otherwise because § 1328(a) uses the term "all debts," rather than specifically enumerating each and every type of debt dischargeable in Chapter 13, flies in the face of clear congressional intent and does nothing to make the majority's "public policy" rationale more palatable.

The erroneous premise underlying the majority's conclusion regarding LeMaire's motivation and sincerity is that LeMaire must be considered a dishonest debtor for whom Chapter 13 is unavailable because of the viciousness of the assault which gave rise to his debt to Handeen. This premise is contrary to the terms of § 1325(a)(3) and finds no support in the case law. As the Seventh Circuit has stressed, § 1325(a)(3) requires that the plan be "'*proposed* in good faith' * * *, not that the debt was incurred in good faith." *Smith*, 848 F.2d at 819. Bankruptcy courts have recognized this important distinction. In order to avoid the error committed by the majority, "'[c]are must be taken not to allow revulsion over a debtor's past deeds to detract from or impair a finding of good faith where that debtor is making an effort to satisfy past obligations to the extent possible and still embark upon a fresh start.'" *In re Belt*, 106 B.R. 553, 565 (Bankr. N.D.Ind.1989) (quoting *In re Chura*, 33 B.R. 558, 560 (Bankr. D.Colo.1983)). The bankruptcy court found that LeMaire was making just such an effort in his proposed plan. Yet, the majority's preoccupation with the heinous nature of LeMaire's crime leads it to ignore this finding and invoke "public policy" as grounds for rejecting the court's determination of LeMaire's motivation and sincerity in proposing his plan. The majority's use of this "public policy" rationale not only stems from an erroneous premise, it also misapprehends the fundamental purposes of Chapter 13 and accords no deference to the bankruptcy court's judgment that LeMaire's plan satisfies those purposes. * * *

II.

The majority bases its decision on the bankruptcy court's treatment of two of the *Estus* factors: (1) whether the plan includes a debt that is nondischargeable in Chapter 7, and (2) the debtor's motivation and sincerity in seeking Chapter 13 relief. However, with respect to both factors, the majority cites a single error: the bankruptcy court's failure to accord sufficient weight to a "public policy" against the discharge of debts such as that owed to Handeen.[17] The majority does attempt to show that the court also erred in its treatment of other factors, but as will be seen, this attempt is anything but persuasive. More-

[17] The majority wisely declines to find any error in the bankruptcy court's determinations regarding LeMaire's financial dealings with his parents. These determinations are fully supported by the record. After hearing lengthy testimony on LeMaire's financial relationship with his parents, the court expressly found that there was no collusion in LeMaire's agreeing to pay his parents rent. "Furthermore, what Handeen asks is not for the debtor to make further financial sacrifices, but that his parents be required to make further financial sacrifices by waiving any rent. I do not think that that is a proper purpose of Chapter 13 nor a proper inquiry by a court in this context." I agree.

over, it is mere window dressing because the majority leaves no doubt that it holds "public policy" alone requires reversal in this case. * * *

The majority believes the bankruptcy court erred by not addressing the argument that LeMaire's failure to list a contingent debt to the United States Public Health Service in his plan demonstrated a lack of good faith. * * * The bankruptcy court found that LeMaire had made no attempt to mislead the court. This finding is clearly correct because the evidence establishes that the inaccuracy here was simply the result of an honest mistake. LeMaire testified that he was receiving a stipend from the federal government as part of a specialized program to train scientists who will go on to do research into drug abuse. The stipend was to continue until the conclusion of his three-year postdoctoral research fellowship. LeMaire testified that, under his agreement with the federal government, a year of the stipend would then be forgiven for each year he worked as a research scientist in the drug abuse field. LeMaire stated further that he expected his fellowship to be renewed for a third year and that he had already been offered a post-fellowship research position with a University of Minnesota scientist at a yearly salary of $18,500. LeMaire testified that he did not list his stipend as a debt because he fully intended to accept this position, which would allow him to satisfy his obligation under the federal program without paying back any of the stipend. LeMaire's attorney told the bankruptcy court that in retrospect he felt a mistake had been made in the schedules, a mistake for which he was responsible, and explained that the contingent debt was not listed in the schedules because of LeMaire's long-standing intention to continue on with his research career. The majority seems to think that LeMaire's frank and open testimony regarding his contingent liability under the federal training program is evidence of bad faith. I disagree completely. It strikes me as utterly implausible that such testimony could in any way be construed as an attempt to mislead the bankruptcy court.

* * *

The majority's final attempt to show that the bankruptcy court committed additional errors (beyond its alleged failure to adequately consider "public policy") is equally unavailing. The majority concedes the bankruptcy court "examined in detail" each of the relevant factors we set forth in *Estus*. After carefully considering these factors and "all the circumstances of this case," the court was "convinced that the debtor's plan is not an abuse of the provisions, purpose or spirit of Chapter 13 and is proposed in good faith." This is precisely the inquiry required by *Estus*. Nevertheless, the majority concludes that the bankruptcy court erred because its order does not specifically discuss whether LeMaire has attempted to "unfairly manipulate the Bankruptcy Code." This phrase is taken from our decision in *Zellner*, which, as the majority acknowledges, "preserved the traditional 'totality of circumstances' approach with respect to *Estus* factors not addressed by the [1984] legislative amendments." * * * It is clear that the phrase "unfairly manipulated the Bankruptcy Code" was either another expression for the abuse of Chapter 13 under the totality of the circumstances * * * or was simply a shorthand reference to some of the *Estus* factors that remained applicable after the 1984 amendments to Chapter 13. The majority, however, suggests that our use of this phrase in *Zellner* established a new and independent factor that the bankruptcy court must expressly consider in examining a debtor's good faith. This is a distortion of our holding in that case. * * * The bankruptcy court's determination that LeMaire's proposed plan was not an abuse of the bankruptcy laws obviously included an implicit finding that he had not unfairly manipulated those laws.

Ultimately, the most disturbing aspect of the majority's decision is the invocation of "public policy" to justify its holding that the bankruptcy court's finding of good faith under § 1325(a)(3) is clearly erroneous. Citing no authority to support its position, the majority purports to find the source of this controlling "public policy" in § 523(a)(6), which prohibits the discharge of debts for willful and malicious injury in Chapter 7 cases. By its own terms, § 523(a) does not extend to a discharge under § 1328(a) in Chapter 13. In § 1328(a), Congress explicitly enacted a policy that permits the discharge of debts for willful and malicious injury in Chapter 13 cases. Section 1328(a) makes "all debts" dischargeable in Chapter 13 outside of a short list of exceptions.[21] On the basis of the clear congressional intent embodied in §§ 523(a) and 1328(a), I reject the majority's conclusion that the policy expressed in § 523(a)(6) can compel a finding that a Chapter 13 plan such as LeMaire's was proposed in bad faith. * * * The majority clearly believes that the confirmation of LeMaire's plan was unjust in light of the vicious nature of his attack on Handeen. However, the remedy lies with Congress, not the judiciary.

[21] That Congress specifically intended to make debts covered by § 523(a)(6) dischargeable under § 1328(a) is further evidenced by § 1328(c), which expressly provides that any debt specified in § 523(a) is not included within the hardship discharge of § 1328(b).

Questions

1. Is the dissent correct that the majority imposed its own policy preferences on the Code?

2. Should Gregory LeMaire and other debtors be able to escape full liability for their actions through the vehicle of bankruptcy? If not, is some measure of "fresh start" appropriate? How much of a fresh start? When has a fresh start become a head start? Has the majority struck the proper balance between the interests of this debtor and creditor?

3. Are some obligations based on conduct so egregious that discharge should not be permissible? Is this such a case? Should the debtor's remorse and "rehabilitation" be relevant to the scope of discharge?

4. Recall Dr. Solomon from Chapter 3, Section D of this casebook. Is the outcome in this case relevant to the viewpoints expressed by the majority and dissenting opinions in *Solomon*?

B. DEBTORS ENTITLED TO DISCHARGE

1. IN GENERAL

The Bankruptcy Code distinguishes denial of discharge from exceptions to discharge. If discharge is denied, all of the debtor's obligations remain fully due and owing after the bankruptcy case is over. Section 727, which governs denial of discharge, is applicable primarily in Chapter 7 cases (except to the limited extent that § 1141(d)(3) imports it into Chapter 11). Thus, when discharge is denied, the Chapter 7 debtor's nonexempt property will be gone and the debts will not—a decidedly unhappy outcome. Exceptions to discharge, on the other hand, are governed primarily by § 523 (which is imported into Chapter 13 by § 1328(a) and into Chapter 11 by § 1141(d)(2)).

We will hold our discussions about discharge exceptions for Section C of this Chapter. We begin here by considering those circumstances under which discharge might be denied altogether. Read §§ 727(a) and 1141(d) and answer the following Problems.

Problems

1. Debtor Corp. filed a Chapter 7 bankruptcy petition. Is it entitled to discharge?

2. Joe Smith filed a Chapter 7 bankruptcy petition in 1994 and received a discharge in June of 1995. If Joe files another Chapter 7 in February of 2001, can he receive a discharge? Does your answer change if Joe's second bankruptcy petition is necessitated by catastrophic, uninsured medical expenses? Does your answer change if Joe's creditors file the second petition?

3. Jane Jones filed a Chapter 13 bankruptcy petition in 1994. Her three-year plan, which was confirmed in June of 1995, provided a dividend of 40% to her unsecured creditors. She completed payments under the plan in 1998. If Jane files a Chapter 7 in February of 2001, can she receive a discharge?

4. Mike Moore had a good job and substantial savings, but he was addicted to gambling. He loved Las Vegas and made several trips there every year. Mike hit an unlucky streak, lost everything he owned, and filed Chapter 7. Assuming that he reveals his losses on his bankruptcy schedules, can he receive a discharge?

5. Assume that Mike Moore's gambling habit runs toward betting on sporting events, which is illegal in Mike's state. How can Mike get the benefit of a bankruptcy discharge without exposing himself to criminal sanctions?

6. Debtor filed a Chapter 13 petition in November 2000 and proposed a plan that met the requirements of §§ 1322 and 1325. One of the creditors, however, objected to confirmation of the plan on the ground that Debtor had previously filed a Chapter 13 petition—in May of 1995. A three-year plan had been confirmed, paid in full, and a discharge granted in July of 1998. Is this a valid objection? See *Matter of Ciotta*, 4 B.R. 253 (Bankr. E.D.N.Y.1980).

7. Easterly Airlines, Inc., which filed a Chapter 11 petition, tried to confirm a plan to reorganize the company. When that proved impossible, Easterly proposed a plan under which all of its assets will be sold for the benefit of its creditors, shareholders will receive nothing, and its operations will shut down. Will Easterly receive a discharge upon confirmation of this plan?

8. Second Time, Inc. filed a Chapter 11 case in June of 1994 and confirmed its plan of reorganization in August of 1995. The plan provided for payments over five years, but Second Time was unable to meet all of the payments during the last year of the plan. Thus, Second Time filed another Chapter 11 petition in January of 2001. It proposed a reorganization plan under which its obligations would be paid over a longer period of time. If Second Time is able to propose a confirmable plan, will it be entitled to a discharge in its second bankruptcy?

9. When, if ever, is it in a creditor's interest to file an objection to a debtor's discharge?

DAVIS v. DAVIS (IN RE DAVIS)

United States Court of Appeals, Eleventh Circuit, 1990.
911 F.2d 560.

PER CURIAM.

This is an appeal from the district court's order affirming the bankruptcy court's order which denied the Debtor/Appellant's discharge. We affirm.

In 1983, the Appellee, Roe Davis, and the Debtor/Appellant, Don Davis, opened a pharmacy business. Roe Davis owned fifty-one percent of the stock, while Don Davis owned the remaining forty-nine percent. Both Roe and Don Davis, who are unrelated, individually signed promissory notes for the money they borrowed to operate the business. The business failed and was closed in October 1985. The final bank loan used to finance the pharmacy was payable in October 1986. Two days after the due date, the Debtor/Appellant discussed with his attorney his inability to pay this note and his concern about possibly losing his home. At the suggestion of his attorney, the Debtor/Appellant deeded his one-half interest in his home to his wife. Shortly thereafter, in November 1986, Appellee Roe Davis paid off the outstanding balance on the bank note, amounting to $118,395.24.

Appellee Roe Davis sued the Debtor/Appellant for contribution and obtained a default judgment for $58,694.24. Two days after obtaining this judgment, the Appellee filed a fraudulent conveyance action against the Debtor/Appellant seeking to set aside the transfer of the Debtor's interest in his home to his wife. Upon service of this complaint, the Debtor/Appellant consulted his attorney, who advised him to see a bankruptcy lawyer. The Debtor/Appellant did so, and was advised to reverse the transfer of his home to his wife. The necessary deed was prepared, executed and recorded. The day following recordation, the Debtor/Appellant filed for bankruptcy protection under Chapter 7 of the Bankruptcy Code.

In his bankruptcy schedules, the Debtor/Appellant disclosed the existence of these transfers, which had taken place within one year of the bankruptcy filing. In April 1987, the Appellee filed an adversary proceeding seeking to deny the Debtor/Appellant's discharge under § 727(a)(2)(A) of the Code. * * *

The matter was tried in December 1987. The bankruptcy court found that the transfer of property of the Debtor/Appellant to his wife was made with the intent to hinder, delay or defraud a creditor as proscribed by § 727(a)(2)(A), notwithstanding retransfer of the property completed the day before the petition was filed. The Debtor/Appellant contended that discharge should not be denied under § 727(a)(2)(A), since the transfer in question did not in fact diminish the assets available to creditors. In a subsequent memorandum opinion, the bankruptcy court rejected this argument, relying chiefly on *Future Time, Inc. v. Yates*, 26 B.R. 1006 (M.D.Ga.), *aff'd mem.*, 712 F.2d 1417 (11th Cir.1983), and denied the Debtor/Appellant a discharge. Debtor/Appellant Davis appealed this order to the district court, which affirmed.

In his appeal to this court, the Debtor/Appellant identifies two issues. First, the Debtor/Appellant argues the district court erred in affirming the denial of discharge in light of the fact that the Debtor/Appellant's transfer of property to his wife did not in fact reduce the assets available to creditors. We disagree in light of *Future Time*. In *Future Time*, the district court affirmed the denial of the debtor's discharge under § 727(a)(2)(A) despite the fact that mortgages and tax liens on the property transferred exceeded its fair market value so that, even without the transfer, the creditors were deprived of no assets since the debtor had no equity in the property.[2] That court reasoned:

> When appellant transferred his interest in the residence to his wife, he obviously intended to shield what he thought was valuable property from the claims of his creditors. To hold now that there occurred no transfer of property with the intent to hinder creditors merely because the debts on the residence exceeded its estimated fair market value would be to reward appellant for his wrongdoing, which the court refuses to do.

26 B.R. at 1009.

The Debtor/Appellant next argues the district court erred in affirming the denial of the Debtor/Appellant's discharge under § 727(a)(2)(A) since the property fraudulently conveyed to his wife was recovered prior to his filing bankruptcy. The Debtor/Appellant relies

---

2 * * *

We point out that in cases such as this one, the creditor is harmed whether or not any equity exists in the property transferred that may come into the estate. The creditor presumably incurred legal fees and expenses when he brought an action challenging the fraudulent transfer.

principally on *In re Adeeb*, 787 F.2d 1339 (9th Cir.1986), for the proposition that, as used in § 727(a)(2)(A), the word "transferred" should be read to mean "transferred and remained transferred" at the time a debtor files his bankruptcy petition. Despite the clear, unambiguous language used in the statute, the *Adeeb* court reasoned that its reading of "transferred" was "most consistent with the legislative purpose of the section." *Id.* at 1344. The court wrote that such a reading would "encourage honest debtors to recover property they have transferred during the year preceding bankruptcy" and serve to facilitate "the equitable distribution of assets among creditors by ensuring that the trustee has possession of all of the debtor's assets." *Id.* at 1345. The court added that this readily allowed the "honest debtor to undo his mistakes and receive his discharge." *Id.* Finally, the court noted its reliance on the practical aspects of such a situation:

> It is not uncommon for an uncounseled or poorly counseled debtor faced with mounting debts and pressure from his creditors to attempt to protect his property by transferring it to others. Upon later reflection or upon obtaining advice from experienced bankruptcy counsel, the debtor may realize that his original transfer of the property was a mistake. If the debtor is informed that his mistake bars him from a discharge in bankruptcy, he will have no incentive to attempt to recover the property or to reveal its existence to his creditors. Rather, he will have a strong incentive to continue to hide his assets.

Id.[3]

Normally, a court should interpret a statute in a manner consistent with the plain meaning of the language used in the statute. The statutory language of § 727(a)(2)(A) is plain and unambiguous. Congress certainly was capable of drafting a statute which would deny a discharge only when assets were fraudulently transferred and remained transferred at the time of filing of bankruptcy proceedings, but it did not. We are a court and not a legislative body; therefore, we are not free to create by interpretation an exception in a statute which is plain on its face. We therefore reject the approach initiated by the Ninth Circuit in *Adeeb*. We recognize that our holding may work

---

[3] Even among courts that follow *Adeeb*, and indeed in that case itself, it has been held that reliance on an attorney's bad advice to transfer assets to avoid losing them to creditors can be asserted to avoid denial of discharge only when that advice is sought in good faith.

hardship in some cases, perhaps this one, but we are compelled to apply statutory law as enacted by Congress.

AFFIRMED.

Questions

1. Apart from § 727(a)(2), the Code's "cure" for a fraudulent conveyance is recovery of the property or its value from the transferee. In *Davis*, the debtor "cured" the fraudulent conveyance by recovering the property before filing bankruptcy. Why was that not sufficient? Which is better bankruptcy policy—the result reached by *Davis* or by *Adeeb*?

2. In response to Don Davis's argument that creditors were not harmed because the property was returned, the court pointed to Roe Davis's litigation costs. Would it have made more sense for the court to have required Don to reimburse Roe for his expenses, rather than denying Don a discharge? Does a court have the power to require such reimbursement under the Code?

3. Do you have any reactions to the quality of the advice given to Don Davis in October of 1986 by his first attorney? Does Davis have a malpractice action? If so, is it an asset of the estate? What is the value of that asset?

4. Is Chapter 13 the solution for the debtor in *Davis v. Davis*?

5. The First Circuit decided a similar issue in *Martin v. Bajgar (In re Bajgar)*, 104 F.3d 495 (1st Cir.1997). In *Bajgar*, the debtor conveyed his interest in real estate to his wife as a belated engagement gift—delayed by 23 years—receiving "love and affection" in exchange. He was facing several foreclosures and a collection action at the time. Less than a year later, he filed a Chapter 7 petition and disclosed the transfer. He and his wife volunteered at the creditors' meeting to reconvey the property. The property was reconveyed three months later, after a creditor filed an objection to discharge. The court distinguished *Adeeb*, which involved an involuntary bankruptcy petition and a prepetition reconveyance, denying the debtor a discharge under § 727(a)(2)(A).

6. Debtor was guarantor on a note owed by his closely-held corporation. When the note went into default, Payee filed suit against Debtor and served notice that he would apply for a protective order prohibiting Debtor from removing money from any deposit account other than in the ordinary course of business. Before the court could enter the protective order, Debtor withdrew $60,000 from a deposit account and took the cash home. At the time Payee obtained the order and levied on Debtor's account, it had a balance of $1,300. Two months later, Payee obtained a judgment against Debtor for $85,000. Debtor promptly filed a bankruptcy petition. The cash was spent on lavish vacations and gambling trips. Can you think of an argument Debtor

might use to avoid loss of his discharge under § 727(a)(2)(A), even though he admits an intent to hinder Payee's collection efforts? See *Bernard v. Sheaffer (In re Bernard)*, 96 F.3d 1279 (9th Cir.1996).

2. EXEMPTION PLANNING AS ACTUAL FRAUD

A debtor, particularly one living in a state with generous exemptions, is understandably interested in taking maximum advantage of those exemptions. The debtor's assets might not be configured in a way that permits enjoyment of the maximum dollar value of the allowable exemptions, however. In that situation, the debtor may want to convert nonexempt assets into exempt assets before filing the bankruptcy petition. As the following case indicates, such prebankruptcy planning seems to be permitted by the Code's legislative history. The problem is that such a conversion of assets may be difficult to distinguish from an "intent to hinder, delay or defraud" creditors, which carries two rather unpleasant consequences: it renders a transfer avoidable as a fraudulent conveyance under either state law, via § 544(b), or § 548(a)(1)(A); and it provides grounds for denial of discharge under § 727(a)(2).

NORWEST BANK NEBRASKA, N.A. v. TVETEN (IN RE TVETEN)

United States Court of Appeals, Eighth Circuit, 1988.
848 F.2d 871.

TIMBERS, Circuit Judge.

Appellant Omar A. Tveten, a physician who owed creditors almost $19,000,000, mostly in the form of personal guaranties on a number of investments whose value had deteriorated greatly, petitioned for Chapter 11 bankruptcy. He had converted almost all of his nonexempt property, with a value of about $700,000, into exempt property that could not be reached by his creditors. The bankruptcy court, on the basis of its findings of fact and conclusions of law, entered an order on February 27, 1987, denying a discharge in view of its finding that Tveten intended to defraud, delay, and hinder his creditors. The district court, in an order entered July 10, 1987 in the District of Minnesota, Diana E. Murphy, *District Judge*, affirmed the bankruptcy court's order. On appeal, Tveten asserts that his transfers merely constituted astute pre-bankruptcy planning. We hold that the bankruptcy court was not clearly erroneous in inferring fraudulent intent on the part of Tveten. We affirm.

I.

We shall summarize only those facts and prior proceedings believed necessary to an understanding of the issues raised on appeal.

Tveten is a 59 year old physician in general practice. He is the sole shareholder of Omar A. Tveten, P.A., a professional corporation. He has no dependents. He began investing in various real estate developments. These investments initially were quite successful. Various physician friends of Tveten joined him in organizing a corporation to invest in these ventures. These investments were highly leveraged. The physicians, including Tveten, personally had guaranteed the debt arising out of these investments. In mid–1985, Tveten's investments began to sour. He became personally liable for an amount close to $19,000,000—well beyond his ability to pay. Appellees Norwest Bank Nebraska, N.A. ("Norwest Bank"), Business Development Corporation of Nebraska ("Business Development"), and Harold J. Panuska ("Panuska") as trustee of the Harold J. Panuska Profit Sharing Trust and the Harold J. Panuska Employee Trust Fund, became creditors of Tveten as a result of his various investment ventures.

Tveten filed a Chapter 11 petition on January 7, 1986. Meanwhile, several creditors already had commenced lawsuits against him. Panuska had obtained a $139,657 judgment against him on October 9, 1985. Norwest Bank and Business Development had commenced an action against him but had not obtained judgment when Tveten filed for bankruptcy. On the date the Chapter 11 petition was filed, Tveten owed his creditors close to $19,000,000.

Before filing for bankruptcy, Tveten consulted counsel. As part of his pre-bankruptcy planning, he liquidated almost all of his non-exempt property, converting it into exempt property worth approximately $700,000. This was accomplished through some seventeen separate transfers. The non-exempt property he liquidated included land sold to his parents and his brother, respectively, for $70,000 and $75,732 in cash; life insurance policies and annuities with a for-profit company with cash values totalling $96,307.58; his net salary and bonuses of $27,820.91; his KEOGH plan and individual retirement fund of $20,487.35; his corporation's profit-sharing plan worth $325,774.51; and a home sold for $50,000.[1] All of the liquidated property was converted into life insurance or annuity contracts with the Lutheran Brotherhood, a fraternal benefit association, which, under

[1] There were no claims that these transfers were for less than market value.

Minnesota law, cannot be attached by creditors. Tveten concedes that the purpose of these transfers was to shield his assets from creditors. Minnesota law provides that creditors cannot attach *any* money or other benefits payable by a fraternal benefit association. Unlike most exemption provisions in other states, the Minnesota exemption has no monetary limit. Indeed, under this exemption, Tveten attempted to place $700,000 worth of his property out of his creditors' reach.

Tveten sought a discharge with respect to $18,920,000 of his debts. Appellees objected to Tveten's discharge. In its order of February 27, 1987, the bankruptcy court concluded that, although Tveten's conversion of non-exempt property to exempt property just before petitioning for bankruptcy, standing alone, would not justify denial of a discharge, his inferred intent to defraud would. The bankruptcy court held that, even if the exemptions were permissible, Tveten had abused the protections permitted a debtor under the Bankruptcy Code (the "Code"). His awareness of Panuska's judgment against him and of several pending lawsuits, his rapidly deteriorating business investments, and his exposure to extensive liability well beyond his ability to pay, all were cited by the court in its description of the circumstances under which Tveten converted his property. Moreover, the court concluded that Tveten intended to hinder and delay his creditors. Accordingly, the bankruptcy court denied Tveten a discharge.

Tveten appealed from the bankruptcy court order to the federal district court. In a memorandum opinion and order entered July 10, 1987, the district court affirmed the denial of a discharge, concluding that the bankruptcy court's finding as to Tveten's intent was not clearly erroneous.

The instant appeal followed. Basically, Tveten asserts on appeal that as a matter of law we should reject the factors relied on by the bankruptcy court to infer that Tveten intended to delay, hinder and defraud creditors. We disagree. We affirm.

II.

The sole issue on appeal is whether Tveten properly was denied a discharge in view of the transfers alleged to have been in fraud of creditors.

At the outset, it is necessary to distinguish between (1) a debtor's right to exempt certain property from the claims of his creditors and (2) his right to a discharge of his debts. The Code permits a debtor to exempt property either pursuant to the provisions of the Code if not forbidden by state law, § 522(b) & (d), or pursuant to the provisions of state law and federal law other than the minimum allowances in the Code. § 522(b)(2). When the debtor claims a state-created exemption, the scope of the claim is determined by state law. It is well established that under the Code the conversion of non-exempt to exempt property for the purpose of placing the property out of the reach of creditors, without more, will not deprive the debtor of the exemption to which he otherwise would be entitled. Both the House and Senate Reports regarding the debtor's right to claim exemptions state:

> As under current law, the debtor will be permitted to convert nonexempt property into exempt property before filing a bankruptcy petition. The practice is not fraudulent as to creditors, and permits the debtor to make full use of the exemptions to which he is entitled under the law.

H.R. Rep. No. 95–595 at 361, *reprinted in* 1978 U.S.C.C.A.N. at 6317; S. Rep. No. 95–989 at 76, *reprinted in* 1978 U.S.C.C.A.N. at 5862. The rationale behind this policy is that "[t]he result which would obtain if debtors were not allowed to convert property into allowable exempt property would be extremely harsh, especially in those jurisdictions where the exemption allowance is minimal." 3 Collier on Bankruptcy, ¶ 522.08[4], at 40 (15th ed. 1984). This blanket approval of conversion is qualified, however, by denial of discharge if there was extrinsic evidence of the debtor's intent to defraud creditors.

A debtor's right to a discharge, however, unlike his right to an exemption, is determined by *federal*, not state, law. The Code provides that a debtor may be denied a discharge under Chapter 7 if, among other things, he has transferred property "with intent to hinder, delay, or defraud a creditor" within one year before the date of the filing of the petition. § 727(a)(2). Although Tveten filed for bankruptcy under Chapter 11, the proscription against discharging a debtor with fraudulent intent in a Chapter 7 proceeding is equally applicable against a debtor applying for a Chapter 11 discharge. The reason for this is that the Code provides that confirmation of a plan does not discharge a Chapter 11 debtor if "the debtor would be denied a discharge under § 727(a) of this title if the case were a case under chapter 7 of this title." § 1141(d)(3)(C).

Although the determination as to whether a discharge should be granted or denied is governed by federal law, the standard applied consistently by the courts is the same as that used to determine whether an exemption is permissible, i.e. absent extrinsic evidence of fraud, mere conversion of non-exempt property to exempt property is not fraudulent as to creditors even if the motivation behind the conversion is to place those assets beyond the reach of creditors.

As the bankruptcy court correctly found here, therefore, the issue in the instant case revolves around whether there was extrinsic evidence to demonstrate that Tveten transferred his property on the eve of bankruptcy with intent to defraud his creditors. The bankruptcy court's finding that there was such intent to defraud may be reversed by us only if clearly erroneous.

There are a number of cases in which the debtor converted non-exempt property to exempt property on the eve of bankruptcy and was granted a discharge because there was no extrinsic evidence of the debtor's intent to defraud. In *Forsberg v. Security State Bank*, 15 F.2d 499 (8th Cir.1926), an old decision of our Court, a debtor was granted a discharge despite his trade of non-exempt cattle for exempt hogs while insolvent and in contemplation of bankruptcy. Although we found that the trade was effected so that the debtor could increase his exemptions, the debtor "should [not] be penalized for merely doing what the law allows him to do." *Id.* at 501. We concluded that "before the existence of such fraudulent purpose can be properly found, there must appear in evidence some facts or circumstances which are extrinsic to the mere facts of conversion of nonexempt assets into exempt and which are indicative of such fraudulent purpose." *Id.* at 502.

There also are a number of cases, however, in which the courts have denied discharges after concluding that there was extrinsic evidence of the debtor's fraudulent intent. In *Ford v. Poston*, 773 F.2d 52 (4th Cir.1985), the debtor had executed a deed of correction transferring a tract of land to himself and his wife as tenants by the entirety. The debtor had testified that his parents originally had conveyed the land to the debtor alone, and that this was a mistake that he corrected by executing a deed of correction. Under relevant state law, the debtor's action removed the property from the reach of his creditors who were not also creditors of his wife. The Fourth Circuit, in upholding the denial of a discharge, found significant the fact that this "mistake" in the original transfer of the property was "corrected" the day after an unsecured creditor obtained judgment against the debtor. *Id.* at 55. The Fourth Circuit held that the bankruptcy court, in denying a discharge, was not clearly erroneous in finding the requisite intent to defraud, after "[h]aving heard * * * [the debtor's] testimony at trial and having considered the circumstances surrounding the transfer". *Id.* In *In re*

Reed, 700 F.2d 986 (5th Cir.1983), shortly after the debtor had arranged with his creditors to be free from the payment obligations until the following year, he rapidly had converted non-exempt assets to extinguish one home mortgage and to reduce another four months before bankruptcy, and had diverted receipts from his business into an account not divulged to his creditors. The Fifth Circuit concluded that the debtor's "whole pattern of conduct evinces that intent." *Id.* at 991. The court went further and stated:

> It would constitute a perversion of the purposes of the Bankruptcy Code to permit a debtor earning $180,000 a year to convert every one of his major nonexempt assets into sheltered property on the eve of bankruptcy with actual intent to defraud his creditors and then emerge washed clean of future obligation by carefully concocted immersion in bankruptcy waters.

Id. at 992.

In most, if not all, cases determining whether discharge was properly granted or denied to a debtor who practiced "pre-bankruptcy planning", the point of reference has been the state exemptions if the debtor was claiming under them. Although discharge was not denied if the debtor merely converted his non-exempt property into exempt property as permitted under state law, the exemptions involved in these cases comported with federal policy to give the debtor a "fresh start"—by limiting the monetary value of the exemptions. This policy has been explicit, or at least implicit, in these cases. In *Forsberg*, for example, we stated that it is not fraudulent for an individual who knows he is insolvent to convert non-exempt property into exempt property, thereby placing the property out of the reach of creditors

> because the statutes granting exemptions have made no such exceptions, and because the policy of such statutes is to favor the debtors, at the expense of the creditors, *in the limited amounts allowed to them, by preventing the forced loss of the home and of the necessities of subsistence*, and because such statutes are construed liberally in favor of the exemption.

15 F.2d at 501 (emphasis added). * * *

In the instant case, however, the state exemption relied on by Tveten was unlimited, with the potential for unlimited abuse. Indeed, this case presents a situation in which the debtor liquidated almost his entire net worth of $700,000 and converted it to non-exempt property in seventeen transfers on the eve of bankruptcy while his creditors, to whom he owed close to $19,000,000, would be left to divide the little that remained in his estate. Borrowing the phrase used by another court, Tveten "did not want a mere *fresh* start, he wanted a *head* start." *In re Zouhar*, 10 B.R. 154, 156 (Bankr. D.N.M.1981) (emphasis in original). His attempt to shield property worth approximately $700,000 goes well beyond the purpose for which exemptions are permitted. Tveten's reliance on his attorney's advice does not protect him here, since that protection applies only to the extent that the reliance was reasonable.

The bankruptcy court, as affirmed by the district court, examined Tveten's entire pattern of conduct and found that he had demonstrated fraudulent intent. We agree. While state law governs the legitimacy of Tveten's exemptions, it is federal law that governs his discharge. Permitting Tveten, who earns over $60,000 annually, to convert all of his major non-exempt assets into sheltered property on the eve of bankruptcy with actual intent to defraud his creditors "would constitute a perversion of the purposes of the Bankruptcy Code". *In re Reed*, 700 F.2d at 992. Tveten still is entitled to retain, free from creditors' claims, property rightfully exempt under relevant state law.

We distinguish our decision in *Hanson v. First National Bank*, 848 F.2d 866 (8th Cir.1988), decided today. *Hanson* involves a creditor's objection to two of the debtors' claimed exemptions under South Dakota law, a matter governed by state law. The complaint centered on the Hansons' sale, while insolvent, of non-exempt property to family members for fair market value and their use of the proceeds to prepay their preexisting mortgage and to purchase life insurance policies in the limited amounts permissible under relevant state law. The bankruptcy court found no extrinsic evidence of fraud. The district court, in a memorandum opinion and order entered June 15, 1987, affirmed. We also affirmed, concluding that the case fell within the myriad of cases which have permitted such a conversion on the eve of bankruptcy.

III.

To summarize:

We hold that the bankruptcy court was not clearly erroneous in inferring fraudulent intent on the part of the debtor, rather than astute pre-bankruptcy planning, with respect to his transfers on the eve of bankruptcy which were intended to defraud, delay and hinder his creditors.

Affirmed.

ARNOLD, Circuit Judge, dissenting.

The Court reaches a result that appeals to one's general sense of righteousness. I believe, however, that it is contrary to clearly established law, and I therefore respectfully dissent.

Dr. Tveten has never made any bones about what he is doing, or trying to do, in this case. He deliberately set out to convert as much property as possible into a form exempt from attachment by creditors under Minnesota law. Such a design necessarily involves an attempt to delay or hinder creditors, in the ordinary, non-legal sense of those words, but, under long-standing principles embodied both in judicial decisions and in statute, such a purpose is not unlawful. The governing authority in this Court is *Forsberg v. Security State Bank*, 15 F.2d 499 (8th Cir.1926). There we said:

> It is well settled that it is not a fraudulent act by an individual who knows he is insolvent to convert a part of his property which is not exempt into property which is exempt, for the purpose of claiming his exemptions therein, and of thereby placing it out of the reach of his creditors.

Id. at 501. Thus, under the controlling law of this Circuit, someone who is insolvent may convert property into exempt form for the very purpose of placing that property beyond the reach of his creditors.

A debtor's right to make full use of statutory exemptions is fundamental to bankruptcy law. To unsecured creditors, a debtor's conversion of his assets into exempt categories of property will always appear unfair, but this apparent unfairness is simply a consequence of the existence of exemptions under the jurisdiction's bankruptcy law. In an early case in this Circuit, Judge Walter H. Sanborn, one of the patriarchs of this Court, explained:

> An insolvent debtor may use with impunity any of his property that is free from the liens and equitable interests of his creditors to purchase a homestead. * * * If he takes property that is not exempt from judicial sale and applies it to this purpose, he merely avails himself of a plain provision of the constitution or the statute enacted for [his] benefit. * * * He takes nothing from the creditors by this action in which they have any vested right. The constitution or statute exempting the homestead from

> the judgments of creditors is in force when they extend the credit to him, and they do so in the face of the fact that he has this right. *Nor can the use of property that is not exempt from execution to procure a homestead be held to be a fraud upon the creditors * * *, because that which the law expressly sanctions and permits cannot be a legal fraud.*

First National Bank of Humboldt v. Glass, 79 F. 706, 707 (8th Cir.1897) (emphasis added).

The same principle was confirmed by Congress when it enacted the Bankruptcy Code of 1978. The report of the House Judiciary Committee states as follows:

> As under current law, the debtor will be permitted to convert nonexempt property into exempt property before filing a bankruptcy petition. The practice is not fraudulent as to creditors, and permits the debtor to make full use of the exemptions to which he is entitled under the law.

H.R. Rep. No. 95–595 at 361, *reprinted in* 1978 U.S.C.C.A.N. at 6317. The same language appears in S. Rep. No. 95–989 at 76, *reprinted in* 1978 U.S.C.C.A.N. at 5862. In the hearings referred to in the House Committee Report, two federal judges, concerned about the "outrageous" implications of existing law, specifically urged Congress to incorporate provisions in the new Bankruptcy Code which would make pre-bankruptcy conversion of assets fraudulent as a matter of federal law. The fact that Congress declined to change existing law, when presented with the same objections to the propriety of debtor tactics like Tveten's that the Court now expresses, indicates that Congress did not intend § 727(a)(2) to proscribe such conduct. The House Report's language plainly says that debtors may convert nonexempt property into exempt property, that doing so is not fraudulent, and that debtors may make "full use" of any applicable exemption. Recent cases in our Court have reiterated this principle.

To be sure, if there is extrinsic evidence of fraud, or of a purpose to hinder or delay creditors, discharge may and should be denied, but "extrinsic," in this context, must mean something beyond the mere conversion of assets into exempt form for the purpose of putting them out of the reach of one's creditors. If Tveten had lied to his creditors, like the debtor in *McCormick v. Security State Bank*, 822 F.2d 806 (8th Cir.1987), or misled them in some way, like the debtor in *In re Reed*, 700 F.2d 986 (5th Cir.1983), or transferred property for less than fair value to a third party, like the debtor in *Ford v. Poston*, 773 F.2d 52 (4th Cir.1985), we would have a very different case. There is absolutely no evidence of that sort of misconduct in this record, and the Court's opinion filed today cites none.

One is tempted to speculate what the result would have been in this case if the amount of assets converted had been $7,000, instead of $700,000. Indeed, the large amount of money involved is the only difference I can see between this case and *Forsberg*. It is true that the *Forsberg* opinion referred to "the limited amounts allowed to" debtors by exemptions, but whether exemptions are limited in amount is a legislative question ordinarily to be decided by the people's elected representatives, in this case the Minnesota Legislature. Where courts punish debtors simply for claiming exemptions within statutory limits, troubling problems arise in separating judicial from legislative power. * * *

If there ought to be a dollar limit, and I am inclined to think that there should be, and if practices such as those engaged in by the debtor here can become abusive, and I admit that they can, the problem is simply not one susceptible of a judicial solution according to manageable objective standards. A good statement of the kind of judicial reasoning that must underlie the result the Court reaches today appears in *In re Zouhar*, 10 B.R. 154 (Bankr. D.N.M.1981), where the amount of assets converted was $130,000. The Bankruptcy Court denied discharge, stating, among other things, that "'there is a principle of too much; phrased colloquially, when a pig becomes a hog it is slaughtered.'" *Id.* at 157. If I were a member of the Minnesota Legislature, I might well vote in favor of a bill to place an over-all dollar maximum on any exemption. But sitting as a judge, by what criteria do I determine when this pig becomes a hog? If $700,000 is too much, what about $70,000? Would it matter if the debtor were a farmer, as in *Forsberg*, rather than a physician? (I ask the question because the appellee creditor's brief mentions the debtor's profession, which ought to be legally irrelevant, several times.)

Debtors deserve more definite answers to these questions than the Court's opinion provides. In effect, the Court today leaves the distinction between permissible and impermissible claims of exemption to each bankruptcy judge's own sense of proportion. As a result, debtors will be unable to know in advance how far the federal courts will allow them to exercise their rights under state law.

Where state law creates an unlimited exemption, the result may be that wealthy debtors like Tveten enjoy a windfall that appears unconscionable, and contrary to the policy of the bankruptcy law. I fully agree with Judge Kishel, however, that

> [this] result * * * cannot be laid at [the] Debtor's feet; it must be laid at the feet of the state legislature. Debtor did nothing more than exercise a prerogative that was fully his under law. It cannot be said that his actions have so tainted him or his bankruptcy petition as to merit denial of discharge.

In re Johnson, 80 B.R. 953, 963 (Bankr. D.Minn.1987) (footnote omitted). I submit that Tveten did nothing more fraudulent than seek to take advantage of a state law of which the federal courts disapprove.

I would reverse this judgment and hold that the debtor's actions in converting property into exempt form do not bar a discharge in bankruptcy.

Notes and Questions

1. Can you distinguish between an intent to enjoy the full benefit of available exemptions and an intent to "hinder" or "delay" creditors?

2. The irreconcilability of cases on this issue is nowhere better illustrated than by *Tveten* and two other decisions of the Eighth Circuit—*Hanson v. First National Bank*, 848 F.2d 866 (8th Cir.1988), and *Panuska v. Johnson (In re Johnson)*, 880 F.2d 78 (8th Cir.1989). (The dissent in *Tveten* quoted the bankruptcy judge's opinion in *Johnson*.)

Hanson was heard by the same three-judge panel of the Eighth Circuit and decided on the same day as *Tveten*. Hanson was a farmer rather than a doctor, and he tried to shelter $34,000 rather than $700,000. Hanson and his wife did not sell everything they owned, unlike Dr. Tveten, and the life insurance policies they bought were exemptable only up to $20,000 under state law. The bankruptcy court found no fraud and the Eighth Circuit affirmed.

Dr. Johnson was involved in the same real estate investments that brought financial doom to Dr. Tveten. He also owed his creditors $19 million and sold nonexempt assets in order to purchase annuities and life insurance from a fraternal benefit organization. Each of these debtors employed the same lawyer, faced the same opposing counsel, and admitted to attempting to put their assets beyond the reach of their creditors (although Dr. Johnson sought to shelter $400,000, rather than $700,000). Dr. Johnson's asset conversions were found permissible by the bankruptcy court, however, and Dr. Tveten's were not. The Eighth Circuit affirmed both bankruptcy court decisions. (*Johnson* was remanded, however, because the bankruptcy court believed—erroneously, as the Eighth Circuit concluded—that fraudulent intent could never as a matter of law be established by the size of the exemption. On remand, the bankruptcy court found fraudulent intent on the basis of several facts: first, that the debtor, who had no dependents and already had term life insurance coverage, bought whole life coverage with a cash surrender value below the maximum exemptable amount and surrendered it soon after bankruptcy was filed; and second, that the debtor traded nonexempt assets for an exempt harpsichord and grand piano when he could not play, one instrument remained in storage, and his live-in girlfriend did not know the other was in the house.)

What explains the outcomes in exemption planning cases? The openness or lack thereof with which the debtor acted? (If so, why is it fraudulent to conceal something that is not itself fraudulent?) The amount of money involved? (Did you notice that the majority mentioned the amount of Dr. Tveten's debt five times in the course of its opinion?) Use of an exemption with an unlimited dollar amount? Prior consultation with a bankruptcy attorney? The result reached by the bankruptcy court? Would it matter if property were converted from nonexempt into exempt form just as a judgment creditor is preparing to execute?

3. Remember, conversion is particularly attractive in states with generous exemptions. If a court disapproves of conversion, is the court disturbed by the conversion itself or is the court really expressing dissatisfaction with the generosity of state exemptions? If the latter, is the draconian remedy of denial of discharge appropriate, in light of Congress's decision to adopt state exemption schemes in bankruptcy?

4. The court in *In re Schwarb*, 150 B.R. 470 (Bankr. M.D.Fla.1992), gave a different view of the passage in the legislative history, cited in *Tveten* and elsewhere, that seems to approve of pre-bankruptcy planning:

> [T]he "Hearings" referred to in the Committee Report consist of a letter from Bankruptcy Judge Phelps and comments on same by Committee Members and witnesses, condemning bankruptcy planning in the strongest terms. Judge Phelps' letter states that case law on the subject of bankruptcy planning "is in a state of utter confusion;" notes "that the conversion of non-exempt assets into exempt assets on the eve of bankruptcy is not, standing alone, fraudulent," and "that the payment of regular monthly payments on a debtor's homestead * * * or various such payments in the usual manner of living of the bankrupt, are perfectly appropriate;" but damns "the deliberate enlargement of exemptions out of the usual and customary manner of living and in contemplation of bankruptcy" as "cheating" which "shocks one's conscience" and "bring[s] the whole bankruptcy process into disrepute."
>
> Judge Phelps observed, "To have the bankrupt form the decision that he will file * * * bankruptcy proceedings and thereafter, with

> guidance from his attorney, to convert his salable assets into cash and then use that cash in such a way to hide it from his creditors, even while his attorney is busy typing up the bankruptcy schedules, appears to me to be fraudulent." Judge Phelps used the word "hide" to mean "shelter," not "conceal"; for he offered an example illustrated by a debtor's own statement of affairs. Former Bankruptcy Judge Cyr, now Judge of the First Circuit Court of Appeals, agreed that such conduct by debtors is "outrageous" and especially will be more prevalent as exemptions become more generous.
>
> Thus, there is scant, if any support for the notion that bankruptcy planning was approved without reservation by Congress. In fact, the Committee Report often cited seems to have been merely an artless paraphrase of Judge Phelps' letter; and the real sense of the Committee should be found in Judge Phelps' letter, rather than the oft-sited [sic] quote seemingly giving a carte blanche approval of pre-bankruptcy planning. Judge Phelps' letter also made it clear that advice of counsel is no excuse for such conduct, but rather may be considered part of the very essence of the offensive conduct.

Id. at 471–72. Do you agree with this view? If so, what makes bankruptcy planning improper, while tax planning remains the great American pastime?

5. How would you advise a client, contemplating bankruptcy, whose assets are not presently configured so as to take maximum advantage of available exemptions? Do you have to outline the possibilities for pre-bankruptcy planning in order to represent your client zealously? When has an attorney gone too far? *Cf. United States v. Zimmerman*, 943 F.2d 1204 (10th Cir.1991); *United States v. Brown*, 943 F.2d 1246 (10th Cir.1991).

C. DEBTS EXCEPTED FROM DISCHARGE

Section 727(a) bars any discharge at all and applies only in Chapter 7 *unless* incorporated into other chapters by specific provisions. See § 1141(d)(3)(C). Section 523(a), on the other hand, excepts particular debts from discharge and applies in cases under all chapters *unless* specific provisions in those chapters provide to the contrary. Chapters 11 and 12 do not have any provisions to the contrary, but Chapter 13 does. Compare §§ 1141(d) and 1228(a) with § 1328(a).

The types of debts excepted from discharge by § 523 vary. Some of the exceptions, such as those for taxes and support obligations, depend upon the nature of the debt and Congress's view that these sorts of obligations have a special "deservingness." Other exceptions, such as those for debts incurred by fraud or breach of fiduciary duty, depend upon the debtor's misconduct. (And, of course, some of the exceptions can be explained by nothing loftier than an ability to influence the political process enough to get a special-interest provision passed.)

1. SECTION 523(a)(1)—TAX OBLIGATIONS

Section 523(a)(1), which excepts certain tax debts from discharge, requires a little patience because of its cross references to § 507(a) (which deals with priorities) and its use of tax law terms of art. The simplest and perhaps most important rule is that a tax claim entitled to priority under § 507(a)(8) is also not dischargeable under § 523-(a)(1)(A). That simple statement, however, is merely the tip of the iceberg.

Problems

1. Debtor filed a Chapter 7 petition on January 22, 2001. Debtor never filed income tax returns for the 1997 and 1998 tax years. Which, if any, of those tax obligations are nondischargeable?

2. Debtor filed income tax returns for the 1997 and 1998 tax years on January 20, 2001, but did not enclose a check, and then filed a bankruptcy petition two days later. Which, if any, of these tax obligations are nondischargeable?

3. Debtor obtained an extension for filing her 1997 federal income tax return to October 15, 1998. She filed the return on October 7, 1998, but did not enclose a check. She filed Chapter 7 on October 10, 2001. Is this tax obligation dischargeable?

4. Debtor is the president and sole shareholder of Corporation. When they both went into bankruptcy, Corporation owed $150,000 to the federal government for amounts withheld from its employees' wages for social security and federal income taxes. Most of this amount related to the three years before Corporation's bankruptcy was filed, but $25,000 of it was for obligations five years old. Debtor is worried because he is a "responsible person" who is liable for these taxes. What amount, if any, of these tax obligations is nondischargeable in Debtor's bankruptcy?

5. Debtor filed a timely return for the 1997 tax year and included a check for the amount he believed was due. The IRS audited the return and sent Debtor a letter in September 2000 claiming a deficiency. Two months later the IRS sent Debtor Form 3552, claiming that he owed $33,000 in additional taxes, $5,000 in penalties and $12,000 in interest. Debtor filed a bankruptcy petition in June of 2001. Which, if any, of these amounts are nondischargeable? See *Hartman v. United States (In re Hartman)*, 110 B.R. 951 (Bankr. D.Kan.1990).

6. Debtor owed $6,000 in federal income taxes for the 2000 tax year, but did not have the money to pay when April 15, 2001 rolled around. So, a few days before the return was due, Debtor obtained a $6,000 cash advance on her American Express card and used the funds to pay her taxes. She filed a Chapter 7 petition in late July, 2001 and had no assets available to pay unsecured creditors, such as American Express. Can American Express prevent the discharge of its debt? See § 523(a)(14).

2. SECTION 523(a)(2)—OBLIGATIONS INCURRED BY FRAUD

Subsection 523(a)(2)(A) applies to value obtained by a false representation or by fraud *other than* a financial statement regarding the debtor. Subsection 523(a)(2)(B) applies to the use of false written financial statements on which the creditor reasonably relied.

Subsection (a)(2)(C) provides a presumption, for the purposes of (a)(2)(A) *only*, that certain categories of debts are nondischargeable—consumer debts for "luxury goods or services" over $1,000 owed to one creditor and incurred in the 60 days before bankruptcy, and cash advances exceeding $1,000 under open-ended consumer credit plans.

Some commentators feared that (a)(2)(C) would be interpreted to support the dischargeability of any debt not within its categories—that is, that nondischargeability under (a)(2)(A) would be limited to the categories of debts listed in (a)(2)(C). That fear has proved unfounded. Any credit obtained without an intention of repaying and in contemplation of bankruptcy may be nondischargeable under § 523(a)(2)(A). The only difference is that, for fact patterns not within (a)(2)(C), no presumption helps the creditor establish nondischargeability.

Problems

1. Debtor purchased a Chevy Lumina from Creditor, on credit, two weeks before filing a Chapter 7 petition. The car is equipped with air conditioning, power brakes, power windows, power steering, power door locks, cruise control and a sunroof. Is this obligation nondischargeable under § 523(a)(2)? Does it matter whether Debtor intended to pay for the car at the time of purchase? See *GMAC v. McDonald (In re McDonald)*, 129 B.R. 279 (Bankr. M.D.Fla.1991).

2. Debtor obtained a $200 cash advance on her Visa card ten days before bankruptcy. Is the obligation dischargeable? Does dischargeability depend on how the money is used—that is, would it matter whether the money was used to buy groceries or to pay for a night on the town?

3. Debtor obtained a loan from his mother-in-law, but did not mention that he was about to divorce her daughter. Is this obligation nondischargeable under § 523(a)(2) in Debtor's Chapter 7 bankruptcy? See *Caspers v. Van Horne (In re Van Horne)*, 823 F.2d 1285 (8th Cir.1987).

4. Josephine Jones obtained a loan from Bank by intentionally misstating the value of her assets on the loan application form. When Bank discovered what happened, it accelerated the loan and threatened her with an immediate lawsuit if she did not pay the balance at once. She does not have the money to do so. Josephine is a friend of Sheldon Toibb and knows that individuals can file Chapter 11. Can she discharge her debt to Bank by filing a bankruptcy petition under Chapter 11? See § 1141(d).

5. In his application for a $15,000 loan from Creditor, Debtor omitted reference on his financial statement to substantial obligations on an out-of-state land development deal because Debtor knew that the information would lead Creditor to reject the application. Creditor did the usual credit checks, learned nothing untoward, and made the loan. Debtor later applied for a second loan, submitting a similarly-false application. Since Debtor's interest payments on the first loan were current, Creditor filed the second loan application without reading it and loaned an additional $12,000. Debtor defaulted and Creditor agreed to forebear if Debtor would give Creditor a mortgage to secure both obligations. Debtor did so. Six months later Debtor defaulted again; Creditor foreclosed and sold the property for $12,300. Debtor filed a bankruptcy petition and Creditor objected to discharge of the remaining obligation ($14,700). How much, if any, is nondischargeable? See *Jennen v. Hunter (In re Hunter)*, 771 F.2d 1126 (8th Cir.1985).

6. Debtor owed Creditor $5,700 on an obligation that had been outstanding for a couple of years. Needing additional credit, she submitted an application that omitted several other debts. Creditor agreed to refinanced by lending Debtor an additional $9,200. From that amount, $5,700 was credited to the existing loan and $3,500 was given to Debtor. Debtor later filed a Chapter 7 petition and Creditor proved that it had relied on her fraudulent application. What amount is nondischargeable—$3,500 or $9,200? See *Matter of McFarland*, 84 F.3d 943 (7th Cir.), *cert. denied sub nom. South Div. Credit Union v. McFarland*, 519 U.S. 931, 117 S.Ct. 302, 136 L.Ed.2d 220 (1996).

AT&T UNIVERSAL CARD SERVICES v. ELLINGSWORTH (IN RE ELLINGSWORTH)

United States Bankruptcy Court, Western District of Missouri, 1997.
212 B.R. 326.

ARTHUR B. FEDERMAN, Bankruptcy Judge.

AT&T Universal Card Services (UCS) filed this adversary proceeding to determine the dischargeability of its debt against Chapter

7 debtor Deborah Ann Ellingsworth. * * * For the reasons set forth below, I find the debt to be dischargeable in part and nondischargeable in part.

FACTUAL BACKGROUND

Ms. Ellingsworth and her husband filed their joint bankruptcy petition on November 25, 1996. According to their bankruptcy schedules Ms. Ellingsworth was indebted to UCS for the sum of $4,038.11 at the time of filing. UCS issued a pre-approved credit card to Ms. Ellingsworth on October 19, 1995, with a credit limit of $4000. * * *

* * *

Don Carter, an employee, testified on behalf of UCS. He admitted that UCS contacted Ms. Ellingsworth in 1995 and informed her that she had been pre-approved for a card. She responded by telephone and was sent a credit card and a Universal Bank Credit Agreement (the Agreement). She never filled out an application for the card. Apparently she only verified by phone her income and employment. She was not asked about other liabilities. According to her bankruptcy schedules and the credit bureau report admitted at the trial, Ms. Ellingsworth and her husband already possessed at least 16 credit cards when she was offered the UCS card. Mr. Carter stated that UCS pre-approved Ms. Ellingsworth for its card based upon a credit score it obtained from a credit bureau. He stated that UCS obtained a Fair, Issacs Credit Bureau Score (a FICO score) of 759 on Ms. Ellingsworth prior to issuing her the card, and that any score above 680 merits consideration for a pre-approved card. He stated that UCS has developed some internal indicators that it uses in addition to the FICO score, but he was not certain of how the internal analysis is performed. And, other than the FICO score and the information provided by the customer as to her income and employment, it appears UCS had no other information available to it prior to issuing the card. According to Mr. Carter, once a card is issued to a customer, it is UCS policy to obtain a FICO score not less than every quarter, and to consider raising or lowering the credit limit or revoking the card, based on any changes. He said full credit bureau reports are not obtained prior to issuing cards because analyzing the credit bureau report itself would be too time consuming.

Mr. Carter testified that a full credit bureau report was generated on Ms. Ellingsworth on July 2, 1997, in preparation for this trial. That report showed her various obligations in detail. A casual reading of the report indicates that Ms. Ellingsworth is insolvent and unable to meet her obligations. UCS did not present any evidence that a quarterly credit score had been obtained on Ms. Ellingsworth between October of 1995, when she received the card, and July 2, 1997, when the credit bureau report was obtained.

UCS claims that Ms. Ellingsworth represented with each purchase and cash advance that she had the ability and the intent to repay her obligation to UCS. It also claims that any cash advances she took within 60 days of the bankruptcy filing aggregating more than $1000 are presumed nondischargeable.

DISCUSSION

A. *Introduction*

The dischargeability of credit card debt is but one small piece in the puzzle that represents unsecured lending today because the use of credit cards is, in fact, a form of unsecured lending. The following scenario illustrates this point. Assume you are a loan officer for a large metropolitan bank. A woman walks in one day and says she wants to borrow $60,000 on her signature. She willingly fills out a financial statement which shows that she already has $300,000 in unsecured debt, but she needs these additional funds for a business trip. She also shows one asset, a heavily encumbered apartment building that is being foreclosed. Of course, she promises to repay the loan if one is made to her. Would a bank that makes such a loan be found to have justifiably relied on her promise? Of course not. But, what if, instead, the bank made the loan without bothering to ask her basic information about assets, liabilities, and income? And what if she did not make an express promise to repay the loan? Should this bank be allowed to claim that it justifiably relied on her implied promises to pay? One would think not. However, those are the very facts of a recent bankruptcy opinion, except that rather than a face to face encounter with a bank officer, the debt was incurred through use of a credit card.[1] In *In re Hashemi* the debtor used his American Express Card to run up over $60,000 in debt while vacationing in France with his family. Dr. Hashemi then came home and filed for bankruptcy protection. The Ninth Circuit held that the debt was nondischargeable. The opinion pays scant attention to whether American Express acted justifiably in relying on debtor's promise to pay, whether express or implied. The Court found only that when Dr. Hashemi began his spending spree his account balance was

---

1 *American Express Travel Related Services Co., Inc. v. Hashemi (In re Hashemi)*, 104 F.3d 1122 (9th Cir.), *cert. denied*, 520 U.S. 1230, 117 S.Ct. 1824, 137 L.Ed.2d 1031 (1997).

$227.00, and that he had often repaid balances in excess of $60,000 in the past. Nonetheless, surely if American Express had been aware of Dr. Hashemi's current situation, it would not have extended the credit. And, if it was not aware that Dr. Hashemi was insolvent, then it should have taken some steps to find out before extending such a large amount of credit. If no lender would have made that loan in a face to face transaction, why are American Express' unreasonable lending practices afforded special protection under the Bankruptcy Code? Is there something in the Bankruptcy Code that treats credit card loans differently from face to face loans? Congress has created certain presumptions of nondischargeability as to credit card debt.[3] To the extent those presumptions are applicable, a portion of Ms. Ellingsworth's debt is nondischargeable. However, to the extent there is not a presumption of nondischargeability, the conduct of UCS in making credit available to her is a significant factor, which renders that portion of her debt dischargeable. * * *

B. *The Growth of Credit Card Use*

In 1995 2.7 billion unrequested solicitations for credit cards were mailed to American consumers. That amounts to about 17 offers per adult. The average card has a spending limit of $6007, therefore, if a consumer accepted every offer, she would end up with a potential credit line of $102,119. And, while the industry average for charging off credit card debt is 6 percent, bank profits have hit the highest levels in more than half a century, thanks primarily to the profits from credit cards. The average household carries about $4000 a month in card debt, a total of $367 billion, and banks earned approximately $35 billion in interest on this total in 1995. Since credit cards are so profitable, and the profits derive from having a very large customer base, issuers such as UCS may choose to ignore the usual standards of credit worthiness. Additionally, the creditors actively seek out undisciplined spenders who carry large unpaid balances from month to month. They dangle large credit lines in front of these consumers, and offer come-ons like lower interest rates for the first few months, as well as pre-printed cash advance checks. Some banks have even started to penalize consumers who pay their accounts in full each month. In their eagerness to capture market share, banks spend little time gathering financial information about their potential credit card customers. Prior to a mass mailing, creditors such as UCS obtain lists from credit bureaus with the names of candidates and a "credit score" for each person on the list. These scores relate generally to past card use, whether the candidate

[3] § 523(a)(2)(C).

pays the minimum monthly balance on current cards, and whether there are any delinquencies or bankruptcies on record. Car loans, medical bills, and mortgages are not included in the credit score, nor are income, job history, marital status, and assets.

The credit score, which can range from 450 to 850, is a supposedly scientific way of assessing the likelihood that a debtor will repay a loan. The computer credit model upon which most lenders rely today was developed by Fair, Issacs, and Company in California. The score is based on all credit-related data in a credit bureau report, but it is not a measure of a borrower's income, assets, or bank accounts. Fair Issacs, which is the service that UCS uses, identifies credit patterns, each of which corresponds to the probability that a lender [sic] will make payments. * * * In other words, as long as you use a credit card instead of a financial statement to obtain an unsecured loan, you do not have to indicate any form of credit-worthiness, other than the fact that, until now, you have paid your bills on time. Unfortunately, this tactic guarantees that borrowers who are encouraged to use credit cards until they acquire unsecured debt that far exceeds their income will ultimately not be able to pay their bills on time.

Banks use other techniques as well to encourage consumers to keep large balances on their credit cards. For example, VISA and MASTERCARD issuer Citibank offer credit cards that give a 2 percent interest rate break to customers who keep a balance of more than $2,500. UCS, the plaintiff here, rewards customers with bonus points if they carry a large balance. More disturbing, credit card companies flood college campuses with sign-up tables to hook customers early in adulthood. It is not unusual for college students with no income at all to accumulate 10 to 15 cards while in college. Why do the credit card companies solicit college students who have no regular job, little income, and no credit history? Because market research indicates that consumers are likely to hang onto the first credit card they obtain and use it long after graduation. Moreover, they will make 77 percent of their monthly purchases with that card.

* * *

C. *Section 523(a)(2)(A)*

* * * The United States Supreme Court recently held that § 523(a)(2)(A) encompasses common law misrepresentation or actual fraud.[37] This approach confirms * * * that the three torts [false pre-

[37] *Field v. Mans*, 516 U.S. 59, 116 S.Ct. 437, 444, 133 L.Ed.2d 351 (1995).

tenses, false representations and actual fraud] are all subject to the single action test of actual fraud. To prove actual or common law fraud, a creditor must prove the following:

(1) the debtor made a false representation;

(2) at the time the representation was made the debtor knew it was false;

(3) debtor subjectively intended to deceive the creditor at the time he made the representation;

(4) the creditor justifiably relied upon the representation; and

(5) [the] creditor was damaged.

While case law makes much of these five elements, most cases turn on whether debtor's use of a credit card is an actual representation that she intends to repay the money borrowed, and whether the creditor justifiably relied on debtor's representation that she intended to repay. * * *

* * * In the past, courts have held that a debtor makes an implied representation with each use of a credit card that she has both the ability and intent to repay the debt. But, fraud can be based on any type of conduct calculated to convey a misleading impression, thus, it is not relevant whether the representation is express or implied. The Court in *Chevy Chase Bank v. Briese (In re Briese)* found that "debtors do not commit fraud just by using their credit cards, even when they are heavily in debt. * * * To permit credit card plaintiffs to benefit from 'implications' is to engage in impermissible burden-shifting."[44]

The implied representation theory developed due to the unique nature of credit card transactions. Since a debtor presents a credit card to a third party merchant when making a purchase, not the issuer, courts held that there could be no direct representation or contemporaneous reliance with each use of the card. Courts, therefore, held that with each use of the card, a debtor made an implied representation that she had the ability and intent to repay the debt. With the advent of electronic transmission of credit card transactions, creditors are now instantly aware when a debtor uses its card. Therefore, debtors make an

---

44 196 B.R. 440, 449 (Bankr. W.D.Wis.1996).

express representation to the issuer each time they use the card that they intend to repay the debt. It is not clear if debtors ever made a representation of an ability to repay. However, as was recently pointed out by the Honorable Leif M. Clark, in the real world very few people who use credit cards represent a present ability to pay.[50] They are using a credit card instead of cash precisely because they do not have the present ability to pay. It is this condition that allows card issuers to charge the interest and finance charges that make the credit card business so profitable. Judge Clark noted, ironically, that "an ability to repay is inferred to protect an industry that purposefully solicits customers who generally lack such ability."[52]

A minority of Courts hold that the credit card company assumes the risk of non-payment with the use of the card, unless the issuer told the debtor to stop using its card.[53] Both the assumption of the risk theory and the implied representation theory were developed at a time when there was a significant lag between the time the card was used and the transaction was actually recorded with the issuer. Neither theory is as relevant today when most credit transactions are automatically recorded electronically at the instant the card is used. The issuer has the technology to refuse to accept the transaction before the merchant completes the sale. In fact, most merchants today will not complete the sale until they receive a code accepting the card. Likewise, if an issuer wishes to terminate the use of a card it can do so automatically. It does not have to inform the debtor to stop using the card, and then wait for it to be mailed back. I, therefore, find that debtors make [an] express representation that they intend to repay the obligation each time they use a credit card.

With these fictional theories removed from the analysis, I must decide two things. Did Ms. Ellingsworth falsely represent to UCS that she intended to repay her obligation to UCS at the time she used the credit card, and did UCS justifiably rely on that representation.

Direct proof of an individual's actual intention and purpose is nearly impossible to find. Therefore, case law has developed a list of

---

50 *Sears, Roebuck and Co. v. Hernandez (In re Hernandez)*, 208 B.R. 872, 880 (Bankr. W.D.Tex.1997).

52 *Id.*

53 *See, e.g., First Nat'l Bank of Mobile v. Roddenberry (In re Roddenberry)*, 701 F.2d 927, 932-33 (11th Cir.1983).

circumstantial factors which a creditor might use to infer intent.[55] These objective or circumstantial factors, much like the "badges of fraud," are:

1. The length of time between the charges made and the filing of bankruptcy;

2. Whether or not an attorney has been consulted concerning the filing of bankruptcy before the charges were made;

3. The number of charges made;

4. The amount of the charges;

5. The financial condition of the debtor at the time the charges are made;

6. Whether the charges were above the credit limit of the account;

7. Did the debtor make multiple charges on the same day;

8. Whether or not the debtor was employed;

9. The debtor's prospects for employment;

10. The debtor's financial sophistication;

11. Whether there was a sudden change in the debtor's buying habits; and

12. Whether the purchases were made for luxuries or necessities.

The goal in applying these factors is not to determine whether a reasonable debtor should have known that she was in over her head, and would not be able to pay her obligations. Instead, these factors are an aid in determining whether this debtor knew she would actually be unable to repay this debt. If so, the debtor incurred the debt with the intent not to repay it.

---

[55] *Citibank South Dakota N.A. v. Dougherty (In re Dougherty)*, 84 B.R. 653, 657 (B.A.P. 9th Cir.1988).

Here, the Ellingsworths filed their Chapter 7 petition within 75 days of using the credit card for the first time. The majority of the cash advances were taken within 60 days of the filing. Between September 11, 1996, and October 15, 1996, Ms. Ellingsworth made 16 cash advance and 8 purchases totaling approximately $4000. According to the bankruptcy schedules, the debtors had over $70,000 in unsecured debt at the time of filing. Ms. Ellingsworth testified that all of the other credit cards were "maxed out" when she began to use the UCS card, therefore, she and her husband had at least $65,000 in debt when the charges were made. Ms. Ellingsworth testified that she did not contact an attorney until she stopped using the UCS card. She did, however, state that she realized on October 15, 1996, that they could not go on using credit cards to meet their expenses, and that they needed credit counseling. She stated she and Mr. Ellingsworth made an appointment with Consumer Credit Counseling on October 18, 1996. The counselor at Consumer Credit Counseling told the debtors that they could not cut their expenses enough to service their debt, and that they should consider filing bankruptcy. According to the worksheet prepared by debtors and the counselor, debtors had net income of $4180 and minimum living expenses of $3383 leaving disposable income of $797. They needed $1465 a month to pay the minimum on their credit cards. Ms. Ellingsworth testified that she voluntarily ceased using the UCS card before she went to credit counseling. I note, however, that she stopped using the card when she reached the credit limit. I also note that Mr. Ellingsworth testified that he contacted Consumer Credit Counseling long enough before their appointment to allow debtors to fill out all the financial information and return it to the counselor five days before their appointment. It appears, therefore, that debtors had determined they at least needed professional advice before they ceased using the UCS card.

Debtor's employment is not at issue here, as she has been employed as a school teacher for 18 years. Though both Mr. and Mrs. Ellingsworth claim that Mr. Ellingsworth's job change was the straw that broke their financial backs, they did not well substantiate that claim. Mr. Ellingsworth claimed he took a decrease in salary, but the decrease seems to be related to the loss of a potential bonus he may have received as a buyer. He also made up for some of the decrease in pay by eliminating a voluntary contribution he was making to a 401(k) plan in the amount of $175.50 a month. Mr. Ellingsworth stated his employer had provided him with a car when he was a buyer, and now he had to provide his own transportation. The car expense represented the largest increased expense after this job change. Ms. Ellingsworth testified that they pay $187 a month for the car plus car insurance and gasoline. His job change was effective in August of 1997. They both insisted at trial that all of the charges were made for necessities. But, Ms. Ellingsworth could not explain a charge in the amount of $63.46 at Dave's Guns in Pataskala, Ohio, nor could she explain a charge in the amount of $217.23 at Golf Discount Campbell in Springfield, Missouri. Ms. Ellingsworth attempted to explain the medical expenses she encounters with three children, but she again failed to document these expenses. She admitted that they have health insurance that pays 80 percent of their health costs, and she did not refer to any specific illness that accounted for some of the funds she obtained with the UCS card.

Finally, I note that the debtors are intelligent and articulate people. They were not convincing when they said that, even though they had over $70,000 in unsecured debt, a second mortgage on their home, and had been using credit cards for six years to make ends meet, they didn't realize the extent of their financial difficulty until they went to client counseling. I especially note that the charges on the UCS card were made over a very short period of time and debtors stopped using the card as soon as the limit was reached. I, therefore, find that when Ms. Ellingsworth used the UCS card she knew that she would be unable to ever repay the debt, and she, therefore, did not intend to repay the debt.

A determination of intent, however, deals only with the debtor's conduct. I turn next to whether UCS proved that it justifiably relied upon Ms. Ellingsworth's representation of her intent to repay. The Supreme Court attempted to distinguish reasonable and justifiable reliance in *Field v. Mans* as follows. Reliance may be justifiable even if it does not conform to the standard of a reasonable man. For example, a creditor may justifiably rely on a debtor's statement that his house is free and clear of liens, without going to the recorder of deeds office to check for itself. On the other hand, a creditor is "required to use his senses, and cannot recover if he blindly relies upon a misrepresentation the falsity of which would be patent to him if he had utilized his opportunity to make a cursory examination or investigation."[64] For example, the Supreme Court stated, if a seller represents that a horse is sound when it is apparent that it has one eye, the buyer cannot be said to have justifiably relied upon the representation. This clarification is not always apparent in the credit card context. The **Restatement (Second) of Torts** does instruct, however, that "justification is a matter of the qualities and characteristics of a particular plaintiff, and the circum-

[64] 516 U.S. at 71 (*quoting* Restatement (Second) of Torts, § 541A, Comment a (1976)).

stances of a particular case, rather than of the application of a community standard of conduct in all cases." * * * [I]t becomes clear that UCS had access to much of the same information emphasized in the *Dougherty* factors that is now available to this Court. Credit card issuers have come to rely on these factors when determining whether to object to the discharge of their debt after someone files for bankruptcy relief. Interestingly, rarely do creditors consider these factors prior issuing a card. * * *

Credit card issuers are very sophisticated creditors. They have instant electronic access each time a credit card is used now. They know the number of charges made in a given day, they know the amount of those charges, and they know when a customer exceeds his credit limit. While they do not know with each use whether a debtor is employed, the issuers could, and often choose not to, obtain updated information about debtor's employment status. Moreover, the issuers elect not to obtain any other financial information, including assets and liabilities, about potential customers at the time a pre-approved card is issued. Often the reaction of a creditor at the time a user exceeds the credit limit on his account is to increase the limit. * * *

* * *

* * * [Issuers] make their decisions to offer customers credit cards not out of some altruistic notion of helping society, but because credit cards are very profitable. They carefully solicit customers who are most likely to use their services in a manner that increases those profits. They don't seek out or want customers who demonstrate an ability to pay by paying their other accounts in full each month. Judge Clark noted in *In re Hernandez* that one large credit card company (not UCS) makes $318 a year on the typical customer who carries a balance, while it loses $30 a year on customers who pay their monthly balance each month.[76] A credit score demonstrates a likelihood a debtor will not default. It is not based upon an analysis of one's assets, secured liabilities, and living expenses. Mr. Carter admitted that credit scoring will not eliminate potential customers who are insolvent. In fact, Ms. Ellingsworth received a credit score, which was acceptable to UCS, at a time when, according to her bankruptcy schedules, the credit bureau report, and the information sheet from Consumer Client Counseling, her expenses exceeded her income by at least $500.00 a month.

* * * Offering this customer a pre-approved card, without making any individual inquiry into her financial status, is the equivalent

[76] 208 B.R. 872, 879 (Bankr. W.D.Tex.1997).

of buying a horse with one eye. If the credit card issuers choose to continue this profitable technique to increase their customer base, they cannot claim that they justifiably relied upon any representation the customer made at the time the card was issued. * * * Moreover, if UCS did not justifiably rely upon Ms. Ellingsworth's representations at the time the card was issued, reliance cannot then attach when the card is used. I find, therefore, that the credit in this case was extended to Ms. Ellingsworth without justifiable consideration of her ability to repay. If UCS did not consider her ability to repay, it certainly cannot now claim that it relied on her intent. Indeed, to hold otherwise only encourages creditors to continue to act irresponsibly. * * *

D. *Section 523(a)(2)(C)*

Section 523(a)(2)(C) presumes the nondischargeability of cash advances exceeding a total of $1000 taken within 60 days of filing: *[the court quoted the subsection]*.

* * * Congress adopted this provision to address what it considered an especially egregious form of behavior referred to as "loading up."[83] Loading up is defined as "going on a buying spree in contemplation of bankruptcy." The Court in *In re Cox* found that the presumption in § 523(a)(2)(C) is the exclusive remedy against loading up.[85] * * * The legislative history indicates that the presumption shifts the burden to the debtor to prove the dischargeability of a debt, as opposed to the burden resting squarely on the creditor to prove the nondischargeability of a debt incurred outside the presumption period. This shift of the burden means "the reliance element inherent in § 523(a)(2)(A) is not relevant in the context of subsection 523(a)(2)(C)."[89] Thus, if the debt is subject to the presumption, Congress has determined that it is the debtor's intent alone, and not the creditor's conduct, which determines dischargeability.

[The court held the amount of cash advances taken within 60 days of filing—a total of $2,058—nondischargeable.]

* * *

---

[83] S. Rep. No. 65, 98th Cong., 1st Sess. 58 (1985).

[85] *GM Card v. Cox (In re Cox)*, 182 B.R. 626, 635 (Bankr. D.Mass.1995).

[89] *Sears Roebuck and Co. v. Hernandez (In re Hernandez)*, 208 B.R. 872, 881 n.17 (Bankr. W.D.Tex.1997).

Questions and Problems

1. Could you not interpret Ms. Ellingsworth's actions in going to credit counseling and not using her cards anymore as a demonstration of responsibility? Why, then, did the court interpret these actions as indicative of a fraudulent intent not to repay?

2. Is the court's analysis of how credit card issuers conduct their business correct, when measured against the requirement of justifiable reliance? Or is the court inappropriately curbing the ability of credit card issuers to function in the marketplace?

3. Debtors, who had recently bought a new home, received an unsolicited application from Bank for a credit card. They filled it out and, after completing a credit check, Bank issued Debtors a credit card with a $10,000 limit. Debtors paid for home repairs and improvements, furniture, appliances, dinners and concert tickets with the card, eventually running up a large obligation. They filed Chapter 7 and Bank challenged discharge of their credit card debt. The evidence showed Debtors to be unsophisticated in money matters, easily swayed by Bank's advertising, and unaware that their income would not support payments on the amount of debt they were amassing. Is their obligation to Bank dischargeable? See *Chevy Chase Federal Savings Bank v. Hoffman (In re Hoffman)*, 1991 U.S. App. LEXIS 11231 (4th Cir.1991).

4. West fraudulently obtained $100,000 from Oltman. In exchange for West's promissory note in the amount of $75,000, Oltman executed a general release and covenant not to sue except on the note. West filed a bankruptcy petition ten months later and listed the obligation on the note as an

unsecured claim. Oltman opposed discharge of the obligation on the grounds of § 523(a)(2). What result? See *Matter of West*, 22 F.3d 775 (7th Cir.1994).

5. The first hint that Mary Colvin, a customer business representative with Union Electric, had a problem came when she stayed home from work to await a call from the President awarding her a Nobel Prize. On advice from her employer, to whom she told this tale, she obtained psychiatric treatment for manic depressive disorder. During a relapse a year later she went to Plaza Motors and filled out a standard financial statement indicating that she was a vice president of Union Electric, earning $100,000 a year. The dealer verified employment and credit rating, but not income or job description—that took too long and customers were typically unwilling to wait. Thus, debtor traded in her 1983 Mercury Cougar, worth $8,000, and drove away in a new red Mercedes 560 SL Coupe worth $66,000. Debtor later realized that she was becoming ill again. She returned the car to Plaza Motors, with 1,300 miles on it. Plaza Motors resold the car and sought to recover a deficiency of $3,600, arguing nondischargeability under § 523(a)(2)(B). What result? See *In re Colvin*, 117 B.R. 484 (Bankr. E.D.Mo.1990).

COHEN v. DE LA CRUZ

United States Supreme Court, 1998.
523 U.S. 213, 118 S.Ct. 1212, 140 L.Ed.2d 341.

JUSTICE O'CONNOR delivered the opinion for a unanimous Court.

Section 523(a)(2)(A) of the Bankruptcy Code excepts from discharge in bankruptcy "any debt * * * for money, property, services, or an extension, renewal, or refinancing of credit, to the extent obtained by * * * false pretenses, a false representation, or actual fraud." The issue in this case is whether § 523(a)(2)(A) bars the discharge of treble damages awarded on account of the debtor's fraudulent acquisition of "money, property, services, or * * * credit," or whether the exception only encompasses the value of the "money, property, services, or * * * credit" the debtor obtains through fraud. We hold that § 523(a)(2)(A) prevents the discharge of all liability arising from fraud, and that an award of treble damages therefore falls within the scope of the exception.

I

Petitioner owned several residential properties in and around Hoboken, New Jersey, one of which was subject to a local rent control ordinance. In 1989, the Hoboken Rent Control Administrator determined that petitioner had been charging rents above the levels permitted by the ordinance, and ordered him to refund to the affected tenants, who are respondents in this Court, $31,382.50 in excess rents charged. Petitioner did not comply with the order.

Petitioner subsequently filed for relief under Chapter 7 of the Bankruptcy Code, seeking to discharge his debts. The tenants filed an adversary proceeding against petitioner in the Bankruptcy Court, arguing that the debt owed to them arose from rent payments obtained by "actual fraud" and that the debt was therefore nondischargeable under § 523(a)(2)(A). They also sought treble damages and attorney's fees and costs pursuant to the New Jersey Consumer Fraud Act.

Following a bench trial, the Bankruptcy Court ruled in the tenants' favor. The court found that petitioner had committed "actual fraud" within the meaning of § 523(a)(2)(A) and that his conduct amounted to an "unconscionable commercial practice" under the New Jersey Consumer Fraud Act. As a result, the court awarded the tenants treble damages totaling $94,147.50, plus reasonable attorney's fees and costs. Noting that courts had reached conflicting conclusions on whether § 523(a)(2)(A) excepts from discharge punitive damages (such as the treble damages at issue here), the Bankruptcy Court sided with those decisions holding that § 523(a)(2)(A) encompasses all obligations arising out of fraudulent conduct, including both punitive and compensatory damages.* The District Court affirmed.

The Court of Appeals for the Third Circuit affirmed in a divided opinion. After accepting the finding of the Bankruptcy Court that petitioner had committed fraud under § 523(a)(2)(A) and the New Jersey Consumer Fraud Act, the Court of Appeals turned to whether the treble damages portion of petitioner's liability represents a "debt * * * for money, property, services, or * * * credit, to the extent obtained by * * * actual fraud." § 523(a)(2)(A). The court observed that the term "debt," defined in the Code as a "right to payment," § 101(5)(A), plainly encompasses all liability for fraud, whether in the form of punitive or compensatory damages. And the phrase "to the extent obtained by," the court reasoned, modifies "money, property, services, or * * * credit," and therefore distinguishes not between compensatory and punitive damages awarded for fraud but instead between money or property obtained through fraudulent means and money or property obtained

* The Bankruptcy Court characterized an award of treble damages under the New Jersey Consumer Fraud Act as punitive in nature, and the Court of Appeals assumed as much without deciding the question. That issue does not affect our analysis, and we have no occasion to revisit it here.

through nonfraudulent means. Here, the court concluded, the entire award of $94,147.50 (plus attorney's fees and costs) resulted from money obtained through fraud and is therefore nondischargeable. Judge Greenberg dissented, concluding that treble damages are not encompassed by § 523(a)(2)(A) because they "do not reflect money, property, or services the debtor 'obtained.'"

As the Court of Appeals recognized, its interpretation of § 523(a)(2)(A) is in accord with that of the Eleventh Circuit but in conflict with that of the Ninth Circuit. Compare *In re St. Laurent*, 991 F.2d 672 (CA11 1993), with *In re Levy*, 951 F.2d 196 (CA9 1991). Bankruptcy courts have likewise reached differing conclusions on whether § 523(a)(2)(A) prevents the discharge in bankruptcy of punitive damages awarded on account of fraud. We noted the issue without resolving it in *Grogan v. Garner*, 498 U.S. 279, 282 n.2 (1991). We granted certiorari to address the conflict in the lower courts, and we now affirm.

II

The Bankruptcy Code has long prohibited debtors from discharging liabilities incurred on account of their fraud, embodying a basic policy animating the Code of affording relief only to an "honest but unfortunate debtor." *Grogan v. Garner*, *supra*, at 287 (internal quotation marks omitted); *Brown v. Felsen*, 442 U.S. 127 (1979). Section 523(a)(2)(A) continues the tradition, excepting from discharge "any debt * * * for money, property, services, or an extension, renewal, or refinancing of credit, to the extent obtained by * * * false pretenses, a false representation, or actual fraud."

The most straightforward reading of § 523(a)(2)(A) is that it prevents discharge of "any debt" respecting "money, property, services, or * * * credit" that the debtor has fraudulently obtained, including treble damages assessed on account of the fraud. See *Field v. Mans*, 516 U.S. 59, 61, 64 (1995) (describing § 523(a)(2)(A) as barring discharge of debts "resulting from" or "traceable to" fraud). First, an obligation to pay treble damages satisfies the threshold condition that it constitute a "debt." A "debt" is defined in the Code as "liability on a claim," § 101(12), a "claim" is defined in turn as a "right to payment," § 101(5)(A), and a "right to payment," we have said, "is nothing more nor less than an enforceable obligation." *Pennsylvania Dept. of Public Welfare v. Davenport*, 495 U.S. 552, 559 (1990). Those definitions "reflect Congress' broad * * * view of the class of obligations that qualify as a 'claim' giving rise to a 'debt,'" *id.* at 558, and they plainly encompass treble damages: An award of treble damages is an "enforceable obligation" of the debtor, and the creditor has a corresponding "right to payment."

Moreover, the phrase "to the extent obtained by" in § 523-(a)(2)(A), as the Court of Appeals recognized, does not impose any limitation on the extent to which "any debt" arising from fraud is excepted from discharge. "To the extent obtained by" modifies "money, property, services, or * * * credit"—not "any debt"—so that the exception encompasses "any debt * * * for money, property, services, or * * * credit, to the extent [that the money, property, services, or * * * credit is] obtained by" fraud. The phrase thereby makes clear that the share of money, property, etc., that is obtained by fraud gives rise to a nondischargeable debt. Once it is established that specific money or property has been obtained by fraud, however, "any debt" arising therefrom is excepted from discharge. In this case, petitioner received rent payments from respondents for a number of years, of which $31,382.50 was obtained by fraud. His full liability traceable to that sum—$94,147.50 plus attorney's fees and costs—thus falls within the exception.

Petitioner does not dispute that the term "debt" encompasses treble damages or that the phrase "to the extent obtained by" modifies "money, property, services, or * * * credit." He nonetheless contends that "any debt * * * for money, property, services, or * * * credit, to the extent obtained by" fraud does not include treble damages awarded in a fraud action. Petitioner submits that § 523(a)(2)(A) excepts from discharge only the portion of the damages award in a fraud action corresponding to the *value* of the "money, property, services, or * * * credit" the debtor obtained by fraud. The essential premise of petitioner's argument is that a "debt for" money, property, or services obtained by fraud is necessarily limited to the value of the money, property, or services received by the debtor. Petitioner, in this sense, interprets "debt for"—or alternatively, "liability on a claim for"—in § 523(a)(2)(A) to mean "liability on a claim to obtain," i.e. "liability on a claim to obtain the money, property, services, or credit obtained by fraud," thus imposing a restitutionary ceiling on the extent to which a debtor's liability for fraud is nondischargeable.

Petitioner's reading of "debt for" in § 523(a)(2)(A), however, is at odds with the meaning of the same phrase in parallel provisions. Section 523(a) defines several categories of liabilities that are excepted from discharge, and the words "debt for" introduce many of them, viz., "debt * * * for a tax or a customs duty * * * with respect to which a return * * * was not filed," § 523(a)(1)(B)(i), "debt * * * for fraud or defalcation while acting in a fiduciary capacity, embezzlement, or larceny," § 523(a)(4), "debt * * * for willful and malicious injury by the debtor to another entity," § 523(a)(6), and "debt * * * for death or personal injury caused by the debtor's operation of a motor vehicle if such operation was unlawful because the debtor was intoxicated," § 523(a)(9). None of these use "debt for" in the restitutionary sense of "liability on a claim to obtain"; it makes little sense to speak of "liability on a claim to obtain willful and malicious injury" or "liability on a claim to obtain fraud or defalcation." Instead, "debt for" is used throughout to mean "debt as a result of," "debt with respect to," "debt by reason of," and the like, see Black's Law Dictionary 644 (6th ed. 1990), connoting broadly any liability arising from the specified object; *Davenport*, *supra*, at 563 (characterizing § 523(a)(7), which excepts from discharge certain debts "for a fine, penalty, or forfeiture" as encompassing "debts arising from a 'fine, penalty, or forfeiture'").

Because each use of "debt for" in § 523(a) serves the identical function of introducing a category of nondischargeable debt the presumption that equivalent words have equivalent meaning when repeated in the same statute has particular resonance here. And contrary to petitioner's submission, it is of no moment that "debt for" in § 523(a)(2)(A) has as its immediate object a commodity (money, property, etc.), but in some of the other exceptions has as its immediate object a description of misconduct, e.g., § 523(a)(4) ("debt for fraud or defalcation [by a] fiduciary"). Section 523(a)(2)(A) also describes misconduct ("false pretenses, a false representation, or actual fraud"), even if it first specifies the result of that conduct (money, property, etc., obtained). The exception in § 523(a)(9) is framed in the same way, initially specifying an outcome as the immediate object of "debt for" ("death or personal injury"), and subsequently describing the misconduct giving rise to that outcome ("operation of a motor vehicle [while] intoxicated"). It is clear that "debt for" in that provision means "debt arising from" or "debt on account of," and it follows that "debt for" has the same meaning in § 523(a)(2)(A). When construed in the context of the statute as a whole, then, § 523(a)(2)(A) is best read to prohibit the discharge of any liability arising from a debtor's fraudulent acquisition of money, property, etc., including an award of treble damages for the fraud.

The history of the fraud exception reinforces our reading of § 523(a)(2)(A). The Bankruptcy Act of 1898 prohibited discharge of "judgments in actions for frauds, or obtaining property by false pretenses or false representations," and an award of punitive damages for fraud plainly fits in the category of "judgments in actions for fraud."

The exception was broadened in 1903 to include all "liabilities for obtaining property by false pretenses or false representations," language that, *a fortiori*, encompasses liability for punitive damages. See *Brown*, 442 U.S. at 138 (interpreting the provision as prohibiting discharge of "all debts arising out of conduct specified" therein); *In re St. Laurent*, 991 F.2d at 679 (noting "practice of holding debts for punitive damages nondischargeable" under this exception "if the compensatory damages * * * were themselves nondischargeable"). And the Bankruptcy Act of 1978 enacted a "substantially similar" provision, *Brown*, *supra*, at 129, n.1, barring discharge of "any debt * * * for obtaining money, property, services, or * * * credit, by * * * false pretenses, a false representation, or actual fraud." § 523(a)(2)(A) (1982 ed.).

As the result of a slight amendment to the language in 1984, referred to in the legislative history only as a "stylistic change," § 523-(a)(2)(A) now excepts from discharge "any debt * * * for money, property, services, or * * * credit, to the extent obtained by * * * false pretenses, a false representation, or actual fraud." We, however, "will not read the Bankruptcy Code to erode past bankruptcy practice absent a clear indication that Congress intended such a departure," *Davenport*, 495 U.S. at 563, and the change to the language of § 523(a)(2)(A) in 1984 in no way signals an intention to narrow the established scope of the fraud exception along the lines suggested by petitioner. If, as petitioner contends, Congress wished to limit the exception to that portion of the debtor's liability representing a restitutionary—as opposed to a compensatory or punitive—recovery for fraud, one would expect Congress to have made unmistakably clear its intent to distinguish among theories of recovery in this manner. See, *e.g.*, § 523(a)(7) (barring discharge of debts "for a fine, penalty, or forfeiture payable to * * * a governmental unit," but only if the debt "is not compensation for actual pecuniary loss").

The conclusion that § 523(a)(2)(A) bars the discharge of all liability arising from fraud is further borne out by the implications of petitioner's alternative construction. The various exceptions to discharge in § 523(a) reflect a conclusion on the part of Congress "that the creditors' interest in recovering full payment of debts in these categories outweighs the debtors' interest in a complete fresh start." *Grogan*, 498 U.S. at 287. But if, as petitioner would have it, the fraud exception only barred discharge of the value of any money, property, etc., fraudulently obtained by the debtor, the objective of ensuring full recovery by the creditor would be ill served. Limiting the exception to the value of the money or property fraudulently obtained by the debtor could prevent even a compensatory recovery for losses occasioned by fraud. For instance, if a debtor fraudulently represents that he will use a certain grade of shingles to roof a house and is paid accordingly, the cost of repairing any resulting water damage to the house could far exceed the payment to the debtor to install the shingles. See *In re Church*, 69 B. R. 425, 427 (Bankr. N.D.Tex.1987). The United States, as amicus curiae, posits another example along these lines, involving "a debtor who fraudulently represents to aircraft manufacturers that his steel bolts are aircraft quality [and] obtains $5,000" for the bolts, but "the fraud causes a multi-million dollar airplane to crash."

As petitioner acknowledges, his gloss on § 523(a)(2)(A) would allow the debtor in those situations to discharge any liability for losses caused by his fraud in excess of the amount he initially received, leaving the creditor far short of being made whole. And the portion of a creditor's recovery that exceeds the value of the money, property, etc., fraudulently obtained by the debtor—and that hence would be dischargeable under petitioner's view—might include compensation not only for losses brought about by fraud but also for attorney's fees and costs of suit associated with establishing fraud. But see § 523(d) (allowing award of attorney's fees and costs to the *debtor* where a creditor requests dischargeability determination under § 523(a)(2) for a consumer debt that is ultimately found to be dischargeable). Those sorts of results would not square with the intent of the fraud exception. As we have observed previously in addressing different issues surrounding the scope of that exception, it is "unlikely that Congress * * * would have favored the interest in giving perpetrators of fraud a fresh start over the interest in protecting victims of fraud." *Grogan*, *supra*, at 287.

In short, the text of § 523(a)(2)(A), the meaning of parallel provisions in the statute, the historical pedigree of the fraud exception, and the general policy underlying the exceptions to discharge all support our conclusion that "any debt * * * for money, property, services, or * * * credit, to the extent obtained by" fraud encompasses any liability arising from money, property, etc., that is fraudulently obtained, including treble damages, attorney's fees, and other relief that may exceed the value obtained by the debtor. Under New Jersey law, the debt for fraudulently obtaining $31,382.50 in rent payments includes treble damages and attorney's fees and costs, and consequently, petitioner's entire debt of $94,147.50 (plus attorney's fees and costs) is nondischargeable in bankruptcy. Accordingly, we affirm the judgment of the Court of Appeals.

It is so ordered.

Questions

1. Do you agree with the Supreme Court's statutory analysis?

2. Without regard to the statutory exegesis, is this result consistent with good bankruptcy policy?

3. SECTION 523(a)(3)—UNSCHEDULED DEBTS

Section 523(a)(3) is designed primarily to protect the interests of creditors who have not received adequate notice that their rights are being affected by a bankruptcy filing.

This subsection may become a trap for the unwary debtor, as *Duerkop v. Jongquist (In re Jongquist)*, 125 B.R. 558 (Bankr. D.Minn. 1991), illustrates. In that case, debtors' Chapter 7 was originally noticed as a no-asset case and creditors were instructed not to file claims. The trustee later found $390 and sent notice to scheduled creditors to file claims. The $390 was applied as follows: $212 to reimburse the trustee for expenses; $58.50 for the trustee's fees; and $65.50 for court costs. Only $54 was available for distribution to unsecured creditors. Duerkop, who was owed $29,999, was omitted from debtors' schedules and received no notice. The court held that § 523(a)(3) protects a creditor's right to file a timely claim and makes no distinction between minimal asset cases and those in which substantial distributions are made to creditors. The entire debt was held nondischargeable despite the fact that Duerkop would have received only a few dollars if he had received proper notice and had filed a timely claim.

4. SECTION 523(a)(4)—BREACH OF FIDUCIARY DUTY

Section 523(a)(4) excepts from discharge debts procured by fraud or defalcation while the debtor was acting in a fiduciary capacity, and debts that arose from embezzlement or larceny.

Several cases have discussed the requirements for finding that the debtor was acting in a fiduciary capacity—a concept ordinarily associated with trust relationships. In *Matter of Marchiando*, 13 F.3d 1111 (7th Cir.), *cert. denied sub nom. Illinois Dep't of the Lottery v. Marchiando*, 114 S.Ct. 2675, 12 L.Ed.2d 810 (1994), debtor owned a convenience store that sold lottery tickets. State law provided that the proceeds of ticket sales "shall constitute a trust fund until paid to the Department." When debtor filed her bankruptcy petition, she owed the state $17,000 in proceeds that she had used in an effort to keep the business afloat. The state argued that the debt was nondischargeable under § 523(a)(4), but the Seventh Circuit disagreed:

> [E]xtension of the fiduciary concept—the use of the concept of "constructive trust" (where "constructive" bears its usual legal meaning of "no") to impose the fiduciary duty of a trustee on a person who is not a trustee—has been held not to come within the reach of § 523(a)(4). * * * To complicate the picture further, the cases are divided over the question whether a statute that, as in our case, deems a debtor a fiduciary in order to enlarge the remedies for default makes the debtor a "fiduciary" for purposes of § 523(a)(4). * * *
>
> The key to knitting the cases into a harmonious whole is the distinction * * * between a trust or other fiduciary relation that has an existence independent of the debtor's wrong and a trust or other fiduciary relation that has no existence before the wrong is committed. A lawyer's fiduciary duty to his client, or a director's duty to his corporation's shareholders, pre-exists any breach of the duty, while in the case of a constructive or resulting trust there is no fiduciary duty until a wrong is committed. The intermediate case, but closer we think to the constructive or resulting trust pole, is that of a trust that has a purely nominal existence until the wrong is committed. Technically, Marchiando became a trustee as soon as she received her license to sell lottery tickets. Realistically, the trust did not begin until she failed to remit ticket receipts. For until then she had no duties of a fiduciary character toward the Department of Lottery or anything or anyone else. Until then, she was just a ticket agent. The state, afraid that she might be a disloyal agent, required her to keep the proceeds of her ticket sales separate from her other funds and threatened her with criminal punishment if she did not. These were devices by which the state sought to establish and enforce a lien in the proceeds, the better to collect them securely. * * *
>
> If we probe more deeply the distinction between the fiduciary relation that imposes real duties in advance of the breach and the fiduciary relation that does not we find that the first group of cases involve a difference in knowledge or power between fiduciary and principal which * * * gives the former a position of ascendancy over the latter. * * *

* * *

> If * * * a fiduciary is anyone whom a state calls a fiduciary—the only principle on which the discharge of Marchiando's debt could be refused—states will have it in their power to deny a fresh start to their debtors by declaring all contractual relations fiduciary. * * * Libertarians may smile approvingly at the state's equating its bureaucracies to the children and other incompetents who are the classic trust beneficiaries, but we do not think Congress would. The convenience-store keeper who commingles the proceeds of her lottery ticket sales with her other receipts is at a considerable remove from the lawyer who converts money in his clients' escrow accounts or the bank trust department that invests someone's retirement fund recklessly.
>
> Marchiando, moreover, is playing a risky game, which makes it unlikely that our decision will endanger legitimate state interests. By successfully challenging the state's effort to prevent her from discharging her debt to it, she invites it to bring a criminal proceeding against her, since any fine levied in such a proceeding would be nondischargeable. § 523(a)(7). * * * The possibility of criminal prosecution of disloyal ticket agents is the lawful alternative, denied most creditors, to the State of Illinois' foredoomed effort to squeeze its lottery law into the nondischarge provision.

Id. at 1115–17.

5. SECTIONS 523(a)(5) AND (a)(15)—FAMILY-RELATED OBLIGATIONS

The discharge exception for support obligations, found in § 523(a)(5), is one of the few discharge exceptions that applies in all chapters. This reflects the importance Congress placed on such obligations as a matter of policy.

The reason for the exception is the deservingness of the "creditors." Obligors (who are usually fathers and ex-husbands, despite the gender-neutrality of the statutory language) do not win many of these cases. Think about it—how sympathetic a view is a court likely to take of a father who is trying to avoid paying for the support of his children?

Before the 1994 Amendments added § 523(a)(15), the major challenge was to distinguish between support obligations, which are not dischargeable under § 523(a)(5), and obligations arising under a property settlement, which were dischargeable. Generally speaking, bankruptcy courts did not reclassify as a dischargeable property settlement any payment identified as support in a marital dissolution decree or in the parties' separation agreement. But courts routinely recharacterized, as a nondischargeable support obligation, payments the parties labeled a property settlement.

Although property settlements are now (possibly) nondischargeable under § 523(a)(15), the need to distinguish support obligations from property settlements has not disappeared. The distinction remains important because of the exception in (a)(15) that permits discharge of nonsupport obligations if "the debtor does not have the ability to pay." Debtors are likely to continue trying to characterize their obligations as property settlements, and to make the additional showing of inability to pay, in order to obtain discharge.

Also note § 523(a)(18), which was added in 1996 in order to resolve a split of authority among the circuit courts. It bars discharge of a support obligation, owed under state law to a state or municipality, that is enforceable under the Social Security Act.

MATTER OF CROSSWHITE

United States Court of Appeals, Seventh Circuit, 1998.
148 F.3d 879.

RIPPLE, Circuit Judge.

The question before us, in this bankruptcy appeal, is whether the two debts that Maurice Crosswhite agreed to assume and pay under a property settlement agreement are dischargeable in bankruptcy pursuant to § 523(a)(15). The bankruptcy court held that the obligations were dischargeable and entered judgment for the debtor Crosswhite. The district court affirmed. For the reasons set forth in the following opinion, we vacate the judgment of the district court and remand for further proceedings consistent with this opinion.

I

BACKGROUND

When the marriage of Maurice and Terry Crosswhite was dissolved on August 16, 1994, Mr. Crosswhite was ordered to pay child support for their two children. Under the terms of the property settlement agreement incorporated into the divorce decree, Mr. Crosswhite kept possession of the marital residence and agreed to pay Terry (now Terry Crosswhite Ginter) $8,000 as a property equalization payment. In addition, Mr. Crosswhite agreed to assume, pay and hold Ms. Ginter harmless on two joint debts, $3,489 to Merchants Bank (to purchase Mr. Crosswhite's boat) and $1,700 to the General Federal Credit Union (to improve the real estate retained by Mr. Crosswhite).

This appeal focuses on the debts owed to the bank and the credit union. Mr. Crosswhite did not pay those marital obligations. Instead, on November 21, 1994, he filed a bankruptcy petition, as "Crosswhite d/b/a Morrie's Automotive Specialists," for relief under Chapter 7 of the United States Bankruptcy Code. When the bank brought suit, Ms. Ginter paid the debt. When the credit union threatened to sue, Ms. Ginter restructured the loan and made monthly payments to pay it. Then Ms. Ginter initiated an adversary proceeding in Mr. Crosswhite's bankruptcy by filing a complaint to determine the dischargeability of Mr. Crosswhite's property settlement agreement obligations under § 523(a)(15).

The bankruptcy court held that debtor Crosswhite's property settlement obligations to Ms. Ginter were dischargeable under § 523(a)(15)(B). The district court affirmed the bankruptcy court's decision. Ms. Ginter has appealed that judgment * * * .

II

DISCUSSION

A.

Section 523(a) of the Bankruptcy Code lists eighteen categories of debts that are excepted from a debtor's discharge, i.e., that are not dischargeable. When deciding whether a particular debt falls within a § 523 exception, courts generally construe the statute strictly against the objecting creditor and liberally in favor of the debtor in order to give the debtor a better chance at a fresh start. Consequently, the party claiming an exception to discharge usually bears the burden of proving by a preponderance of the evidence that the debt is not dischargeable. That policy of protecting and favoring the debtor is tempered, however, when the debt arises from a divorce or separation agreement. Bankruptcy law has had a longstanding corresponding policy of protecting a debtor's spouse and children when the debtor's support is required. This policy is manifest in the Bankruptcy Code's § 523(a)(5) * * * . This exception therefore expresses Congress' determination to protect former spouses in matters of alimony, maintenance, and support despite the

Bankruptcy Code's general policy of providing a debtor with a fresh start. Because of this Congressional determination, a § 523(a)(5) exception from discharge is construed more liberally than other § 523 exceptions.

Subsection (15) of § 523(a) was added to the Bankruptcy Code in the Bankruptcy Reform Act of 1994 to expand the § 523(a)(5) exception to discharge for marital debts. [*The court quoted § 523(a)(15).*] This section is intended to cover divorce-related debts such as those in property settlement agreements that "should not justifiably be discharged." 4 Lawrence P. King, Collier on Bankruptcy ¶ 523.21 (15th ed. rev. 1998). The legislative history of this section reflects the same policy interest in protecting ex-spouses and children that is found in § 523(a)(5) by treating property settlement debts as nondischargeable.

Many courts (including the bankruptcy and district courts reviewing Ms. Ginter's adversary proceeding in Mr. Crosswhite's bankruptcy) have criticized this provision for its lack of clarity. However, we believe that a careful parsing of the provision eliminates some of the confusion. Section 523 provides the general scheme for establishing exceptions from discharge, and two subsections provide specific protection to the debtor's children, spouse and former spouse. Subsection (5) establishes as nondischargeable the debtor's obligations of alimony, maintenance and support; subsection (15) sets forth as nondischargeable any marital debt other than alimony, maintenance or support that is incurred in connection with a divorce or separation. Subsection (15) then offers two exceptions to that rule of nondischargeability under subsubsections, or sub-parts, (A) and (B). Therefore, a subsection (15) property settlement debt is not dischargeable *unless*, under (A), the debtor does not have the ability to pay the debt from disposable income, or, under (B), the benefit to the debtor in discharging the debt outweighs the detrimental consequences to the debtor's former spouse or child.

B.

In the case before us, the bankruptcy court first considered Mr. Crosswhite's ability to pay the property settlement obligations pursuant to § 523(a)(15)(A). It held that the debtor Crosswhite, despite his current inability to pay his debts to Ms. Ginter, had the capability to pay the marital debts because he is a skilled and experienced mechanic who is reasonably able to earn more than he now does. The bankruptcy court placed on the debtor the burden of proving that he did not have the ability to pay his marital debts and concluded that Mr. Crosswhite failed to make that showing. As a result, the court concluded that the debtor did not qualify for the discharge exception provided under § 523(a)(15)(A). (That finding was not disputed in the district court and is not an issue before us.) The bankruptcy court then turned to Mr. Crosswhite's alternative possibility for excepting the property settlement debts under subpart (B). The bankruptcy court noted that Congress gave no guidance on how to balance the debtor's benefit against the creditor's detriment in its analysis of § 523(a)(15)(B). It chose to follow a "totality of the circumstances" approach which required both parties to proffer evidence: The debtor must present evidence demonstrating the benefits he would receive from a discharge of the debt, and the creditor must produce evidence of the detrimental consequences to her if the debt were discharged. According to the court, its role was to "balance one party's economic benefit against another party's economic detriment," but not to "inquire into which of the two parties before the court is better able to pay." It announced that it would consider only financial factors—the income, expenses, and economic circumstances of each party and of their new spouses—and not non-economic evidence. The court then stated that it had examined the debtor's financial circumstances in connection with its analysis under subpart (A) and that the "analysis required by § 523(a)(15)(B) requires a similar evaluation of his former wife's circumstances."

In its subsequent evaluation, the bankruptcy court noted that Ms. Ginter was remarried, that she and her current husband have full-time jobs and that their income was sufficient to cover more than their monthly obligations. It acknowledged Ms. Ginter's achievements: She "successfully weathered the financial storm created by the Debtor's failure to honor his commitments to hold her harmless from the marital debts he was to pay." It also recognized that her financial stability is due primarily to her new spouse's productive employment and to his inheritance. Accepting as a "given" Mr. Crosswhite's "somewhat parasitic existence" with only a theoretical ability to pay his obligations as a result of his "long term commitment to suboptimal employment," it determined that discharging the debt was appropriate because Ms. Ginter's financial circumstances were better than Mr. Crosswhite's and would not deteriorate in this situation.[5] The bankruptcy court then held that Mr. Crosswhite's obligations to Ms. Ginter were dischargeable because the benefit of discharging the debt to him outweighed the detriment it caused to Ms. Ginter.

[5] The bankruptcy court found it significant that, because Mr. Crosswhite's obligation to pay the $8,000 property equalization award to Ms. Ginter was secured by a judicial lien on Mr. Crosswhite's residence, Ms. Ginter had the opportunity to obtain payment in full. We note, however, that the lien covered only the $8,000 award and not the property settlement debts.

The district court affirmed the bankruptcy court's ruling. * * *

C.

1.

Ms. Ginter, the creditor/nondebtor spouse, does not object to shouldering the initial burden under § 523(a)(15) of proving the existence of a nondischargeable debt—a debt that is not a § 523(a)(5) debt, but is one incurred by the debtor in the course of the divorce. Ms. Ginter does object, however, to what she believes is the additional burden placed on her by the bankruptcy and district courts: Under subpart (B), the statute requires, according to Ms. Ginter, that the creditor first prove that the nature of the debt is one encompassed under subsection (15); then the debtor must establish, as an affirmative defense, either that the debtor cannot pay the debt or that the benefit to the debtor of discharging the debt outweighs the resulting detriment to the nondebtor spouse. If the burden of proof had been placed on Mr. Crosswhite, she contends, the court would have found the debt nondischargeable because Mr. Crosswhite could not show that the benefit to him outweighed the harm to his former wife. Ms. Ginter therefore urges this court to place the burden of proving § 523(a)(15)(B) on the debtor.

Upon consideration of the statutory language, the structure of the statute, the legislative history and the case law, we conclude that there is a clear shift in the burden of proof under § 523(a)(15). The burden of proving initially that she holds a subsection (15) claim against the debtor should be borne by the creditor (nondebtor/former spouse). To make that showing, the creditor must establish that the debt is within the purview of subsection (15) by demonstrating that it does not fall under § 523(a)(5) and that it nevertheless was incurred by the debtor in the course of the divorce or in connection with a divorce decree or similar agreement. Once that showing has been established, the burden of proving that he falls within either of the two exceptions to nondischargeability rests with the debtor. In short, once the creditor's initial proof is made, the debt is excepted from discharge and the debtor is responsible for the debt unless either of the two exceptions, subpart (A), the "ability to pay" test, or (B), the "detriment" test, can be proven by the debtor.

* * *

It is true that the burden-of-proof analysis is more complex under subpart (B) because the court must consider the equity of the discharge by weighing its effect on each party. * * * To be sure, each party must come forward with the information necessary to make that final assessment: The debtor alone can show how beneficial the discharge of that debt would be; the creditor alone can demonstrate how detrimental the discharge of that debt would be. Nevertheless, the statute clearly places the ultimate burden on the debtor to prove to the court, in the manner of an affirmative defense, that the debt should be discharged under subpart (A) because he is unable to pay or under subpart (B) because the benefit to him outweighs the harm to the creditor.

* * *

2.

Application of these principles to the case before us is no easy task. As the bankruptcy court noted at some length in its thoughtful opinion, § 523(a)(15) is a difficult provision to apply in the practical setting of bankruptcy administration. Yet, it embodies important Congressional policy determinations that we are bound to acknowledge and to enforce. As the bankruptcy court and, in turn, the district court grappled with the jello-like statutory language, both appeared to acknowledge, at one point, that the burden of establishing the exception is on the debtor. However, a reading of both opinions in their entirety leaves us with grave doubt as to whether abstract verbalization of the correct standard actually was applied in the courts' analyses. Rather, it appears to us that these courts may well have placed improperly the burden of satisfying the test under § 523(a)(15)(B) on the creditor, Ms. Ginter, rather than on the debtor, Mr. Crosswhite.

* * * Both courts quite correctly understood that each party has the responsibility to supply the information within its exclusive control to the court in order that the court may engage in the comparative analysis of the circumstances of the debtor and the creditor called for by subpart (B). But they do not seem to have placed the ultimate burden of persuasion on the debtor as the subpart requires.

The courts' failure to place the ultimate burden of persuasion on the debtor, Mr. Crosswhite, may stem in part from the bankruptcy court's exclusive focus on what it termed the "economic" considerations, a term the court left largely undefined. We agree that the appropriate inquiry under subpart (B) is the economic impact that the exception of these debts would have on the debtor and the creditor, but we believe that this economic impact must take into consideration the clear intent of the Congress, in enacting § 523(a)(15), to broaden the types of marital debts that are nondischargeable beyond those described in subsection (a)(5). * * * The Bankruptcy Code, by adding § 523(a)(15), has set forth two subsections that are mutually exclusive: Subsection (5) encompasses alimony, maintenance and support, and subsection (15) applies only to debts "not of a kind described in paragraph (5)." Both bankruptcy provisions except marital debts from discharge, however, and together they were intended by the Congress "to rectify the perceived inequity resulting in many cases decided under § 523(a)(5)." Bernice B. Donald & Jennie D. Latta, *The Dischargeability of Property Settlement and Hold Harmless Agreements in Bankruptcy: An Overview of § 523(a)(15)*, 31 Fam. L.Q. 409, 414 (1997). In light of the Congress' desire to uphold a state court's effort to effect economic justice between the parties to a marriage, bankruptcy courts must consider this clear intent when making the economic determination required by subpart (B).

For this reason, we cannot agree with the proposition, expressed succinctly by the district court, that the bankruptcy court's judgment, which "appears to be harsh," and "rewards [the debtor's] irresponsibility," was "mandated by Congress." Congress, by enacting § 523(a)(15), made it clear that, even if the state courts did not use the traditional devices of alimony and support, the long-term responsibilities of the debtor to those with whom he once had a familial relationship and to those who are dependent upon him because of that familial relationship are economic factors that must be weighed. Here, the court failed to require Mr. Crosswhite to demonstrate whether "the benefit to Debtor * * * outweighs the detriment to Plaintiff."[14] Subparts (A) and (B) are

[14] Concerning Mr. Crosswhite's financial situation, we note that the record reflects that Mr. Crosswhite is a self-employed auto mechanic. He lives in the marital home with his girlfriend; he gives her his income and she makes up the deficiency in the monthly bills. Under the subpart (A) analysis, the bankruptcy court criticized Mr. Crosswhite for remaining self-employed and for choosing "a lifestyle that cannot be sustained without the continual financial assistance of third parties." The court concluded:

> Instead of working for someone else who would pay him enough money to provide for himself and pay his debts, Debtor has chosen to remain self-employed in order to pursue a business that has historically been unprofitable and which will continue to be so for the foreseeable future. Debtor is reasonably capable of earning more, if he took advantage of the opportunities available to him. Debtor has failed to prove that he does not have the ability to pay his debts to Plaintiff.

In the subpart (B) analysis, however, although the bankruptcy court again referenced Mr. Crosswhite's "suboptimal employment" and "somewhat parasitic existence," it did

two separate tests; however, the debtor has the burden of proof with respect to each. We therefore must vacate the decision of the district court and remand the case to that court with instructions to remand it to the bankruptcy court for new factual findings made under the proper burden of proof.

D.

Ms. Ginter also contends that the bankruptcy court misapplied the factors it used in the "totality of circumstances" test when balancing the equities under § 523(a)(15)(B). In particular, she asserts that the bankruptcy court's benefits-detriments analysis was incorrect because it took into account her new husband's significant contribution to her financial improvements but failed to consider the financial contribution made by the debtor's "spousal equivalent," his live-in girlfriend. According to Ms. Ginter, Mr. Crosswhite's deliberate failure to pay his property settlement obligations has created personal and financial hardships on her and on their children. She notes that she works full time as a sales assistant, that she earns about $25,000 to support herself and the debtor's two children, and that she must live in a mobile home while he lives in the family residence. In her view, Congress clearly intended such debts to be nondischargeable unless the debtor, not the nondebtor, proved otherwise, and the record clearly shows that the debtor did not accomplish such a showing.

We appreciate the difficult role that this statute imposes on courts that are charged with applying that equitable balancing test. Bankruptcy courts have expressed their frustration over the lack of guidance from Congress with respect to this responsibility for balancing the benefit and the detriment in order to reach an equitable resolution. In an effort to meet this difficult responsibility, the bankruptcy courts have developed a "totality of the circumstances" test as the general method for weighing benefit and detriment; however, they use a number of different approaches for applying that umbrella test.[16]

not reconsider the factor so important under subpart (A)—that Mr. Crosswhite "is reasonably capable of earning more." Nor (as we discuss later) did the bankruptcy court consider such other factors as the financial contributions of Mr. Crosswhite's live-in girlfriend.

[16] Some courts, like the bankruptcy court in this case, follow a finances-based test; others incorporate intangible non-economic factors into their analyses. Some bankruptcy courts count a spouse's contributions under subpart (B). Some count the contributions of live-in companions on the ground that all income that is part of the debtor's household should be considered when weighing the equities. Other courts focus only on the debtor and creditor and do not take into consideration a spouse's or companion's

In this case, we need not set forth in detail an exhaustive methodology applicable in each and every case. Indeed, the equitable nature of the inquiry renders futile an attempt to impose such a universal formula. We believe that the bankruptcy court set the correct course when it adopted a "totality of the circumstances" approach to its inquiry. Its later deviation from that course, when it omitted from its analysis an evaluation of factors that could have a real impact on the actual overall economic condition of Mr. Crosswhite, compounded its earlier failure to place upon him the ultimate burden of qualifying for the exception. The bankruptcy court determined that it ought not take into account the contribution of his live-in girlfriend to his economic condition. However, economic interdependence can indeed result in a significant alteration of economic realities.[17] To the extent that her contribution to household living expenses actually improved Mr. Crosswhite's economic picture, it was not, we believe, a factor that ought to have been eliminated from any consideration.

CONCLUSION

Because the bankruptcy court did not take into account all of the factors that it ought to have weighed and because it did not place the ultimate burden of establishing the § 523(a)(15)(B) exception on the debtor, we must vacate the decision of the district court and remand the case to that court with instructions to remand it to the bankruptcy court for new factual findings made under the proper burden of proof.

MANION, Circuit Judge, dissenting.

I agree with much of the court's thorough analysis, but I differ on a couple of important points that lead me to a different conclusion. Thus, I respectfully dissent.

Resolving this appeal is problematic because not only do we face issues of first impression in any circuit court, but the debtor, who prevailed in the bankruptcy court, did not defend his victory in the

---

income. There is disagreement, as well, about whether the court should take into account the parties' future possible income and expenses in its balancing. * * *

[17] We leave to the bankruptcy judge the task of determining whether there has been a sufficient degree of economic interdependence to have altered Mr. Crosswhite's economic situation. In arriving at this judgment, the bankruptcy judge ought to consider such factors as the period of time the individuals have lived as a single economic unit and the degree to which they have commingled their assets.

district court or here. So we have only the appellant's brief and the lower court opinions to help us decide this appeal.

I fully agree with the court and both lower courts on the burden of proof. * * *

Under the balancing required by subsection (a)(15)(B), there are three possible outcomes: the creditor's detriment outweighs the debtor's benefit; the creditor's detriment equals the debtor's benefit; or the creditor's detriment is less than the debtor's benefit. The statute's text makes clear that only in the third case would the debt be dischargeable under (a)(15)(B) because the debtor's "benefit" must "outweigh" the creditor's "detrimental consequences." This determination depends mostly on how the bankruptcy court weighs the facts and circumstances of the case. While the debtor has the burden of proving that the harms balance in his favor, most of the analysis must focus on what the bankruptcy court actually found.

Both of the lower courts stated the appropriate burden of proof, but this court remands because it questions whether they actually applied that burden. I conclude that they did apply the burden they recited, leaving the key question of whether the bankruptcy court abused its discretion in balancing the harms under (a)(15)(B) in favor of Crosswhite. In my view it did not, and therefore I would affirm. Even if one considers Crosswhite's girlfriend's contribution—which as I address below I would not—his economic position is still worse than Ginter's. * * * Under this statute, who bears the burden of proof tells us who wins ties. Because of the way the law is written, this is not even a close case, much less a tie.

Back to Crosswhite's girlfriend. The court concludes that the bankruptcy court erred by not considering the income of his live-in girlfriend as part of the totality of the circumstances that had to be weighed. There is no question that the income of a debtor's new spouse should be considered just as the income of a creditor's new spouse should be. But generally a live-in girlfriend (or boyfriend) is not a "spousal equivalent." Crosswhite's girlfriend can leave him whenever she tires of his "somewhat parasitic existence," and he would have no claim for continued support; that is not true of Ginter's new husband. There may be unusual situations in which a non-spouse is a "spousal equivalent." *See In re Bicsak*, 207 B.R. 657, 658 (Bkr. W.D.Mo.1997) (involving couple who lived together for five years, were married and had child together but marriage was annulled because wife's prior marriage had not been properly dissolved). The extent that a nonmarriage relationship is marriage-like should be a fact for the bankruptcy court to find, and how that fact weighs into the balance should then be within the bankruptcy court's discretion. Even giving the girlfriend's contribution zero weight—as the bankruptcy court did here—would not necessarily be an abuse of discretion without some specific determination that indicates some extra-marital bond (for example, a child, joint title to real estate, or some contractual obligation). Otherwise, the girlfriend could be gone at a moment's notice with no purse strings attached.

The bankruptcy court's finding that Crosswhite did not satisfy the requirements of § 523(a)(15)(A) is not before us because Crosswhite did not contest this appeal in this court or the district court, much less file a cross-appeal. But given the court's remand, I question the bankruptcy court's imputing of potentially earned income to Crosswhite. This appears to be wrong as a matter of law but the court seems to leave open the question of whether under the balancing of harms analysis of § 523(a)(15)(B), the bankruptcy court could or should impute to a debtor income he could earn if he were not engaged in "suboptimal employment." * * * It is certainly possible, even likely, that someone else with comparable skills could obtain a job paying considerably more than Crosswhite earns. But the cold fact is that Crosswhite does not have such a job, which is probably why he is in bankruptcy rather than paying off his debts. Perhaps he works for himself because he cannot work for others; this raises issues of Crosswhite's personality, disposition, and work ethic, which would have to be put in the record. And because under (a)(15)(B) the bankruptcy court must look into the totality of the circumstances, if Crosswhite's potential employment is to be considered, so would Ginter's and her new husband's potential for more income. Inquiring into what Crosswhite could earn invites multiple layers of speculation. Moreover, most people are engaged in "suboptimal employment" if that term means nothing more than that they could earn more doing something else (or in addition to) what they actually do. * * * It would be a different issue if a debtor intentionally sought employment far below his potential simply to go bankrupt and defraud his creditors; such a finding could amount to bad faith or substantial abuse and justify dismissing the bankruptcy petition all together.

Finally, it is not necessary to delve into the legislative history of § 523(a)(5) and (a)(15) because—at least to the extent necessary to resolve this appeal—the legislative intent and policy are clear from the text of the statute itself. * * * And the statute clearly expresses the legislative intent to treat creditors less favorably under (a)(15) than under (a)(5) because (a)(5) has no exceptions to non-dischargeability while (a)(15)'s two exceptions benefit the debtor at the expense of the creditor. If anything, the legislative history only confirms what is clear from the text. This policy choice is rational: support debts can be considered more important and so it would make no sense to load a debtor up with property settlement debts to the point that he could not pay his support debts. To the extent this policy choice is debatable—and the court notes numerous commentators who disagree with it—the wisdom of that choice is a matter for the political branches.

Certainly the outcome here does not seem fair. Ginter and her new husband, with decent jobs, are easily better off than Crosswhite, who is underemployed and partially dependent on a live-in girlfriend who could be gone tomorrow. But given that equation, "discharging [the] debt would result in a benefit to [Crosswhite] that outweighs the detrimental consequences to [Ginter]." While we can question the efficacy of such a law, we cannot rewrite it to make it more equitable. * * *

I would affirm the lower courts.

Notes

1. Domestic relations lawyers have long taken tax considerations into account when preparing settlement agreements in divorce cases. Obviously, family lawyers need to know a little bankruptcy, too.

2. Recall the discussion of § 522(f) and *Farrey v. Sanderfoot*, 500 U.S. 291, 111 S.Ct. 1825, 114 L.Ed.2d 337 (1991), in Chapter 5 of this casebook. *Farrey* held that a debtor can avoid "the fixing of a lien" that impairs an exemption under § 522(f) only if the debtor had an interest in the property before the lien attached.

3. Sections 523(a)(5) and (a)(15) work in tandem with several other Code provisions we have already seen: § 362(b)(2), which provides an exception to the automatic stay for actions to establish paternity, to obtain or modify a support order, or to collect spousal or child support from non-estate property; § 507(a)(7), which provides a seventh-level priority for spousal or child support; § 522(f)(1), which bars the avoidance of judicial liens securing spousal or child support obligations; and § 547(c)(7), which excepts payments for spousal or child support from preference avoidance. Taken together, these provisions make support obligees the most favored creditors in bankruptcy.

6. SECTION 523(a)(6)—WILLFUL AND MALICIOUS INJURIES

Most of the cases brought under § 523(a)(6) fall into two categories—allegations by a secured creditor that the debtor has sold encumbered collateral without authority, and personal injury caused by the debtor to another. Before § 523(a)(9) was enacted in 1984, arguments were sometimes raised that debts for injuries caused by the debtor while driving under the influence were nondischargeable under § 523(a)(6).

C.I.T. FINANCIAL SERVICES, INC. v. POSTA (IN RE POSTA)

United States Court of Appeals, Tenth Circuit, 1989.
866 F.2d 364.

PER CURIAM.

* * *

C.I.T. Financial Services, Inc. appeals the dismissal of its complaint objecting to the discharge in bankruptcy of a debt of Gregory Alyan Posta and Mary Jones Posta. CIT argues that the Postas' debt to CIT, secured by a mobile travel trailer, is nondischargeable under § 523(a)(6) of the Bankruptcy Code, because the Postas sold the trailer in violation of the terms of CIT's security agreement. In dismissing CIT's complaint, the bankruptcy court found that the Postas had not willfully disregarded CIT's rights by selling the trailer and that their debt to CIT was properly dischargeable. On appeal, the district court affirmed. We likewise affirm.

In 1983, the Postas purchased a mobile travel trailer from Washburn Enterprises in Lakewood, Colorado, financing $23,631 of the purchase price through CIT. The Postas executed a security agreement with CIT, granting CIT a security interest in the trailer. The agreement provided that the Postas could not sell, rent, or transfer the trailer, or move it from their home address unless CIT agreed in writing. The bankruptcy court found that neither Mr. nor Mrs. Posta read the security agreement before signing it.

Within a year after this purchase, payments on the trailer began to strain the Postas' finances. The couple determined that they would be unable to meet their other financial obligations and continue to make the payments on the trailer. Consequently, they moved the trailer from their home in Ridgeway, Colorado, to a dealership in Denver, attempting to lease it through the dealer. They also advertised the trailer for sale in Denver newspapers.

On October 7, 1984, the Postas were contacted by Mr. Ronald Swartz, who indicated that he was interested in buying the trailer. Mr. Swartz met with the Postas that day and, after some negotiation, agreed to purchase the trailer. That evening, the parties signed a sales agreement prepared by Mr. Swartz. As provided in the agreement, Mr. Swartz delivered $962.65 in cash to the Postas (representing their equity in the trailer plus the next monthly payment) and a promissory note for $22,245.00 (the remaining balance on their loan from CIT). To secure the note, Mr. Swartz executed a second deed of trust on certain condominium property located in Grand County, Colorado. He also purchased an insurance policy on the trailer, naming the Postas as additional insureds.

Mr. Swartz left that evening with the trailer. He returned the following morning to deliver a copy of the sales agreement and two football tickets which he had promised to Mr. Posta. After that morning, however, neither he nor the trailer were ever seen again. Mr. Swartz defaulted on his payments on the promissory note, and the Postas discovered that Mr. Swartz did not hold record interest in the property subject to the deed of trust securing the note. Despite their efforts, the couple was unable to locate Mr. Swartz at any of the addresses he had given them. They reported the incident to the appropriate authorities and to CIT, and unsuccessfully attempted to recover on the insurance policy covering the trailer. The Postas were then forced to default on their loan payments to CIT, and shortly thereafter they filed for bankruptcy.

CIT instituted the instant action in bankruptcy court on November 20, 1985, objecting to the discharge of the Postas' debt secured by the trailer. CIT alleged that, under § 523(a)(6) of the Bankruptcy Code, the debt was not dischargeable because the Postas had willfully and maliciously converted the travel trailer. * * * After a hearing on the matter, the bankruptcy court ruled that the Postas' sale of the trailer was merely a technical conversion. It found no evidence that the Postas' actions were taken in conscious disregard of the rights of CIT and held that the conversion was not malicious. The district court affirmed on appeal * * *.

* * * The only issue before us is whether the bankruptcy court properly construed the term "malicious" under § 523(a)(6) of the Bankruptcy Code. CIT argues that the Postas' intentional sale of the trailer in violation of the terms of the security agreement was, by its nature, malicious. We disagree.

We begin by examining the relevant provision of the Bankruptcy Code. Section 523(a)(6) of the Code excepts from discharge any debt "for willful and malicious injury by the debtor to another entity or the property of another entity." Such injury includes the conversion of property subject to a creditor's security interest. For a debt to be nondischargeable under this section, however, the debtor's conversion of property must be both "willful" and "malicious." The creditor objecting to the discharge has the burden of proving both of these elements by clear and convincing evidence.

The "willful" element is straightforward. It simply addresses whether the debtor intentionally performed the basic act complained of. "Willful" conduct is conduct that is volitional and deliberate and over which the debtor exercises meaningful control, as opposed to unintentional or accidental conduct. Thus, acts caused by the debtor's negligence or recklessness are not encompassed by this exception.

In this case, there seems to be little question but that the Postas voluntarily and intentionally sold the trailer; so their conduct was "willful." The issue is, instead, whether in doing so, they acted maliciously. CIT asserts that when a debtor intends to do an act which results in harm to his creditor, such conduct is "malicious." Consequently, because the Postas intentionally sold the trailer, and because the sale was in violation of the security agreement and ultimately harmed CIT, CIT contends that the "malicious" element is satisfied. We disagree.

Were we to accept CIT's argument, nearly any intentional conduct would fall within this exception to discharge, and the word "malicious" in this section would be rendered meaningless. Statutes should be construed to give effect to every word Congress has used. Although we agree that conduct which violates the rights of a creditor is wrongful, we refuse to infer that it is, by its very nature, "malicious." Instead, the focus of the "malicious" inquiry is on the debtor's actual knowledge or the reasonable foreseeability that his conduct will result in injury to the creditor, "not on abstract and perhaps moralistic notions of the 'wrongfulness' of the debtor's act." *In re Egan*, 52 B.R. 501, 507 n.4 (Bankr. D.Minn.1985). Thus, the Postas' sale of the trailer was not "malicious" simply because it violated the terms of the security agreement.

Under § 523(a)(6), the debtor's malicious intent can be shown in two ways. In the rare instances in which there is direct evidence that the debtor's conduct was taken with the specific intent to harm the creditor, the malice requirement is easily established. More commonly, however, malicious intent must be demonstrated by evidence that the debtor had knowledge of the creditor's rights and that, with that knowledge, proceeded to take action in violation of those rights. Such knowledge can be inferred from the debtor's experience in the business, his concealment of the sale, or by his admission that he has read and understood the security agreement.

We are not persuaded by CIT's argument that the bankruptcy court misconstrued the term "malicious" as to require actual malice, or a specific intent to harm the creditor. Rather, the court correctly looked to whether the Postas had willfully disregarded the rights of CIT in making the sale. The court noted that the Postas were relatively inexperienced in business matters, that they had difficulty in understanding business concepts, and that they had not read the security agreement. The evidence shows that, at all times, the Postas intended to fulfill their loan obligations to CIT by applying the proceeds of Mr. Swartz' note to the loan. They did not conceal the sale from CIT and, in fact, requested CIT's assistance when it appeared their arrangement with Mr. Swartz had gone sour. We agree with the bankruptcy court that, in light of these facts, at most, all that occurred was a "technical conversion." Technical conversions do not fall within the § 523(a)(6) exception to discharge.

CIT attempts to distinguish this case from other cases involving technical conversions by arguing that, because it did not acquiesce in any way in the Postas' sale of the trailer, the court may not excuse the Postas' disregard of the terms of the security agreement. This attempted distinction is illusory. The issue of a creditor's acquiescence comes into play only in those cases in which the debtor has knowledge of the creditor's limitations on the sale of its collateral but, because of some conduct by the creditor, is led to believe the sale would nevertheless be permissible. In this case, however, the threshold question, as noted above, is whether the Postas had *any* knowledge that the sale would violate the terms of the security agreement. The district court found that the Postas had no knowledge of such terms of the security agreement. It properly concluded that, because they did not knowingly violate CIT's rights by selling the trailer, the Postas' conversion of CIT's property was not "malicious." That CIT did not acquiesce in the sale was therefore irrelevant.

The order of the United States District Court for the District of Colorado is AFFIRMED.

Questions and Problems

1. Assume that the creditor in *Posta* had failed to perfect its security interest under state law. Would that render § 523(a)(6) inapplicable? See *Hardwick v. Petsch (Matter of Petsch)*, 82 B.R. 605 (Bankr. M.D.Fla. 1988).

2. Debtor is the president of a closely held corporation. Bank loaned money to the corporation, secured by the corporation's accounts receivable and backed by Debtor's personal guaranty. Proceeds of accounts receivable were supposed to be deposited into a special bank account and thereby made available to Bank to pay the loan. When the corporation encountered financial problems, however, Debtor diverted proceeds into another account and used the funds to try to keep the business running. Those efforts failed and both Debtor and the corporation ended up in bankruptcy. Can Bank, under § 523(a)(6), block discharge of the amount Debtor diverted? See *Barclays American Business Credit, Inc. v. Long (In re Long)*, 774 F.2d 875 (8th Cir.1985).

3. Debtors borrowed $3,600 from Creditor and gave a security interest in personal property then worth $1,300. Debtors later sold the personalty at a rummage sale, without Creditor's permission, for $120. The fair market value of the property was then $865. If the court finds that Creditor has a nondischargeable claim under § 523(a)(6), what amount is nondischargeable—$120? $865? $1,300? $3,600? See *Friendly Financial Service Mid-City, Inc. v. Modicue (In re Modicue)*, 926 F.2d 452 (5th Cir.1991).

As indicated above, § 523(a)(6) also applies when the debtor has caused personal injury to another person. When injury results from an intentional tort, § 523(a)(6)'s application is straightforward. (Recall *Handeen v. LeMaire*, in Section A of this Chapter.) When the debtor's conduct was reckless or grossly negligent, however, courts have struggled with the phrase "willful and malicious."

One of the early leading cases, *Perkins v. Scharffe*, 817 F.2d 392 (6th Cir.1987), *cert. denied*, 484 U.S. 853, 108 S.Ct. 156, 98 L.Ed.2d 112 (1987), arose out of "absolutely appalling" medical treatment rendered by a doctor in treating a patient's foot infection. The Sixth Circuit characterized the issue as whether § 523(a)(6) "requires an intentional act that results in injury or an act with intent to cause injury." The court concluded that "'willful' means 'deliberate or intentional'" and that "'willful' and 'malicious' requires the intentional doing of an act that necessarily leads to injury." *Id.* at 394. The court quoted Collier's discussion of § 523(a)(6), in support of adopting the "looser standard":

> In order to fall within the exception of § 523(a)(6), the injury to an entity or property must have been willful and malicious. An injury to an entity or property may be a malicious injury within this provision if it was wrongful and without just cause or excessive, even in the absence of personal hatred, spite, or ill-will. The word "willful" means "deliberate or intentional," a deliberate and intentional act which necessarily leads to injury. Therefore, a wrongful act done intentionally, which necessarily produces harm and is without just cause or excuse, may constitute a willful and malicious injury.

Id., quoting 3 Collier on Bankruptcy ¶ 523–111 (15th ed. 1986). The Supreme Court finally took the issue, in a case with facts eerily similar to those in *Perkins*:

KAWAAUHAU v. GEIGER

United States Supreme Court, 1998.
523 U.S. 57, 118 S.Ct. 974, 140 L.Ed.2d 90.

JUSTICE GINSBURG delivered the opinion for a unanimous Court.

Section 523(a)(6) of the Bankruptcy Code provides that a debt "for willful and malicious injury by the debtor to another" is not dischargeable. The question before us is whether a debt arising from a medical malpractice judgment, attributable to negligent or reckless conduct, falls within this statutory exception. We hold that it does not and that the debt is dischargeable.

I

In January 1983, petitioner Margaret Kawaauhau sought treatment from respondent Dr. Paul Geiger for a foot injury. Geiger examined Kawaauhau and admitted her to the hospital to attend to the risk of infection resulting from the injury. Although Geiger knew that intravenous penicillin would have been more effective, he prescribed oral penicillin, explaining in his testimony that he understood his patient wished to minimize the cost of her treatment.

Geiger then departed on a business trip, leaving Kawaauhau in the care of other physicians, who decided she should be transferred to an infectious disease specialist. When Geiger returned, he canceled the transfer and discontinued all antibiotics because he believed the infection had subsided. Kawaauhau's condition deteriorated over the next few days, requiring the amputation of her right leg below the knee.

Kawaauhau, joined by her husband Solomon, sued Geiger for malpractice. After a trial, the jury found Geiger liable and awarded the Kawaauhaus approximately $355,000 in damages. Geiger, who carried no malpractice insurance,[2] moved to Missouri, where his wages were garnished by the Kawaauhaus. Geiger then petitioned for bankruptcy. The Kawaauhaus requested the Bankruptcy Court to hold the malpractice judgment nondischargeable on the ground that it was a debt "for willful and malicious injury" excepted from discharge by § 523(a)(6). The Bankruptcy Court concluded that Geiger's treatment fell far below the appropriate standard of care and therefore ranked as "willful and malicious." Accordingly, the Bankruptcy Court held the debt nondischargeable. In an unpublished order, the District Court affirmed.

A three-judge panel of the Court of Appeals for the Eighth Circuit reversed, and a divided en banc court adhered to the panel's position. Section 523(a)(6)'s exemption from discharge, the en banc court held, is confined to debts "based on what the law has for generations called an intentional tort." On this view, a debt for malpractice, because it is based on conduct that is negligent or reckless, rather than intentional, remains dischargeable.

The Eighth Circuit acknowledged that its interpretation of § 523(a)(6) diverged from previous holdings of the Sixth and Tenth Circuits (citing *Perkins v. Scharffe*, 817 F.2d 392, 394 (CA6), cert. denied, 484 U.S. 853 (1987), and *In re Franklin*, 726 F.2d 606, 610 (CA10 1984)). We granted certiorari to resolve this conflict, and now affirm the Eighth Circuit's judgment.

II

[The Court quoted § 523(a)(6).] The Kawaauhaus urge that the malpractice award fits within this exception because Dr. Geiger inten-

---

[2] Although the record is not clear on this point, it appears that Dr. Geiger was not required by state law to carry medical malpractice insurance.

tionally rendered inadequate medical care to Margaret Kawaauhau that necessarily led to her injury. According to the Kawaauhaus, Geiger deliberately chose less effective treatment because he wanted to cut costs, all the while knowing that he was providing substandard care. Such conduct, the Kawaauhaus assert, meets the "willful and malicious" specification of § 523(a)(6).

We confront this pivotal question concerning the scope of the "willful and malicious injury" exception: Does § 523(a)(6)'s compass cover acts, done intentionally,[3] that cause injury (as the Kawaauhaus urge), or only acts done with the actual intent to cause injury (as the Eighth Circuit ruled)? The words of the statute strongly support the Eighth Circuit's reading.

The word "willful" in (a)(6) modifies the word "injury," indicating that non-dischargeability takes a deliberate or intentional *injury*, not merely a deliberate or intentional *act* that leads to injury. Had Congress meant to exempt debts resulting from unintentionally inflicted injuries, it might have described instead "willful acts that cause injury." Or, Congress might have selected an additional word or words, *i.e.*, "reckless" or "negligent," to modify "injury." Moreover, as the Eighth Circuit observed, the (a)(6) formulation triggers in the lawyer's mind the category "intentional torts," as distinguished from negligent or reckless torts. Intentional torts generally require that the actor intend "the *consequences* of an act," not simply "the act itself." Restatement (Second) of Torts § 8A, comment a, p. 15 (1964) (emphasis added).

The Kawaauhaus' more encompassing interpretation could place within the excepted category a wide range of situations in which an act is intentional, but injury is unintended, *i.e.*, neither desired nor in fact anticipated by the debtor. Every traffic accident stemming from an initial intentional act—for example, intentionally rotating the wheel of an automobile to make a left-hand turn without first checking oncoming traffic—could fit the description. A "knowing breach of contract" could also qualify. A construction so broad would be incompatible with the "well-known" guide that exceptions to discharge "should be confined to those plainly expressed." *Gleason v. Thaw*, 236 U.S. 558, 562 (1915).

---

3 The word "willful" is defined in Black's Law Dictionary as "voluntary" or "intentional." Black's Law Dictionary 1434 (5th ed. 1979). Consistently, legislative reports note that the word "willful" in § 523(a)(6) means "deliberate or intentional." See S. Rep. No. 95-989, p. 79 (1978); H. R. Rep. No. 95-595, p. 365 (1977).

Furthermore, "we are hesitant to adopt an interpretation of a congressional enactment which renders superfluous another portion of that same law." *Mackey v. Lanier Collection Agency & Service, Inc.*, 486 U.S. 825, 837 (1988). Reading § 523(a)(6) as the Kawaauhaus urge would obviate the need for § 523(a)(9), which specifically exempts debts "for death or personal injury caused by the debtor's operation of a motor vehicle if such operation was unlawful because the debtor was intoxicated from using alcohol, a drug, or another substance." See also § 523(a)(12) (exempting debts for "malicious or reckless failure" to fulfill certain commitments owed to a federal depository institutions regulatory agency).[4]

The Kawaauhaus heavily rely on *Tinker v. Colwell*, 193 U.S. 473 (1904), which presented this question: Does an award of damages for "criminal conversation" survive bankruptcy under the 1898 Bankruptcy Act's exception from discharge for judgments in civil actions for "'willful and malicious injuries to the person or property of another'"? The *Tinker* Court held such an award a nondischargeable debt. The Kawaauhaus feature certain statements in the *Tinker* opinion, in particular: "[An] act is willful * * * in the sense that it is intentional and voluntary" even if performed "without any particular malice"; an act that "necessarily causes injury and is done intentionally, may be said to be done willfully and maliciously, so as to come within the [bankruptcy discharge] exception"; the statute exempts from discharge liability for "'a wrongful act, done intentionally, without just cause or excuse'" (quoting from definition of malice in *Bromage v. Prosser*, 4 Barn. & Cress. 247, 107 Eng. Rep. 1051 (K.B. 1825)).

The exposition in the *Tinker* opinion is less than crystalline. Counterbalancing the portions the Kawaauhaus emphasize, the *Tinker* Court repeatedly observed that the tort in question qualified in the common law as trespassory. Indeed, it ranked as "trespass vi et armis." Criminal conversation, the Court noted, was an action akin to a master's "action of trespass and assault * * * for the battery of his servant." *Tinker* thus placed criminal conversation solidly within the traditional intentional tort category, and we so confine its holding. That decision, we clarify, provides no warrant for departure from the current statutory instruction that, to be nondischargeable, the judgment debt must be "for willful and malicious *injury*."

---

[4] Sections 523(a)(9) and (12) were added to the Bankruptcy Code in 1984 and 1990 respectively.

* * *

Finally, the Kawaauhaus maintain that, as a policy matter, malpractice judgments should be excepted from discharge, at least when the debtor acted recklessly or carried no malpractice insurance. Congress, of course, may so decide. But unless and until Congress makes such a decision, we must follow the current direction § 523(a)(6) provides.

* * *

We hold that debts arising from recklessly or negligently inflicted injuries do not fall within the compass of § 523(a)(6). For the reasons stated, the judgment of the Court of Appeals for the Eighth Circuit is

Affirmed.

Questions

1. Given the Court's reading of "willful," what role is left for the additional requirement that the injury be "malicious"?

2. Section 523(a)(9) was added to the Code largely because § 523(a)(6)'s application in drunk driving cases was uncertain. In light of that fact, is the Court's use of § 523(a)(9) a bit disingenuous?

7. SECTION 523(a)(7)—FINES PAYABLE TO GOVERNMENTAL UNITS

The legislative history to the 1978 Code suggests that Congress was thinking primarily about tax penalties in connection with § 523(a)(7). The provision also applies to criminal restitution obligations, however, as the next case demonstrates.

KELLY v. ROBINSON

United States Supreme Court, 1986.
479 U.S. 36, 107 S.Ct. 353, 93 L.Ed.2d 216.

JUSTICE POWELL delivered the opinion of the Court.

We granted review in this case to decide whether restitution obligations, imposed as conditions of probation in state criminal proceedings, are dischargeable in proceedings under Chapter 7 of the Bankruptcy Code.

I

In 1980, Carolyn Robinson pleaded guilty to larceny in the second degree. The charge was based on her wrongful receipt of $9,932.95 in welfare benefits from the Connecticut Department of Income Maintenance. On November 14, 1980, the Connecticut Superior Court sentenced Robinson to a prison term of not less than one year nor more than three years. The court suspended execution of the sentence and placed Robinson on probation for five years. As a condition of probation, the judge ordered Robinson to make restitution to the State of Connecticut Office of Adult Probation (Probation Office) at the rate of $100 per month, commencing January 16, 1981, and continuing until the end of her probation.[2]

On February 5, 1981, Robinson filed a voluntary petition under Chapter 7 of the Bankruptcy Code in the United States Bankruptcy Court for the District of Connecticut. That petition listed the restitution obligation as a debt. On February 20, 1981, the Bankruptcy Court notified both of the Connecticut agencies of Robinson's petition and informed them that April 27, 1981, was the deadline for filing objections to discharge. The agencies did not file proofs of claim or objections to discharge, apparently because they took the position that the bankruptcy would not affect the conditions of Robinson's probation. Thus, the agencies did not participate in the distribution of Robinson's estate. On May 14, 1981, the Bankruptcy Court granted Robinson a discharge. See § 727.

At the time Robinson received her discharge in bankruptcy, she had paid $450 in restitution. On May 20, 1981, her attorney wrote the Probation Office that she believed the discharge had altered the conditions of Robinson's probation, voiding the condition that she pay restitution. Robinson made no further payments.

The Connecticut Probation Office did not respond to this letter until February 1984, when it informed Robinson that it considered the obligation to pay restitution nondischargeable. Robinson responded by filing an adversary proceeding in the Bankruptcy Court, seeking a

---

[2] There is some uncertainty about the total amount Robinson was ordered to pay. Although the judge imposed restitution in a total amount of $9,932.95, five years of payments at $100 a month total only $6,000.

declaration that the restitution obligation had been discharged, as well as an injunction to prevent the State's officials from forcing Robinson to pay.

After a trial, the Bankruptcy Court entered a memorandum and proposed order, concluding that the 1981 discharge in bankruptcy had not altered the conditions of Robinson's probation. The court adopted the analysis it had applied in a similar case decided one month earlier, *In re Pellegrino (Pellegrino* v. *Division of Criminal Justice)*, 42 B.R. 129 (Bankr.D.Conn.1984). In *Pellegrino*, the court began with the Bankruptcy Code's definitional sections. First, [§ 101(12)] defines a "debt" as a "liability on a claim." In turn, [§ 101(5)] defines a "claim" as a "right to payment, whether or not such right is reduced to judgment, liquidated, unliquidated, fixed, contingent, matured, unmatured, disputed, undisputed, legal, equitable, secured, or unsecured." Finally, [§ 101(10)] defines a "creditor" as an "entity that has a claim against the debtor that arose at the time of or before the order for relief concerning the debtor."

The *Pellegrino* court then examined the statute under which the Connecticut judge had sentenced the debtor to pay restitution. Restitution appears as one of the conditions of probation enumerated in Conn. Gen. Stat. § 53a–30 (1985). Under that section, restitution payments are sent to the Probation Office. The payments then are forwarded to the victim. Although the Connecticut penal code does not provide for enforcement of the probation conditions by the victim, it does authorize the trial court to issue a warrant for the arrest of a criminal defendant who has violated a condition of probation. Because the Connecticut statute does not allow the victim to enforce a right to receive payment, the court concluded that neither the victim nor the Probation Office had a "right to payment," and hence neither was owed a "debt" under the Bankruptcy Code. It argued: "Unlike an obligation which arises out of a contractual, statutory or common law duty, here the obligation is rooted in the traditional responsibility of a state to protect its citizens by enforcing its criminal statutes and to rehabilitate an offender by imposing a criminal sanction intended for that purpose." The court acknowledged the tension between its conclusion and the Code's expansive definition of debt, but found an exception to the statutory definition in "the long-standing tradition of restraint by federal courts from interference with traditional functions of state governments." The court concluded that, even if the probation condition was a debt subject to bankruptcy jurisdiction, it was nondischargeable under § 523(a)(7) of the Code. That subsection provides that a discharge in bankruptcy does not affect any debt that "is for a fine, penalty, or forfeiture payable to and for the benefit of a governmental unit, and is not compensation for actual pecuniary loss."

The court also concluded that the purpose of the restitution condition was "to promote the rehabilitation of the offender, not to compensate the victim." It specifically rejected the argument that the restitution must be deemed compensatory because the amount precisely matched the victim's loss. It noted that the state statute allows an offender to "make restitution of the fruits of his offense or make restitution, in an amount he can afford to pay or provide in a suitable manner, for the loss or damage caused thereby." In its view, the Connecticut statute focuses "upon the offender and not on the victim, and * * * restitution is part of the criminal penalty rather than compensation for a victim's actual loss." Thus, the Bankruptcy Court held that the bankruptcy discharge had not affected the conditions of Pellegrino's probation. The United States District Court for the District of Connecticut adopted the Bankruptcy Court's proposed dispositions of *Pellegrino* and this case without alteration.

The Court of Appeals for the Second Circuit reversed. It first examined the Code's definition of debt. Although it recognized that most courts had reached the opposite conclusion, the court decided that a restitution obligation imposed as a condition of probation is a debt. It relied on the legislative history of the Code that evinced Congress' intent to broaden the definition of "debt" from the much narrower definition of the Bankruptcy Act of 1898. The court also noted that anomalies might result from a conclusion that such an obligation is not a debt. Most importantly, nondebt status would deprive a State of the opportunity to participate in the distribution of the debtor's estate.

Having concluded that restitution obligations are debts, the court turned to the question of dischargeability. The court stated that the appropriate Connecticut agency probably could have avoided discharge of the debt if it had objected under §§ 523(a)(2) or 523(a)(4) of the Code. As no objections to discharge were filed, the court concluded that the State could rely only on § 523(a)(7), the subsection that provides for automatic nondischargeability for certain debts. The court then looked to the text of the Connecticut statute to determine whether Robinson's probation condition was "compensation for actual pecuniary loss" within the meaning of § 523(a)(7). But where the Bankruptcy Court had considered the entire state probation system, the Court of Appeals focused only on the language that allows a restitution order to be assessed "for the loss or damage caused [by the crime]." The court thought this language compelled the conclusion that the probation condition was "compensation for actual pecuniary loss." It held, therefore, that this particular condition of Robinson's probation was not protected from discharge by § 523(a)(7). Accordingly, it reversed the District Court.

We granted the State's petition for a writ of certiorari. * * * We reverse.

II

The Court of Appeals' decision focused primarily on the language of §§ 101 and 523 of the Code. Of course, the "starting point in every case involving construction of a statute is the language itself." *Blue Chip Stamps* v. *Manor Drug Stores*, 421 U.S. 723, 756 (1975) (POWELL, J., concurring). But the text is only the starting point. * * * In this case, we must consider the language of §§ 101 and 523 in light of the history of bankruptcy court deference to criminal judgments and in light of the interests of the States in unfettered administration of their criminal justice systems.

A

* * *

Congress enacted the Code in 1978 against the background of an established judicial exception to discharge for criminal sentences, including restitution orders, an exception created in the face of a statute drafted with considerable care and specificity.

Just last Term we declined to hold that the new Bankruptcy Code silently abrogated another exception created by courts construing the old Act. In *Midlantic National Bank* v. *New Jersey Dept. of Environmental Protection*, 474 U.S. 494 (1986), a trustee in bankruptcy asked us to hold that the 1978 Code had implicitly repealed an exception to the trustee's abandonment power. Courts had created that exception out of deference to state health and safety regulations, a consideration comparable to the States' interests implicated by this case. We stated:

> "The normal rule of statutory construction is that if Congress intends for legislation to change the interpretation of a judicially created concept, it makes that intent specific. The Court has followed this rule with particular care in construing the scope of bankruptcy codifications. If Congress wishes to grant the

trustee an extraordinary exemption from nonbankruptcy law, 'the intention would be clearly expressed, not left to be collected or inferred from disputable considerations of convenience in administering the estate of the bankrupt.'" *Id.* at 501 (quoting *Swarts* v. *Hammer*, 194 U.S. 441, 444 (1904)) (citations omitted).

B

Our interpretation of the Code also must reflect the basis for this judicial exception, a deep conviction that federal bankruptcy courts should not invalidate the results of state criminal proceedings. The right to formulate and enforce penal sanctions is an important aspect of the sovereignty retained by the States. This Court has emphasized repeatedly "the fundamental policy against federal interference with state criminal prosecutions." *Younger* v. *Harris*, 401 U.S. 37, 46 (1971). The Court of Appeals nevertheless found support for its holding in the fact that Connecticut officials probably could have ensured continued enforcement of their court's criminal judgment against Robinson had they objected to discharge under § 523(c). Although this may be true in many cases, it hardly justifies an interpretation of the 1978 Act that is contrary to the long-prevailing view that "fines and penalties are not affected by a discharge," 1A Collier on Bankruptcy ¶ 17.13, p. 1610 (14th ed. 1978).

Moreover, reliance on a right to appear and object to discharge would create uncertainties and impose undue burdens on state officials. In some cases it would require state prosecutors to defend particular state criminal judgments before federal bankruptcy courts. As JUSTICE BRENNAN has noted, federal adjudication of matters already at issue in state criminal proceedings can be "an unwarranted and unseemly duplication of the State's own adjudicative process." *Perez* v. *Ledesma*, 401 U.S. 82, 121 (1971) (opinion concurring in part and dissenting in part).

Also, as Robinson's attorney conceded at oral argument, some restitution orders would not be protected from discharge even if the State did appear and enter an objection to discharge. For example, a judge in a negligent homicide case might sentence the defendant to probation, conditioned on the defendant's paying the victim's husband compensation for the loss the husband sustained when the defendant killed his wife. It is not clear that such a restitution order would fit the terms of any of the exceptions to discharge listed in § 523 other than § 523-(a)(7). Thus, this interpretation of the Code would do more than force state prosecutors to defend state criminal judgments in federal bankruptcy court. In some cases, it could lead to federal remission of judgments imposed by state criminal judges.

This prospect, in turn, would hamper the flexibility of state criminal judges in choosing the combination of imprisonment, fines, and restitution most likely to further the rehabilitative and deterrent goals of state criminal justice systems. We do not think Congress lightly would limit the rehabilitative and deterrent options available to state criminal judges.

* * * This Court has recognized that the States' interest in administering their criminal justice systems free from federal interference is one of the most powerful of the considerations that should influence a court considering equitable types of relief. This reflection of our federalism also must influence our interpretation of the Bankruptcy Code in this case.

III

In light of the established state of the law—that bankruptcy courts could not discharge criminal judgments—we have serious doubts whether Congress intended to make criminal penalties "debts" within the meaning of [§ 101(5)]. But we need not address that question in this case, because we hold that § 523(a)(7) preserves from discharge any condition a state criminal court imposes as part of a criminal sentence.

* * * On its face, § 523(a)(7) certainly does not compel the conclusion reached by the Court of Appeals, that a discharge in bankruptcy voids restitution orders imposed as conditions of probation by state courts. Nowhere in the House and Senate Reports is there any indication that this language should be read so intrusively.[13] If Congress had intended, by § 523(a)(7) or by any other provision, to discharge state criminal sentences, "we can be certain that there would

[13] * * *

It seems likely that the limitation of § 523(a)(7) to fines assessed "for the benefit of a governmental unit" was intended to prevent application of that subsection to wholly private penalties such as punitive damages. See H.R. Doc. No. 93–137, pt. 2, pp. 116, 141 (1973). As for the reference to "compensation for actual pecuniary loss," the Senate Report indicates that the main purpose of this language was to prevent § 523(a)(7) from being applied to tax penalties. S. Rep. No. 95–989 at 79, *reprinted in* 1978 U.S.C.C.A.N. at 5865.

* * *

have been hearings, testimony, and debate concerning consequences so wasteful, so inimical to purposes previously deemed important, and so likely to arouse public outrage," *TVA* v. *Hill*, 437 U.S. 153, 209 (1978) (POWELL, J., dissenting).

Our reading of § 523(a)(7) differs from that of the Second Circuit. On its face, it creates a broad exception for all penal sanctions, whether they be denominated fines, penalties, or forfeitures. Congress included two qualifying phrases; the fines must be both "to and for the benefit of a governmental unit," and "not compensation for actual pecuniary loss." Section 523(a)(7) protects traditional criminal fines; it codifies the judicially created exception to discharge for fines. We must decide whether the result is altered by the two major differences between restitution and a traditional fine. Unlike traditional fines, restitution is forwarded to the victim, and may be calculated by reference to the amount of harm the offender has caused.

In our view, neither of the qualifying clauses of § 523(a)(7) allows the discharge of a criminal judgment that takes the form of restitution. The criminal justice system is not operated primarily for the benefit of victims, but for the benefit of society as a whole. Thus, it is concerned not only with punishing the offender, but also with rehabilitating him. Although restitution does resemble a judgment "for the benefit of" the victim, the context in which it is imposed undermines that conclusion. The victim has no control over the amount of restitution awarded or over the decision to award restitution. Moreover, the decision to impose restitution generally does not turn on the victim's injury, but on the penal goals of the State and the situation of the defendant. * * *

This point is well illustrated by the Connecticut statute under which the restitution obligation was imposed. The statute authorizes a judge to impose any of eight specified conditions of probation, as well as "any other conditions reasonably related to his rehabilitation." Conn. Gen. Stat. § 53a–30(a)(9) (1985). Clause (4) of that section authorizes a judge to require that the defendant

> "make restitution of the fruits of his offense or make restitution, in an amount he can afford to pay or provide in a suitable manner, for the loss or damage caused thereby and the court may fix the amount thereof and the manner of performance."

This clause does not require imposition of restitution in the amount of the harm caused. Instead, it provides for a flexible remedy tailored to the defendant's situation.

Because criminal proceedings focus on the State's interests in rehabilitation and punishment, rather than the victim's desire for compensation, we conclude that restitution orders imposed in such proceedings operate "for the benefit of" the State. Similarly, they are not assessed "for * * * compensation" of the victim. The sentence following a criminal conviction necessarily considers the penal and rehabilitative interests of the State. Those interests are sufficient to place restitution orders within the meaning of § 523(a)(7).

In light of the strong interests of the States, the uniform construction of the old Act over three-quarters of a century, and the absence of any significant evidence that Congress intended to change the law in this area, we believe this result best effectuates the will of Congress. Accordingly, the decision of the Court of Appeals for the Second Circuit is

Reversed.

JUSTICE MARSHALL, with whom JUSTICE STEVENS joins, dissenting.

Petitioners failed to assert timely objections to the discharge of respondent Robinson's restitution debt, and the majority goes to considerable lengths to excuse this default. Respondent concedes that the restitution obligation would not have been discharged had petitioners objected in a timely fashion. * * *

The Court charitably attributes petitioners' inaction to the fact that from the start petitioners took the position they assert here. But their representations at oral argument suggest only that they failed to object because "state agencies were admittedly somewhat confused on how to handle it" and were "a little perplexed because this was the first time it happened." Petitioners seek a broad construction of the statute to excuse their confusion-induced waiver of the right to object and thereby guarantee that Robinson's restitution obligation would not be discharged. In my opinion, however, the statute cannot fairly be read to arrive at the result the majority reaches today.

The Court concludes that a criminal restitution obligation is nondischargeable under § 523(a)(7) because it is "a fine, penalty, or forfeiture payable to and for the benefit of a governmental unit, and is not compensation for actual pecuniary loss." I find unconvincing the majority's conclusion that the criminal restitution order at issue here is not "compensation for actual pecuniary loss."[2] While restitution imposed as a condition of probation under the Connecticut statute is in part a penal sanction, it is also intended to compensate victims for their injuries. * * * Were the restitution order purely penal, the statute would not connect the amount of restitution to the damage imposed. Tying the amount of restitution to the amount of actual damage sustained by the victim strongly suggests that the payment is meant to compensate the victim. This comports with the theory underlying restitution sanctions. Restitution is not simply a punishment that incidentally compensates the victim. Indeed, compensation is an essential element of a restitution scheme * * *.

Nor do I accept that we can avoid the consequences of respondent's discharge in bankruptcy by finding that the restitution obligation was not a "debt." First, the scope of debts under the Code is expansive. "Debt" is defined in [§ 101(12)] as "liability on a claim," and "claim" is defined in [§ 101(5)] as a "right to payment." The legislative history of the Code indicates that "claim" was to be given the "broadest possible definition." H.R. Rep. No. 95–595 at 309, *reprinted in* 1978 U.S.C.C.A.N. at 6266; S. Rep. No. 95–989 at 22, *reprinted in* 1978 U.S.C.C.A.N. at 5808. In light of the broad scope of "debt" under the Code, I agree with the Court of Appeals that the Probation Office had a right to payment, notwithstanding "that the right is enforceable by the threat of revocation of probation and incarceration rather than by the threat of levy and execution on the debtor's property. The right is not the less cognizable because the obligor must suffer loss of freedom rather than loss of property upon failure to pay."[4]

The definition of "debt" is intentionally broad not only to ensure the debtor a meaningful discharge but also to guarantee as many

[2] * * * The majority contends that "Congress enacted the Code in 1978 against the background of an established judicial exception to discharge for criminal sentences," and that Congress should not be deemed to abrogate judicially created law unless it makes explicit the intent to do so. But, far from abrogating judicially created law making fines and penalties nondischargeable as a general matter, Congress has codified that law *and* added the requirements of § 523(a)(7). The historical basis of the exception does not negate the additional limitations expressed in the statute.

[4] Though Connecticut does not permit the victim to enforce the restitution order as a civil judgment, other jurisdictions do. Under such statutes, it would be even more difficult to argue that a criminal restitution order does not create a "right to payment" and is consequently not a "debt."

creditors as possible the right to participate in the distribution of the property of the estate. * * * As the Court of Appeals observed, a conclusion that the restitution obligation was not a debt "would produce the anomalous result that no holder of a right to restitution could participate in the bankruptcy proceeding or receive any distributions of the debtor's assets in liquidation. There is no evidence that Congress intended such a result." On the contrary, Congress plainly intended that fines, penalties, and forfeitures be deemed debts eligible to participate in the distribution of the bankruptcy estate, and the statute provides explicitly for that participation. See § 726(a)(4). The very fact that fines, penalties, and forfeitures are made nondischargeable under § 523(a)(7) indicates that they were deemed "debts"; if they were not debts, they would not be affected by discharge, see § 524, and there would be no need to make them nondischargeable.

* * *

Notes and Questions

1. Although the Court said it was unnecessary to decide whether criminal penalties are "debts," did the Court decide that question anyway?

2. What is the consequence in the context of *Kelly* if criminal restitution obligations are "debts"?

3. Read § 523(c)(1) and look again at §§ 523(a)(2) and (a)(4). Did the Court save the State when the State failed to take available steps to protect itself? Is the Court's explanation on this point convincing?

4. The Court decided in *Pennsylvania Department of Public Welfare v. Davenport*, 495 U.S. 552, 110 S.Ct. 2126, 109 L.Ed.2d 588 (1990), that restitution obligations, imposed by state courts as a condition of probation, are "debts" as defined by § 101(12), and thus are dischargeable in Chapter 13. Does this conclusion in *Davenport* undercut *Kelly*?

Congress legislatively overruled *Davenport* by enacting § 1328(a)(3), but that subsection does not affect *Davenport's* interpretation of "debt."

8. SECTION 523(a)(8)—EDUCATIONAL LOANS

Congress had before it, in 1978, a few anecdotes about debtors who had incurred substantial loan obligations while attending medical or law school, and who had then discharged those obligations in bankruptcy immediately upon graduating and before commencing lucrative jobs. Section 523(a)(8) was included in the Code in order to deal with such cases, continuing the nondischargeability first enacted as part of the Higher Education Act of 1965. Ironically, the subsection does not seem to catch the high-flying debtors Congress had in mind. Rather, it arises most often when debtors have attended trade schools that either have failed to equip their students with marketable skills or have closed their doors before students have completed the course of study.

Section 523(a)(8) has been repeatedly amended, and each change has made it more difficult for debtors to discharge educational loans. Originally, § 523(a)(8) barred the discharge only of governmentally-sponsored loans that had been outstanding for less than five years. Over the years, the subsection was amended to include educational loans from additional sources and to extend, and then eliminate, the time period. During that process, § 1328(a)(2) was also amended to make student loans nondischargeable in Chapter 13.

Section 523(a)(8) permits discharge if its denial would present an "undue hardship" to the debtor or the debtor's dependents. Courts have interpreted this exception quite narrowly, generally following a three-part test:

1) the debtor cannot maintain a minimal standard of living, based on current income and expenses, if required to repay the loan;

2) this circumstance is likely to continue for a significant portion of the loan repayment period; and

3) the debtor has made good faith efforts to repay the loan.

See, e.g., Brunner v. New York State Higher Educational Services Corp., 831 F.2d 395 (2d Cir.1987). *Accord, Matter of Roberson*, 999 F.2d 1132 (7th Cir.1993); *Pennsylvania Higher Education Assistance Agency v. Faish (In re Faish)*, 72 F.3d 298 (3d Cir.1995), *cert. denied*, 518 U.S. 1009, 116 S.Ct. 2532, 135 L.Ed.2d 1055 (1996) (describing and rejecting two other tests in favor of the *Brunner* test).

Problems

1. Debtor graduated from a state university with a degree in psychology, owing $25,000 in student loans. He looked for a position in employment relations, doing job placement testing, for six months but found nothing. Although Debtor can type, he has not looked for a secretarial position. When the university began pressing for him to begin repayment, he scraped together

a few hundred dollars. He filed a bankruptcy petition and seeks to discharge the balance of the loan obligation. What result?

2. Debtor borrowed $100,000 to finance her son's education at a fine private university. She maintained a repayment schedule for about a year, but encountered financial problems and filed bankruptcy. Assuming that Debtor cannot establish undue hardship, is there some other argument she might use to avoid nondischargeability under § 523(a)(8)? Compare *In re Pelkowski*, 990 F.2d 737 (3d Cir.1993), with *Northwestern University Student Loan Office v. Behr (In re Behr),* 80 B.R. 124 (Bankr.N.D.Iowa 1987).

9. ISSUE PRECLUSION

Principles of issue preclusion, applicable in other cases, are also applicable in bankruptcy. In *Grogan v. Garner*, 498 U.S. 279, 111 S.Ct. 654, 112 L.Ed.2d 755 (1991), Creditor sued Debtor in state court for fraud in connection with the sale of corporate securities, proved the case under a preponderance of the evidence standard, and obtained a judgment. When Debtor filed bankruptcy and sought to discharge the judgment, Creditor argued that collateral estoppel required a holding of nondischargeability under § 523. The issue in *Grogan* was whether the discharge exceptions must be established by a preponderance of the evidence, rather than by clear and convincing evidence. In the course of finding a preponderance standard appropriate, the Supreme Court recognized the applicability of collateral estoppel:

> Our prior cases have suggested, but have not formally held, that the principles of collateral estoppel apply in bankruptcy proceedings under the current Bankruptcy Act [sic]. * * * We now clarify that collateral estoppel principles do indeed apply in discharge exception proceedings pursuant to § 523(a).

Id. at 284–85 n.11, 111 S.Ct. at 658 n.11, 112 L.Ed.2d at 763 n.11.

Issue preclusion requires that: 1) the issue under consideration be identical to that involved in a prior action; 2) the issue was actually litigated in the prior action; and 3) determination of the issue was necessary to the judgment entered in the prior action. See *Sheerin v. Davis (Matter of Davis)*, 3 F.3d 113 (5th Cir.1993). If these requirements are satisfied, then a state court judgment finding that the debtor, for example, obtained the debt by fraud or breached a fiduciary obligation, will preclude the debtor from contesting nondischargeability of the debt under the appropriate subsection of § 523. See *Bush v. Balfour Beatty Bahamas, Ltd. (In re Bush)*, 62 F.3d 1319 (11th Cir.1995) (holding debtor precluded from litigating issue of fraud when "he engaged in dilatory and deliberately obstructive conduct" in earlier state court proceedings, but ultimately chose to suffer a default).

D. EFFECT OF DISCHARGE

1. GENERALLY

Only the debtor's personal liability is affected by bankruptcy; liens that survive bankruptcy can later be enforced against the encumbered property. This doctrine, first established in *Long v. Bullard*, 117 U.S. 617, 6 S.Ct. 917, 29 L.Ed. 1004 (1886), is today reflected in at least two places in the Code. First, § 522(c) provides that liens may be enforced against exempt property after the case. Second, § 524(a) provides an injunction that bars the collection of prepetition debts "as a personal liability of the debtor." As enacted in 1978, § 524(a) provided that discharge enjoined efforts to collect a prepetition debt "as a personal liability of the debtor, or from property of the debtor." The latter phrase was dropped in 1984 to avoid any mistaken belief that discharge prevents postpetition enforcement of valid liens.

Problems

1. Creditor obtained a $5,000 judgment against Debtor on an unsecured loan obligation. Debtor filed a bankruptcy petition, listed the debt owed to Creditor on the schedules, and received a discharge under § 727. Debtor had no nonexempt assets, so Creditor did not file a claim. (See Rule 2002(e).) After the bankruptcy case was closed, Creditor brought suit to collect the debt in state court. Debtor appeared and moved for summary judgment, asserting the discharge. What result? Would the result change if Debtor had not appeared and a default judgment had been entered against Debtor by the state court?

2. Assume the same facts as in Problem # 1, except that Creditor argued in the subsequent state court proceeding that the loan had been procured by fraud and was therefore nondischargeable under § 523(a)(2). What result? See § 523(c)(1).

3. Creditor sustained injuries when Debtor's car jumped the curb and hit Creditor as she was walking on the sidewalk. Debtor filed a bankruptcy petition, listed the debt owed to Creditor on the schedules, and received a discharge under § 727. Debtor had no nonexempt assets, so Creditor did not file a claim. After the bankruptcy case was closed, Creditor sued in state court and argued that the debt was not discharged because Debtor had been intoxicated at the time of the accident. Debtor asserted the discharge injunction. What result?

4. Assume the same facts as in Problem # 3, except that Creditor wants to collect from Debtor's insurance carrier. Debtor, however, must be named as defendant under local rules. Does § 524(a) bar the filing of this suit postbankruptcy? See § 524(e).

5. Debtor, Eugene Andrus, discharged a $20,000 obligation owed to Stanley Stann, who lived two doors away. In a rage, Stann posted a sign in his front yard that read: "GENE ANDRUS IS A DEADBEAT! THIS IS A PUBLIC SERVICE ANNOUNCEMENT!" Has Stann violated § 524(a)? Is this protected speech? See *In re Andrus*, 189 B.R. 413 (N.D.Ill.1995).

6. Debtor wrote a check in payment for goods purchased from Seller. The check bounced and Seller filed a claim in Debtor's subsequent bankruptcy. Seller received a dividend of 10 cents on the dollar and, after closing of the bankruptcy case, filed a state criminal complaint against Debtor for writing a bad check. What result if the criminal statute makes repayment an affirmative defense to the crime? Would the result change if the statute includes no such affirmative defense but the local prosecutor as a matter of policy will not pursue a case if restitution has been made?

7. Can Creditor in Problem # 6 merely telephone Debtor and threaten to initiate criminal proceedings if the balance of the obligation is not paid?

8. Debtor, who was a major shareholder of a Hong Kong company, personally guaranteed the corporation's $24 million obligation to Hong Kong Bank. Debtor came to the United States and filed a Chapter 7 petition. Hong Kong Bank filed a proof of claim in the case and Debtor later received a discharge. Bank then sought to collect from Debtor in Hong Kong. Is that a violation of § 524? If so, what can the U.S. court do about it? See *Hong Kong & Shanghai Banking Corp., Ltd. v. Simon (In re Simon)*, 153 F.3d 991 (9th Cir.1998), *cert. denied*, 525 U.S. 1141, 119 S.Ct. 1032, 143 L.Ed.2d 41 (1999).

2. EFFECT OF DISCHARGE ON EXEMPT PROPERTY

Since a debtor may have only exempt property remaining after the case is over, an important question is whether creditors can reach that property after bankruptcy. Sections 524 and 522(c) address this question. Do you see the influence of *Long v. Bullard* in them?

Problems

Debtor filed a Chapter 7 case in which unsecured creditors received nothing. Debtor exempted all of his household goods, which have negligible value, under § 522(d)(3), and exempted a car, which is worth $2,400, under § 522(d)(2). Debtor received a discharge and the bankruptcy case was closed.

Under § 522(c), which of the following creditors, if any, can use state collection proceedings to levy on the car in order to satisfy prepetition obligations?

1. Local Utility Company, which was owed $150 for electric services.

2. Debtor's ex-wife, who was owed $2,000 for child support for the two months preceding the filing of the case.

3. First National Bank, which was owed $6,000 on an educational loan excepted from discharge under § 523(a)(8).

4. GMAC, which was owed S4,500 and which held a security interest in the car.

5. IRS, which was owed $3,000 and which filed notice of a tax lien four months before Debtor filed bankruptcy.

The following case deals with § 522(c) and its interaction with family support obligations that are nondischargeable under § 523(a)(5).

DAVIS v. DAVIS (MATTER OF DAVIS)

United States Court of Appeals, Fifth Circuit, 1999.
170 F.3d 475 (en banc), *cert. denied*, 120 S.Ct. 67, 145 L.Ed.2d 57 (1999).

EDITH H. JONES, Circuit Judge.

In 1987, Cullen and Karen Davis filed for bankruptcy relief and claimed as their exempt Texas homestead a residence valued at $500,000 which they owned free and clear. Cullen's former wife Sandra obtained a judgment from the bankruptcy court declaring that her $250,000-plus claim for alimony, child support, and maintenance was nondischargeable under § 523(a)(5). To enforce the nondischargeability judgment, Sandra sought turnover relief in the form of an order permitting her to foreclose on Cullen's and Karen's homestead. The bankruptcy court and the district court held that she could not levy on the debtors' homestead because it is protected from execution under Texas law, and § 522(c)(1), a provision of the Bankruptcy Code, did not preempt the debtors' state-law rights. A split panel of this court reversed the lower courts. This case was selected for en banc rehearing because of its importance to federal bankruptcy law and to state exemption rules. We conclude that the lower courts were essentially correct and affirm their judgments denying Sandra the relief she seeks.

FACTUAL AND PROCEDURAL HISTORY

When Sandra and Cullen divorced in 1968, they executed a property settlement, support and child custody agreement, and divorce judgment (collectively "divorce judgment"), and Cullen agreed to make monthly payments to Sandra through January 1, 1991, with certain contingent payments thereafter. In 1979, Cullen married Karen Davis. In 1984, Cullen and Karen purchased a house and lot for $750,000.

In 1987, Cullen and Karen stopped making payments to Sandra as required by the divorce judgment and filed for Chapter 7 bankruptcy relief, followed later by conversion to Chapter 11. As has been noted, Cullen's and Karen's costly, lien-free home was claimed as exempt property pursuant to § 522(b)(2)(A) and valued at $500,000 on their schedules.

Armed with the bankruptcy court's judgment that Cullen owed her $300,000 in nondischargeable alimony, maintenance and child support obligations and associated attorneys' fees, Sandra requested that the bankruptcy court seize and sell the debtors' homestead * * *. Because a debtor's homestead is exempt from attachment, execution, or seizure under Tex. Const. art. XVI § 50 and Texas Property Code § 41.002(a), the bankruptcy court determined that the debtors' homestead was not subject to the Texas turnover statute. In so doing, the court rejected Sandra's argument that § 522(c)(1) of the Bankruptcy Code preempted the Texas homestead exemption for nondischargeable debts related to family support as defined in § 523(a)(5). Sandra appealed this ruling to the district court, which affirmed for substantially the same reasons. Sandra timely appealed to this court. We review the lower courts' interpretation of the Bankruptcy Code *de novo*.

THE BANKRUPTCY EXEMPTION STATUTE

At issue in this case are the meaning and preemptive force, if any, of § 522(c), a provision that is part of the Bankruptcy Code's framework for the treatment of exempt property. * * *

* * *

In order to prevail in this case, Sandra must demonstrate that § 522(c) creates a basis for execution on Cullen's homestead to enforce her nondischargeable divorce judgment and that, in enacting this provision, Congress expressly or impliedly preempted the Texas homestead law.

Sandra's argument as to § 522(c) is simple. She reads the section to say that property exempt from payment of discharged debts is "liable" for the types of debts listed as exceptions. But the statute does not say this. Rather, it states that exempt property "is not liable * * * for any debt * * * except * * * [a nondischargeable divorce judgment]." Her argument did not persuade the bankruptcy court, who wrote:

> [Section 522(c)] does not create or establish liability. It enjoins most liability imposed by non-bankruptcy law upon exempt property but does not enjoin all liability for all debts. While it does not impose an injunction against liability on exempt property for § 523(a)(1) or (a)(5) debts, it also does not prevent non-bankruptcy law from imposing such an injunction. Indeed, Texas has done so.

At best, the statutory language is ambiguous from the standpoint of imposing the liability Sandra seeks. Viewed in light of the exemption framework outlined above, however, [the bankruptcy court's] explanation is more plausible than Sandra's. In other words, § 522(c) sought to leave exempt property exposed to post-bankruptcy liability only to the extent it would have been exposed if the bankruptcy had not occurred. This interpretation is the most plausible reading of § 522(c) for several reasons.

Unless Congress expressly legislates otherwise, *see infra*, the policies of bankruptcy law have little bearing on property after it is exempt from the debtor's estate. Such property is no longer available for distribution to creditors, and it is not subject to charge for bankruptcy administrative fees. The debtor may use the exempt property without claims of pre-petition creditors hanging over his head. Of course, Congress deemed necessary some narrow exceptions to this policy of a fresh start for the debtor's exempt property. Thus, purchase money liens on exempt property had to be protected to insure a free flow of credit for purchases of property in markets like residential real estate. Further, tax liens were preserved against exempt property because the contrary result—voiding, e.g., school tax liens on a homestead—is unthinkable. Section 522(c)(2) deals with these claims by simply leaving them unaltered on exempt property. The section does not "create" or "impose" liability, nor does it override or add to state law or federal tax law. The holders of those sorts of unaltered claims would have to proceed via applicable non-bankruptcy collection schemes to realize on their security against exempt property.

Yet the same introductory language to § 522(c) that leaves these liens and underlying state and federal law collection schemes unaltered is argued to have a different meaning with respect to Sandra's nondischargeable divorce judgment. When Sandra contends that the language "creates" a "liability" over and above the protection her lien is accorded in state law, she means that the bankruptcy court can order execution on the homestead to satisfy the divorce judgment. This contention flatly contradicts standard canons of statutory interpretation, for the same language in a single statutory provision cannot have two different meanings.

Sandra's position is also hard to justify if applied to nondischargeable tax debts, the other non-lien debts specified in § 522(c)(1). That is, while a sense of compassion for ex-spouses and children, who are the obligees of nondischargeable family support obligations, provides impetus for "creation" of liability against exempt property, the balance is not so easily struck in favor of "creating" liability of exempt property to pay nondischargeable, non-liened tax debts. Congress might have made the choice to "create" liability of exempt property for both types of nondischargeable debt, but this is unlikely. Taxing authorities benefit from favorable lien laws and other extraordinary enforcement sanctions and penalties, and these prerequisites render additional protections in § 522(c) superfluous. Linguistically, Sandra's argument must furnish the same protection to nondischargeable non-liened tax obligations as she asserts it does for nondischargeable family support obligations. But the mandated linguistic parallelism exposes an illogical result.

Notwithstanding our view that Sandra's construction of § 522(c) creates internal inconsistencies in that provision, bits of legislative history and the import of § 522(f) may be cited to bolster her position. These arguments are not without force, but they are ultimately unconvincing.

In 1990, Congress amended § 522(c)(3), creating an exception designed to prevent "bank insider kingpins" from hiding behind state exemptions to retain their "ill gotten gains." A statement of Senator Biden during Senate consideration of the provision suggests that the proposed legislative language

> specifically pre-empts State homestead laws, which would otherwise allow S&L crooks to retain lavish homes through the excessive protections in some State bankruptcy laws.

136 Cong. Rec. S17,602 (daily ed. Oct. 27, 1990). Isolated statements of individual legislators represent neither the intent of the legislature as a whole nor definitive interpretations of the language enacted by Congress. Further, these particular statements post-date by twelve years the enactment of the prefatory language in § 522(c) with which we are here concerned. For that additional reason, they are not probative.

Sandra also contends that § 522(c)(1) is not intended to serve simply as a lien preservation provision, because that purpose is fulfilled by § 522(f), which provides in part that while a debtor may avoid the fixing of a lien on exempt property, the debtor may not avoid a judicial lien for alimony or family support. If § 522(c)(1) does not have the broader purpose of permitting execution against exempt property, then it is allegedly redundant of the lien preservation function of § 522-(f)(1)(A)(i). But § 522(c) is not duplicative of § 522(f)(1)(A). The former provision states the effect of an exemption on liability for each kind of debt specified, while the latter provision states when a party may avoid the fixing of a pre-petition lien on exempt property. The two sections overlap in part, but their scope and purpose differ.

Nor does the Supreme Court's interpretation of § 522(f) shed light on the relation between that provision and § 522(c), at least not in any sense helpful to Sandra. In *Owen v. Owen*, 500 U.S. 305 (1991), the Supreme Court discussed whether under § 522(f) a state homestead exemption (with its state law limitation) should be treated differently from the federal exemption insofar as the § 522(f) federal lien avoidance provision is concerned. The Court concluded that "nothing in the text of § 522(f) remotely justifies treating the two categories of exemptions differently." *Id.* at 313. In this case, the provision in § 522(c)(1) for continuing liability for certain debts applies equally to both federal and state exemption schemes; in each scenario, liability persists after bankruptcy to the same extent it did before. It is only with respect to the enforcement of such liability, a matter which Congress has left to state mechanisms, that the results differ.

A holistic reading of § 522(c)(1) undermines Sandra's theory that the provision is literally self-executing. She has confused her right with her remedy. This error is exposed by applying her reasoning to other debts that § 522(c) preserves notwithstanding property exemptions, i.e. certain tax debts, federal depository regulators' debts, and debts already secured by a valid lien. If Sandra's reading of § 522(c) is correct, then a homestead could be sold to repay non-liened tax debt, made nondischargeable according to § 523(a)(1), or indeed to pay off an obligation owed to the FDIC without recourse to federal or state lien or homestead protection laws. The impact of such a construction would put the preferred creditors in a better position after the debtor has filed bankruptcy than before and may create an incentive for filing involuntary bankruptcies. In effect, Sandra's proffered construction of § 522(c) does not merely withhold any special protection offered by bankruptcy law, but overrides non-bankruptcy law and has the effect of denying the debtor even exemptions that would have been available outside of bankruptcy. Further, this interpretation seriously disadvantages a debtor subject to the listed obligations, and it actively discourages a large number of potential debtors who are faced with the types of obligations excepted from § 522(c) from seeking bankruptcy relief. Congress surely would not have reached this consequential result without legislating more explicitly.

For all these reasons, we conclude that § 522(c)(1) does not "create" "liability" of exempt property for specified debts following bankruptcy. Instead, the section permits creditors holding such claims to proceed against the property after bankruptcy based on the rights and remedies they would have had under state law if bankruptcy had not been filed.

PREEMPTION

To prevail in her approach to § 522(c), Sandra must show that it preempts Texas law, thus subjecting Cullen's homestead to seizure and sale to satisfy her nondischargeable divorce judgment, despite the express prohibition on such foreclosure contained in the Texas constitution and statutes.

* * * Sandra has attempted to demonstrate (1) express preemption; (2) that §§ 523(a)(5) and 522(c) of the Bankruptcy Code create so pervasive a set of regulations as to impliedly preempt state laws regarding exempt property; and (3) that § 522(c) conflicts irreconcilably with the Texas homestead exemption. Express preemption is precluded by our rejection of Sandra's proffered interpretation of § 522(c).

The Bankruptcy Code's "policy" of strengthening enforcement of family support obligations is a weak reed on which to support implied preemption. Although § 522(c) entitles these obligations to special status against property otherwise exempt in bankruptcy, neither that provision nor § 523(a)(5), the provision for nondischargeability of family support obligations, which § 522(c) incorporates, expresses the full intent of the Code. A debtor who owes family support obligations is afforded a great deal of latitude and protection. First, the filing of the bankruptcy case automatically stays payments of support obligations, as it does all other payments to pre-petition creditors. *See* § 362(a). An ex-spouse deprived of certain family support payments must file an adversary proceeding in bankruptcy court to enforce nondischargeability, and even then, the court may order reduction of certain payments if it finds that the defaulting spouse would suffer "hardship." *See* §§ 523(c), 523(a)(15). A debtor may obtain a Chapter 7 discharge or confirm a Chapter 13 plan without being current in family support obligations. Bankruptcy law presently contains neither a pervasive or consistent approach toward family support obligations.

Reliance on the exemption provision of the Code as a source of implied preemption is also misplaced. Congress specifically preserved state exemptions under § 522(b), rejecting a proposal for uniform federal exemptions. Congress allowed states to define the existence and limits of exemptions. By expressly preserving a role for the state law in the Bankruptcy Code, it is clear that Congress has not devised a policy on federal exemptions so pervasive as to leave no room for a state to supplement bankruptcy law with respect to exemptions.

Even more important, there is no direct conflict between compliance with the Bankruptcy Code and the Texas homestead law. We concluded earlier that in specifying certain debts for which the exempt property is still liable, § 522(c) leaves the parties to their state law collection rights. To execute a judgment against Texas property, a judgment creditor must rely on the state mechanism for enforcement. Although Texas law does not permit the seizure of a homestead for a family support obligation, Sandra can still perfect a judgment lien against the property in question, even if it is a homestead. The property is thus liable, although it is immune from seizure while it is a homestead. This is all § 522(c)(1) requires. Section 522(c)(1) assures that the debtor remains ultimately liable, and the property or proceeds from the sale of property may be subject to seizure if the property ever ceases to be the debtor's homestead. Because the Texas homestead law does not bar the attachment of a perfected lien to homestead property, it does not conflict with § 522(c)(1).

Section 522(c) also fails to conflict with Texas law because it is not self-executing, it provides no means for enforcing the creditor's right. Fed. R. Civ. P. 69(a) explains why:

> Process to enforce a judgment for the payment of money shall be a writ of execution * * * . The procedure on execution, in proceedings on and in aid of a judgment, and in proceedings on

> and in aid of execution *shall be in accordance with the practice and procedure of the state in which the district court is held,* existing at the time the remedy is sought, *except that any statute of the United States governs to the extent that it is applicable.*

(Emphasis added). Pursuant to Rule 69(a), incorporated by Bankr. R. 7069, Texas's enforcement mechanisms govern in bankruptcy court in the absence of a federal execution statute. The Texas turnover statute does not permit seizure and sale of a homestead to satisfy a family support obligation.

CONCLUSION

Cullen and Karen Davis were entitled to exempt their homestead from claims of creditors under Texas and federal bankruptcy law, and they did so. Sandra is entitled, under § 522(c)(1), to enforce her nondischargeable judgment for family support obligations notwithstanding the exemption claim, but her remedy must be in accord with Texas law, since § 522(c) is not an execution statute and does not preempt relevant Texas law. Either Texas or, perhaps, the U.S. Congress could alter this situation, but it is our duty to enforce the present statute.

The judgment of the district court, affirming the judgment of the bankruptcy court, is AFFIRMED.

DENNIS, Circuit Judge, with whom POLITZ and ROBERT M. PARKER, Circuit Judges, join, dissenting:

"Property that is properly exempted under § 522 [of the Bankruptcy Code] is (*with some exceptions*) immunized against liability for prebankruptcy debts. § 522(c)." *Owen v Owen,* 500 U.S. 305, 308 (1991) (emphasis added). The issue in this case is whether the bankruptcy court's judgment in favor of the debtor's former spouse against the debtor for unpaid alimony, maintenance, and child support debts falls within one of § 522(c)'s exceptions so that the debtor's otherwise exempted property is not immunized against liability, seizure and sale for their payment. Because the majority opinion decides this question in diametric contradiction to § 522(c)'s clear language, and in conflict with the decisions of the Supreme Court, other circuits, and numerous bankruptcy courts in this and other circuits that have followed the panel opinion in this case, I respectfully dissent.

* * *

II. Discussion

* * *

Property that is exempted under § 522 and therefore immune from all other liability is liable for and may be seized to pay nondischargeable alimony, maintenance, and child support debts and other obligations excepted from § 522(c) protection. *See Owen, 500 U.S. at 308* ("Property that is properly exempted under § 522 is (*with some exceptions*) immunized against liability for prebankruptcy debts.") (emphasis added); RESNICK, WEINTRAUB & RESNICK, BANKRUPTCY LAW MANUAL ¶ 4.08 at 4-54 (4th ed. 1996) ("Exempt property may be seized to pay nondischargeable tax liabilities and obligations to pay alimony, maintenance, or support.") * * *.

This reading of § 522 is in accord with its legislative history. Referring to that section the Senate report, with which the House report is virtually identical, reads:

> Subsection (c) insulates exempt property from prepetition claims other than tax claims (whether or not dischargeable), and other than alimony, maintenance, or support claims that are excepted from discharge. The rule of *Long v. Bullard*, 117 U.S. 617 (1886), is accepted with respect to the enforcement of valid liens on nonexempt property as well as on exempt property.

S. Rep. No. 95-989, *reprinted in* 1978 U.S.C.C.A.N. 5787, 5862; *see* H.R. Rep. No. 95-595, *reprinted in* 1978 U.S.C.C.A.N. 6317. The drafters of the exemption section thus were aware that exempt property would be protected against some, but not all, nondischargeable debts.

In the present case, the panel opinion's interpretation of § 522(c) is confirmed by the legislative history of § 522(c)(3), the third exception added by the Crime Control Act of 1990, Pub. L. No. 101-647, relating to the enforcement of certain nondischargeable debts owed to a federal depository institutions regulatory agency acting as a conservator, receiver, or liquidating agent. Referring to that new exception, the section-by-section analysis pursuant to the remarks of Representative Charles Schumer on the Banking Law Enforcement section of the Crime Control Act of 1990 provides:

> *Currently, § 522(c) provides that the property exemptions described elsewhere in § 522 do not apply in the case of tax obligations, alimony and child support responsibilities*, or

> security agreements in which the otherwise exempt property is pledged as collateral. The new exception would apply to certain debts owed by institution-affiliated parties to federal depositary institutions regulatory agencies acting in their capacity as receiver, conservator, or liquidating agent. * * *

136 Cong. Rec. E3687 (Nov. 2, 1990) (emphasis added). Also, Senator Biden, Chairman of the Senate Judiciary Committee, remarked:

> I accepted changes drafted by the House only because they maintained the core Senate-passed bankruptcy language that prevents all S&L wrongdoers from discharging their debts by filing for bankruptcy. *The final language specifically preempts State homestead laws, which would otherwise allow S&L crooks to retain lavish homes through the excessive protections in some State bankruptcy laws.*
>
> * * *

136 Cong. Rec. S17602 (Oct. 27, 1990) (emphasis added).

Bankruptcy courts consistently have interpreted the tax and tax lien provisions of §§ 522(c)(1) and (2), correlative to the alimony provision of § 522(c)(1), to authorize creditors and lienholders to reach the exempted property of the debtor to satisfy tax liabilities.

Section 522(c)(1) was not intended, as the majority asserts, merely to preserve judgments and judicial liens securing alimony, maintenance, and child support debts against exempted property. That purpose is effectuated by § 522(f)(1), which excepts from the debtor's right under § 522 to avoid the impairment of the fixing of liens on exempted property, *inter alia*, judicial liens securing alimony, maintenance, and child support debts. Nor was § 522(c)(1) intended merely to put alimony or child support judgment creditors on the same footing with other creditors holding nondischargeable claims. That result is expressly accomplished by § 523(a)(5). The context in which § 522(c)(1) occurs, the text of the Bankruptcy Code as a whole, including particularly §§ 522(b), (c) and (f) and § 523(a)(5), *in pari materia*, and the legislative history of those provisions, clearly show that § 522(c)(1) does not redundantly duplicate the lien preservation function of § 522(f)(1)(A)(i) or the exception to discharge function of § 523(a)(5). By § 522(c)(1), Congress clearly intended to insulate nondischargeable alimony, child support, and maintenance debts from the effects of the debtor's exemptions.

The en banc majority erroneously concludes that the Bankruptcy Code does not preempt the state homestead exemption laws. They fail to recognize the scope of the federal preemption of the field of bankruptcy law or the exclusivity of the federal-law basis of the debtor's qualified right to exempt property from the bankruptcy estate. The power of Congress to establish uniform laws on the subject of bankruptcies throughout the United States is unrestricted and paramount. U.S. CONST. art. I, § 8, cl. 4; *International Shoe Co. v. Pinkus*, 278 U.S. 261, 265 (1929). Congress exercised this power by enacting national, uniform bankruptcy laws, the most recent of which is the Bankruptcy Code, which necessarily exclude or displace any conflicting state regulation. *International Shoe*, 278 U.S. at 265. Consequently, states may not pass or enforce laws to interfere with or complement the Bankruptcy Code or to provide additional or auxiliary regulations.

* * *

B. Response to Majority's Erroneous Reasoning

The majority's decision is based on two arguments: (1) that § 522(c) of the Bankruptcy Code is ambiguous as to whether the types of creditors' claims that §§ 522(c)(1)-(3) except from immunization of exempted property against liability may be enforced against exempted property after bankruptcy; and (2) that the most plausible interpretation of § 522(c) is that it "leaves exempt property exposed to post-bankruptcy liability only to the extent it would have been exposed if the bankruptcy had not occurred." Both arguments are incorrect for the many reasons discussed below.

Perhaps the best short refutation of the majority's arguments is contained in Professor Resnick's explanation of how § 522(c) is designed to protect the debtor's exempted property from most, but not all, nondischarged creditors' claims:

> It is easy to see that if property that is exempt under the Code but not under state law is available to creditors with nondischargeable claims, the effect of the exemption may be wiped out.
>
> Congress was aware of this problem, and, for this reason, the Code provides that exempt property may not be levied upon for any prepetition debt, whether or not the debt is discharged. There are, however, several exceptions. Exempt property may be seized to pay nondischargeable tax liabilities

> and obligations to pay alimony, maintenance, or support. Moreover, valid liens that may not be avoided under the trustee's powers and certain tax liens in exempt property are not affected by the bankruptcy. A third exception was added in 1990 relating to the enforcement of certain nondischargeable debts owed to a federal depository institutions regulatory agency acting as a conservator, receiver, or liquidating agent.

RESNICK, *supra* ¶ 4.08[1], at 4-53 to 4-54 (footnotes omitted).

Thus, § 522(c) is designed to perform two essential functions. In general, it shields exempted property from liability to seizure and sale for the payment of nondischargeable debts. As exceptions to that general rule, it allows piercings of the shield and permits levies upon exempted property for the payment of a small number of certain types of nondischargeable debts. The exceptions are narrowly and carefully drawn to uniformly further several policies deemed by Congress to be of national importance.

The indiscriminate rendering of § 522(c) by the majority opinion erroneously obliterates the important distinction Congress drew between the small class of particular types of nondischargeable debts specified by §§ 522(c)(1)-(3) and all other nondischargeable debts listed in § 523(a). The majority wrongfully relegates needy former spouses with unpaid alimony and child support claims, and other claimants given legislated preference by §§ 522(1)-(3), to the ordinary nondischargeable creditor class, forces them to compete with all comers for basic sustenance from the scarce non-exempt assets of the debtor, and defeats the goals envisioned by Congress in its well thought out and deliberately crafted legislation.

The majority opinion does not follow the plain meaning of the Bankruptcy Code's words. Section 522(c) is not ambiguous, especially when it is read within the context of the Code as a whole. Contrary to the majority opinion, § 522(c)'s exception of specific debts named therein from the effects of the debtor's exemptions is not qualified according to whether the debt is accompanied by a lien. The majority's attempt to read such a qualification or distinction into § 522(c) is an unconcealed attempt to substitute its own policy making for that of Congress. When the words of § 522(c) are applied as written and within the context of the Code as a whole, they clearly and unambiguously conflict with and preempt the state homestead exemption laws with respect to the debtor's alimony, child support, and maintenance obligations. Section 105 of the Bankruptcy Code unquestionably authorizes a bankruptcy court to issue any order, process, or judgment necessary to carry out the provisions of the Code, including an order to seize and sell the debtor's property to satisfy the bankruptcy court's judgment. Federal Rule of Civil Procedure 69(a) must be used by federal courts in accordance with other applicable statutes of the United States to enforce, not thwart, federal court judgments. The majority is clearly wrong in ignoring § 105 of the Bankruptcy Code and in misapplying Federal Rule of Civil Procedure 69(a) to unpreempt and exalt the state homestead exemption laws over the Bankruptcy Code and to defeat the enforcement of the bankruptcy court's judgment.

1. The Meaning of "Exemption" and "Liability"

Section 522(c) is not "ambiguous" as the majority contends. The plain meaning of the term "exemption," as used in § 522 of the Bankruptcy Code, refutes the majority's argument that the term "liable," as used in that section, means that a debtor's property is only subject to a judgment lien, and remains immune from seizure and sale.

The Supreme Court has defined "exemption" as the "right * * * which withdraws the property from *levy and sale under judicial process*." *White v. Stump*, 266 U.S. 310, 313 (1924) (emphasis added). This court has defined "exemption" as "the freedom of property of debtors *from liability to seizure and sale under legal process for the payment of their debts*." *Clark v. Nirenbaum*, 8 F.2d 451, 452 (5th Cir. 1925) (emphasis added), *cert. denied*, 270 U.S. 649 (1926). * * *

This definition of exemption is critical to an understanding of the meaning of the word "liable" in § 522:

> (c) Unless the case is dismissed, *property exempt under this section is not liable* during or after the case for any debt of the debtor that arose, or that is determined under § 502 of this title as if such debt had arisen, before the commencement of the case, *except*—
>
> > (1) a debt of a kind specified in section * * * 523(a)(5) of this title.

The word "liable," as used in the section of the Bankruptcy Code entitled "Exemptions," means "liable to levy and sale on execution or attachment." More specifically, the statutory reference to "liable," in the context of exemptions, means that property exempted by a debtor under "Federal law" or "State or local law" pursuant to § 522-

(b)(2)(A) is free from liability for seizure and sale by his or her creditor under judicial process *unless* the debt is, *inter alia*, a debt "to a spouse, former spouse, or child of the debtor, for alimony to, maintenance for, or support of such spouse or child, in connection with a separation agreement, divorce decree or other order of a court of record." § 523-(a)(5). Because alimony and child support debts are an exception to the debtor's privilege to exempt certain property from seizure and sale (*see* discussion *infra* of "exceptions to exemptions"), it follows that the property is liable for seizure and sale by a former spouse with a judgment for alimony and child support that is nondischargeable under § 523(a)(5).

The majority asserts without any support in federal law that "liable" in § 522(c)(1) means only that an alimony and child support creditor can "perfect a judgment lien against the property * * * although it is immune from seizure." The majority cites only Texas law for the proposition that Congress intended "liable" in § 522(c)(1) as an esoteric proxy for "nondischargeable debt" and "nonavoidable lien." "Liable" taken in its usual sense and as used in § 522, however, means "liable for seizure and sale" and not merely "liable to attachment by a nonavoidable but unenforceable lien." Section 522(c) of the Bankruptcy Code *expressly* abrogates a debtor's privilege allowed by state law by which he may hold property free from all liability to levy and sale under legal process for the payment of debts defined by § 523(a)(5). By denying the debtor this privilege of exemption for certain nondischargeable debts, § 522(c) permits the property to be seized and sold to satisfy these obligations.

2. Section 522's "Exception to Exemptions" For Family Support Debts

The Bankruptcy Code does not confer upon a debtor an absolute or unqualified right to exempt property from seizure and sale. Section 522 expressly makes nondischargeable debts for alimony, maintenance or child support an *exception* to the debtor's general privilege to exempt certain property from liability for seizure and sale. Thus, property exempted under § 522 is nevertheless liable for seizure and sale to satisfy debts specified in § 523(a)(1) (tax obligations) and § 523(a)(5) (child and spousal support). The majority uses circular and obverse reasoning in an attempt to show that Texas state exemption law (by virtue of Fed. R. Civ. P. 69(a)) "reverse preempts" federal court enforcement of judgments for nondischargeable alimony and support debts under § 522(c) of the Bankruptcy Code. To the contrary, however, Congress, by the specific terms of § 522 and its constitutional power, has superseded and preempted the effect of the state exemption law upon this particular kind of debt. While the Bankruptcy Code allows a debtor to claim state exemptions, it also revokes this privilege as to the debtor's nondischargeable child and spousal support obligations.

* * *

3. Preemption

* * *

* * * I recognize that Congress afforded significant deference to state law by allowing bankruptcy debtors to choose state exemptions and by further allowing states to opt out of the federal exemption scheme entirely. Yet, such deference does not warrant the conclusion that the detailed exceptions in § 522(c) to the general immunity from liability of the "property exempted" provided for by the same section must yield to or be controlled by the state exemption laws. As the Supreme Court recognized in discussing the interplay between § 522(f) and state exemption exceptions in *Owen*, the state's ability to define its exemptions is not absolute and must yield to conflicting policies in the Bankruptcy Code.

Only by adding a heavy Texas spin to gloss over the plain words and meaning of § 522(c) is the majority able to close its eyes to the obvious conflict between the state laws that exempt homestead property from liability to seizure and sale for alimony and child support debts and § 522(c)(1), which excepts nondischargeable alimony and child support debts from the effects of that exemption. The majority struggles to avoid acknowledging the conflict by theorizing that § 522(c)(1) does not mean what it says but strangely enough has a meaning that produces substantially the same result Texas courts have reached when a Texas court judgment creditor seeks to enforce her alimony and child support decree based solely on state law against the judgment debtor's homestead: The former spouse may have her lien attached to the property but she cannot enforce it until the debtor dies or abandons his homestead. In fact, as we have learned during the course of this case, under Texas law, she cannot enforce it against the proceeds of his sale of the homestead if he invests them in another Texas homestead within six months of the sale.

The conflict between the Bankruptcy Code and the Texas homestead exemption laws, however, is too sharp and too real to be covered up by any amount of ingenious judicial gloss. The state laws provide for an exemption of property from liability to seizure and sale for the owner's alimony and child support debts. The federal bankruptcy law in § 522(c)(1) provides for an exception to that exemption of the same property from liability to seizure and sale for the debtor-owner's alimony and child support debts.

Consequently, there is a conflict between the state and federal laws. Therefore, it must be concluded that the state homestead laws are preempted by the federal Bankruptcy Code. State law is void to the extent it is in conflict with a federal statute.

4. Bankruptcy Court's Broad Enforcement Powers Under § 105

The majority insists that the Bankruptcy Code provides no means by which federal courts can enforce a final judgment rendered by a bankruptcy court.

Section 105 of the Bankruptcy Code, however, plainly states: [*the dissent quoted § 105*].

* * *

One leading commentator on bankruptcy law characterizes § 105 as "an omnibus provision phrased in such general terms as to be the basis for a broad exercise of power in the administration of a bankruptcy case. The basic purpose of § 105 is to assure the bankruptcy courts power to take whatever action is appropriate or necessary in aid of the exercise of its jurisdiction." 2 L. KING, COLLIER ON BANKRUPTCY § 105.01, at 105-3 (1996). The second sentence of § 105(a) was expressly intended to broaden the authority of bankruptcy courts to act, sua sponte, to promote the Code's provisions.

* * *

The broad grant of authority conferred upon bankruptcy courts and district courts by § 105 permits these courts to issue "any order, process, or judgment that is necessary or appropriate to carry out the provisions of this title." Therefore, § 105 provides federal courts with a means of enforcing the bankruptcy court's judgment based on nondischargeable alimony, maintenance, and child support debts by ordering the debtor's homestead seized and sold to satisfy this nondischargeable, nonexemptible debt.

5. Assimilation of State Practices and Procedures

Federal Rule of Civil Procedure 69(a) provides that the procedure "on execution, in proceedings supplementary to and in aid of a judgment, and in proceedings on and in aid of execution shall be in accordance with the practice and procedure of the state in which the district court is held, existing at the time the remedy is sought, *except that any statute of the United States governs to the extent that it is applicable*." Fed. R. Civ. P. 69(a) (emphasis added). Thus, the emphasized exception makes any applicable federal statute controlling, as well as any relevant civil rule, because those rules have the force of a statute.

Section 105 of the Bankruptcy Code is a fitting, fully applicable, and, therefore, controlling federal statute authorizing the bankruptcy court to enforce its judgment. Consequently, Federal Rule of Civil Procedure 69(a), and state practice and procedure adopted thereby, do not prevent a federal court from using whatever means are necessary to guarantee compliance with its judgments. The Fourth Circuit aptly summed up the relationship between state procedural vehicles and federal statutes as follows:

> Even though we look to state law to determine the practice and procedure to be followed in the execution of a judgment, we do so in furtherance of federal law, giving effect to rules entitling parties to enforce federal judgments in federal courts. *Consequently, any aspects of the assimilated practices and procedures that are uniquely designed to enforce state judgments are not assimilated, nor is any aspect that may be inconsistent with the federal policy of affording judgment creditors the right to a writ of execution to enforce money judgments in federal courts.*

United States v. Harkins Builders, Inc., 45 F.3d 830, 833 (4th Cir. 1995) (emphasis added). Consequently, a debtor cannot accomplish "through the back door," ostensibly under Rule 69(a), what cannot be accomplished under the federal Bankruptcy Code: invoking state exemption laws to immunize or protect homestead property from seizure and sale to satisfy nondischargeable, nonexemptible child and spousal support debts.

III. Conclusion

The Bankruptcy Code provides that the commencement of a voluntary bankruptcy case creates an estate comprised of legal and equitable interests of the debtor in property, wherever located and by whomever held. § 541. Under the Code, an individual debtor has a qualified right, under defined circumstances, to exempt from the estate the same property that is exempt from levy under state, local, and non-bankruptcy federal law. § 522(b)(2)(A). Property that is exempted from the estate is immunized against liability for prebankruptcy debts, subject to the exception of, *inter alia*, debts for alimony, maintenance, child support, taxes and other liabilities specified by the Code. § 522(c). The debtor's qualified right to exempt property from the estate, and the relationships between the debtor, his creditors, and exempted or non-exempted property with regard to prebankruptcy debts, are governed exclusively by federal law. Consequently, it is clear that the provisions of the state homestead exemption law that seek to immunize the debtor's homestead against liability to seizure and sale for nondischargeable alimony and support debts conflict with and have been superseded by the Bankruptcy Code. The state law cannot alter the obligations of a bankruptcy debtor and his creditors as provided for by federal bankruptcy law. For these reasons, the state homestead exemption laws are inoperative against the debtor's former spouse in this case and she is entitled under the Bankruptcy Code to proceed against the debtor's otherwise exempted property to satisfy her alimony, maintenance, and child support judgment. Accordingly, the judgments below should be vacated and the case should be remanded to the bankruptcy court with directions to allow the appellant to obtain a writ of execution and all other relief to which she is entitled by law.

Note

This case involved Cullen Davis's first wife, Sandra, from whom he was divorced in 1968. His legal problems involving his estranged second wife, Priscilla, are even more interesting.

In 1976, when Cullen controlled an international oil empire worth approximately $400 million, a masked gunman wearing a woman's black shoulder-length wig entered Cullen's 19,000-square-foot estate in Fort Worth. Four people were shot. Priscilla's boyfriend, Stan Farr, a former basketball player at Texas Christian University, was killed, along with Priscilla's daughter from a previous marriage, Andrea Wilborn. Priscilla and a family friend were wounded in the attack; a fifth person escaped without injuries. All three survivors named Cullen as the trigger man and prosecutors cited rancorous divorce proceedings with Priscilla as his motive for murder. A first trial ended in a hung jury and Cullen was acquitted in the second trial. Karen, who was then Cullen's mistress, was an alibi witness.

Priscilla later obtained a $5 million settlement from Cullen in a personal injury and wrongful death suit, but it was never paid. Cullen settled a wrongful death suit filed by Farr's children for $250,000. Cullen was also indicted and later acquitted on charges that he tried to hire a hit man to kill the judge assigned to hear his divorce case with Priscilla.

Four books have been written about these incidents. One of them, Gary Cartwright's Blood Will Tell, published in 1978, became the basis of a 1995 TV miniseries, "Texas Justice." Heather Locklear starred as Priscilla.

Cullen and Karen lived in the mansion where the murders took place until 1984, when Cullen's criminal and financial problems forced them to move. The mansion, which stood empty for years, was refurbished and opened as The Stonegate Mansion Restaurant in 1996. They have been frequent patrons.

Cullen and Karen have announced their collaboration on a book that will assert Cullen's innocence in the shootings.

E. REAFFIRMATION

"Reaffirmation" is the making of a new agreement to repay a debt. Unlike redemption, which we encountered in Chapter 4, reaffirmation is consensual—both debtor and creditor must agree to it. Such an agreement is an enforceable contract under common law, despite the lack of fresh consideration to support the new promise to pay. Restatement of Contracts (Second) § 83. Thus, reaffirmation waives the discharge as far as that debt is concerned, and subjects the debtor to later collection efforts by the creditor if the debtor defaults.

Research done before enactment of the Code revealed that a large percentage of Chapter 7 debtors reaffirmed some debts: for example, 48% reaffirmed debts for appliances or furniture, and 30% reaffirmed debts for cars.

Congress believed that reaffirmations seriously threaten the fresh start bankruptcy is supposed to provide, and some efforts were made to ban reaffirmations completely. Those efforts were unsuccessful, but a compromise was reached that surrounds reaffirmations with procedural safeguards. Read §§ 524(c) and (d) and apply those subsections to the following Problems.

Questions and Problems

1. You represent Debtor, who lives out in the country. Debtor's only source of income is disability benefits of $400 per month. Debtor wants to reaffirm a $5,000 debt owed to GMAC, which has a purchase money security

interest in Debtor's car. It is Debtor's sole means of transportation to the doctor's office and grocery store. The car is currently worth only $3,500 and the monthly payment on the reaffirmed debt would be $220. Would you sign the affidavit required by § 524(c)(3)? Cf. *In re Delano*, 7 B.R. 72 (Bankr. D.Me.1980). If you refuse, what happens?

2. Debtor, who is represented by counsel, has signed an agreement reaffirming a debt. Debtor is notified of the reaffirmation hearing, but fails to appear. Is the reaffirmation enforceable? Compare *Sweet v. Bank of Oklahoma*, 954 F.2d 610 (10th Cir.1992), with *In re Fisher*, 113 B.R. 714 (Bankr. N.D.Okla.1990).

3. Why did Congress not prohibit all reaffirmations? Can you see a reason for a debtor to reaffirm a debt owed an employer? A debt co-signed by a good friend? A debt nondischargeable under § 523(a)? A debt secured by a purchase money security interest in household goods?

Note on the Sears Reaffirmation Scandal

On November 14, 1996, Francis Latanowich sent a letter, handwritten on a yellow legal pad, to the bankruptcy court that had granted him a discharge in his Chapter 7 case the preceding April. He said:

> I took advice from a lawyer friend and he told me to keep some of my debts so I could start getting my credit back. * * * I have tried to meet the payment every month but it is keeping food off the table for my kids. I would like to know if you could reopen my case so I could get rid of all my debt forever.

Thus began a process that ultimately cost Sears almost half a billion dollars. It also uncovered a nationwide, decade-long practice by Sears, as well as other retailers, systematically and deliberately to ignore the requirements of § 524(c).

Latanowich owed Sears $1,161 when he filed bankruptcy. The obligation was secured by an automobile battery worth $75 and a television set worth $403. Sears told him he either had to return the items or reaffirm, and it offered to extend him an additional $200 in credit if he chose reaffirmation. He signed. In the following seven months he charged purchases of $339 to his Sears card and made $375 in payments. With interest accruing on the prepetition debt, however, he owed Sears $160 more in November, when he wrote the letter, than he did when he filed his petition.

The bankruptcy judge who got Latanowich's letter wanted to know why no reaffirmation to Sears was in the court's file. Dissatisfied with the proffered explanations, she ordered Sears to file a list of every case in the District of Massachusetts, from January 1, 1995 through January 29, 1997, in which Sears had obtained a reaffirmation agreement but had failed to file it with the court. Sears ultimately filed a list with an astonishing 2,733 cases on it. See *In re Latanowich*, 207 B.R. 326 (Bankr. D.Mass.1997). When full investigations were completed, it was learned that Sears had improperly collected $110 million from 187,000 customers across the United States.

The company reacted by taking responsibility, cooperating with investigators, and making restitution to all affected customers. Almost $300 million went to debtors, both as refunds (plus interest) of $1.40 for every $1.00 improperly collected, and as forgiveness of debts for additional items they purchased. Sears also paid over $40 million in civil penalties to the 50 states and $60 million to settle criminal bankruptcy fraud charges. In addition, the company settled a suit brought by shareholders who asserted that the scandal had hurt the value of their stock. Adding in legal fees and costs of researching its records, the scandal cost Sears approximately $475 million.

F. DISCRIMINATORY TREATMENT

When it was enacted in 1978, the Code contained only the prohibition against discrimination now found in § 525(a). Although limitation to governmental units and to discrimination *solely* on the basis of prior bankruptcy rendered the provision quite narrow, it was intended to codify *Perez v. Campbell,* 402 U.S. 637, 91 S.Ct. 1704, 29 L.Ed.2d 233 (1971). *Perez* is discussed in the next case.

Two subsequent additions to § 525 have made the Code somewhat more protective of former debtors: subsection (b), added in 1984, which prohibits discrimination in private employment solely because of prior bankruptcy; and subsection (c), added in 1994, which prohibits denial of a student loan on the ground of bankruptcy.

DUFFEY v. DOLLISON

United States Court of Appeals for the Sixth Circuit, 1984.
734 F.2d 265.

ENGEL, CIRCUIT JUDGE.

The precise issue presented by this appeal is whether Ohio's Motor Vehicle Financial Responsibility Act, as it has been applied to the Duffeys, conflicts with § 525 of the Bankruptcy Act of 1978, thereby violating the Supremacy Clause of the United States Constitution.

Motor vehicle financial responsibility laws, which require motorists to maintain some type of automobile insurance or otherwise to furnish proof of financial responsibility, have been enacted in nearly all states. Some states compel all drivers to furnish proof that they are adequately insured as a precondition to the issuance of driver's or automobile licenses. Other states, such as Ohio, have enacted less comprehensive laws which require proof of financial responsibility only when a driver has failed, within a reasonable time, to satisfy a judgment for damages arising from an automobile accident or has been convicted of certain serious traffic offenses. The public benefit from such laws has long been recognized. The Supreme Court has established that states may constitutionally require all motorists to carry liability insurance or post security before they are issued driver's licenses. *Bell v. Burson,* 402 U.S. 535, 539 (1971).

The validity of the Ohio statute is a matter of great concern to those interested in keeping irresponsible drivers off the highways as well as to those individuals who, voluntarily or involuntarily, go into bankruptcy. While we have been furnished no Ohio statistics, the general pervasiveness of the problem is well illustrated by the stipulated findings in *Henry v. Heyison,* 4 B.R. 437 (E.D.Pa.1980). There, the court noted that in one year, 12,000 drivers in Pennsylvania had their driver's licenses suspended as the result of unsatisfied motor vehicle tort judgments. Of those 12,000 drivers, 300 had reported that their motor vehicle tort judgments were discharged in bankruptcy proceedings.

This appeal is particularly important because several bankruptcy courts that have considered whether the Ohio Motor Vehicle Financial Responsibility Act unconstitutionally conflicts with federal bankruptcy laws have reached opposite conclusions. * * *

Finally, the present controversy is significant because it involves a potential conflict between important state and federal interests: state concern for public safety and federal concern for establishing uniform bankruptcy laws. Clearly if these competing interests are incompatible, the Supremacy Clause dictates that we resolve the conflict in favor of federal law. Good policy and good sense, however, suggest the desirability of accommodating both interests if this can reasonably be achieved.

I.

The facts here are stipulated. On June 18, 1979, a judgment of $912.76, arising from an auto accident, was entered against George Duffey in the Municipal Court of Franklin County, Ohio. This judgment was not satisfied within 30 days and, consequently, Mr. Duffey's operator's license and vehicle registration were suspended on July 28,

1980, by the Registrar of Motor Vehicles, Dean Dollison * * *. On May 23, 1980, a judgment of $1,131.90, arising from an auto accident, was entered against Shari Duffey in the Franklin County Municipal Court. This judgment also was not satisfied within 30 days, resulting in the suspension of Mrs. Duffey's driving privileges on October 28, 1980.

The Duffeys, on January 27, 1981, filed a voluntary joint bankruptcy petition under Chapter 7 of the Bankruptcy Act. A copy of their bankruptcy petition, which listed the unsatisfied accident-related judgments in the schedule of debts, was sent by the Duffeys to Registrar Dollison with the request that he reinstate their driving privileges. Dollison, while recognizing that the judgment debts were subject to discharge and that the Duffeys could not be required to satisfy or reaffirm the debt as a condition to reobtaining their licenses, nevertheless refused to vacate the order of suspension until the Duffeys had filed evidence of financial responsibility * * *.

On February 24, 1981, the Duffeys brought suit in bankruptcy court in the Southern District of Ohio for reinstatement of their driving privileges. In that action the Duffeys argued that Ohio's requirement of proof of financial responsibility, as it applies to individuals whose unsatisfied tort judgments have been stayed or discharged by bankruptcy, unconstitutionally conflicts with the federal bankruptcy provision prohibiting the discriminatory treatment of bankrupts, § 525. The bankruptcy judge agreed that the challenged provisions of the Ohio Motor Vehicle Financial Responsibility Act conflict with the Bankruptcy Act and ordered the Registrar to reinstate the Duffeys' driving privileges. The Registrar appealed this decision to the United States District Court for the Southern District of Ohio. In a carefully considered opinion, United States District Judge John D. Holschuh reversed the decision of the bankruptcy court and held that Ohio's financial responsibility requirement does not violate § 525 of the Bankruptcy Act because the state statute applies equally to bankrupts and nonbankrupts. We affirm.

II.

The Supreme Court, in *Perez v. Campbell,* 402 U.S. 637 (1971), stated that "[d]eciding whether a state statute is in conflict with a federal statute and hence invalid under the Supremacy Clause is essentially a two-step process of first ascertaining the construction of the two statutes and then determining the constitutional question whether they are in conflict." *Id.* at 644. In making this decision a reviewing court must "determine whether a challenged state statute 'stands as an obstacle to the accomplishment and execution of the full purposes and objectives of Congress.'" *Id.* at 649 (quoting *Hines v. Davidowitz,* 312 U.S. 52, 67 (1941)). Applying the *Perez* approach, we therefore first ascertain the construction of the Ohio Motor Vehicle Financial Responsibility Act and § 525 of the Bankruptcy Act, and then determine whether the statutes conflict.

A.

The Ohio Motor Vehicle Financial Responsibility Act provides that "[w]henever any person fails within thirty days to satisfy a judgment rendered within this state, upon written request of the judgment creditor or his attorney," the court must forward a certified copy of the judgment to the registrar of motor vehicles. Upon receipt of a certified copy of the unsatisfied judgment, the registrar shall "suspend the license and registration and nonresident's operating privilege of any person against whom such judgment was rendered * * *." Driving privileges must remain suspended for seven years; however, "[t]he registrar shall vacate the order of suspension *upon proof that such judgment is stayed,* or satisfied in full * * * *and upon such person's filing with the registrar of motor vehicles evidence of financial responsibility* * * *." (Emphasis added). Proof of financial responsibility must be maintained for three years and may be given by filing a certificate of insurance, a surety bond, a certificate of deposit, or a certificate of self-insurance.

* * * Following the United States Supreme Court's decision in *Perez,* the former version of Ohio's Motor Vehicle Financial Responsibility Act was declared unconstitutional to the extent that it required payment of a tort judgment as a condition to restoration of driving privileges, even though the underlying judgment was stayed, or discharged in bankruptcy. *Weaver v. O'Grady,* 350 F.Supp. 403, 407 (S.D.Ohio 1972). The Act as it is now written cures that defect. However, bankruptcy does not relieve the judgment debtor of the requirement of posting proof of future financial responsibility.

The Ohio Act has as its object the protection of the public from financially irresponsible motorists who have proved unwilling or unable to satisfy a judgment arising from an automobile accident. The statute embodies a "one-bite" approach to achieving this purpose by permitting motorists the privilege of driving without any proof of financial responsibility until they incur an accident-related judgment and fail to satisfy it within 30 days.

B.

Section 525[(a)] of the Bankruptcy Act of 1978 * * * has yet to be authoritatively construed by the United States Supreme Court. However, the legislative history indicates that § 525, "codifies the result of *Perez v. Campbell,* 402 U.S. 637 (1971), which held that a State would frustrate the Congressional policy of a fresh start for a debtor if it were permitted to refuse to renew a drivers license because a tort judgment resulting from an automobile accident had been unpaid as a result of a discharge in bankruptcy." S.Rep. No. 95–989 at 81, *reprinted in* 1978 U.S.C.C.A.N. at 5867. Therefore when construing § 525[(a)], it is helpful to examine the *Perez* holding.

In *Perez,* the petitioners filed a voluntary bankruptcy petition two days before judgment was entered against them for personal injuries and property damages which arose from an automobile collision. The judgment was discharged in bankruptcy by order of the district court. Nevertheless, the State of Arizona suspended the Perezes' driving privileges pursuant to a statute which provided for such suspension when an accident-related judgment went unsatisfied for 60 days. In order to regain their privileges, the Perezes were required to satisfy the judgment and give proof of future financial responsibility. Unlike the Ohio Act, the Arizona statute required satisfaction of the judgment even though it was discharged in bankruptcy or its collection stayed.

In considering whether the Arizona law unconstitutionally conflicted with the Bankruptcy Act, the Court noted that "the validity of [the] limited requirement that some drivers post evidence of financial responsibility for the future in order to regain driving privileges is not questioned here." 402 U.S. at 642. The only issue the Court examined was whether a State may enact a statute "providing that a discharge in bankruptcy of [an] automobile accident tort judgment shall have no effect on the judgment debtor's obligation to repay the judgment creditor, at least insofar as such repayment may be enforced by the withholding of driving privileges by the State." *Id.* at 643. The majority determined that the statute jeopardized the "fresh start" objectives of the Bankruptcy Act by providing creditors leverage for collection of judgments which had been discharged in bankruptcy. In the majority's view, one of the primary purposes of the Bankruptcy Act "is to give debtors 'a new opportunity in life and a clear field for future effort, unhampered by the pressure and discouragement of preexisting debt.'" *Id.* at 648 (quoting *Local Loan Co. v. Hunt,* 292 U.S. 234, 244 (1934)). Because the Arizona law obstructed these objectives, it was found to be invalid under the Supremacy Clause.

Thus the *Perez* decision, which § 525[(a)] of the Bankruptcy Act codifies, specifically left open the issue we now consider: whether bankrupts who have discharged an accident-related judgment can be required, as a condition to the restoration of driving privileges suspended prior to the bankruptcy, to post evidence of financial responsibility. The legislative history indicates that § 525[(a)] was intended by Congress to incorporate further refinements of the *Perez* doctrine:

> [T]he enumeration of various forms of discrimination against former bankrupts is not intended to permit other forms of discrimination. The courts have been developing the *Perez* rule. This section permits further development to prohibit actions by governmental or quasi-governmental organizations that perform licensing functions, such as a State bar association or a medical society, or by other organizations that can seriously affect the debtors' livelihood or fresh start. * * *

S.Rep. No. 95–989 at 81, *reprinted in* 1978 U.S.C.C.A.N. at 5867. It appears that § 525 is intended to ensure that bankrupts are not deprived of a "fresh start" because of governmental discrimination against them, based "solely" on the bankruptcy. Senate Report 95–989 specifies that "the effect of * * * [§ 525], and of further interpretations of the *Perez* rule, is to strengthen the anti-reaffirmation policy found in § 524(b). Discrimination based solely on nonpayment could encourage reaffirmations, contrary to the expressed policy." *Id.* The House further noted regarding § 525[(a)]:

> [T]he purpose of the section is to prevent an automatic reaction against an individual for availing himself of the protection of the bankruptcy laws. Most bankruptcies are caused by circumstances beyond the debtor's control. To penalize a debtor by discriminatory treatment as a result is unfair and undoes the beneficial effects of the bankruptcy laws. However, in those cases where the causes of a bankruptcy are intimately connected with the license, grant, or employment in question, an examination into the circumstances surrounding the bankruptcy will permit governmental units to pursue appropriate regulatory policies and take appropriate action without running afoul of bankruptcy policy.

H.R.Rep. No. 95–595 at 165, *reprinted in* 1978 U.S.C.C.A.N. at 6126 (footnote omitted). Therefore, we agree with the district court's conclusion that "the primary purpose of § 525[(a)] of the Bankruptcy Code is to prevent the government either from denying privileges to individuals solely as a reaction to their filing bankruptcy or from conditioning the grant of privileges on the bankrupt's reaffirmation of certain debts." It is thus necessary to determine whether the Ohio Financial Responsibility Act impedes the accomplishment of, or frustrates, these Congressional objectives.

III.

* * *

The Duffeys contend that Ohio law requires them to post proof of financial responsibility "solely" because they have not paid a debt that is dischargeable in bankruptcy. Therefore in the Duffeys' view, the Ohio Act violates § 525 of the Bankruptcy Act because § 525[(a)] specifically prohibits states from using the failure to pay a debt as the basis for denying a driver's license.

We agree with the district court that the Duffeys misinterpret both § 525[(a)] and the Ohio Act. Of course, the former Ohio statute, by requiring payment of the judgment notwithstanding bankruptcy, would indeed violate § 525[(a)]; as the legislative history of § 525 indicates, this would be "the *Perez* situation." S.Rep. No. 95–989 at 81, *reprinted in* 1978 U.S.C.C.A.N. at 5867. However, since the present Ohio Act provides that a judgment stayed or discharged in bankruptcy need not be satisfied by the judgment debtor as a condition to the restoration of driving privileges, it clearly is consistent with the immediate holding in *Perez:* the Act neither provides creditors "leverage for the collection of damages," nor under the facts here does it coerce bankrupts into reaffirming discharged debts. 402 U.S. at 646–47.

We recognize that the portion of the Ohio Act which suspends motorists' driving privileges for failure to satisfy a judgment is not triggered unless a judgment creditor requests in writing that a certified copy of the unsatisfied judgment be forwarded to the Registrar. It is conceivable that under certain circumstances not present here, a creditor might attempt to use this ability to initiate license suspension proceedings to coerce a debtor into reaffirming all or part of a judgment that is stayed by the Bankruptcy Act.

However under the facts of this case, the Duffeys could not have been coerced into reaffirming the stayed judgments because the judgments had been certified to the Registrar and the requirement of furnishing proof of financial responsibility had been fixed *before* the Duffeys filed in bankruptcy. Once the judgment[s] were certified, the

Duffeys could not have regained their driving privileges without furnishing proof of financial responsibility even by paying the judgments. Thus, at that juncture, the judgment creditors could do nothing further to benefit or inconvenience the Duffeys; there was no leverage which could have induced the Duffeys to reaffirm their debts. As applied here the Ohio Act, which depends on judgment creditors to initiate license suspension proceedings, employs a reasonable method for relieving the state of the burden of policing every accident-related judgment. Ohio simply has chosen in civil cases to place the responsibility for reporting unsatisfied tort judgments on the party in the best position to know whether a judgment has been satisfied, and with the greatest incentive to notify the Registrar of nonpayment.

The Duffeys would have us hold that the Ohio Motor Vehicle Financial Responsibility Act violates § 525 because the Act fails to treat a bankrupt as though he or she had never incurred a dischargeable, accident-related tort judgment. Under such an interpretation, once a judgment is discharged or stayed, states would be absolutely prohibited from imposing or continuing any burden, whether a reaffirmation of liability or the imposition of financial responsibility requirements. We believe that this reads more into § 525[(a)] than Congress intended.

As the district court correctly noted:

> [N]either the language of the statute nor its legislative history indicates that § 525 was intended by Congress to erase all traces of a discharged debt and thereby foreclose the imposition of any future responsibility requirements. To the contrary, the legislative history of § 525 contemplates both the consideration of the circumstances surrounding bankruptcy and the valid imposition of future financial responsibility requirements.

This conclusion is amply supported by the legislative history. Senate Report 95–989 specifically observes that § 525 "does not prohibit consideration of other factors, *such as future financial responsibility or ability,* and does not prohibit imposition of requirements such as net capital rules, if applied nondiscriminatorily." S.Rep. No. 95–989 at 81, *reprinted in* 1978 U.S.C.C.A.N. at 5867 (emphasis added). House Report No. 95–595 makes this point even more emphatically:

> [T]he prohibition [of § 525] *does not extend so far as to prohibit examination of the factors surrounding bankruptcy, the imposition of financial responsibility rules if they are not imposed only on former bankrupts,* or the examination of prospective

> financial condition or managerial ability. * * * [I]n those cases where the causes of a bankruptcy are intimately connected with the license, grant, or employment in question, an examination into the circumstances surrounding the bankruptcy will permit governmental units to pursue appropriate regulatory policies and take appropriate action without running afoul of bankruptcy policy.

H.R.Rep. No. 95–595 at 165, *reprinted in* 1978 U.S.C.C.A.N. at 6126 (emphasis added). Thus, Congress has evinced a clear intent to permit the imposition of financial responsibility requirements, so long as they are not discriminatorily applied to bankrupts.

The Ohio Financial Responsibility Act in no way discriminates against bankrupts, or penalizes them for filing in bankruptcy. The Act provides that "any person" who fails to satisfy an accident-related judgment within 30 days shall have his or her driving privileges suspended by the Registrar. The statute applies without exception to *any* person who fails to satisfy a judgment for whatever reason, whether because of unwillingness, inadvertence, or inability to pay. Once a judgment has been certified to the Registrar for non-payment, the debtor's obligation to furnish proof of financial responsibility becomes fixed. Thereafter, neither payment of the debt, reaffirmation, nor bankruptcy can relieve the debtor of this requirement. Judgment debtors such as the Duffeys who seek relief under the bankruptcy laws are therefore treated no differently from any other judgment debtor. Indeed it is this lack of discrimination to which the Duffeys take exception. By arguing that bankrupts who have proved to be irresponsible drivers should be excused from the requirement of posting proof of financial responsibility, the Duffeys in effect ask this court "to go beyond the fresh start policy of *Perez* and * * * give a debtor a head start over persons who are able to satisfy their unpaid judgment debts without resort to a discharge in bankruptcy." *In re Cerny,* 17 B.R. 221, 224 (Bankr.N.D.Ohio 1982). We do not believe that § 525[(a)] was intended by Congress to afford debtors in bankruptcy such preferential treatment.

We therefore hold that Ohio's "one-bite" approach to the imposition of financial responsibility requirements, as applied to the Duffeys, violates neither the *Perez* holding nor its statutory codification, § 525[(a)] of the Bankruptcy Act. As Judge Holschuh persuasively reasoned,

> [i]t is undisputed that Ohio may require all motorists to carry liability insurance or post security before they are issued

operator's licenses. If the State may legitimately establish such a prerequisite to the grant of driving privileges, a less stringent requirement should *a fortiori* be valid. The challenged Ohio statutes afford individuals the opportunity of driving without any showing of financial responsibility until they incur a judgment which they are unable to pay. This "one-bite" approach undoubtedly makes it possible for many individuals who otherwise could not afford insurance to obtain driving privileges. [The Duffeys] argue that because Ohio has used this more lenient approach, it is forbidden to suspend their driving privileges, despite the fact that they have demonstrated irresponsibility as a driver coupled with an inability to satisfy a resulting judgment. [This] argument, however, ignores the potential consequences to the victims of an accident caused by an individual who is an irresponsible driver.

Our ruling here is a relatively narrow one. We uphold the Ohio Act where the requirement to furnish proof of financial responsibility has become fixed, through certification to the Registrar, prior to bankruptcy. Where the obligation has thus become fixed, neither payment of the judgment, nor arrangement with the creditor, nor bankruptcy can relieve the debtor of the requirement of furnishing proof of financial responsibility. In this respect the Ohio Act does not have the effect of discriminating between those who are bankrupt and those who are not. It cannot induce the bankrupt to reaffirm a discharged debt, or to pay thereafter, for neither action can affect the legal requirement to post proof of financial responsibility.

The judgment of the district court is AFFIRMED.

HICKS v. FIRST NATIONAL BANK OF HARRISON (IN RE HICKS)

United States Bankruptcy Court, Western District of Arkansas, 1986.
65 B.R. 980.

ROBERT F. FUSSELL, CHIEF JUDGE.

On July 18, 1986 a hearing was held on the Complaint of debtor Kathryn A. Hicks alleging that the First National Bank of Harrison, Arkansas, (Bank) has acted in violation of § 525, the debtor discrimination statute. In her complaint the plaintiff seeks reinstatement of her position with the Bank as teller for the Bank's window position number two, with all of the responsibilities and duties she had with the Bank prior to October 24, 1985. Mrs. Hicks also requests attorney's fees and the costs of the action.

* * *

FACTS

Mrs. Hicks was employed as a teller by the Bank in December, 1983 and began working full time on January 13, 1984. Prior to her employment with the Harrison Bank, she had worked as a teller for the First National Bank in Chandler, Oklahoma, for approximately five years.

On October 22, 1985, while Mrs. Hicks was working as a teller for the defendant Bank, she and her husband, Carson L. Hicks, filed a chapter 7 bankruptcy petition. The following day, Wednesday, October 23, 1985, a news item appeared on page 8 of the "Harrison (Ark.) Daily Times." It stated:

Omaha Couple File Petition

> LITTLE ROCK—Carson L. and Kathryn Hicks of Omaha, Ark., filed a chapter 7 liquidation petition in Bankruptcy Court Tuesday, listing debts of more than $209,000 and assets of more than $174,000.
>
> Hicks owned Carson's Motors in Harrison.
>
> Under Chapter 7, a trustee will be appointed by the court to sell off their assets and pay their creditors.
>
> The petition listed nine debts including six loans from First National Bank at Harrison totalling more than $189,000. The loans were secured by the couple's residence, land, cattle and vehicles for the motor company.

Debra Keef, Kathryn Hicks' supervisor, saw the article around 3:00 p.m. on that same day. The next morning Mrs. Keef informed Mrs. Hicks that she would be transferred to the Bank's bookkeeping department until the bankruptcy proceedings were complete. At that same meeting Mrs. Hicks was asked to sign an affidavit presented to her which had already been signed on behalf of the Bank by Mrs. Keef and Doris Arnold, another vice president. The affidavit, introduced as Plaintiff's Exhibit # 2, stated:

> IT IS understood and agreed by the undersigned, that KATHY HICKS is being transferred to a non-contact position within FIRST NATIONAL BANK OF HARRISON, as a result of attached EXHIBIT A.[1]
>
> It is further understood that said transfer is made in an effort to protect the image and maintain customer confidence of First National Bank of Harrison while removing said employee from a compromising position. It is also understood that said transfer in no way reflects on the employee's job performance.
>
> Said transfer is effective this 24th day of October, 1985 and will remain in effect until such time condition mentioned in Exhibit A has been resolved.

Mrs. Hicks refused to sign.

Mrs. Keef, whose duties at the time of Mrs. Hicks' transfer included supervising customer relations, testified that the Bank's decision to remove Mrs. Hicks from the teller window was prompted by "the bankruptcy notice the day before" the transfer. Mrs. Hicks' protests about the transfer were to no avail. She has remained in the bookkeeping department since her transfer the day after the notice of the bankruptcy appeared in the Harrison paper. Mrs. Keef testified that the Bank had three reasons for transferring Mrs. Hicks. According to Mrs. Keef, the Bank's first and foremost reason for wanting to move Mrs. Hicks "from her position of cash handling to one without was for Kathy herself," to prevent her embarassment [sic]. Mrs. Hicks testified that she had explained to the Bank that she would not be embarassed [sic] to remain as a teller and the credible testimony showed that Mrs. Hicks remained unwaivering in her insistence that she be allowed to keep her position. In light of Mrs. Hicks' testimony, the Bank's first "reason" provided no justification for the transfer. The second reason the Bank gave for the transfer was its fear of possible harm to customer relations and public confidence if Mrs. Hicks were allowed to remain at the teller window. Mrs. Keef testified in that regard as follows:

> Public confidence is difficult to measure and hard to maintain. * * * Banking is extremely competitive in Harrison and having [good] customer relations very important.

---

[1] Exhibit A was a copy of the article that appeared in the Harrison newspaper giving notice of Mrs. Hicks' bankruptcy filing.

> Personal contact is extremely important for First National Bank. And without confidence, we have no business.
>
> We felt that, upon the notice [of Mrs. Hicks' bankruptcy] in the paper, there was no confidence as before.

Except for Mrs. Keef's self-serving testimony on point, to which the Court finds no weight should be given, the record is devoid of evidence that customer relations or public confidence was in fact harmed in any way. Mrs. Keef testified further that the move was necessary because the Bank could not bond a teller who had financial difficulties. However, there was no other evidence offered to support such contention, and the Court does not credit Mrs. Keef's statement on point.

The evidence reveals that Mrs. Hicks was a good employee who had received raises in her position as teller and special recognition for having a perfect quarter, i.e., for being totally balanced at the teller window throughout a three-month period.

It is uncontroverted that the transfer did not involve a decrease in pay. In fact, Mrs. Hicks has received a raise of 5%—the highest given—since her transfer to the bookkeeping department. The credible evidence on point also shows that the bookkeeping department and the in-take, or teller, department at the Bank are set up on the same pay scale with identical advancement opportunities.

ISSUES

1. Was Mrs. Hicks the victim of discrimination by the Bank because of her bankruptcy?

2. If so, was the discrimination solely because she had filed bankruptcy?

3. If a § 525(b) violation is found, is Mrs. Hicks entitled to her old position and to attorneys fees and costs?

CONCLUSIONS OF LAW

1. DISCRIMINATION

One of the specific purposes of the federal system of bankruptcy is to provide the debtor "a fresh start in life, free from debts, except of a certain character." *Stellwagen v. Clum*, 245 U.S. 605, 617

(1918). The "fresh start" policy was first strenghtened [sic] by the United States Supreme Court in *Perez v. Campbell*, 402 U.S. 637 (1971), when it restricted the discrimination that could be practiced against discharged debtors. The Bankruptcy Reform Act of 1978 codified *Perez* in what is now § 525(a) of the Code * * * . In the Bankruptcy Amendments and Federal Judgeship Act of 1984, Congress extended the anti-discrimination provisions to the private sector by adding a new subsection to the Code [§ 525(b)] * * * . The only reported case under the new subsection, deals with a situation in which the debtor was fired by her private employer as a result of her bankruptcy filing. *In re Hopkins*, 66 B.R. 828 (Bankr. W.D.Ark.1986). In *Hopkins* the Court found a § 525(b) violation.

There is no question but that, through her involuntary transfer to a non-public contact department, Mrs. Hicks has been treated differently than the Bank's other efficient, qualified tellers. The real issue becomes whether the discriminatory treatment of Mrs. Hicks is the type the Code was designed to prohibit. A recent law journal article has analyzed § 525(b) and concludes:

> It would appear that discrimination for proscribed reasons having the effect of not only terminating an individual's employment, but also affecting his or her promotions, salary increases, job duties, discipline or any terms or conditions of employment, can be said to come within the protections afforded individuals.

Chobot, "Anti–Discrimination Under the Bankruptcy Laws," 60 Am. Bankr. L.J. 185, 197 (1986). This Court agrees that the discrimination prohibition of § 525(b) is violated when the debtor/employee's job duties are affected by the employer's actions, even though there are no adverse economic consequences as a result of the change in duties. In the case now before the Court it is undisputed that Mrs. Hicks' duties were changed from one of dealing with the public and handling cash to one with little or no customer contact and no handling of cash transactions. Therefore, the Court concludes that the Bank did discriminate against Mrs. Hicks with respect to her employment.

2. "Solely Because Such Debtor * * * Is a Debtor"

Even though discrimination is present, in order to prevail under § 525, Mrs. Hicks must provide sufficient evidence to establish that the discriminatory treatment resulted solely because of her bankruptcy status.

Mrs. Keef, Mrs. Hicks' supervisor, admitted that Mrs. Hicks' transfer away from the teller window was made because of the notice of the bankruptcy in the paper and the Bank's fear that customer relations could be harmed if Mrs. Hicks remained in that position. As the facts set out above show, the Bank had confidence in Mrs. Hicks as a teller and had given her raises and rewards in that job. Further, there was no evidence that customer relations had been harmed. If an employee [sic] were allowed to change an employee's duties and position upon the premise of anticipated harm to customer relations, § 525(b) would no longer provide protection against discrimination for the debtor employee. For example, "[a]n employer could always avoid this subsection by claiming that he anticipates a loss of public confidence by allowing a debtor to remain employed." *In re Hopkins*, 66 B.R. 828, 832 (Bankr. W.D.Ark.1986).

In addition, there was no evidence that the Bank had any valid concern for Mrs. Hicks' possible dishonesty if she were allowed to remain as a teller. Further, no reason except the newspaper bankruptcy article was given for the transfer. In fact, Mrs. Keef indicated the transfer would be undone and Mrs. Hicks would again be given a position as teller once the bankruptcy proceedings end.

The facts surrounding Mrs. Hicks' transfer to the accounting department clearly establish that the decision to move her was based solely on her bankruptcy filing.

3. Remedies

(a) Position

Mrs. Hicks has requested that the Bank return her to her position as teller. Section 525(b) itself provides no remedy for violation by a private employer. As yet, there are no published cases under that new provision providing guidance for appropriate remedies. Section 525, as it appeared in the Bankruptcy Reform Act of 1978, was also devoid of any provision for remedy for governmental discrimination. Nevertheless, courts finding violations of the governmental discrimination provision have considered and awarded a variety of remedies. *See, e.g., In re Goldrich*, 45 B.R. 514 (Bankr. E.D.N.Y.1984) (injunction granted against denial of financial assistance to debtor; affirmative direction granted requiring defendants to process debtor's applications for financial assistance); *and see In re Terry*, 7 B.R. 880 (Bankr. E.D.Va.1980) (termination of employment for cause; no violation of § 525; restoration of employment considered but not justified because no violation);

In re William Tell II, Inc., 38 B.R. 327 (Bankr. N.D.Ill.1983) (affirmed bankruptcy court award ordering renewal of liquor license); *In re Aegean Fare, Inc.*, 35 B.R. 923, 929 (D.Mass.1983) (governmental agency admonished that "appropriate sanctions exist for the violation" of § 525).

Presumably the remedies awarded are derived from § 105(a) which grants the bankruptcy court the power to enforce provisions of the Bankruptcy Code.

The requested remedy in this case is in line with the remedies considered by courts under the provision regarding governmental discrimination. The Court finds that an order restoring Mrs. Hicks to her position as teller is appropriate under § 525(b) and determines that it has the power to enter such an order under § 105(a).

(b) Attorney's Fees and Costs

There is no authority in § 525 for an award of attorney's fees to the prevailing party. * * * If Congress had desired to sanction or encourage fee awards in cases under § 525, it could easily have granted the courts discretion to make such awards. It did not do so.

In the absence of specific statutory authority, a court ordinarily has no power to award attorney fees. * * * There is no reason under the facts of this case to cause an exception to the general rule that each party must bear his own costs of litigation.

* * *

Questions and Problems

1. Would *Hicks* have turned out differently if the bank had been able to establish that bank customers did not want Mrs. Hicks to handle their money because she was the debtor in a bankruptcy case?

2. Note that First National Bank of Harrison was the Hicks's principal creditor. Do you suppose that fact had any influence on the Bank's actions?

3. Colleges have, on occasion, refused to release copies of transcripts to students whose loans remain unpaid. Compare *In re Heath,* 3 B.R. 351 (Bankr.N.D.Ill.1980), with *Johnson v. Edinboro State College,* 728 F.2d 163 (3d Cir.1984). Transcripts, unlike new loan funds, have no intrinsic value to the college or university. What purpose other than collection could be furthered by refusing to release the transcript? Is that a basis for distinguishing

cases in which debtors are seeking transcripts from cases in which debtors are seeking new loans?

4. Does it matter, when debtors request copies of their college transcripts, whether the prior educational loan was discharged or was excepted from discharge?

5. May a state Board of Bar Examiners take a bankruptcy filing into account when assessing the fitness of an applicant to practice law? Cf. *Florida Board of Bar Examiners v. G.W.L.,* 364 So.2d 454 (Fla.1978); *Application of Gahan,* 279 N.W.2d 826 (Minn. 1979).

6. An architectural firm filed bankruptcy while in the process of negotiating with a general contractor to obtain a subcontract for work on a people-mover to be built at O'Hare Airport. Negotiations ceased and the debtor sought an injunction to prevent the general contractor from hiring another architect. What result under § 525? See *In re Madison Madison International of Illinois, P.C.*, 77 B.R. 678 (Bankr. E.D.Wis.1987).

7. The General Services Administration, a federal agency, advertised used cars for sale. Small print at the bottom of the ad said "Credit terms available." When Michael Brown offered to buy a car, the GSA demanded cash because Brown had just come out of bankruptcy. Has the GSA violated § 525?

8. Debtor is a sergeant in the armed forces with a top security clearance. If he is denied a transfer to the staff of the Joint Chiefs, solely on the grounds that he filed a bankruptcy petition, is § 525 violated? See *Applegate v. March (In re Applegate)*, 64 B.R. 448 (Bankr. E.D.Va. 1986).

Chapter 8

REORGANIZATION

A. INTRODUCTION

Chapter 11 is designed to accomplish the financial rehabilitation of, chiefly, business enterprises. (But remember *Toibb v. Radloff*!) Its underlying premise is that the assets of a particular enterprise are best used by being kept together so that the value of the going concern can be preserved. Given that premise, it may come as a shock to learn that most Chapter 11 cases do not culminate in the confirmation of a plan, much less its successful performance. One can only speculate as to why. Many of these firms, most likely, never belonged in Chapter 11 in the first place for one reason or another—they were bad business ideas from the beginning, or they were too far gone for resuscitation by the time bankruptcy was filed. Immediate liquidation, however, rarely serves a corporate debtor. Management personnel can remain in control as debtor-in-possession, preserving jobs for employees (and for themselves) while trying to reorganize, and they may also be able to preserve something for shareholders. Since many, if not most, Chapter 11 debtors are closely held corporations, managers *are* shareholders. If the corporation is insolvent, the reorganization effort will be made with other people's money. The manager-shareholders will enjoy the upside benefit of a successful reorganization, but they carry none of the downside risk. Failure in the reorganization effort costs them nothing.

Another explanation, currently in vogue, for Chapter 11's failure rate is that Chapter 11 is itself fundamentally flawed. See Michael Bradley & Michael Rosenzweig, *The Untenable Case for Chapter 11*, 101 Yale L.J. 1043 (1992). But see Donald R. Korobkin, *The Unwarranted Case Against Corporate Reorganization: A Reply to Bradley and Rosenzweig*, 78 Iowa L. Rev. 669 (1993); Lynn M. LoPucki, *Strange Visions in a Strange World: A Reply to Professors Bradley and Rosenzweig*, 91 Mich. L. Rev. 79 (1992); Elizabeth Warren, *The Untenable Case for Repeal of Chapter 11*, 102 Yale. L.J. 437 (1992).

Whatever the reason for the failures, Chapter 11 has brought us some remarkable (and sometimes successful) cases—A.H. Robins, Johns–Manville, LTV, Texaco and Eastern Airlines, just to name a few. Recall why these particular debtors filed bankruptcy and you will begin to appreciate the power and flexibility of Chapter 11: Robins and Manville were faced with enormous tort liabilities; LTV owed substantial environmental and pension plan obligations; Texaco could not afford the supersedeas bond necessary to stay Pennzoil's collection of its multi-billion dollar judgment during appeal; and Eastern had union troubles (among others). In cases such as these, Chapter 11 is theater, too.

B. AUTOMATIC STAY

Although you have already become familiar with the automatic stay, a few special applications arise in the context of a reorganization case. The next case illustrates the possibilities.

GAF CORP. v. JOHNS–MANVILLE CORP. (MATTER OF JOHNS–MANVILLE CORP.)

United States Bankruptcy Court, Southern District of New York, 1983.
26 B.R. 405, *affirmed sub nom. Johns–Manville Corp. v. Asbestos Litigation Group (In re Johns–Manville Corp.)*, 40 B.R. 219 (S.D.N.Y.1984).

BURTON R. LIFLAND, Bankruptcy Judge.

I. BACKGROUND FACTS

Plaintiffs in this declaratory judgment action are inviting this Court pursuant to its equitable powers to broaden the automatic stay afforded the debtor under § 362 to include the non-debtor plaintiffs. Essentially, these plaintiffs request by motion for summary judgment that this Court make a ruling which would be the ultimate determination for all courts across the country as to the indispensable nature of Manville in asbestos litigation pending in various state and federal forums.

The plaintiffs are co-defendants of Johns–Manville, Inc. ("Manville") in approximately 11,000 asbestos-related personal injury and property damage suits to which Manville or any of its affiliates is a party. * * *

II. FACTS REGARDING THE INSTANT PROCEEDING

On August 26, 1982, Manville filed a petition within the framework of Chapter 11 of the Bankruptcy Code (the "Code"). Pursuant to § 362(a) of the Code, the filing of the petition triggered an automatic stay of the commencement or continuation of all proceedings against Manville that had been or could have been commenced prior to the bringing of Manville's Chapter 11 petition. On the same date, this Court entered a restraining order substantially identical to the § 362 stay.

Seeking to broaden the Manville stay so as to include them, the co-defendants assert that such an order is vital for the orderly liquidation of claims against Manville. They point out that courts throughout the country have reached inconsistent results with respect to the effects of the stay on co-defendants. They further contend that they have unliquidated and contingent claims against Manville for contribution or idemnification [sic] relating to the asbestos cases. They argue that a stay order applicable to them is necessary to facilitate the equitable administration of the Manville estate and to allow all parties to concentrate on a plan of reorganization rather than to apply their resources to duplicative and protracted litigation. They submit that this Chapter 11 case is so extraordinary and the debtors['] involvement in the subject litigation is so inextricably bound up with the rights and responsibilities of the co-defendants and the class they represent that this Court must exercise its power pursuant to § 105 of the Code in the interest of facilitating a comprehensive plan of reorganization which will resolve on a global basis this mammoth problem.

* * *

The co-defendants argue that this relief would facilitate the resolution and liquidation of claims, relieve this Court of the burden of trying the many asbestos cases now pending throughout the country, allow equitable treatment of all Manville's creditors and avoid duplicative litigation.

* * *

III. Issues Presented

The issues presented are: (1) whether this Court should take the unprecedented step of exercising its discretion pursuant to § 105 of the Code to extend the § 362 automatic stay so as to encompass the co-defendants herein * * *.

IV. Discussion of Law

Upon examination of the actual wording and legislative history of §§ 362 and 105 and the relevant case law, it is the determination of this court not to extend Manville's § 362 automatic stay on a global basis so as to prohibit the pursuance of all claims against all co-defendants in every case now pending throughout the country. Rather, the determination of this issue must remain lodged with the court before whom each individual case is pending.

The co-defendants have argued at various times during these proceedings that this court consider their plea that a universal stay will have the effect of creating an atmosphere within the Manville reorganization that could accommodate an industry-wide solution of the entire asbestos health-related problem. They hypothesize a suspension of the enormous litigation nationwide which would facilitate the creation of: a superfund or pool to which they, the insurance industry and Manville would contribute; and, a delivery system to the health claimants. To the extent that the co-defendants purported goal is to join in the creation of an expedient, efficient and fair compensatory delivery system to asbestos victims, their aim is indeed laudable, notwithstanding their self-advancing motivations. The co-defendants assert that extending the stay will shift the focus from asbestos lawsuits and render the asbestos claimants more amenable to cooperate with the debtors and others, including the insurance industry, to achieve a successful reorganization that could include present claimants, as well as future victims who have not as yet manifested symptoms of asbestos-related disease. Indeed, this suspension of the litigation might well serve the purposes urged by the co-defendants.

However, such a pervasive stay, while tempting, is not within this Court's power at this juncture because, as fully discussed *infra*, the scope of § 362 is narrowly focused on protection of the debtor only. Such a pervasive extension of the stay may not be accomplished by judicial fiat. Thus, I am constrained to declare that so broad an extension of the automatic stay must either be accomplished by legislation or conceivably as part of an eventual reorganization plan.

* * *

A. The Main Relief Sought

1. The Scope of § 362 of the Bankruptcy Code

* * *

The language of § 362 clearly refers only to actions against the debtor and does not relate to any other interparty claims. * * *

Furthermore, the legislative history of § 362 indicates that the automatic stay protects creditors from the injustice of a race for the *debtor's* assets:

> The automatic stay also provides creditor protection. Without it, certain creditors would be able to pursue their own remedies against the *debtor's* property. Those who acted first would obtain payment of the claims in preference to and to the detriment of other creditors. Bankruptcy is designed to provide an orderly liquidation procedure under which all creditors are treated equally. A race of diligence by creditors for the *debtor's* assets prevents that.

H.R. Rep. No. 95–595 at 340, *reprinted in* 1978 U.S.C.C.A.N. at 6297 (emphasis added).

The legislative history also notes that § 362 is designed to protect the debtor:

> The automatic stay is one of the fundamental debtor protections provided by the bankruptcy laws. It gives the debtor a breathing spell from his creditors. It stops all collection efforts, all

> harassment, and all foreclosure actions. It permits the debtor to attempt a repayment or reorganization plan, or simply to be relieved of the financial pressures that drove him into bankruptcy.

S. Rep. No. 95–989 at 54–55, *reprinted in* 1978 U.S.C.C.A.N. at 5840–41.

Notwithstanding this limited focus of § 362, the co-defendants urge the Court to use its discretionary powers to include them under the penumbra of § 362's protection. However, although I find their arguments attractive, I do not find their request for such an extension of the automatic stay supportable at law. This holding is formulated against a background of authority denying such relief in bankruptcy cases generally as well as in other courts' decisions in the Manville and United Asbestos and Rubber Co. ("Unarco") bankruptcy cases.

* * *

Courts across the country have been faced with the dilemma of whether to proceed in asbestos litigation in the absence of a co-defendant which has filed for Chapter 11. These courts have reached differing conclusions depending upon the individual facts in each case. Some courts have allowed the actions to continue against co-defendants in the absence of Manville or Unarco. *See, e.g.*, *In re Related Asbestos Cases*, 23 B.R. 523 (N.D.Cal.1982), where the court held that § 362 does not apply to claims against non-bankrupt co-defendants. In this California case, Chief Judge Peckham ordered the severance of the claims against Manville and Unarco and allowed the cases against the co-defendants to continue. He held that FRCP Rule 19 is no impediment to the continuation of these suits because joint tortfeasors are not indispensable parties.

The courts in the above-cited cases have * * * relied on the plain language of § 362(a) which acts as a stay of actions against the debtor only. These courts also note that the legislative history supports this construction and rely on the comparison between the specific statutory provision for extension of the stay to co-debtors in Chapter 13[a] and the absence of any counterpart to it in Chapter 11.[3]

---

[a] Section 1301(a). Eds.

[3] It is true, as the co-defendants indicate, that some courts have stayed the actions as to all defendants until further order of the court. * * * In the instances where trial courts have prohibited suits from going forward without Manville or Unarco, there

* * *

In light of the clear language and legislative history of § 362(a), the promulgation of a specific provision to stay proceedings against co-defendants of Chapter 13 debtors and case law interpretation, this court holds that § 362 is limited in scope to the debtor and does not operate to stay actions against the co-defendants of this debtor.

Moreover, it cannot be held that as a matter of law Manville is an indispensable party to the asbestos litigation. Under federal law, joint tortfeasors are not considered indispensable parties.

Further, a universal finding that Manville is an indispensable party to all the thousands of cases in which it is currently a defendant is not possible on the facts before the court today. * * *

[T]he determination of indispensability must be made on a case-by-case basis by the courts across the country where the asbestos litigation is pending. The facts of a particular case may render Manville an indispensable party. For example, if Manville supplied the major portion of asbestos products in a particular location it could be held to be unfair to proceed in Manville's absence. That the indispensability is best determined on a case-by-case basis is illustrated by the divergent results reached by courts in applying a FRCP Rule 19 analysis. It would be most inappropriate for this court, without detailed knowledge of the specific factual contexts, to issue a sweeping ruling on Manville's indispensability. This ruling is properly lodged with each individual trial court. This holding should not be construed to preclude consideration of stay extension to non-debtor parties in a narrower setting where something more than the filing of a bankruptcy petition by a party is shown.

2. Scope of § 105 of the Bankruptcy Code Where No Statutory Basis Exists for the Grant of Stay Relief

Notwithstanding the limited focus of § 362, the co-defendants propose that the Court use its powers under § 105 of the Code so as to provide them with injunctive relief unavailable to them under § 362. The issue thereby presented is whether the All Writs Statute embodied in § 105 can be used where no statutory basis exists to grant stay relief.

---

were either specific trial court findings of indispensability or the stay was ordered separate and apart from § 362. Accordingly, these asbestos cases cited by the co-defendants do not support the instant application for a broad and blanket extension of the automatic stay to cover all co-defendants in all suits on a global basis.

Although § 105 may be used to extend the stay, § 105 does not have a life of its own and this extension may only be accomplished within the proper boundaries of § 362. That is, unless this extension is designed to protect the debtor's interests, it cannot be granted.

* * *

Section 105 of the Code was not intended to grant the bankruptcy court powers without bounds, and the court's equitable powers thereunder are not unrestricted.

The crux of the matter before this Court is whether the injunctive relief sought by the co-defendants under § 105(a) is "necessary or appropriate" in order to achieve the goals of a Chapter 11 reorganization. A request for an injunction pending confirmation of the debtor's plans, such as the one requested by the co-defendants, is deemed a request for a preliminary injunction.

* * *

Therefore, * * * [t]he co-defendants here must show that without the sought-after relief, they will suffer irreparable injury and that they are likely to prevail on the merits. * * *

The co-defendants argue that they will suffer irreparable injury if § 105(a) of the Code is not employed by this Court to expand the stay afforded the debtor by virtue of § 362 to encompass co-defendants. It therefore follows, they argue, that because the co-defendants will suffer irreparable injury without the presence of Manville, Manville is an indispensable party to all of the litigation pending throughout the nation.

The co-defendants indicate a number of specific examples of the injuries they claim they will suffer without injunctive relief. First, they allege that there will be a multiplicity of actions resulting in an increased risk of inconsistent verdicts and a great increase in litigation costs to the co-defendants. Second, they claim that the asbestos lawsuits contain issues of comparative negligence, apportionment among joint tortfeasors, and primary and secondary liability with respect to sellers of asbestos products and suppliers of raw asbestos itself. They argue that without Manville as a party to the litigation, each defendant will not be able fairly to determine its share of liability. Third, the co-defendants contend that their ability to obtain discovery and production of documents from Manville has been severely impaired by Manville's filing. Fourth, they argue that long-established coordinated defense efforts between Manville and the co-defendants will be devastated if the relief sought is not granted. Finally, the co-defendants point out that Manville is currently in litigation with a number of insurance companies regarding questions of insurance coverage of asbestos-related claims. The co-defendants urge that should it be established that Manville is covered by insurance for some or all of the asbestos claims, then Manville's defense of these cases in the courts in which they arose would be able to go forward without a substantial detrimental effect on property of the estate.

The co-defendants rely upon *In re Otero Mills, Inc.*, 21 B.R. 777 (Bankr. D.N.M.), *aff'd sub nom. Otero Mills, Inc. v. Security Bank & Trust (In re Otero Mills, Inc.)*, 25 B.R. 1018 (D.N.M.1982), in their attempt to employ § 105 to enjoin actions not directly covered by § 362. In *Otero*, the debtor had executed a number of promissory notes which were guaranteed by its president. The holder of the notes brought suit against the president of the corporation to collect on the notes. The debtor argued that irreparable harm would result if the foreclosure were allowed because the property subject to the foreclosure was property which the president planned to sell with the intention that the proceeds be contributed to the debtor for the payment of corporate debts. The court agreed and extended the stay to encompass the debtor's president.

While it is true that in *Otero* a creditor was stayed from continuing an action against a non-debtor party, the case does not support the ubiquitous relief sought by the co-defendants. *Otero* sets forth the following standards for a court to employ in deciding whether to prohibit the continuance of a suit against a non-debtor party:

> The power to enjoin extends to some cases of a creditor's action against a co-debtor or guarantor, but only in limited circumstances. To so enjoin a creditor's actions against a third party, the court must find that failure to enjoin would affect the bankruptcy estate and would adversely or detrimentally influence and pressure the debtor through that third party. * * * This power to enjoin assures that a creditor may not do indirectly that which he is forbidden to do directly. Accordingly, § 105 permits this Court to enjoin a creditor's action against a third party co-debtor or guarantor when the proper showing is made by the party requesting the injunction. * * * [Therefore, to obtain such a stay] the debtor must show:

> 1. Irreparable harm to the bankruptcy estate if the injunction does not issue;
>
> 2. Strong likelihood of success on the merits; and
>
> 3. No harm or minimal harm to the other party or parties.

21 B.R. at 778–79 (citations omitted).

While these standard[s] were met in *Otero*, it is abundantly clear that the first requirement cannot be met in the instant case. That Manville is basically indifferent to the co-defendants' requested relief is suggestive of a perception of a lack of irreparable harm to the debtor's estate if the injunction does not issue. Failure to extend the stay herein would not adversely or detrimentally influence or pressure Manville through the co-defendants. This is because the interests of Manville and the co-defendants at the individual trial level are not so interwoven as to create that undue influence. Thus, at least conceptually, a creditor does not impact Manville indirectly by proceeding against the co-defendants.

In addition, the co-defendants have made no showing with regard to the second requirement. Moreover, the third requirement cannot be met. The asbestos victims will certainly suffer by the total frustration of their opportunity for a day in court. As Chief Judge Peckham stated in the context of asbestos litigation:

> Such delay is not costless to these plaintiffs, many of whom are suffering financial hardships and who seek damages to redress their injuries and some of whom are dying and whose testimony must be perpetuated. The defendants may be inconvenienced by expeditious resumption of the actions against them. However, under *Landis*, the balance of hardship weighs in favor of the injured plaintiffs.

In re Related Asbestos Cases, 23 B.R. 523, 531–32 (N.D.Cal.1982) (citing *Landis v. North American Co.*, 299 U.S. 248 (1936)).

* * *

In sum, § 105 of the Code cannot operate here to expand the scope of § 362. Because § 105 can only be used to allow a court to issue all "necessary or appropriate" orders to carry out the provisions of Title 11, it cannot be used to carry out an order in contravention of the narrow focus of § 362. In an appropriate case, where the proposed extension of the stay is designed to cover actions against entities that truly are inextricably interwoven with the debtor or which affect property of the debtor's estate, § 105 may be used. In the instant case, such is not the situation as any liability of these co-defendants is not directly attributable to the debtor as it would be if these co-defendants were, for example, key employees of the debtor. In order for these key employees to be covered by the stay, it would have to be shown that they are prevented from carrying out their reorganization duties of plan formulation because of participation in the litigation. Co-defendants have not met their burden of proof in satisfying the injunctive relief standards for extending the stay by means of § 105 of the Code.

* * *

Questions

1. Is the reach of §§ 362(a) or 105 equivalent to a determination of indispensability under the Federal Rules of Civil Procedure? If so, why are the co-defendants arguing this issue in bankruptcy court?

2. Is the court in *Manville* suggesting that § 105 is coextensive with a request for injunctive relief? If so, is § 105 necessary—that is, could a party obtain an injunction under generally applicable law even in the absence of § 105?

3. The court said that industry-wide relief "must either be accomplished by legislation or conceivably as part of an eventual reorganization plan." If a court has no power to fashion industry-wide relief under §§ 105 and 362, why can it grant such relief as part of a reorganization plan?

4. Recall that in 1994 Congress added § 524(g), which codifies the trust device created in *Manville* and the channeling injunction that effectuated it. Would § 524(g) control the result in the principal case if it were to arise now?

5. Section 105 has been invoked not only to protect nondebtors under the automatic stay; it has also been relied upon by proponents of plan provisions that would release nondebtors and permanently enjoin any actions against them. A provision in the Continental Airlines reorganization plan, for example, enjoined shareholder suits against certain present and former directors and officers who were not themselves in bankruptcy. The bankruptcy and district courts upheld the provision, but the Third Circuit reversed, finding the provision legally and factually unsupportable. *Gillman v. Continental Airlines (In re Continental Airlines)*, 203 F.3d 203 (3d Cir.2000). The court recognized that other courts have "adopted a more flexible approach," notably in the

Drexel, Manville and Robins bankruptcies, but the plans in those cases established trusts through which consideration was paid to the affected parties:

> A central focus of these three reorganizations was the global settlement of massive liabilities against the debtors and co-liable parties. Substantial debtor co-liable parties provided compensation to claimants in exchange for the release of their liabilities and made these reorganizations feasible.
>
> * * *
>
> * * * [T]he provision in the Continental Debtors' plan releasing and permanently enjoining Plaintiffs; lawsuits against the non-debtor D&O defendants does not pass muster under even the most flexible tests for the validity of non-debtor releases. The hallmarks of permissible non-consensual releases—fairness, necessity to the reorganization, and specific factual findings to support these conclusions—are all absent here.

Id. at 212-214 (footnote omitted). The court declined to take the opportunity to set out the circumstances under which such an injunction might be upheld.

Note on Single Asset Real Estate Cases

Single asset real estate cases (often called "SAREs," for short) are those in which the debtor's principal asset is a single piece of real property (frequently, a not-yet-completed development project) and the only large creditor is the undersecured mortgagee. Such debtors may have few, if any, employees, and only a small amount of unsecured debt. These debtors may be newly-created corporate entities, formed solely to act as transferee of the property at issue. Transfer of the property to a new corporation enables the transferor to insulate its other assets from bankruptcy and to obtain the benefits of the automatic stay for the troubled parcel. For this reason, these fact patterns have become known as the "new debtor syndrome." *In re N.R. Guaranteed Retirement, Inc.,* 112 B.R. 263, 273 (Bankr.N.D.Ill.), affirmed 119 B.R. 149 (N.D.Ill.1990). Bankruptcy cases with this fact pattern are not new, but large numbers of them began to appear in the 1980s when the value of heavily encumbered parcels of land tumbled.

These cases raise questions that go to the heart of bankruptcy, chiefly because they do not present the "common pool" problem often identified as Chapter 11's fundamental jurisprudential justification. (Recall the Jackson excerpt in Chapter 2, Section A, of this casebook.) Instead, they involve the type of dispute, between a debtor and one creditor, for which state law remedies were designed. When these disputes are brought into bankruptcy, therefore, they raise serious questions regarding "good faith" and, ultimately, the appropriate function of bankruptcy. *See, e.g., Phoenix Piccadilly v. Life Insurance Co. of Virginia (In re Phoenix Piccadilly),* 849 F.2d 1393 (11th

Cir.1988) (reprinted in Chapter 2, Section B.3 of this casebook); *Little Creek Development Co. v. Commonwealth Mortgage Corp. (Matter of Little Creek Development Co.),* 779 F.2d 1068 (5th Cir.1986); H. Miles Cohn, *Good Faith and the Single–Asset Debtor,* 62 Am.Bankr.L.J. 131 (1988); Brian S. Katz, *Single–Asset Real Estate Cases and the Good Faith Requirement: Why Reluctance to Ask Whether a Case Belongs in Bankruptcy May Lead to the Incorrect Result,* 9 Bankr.Dev.J. 77 (1992).

Apparently Congress has decided that single asset real estate cases should not be excluded from bankruptcy (despite the conclusion by the court in *Phoenix Piccadilly* that a SARE should be dismissed for bad faith), given the addition to the Code in 1994 of an automatic stay provision addressed to them. The next case deals with at least two of the questions the provision raises.

IN RE OCEANSIDE MISSION ASSOCIATES

United States Bankruptcy Court, Southern District of California, 1996.
192 B.R. 232.

PETER W. BOWIE, Judge.

The senior secured creditor contends that this is a "single asset real estate" case and that the debtor must be held to the requirements of newly enacted § 362(d)(3).

* * *

FACTS

The debtor, a limited partnership, owns undeveloped real property which generates no income. The property is subject to secured claims which exceed $4,000,000, but may be worth less than $4,000,000. The senior secured creditor has asked for relief from the automatic stay in part on the grounds that the property is "single asset real estate" and that the debtor has failed to comply with § 362(d)(3).

ANALYSIS

Section 218 of the Bankruptcy Reform Act of 1994 added two new subsections to the Bankruptcy Code to deal with the "single asset real estate" case. Section 101(51B) defines "single asset real estate" and § 362(d)(3) provides that the court shall grant relief from stay with respect to an act against "single asset real estate" unless the debtor has filed a plan or commenced interest payments within 90 days of the petition. It is undisputed that the debtor has failed to file a plan or commence payments within 90 days. The issue is whether the property is "single asset real estate."

[The court quoted § 101(51B).] The parties agree that the property is a "single property or project, other than residential real property with fewer than 4 residential units." The parties disagree as to whether § 101(51B) includes undeveloped or raw land that generates no income and, if so, whether the $4,000,000 limit on secured debts takes into account the value of the property; i.e., does one aggregate all asserted secured claims or only those which would be a "secured claim" under § 506(a)?

1. Must the Real Property Generate Income?

The definition of "single asset real estate" is limited to real property "which generates substantially all of the gross income of a debtor and on which no substantial business is being conducted by a debtor other than the business of operating the real property." Congress has obviously attempted to exclude certain debtors, but which ones? Section 101(51B) is clearly designed to exclude debtors that, although they own a single piece of property, have other income generating operations. The question is whether it is also meant to exclude debtors that own undeveloped land that generates no income. The language of the statute is, unfortunately, ambiguous.

Reading the first, or "gross income," clause to *include* raw land that generates no income is awkward but possible. If the debtor has no income, then substantially all of its income could be said to be generated by the property; i.e., substantially all of nothing is nothing. In addition to the awkwardness, this interpretation seems to render the second clause, "and on which no substantial business is being conducted by a debtor other than the business of operating the real property," superfluous. If the debtor has no "gross income", then the debtor is obviously not conducting "substantial business" on the property, or anywhere else for that matter. Conversely, a debtor operating a substantial business would not derive substantially all of its income from the property and would thus be excluded under either clause. It is well settled that statutes are to be interpreted so as to avoid rendering any portion superfluous. Thus, one might conclude that the two clauses are designed to exclude different types of property: the "gross income" clause to exclude property which generates no income and the "substantial business" clause to exclude restaurants, hotels, and the like. There are, however, problems with this interpretation.

Interpreting the statute to *exclude* raw land does not appear to serve the purpose of the statutory scheme. Sections 101(51B) and 362(d)(3) are designed to require debtors with "single asset real estate" to act in an expedited fashion. § 362(d)(3). The consequence of not acting quickly is that the automatic stay may be lifted without further ado. There is no apparent purpose for Congress to have excused debtors who own only raw land from this expedited program: If a debtor who owns an apartment complex is forced to act quickly why not a debtor who owns raw land? Legislative enactments are not to be construed as establishing statutory schemes that defeat the purpose of the statutes. Rather, appropriate statutory construction favors the more reasonable result. It is much more plausible that the "gross income" clause and the "substantial business" clause were both meant to exclude debtors who happen to own real property but who are also involved in income generating businesses in addition to ownership of the real property.

Since the language of § 101(51B) is unclear it is appropriate to look to the legislative history. With the Reform Act, Congress provided a "Section-By-Section Description" in which it paraphrased the definition of "single asset real estate":

> *Section 218. Single asset real estate*
>
> This section will add a new definition to the Code for "single asset real estate," meaning real property * * * which generates substantially all of the gross income of the debtor and has aggregate noncontingent, liquidated secured debts in an amount up to $4 million.

H.R. Rep. No. 835, 103rd Cong., 2nd Sess. (1994), *reprinted in* 1994 U.S.C.C.A.N. at 3340. In describing the scope of "single asset real estate" Congress apparently found it unnecessary to use the "substantial business" clause. If the two clauses were meant to exclude different types of debtor, then the "substantial business" clause would have had to have been included in the paraphrase. Since it was not, one might conclude that both clauses were meant to exclude debtors with income generating operations beyond the real property. Other legislative history supports this conclusion.

Section 218 of the Reform Act can be traced back to § 211 of S. 1985 which provided:

> "single asset real estate" means real property, other than residential real property with fewer than 4 residential units,

> which generates substantially all of the gross income of a debtor and on which no substantial business is being conducted by a debtor other than the business of operating the real property and activities incidental thereto * * * .

S. 1985, 102nd Cong., 2d Sess. § 211(a)(2) (1992). Senate Report 279 explained that "single asset real estate" was to be "limited to investment property of the debtor." S.Rep. No. 279, 102nd Cong., 2d Sess., May 7, 1992. Surely if any property is considered "investment property," raw, undeveloped land would be.

When faced with the task of interpreting "single asset real estate" the court in *In re Philmont Development Co.*, 181 Bankr. 220 (Bankr.E.D.Pa.1995), found that the legislative history which accompanied the Reform Act was not particularly "illuminating." The court noted, however, that:

> The terms single asset case, or single asset real estate case, are well-known and often used colloquialisms which essentially refer to real estate entities attempting to cling to ownership of real property in a depressed market * * * rather than businesses involving manufacturing, sales or services. * * * The drafters of sections of (sic) 101(51B) and 362(d)(3) were aware of the colloquial use of the phrase "single asset real estate," and the Court believes that their intention in using that phrase grew out of its previous colloquial and common usage.

Id. at 223 (citations omitted.) It is well settled that where Congress uses terms that have accumulated settled meaning under the common law, a court should infer, unless the statute otherwise dictates, that Congress meant to incorporate the established meaning of these terms. In *In re KKEMKO, Inc.*, 181 B.R. 47 (Bankr.S.D.Ohio 1995), the court also looked to the history of the usage of the term "single asset real estate" and stated, albeit in dicta, that the definition in § 101(51B) did include raw land.

This Court has reviewed many of the cases that used the phrase "single asset real estate," and discovered several in which the phrase was applied to raw, undeveloped land.

If Congress intended to exclude raw land from the definition they would have done so specifically or at least explained in the comments that the definition was meant to exclude raw land. Without such an express exclusion this court does not believe that Congress meant for "single asset real estate" to mean less than it did before the sections were enacted. Although it requires a bit of a tortured reading, based upon the statutory purpose of the new sections, the limited legislative history, the usage of the term "single asset real estate" in prior case law and the fact that excluding raw land would simply not make sense, this Court concludes that "single asset real estate" includes undeveloped real property which generates no income.

2. Should the Calculation of the Amount of the Secured Debt Take Into Consideration the Value of the Property?

Section 101(51B) is limited to debtors with "aggregate non-contingent, liquidated secured debts in an amount no more than $4,000,000." Debtors with secured debts exceeding $4,000,000 are excused from compliance with the expedited schedule of § 362(d)(3). Presumably Congress decided that cases of a certain magnitude ought to be afforded more than 90 days to file a plan or begin making interest payments. The Debtor has scheduled secured claims in excess of $4,000,000 and argues that it ought to be excused. The secured creditor argues that secured claims cannot exceed the value of the collateral and since the property is worth less than $4,000,000 the secured claims cannot exceed $4,000,000. The Debtor, argues the secured creditor, is, therefore, required to comply with § 362(d)(3) or relief must be granted.

The $4,000,000 limitation is not explained in the legislative history, nor is there prior case law from which it was derived. The determination of whether the secured claims exceed the cap must be made in a way which is consistent with other provisions of the Code: statutory construction is a holistic endeavor.

[The court quoted § 506(a).] Congress explained that the effect of § 506(a) is that an undersecured creditor "has a secured claim to the extent of the value of his collateral; and he has an unsecured claim for the balance of his claim." S. Rep. No. 95-989, *reprinted in* 1978 U.S.C.C.A.N. at 5854. Looking only to this section one might conclude that secured claims are limited to the value of the collateral. However, secured claim is given a different meaning in other sections.

In *Dewsnup v. Timm*, 502 U.S. 410 (1992), the court determined that "allowed secured claim" used in § 506(d) means the full allowed amount of the creditor's claim regardless of the value of the collateral.

Similarly, in § 1129(b)(2) Congress clearly distinguished between the amount of a secured claim and the value of the creditor's interest in collateral. *[The court quoted § 1129(b)(2)(A)(i)(II).]* Congress provided an example of the application of § 1129(b)(2)(A)(i)(II):

> For example, if a creditor loaned $15,000,000 to a debtor secured by real property worth $18,000,000 and the value of the real property had dropped to $12,000,000 by the date when the debtor commenced a proceeding under chapter 11, the plan could be confirmed notwithstanding the dissent of the creditor as long as the lien remains on the collateral to secure a $15,000,000 debt, the face amount of present or extended payments to be made to the creditor under the plan is at least $15,000,000, and the present value of the present or deferred payments is not less than $12,000,000.

124 Cong. Rec. H. 11102 (Sept. 28, 1978). If Congress meant for the amount of a secured claim to be limited to the value of the collateral then there were would be no difference between the first reference "the allowed amount of such claim" and the second reference "the value of such holder's interest in the estate's interest in such property." The first requirement would be superfluous because a string of payments with a certain present value will always total at least the amount of such value.[1] * * *

The first requirement in § 1129(b)(2)(A)(i)(II) is not, however, superfluous because a secured creditor, in most instances, is allowed to elect to have his entire claim treated as secured notwithstanding the value of the property. § 1111(b). If such an election is made, then notwithstanding § 506(a), such claim is a secured claim to the extent that such claim is allowed.[b]

The clause "aggregate non-contingent, liquidated secured debts in an amount no more than $4,000,000," is, then, open to at least two interpretations both of which find support elsewhere in the Code. Given this ambiguity and lack of legislative history, the determination

---

[1] For example if present value of several payments made over ten years is $1,000 then the total of all the payments will always be greater than $1,000. Money received tomorrow is always worth less than the same amount received today. Theoretically, this would not be true in times of deflation where a bank would say "we're not going to accept your money today and pay you the same amount tomorrow because tomorrow the money will be worth more than it is today." In such case, and only such case, the total of the payments would be greater than the present value. This Court is, however, aware of no time in history when such has been the case and does not anticipate deflation in the foreseeable future.

[b] We will study § 1111(b) in Section F.1 of this Chapter. Eds.

turns on which of the viable possibilities best gives effect to the purpose of the statute. One purpose of the statutory scheme of §§ 101(51B) and 362(d) is to place these "single asset real estate" cases on a sort of a "fast-track" program. *In re Philmont Development*, 181 B.R. at 223. Another purpose is to afford secured creditors a relatively easy way to obtain relief from stay: all they have to do is show that the debtor has failed to perform under § 362(d)(3) rather than engaging an appraiser and fighting over value. *In re KKEMKO, Inc.*, 181 B.R. at 49. If we interpret § 101(51B) to limit the amount of secured claims to the value of the property then we are inviting valuation disputes at an early stage of the case. To require such a valuation would thwart the expedient resolution of the case and introduce unnecessary costs to a case that may go quietly away in 90 days.

Furthermore, limiting the claims to the value of the property could result in a debtor who in good faith believes his property to be worth more than $4,000,000 inadvertently missing the 90-day deadline. One can imagine a case in which a debtor schedules secured claims of more than $4,000,000 and real property worth more than $4,000,000. A secured creditor moves for relief from stay for cause such as lack of adequate protection. A valuation, decided after 90 days after the commencement of the case, discloses that the value of the property is actually less than $4,000,000. Whether or not the creditor was adequately protected the court would be compelled to lift the stay since the debtor did not comply, because he did not think he had to, with § 362(d).

The clear intent of Congress is to move these single asset cases in and, if appropriate, out of bankruptcy without wasting time and resources. The interpretation which best suits this purpose is that "aggregate non-contingent, liquidated secured debts in an amount no more than $4,000,000," refers to the total amount of all secured claims without regard to the value of the property.

CONCLUSION

For the reasons set forth above this Court concludes that the definition of "single asset real estate" in § 101(51B) includes undeveloped real property which generates no income, and that the calculation of the amount of "aggregate non-contingent, liquidated secured debts" is to be based upon the full amount of asserted secured claims without respect to the value of the property.

Accordingly, the secured creditor's motion for relief from stay, to the extent it is based on the asserted failure of the debtor to comply with § 362(d)(3), is denied.

IT IS SO ORDERED.

Note

The court thought that identification of undersecured claims for purposes of bifurcation would unduly delay the case. Note the number of issues (some of which we have already seen and others of which will arise later in this Chapter) that turn on the valuation of property securing claims, but that also must be confronted early in the case. These might include, for example, requests for use of cash collateral under § 363, efforts to obtain credit under § 364, and requests for relief from stay under § 362(d)(2). If courts are handling these issues early-on in other cases, one might wonder why valuation presents such an obstacle in the context of § 362(d)(3).

C. CONTROLLING THE DEBTOR

Appointment of a trustee is unusual in a Chapter 11 case. Ordinarily, the debtor becomes debtor-in-possession and the old managers stay in place. Section 1104(a) sets out two grounds for appointment of a trustee, however—for "cause" and "in the interests of creditors," etc. Cases interpreting § 1104(a) have not developed hard and fast rules; rather, courts look to the effect that appointment, or refusal to appoint, will have on the reorganization effort. Under that kind of standard, the outcome in the following case is unsurprising.

IN RE MARVEL ENTERTAINMENT GROUP, INC.

United States Court of Appeals, Third Circuit, 1998.
140 F.3d 463.

ALDISERT, Circuit Judge.

These expedited and consolidated appeals require us to decide if the district court properly exercised its discretion by appointing a trustee in the bankruptcy of Marvel Entertainment Group, Inc., because of the extreme acrimony between the debtor-in-possession and the creditors. * * * We will affirm the appointment of the trustee * * * .

I.

Marvel and various corporate affiliates filed chapter 11 petitions on December 27, 1996 and continued to run Marvel as debtor-in-possession. Approximately 1,700 creditors held $1 billion in claims against the Marvel estate.

Both before and after the filing of the petitions, Westgate International, L.P. and High River Limited Partnership, each controlled by Carl Icahn, (the "Icahn interests"), purchased at a discount a substantial number of pre-petition debt claims and bonds which had been issued by several holding companies owning all or substantially all of Marvel's stock. These holding companies, under the control of Ronald Perelman, had pledged their Marvel stock as security for the bonds. Two groups loomed large in the bankruptcy proceedings: one was an Official Bondholders' Committee and an indenture trustee, LaSalle National Bank, chosen to act primarily on behalf of the Icahn interests; the other, various creditors of Marvel, known as "the Lenders," who held over $600 million in debt claims at the time of the filings, secured by all of Marvel's assets.

From the start of the proceedings, disputes arose among the various parties, especially between the Icahn interests and the Lenders. The Icahn interests opposed an initial bankruptcy financing plan submitted by the Perelman holding companies, under which the holding companies would have infused $100 million into Marvel in return for priority recognition of the Lenders' debt claims. The Icahn interests contended that the Perelman-controlled Marvel debtors were favoring their "lender accomplices" to ensure that "Perelman re-acquires control of Marvel, without competitive bidding, for an obscenely low price." Notwithstanding the Icahn interests' objections, the bankruptcy court approved the financing plan.

From January through June of 1997, tension arose between the Lenders and the Icahn interests. The Icahn interests fought to take control of the Marvel board of directors. Substantial litigation went forward. On January 13, 1997, the Icahn interests moved the bankruptcy court to lift the automatic bankruptcy stay, § 362(a)(3), so they could foreclose on the holding companies' defaulted bonds and vote the pledged stock. Marvel sought a temporary restraining order from the bankruptcy court to enjoin the Icahn interests from voting the stock and replacing Marvel's board of directors. The bankruptcy court issued the order on March 24, 1997. On the same day, the Lenders moved the bankruptcy court for an order appointing a responsible officer to take control of the bankruptcy, or in the alternative a trustee. That same month, the Icahn interests took significant steps toward gaining control of Marvel. They offered to infuse $365 million into Marvel, partially for operation of its business but mostly to repay $300 million of its secured debt, in return for "exclusive" control of Marvel's operations. Through their agent Chase Manhattan Bank, the Lenders vigorously opposed this plan, explaining that the Icahn interests had presented no "concrete turn-around strategy * * * or a management team capable of executing one."

On May 14, 1997, the district court vacated the bankruptcy court's temporary restraining order, permitting the Icahn interests to vote the pledged stock. With the lifting of the restraining order, the litigation ended and the inevitable took place—on June 20, 1997, the Icahn interests took control of Marvel. Thus, an anomaly arose. The Icahn interests began to wear two hats—one as creditors of the holding companies that controlled Marvel; the other as the debtor-in-possession of Marvel.

Settlement negotiations proceeded throughout the summer of 1997. The new Icahn-controlled debtor-in-possession proposed a settlement in which the Icahn interests would control a newly-organized Marvel company merged with its affiliate Toy Biz, and would purchase the Lenders' claims at a substantial discount. To consummate the settlement, it was necessary to obtain the approval of two-thirds of all creditors as required under the Bankruptcy Code, § 1126(c). The Lenders were not successful in obtaining this approval.

The parties tried again. Another proposed settlement was attempted by the Icahn interests, this time with Chase directly as one of the Lenders. The terms were similar to those contained in the first effort, but this time Chase was required to sell its claims to the Icahn interests for even less than what was offered under the former proposal. Moreover, the settlement proposal required the creditors to support the Icahn interests' control of all Marvel entities and to agree to place High River's and Westgate's debt claims into a priority secured position. The necessary two-thirds approval not forthcoming, the settlement negotiations collapsed in October 1997.

On October 30, 1997, the Icahn-controlled debtor-in-possession commenced adverse litigation in the district court against the Perelman holding companies, the Lenders and other creditors in the Marvel bankruptcy (the "Perelman litigation"). It asserted 19 causes of action alleging breach of fiduciary duty, fraudulent conveyance, preferential transfer and breach of contract. The complaint sought to void the Lenders' claims or to subordinate them to the claims of High River and Westgate. The complaint described an alleged conspiracy between Toy Biz, the former Marvel board and the Lenders to "sabotage" the new Icahn-controlled debtor-in-possession's reorganization efforts. At the same time, the Icahn interests moved the district court for an order withdrawing the chapter 11 petitions and all related matters in the bankruptcy court and removing them to the district court to be heard in conjunction with the Perelman litigation. The Lenders opposed this withdrawal and renewed their motion before the bankruptcy court for the appointment of a trustee.

* * *

At a district court hearing on November 13, 1997, all parties agreed to the withdrawal of the Marvel cases from the bankruptcy court and their transfer to the district court. The district court then heard argument on whether a trustee should be appointed. The argument was summarized by the court:

> In opposing the motion, the Debtors accuse the Lenders, and specifically Chase, of flip-flopping on positions throughout the life of this proceeding, whenever it suits their purposes. The Debtors describe the reorganization plan of the Lenders and Toy Biz as illegal, and claim that the Lenders have no desire that a neutral trustee be appointed. * * * They claim that the Lenders have put a strangle-hold on the Debtor's financing, and that the Lenders are responsible for failure of both the Settlement and the Second Settlement. They also repeat many of the allegations made in the Perelman litigation. * * *
>
> The Creditors Committee describes the relationship between the Icahn interests and the Lenders as having reached an "impasse." * * *
>
> In support of their motion, the Lenders accuse the Icahn interests of an elaborate scheme to take over Marvel at a discount price while diminishing the value of the Lender's claims on the company as creditors. They claim that the Perelman litigation is part of that scheme, and was brought, at least in part, as a weapon to punish the Lenders for not consummating the two Settlements. * * * The Lenders claim that the present board is incapable of neutrality, and is guilty of breaching its fiduciary duties to creditors.

On December 12, 1997, the district court granted the motion authorizing the United States Trustee to appoint a trustee. Appealing that order are Marvel and the Icahn interests which control it.

* * *

III.

Under the Bankruptcy Code, the district court was empowered to appoint a trustee: *[the court quoted § 1104(a)]*. The party moving for appointment of a trustee, in this case the Lenders, must prove the need for a trustee under either subsection by clear and convincing evidence. "It is settled that appointment of a trustee should be the exception, rather than the rule." *In re Sharon Steel Corp.*, 871 F.2d 1217, 1225 (3d Cir.1989). In the usual chapter 11 proceeding, the debtor remains in possession throughout reorganization because "current management is generally best suited to orchestrate the process of rehabilitation for the benefit of creditors and other interests of the estate." *In re V. Savino Oil & Heating Co.*, 99 B.R. 518, 524 (Bankr. E.D.N.Y. 1989). Thus, the basis for the strong presumption against appointing an outside trustee is that there is often no need for one: "The debtor-in-possession is a fiduciary of the creditors and, as a result, has an obligation to refrain from acting in a manner which could damage the estate, or hinder a successful reorganization." *Petit v. New England Mort. Servs.*, 182 B.R. 64, 69 (D.Me.1995) (internal quotations omitted). The strong presumption also finds its basis in the debtor-in-possession's usual familiarity with the business it had already been managing at the time of the bankruptcy filing, often making it the best party to conduct operations during the reorganization. The facts here, however, militate against invoking this presumption. The Icahn interests took control over Marvel's management six months after the chapter 11 filing. We are not confronted with a debtor who possesses extensive familiarity with the company's operations. It is therefore inappropriate to suggest that the usual presumption should be applied to a Johnny-come-lately debtor-in-possession, especially one that is also a substantial creditor.

The district court determined that the Icahn interests were "unable to resolve conflicts" with creditors of the estate. On the basis of this acrimony, it ordered the appointment of a trustee. We hold that the district court did not abuse its discretion because (A) this acrimony rises to the level of "cause" under § 1104(a)(1), and (B) a trustee would serve the best interests of the parties and estate.

A.

We have not heretofore addressed the question of whether acrimony between debtor and creditor in a bankruptcy case may rise to the level of "cause" necessitating the appointment of a trustee under § 1104(a)(1). Cf. *Sharon Steel*, 871 F.2d at 1228 (finding "cause" due to debtor-in-possession's gross mismanagement of estate and internal conflicts of interest). * * * A review of cases from other circuits, as well as the policies behind the appointment of a trustee, demonstrates that the district court here properly exercised its discretion by invoking § 1104(a)(1) to reach its conclusion.

It is significant that the language of § 1104(a)(1) does not promulgate an exclusive list of causes for which a trustee must be appointed, but rather provides that a trustee shall be appointed "for cause, including fraud, dishonesty, incompetence, or gross mismanagement * * * or similar cause". The Court of Appeals for the Fourth Circuit has recognized that "the concepts of incompetence, dishonesty, gross mismanagement and even fraud all cover a wide range of conduct," and courts must be given the discretion necessary to determine if the debtor-in-possession's "conduct shown rises to a level sufficient to warrant the appointment of a trustee." *Committee of Dalkon Shield Claimants v. A.H. Robins Co.*, 828 F.2d 239, 242 (4th Cir.1987) (internal quotation omitted). This discretionary authority is consistent with a "policy of flexibility" permeating the Bankruptcy Code's overall aim of protecting creditors while giving debtors a second chance. The Code itself, therefore, does not prohibit the appointment of a trustee based on a finding of acrimony between debtor and creditor, parties whose interests must be balanced and protected under the discretion of the courts.

Moreover, we are impressed by the persuasive reasoning in *In re Cajun Elec. Power Coop., Inc.*, 74 F.3d 599, 600 (5th Cir.) (adopting on rehearing the opinion of dissent in 69 F.3d at 751), *cert. denied*, 136 L.Ed.2d 15, 117 S.Ct. 51 (1996), in which the court upheld a trustee appointment based on a finding of acrimony. In that case, the debtor-in-possession's interests conflicted with those of its creditors to such an extent that "the appointment of a trustee may be the only effective way to pursue reorganization." The debtor-in-possession was a utility cooperative whose board members were faced with a federal agency order lowering its utility rates. The debtor-in-possession's board members, themselves managers or members of the debtor-in-possession's individual member utility companies, were required to decide whether to appeal the agency order, seeking to maintain the high rates charged to the individual member companies and thus to better enable the debtor-in-possession to meet its debt obligations to its creditors in bankruptcy, or to take no action and charge less to their individual companies. The court recognized that the debtor-creditor conflict went "beyond the 'inherent' conflicts under which all healthy cooperatives operate." 74 F.3d at 600 (adopting dissent at 69 F.3d at 751). The extent of this conflict alone provided sufficient cause for the appointment of a trustee under § 1104(a)(1).

In *Cajun Electric*, the court recognized that all cooperatives operate amidst certain "inherent" conflicts of interest, but rejected the notion that its holding created a "'per se rule' under which any cooperative seeking Chapter 11 protection would be automatically subject to the appointment of a trustee." Rather, the teachings of this case are that a district court may find cause to appoint a trustee for "acrimony" only on a case-by-case basis, when the inherent conflicts extend beyond the healthy conflicts that always exist between debtor and creditor, or as it found in that case, when the parties "begin working at cross-purposes".

We therefore adopt the reasoning in *Cajun Electric*, and apply its teachings to the case at bar. Here the district court found that "the Debtors, as controlled by the Icahn interests, and the Lenders, take dramatically different stances on many issues." Citing (1) the debtor-in-possession's institution of several adversary actions, (2) the unconsummated settlements, (3) the U.S. Trustee's opinion "that the parties seem to be unable to reach a consensus" and (4) its observations that "the Debtors and the Lenders have flung accusations at each other, and have failed to demonstrate any ability to resolve matters cooperatively," the district court concluded that "there is no reasonable likelihood of any cooperation between the parties in the near future." As in *Cajun Electric*, the district court did not clearly err, based on its review of these events, when it found a deep conflict to exist between the Icahn-controlled debtor-in-possession and the creditors in bankruptcy. Also like *Cajun Electric*, "this is a large and messy bankruptcy that promises to get worse without a disinterested administrator at the helm."

We expressly hold that there is no per se rule by which mere conflicts or acrimony between debtor and creditor mandate the appointment of a trustee. In this case, rather, we are faced with circumstances in which the Icahn interests, themselves creditors of the Perelman holding companies, are currently in control of the debtor at the same time that the debtor proposes reorganization plans. In this position, although the Icahn interests are technically and officially fiduciaries to all creditors, they would also be placed in an awkward position of evaluating their own indenture and debt claims. Having found that this unhealthy conflict of interest was manifest in the "deep-seeded conflict and animosity" between the Icahn-controlled debtor and the Lenders and in the lack of confidence all creditors had in the Icahn interests' ability to act as fiduciaries, the district court did not depart from the proper exercise of discretion when it determined sufficient cause existed under § 1104-(a)(1) to appoint a neutral trustee to facilitate reorganization.

We reject the Icahn interests' argument that unhappy creditors involved in future bankruptcies could remove the debtors-in-possession by their obstinate refusal to cooperate. We are not impressed by this *argumentum ad terrorem*. In the view we take, it is within the district court's sound discretion to make a determination of cause, and this requires fact-finding and application of the facts to relevant precepts. The district court here determined that the Icahn interests were not entirely without blame for the breakdown of reorganization efforts with the Lenders * * * .

Finally, the policies behind the appointment of a trustee support our conclusion. The appointment of a trustee is the installation of a court officer charged with fiduciary duties. The district court's determination that cause existed to appoint an independent trustee based on the Icahn interests' actions is a recognition of their failure to assume these duties. When the chapter 11 petition was filed in this case, the debtor-in-possession assumed the same fiduciary duties as would an appointed trustee; the Icahn interests later stepped into this fiduciary position when they took control of Marvel. These obligations include "open, honest and straightforward disclosure to the Court and creditors." *See V. Savino Oil*, 99 B.R. at 526. The Icahn interests' actions surrounding the Perelman litigation fall short of this fiduciary benchmark. Also among the fiduciary obligations of a debtor-in-possession is the "duty to protect and conserve property in its possession for the benefit of creditors." *In re Ionosphere Clubs, Inc.*, 113 B.R. 164, 169 (Bankr.S.D.N.Y.1990). The intense and high-stakes bickering between the Icahn interests and the Lenders does not instill confidence that the Icahn interests could fairly negotiate with the creditors to whom they owe these duties, nor that reorganization will occur effectively.

As one bankruptcy court has noted:

> The willingness of Congress to leave a debtor-in-possession is premised on an expectation that current management can be depended upon to carry out the fiduciary responsibilities of a trustee. And if the debtor-in-possession defaults in this respect,

> § 1104(a)(1) commands that the stewardship of the reorganization effort must be turned over to an independent trustee.

V. *Savino Oil*, 99 B.R. at 526. Here, the district court acted within the proper bounds of discretion in appointing a trustee under § 1104(a)(1) because of the Icahn interests' contribution to the acrimony with Marvel's creditors.

B.

Unlike § 1104(a)(1), which provides for mandatory appointment upon a specific finding of cause, § 1104(a)(2) "envisions a flexible standard." It gives the district court discretion to appoint a trustee "when to do so would serve the parties' and estate's interests." *Sharon Steel*, 871 F.2d at 1226. Here the court found that "deep seeded conflict and animosity between a debtor and its creditors" is at the heart of this bankruptcy case, thus "the selection of a plan, whatever its details, is in the best interests of all parties, and the best way to achieve that result is to appoint a trustee." Even if we were of the view that the appointment of a trustee was not mandated by the analysis required in § 1104(a)(1), we are satisfied that the district court's determination would come within proper exercise of discretion under the flexible § 1104(a)(2) standard. The level of acrimony found to exist in this case certainly makes the appointment of a trustee in the best interests of the parties and the estate.

* * *

We also reject the Icahn interests' arguments that the district court must apply a strict cost-benefit analysis when deciding to appoint a trustee. This is a case of profound financial magnitude, involving approximately $1 billion in claims against the estate. *See In re Sharon Steel Corp.*, 86 B.R. 455, 466 (W.D.Pa.1988) ("In a case of this magnitude, the cost of having a trustee in place is insignificant when compared with the other costs of administration and when compared with the enormous benefit to be achieved by the establishment of trust and confidence in * * * management.").

Neither did the court abuse its discretion by deciding not to appoint an examiner in the trustee's stead: "I'm just not convinced that an examiner is going to get done what needs to get done here. I think we need a decision-maker to come in and make some decisions." Under the Bankruptcy Code, a trustee is given all the powers of an examiner to analyze and report on the interests of the parties and actions of the debtor, but is also given the power to act on behalf of the estate, including the filing of a reorganization plan. §§ 1106(a)(5), (b).

An examiner is not a substitute for a trustee. The district court need not have favored the appointment of an examiner here, especially after finding that a trustee is the more appropriate position.

Whether viewed from § 1104(a)(1) or (a)(2), the district court acted within appropriate bounds of discretion in appointing a trustee to act as a neutral and efficient fiduciary in this complicated bankruptcy under the circumstances of the strife-ridden history presented here.

* * *

Questions

1. Why did the court find that both §§ 1104(a)(1) and (a)(2) were satisfied? Do you understand the differences between the two subsections?

2. Is it so clearly correct that unhappy creditors could not obtain the appointment of a trustee "by their obstinate refusal to cooperate" with the debtor-in-possession? Consider the situation in the Eastern Airlines bankruptcy, described by the court in *In re Ionosphere Clubs, Inc.*, 113 B.R. 164 (Bankr.S.D.N.Y.1990). There, the creditors (including labor unions) became disaffected with the leadership of Frank Lorenzo, who was in charge of Eastern, as huge operating losses were coupled with an inability to make operating projections and to formulate a long-range business plan. Some commentators might describe the stance taken by those creditors as an "obstinate refusal to cooperate;" others—including the creditors themselves—would no doubt take the position that ample reasons were presented. Where is the line between a good faith throwing in of the towel, and "obstinate refusal"?

Old managers are not the only ones in control of the debtor-in-possession. The managers are themselves controlled by the corporation's board of directors. Board members, in turn, must answer to the shareholders, *if* the shareholders can get a shareholders' meeting called.

MANVILLE CORP. v. EQUITY SECURITY HOLDERS COMMITTEE (IN RE JOHNS–MANVILLE CORP.)

United States Court of Appeals, Second Circuit, 1986.
801 F.2d 60.

MAHONEY, Circuit Judge.

This action, one segment in a long-running Chapter 11 reorganization proceeding, arose in consequence of the competing interests of creditors, stockholders, and the board of directors in the development of rehabilitation plans for appellee, the Manville Corporation ("Manville"), formerly Johns–Manville Corporation. Appellants are the Equity Security Holders Committee and individual members of that committee (collectively the "Equity Committee"), appointed by the bankruptcy court to represent the interests of stockholders in Manville's reorganization. The Securities and Exchange Commission, although technically an appellee, shares the interests of the Equity Committee in the matter at hand. Manville is aligned for purposes of this appeal with the Committee of Asbestos Health Related Claimants and/or Creditors (the "Asbestos Health Committee"), which represents the interests of the victims of diseases resulting from exposure to asbestos who have presently existing claims in tort against Manville, and with the Legal Representative, who represents the interests of future claimants who have not yet manifested such diseases.

The instant conflict arises in part because each of the committees representing the various interests in Manville must depend upon the Manville board of directors to advance those interests in the bankruptcy court at this stage of the rehabilitation proceedings. As debtor, Manville had the exclusive right under the Bankruptcy Code to file rehabilitation plans for the first 120 days of reorganization, and the bankruptcy court in these proceedings has granted Manville several extensions prolonging its exclusive filing period. Therefore, although in theory each of the committees may one day have the opportunity to submit a rehabilitation plan to the bankruptcy court if Manville's own proposals are rejected or if a trustee is appointed to replace the Manville board, *see* § 1121(c), Manville has for three or four years enjoyed the exclusive right, after negotiating with the committees, to file proposed plans. And although any of the committees may decline to accept a plan submitted to the bankruptcy court for confirmation, the power to formulate such plans in the first instance or at least to exercise a voice in their formulation is clearly a desideratum under the program laid down by the Bankruptcy Code, because the bankruptcy court may confirm a plan with or without the acquiescence of all classes of claims. * * *

In order to channel negotiations toward acceptable plans, the various factions interested in Manville's rehabilitation have formed *ad hoc* alliances when the occasion has called for them. The challenge all the committees have faced is to fashion a plan that will preserve Manville's capacity to generate enough revenue to pay existing creditors, to cover its liabilities to present and future tort claimants where liability is certain though its precise extent is unknown, and to satisfy Manville's shareholders. The seemingly strange bedfellows in the instant litigation, Manville and the committees representing present and future tort claimants, have long struggled to devise a reorganization plan acceptable to each. Along the way they have at times been antagonists rather than allies. * * *

To their credit, Manville and the Legal Representative finally came to terms in August of 1985, formulating a plan that would earmark billions of dollars for payment to present and future asbestosis victims as well as to others damaged by the asbestos products that Manville once manufactured and sold. They have now received the blessing of the Asbestos Health Committee and apparently of the other creditor committees. Having reconciled their differences, however, they encountered opposition from the Equity Committee immediately following their breakthrough, on the eve of their submission of the plan to the bankruptcy court for confirmation. Under protest, the Equity Committee had been cut out of the negotiations that led to their plan, and if the product of Manville's new understanding with the tort claimants and other creditors is confirmed, equity may be diluted by 90% or more. Displeased with that prospect, which the Equity Committee views as evidence of the Manville board's abdication of its responsibilities to the shareholders, the Equity Committee brought an action in Delaware state court seeking to compel Manville to hold a shareholders' meeting, pursuant to § 211(c) of Delaware's General Corporation Law. The Equity Committee's avowed purpose was to replace Manville directors, so that new directors might reconsider submitting the proposed plan.

Manville countered with the instant action. At Manville's behest, the bankruptcy court issued an injunction prohibiting the Equity Committee from pursuing the Delaware action on the ground that the holding of a shareholders' meeting would obstruct Manville's reorganization. Denying the Equity Committee's motion for summary judgment, the bankruptcy court granted summary judgment to Manville *sua sponte*. The district court affirmed. On appeal, the Equity Committee argues that the district court erred in affirming the decision to enjoin, in affirming the grant of summary judgment to Manville, and in finding that the bankruptcy court had jurisdiction to issue the injunction.

* * *

THE INJUNCTION AND THE GRANT OF SUMMARY JUDGMENT

Turning, then, to the decision to enjoin, we first encounter the well-settled rule that the right to compel a shareholders' meeting for the purpose of electing a new board subsists during reorganization proceedings. As a consequence of the shareholders' right to govern their corporation, a prerogative ordinarily uncompromised by reorganization, "a bankruptcy court should not lightly employ its equitable power to block an election of a new board of directors." *In re Potter Instrument Co.*, 593 F.2d 470, 475 (2d Cir.1979). In accordance with this rule, the parties and the lower courts agree that the Equity Committee's right to call a meeting may be impaired only if the Equity Committee is guilty of "clear abuse" in attempting to call one. The Equity Committee's principal argument is that the "clear abuse" standard was not satisfied. In addition, however, the Equity Committee seems to argue that the district court's analysis was incomplete; *i.e.*, the Equity Committee contends that in reviewing the bankruptcy court's decision to issue the injunction, the district court should have required, in addition to a showing of clear abuse, the usual showing of irreparable injury.

An examination of both lower court decisions will clarify the analysis that follows. The bankruptcy court found that "any shareholder meeting and ensuing proxy fight has the potential to derail the entire Manville reorganization with devastating consequences or at least to delay or halt plan negotiations." Reviewing the bankruptcy court's findings, the district court concluded that the Equity Committee intended either to "torpedo" the reorganization or to acquire a bargaining chip in aid of its negotiation power. In either case, the district court reasoned, the bankruptcy court did not err in concluding that the Equity Committee was guilty of clear abuse.

Taking the district court's latter point first, we cannot agree that the Equity Committee's professed desire to arrogate more bargaining power in the negotiation of a plan—in contrast to some secret desire to destroy all prospects for reorganization—may in itself constitute clear abuse. The law of this circuit directs that the shareholders' natural wish to participate in this matter of corporate governance be respected. In *In re Bush Terminal Co.*, 78 F.2d 662 (2d Cir.1935), for example, this court reversed an order enjoining a shareholders' meeting to be called for the purpose of advancing a rehabilitation plan more favorable to equity. Expressly upholding the right of a majority shareholder to try to replace board members for that purpose, the court reasoned:

> [T]he debtor is given the right to be heard on all questions. Obviously, the stockholders should have the right to be adequately represented in the conduct of the debtor's affairs, especially in such an important matter as the reorganization of the debtor. Such representation can be obtained only by having

> as directors persons of their choice. * * * [T]he debtor is given the power to propose a plan of reorganization. No reason is advanced why stockholders, if they feel that the present board of directors is not acting in their interest, or has caused an unsatisfactory plan to be filed on behalf of the debtor, should not cause a new board to be elected which will act in conformance with the stockholders' wishes.

Id. at 664.

* * * Under this analysis, the shareholders' mere intention to exercise bargaining power—whether by actually replacing the directors or by "bargaining away" their chip without replacing the board, as the district court suggests they may have wished to do—cannot without more constitute clear abuse. Unless the Equity Committee were to bargain in bad faith—*e.g.*, to demonstrate a willingness to risk rehabilitation altogether in order to win a larger share for equity—its desire to negotiate for a larger share is protected. Moreover, if rehabilitation is placed at risk as a result of the other committees' intransigent unwillingness to negotiate with the Equity Committee, as opposed to their real inability, within some reasonable amount of time, to formulate any confirmable plan more satisfactory to equity, the Equity Committee should not alone bear the consequences of a stalemate by being deemed guilty of clear abuse.[6]

In re Lionel Corp., 30 B.R. 327 (Bankr.S.D.N.Y.1983), buttresses our conclusion that shareholders' desire for leverage is not a basis for denying them an election, so long as leverage means only the improvement of their bargaining position or the assurance of their participation in negotiations. In *In re Lionel Corp.* the bankruptcy court held that the record failed to demonstrate how reorganization would be impeded merely because the shareholders might be successful in their quest to cause the reorganization to "take an entirely different turn." *Id.* at 330. Surely if the Equity Committee is permitted to elect new directors in order to redirect or alter the course of a reorganization—and the district court here explicitly recognized that the committee is permitted to do that—the Equity Committee should be permitted, in the district court's words of disapproval, to "use the threat of a new board as a lever vis-a-vis other interested constituencies and vis-a-vis the current Manville board." The Equity Committee denies that there is evidence tending to show that it meant to use any "threat" as a "lever," but if

[6] We note that if Manville were determined to be insolvent, so that the shareholders lacked equity in the corporation, denial of the right to call a meeting would likely be proper, because the shareholders would no longer be real parties in interest. * * *

there is any such evidence, it would suggest only that the Equity Committee might be willing to back away from replacing the directors if it were to find the board more responsive to its interests. For related reasons, we are not persuaded that the Equity Committee's failure to call for a meeting at an earlier stage in the negotiations places its desire for leverage in a different light. If dissatisfaction with the board's representation of shareholders is a legitimate ground for calling a meeting, the Equity Committee did not waive the right to call a meeting by waiting until it became dissatisfied.[7]

Finally, we reject appellees' suggestion that the availability to the Equity Committee of other means with which to oppose Manville's plan robs the Equity Committee of its chosen means. It is true that the Equity Committee could have sought the appointment of a trustee to displace Manville as the sole author of proposed plans and that it may later object to the confirmation of any plan Manville submits to the bankruptcy court. But those correctives provide only imperfect substitutes for a voice in the original formulation of a plan. More to the present point, perhaps, those avenues to shareholder satisfaction cannot be said to be exclusive in light of this circuit's legitimation of the shareholders' right to elect new directors for the frank purpose of advancing a plan they prefer.

* * *

We now reach the district court's alternative ground for affirming the grant of summary judgment. The bankruptcy court's finding that the proposed stockholders' meeting might jeopardize the reorganization process, "or at least * * * delay or halt plan negotiations," a finding reflected in the district court's view that the Equity Committee might have intended to "torpedo" the reorganization, poses an issue more difficult than the question of the stockholders' desire for a voice in negotiations. While delay to rehabilitation would not by itself provide a

---

[7] We do not suggest, of course, that an equity committee's delay in calling a shareholders' meeting may never contribute to a finding of clear abuse. As the Securities and Exchange Commission pointed out in its brief, an attempt to call a shareholders' meeting after a plan has been submitted to the bankruptcy court and after confirmation hearings have begun would usually be more disruptive to the proceedings than an earlier attempt would be. Such an attempt might also indicate bad faith and a willingness to risk jeopardy to rehabilitation. On the other hand, a rule that required a call before dissatisfaction had crystallized would only encourage preemptive efforts that might otherwise be avoided by negotiation. In this case, the Equity Committee apparently acted promptly upon learning of Manville's proposed plan and is certainly not accountable for any movement toward confirmation that may have occurred thereafter over its objections.

ground for overriding the shareholders' right to govern Manville—delay being a concomitant of the right to change boards—real jeopardy to reorganization prospects would provide such a ground.

In *In re Potter Instrument Co.*, 593 F.2d 470 (2d Cir.1979), this court upheld the bankruptcy court's refusal, upon a finding of clear abuse, to order a shareholders' meeting to be called for the purpose of electing new directors. We reasoned that "such an election might result in unsatisfactory management and would probably jeopardize both [the debtor's] rehabilitation and the rights of creditors and stockholders—sounding the 'death knell' to the debtor as well as to appellant himself." *Id.* at 475. * * *

The Equity Committee persuasively calls into question whether the bankruptcy court had any basis for concluding here that an election would jeopardize the reorganization process, particularly since the bankruptcy court's articulated basis appears to have been colored by an unsubstantiated suspicion that the Equity Committee affirmatively wished to jeopardize reorganization. Perhaps Potter was willing to embark on a suicide mission, "sounding the 'death knell' to * * * himself" along with the debtor. But as the Equity Committee argues, the lower courts in this case pointed to no evidence to support any finding that it wished to "torpedo" the reorganization, which the Equity Committee contends would be an irrational goal from its perspective.

* * *

CONCLUSION

Whether the Equity Committee's call for a shareholders' meeting constitutes clear abuse and whether such a meeting would cause irreparable harm to Manville's reorganization are triable issues of fact. The summary judgment award to Manville is therefore reversed. On remand, the court should undertake a more elaborate inquiry into clear abuse and irreparable harm. Rather than focusing on the Equity Committee's conceded desire to enhance its bargaining position, the court should analyze the real risks to rehabilitation posed by permitting the Equity Committee to call a meeting of shareholders for the purpose of compelling reconsideration of Manville's presently proposed plan. We emphasize, however, that given its greater knowledge about this complex and perhaps fragile reorganization, the bankruptcy court may exercise its legitimate injunctive powers to control the future course of rehabilitation pursuant to appropriate legal standards and evidentiary showings.

OAKES, Circuit Judge (dissenting).

I am unclear what the majority intends to accomplish by the reversal and remand, except to compel bankruptcy judges and district courts to make more precise findings in support of their orders. Ordinarily I would support such a limited remand, especially where, as here, the bankruptcy court's reasoning required supplementation by the district court. But here confirmation of a plan in one of the most complicated and difficult bankruptcy reorganizations in history is well under way, and I fear that the court's opinion will not only unnecessarily duplicate, but it will, if not derail, at least delay the confirmation proceedings.

After all, the proposed plan had been in heated, tricky, combative negotiation for some three years prior to the Equity Committee's actions. If the plan is indeed biased, the Equity Committee has ample opportunity to oppose confirmation and to prove discrimination or unfairness to it.

Under *In re Potter Instrument Co.*, 593 F.2d 470, 475 (2d Cir.1979), the court has a duty to refuse to order a shareholder's meeting upon a showing of clear abuse which "would probably jeopardize both [the debtor's] rehabilitation and the rights of creditors and stockholders." To seek a shareholders' meeting at this late date, it seems to me, is just such a clear abuse. The Equity Committee, if it has its way, would set this reorganization back to square one. Apparently satisfied with the Board of Directors for three years following the filing of the bankruptcy petition, the committee waited until the directors finally proposed a plan to object, not only to the plan, but to the directors themselves. In addition to seeking to upset the plan, it is now trying to replace the directors, a result that would require negotiations to recommence from the beginning. In such a complex and lengthy proceeding as this one, the Equity Committee's actions seem to me to be the very essence of abuse. Moreover, the bankruptcy court's determination that a shareholders' meeting would lead to "waste of this estate's resources and thereby jeopardize the reorganization process" and that it "has the potential to derail the entire Manville reorganization with devastating consequences or at least to delay or halt plan negotiations" adequately supports its conclusion of irreparable harm.

But there is an entirely different reason that argues for affirmance. The bankruptcy judge has been living with this reorganization for a long time. He is fully sensitive to the enormity of the problems imposed by billions of dollars of future claims, as well as by billions of dollars of present claims for personal injury, death, and property damage—claims on a scale never before to hit the courts—as well as claims for punitive damages that, given those that have so far been imposed in the tiny fraction of cases that have been decided, are staggering to say the least. I repeat, no more complex reorganization has ever come before any bankruptcy court, and I include the railroad reorganization of recent past as well as of yore. I would here, as seldom elsewhere, defer to the bankruptcy court's discretion.

Yet a third reason calls for no further delay in the name of abstract stockholders' rights. There are innocent injured people, some of whom are survivors of deceased persons, whose recoveries have already been unduly delayed by the reorganization proceedings. Further delay will in many instances be unconscionable.

I would affirm outright and leave the Equity Committee to its usual remedy of objecting to the plan and its fairness in the confirmation proceeding.

Accordingly, I respectfully dissent.

Questions

1. What provision of the Code gives the bankruptcy court power to enjoin a state court proceeding?

2. Where would the Second Circuit draw the line between permissible and impermissible efforts to replace a reorganizing debtor's management?

3. In footnote 6, the *Manville* court suggested that a different result might be reached if a debtor were insolvent "because the shareholders would no longer be real parties in interest." Why is that so?

4. On remand, and after trial, the bankruptcy court found that a shareholders' meeting posed a "serious threat and real jeopardy" to Manville's reorganization. 66 B.R. 517, 534 (Bankr. S.D.N.Y.1986). The court found "that it has always been and still remains the *in terrorem* intent of [one shareholder group] to call a shareholders meeting, *with a full awareness of the devastating consequences to the fabric of the reorganization*, in order to elect a new Board of Directors *who will withdraw or substantially modify the present plan of reorganization*." *Id.* at 535. In light of doubt that new directors could achieve a consensual plan within a reasonable time, the court found that the call for a shareholders' meeting was a "clear abuse." *Id.* at 541. So perhaps the dissent was right—remand accomplished little more than requiring clarity in the bankruptcy court's order.

5. Did you notice, in *Marvel Entertainment*, that the Icahn interests took control after waging a battle—successfully, in that case—to call a shareholders' meeting?

D. OPERATING THE BUSINESS

The effort to reorganize would halt in its tracks if the debtor-in-possession could not operate its business during the bankruptcy proceeding. That, however, requires money and the use of property in which creditors have an interest. Sections 363 and 364 address the debtor-in-possession's needs in this regard.

1. USE OF CASH COLLATERAL

"Cash collateral" is collateral (that is, property in which "an entity other than the estate [has] an interest") in a particularly liquid form ("cash, negotiable instruments, * * * deposit accounts, or other cash equivalents"). § 363(a). These assets are probably needed for daily operations and can very easily slip away from creditors. The Code prohibits the use of cash collateral without the creditor's consent or the court's authorization. § 363(c)(2). Is that sufficient protection for the creditor?

MBANK DALLAS, N.A. v. O'CONNOR (IN RE O'CONNOR)

United States Court of Appeals, Tenth Circuit, 1987.
808 F.2d 1393.

JOHN P. MOORE, Circuit Judge.

* * *

The controversy under consideration evolves from a voluntary petition for reorganization filed by Mr. William Joseph O'Connor and Mrs. Jane Elizabeth O'Connor, husband and wife, (Debtors) pursuant to Chapter 11 of the Bankruptcy Reform Act of 1978 (Code). During administration of the case, the Debtors sought leave from the bankruptcy court to use certain cash on deposit in a court-controlled bank account to drill 3 gas wells in areas previously leased by a limited partnership in which Mr. O'Connor was the general partner. To protect creditors claiming interests in the subject cash, Debtors offered replacement liens on the well proceeds and on other unencumbered regular monthly income received by Mr. O'Connor. MBank Dallas, N.A. (Bank) asserted a security interest in the cash and objected to the Debtors' proposal.

After notice and a hearing at which the bankruptcy court took evidence regarding the value of the revenue that would be generated by the drilling project and the prospects for success, as well as the value of the monthly income offered as an additional replacement lien, the court made findings of fact and concluded it would be in the best interest of the estate to grant the leave requested. The court further concluded that the Bank would be adequately protected by the replacement liens offered by the Debtors.

The Bank appealed this decision to the district court which set bond and stayed the use of the cash. The district court ultimately reversed the bankruptcy court, concluding the bankruptcy court erred in finding the Bank would be adequately protected. Relying upon *Rader v. Boyd,* 267 F.2d 911 (10th Cir.1959), the district court concluded that the replacement liens were too speculative to provide the adequate protection required by § 363(e). * * *

The record indicates the Debtors had cash available from operations in the amount of $721,600. Since that cash represented proceeds from property on which the Bank claimed a security interest, it asserted the funds were subject to a proceeds lien and were "cash collateral" within the meaning of § 363. * * *

At the hearing before the bankruptcy court, the Debtors offered evidence that in the area in which Debtors proposed to drill, Mr. O'Connor's limited partnership had 150 proven wells, 148 of which were still producing. Mr. O'Connor testified that the 3 proposed wells would be drilled "on the inside of what we have already established as producing wells, therefore putting the risk down to a very nominal level." He also testified that purchasers of the gas to be produced were already available and that there was presently a ready market for that gas which would extend well into the future. The Debtors' expert testified that future cash flow could be expected from the project in the sum of $6,774,862 and that the O'Connor share of that expectation was $5,284,392. In the opinion of the expert, the Debtors' interest, discounted to present value, was worth $3,674,071 at the time of the hearing. Although the Bank offered contrary evidence, the bankruptcy court rejected the Bank's assertions.

On the basis of the disputed evidence, the bankruptcy court found that "future net revenues attributable to Debtors' interest in the wells will be $5.2 million and that the present value of those revenues is in excess of $2.8 million." The court further found that Debtors had additional unencumbered property with "a present value of $10,000 per month." The bankruptcy court concluded that the Bank was adequately protected by the replacement liens in the properties having these values and, as a consequence, "granting the motion would be in the best interest of the estate and its creditors."

In its appeal to the district court and in its brief here, the Bank has advanced many reasons why the bankruptcy court reached the wrong decision but gives only passing treatment to the issue of consequence; that is, whether the bankruptcy court's findings are clearly erroneous. We have not considered the issue before, but we are convinced that whether a creditor is adequately protected is a question of fact.

In recognition of the powers created in bankruptcy law to adjust debts and creditors' interests, Congress realized the need to protect creditors from unfair treatment. Hence, it codified the concept of adequate protection into the several aggressive remedies available to debtors and bankruptcy trustees. The whole purpose in providing adequate protection for a creditor is to insure that the creditor receives the value for which the creditor bargained prebankruptcy. * * * Since value is a function of many factual variables, it logically follows that adequate protection is a question of fact. As a question of fact, the bankruptcy court's determination that adequate protection exists or fails to exist can be reversed on appeal only if it is clearly erroneous. We have said that a clearly erroneous finding is one that leaves the reviewing court with the distinct and firm conviction that a mistake was made. We are left with no such conviction here.

* * *

The question of adequacy was examined and decided by the bankruptcy court on disputed but sufficient evidence. Mr. O'Connor testified that the wells were going to be drilled in a proven area in which all his previous attempts had been successful. He explained that he had drilled 150 wells and all were still producing except for 2 which had experienced mechanical failure. In addition, Debtors' expert witness testified that ready buyers existed to buy the product of the proposed wells in a quantity to provide a cash flow more than sufficient to protect the Bank's proceeds lien. * * *

In this case, Debtors, in the midst of a Chapter 11 proceeding, have proposed to deal with cash collateral for the purpose of enhancing the prospects of reorganization. This quest is the ultimate goal of Chapter 11. Hence, the Debtors' efforts are not only to be encouraged, but also their efforts during the administration of the proceeding are to be measured in light of that quest. Because the ultimate benefit to be achieved by a successful reorganization inures to all the creditors of the estate, a fair opportunity must be given to the Debtors to achieve that end. Thus, while interests of the secured creditor whose property rights are of concern to the court, the interests of all other creditors also have bearing upon the question of whether use of cash collateral shall be permitted during the early stages of administration.

The first effort of the court must be to insure the value of the collateral will be preserved. Yet, prior to confirmation of a plan of reorganization, the test of that protection is not by the same measurements applied to the treatment of a secured creditor in a proposed plan. In order to encourage the Debtors' efforts in the formative period prior to the proposal of a reorganization, the court must be flexible in applying the adequate protection standard. In doing so, however, care must be exercised to insure that the vested property rights of the secured creditor and the values and risks bargained for by that creditor prior to bankruptcy are not detrimentally affected.

Here, the creditor had a proceeds lien in cash worth $721,600. The Debtors proposed to use the cash thereby reducing the *value* of the creditor's security interest by $721,600, but in exchange, the Debtors proposed to give the creditor a *new* proceeds lien in property presently worth over five times that sum. The only distinction between the security interest the Bank had in the cash and the substitute security interest in the new wells is the risk inherent in drilling a dry hole.[6] Yet, the flexibility in judging whether that risk was significant or insignificant is what distinguishes this case from *Rader*.

The bankruptcy court found, in effect, that because the wells were to be drilled in proven areas, the risk to the Bank was not significant. That determination is supported by substantial evidence, and it is critical to the issue of adequate protection that exists in this case.

---

6 This risk is set off somewhat, however, by the additional substitute lien in the $10,000 per month income received by Mr. O'Connor. There is nothing in the record indicating this income is speculative, and its present worth is more than half the value of the cash collateral Debtors wanted to use.

The Bank argued and continues to argue strenuously that granting the Debtors' motion was improper because the effect was contrary to the "reorganizational effect" of the plan it had proposed. The bankruptcy court found that the Bank's plan was nothing more than a program for liquidation of the Debtors' assets and concluded it was more appropriate at that stage of the proceedings to allow the Debtors an opportunity to reorganize. We agree with that conclusion.

The judgment of the district court is REVERSED. The case is REMANDED * * * to the bankruptcy court for reinstitution of its order granting leave to use cash collateral.

Notes and Questions

1. In exchange for the use of $721,000 of its collateral, the creditor in this case is being given an interest in the proceeds of a gas well, with a projected present value of $3,675,000, and an interest in the nonspeculative $10,000 monthly income of one of the debtors, with a present value of more than $360,000. Yet the creditor is arguing lack of adequate protection. Does this say anything to you about "the risk inherent in drilling a dry hole"?

2. An attorney representing the debtor-in-possession must pay attention to the use of cash collateral. In *Midwest Properties No. Two v. Big Hill Investment Co.*, 93 B.R. 357 (N.D.Tex.1988), the debtor-in-possession failed to establish a separate account and to account for cash collateral, in violation of § 363(c)(4). The bankruptcy court imposed sanctions on the debtor's president and on the corporation's attorney; if the sanctions were not paid by a specified date, the court imposed a 10% penalty and ordered that the parties be imprisoned until they made payment. The district court, on appeal, approved the imposition of sanctions, but reversed and remanded for more detailed findings on how the amounts were calculated.

2. OBTAINING POSTPETITION CREDIT

Section 364 authorizes the debtor-in-possession to borrow postpetition on a series of terms, each more onerous and potentially detrimental to existing interests than the one before. Subsection (a) gives administrative expense priority to obligations incurred in the ordinary course of business (and obligations not in the ordinary course, but authorized by the court under § 364(b)).

If credit cannot be obtained on those terms, subsection (c)(1) permits the court to authorize a priority that trumps both § 503(b) administrative expense claims and those claims for inadequate adequate protection given a superpriority under § 507(b). That makes the § 363-(c)(1) claim a "super-superpriority."

If credit is still unobtainable, the court can authorize the granting of a lien on previously unencumbered property, (c)(2), or the granting of a junior lien in property already subject to encumbrance, (c)(3).

The last resort is § 364(d), which permits the court to authorize postpetition credit secured by a lien that is equal or senior in priority to an existing lien. Existing secured creditors are entitled to adequate protection of their interests.

A few creditors have seen a way to obtain collateral not only for their postpetition loans, but also for prepetition unsecured debts. *Saybrook Manufacturing* is the leading case dealing with this so-called "cross-collateralization."

SHAPIRO v. SAYBROOK MANUFACTURING CO. (MATTER OF SAYBROOK MANUFACTURING CO.)

United States Court of Appeals, Eleventh Circuit, 1992.
963 F.2d 1490.

COX, Circuit Judge.

Seymour and Jeffrey Shapiro, unsecured creditors, objected to the bankruptcy court's authorization for the Chapter 11 debtors to "cross-collateralize" their pre-petition debt with unencumbered property from the bankruptcy estate. The bankruptcy court overruled the objection and also refused to grant a stay of its order pending appeal. The Shapiros appealed to the district court, which dismissed the case as moot under § 364(e) of the Bankruptcy Code because the Shapiros had failed to obtain a stay. We conclude that this appeal is not moot and that cross-collateralization is not authorized under the Bankruptcy Code. Accordingly, we reverse and remand.

I. FACTS AND PROCEDURAL HISTORY

Saybrook Manufacturing Co., Inc., and related companies (the "debtors"), initiated proceedings seeking relief under Chapter 11 of the Bankruptcy Code on December 22, 1988. On December 23, 1988, the debtors filed a motion for the use of cash collateral and for authorization to incur secured debt. The bankruptcy court entered an emergency financing order that same day. At the time the bankruptcy petition was filed, the debtors owed Manufacturers Hanover approximately $34 million. The value of the collateral for this debt, however, was less than $10 million. Pursuant to the order, Manufacturers Hanover agreed to lend the debtors an additional $3 million to facilitate their reorganization. In exchange, Manufacturers Hanover received a security interest in all of the debtors' property—both property owned prior to filing the bankruptcy petition and that which was acquired subsequently. This security interest not only protected the $3 million of post-petition credit but also secured Manufacturers Hanover's $34 million pre-petition debt.

This arrangement enhanced Manufacturers Hanover's position vis-a-vis other unsecured creditors, such as the Shapiros, in the event of liquidation. Because Manufacturers Hanover's pre-petition debt was undersecured by approximately $24 million, it originally would have shared in a pro rata distribution of the debtors' unencumbered assets along with the other unsecured creditors. Under the financing order, however, Manufacturers Hanover's pre-petition debt became fully secured by all of the debtors' assets. If the bankruptcy estate were liquidated, Manufacturers Hanover's entire debt—$34 million pre-petition and $3 million post-petition—would have to be paid in full before any funds could be distributed to the remaining unsecured creditors.

Securing pre-petition debt with pre- and post-petition collateral as part of a post-petition financing arrangement is known as cross-collateralization. The Second Circuit aptly defined cross-collateralization as follows:

> [I]n return for making new loans to a debtor in possession under Chapter XI, a financing institution obtains a security interest on all assets of the debtor, both those existing at the date of the order and those created in the course of the Chapter XI proceeding, not only for the new loans, the propriety of which is not contested, but [also] for existing indebtedness to it.

Otte v. Manufacturers Hanover Commercial Corp. (In re Texlon Corp.), 596 F.2d 1092, 1094 (2d Cir.1979).

Because the Second Circuit was the first appellate court to describe this practice in *In re Texlon*, it is sometimes referred to as *Texlon*-type cross-collateralization. Another form of cross-collateralization involves securing post-petition debt with pre-petition collateral. This form of non-*Texlon*-type cross-collateralization is not at issue in this appeal. The Shapiros challenge only the cross-collateralization of the lenders' pre-petition debt, not the propriety of collateralizing the post-petition debt.

The Shapiros filed a number of objections to the bankruptcy court's order on January 13, 1989. After a hearing, the bankruptcy court overruled the objections. The Shapiros then filed a notice of appeal and a request for the bankruptcy court to stay its financing order pending appeal. The bankruptcy court denied the request for a stay on February 23, 1989.

The Shapiros subsequently moved the district court to stay the bankruptcy court's financing order pending appeal; the court denied the motion on March 7, 1989. On May 20, 1989, the district court dismissed the Shapiros' appeal as moot under § 364(e) because the Shapiros had failed to obtain a stay of the financing order pending appeal, rejecting the argument that cross-collateralization is contrary to the Code. The Shapiros then appealed to this court.

II. Issues on Appeal

1. Whether the appeal to the district court and the appeal to this court are moot under § 364(e) of the Bankruptcy Code because the Shapiros failed to obtain a stay of the bankruptcy court's financing order.

2. Whether cross-collateralization is authorized under the Bankruptcy Code.

* * *

V. Discussion

A. Mootness

We begin by addressing the lenders' claim that this appeal is moot under § 364(e) of the Bankruptcy Code. * * * The purpose of this provision is to encourage the extension of credit to debtors in bankruptcy by eliminating the risk that any lien securing the loan will be modified on appeal.

The lenders suggest that we assume cross-collateralization is authorized under § 364 and then conclude the Shapiros' appeal is moot under § 364(e). This is similar to the approach adopted by the Ninth Circuit in *Burchinal v. Central Washington Bank (In re Adams Apple, Inc.)*, 829 F.2d 1484 (9th Cir.1987). That court held that cross-collateralization was "authorized" under § 364 for the purposes of § 364(e) mootness but declined to decide whether cross-collateralization was illegal per se under the Bankruptcy Code. *See also Unsecured Creditors' Committee v. First National Bank & Trust Co. (In re Ellingsen MacLean Oil Co.)*, 834 F.2d 599 (6th Cir.1987), *cert. denied*, 488 U.S. 817 (1988).

We reject the reasoning of *In re Adams Apple* and *In re Ellingsen* because they "put the cart before the horse." By its own terms, § 364(e) is only applicable if the challenged lien or priority was authorized under § 364. *See* Charles J. Tabb, *Lender Preference Clauses and the Destruction of Appealability and Finality: Resolving a Chapter 11 Dilemma*, 50 Ohio St. L.J. 109, 116–35 (1989) (criticizing *In re Adams Apple, In re Ellingsen*, and the practice of shielding cross-collateralization from appellate review via mootness under § 364(e)). We cannot determine if this appeal is moot under § 364(e) until we decide the central issue in this appeal—whether cross-collateralization is authorized under § 364. Accordingly, we now turn to that question.

B. Cross–Collateralization and § 364

Cross-collateralization is an extremely controversial form of Chapter 11 financing. Nevertheless, the practice has been approved by several bankruptcy courts. Even the courts that have allowed cross-collateralization, however, were generally reluctant to do so.

In *In re Vanguard Diversified, Inc.*, 31 B.R. 364 (Bankr. E.D.N.Y.1983), for example, the bankruptcy court noted that cross-collateralization is "a disfavored means of financing" that should only be used as a last resort. *Id.* at 366. In order to obtain a financing order including cross-collateralization, the court required the debtor to demonstrate (1) that its business operations would fail absent the proposed financing, (2) that it is unable to obtain alternative financing on acceptable terms, (3) that the proposed lender will not accept less preferential terms, and (4) that the proposed financing is in the general creditor body's best interest. This four-part test has since been adopted by other bankruptcy courts which permit cross-collateralization.

* * *

Cross-collateralization is not specifically mentioned in the Bankruptcy Code. We conclude that cross-collateralization is inconsistent with bankruptcy law for two reasons. First, cross-collateralization is not authorized as a method of post-petition financing under

§ 364. Second, cross-collateralization is beyond the scope of the bankruptcy court's inherent equitable power because it is directly contrary to the fundamental priority scheme of the Bankruptcy Code. *See generally* Charles J. Tabb, *A Critical Reappraisal of Cross–Collateralization in Bankruptcy*, 60 S. Cal. L. Rev. 109 (1986).

Section 364 authorizes Chapter 11 debtors to obtain secured credit and incur secured debt as part of their reorganization. It provides, in relevant part, that:

> (c) If the trustee is unable to obtain unsecured credit allowable under § 503(b)(1) of this title as an administrative expense, the court, after notice and a hearing, *may authorize the obtaining of credit or the incurring of debt*—
>
> (1) with priority over any or all administrative expenses of the kind specified in § 503(b) or 507(b) of this title;
>
> (2) secured by a lien on property of the estate that is not otherwise subject to a lien; or
>
> (3) secured by a junior lien on property of the estate that is subject to a lien.
>
> (d)(1) The court, after notice and a hearing, *may authorize the obtaining of credit or incurring of debt* secured by a senior or equal lien on property of the estate that is subject to a lien only if—
>
> (A) the trustee is unable to obtain such credit otherwise; and
>
> (B) there is adequate protection of the interest of the holder of the lien on the property of the estate on which such senior or equal lien is proposed to be granted.
>
> (2) In any hearing under this subsection, the trustee has the burden of proof on the issue of adequate protection.

§§ 364(c) & (d) (emphasis added). By their express terms, §§ 364(c) & (d) apply only to future—i.e., post-petition—extensions of credit. They do not authorize the granting of liens to secure pre-petition loans.

* * *

Given that cross-collateralization is not authorized by § 364, we now turn to the lenders' argument that bankruptcy courts may permit the practice under their general equitable power. Bankruptcy courts are indeed courts of equity, and they have the power to adjust claims to avoid injustice or unfairness. This equitable power, however, is not unlimited. * * *

Section 507 of the Bankruptcy Code fixes the priority order of claims and expenses against the bankruptcy estate. Creditors within a given class are to be treated equally, and bankruptcy courts may not create their own rules of superpriority within a single class. Cross-collateralization, however, does exactly that. As a result of this practice, post-petition lenders' unsecured pre-petition claims are given priority over all other unsecured pre-petition claims. The Ninth Circuit recognized that "[t]here is no * * * applicable provision in the Bankruptcy Code authorizing the debtor to pay certain pre-petition unsecured claims in full while others remain unpaid. To do so would impermissibly violate the priority scheme of the Bankruptcy Code." *Transamerica Commercial Finance Corp. v. Citibank (In re Sun Runner Marine, Inc.)*, 945 F.2d 1089, 1094 (9th Cir.1991) (citations omitted).

The Second Circuit has noted that, if cross-collateralization were initiated by the bankrupt while insolvent and shortly before filing a petition, the arrangement "would have constituted a voidable preference." *In re Texlon*, 596 F.2d at 1097. The fundamental nature of this practice is not changed by the fact that it is sanctioned by the bankruptcy court. We disagree with the district court's conclusion that, while cross-collateralization may violate some policies of bankruptcy law, it is consistent with the general purpose of Chapter 11 to help businesses reorganize and become profitable. Rehabilitation is certainly the primary purpose of Chapter 11. This end, however, does not justify the use of any means. Cross-collateralization is directly inconsistent with the priority scheme of the Bankruptcy Code. Accordingly, the practice may not be approved by the bankruptcy court under its equitable authority.

VI. Conclusion

* * * Because *Texlon*-type cross-collateralization is not explicitly authorized by the Bankruptcy Code and is contrary to the basic priority structure of the Code, we hold that it is an impermissible means of obtaining post-petition financing. The judgment of the district court is REVERSED and the case is REMANDED for proceedings not inconsistent with this opinion.

Questions

1. Isn't this sort of inquiry exactly what § 364(e) was intended to prevent?

2. What relief is appropriate? Return of the new money and elimination of the new lien? Assuming that the debtor has spent a good bit of the new loan (a safe bet!), will the bank be forced to relinquish its new security interest and become unsecured for an additional $3 million?

3. ADEQUATE PROTECTION

A creditor whose collateral is jeopardized in some way—such as use by the debtor-in-possession in its reorganization effort, or loss of priority to a postpetition lender—is entitled to adequate protection. Section 361 lists ways in which adequate protection can be given.

Problems

1. Debtor Corp. was in the business of hauling goods interstate. The trucks in its fleet were financed by Bank, which held perfected security interests in all of Debtor Corp.'s equipment. Debtor Corp. filed a Chapter 11 petition on February 1 and continued using the trucks while attempting to reorganize. Bank filed a motion for adequate protection on August 1 of the next year and it was heard on November 1. Bank presented very convincing evidence that the fleet of trucks had depreciated and continued to depreciate at the rate of $10,000 per month. Bank sought an order that Debtor Corp. pay $210,000 in adequate protection payments for the period since bankruptcy began, and $10,000 every month until confirmation of a plan. Is Bank entitled to such an order?

2. Debtor, Inc. operated a retail store in an area of town suffering progressive urban blight. Debtor, Inc.'s premises were subject to a first mortgage for $350,000, owed to First Bank, and a second mortgage for $200,000, owed to Second Bank. The property was worth $450,000 when Debtor, Inc. filed a bankruptcy petition six months ago, but it is declining in value at the rate of about $1,000 per month. First Bank's loan accrues interest of $2,300 per month. Assuming that both First Bank and Second Bank act aggressively to preserve their interests, what amounts of adequate protection payments can each of them claim at the time of bankruptcy? Will those amounts change as the bankruptcy case progresses?

The following case, while difficult, raises two important statutory issues surrounding the § 507(b) superpriority to which a creditor is entitled when an award of adequate protection turns out to be inadequate. The case also demonstrates, arithmetically, the practical problems a creditor faces in proving its entitlement under § 507(b).

IN RE CALLISTER

United States Bankruptcy Court, District of Utah, 1981.
15 B.R. 521.

RALPH R. MABEY, Bankruptcy Judge.

FACTUAL AND PROCEDURAL BACKGROUND

This case raises issues concerning the superpriority provision of § 507(b).

Debtor, the sole proprietor of a trucking business, filed a petition under Chapter 11 on December 12, 1980. Ingersoll–Rand Financial Corporation (Rand), which holds a security interest in three tractors and two trailers, filed a complaint seeking relief from the automatic stay on January 2, 1981. A hearing was held January 23. At that time, the parties stipulated that the collateral was worth $129,000, that the debt owing was $106,248, and that debtor would pay $1,232 per month beginning February 1 to Rand. Debtor also agreed to insure the equipment as required in the security agreements. A procedure was established for lifting the stay in the event of default. The court ruled that Rand was adequately protected under this arrangement. Two payments were made, but debtor defaulted May 1, and the stay was lifted June 5. The case was converted to Chapter 7 on August 5.

Meanwhile, counsel for debtor filed an application for allowance and payment of fees in the amount of $9,052 under § 331. Counsel for the unsecured creditors committee likewise requested fees in the amount of $2,994. Rand objected, claiming that the fees might be allowed but not paid because it was entitled to a superpriority under 507(b).

Hearings were held August 18 and 19. The evidence showed that two of the three tractors underwent repair from January to June and therefore conferred no benefit on the estate. The third tractor was used for approximately three weeks but it caught fire and was destroyed. Through inadvertence, no insurance was in force to indemnify this casualty. The trailers were used without mishap.

Debtor values the collateral, as of June 5, at $89,600. This is the value "as is" without repairs or payment of repair bills. In his view, with the exception of the burned tractor, minimal depreciation has occurred. The decline in value is attributable to the uninsured loss and depression in prices.

Rand values the collateral, as of the same time, and also "as is," at $63,900. In its view, substantial depreciation, independent of the accident, has taken place.

The court values the collateral as of June 5 at $68,900. Subtracting costs of repair in the amount of $7,097 leaves $61,803. Hence, the collateral has dwindled in worth by $67,197. At least four factors account for this decrease. The uninsured loss equals $19,411.[14] Error in the stipulation is responsible for $33,447.[15] Market forces caused a loss of $7,993.[16] Use caused a loss of $6,346.[17] Because of the error in

---

[14] The burned tractor had a stipulated value of $30,000 on January 23. It was worth $5,000 on June 5. The entire difference of $25,000, however, is not attributable to the accident. A portion, $5,589, is due to the error in the stipulation. *See infra* note 15. No share of the loss through market forces is allocated to the burned tractor.

[15] The security agreements, executed in June, 1980, show that the equipment was financed for $110,450. It is unclear whether this was the price or whether, and in what amount, a down payment may have been made. Hughes [the dealer from whom debtor purchased the equipment] testified that the 1978 tractor was sold for $44,850, the 1977 tractors for $28,750 each, and the trailers for $10,450 each, for a total of $123,250. The equipment was valued by stipulation in January, 1981, after approximately eight months of use, at $129,000. Thus, there was a difference between the Hughes price and the stipulated value of $5,750. Since there was no evidence that this type of equipment appreciates in value, and since an escalation in value is improbable, this amount represents a mistake in the stipulation. But even this amount is understated since it does not account for depreciation through use between June and January. Monthly payments under the security agreements, which are ordinarily keyed to depreciation, were $3,866. This amount, however, includes interest which was per diem $51.38 * * * or for thirty days $1,541. This would make monthly principal payments of $2,325 or for eight months $18,600. (In contrast, the stipulated figure of $1,232 for eight months yields $9,856.) Thus, the mistake in price of $5,750 and depreciation of $18,600 equals $24,350. The stipulated value of $129,000 contained two additional errors. First, it did not account for the cost of repairs at $7,097. Second, it did not account for the value of siding which debtor placed on but later removed from one trailer at $2,000. Cumulative error equals $33,447.

[16] This figure is deduced by elimination. It is the difference between the decline in worth of the collateral and all other items of loss.

[17] The trailers were the only equipment which depreciated through use. They had a stipulated worth of $22,000 on January 23 and were valued at $11,400 on June 5 for a difference of $10,600. The entire difference, however, is not attributable to depreciation through use. A portion, $4,254, is due to error in the stipulation. *See supra* note

the stipulation, the allowed secured claim on January 23 was $95,553, not $106,248. The allowed secured claim on June 5 was $61,803, for a reduction of $33,750.

These facts raise several issues which may be classified under the headings of statutory construction, allowance, and rank. Under statutory construction: May a creditor ineligible for an administrative claim under § 503(b) qualify for superpriority status under 507(b)? Under allowance: Are losses caused by failure to obtain insurance, an error in the stipulation, market forces, and depreciation recompensable under 507(b)? Under rank: Does the superpriority take precedence over interim fees under 331? Under what, if any, circumstances may fees be paid notwithstanding the existence of or potential for a superpriority? These questions are discussed below.

IS THE SUPERPRIORITY AN ADMINISTRATIVE EXPENSE OR SOMETHING MORE?

* * *

Debtor maintains that only creditors who have claims under 503(b) *and* who lose adequate protection may enjoy the benefit of 507(b). This view draws support from the face of 507(b) which speaks of "a claim allowable under subsection (a)(1) of this section" which in turn refers to 503(b).[20] But 507(b), on closer analysis, is the proverbial prism in the fog. A review of its language, history, and relation to adequate protection, however, may elucidate its meaning.

The Language of 507(b)

The use of property for the estate creates an administrative claim under 503(b). Curbing repossession of property through the stay, without more, may not lead to the same result. Section 507(b), however, treats property used and property subject to the stay, implying that both, so long as they lose adequate protection, meet the standards of 503(b). Indeed, commentators appear to equate inadequate protection with allowability under 503(b). *See, e.g.*, 3 Collier on Bankruptcy ¶ 507.05 at 507–46 (15th ed. 1980) ("In essence, [507(b)] affords a superpriority to post-petition creditors in whose case the protection

15. No share of the loss through market forces is allocated to the trailers.

20 Rand argues that whether it qualifies for an administrative claim under 503(b) is irrelevant. The use of the trailers, in any event, was probably an actual, necessary cost of preserving the estate. The uninsured loss may likewise fit this category.

given by the trustee is inadequate to protect the creditor's interest *thereby resulting in an administrative expense claim under § 503(b)(1)(A)* ") (emphasis supplied).[20a] The facts, however, may belie this assumption. Here, for example, debtor needed the equipment, but circumstance, for the most part, kept it idle. If the equipment has not been an "actual, necessary cost * * * of preserving the estate," does it nevertheless qualify as a superpriority because its *use is implicit* in 507(b)?

History of the Superpriority

The superpriority may be difficult to articulate by statute, because it is equitable in origin and genealogy. The Commission would have permitted the trustee to use collateral subject to a request "to modify the stay by imposing such conditions on the use of the property or the proceeds thereof as will adequately protect the secured party." Report of the Commission on the Bankruptcy Laws of the United States, H. Doc. No. 93–137, pt. II, § 7–203(b)(2) (1973). Granting administrative priority was an appropriate condition "if it is clear that the proceeds of the liquidation of property of the estate available to pay the claim will be sufficient." *Id.* at Note 3.

The authority for this proposal was *In re Yale Express System, Inc.*, 384 F.2d 990 (2d Cir.1967). In *Yale Express*, the creditor held a security interest in truck bodies and trailers sold to a freight carrier. It sought reclamation of the collateral. The district court * * * [denied reclamation and] the second circuit upheld the order because it was "unable to conclude that the court had abused its equitable discretion." *Id.* at 992. The opinion relied upon findings that the equipment was essential to the business and that reorganization was "not a mere will-o'-the wisp" but a "reasonable possibility." Applications for payment of rent were also denied on the ground that, if the debtor paid rent to this

[20a] This conclusion may be based upon the belief that 503(b) is not, in fact, limited to "actual, necessary" costs of administration: "While it is true that the court is not free to fashion additional priorities nor to determine among the priorities the order of payment save as Congress provided for such order, it ought not be assumed that the six designations are necessarily exclusive nor designed to cover every conceivable situation. Thus, the phrase in § 503(b)(1) 'actual, necessary costs and expenses of preserving the estate' should not be thought to preclude a court from determining whether or not a certain claim offered as an expense of administration should not be within the meaning of such phrase. * * * What is meant, however, by the provisions of § 503(b) is that however a court might construe any of the particular phrases, the court's ultimate determination to allow a claim as an administrative expense is dependent upon the subsections of § 503(b). Unless a claim is allowed as an administrative expense, it is not within this section and, therefore, is not entitled to the priority given such administrative claims by § 507(a)." 3 Collier on Bankruptcy, *supra* ¶ 503.03 at 503–11—503–12.

creditor, it would have to pay rent to all which would "nullify the reorganization as effectively as granting the petition for reclamation." *Id.* As an afternote, the court remarked that it had not "overlooked [the creditor's] contention that equitable considerations compel a favorable ruling in its behalf because the vehicles in which it claims a security interest are depreciating. *But to such extent as [the creditor] has been damaged by the use of its property pending the reorganization, it is entitled to equitable consideration in the reorganization plan* [citation omitted]." *Id.* (emphasis supplied).

Yale Express alarmed lenders and they mounted an attack on its codification. One observer wrote that "granting a priority just postpones the day of reckoning until the date of confirmation of the debtor's plan and, in turn, presupposes that a plan will be confirmed." It is "granting an ephemeral future priority as a device for avoiding present reality." Murphy, "Use of Collateral in Business Rehabilitation: A Suggested Redrafting of § 7–203 of the Bankruptcy Reform Act," 63 Cal. L. Rev. 1483, 1505 (1975).

Notwithstanding this critique, the concept of an administrative priority as a means of providing adequate protection was written into § 361(3) of H.R. 8200. *See* H.R. 8200, 95th Cong., 1st Sess. (1977). The House Report cautioned that "this method, more than the others, requires a prediction as to whether the unencumbered assets that will remain if the case is converted from reorganization to liquidation will be sufficient to pay the protected entity in full. It is clearly the most risky, from the entity's perspective, and should be used only when there is relative certainty that administrative expenses will be able to be paid in full in the event of liquidation." H.R. Rep. No. 95–595 at 340, *reprinted in* 1978 U.S.C.C.A.N. at 6296. The Senate disagreed and omitted the concept of an administrative priority as a means of providing adequate protection "because such protection is too uncertain to be meaningful." S. Rep. No. 95–989 at 54, *reprinted in* 1978 U.S.C.C.A.N. at 5840.

As enacted, § 361 dropped subsection (3) of H.R. 8200 because "in every case there is the uncertainty that the estate will have sufficient property to pay administrative expenses in full." 124 Cong. Rec. H11,092 (daily ed., September 28, 1978). Language forbidding use of administrative priorities in fashioning adequate protection took its place. The concept, however, was not entirely abandoned. It was grafted on to 507 so that "to the extent the protection [under § 361] proves to be inadequate after the fact, the creditor is entitled to a first priority administrative expense." *Id.* Floor leaders commented further that "§ 507(b) * * * is new and is derived from the compromise contained in the House with respect to adequate protection under § 361. Subsection (b) provides that to the extent adequate protection of the interest of a holder of a claim proves to be inadequate, then the creditor's claim is given priority over every other allowable claim entitled to distribution under § 507(a)." *Id.* at 11,095.

The Superpriority and Adequate Protection

The superpriority is the stepchild of adequate protection and they enjoy a symbiotic relationship. * * *

[W]hereas adequate protection shields the creditor in the first instance from impairment in the value of his "interest in property," the superpriority was intended to recapture value unexpectedly lost during the course of a case: "It establishes a statutory fail-safe system in recognition of the ultimate reality that protection previously determined the 'indubitable equivalent' * * * may later prove inadequate." *In re Marine Optical, Inc.*, 10 B.R. 893 (1st Cir. BAP 1981).

Guidelines for Allowance of a Superpriority

Guidelines for allowing a superpriority may be distilled from 507(b), its language, history, and relation to adequate protection. The language of 507(b), especially in relation to 503(b), is difficult to plumb. Indeed, 503(b) and 507(b) may be at odds. One is keyed to preserving the estate, the other is designed to protect secured creditors. Coincidentally, they reflect the tension of interests in this case between counsel who request fees and Rand which demands superpriority. If 507(b) is faithful to one of these purposes, it may be untrue to the other.

The history of the superpriority and its relation to adequate protection share this ambivalence. If the Commission proposal, *Yale Express*, and H.R. 8200 are the antecedents of 507(b), then 503(b) with its criteria of need and usefulness to the estate has relevance. But Congress may have discounted these views, establishing a "statutory fail-safe" to reimburse creditors where there is a shortfall in adequate protection. This reimbursement may not be reducible to the ambit of 503(b). Indeed, if only administrative expenses qualify under 507(b), the measure of allowance may be fair rental value, or some other indicia of use. A different yardstick, however, may gauge the miscarriage of adequate protection.[23]

---

[23] One commentator has flagged this ambiguity. After quoting the legislative history

The parties seek a ruling that the superpriority must be allowed either as an administrative expense or as a guarantee of adequate protection. But neither approach is satisfactory. The statute is a confederation of principles; it cannot be "construed" to favor one at the expense of another; it should be interpreted to account for the merits of all. Hence, equitable considerations, arising from the facts of each case, should be examined. The rights and importance of other interests must be weighed. The manner in which adequate protection was provided and the role of the superpriority as a "backstop" should be considered.

PROBLEMS OF ALLOWANCE

The Uninsured Loss

Rand argues that adequate protection in the form of a stipulation to procure insurance was afforded; noncompliance resulted in the uninsured destruction of the tractor; therefore adequate protection failed and 507(b) comes into play.

True, the superpriority is born when adequate protection fails. But whether adequate protection has failed depends upon whether and how it has been provided. In this regard, Rand may misconceive the purpose of adequate protection which shelters creditors "from any impairment in value attributable to the stay. The stay does not cause, but it may forestall a creditor from preventing or mitigating a decline in value. Some harm to collateral however may be unavoidable with or without the stay. Likewise, creditors may acquiesce in some harm to collateral for business or other reasons notwithstanding the stay. In

---

which "implies that the entire deficiency sustained by the creditor is entitled to superpriority status," he observes that "the language of the subsection itself seems to say something quite different. Unlike the legislative history, subsection 507(b) does not speak in terms of the 'creditor's claim,' but rather of the 'claim allowable under subsection (a)(1) of this section * * * arising from the * * * stay of action, use, sale, or lease, * * * or granting of a lien' on the property in question. The language of the statute, therefore, seems to limit the superpriority by two factors. First, it would seem to apply only to that portion of the deficiency actually incurred as a cost of administration; i.e., the portion incurred *subsequent* to commencement of the proceeding. This could be measured by the interest accrued during that period, or perhaps by the fair rental value of the use of the property during the period—but clearly would not include the entire deficiency claim. The subsection also seems to limit the super-priority to the amount by which the collateral actually decreased in value during the period of administration. The court could well determine that only a small portion of the total deficiency was caused by post-petition decrease in value. Here again, the amount entitled to a subsection 507(b) priority would be only a portion of the entire deficiency." Levit, "Use and Disposition of Property Under Chapter 11 of the Bankruptcy Code: Some Practical Concerns," 53 Am. Bank. L.J. 275, 290 (1979) (emphasis in original).

these situations and others which may arise, any impairment in value may not be attributable to the stay. Hence, not every decline in value must be recompensed, only those which, but for the stay, could be and probably would be prevented or mitigated." *In re Alyucan Interstate Corp.*, 12 B.R. 803, 808 (Bankr. D. Utah 1981).

The uninsured loss may not have been attributable to the stay for at least two reasons. First, the risk occasioned by the stay, and for which protection in the form of insurance was afforded, was that the tractor, before repossession, would be damaged. There was, however, another risk at work, *viz.*, the risk of inadvertently failing to obtain insurance. Protection against this risk was not and indeed could not have been afforded.

If this risk were allocated between debtor and Rand outside bankruptcy, naturally, it would be borne by debtor, who, as between the two innocent parties, was in a better position to prevent the inadvertence. But the risk must be allocated not only between debtor and Rand, but also between Rand and other administrative claimants. As between these parties, Rand was in a better position to prevent the mistake and therefore arguably it should suffer the loss.

Second, the loss which flowed, not from the accident, but from the oversight, while unprotectible under 361, was preventable by Rand. The security agreements permit Rand, when the debtor does not obtain insurance, to pay the premium and charge the account. Under § 506(b), when the creditor is oversecured, this supplements the allowed secured claim, increasing the lien entitled to protection. Although the fact of reorganization invites more than ordinary diligence by creditors, Rand did not ascertain whether insurance was bought, nor did it exercise its right to default under the stipulation. Indeed, Rand, from one view, may have "acquiesced" in the harm to its collateral.

Nevertheless, deciding whether loss is attributable to the stay, using the abstraction of "cause," in this case, is speculative. The conflict between debtor, Rand, and administrative claimants may be overdrawn. The debtor is a debtor in possession, the fiduciary representative of the estate. The interest of administrative claimants is his stewardship. Even absent court order, this includes the procurement of insurance. A rule which might relax this duty, where possible, should be avoided. The assertion that the failure to insure was preventable, while compelling under other circumstances, is not convincing on these facts. A degree of reliance upon stipulations is warranted, and Rand, with less than a month to act, did not sleep on its rights. These considerations mandate allowance of the uninsured loss as a superpriority.

Error in the Stipulation

Stipulations raise another complex of problems. On one hand, they show cooperation between creditors and the estate which should be requited. They reduce costs otherwise incurred in litigation and permit a constructive allocation of resources. They lessen the judicial burden of administering the estate, an important principle of the Reform Act.

* * * Equity rewards diligence, and a creditor careless in negotiating a stipulation has no standing in chancery. This is especially true where the rights of other parties may be impaired.

On balance, Rand is not entitled to a superpriority for the loss attributable to the error in the stipulation. Disallowance under these circumstances will not discourage stipulations. Rather, it will further care in their formulation. Rand was less the cooperative creditor than reluctant caretaker of its collateral. Hence, its motive in stipulating is not an equitable consideration in its favor. Given the incalculability of values, some misapprehension is expected; but this error was not the product of excusable neglect. It was a gross miscalculation which could have been easily detected. Indeed, the disparity between the price and stipulation should have warned Rand that something was amiss, prompting investigation, and discovery of the trailer siding and unpaid repair bills. Rand is experienced with this type of collateral, familiar with values and industry trends. Given its sophistication and leverage under the Code, it enjoys substantial bargaining power with debtor. Thus, its claim that it relied upon the representations of debtor in arriving at the stipulated value is unpersuasive. Under these circumstances, equity will look past the form of the stipulation to the substance of the value. The value of $129,000 was a fiction. The loss of $33,447 was no loss. This amount should not be credited toward a superpriority.

Market Forces

Both sides acknowledge the interposition of the market: several carriers have folded and are liquidating their equipment; newer models are more attractive to entrepreneurs. This combination of circumstances has lowered prices.

The property at stake and its susceptibility to market forces are factors to be considered in determining adequate protection. Arguably,

Rand should have accounted for these forces in negotiating the stipulated interim payments. But the collapse of freighters and the inauguration of products are not readily foreseeable. In this regard, Rand, like debtor, is at the mercy of events beyond its control. Rand did not speculate on the market at the expense of the estate; it was reasonably prompt in obtaining relief from the stay and mitigating damage. The loss resulting from market forces therefore "ought not equitably to be saddled on [Rand] but on [the estate] for whose supposed benefit the restraint was imposed." *In re New York, New Haven & Hartford R. Co.*, 147 F.2d 40, 48 (2d Cir.1945).

Depreciation Through Use

Since the trailers were used and useful to the estate, debtor, in principle, should not object to loss through depreciation as a superpriority. The question is how much loss. The stipulation provided for interim payments, which if paid, from February to May, would have totalled $4,928. Actual depreciation equalled $6,346. *See supra* note 17. Should Rand receive the amount it bargained for in the stipulation or the amount of real loss? Equity recommends the former. Rand was not bereft in bankruptcy. It had the background and tools to insure that payments were commensurate with depreciation. Indeed, if it had calculated depreciation based upon the security agreements, *see supra* note 15, the amount would have been $9,300. This figure, unlike the stipulated payments, approximates the real loss. The court is reluctant to penalize the estate for an error which could have been remedied by Rand. The depreciation allocable to superpriority is therefore $4,928, minus payments received in the amount of $2,464, or $2,464.

Calculating the Superpriority

In principle, calculation of the superpriority is straightforward; the error in the stipulation, however, complicates the figures in this case. Ordinarily, the loss eligible for superpriority status should be deducted from the value of the collateral at the adequate protection hearing. The extent to which this erodes the allowed secured claim on that date constitutes the allowed super-priority. Here, eligible loss equalled $19,411 for the burned tractor, $7,993 for market decline, and $2,464 for depreciation, for a total of $29,868. The value of the collateral and the allowed secured claim on January 23, making adjustments for the error in the stipulation, was $95,553; the value of the collateral and the allowed secured claim on June 5 was $61,803, for a reduction of $33,750. The allowed secured claim is diminished by more than the eligible loss. The difference of $3,882 is the ineligible loss attributable to depreciation through use. Hence, the eligible loss is the allowed superpriority.

If adjustments were not made for the error in the stipulation, the result would be different. The loss of $29,868 would be subtracted from $129,000, *i.e.* it would be charged against the "equity cushion" which existed on that date. The brunt of the loss would be borne by the estate, and would erode the allowed secured claim ($106,248) by only $7,116. This would be the allowed superpriority.

Since the stipulated value was not credited for purposes of determining loss, however, it should not be a factor in calculating the superpriority. The adjusted figures are therefore used, yielding a superpriority of $29,868.

PROBLEMS OF RANK

Rand argues that the superpriority has precedence over claims allowed under 503(b). Attorneys fees may be allowed under 503(b)(2). Thus no fees may be paid until the superpriority is satisfied. This argument is flawed, however, for several reasons.

Fees are allowed under § 330 and classified as administrative expenses under 503(b)(2). But while other administrative expenses must wait until confirmation, § 1129(a)(9), or liquidation, § 726, for reimbursement, fees are payable on an interim and therefore a preeminent basis under 331. Not only the statutory scheme but also reasons of policy support this preeminence of fees under 331.[38a]

Lenders like Rand may be involuntarily harnessed to the ordeal of reorganization, but fee claimants voluntarily contribute to the ideal of rehabilitation. Section 331 encourages this volunteerism and, as an inducement to work for the estate, is a vital provision of the Reform Act which places the burden of administration upon trustees, creditor committees, and their professional representatives. Absent this incentive, it would be difficult to assure continued efficient management. Requests for adequate protection in Chapter 11 are ubiquitous; each raises the spectre of a superpriority. If the superpriority, in turn, might preempt

[38a] Section 507(b) gives the superpriority precedence over claims allowed under 507(a), or in other words, over claims allowed under 503(b). Fees, however, may be allowed under 330 and 331. When allowed under these provisions, instead of 503(b)(2), they are not subject to the regimen of 507. Moreover, as indicated in the text, fees are not only allowed but also payable under 331. Section 507(b), in contrast, is silent respecting payment. This gives a *de facto* preeminence to fees.

interim fees, it would jeopardize the further provision of services. The result would not be attractive. The administrators might mutiny: but the case, whether in Chapter 11 or in a superseding Chapter 7, would not care for itself. They might cut corners: but this would cause delay, which is anathema to creditors, especially those holding a superpriority who are waiting for confirmation or liquidation. They might demand exorbitant retainers at the beginning of each case: but for most debtors this either would be impossible or would decrease their chances for rehabilitation.[40]

These dangers do not dictate that in every instance fees must be paid ahead of the superpriority. Section 331 says that fees "may" be paid on an interim basis. There is a presumption, for the reasons outlined above, that they will be paid notwithstanding the existence of a superpriority. * * * But it is rebuttable under appropriate equitable circumstances. These circumstances, however, are not present in this case.

IT IS THEREFORE ORDERED:

1. Rand is allowed a superpriority in the amount of $29,868.

2. Fees of counsel for debtor and the unsecured creditors committee which have been previously allowed shall be paid forthwith.

Questions

1. One of the statutory issues in *Callister* is whether a creditor must be entitled to an administrative expense claim under § 503(b) (because its collateral was actually used by the debtor-in-possession) in order to obtain a superpriority claim under § 507(b). How did the court answer that question?

2. The other statutory issue in *Callister* is whether the superpriority must be paid before interim attorneys' fees. The sequence of payment will be of no consequence, ultimately, if the estate is sufficient to pay all administrative expense claims. But what if assets are insufficient? What would be the result of *Callister*'s holding in such a case? Did the court apply its own notions of sensible bankruptcy policy, rather than the words of the statute?

---

[40] It is likewise unfair, if not unrealistic, to expect counsel to underwrite the reorganization. This would drive experienced and expert counsel to more reliably lucrative fields of practice.

4. SALE OF PROPERTY

Section 363 permits the trustee not only to use property in which a creditor has an interest, but also to sell or lease it. When the sale of such property is part of the debtor's ordinary course of business, as the sale of inventory from a store's shelves, no court authorization is needed. § 363(c). In that event, the creditor's protection is its interest in the proceeds. § 363(c)(2).

Sales outside the ordinary course of business, especially if free of lien, are of more concern. The next case addresses whether a significant portion of the debtor's assets may be sold outside of the plan. The case following it addresses the question of price.

COMMITTEE OF EQUITY SECURITY HOLDERS v. LIONEL CORP. (IN RE LIONEL CORP.)

United States Court of Appeals, Second Circuit, 1983.
722 F.2d 1063.

CARDAMONE, Circuit Judge.

This expedited appeal is from an order of United States District Judge Dudley B. Bonsal dated September 7, 1983, approving an order entered earlier that day by the United States Bankruptcy Court for the Southern District of New York (Ryan, J.). The order authorized the sale by Lionel Corporation, a Chapter 11 debtor in possession, of its 82% common stock holding in Dale Electronics, Inc. to Peabody International Corporation for $50 million.

I. FACTS

On February 19, 1982 the Lionel Corporation—toy train manufacturer of childhood memory—and two of its subsidiaries, Lionel Leisure, Inc. and Consolidated Toy Company, filed joint petitions for reorganization under Chapter 11 of the Bankruptcy Code. Resort to Chapter 11 was precipitated by losses totalling $22.5 million that Lionel incurred in its toy retailing operation during the two year period ending December 1982.

There are 7.1 million shares of common stock of Lionel held by 10,000 investors. Its consolidated assets and liabilities as of March 31,

1983 were $168.7 million and $191.5 million, respectively, reflecting a negative net worth of nearly $23 million. Total sales for 1981 and 1982 were $295.1 million and $338.6 million. Lionel's creditors hold approximately $135.6 million in pre-petition claims, and they are represented in the ongoing bankruptcy proceedings by an Official Creditors' Committee whose 13 members hold $80 million of those claims. The remaining $55 million is scattered among thousands of small creditors.

Lionel continues to operate its businesses and manage its properties * * * .

Lionel's most important asset and the subject of this proceeding is its ownership of 82% of the common stock of Dale, a corporation engaged in the manufacture of electronic components. Dale is not a party to the Lionel bankruptcy proceeding. Public investors own the remaining 18 percent of Dale's common stock, which is listed on the American Stock Exchange. Its balance sheet reflects assets and liabilities as of March 31, 1983 of $57.8 million and $29.8 million, respectively, resulting in shareholders equity of approximately $28.0 million. Lionel's stock investment in Dale represents approximately 34 percent of Lionel's consolidated assets, and its interest in Dale is Lionel's most valuable single asset. Unlike Lionel's toy retailing operation, Dale is profitable. For the same two-year period ending in December 1982 during which Lionel had incurred its substantial losses, Dale had an aggregate operating profit of $18.8 million.

On June 14, 1983 Lionel filed an application under § 363(b) seeking bankruptcy court authorization to sell its 82% interest in Dale to Acme-Cleveland Corporation for $43 million in cash. Four days later the debtor filed a plan of reorganization conditioned upon a sale of Dale with the proceeds to be distributed to creditors. Certain issues of the reorganization remain unresolved, and negotiations are continuing; however, a solicitation of votes on the plan has not yet begun. On September 7, 1983, following the Securities and Exchange Commission's July 15 filing of objections to the sale, Bankruptcy Judge Ryan held a hearing on Lionel's application. At the hearing, Peabody emerged as the successful of three bidders with an offer of $50 million for Lionel's interest in Dale.

The Chief Executive Officer of Lionel and a Vice-President of Salomon Brothers were the only witnesses produced and both testified in support of the application. Their testimony established that while the price paid for the stock was "fair," Dale is not an asset "that is wasting away in any sense." Lionel's Chief Executive Officer stated that there was no reason why the sale of Dale stock could not be accomplished as part of the reorganization plan, and that the sole reason for Lionel's application to sell was the Creditors' Committee's insistence upon it. The creditors wanted to turn this asset of Lionel into a "pot of cash," to provide the bulk of the $70 million required to repay creditors under the proposed plan of reorganization.

In confirming the sale, Judge Ryan made no formal findings of fact. He simply noted that cause to sell was sufficiently shown by the Creditors' Committee's insistence upon it. Judge Ryan further found cause—presumably from long experience—based upon his own opinion that a present failure to confirm would set the entire reorganization process back a year or longer while the parties attempted to restructure it.

The Committee of Equity Security Holders, statutory representatives of the 10,000 public shareholders of Lionel, appealed this order claiming that the sale, prior to approval of a reorganization plan, deprives the equity holders of the Bankruptcy Code's safeguards of disclosure, solicitation and acceptance and divests the debtor of a dominant and profitable asset which could serve as a cornerstone for a sound plan. The SEC also appeared and objected to the sale in the bankruptcy court and supports the Equity Committee's appeal, claiming that approval of the sale side-steps the Code's requirement for informed suffrage which is at the heart of Chapter 11.

The Creditors' Committee favors the sale because it believes it is in the best interests of Lionel and because the sale is expressly authorized by § 363(b) of the Code. Lionel tells us that its ownership of Dale, a non-operating asset, is held for investment purposes only and that its sale will provide the estate with the large block of the cash needed to fund its plan of reorganization.

From the oral arguments and briefs we gather that the Equity Committee believes that Chapter 11 has cleared the reorganization field of major pre-plan sales—somewhat like the way Minerva routed Mars—relegating § 363(b) to be used only in emergencies. The Creditors' Committee counters that a bankruptcy judge should have absolute freedom under § 363(b) to do as he thinks best. Neither of these arguments is wholly persuasive. Here, as in so many similar cases, we must avoid the extremes, for the policies underlying the Bankruptcy Reform Act of 1978 support a middle ground—one which gives the bankruptcy judge considerable discretion yet requires him to articulate sound business justifications for his decisions.

II. DISCUSSION

The issue now before this Court is to what extent Chapter 11 permits a bankruptcy judge to authorize the sale of an important asset of the bankrupt's estate, out of the ordinary course of business and prior to acceptance and outside of any plan of reorganization. Section 363(b), the focal point of our analysis, provides that "the trustee, after notice and a hearing, may use, sell, or lease, other than in the ordinary course of business, property of the estate."

On its face, § 363(b) appears to permit disposition of any property of the estate of a corporate debtor without resort to the statutory safeguards embodied in Chapter 11 of the Bankruptcy Code. Yet, analysis of the statute's history and over seven decades of case law convinces us that such a literal reading of § 363(b) would unnecessarily violate the congressional scheme for corporate reorganizations.

A. *Bankruptcy Act of 1867—the "Perishable" Standard*

An early statutory reference providing for the sale of a debtor's property prior to final liquidation of the estate in limited circumstances was § 25 of the Bankruptcy Act of 1867. Congress there stated:

> "*And be it further enacted*, That when it appears to the satisfaction of the court that the estate of the debtor, or any part thereof, is of a *perishable nature*, or *liable to deteriorate in value*, the court may order the same to be sold, in such manner as may be deemed most expedient, under the direction of the messenger or assignee, as the case may be, who shall hold the funds received in place of the estate disposed of * * * ." (emphasis added and in original).

The 1867 Act did not provide for reorganizations; nevertheless, the requirements that the property be of a perishable nature or liable to deteriorate in value and that there be loss if the same is not sold immediately were also found in General Bankruptcy Order No. XVIII(3), adopted by the Supreme Court in 1898.

From 1898 through 1937, the Bankruptcy Act did not contain a specific provision permitting pre-adjudication sales of a debtor's property. But, pursuant to General Order XVIII, this Circuit over fifty years ago upheld an order that approved a private, pre-adjudication sale of a bankrupt's stock of handkerchiefs. Not only was merchandise sold at a price above its appraised value, but Christmas sales had commenced and the sale of handkerchiefs would decline greatly after the holidays. Our court held that the concept of "perishable" was not limited to its physical meaning, but also included property liable to deteriorate in price and value. *In re Pedlow*, 209 F. 841, 842 (2d Cir.1913).

B. *Chandler Act of 1938—The "Upon Cause Shown" Standard*

Section 116(3) of the 1938 Act, which was the immediate predecessor of § 363(b) * * * provided:

> "Upon the approval of a petition, the judge may, in addition to the jurisdiction, powers and duties hereinabove and elsewhere in this chapter conferred and imposed upon him and the court * * * (3) authorize a receiver or a trustee or a debtor in possession, upon such notice as the judge may prescribe and upon cause shown, to lease or sell any property of the debtor, whether real or personal, upon such terms and conditions as the judge may approve."

This section applied in Chapter X proceedings, and a similar provision, § 313(2), pertained to Chapter XI cases. Thus, when reorganization became part of the bankruptcy law, the long established administrative powers of the court to sell a debtor's property prior to adjudication were extended to cover reorganizations with a debtor in possession under Chapter XI pursuant to § 313(2), as well as a trustee in control under Chapter X pursuant to § 116(3). These sections, as their predecessors, were designed to handle leases or sales required during the time lag between the filing of a petition for reorganization and the date when the plan was approved.[2]

The Rules of Bankruptcy Procedure applicable in Chapters X and XI, the Act's reorganization procedures, provided for a sale of all or part of a bankrupt's property after application to the court and "upon cause shown." Despite the provisions of this Rule, the "perishable" concept, expressed in the view that a pre-confirmation or pre-adjudica-

[2] A letter from a district judge in California addressed to the House Committee holding hearings on these sections illustrates one of the reasons for the addition in 1937 of rules permitting pre-confirmation sales. The letter recounted the difficulty the writer had in a reorganization involving a California land company whose business consisted of selling real property. Because of the lack of clear authority to sell, title companies refused to certify title to the land during the time interval after a petition had been filed and prior to plan approval. The writer therefore recommended adoption of legislation that would grant the bankruptcy judge authority to issue orders during the time from filing to approval permitting the sale or lease of the debtor's property.

tion sale was the exception and not the rule, persisted. As one commentator stated, "ordinarily, in the absence of perishable goods, or depreciation of assets, or actual jeopardy of the estate, a sale will not be ordered, particularly prior to adjudication." 1 *Collier on Bankruptcy* ¶ 2.28(3) (14th ed. 1978) (footnotes omitted).

Thirty years after *Pedlow*, in *Frank v. Drinc-O-Matic, Inc.*, 136 F.2d 906 (2d Cir.1943), we upheld the sale of a debtor's 19 vending machines that were subject to a vendor's lien and in the possession of their manufacturer. We noted that the trustee had no funds with which to redeem the machines and that six months had passed from the filing of the petition without proposal of a reorganization plan. Finally, we stated that appellate review of the power exercised by a lower court in directing a sale pursuant to § 116(3) was limited to whether the district court had abused its discretion.

Citing § 116(3) of the Act, we next affirmed an order of a sale of vats, kettles and other brewing machinery which, with "the approach of warm weather * * * will, because of lack of use and refrigeration, deteriorate rapidly and lose substantially all their value." *In re V. Loewer's Gambrinus Brewery Co.*, 141 F.2d 747, 748 (2d Cir.1944). While the court acknowledged the viability of the "perishable" property concept, it upheld the sale even though virtually all of the income producing assets of the debtor were involved. The same proceeding, then entitled *Patent Cereals v. Flynn*, 149 F.2d 711 (2d Cir.1945), came before us the following year. We said it made no difference whether sale of a debtor's property preceded or was made part of a plan of reorganization. Nothing, we continued, in former § 216 (providing for the sale of a reorganizing debtor's property pursuant to a plan) precluded approval of a plan after a sale of all or a substantial part of the debtor's property. Section 216 merely permitted a plan providing for such sale and did not forbid a plan after such a sale has already taken place.

Judge Ryan, in authorizing the sale of the Dale stock cited *Patent Cereals* as his authority. Appellees here cite *Patent Cereals* for the proposition that this court has abandoned the perishable property or emergency concept. We reject such a broad reading of *Patent Cereals* for several reasons. First, the decision involved an appeal from a denial of confirmation of a plan of reorganization, *i.e.*, the sale in that case was a fait accompli, it was not as here an appeal from an authorization of sale. Second, the earlier decision in *Loewer's Gambrinus Brewery*, indicates that the court did view the original sale as involving perishable property. Third, subsequent cases in this Circuit confirm the misapprehension in appellees' and Judge Ryan's broad interpretation.

The Third Circuit took an even stricter view in *In re Solar Mfg. Corp.*, 176 F.2d 493 (3d Cir.1949). Acknowledging that a sale of corporate assets could occur outside and prior to a plan, yet expressing concern that sales of that nature do not adequately "protect the interests of those whose money is tied up in the tottering enterprise," the court concluded that pre-confirmation sales should be "confined to emergencies where there is imminent danger that the assets of the ailing business will be lost if prompt action is not taken." *Id.* at 494. This "emergency" approach was so appealing that our court cited *Solar Mfg. Corp.* with approval and held in *In re Pure Penn Petroleum Co.*, 188 F.2d 851 (2d Cir.1951), that the debtor must plead and prove "the existence of an emergency involving imminent danger of loss of the assets if they were not promptly sold." *Id.* at 854.

Finally, in *In re Sire Plan, Inc.*, 332 F.2d 497 (2d Cir.1964), corporate owners of a seven-story skeletal building then under construction filed for reorganization under Chapter X of the Act. Because of the site's close proximity to the impending 1964 World's Fair, Holiday Inns felt it was a favorable location for a hotel and accordingly offered to purchase it. The sale to Holiday Inns was affirmed under the *Patent Cereal* rationale. The Court stated that there is no requirement that the sale be in aid of a reorganization; but we further noted, as in *Pure Penn*, that the evidence demonstrated that in its exposed state a "partially constructed building is a 'wasting asset' [that] can only deteriorate in value the longer it remains uncompleted." *Id.* at 499.

More recently, other circuits have upheld sales prior to plan approval under the Bankruptcy Act where the bankruptcy court outlined the circumstances in its findings of fact indicating why the sale was in the best interest of the estate. In essence, these cases evidence the continuing vitality under the old law of an "emergency" or "perishability" standard. As we shall see, the new Bankruptcy Code no longer requires such strict limitations on a bankruptcy judge's authority to order disposition of the estate's property; nevertheless, it does not go so far as to eliminate all constraints on that judge's discretion.

C. *The Bankruptcy Reform Act of 1978*

Section 363(b) of the Code seems on its face to confer upon the bankruptcy judge virtually unfettered discretion to authorize the use, sale or lease, other than in the ordinary course of business, of property of the estate. Of course, the statute requires that notice be given and a hearing conducted, but no reference is made to an "emergency" or "perishability" requirement nor is there an indication that a debtor in possession or trustee contemplating sale must show "cause." Thus, the language of § 363(b) clearly is different from the terms of its statutory predecessors. And, while Congress never expressly stated why it abandoned the "upon cause shown" terminology of § 116(3), arguably that omission permits easier access to § 363(b). Various policy considerations lend some support to this view.

First and foremost is the notion that a bankruptcy judge must not be shackled with unnecessarily rigid rules when exercising the undoubtedly broad administrative power granted him under the Code. As Justice Holmes once said in a different context, "some play must be allowed for the joints of the machine . . . " *Missouri, Kansas & Texas Ry. Co. v. May*, 194 U.S. 267, 270 (1904). To further the purposes of Chapter 11 reorganization, a bankruptcy judge must have substantial freedom to tailor his orders to meet differing circumstances. This is exactly the result a liberal reading of § 363(b) will achieve.

Support for this policy is found in the rationale underlying a number of earlier cases that had applied § 116(3) of the Act. In particular, this Court's decision in *Sire Plan* was not hinged on an "emergency" or "perishability" concept. Lip service was paid to the argument that a partially constructed building is a "wasting asset;" but the real justification for authorizing the sale was the belief that the property's value depended on whether a hotel could be built in time for the World's Fair and that an advantageous sale after the opening of the World's Fair seemed unlikely. Thus, the reason was not solely that a steel skeleton was deteriorating, but rather that a good business opportunity was presently available, so long as the parties could act quickly. In such cases therefore the bankruptcy machinery should not straightjacket the bankruptcy judge so as to prevent him from doing what is best for the estate.

Just as we reject the requirement that only an emergency permits the use of § 363(b), we also reject the view that § 363(b) grants the bankruptcy judge carte blanche. Several reasons lead us to this conclusion: the statute requires notice and a hearing, and these procedural safeguards would be meaningless absent a further requirement that reasons be given for whatever determination is made; similarly, appellate review would effectively be precluded by an irreversible order; and, finally, such construction of § 363(b) swallows up Chapter 11's safeguards. In fact, the legislative history surrounding the enactment of Chapter 11 makes evident Congress' concern with rights of equity interests as well as those of creditors.[3]

---

[3] The Commission on the Bankruptcy Laws of the United States submitted a draft

Chapter 5 of the House bill dealing with reorganizations states that the purpose of a business reorganization is to restructure a business' finances to enable it to operate productively, provide jobs for its employees, pay its creditors and produce a return for its stockholders. The automatic stay upon filing a petition prevents creditors from acting unilaterally or pressuring the debtor. The plan of reorganization determines how much and in what form creditors will be paid, whether stockholders will continue to retain any interests, and in what form the business will continue. Requiring acceptance by a percentage of creditors and stockholders for confirmation forces negotiation among the debtor, its creditors and its stockholders. A fair analysis of the House bill reveals that reorganization under the 1938 Chandler Act, though designed to protect creditors had, over the years, often worked to their detriment and to the detriment of shareholders as well. The primary reason reorganization under the Act had not served well was that disclosure was minimal and reorganization under the Act was designed to deal with trade debt, not secured or public debt or equity. The present bill, it was believed, provides some form of investor protection to make it a "fairer reorganization vehicle." The key to the reorganization Chapter, therefore, is disclosure. * * *

The Senate hearings similarly reflect a concern as to how losses are to be apportioned between creditors and stockholders in the reorganization of a public company. Noting that "the most vulnerable today are public investors," the Senate Judiciary Committee Report states that the bill is designed to counteract "the natural tendency of a debtor in distress to pacify large creditors with whom the debtor would expect to do business, at the expense of small and scattered public investors." S. Rep. No. 95-989, 95th Cong. 2d Sess. 10 (1978). The Committee believed that investor protection is most critical when the public company is in such financial distress as to cause it to seek aid under the bankruptcy laws. The need for this protection was plain. Reorganization under the 1938 Act was often unfair to public investors who lacked bargaining power, and these conditions continued. Echoing the conclusion of the House Committee, the Senate Committee believed that the bill would promote fairer and more equitable reorganizations granting to public investors the last chance to conserve values that corporate insolvency has jeopardized.

---

provision that would have permitted resort to § 363(b) in the absence of an emergency, even in the case of "all or substantially all the property of the estate." Congress eventually deleted this provision without explanation, an action which we hardly consider dispositive of the issue before us here.

III. CONCLUSION

The history surrounding the enactment in 1978 of current Chapter 11 and the logic underlying it buttress our conclusion that there must be some articulated business justification, other than appeasement of major creditors, for using, selling or leasing property out of the ordinary course of business before the bankruptcy judge may order such disposition under § 363(b).

The case law under § 363's statutory predecessors used terms like "perishable," "deteriorating," and "emergency" as guides in deciding whether a debtor's property could be sold outside the ordinary course of business. The use of such words persisted long after their omission from newer statutes and rules. The administrative power to sell or lease property in a reorganization continued to be the exception, not the rule. In enacting the 1978 Code Congress was aware of existing case law and clearly indicated as one of its purposes that equity interests have a greater voice in reorganization plans—hence, the safeguards of disclosure, voting, acceptance and confirmation in present Chapter 11.

Resolving the apparent conflict between Chapter 11 and § 363(b) does not require an all or nothing approach. Every sale under § 363(b) does not automatically short-circuit or side-step Chapter 11; nor are these two statutory provisions to be read as mutually exclusive. Instead, if a bankruptcy judge is to administer a business reorganization successfully under the Code, then—like the related yet independent tasks performed in modern production techniques to ensure good results—some play for the operation of both § 363(b) and Chapter 11 must be allowed for.

The rule we adopt requires that a judge determining a § 363(b) application expressly find from the evidence presented before him at the hearing a good business reason to grant such an application. In this case the only reason advanced for granting the request to sell Lionel's 82 percent stock interest in Dale was the Creditors' Committee's insistence on it. Such is insufficient as a matter of fact because it is not a sound business reason and insufficient as a matter of law because it ignores the equity interests required to be weighed and considered under Chapter 11. The court also expressed its concern that a present failure to approve the sale would result in a long delay. As the Supreme Court has noted, it is easy to sympathize with the desire of a bankruptcy court to expedite bankruptcy reorganization proceedings for they are frequently protracted. "The need for expedition, however, is not a justification for abandoning proper standards." *Protective Committee for Independent Stockholders of TMT Trailer Ferry, Inc. v. Anderson*, 390 U.S. 414, 450 (1968). Thus, the approval of the sale of Lionel's 82 percent interest in Dale was an abuse of the trial court's discretion.

In fashioning its findings, a bankruptcy judge must not blindly follow the hue and cry of the most vocal special interest groups; rather, he should consider all salient factors pertaining to the proceeding and, accordingly, act to further the diverse interests of the debtor, creditors and equity holders, alike. He might, for example, look to such relevant factors as the proportionate value of the asset to the estate as a whole, the amount of elapsed time since the filing, the likelihood that a plan of reorganization will be proposed and confirmed in the near future, the effect of the proposed disposition on future plans of reorganization, the proceeds to be obtained from the disposition vis-a-vis any appraisals of the property, which of the alternatives of use, sale or lease the proposal envisions and, most importantly perhaps, whether the asset is increasing or decreasing in value. This list is not intended to be exclusive, but merely to provide guidance to the bankruptcy judge.

Finally, we must consider whether appellants opposing the sale produced evidence before the bankruptcy court that such sale was not justified. While a debtor applying under § 363(b) carries the burden of demonstrating that a use, sale or lease out of the ordinary course of business will aid the debtor's reorganization, an objectant, such as the Equity Committee here, is required to produce some evidence respecting its objections. Appellants made three objections below: First, the sale was premature because Dale is not a wasting asset and there is no emergency; second, there was no justifiable cause present since Dale, if anything, is improving; and third, the price was inadequate. No proof was required as to the first objection because it was stipulated as conceded. The second and third objections are interrelated. Following Judge Ryan's suggestion that objections could as a practical matter be developed on cross-examination, Equity's counsel elicited testimony from the financial expert produced by Lionel that Dale is less subject than other companies to wide market fluctuations. The same witness also conceded that he knew of no reason why those interested in Dale's stock at the September 7, 1983 hearing would not be just as interested six months from then.[4] The only other witness who testified was the Chief Executive Officer of Lionel, who stated that it was only at the

---

[4] As noted, the bidding for Dale started with a $43 million offer from Acme-Cleveland and has since jumped to $50 million. There is no indication that this trend will reverse itself.

insistence of the Creditors' Committee that Dale stock was being sold and that Lionel "would very much like to retain its interest in Dale." These uncontroverted statements of the two witnesses elicited by the Equity Committee on cross-examination were sufficient proof to support its objections to the present sale of Dale because this evidence demonstrated that there was no good business reason for the present sale. Hence, appellants satisfied their burden.

Accordingly, the order appealed from is reversed and the matter remanded to the district court with directions to remand to the bankruptcy court for further proceedings consistent with this opinion.

WINTER, CIRCUIT JUDGE, dissenting:

In order to expedite the decision in this matter, I set forth my dissenting views in summary fashion.

The following facts are undisputed as the record presently stands: (i) Lionel sought a buyer for the Dale stock willing to condition its purchase upon confirmation of a reorganization plan. It was unsuccessful since, in the words of the bankruptcy judge, "the confirmation of any plan is usually somewhat iffy," and few purchasers are willing to commit upwards of $50 million for an extended period without a contract binding on the other party; (ii) every feasible reorganization plan contemplates the sale of the Dale stock for cash; (iii) a reorganization plan may be approved fairly soon if the Dale stock is sold now. If the sale is prohibited, renewed negotiations between the creditors and the equity holders will be necessary, and the submission of a plan, if any, will be put off well into the future; and (iv) the Dale stock can be sold now at or near the same price as it can be sold later.

The effect of the present decision is thus to leave the debtor in possession powerless as a legal matter to sell the Dale stock outside a reorganization plan and unable as an economic matter to sell it within one. This, of course, pleases the equity holders who, having introduced no evidence demonstrating a disadvantage to the bankrupt estate from the sale of the Dale stock, are now given a veto over it to be used as leverage in negotiating a better deal for themselves in a reorganization.

The likely results of today's decision are twofold: (i) The creditors will at some point during the renewed protracted negotiations refuse to extend more credit to Lionel, thus thwarting a reorganization entirely; and (ii) notwithstanding the majority decision, the Dale stock will be sold under § 363(b) for exactly the same reasons offered in support of the present proposed sale. However, the ultimate reorganization plan will be more favorable to the equity holders, and they will not veto the sale.

It seems reasonably obvious that result (i) is something that the statutory provisions governing reorganizations, including § 363(b), are designed to avoid. Result (ii) not only is contrary to the purpose of the reorganization provisions in causing delay and further economic risk but also suffers from the legal infirmity which led the majority to reject the proposed sale, the only difference between the two sales being the agreement of the equity holders.

The equity holders offered no evidence whatsoever that the sale of Dale now will harm Lionel or that Dale can in fact be sold at a reasonable price as part of a reorganization plan. The courts below were quite right in not treating their arguments seriously for they are the legal equivalent of the "Hail Mary pass" in football.

IN RE BEKER INDUSTRIES CORP.

United States Bankruptcy Court, Southern District of New York, 1986.
63 B.R. 474.

HOWARD C. BUSCHMAN, III, Bankruptcy Judge.

This matter presents the issue of whether property that is subject to junior and senior liens not disputed on this motion may be sold pursuant to § 363(f) by a debtor-in-possession free and clear of such liens for less than the aggregate amount of the liens over the objection of the junior lienholders.

I.

Among the creditors of Beker Industries Corp. ("Beker" or the "Debtor") who found themselves before the bankruptcy court for this district when Beker filed its petition for reorganization under Chapter 11 of the Bankruptcy Code are the holders of Beker's 15-7/8% Secured Subordinated Debentures issued in 1983 and due July 1, 2003 (the "debentures"). A committee has been appointed to represent their interests (the "Committee"). Payment of the debentures is secured by liens on Beker's fertilizer plant at Conda, Idaho and Beker's interest in a partnership which owns, *inter alia*, an adjacent phosphate mine, a rock beneficiation plant and mineral interest (the "Conda Assets"). These liens are subject to a $10 million senior lien in favor of certain banks.

That lien was imposed by this Court pursuant to § 364(d) upon granting Beker's motion for an order permitting it to enter into a loan agreement. The debenture holders claim to be owed in excess of $72 million.

By order to show cause dated July 14, 1986, the Debtor seeks permission pursuant to § 363 to sell the Conda Assets free and clear of the senior and junior liens by public auction to be held on August 1, 1986. The liens are to attach to the proceeds. A hearing to consider whether the auction sale should proceed under *Committee of Equity Security Holders v. Lionel Corp. (In re Lionel Corp.)*, 722 F.2d 1063 (2d Cir.1983), and whether reasonable contacts had been made within the industry to identify and interest purchasers who might be interested in acquiring the Conda Assets was scheduled for July 23, 1986. All parties assume that the sale price will be less than the aggregate amount of the various liens. Upon the complaint of the Committee that it had been frustrated in obtaining discovery, its assertion that it needed time to develop expert testimony and its claim that the sale was barred by § 363(f)(3), the Court adjourned the July 23, 1986 hearing and sale *sine die* pending resolution of the instant issue.

II.

* * * Section 363(f) provides for sale over the objection of [a] secured creditor only under certain conditions, two of which are in issue here:

> (3) * * * the price at which such property is to be sold is greater than the aggregate *value* of all liens on such property;
>
> * * *
>
> (5) such entity could be compelled in a legal or equitable proceeding, to accept a money satisfaction of such interest.

§§ 363(f)(3) and (5) (emphasis added).

It is well settled that in construing statutory language, terms of particular meaning to the subject matter of the statute are to be interpreted in line with that meaning and in light of other provisions of the statute.

Here, the term "value" has such meaning. That term is employed in the same context in § 506(a). There it is provided that

> An allowed claim of a creditor secured by a lien on property [of the estate] * * * is a secured claim to the extent of the *value* of such creditor's interest in the estate's interest in such property * * * and is an unsecured claim to the extent that the *value* of such creditor's interest * * * is less than the amount of such allowed claim. Such *value* shall be determined in light of the purpose of the valuation and of the proposed disposition or use of such property, and in conjunction with any hearing on such disposition or use or on a plan affecting such creditor's interest.

(Emphasis added.) It is thus plainly indicated that the term "value", as used in § 506(a) with respect to the interest of a secured creditor, means its actual value as determined by the Court, as distinguished from the amount of the lien. That indication and the last sentence of § 506(a) requiring determination of value upon disposition of an asset standing as collateral strongly support the conclusion that the term "value", as employed in § 363(f)(3) is to be similarly interpreted.

We reach this conclusion notwithstanding the statement in the House and Senate reports that "[t]he trustee may sell free and clear if * * * the sale price of the property is greater than the *amount* secured by the lien." H.R. Rep. No. 95–595 at 345, *reprinted in* 1978 U.S.C.C.A.N. at 6301–02; S. Rep. No. 95–989 at 56, *reprinted in* 1978 U.S.C.C.A.N. at 5842 (1978) (emphasis added). But it is not at all clear that this language is anything more than colloquial or that the authors of these reports focused on the distinction between value and amount. Moreover, Congress, in enacting the Code, maintained that it is the value of the collateral that is protected by the Code. In discussing the adequate protection afforded a secured creditor under § 361 and linking that concept to value, the Senate Report emphasized: "This is consistent with the view expressed in *Wright v. Union Central Life Insurance Co.*, 311 U.S. 273 (1940), where the Court suggested that it was the value of the secured creditor's collateral, and not necessarily his rights in the specific collateral, that was entitled to protection." S. Rep. No. 95–989 at 54, *reprinted in* 1978 U.S.C.C.A.N. at 5840.

Our function is not to determine merely what the legislative history says. Rather, the inquiry concerns what the statute means. Here, the statutory language and scheme are patently clear enough; they control. We thus conclude that § 363(f)(3) is to be interpreted to mean what it says: the price must be equal to or greater than the aggregate value of the liens asserted against it, not their amount.

* * *

Furthermore, it is undisputed that collateralized property can be sold for less than the amount of the lien at confirmation by cramming down a secured creditor. Section 1129(b)(2)(A)(ii) so provides without any references to the protections of § 363(f), so long as the lien attaches to the proceeds or the secured creditor can bid in its lien pursuant to § 363(k). Moreover, if a debtor desires to retain the property subject to the lien, it need pay only the allowed amount of the secured claim. § 1129(b)(2)(A)(i). As noted, § 506(a) limits such a claim to the value of the collateral as determined by the bankruptcy court. § 1129-(b)(2)(A)(i). No constitutional provision bars such an exercise. * * *

But the power to sell speaks only little as to its exercise, particularly in the case of a major asset. Under the former Bankruptcy Act, it was repeatedly said that "as a general rule" a bankruptcy court should not order property subject to one or more liens sold free and clear unless the sale proceeds will produce full compensation for secured creditors and produce equity for the estate. A "general rule" implies that there are exceptions. Thus, the court in *In re Bernhard Altmann International Corp.*, 226 F.Supp. 201, 205–07 (S.D.N.Y.1963), although also stating the general practice, observed that collateralized property might be sold for less than the amount of a lien over the objection of a secured creditor where justified by special circumstances to be developed at an evidentiary hearing and upon the court valuing the property. It held:

> The Bankruptcy Court was required to ascertain the facts as to the value of the property to be sold and the value of all the security held by the lienor so as to determine the respective interests of the lienor and the general creditors in the security, whether the estate had any equity in it and whether there might be provable claims for a deficiency which might affect the rights of the general creditors. Any other circumstances bearing on the question of the relative interests of the lienor and the general creditors, or the advantages or disadvantages to either or both of the proposed methods of disposition, should have been considered also.
>
> It was only then that the referee could exercise his sound discretion to determine whether the proposed sale by [the mortgagee] to [a third party] coupled with the waiver of deficiency conditioned upon [such] sale * * * or a public sale, furnished adequate protection to the rights of the mortgagee and was in the best interests of the bankrupt estate. He was not

> bound to approve either of such sales unless he found that these conditions had been satisfied.

Id. at 206–07. Thus, some flexibility in the reorganization process will be retained and the creditor given a high measure of protection.

Because of the vagaries of the valuation process, particularly for assets like those at issue here, the proper exercise of discretion would require that those circumstances be compelling and that it be found, as in *In re Hatfield Homes, Inc.*, 30 B.R. 353, 355 (Bankr. E.D.Pa.1983), that "the proposed sales price is the best price obtainable under the circumstances of a particular case." Since property in which there is no equity for the general estate "in practical essence * * * belong[s] to the secured creditors," *Bernhard Altmann*, 226 F.Supp. at 207, they, absent compelling circumstances, should sell it themselves if they object to the sale.

Of course, the Debtor might assert that, were the property to deteriorate in value in the hands of the secured creditors, their deficiency claims might increase to the detriment of the estate. But the Court can consider this factor along with others. One might suspect, moreover, that such a creditor could be estopped from claiming a deficiency greater than that proposed by the Debtor.

In determining whether there are special circumstances, it is to be remembered that the purpose of the general rule is to protect the secured creditor from a debtor cashing out its collateral and leaving it with an unsecured deficiency claim in the absence of special circumstances, and the determinations noted above. The cases that invoke the general rule usually concern secured creditors who desire foreclosure. But if a secured creditor does not desire to take the property for itself and yet refuses to consent to a sale at less than the amount of its lien, it is effectively insisting that others, including the debtor at the expense of its own cash flow and of its general creditors, continue to fund the property without a firm prospect for return. Such might be a special circumstance in the context of a particular case and in light of other evidence.

III.

None of these considerations are altered by § 363(f)(5) which the Debtor claims enables it to sell the property without constraint. As noted, that section enables a debtor-in-possession to sell property free and clear of the interest of another entity if that entity could be compelled to take a money satisfaction in a legal and equitable proceeding.

Relying on *In re Hunt Energy Co. Inc.*, 48 B.R. 472, 485 (Bankr. N.D. Ohio 1985), and *In re Red Oak Farms, Inc.*, 36 B.R. 856, 858 (Bankr. W.D.Mo.1984), the Debtor claims that since a secured creditor could be crammed down pursuant to § 1129(b)(2), that section is satisfied.

We disagree if by this assertion the Debtor is claiming that such property can be sold for less than the aggregate amount of all liens without the protections noted above. First, one would think that Congress, in authoring the Bankruptcy Code, could have easily found the words necessary to refer to § 1129(b)(2) of the Code had that been its intent. Rather, § 363(f)(5) is to be interpreted, in our judgment, as referring to those few interests in property that can, by operation of law, be reduced to dollars. Liens are addressed directly in § 363(f)(3) and it is that section which is to be applied. To interpret § 363(f)(5) in the fashion suggested by the Debtor would "swallow-up (f)(1)-(f)(4)." *Matter of Stroud Wholesale, Inc.*, 47 B.R. 999, 1003 (E.D.N.C.1985).

Second, in *Hunt*, the court seemingly applied the cram-down theory in selling a major asset on the basis of its finding that the Debtor had valid business reasons as required by *Lionel*. But it ignored the policies of the general rule noted above and also that *Lionel* did not concern the sale of collateral over the objection of a secured creditor. Furthermore, at confirmation, the overall interest of all creditors and the Debtor becomes so strong that statutory cram-down on a dissenting secured creditor is justified by the need to confirm. Absent the existence of special circumstances prior to confirmation, the secured creditor should be protected as noted above.

Consequently, it appears that an evidentiary hearing is to be held to determine whether the Debtor has equity in the property and, if not, whether circumstances exist warranting sale of the property. * * *

Questions and Problems

1. Does an undersecured junior creditor have an incentive to block a sale, if possible, in every case in which the sale price will not be sufficient to pay that creditor's claim? If so, should this incentive influence a court in deciding whether to approve the sale?

2. What does the court mean by "value"? By "amount"?

3. Does the court's reading of (f)(3) make sense in light of the other subsections of § 363(f)?

4. Although *Beker* remains, perhaps, the leading case on this side of the issue, courts have yet to agree on the meaning of the phrase "value of all liens." In *In re Feinstein Family Partnership*, 247 B.R. 502 (Bankr. M.D.Fla. 2000), the court took issue with the *Beker* line of cases:

> All these case[s] treated motions to sell property pursuant to § 363-(f)(3) in the context of § 506(a). Section 506(a) is designed to determine secured status. This Section was designed to serve a twofold purpose: (1) to limit the estate's liability on a claim filed as a secured [claim] to payment up to the actual value of the collateral; and (2) to bifurcate the claim and permit an undersecured creditor to have an allowed unsecured claim and share on par with the other allowed unsecured claims. In sum, § 506(a) was designed for the purpose of determining the allowance of secured claims and not for the purpose of selling encumbered property without satisfying in full all liens from the sale proceeds. This conclusion is further fortified by Subclause (d) which provides that to the extent a lien secures a claim against the debtor that is not an allowed secured claim, such lien is void. It is evident that § 506 was designed to deal only with claims actually filed. It is elementary that secured creditors are not required to file proofs of claim in a Chapter 7 case. Consequently, their claims cannot be disallowed and, in turn, their liens voided pursuant to § 506(d). It follows that the reliance on the provisions of § 506 is misplaced and they are irrelevant to a § 362(f)(3) sale. Thus, the Trustee cannot use § 506 to justify the sale of encumbered property without complying with the requirements of § 363(f)(3), that is the full satisfaction of all valid liens encumbering the Property. To conclude otherwise would render Subclause (5) superfluous. This Section permits a cramdown if the secured creditor could be compelled in a legal or equitable proceeding to accept money satisfaction of the interest of the lien holder.

Id. at 509. Which court has the better argument?

5. Does the disagreement among cases dealing with this issue arise from disagreement about the nature of secured creditors' rights in bankruptcy? That is, does the *Beker* court implicitly accept that a secured creditor is entitled to the value of its collateral and nothing more?

6. Debtor went broke while attempting to develop and market a subdivision comprised of 25 lots. The subdivision was subject to a blanket mortgage in favor of Developers' Bank, securing an obligation of $2 million. After filing a Chapter 11 petition, Debtor found buyers for two lots. Each of them was willing to pay $100,000 for a lot, but both required that Debtor deliver title free of Bank's lien. Bank will release its lien voluntarily only upon compliance with the terms of the note—that is, upon payment of $2 million. Can Debtor obtain a court order requiring Bank to release its lien on those two lots?

See *Seidle v. Modular Paving, Inc. (In re 18th Avenue Development Corp.)*, 14 B.R. 862 (Bankr. S.D.Fla.1981).

7. Whittaker frequented bankruptcy sales, knowing that some wonderful bargains were sometimes available. Recently, Whittaker bought a luxury recreational vehicle from an individual's Chapter 11 estate, paying only about 60% of the retail price. The sale was authorized by the bankruptcy court and possession was given to Whittaker. An irate man, who introduced himself as Adams, visited Whittaker two weeks later. Adams claimed that the RV belonged to him and was merely parked for safe-keeping at the debtor's home, while Adams was on an extended trip. Adams demanded possession. Must Whittaker hand Adams the keys? See *In re Sax*, 796 F.2d 994 (7th Cir.1986).

E. VALUATION OF THE FIRM

A court may have to determine the value of a reorganizing corporation in order to resolve several different issues—for example, whether a creditor is entitled to adequate protection or whether the proposed plan pays a particular creditor or group of creditors the minimum amount required by the Code. The valuation method does not seem dependent upon the context of the issue to be decided. The following case arose from creditors' motions for relief from stay.

IN RE ASCHER

United States Bankruptcy Court, Northern District of Illinois, 1992.
146 B.R. 764.

JACK B. SCHMETTERER, Bankruptcy Judge.

Michael Brogan, Edward Long, and James Kelly (the "Movants") moved for relief from the automatic stay pursuant to § 362(d). They seek to remain in possession of the commercial laundry facility located in Harvard, Illinois, doing business as Royal Laundry Systems, in order to realize the value of their security interest. * * * The motion was opposed by the Debtor Walter Ascher ("Ascher") and the Chapter 11 Trustee David Grochocinski. * * *

FINDINGS OF FACT

1. All–American Laundry Service, Inc. ("All–American") was formed as a Corporation under Illinois law in 1988 for the purpose of acquiring the assets of Royal Laundry Systems ("Royal") and operating Royal's commercial laundry facility in Harvard, Illinois (the "Laun-

dry"). Ascher was the president of All–American, and he also claims to be the company's sole shareholder.

Calculation of Movant's Secured Claim

[Bank lent All–American $668,000 to finance the purchase of Royal's assets. Bank perfected liens on all of Royal's real and personal property as security for the loan. As additional security, Ascher pledged stock in All–American and Movants pledged stock in UPS. When the loan went into default 18 months later and Bank took steps to sell the UPS stock, Movants paid the balance due. Bank assigned the note and liens to Movants and their nominee, Laundry Credit Corp.

Movants ousted Ascher and took physical possession of the laundry. They were required to advance $41,357 in additional funds to cover payroll, accounting services and operating expenses. They also incurred $5,000 in legal fees recoverable under the terms of the note.

When the bankruptcy petition was filed, $625,000 in principal was due on the note. The parties disagreed regarding the applicable interest rate. If the contract postmaturity rate of 11% were used, as Movants advocated, $347,196 in interest had accrued as of bankruptcy. If the contract prematurity rate of 2% over prime were used, as the trustee argued, $184,417 in interest had accrued as of bankruptcy.]

* * *

14. Therefore, the total secured debt owed to Movants is either $855,774.12 or $1,018,553.43, depending on whether one accepts the Trustee's or the Movants' theory on which interest rate to apply to the balance due.

Calculation of the Laundry's Value

15. Expert testimony was offered as to the value of the Laundry. The net capitalized earnings (or discounted cash flow) is found to be the proper approach to determining value of the Laundry, because it is a going entity and is expected to remain as such by all the Parties to this litigation. Under this approach, the valuation is conducted by predicting the future earnings for the company, and then discounting those earnings by a capitalization (or discount) rate which is the rate of return required by a potential investor in order for his or her investment to be worthwhile. The following formula is applied to reach a prediction as to value:

$$\frac{\text{Predicted earnings per year}}{\text{Capitalization rate}} = \text{Value of Company's future net earnings to investors}$$

16. The Laundry is currently controlled through the Laundry Credit Corporation which is an Illinois corporation wholly owned by Movants. Management and sales services are provided by Mr. John Eakes, a principal of Royal (the Laundry's former owner) and his subordinates through an agreement with Professional Laundry Service Consultants, Inc., an Illinois corporation owned by Mr. Eakes. Mr. Eakes was hired because Movants' only business experience related to their jobs as executives at UPS, and they needed a person with experience in the commercial laundry industry to manage the Laundry. The management fees paid to Mr. Eakes and Professional Laundry Service Consultants are a reasonable and necessary component of the Laundry's expenses, and would be paid by a future investor.

17. The Movants also hired Mr. Brogan's son Steve to work at the Laundry as accounts payable and receivables clerk at a salary of about $36,000 a year. The Trustee and Debtor maintain that his salary is excessive and that his salary expenses cannot be attributable to the business in calculating its net profits. However, since these parties presented insufficient evidence by which the Court could judge the reasonableness of Steve's salary, this argument was not established.

18. The Management fees and Steve Brogan's salary shall be attributed to the business in calculating net profits. Management fees represent the costs of retaining competent management for the business, and Steve Brogan's salary represents the cost of keeping an owner's agent on the premises who has undivided loyalty to the owner. A future owner-manager might not need such agents, but owner-managers represent only a portion of the potential investors who could buy the Laundry. Thus, the assumption of management fees and on-site agent salary costs are necessary to find the real value of the laundry to potential investors.

19. Debtor further asks the Court to discount non-cash expenses, such as depreciation, when calculating the Laundry's net profits. The equipment used in the Laundry's operation wears down and needs to be replaced periodically, and depreciation accounts for this real cost of doing business. Thus, an accounting of profits without any provision for depreciation is, in effect, borrowing against the company's future. Since it is not rational to assume that any future investor would desire to run the business into the ground in an effort to maximize his first year's profits, Debtor's argument is rejected.

20. Annualizing the Laundry's net profits for the first half of 1992 (at $181,464) provides the most accurate basis for prediction of the Laundry's future earnings potential. This conclusion is made for several reasons:

a. In the first six months of 1992 the Laundry netted $90,732. The evidence shows that this figure is representative of the whole year.

b. The net earnings history of the Laundry is as follows: In 1990, the Laundry lost $58,754. In 1991, the Laundry lost $4,973. However, the Laundry was in a state of upheaval from 1989 to 1991. Management had changed hands several times, and several customers were lost. The business had only recovered to a stable condition in the latter half of 1991. Prior to the sale of the business in late 1988, the Laundry netted annual profits around $450,000.

c. Mr. Eakes testified that the Laundry is currently operating at or near capacity and that expenses have been reduced over the past year to an efficient level. Thus, earnings are not likely to increase, and expenses are not likely to decrease, beyond their current levels.

21. The Laundry's business consists of cleaning sheets, towels, and other washable items under contracts with hotels and hospitals. The business faces several risks in its operations:

a. All of the Laundry's business comes from five or six clients, and most of these clients have no contractual relationship with the Laundry itself. They have contracts with Mr. Eakes who then allocates the business to the Laundry. Over two-thirds of the laundry to be processed comes from these contracts with Mr. Eakes. Therefore, any new investor in the Laundry would be dependent on him until new business could be developed.

b. There is a dispute with the Internal Revenue Service over allegedly unpaid payroll taxes in the amount of $203,630. While this problem has not reached a critical stage, this threat of liability is apparently still outstanding.

c. The Laundry is likely to incur new expenses as a result of new regulations promulgated by the Occupational

Safety and Health Administration which will require the laundry workers to wear protective clothing to prevent the spread of AIDS and hepatitis.

d. The local water supply contains a high iron content which occasionally causes rust-colored stains to appear on the processed laundry. An iron-removal system was installed by the Movants, but the problem has returned intermittently, and limits the Laundry's efforts to compete for certain clients. Related to this iron problem is a dispute over unpaid bills with the Village of Harvard which provides the water. An unpaid municipal water bill of $69,050 is currently outstanding. This dispute has not been formally settled, but Mr. Eakes reached an accommodation with the Village which defers the issue and may resolve it.

e. Workmen's Compensation insurance is likely to rise due to increased concern about AIDS and hepatitis. Mr. Eakes testified that the Laundry's current provider has demanded a significant increase in premiums in order to renew its policy.

f. The labor force of the business consists primarily of recent immigrants to this country. In August 1991, the Immigration and Naturalization Service paid the Laundry facility a visit, and half of its workers were taken away. This temporarily disrupted operations, but it did not cause any long term damage. The Laundry was able to replace lost workers quickly, but whether it has potential liability under federal law for hiring illegal aliens is unknown and was not addressed at trial.

g. Other risks may exist concerning environmental problems and possible competition between washable and disposable items. However, the potential liability for these speculative risks has not been quantified.

22. The estimate by the Trustee's expert for the required return for a putative equity investor in the Laundry is reasonable. Such an investor would require a 25% return on the equity investment in order to provide a reasonable profit and compensate for risks inherent in owning this business.

23. The Court further agrees with the Trustee's expert that an acquisition of the Laundry can partly be accomplished with debt financing. This expert found, and the Court agrees, that a lender would fi-

nance 45% of the purchase price. Based on this expert's testimony, the Court finds that the required return for this lender would be 12%. Thus, a capitalization rate for this estimation of value would be 19% to 19.5%.[2]

24. Therefore, the Court applies an income estimate of about $180,000 a year and a capitalization rate of 19% to 19.5% to reach a finding of value in the range of $945,000 to $925,000.

25. The above valuation must be discounted by 10% to account for the broker costs, sales expenses, and risks inherent in selling the business. This leaves a net value to the owners, creditors, and estate of $850,500 to $832,500.

26. The Laundry's value is highly uncertain and there is no equity cushion over debt. Furthermore, the risk that the business value will fluctuate falls most heavily on Movants. Therefore, Movants are not adequately protected by equity cushion, and there is no suggestion that Movants will receive adequate protection payments.

27. Mr. Ascher filed for his petition for relief under Chapter 11 of the Bankruptcy Code on June 8, 1990. On August 1, 1990, he consented to entry of an Order by this Court for appointment of a Chapter 11 Trustee. Mr. David Grochocinski was subsequently appointed. No Plan of Reorganization was proffered at trial, nor is there any indication that a plan is in the offing, other than a liquidat[ing] plan.

* * *

CONCLUSIONS OF LAW

* * *

2. Section 362(d) of the Bankruptcy Code provides that the automatic stay may be modified to permit an action against debtor's property when the debtor has no equity in that property, and it is not necessary for an effective reorganization. § 362(d)(2).

2

Equity return (25%)	×	percentage of total investment (55%)	=	13.75%
Debt return (12%)	×	percentage of total investment (45%)	=	5.4%
		Capitalization Rate	=	19.5%

3. The Movants have the burden of proving by a preponderance of evidence that Debtor has no equity in the property. § 362(g). The parties opposing the motion have the burden of proof on all other issues. § 362(g). To establish that the property is necessary to an effective reorganization, Ascher and the Trustee must show that there is "a reasonable possibility of a successful reorganization within a reasonable time." *United Savings Assoc. v. Timbers*, 484 U.S. 365, 376 (1988).

4. The Movants have met their burden on the issue of Debtor's equity in the Laundry. The value of the Laundry business as a going entity to the Movants and to the estate is in the range of $850,500 to $832,500, and, even accepting the Trustee's theory on interest rates, the amount owed is $855,774.12. Therefore, Debtor has no equity in the Laundry.

5. Since the payments made by Brogan to fund the payroll and pay other expenses were necessary for the preservation of the Laundry as a going entity, Movants are entitled to recover these funds from the proceeds of the sale of the Laundry under § 506(c). With a super priority claim under § 506(c), Movants are entitled to payment of this claim ahead of any other claimant including the Trustee, and this claim may be recovered directly from the property. Therefore, the payments made by Brogan, as discussed in the Findings, are included in the calculation of Movant's secured claim against the Debtor's property.

* * *

7. The parties opposing [lifting] the stay have not met their burden to show that a plan of reorganization is reasonably in prospect or that the Laundry would be necessary for Debtor's reorganization. Therefore, Movants are entitled to judgment on the motion to modify the stay.

8. Relief from the stay may be granted by "terminating, annulling, modifying, or conditioning such stay." § 362(d). Therefore, the Court has considerable flexibility to fashion relief that protects the interest of the Movants, Debtor, and the estate.

CONCLUSION

The evidence is clearly in favor of the Movants on all issues in this case, and judgment will be entered in their favor on the motion to modify the stay. However, the actual value of the laundry remains uncertain and dependent on what offers the market will bring. In entering an order in this case, the Court has only modified the stay to allow the Movants to sell the Laundry, and several conditions are incorporated into the order to ensure that they make prompt and significant efforts to market and sell the property.

Notes

1. *Ascher* uses the "income capitalization approach" to value the business. The court in *In re SM 104 Ltd.*, 160 B.R. 202 (Bankr. S.D.Fla.1993), characterized this approach as follows:

> This method gives recognition to the view that investors do not buy the bricks and mortar of a building. Rather, they buy the earnings the bricks and mortar will produce in the future. Measuring the fair market value of collateral under the income capitalization approach is a two-step analysis. First, the future net operating income of the property is estimated. Next, that income is divided by a capitalization rate ("capitalized") to obtain the fair market value of the property.
>
> The capitalization rate is computed by determining the annual rate of return a hypothetical investor would be looking for in deciding whether to buy the property. More specifically, the capitalization rate equals the risk-free interest rate available in the marketplace plus some risk premium the hypothetical investor would require to induce her to make the investment.

Id. at 211–12. (Another portion of the opinion in *SM 104* appears later in this chapter.)

2. Valuation on the basis of predicted future earnings is known as "going concern" or "enterprise" valuation. It requires either capitalization of the earning stream or a discounting of predicted future earnings back to present value.

The Supreme Court endorsed enterprise valuation in a decision under the 1898 Act, *Consolidated Rock Products Co. v. Du Bois*, 312 U.S. 510, 61 S.Ct. 675, 85 L.Ed. 982 (1941):

> As Mr. Justice Holmes said in *Galveston, H. & S.A. Ry. Co.* v. *Texas*, 210 U.S. 217, 226, "the commercial value of property consists in the expectation of income from it." Such criterion is the appropriate one here, since we are dealing with the issue of solvency arising in connection with reorganization plans involving productive properties. * * * The criterion of earning capacity is the essential one if the enterprise is to be freed from the heavy hand of past errors, miscalculations or disaster, and if the allocation of securities among the various claimants is to be fair and equitable. Since its application

> requires a prediction as to what will occur in the future, an estimate, as distinguished from mathematical certitude, is all that can be made. But that estimate must be based on an informed judgment which embraces all facts relevant to future earning capacity and hence to present worth, including, of course, the nature and condition of the properties, the past earnings record, and all circumstances which indicate whether or not that record is a reliable criterion of future performance.

Id. at 526, 61 S.Ct. at 685, 85 L.Ed. at 993–94.

3. Two other valuation methods are also used on occasion. Under the "comparable sales approach," an appraiser compares recent sales prices of similar properties, adjusting for differences between comparable properties and the one at issue. The "replacement cost approach" determines the cost of constructing similar property. *SM 104,* which is quoted in note 1, also discusses these additional valuation methods.

F. CONFIRMATION OF THE PLAN

Section 1129(a) sets out requirements that a plan must meet in order to be confirmed, and we will deal with the most important of them in this section. Note as we proceed through these materials that many of § 1129(a)'s requirements are triggered only if a creditor does not consent to the plan.

The debtor-in-possession begins the process of plan negotiation with a fair amount of control because, in cases not involving small businesses, only the debtor may file a plan for the first 120 days after the order for relief. § 1121(b). Courts have been so willing to extend this "exclusivity period," often for years, that the 1994 Amendments added § 1121(e). It applies only to a small business, which is defined in § 101(51C) as one with noncontingent liquidated debts of less than $2 million. Section 1121(e) gives a shorter exclusivity period initially (100 days), requires all plans to be filed within 160 days, permits shortening of these periods for cause, and permits extensions only in circumstances beyond the debtor's control. It remains to be seen whether these changes significantly affect the balance of power between debtors and creditors as they negotiate plan provisions.

You should be aware that most Chapter 11 plans are consensual, often having evolved through protracted negotiation. Perhaps after our study you will see why the parties may have an incentive to avoid litigation over these complicated issues!

We begin with classification.

1. CLASSIFICATION AND VOTING

Chapter 11 plans deal with creditors by classes. Section 1129(a) requires as a condition of confirmation that, if any class is impaired (a matter we will turn to momentarily), at least one impaired class has voted for the plan. § 1129(a)(10). Debtors often expend a great deal of effort to meet this requirement and no cases paint the issue more starkly than the single asset real estate cases. In order to follow the next two cases, however, you need an introduction to one of the most infamous sections in the Code—§ 1111(b).

Note on § 1111(b)

Section 1111(b) was enacted in response to the decision in *In re Pine Gate Associates, Ltd.*, 2 B.C.D. 1478 (Bankr. N.D.Ga.1976). The reorganizing debtor in *Pine Gate* owned an apartment project. Creditors holding an undersecured nonrecourse mortgage insisted that their debts be paid in full or that the property be turned over to them. The court, however, permitted the debtor to pay the appraised value of the collateral, rather than the full amount of the debt, and to keep the property free and clear of liens. Creditors were unhappy about *Pine Gate* because they could not bid in the amount of the debt, in the absence of a public sale, and they could not assert deficiency claims, when loans are nonrecourse.

Section 1111(b) addresses both of these complaints. First, it treats all liens as recourse, even though the obligation under state law can be asserted only against the debtor's property, thereby operating as an exception to the usual bifurcation rules of § 506(a). The consequence of this treatment is that the creditor, with no recourse under state law, will have in bankruptcy a secured claim measured by the value of the collateral and an unsecured claim for the deficiency. This unsecured claim will give the creditor "a voice in the Chapter 11 process" because the creditor may be able to "dominate the vote within the unsecured class." *In re 500 Fifth Avenue Associates*, 148 B.R. 1010, 1021 (Bankr. S.D.N.Y.1993).

Second, § 1111(b) permits an undersecured creditor to "elect" to have a secured claim measured by the amount of the debt rather than the value of the collateral. Thus, the creditor may waive its unsecured claim (whether it came by the claim as a recourse creditor under state law or as a nonrecourse creditor given the claim by § 1111(b)) and be treated as a fully secured creditor. A restriction, which will be applicable to a creditor completely under water, is that a creditor may not make the election if its interest in the collateral is of inconsequential value.

Be careful not to jump to the conclusion that an undersecured creditor would always choose to have an allowed secured claim in the amount of the debt. For one thing, as the court in *500 Fifth Avenue Associates* pointed out, the electing creditor gives up what may be a sizeable, and therefore influential, unsecured claim.

PHOENIX MUTUAL LIFE INSURANCE CO. v. GREYSTONE III JOINT VENTURE (MATTER OF GREYSTONE III JOINT VENTURE)

United States Court of Appeals, Fifth Circuit, 1991.
995 F.2d 1274, *cert. denied*, 506 U.S. 821, 113 S.Ct. 72, 121 L.Ed.2d 37 (1992).

[As amended on Petition for Rehearing, February 27, 1992.]

EDITH H. JONES, Circuit Judge.

This appeal pits a debtor whose only significant asset is an office building in the troubled Austin, Texas real estate market against a lender who possesses a multi-million dollar lien on the property. After obtaining bankruptcy relief under Chapter 11, Greystone III proposed a "cramdown" plan of reorganization, hoping to force a write-down of over $3,000,000 on the secured lender's note and to retain possession and full ownership of the property. Over the secured lender's strenuous objections, the bankruptcy court confirmed the debtor's plan. On appeal, the district court upheld the bankruptcy court's judgment.

For two reasons, we must reverse. First, the Greystone plan impermissibly classified like creditors in different ways and manipulated classifications to obtain a favorable vote. * * *

I.

Appellant Phoenix Mutual Life Insurance Corporation ("Phoenix") lent $8,800,000, evidenced by a non-recourse promissory note secured by a first lien, to Greystone to purchase the venture's office building. When Greystone defaulted on the loan, missing four payments, Phoenix posted the property for foreclosure. Greystone retaliated by filing a Chapter 11 bankruptcy reorganization petition.

At the date of bankruptcy Greystone owed Phoenix approximately $9,325,000, trade creditors approximately $10,000, and taxing authorities approximately $145,000. The bankruptcy court valued Phoenix's secured claim at $5,825,000, the appraised value of the office building, leaving Phoenix an unsecured deficiency of approximately $3,500,000—the difference between the aggregate owed Phoenix and its secured claim.

As filed, Greystone's Second Amended Plan of Reorganization (the "Plan"), the confirmation of which is challenged in this appeal, separately classified the Code-created unsecured deficiency claim of Phoenix Mutual, *see* § 1111(b), and the unsecured claims of the trade creditors. The Plan proposed to pay Phoenix and the trade creditors slightly less than four cents on the dollar for their unsecured claims, but it also provided that Greystone's general partner would satisfy the balance of the trade creditors' claims after confirmation of the Plan.

In a separate class, the Plan further provided for security deposit "claims" held by existing tenants of the office building. These claimants were promised, notwithstanding the debtor's eventual assumption of their leases, 25% of their deposits upon approval of the Plan and 50% of their deposits at the expiration of their respective leases. The Plan stipulated that the general partner would "retain its legal obligations and * * * pay the [tenant] * * * creditors the balance of their claims upon confirmation."

Finally, Greystone's Plan contemplated a $500,000 capital infusion by the debtor's partners, for which they would reacquire 100% of the equity interest in the reorganized Greystone.

Unsurprisingly, Phoenix rejected this Plan, while the trade creditors and the class of holders of tenant security deposits voted to accept it. On January 27, 1989, the bankruptcy court held a confirmation hearing at which the Debtor orally modified its Plan to delete the statements that the general partner would pay the balance of trade debt and tenant security deposit claims after confirmation. A Phoenix representative testified that the insurance company was willing to fund its own plan of reorganization by paying off all unsecured creditors in cash in full after confirmation. The bankruptcy court refused to consider this proposal and then confirmed Greystone's modified Plan. The district court upheld the confirmation.

Phoenix Mutual now appeals * * * .

II.

Phoenix first attacks Greystone's classification of its unsecured deficiency claim in a separate class from that of the other unsecured claims against the debtor. This issue benefits from some background explanation.

Chapter 11 requires classification of claims against a debtor for two reasons. Each class of creditors will be treated in the debtor's plan of reorganization based upon the similarity of its members' priority status and other legal rights against the debtor's assets. § 1122. Proper classification is essential to ensure that creditors with claims of similar priority against the debtor's assets are treated similarly. Second, the classes must separately vote whether to approve a debtor's plan of reorganization. § 1129(a)(8), (10). A plan may not be confirmed unless either (1) it is approved by two-thirds in amount and more than one-half in number of each "impaired" class, §§ 1126(c), 1129(a)(8); or (2) at least one impaired class approves the plan, § 1129(a)(10), and the debtor fulfills the cramdown requirements of § 1129(b) to enable confirmation notwithstanding the plan's rejection by one or more impaired classes. Classification of claims thus affects the integrity of the voting process, for, if claims could be arbitrarily placed in separate classes, it would almost always be possible for the debtor to manipulate "acceptance" by artful classification.

In this case, Greystone's plan classified the Phoenix claim in separate secured and unsecured classes, a dual status afforded by § 1111(b) despite the nonrecourse nature of Phoenix's debt. Because of Phoenix's opposition to a reorganization, Greystone knew that its only hope for confirmation lay in the Bankruptcy Code's cramdown provision. § 1129(b). The substantive impact of cramdown will be discussed later. Procedurally, Greystone faced a dilemma in deciding how to obtain the approval of its cramdown plan by *at least one* class of "impaired" claims, as the Code requires. § 1129(a)(10). Greystone anticipated an adverse vote of Phoenix's secured claim. If the Phoenix $3.5 million unsecured deficiency claim shared the same class as Greystone's other unsecured trade claims, it would swamp their $10,000 value in voting against confirmation. The only other arguably impaired class consisted of tenant security deposit claims, which, the bankruptcy court found, were not impaired at all.

Greystone surmounted the hurdle by classifying Phoenix's unsecured deficiency claim separately from the trade claims, although both classes were to be treated alike under the plan and would receive a cash payment equal to 3.42% of each creditor's claim. Greystone then achieved the required favorable vote of the trade claims class.

Phoenix contends that Greystone misapplied § 1122 by classifying its unsecured claim separately from those of trade creditors. The lower courts rejected Phoenix's argument in three steps. First, they held that § 1122 of the Code does not unambiguously prevent classification of like claims in separate classes. The only question is what types of class differentiations among like claims are acceptable. Second, Greystone's [sic] unsecured deficiency claim is "legally different" from that of the trade claims because it arises statutorily, pursuant to § 1111(b). Third, "good business reasons" justify the separate classification of these unsecured claims. We must address each of these arguments.

Section 1122 prescribes classification of claims for a reorganization * * *. We observe from this language that the lower courts' suggestion that § 1122 does not prevent classification of like claims in separate classes is oversimplified. It is true that § 1122(a) in terms only governs permissible *inclusions* of claims in a class rather [than] requiring that all similar claims be grouped together. One cannot conclude categorically that § 1122(a) prohibits the formation of different classes from similar types of claims. But if § 1122(a) is wholly permissive regarding the creation of such classes, there would be no need for § 1122(b) specifically to authorize a class of smaller unsecured claims, a common feature of plans in reorganization cases past and present. The broad interpretation of § 1122(a) adopted by the lower courts would render § 1122(b) superfluous, a result that is anathema to elementary principles of statutory construction.

Section 1122 consequently must contemplate some limits on classification of claims of similar priority. A fair reading of both subsections suggests that ordinarily "substantially similar claims," those which share common priority and rights against the debtor's estate, should be placed in the same class. Section 1122(b) expressly creates one exception to this rule by permitting small unsecured claims to be classified separately from their larger counterparts if the court so approves for administrative convenience. The lower courts acknowledged the force of this narrow rather than totally permissive construction of § 1122 by going on to justify Greystone's segregation of the Phoenix claim. Put otherwise, the lower courts essentially found that Phoenix's unsecured deficiency claim is not "substantially similar" to those of the trade creditors.

Those courts did not, however, adhere to the one clear rule that emerges from otherwise muddled caselaw on § 1122 claims classification: thou shalt not classify similar claims differently in order to gerrymander an affirmative vote on a reorganization plan. As the Sixth Circuit observed:

> [T]here must be some limit on a debtor's power to classify creditors in such a manner. * * * Unless there is some requirement

> of keeping similar claims together, nothing would stand in the way of a debtor seeking out a few impaired creditors (or even one such creditor) who will vote for the plan and placing them in their own class.

In re U.S. Truck Co., 800 F.2d 581, 586 (6th Cir.1986). We agree with this rule, and if Greystone's proffered "reasons" for separately classifying the Phoenix deficiency claim simply mask the intent to gerrymander the voting process, that classification scheme should not have been approved.

* * * We conclude that if § 1122(a) permits classification of "substantially similar" claims in different classes, such classification may only be undertaken for reasons independent of the debtor's motivation to secure the vote of an impaired, assenting class of claims. To those proffered reasons we now turn.

Greystone contends that the "legal difference" between Phoenix's deficiency claim and the trade creditors' claims is sufficient to sustain its classification scheme. The alleged distinction between the legal attributes of the unsecured claims is that under state law Phoenix has no recourse against the debtor personally. However, state law is irrelevant where, as here, the Code has eliminated the legal distinction between non-recourse deficiency claims and other unsecured claims.

The purpose of § 1111(b) is to provide an undersecured creditor an election with respect to the treatment of its deficiency claim. Generally, the creditor may elect recourse status and obtain the right to vote in the unsecured class, or it may elect to forego recourse to gain an allowed secured claim for the entire amount of the debt. If separate classification of unsecured deficiency claims arising from non-recourse debt were permitted solely on the ground that the claim is non-recourse under state law, the right to vote in the unsecured class would be meaningless. Plan proponents could effectively disenfranchise the holders of such claims by placing them in a separate class and confirming the plan over their objection by cramdown. With its unsecured voting rights effectively eliminated, the electing creditor's ability to negotiate a satisfactory settlement of either its secured or unsecured claims would be seriously undercut. It seems likely that the creditor would often have to "elect" to take an allowed secured claim under § 1111(b)(2) in the hope that the value of the collateral would increase after the case is closed.[6]

---

[6] In this case, for example, Greystone proposed to extinguish Phoenix's $3,500,000 deficiency claim by the promised payment of $140,000. Under the valuation process,

Thus, the election under § 1111(b) would be essentially meaningless. We believe Congress did not intend this result.

As the bankruptcy court viewed this issue, the debtor's ability to achieve a cramdown plan should be preferred over the creditor's § 1111(b) election rights because of the Code's policy of facilitating reorganization. The bankruptcy court resorted to policy considerations because it believed Congress did not foresee the potential impact of an electing creditor's deficiency claim on the debtor's aspiration to cramdown a plan. We disagree with this approach for three reasons. First, it results here in violating § 1122, by gerrymandering the plan vote, for the sake of allegedly effectuating a § 1129(b) cramdown. "Policy" considerations do not justify preferring one section of the Code, much less elevating its implicit "policies" over other sections, where the statutory language draws no such distinctions. Second, as shown, it virtually eliminates the § 1111(b) election for secured creditors in this type of case. Third, the bankruptcy court's concern for the viability of cramdown plans is overstated. If Phoenix's unsecured claim were lower and the trade debt were higher, or if there were other impaired classes that favored the plan, a cramdown plan would be more realistic. That Greystone's cramdown plan may not succeed on the facts before us does not disprove the utility of the cramdown provision. The state law distinction between Code-created unsecured deficiency claims and other unsecured claims does not alone warrant separate classification.

Greystone next argues that separate classification was justified for "good business reasons." The bankruptcy court found that the debtor "need[s] trade to maintain good will for future operations." The court further reasoned:

> [I]f the expectation of trade creditors is frustrated * * * [they] have little recourse but to refrain from doing business with the enterprise. The resulting negative reputation quickly spreads in the trade community, making it difficult to obtain services in the future on any but the most onerous terms.

---

it confined Phoenix's secured claim to $5.8 million. § 506(a). Phoenix obviously objects to this arrangement because, in the future, it might ultimately receive more than the written-down value of the office building in a liquidation following foreclosure. Yet, with its voting rights effectively eliminated by separate classification, Phoenix has no leverage to persuade the Debtor to consider a more reasonable settlement. Had this scenario triumphed, Phoenix's most realistic option might have been to take an allowed secured claim in the hope that eventually the market value of the office building will increase by more than $140,000 over the presently estimated value of the collateral.

Greystone argues that the "realities of business" more than justify separate classification of the trade debt from Phoenix's deficiency claim. This argument is specious, for it fails to distinguish between the *classification* of claims and the *treatment* of claims. Greystone's justification for separate classification of the trade claims might be valid if the trade creditors were to receive different treatment from Phoenix. Indeed, Greystone initially created a separate class of unsecured creditors that could be wooed to vote for the plan by the promise to pay their remaining claims in full *outside the plan*. Greystone then changed course and eliminated its promise. Because there is no separate treatment of the trade creditors in this case, we reject Greystone's "realities of business" argument.

Even if Greystone's Plan had treated the trade creditors differently from Phoenix, the classification scheme here is still improper. At the confirmation hearing, none of the Debtor's witnesses offered any reason for classifying the trade debt separately from Phoenix's unsecured deficiency claim. There is no evidence in the record of a limited market in Austin for trade goods and services. Nor is there any evidence that Greystone would be unable to obtain any of the trade services if the trade creditors did not receive preferential treatment under the Plan. Thus, the bankruptcy court's finding that there were good business reasons for separate classification is without support in the record and must be set aside as clearly erroneous.

Phoenix's unsecured deficiency claim approximates $3,500,000, while the claims of the unsecured trade creditors who voted to accept the Plan total less than $10,000. Greystone's classification scheme, which effectively disenfranchised Phoenix's Code-created deficiency claim, is sanctioned neither by the Code nor by caselaw. The lower courts erred in approving it.

* * *

V.

For the foregoing reasons, the judgment of the district court affirming the bankruptcy court's confirmation of Greystone's plan of reorganization is REVERSED. The case is REMANDED for proceedings consistent with this opinion.

* * *

IN RE SM 104 LTD.

United States Bankruptcy Court, Southern District of Florida, 1993.
160 B.R. 202.

ROBERT E. GINSBERG, Bankruptcy Judge.

[Debtor owned and operated an office complex in Fort Lauderdale, Florida. At the time of bankruptcy, the property was worth $2.27 million. A first mortgage, securing a nonrecourse debt of $5.5 million, was held by EquiVest, Inc. Debtor's proposed plan classified EquiVest's deficiency claim, created by § 1111(b), in Class 3. Trade creditors, owed a total of $175,000, were placed in Class 5. Debtor gave no business reason to justify separate classification and proposed to pay both classes a dividend of 8.5%. EquiVest voted to reject the plan; Class 5 voted to accept it.]

* * * Given the size of EquiVest's § 1111(b) unsecured deficiency claim relative to the other unsecured claims and EquiVest's opposition to the plan, it is obvious the reason the Debtor seeks to separately classify EquiVest's § 1111(b) deficiency claim from the claims of other unsecured creditors is to satisfy the requirements of § 1129(a)(10); i.e., to get one impaired class to accept the plan. EquiVest claims that the Debtor's apparently manipulative motive is improper, and that EquiVest's unsecured deficiency claim should be placed in the same class as the claims of the general unsecured creditors. If the court accepts EquiVest's argument that it should be classified with the other general unsecured creditors in a single class and EquiVest's argument that the Class 5 unsecured creditors were the only impaired class to accept the plan, such a joint classification would be the death knell for the Debtor's plan because the Debtor could no longer satisfy the requirements of § 1129(a)(10). EquiVest's deficiency claim would be large enough to overwhelm the claims of the other members of that single class, and, by voting no, EquiVest could prevent the plan from being accepted by two-thirds in amount of the total unsecured claims. *See* § 1126(c).

* * *

(2) May a plan classify an unsecured deficiency claim created by § 1111(b) separately from other general unsecured claims ?[28]

---

[28] This section considers only the propriety of the separate classification of unsecured deficiency claims of nonrecourse creditors, which are created by § 1111(b). The court does not consider the propriety of separate classification of the unsecured deficiency

In general, the proponent of a Chapter 11 plan has broad discretion to classify claims and interests in the plan according to the particular facts and circumstances of each case. The provision in Chapter 11 governing classification is § 1122 * * *.

Section 1122(a) expressly provides that only substantially similar claims may be placed in the same class. It does not expressly require that all substantially similar claims be placed in the same class, nor does it expressly prohibit substantially similar claims from being classified separately. Nevertheless, many courts, including five circuit courts of appeal, while recognizing that § 1122 does not explicitly forbid a plan proponent from placing similar claims in separate classes, have imposed significant limits on the ability of a plan proponent to do so. *See, e.g., Hancock Mutual Life Insur. Co. v. Route 37 Business Park Assoc.*, 987 F.2d 154, 159–60 (3d Cir.1993); *In re Lumber Exchange Bldg. Ltd.*, 968 F.2d 647, 649 (8th Cir.1992); *In re Bryson Properties XVIII*, 961 F.2d 496, 502 (4th Cir.), *cert. denied*, 113 S.Ct. 191 (1992); *Matter of Greystone III Joint Venture*, 995 F.2d 1274, 1278–79 (5th Cir.1991); *In re U.S. Truck Co.*, 800 F.2d 581, 586 (6th Cir.1986). The majority of lower courts have followed suit.

In *Greystone*, the Fifth Circuit held that "one clear rule" has emerged from the otherwise muddled § 1122 caselaw: "thou shalt not classify similar claims differently in order to gerrymander an affirmative vote on a reorganization plan." The court reasoned that if § 1122(a) were wholly permissive regarding the formation of different classes from similar types of claims, there would be no need for § 1122(b) to authorize a class of smaller, unsecured claims. The *Greystone* court then held that a broad interpretation of the powers to classify similar claims separately under § 1122(a) "would render § 1122(b) superfluous, a result that is anathema to elementary principles of statutory construction." Consequently, the *Greystone* court held that § 1122 must contemplate some limits on classification of claims of similar rights.

However, while *Greystone* and the other cases have paid lip service to principles of statutory construction and the language of § 1122, they have turned more on notions of basic fairness and good faith. Indeed, most courts seem to base their rulings less on the language of § 1122 than on their view that separate classification is usually done to manipulate the voting to insure that at least one impaired class of creditors accepts the plan, and thus that the plan meets the requirements of

claims of recourse creditors, which are created by contract.

§ 1129(a)(10).[32] Such manipulation is viewed as some sort of "abuse" of Chapter 11. As the Eleventh Circuit noted, "[t]here must be some limit on a debtor's power to classify creditors. * * * The potential for abuse would be significant otherwise." *In re Holywell Corp.*, 913 F.2d 873, 880 (11th Cir.1990). Courts subscribing to this view have rejected any plan where the classification scheme "is designed to manipulate class voting, or violates basic priority rights." *Id.* Under such an analysis, the courts in *Route 37*, *Lumber Exchange*, *Bryson*, and *Greystone* have held that separate classification of an unsecured deficiency claim created by § 1111(b) from general unsecured claims solely to gerrymander to create [an] impaired accepting creditor class (i.e. the general unsecured creditors) is impermissible.

Obviously, one premise for the rulings in *Route 37*, *Lumber Exchange*, *Bryson*, and *Greystone* has been that unsecured deficiency claims created by § 1111(b) are substantially similar to general unsecured claims. Indeed, if the claims are not substantially similar, § 1122(a) would bar them from being put in the same class. However, a few lower courts have rejected this conclusion and held that unsecured deficiency claims created by § 1111(b) are not substantially similar to other unsecured claims, and thus that separate classification of those claims is not only permissible, but mandatory. *See In re D & W Realty Corp.*, 156 B.R. 140, 144 (Bankr. S.D.N.Y.1993); *In re Aztec Co.*, 107 B.R. 585, 587 (Bankr. M.D.Tenn.1989).[33]

These latter courts rely on two lines of reasoning to support their conclusion. First, some of these courts believe that general unsecured claims and unsecured deficiency claims created by § 1111(b) are legally distinct because the former are recourse claims cognizable under state law, while the latter exist only within the Chapter 11 bankruptcy case and are not cognizable under state law. The circuit courts have largely rejected this argument, holding that § 1111(b) has largely eliminated the legal distinction between nonrecourse deficiency claims for purposes of Chapter 11.

---

[32] In fact, *Greystone* directly stated that separate classification was proper if "for reasons independent of the debtor's motivation to secure the vote of an impaired, assenting class." Indeed, separate classification for valid business reasons is uniformly accepted.

[33] Because this court holds below that an unsecured deficiency claim created by § 1111(b) is not substantially similar to other general unsecured claims, this court need not address whether separate classification of substantially similar claims solely to gerrymander an accepting impaired class is permissible under the Code.

In addition, the minority of courts supporting the proposition that the separate classification of unsecured deficiency claims created by § 1111(b) is either proper or required often argue that separate classification is permissible on the grounds that the vote of such claims will be uniquely affected by the plan's proposed treatment of the secured claim held by the creditor. Thus, for example, the court in *Aztec* reasoned that the undersecured mortgagee would have "every incentive to vote its large deficiency claim to affect the treatment of its secured claim by defeating confirmation of any plan" if classified with other unsecured creditors. 107 B.R. at 587. Such a rationale is highly persuasive when viewed in light of the logic underlying § 1129(a)(10). Section 1129(a)(10) was intended not to give the real estate lobby a veto power, but merely to require "some indicia of creditor support" for confirmation of a proposed Chapter 11 plan.

* * *

Fortunately, this court does not have to sort out the validity of the various lines of reasoning enunciated by those courts considering separate classification of unsecured deficiency claims created by § 1111(b). Instead, this court believes that the lines of reasoning articulated by the circuit courts and the majority of district and bankruptcy courts have missed the forests for the trees. Section 1122(a) allows joint classification of claims *only* if the claims are substantially similar in terms of their legal rights. There are, however, significant differences between the legal rights of a general unsecured claim and an unsecured deficiency claim created for the nonrecourse lender by § 1111(b). Thus, an unsecured deficiency claim created by § 1111(b) is not substantially similar to general unsecured claims, and, under § 1122(a), the two types of claims *cannot* be classified together.

The most obvious difference between a general unsecured claim and an unsecured deficiency claim created by § 1111(b) is that the former exists regardless of what chapter of the Bankruptcy Code the case is in, while the latter exists only so long as the case remains in Chapter 11. *See* § 103(f). If the Chapter 11 case is converted to Chapter 7, the nonrecourse lender is confined to its collateral for recovery. It has no deficiency claim against the Chapter 7 estate. *See* § 502(b)(1). This distinction is significant.

One area in which the distinction between the rights of holders of general unsecured claims and the rights of § 1111(b) deficiency claimants can be seen clearly is in the application of the "best interests" test of § 1129(a)(7). Section 1129(a)(7) sets out the financial minimum that assenting creditors in an assenting class can impose on dissenting creditors within that class. * * *

Thus, the majority in a class can never force the minority in that class to take less in present value terms than the minority would receive in a Chapter 7 liquidation case involving the debtor.

The application of this standard to a class consisting of both general unsecured claims and § 1111(b) deficiency claims can lead to anomalous results. A simple example shows why. Suppose that an unsecured deficiency claim created by § 1111(b) is placed in the same class as the general unsecured claims, and that the plan provides for that class to receive a 25% payment of claims on the effective date of the plan. Suppose further that, in a Chapter 7 liquidation, the holders of general unsecured claims would be paid a 35% dividend. The plan would fail the best interests of the creditors test as to the general unsecured creditors, and the plan could not be confirmed unless each general unsecured claim voted for the plan. *See* § 1129(a)(7). This would be true even if a majority in number and two-thirds in amount of the claims in the class that voted on the plan voted to accept. *See* § 1126(c). On the other hand, the plan would propose to give the unsecured deficiency claim created by § 1111(b) more than it would receive in a hypothetical Chapter 7 liquidation: in a Chapter 7 case, the unsecured deficiency claim created by § 1111(b) would not exist and would not be paid at all.

All that is ever required to satisfy the best interests test as to a § 1111(b) nonrecourse deficiency claim is for the claimholder to receive the present value of the collateral.[36] Nevertheless, as long as joint classification is utilized, the holder of a § 1111(b) deficiency claim can hold out for a dividend equal to what the general unsecured claims are being paid to satisfy the best interests of the creditors test as to such creditors, even though the undersecured nonrecourse claim is never entitled to any payment in a Chapter 7 case for the amount by which the value of its collateral is less than it is owed. This is because § 1123(a)(4) requires a plan to provide for the same treatment of all claims in a class, unless the holder of a claim agrees to less favorable treatment. Thus, in the hypothetical above, if the plan were amended to satisfy the best interests of the creditors test by giving the holders of general unsecured claims a 35% dividend, the holder of the § 1111(b) nonrecourse deficiency claim could, as long as the claims are jointly classified, insist on the same 35% dividend, or block confirmation of the

---

[36] This result is made clear by § 1129(a)(7)(B) * * *.

plan. It would be hard to believe that the drafters of the Bankruptcy Code intended such an absurd result.

There are other significant disparities between the legal rights of the holder of a general unsecured claim and the holder of a § 1111(b) nonrecourse deficiency claim. For example, if the debtor is a partnership, the general partners are liable for the debts of the partnership in the event the case converts to one under Chapter 7. *See* § 723. If the Chapter 11 case shows signs of possible failure, the general unsecured creditors could seek equitable relief to prevent dissipation of the assets of the general partners pending resolution of the Chapter 11 case. It is unlikely that the holder of a § 1111(b) nonrecourse deficiency claim could pursue such relief, since the nonrecourse lender is confined to its collateral as a source of payment in Chapter 7. It has no deficiency claim against either the estate or the general partners.

It is clear that the legal rights of creditors holding unsecured deficiency claims created by § 1111(b) and general unsecured creditors are, for classification purposes, substantially dissimilar. Therefore, separate classification of unsecured deficiency claims created by § 1111(b) and general unsecured claims is not only permissible, but mandatory.

The conclusion that an unsecured deficiency claim created by § 1111(b) cannot be placed in the same class with general unsecured claims is further supported by the language of § 1111(b) itself. In fact, the plain meaning of § 1111(b) clearly leads to the conclusion that the § 1111(b) claim must be placed in a class by itself or with only other § 1111(b) claims. The drafters of the Bankruptcy Code provided that the § 1111(b)(2) election is to be made not by the individual § 1111(b) claimants, but by "the class of which such claim is a part." *See* § 1111(b)(1)(A)(i). If the § 1111(b) claim is placed in the same class as general unsecured claims, the literal language of the statute would afford the general unsecured creditors the opportunity to vote on whether their classmate, the § 1111(b) claimholder, should be permitted to make the § 1111(b)(2) election. *See D & W Realty*, 156 B.R. at 144. In fact, the general unsecured creditors could easily block the § 1111(b)(2) election by denying the § 1111(b) creditor the approval of the election by a majority in number of claim holders in the class required by § 1111. Obviously, the drafters of the Bankruptcy Code did not intend such an absurd result. More importantly, the § 1111(b) election process makes perfect sense if § 1111(b) is read to require that an § 1111(b) unsecured deficiency claim must be placed either in a class by itself or in a class with only other § 1111(b) claims.

By the same token, § 1111(b)(1)(B) denies the right to make the election to "[a] class of claims" if, *inter alia*, the lien claims of the members of the class are of "inconsequential value." By definition, the general unsecured creditors have no lien claims. If the analysis is on a class-wide basis, as the statute clearly mandates, and the § 1111(b) claim and the general unsecured claims are placed in a single class, the general unsecured creditors theoretically could ride the § 1111(b) claimholder's coattails and participate in the § 1111(b) election process, since the collateral held by all of the members of the class collectively is not of inconsequential value. Again, such an absurd result can be avoided by simply reading § 1111(b) as its plain meaning provides; that is, by reading § 1111(b) to require that a § 1111(b) claim be placed in a class by itself or in a class with only other § 1111(b) claims.

Thus, this court rules that the Debtor's separate classification of EquiVest's Class 3 unsecured deficiency claim and the claims of the Class 5 general unsecured creditors is permissible. Indeed, such separate classification is required by § 1122(a). Since separate classification is required by § 1122(a), the Debtor's motive in separately classifying the § 1111(b) claim and the general unsecured claims is irrelevant.

* * *

Notes and Questions

1. At the time it was decided, *SM 104* was in a minority. The court could cite only a few other cases also finding separate classification mandatory, and one of them, *In re D & W Realty Corp.*, 156 B.R. 140 (Bankr. S.D.N.Y.1993), was reversed on appeal, 165 B.R. 127 (S.D.N.Y. 1994). In addition, the Second Circuit joined the majority, with its decision in *Boston Post Road Limited Partnership v. FDIC (In re Boston Post Road Limited Partnership)*, 21 F.3d 477 (2d Cir.1994). The Seventh Circuit, however, in *Matter of Woodbrook Associates*, 19 F.3d 314 (7th Cir.1994), criticized *Greystone* for its implicit proposition "that separate classification of a § 1111(b) claim is nearly conclusive evidence of a debtor's intent to gerrymander an affirmative vote for confirmation. The court gave a list of reasons, much like *SM 104*'s, why § 1111(b) claims are significantly different from general unsecured claims.

2. Do you see enough difference between an undersecured creditor's deficiency claim and other unsecured claims to justify the conclusion that they are not "substantially similar" within § 1122(a)? Does that difference exist only when the undersecured creditor's unsecured claim arises under § 1111(b)—that is, when the undersecured creditor has no recourse under state law?

3. Which case does a better job of interpreting the statute—*SM 104* or *Greystone*? Have the cases in the majority "turned more on notions of basic fairness and good faith" and "missed the forest for the trees," as *SM 104* charged? What, exactly, is the "fair" result in these single-asset real estate cases?

2. IMPAIRMENT OF CLAIMS AND INTERESTS

The Code only permits creditors whose interests are "impaired" within the meaning of § 1124 to vote on the plan by conclusively presuming that unimpaired creditors have accepted the plan, § 1126(f). Since only classes that reject the plan can obtain the protections of cramdown under § 1129(b), the concept of impairment is important.

A claim is "impaired" under § 1124 unless it fits within one of the two listed exceptions. Read § 1124 and apply it to the following Problems.

Problems

1. Debtor owed $150,000 to Bank, secured by Debtor's inventory and accounts receivable. That collateral was worth $200,000 at the time of bankruptcy. Debtor's plan put Bank in a class by itself and provided that Bank would receive substitute collateral in the form of a second mortgage on Debtor's real estate. The real property was worth $750,000 and was encumbered by a first mortgage of $250,000. Is Bank's $150,000 claim impaired?

2. Debtor owed $300,000 to various trade creditors who had sold goods to Debtor on a net 30–days basis. The entire sum was past due as of the date of bankruptcy. Debtor's plan classified them together and proposed to pay 95% of the face amount of the debts, over the course of three years. Is the class of trade claims impaired?

3. Lender had a mortgage on Debtor's premises, worth $200,000, that secured a debt of $200,000. The parties' note entitled Lender to receive $2,500 per month, plus 8% interest, and 80 months remained in the loan term. Debtor was not in default at the time of bankruptcy, but made no payments to Lender during the 4–year pendency of the case. Debtor's plan separately classified Lender's claim and proposed to pay $2,500 per month, plus 8%, for a term of 80 months beginning the month after confirmation. Lender is upset about the four years during which nothing was paid on the loan and wants to vote against this plan. Is Lender's claim impaired?

3. BEST INTERESTS TEST AND FEASIBILITY

The so-called "best interests" test of § 1129(a)(7) is designed to protect individual dissenting creditors—not *classes* of creditors, but individual creditors—by requiring that each dissenting creditor receive under the proposed plan at least as much as that dissenter would have received in a Chapter 7 case. The protections of § 1129(a)(7) apply even though the dissenter is outvoted by other members of the class and, as a result, the class of which the dissenter is a part accepts the plan.

Subsection (a)(7) requires the court to conduct a hypothetical liquidation analysis and to compare the dissenter's hypothetical dividend with the plan's proposed payment. *In re Merrimack Valley Oil Co.*, 32 B.R. 485 (Bankr. D.Mass.1983), illustrates this process. Debtors in that case were in the business of selling oil. Their plan provided for a 35% dividend to unsecured creditors to be paid over three years, with an extra 5% to Belcher, their major supplier. The court, in determining whether the best interests test was met, began by listing and valuing the debtors' assets and liabilities:

> The liquidation values are found to be as follows:
>
> | | |
> |---|---|
> | Cash | $ 310,900 |
> | Inventories | 63,600 |
> | Real Estate—Business | 100,000 |
> | Real Estate—Residential | 340,000 |
> | Transportation Equipment | 294,000 |
> | Furniture and Fixtures | 10,000 |
> | Race Horses | 173,000 |
> | Accounts Receivable | 282,400 |
> | Other Assets | 14,000 |
> | TOTAL NET REALIZABLE VALUE | $1,587,900 |
>
> The value of goodwill and customer list is found to be highly speculative in the light of the restrictions and covenants required for their sale to be of any consequence.
>
> The secured and priority claims are as follows:
>
> | | |
> |---|---|
> | Notes and mortgages | $126,100 |
> | Chapter 11 fees and expenses | 157,500 |
> | Priority claims under Chapter 11 | 113,100 |
> | Post-filing debt | 394,900 |
> | Estimated Chapter 7 expenses | 160,000 |
> | TOTAL | $951,600 |

> The net amount available on liquidation is therefore $636,000 or approximately twenty per cent (20%) of unsecured debt of $3,193,975.
>
> The plan provides for thirty-five per cent (35%) to unsecured creditors and forty per cent (40%) to Belcher for its allowed claim. The present value of said payments is twenty-nine per cent (29%) (32% to Belcher). In liquidation, payment would not be made for at least six months of conversion to Chapter 7 because creditors have six months to file proofs of claims pursuant to Bankruptcy Rule 302(e). Secured creditors and administrative claimants are not impaired under the plan. Accordingly, I find that the debtors' plan which offers creditors 35% to 40% over three years, which amounts to a present value of 29% to 32%, is in the best interests of creditors, and complies with the requirements of § 1129(a)(7).

Id. at 487.

Section 1129(a)(11) imposes the so-called "feasibility" test, requiring a finding that "the plan is not likely to be followed by the liquidation, or the need for further financial reorganization, of the debtor." According to *Merrimack Valley,* a court must determine, on a case-by-case basis, "that the plan offers a reasonably workable prospect of success and is not a visionary scheme." 32 B.R. at 488. The court considers factors such as "(1) the adequacy of the capital structure; (2) the earning power of the business; (3) economic conditions; and (4) the ability of management." *Id.*

4. CRAMDOWN

a. Fair and Equitable Test

Section 1129(b)(1) requires that a plan be "fair and equitable" if it is to be confirmed over the objection of nonconsenting classes. This is "cramdown." Subsection (b)(2) elaborates the meaning of "fair and equitable" in three subsections, applicable respectively to secured classes, unsecured classes and classes of "interests" (that is, shareholders).

We will begin where § 1129(b)(2) does—with secured claims. To effect cramdown in the case of secured creditors, the plan can do one of three things. First, it can provide that the creditor retain its lien and receive payments that meet certain requirements. § 1129-

(b)(2)(A)(i). Second, it can provide for sale of the property, subject to § 363(k), with the lien to attach to proceeds of the sale. § 1129-(b)(2)(A)(ii). Third, it can provide that the creditor receive the "indubitable equivalent" of its claim. § 1129(b)(2)(A)(iii). This alternative was derived from *In re Murel Holding Corp.*, 75 F.2d 941 (2d Cir. 1935), a well-known opinion written by Judge Learned Hand. (You may remember the Court's discussion of *Murel* in *Timbers*, which appears in Chapter 4, Section B of this casebook.)

For our purposes, the first of these alternatives is the most important—the creditor must retain its lien and receive a stream of payments that meets two criteria: 1) "deferred cash payments totaling at least the allowed amount of such claim"—a "principal amount" test; and 2) "of a value, as of the effective date of the plan, of at least the value of such holder's interest in the estate's interest in such property"—a "present value" test. For example, assume that Debtor owes Creditor $25,000 and that the obligation is secured by a lien on collateral worth $10,000. Creditor's secured claim is measured by the value of the collateral under § 506(a)—$10,000. These tests require Debtor 1) to make a stream of payments having a face amount of at least the value of the secured claim ($10,000), and 2) to pay Creditor an amount equal to the present value of its collateral ($10,000 plus interest).

These tests look decidedly strange in light of § 506(a) bifurcation. Why require that the face amount of the stream of payments be at least as much as the value of the secured claim *and* require that the creditor receive the value of the collateral plus appropriate interest? Satisfying the latter will necessarily satisfy the former, or so it seems. The key to understanding the statutory wording lies in § 1111(b).

The election under § 1111(b), rather than bifurcation under § 506(a), determines the amount of the allowed secured claim for purposes of § 1129(b)(2)(A)(i)(II). Returning to our prior example, assume that Creditor, whose collateral was worth $10,000, elected to have a secured claim in the amount of the debt—$25,000. The tests now require Debtor 1) to make a stream of payments having a face amount of at least the value of the secured claim ($25,000), and 2) to pay Creditor an amount equal to the present value of its collateral ($10,000 plus interest).

Although this looks good for the undersecured creditor at first, be aware that the creditor need be paid no more, *in terms of economic value*, than an amount equal to the value of the collateral *even if the creditor makes the § 1111(b) election*. If payments are stretched out for a sufficient period of time, the present value of payments having a face amount equal to the debt ($25,000) can, in fact, be made to equal the value of the collateral ($10,000). Assume, for example, that Debtor's plan proposes to pay Creditor interest only, annually, at the rate of 10% for 15 years, with a balloon payment of $10,000 at the end of that time. If the court finds that 10% is the appropriate rate and confirms the plan, Debtor will make a stream of payments with a face amount of $25,000 ($1,000 per year for 15 years, plus a balloon of $10,000); the present value of that stream of payments as of the time of confirmation, however, is only $10,000.

Clearly, identification of the appropriate discount rate is critical in determining whether the "present value" test of § 1129(b)(2)(A)(i)(II) is satisfied by a debtor's proposed plan. The next two cases deal with this issue. As you will note, the statutory issue is very much like that encountered in Chapter 4 of this casebook, where the principal cases dealt with § 1325(a)(5).

MATTER OF LANDMARK AT PLAZA PARK, LTD.

United States Bankruptcy Court, District of New Jersey, 1980.
7 B.R. 653.

RICHARD W. HILL, Bankruptcy Judge.

* * *

Debtor, Landmark at Plaza Park, Ltd., is a limited partnership whose only substantial asset is a 200–unit garden apartment complex located in Morrisville, Pennsylvania. City Federal (hereafter City) holds a first mortgage on this property in the face amount of $2,250,000. The mortgage bears an interest rate of 9.5% and is due and payable on October 1, 1986. On October 2, 1980, this Court issued a written decision denying City's request for relief from the automatic stay provisions of § 362 of the Bankruptcy Code, and continuing the stay until the conclusion of the hearing on confirmation of the debtor's plan. This opinion deals with debtor's plan as it affects City, the only objecting class of creditors. As to all other classes of creditors, there is no dispute and the Court is satisfied that the confirmation standards specified in § 1129 have been met.

Before discussing the merits of debtor's plan three things should be noted. First, the parties have stipulated that the record from the § 362 hearing is part of the record herein. Second, the parties have stipulated that for the purpose of the confirmation hearing $2,260,000 is the fair market value of the property. This value was fixed by the Court after lengthy testimony was presented at the § 362 hearing. And third, City has made an election pursuant to § 1111(b)(2) of the Code. Thus, its claim in the amount of $2,512,457 will be treated as fully secured.

I. THE PLAN AS MODIFIED

Crucial to an understanding of the Court's decision is a discussion of the plan and how it affects City. Contractually, City is a first mortgagee without recourse. It has possession of the property and is collecting the rents pursuant to a rent assignment agreement. The mortgage has been in default since at least December, 1979. City is undersecured and wants to complete its foreclosure action.

The debtor has proposed in substance the following plan:

1. City is to redeliver possession of the property to the debtor.

2. On the 16th month after the effective date of the plan and through the 36th month debtor will commence monthly interest payments at the rate of 12.5% computed on the value of the property—$2,260,000.

3. Debtor will deliver to City a non-recourse note, payable in three years in the face amount of $2,705,820.31, in substitution of all existing liabilities.

4. The existing mortgage will secure the note set forth in paragraph 3, except to the extent that it is inconsistent with or modified by the plan.

5. City is the only member of the class of creditors to which it has been assigned.

The face amount of the note is derived as follows:

a. Current value of collateral	$2,260,000.00
b. Unpaid interest: months 1–15 @ 12.5%	353,125.00
c. Interest on unpaid interest: 21 months @ 15%	92,695.31
Face amount of note	$2,705,820.31

The debtor's principal theory is that the note will be paid off at the end of 36 months by a combination of refinancing and accumulation of cash from the project, all of which will subsequently be discussed at length. The key to the debtor's plan is a proposal to obtain a new first mortgage in three years in the face amount of $2,400,000.

It is undisputed that pursuant to this plan City is impaired within the meaning of § 1124 of the Code. City has rejected the plan.

II. THE ISSUES

Confirmation standards under the Code are set forth in § 1129. Clearly, the debtor has complied with all provisions of that section except for the following subsections: (a)(7)(B); (a)(8); (a)(11); (b)(1); and (b)(2)(A). Actually the list is much shorter. The requirements of (a)(7)(B) are, in effect, carried forward in (b)(1) and (b)(2). Thus if the requirement of subsections (b)(1) and (b)(2) are met, (a)(7)(B) will also have been met. Similarly, the requirements of (a)(8) are waived by the specific language of (b)(1) if other requirements of (b)(1) and (b)(2) are met. That leaves at issue the debtor's compliance with subsections (a)(11), (b)(1) and (b)(2). Subsection (a)(11) of § 1129 is the feasibility requirement and, in a general sense, deals with whether the debtor can and will accomplish what it has proposed. Subsection (b) of § 1129 is the "cram-down" provision of the Code. It describes those circumstances in which a class of creditors or interests may over its objection be involuntarily subjected to the provisions of a plan. Each of these sections will be discussed at length. The provisions of subsection (b) will be discussed first because certain determinations made there bear on the feasibility determination required by subsection (a)(11).

III. THE REQUIREMENTS OF § 1129(B)(1) AND (2)

The provisions of § 1129(b) specify the circumstances under which a class of creditors or interests may be involuntarily subjected to a plan of reorganization. [*The court quoted §§ 1129(b)(1) and (b)(2).*]

The concept that a plan is fair and equitable is not fully defined in the Code. Section 1129(b)(2)(A), (B) & (C) states several factors which are included in that requirement but the legislative history accompanying that section makes clear that other factors fundamental to fair and equitable treatment of a dissenting class were omitted to "avoid complexity." 124 *Cong. Rec. H* 11,103 (daily ed. Sept. 28, 1978) (remarks of Rep. Don Edwards). Given the present posture of this case the Court is satisfied that the factors set forth in § 1129-(b)(2)(A)(i), dealing with the cram down of a secured creditor, adequately deal with the question of whether the plan, as to City, is fair and equitable, and the Court will limit its consideration to those factors.

To meet the requirements of § 1129(b)(2)(A)(i) the debtor's plan must do three things. First, it must provide for retention by the creditor of its lien. Second, the total stream of deferred cash payments proposed by the plan must at least total the amount of the secured claim. Third, the total stream of payments must have a value equal to the value of the property. The plan before the Court satisfies the first two requirements, but may not satisfy the third.[5]

The third requirement is found in that portion of § 1129-(b)(2)(A)(i)(II) stating that "each holder of a claim * * * receive * * * deferred cash payments * * * of a value * * * of at least the value of such holder's interest in the estate's interest in such property." This provision requires the Court to determine the present value of the payments to be made under the plan. Here the total stream of payments under the plan is $3,200,195.17. The discounted value of these payments must equal $2,260,000, the value of the value of the property.

The debtor's construct for meeting subsection (b)(2)(A)(i)(II) is simple. It assumes that the value of the property constitutes the principal amount of a loan and purports to repay to City that principal amount together with interest at 12.5% per annum. Thus, the debtor argues that if the interest rate fixed is adequate the discounted value of the principal plus interest must equal the present value of the property. To support the fixing of a 12.5% interest rate debtor presented evidence that at the time of the confirmation hearing certain institutional investors would provide first mortgage loans on similar property at that rate. The testimony also revealed, however, that 12.5% is at the low end of the interest range.

City strongly rejects the present value approach asserted by the debtor. It focuses on the question of whether the stream of payments offered by the debtor could be sold as of the effective date of the plan for a price at least equal to $2,260,000. City presented expert testimony that attempted to establish two facts: (1) that even assuming that the

---

[5] For purposes of this opinion the allowed amount of the secured claim is $2,512,457. The total stream of payments is $3,200,195.17 consisting of the face amount of the note, $2,705,820.31, plus 21 months interest totaling $494,374.86. Requirement (2) is thus satisfied. classification of unsecured deficiency claims of nonrecourse creditors, which are created by § 1111(b). The court does not consider the propriety of separate classification of the unsecured deficiency claims of recourse creditors, which are created by contract.

property was in good condition and under capable management, the only market for debtor's proposed payment stream would be the secondary mortgage market with the purchase price being 50 to 60 percent of the value of the collateral. It is City's contention that regardless of the interest rate offered the value of the payment stream will be less than the value of the property; (2) that with income producing property, a non-recourse note in excess of the value of the property would always be worth less than the value of the property because an investor would always prefer the property to the note. City's expert grudgingly conceded that his opinion of the value of the note would change if he had confidence in management and believed that future income projections would in fact be sufficient to pay off the note. The expert, however, then backtracked and concluded that mortgage loans could not be made in reliance on future income projections.

In the Court's view, City's expert so overstated his position that his opinion on saleability and value cannot be considered. Succinctly stated, the Court is satisfied that a non-recourse note in excess of the value of the property can be worth at least the value of the property if sufficient interest is paid on the note and repayment is sufficiently certain. The question in the present case becomes whether the 12.5% interest rate offered by the debtor is adequate and whether repayment is sufficiently certain.

Conceptually, the modified plan seeks to force City to make a $2,260,000 loan, repayable in three years, with the first 15 months of interest deferred. There is no amortization over the term of the loan. Since there is currently no equity in the property the debtor is asking City to make a 100% loan. The rate of interest on a loan of this type should correspond to the rate of interest which would be charged or obtained by a creditor making a loan to a third party with similar terms, duration, collateral and risk. Although the rate of interest may be identical to the market rate of interest, this will often not be the case because of the particular risk involved.[8]

It appears clear to the Court that the forced loan proposed by the debtor includes terms less favorable to City than would typically be found in the market and that any confirmable plan must compensate City for this deficiency. Testimony presented at the confirmation hear-

---

[8] Although risk is a factor in determining rates of interest, its importance must not be overstated. We must assume when fixing an interest rate that the plan will be confirmed. If risk of repayment is too great the plan will not be confirmed because the debtor has not met the requirements of § 1129(a)(11). The question of an interest rate would therefore become irrelevant.

ing revealed that institutions such as thrifts, life insurance companies and pension funds would make first mortgage loans on garden apartments with an interest rate ranging from 12.5 to 14 percent. The typical first mortgage loan would have a term of three to ten years, with amortization calculated on a 25 year payout and a 75% maximum loan to value ratio. Secondary mortgage financing would be available for additional borrowing requirements at five points over the prime rate (which was 14% at the time of the confirmation hearing). For interest rate purposes, therefore, it appears appropriate to treat City as the forced holder of two mortgages: a first mortgage to the extent of 75% of the loan and a second mortgage to the extent of 25% of the loan. The Court believes that the first 75% of the loan should bear an interest rate between 13.5% and 14%, the high end of the range for a typical garden apartment loan. Although the three year term is consistent with that in the marketplace, the deferral of interest and the lack of amortization requires a higher interest rate. The remaining 25% of the loan should bear an interest rate at least consistent with that charged in the commercial secondary mortgage market. Testimony at trial indicated that interest on such mortgages is generally five points over prime. With the prime rate approximately 14% at the time of confirmation, the Court believes that 19% is the miminum [sic] interest rate on this portion of the loan. A composite loan rate of 15% is then arrived at, computed as follows:

.75(.135)	=	.1013
.25(.19)	=	.0475
		.1488
.75(.14)	=	.1050
.25 (.19)	=	.0475
		.1525
		Say 15%

Thus, if a note and interest payments were offered to City by debtor at a 15% rate debtor would appear to meet the requirement that the discounted stream of payments equal the value of the property. Because the 12.5% rate proposed by debtor is below the 15% minimum rate established by the Court the plan as presented does not comply with § 1129(b)(2)(A)(i)(II) and, therefore, cannot be confirmed. * * *

IN RE VILLA DIABLO ASSOCIATES

United States Bankruptcy Court, Northern District of California, 1993.
156 B.R. 650.

JAMES R. GRUBE, Bankruptcy Judge.

I. INTRODUCTION.

This case involves a dispute between the debtor and its principal secured creditor over how present value should be calculated for purposes of "cramming down" a plan of reorganization under § 1129(b).

II. PROCEDURAL BACKGROUND.

Villa Diablo filed its Chapter 11 petition on July 13, 1992. Its primary asset is a 48 unit apartment complex located in Concord, California. Citibank holds a note secured by a first deed of trust on the property. At the time of the filing it was owed $2,259,069. The debtor has been unsuccessfully trying to sell the property since well before the case was filed.

[Citibank, which was undersecured, moved for relief from the stay in February 1993. The court continued the stay in effect on the condition that the debtor file a plan by a designated date. The debtor did so.]

The plan provides that Citibank will retain its lien on the property and accrue interest on its secured claim at the rate of 4.13%. The plan also provides for a minimum payment of $14,000 per month to Citibank, which calculates to an effective interest rate of 7.99% on the amount of Citibank's secured claim as calculated by the debtor. The property is to be sold within five years of confirmation. If it is not sold within five years, or if the debtor has failed to promptly cure any default, Citibank will be free to foreclose without further order of the court.

At the June 17th hearing, Citibank raised a variety of objections to the disclosure statement and plan. Among the objections was Citibank's contention that the debtor's proposed interest rate of 4.13% does not provide it with present value, and that the plan therefor fails to satisfy the fair and equitable test of § 1129(b). The debtor indicated that it might be willing to increase the interest rate but also admitted that its cash flow could not support an interest rate higher than 9%. However, in examining the cash flow from the property, it appears that if an interest rate higher than 8% is required, the debtor will not be able to confirm a plan. The court therefore severed the present value issue and set it for hearing on June 29th.

The plan and disclosure statement do not describe the manner in which the 4.13% interest rate was chosen. In its response to Citibank's objections, the debtor stated that it chose the one year Treasury Bill rate, 3.13% at the time the disclosure statement was filed, as an index to which it apparently added 1%. In a subsequent declaration filed in connection with the present value hearing, the debtor indicated that an appropriate interest rate might be in the range of 6.671% to 6.921%. This was calculated by using the Eleventh District Cost of Funds as an index and adding to that index 250 to 275 basis points.[2] Even if the debtor were to amend its plan to increase the interest rate, Citibank contends that the proposed rate is still artificially low and fails to satisfy the requirements of § 1129(b).

III. Determining Present Value.

A. The Law In The Ninth Circuit.

The Ninth Circuit has adopted a case by case market approach for determining present value payments under § 1129(a)(9)(C) or § 1129(b)(2)(A)(i)(II). While a market rate approach is to be utilized, two approaches have developed in the case law as to how the market rate may be found. The first approach is for the court to determine the current market interest rate for similar loans in the geographical area based upon evidence regarding such rates. From that evidence the court should evaluate the nature and quality of the collateral, the loan to value ratio, the debt coverage ratio, and other relevant risk factors to determine an interest rate the market would assign to the subject loan.

The second approach determines the market rate through the use of a formula. The Ninth Circuit has specifically approved the formula approach suggesting that the building of a formula rate is similar to the creation of a presumption which can then be tested by the introduction of evidence regarding market rates in the geographical area. The formula approach is nothing more than an alternative procedure which can be used to determine a market rate.

---

[2] A basis point is one-hundredth of a percent.

If, for example, a debtor wanted to rewrite a loan for an apartment building with a loan to value ratio of 70% and a debt coverage ratio of 1.2, the first approach would make the most sense because the market has information readily available regarding the terms and conditions of such a loan including the available interest rate. But where the loan to be rewritten is outside normal underwriting criteria, such as a 100% loan to value ratio, the first approach is difficult because there is no reliable market data for comparison. The formula approach is therefore often a more useful tool in such circumstances.

The formula approach nevertheless seeks a market rate. * * *

* * * Simply stated, there is no authority suggesting that a Chapter 11 debtor is entitled to a more favorable interest rate than a fully qualified borrower in the marketplace.

B. Application Of The Formula Approach.

Villa Diablo seeks to utilize the formula approach. This begins with the establishment of a "base rate" utilizing the rate on treasury obligations, the prime rate, or some other established index. The debtor now proposes to use the Eleventh District Cost of Funds as its "base rate". The Eleventh District Cost of Funds for June 1993 was 4.171%. Once the "base rate" is established, it is then adjusted based upon several factors relating to the nature of the loan, the security, and the risk of default.

1. Factors affecting the base rate.

a. The size and term of the loan.

This factor examines the manner in which the marketplace structures loans in similar situations, that is, for similar types of properties without taking into consideration the borrower's status as a Chapter 11 debtor. Stated another way, has the debtor proposed a loan structure consistent with the practices in the marketplace?

The evidence before the court supports a finding that loans on apartment complexes of more than 37 units, secured by a first deed of trust, will generally be based on a loan to value ratio of about 70%, have a debt coverage ratio of between 1.15 and 1.3, have a term of three to ten years, and provide for a variable rate of interest. The debtor's suggested amendment to the plan involves a five year loan with a variable interest rate. This is consistent with normal practices in the marketplace, at least for the portion of the loan up to 70% of the value of the property. For this portion of the loan there is actually a market which can and should be utilized to guide the formula.

The debtor and Citibank presented a survey of rates quoted by various lenders * * *. In examining the quoted rates, the court finds the "center of gravity" of the market to be 7.00%. The initial index must then be adjusted for that portion of the loan which can be measured accurately in the marketplace. The "base rate" of 4.171% thus becomes 7.00%. This is the rate that would likely be offered a qualified borrower for a similar property having a 70% loan to value ratio and a debt coverage ratio of 1.15 to 1.3.

b. Whether the loan is secured.

This factor is considered because the present value concept encompasses the payment of tax obligations under § 1129(a)(9)(C) which are often unsecured. In an unsecured setting an upward adjustment is normally appropriate. This factor is also relevant in a secured setting where there is a 100% loan to value ratio.

The "center of gravity" rate of 7.00% assumes a loan to value ratio of 70%. This 30% equity cushion protects the lender against the expenses necessarily incurred in the event it must foreclose on the property. The court recognizes that if Citibank's claim is split into allowed secured and unsecured claims, the allowed secured claim will be fully collateralized at the time of confirmation.

However, confirmation does not guarantee performance under the plan. There is at least some risk of a future default which would result in Citibank incurring certain costs to realize on its collateral. This could result in Citibank's recovery being less than 100% of its allowed secured claim. The court finds that this risk of less than full recovery requires an upward adjustment of 100 basis points.

c. The quality of the security.

This factor examines the quality of the collateral for the loan not only at the present time, but prospectively during the term of the plan. The parties agree that the apartment complex has had a troubled past and is located in a neighborhood that has had high levels of crime and drug use. While the area shows some signs of improvement, the overall quality of the security remains in a range of average to poor. When examining the quality of the security for a loan, underwriters may add or subtract from 25 to 50 basis points to the initial rate which the court has characterized as being at the "center of gravity" of the real estate loan market. The overall quality of the security here is poor and the court finds that an increase of 50 basis points is appropriate.

d. The risk of default.

(1) General factors.

Virtually every loan in a bankruptcy setting will have some risk of default. Where there is substantial equity in a property and the debtor's cash flow is strong, the risk may be slight, but such is not the case here. First, this proposed transaction involves a 100% loan to value ratio. This lack of equity increases the possibility of less than full repayment to Citibank. There is no possibility of additional borrowing on the part of the debtor. While the debtor has an investment of time and money which it hopes to recoup, it does not have existing equity to protect. This may reduce the motivation to perform over time. This additional performance risk requires an upward adjustment of 75 basis points.

The apartment complex also has a cash flow that is, at best, marginal. The debtor's April and May income statements reveal that at 100% occupancy, excluding expenses for bankruptcy counsel, the property generates between $14,000 and $14,500 per month. The debtor's plan provides for a minimum monthly payment of $14,000. In essence, the debtor proposes to give all its available monthly cash flow to Citibank as its payment. The apartment complex presently has 100% occupancy. There is no room in the debtor's proposal for a reserve for vacancies. A vacancy factor is a normal part of any projection for an apartment operation and the risk it represents is very real. There is likewise no projected cash available for deferred maintenance or emergencies. Such reserves are essential in any normal lending situation.

The debt coverage ratio normally required simply does not exist. This lack of cash reserves, and the possibility of a cash shortfall in the future requires an upward adjustment of 125 basis points.

(2) Effect of the confirmation process.

Citibank's expert, Price Waterhouse, indicates that the risks associated with these factors might cause a hypothetical investor to demand a rate of return of 18% to 20% for that portion of the loan exceeding 70% of value. However, creating a hypothetical investor in the marketplace is speculative and ignores the protection afforded by the confirmation process.

There is, in fact, no market which can quote terms for this portion of the loan, or any of the "cram down" loans Congress provided for in Chapters 11, 12 and 13 of the Bankruptcy Code. In essence, the structure of these loans is one created by statute with the terms to be determined, to the extent possible, in light of common practices in the marketplace. With respect to aspects of a loan for which no reliable market data is available, the underwriting function of private lenders is replaced by the protection afforded to creditors in the Code. In particular, confirmation requires that the court find a plan to be "feasible" under § 1129(a)(11) and, where a secured creditor objects, that the plan be "fair and equitable" to that creditor pursuant to § 1129(b). The confirmation process for this statutory loan scrutinizes the risks in a manner similar to that of an underwriter. Because of these stringent requirements, assuming the debtor could satisfy them, the risk of default after confirmation is not as great as Citibank would suggest. In light of the protection afforded by the confirmation process, the court believes that a reduction of 50 basis points is justified.

2. The proper rate.

Based on the above analysis, the court finds that the plan would have to provide Citibank 10.00% interest on its allowed secured claim to satisfy the present value requirement of § 1129(b). The rate would also have to be adjustable at reasonable intervals to allow for fluctuations to the base of the rate, the Eleventh District Cost of Funds.

IV. CONCLUSION.

Since the payment of present value to Citibank requires an interest rate of 10.00%, there is no possibility that the debtor can propose a feasible plan as required by § 1129(a)(11). There is, therefor[e], no basis for continuing to stay the termination of the automatic stay as provided for in the court's prior order.

Questions and Problems

1. *Landmark at Plaza Park* uses a "market" rate of interest, while *Villa Diablo* constructs an adjusted risk-free rate. How do the two differ? Does either approach consistently favor the debtor-in-possession? The creditor?

2. Bank extended a line of credit to Debtor several years before bankruptcy. The debt was secured by Debtor's inventory. The loan agreement provided that the rate of interest would be adjusted every six months, in light of the prime rate and Debtor's performance. At the time of bankruptcy, the contract rate was 10.5% and Debtor owed Bank $650,000. Debtor's plan proposed to pay Bank an interest rate of only 7%, because prevailing market rates had fallen since the parties last adjusted the contract rate. Bank objected to confirmation of the plan on the grounds that the contract rate should control. What result?

3. Assume the same facts as in Problem # 2, except that the market rate has risen sharply since Debtor filed a bankruptcy petition. Debtor's plan proposed to pay Bank at the contract rate in effect at the time of filing. Bank objected to confirmation of the plan on the grounds that the higher market rate should control. What result? Would your answer change if the parties' agreement did not provide for periodic adjustment in the interest rate?

4. Recall that payment, over time, of the present value of the secured claim is only one of the ways that a secured creditor's claim may be satisfied under the plan. The other alternatives are, first, sale of the property pursuant to § 363(k), with a lien attaching to the proceeds, § 1129(b)(2)(A)(ii), and second, "realization by [the secured creditor] of the indubitable equivalent of" the claim, § 1129(b)(2)(A)(iii).

The second of these alternatives has presented interpretive problems when a debtor has proposed transferring property to the secured creditor in satisfaction of the claim, but without exposing the property to a marketplace valuation. In *Arnold & Baker Farms v. U.S. (In re Arnold and Baker Farms)*, 85 F.3d 1415 (9th Cir.1996), for example, the debtor partnership proposed what is known as a "dirt for debt" plan. The debtor's obligation to the Farmers Home Administration (FmHA) was secured by a lien on 1,320 acres of the debtor's land. The debtor proposed to convey 566.5 acres to FmHA as the "indubitable equivalent" of the obligation, on the basis of the bankruptcy court's finding that the land was worth $7,300 per acre. FmHA objected on the grounds that the land was only worth $1,381 per acre. This valuation was based, in part, on disagreement about the highest and best use of the land. In addition, the Resolution Trust Corporation had acquired several thousand acres near the debtor's property and was offering large parcels for sale at no more than $2,105 per acre.

The bankruptcy court confirmed the plan, but the BAP, affirmed by the Ninth Circuit, reversed:

> The bankruptcy court found the value of each acre to be $7,300, and thus the value of the 566.5 acres to be transferred to FmHA to be $4,135,450 ($7,300 × 566.5). We must decide, therefore, whether a distribution of land with an estimated value of $4,135,450 constitutes the indubitable equivalent of a $3,837,618

claim secured by 1,320 acres. Under the circumstances of this case, we conclude that it does not.

> The partial distribution of 566.5 acres to FmHA will not insure the safety of or prevent jeopardy to the principal. FmHA originally lent funds to Arnold and Baker secured by 1320 acres of land. If Arnold and Baker defaulted on the terms of the note, FmHA bargained for the right to foreclose on the entire 1320 acres of land in order to satisfy the outstanding obligation. In this situation, the principal is protected to the extent of the entire 1320 acres held as security.
>
> If FmHA subsequently sells the property for less than the value calculated by the bankruptcy court, FmHA has no recourse to the remaining collateral to satisfy the deficiency. As a result, the distribution to FmHA may not be "completely compensatory."

Id. at 1422, *quoting* 177 B.R. 648, 661-62 (9th Cir. BAP 1994). Under what circumstances do you think the Ninth Circuit would approve a "dirt for debt" plan?

b. Absolute Priority Rule

To effect cramdown in the case of unsecured creditors, a plan must comply with § 1129(b)(2)(B). That subsection provides two alternatives, the first of which is payment of the full amount of the allowed claim. That alternative is seldom chosen, given that the amount of the allowed unsecured claim is usually the full debt. A debtor who can pay that much is unlikely to need bankruptcy. The second alternative comes into play when debtors do not propose to pay their obligations in full. It provides that, if an unsecured class is not paid in full, then classes of claims or interests junior to the unsecured class will receive nothing. In other words, equity interests must be cut out completely if unsecured creditors are paid less than 100%. This is the absolute priority rule, and it is a substantial obstacle for shareholders who want to retain ownership.

An issue that continues to be hotly debated is whether a junior class—typically, owners of the prebankruptcy firm—can contribute new value to the reorganized firm in order to retain some interest in it. (Section 1129(b)(2)(B)(ii)'s prohibition, after all, is only as to what a junior class may retain "on account of" their claim or interest.) This so-called "new value exception" to the absolute priority rule raises two interrelated questions. The first question—whether any such exception actually exists—is one that the Supreme Court has avoided time after time. The Court has, instead, presumed the existence of the exception and addressed the second question—what sort of contribution suffices as new value.

We will address the first question first, with a case that decided the issue head-on, and then turn to the Supreme Court cases addressing the sort of contribution that is necessary.

BONNER MALL PARTNERSHIP v. U.S. BANCORP MORTGAGE CO. (IN RE BONNER MALL PARTNERSHIP)

United States Court of Appeals, Ninth Circuit, 1993.
2 F.3d 899.

REINHARDT, Circuit Judge:

This case requires us to decide whether the new value "exception" to the absolute priority rule survives the enactment of the Bankruptcy Reform Act of 1978 (better known as the Bankruptcy Code), which replaced the Bankruptcy Act of 1898. The new value exception allows the shareholders of a corporation in bankruptcy to obtain an interest in the reorganized debtor in exchange for new capital contributions over the objections of a class of creditors that has not received full payment on its claims. Whether this doctrine is viable under the Bankruptcy Code has significant implications for the relative bargaining power of debtors and creditors in Chapter 11 cases. Although no circuit court has taken a definitive position on this question, *dicta* in several opinions demonstrate intra and inter-circuit disagreements. District and bankruptcy courts are sharply divided on the question, as are the commentators. The question will in all probability ultimately be decided by the Supreme Court. In the meantime, we conclude that the new value exception remains a vital principle of bankruptcy law.

I. Background

In 1984–85, Northtown Investments built Bonner Mall. The project was financed by a $6.3 million loan, secured by the mall property, from First National Bank of North Idaho, which later sold the note and deed of trust to appellant U.S. Bancorp Mortgage Co. ("Bancorp"). In October 1986 the mall was purchased by appellee Bonner Mall Partnership ("Bonner"), subject to the lien acquired by Bancorp. Bonner is composed of six partners, five trusts and one individual investor, and was formed for the express purpose of buying the mall. Unfortunately, the cash-flow from the mall was much smaller than Bonner expected. When Bonner failed to pay its real estate taxes to Bonner County, Idaho, Bancorp commenced a nonjudicial foreclosure action. After several unsuccessful attempts to renegotiate and restructure Bonner's debt, Bancorp set a trustee's sale for March 14, 1991.

[Bonner filed a petition under Chapter 11 on March 13, 1991 and proposed a plan that relied on the new value exception. Bancorp sought relief from the stay, arguing that the exception did not survive enactment of the Code. The bankruptcy judge agreed with Bancorp and granted its motion for relief from the stay.]

On appeal, the district judge determined that the only issue before him was whether the Bankruptcy Code had eliminated the new value exception. He found that it had not. * * * Bancorp filed a timely appeal to this court. Like the district court, we resolve only the question whether the new value exception survives. * * *

III. Bonner's Plan, Confirmation, and the New Value Exception

* * *

The issue before the bankruptcy judge in deciding whether to grant Bancorp's motion for relief from the stay was whether Bonner's Plan had a reasonable possibility of confirmation in a cramdown, *i.e.*, whether the standards set forth in § 1129(b)(1) could feasibly be satisfied.

The resolution of this question turns on whether there is a reasonable possibility that a bankruptcy judge could find Bonner's Plan "fair and equitable." Section 1129(b)(2) of the Code defines "fair and equitable" as *including* several enumerated *requirements*. * * * Section 1129(b)(2)(B) is a two-part codification of the judge-made absolute priority rule, compliance with which was a prerequisite to any determination that a plan was "fair and equitable" under the Bankruptcy Act.

Here, each of the unsecured claims against Bonner will not be paid in full on the effective date of the Plan. As a result, § 1129(b)(2)(B)(i) cannot be satisfied. Therefore, Bonner's Plan cannot be held to be "fair and equitable" unless it complies with the provisions of § 1129(b)(2)(B)(ii). If it fails to meet the requirements of that section it is unconfirmable as a matter of law. A critical area of dispute in this case is whether Bonner's Plan violates § 1129(b)(2)(B)(ii) and, in turn, the absolute priority rule and the "fair and equitable" principle.

Under pre-Code Bankruptcy Act practice, a plan that allowed stockholders in the business that had filed for bankruptcy protection (old equity) to receive stock in the reorganized debtor in exchange for contributions of added capital (new value) could under certain conditions satisfy the absolute priority rule and be considered "fair and equitable" even though a senior class was not paid in full. *See Case v. Los Angeles Lumber Products Co.*, 308 U.S. 106, 121 (1939). That set of conditions became known collectively as the "new value exception" to the absolute priority rule; the terms of that "exception" will be discussed below.

Although the question we must ultimately answer is whether the new value exception survived the enactment of the Bankruptcy Code, we should note, preliminarily, that the term "exception" is misleading. The doctrine is not actually an exception to the absolute priority rule but is rather a corollary principle, or, more simply a description of the limitations of the rule itself. It is, as indicated above, the set of conditions under which former shareholders may lawfully obtain a priority interest in the reorganized venture. The Supreme Court appeared to recognize as much in *Case v. Los Angeles Lumber* when it stated that if a new capital contribution satisfies certain conditions "the creditor cannot complain that he is not accorded full right of priority against the corporate assets." *Id.* at 122 (internal quotation omitted). More properly, the new value exception should be called something like the "new capital-infusion doctrine" or as one commentator has suggested, "the scrutinize old equity participation rule." Elizabeth Warren, *A Theory of Absolute Priority*, 1991 Annual Survey of American Law 9, 42.

The question whether the adoption of the Code served to eliminate the new value exception was before the Supreme Court in *Norwest Bank Worthington v. Ahlers*, 485 U.S. 197 (1988). While there is language in the opinion questioning the viability of the doctrine, the Court explicitly stated that it was not deciding the issue. Instead, the Court assumed that the doctrine existed but found that all of its requirements were not satisfied under the facts of that case. Since *Ahlers*, several court[s] of appeals have avoided a direct holding on the viability of the "exception" by using the same stratagem.

* * *

While there is a division in the district and bankruptcy courts of our circuit and nationwide, the majority of courts that have considered the question have held that the new value exception is alive and well. We share the view that the doctrine remains a vital legal principle. Accordingly, we hold that the Code permits the confirmation of a reorganization plan that provides for the infusion of capital by the shareholders of the bankrupt corporation in exchange for stock if the plan meets the conditions that plans were required to meet prior to the Code's adoption.

IV. The New Value Exception and the Code

Our explanation of why we hold that the new value exception survives will address several distinct but related issues. First, we determine that the Code provision codifying the absolute priority rule does not prohibit confirmation of a new value plan. Second, we decide that Congress' failure expressly to include the new value doctrine as a standard to be considered in applying the "fair and equitable" principle does not reflect an intent to eliminate the exception. Finally, we conclude that the new value exception is fully consistent with the structure and underlying policies of Chapter 11.

A. The Codification of the Absolute Priority Rule Does Not Serve to Eliminate the New Value Exception.

The parties take diametrically opposed positions as to the consistency of the new value exception with § 1129(b)(2)(B)(ii). Bancorp argues that * * * the plain meaning of § 1129(b)(2)(B)(ii) demonstrates that the new value exception did not survive the enactment of the Code. Bonner contends that: 1) the infusion of new capital from a source outside the bankruptcy estate, even if the source is a former equity holder, is an independent act that does not violate the absolute priority rule; and 2) § 1129(b)(2)(B)(ii) does not forbid confirmation of plans that meet the requirements of the new value exception.

In determining whether § 1129(b)(2)(B)(ii) abolishes the new value exception we apply the traditional tools of statutory construction. * * * Applying these familiar rules, we conclude that the plain language of § 1129(b)(2)(B)(ii) demonstrates that Bonner's, and not Bancorp's, reading of the provision is correct.

1. Because Qualifying New Value Plans Do Not Give Old Equity Holders Stock in the Reorganized Debtor "On Account Of" Their Prior Ownership Interests, They Do Not Violate § 1129(b)(2)(B)(ii).

Section 1129(b)(2)(B)(ii) requires that a plan provide that with respect to a class of unsecured claims that has not received full payment—

> the holder of any claim or interest that is junior to the claims of such class will not receive or retain under the plan *on account of such junior claim or interest* any property. (Emphasis added.)

In plainer English the provision bars old equity from receiving any property via a reorganization plan "*on account of*" its prior equitable ownership when all senior claim classes are not paid in full. The central inquiry in determining the reach of the prohibition is the meaning of the critical words "on account of".

We have no difficulty in reconciling the "on account of" language with the new value exception. Under Bankruptcy Act practice, old equity was required to meet several requirements in order to take advantage of that doctrine. Former equity owners were required to offer value that was 1) new, 2) substantial, 3) money or money's worth, 4) necessary for a successful reorganization[,] and 5) reasonably equivalent to the value or interest received. *Case v. Los Angeles Lumber*, 308 U.S. at 121–22. Several courts have concluded that if a proposed plan satisfies all of these requirements, *i.e.* the new value exception, it will not violate § 1129(b)(2)(B)(ii) of the Code and the absolute priority rule. Such a plan, they reason, will *not* give old equity property "*on account of* " prior interests, but instead will allow the former owners to participate in the reorganized debtor *on account of* a substantial, necessary, and fair new value contribution. We agree with their analysis.

We recognize that in some larger sense the reason that former owners receive new equity interests in reorganized ventures is that they are former owners. But it is also true that in new value transactions old equity owners receive stock in exchange for the additional capital they invest. Causation for any event has many and varied levels. Here, the answer to the meaning of the phrase "on account of" lies in the level of causation Congress had in mind when it prohibited old equity owners from receiving property "on account of" their prior interests. A reading of the full text of § 1129(b)(2)(B)(ii) makes it clear that what Congress had in mind was direct or immediate causation rather than a more remote variety, and that it did not intend to prohibit persons who receive stock because they have provided new capital from becoming participants in the reorganized debtor simply because they were also owners of the original enterprise.[23]

Had Congress intended that old equity never receive any property under a reorganization plan where senior claim classes are not paid in full, it could simply have omitted the "on account of" language from § 1129(b)(2)(B)(ii). We would then be left with an absolute prohibition against former equity owners' receiving or retaining property in the reorganized debtor in such circumstances. The expansive reading of the phrase "on account of such junior claim or interest" suggested by Bancorp would lead to the identical result, thus rendering the disputed phrase superfluous. Under that interpretation any distribution to old equity would always be "on account of" its former interest in some sense. We decline Bancorp's invitation to nullify Congress' deliberate use of the term "on account of such junior claim or interest", particularly since nearly identical language can be found throughout the Code.[24] Congress must have intended the "on account of" language to have some significant meaning as well as some particular limiting effect.

We believe that Congress intended the "on account of" phrase in § 1129(b)(2)(B)(ii) to require bankruptcy courts to determine whether a reorganization plan that gives stock to former equity holders does so primarily because of their old interests in the debtor or for legitimate business reasons. The new value doctrine provides the means by which a court can discover whether a particular new capital transaction is proposed "on account of" old equity's prior ownership or "on account of" its new contribution. In other words, in evaluating whether a reorganization plan satisfies the requirements of the new value exception a court is in fact determining whether old equity is unjustifiably attempting to retain its corporate ownership powers in violation of the absolute

---

[23] Professor Warren has stated:

> The Code does not prohibit old equity from becoming a post-petition financer of the business or a post-plan owner of the business. The Code leaves old equity in the same position as any other potential investor: it may offer to buy any of the assets of the estate on the same terms as any other buyer.

A Theory of Absolute Priority at 39. *Accord* Raymond T. Nimmer, *Negotiated Bankruptcy Reorganization Plans: Absolute Priority and New Value Contributions*, 36 Emory L.J. 1009, 1051 (1987); Bruce A. Markell, *Owners, Auctions, and Absolute Priority in Bankruptcy Reorganizations*, 44 Stan. L. Rev. 69, 96–102 (1991).

[24] For example, § 1129 alone uses a variant of the "on account of such claim or interest" language seven times.

priority rule or whether there is genuine and fair exchange of new capital for an equity interest.

Contrary to Bancorp's contentions, § 1129(b)(2)(B)(ii) does not by its terms eliminate, or even refer to, the new value exception. Rather, the language of that section and the requirements of the new value principle complement each other. Consequently, the fact that a reorganization plan provides for a new value transaction does not in and of itself violate § 1129(b)(2)(B)(ii) and the absolutely [sic] priority rule.

2. The "On Account Of" Language of § 1129(b)(2)(B)(ii) Does Not Bar Plans That Give Old Equity Alone the Opportunity to Acquire Stock for a New Capital Contribution.

As Bancorp notes, several courts have held that where a reorganization plan gives old equity *alone* the right to obtain an interest in the reorganized debtor in exchange for new value, as Bonner's Plan does, the old equity holders are given "property" *on account of their prior ownership interests* and the absolute priority rule is violated. * * * Under this analysis the "property" given to old equity in violation of the absolute priority rule is *not* the stock in the reorganized debtor received in exchange for a new value contribution. Rather "*[the] exclusive right* of [the] Debtor's existing partners to obtain equity interests in [the] Debtor itself constitutes property that the partners retain 'on account of' their existing interests." *In re Outlook/Century, Ltd.*, 127 B.R. 650, 654 (Bankr. N.D.Cal.1991) (emphasis added).

We disagree with this analysis. Even assuming that an exclusive opportunity is "property", it does not follow that such an opportunity is property received or retained "on account of" old equity's prior ownership interests in the debtor. A proposed reorganization plan may give old equity the exclusive opportunity to purchase stock in exchange for new capital for other reasons. Exclusivity may be given because the plan proponent may believe that the participation of old equity in the new business will enhance the value of the business after reorganization. It is possible the debtor will conclude that additional funding will be easier to obtain if the old owners, the most likely investors, know in advance that their partners will all be familiar faces. Even more important, it may be apparent to the proponents of the plan that there will be no other legitimate investors who would be willing to put substantial capital into a business that is just emerging from Chapter 11 protection. * * * The proponent of a plan may have good reason to believe that old equity would not participate without the incentive of an exclusive opportunity.

As stated earlier, whether a particular plan gives old equity a property interest "on account of" its old ownership interests in violation of the absolute priority rule or for another, permissible reason is a factual question. The answer depends upon whether the requirements of the new value exception are met. We believe that this same analysis applies whether a plan gives old equity an exclusive or non-exclusive right of participation in a new value transaction. What matters instead is whether the proposed transaction meets the criterion "necessary to the success of the reorganization". In other words, if an exclusive participation plan satisfies that requirement, then it allows the partners the sole right to participate in a new value transaction not because of illegitimate collusion between old equity and the plan proponent but because such participation is necessary for a successful reorganization and in the best interests of all concerned. Of course, any exclusive participation plan must also fulfill the new value doctrine's four other requirements as well.

In sum, where the strictures of the new value exception are met, there is simply no violation of the absolute priority rule, whether the plan provides for exclusive or non-exclusive participation, because old equity will not retain or receive property "on account of" its old ownership interests in violation of § 1129(b)(2)(B)(ii).

B. Congress' Failure to List the New Value Exception as a Specific Doctrine Permitted under the "Fair and Equitable" Principle Does Not Demonstrate an Intent to Eliminate It.

While the absolute priority rule clearly does not *prohibit* confirmation of a new value exception plan in a cramdown, this does not necessarily mean that the "fair and equitable" provisions of the Code should be interpreted as *permitting* confirmation of such a plan. Bancorp argues that Congress' failure expressly to provide for the continuation of the new value exception in the provision setting forth the requirements of the "fair and equitable" principle must be interpreted as an implicit statement that it did not intend the doctrine to survive the adoption of the Code. Recognizing that the Code does not unambiguously allow for new capital contribution plans, Bonner argues that such plans are consistent with the "fair and equitable" principle and that despite the absence of an express provision, Congress intended to maintain the new value exception.

Bonner relies upon "the normal rule of statutory construction * * * that if Congress intends for legislation to change the interpretation of a judicially created concept, it makes that intent specific." *Midlantic*

Nat'l. Bank v. New Jersey Dept. of Envtl. Protection, 474 U.S. 494, 501 (1986) (citations omitted); *Kelly v. Robinson*, 479 U.S. 36 (1988). This rule is followed with particular care in construing the Bankruptcy Code. When Congress amends the bankruptcy laws, it does not start from scratch. The Bankruptcy Code should not be read to abandon past bankruptcy practice absent a clear indication that Congress intended to do so.

* * *

There is simply no question that the new value exception was an established pre-Code Bankruptcy practice of which Congress would have had (and did have) knowledge. First, several Supreme Court cases had mentioned the principle, albeit the last time in 1946. Second, several appellate court cases recognized the new value doctrine after 1946. Finally, a proposal to broaden the new value exception was put before Congress during the drafting of the Code. While the proposal was rejected, that action demonstrates that Congress knew of the doctrine when it enacted the Code.

Once it has been shown that Congress was aware of a pre-Code practice, the remaining inquiry * * * is whether it has made clear its intent to change that practice. Bancorp argues that the codification of the formerly judicially-defined concept of "fair and equitable" without a reference to the new value exception shows Congress' clear intent to eliminate the doctrine. However, § 1129(b)(2) explicitly defines the term "fair and equitable" as merely *including* the general requirements listed in the Code and expressly leaves room for additional factors to be considered in applying the principle in other particular circumstances. *See* § 102(3) (defining "includes" as "not limiting"). There is nothing in the language of the Code that suggests that courts cannot continue to apply the requirements of the new value exception in determining whether a plan that affords old equity a property interest in exchange for a capital contribution is "fair and equitable". In any event, the text of § 1129(b)(2) does not evidence the clear intent necessary to support a conclusion that Congress decided to eliminate the new value doctrine; silence is not a sufficient basis from which we may infer such a purpose.

Where the text of the Code does not unambiguously abrogate pre-Code practice, courts should presume that Congress intended it to continue unless the legislative history dictates a contrary result. It does not do so here. If anything, the legislative history of the Code supports the continued existence of the new value doctrine. It contains statements by sponsors of the Code that although § 1129(b)(2) lists several specific factors interpreting "fair and equitable", others were omitted to avoid statutory complexity and because courts would independently find that they were fundamental to "fair and equitable treatment".[33] This legislative history is evidence that Congress enacted the Code with knowledge that other, judicially-created standards governing the application of the "fair and equitable" principle existed and that it failed to include such standards for reasons other than an intent to eliminate them.

* * * Congress rejected a proposal by the Bankruptcy Commission to expand the new value exception significantly. That proposal would have eliminated the "money or money's worth" requirement set forth in *Case v. Los Angeles Lumber* and permitted new "important" contributions, including contributions of management, to suffice. Congress' rejection of the Bankruptcy Commission's proposal shows only that it did not want to broaden the exception; it does not indicate rejection of the exception itself. Indeed, "the Commission's proposal presupposed the existence of the new value exception, and Congress's rejection of the modification could just as easily be construed as an endorsement of the status quo." *Snyder v. Farm Credit Bank of St. Louis (In re Snyder)*, 967 F.2d 1126, 1130 (7th Cir.1992).

* * * Given that there is no evidence of a clear intent on the part of Congress to eliminate the new value exception in either the statutory text or the legislative history, under *Dewsnup* and *Davenport* pre-Code practice continues to apply.

C. Congress' Overhaul of the Reorganization Process Does Not Justify a Conclusion that the New Value Exception was Abolished.

Bancorp contends that where the Code totally revamps an area of bankruptcy law, pre-Code practice may appropriately be ignored. Bancorp relies on *Union Bank v. Wolas*, 112 S.Ct. 527 (1992), in support of this proposition. In *Wolas* the Court unanimously found that the text of the Code sharply limited the pre-Code practice at issue. * * * While the *Wolas* Court relied in part upon the major changes made to the statutory framework by the enactment of the Code, it did so only as a *confirmation* of its earlier conclusion that the plain text of the Code provision altered pre-Code practice. Here, and as shown above, the lan-

---

[33] One example of a well-established component of "fair and equitable" that was not included was the concept that no senior class is to receive more than 100 percent of the amount of its claims. * * *

guage of the text at issue, § 1129(b)(2), does not by its terms affect the new value exception in any respect.

* * *

Bancorp also contends that the Code meant to give creditors, not the bankruptcy court, the power to decide when to waive the absolute priority rule. It is true that § 1126(c) allows creditors to consent to confirmation of a plan that does not comply with the absolute priority rule. However, that section permits creditors to waive a priority *they* possess. The new value exception allows bankruptcy courts to afford a priority to *others* over the creditors. There is simply no logical analysis that would allow us to conclude that by permitting creditors to waive their own priority Congress demonstrated the intent to deprive bankruptcy courts of *their* power to afford investors of new capital a priority over an impaired class of creditors. Moreover, the very purpose of the Code's cramdown provision, § 1129(b), which had no direct equivalent under the Act, is to allow the court, and not the creditors, to decide whether a "fair and equitable" plan should be confirmed over creditor objections. While creditor autonomy is certainly an important aspect of the reorganization process, the argument that the new value exception impedes that autonomy is really a complaint against the practice of confirmation by cramdown. That grievance cannot be addressed here.

Finally, Bancorp argues that the Code's creation of the entity of the debtor-in-possession to run the business in lieu of a trustee would cause self-dealing by insiders if the new value exception were still allowed. However, the very purpose of the Code's creation of the debtor-in-possession was to increase the power of those in control of the debtor during the reorganization process. Bankruptcy law is very formalistic in that it treats the debtor, the debtor-in-possession, and old equity as legally distinct entities when in reality they may all be one and the same. The risk of self-dealing among these entities at the expense of creditors is a risk created by the Code itself. The stringent requirements of the new value exception are designed to mitigate that risk. The enactment in the Code of changes that aggravate the self-dealing problem constitutes good reason for courts to make certain that a proposed new value plan strictly adheres to the requirements of the exception. The modifications to the reorganization process are not, however, cause for us to ignore several decades of bankruptcy practice in determining Congress' intent with respect to the new value exception.

Despite all of the differences between the Act and the Code, the primary rationale for the new value exception has not been eliminated by any statutory alteration to the confirmation process. The new value exception is based on "practical necessit[y]", on the recognition that new money frequently could not be obtained for the reorganized debtor in the absence of that doctrine. *See Mason v. Paradise Irrigation Dist.*, 326 U.S. 536, 542 (1946). That practical necessity remains just as pertinent under the Code. * * *

D. The New Value Exception is Consistent with the Underlying Policies of Chapter 11.

In interpreting statutory language we are not confined to the specific provision at issue but may look to the structure of the law as a whole and to its object and policy. Chapter 11 has two major objectives[:] 1) to permit successful rehabilitation of debtors; and 2) to maximize the value of the estate. The new value exception, properly applied, serves both goals. By permitting prior stockholders to contribute new money in exchange for participation in the reorganized company, the debtor is given an additional source of capital. The new contribution increases the amount available for the estate to use both in its reorganization and in funding the plan and paying creditors. Without the inducement of participation in the reorganized debtor, the new money may be unavailable. All parties involved, including the creditors, benefit from an increase in the assets of the estate.

"Prior owners are a source of capital different in kind from new investors in that they have an ongoing role in the reorganization and a prior investment in the company." *Prudential Ins. Co. v. F.A.B. Indus. (In re F.A.B. Indus.)*, 147 B.R. 763, 769 n. 13 (C.D.Cal.1992) [internal quotations deleted]. Moreover, in many situations the new value exception allows control and management of the company to remain with the original owners, who arguably can best reestablish a profitable business. Old owners may have valuable expertise and experience that outside investors lack. Some studies demonstrate that reorganizations have been more successful when former management was allowed to use its expertise in running the business.

It has been argued that the new value exception allows old equity to repurchase the business at a bargain price, while superior creditors go unpaid, and that this result is contrary to the Chapter 11 policy of protecting creditor interests. We believe that this argument is incorrect in two respects. First, while the protection of creditors' interests is an important purpose under Chapter 11, the Supreme Court has made clear that successful debtor reorganization and maximization of the value of the estate are the primary purposes.[37] Chapter 11 is designed to avoid liquidations under Chapter 7, since liquidations may have a negative impact on jobs, suppliers of the business, and the economy as a whole. The ability of stockholders to remain in possession and control of operations, rehabilitate the business, and retain ownership through the new value exception encourages debtors to attempt Chapter 11 reorganization instead of simply liquidating their assets and starting over.

Second, we believe that if the new value exception's requirements are properly applied, creditors' interests will generally be benefited as well. The strictures of the new value doctrine provide creditors with significant safeguards against collusion between the proponent of the reorganization plan and the old equity owners.[38] Although the new value exception has been criticized as a subversion of the absolute priority rule, its requirements actually enhance the rule. As we noted earlier, they constitute guidelines by which a court can ensure that old equity will *not* acquire an interest in the reorganized debtor or other property *on account of* its old ownership interests. In fact, the new value exception puts limits on the power of old equity to gain an interest in the reorganized business beyond that provided in the explicit language of the Code. * * *

VI. Conclusion

Viewed properly, "the new value exception" may be seen as a rule of construction, or a rule that serves to define the meaning of the absolute priority rule and determine when it has been satisfied. As such it is as pertinent today as it was under pre-Code bankruptcy practice. The arguments that Bancorp advances do not persuade us that Congress would have had any reason to disregard a beneficial rule of construction that assists courts in implementing an important bankruptcy doctrine at the very time it was incorporating that doctrine into the Bankruptcy Code.

---

[37] From one perspective, the debate over the survival of the new value exception is a division between those who perceive the paramount objective of Chapter 11 to be successful reorganization of the debtor and those who believe it should be protection of creditors' interests.

[38] If old equity contributes a substantial amount of new capital to the business undergoing reorganization, then the risk of a later failure falls more heavily on stockholders than creditors.

Nothing in the text of the Code prohibits the confirmation of plans that properly employ the new value doctrine. Nor does the legislative history demonstrate that Congress intended to abrogate this judicially created, pre-Code legal principle. Therefore, we conclude that the new value "exception", with its stringent requirements, survives. We recognize that, if applied carelessly, the doctrine has the potential to subvert the interests of creditors and allow debtors and old equity to abuse the reorganization process. The proper answer to these concerns is vigilance on the part of bankruptcy courts in ensuring that all of the requirements of the new value exception are met in every case. Here, it is unclear whether Bonner's plan can meet all of the requirements of the doctrine and achieve confirmation. Nevertheless, it may well be within the realm of potentially confirmable plans and thereby survive Bancorp's motion for relief from the automatic stay. The bankruptcy court must make that determination initially.

The judgment of the district court is AFFIRMED and the case is REMANDED to the bankruptcy court for further proceedings consistent with this opinion.

Notes and Questions

1. The Supreme Court granted certiorari in *Bonner Mall*, but the parties reached a settlement soon thereafter. The issue on appeal to the Supreme Court then became whether the Ninth Circuit's opinion should be vacated. The Court held that mootness by reason of settlement does not justify vacatur. *U.S. Bancorp Mortgage Co. v. Bonner Mall Partnership,* 513 U.S. 18, 115 S.Ct. 386, 130 L.Ed.2d 233 (1994). Thus, the Ninth Circuit's opinion in the case retains precedential force. In addition, as the Ninth Circuit suggested, the question whether the new value exception survives in the Code remained ripe for Supreme Court consideration.

2. Was the outcome in *Bonner Mall* driven by the rules of statutory interpretation that the court followed? Would other approaches to statutory construction have supported a different result?

3. Is the difference in opinion expressed by various courts on this issue "a division between those who perceive the paramount objective of Chapter 11 to be successful reorganization of the debtor and those who believe it should be protection of creditors' interests," as the court speculated in footnote 37?

4. As the court in *Bonner Mall* noted, the Supreme Court held in *Case v. Los Angeles Lumber Products Co.*, 308 U.S. 106, 60 S.Ct. 1, 84 L.Ed. 110 (1939), that the stockholder of an insolvent debtor may participate in the plan of re-

organization if that participation is "based on a contribution in money or money's worth, reasonably equivalent in view of all the circumstances to the participation of the stockholder." *Id.* at 121-22. When asked in *Norwest Bank Worthington v. Ahlers*, 485 U.S. 197, 108 S.Ct. 963, 99 L.Ed.2d 169 (1988), to determine whether that "new value exception" to the absolute priority rule had survived in the Code, the Supreme Court declined to reach the issue. The Court held instead that the exception did not encompass a promise by the respondent-shareholders to contribute their future "labor, experience, and expertise" to the reorganized entity:

> *Los Angeles Lumber* itself rejected an analogous proposition, finding that the promise of the existing shareholders to pledge their "financial standing and influence in the community" and their "continuity of management" to the reorganized enterprise was "[in]adequate consideration" that could not possibly be deemed "money's worth." *Id.* at 122. No doubt, the efforts promised by the *Los Angeles Lumber* equity holders—like those of respondents—had "value" and would have been of some benefit to any reorganized enterprise. But ultimately, as the Court said in *Los Angeles Lumber*, "[t]hey reflect merely vague hopes or possibilities." *Id.* at 122–23. The same is true of respondents' pledge of future labor and management skills.
>
> Viewed from the time of approval of the plan, respondents' promise of future services is intangible, inalienable, and, in all likelihood, unenforceable. It "has no place in the asset column of the balance sheet of the new [entity]." *Id.* Unlike "money or money's worth," a promise of future services cannot be exchanged in any market for something of value to the creditors *today*. In fact, no decision of this Court or any Court of Appeals, other than the decision below, has ever found a promise to contribute future labor, management, or expertise sufficient to qualify for the *Los Angeles Lumber* exception to the absolute priority rule. In short, there is no way to distinguish between the promises respondents proffer here and those of the shareholders in *Los Angeles Lumber*; neither is an adequate contribution to escape the absolute priority rule.

485 U.S. at 204-05, 108 S.Ct. at 967, 99 L.Ed.2d at 178.

The Supreme Court had another chance, in the following case, to address the question whether the new value exception to the absolute priority rule survives in the Bankruptcy Code. Again, the Court ducked the question.

BANK OF AMERICA NATIONAL TRUST & SAVINGS ASSOCIATION v. 203 NORTH LASALLE STREET PARTNERSHIP

United States Supreme Court, 1999.
526 U.S. 434, 119 S. Ct. 1411, 143 L.Ed. 2d 607

JUSTICE SOUTER delivered the opinion of the Court.

The issue in this Chapter 11 reorganization case is whether a debtor's prebankruptcy equity holders may, over the objection of a senior class of impaired creditors, contribute new capital and receive ownership interests in the reorganized entity, when that opportunity is given exclusively to the old equity holders under a plan adopted without consideration of alternatives. We hold that old equity holders are disqualified from participating in such a "new value" transaction by the terms of § 1129(b)(2)(B)(ii), which in such circumstances bars a junior interest holder's receipt of any property on account of his prior interest.

I

Petitioner, Bank of America National Trust and Savings Association (Bank), is the major creditor of respondent, 203 North LaSalle Street Partnership (Debtor or Partnership), an Illinois real estate limited partnership. The Bank lent the Debtor some $93 million, secured by a nonrecourse first mortgage on the Debtor's principal asset, 15 floors of an office building in downtown Chicago. In January 1995, the Debtor defaulted, and the Bank began foreclosure in a state court.

In March, the Debtor responded with a voluntary petition for relief under Chapter 11 of the Bankruptcy Code, which automatically stayed the foreclosure proceedings, see § 362(a). The Debtor's principal objective was to ensure that its partners retained title to the property so as to avoid roughly $20 million in personal tax liabilities, which would fall due if the Bank foreclosed. * * *

The value of the mortgaged property was less than the balance due the Bank, which elected to divide its undersecured claim into secured and unsecured deficiency claims under § 506(a) and § 1111(b). Under the plan, the Debtor separately classified the Bank's secured claim, its unsecured deficiency claim, and unsecured trade debt owed to other creditors. See § 1122(a). The Bankruptcy Court found that the Debtor's available assets were prepetition rents in a cash account of $3.1 million and the 15 floors of rental property worth $54.5 million.

The secured claim was valued at the latter figure, leaving the Bank with an unsecured deficiency of $38.5 million.

So far as we need be concerned here, the Debtor's plan had these further features:

(1) The Bank's $54.5 million secured claim would be paid in full between 7 and 10 years after the original 1995 repayment date.

(2) The Bank's $38.5 million unsecured deficiency claim would be discharged for an estimated 16% of its present value.

(3) The remaining unsecured claims of $90,000, held by the outside trade creditors, would be paid in full, without interest, on the effective date of the plan.

(4) Certain former partners of the Debtor would contribute $6.125 million in new capital over the course of five years (the contribution being worth some $4.1 million in present value), in exchange for the Partnership's entire ownership of the reorganized debtor.

The last condition was an exclusive eligibility provision: the old equity holders were the only ones who could contribute new capital.[11]

The Bank objected and, being the sole member of an impaired class of creditors, thereby blocked confirmation of the plan on a consensual basis. See § 1129(a)(8). The Debtor, however, took the alternate route to confirmation of a reorganization plan, forthrightly known as the judicial "cramdown" process for imposing a plan on a dissenting class. § 1129(b).

There are two conditions for a cramdown. First, all requirements of § 1129(a) must be met (save for the plan's acceptance by each impaired class of claims or interests, see § 1129(a)(8)). Critical among them are the conditions that the plan be accepted by at least one class of impaired creditors, see § 1129(a)(10), and satisfy the "best-interest-of-creditors" test, see § 1129(a)(7). Here, the class of trade creditors with

[11] The plan eliminated the interests of noncontributing partners. More than 60% of the Partnership interests would change hands on confirmation of the plan. The new Partnership, however, would consist solely of former partners, a feature critical to the preservation of the Partnership's tax shelter.

impaired unsecured claims voted for the plan, and there was no issue of best interest. Second, the objection of an impaired creditor class may be overridden only if "the plan does not discriminate unfairly, and is fair and equitable, with respect to each class of claims or interests that is impaired under, and has not accepted, the plan." § 1129(b)(1). As to a dissenting class of impaired unsecured creditors, such a plan may be found to be "fair and equitable" only if the allowed value of the claim is to be paid in full, § 1129(b)(2)(B)(i), or, in the alternative, if "the holder of any claim or interest that is junior to the claims of such [impaired unsecured] class will not receive or retain under the plan on account of such junior claim or interest any property," § 1129(b)(2)(B)(ii). That latter condition is the core of what is known as the "absolute priority rule."

The absolute priority rule was the basis for the Bank's position that the plan could not be confirmed as a cramdown. As the Bank read the rule, the plan was open to objection simply because certain old equity holders in the Debtor Partnership would receive property even though the Bank's unsecured deficiency claim would not be paid in full. The Bankruptcy Court approved the plan nonetheless, and accordingly denied the Bank's pending motion to convert the case to Chapter 7 liquidation, or to dismiss the case. The District Court affirmed, as did the Court of Appeals.

* * *

We granted certiorari to resolve a Circuit split on the issue. The Seventh Circuit in this case joined the Ninth in relying on a new value corollary to the absolute priority rule to support confirmation of such plans. See *In re Bonner Mall Partnership*, 2 F.3d 899, 910-916 (CA9 1993), cert. granted, 510 U.S. 1039, vacatur denied and appeal dism'd as moot, 513 U.S. 18 (1994). The Second and Fourth Circuits, by contrast, without explicitly rejecting the corollary, have disapproved plans similar to this one. See *In re Coltex Loop Central Three Partners, L.P.*, 138 F.3d 39, 44-45 (CA2 1998); *In re Bryson Properties, XVIII*, 961 F.2d 496, 504 (CA4), cert. denied, 506 U.S. 866 (1992).[15] We do not decide whether the statute includes a new value corollary or exception, but hold that on any reading respondent's proposed plan fails to satisfy the statute, and accordingly reverse.

---

[15] All four of these cases arose in the single-asset real estate context, the typical one in which new value plans are proposed.

II

The terms "absolute priority rule" and "new value corollary" (or "exception") are creatures of law antedating the current Bankruptcy Code, and to understand both those terms and the related but inexact language of the Code some history is helpful. The Bankruptcy Act preceding the Code contained no such provision as subsection (b)(2)(B)(ii), its subject having been addressed by two interpretive rules. The first was a specific gloss on the requirement of § 77B (and its successor, Chapter X) of the old Act, that any reorganization plan be "fair and equitable." The reason for such a limitation was the danger inherent in any reorganization plan proposed by a debtor, then and now, that the plan will simply turn out to be too good a deal for the debtor's owners. * * * Hence the pre-Code judicial response known as the absolute priority rule, that fairness and equity required that "the creditors * * * be paid before the stockholders could retain [equity interests] for any purpose whatever." *Northern Pacific R. Co. v. Boyd*, 228 U.S. 482, 508 (1913).

The second interpretive rule addressed the first. Its classic formulation occurred in *Case v. Los Angeles Lumber Products Co.*, in which the Court spoke through Justice Douglas in this dictum:

> "It is, of course, clear that there are circumstances under which stockholders may participate in a plan of reorganization of an insolvent debtor * * * . Where the necessity [for new capital] exists and the old stockholders make a fresh contribution and receive in return a participation reasonably equivalent to their contribution, no objection can be made * * * .
>
> "We believe that to accord 'the creditor his full right of priority against the corporate assets' where the debtor is insolvent, the stockholder's participation must be based on a contribution in money or in money's worth, reasonably equivalent in view of all the circumstances to the participation of the stockholder." 308 U.S. at 121-122.

Although counsel for one of the parties here has described the *Case* observation as " 'black-letter' principle," it never rose above the technical level of dictum in any opinion of this Court, which last addressed it in *Norwest Bank Worthington v. Ahlers*, 485 U.S. 197 (1988), holding that a contribution of " 'labor, experience, and expertise' " by a junior interest holder was not in the " 'money's worth' " that the *Case* observation required. *Id.* at 203-205. Nor, prior to the enactment of the current Bankruptcy Code, did any court rely on the *Case* dictum to approve a plan that gave old equity a property right after reorganization. Hence the controversy over how weighty the *Case* dictum had become, as reflected in the alternative labels for the new value notion: some writers and courts (including this one, see *Ahlers*, supra, at 203, n.3) have spoken of it as an exception to the absolute priority rule, while others have characterized it as a simple corollary to the rule, see, *e.g.*, *In re Bonner Mall Partnership*, 2 F.3d at 906.

Enactment of the Bankruptcy Code in place of the prior Act might have resolved the status of new value by a provision bearing its name or at least unmistakably couched in its terms, but the Congress chose not to avail itself of that opportunity. In 1973, Congress had considered proposals by the Bankruptcy Commission that included a recommendation to make the absolute priority rule more supple by allowing nonmonetary new value contributions. Although Congress took no action on any of the ensuing bills containing language that would have enacted such an expanded new value concept, each of them was reintroduced in the next congressional session. After extensive hearings, a substantially revised House bill emerged, but without any provision for nonmonetary new value contributions. After a lengthy mark-up session, the House produced H. R. 8200, which would eventually become the law. It had no explicit new value language, expansive or otherwise, but did codify the absolute priority rule in nearly its present form.

* * *

The upshot is that this history does nothing to disparage the possibility apparent in the statutory text, that the absolute priority rule now on the books as subsection (b)(2)(B)(ii) may carry a new value corollary. Although there is no literal reference to "new value" in the phrase "on account of such junior claim," the phrase could arguably carry such an implication in modifying the prohibition against receipt by junior claimants of any interest under a plan while a senior class of unconsenting creditors goes less than fully paid.

III

Three basic interpretations have been suggested for the "on account of" modifier. The first reading is proposed by the Partnership, that "on account of" harks back to accounting practice and means something like "in exchange for," or "in satisfaction of." On this view, a plan would not violate the absolute priority rule unless the old equity holders received or retained property in exchange for the prior interest, without any significant new contribution; if substantial money passed from them as part of the deal, the prohibition of subsection (b)(2)(B)(ii) would not stand in the way, and whatever issues of fairness and equity there might otherwise be would not implicate the "on account of" modifier.

This position is beset with troubles, the first one being textual. Subsection (b)(2)(B)(ii) forbids not only receipt of property on account of the prior interest but its retention as well. See also §§ 1129-(a)(7)(A)(ii), (a)(7)(B), (b)(2)(B)(i), (b)(2)(C)(i), (b)(2)(C)(ii). A common instance of the latter would be a debtor's retention of an interest in the insolvent business reorganized under the plan. Yet it would be exceedingly odd to speak of "retaining" property in exchange for the same property interest, and the eccentricity of such a reading is underscored by the fact that elsewhere in the Code the drafters chose to use the very phrase "in exchange for," § 1123(a)(5)(J) (a plan shall provide adequate means for implementation, including "issuance of securities of the debtor * * * for cash, for property, for existing securities, or in exchange for claims or interests"). It is unlikely that the drafters of legislation so long and minutely contemplated as the 1978 Bankruptcy Code would have used two distinctly different forms of words for the same purpose.

The second difficulty is practical: the unlikelihood that Congress meant to impose a condition as manipulable as subsection (b)(2)(B)(ii) would be if "on account of" meant to prohibit merely an exchange unaccompanied by a substantial infusion of new funds but permit one whenever substantial funds changed hands. "Substantial" or "significant" or "considerable" or like characterizations of a monetary contribution would measure it by the Lord Chancellor's foot, and an absolute priority rule so variable would not be much of an absolute. Of course it is true (as already noted) that, even if old equity holders could displace the rule by adding some significant amount of cash to the deal, it would not follow that their plan would be entitled to adoption; a contested plan would still need to satisfy the overriding condition of fairness and equity. But that general fairness and equity criterion would apply in any event, and one comes back to the question why Congress would have bothered to add a separate priority rule without a sharper edge.

Since the "in exchange for" reading merits rejection, the way is open to recognize the more common understanding of "on account of" to mean "because of." This is certainly the usage meant for the phrase at other places in the statute, see § 1111(b)(1)(A) (treating certain claims as if the holder of the claim "had recourse against the debtor on account of such claim"); § 522(d)(10)(E) (permitting debtors to exempt payments under certain benefit plans and contracts "on account of illness, disability, death, age, or length of service"); § 547(b)(2) (authorizing trustee to avoid a transfer of an interest of the debtor in property "for or on account of an antecedent debt owed by the debtor"); § 547(c)(4)(B) (barring trustee from avoiding a transfer when a creditor gives new value to the debtor "on account of which new value the debtor did not make an otherwise unavoidable transfer to * * * such creditor"). So, under the commonsense rule that a given phrase is meant to carry a given concept in a single statute, the better reading of subsection (b)(2)(B)(ii) recognizes that a causal relationship between holding the prior claim or interest and receiving or retaining property is what activates the absolute priority rule.

The degree of causation is the final bone of contention. We understand the Government, as *amicus curiae*, to take the starchy position not only that any degree of causation between earlier interests and retained property will activate the bar to a plan providing for later property, but also that whenever the holders of equity in the Debtor end up with some property there will be some causation; when old equity, and not someone on the street, gets property the reason is *res ipsa loquitur*. An old equity holder simply cannot take property under a plan if creditors are not paid in full.

There are, however, reasons counting against such a reading. If, as is likely, the drafters were treating junior claimants or interest holders as a class at this point, then the simple way to have prohibited the old interest holders from receiving anything over objection would have been to omit the "on account of" phrase entirely from subsection (b)(2)(B)(ii). On this assumption, reading the provision as a blanket prohibition would leave "on account of" as a redundancy, contrary to the interpretive obligation to try to give meaning to all the statutory language. One would also have to ask why Congress would have desired to exclude prior equity categorically from the class of potential owners following a cramdown. Although we have some doubt about the Court of Appeals's assumption that prior equity is often the only source of significant capital for reorganizations, old equity may well be in the best position to make a go of the reorganized enterprise and so may be the party most likely to work out an equity-for-value reorganization.

A less absolute statutory prohibition would follow from reading the "on account of" language as intended to reconcile the two recognized policies underlying Chapter 11, of preserving going concerns and maximizing property available to satisfy creditors. Causation between the old equity's holdings and subsequent property substantial enough to disqualify a plan would presumably occur on this view of things whenever old equity's later property would come at a price that failed to provide the greatest possible addition to the bankruptcy estate, and it would always come at a price too low when the equity holders obtained or preserved an ownership interest for less than someone else would have paid.[26] A truly full value transaction, on the other hand, would pose no threat to the bankruptcy estate not posed by any reorganization, provided of course that the contribution be in cash or be realizable money's worth, just as *Ahlers* required for application of *Case*'s new value rule.

IV

Which of these positions is ultimately entitled to prevail is not to be decided here, however, for even on the latter view the Bank's objection would require rejection of the plan at issue in this case. It is doomed, we can say without necessarily exhausting its flaws, by its provision for vesting equity in the reorganized business in the Debtor's partners without extending an opportunity to anyone else either to compete for that equity or to propose a competing reorganization plan. Although the Debtor's exclusive opportunity to propose a plan under § 1121(b) is not itself "property" within the meaning of subsection (b)(2)(B)(ii), the respondent partnership in this case has taken advantage of this opportunity by proposing a plan under which the benefit of equity ownership may be obtained by no one but old equity partners. Upon the court's approval of that plan, the partners were in the same position that they would have enjoyed had they exercised an exclusive option under the plan to buy the equity in the reorganized entity, or contracted to purchase it from a seller who had first agreed to deal with no one else. It is quite true that the escrow of the partners' proposed investment eliminated any formal need to set out an express option or exclusive dealing provision in the plan itself, since the court's approval that created the opportunity and the partners' action to obtain its advantage were simultaneous. But before the Debtor's plan was accepted no

---

[26] Even when old equity would pay its top dollar and that figure was as high as anyone else would pay, the price might still be too low unless the old equity holders paid more than anyone else would pay, on the theory that the "necessity" required to justify old equity's participation in a new value plan is a necessity for the participation of old equity as such. On this interpretation, disproof of a bargain would not satisfy old equity's burden; it would need to show that no one else would pay as much. No such issue is before us, and we emphasize that our holding here does not suggest an exhaustive list of the requirements of a proposed new value plan.

one else could propose an alternative one, and after its acceptance no one else could obtain equity in the reorganized entity. At the moment of the plan's approval the Debtor's partners necessarily enjoyed an exclusive opportunity that was in no economic sense distinguishable from the advantage of the exclusively entitled offeror or option holder. This opportunity should, first of all, be treated as an item of property in its own right. While it may be argued that the opportunity has no market value, being significant only to old equity holders owing to their potential tax liability, such an argument avails the Debtor nothing, for several reasons. It is to avoid just such arguments that the law is settled that any otherwise cognizable property interest must be treated as sufficiently valuable to be recognized under the Bankruptcy Code. Even aside from that rule, the assumption that no one but the Debtor's partners might pay for such an opportunity would obviously support no inference that it is valueless, let alone that it should not be treated as property. And, finally, the source in the tax law of the opportunity's value to the partners implies in no way that it lacks value to others. It might, indeed, be valuable to another precisely as a way to keep the Debtor from implementing a plan that would avoid a Chapter 7 liquidation.

Given that the opportunity is property of some value, the question arises why old equity alone should obtain it, not to mention at no cost whatever. The closest thing to an answer favorable to the Debtor is that the old equity partners would be given the opportunity in the expectation that in taking advantage of it they would add the stated purchase price to the estate. But this just begs the question why the opportunity should be exclusive to the old equity holders. If the price to be paid for the equity interest is the best obtainable, old equity does not need the protection of exclusiveness (unless to trump an equal offer from someone else); if it is not the best, there is no apparent reason for giving old equity a bargain. There is no reason, that is, unless the very purpose of the whole transaction is, at least in part, to do old equity a favor. And that, of course, is to say that old equity would obtain its opportunity, and the resulting benefit, because of old equity's prior interest within the meaning of subsection (b)(2)(B)(ii). Hence it is that the exclusiveness of the opportunity, with its protection against the market's scrutiny of the purchase price by means of competing bids or even competing plan proposals, renders the partners' right a property interest extended "on account of" the old equity position and therefore subject to an unpaid senior creditor class's objection.

It is no answer to this to say that the exclusive opportunity should be treated merely as a detail of the broader transaction that would follow its exercise, and that in this wider perspective no favoritism may be inferred, since the old equity partners would pay something, whereas no one else would pay anything. If this argument were to carry the day, of course, old equity could obtain a new property interest for a dime without being seen to receive anything on account of its old position. But even if we assume that old equity's plan would not be confirmed without satisfying the judge that the purchase price was top dollar, there is a further reason here not to treat property consisting of an exclusive opportunity as subsumed within the total transaction proposed. On the interpretation assumed here, it would, of course, be a fatal flaw if old equity acquired or retained the property interest without paying full value. It would thus be necessary for old equity to demonstrate its payment of top dollar, but this it could not satisfactorily do when it would receive or retain its property under a plan giving it exclusive rights and in the absence of a competing plan of any sort.[27] Under a plan granting an exclusive right, making no provision for competing bids or competing plans, any determination that the price was top dollar would necessarily be made by a judge in bankruptcy court, whereas the best way to determine value is exposure to a market. This is a point of some significance, since it was, after all, one of the Code's innovations to narrow the occasions for courts to make valuation judgments, as shown by its preference for the supramajoritarian class creditor voting scheme in § 1126(c), see *Ahlers, supra*, at 207 ("The Code provides that it is up to the creditors—and not the courts—to accept or reject a reorganization plan which fails to provide them adequate protection or fails to honor the absolute priority rule"). In the interest of statutory coherence, a like disfavor for decisions untested by competitive choice ought to extend to valuations in administering subsection (b)(2)(B)(ii) when some form of market valuation may be available to test the adequacy of an old equity holder's proposed contribution.

Whether a market test would require an opportunity to offer competing plans or would be satisfied by a right to bid for the same interest sought by old equity, is a question we do not decide here. It is enough to say, assuming a new value corollary, that plans providing junior interest holders with exclusive opportunities free from competition and without benefit of market valuation fall within the prohibition of § 1129(b)(2)(B)(ii).

---

[27] The dissent emphasizes the care taken by the Bankruptcy Judge in examining the valuation evidence here, in arguing that there is no occasion for us to consider the relationship between valuation process and top-dollar requirement. While we agree with the dissent as to the judge's conscientious handling of the matter, the ensuing text of this opinion sets out our reasons for thinking the Act [sic] calls for testing valuation by a required process that was not followed here.

The judgment of the Court of Appeals is accordingly reversed, and the case is remanded for further proceedings consistent with this opinion.

It is so ordered.

[The opinion of JUSTICES THOMAS *and* SCALIA, *concurring in the judgment but taking great exception to the majority's approach to statutory interpretation, is omitted.]*

JUSTICE STEVENS, dissenting.

Prior to the enactment of the Bankruptcy Reform Act of 1978, this Court unequivocally stated that there are circumstances under which stockholders may participate in a plan of reorganization of an insolvent debtor if their participation is based on a contribution in money, or in money's worth, reasonably equivalent in view of all the circumstances to their participation. As we have on two prior occasions,[2] we granted certiorari in this case to decide whether § 1129(b)(2)(B)(ii) of the 1978 Act preserved or repealed this "new value" component of the absolute priority rule. I believe the Court should now definitively resolve the question and state that a holder of a junior claim or interest does not receive property "on account of" such a claim when its participation in the plan is based on adequate new value.

The Court today wisely rejects the Government's "starchy" position that an old equity holder can never receive an interest in a reorganized venture as a result of a cramdown unless the creditors are first paid in full. Nevertheless, I find the Court's objections to the plan before us unsupported by either the text of § 1129(b)(2)(B)(ii) or the record in this case. I would, therefore, affirm the judgment of the Court of Appeals.

I

Section 1129 of Chapter 11 sets forth in detail the substantive requirements that a reorganization plan must satisfy in order to qualify for confirmation. In the case of dissenting creditor classes, a plan must conform to the dictates of § 1129(b). With only one exception, the requirements of §§ 1129(a) and 1129(b) are identical for plans submitted by stockholders or junior creditors and plans submitted by

---

[2] See *Norwest Bank Worthington v. Ahlers*, 485 U.S. 197, 203 n.3 (1988); *U.S. Bancorp Mortgage Co. v. BonnerMall Partnership*, 513 U.S. 18 (1994).

other parties. That exception is the requirement in § 1129(b)(2)(B)(ii) that no holder of a junior claim or interest may receive or retain any property "on account of such junior claim or interest."

When read in the light of Justice Douglas' opinion in *Case v. Los Angeles Lumber Products Co.*, 308 U.S. 106 (1939), the meaning of this provision is perfectly clear. Whenever a junior claimant receives or retains an interest for a bargain price, it does so "on account of" its prior claim. On the other hand, if the new capital that it invests has an equivalent or greater value than its interest in the reorganized venture, it should be equally clear that its participation is based on the fair price being paid and that it is not "on account of" its old claim or equity.

Of course, the fact that the proponents of a plan offer to pay a fair price for the interest they seek to acquire or retain does not necessarily mean that the bankruptcy judge should approve their plan. Any proposed cramdown must satisfy all of the requirements of § 1129 including, most notably, the requirement that the plan be "fair and equitable" to all creditors whose claims are impaired. Moreover, even if the old stockholders propose to buy the debtor for a fair price, presumably their plan should not be approved if a third party, perhaps motivated by unique tax or competitive considerations, is willing to pay an even higher price. Cf. § 1129(c).

In every reorganization case, serious questions concerning the value of the debtor's assets must be resolved. Nevertheless, for the purpose of answering the legal question presented by the parties to this case, I believe that we should assume that all valuation questions have been correctly answered. If, for example, there had been a widely advertised auction in which numerous bidders participated, and if the plan proposed by respondents had been more favorable by a wide margin than any competing proposal, would § 1129(b)(2)(B)(ii) require rejection of their plan simply because it provides that they shall retain 100% of the equity?

Petitioner and the Government would reply "yes" because they think § 1129(b)(2)(B)(ii) imposes an absolute ban on participation by junior claimants without the consent of all senior creditors. The Court correctly rejects this extreme position because it would make the words "on account of" superfluous, and because there is no plausible reason why Congress would have desired such a categorical exclusion, given that in some cases old equity may be the most likely source of new capital. Indeed, the dissenting judge in the Court of Appeals thought "such a result would border on the absurd." Thus, neither the dissenting judge in the Court of Appeals nor the Court appears to be in doubt about the proper answer to my hypothetical question. Instead, the decision is apparently driven by doubts concerning the procedures followed by the Bankruptcy Judge in making his value determinations, implicitly suggesting that the statute should be construed to require some form of competitive bidding in cases like this.

Perhaps such a procedural requirement would be a wise addition to the statute, but it is surely not contained in the present text of § 1129(b)(2)(B)(ii). Indeed, that subsection is not a procedural provision at all. Section 1129 defines the substantive elements that must be met to render plans eligible for confirmation by the bankruptcy judge after all required statutory procedures have been completed. Because * * * petitioner does not now challenge either the procedures followed by the Bankruptcy Judge or any of his value determinations, neither the record nor the text of § 1129(b)(2)(B)(ii) provides any support for the Court's disposition of this case.

* * *

Since the Court of Appeals correctly interpreted § 1129-(b)(2)(B)(ii), its judgment should be affirmed.

Accordingly, I respectfully dissent.

Questions

1. What was the basis for the disagreement between the majority and dissent regarding the confirmation procedures required by the Code?

2. What do you think the Court would do if confronted with a plan, reached through a process open to third parties, under which equity holders, the only bidders, were to contribute new value for new equity? In other words, *is* there a new value exception (or corollary) to the absolute priority rule?

3. How does the absolute priority rule operate in an individual's Chapter 11 case?

c. Tax Claims

We end this Chapter where we began—with a debate about the limits of a bankruptcy court's power under § 105. Although the creditor involved in the following case, the IRS, is not a sympathetic character to many of us, perhaps general creditors stand to lose the most under the Supreme Court's holding.

UNITED STATES v. ENERGY RESOURCES CO.

United States Supreme Court, 1990.
495 U.S. 545, 110 S.Ct. 2139, 109 L.Ed.2d 580.

JUSTICE WHITE delivered the opinion of the Court.

In this case, we decide that a bankruptcy court has the authority to order the Internal Revenue Service (IRS) to treat tax payments made by Chapter 11 debtor corporations as trust fund payments where the bankruptcy court determines that this designation is necessary for the success of a reorganization plan.

I

The Internal Revenue Code requires employers to withhold from their employees' paychecks money representing employees' personal income taxes and Social Security taxes. Because federal law requires employers to hold these funds in "trust for the United States," these taxes are commonly referred to as "trust fund" taxes. Should employers fail to pay trust fund taxes, the Government may collect an equivalent sum directly from the officers or employees of the employer who are responsible for collecting the tax. 26 U.S.C. § 6672. These individuals are commonly referred to as "responsible" individuals.

This case involves corporations that have filed petitions for reorganization under Chapter 11 of the Bankruptcy Code. *[Both debtors, Newport Offshore and Energy Resources, proposed plans under which tax claims would be paid over time, with payments to be allocated first to satisfy trust fund taxes. The bankruptcy court confirmed Newport Offshore's plan, but the Rhode Island district court reversed. Newport Offshore appealed to the First Circuit. The IRS refused to apply Energy Resources's payments as the plan provided and the bankruptcy court ordered the IRS to do so. The Massachusetts district court affirmed and the government appealed to the First Circuit.]*

Consolidating the two cases, the First Circuit reversed in *In re Newport Offshore Ltd.* and affirmed in *In re Energy Resources Co.* The court first considered whether a tax payment made pursuant to a Chapter 11 reorganization plan is "voluntary" or "involuntary" as those terms are used in the IRS' own rules. IRS policy permits taxpayers who "voluntarily" submit payments to the IRS to designate the tax liability to which the payment will apply. The taxpayer corporations argued that tax payments within a Chapter 11 reorganization are best characterized as "voluntary" and therefore that the IRS' own rules bind the agency to respect the debtors' designation of the tax payments. Granting deference to the agency's interpretation of its own rules, the First Circuit accepted the IRS' view that payments made pursuant to the Chapter 11 plan are involuntary for purposes of the IRS' rules. The First Circuit concluded, however, that even if the payments were properly characterized as involuntary under the IRS' regulations, the Bankruptcy Courts nevertheless had the authority to order the IRS to apply an "involuntary" payment made by a Chapter 11 debtor to trust fund tax liabilities if the Bankruptcy Court concluded that this designation was necessary to ensure the success of the reorganization.

We granted certiorari because the First Circuit's conclusion on this issue conflicts with decisions in other Circuits. We affirm the judgment below, for whether or not the payments at issue are rightfully considered to be involuntary, a bankruptcy court has the authority to order the IRS to apply the payments to trust fund liabilities if the bankruptcy court determines that this designation is necessary to the success of a reorganization plan.

II

The Bankruptcy Code does not explicitly authorize the bankruptcy courts to approve reorganization plans designating tax payments as either trust fund or nontrust fund. The Code, however, grants the bankruptcy courts residual authority to approve reorganization plans including "any * * * appropriate provision not inconsistent with the applicable provisions of this title." § 1123(b)(5); see also § 1129. The Code also states that bankruptcy courts may "issue any order, process, or judgment that is necessary or appropriate to carry out the provisions" of the Code. § 105(a). These statutory directives are consistent with the traditional understanding that bankruptcy courts, as courts of equity, have broad authority to modify creditor-debtor relationships.

The Government suggests that, in this case, the Bankruptcy Courts have transgressed one of the limitations on their equitable power. Specifically, the Government contends that the orders conflict with the Code's provisions protecting the Government's ability to collect delinquent taxes. As the Government points out, the Code provides a priority for specified tax claims, including those at issue in this case, and makes those tax debts nondischargeable. See §§ 507(a)(7), 523(a)(1)(A). The Code, moreover, requires a bankruptcy court to assure itself that reorganization will succeed, § 1129(a)(11), and therefore that the IRS, in all likelihood, will collect the tax debt owed. The tax debt must be paid off within six years. § 1129(a)(9)(C).

It is evident that these restrictions on a bankruptcy court's authority do not preclude the court from issuing orders of the type at issue here, for those restrictions do not address the bankruptcy court's ability to designate whether tax payments are to be applied to trust fund or non-trust-fund tax liabilities. The Government is correct that, if it can apply a debtor corporation's tax payments to non-trust-fund liability before trust fund liability, it stands a better chance of debt discharge because the debt that is not guaranteed will be paid off before the guaranteed debt. While this result might be desirable from the Government's standpoint, it is an added protection not specified in the Code itself: Whereas the Code gives it the right to be assured that its taxes will be paid in six years, the Government wants an assurance that its taxes will be paid even if the reorganization fails—*i.e.*, even if the bankruptcy court is incorrect in its judgment that the reorganization plan will succeed.

Even if consistent with the Code, however, a bankruptcy court order might be inappropriate if it conflicted with another law that should have been taken into consideration in the exercise of the court's discretion. The Government maintains that the orders at issue here contravene § 6672 of the Internal Revenue Code, the provision permitting the IRS to collect unpaid trust fund taxes directly from the personal assets of "responsible" individuals. The Government contends that § 6672 reflects a congressional decision to protect the Government's tax revenues by ensuring an additional source from which trust fund taxes might be collected. It is true that § 6672 provides that, if the Government is unable to collect trust fund taxes from a corporate taxpayer, the Government has an alternative source for this revenue. Here, however, the Bankruptcy Courts' orders do not prevent the Government from collecting trust fund revenue; to the contrary, the orders require the Government to collect trust fund payments before collecting non-trust-fund payments. As the Government concedes, § 6672 remains both during and after the corporate Chapter 11 filing as an alternative collection source for trust fund taxes.

The Government nevertheless contends that the Bankruptcy Courts' orders contravene § 6672 because, if the IRS cannot designate a debtor corporation's tax payments as non-trust-fund, the debtor might be able to pay only the guaranteed debt, leaving the Government at risk for non-trust-fund taxes. This may be the case, but § 6672, by its terms, does not protect against this eventuality. That section plainly does not require us to hold that the orders at issue here, otherwise wholly consistent with a bankruptcy court's authority under the Bankruptcy Code, were nonetheless improvident.

III

In this case, the Bankruptcy Courts have not transgressed any limitation on their broad power. We therefore hold that they may order the IRS to apply tax payments to offset trust fund obligations where it concludes that this action is necessary for a reorganization's success. The judgment of the Court of Appeals is therefore

Affirmed.

JUSTICE BLACKMUN dissents.

Questions

1. What incentives has the Supreme Court created for individuals personally responsible for certain corporate taxes to look longingly at bankruptcy?

2. Does *Energy Resources* have any limiting principle? What solace can you offer a creditor who is concerned that corporate assets will be used, through a reorganization plan, to pay taxes for which corporate insiders are personally liable?

Index

References are to Pages